Middle-Length Discourses of the Buddha (Majjhima Nikaya): Translation and Transliteration

Bodhi Path Press

GRAPEVINE INDIA

Published by

GRAPEVINE INDIA PUBLISHERS PVT LTD

www.grapevineindia.com

Delhi | Mumbai

email: grapevineindiapublishers@gmail.com

Ordering Information:

Quantity sales: Special discounts are available on quantity purchases by corporations, associations, and others. For details, reach out to the publisher.

First published by Grapevine India 2024

MULAPANNASAPALI

PART ONE: THE ROOT FIFTY DISCOURSES

MULAPARIYAYAVAGGA

THE DIVISION OF THE DISCOURSE ON THE ROOT

1 Mulapariyayasutta:

The Root of All Things

Evaṁ me sutaṁ—

So I have heard.

ekaṁ samayaṁ bhagavā ukkaṭṭhāyaṁ viharati subhagavane sālarājamūle.

At one time the Buddha was staying near Ukkaṭṭhā, in the Subhaga Forest at the root of a magnificent sal tree.

Tatra kho bhagavā bhikkhū āmantesi:

There the Buddha addressed the mendicants,

"bhikkhavo"ti.

"Mendicants!"

"Bhadante"ti te bhikkhū bhagavato paccassosuṁ.

"Venerable sir," they replied.

Bhagavā etadavoca:

The Buddha said this:

"sabbadhammamūlapariyāyaṁ vo, bhikkhave, desessāmi.

"Mendicants, I will teach you the explanation of the root of all things.

Taṁ suṇātha, sādhukaṁ manasi karotha, bhāsissāmī"ti.

Listen and pay close attention, I will speak."

"Evaṁ, bhante"ti kho te bhikkhū bhagavato paccassosuṁ.

"Yes, sir," they replied.

Bhagavā etadavoca:

The Buddha said this:

"Idha, bhikkhave, assutavā puthujjano ariyānaṁ adassāvī ariyadhammassa akovido ariyadhamme avinīto, sappurisānaṁ adassāvī sappurisadhammassa akovido sappurisadhamme avinīto—

"Take an unlearned ordinary person who has not seen the noble ones, and is neither skilled nor trained in the teaching of the noble ones. They've not seen good persons, and are neither skilled nor trained in the teaching of the good persons.

pathaviṁ pathavito sañjānāti;

They perceive earth as earth.

pathaviṁ pathavito saññatvā pathaviṁ maññati, pathaviyā maññati, pathavito maññati, pathaviṁ meti maññati, pathaviṁ abhinandati.

But then they identify with earth, they identify regarding earth, they identify as earth, they identify that 'earth is mine', they take pleasure in earth.

Taṁ kissa hetu?

Why is that?

'Apariññātaṁ tassā'ti vadāmi.

Because they haven't completely understood it, I say.

Āpaṁ āpato sañjānāti;

They perceive water as water.

āpaṁ āpato saññatvā āpaṁ maññati, āpasmiṁ maññati, āpato maññati, āpaṁ meti maññati, āpaṁ abhinandati.

But then they identify with water …

Taṁ kissa hetu?

Why is that?

'Apariññātaṁ tassā'ti vadāmi.

Because they haven't completely understood it, I say.

Tejaṁ tejato sañjānāti;

They perceive fire as fire.

tejaṁ tejato saññatvā tejaṁ maññati, tejasmiṁ maññati, tejato maññati, tejaṁ meti maññati, tejaṁ abhinandati.

But then they identify with fire …

Taṁ kissa hetu?

Why is that?

'Apariññātaṁ tassā'ti vadāmi.

Because they haven't completely understood it, I say.

Vāyaṁ vāyato sañjānāti;

They perceive air as air.

vāyaṁ vāyato saññatvā vāyaṁ maññati, vāyasmiṁ maññati, vāyato maññati, vāyaṁ meti maññati, vāyaṁ abhinandati.

But then they identify with air …

Taṁ kissa hetu?

Why is that?

'Apariññātaṁ tassā'ti vadāmi.

Because they haven't completely understood it, I say.

Bhūte bhūtato sañjānāti;

They perceive creatures as creatures.

bhūte bhūtato saññatvā bhūte maññati, bhūtesu maññati, bhūtato maññati, bhūte meti maññati, bhūte abhinandati.

But then they identify with creatures …

Taṁ kissa hetu?

Why is that?

'Apariññātaṁ tassā'ti vadāmi.

Because they haven't completely understood it, I say.

Deve devato sañjānāti;

They perceive gods as gods.

deve devato saññatvā deve maññati, devesu maññati, devato maññati, deve meti maññati, deve abhinandati.

But then they identify with gods …

Taṁ kissa hetu?

Why is that?

'Apariññātaṁ tassā'ti vadāmi.

Because they haven't completely understood it, I say.

Pajāpatiṁ pajāpatito sañjānāti;

They perceive the Creator as the Creator.

pajāpatiṁ pajāpatito saññatvā pajāpatiṁ maññati, pajāpatismiṁ maññati, pajāpatito maññati, pajāpatiṁ meti maññati, pajāpatiṁ abhinandati.

But then they identify with the Creator …

Taṁ kissa hetu?

Why is that?

'Apariññātaṁ tassā'ti vadāmi.

Because they haven't completely understood it, I say.

Brahmaṁ brahmato sañjānāti;

They perceive Brahmā as Brahmā.

brahmaṁ brahmato saññatvā brahmaṁ maññati, brahmasmiṁ maññati, brahmato maññati, brahmaṁ meti maññati, brahmaṁ abhinandati.

But then they identify with Brahmā …

Taṁ kissa hetu?

Why is that?

'Apariññātaṁ tassā'ti vadāmi.

Because they haven't completely understood it, I say.

Ābhassare ābhassarato sañjānāti;

They perceive the gods of streaming radiance as the gods of streaming radiance.

ābhassare ābhassarato saññatvā ābhassare maññati, ābhassaresu maññati, ābhassarato maññati, ābhassare meti maññati, ābhassare abhinandati.

But then they identify with the gods of streaming radiance …

Taṁ kissa hetu?

Why is that?

'Apariññātaṁ tassā'ti vadāmi.

Because they haven't completely understood it, I say.

Subhakiṇhe subhakiṇhato sañjānāti;

They perceive the gods replete with glory as the gods replete with glory.

subhakiṇhe subhakiṇhato saññatvā subhakiṇhe maññati, subhakiṇhesu maññati, subhakiṇhato maññati, subhakiṇhe meti maññati, subhakiṇhe abhinandati.

But then they identify with the gods replete with glory …

Taṁ kissa hetu?

Why is that?

'Apariññātaṁ tassā'ti vadāmi.

Because they haven't completely understood it, I say.

Vehapphale vehapphalato sañjānāti;

They perceive the gods of abundant fruit as the gods of abundant fruit.

vehapphale vehapphalato saññatvā vehapphale maññati, vehapphalesu maññati, vehapphalato maññati, vehapphale meti maññati, vehapphale abhinandati.

But then they identify with the gods of abundant fruit …

Taṁ kissa hetu?

Why is that?

'Apariññātaṁ tassā'ti vadāmi.

Because they haven't completely understood it, I say.

Abhibhuṁ abhibhuto sañjānāti;

They perceive the Overlord as the Overlord.

abhibhuṁ abhibhuto saññatvā abhibhuṁ maññati, abhibhusmiṁ maññati, abhibhuto maññati, abhibhuṁ meti maññati, abhibhuṁ abhinandati.

But then they identify with the Overlord …

Taṁ kissa hetu?

Why is that?

'Apariññātaṁ tassā'ti vadāmi.

Because they haven't completely understood it, I say.

Ākāsānañcāyatanaṁ ākāsānañcāyatanato sañjānāti;

They perceive the dimension of infinite space as the dimension of infinite space.

ākāsānañcāyatanaṁ ākāsānañcāyatanato saññatvā ākāsānañcāyatanaṁ maññati, ākāsānañcāyatanasmiṁ maññati, ākāsānañcāyatanato maññati, ākāsānañcāyatanaṁ meti maññati, ākāsānañcāyatanaṁ abhinandati.

But then they identify with the dimension of infinite space …

Taṁ kissa hetu?

Why is that?

'Apariññātaṁ tassā'ti vadāmi.

Because they haven't completely understood it, I say.

Viññāṇañcāyatanaṁ viññāṇañcāyatanato sañjānāti;

They perceive the dimension of infinite consciousness as the dimension of infinite consciousness.

viññāṇañcāyatanaṁ viññāṇañcāyatanato saññatvā viññāṇañcāyatanaṁ maññati, viññāṇañcāyatanasmiṁ maññati, viññāṇañcāyatanato maññati, viññāṇañcāyatanaṁ meti maññati, viññāṇañcāyatanaṁ abhinandati.

But then they identify with the dimension of infinite consciousness …

Taṁ kissa hetu?

Why is that?

'Apariññātaṁ tassā'ti vadāmi.

Because they haven't completely understood it, I say.

Ākiñcaññāyatanaṁ ākiñcaññāyatanato sañjānāti;

They perceive the dimension of nothingness as the dimension of nothingness.

ākiñcaññāyatanaṁ ākiñcaññāyatanato saññatvā ākiñcaññāyatanaṁ maññati, ākiñcaññāyatanasmiṁ maññati, ākiñcaññāyatanato maññati, ākiñcaññāyatanaṁ meti maññati, ākiñcaññāyatanaṁ abhinandati.

But then they identify with the dimension of nothingness …

Taṁ kissa hetu?

Why is that?

'Apariññātaṁ tassā'ti vadāmi.

Because they haven't completely understood it, I say.

Nevasaññānāsaññāyatanaṁ nevasaññānāsaññāyatanato sañjānāti;

They perceive the dimension of neither perception nor non-perception as the dimension of neither perception nor non-perception.

nevasaññānāsaññāyatanaṁ nevasaññānāsaññāyatanato saññatvā nevasaññānāsaññāyatanaṁ maññati, nevasaññānāsaññāyatanasmiṁ maññati, nevasaññānāsaññāyatanato maññati, nevasaññānāsaññāyatanaṁ meti maññati, nevasaññānāsaññāyatanaṁ abhinandati.

But then they identify with the dimension of neither perception nor non-perception …

Taṁ kissa hetu?

Why is that?

'Apariññātaṁ tassā'ti vadāmi.

Because they haven't completely understood it, I say.

Diṭṭhaṁ diṭṭhato sañjānāti;

They perceive the seen as the seen.

diṭṭhaṁ diṭṭhato saññatvā diṭṭhaṁ maññati, diṭṭhasmiṁ maññati, diṭṭhato maññati, diṭṭhaṁ meti maññati, diṭṭhaṁ abhinandati.

But then they identify with the seen …

Taṁ kissa hetu?

Why is that?

'Apariññātaṁ tassā'ti vadāmi.

Because they haven't completely understood it, I say.

Sutaṁ sutato sañjānāti;

They perceive the heard as the heard.

sutaṁ sutato saññatvā sutaṁ maññati, sutasmiṁ maññati, sutato maññati, sutaṁ meti maññati, sutaṁ abhinandati.

But then they identify with the heard …

Taṁ kissa hetu?

Why is that?

'Apariññātaṁ tassā'ti vadāmi.

Because they haven't completely understood it, I say.

Mutaṁ mutato sañjānāti;

They perceive the thought as the thought.

mutaṁ mutato saññatvā mutaṁ maññati, mutasmiṁ maññati, mutato maññati, mutaṁ meti maññati, mutaṁ abhinandati.

But then they identify with the thought …

Taṁ kissa hetu?

Why is that?

'Apariññātaṁ tassā'ti vadāmi.

Because they haven't completely understood it, I say.

Viññātaṁ viññātato sañjānāti;

They perceive the known as the known.

viññātaṁ viññātato saññatvā viññātaṁ maññati, viññātasmiṁ maññati, viññātato maññati, viññātaṁ meti maññati, viññātaṁ abhinandati.

But then they identify with the known …

Taṁ kissa hetu?

Why is that?

'Apariññātaṁ tassā'ti vadāmi.

Because they haven't completely understood it, I say.

Ekattaṁ ekattato sañjānāti;

They perceive oneness as oneness.

ekattaṁ ekattato saññatvā ekattaṁ maññati, ekattasmiṁ maññati, ekattato maññati, ekattaṁ meti maññati, ekattaṁ abhinandati.

But then they identify with oneness …

Taṁ kissa hetu?

Why is that?

'Apariññātaṁ tassā'ti vadāmi.

Because they haven't completely understood it, I say.

Nānattaṁ nānattato sañjānāti;

They perceive diversity as diversity.

nānattaṁ nānattato saññatvā nānattaṁ maññati, nānattasmiṁ maññati, nānattato maññati, nānattaṁ meti maññati, nānattaṁ abhinandati.

But then they identify with diversity …

Taṁ kissa hetu?

Why is that?

'Apariññātaṁ tassā'ti vadāmi.

Because they haven't completely understood it, I say.

Sabbaṁ sabbato sañjānāti;

They perceive all as all.

sabbaṁ sabbato saññatvā sabbaṁ maññati, sabbasmiṁ maññati, sabbato maññati, sabbaṁ meti maññati, sabbaṁ abhinandati.

But then they identify with all …

Taṁ kissa hetu?

Why is that?

'Apariññātaṁ tassā'ti vadāmi.

Because they haven't completely understood it, I say.

Nibbānaṁ nibbānato sañjānāti;

They perceive extinguishment as extinguishment.

nibbānaṁ nibbānato saññatvā nibbānaṁ maññati, nibbānasmiṁ maññati, nibbānato maññati, nibbānaṁ meti maññati, nibbānaṁ abhinandati.

But then they identify with extinguishment, they identify regarding extinguishment, they identify as extinguishment, they identify that 'extinguishment is mine', they take pleasure in extinguishment.

Taṁ kissa hetu?

Why is that?

'Apariññātaṁ tassā'ti vadāmi.

Because they haven't completely understood it, I say.

Puthujjanavasena paṭhamanayabhūmiparicchedo niṭṭhito.

Yopi so, bhikkhave, bhikkhu sekkho appattamānaso anuttaraṁ yogakkhemaṁ patthayamāno viharati, sopi pathaviṁ pathavito abhijānāti;

A mendicant who is a trainee, who hasn't achieved their heart's desire, but lives aspiring to the supreme sanctuary, directly knows earth as earth.

pathaviṁ pathavito abhiññāya pathaviṁ mā maññi, pathaviyā mā maññi, pathavito mā maññi, pathaviṁ meti mā maññi, pathaviṁ mābhinandi.

But they shouldn't identify with earth, they shouldn't identify regarding earth, they shouldn't identify as earth, they shouldn't identify that 'earth is mine', they shouldn't take pleasure in earth.

Taṁ kissa hetu?

Why is that?

'Pariññeyyaṁ tassā'ti vadāmi.

So that they may completely understand it, I say.

Āpaṁ …pe…

They directly know water …

tejaṁ …

fire …

vāyaṁ …

air …

bhūte …

creatures ...

deve ...

gods ...

pajāpatiṁ ...

the Creator ...

brahmaṁ ...

Brahmā ...

ābhassare ...

the gods of streaming radiance ...

subhakiṇhe ...

the gods replete with glory ...

vehapphale ...

the gods of abundant fruit ...

abhibhuṁ ...

the Overlord ...

ākāsānañcāyatanaṁ ...

the dimension of infinite space ...

viññāṇañcāyatanaṁ ...

the dimension of infinite consciousness ...

ākiñcaññāyatanaṁ ...

the dimension of nothingness ...

nevasaññānāsaññāyatanaṁ ...

the dimension of neither perception nor non-perception ...

diṭṭhaṁ ...

the seen ...

sutaṁ ...

the heard ...

mutaṁ …

the thought …

viññātaṁ …

the known …

ekattaṁ …

oneness …

nānattaṁ …

diversity …

sabbaṁ …

all …

nibbānaṁ nibbānato abhijānāti;

They directly know extinguishment as extinguishment.

nibbānaṁ nibbānato abhiññāya nibbānaṁ mā maññi, nibbānasmiṁ mā maññi, nibbānato mā maññi, nibbānaṁ meti mā maññi, nibbānaṁ mābhinandi.

But they shouldn't identify with extinguishment, they shouldn't identify regarding extinguishment, they shouldn't identify as extinguishment, they shouldn't identify that 'extinguishment is mine', they shouldn't take pleasure in extinguishment.

Taṁ kissa hetu?

Why is that?

'Pariññeyyaṁ tassā'ti vadāmi.

So that they may completely understand it, I say.

Sekkhavasena dutiyanayabhūmiparicchedo niṭṭhito.

Yopi so, bhikkhave, bhikkhu arahaṁ khīṇāsavo vusitavā katakaraṇīyo ohitabhāro anuppattasadattho parikkhīṇabhavasaṁyojano sammadaññāvimutto, sopi pathaviṁ pathavito abhijānāti;

A mendicant who is perfected—with defilements ended, who has completed the spiritual journey, done what had to be done, laid down the burden, achieved their own true goal, utterly ended the fetters of rebirth, and is rightly freed through enlightenment—directly knows earth as earth.

pathaviṁ pathavito abhiññāya pathaviṁ na maññati, pathaviyā na maññati, pathavito na maññati, pathaviṁ meti na maññati, pathaviṁ nābhinandati.

But they don't identify with earth, they don't identify regarding earth, they don't identify as earth, they don't identify that 'earth is mine', they don't take pleasure in earth.

Taṁ kissa hetu?

Why is that?

'Pariññātaṁ tassā'ti vadāmi.

Because they have completely understood it, I say.

Āpaṁ …pe…

They directly know water …

tejaṁ …

fire …

vāyaṁ …

air …

bhūte …

creatures …

deve …

gods …

pajāpatiṁ …

the Creator …

brahmaṁ …

Brahmā …

ābhassare …

the gods of streaming radiance …

subhakiṇhe …

the gods replete with glory …

vehapphale …

the gods of abundant fruit …

abhibhuṁ …

the Overlord …

ākāsānañcāyatanaṁ …

the dimension of infinite space …

viññāṇañcāyatanaṁ …

the dimension of infinite consciousness …

ākiñcaññāyatanaṁ …

the dimension of nothingness …

nevasaññānāsaññāyatanaṁ …

the dimension of neither perception nor non-perception …

diṭṭhaṁ …

the seen …

sutaṁ …

the heard …

mutaṁ …

the thought …

viññātaṁ …

the known …

ekattaṁ …

oneness …

nānattaṁ …

diversity …

sabbaṁ …

all …

nibbānaṁ nibbānato abhijānāti;

They directly know extinguishment as extinguishment.

nibbānaṁ nibbānato abhiññāya nibbānaṁ na maññati, nibbānasmiṁ na maññati, nibbānato na maññati, nibbānaṁ meti na maññati, nibbānaṁ nābhinandati.

But they don't identify with extinguishment, they don't identify regarding extinguishment, they don't identify as extinguishment, they don't identify that 'extinguishment is mine', they don't take pleasure in extinguishment.

Taṁ kissa hetu?

Why is that?

'Pariññātaṁ tassā'ti vadāmi.

Because they have completely understood it, I say.

Khīṇāsavavasena tatiyanayabhūmiparicchedo niṭṭhito.

Yopi so, bhikkhave, bhikkhu arahaṁ khīṇāsavo vusitavā katakaraṇīyo ohitabhāro anuppattasadattho parikkhīṇabhavasaṁyojano sammadaññā vimutto, sopi pathaviṁ pathavito abhijānāti;

A mendicant who is perfected—with defilements ended, who has completed the spiritual journey, done what had to be done, laid down the burden, achieved their own true goal, utterly ended the fetters of rebirth, and is rightly freed through enlightenment—directly knows earth as earth.

pathaviṁ pathavito abhiññāya pathaviṁ na maññati, pathaviyā na maññati, pathavito na maññati, pathaviṁ meti na maññati, pathaviṁ nābhinandati.

But they don't identify with earth, they don't identify regarding earth, they don't identify as earth, they don't identify that 'earth is mine', they don't take pleasure in earth.

Taṁ kissa hetu?

Why is that?

Khayā rāgassa, vītarāgattā.

Because they're free of greed due to the ending of greed.

Āpaṁ ...pe...

They directly know water ...

tejaṁ ...

fire ...

vāyaṁ ...

air ...

bhūte ...

creatures …

deve …

gods …

pajāpatiṁ …

the Creator …

brahmaṁ …

Brahmā …

ābhassare …

the gods of streaming radiance …

subhakiṇhe …

the gods replete with glory …

vehapphale …

the gods of abundant fruit …

abhibhuṁ …

the Overlord …

ākāsānañcāyatanaṁ …

the dimension of infinite space …

viññāṇañcāyatanaṁ …

the dimension of infinite consciousness …

ākiñcaññāyatanaṁ …

the dimension of nothingness …

nevasaññānāsaññāyatanaṁ …

the dimension of neither perception nor non-perception …

diṭṭhaṁ …

the seen …

sutaṁ …

the heard …

mutaṁ …

the thought …

viññātaṁ …

the known …

ekattaṁ …

oneness …

nānattaṁ …

diversity …

sabbaṁ …

all …

nibbānaṁ nibbānato abhijānāti;

They directly know extinguishment as extinguishment.

nibbānaṁ nibbānato abhiññāya nibbānaṁ na maññati, nibbānasmiṁ na maññati, nibbānato na maññati, nibbānaṁ meti na maññati, nibbānaṁ nābhinandati.

But they don't identify with extinguishment, they don't identify regarding extinguishment, they don't identify as extinguishment, they don't identify that 'extinguishment is mine', they don't take pleasure in extinguishment.

Taṁ kissa hetu?

Why is that?

Khayā rāgassa, vītarāgattā.

Because they're free of greed due to the ending of greed.

Khīṇāsavavasena catutthanayabhūmiparicchedo niṭṭhito.

Yopi so, bhikkhave, bhikkhu arahaṁ khīṇāsavo vusitavā katakaraṇīyo ohitabhāro anuppattasadattho parikkhīṇabhavasaṁyojano sammadaññāvimutto, sopi pathaviṁ pathavito abhijānāti;

A mendicant who is perfected—with defilements ended, who has completed the spiritual journey, done what had to be done, laid down the burden, achieved their own true goal, utterly ended the fetters of rebirth, and is rightly freed through enlightenment—directly knows earth as earth.

pathaviṁ pathavito abhiññāya pathaviṁ na maññati, pathaviyā na maññati, pathavito na maññati, pathaviṁ meti na maññati, pathaviṁ nābhinandati.

But they don't identify with earth, they don't identify regarding earth, they don't identify as earth, they don't identify that 'earth is mine', they don't take pleasure in earth.

Taṁ kissa hetu?

Why is that?

Khayā dosassa, vītadosattā.

Because they're free of hate due to the ending of hate.

Āpaṁ …pe…

They directly know water …

tejaṁ …

fire …

vāyaṁ …

air …

bhūte …

creatures …

deve …

gods …

pajāpatiṁ …

the Creator …

brahmaṁ …

Brahmā …

ābhassare …

the gods of streaming radiance …

subhakiṇhe …

the gods replete with glory …

vehapphale …

the gods of abundant fruit …

abhibhuṁ …

the Overlord …

ākāsānañcāyatanaṁ …

the dimension of infinite space …

viññāṇañcāyatanaṁ …

the dimension of infinite consciousness …

ākiñcaññāyatanaṁ …

the dimension of nothingness …

nevasaññānāsaññāyatanaṁ …

the dimension of neither perception nor non-perception …

diṭṭhaṁ …

the seen …

sutaṁ …

the heard …

mutaṁ …

the thought …

viññātaṁ …

the known …

ekattaṁ …

oneness …

nānattaṁ …

diversity …

sabbaṁ …

all …

nibbānaṁ nibbānato abhijānāti;

They directly know extinguishment as extinguishment.

nibbānaṁ nibbānato abhiññāya nibbānaṁ na maññati, nibbānasmiṁ na maññati, nibbānato na maññati, nibbānaṁ meti na maññati, nibbānaṁ nābhinandati.

But they don't identify with extinguishment, they don't identify regarding extinguishment, they don't identify as extinguishment, they don't identify that 'extinguishment is mine', they don't take pleasure in extinguishment.

Taṁ kissa hetu?

Why is that?

Khayā dosassa, vītadosattā.

Because they're free of hate due to the ending of hate.

Khīṇāsavavasena pañcamanayabhūmiparicchedo niṭṭhito.

Yopi so, bhikkhave, bhikkhu arahaṁ khīṇāsavo vusitavā katakaraṇīyo ohitabhāro anuppattasadattho parikkhīṇabhavasaṁyojano sammadaññāvimutto, sopi pathaviṁ pathavito abhijānāti;

A mendicant who is perfected—with defilements ended, who has completed the spiritual journey, done what had to be done, laid down the burden, achieved their own true goal, utterly ended the fetters of rebirth, and is rightly freed through enlightenment—directly knows earth as earth.

pathaviṁ pathavito abhiññāya pathaviṁ na maññati, pathaviyā na maññati, pathavito na maññati, pathaviṁ meti na maññati, pathaviṁ nābhinandati.

But they don't identify with earth, they don't identify regarding earth, they don't identify as earth, they don't identify that 'earth is mine', they don't take pleasure in earth.

Taṁ kissa hetu?

Why is that?

Khayā mohassa, vītamohattā.

Because they're free of delusion due to the ending of delusion.

Āpaṁ ...pe...

They directly know water ...

tejaṁ ...

fire ...

vāyaṁ ...

air ...

bhūte ...

creatures …

deve …

gods …

pajāpatiṁ …

the Creator …

brahmaṁ …

Brahmā …

ābhassare …

the gods of streaming radiance …

subhakiṇhe …

the gods replete with glory …

vehapphale …

the gods of abundant fruit …

abhibhuṁ …

the Overlord …

ākāsānañcāyatanaṁ …

the dimension of infinite space …

viññāṇañcāyatanaṁ …

the dimension of infinite consciousness …

ākiñcaññāyatanaṁ …

the dimension of nothingness …

nevasaññānāsaññāyatanaṁ …

the dimension of neither perception nor non-perception …

diṭṭhaṁ …

the seen …

sutaṁ …

the heard …

mutaṁ …

the thought …

viññātaṁ …

the known …

ekattaṁ …

oneness …

nānattaṁ …

diversity …

sabbaṁ …

all …

nibbānaṁ nibbānato abhijānāti;

They directly know extinguishment as extinguishment.

nibbānaṁ nibbānato abhiññāya nibbānaṁ na maññati, nibbānasmiṁ na maññati, nibbānato na maññati, nibbānaṁ meti na maññati, nibbānaṁ nābhinandati.

But they don't identify with extinguishment, they don't identify regarding extinguishment, they don't identify as extinguishment, they don't identify that 'extinguishment is mine', they don't take pleasure in extinguishment.

Taṁ kissa hetu?

Why is that?

Khayā mohassa, vītamohattā.

Because they're free of delusion due to the ending of delusion.

Khīṇāsavavasena chaṭṭhanayabhūmiparicchedo niṭṭhito.

Tathāgatopi, bhikkhave, arahaṁ sammāsambuddho pathaviṁ pathavito abhijānāti;

The Realized One, the perfected one, the fully awakened Buddha directly knows earth as earth.

pathaviṁ pathavito abhiññāya pathaviṁ na maññati, pathaviyā na maññati, pathavito na maññati, pathaviṁ meti na maññati, pathaviṁ nābhinandati.

But he doesn't identify with earth, he doesn't identify regarding earth, he doesn't identify as earth, he doesn't identify that 'earth is mine', he doesn't take pleasure in earth.

Taṁ kissa hetu?

Why is that?

'Pariññātantaṁ tathāgatassā'ti vadāmi.

Because the Realized One has completely understood it to the end, I say.

Āpaṁ ...pe...

He directly knows water ...

tejaṁ ...

fire ...

vāyaṁ ...

air ...

bhūte ...

creatures ...

deve ...

gods ...

pajāpatiṁ ...

the Creator ...

brahmaṁ ...

Brahmā ...

ābhassare ...

the gods of streaming radiance ...

subhakiṇhe ...

the gods replete with glory ...

vehapphale ...

the gods of abundant fruit ...

abhibhuṁ ...

the Overlord ...

ākāsānañcāyatanaṁ ...

the dimension of infinite space …

viññāṇañcāyatanaṁ …

the dimension of infinite consciousness …

ākiñcaññāyatanaṁ …

the dimension of nothingness …

nevasaññānāsaññāyatanaṁ …

the dimension of neither perception nor non-perception …

diṭṭhaṁ …

the seen …

sutaṁ …

the heard …

mutaṁ …

the thought …

viññātaṁ …

the known …

ekattaṁ …

oneness …

nānattaṁ …

diversity …

sabbaṁ …

all …

nibbānaṁ nibbānato abhijānāti;

He directly knows extinguishment as extinguishment.

nibbānaṁ nibbānato abhiññāya nibbānaṁ na maññati, nibbānasmiṁ na maññati, nibbānato na maññati, nibbānaṁ meti na maññati, nibbānaṁ nābhinandati.

But he doesn't identify with extinguishment, he doesn't identify regarding extinguishment, he doesn't identify as extinguishment, he doesn't identify that 'extinguishment is mine', he doesn't take pleasure in extinguishment.

Taṁ kissa hetu?

Why is that?

'Pariññātantaṁ tathāgatassā'ti vadāmi.

Because the Realized One has completely understood it to the end, I say.

Tathāgatavasena sattamanayabhūmiparicchedo niṭṭhito.

Tathāgatopi, bhikkhave, arahaṁ sammāsambuddho pathaviṁ pathavito abhijānāti;

The Realized One, the perfected one, the fully awakened Buddha directly knows earth as earth.

pathaviṁ pathavito abhiññāya pathaviṁ na maññati, pathaviyā na maññati, pathavito na maññati, pathaviṁ meti na maññati, pathaviṁ nābhinandati.

But he doesn't identify with earth, he doesn't identify regarding earth, he doesn't identify as earth, he doesn't identify that 'earth is mine', he doesn't take pleasure in earth.

Taṁ kissa hetu?

Why is that?

'Nandī dukkhassa mūlan'ti—

Because he has understood that relishing is the root of suffering,

iti viditvā 'bhavā jāti bhūtassa jarāmaraṇan'ti.

and that rebirth comes from continued existence; whoever has come to be gets old and dies.

Tasmātiha, bhikkhave, 'tathāgato sabbaso taṇhānaṁ khayā virāgā nirodhā cāgā paṭinissaggā anuttaraṁ sammāsambodhiṁ abhisambuddho'ti vadāmi.

That's why the Realized One—with the ending, fading away, cessation, giving up, and letting go of all cravings—has awakened to the supreme perfect Awakening, I say.

Āpaṁ …pe…

He directly knows water …

tejaṁ …

fire …

vāyaṁ …

air …

bhūte …

creatures …

deve …

gods …

pajāpatiṁ …

the Creator …

brahmaṁ …

Brahmā …

ābhassare …

the gods of streaming radiance …

subhakiṇhe …

the gods replete with glory …

vehapphale …

the gods of abundant fruit …

abhibhuṁ …

the Overlord …

ākāsānañcāyatanaṁ …

the dimension of infinite space …

viññāṇañcāyatanaṁ …

the dimension of infinite consciousness …

ākiñcaññāyatanaṁ …

the dimension of nothingness …

nevasaññānāsaññāyatanaṁ …

the dimension of neither perception nor non-perception …

diṭṭhaṁ …

the seen …

sutaṁ …

the heard …

mutaṁ …

the thought …

viññātaṁ …

the known …

ekattaṁ …

oneness …

nānattaṁ …

diversity …

sabbaṁ …

all …

nibbānaṁ nibbānato abhijānāti;

He directly knows extinguishment as extinguishment.

nibbānaṁ nibbānato abhiññāya nibbānaṁ na maññati, nibbānasmiṁ na maññati, nibbānato na maññati, nibbānaṁ meti na maññati, nibbānaṁ nābhinandati.

But he doesn't identify with extinguishment, he doesn't identify regarding extinguishment, he doesn't identify as extinguishment, he doesn't identify that 'extinguishment is mine', he doesn't take pleasure in extinguishment.

Taṁ kissa hetu?

Why is that?

'Nandī dukkhassa mūlan'ti—

Because he has understood that relishing is the root of suffering,

iti viditvā 'bhavā jāti bhūtassa jarāmaraṇan'ti.

and that rebirth comes from continued existence; whoever has come to be gets old and dies.

Tasmātiha, bhikkhave, 'tathāgato sabbaso taṇhānaṁ khayā virāgā nirodhā cāgā paṭinissaggā anuttaraṁ sammāsambodhiṁ abhisambuddho'ti vadāmī'ti.

That's why the Realized One—with the ending, fading away, cessation, giving up, and letting go of all cravings—has awakened to the supreme perfect Awakening, I say."

Tathāgatavasena aṭṭhamanayabhūmiparicchedo niṭṭhito.

Idamavoca bhagavā.

That is what the Buddha said.

Na te bhikkhū bhagavato bhāsitaṁ abhinandunti.

But the mendicants were not happy with what the Buddha said.

Mūlapariyāyasuttaṁ niṭṭhitaṁ paṭhamaṁ.

2 Sabbasavasutta:

All the Defilements

Evaṁ me sutaṁ—

So I have heard.

ekaṁ samayaṁ bhagavā sāvatthiyaṁ viharati jetavane anāthapiṇḍikassa ārāme.

At one time the Buddha was staying near Sāvatthī in Jeta's Grove, Anāthapiṇḍika's monastery.

Tatra kho bhagavā bhikkhū āmantesi:

There the Buddha addressed the mendicants,

"bhikkhavo"ti.

"Mendicants!"

"Bhadante"ti te bhikkhū bhagavato paccassosuṁ.

"Venerable sir," they replied.

Bhagavā etadavoca:

The Buddha said this:

"sabbāsavasaṁvarapariyāyaṁ vo, bhikkhave, desessāmi.

"Mendicants, I will teach you the explanation of the restraint of all defilements.

Taṁ suṇātha, sādhukaṁ manasi karotha, bhāsissāmī"ti.

Listen and pay close attention, I will speak."

"Evaṁ, bhante"ti kho te bhikkhū bhagavato paccassosuṁ.

"Yes, sir," they replied.

Bhagavā etadavoca:

The Buddha said this:

"Jānato ahaṁ, bhikkhave, passato āsavānaṁ khayaṁ vadāmi, no ajānato no apassato.

"Mendicants, I say that the ending of defilements is for one who knows and sees, not for one who does not know or see.

Kiñca, bhikkhave, jānato kiñca passato āsavānaṁ khayaṁ vadāmi?

For one who knows and sees what?

Yoniso ca manasikāraṁ ayoniso ca manasikāraṁ.

Proper attention and improper attention.

Ayoniso, bhikkhave, manasikaroto anuppannā ceva āsavā uppajjanti, uppannā ca āsavā pavaḍḍhanti;

When you pay improper attention, defilements arise, and once arisen they grow.

yoniso ca kho, bhikkhave, manasikaroto anuppannā ceva āsavā na uppajjanti, uppannā ca āsavā pahīyanti.

When you pay proper attention, defilements don't arise, and those that have already arisen are given up.

Atthi, bhikkhave, āsavā dassanā pahātabbā, atthi āsavā saṁvarā pahātabbā, atthi āsavā paṭisevanā pahātabbā, atthi āsavā adhivāsanā pahātabbā, atthi āsavā parivajjanā pahātabbā, atthi āsavā vinodanā pahātabbā, atthi āsavā bhāvanā pahātabbā.

Some defilements should be given up by seeing, some by restraint, some by using, some by enduring, some by avoiding, some by dispelling, and some by developing.

1. Dassanapahatabbaasava

1. Defilements Given Up by Seeing

Katame ca, bhikkhave, āsavā dassanā pahātabbā?

And what are the defilements that should be given up by seeing?

Idha, bhikkhave, assutavā puthujjano ariyānaṁ adassāvī ariyadhammassa akovido ariyadhamme avinīto, sappurisānaṁ adassāvī sappurisadhammassa akovido sappurisadhamme avinīto—

Take an unlearned ordinary person who has not seen the noble ones, and is neither skilled nor trained in the teaching of the noble ones. They've not seen good persons, and are neither skilled nor trained in the teaching of the good persons.

manasikaraṇīye dhamme nappajānāti, amanasikaraṇīye dhamme nappajānāti.

They don't understand to which things they should pay attention and to which things they should not pay attention.

So manasikaraṇīye dhamme appajānanto amanasikaraṇīye dhamme appajānanto, ye dhammā na manasikaraṇīyā, te dhamme manasi karoti, ye dhammā manasikaraṇīyā te dhamme na manasi karoti.

So they pay attention to things they shouldn't and don't pay attention to things they should.

Katame ca, bhikkhave, dhammā na manasikaraṇīyā ye dhamme manasi karoti?

And what are the things to which they pay attention but should not?

Yassa, bhikkhave, dhamme manasikaroto anuppanno vā kāmāsavo uppajjati, uppanno vā kāmāsavo pavaḍḍhati;

They are the things that, when attention is paid to them, give rise to unarisen defilements and make arisen defilements grow: the defilements of sensual desire,

anuppanno vā bhavāsavo uppajjati, uppanno vā bhavāsavo pavaḍḍhati;

desire to be reborn,

anuppanno vā avijjāsavo uppajjati, uppanno vā avijjāsavo pavaḍḍhati—

and ignorance.

ime dhammā na manasikaraṇīyā ye dhamme manasi karoti.

These are the things to which they pay attention but should not.

Katame ca, bhikkhave, dhammā manasikaraṇīyā ye dhamme na manasi karoti?

And what are the things to which they do not pay attention but should?

Yassa, bhikkhave, dhamme manasikaroto anuppanno vā kāmāsavo na uppajjati, uppanno vā kāmāsavo pahīyati;

They are the things that, when attention is paid to them, do not give rise to unarisen defilements and give up arisen defilements: the defilements of sensual desire,

anuppanno vā bhavāsavo na uppajjati, uppanno vā bhavāsavo pahīyati;

desire to be reborn,

anuppanno vā avijjāsavo na uppajjati, uppanno vā avijjāsavo pahīyati—

and ignorance.

ime dhammā manasikaraṇīyā ye dhamme na manasi karoti.

These are the things to which they do not pay attention but should.

Tassa amanasikaraṇīyānaṁ dhammānaṁ manasikārā manasikaraṇīyānaṁ dhammānaṁ amanasikārā anuppannā ceva āsavā uppajjanti uppannā ca āsavā pavaḍḍhanti.

Because of paying attention to what they should not and not paying attention to what they should, unarisen defilements arise and arisen defilements grow.

So evaṁ ayoniso manasi karoti:

This is how they attend improperly:

'ahosiṁ nu kho ahaṁ atītamaddhānaṁ? Na nu kho ahosiṁ atītamaddhānaṁ? Kiṁ nu kho ahosiṁ atītamaddhānaṁ? Kathaṁ nu kho ahosiṁ atītamaddhānaṁ? Kiṁ hutvā kiṁ ahosiṁ nu kho ahaṁ atītamaddhānaṁ?

'Did I exist in the past? Did I not exist in the past? What was I in the past? How was I in the past? After being what, what did I become in the past?

Bhavissāmi nu kho ahaṁ anāgatamaddhānaṁ? Na nu kho bhavissāmi anāgatamaddhānaṁ? Kiṁ nu kho bhavissāmi anāgatamaddhānaṁ? Kathaṁ nu kho bhavissāmi anāgatamaddhānaṁ? Kiṁ hutvā kiṁ bhavissāmi nu kho ahaṁ anāgatamaddhānan'ti?

Will I exist in the future? Will I not exist in the future? What will I be in the future? How will I be in the future? After being what, what will I become in the future?'

Etarahi vā paccuppannamaddhānaṁ ajjhattaṁ kathaṅkathī hoti:

Or they are undecided about the present thus:

'ahaṁ nu khosmi? No nu khosmi? Kiṁ nu khosmi? Kathaṁ nu khosmi? Ayaṁ nu kho satto kuto āgato? So kuhiṁ gāmī bhavissatī'ti?

'Am I? Am I not? What am I? How am I? This sentient being—where did it come from? And where will it go?'

Tassa evaṁ ayoniso manasikaroto channaṁ diṭṭhīnaṁ aññatarā diṭṭhi uppajjati.

When they attend improperly in this way, one of the following six views arises in them and is taken as a genuine fact.

'Atthi me attā'ti vā assa saccato thetato diṭṭhi uppajjati;

The view: 'My self exists in an absolute sense.'

'natthi me attā'ti vā assa saccato thetato diṭṭhi uppajjati;

The view: 'My self does not exist in an absolute sense.'

'attanāva attānaṁ sañjānāmī'ti vā assa saccato thetato diṭṭhi uppajjati;

The view: 'I perceive the self with the self.'

'attanāva anattānaṁ sañjānāmī'ti vā assa saccato thetato diṭṭhi uppajjati;

The view: 'I perceive what is not-self with the self.'

'anattanāva attānaṁ sañjānāmī'ti vā assa saccato thetato diṭṭhi uppajjati;

The view: 'I perceive the self with what is not-self.'

atha vā panassa evaṁ diṭṭhi hoti:

Or they have such a view:

'yo me ayaṁ attā vado vedeyyo tatra tatra kalyāṇapāpakānaṁ kammānaṁ vipākaṁ paṭisaṁvedeti so kho pana me ayaṁ attā nicco dhuvo sassato avipariṇāmadhammo sassatisamaṁ tatheva ṭhassatī'ti.

'This self of mine is he, the speaker and feeler who experiences the results of good and bad deeds in all the different realms. This self is permanent, everlasting, eternal, and imperishable, and will last forever and ever.'

Idaṁ vuccati, bhikkhave, diṭṭhigataṁ diṭṭhigahanaṁ diṭṭhikantāraṁ diṭṭhivisūkaṁ diṭṭhivipphanditaṁ diṭṭhisaṁyojanaṁ.

This is called a misconception, the thicket of views, the desert of views, the trick of views, the evasiveness of views, the fetter of views.

Diṭṭhisaṁyojanasaṁyutto, bhikkhave, assutavā puthujjano na parimuccati jātiyā jarāya maraṇena sokehi paridevehi dukkhehi domanassehi upāyāsehi;

An unlearned ordinary person who is fettered by views is not freed from rebirth, old age, and death, from sorrow, lamentation, pain, sadness, and distress.

'na parimuccati dukkhasmā'ti vadāmi.

They're not freed from suffering, I say.

Sutavā ca kho, bhikkhave, ariyasāvako—

ariyānaṁ dassāvī ariyadhammassa kovido ariyadhamme suvinīto, sappurisānaṁ dassāvī sappurisadhammassa kovido sappurisadhamme suvinīto—

But take a learned noble disciple who has seen the noble ones, and is skilled and trained in the teaching of the noble ones. They've seen good persons, and are skilled and trained in the teaching of the good persons.

manasikaraṇīye dhamme pajānāti amanasikaraṇīye dhamme pajānāti.

They understand to which things they should pay attention and to which things they should not pay attention.

So manasikaraṇīye dhamme pajānanto amanasikaraṇīye dhamme pajānanto ye dhammā na manasikaraṇīyā te dhamme na manasi karoti, ye dhammā manasikaraṇīyā te dhamme manasi karoti.

So they pay attention to things they should and don't pay attention to things they shouldn't.

Katame ca, bhikkhave, dhammā na manasikaraṇīyā ye dhamme na manasi karoti?

And what are the things to which they don't pay attention and should not?

Yassa, bhikkhave, dhamme manasikaroto anuppanno vā kāmāsavo uppajjati, uppanno vā kāmāsavo pavaḍḍhati;

They are the things that, when attention is paid to them, give rise to unarisen defilements and make arisen defilements grow: the defilements of sensual desire,

anuppanno vā bhavāsavo uppajjati, uppanno vā bhavāsavo pavaḍḍhati;

desire to be reborn,

anuppanno vā avijjāsavo uppajjati, uppanno vā avijjāsavo pavaḍḍhati—

and ignorance.

ime dhammā na manasikaraṇīyā, ye dhamme na manasi karoti.

These are the things to which they don't pay attention and should not.

Katame ca, bhikkhave, dhammā manasikaraṇīyā ye dhamme manasi karoti?

And what are the things to which they do pay attention and should?

Yassa, bhikkhave, dhamme manasikaroto anuppanno vā kāmāsavo na uppajjati, uppanno vā kāmāsavo pahīyati;

They are the things that, when attention is paid to them, do not give rise to unarisen defilements and give up arisen defilements: the defilements of sensual desire,

anuppanno vā bhavāsavo na uppajjati, uppanno vā bhavāsavo pahīyati;

desire to be reborn,

anuppanno vā avijjāsavo na uppajjati, uppanno vā avijjāsavo pahīyati—

and ignorance.

ime dhammā manasikaraṇīyā ye dhamme manasi karoti.

These are the things to which they do pay attention and should.

Tassa amanasikaraṇīyānaṁ dhammānaṁ amanasikārā manasikaraṇīyānaṁ dhammānaṁ manasikārā anuppannā ceva āsavā na uppajjanti, uppannā ca āsavā pahīyanti.

Because of not paying attention to what they should not and paying attention to what they should, unarisen defilements don't arise and arisen defilements are given up.

So 'idaṁ dukkhan'ti yoniso manasi karoti, 'ayaṁ dukkhasamudayo'ti yoniso manasi karoti, 'ayaṁ dukkhanirodho'ti yoniso manasi karoti, 'ayaṁ dukkhanirodhagāminī paṭipadā'ti yoniso manasi karoti.

They properly attend: 'This is suffering' … 'This is the origin of suffering' … 'This is the cessation of suffering' … 'This is the practice that leads to the cessation of suffering'.

Tassa evaṁ yoniso manasikaroto tīṇi saṁyojanāni pahīyanti—

And as they do so, they give up three fetters:

sakkāyadiṭṭhi, vicikicchā, sīlabbataparāmāso.

identity view, doubt, and misapprehension of precepts and observances.

Ime vuccanti, bhikkhave, āsavā dassanā pahātabbā.

These are called the defilements that should be given up by seeing.

2. Saṁvarapahatabbaasava

2. Defilements Given Up by Restraint

Katame ca, bhikkhave, āsavā saṁvarā pahātabbā?

And what are the defilements that should be given up by restraint?

Idha, bhikkhave, bhikkhu paṭisaṅkhā yoniso cakkhundriyasaṁvarasaṁvuto viharati.

Take a mendicant who, reflecting properly, lives restraining the faculty of the eye.

Yañhissa, bhikkhave, cakkhundriyasaṁvaraṁ asaṁvutassa viharato uppajjeyyuṁ āsavā vighātapariḷāhā, cakkhundriyasaṁvaraṁ saṁvutassa viharato evaṁsa te āsavā vighātapariḷāhā na honti.

For the distressing and feverish defilements that might arise in someone who lives without restraint of the eye faculty do not arise when there is such restraint.

Paṭisaṅkhā yoniso sotindriyasaṁvarasaṁvuto viharati ...pe...

Reflecting properly, they live restraining the faculty of the ear ...

ghānindriyasaṁvarasaṁvuto viharati ...pe...

the nose ...

jivhindriyasaṁvarasaṁvuto viharati ...pe...

the tongue ...

kāyindriyasaṁvarasaṁvuto viharati ...pe...

the body ...

manindriyasaṁvarasaṁvuto viharati.

the mind.

Yañhissa, bhikkhave, manindriyasaṁvaraṁ asaṁvutassa viharato uppajjeyyuṁ āsavā vighātapariḷāhā, manindriyasaṁvaraṁ saṁvutassa viharato evaṁsa te āsavā vighātapariḷāhā na honti.

For the distressing and feverish defilements that might arise in someone who lives without restraint of the mind faculty do not arise when there is such restraint.

Yañhissa, bhikkhave, saṁvaraṁ asaṁvutassa viharato uppajjeyyuṁ āsavā vighātapariḷāhā, saṁvaraṁ saṁvutassa viharato evaṁsa te āsavā vighātapariḷāhā na honti.

For the distressing and feverish defilements that might arise in someone who lives without restraint do not arise when there is such restraint.

Ime vuccanti, bhikkhave, āsavā saṁvarā pahātabbā.

These are called the defilements that should be given up by restraint.

3. Patisevanapahatabbaasava

3. Defilements Given Up by Using

Katame ca, bhikkhave, āsavā paṭisevanā pahātabbā?

And what are the defilements that should be given up by using?

Idha, bhikkhave, bhikkhu paṭisaṅkhā yoniso cīvaraṁ paṭisevati:

Take a mendicant who, reflecting properly, makes use of robes:

'yāvadeva sītassa paṭighātāya, uṇhassa paṭighātāya, ḍaṁsamakasavātātapasarīsapasamphassānaṁ paṭighātāya, yāvadeva hirikopīnappaṭicchādanatthaṁ'.

'Only for the sake of warding off cold and heat; for warding off the touch of flies, mosquitoes, wind, sun, and reptiles; and for covering up the private parts.'

Paṭisaṅkhā yoniso piṇḍapātaṁ paṭisevati:

Reflecting properly, they make use of almsfood:

'neva davāya, na madāya, na maṇḍanāya, na vibhūsanāya, yāvadeva imassa kāyassa ṭhitiyā yāpanāya, vihiṁsūparatiyā, brahmacariyānuggahāya, iti purāṇañca vedanaṁ paṭihaṅkhāmi navañca vedanaṁ na uppādessāmi, yātrā ca me bhavissati anavajjatā ca phāsuvihāro ca'.

'Not for fun, indulgence, adornment, or decoration, but only to sustain this body, to avoid harm, and to support spiritual practice. In this way, I shall put an end to old discomfort and not give rise to new discomfort, and I will live blamelessly and at ease.'

Paṭisaṅkhā yoniso senāsanaṁ paṭisevati:

Reflecting properly, they make use of lodgings:

'yāvadeva   sītassa   paṭighātāya,   uṇhassa   paṭighātāya, ḍaṁsamakasavātātapasarīsapasamphassānaṁ   paṭighātāya,   yāvadeva utuparissayavinodanapaṭisallānārāmatthaṁ'.

'Only for the sake of warding off cold and heat; for warding off the touch of flies, mosquitoes, wind, sun, and reptiles; to shelter from harsh weather and to enjoy retreat.'

Paṭisaṅkhā yoniso gilānappaccayabhesajjaparikkhāraṁ paṭisevati:

Reflecting properly, they make use of medicines and supplies for the sick:

'yāvadeva   uppannānaṁ   veyyābādhikānaṁ   vedanānaṁ   paṭighātāya, abyābajjhaparamatāya'.

'Only for the sake of warding off the pains of illness and to promote good health.'

Yañhissa, bhikkhave, appaṭisevato uppajjeyyuṁ āsavā vighātaparilāhā, paṭisevato evaṁsa te āsavā vighātaparilāhā na honti.

For the distressing and feverish defilements that might arise in someone who lives without using these things do not arise when they are used.

Ime vuccanti, bhikkhave, āsavā paṭisevanā pahātabbā.

These are called the defilements that should be given up by using.

4. Adhivasanapahatabbaasava

4. Defilements Given Up by Enduring

Katame ca, bhikkhave, āsavā adhivāsanā pahātabbā?

And what are the defilements that should be given up by enduring?

Idha, bhikkhave, bhikkhu paṭisaṅkhā yoniso khamo hoti sītassa uṇhassa, jighacchāya pipāsāya. Ḍaṁsamakasavātātapasarīsapasamphassānaṁ, duruttānaṁ durāgatānaṁ vacanapathānaṁ, uppannānaṁ sārīrikānaṁ vedanānaṁ dukkhānaṁ tibbānaṁ kharānaṁ kaṭukānaṁ asātānaṁ amanāpānaṁ pāṇaharānaṁ adhivāsakajātiko hoti.

Take a mendicant who, reflecting properly, endures cold, heat, hunger, and thirst. They endure the touch of flies, mosquitoes, wind, sun, and reptiles. They endure rude and unwelcome criticism. And they put up with physical pain—sharp, severe, acute, unpleasant, disagreeable, and life-threatening.

Yañhissa, bhikkhave, anadhivāsayato uppajjeyyuṁ āsavā vighātaparil̤āhā, adhivāsayato evaṁsa te āsavā vighātaparil̤āhā na honti.

For the distressing and feverish defilements that might arise in someone who lives without enduring these things do not arise when they are endured.

Ime vuccanti, bhikkhave, āsavā adhivāsanā pahātabbā.

These are called the defilements that should be given up by enduring.

5. Parivajjanapahatabbaasava

5. Defilements Given Up by Avoiding

Katame ca, bhikkhave, āsavā parivajjanā pahātabbā?

And what are the defilements that should be given up by avoiding?

Idha, bhikkhave, bhikkhu paṭisaṅkhā yoniso caṇḍaṁ hatthiṁ parivajjeti, caṇḍaṁ assaṁ parivajjeti, caṇḍaṁ goṇaṁ parivajjeti, caṇḍaṁ kukkuraṁ parivajjeti, ahiṁ khāṇuṁ kaṇṭakaṭṭhānaṁ sobbhaṁ papātaṁ candanikaṁ oḷigallaṁ.

Take a mendicant who, reflecting properly, avoids a wild elephant, a wild horse, a wild ox, a wild dog, a snake, a stump, thorny ground, a pit, a cliff, a swamp, and a sewer.

Yathārūpe anāsane nisinnaṁ yathārūpe agocare carantaṁ yathārūpe pāpake mitte bhajantaṁ viññū sabrahmacārī pāpakesu ṭhānesu okappeyyuṁ, so tañca anāsanaṁ tañca agocaraṁ te ca pāpake mitte paṭisaṅkhā yoniso parivajjeti.

Reflecting properly, they avoid sitting on inappropriate seats, walking in inappropriate neighborhoods, and mixing with bad friends—whatever sensible spiritual companions would believe to be a bad setting.

Yañhissa, bhikkhave, aparivajjayato uppajjeyyuṁ āsavā vighātapariḷāhā, parivajjayato evaṁsa te āsavā vighātapariḷāhā na honti.

For the distressing and feverish defilements that might arise in someone who lives without avoiding these things do not arise when they are avoided.

Ime vuccanti, bhikkhave, āsavā parivajjanā pahātabbā.

These are called the defilements that should be given up by avoiding.

6. Vinodanapahatabbaasava

6. Defilements Given Up by Dispelling

Katame ca, bhikkhave, āsavā vinodanā pahātabbā?

And what are the defilements that should be given up by dispelling?

Idha, bhikkhave, bhikkhu paṭisaṅkhā yoniso uppannaṁ kāmavitakkaṁ nādhivāseti pajahati vinodeti byantīkaroti anabhāvaṁ gameti, uppannaṁ byāpādavitakkaṁ ...pe... uppannaṁ vihiṁsāvitakkaṁ ...pe... uppannuppanne pāpake akusale dhamme nādhivāseti pajahati vinodeti byantīkaroti anabhāvaṁ gameti.

Take a mendicant who, reflecting properly, doesn't tolerate a sensual, malicious, or cruel thought that has arisen, but gives it up, gets rid of it, eliminates it, and obliterates it. They don't tolerate any bad, unskillful qualities that have arisen, but give them up, get rid of them, eliminate them, and obliterate them.

Yañhissa, bhikkhave, avinodayato uppajjeyyuṁ āsavā vighātapariḷāhā, vinodayato evaṁsa te āsavā vighātapariḷāhā na honti.

For the distressing and feverish defilements that might arise in someone who lives without dispelling these things do not arise when they are dispelled.

Ime vuccanti, bhikkhave, āsavā vinodanā pahātabbā.

These are called the defilements that should be given up by dispelling.

7. Bhavanapahatabbaasava

7. Defilements Given Up by Developing

Katame ca, bhikkhave, āsavā bhāvanā pahātabbā?

And what are the defilements that should be given up by developing?

Idha, bhikkhave, bhikkhu paṭisaṅkhā yoniso satisambojjhaṅgaṁ bhāveti vivekanissitaṁ virāganissitaṁ nirodhanissitaṁ vossaggapariṇāmiṁ;

It's when a mendicant, reflecting properly, develops the awakening factors of mindfulness, paṭisaṅkhā yoniso dhammavicayasambojjhaṅgaṃ bhāveti …pe…

investigation of principles,

vīriyasambojjhaṅgaṃ bhāveti …

energy,

pītisambojjhaṅgaṃ bhāveti …

rapture,

passaddhisambojjhaṅgaṃ bhāveti …

tranquility,

samādhisambojjhaṅgaṃ bhāveti …

immersion,

upekkhāsambojjhaṅgaṃ bhāveti vivekanissitaṃ virāganissitaṃ nirodhanissitaṃ
vossaggapariṇāmiṃ.

and equanimity, which rely on seclusion, fading away, and cessation, and ripen
as letting go.

Yañhissa, bhikkhave, abhāvayato uppajjeyyuṃ āsavā vighātapariḷāhā, bhāvayato
evaṃsa te āsavā vighātapariḷāhā na honti.

For the distressing and feverish defilements that might arise in someone who lives
without developing these things do not arise when they are developed.

Ime vuccanti, bhikkhave, āsavā bhāvanā pahātabbā.

These are called the defilements that should be given up by developing.

Yato kho, bhikkhave, bhikkhuno ye āsavā dassanā pahātabbā te dassanā pahīnā
honti, ye āsavā saṃvarā pahātabbā te saṃvarā pahīnā honti, ye āsavā paṭisevanā
pahātabbā te paṭisevanā pahīnā honti, ye āsavā adhivāsanā pahātabbā te adhivāsanā
pahīnā honti, ye āsavā parivajjanā pahātabbā te parivajjanā pahīnā honti, ye āsavā
vinodanā pahātabbā te vinodanā pahīnā honti, ye āsavā bhāvanā pahātabbā te
bhāvanā pahīnā honti;

Now, take a mendicant who, by seeing, has given up the defilements that should
be given up by seeing. By restraint, they've given up the defilements that should
be given up by restraint. By using, they've given up the defilements that should be
given up by using. By enduring, they've given up the defilements that should be
given up by enduring. By avoiding, they've given up the defilements that should
he given up by avoiding. By dispelling, they've given up the defilements that
should be given up by dispelling. By developing, thcy've given up the defilements
that should be given up by developing.

ayaṁ vuccati, bhikkhave: 'bhikkhu sabbāsavasaṁvarasaṁvuto viharati, acchecchi taṇhaṁ, vivattayi saṁyojanaṁ, sammā mānābhisamayā antamakāsi dukkhassā'"ti.

They're called a mendicant who lives having restrained all defilements, who has cut off craving, untied the fetters, and by rightly comprehending conceit has made an end of suffering."

Idamavoca bhagavā.

That is what the Buddha said.

Attamanā te bhikkhū bhagavato bhāsitaṁ abhinandunti.

Satisfied, the mendicants were happy with what the Buddha said.

Sabbāsavasuttaṁ niṭṭhitaṁ dutiyaṁ.

3 Dhammadayadasutta:

Heirs in the Teaching

Evaṁ me sutaṁ—

So I have heard.

ekaṁ samayaṁ bhagavā sāvatthiyaṁ viharati jetavane anāthapiṇḍikassa ārāme.

At one time the Buddha was staying near Sāvatthī in Jeta's Grove, Anāthapiṇḍika's monastery.

Tatra kho bhagavā bhikkhū āmantesi:

There the Buddha addressed the mendicants,

"bhikkhavo"ti.

"Mendicants!"

"Bhadante"ti te bhikkhū bhagavato paccassosuṁ.

"Venerable sir," they replied.

Bhagavā etadavoca:

The Buddha said this:

"Dhammadāyādā me, bhikkhave, bhavatha, mā āmisadāyādā.

"Mendicants, be my heirs in the teaching, not in material things.

Atthi me tumhesu anukampā:

Out of compassion for you, I think,

'kinti me sāvakā dhammadāyādā bhaveyyuṁ, no āmisadāyādā'ti.

'How can my disciples become heirs in the teaching, not in material things?'

Tumhe ca me, bhikkhave, āmisadāyādā bhaveyyātha no dhammadāyādā, tumhepi tena ādiyā bhaveyyātha:

If you become heirs in material things, not in the teaching, they'll point to you, saying,

'āmisadāyādā satthusāvakā viharanti, no dhammadāyādā'ti;

'The Teacher's disciples live as heirs in material things, not in the teaching.'

ahampi tena ādiyo bhaveyyaṁ:

And they'll point to me, saying,

'āmisadāyādā satthusāvakā viharanti, no dhammadāyādā'ti.

'The Teacher's disciples live as heirs in material things, not in the teaching.'

Tumhe ca me, bhikkhave, dhammadāyādā bhaveyyātha, no āmisadāyādā, tumhepi tena na ādiyā bhaveyyātha:

If you become heirs in the teaching, not in material things, they'll point to you, saying,

'dhammadāyādā satthusāvakā viharanti, no āmisadāyādā'ti;

'The Teacher's disciples live as heirs in the teaching, not in material things.'

ahampi tena na ādiyo bhaveyyaṁ:

And they'll point to me, saying,

'dhammadāyādā satthusāvakā viharanti, no āmisadāyādā'ti.

'The Teacher's disciples live as heirs in the teaching, not in material things.'

Tasmātiha me, bhikkhave, dhammadāyādā bhavatha, mā āmisadāyādā.

So, mendicants, be my heirs in the teaching, not in material things.

Atthi me tumhesu anukampā:

Out of compassion for you, I think,

'kinti me sāvakā dhammadāyādā bhaveyyuṁ, no āmisadāyādā'ti.

'How can my disciples become heirs in the teaching, not in material things?'

Idhāhaṁ, bhikkhave, bhuttāvī assaṁ pavārito paripuṇṇo pariyosito suhito yāvadattho;

Suppose that I had eaten and refused more food, being full, and having had as much as I needed.

siyā ca me piṇḍapāto atirekadhammo chaḍḍanīyadhammo.

And there was some extra almsfood that was going to be thrown away.

Atha dve bhikkhū āgaccheyyuṁ jighacchādubbalyaparetā.

Then two mendicants were to come who were weak with hunger.

Tyāhaṁ evaṁ vadeyyaṁ:

I'd say to them,

'ahaṁ khomhi, bhikkhave, bhuttāvī pavārito paripuṇṇo pariyosito suhito yāvadattho;

'Mendicants, I have eaten and refused more food, being full, and having had as much as I need.

atthi ca me ayaṁ piṇḍapāto atirekadhammo chaḍḍanīyadhammo.

And there is this extra almsfood that's going to be thrown away.

Sace ākaṅkhatha, bhuñjatha, no ce tumhe bhuñjissatha, idānāhaṁ appaharite vā chaḍḍessāmi, appāṇake vā udake opilāpessāmī'ti.

Eat it if you like. Otherwise I'll throw it out where there is little that grows, or drop it into water that has no living creatures.'

Tatrekassa bhikkhuno evamassa:

Then one of those mendicants thought,

'bhagavā kho bhuttāvī pavārito paripuṇṇo pariyosito suhito yāvadattho;

'The Buddha has eaten and refused more food.

atthi cāyaṁ bhagavato piṇḍapāto atirekadhammo chaḍḍanīyadhammo.

And he has some extra almsfood that's going to be thrown away.

Sace mayaṁ na bhuñjissāma, idāni bhagavā appaharite vā chaḍḍessati, appāṇake vā udake opilāpessati.

If we don't eat it he'll throw it away.

Vuttaṁ kho panetaṁ bhagavatā:

But the Buddha has also said:

"dhammadāyādā me, bhikkhave, bhavatha, mā āmisadāyādā"ti.

"Be my heirs in the teaching, not in material things."

Āmisaññataraṁ kho panetaṁ, yadidaṁ piṇḍapāto.

And almsfood is a kind of material thing.

Yannūnāhaṁ imaṁ piṇḍapātaṁ abhuñjitvā imināva jighacchādubbalyena evaṁ imaṁ rattindivaṁ vītināmeyyan'ti.

Instead of eating this almsfood, why don't I spend this day and night weak with hunger?'

So taṁ piṇḍapātaṁ abhuñjitvā teneva jighacchādubbalyena evaṁ taṁ rattindivaṁ vītināmeyya.

And that's what they did.

Atha dutiyassa bhikkhuno evamassa:

Then the second of those mendicants thought,

'bhagavā kho bhuttāvī pavārito paripuṇṇo pariyosito suhito yāvadattho;

'The Buddha has eaten and refused more food.

atthi cāyaṁ bhagavato piṇḍapāto atirekadhammo chaḍḍanīyadhammo.

And he has some extra almsfood that's going to be thrown away.

Sace mayaṁ na bhuñjissāma, idāni bhagavā appaharite vā chaḍḍessati, appāṇake vā udake opilāpessati.

If we don't eat it he'll throw it away.

Yannūnāhaṁ imaṁ piṇḍapātaṁ bhuñjitvā jighacchādubbalyaṁ paṭivinodetvā evaṁ imaṁ rattindivaṁ vītināmeyyan'ti.

Why don't I eat this almsfood, then spend the day and night having got rid of my hunger and weakness?'

So taṁ piṇḍapātaṁ bhuñjitvā jighacchādubbalyaṁ paṭivinodetvā evaṁ taṁ rattindivaṁ vītināmeyya.

And that's what they did.

Kiñcāpi so, bhikkhave, bhikkhu taṁ piṇḍapātaṁ bhuñjitvā jighacchādubbalyaṁ paṭivinodetvā evaṁ taṁ rattindivaṁ vītināmeyya, atha kho asuyeva me purimo bhikkhu pujjataro ca pāsaṁsataro ca.

Even though that mendicant, after eating the almsfood, spent the day and night rid of hunger and weakness, it is the former mendicant who is more worthy of respect and praise.

Taṁ kissa hetu?

Why is that?

Tañhi tassa, bhikkhave, bhikkhuno dīgharattaṁ appicchatāya santuṭṭhiyā sallekhāya subharatāya vīriyārambhāya saṁvattissati.

Because for a long time that will conduce to that mendicant being of few wishes, content, self-effacing, unburdensome, and energetic.

Tasmātiha me, bhikkhave, dhammadāyādā bhavatha, mā āmisadāyādā.

So, mendicants, be my heirs in the teaching, not in material things.

Atthi me tumhesu anukampā:

Out of compassion for you, I think,

'kinti me sāvakā dhammadāyādā bhaveyyuṁ, no āmisadāyādā'"ti.

'How can my disciples become heirs in the teaching, not in material things?'"

Idamavoca bhagavā.

That is what the Buddha said.

Idaṁ vatvāna sugato uṭṭhāyāsanā vihāraṁ pāvisi.

When he had spoken, the Holy One got up from his seat and entered his dwelling.

Tatra kho āyasmā sāriputto acirapakkantassa bhagavato bhikkhū āmantesi:

Then soon after the Buddha left, Venerable Sāriputta said to the mendicants,

"āvuso bhikkhave"ti.

"Reverends, mendicants!"

"Āvuso"ti kho te bhikkhū āyasmato sāriputtassa paccassosuṁ.

"Reverend," they replied.

Āyasmā sāriputto etadavoca:

Sāriputta said this:

"Kittāvatānu kho, āvuso, satthu pavivittassa viharato sāvakā vivekaṁ nānusikkhanti, kittāvatā ca pana satthu pavivittassa viharato sāvakā vivekamanusikkhantī"ti?

"Reverends, how do the disciples of a Teacher who lives in seclusion not train in seclusion? And how do they train in seclusion?"

"Dūratopi kho mayaṁ, āvuso, āgacchāma āyasmato sāriputtassa santike etassa bhāsitassa atthamaññātuṁ.

"Reverend, we would travel a long way to learn the meaning of this statement in the presence of Venerable Sāriputta.

Sādhu vatāyasmantaṁyeva sāriputtaṁ paṭibhātu etassa bhāsitassa attho;

May Venerable Sāriputta himself please clarify the meaning of this.

āyasmato sāriputtassa sutvā bhikkhū dhāressantī"ti.

The mendicants will listen and remember it."

"Tena hāvuso, suṇātha, sādhukaṁ manasi karotha, bhāsissāmī"ti.

"Well then, reverends, listen and pay close attention, I will speak."

"Evamāvuso"ti kho te bhikkhū āyasmato sāriputtassa paccassosuṁ.

"Yes, reverend," they replied.

Āyasmā sāriputto etadavoca:

Sāriputta said this:

"Kittāvatā nu kho, āvuso, satthu pavivittassa viharato sāvakā vivekaṁ nānusikkhanti?

"Reverends, how do the disciples of a Teacher who lives in seclusion not train in seclusion?

Idhāvuso, satthu pavivittassa viharato sāvakā vivekaṁ nānusikkhanti,

The disciples of a teacher who lives in seclusion do not train in seclusion.

yesañca dhammānaṁ satthā pahānamāha, te ca dhamme nappajahanti,

They don't give up what the Teacher tells them to give up.

bāhulikā ca honti, sāthalikā, okkamane pubbaṅgamā, paviveke nikkhittadhurā.

They're indulgent and slack, leaders in backsliding, neglecting seclusion.

Tatrāvuso, therā bhikkhū tīhi ṭhānehi gārayhā bhavanti.

In this case, the senior mendicants should be criticized on three grounds.

'Satthu pavivittassa viharato sāvakā vivekaṁ nānusikkhantī'ti—

'The disciples of a teacher who lives in seclusion do not train in seclusion.'

iminā paṭhamena ṭhānena therā bhikkhū gārayhā bhavanti.

This is the first ground.

'Yesañca dhammānaṁ satthā pahānamāha te ca dhamme nappajahantī'ti—

'They don't give up what the Teacher tells them to give up.'

iminā dutiyena ṭhānena therā bhikkhū gārayhā bhavanti.

This is the second ground.

'Bāhulikā ca, sāthalikā, okkamane pubbaṅgamā, paviveke nikkhittadhurā'ti—

'They're indulgent and slack, leaders in backsliding, neglecting seclusion.'

iminā tatiyena ṭhānena therā bhikkhū gārayhā bhavanti.

This is the third ground.

Therā, āvuso, bhikkhū imehi tīhi ṭhānehi gārayhā bhavanti.

The senior mendicants should be criticized on these three grounds.

Tatrāvuso, majjhimā bhikkhū …pe…

In this case, the middle mendicants

navā bhikkhū tīhi ṭhānehi gārayhā bhavanti.

and the junior mendicants should be criticized on the same three grounds.

'Satthu pavivittassa viharato sāvakā vivekaṁ nānusikkhantī'ti—

iminā paṭhamena ṭhānena navā bhikkhū gārayhā bhavanti.

'Yesañca dhammānaṁ satthā pahānamāha te ca dhamme nappajahantī'ti—

iminā dutiyena ṭhānena navā bhikkhū gārayhā bhavanti.

'Bāhulikā ca honti, sāthalikā, okkamane pubbaṅgamā, paviveke nikkhittadhurā'ti—

iminā tatiyena ṭhānena navā bhikkhū gārayhā bhavanti.

Navā, āvuso, bhikkhū imehi tīhi ṭhānehi gārayhā bhavanti.

Ettāvatā kho, āvuso, satthu pavivittassa viharato sāvakā vivekaṁ nānusikkhanti.

This is how the disciples of a Teacher who lives in seclusion do not train in seclusion.

Kittāvatā ca panāvuso, satthu pavivittassa viharato sāvakā vivekamanusikkhanti?

And how do the disciples of a teacher who lives in seclusion train in seclusion?

Idhāvuso, satthu pavivittassa viharato sāvakā vivekamanusikkhanti—

The disciples of a teacher who lives in seclusion train in seclusion.

yesañca dhammānaṁ satthā pahānamāha te ca dhamme pajahanti;

They give up what the Teacher tells them to give up.

na ca bāhulikā honti, na sāthalikā okkamane nikkhittadhurā paviveke pubbaṅgamā.

They're not indulgent and slack, leaders in backsliding, neglecting seclusion.

Tatrāvuso, therā bhikkhū tīhi ṭhānehi pāsaṁsā bhavanti.

In this case, the senior mendicants should be praised on three grounds.

'Satthu pavivittassa viharato sāvakā vivekamanusikkhantī'ti—

'The disciples of a teacher who lives in seclusion train in seclusion.'

iminā paṭhamena ṭhānena therā bhikkhū pāsaṁsā bhavanti.

This is the first ground.

'Yesañca dhammānaṁ satthā pahānamāha te ca dhamme pajahantī'ti—

'They give up what the Teacher tells them to give up.'

iminā dutiyena ṭhānena therā bhikkhū pāsaṁsā bhavanti.

This is the second ground.

'Na ca bāhulikā, na sāthalikā okkamane nikkhittadhurā paviveke pubbaṅgamā'ti—

'They're not indulgent and slack, leaders in backsliding, neglecting seclusion.'

iminā tatiyena ṭhānena therā bhikkhū pāsaṁsā bhavanti.

This is the third ground.

Therā, āvuso, bhikkhū imehi tīhi ṭhānehi pāsaṁsā bhavanti.

The senior mendicants should be praised on these three grounds.

Tatrāvuso, majjhimā bhikkhū …pe…

In this case, the middle mendicants

navā bhikkhū tīhi ṭhānehi pāsaṁsā bhavanti.

and the junior mendicants should be praised on the same three grounds.

'Satthu pavivittassa viharato sāvakā vivekamanusikkhantī'ti—

iminā paṭhamena ṭhānena navā bhikkhū pāsaṁsā bhavanti.

'Yesañca dhammānaṁ satthā pahānamāha te ca dhamme pajahantī'ti—

iminā dutiyena ṭhānena navā bhikkhū pāsaṁsā bhavanti.

'Na ca bāhulikā, na sāthalikā okkamane nikkhittadhurā paviveke pubbaṅgamā'ti—

iminā tatiyena ṭhānena navā bhikkhū pāsaṁsā bhavanti.

Navā, āvuso, bhikkhū imehi tīhi ṭhānehi pāsaṁsā bhavanti.

Ettāvatā kho, āvuso, satthu pavivittassa viharato sāvakā vivekamanusikkhanti.

This is how the disciples of a Teacher who lives in seclusion train in seclusion.

Tatrāvuso, lobho ca pāpako doso ca pāpako.

The bad thing here is greed and hate.

Lobhassa ca pahānāya dosassa ca pahānāya atthi majjhimā paṭipadā cakkhukaraṇī ñāṇakaraṇī upasamāya abhiññāya sambodhāya nibbānāya saṁvattati.

There is a middle way of practice for giving up greed and hate. It gives vision and knowledge, and leads to peace, direct knowledge, awakening, and extinguishment.

Katamā ca sā, āvuso, majjhimā paṭipadā cakkhukaraṇī ñāṇakaraṇī upasamāya abhiññāya sambodhāya nibbānāya saṁvattati?

And what is that middle way of practice?

Ayameva ariyo aṭṭhaṅgiko maggo, seyyathidaṁ—

It is simply this noble eightfold path, that is:

sammādiṭṭhi sammāsaṅkappo sammāvācā sammākammanto sammāājīvo sammāvāyāmo sammāsati sammāsamādhi.

right view, right thought, right speech, right action, right livelihood, right effort, right mindfulness, and right immersion.

Ayaṁ kho sā, āvuso, majjhimā paṭipadā cakkhukaraṇī ñāṇakaraṇī upasamāya abhiññāya sambodhāya nibbānāya saṁvattati.

This is that middle way of practice, which gives vision and knowledge, and leads to peace, direct knowledge, awakening, and extinguishment.

Tatrāvuso, kodho ca pāpako upanāho ca pāpako ...pe...

The bad thing here is anger and hostility. ...

makkho ca pāpako paḷāso ca pāpako,

disdain and contempt ...

issā ca pāpikā maccherañca pāpakaṁ,

jealousy and stinginess ...

māyā ca pāpikā sāṭheyyañca pāpakaṁ,

deceit and deviousness ...

thambho ca pāpako sārambho ca pāpako,

obstinacy and aggression ...

māno ca pāpako atimāno ca pāpako,

conceit and arrogance ...

mado ca pāpako pamādo ca pāpako.

vanity and negligence.

Madassa ca pahānāya pamādassa ca pahānāya atthi majjhimā paṭipadā cakkhukaraṇī ñāṇakaraṇī upasamāya abhiññāya sambodhāya nibbānāya saṁvattati.

There is a middle way of practice for giving up vanity and negligence. It gives vision and knowledge, and leads to peace, direct knowledge, awakening, and extinguishment.

Katamā ca sā, āvuso, majjhimā paṭipadā cakkhukaraṇī ñāṇakaraṇī upasamāya abhiññāya sambodhāya nibbānāya saṁvattati?

And what is that middle way of practice?

Ayameva ariyo aṭṭhaṅgiko maggo, seyyathidaṁ—

It is simply this noble eightfold path, that is:

sammādiṭṭhi sammāsaṅkappo sammāvācā sammākammanto sammāājīvo sammāvāyāmo sammāsati sammāsamādhi.

right view, right thought, right speech, right action, right livelihood, right effort, right mindfulness, and right immersion.

Ayaṁ kho sā, āvuso, majjhimā paṭipadā cakkhukaraṇī ñāṇakaraṇī upasamāya abhiññāya sambodhāya nibbānāya saṁvattatī"ti.

This is that middle way of practice, which gives vision and knowledge, and leads to peace, direct knowledge, awakening, and extinguishment."

Idamavocāyasmā sāriputto.

This is what Venerable Sāriputta said.

Attamanā te bhikkhū āyasmato sāriputtassa bhāsitaṁ abhinandunti.

Satisfied, the mendicants were happy with what Sāriputta said.

Dhammadāyādasuttaṁ niṭṭhitaṁ tatiyaṁ.

4 Bhayabheravasutta:

Fear and Dread

Evaṁ me sutaṁ—

So I have heard.

ekaṁ samayaṁ bhagavā sāvatthiyaṁ viharati jetavane anāthapiṇḍikassa ārāme.

At one time the Buddha was staying near Sāvatthī in Jeta's Grove, Anāthapiṇḍika's monastery.

Atha kho jāṇussoṇi brāhmaṇo yena bhagavā tenupasaṅkami; upasaṅkamitvā bhagavatā saddhiṁ sammodi.

Then the brahmin Jāṇussoṇi went up to the Buddha, and exchanged greetings with him.

Sammodanīyaṁ kathaṁ sāraṇīyaṁ vītisāretvā ekamantaṁ nisīdi. Ekamantaṁ nisinno kho jāṇussoṇi brāhmaṇo bhagavantaṁ etadavoca:

When the greetings and polite conversation were over, he sat down to one side and said to the Buddha:

"yeme, bho gotama, kulaputtā bhavantaṁ gotamaṁ uddissa saddhā agārasmā anagāriyaṁ pabbajitā, bhavaṁ tesaṁ gotamo pubbaṅgamo, bhavaṁ tesaṁ gotamo bahukāro, bhavaṁ tesaṁ gotamo samādapetā;

"Master Gotama, those gentlemen who have gone forth from the lay life to homelessness out of faith in Master Gotama have Master Gotama to lead the way, help them out, and give them encouragement.

bhoto ca pana gotamassa sā janatā diṭṭhānugatiṁ āpajjatī"ti.

And those people follow Master Gotama's example."

"Evametaṁ, brāhmaṇa, evametaṁ, brāhmaṇa.

"That's so true, brahmin! Everything you say is true, brahmin!"

Ye te, brāhmaṇa, kulaputtā mamaṁ uddissa saddhā agārasmā anagāriyaṁ pabbajitā, ahaṁ tesaṁ pubbaṅgamo, ahaṁ tesaṁ bahukāro, ahaṁ tesaṁ samādapetā;

mama ca pana sā janatā diṭṭhānugatiṁ āpajjatī"ti.

"Durabhisambhavāni hi kho, bho gotama, araññavanapatthāni pantāni senāsanāni, dukkaraṁ pavivekaṁ, durabhiramaṁ ekatte,

"But Master Gotama, remote lodgings in the wilderness and the forest are challenging. It's hard to maintain seclusion and hard to find joy in solitude.

haranti maññe mano vanāni samādhiṁ alabhamānassa bhikkhuno"ti.

The forests seem to rob the mind of a mendicant who isn't immersed in samādhi."

"Evametaṁ, brāhmaṇa, evametaṁ, brāhmaṇa.

"That's so true, brahmin! Everything you say is true, brahmin!

Durabhisambhavāni hi kho, brāhmaṇa, araññavanapatthāni pantāni senāsanāni, dukkaraṁ pavivekaṁ, durabhiramaṁ ekatte,

haranti maññe mano vanāni samādhiṁ alabhamānassa bhikkhuno.

Mayhampi kho, brāhmaṇa, pubbeva sambodhā anabhisambuddhassa bodhisattasseva sato etadahosi:

Before my awakening—when I was still unawakened but intent on awakening—I too thought,

'durabhisambhavāni hi kho araññavanapatthāni pantāni senāsanāni, dukkaraṁ pavivekaṁ, durabhiramaṁ ekatte,

'Remote lodgings in the wilderness and the forest are challenging. It's hard to maintain seclusion and hard to find joy in solitude.

haranti maññe mano vanāni samādhiṁ alabhamānassa bhikkhuno'ti.

The forests seem to rob the mind of a mendicant who isn't immersed in samādhi.'

Tassa mayhaṁ, brāhmaṇa, etadahosi:

Then I thought,

'ye kho keci samaṇā vā brāhmaṇā vā aparisuddhakāyakammantā araññavanapatthāni pantāni senāsanāni paṭisevanti, aparisuddhakāyakammantasandosahetu have te bhonto samaṇabrāhmaṇā akusalaṁ bhayabheravaṁ avhāyanti.

'There are ascetics and brahmins with unpurified conduct of body, speech, and mind who frequent remote lodgings in the wilderness and the forest. Those ascetics and brahmins summon unskillful fear and dread because of these defects in their conduct.

Na kho panāhaṁ aparisuddhakāyakammanto araññavanapatthāni pantāni senāsanāni paṭisevāmi;

But I don't frequent remote lodgings in the wilderness and the forest with unpurified conduct of body, speech, and mind.

parisuddhakāyakammantohamasmi.

My conduct is purified.

Ye hi vo ariyā parisuddhakāyakammantā araññavanapatthāni pantāni senāsanāni paṭisevanti tesamahaṁ aññataro'ti.

I am one of those noble ones who frequent remote lodgings in the wilderness and the forest with purified conduct of body, speech, and mind.'

Etamahaṁ, brāhmaṇa, parisuddhakāyakammataṁ attani sampassamāno bhiyyo pallomamāpādiṁ araññe vihārāya.

Seeing this purity of conduct in myself I felt even more unruffled about staying in the forest.

Tassa mayhaṁ, brāhmaṇa, etadahosi:

Then I thought,

'ye kho keci samaṇā vā brāhmaṇā vā aparisuddhavacīkammantā …pe…

aparisuddhamanokammantā …pe…

aparisuddhājīvā araññavanapatthāni pantāni senāsanāni paṭisevanti, aparisuddhājīvasandosahetu have te bhonto samaṇabrāhmaṇā akusalaṁ bhayabheravaṁ avhāyanti.

'There are ascetics and brahmins with unpurified livelihood who frequent remote lodgings in the wilderness and the forest. Those ascetics and brahmins summon unskillful fear and dread because of these defects in their livelihood.

Na kho panāhaṁ aparisuddhājīvo araññavanapatthāni pantāni senāsanāni paṭisevāmi;

But I don't frequent remote lodgings in the wilderness and the forest with unpurified livelihood.

parisuddhājīvohamasmi.

My livelihood is purified.

Ye hi vo ariyā parisuddhājīvā araññavanapatthāni pantāni senāsanāni paṭisevanti tesamahaṁ aññataro'ti.

I am one of those noble ones who frequent remote lodgings in the wilderness and the forest with purified livelihood.'

Etamahaṁ, brāhmaṇa, parisuddhājīvataṁ attani sampassamāno bhiyyo pallomamāpādiṁ araññe vihārāya.

Seeing this purity of livelihood in myself I felt even more unruffled about staying in the forest.

Tassa mayhaṁ, brāhmaṇa, etadahosi:

Then I thought,

'ye kho keci samaṇā vā brāhmaṇā vā abhijjhālū kāmesu tibbasārāgā araññavanapatthāni pantāni senāsanāni paṭisevanti, abhijjhālukāmesutibbasārāgasandosahetu have te bhonto samaṇabrāhmaṇā akusalaṁ bhayabheravaṁ avhāyanti.

'There are ascetics and brahmins full of desire for sensual pleasures, with acute lust ...

Na kho panāhaṁ abhijjhālu kāmesu tibbasārāgo araññavanapatthāni pantāni senāsanāni paṭisevāmi;

anabhijjhālūhamasmi.

I am not full of desire ...'

Ye hi vo ariyā anabhijjhālū araññavanapatthāni pantāni senāsanāni paṭisevanti, tesamahaṁ aññataro'ti.

Etamahaṁ, brāhmaṇa, anabhijjhālutaṁ attani sampassamāno bhiyyo pallomamāpādiṁ araññe vihārāya.

Tassa mayhaṁ, brāhmaṇa, etadahosi:

'ye kho keci samaṇā vā brāhmaṇā vā byāpannacittā paduṭṭhamanasaṅkappā araññavanapatthāni pantāni senāsanāni paṭisevanti, byāpannacittapaduṭṭhamanasaṅkappasandosahetu have te bhonto samaṇabrāhmaṇā akusalaṁ bhayabheravaṁ avhāyanti.

'There are ascetics and brahmins full of ill will, with malicious intentions ...

Na kho panāhaṁ byāpannacitto paduṭṭhamanasaṅkappo araññavanapatthāni pantāni senāsanāni paṭisevāmi;

mettacittohamasmi.

I have a heart full of love …'

Ye hi vo ariyā mettacittā araññavanapatthāni pantāni senāsanāni paṭisevanti tesamahaṁ aññataro'ti.

Etamahaṁ, brāhmaṇa, mettacittataṁ attani sampassamāno bhiyyo pallomamāpādiṁ araññe vihārāya.

Tassa mayhaṁ, brāhmaṇa, etadahosi:

'ye kho keci samaṇā vā brāhmaṇā vā thinamiddhapariyuṭṭhitā araññavanapatthāni pantāni senāsanāni paṭisevanti, thinamiddhapariyuṭṭhānasandosahetu have te bhonto samaṇabrāhmaṇā akusalaṁ bhayabheravaṁ avhāyanti.

'There are ascetics and brahmins overcome with dullness and drowsiness …

Na kho panāhaṁ thinamiddhapariyuṭṭhito araññavanapatthāni pantāni senāsanāni paṭisevāmi;

vigatathinamiddhohamasmi.

I am free of dullness and drowsiness …'

Ye hi vo ariyā vigatathinamiddhā araññavanapatthāni pantāni senāsanāni paṭisevanti tesamahaṁ aññataro'ti.

Etamahaṁ, brāhmaṇa, vigatathinamiddhataṁ attani sampassamāno bhiyyo pallomamāpādiṁ araññe vihārāya.

Tassa mayhaṁ, brāhmaṇa, etadahosi:

'ye kho keci samaṇā vā brāhmaṇā vā uddhatā avūpasantacittā araññavanapatthāni pantāni senāsanāni paṭisevanti, uddhataavūpasantacittasandosahetu have te bhonto samaṇabrāhmaṇā akusalaṁ bhayabheravaṁ avhāyanti.

'There are ascetics and brahmins who are restless, with no peace of mind …

Na kho panāhaṁ uddhato avūpasantacitto araññavanapatthāni pantāni senāsanāni paṭisevāmi;

vūpasantacittohamasmi.

My mind is peaceful …'

Ye hi vo ariyā vūpasantacittā araññavanapatthāni pantāni senāsanāni paṭisevanti, tesamahaṁ aññataro'ti.

Etamahaṁ, brāhmaṇa, vūpasantacittataṁ attani sampassamāno bhiyyo pallomamāpādiṁ araññe vihārāya.

Tassa mayhaṁ, brāhmaṇa, etadahosi:

'ye kho keci samaṇā vā brāhmaṇā vā kaṅkhī vicikicchī araññavanapatthāni pantāni senāsanāni paṭisevanti, kaṅkhivicikicchisandosahetu have te bhonto samaṇabrāhmaṇā akusalaṃ bhayabheravaṃ avhāyanti.

'There are ascetics and brahmins who are doubting and uncertain ...

Na kho panāhaṃ kaṅkhī vicikicchī araññavanapatthāni pantāni senāsanāni paṭisevāmi;

tiṇṇavicikicchohamasmi.

I've gone beyond doubt ...'

Ye hi vo ariyā tiṇṇavicikicchā araññavanapatthāni pantāni senāsanāni paṭisevanti tesamahaṃ aññataro'ti.

Etamahaṃ, brāhmaṇa, tiṇṇavicikicchataṃ attani sampassamāno bhiyyo pallomamāpādiṃ araññe vihārāya.

Tassa mayhaṃ, brāhmaṇa, etadahosi:

'ye kho keci samaṇā vā brāhmaṇā vā attukkaṃsakā paravambhī araññavanapatthāni pantāni senāsanāni paṭisevanti, attukkaṃsanaparavambhanasandosahetu have te bhonto samaṇabrāhmaṇā akusalaṃ bhayabheravaṃ avhāyanti.

'There are ascetics and brahmins who glorify themselves and put others down ...

Na kho panāhaṃ attukkaṃsako paravambhī araññavanapatthāni pantāni senāsanāni paṭisevāmi;

anattukkaṃsako aparavambhīhamasmi.

I don't glorify myself and put others down ...'

Ye hi vo ariyā anattukkaṃsakā aparavambhī araññavanapatthāni pantāni senāsanāni paṭisevanti tesamahaṃ aññataro'ti.

Etamahaṃ, brāhmaṇa, anattukkaṃsakataṃ aparavambhitaṃ attani sampassamāno bhiyyo pallomamāpādiṃ araññe vihārāya.

Tassa mayhaṃ, brāhmaṇa, etadahosi:

'ye kho keci samaṇā vā brāhmaṇā vā chambhī bhīrukajātikā araññavanapatthāni pantāni senāsanāni paṭisevanti, chambhibhīrukajātikasandosahetu have te bhonto samaṇabrāhmaṇā akusalaṃ bhayabheravaṃ avhāyanti.

'There are ascetics and brahmins who are cowardly and craven ...

Na kho panāhaṃ chambhī bhīrukajātiko araññavanapatthāni pantāni senāsanāni paṭisevāmi;

vigatalomahaṃsohamasmi.

I don't get startled ...'

Ye hi vo ariyā vigatalomahaṁsā araññavanapatthāni pantāni senāsanāni paṭisevanti tesamahaṁ aññataro'ti.

Etamahaṁ, brāhmaṇa, vigatalomahaṁsataṁ attani sampassamāno bhiyyo pallomamāpādiṁ araññe vihārāya.

Tassa mayhaṁ, brāhmaṇa, etadahosi:

'ye kho keci samaṇā vā brāhmaṇā vā lābhasakkārasilokaṁ nikāmayamānā araññavanapatthāni pantāni senāsanāni paṭisevanti, lābhasakkārasilokanikāmanasandosahetu have te bhonto samaṇabrāhmaṇā akusalaṁ bhayabheravaṁ avhāyanti.

'There are ascetics and brahmins who enjoy possessions, honor, and popularity ...

Na kho panāhaṁ lābhasakkārasilokaṁ nikāmayamāno araññavanapatthāni pantāni senāsanāni paṭisevāmi;

appicchohamasmi.

I have few wishes ...'

Ye hi vo ariyā appicchā araññavanapatthāni pantāni senāsanāni paṭisevanti tesamahaṁ aññataro'ti.

Etamahaṁ, brāhmaṇa, appicchataṁ attani sampassamāno bhiyyo pallomamāpādiṁ araññe vihārāya.

Tassa mayhaṁ, brāhmaṇa, etadahosi:

'ye kho keci samaṇā vā brāhmaṇā vā kusītā hīnavīriyā araññavanapatthāni pantāni senāsanāni paṭisevanti, kusītahīnavīriyasandosahetu have te bhonto samaṇabrāhmaṇā akusalaṁ bhayabheravaṁ avhāyanti.

'There are ascetics and brahmins who are lazy and lack energy ...

Na kho panāhaṁ kusīto hīnavīriyo araññavanapatthāni pantāni senāsanāni paṭisevāmi;

āraddhavīriyohamasmi.

I am energetic ...'

Ye hi vo ariyā āraddhavīriyā araññavanapatthāni pantāni senāsanāni paṭisevanti tesamahaṁ aññataro'ti.

Etamahaṁ, brāhmaṇa, āraddhavīriyataṁ attani sampassamāno bhiyyo pallomamāpādiṁ araññe vihārāya.

Tassa mayhaṁ, brāhmaṇa, etadahosi:

'ye kho keci samaṇā vā brāhmaṇā vā muṭṭhassatī asampajānā araññavanapatthāni pantāni senāsanāni paṭisevanti, muṭṭhassatiasampajānasandosahetu have te bhonto samaṇabrāhmaṇā akusalaṁ bhayabheravaṁ avhāyanti.

'There are ascetics and brahmins who are unmindful and lack situational awareness …

Na kho panāhaṁ muṭṭhassati asampajāno araññavanapatthāni pantāni senāsanāni paṭisevāmi;

upaṭṭhitassatihamasmi.

I am mindful …'

Ye hi vo ariyā upaṭṭhitassatī araññavanapatthāni pantāni senāsanāni paṭisevanti tesamahaṁ aññataro'ti.

Etamahaṁ, brāhmaṇa, upaṭṭhitassatitaṁ attani sampassamāno bhiyyo pallomamāpādiṁ araññe vihārāya.

Tassa mayhaṁ, brāhmaṇa, etadahosi:

'ye kho keci samaṇā vā brāhmaṇā vā asamāhitā vibbhantacittā araññavanapatthāni pantāni senāsanāni paṭisevanti, asamāhitavibbhantacittasandosahetu have te bhonto samaṇabrāhmaṇā akusalaṁ bhayabheravaṁ avhāyanti.

'There are ascetics and brahmins who lack immersion, with straying minds …

Na kho panāhaṁ asamāhito vibbhantacitto araññavanapatthāni pantāni senāsanāni paṭisevāmi;

samādhisampannohamasmi.

I am accomplished in immersion …'

Ye hi vo ariyā samādhisampannā araññavanapatthāni pantāni senāsanāni paṭisevanti tesamahaṁ aññataro'ti.

Etamahaṁ, brāhmaṇa, samādhisampadaṁ attani sampassamāno bhiyyo pallomamāpādiṁ araññe vihārāya.

Tassa mayhaṁ, brāhmaṇa, etadahosi:

'ye kho keci samaṇā vā brāhmaṇā vā duppaññā eḷamūgā araññavanapatthāni pantāni senāsanāni paṭisevanti, duppaññaeḷamūgasandosahetu have te bhonto samaṇabrāhmaṇā akusalaṁ bhayabheravaṁ avhāyanti.

'There are ascetics and brahmins who are witless and stupid who frequent remote lodgings in the wilderness and the forest. Those ascetics and brahmins summon unskillful fear and dread because of the defects of witlessness and stupidity.

Na kho panāhaṁ duppañño eḷamūgo araññavanapatthāni pantāni senāsanāni paṭisevāmi;

But I don't frequent remote lodgings in the wilderness and the forest witless and stupid.

paññāsampannohamasmi.

I am accomplished in wisdom.

Ye hi vo ariyā paññāsampannā araññavanapatthāni pantāni senāsanāni paṭisevanti tesamahaṁ aññataro'ti.

I am one of those noble ones who frequent remote lodgings in the wilderness and the forest accomplished in wisdom.'

Etamahaṁ, brāhmaṇa, paññāsampadaṁ attani sampassamāno bhiyyo pallomamāpādiṁ araññe vihārāya.

Seeing this accomplishment of wisdom in myself I felt even more unruffled about staying in the forest.

Soḷasapariyāyaṁ niṭṭhitaṁ.

Tassa mayhaṁ, brāhmaṇa, etadahosi:

Then I thought,

'yannūnāhaṁ yā tā rattiyo abhiññātā abhilakkhitā—

'There are certain nights that are recognized as specially portentous:

cātuddasī pañcadasī aṭṭhamī ca pakkhassa—

the fourteenth, fifteenth, and eighth of the fortnight.

tathārūpāsu rattīsu yāni tāni ārāmacetiyāni vanacetiyāni rukkhacetiyāni bhiṁsanakāni salomahaṁsāni tathārūpesu senāsanesu vihareyyaṁ appeva nāmāhaṁ bhayabheravaṁ passeyyan'ti.

On such nights, why don't I stay in awe-inspiring and hair-raising shrines in parks, forests, and trees? In such lodgings, hopefully I might see that fear and dread.'

So kho ahaṁ, brāhmaṇa, aparena samayena yā tā rattiyo abhiññātā abhilakkhitā—

Some time later, that's what I did.

cātuddasī pañcadasī aṭṭhamī ca pakkhassa—

tathārūpāsu rattīsu yāni tāni ārāmacetiyāni vanacetiyāni rukkhacetiyāni bhiṁsanakāni salomahaṁsāni tathārūpesu senāsanesu viharāmi.

Tattha ca me, brāhmaṇa, viharato mago vā āgacchati, moro vā kaṭṭhaṁ pāteti, vāto vā paṇṇakasaṭaṁ ereti;

As I was staying there a deer came by, or a peacock snapped a twig, or the wind rustled the leaves.

tassa mayhaṁ brāhmaṇa etadahosi:

Then I thought,

'etaṁ nūna taṁ bhayabheravaṁ āgacchatī'ti.

'Is this that fear and dread coming?'

Tassa mayhaṁ, brāhmaṇa, etadahosi:

Then I thought,

'kiṁ nu kho ahaṁ aññadatthu bhayapaṭikaṅkhī viharāmi?

'Why do I always meditate expecting that fear and terror to come?

Yannūnāhaṁ yathābhūtaṁ yathābhūtassa me taṁ bhayabheravaṁ āgacchati, tathābhūtaṁ tathābhūtova taṁ bhayabheravaṁ paṭivineyyan'ti.

Why don't I get rid of that fear and dread just as it comes, while remaining just as I am?'

Tassa mayhaṁ, brāhmaṇa, caṅkamantassa taṁ bhayabheravaṁ āgacchati.

Then that fear and dread came upon me as I was walking.

So kho ahaṁ, brāhmaṇa, neva tāva tiṭṭhāmi na nisīdāmi na nipajjāmi, yāva caṅkamantova taṁ bhayabheravaṁ paṭivinemi.

I didn't stand still or sit down or lie down until I had got rid of that fear and dread while walking.

Tassa mayhaṁ, brāhmaṇa, ṭhitassa taṁ bhayabheravaṁ āgacchati.

Then that fear and dread came upon me as I was standing.

So kho ahaṁ, brāhmaṇa, neva tāva caṅkamāmi na nisīdāmi na nipajjāmi. Yāva ṭhitova taṁ bhayabheravaṁ paṭivinemi.

I didn't walk or sit down or lie down until I had got rid of that fear and dread while standing.

Tassa mayhaṁ, brāhmaṇa, nisinnassa taṁ bhayabheravaṁ āgacchati.

Then that fear and dread came upon me as I was sitting.

So kho ahaṁ, brāhmaṇa, neva tāva nipajjāmi na tiṭṭhāmi na caṅkamāmi, yāva nisinnova taṁ bhayabheravaṁ paṭivinemi.

I didn't lie down or stand still or walk until I had got rid of that fear and dread while sitting.

Tassa mayhaṁ, brāhmaṇa, nipannassa taṁ bhayabheravaṁ āgacchati.

Then that fear and dread came upon me as I was lying down.

So kho ahaṁ, brāhmaṇa, neva tāva nisīdāmi na tiṭṭhāmi na caṅkamāmi, yāva nipannova taṁ bhayabheravaṁ paṭivinemi.

I didn't sit up or stand still or walk until I had got rid of that fear and dread while lying down.

Santi kho pana, brāhmaṇa, eke samaṇabrāhmaṇā rattiṁyeva samānaṁ divāti sañjānanti, divāyeva samānaṁ rattīti sañjānanti.

There are some ascetics and brahmins who perceive that it's day when in fact it's night, or perceive that it's night when in fact it's day.

Idamahaṁ tesaṁ samaṇabrāhmaṇānaṁ sammohavihārasmiṁ vadāmi.

This meditation of theirs is delusional, I say.

Ahaṁ kho pana, brāhmaṇa, rattiṁyeva samānaṁ rattīti sañjānāmi, divāyeva samānaṁ divāti sañjānāmi.

I perceive that it's night when in fact it is night, and perceive that it's day when in fact it is day.

Yaṁ kho taṁ, brāhmaṇa, sammā vadamāno vadeyya:

And if there's anyone of whom it may be rightly said that

'asammohadhammo satto loke uppanno bahujanahitāya bahujanasukhāya lokānukampāya atthāya hitāya sukhāya devamanussānan'ti, mameva taṁ sammā vadamāno vadeyya:

a being not liable to delusion has arisen in the world for the welfare and happiness of the people, out of compassion for the world, for the benefit, welfare, and happiness of gods and humans, it's of me that this should be said.

'asammohadhammo satto loke uppanno bahujanahitāya bahujanasukhāya lokānukampāya atthāya hitāya sukhāya devamanussānan'ti.

Āraddhaṁ kho pana me, brāhmaṇa, vīriyaṁ ahosi asallīnaṁ, upaṭṭhitā sati asammuṭṭhā, passaddho kāyo asāraddho, samāhitaṁ cittaṁ ekaggaṁ.

My energy was roused up and unflagging, my mindfulness was established and lucid, my body was tranquil and undisturbed, and my mind was immersed in samādhi.

So kho ahaṁ, brāhmaṇa, vivicceva kāmehi vivicca akusalehi dhammehi savitakkaṁ savicāraṁ vivekajaṁ pītisukhaṁ paṭhamaṁ jhānaṁ upasampajja vihāsiṁ.

Quite secluded from sensual pleasures, secluded from unskillful qualities, I entered and remained in the first absorption, which has the rapture and bliss born of seclusion, while placing the mind and keeping it connected.

Vitakkavicārānaṁ vūpasamā ajjhattaṁ sampasādanaṁ cetaso ekodibhāvaṁ avitakkaṁ avicāraṁ samādhijaṁ pītisukhaṁ dutiyaṁ jhānaṁ upasampajja vihāsiṁ.

As the placing of the mind and keeping it connected were stilled, I entered and remained in the second absorption, which has the rapture and bliss born of immersion, with internal clarity and confidence, and unified mind, without placing the mind and keeping it connected.

Pītiyā ca virāgā upekkhako ca vihāsiṁ, sato ca sampajāno sukhañca kāyena paṭisaṁvedesiṁ; yaṁ taṁ ariyā ācikkhanti: 'upekkhako satimā sukhavihārī'ti tatiyaṁ jhānaṁ upasampajja vihāsiṁ.

And with the fading away of rapture, I entered and remained in the third absorption, where I meditated with equanimity, mindful and aware, personally experiencing the bliss of which the noble ones declare, 'Equanimous and mindful, one meditates in bliss.'

Sukhassa ca pahānā dukkhassa ca pahānā pubbeva somanassadomanassānaṁ atthaṅgamā adukkhamasukhaṁ upekkhāsatipārisuddhiṁ catutthaṁ jhānaṁ upasampajja vihāsiṁ.

With the giving up of pleasure and pain, and the ending of former happiness and sadness, I entered and remained in the fourth absorption, without pleasure or pain, with pure equanimity and mindfulness.

So evaṁ samāhite citte parisuddhe pariyodāte anaṅgaṇe vigatūpakkilese mudubhūte kammaniye ṭhite āneñjappatte pubbenivāsānussatiñāṇāya cittaṁ abhininnāmesiṁ. So anekavihitaṁ pubbenivāsaṁ anussarāmi,

When my mind had become immersed in samādhi like this—purified, bright, flawless, rid of corruptions, pliable, workable, steady, and imperturbable—I extended it toward recollection of past lives. I recollected many kinds of past lives.

seyyathidaṁ—ekampi jātiṁ dvepi jātiyo tissopi jātiyo catassopi jātiyo pañcapi jātiyo dasapi jātiyo vīsampi jātiyo tiṁsampi jātiyo cattālīsampi jātiyo paññāsampi jātiyo jātisatampi jātisahassampi jātisatasahassampi anekepi saṁvaṭṭakappe anekepi vivaṭṭakappe anekepi saṁvaṭṭavivaṭṭakappe: 'amutrāsiṁ evaṁnāmo evaṅgotto evaṁvaṇṇo evamāhāro evaṁsukhadukkhappaṭisaṁvedī evamāyupariyanto, so tato cuto amutra udapādiṁ; tatrāpāsiṁ evaṁnāmo evaṅgotto evaṁvaṇṇo evamāhāro evaṁsukhadukkhappaṭisaṁvedī evamāyupariyanto, so tato cuto idhūpapanno'ti. Iti sākāraṁ sauddesaṁ anekavihitaṁ pubbenivāsaṁ anussarāmi.

That is: one, two, three, four, five, ten, twenty, thirty, forty, fifty, a hundred, a thousand, a hundred thousand rebirths; many eons of the world contracting, many eons of the world expanding, many eons of the world contracting and expanding. I remembered: 'There, I was named this, my clan was that, I looked like this, and that was my food. This was how I felt pleasure and pain, and that was how my life ended. When I passed away from that place I was reborn somewhere else. There, too, I was named this, my clan was that, I looked like this, and that was my food. This was how I felt pleasure and pain, and that was how my life ended. When I passed away from that place I was reborn here.' And so I recollected my many kinds of past lives, with features and details.

Ayaṁ kho me, brāhmaṇa, rattiyā paṭhame yāme paṭhamā vijjā adhigatā,

This was the first knowledge, which I achieved in the first watch of the night.

avijjā vihatā vijjā uppannā, tamo vihato āloko uppanno, yathā taṁ appamattassa ātāpino pahitattassa viharato.

Ignorance was destroyed and knowledge arose; darkness was destroyed and light arose, as happens for a meditator who is diligent, keen, and resolute.

So evaṁ samāhite citte parisuddhe pariyodāte anaṅgaṇe vigatūpakkilese mudubhūte kammaniye ṭhite āneñjappatte sattānaṁ cutūpapātañāṇāya cittaṁ abhininnāmesiṁ.

When my mind had become immersed in samādhi like this—purified, bright, flawless, rid of corruptions, pliable, workable, steady, and imperturbable—I extended it toward knowledge of the death and rebirth of sentient beings.

So dibbena cakkhunā visuddhena atikkantamānusakena satte passāmi cavamāne upapajjamāne hīne paṇīte suvaṇṇe dubbaṇṇe sugate duggate yathākammūpage satte pajānāmi: 'ime vata bhonto sattā kāyaduccaritena samannāgatā vacīduccaritena samannāgatā manoduccaritena samannāgatā ariyānaṁ upavādakā micchādiṭṭhikā micchādiṭṭhikammasamādānā; te kāyassa bhedā paraṁ maraṇā apāyaṁ duggatiṁ vinipātaṁ nirayaṁ upapannā. Ime vā pana bhonto sattā kāyasucaritena samannāgatā vacīsucaritena samannāgatā manosucaritena samannāgatā ariyānaṁ anupavādakā sammādiṭṭhikā sammādiṭṭhikammasamādānā; te kāyassa bhedā paraṁ maraṇā sugatiṁ saggaṁ lokaṁ upapannā'ti. Iti dibbena cakkhunā visuddhena atikkantamānusakena satte passāmi cavamāne upapajjamāne hīne paṇīte suvaṇṇe dubbaṇṇe sugate duggate yathākammūpage satte pajānāmi.

With clairvoyance that is purified and superhuman, I saw sentient beings passing away and being reborn—inferior and superior, beautiful and ugly, in a good place or a bad place. I understood how sentient beings are reborn according to their deeds: 'These dear beings did bad things by way of body, speech, and mind. They spoke ill of the noble ones; they had wrong view; and they chose to act out of that wrong view. When their body breaks up, after death, they're reborn in a place of loss, a bad place, the underworld, hell. These dear beings, however, did good things by way of body, speech, and mind. They never spoke ill of the noble ones; they had right view; and they chose to act out of that right view. When their body breaks up, after death, they're reborn in a good place, a heavenly realm.' And so, with clairvoyance that is purified and superhuman, I saw sentient beings passing away and being reborn—inferior and superior, beautiful and ugly, in a good place or a bad place. I understood how sentient beings are reborn according to their deeds.

Ayaṁ kho me, brāhmaṇa, rattiyā majjhime yāme dutiyā vijjā adhigatā,

This was the second knowledge, which I achieved in the middle watch of the night.

avijjā vihatā vijjā uppannā, tamo vihato āloko uppanno, yathā taṁ appamattassa ātāpino pahitattassa viharato.

Ignorance was destroyed and knowledge arose; darkness was destroyed and light arose, as happens for a meditator who is diligent, keen, and resolute.

So evaṁ samāhite citte parisuddhe pariyodāte anaṅgaṇe vigatūpakkilese mudubhūte kammaniye ṭhite āneñjappatte āsavānaṁ khayañāṇāya cittaṁ abhininnāmesiṁ.

When my mind had become immersed in samādhi like this—purified, bright, flawless, rid of corruptions, pliable, workable, steady, and imperturbable—I extended it toward knowledge of the ending of defilements.

So 'idaṁ dukkhan'ti yathābhūtaṁ abbhaññāsiṁ, 'ayaṁ dukkhasamudayo'ti yathābhūtaṁ abbhaññāsiṁ, 'ayaṁ dukkhanirodho'ti yathābhūtaṁ abbhaññāsiṁ, 'ayaṁ dukkhanirodhagāminī paṭipadā'ti yathābhūtaṁ abbhaññāsiṁ.

I truly understood: 'This is suffering' ... 'This is the origin of suffering' ... 'This is the cessation of suffering' ... 'This is the practice that leads to the cessation of suffering'.

'Ime āsavā'ti yathābhūtaṁ abbhaññāsiṁ, 'ayaṁ āsavasamudayo'ti yathābhūtaṁ abbhaññāsiṁ, 'ayaṁ āsavanirodho'ti yathābhūtaṁ abbhaññāsiṁ, 'ayaṁ āsavanirodhagāminī paṭipadā'ti yathābhūtaṁ abbhaññāsiṁ.

I truly understood: 'These are defilements' ... 'This is the origin of defilements' ... 'This is the cessation of defilements' ... 'This is the practice that leads to the cessation of defilements'.

Tassa me evaṁ jānato evaṁ passato kāmāsavāpi cittaṁ vimuccittha, bhavāsavāpi cittaṁ vimuccittha, avijjāsavāpi cittaṁ vimuccittha.

Knowing and seeing like this, my mind was freed from the defilements of sensuality, desire to be reborn, and ignorance.

Vimuttasmiṁ vimuttamiti ñāṇaṁ ahosi.

When it was freed, I knew it was freed.

'Khīṇā jāti, vusitaṁ brahmacariyaṁ, kataṁ karaṇīyaṁ, nāparaṁ itthattāyā'ti abbhaññāsiṁ.

I understood: 'Rebirth is ended; the spiritual journey has been completed; what had to be done has been done; there is no return to any state of existence.'

Ayaṁ kho me, brāhmaṇa, rattiyā pacchime yāme tatiyā vijjā adhigatā,

This was the third knowledge, which I achieved in the final watch of the night.

avijjā vihatā vijjā uppannā, tamo vihato āloko uppanno, yathā taṁ appamattassa ātāpino pahitattassa viharato.

Ignorance was destroyed and knowledge arose; darkness was destroyed and light arose, as happens for a meditator who is diligent, keen, and resolute.

Siyā kho pana te, brāhmaṇa, evamassa:

Brahmin, you might think:

'ajjāpi nūna samaṇo gotamo avītarāgo avītadoso avītamoho, tasmā araññavanapatthāni pantāni senāsanāni paṭisevatī'ti.

'Perhaps the Master Gotama is not free of greed, hate, and delusion even today, and that is why he still frequents remote lodgings in the wilderness and the forest.'

Na kho panetaṁ, brāhmaṇa, evaṁ daṭṭhabbaṁ.

But you should not see it like this.

Dve kho ahaṁ, brāhmaṇa, atthavase sampassamāno araññavanapatthāni pantāni senāsanāni paṭisevāmi—

I see two reasons to frequent remote lodgings in the wilderness and the forest.

attano ca diṭṭhadhammasukhavihāraṁ sampassamāno, pacchimañca janataṁ anukampamāno"ti.

I see a happy life for myself in the present, and I have compassion for future generations."

"Anukampitarūpā vatāyaṁ bhotā gotamena pacchimā janatā, yathā taṁ arahatā sammāsambuddhena.

"Indeed, Master Gotama has compassion for future generations, since he is a perfected one, a fully awakened Buddha.

Abhikkantaṁ, bho gotama. Abhikkantaṁ, bho gotama.

Excellent, Master Gotama! Excellent, Master Gotama!

Seyyathāpi, bho gotama, nikkujjitaṁ vā ukkujjeyya, paṭicchannaṁ vā vivareyya, mūḷhassa vā maggaṁ ācikkheyya, andhakāre vā telapajjotaṁ dhāreyya: 'cakkhumanto rūpāni dakkhantī'ti; evamevaṁ bhotā gotamena anekapariyāyena dhammo pakāsito.

As if he were righting the overturned, or revealing the hidden, or pointing out the path to the lost, or lighting a lamp in the dark so people with good eyes can see what's there, Master Gotama has made the teaching clear in many ways.

Esāhaṁ bhavantaṁ gotamaṁ saraṇaṁ gacchāmi dhammañca bhikkhusaṅghañca.

I go for refuge to Master Gotama, to the teaching, and to the mendicant Saṅgha.

Upāsakaṁ maṁ bhavaṁ gotamo dhāretu ajjatagge pāṇupetaṁ saraṇaṁ gatan"ti.

From this day forth, may Master Gotama remember me as a lay follower who has gone for refuge for life."

Bhayabheravasuttaṁ niṭṭhitaṁ catutthaṁ.

5 Anaṅganasutta:

Unblemished

Evaṁ me sutaṁ—

So I have heard.

ekaṁ samayaṁ bhagavā sāvatthiyaṁ viharati jetavane anāthapiṇḍikassa ārāme.

At one time the Buddha was staying near Sāvatthī in Jeta's Grove, Anāthapiṇḍika's monastery.

Tatra kho āyasmā sāriputto bhikkhū āmantesi:

There Sāriputta addressed the mendicants:

"āvuso bhikkhave"ti.

"Reverends, mendicants!"

"Āvuso"ti kho te bhikkhū āyasmato sāriputtassa paccassosuṁ.

"Reverend," they replied.

Āyasmā sāriputto etadavoca:

Sāriputta said this:

"Cattārome, āvuso, puggalā santo saṁvijjamānā lokasmiṁ.

"Mendicants, these four people are found in the world.

Katame cattāro?

What four?

Idhāvuso, ekacco puggalo sāṅgaṇova samāno 'atthi me ajjhattaṁ aṅganan'ti yathābhūtaṁ nappajānāti.

One person with a blemish doesn't truly understand: 'There is a blemish in me.'

Idha panāvuso, ekacco puggalo sāṅgaṇova samāno 'atthi me ajjhattaṁ aṅgaṇan'ti yathābhūtaṁ pajānāti.

But another person with a blemish does truly understand: 'There is a blemish in me.'

Idhāvuso, ekacco puggalo anaṅgaṇova samāno 'natthi me ajjhattaṁ aṅgaṇan'ti yathābhūtaṁ nappajānāti.

One person without a blemish doesn't truly understand: 'There is no blemish in me.'

Idha panāvuso, ekacco puggalo anaṅgaṇova samāno 'natthi me ajjhattaṁ aṅgaṇan'ti yathābhūtaṁ pajānāti.

But another person without a blemish does truly understand: 'There is no blemish in me.'

Tatrāvuso, yvāyaṁ puggalo sāṅgaṇova samāno 'atthi me ajjhattaṁ aṅgaṇan'ti yathābhūtaṁ nappajānāti, ayaṁ imesaṁ dvinnaṁ puggalānaṁ sāṅgaṇānaṁyeva sataṁ hīnapuriso akkhāyati.

In this case, of the two persons with a blemish, the one who doesn't understand is said to be worse,

Tatrāvuso, yvāyaṁ puggalo sāṅgaṇova samāno 'atthi me ajjhattaṁ aṅgaṇan'ti yathābhūtaṁ pajānāti, ayaṁ imesaṁ dvinnaṁ puggalānaṁ sāṅgaṇānaṁyeva sataṁ seṭṭhapuriso akkhāyati.

while the one who does understand is better.

Tatrāvuso, yvāyaṁ puggalo anaṅgaṇova samāno 'natthi me ajjhattaṁ aṅgaṇan'ti yathābhūtaṁ nappajānāti, ayaṁ imesaṁ dvinnaṁ puggalānaṁ anaṅgaṇānaṁyeva sataṁ hīnapuriso akkhāyati.

And of the two persons without a blemish, the one who doesn't understand is said to be worse,

Tatrāvuso, yvāyaṁ puggalo anaṅgaṇova samāno 'natthi me ajjhattaṁ aṅgaṇan'ti yathābhūtaṁ pajānāti, ayaṁ imesaṁ dvinnaṁ puggalānaṁ anaṅgaṇānaṁyeva sataṁ seṭṭhapuriso akkhāyatī'ti.

while the one who does understand is better."

Evaṁ vutte, āyasmā mahāmoggallāno āyasmantaṁ sāriputtaṁ etadavoca:

When he said this, Venerable Mahāmoggallāna said to him:

"Ko nu kho, āvuso sāriputta, hetu ko paccayo yenimesaṁ dvinnaṁ puggalānaṁ sāṅgaṇānaṁyeva sataṁ eko hīnapuriso akkhāyati, eko seṭṭhapuriso akkhāyati?

"What is the cause, Reverend Sāriputta, what is the reason why, of the two persons with a blemish, one is said to be worse and one better?

Ko panāvuso sāriputta, hetu ko paccayo yenimesaṁ dvinnaṁ puggalānaṁ anaṅgaṇānaṁyeva sataṁ eko hīnapuriso akkhāyati, eko seṭṭhapuriso akkhāyatī"ti?

And what is the cause, what is the reason why, of the two persons without a blemish, one is said to be worse and one better?"

"Tatrāvuso, yvāyaṁ puggalo sāṅgaṇova samāno 'atthi me ajjhattaṁ aṅgaṇan'ti yathābhūtaṁ nappajānāti, tassetaṁ pāṭikaṅkhaṁ—na chandaṁ janessati na vāyamissati na vīriyaṁ ārabhissati tassaṅgaṇassa pahānāya;

"Reverend, take the case of the person who has a blemish and does not understand it. You can expect that they won't generate enthusiasm, make an effort, or rouse up energy to give up that blemish.

so sarāgo sadoso samoho sāṅgaṇo saṅkiliṭṭhacitto kālaṁ karissati.

And they will die with greed, hate, and delusion, blemished, with a corrupted mind.

Seyyathāpi, āvuso, kaṁsapāti ābhatā āpaṇā vā kammārakulā vā rajena ca malena ca pariyonaddhā.

Suppose a bronze dish was brought from a shop or smithy covered with dirt or stains.

Tamenaṁ sāmikā na ceva paribhuñjeyyuṁ na ca pariyodapeyyuṁ, rajāpathe ca naṁ nikkhipeyyuṁ.

And the owners neither used it or had it cleaned, but kept it in a dirty place.

Evañhi sā, āvuso, kaṁsapāti aparena samayena saṅkiliṭṭhatarā assa malaggahitā"ti?

Over time, wouldn't that bronze dish get even dirtier and more stained?"

"Evamāvuso"ti.

"Yes, reverend."

"Evameva kho, āvuso, yvāyaṁ puggalo sāṅgaṇova samāno 'atthi me ajjhattaṁ aṅgaṇan'ti yathābhūtaṁ nappajānāti, tassetaṁ pāṭikaṅkhaṁ—na chandaṁ janessati na vāyamissati na vīriyaṁ ārabhissati tassaṅgaṇassa pahānāya;

"In the same way, take the case of the person who has a blemish and does not understand it. You can expect that ...

so sarāgo sadoso samoho saṅgaṇo saṅkiliṭṭhacitto kālaṃ karissati.

they will die with a corrupted mind.

Tatrāvuso, yvāyaṃ puggalo saṅgaṇova samāno 'atthi me ajjhattaṃ aṅganan'ti yathābhūtaṃ pajānāti, tassetaṃ pāṭikaṅkhaṃ—chandaṃ janessati vāyamissati vīriyaṃ ārabhissati tassaṅgaṇassa pahānāya;

Take the case of the person who has a blemish and does understand it. You can expect that they will generate enthusiasm, make an effort, and rouse up energy to give up that blemish.

so arāgo adoso amoho anaṅgaṇo asaṅkiliṭṭhacitto kālaṃ karissati.

And they will die without greed, hate, and delusion, unblemished, with an uncorrupted mind.

Seyyathāpi, āvuso, kaṃsapāti ābhatā āpaṇā vā kammārakulā vā rajena ca malena ca pariyonaddhā.

Suppose a bronze dish was brought from a shop or smithy covered with dirt or stains.

Tamenaṃ sāmikā paribhuñjeyyuñceva pariyodapeyyuñca, na ca naṃ rajāpathe nikkhipeyyuṃ.

But the owners used it and had it cleaned, and didn't keep it in a dirty place.

Evañhi sā, āvuso, kaṃsapāti aparena samayena parisuddhatarā assa pariyodātā"ti?

Over time, wouldn't that bronze dish get cleaner and brighter?"

"Evamāvuso"ti.

"Yes, reverend."

"Evameva kho, āvuso, yvāyaṃ puggalo saṅgaṇova samāno 'atthi me ajjhattaṃ aṅganan'ti yathābhūtaṃ pajānāti, tassetaṃ pāṭikaṅkhaṃ—chandaṃ janessati vāyamissati vīriyaṃ ārabhissati tassaṅgaṇassa pahānāya;

"In the same way, take the case of the person who has a blemish and does understand it. You can expect that ...

so arāgo adoso amoho anaṅgaṇo asaṅkiliṭṭhacitto kālaṃ karissati.

they will die with an uncorrupted mind.

Tatrāvuso, yvāyaṃ puggalo anaṅgaṇova samāno 'natthi me ajjhattaṃ aṅganan'ti yathābhūtaṃ nappajānāti, tassetaṃ pāṭikaṅkhaṃ—subhanimittaṃ manasi karissati, tassa subhanimittassa manasikārā rāgo cittaṁ anuddhaṁsessati;

Take the case of the person who doesn't have a blemish but does not understand it. You can expect that they will focus on the feature of beauty, and because of that, lust will infect their mind.

so sarāgo sadoso samoho sāṅgaṇo saṅkiliṭṭhacitto kālaṁ karissati.

And they will die with greed, hate, and delusion, blemished, with a corrupted mind.

Seyyathāpi, āvuso, kaṁsapāti ābhatā āpaṇā vā kammārakulā vā parisuddhā pariyodātā.

Suppose a bronze dish was brought from a shop or smithy clean and bright.

Tamenaṁ sāmikā na ceva paribhuñjeyyuṁ na ca pariyodapeyyuṁ, rajāpathe ca naṁ nikkhipeyyuṁ.

And the owners neither used it or had it cleaned, but kept it in a dirty place.

Evañhi sā, āvuso, kaṁsapāti aparena samayena saṅkiliṭṭhatarā assa malaggahitā"ti?

Over time, wouldn't that bronze dish get dirtier and more stained?"

"Evamāvuso"ti.

"Yes, reverend."

"Evameva kho, āvuso, yvāyaṁ puggalo anaṅgaṇova samāno 'natthi me ajjhattaṁ aṅgaṇan'ti yathābhūtaṁ nappajānāti, tassetaṁ pāṭikaṅkhaṁ—subhanimittaṁ manasi karissati, tassa subhanimittassa manasikārā rāgo cittaṁ anuddhaṁsessati;

"In the same way, take the case of the person who has no blemish and does not understand it. You can expect that ...

so sarāgo sadoso samoho sāṅgaṇo saṅkiliṭṭhacitto kālaṁ karissati.

they will die with a corrupted mind.

Tatrāvuso, yvāyaṁ puggalo anaṅgaṇova samāno 'natthi me ajjhattaṁ aṅgaṇan'ti yathābhūtaṁ pajānāti, tassetaṁ pāṭikaṅkhaṁ—subhanimittaṁ na manasi karissati, tassa subhanimittassa amanasikārā rāgo cittaṁ nānuddhaṁsessati;

Take the case of the person who doesn't have a blemish and does understand it. You can expect that they won't focus on the feature of beauty, and because of that, lust won't infect their mind.

so arāgo adoso amoho anaṅgaṇo asaṅkiliṭṭhacitto kālaṁ karissati.

And they will die without greed, hate, and delusion, unblemished, with an uncorrupted mind.

Seyyathāpi, āvuso, kaṁsapāti ābhatā āpaṇā vā kammārakulā vā parisuddhā pariyodātā.

Suppose a bronze dish was brought from a shop or smithy clean and bright.

Tamenaṁ sāmikā paribhuñjeyyuñceva pariyodapeyyuñca, na ca naṁ rajāpathe nikkhipeyyuṁ.

And the owners used it and had it cleaned, and didn't keep it in a dirty place.

Evañhi sā, āvuso, kaṁsapāti aparena samayena parisuddhatarā assa pariyodātā"ti?

Over time, wouldn't that bronze dish get cleaner and brighter?"

"Evamāvuso"ti.

"Yes, reverend."

"Evameva kho, āvuso, yvāyaṁ puggalo anaṅgaṇova samāno 'natthi me ajjhattaṁ aṅgaṇan'ti yathābhūtaṁ pajānāti, tassetaṁ pāṭikaṅkhaṁ—subhanimittaṁ na manasi karissati, tassa subhanimittassa amanasikārā rāgo cittaṁ nānuddhaṁsessati;

"In the same way, take the case of the person who doesn't have a blemish and does understand it. You can expect that …

so arāgo adoso amoho anaṅgaṇo asaṅkiliṭṭhacitto kālaṁ karissati.

they will die with an uncorrupted mind.

Ayaṁ kho, āvuso moggallāna, hetu ayaṁ paccayo yenimesaṁ dvinnaṁ puggalānaṁ sāṅgaṇānaṁyeva sataṁ eko hīnapuriso akkhāyati, eko seṭṭhapuriso akkhāyati.

This is the cause, this is the reason why, of the two persons with a blemish, one is said to be worse and one better.

Ayaṁ panāvuso moggallāna, hetu ayaṁ paccayo yenimesaṁ dvinnaṁ puggalānaṁ anaṅgaṇānaṁyeva sataṁ eko hīnapuriso akkhāyati, eko seṭṭhapuriso akkhāyatī"ti.

And this is the cause, this is the reason why, of the two persons without a blemish, one is said to be worse and one better."

"Aṅgaṇaṁ aṅgaṇanti, āvuso, vuccati.

"Reverend, the word 'blemish' is spoken of.

Kissa nu kho etaṁ, āvuso, adhivacanaṁ yadidaṁ aṅgaṇan"ti?

But what is 'blemish' a term for?"

"Pāpakānaṁ kho etaṁ, āvuso, akusalānaṁ icchāvacarānaṁ adhivacanaṁ, yadidaṁ aṅgaṇan"ti.

"Reverend, 'blemish' is a term for the spheres of bad, unskillful wishes.

"Ṭhānaṁ kho panetaṁ, āvuso, vijjati yaṁ idhekaccassa bhikkhuno evaṁ icchā uppajjeyya:

It's possible that some mendicant might wish:

'āpattiñca vata āpanno assaṁ, na ca maṁ bhikkhū jāneyyuṁ āpattiṁ āpanno'ti.

'If I commit an offense, I hope the mendicants don't find out!'

Ṭhānaṁ kho panetaṁ, āvuso, vijjati yaṁ taṁ bhikkhuṁ bhikkhū jāneyyuṁ:

But it's possible that the mendicants do find out that that mendicant

'āpattiṁ āpanno'ti.

has committed an offense.

'Jānanti maṁ bhikkhū āpattiṁ āpanno'ti—

Thinking, 'The mendicants have found out about my offense,'

iti so kupito hoti appatīto.

they get angry and bitter.

Yo ceva kho, āvuso, kopo yo ca appaccayo—

And that anger and that bitterness

ubhayametaṁ aṅgaṇaṁ.

are both blemishes.

Ṭhānaṁ kho panetaṁ, āvuso, vijjati yaṁ idhekaccassa bhikkhuno evaṁ icchā uppajjeyya:

It's possible that some mendicant might wish:

'āpattiñca vata āpanno assaṁ, anuraho maṁ bhikkhū codeyyuṁ, no saṅghamajjhe'ti.

'If I commit an offense, I hope the mendicants accuse me in private, not in the middle of the Saṅgha.'

Ṭhānaṁ kho panetaṁ, āvuso, vijjati yaṁ taṁ bhikkhuṁ bhikkhū saṅghamajjhe codeyyuṁ, no anuraho.

But it's possible that the mendicants do accuse that mendicant in the middle of the Saṅgha …

'Saṅghamajjhe maṁ bhikkhū codenti, no anuraho'ti—

iti so kupito hoti appatīto.

Yo ceva kho, āvuso, kopo yo ca appaccayo—

ubhayametaṁ aṅgaṇaṁ.

Ṭhānaṁ kho panetaṁ, āvuso, vijjati yaṁ idhekaccassa bhikkhuno evaṁ icchā uppajjeyya:

It's possible that some mendicant might wish:

'āpattiñca vata āpanno assaṁ, sappaṭipuggalo maṁ codeyya, no appaṭipuggalo'ti.

'If I commit an offense, I hope I'm accused by an equal, not by someone who is not an equal.'

Ṭhānaṁ kho panetaṁ, āvuso, vijjati yaṁ taṁ bhikkhuṁ appaṭipuggalo codeyya, no sappaṭipuggalo.

But it's possible that someone who is not an equal accuses that mendicant …

'Appaṭipuggalo maṁ codeti, no sappaṭipuggalo'ti—

iti so kupito hoti appatīto.

Yo ceva kho, āvuso, kopo yo ca appaccayo—

ubhayametaṁ aṅgaṇaṁ.

Ṭhānaṁ kho panetaṁ, āvuso, vijjati yaṁ idhekaccassa bhikkhuno evaṁ icchā uppajjeyya:

It's possible that some mendicant might wish:

'aho vata mameva satthā paṭipucchitvā paṭipucchitvā bhikkhūnaṁ dhammaṁ deseyya, na aññaṁ bhikkhuṁ satthā paṭipucchitvā paṭipucchitvā bhikkhūnaṁ dhammaṁ deseyyā'ti.

'Oh, I hope the Teacher will teach the mendicants by repeatedly questioning me alone, not some other mendicant.'

Ṭhānaṁ kho panetaṁ, āvuso, vijjati yaṁ aññaṁ bhikkhuṁ satthā paṭipucchitvā paṭipucchitvā bhikkhūnaṁ dhammaṁ deseyya, na taṁ bhikkhuṁ satthā paṭipucchitvā paṭipucchitvā bhikkhūnaṁ dhammaṁ deseyya.

But it's possible that the Teacher will teach the mendicants by repeatedly questioning some other mendicant …

'Aññaṁ bhikkhuṁ satthā paṭipucchitvā paṭipucchitvā bhikkhūnaṁ dhammaṁ deseti, na maṁ satthā paṭipucchitvā paṭipucchitvā bhikkhūnaṁ dhammaṁ desetī'ti—

iti so kupito hoti appatīto.

Yo ceva kho, āvuso, kopo yo ca appaccayo—

ubhayametaṁ aṅgaṇaṁ.

Ṭhānaṁ kho panetaṁ, āvuso, vijjati yaṁ idhekaccassa bhikkhuno evaṁ icchā uppajjeyya:

It's possible that some mendicant might wish:

'aho vata mameva bhikkhū purakkhatvā purakkhatvā gāmaṁ bhattāya paviseyyuṁ, na aññaṁ bhikkhuṁ bhikkhū purakkhatvā purakkhatvā gāmaṁ bhattāya paviseyyun'ti.

'Oh, I hope the mendicants will enter the village for the meal putting me at the very front, not some other mendicant.'

Ṭhānaṁ kho panetaṁ, āvuso, vijjati yaṁ aññaṁ bhikkhuṁ bhikkhū purakkhatvā purakkhatvā gāmaṁ bhattāya paviseyyuṁ, na taṁ bhikkhuṁ bhikkhū purakkhatvā purakkhatvā gāmaṁ bhattāya paviseyyuṁ.

But it's possible that the mendicants will enter the village for the meal putting some other mendicant at the very front ...

'Aññaṁ bhikkhuṁ bhikkhū purakkhatvā purakkhatvā gāmaṁ bhattāya pavisanti, na maṁ bhikkhū purakkhatvā purakkhatvā gāmaṁ bhattāya pavisantī'ti—

iti so kupito hoti appatīto.

Yo ceva kho, āvuso, kopo yo ca appaccayo—

ubhayametaṁ aṅgaṇaṁ.

Ṭhānaṁ kho panetaṁ, āvuso, vijjati yaṁ idhekaccassa bhikkhuno evaṁ icchā uppajjeyya:

It's possible that some mendicant might wish:

'aho vata ahameva labheyyaṁ bhattagge aggāsanaṁ aggodakaṁ aggapiṇḍaṁ, na añño bhikkhu labheyya bhattagge aggāsanaṁ aggodakaṁ aggapiṇḍan'ti.

'Oh, I hope that I alone get the best seat, the best drink, and the best almsfood in the refectory, not some other mendicant.'

Ṭhānaṁ kho panetaṁ, āvuso, vijjati yaṁ añño bhikkhu labheyya bhattagge aggāsanaṁ aggodakaṁ aggapiṇḍaṁ, na so bhikkhu labheyya bhattagge aggāsanaṁ aggodakaṁ aggapiṇḍaṁ.

But it's possible that some other mendicant gets the best seat, the best drink, and the best almsfood in the refectory ...

'Añño bhikkhu labhati bhattagge aggāsanaṁ aggodakaṁ aggapiṇḍaṁ, nāhaṁ labhāmi bhattagge aggāsanaṁ aggodakaṁ aggapiṇḍan'ti—

iti so kupito hoti appatīto.

Yo ceva kho, āvuso, kopo yo ca appaccayo—

ubhayametaṁ aṅgaṇaṁ.

Ṭhānaṁ kho panetaṁ, āvuso, vijjati yaṁ idhekaccassa bhikkhuno evaṁ icchā uppajjeyya:

It's possible that some mendicant might wish:

'aho vata ahameva bhattagge bhuttāvī anumodeyyaṁ, na añño bhikkhu bhattagge bhuttāvī anumodeyyā'ti.

'I hope that I alone give the verses of gratitude after eating in the refectory, not some other mendicant.'

Ṭhānaṁ kho panetaṁ, āvuso, vijjati yaṁ añño bhikkhu bhattagge bhuttāvī anumodeyya, na so bhikkhu bhattagge bhuttāvī anumodeyya.

But it's possible that some other mendicant gives the verses of gratitude after eating in the refectory …

'Añño bhikkhu bhattagge bhuttāvī anumodati, nāhaṁ bhattagge bhuttāvī anumodāmī'ti—

iti so kupito hoti appatīto.

Yo ceva kho, āvuso, kopo yo ca appaccayo—

ubhayametaṁ aṅgaṇaṁ.

Ṭhānaṁ kho panetaṁ, āvuso, vijjati yaṁ idhekaccassa bhikkhuno evaṁ icchā uppajjeyya:

It's possible that some mendicant might wish:

'aho vata ahameva ārāmagatānaṁ bhikkhūnaṁ dhammaṁ deseyyaṁ, na añño bhikkhu ārāmagatānaṁ bhikkhūnaṁ dhammaṁ deseyyā'ti.

'Oh, I hope that I might teach the Dhamma to the monks, nuns, laymen, and laywomen in the monastery, not some other mendicant.'

Ṭhānaṁ kho panetaṁ, āvuso, vijjati yaṁ añño bhikkhu ārāmagatānaṁ bhikkhūnaṁ dhammaṁ deseyya, na so bhikkhu ārāmagatānaṁ bhikkhūnaṁ dhammaṁ deseyya.

'Añño bhikkhu ārāmagatānaṁ bhikkhūnaṁ dhammaṁ deseti, nāhaṁ ārāmagatānaṁ bhikkhūnaṁ dhammaṁ desemī'ti—

iti so kupito hoti appatīto.

Yo ceva kho, āvuso, kopo yo ca appaccayo—

ubhayametaṁ aṅgaṇaṁ.

Ṭhānaṁ kho panetaṁ, āvuso, vijjati yaṁ idhekaccassa bhikkhuno evaṁ icchā uppajjeyya:

'aho vata ahameva ārāmagatānaṁ bhikkhunīnaṁ dhammaṁ deseyyaṁ ...pe...

upāsakānaṁ dhammaṁ deseyyaṁ ...pe...

upāsikānaṁ dhammaṁ deseyyaṁ, na añño bhikkhu ārāmagatānaṁ upāsikānaṁ dhammaṁ deseyyā'ti.

Ṭhānaṁ kho panetaṁ, āvuso, vijjati yaṁ añño bhikkhu ārāmagatānaṁ upāsikānaṁ dhammaṁ deseyya, na so bhikkhu ārāmagatānaṁ upāsikānaṁ dhammaṁ deseyya.

But it's possible that some other mendicant teaches the Dhamma ...

'Añño bhikkhu ārāmagatānaṁ upāsikānaṁ dhammaṁ deseti, nāhaṁ ārāmagatānaṁ upāsikānaṁ dhammaṁ desemī'ti—

iti so kupito hoti appatīto.

Yo ceva kho, āvuso, kopo yo ca appaccayo—

ubhayametaṁ aṅgaṇaṁ.

Ṭhānaṁ kho panetaṁ, āvuso, vijjati yaṁ idhekaccassa bhikkhuno evaṁ icchā uppajjeyya:

It's possible that some mendicant might wish:

'aho vata mameva bhikkhū sakkareyyuṁ garuṁ kareyyuṁ māneyyuṁ pūjeyyuṁ, na aññaṁ bhikkhuṁ bhikkhū sakkareyyuṁ garuṁ kareyyuṁ māneyyuṁ pūjeyyun'ti.

'Oh, I hope that the monks, nuns, laymen, and laywomen will honor, respect, revere, and venerate me alone, not some other mendicant.'

Ṭhānaṁ kho panetaṁ, āvuso, vijjati yaṁ aññaṁ bhikkhuṁ bhikkhū sakkareyyuṁ garuṁ kareyyuṁ māneyyuṁ pūjeyyuṁ, na taṁ bhikkhuṁ bhikkhū sakkareyyuṁ garuṁ kareyyuṁ māneyyuṁ pūjeyyuṁ.

'Aññaṁ bhikkhuṁ bhikkhū sakkaronti garuṁ karonti mānenti pūjenti, na maṁ bhikkhū sakkaronti garuṁ karonti mānenti pūjentī'ti—

iti so kupito hoti appatīto.

Yo ceva kho, āvuso, kopo yo ca appaccayo—

ubhayametaṁ aṅgaṇaṁ.

Ṭhānaṁ kho panetaṁ, āvuso, vijjati yaṁ idhekaccassa bhikkhuno evaṁ icchā uppajjeyya:

'aho vata mameva bhikkhuniyo …pe…

upāsakā …pe…

upāsikā sakkareyyuṁ garuṁ kareyyuṁ māneyyuṁ pūjeyyuṁ, na aññaṁ bhikkhuṁ upāsikā sakkareyyuṁ garuṁ kareyyuṁ māneyyuṁ pūjeyyun'ti.

Ṭhānaṁ kho panetaṁ, āvuso, vijjati yaṁ aññaṁ bhikkhuṁ upāsikā sakkareyyuṁ garuṁ kareyyuṁ māneyyuṁ pūjeyyuṁ, na taṁ bhikkhuṁ upāsikā sakkareyyuṁ garuṁ kareyyuṁ māneyyuṁ pūjeyyuṁ.

But it's possible that some other mendicant is honored, respected, revered, and venerated …

'Aññaṁ bhikkhuṁ upāsikā sakkaronti garuṁ karonti mānenti pūjenti, na maṁ upāsikā sakkaronti garuṁ karonti mānenti pūjentī'ti—

iti so kupito hoti appatīto.

Yo ceva kho, āvuso, kopo yo ca appaccayo—

ubhayametaṁ aṅgaṇaṁ.

Ṭhānaṁ kho panetaṁ, āvuso, vijjati yaṁ idhekaccassa bhikkhuno evaṁ icchā uppajjeyya:

It's possible that some mendicant might wish:

'aho vata ahameva lābhī assaṁ paṇītānaṁ cīvarānaṁ, na añño bhikkhu lābhī assa paṇītānaṁ cīvarānan'ti.

'I hope I get the nicest robes, almsfood, lodgings, and medicines and supplies for the sick, not some other mendicant.'

Ṭhānaṁ kho panetaṁ, āvuso, vijjati yaṁ añño bhikkhu lābhī assa paṇītānaṁ cīvarānaṁ, na so bhikkhu lābhī assa paṇītānaṁ cīvarānaṁ.

But it's possible that some other mendicant gets the nicest robes, almsfood, lodgings, and medicines and supplies for the sick …

'Añño bhikkhu lābhī paṇītānaṁ cīvarānaṁ, nāhaṁ lābhī paṇītānaṁ cīvarānan'ti—

iti so kupito hoti appatīto.

Yo ceva kho, āvuso, kopo yo ca appaccayo—

ubhayametaṁ aṅgaṇaṁ.

Ṭhānaṃ kho panetaṃ, āvuso, vijjati yaṃ idhekaccassa bhikkhuno evaṃ icchā uppajjeyya:

'aho vata ahameva lābhī assaṃ paṇītānaṃ piṇḍapātānaṃ …pe…

paṇītānaṃ senāsanānaṃ …pe…

paṇītānaṃ gilānappaccayabhesajjaparikkhārānaṃ, na añño bhikkhu lābhī assa paṇītānaṃ gilānappaccayabhesajjaparikkhārānan'ti.

Ṭhānaṃ kho panetaṃ, āvuso, vijjati yaṃ añño bhikkhu lābhī assa paṇītānaṃ gilānappaccayabhesajjaparikkhārānaṃ, na so bhikkhu lābhī assa paṇītānaṃ gilānappaccayabhesajjaparikkhārānaṃ.

'Añño bhikkhu lābhī paṇītānaṃ gilānappaccayabhesajjaparikkhārānaṃ, nāhaṃ lābhī paṇītānaṃ gilānappaccayabhesajjaparikkhārānan'ti—

Thinking, 'Some other mendicant has got the nicest robes, almsfood, lodgings, and medicines and supplies for the sick',

iti so kupito hoti appatīto.

they get angry and bitter.

Yo ceva kho, āvuso, kopo yo ca appaccayo—

And that anger and that bitterness

ubhayametaṃ aṅgaṇaṃ.

are both blemishes.

Imesaṃ kho etaṃ, āvuso, pāpakānaṃ akusalānaṃ icchāvacarānaṃ adhivacanaṃ, yadidaṃ aṅgaṇanti.

'Blemish' is a term for these spheres of bad, unskillful wishes.

Yassa kassaci, āvuso, bhikkhuno ime pāpakā akusalā icchāvacarā appahīnā dissanti ceva sūyanti ca, kiñcāpi so hoti āraññiko pantasenāsano piṇḍapātiko sapadānacārī paṃsukūliko lūkhacīvaradharo, atha kho naṃ sabrahmacārī na ceva sakkaronti na garuṃ karonti na mānenti na pūjenti.

Suppose these spheres of bad, unskillful wishes are seen and heard to be not given up by a mendicant. Even though they dwell in the wilderness, in remote lodgings, eat only almsfood, wander indiscriminately for almsfood, wear rag robes, and wear shabby robes, their spiritual companions don't honor, respect, revere, and venerate them.

Taṃ kissa hetu?

Why is that?

Te hi tassa āyasmato pāpakā akusalā icchāvacarā appahīnā dissanti ceva sūyanti ca.

It's because these spheres of bad, unskillful wishes are seen and heard to be not given up by that venerable.

Seyyathāpi, āvuso, kaṁsapāti ābhatā āpaṇā vā kammārakulā vā parisuddhā pariyodātā.

Suppose a bronze dish was brought from a shop or smithy clean and bright.

Tamenaṁ sāmikā ahikuṇapaṁ vā kukkurakuṇapaṁ vā manussakuṇapaṁ vā racayitvā aññissā kaṁsapātiyā paṭikujjitvā antarāpaṇaṁ paṭipajjeyyuṁ.

Then the owners were to prepare it with the carcass of a snake, a dog, or a human, cover it with a bronze lid, and parade it through the market-place.

Tamenaṁ jano disvā evaṁ vadeyya:

When people saw it they'd say:

'ambho, kimevidaṁ harīyati jaññajaññaṁ viyā'ti?

'My good man, what is it that you're carrying like a precious treasure?'

Tamenaṁ uṭṭhahitvā apāpuritvā olokeyya.

So they'd open up the lid for people to look inside.

Tassa sahadassanena amanāpatā ca saṇṭhaheyya, pāṭikulyatā ca saṇṭhaheyya, jegucchatā ca saṇṭhaheyya;

But as soon as they saw it they were filled with loathing, revulsion, and disgust.

jighacchitānampi na bhottukamyatā assa, pageva suhitānaṁ.

Not even those who were hungry wanted to eat it, let alone those who had eaten.

Evameva kho, āvuso, yassa kassaci bhikkhuno ime pāpakā akusalā icchāvacarā appahīnā dissanti ceva sūyanti ca, kiñcāpi so hoti āraññiko pantasenāsano piṇḍapātiko sapadānacārī paṁsukūliko lūkhacīvaradharo, atha kho naṁ sabrahmacārī na ceva sakkaronti na garuṁ karonti na mānenti na pūjenti.

In the same way, when these spheres of bad, unskillful wishes are seen and heard to be not given up by a mendicant ... their spiritual companions don't honor, respect, revere, and venerate them.

Taṁ kissa hetu?

Why is that?

Te hi tassa āyasmato pāpakā akusalā icchāvacarā appahīnā dissanti ceva sūyanti ca.

It's because these spheres of bad, unskillful wishes are seen and heard to be not given up by that venerable.

Yassa kassaci, āvuso, bhikkhuno ime pāpakā akusalā icchāvacarā pahīnā dissanti ceva sūyanti ca, kiñcāpi so hoti gāmantavihārī nemantaniko gahapaticīvaradharo, atha kho nam sabrahmacārī sakkaronti garum karonti mānenti pūjenti.

Suppose these spheres of bad, unskillful wishes are seen and heard to be given up by a mendicant. Even though they dwell within a village, accept invitations to a meal, and wear robes offered by householders, their spiritual companions honor, respect, revere, and venerate them.

Tam kissa hetu?

Why is that?

Te hi tassa āyasmato pāpakā akusalā icchāvacarā pahīnā dissanti ceva sūyanti ca.

It's because these spheres of bad, unskillful wishes are seen and heard to be given up by that venerable.

Seyyathāpi, āvuso, kamsapāti ābhatā āpaṇā vā kammārakulā vā parisuddhā pariyodātā.

Suppose a bronze dish was brought from a shop or smithy clean and bright.

Tamenam sāmikā sālīnam odanam vicitakāḷakam anekasūpam anekabyañjanam racayitvā aññissā kamsapātiyā paṭikujjitvā antarāpaṇam paṭipajjeyyum.

Then the owners were to prepare it with boiled fine rice with the dark grains picked out and served with many soups and sauces, cover it with a bronze lid, and parade it through the market-place.

Tamenam jano disvā evam vadeyya:

When people saw it they'd say:

'ambho, kimevidam harīyati jaññajaññam viyā'ti?

'My good man, what is it that you're carrying like a precious treasure?'

Tamenam uṭṭhahitvā apāpuritvā olokeyya.

So they'd open up the lid for people to look inside.

Tassa saha dassanena manāpatā ca saṇṭhaheyya, appaṭikulyatā ca saṇṭhaheyya, ajegucchatā ca saṇṭhaheyya;

And as soon as they saw it they were filled with liking, attraction, and relish.

suhitānampi bhottukamyatā assa, pageva jighacchitānaṁ.

Even those who had eaten wanted to eat it, let alone those who were hungry.

Evameva kho, āvuso, yassa kassaci bhikkhuno ime pāpakā akusalā icchāvacarā pahīnā dissanti ceva sūyanti ca, kiñcāpi so hoti gāmantavihārī nemantaniko gahapaticīvaradharo, atha kho naṁ sabrahmacārī sakkaronti garuṁ karonti mānenti pūjenti.

In the same way, when these spheres of bad, unskillful wishes are seen and heard to be given up by a mendicant … their spiritual companions honor, respect, revere, and venerate them.

Taṁ kissa hetu?

Why is that?

Te hi tassa āyasmato pāpakā akusalā icchāvacarā pahīnā dissanti ceva sūyanti cā"ti.

It's because these spheres of bad, unskillful wishes are seen and heard to be given up by that venerable."

Evaṁ vutte, āyasmā mahāmoggallāno āyasmantaṁ sāriputtaṁ etadavoca:

When he said this, Venerable Mahāmoggallāna said to him,

"upamā maṁ, āvuso sāriputta, paṭibhātī"ti.

"Reverend Sāriputta, a simile springs to mind."

"Paṭibhātu taṁ, āvuso moggallānā"ti.

"Then speak as you feel inspired," said Sāriputta.

"Ekamidāhaṁ, āvuso, samayaṁ rājagahe viharāmi giribbaje.

"Reverend, at one time I was staying right here in Rājagaha, the Mountainfold.

Atha khvāhaṁ, āvuso, pubbaṇhasamayaṁ nivāsetvā pattacīvaramādāya rājagahaṁ piṇḍāya pāvisiṁ.

Then I robed up in the morning and, taking my bowl and robe, entered Rājagaha for alms.

Tena kho pana samayena samīti yānakāraputto rathassa nemiṁ tacchati.

Now at that time Samīti the cartwright was planing the rim of a chariot wheel.

Tamenaṁ paṇḍuputto ājīvako purāṇayānakāraputto paccupaṭṭhito hoti.

The Ājīvaka ascetic Paṇḍuputta, who used to be a cartwright, was standing by,

Atha kho, āvuso, paṇḍuputtassa ājīvakassa purāṇayānakāraputtassa evaṁ cetaso parivitakko udapādi:

and this thought came to his mind:

'aho vatāyaṁ samīti yānakāraputto imissā nemiyā imañca vaṅkaṁ imañca jimhaṁ imañca dosaṁ taccheyya, evāyaṁ nemi apagatavaṅkā apagatajimhā apagatadosā suddhā assa sāre patiṭṭhitā'ti.

'Oh, I hope Samīti the cartwright planes out the crooks, bends, and flaws in this rim. Then the rim will be rid of crooks, bends, and flaws, and consist purely of the essential core.'

Yathā yathā kho, āvuso, paṇḍuputtassa ājīvakassa purāṇayānakāraputtassa cetaso parivitakko hoti tathā tathā samīti yānakāraputto tassā nemiyā tañca vaṅkaṁ tañca jimhaṁ tañca dosaṁ tacchati.

And Samīti planed out the flaws in the rim just as Paṇḍuputta thought.

Atha kho, āvuso, paṇḍuputto ājīvako purāṇayānakāraputto attamano attamanavācaṁ nicchāresi:

Then Paṇḍuputta expressed his gladness:

'hadayā hadayaṁ maññe aññāya tacchatī'ti.

'He planes like he knows my heart with his heart!'

Evameva kho, āvuso, ye te puggalā assaddhā, jīvikatthā na saddhā agārasmā anagāriyaṁ pabbajitā, saṭhā māyāvino ketabino uddhatā unnaḷā capalā mukharā vikiṇṇavācā, indriyesu aguttadvārā, bhojane amattaññuno, jāgariyaṁ ananuyuttā, sāmaññe anapekkhavanto, sikkhāya na tibbagāravā, bāhulikā sāthalikā, okkamane pubbaṅgamā, paviveke nikkhittadhurā, kusītā hīnavīriyā muṭṭhassatī asampajānā asamāhitā vibbhantacittā duppaññā eḷamūgā, tesaṁ āyasmā sāriputto iminā dhammapariyāyena hadayā hadayaṁ maññe aññāya tacchati.

In the same way, there are those faithless people who went forth from the lay life to homelessness not out of faith but to earn a livelihood. They're devious, deceitful, and sneaky. They're restless, insolent, fickle, scurrilous, and loose-tongued. They do not guard their sense doors or eat in moderation, and they are not dedicated to wakefulness. They don't care about the ascetic life, and don't keenly respect the training. They're indulgent and slack, leaders in backsliding, neglecting seclusion, lazy, and lacking energy. They're unmindful, lacking situational awareness and immersion, with straying minds, witless and stupid. Venerable Sāriputta planes their faults with this exposition of the teaching as if he knows my heart with his heart!

Ye pana te kulaputtā saddhā agārasmā anagāriyaṁ pabbajitā, asaṭhā amāyāvino aketabino anuddhatā anunnaḷā acapalā amukharā avikiṇṇavācā, indriyesu guttadvārā, bhojane mattaññuno, jāgariyaṁ anuyuttā, sāmaññe apekkhavanto, sikkhāya tibbagāravā, na bāhulikā na sāthalikā, okkamane nikkhittadhurā, paviveke pubbaṅgamā, āraddhavīriyā pahitattā upaṭṭhitassatī sampajānā samāhitā ekaggacittā paññavanto aneḷamugā, te āyasmato sāriputtassa imaṁ dhammapariyāyaṁ sutvā pivanti maññe, ghasanti maññe vacasā ceva manasā ca:

But there are those gentlemen who went forth from the lay life to homelessness out of faith. They're not devious, deceitful, and sneaky. They're not restless, insolent, fickle, scurrilous, and loose-tongued. They guard their sense doors and eat in moderation, and they are dedicated to wakefulness. They care about the ascetic life, and keenly respect the training. They're not indulgent or slack, nor are they leaders in backsliding, neglecting seclusion. They're energetic and determined. They're mindful, with situational awareness, immersion, and unified minds; wise, not stupid. Hearing this exposition of the teaching from Venerable Sāriputta, they drink it up and devour it, as it were. And in speech and thought they say:

'sādhu vata, bho, sabrahmacārī akusalā vuṭṭhāpetvā kusale patiṭṭhāpetī'ti.

'It's good, sirs, that he draws his spiritual companions away from the unskillful and establishes them in the skillful.'

Seyyathāpi, āvuso, itthī vā puriso vā daharo yuvā maṇḍanakajātiko sīsaṁnhāto uppalamālaṁ vā vassikamālaṁ vā atimuttakamālaṁ vā labhitvā ubhohi hatthehi paṭiggahetvā uttamaṅge sirasmiṁ patiṭṭhapeyya;

Suppose there was a woman or man who was young, youthful, and fond of adornments, and had bathed their head. After getting a garland of lotuses, jasmine, or liana flowers, they would take them in both hands and place them on the crown of the head.

evameva kho, āvuso, ye te kulaputtā saddhā agārasmā anagāriyaṁ pabbajitā, asaṭhā amāyāvino aketabino anuddhatā anunnaḷā acapalā amukharā avikiṇṇavācā, indriyesu guttadvārā, bhojane mattaññuno, jāgariyaṁ anuyuttā, sāmaññe apekkhavanto, sikkhāya tibbagāravā, na bāhulikā na sāthalikā, okkamane nikkhittadhurā, pavivekē pubbaṅgamā, āraddhavīriyā pahitattā upaṭṭhitassatī sampajānā samāhitā ekaggacittā paññavanto aneḷamūgā, te āyasmato sāriputtassa imaṁ dhammapariyāyaṁ sutvā pivanti maññe, ghasanti maññe vacasā ceva manasā ca:

In the same way, those gentlemen who went forth from the lay life to homelessness out of faith … say:

'sādhu vata, bho, sabrahmacārī akusalā vuṭṭhāpetvā kusale patiṭṭhāpetī'"ti.

'It's good, sirs, that he draws his spiritual companions away from the unskillful and establishes them in the skillful.'"

Itiha te ubho mahānāgā aññamaññassa subhāsitaṁ samanumodiṁsūti.

And so these two spiritual giants agreed with each others' fine words.

Anaṅgaṇasuttaṁ niṭṭhitaṁ pañcamaṁ.

6 Akankheyyasutta:

One Might Wish

Evaṁ me sutaṁ—

So I have heard.

ekaṁ samayaṁ bhagavā sāvatthiyaṁ viharati jetavane anāthapiṇḍikassa ārāme.

At one time the Buddha was staying near Sāvatthī in Jeta's Grove, Anāthapiṇḍika's monastery.

Tatra kho bhagavā bhikkhū āmantesi:

There the Buddha addressed the mendicants,

"bhikkhavo"ti.

"Mendicants!"

"Bhadante"ti te bhikkhū bhagavato paccassosuṁ.

"Venerable sir," they replied.

Bhagavā etadavoca:

The Buddha said this:

"Sampannasīlā, bhikkhave, viharatha sampannapātimokkhā; pātimokkhasaṁvarasaṁvutā viharatha ācāragocarasampannā aṇumattesu vajjesu bhayadassāvino; samādāya sikkhatha sikkhāpadesu.

"Mendicants, live by the ethical precepts and the monastic code. Live restrained in the monastic code, conducting yourselves well and seeking alms in suitable places. Seeing danger in the slightest fault, keep the rules you've undertaken.

Ākaṅkheyya ce, bhikkhave, bhikkhu: 'sabrahmacārīnaṁ piyo ca assaṁ manāpo ca garu ca bhāvanīyo cā'ti, sīlesvevassa paripūrakārī ajjhattaṁ cetosamathamanuyutto anirākatajjhāno vipassanāya samannāgato brūhetā suññāgārānaṁ.

A mendicant might wish: 'May I be liked and approved by my spiritual companions, respected and admired.' So let them fulfill their precepts, be committed to inner serenity of the heart, not neglect absorption, be endowed with discernment, and frequent empty huts.

Ākaṅkheyya ce, bhikkhave, bhikkhu: 'lābhī assaṁ cīvarapiṇḍapātasenāsanagilānappaccayabhesajjaparikkhārānan'ti, sīlesvevassa paripūrakārī ajjhattaṁ cetosamathamanuyutto anirākatajjhāno vipassanāya samannāgato brūhetā suññāgārānaṁ.

A mendicant might wish: 'May I receive robes, almsfood, lodgings, and medicines and supplies for the sick.' So let them fulfill their precepts, be committed to inner serenity of the heart, not neglect absorption, be endowed with discernment, and frequent empty huts.

Ākaṅkheyya ce, bhikkhave, bhikkhu: 'yesāhaṁ cīvarapiṇḍapātasenāsanagilānappaccayabhesajjaparikkhāraṁ paribhuñjāmi tesaṁ te kārā mahapphalā assu mahānisaṁsā'ti, sīlesvevassa paripūrakārī ajjhattaṁ cetosamathamanuyutto anirākatajjhāno vipassanāya samannāgato brūhetā suññāgārānaṁ.

A mendicant might wish: 'May the services of those whose robes, almsfood, lodgings, and medicines and supplies for the sick I enjoy be very fruitful and beneficial for them.' So let them fulfill their precepts ...

Ākaṅkheyya ce, bhikkhave, bhikkhu: 'ye maṁ ñātī sālohitā petā kālaṅkatā pasannacittā anussaranti tesaṁ taṁ mahapphalaṁ assa mahānisaṁsan'ti, sīlesvevassa paripūrakārī ajjhattaṁ cetosamathamanuyutto anirākatajjhāno vipassanāya samannāgato brūhetā suññāgārānaṁ.

A mendicant might wish: 'When deceased family and relatives who have passed away recollect me with a confident mind, may this be very fruitful and beneficial for them.' So let them fulfill their precepts ...

Ākaṅkheyya ce, bhikkhave, bhikkhu: 'aratiratisaho assaṁ, na ca maṁ arati saheyya, uppannaṁ aratiṁ abhibhuyya abhibhuyya vihareyyan'ti, sīlesvevassa paripūrakārī ...pe... brūhetā suññāgārānaṁ.

A mendicant might wish: 'May I prevail over desire and discontent, and may desire and discontent not prevail over me. May I live having mastered desire and discontent whenever they arose.' So let them fulfill their precepts ...

Ākaṅkheyya ce, bhikkhave, bhikkhu: 'bhayabheravasaho assaṁ, na ca maṁ bhayabheravaṁ saheyya, uppannaṁ bhayabheravaṁ abhibhuyya abhibhuyya vihareyyan'ti, sīlesvevassa paripūrakārī ...pe... brūhetā suññāgārānaṁ.

A mendicant might wish: 'May I prevail over fear and dread, and may fear and dread not prevail over me. May I live having mastered fear and dread whenever they arose.' So let them fulfill their precepts ...

Ākaṅkheyya ce, bhikkhave, bhikkhu: 'catunnaṁ jhānānaṁ ābhicetasikānaṁ diṭṭhadhammasukhavihārānaṁ nikāmalābhī assaṁ akicchalābhī akasiralābhī'ti, sīlesvevassa paripūrakārī ...pe... brūhetā suññāgārānaṁ.

A mendicant might wish: 'May I get the four absorptions—blissful meditations in the present life that belong to the higher mind—when I want, without trouble or difficulty.' So let them fulfill their precepts ...

Ākaṅkheyya ce, bhikkhave, bhikkhu: 'ye te santā vimokkhā atikkamma rūpe āruppā, te kāyena phusitvā vihareyyan'ti, sīlesvevassa paripūrakārī ...pe...

brūhetā suññāgārānaṁ.

A mendicant might wish: 'May I have direct meditative experience of the peaceful liberations that are formless, transcending form.' So let them fulfill their precepts …

Ākaṅkheyya ce, bhikkhave, bhikkhu: 'tiṇṇaṁ saṁyojanānaṁ parikkhayā sotāpanno assaṁ avinipātadhammo niyato sambodhiparāyaṇo'ti, sīlesvevassa paripūrakārī …pe… brūhetā suññāgārānaṁ.

A mendicant might wish: 'May I, with the ending of three fetters, become a stream-enterer, not liable to be reborn in the underworld, bound for awakening.' So let them fulfill their precepts …

Ākaṅkheyya ce, bhikkhave, bhikkhu: 'tiṇṇaṁ saṁyojanānaṁ parikkhayā rāgadosamohānaṁ tanuttā sakadāgāmī assaṁ sakideva imaṁ lokaṁ āgantvā dukkhassantaṁ kareyyan'ti, sīlesvevassa paripūrakārī …pe… brūhetā suññāgārānaṁ.

A mendicant might wish: 'May I, with the ending of three fetters, and the weakening of greed, hate, and delusion, become a once-returner, coming back to this world once only, then making an end of suffering.' So let them fulfill their precepts …

Ākaṅkheyya ce, bhikkhave, bhikkhu: 'pañcannaṁ orambhāgiyānaṁ saṁyojanānaṁ parikkhayā opapātiko assaṁ tattha parinibbāyī anāvattidhammo tasmā lokā'ti, sīlesvevassa paripūrakārī …pe… brūhetā suññāgārānaṁ.

A mendicant might wish: 'May I, with the ending of the five lower fetters, be reborn spontaneously and become extinguished there, not liable to return from that world.' So let them fulfill their precepts …

Ākaṅkheyya ce, bhikkhave, bhikkhu: 'anekavihitaṁ iddhividhaṁ paccanubhaveyyaṁ—ekopi hutvā bahudhā assaṁ, bahudhāpi hutvā eko assaṁ; āvibhāvaṁ tirobhāvaṁ; tirokuṭṭaṁ tiropākāraṁ tiropabbataṁ asajjamāno gaccheyyaṁ, seyyathāpi ākāse; pathaviyāpi ummujjanimujjaṁ kareyyaṁ, seyyathāpi udake; udakepi abhijjamāne gaccheyyaṁ, seyyathāpi pathaviyaṁ; ākāsepi pallaṅkena kameyyaṁ, seyyathāpi pakkhī sakuṇo; imepi candimasūriye evaṁmahiddhike evaṁmahānubhāve pāṇinā parāmaseyyaṁ parimajjeyyaṁ; yāva brahmalokāpi kāyena vasaṁ vatteyyan'ti, sīlesvevassa paripūrakārī …pe… brūhetā suññāgārānaṁ.

A mendicant might wish: 'May I wield the many kinds of psychic power: multiplying myself and becoming one again; appearing and disappearing; going unimpeded through a wall, a rampart, or a mountain as if through space; diving in and out of the earth as if it were water; walking on water as if it were earth; flying cross-legged through the sky like a bird; touching and stroking with my hand the sun and moon, so mighty and powerful; controlling the body as far as the Brahmā realm.' So let them fulfill their precepts …

Ākaṅkheyya ce, bhikkhave, bhikkhu: 'dibbāya sotadhātuyā visuddhāya atikkantamānusikāya ubho sadde suṇeyyaṁ—dibbe ca mānuse ca ye dūre santike cā'ti, sīlesvevassa paripūrakārī ...pe... brūhetā suññāgārānaṁ.

A mendicant might wish: 'With clairaudience that is purified and superhuman, may I hear both kinds of sounds, human and divine, whether near or far.' So let them fulfill their precepts ...

Ākaṅkheyya ce, bhikkhave, bhikkhu: 'parasattānaṁ parapuggalānaṁ cetasā ceto paricca pajāneyyaṁ—

A mendicant might wish: 'May I understand the minds of other beings and individuals, having comprehended them with my mind.

sarāgaṁ vā cittaṁ sarāgaṁ cittanti pajāneyyaṁ,

May I understand mind with greed as "mind with greed",

vītarāgaṁ vā cittaṁ vītarāgaṁ cittanti pajāneyyaṁ;

and mind without greed as "mind without greed";

sadosaṁ vā cittaṁ sadosaṁ cittanti pajāneyyaṁ,

mind with hate as "mind with hate",

vītadosaṁ vā cittaṁ vītadosaṁ cittanti pajāneyyaṁ;

and mind without hate as "mind without hate";

samohaṁ vā cittaṁ samohaṁ cittanti pajāneyyaṁ,

mind with delusion as "mind with delusion",

vītamohaṁ vā cittaṁ vītamohaṁ cittanti pajāneyyaṁ;

and mind without delusion as "mind without delusion";

saṅkhittaṁ vā cittaṁ saṅkhittaṁ cittanti pajāneyyaṁ,

constricted mind as "constricted mind",

vikkhittaṁ vā cittaṁ vikkhittaṁ cittanti pajāneyyaṁ;

and scattered mind as "scattered mind";

mahaggataṁ vā cittaṁ mahaggataṁ cittanti pajāneyyaṁ,

expansive mind as "expansive mind",

amahaggataṁ vā cittaṁ amahaggataṁ cittanti pajāneyyaṁ;

and unexpansive mind as "unexpansive mind";

sauttaraṁ vā cittaṁ sauttaraṁ cittanti pajāneyyaṁ,

mind that is not supreme as "mind that is not supreme",

anuttaraṁ vā cittaṁ anuttaraṁ cittanti pajāneyyaṁ;

and mind that is supreme as "mind that is supreme";

samāhitaṁ vā cittaṁ samāhitaṁ cittanti pajāneyyaṁ,

mind immersed in samādhi as "mind immersed in samādhi",

asamāhitaṁ vā cittaṁ asamāhitaṁ cittanti pajāneyyaṁ;

and mind not immersed in samādhi as "mind not immersed in samādhi";

vimuttaṁ vā cittaṁ vimuttaṁ cittanti pajāneyyaṁ,

freed mind as "freed mind",

avimuttaṁ vā cittaṁ avimuttaṁ cittanti pajāneyyan'ti,

and unfreed mind as "unfreed mind".'

sīlesvevassa paripūrakārī …pe… brūhetā suññāgārānaṁ.

So let them fulfill their precepts …

Ākaṅkheyya ce, bhikkhave, bhikkhu: 'anekavihitaṁ pubbenivāsaṁ anussareyyaṁ, seyyathidaṁ—ekampi jātiṁ dvepi jātiyo tissopi jātiyo catassopi jātiyo pañcapi jātiyo dasapi jātiyo vīsampi jātiyo tiṁsampi jātiyo cattālīsampi jātiyo paññāsampi jātiyo jātisatampi jātisahassampi jāti satasahassampi anekepi saṁvaṭṭakappe anekepi vivaṭṭakappe anekepi saṁvaṭṭavivaṭṭakappe—amutrāsiṁ evaṁnāmo evaṅgotto evaṁvaṇṇo evamāhāro evaṁsukhadukkhappaṭisaṁvedī evamāyupariyanto, so tato cuto amutra udapādiṁ; tatrāpāsiṁ evaṁnāmo evaṅgotto evaṁvaṇṇo evamāhāro evaṁsukhadukkhappaṭisaṁvedī evamāyupariyanto, so tato cuto idhūpapannoti. Iti sākāraṁ sauddesaṁ anekavihitaṁ pubbenivāsaṁ anussareyyan'ti,

A mendicant might wish: 'May I recollect many kinds of past lives. That is: one, two, three, four, five, ten, twenty, thirty, forty, fifty, a hundred, a thousand, a hundred thousand rebirths; many eons of the world contracting, many eons of the world expanding, many eons of the world contracting and expanding. May I remember: "There, I was named this, my clan was that, I looked like this, and that was my food. This was how I felt pleasure and pain, and that was how my life ended. When I passed away from that place I was reborn somewhere else. There, too, I was named this, my clan was that, I looked like this, and that was my food. This was how I felt pleasure and pain, and that was how my life ended. When I passed away from that place I was reborn here." May I thus recollect my many kinds of past lives, with features and details.'

sīlesvevassa paripūrakārī ...pe... brūhetā suññāgārānaṁ.

So let them fulfill their precepts ...

Ākaṅkheyya ce, bhikkhave, bhikkhu: 'dibbena cakkhunā visuddhena atikkantamānusakena satte passeyyaṁ cavamāne upapajjamāne hīne paṇīte suvaṇṇe dubbaṇṇe sugate duggate yathākammūpage satte pajāneyyaṁ—ime vata bhonto sattā kāyaduccaritena samannāgatā vacīduccaritena samannāgatā manoduccaritena samannāgatā ariyānaṁ upavādakā micchādiṭṭhikā micchādiṭṭhikammasamādānā, te kāyassa bhedā paraṁ maraṇā apāyaṁ duggatiṁ vinipātaṁ nirayaṁ upapannā; ime vā pana bhonto sattā kāyasucaritena samannāgatā vacīsucaritena samannāgatā manosucaritena samannāgatā ariyānaṁ anupavādakā sammādiṭṭhikā sammādiṭṭhikammasamādānā, te kāyassa bhedā paraṁ maraṇā sugatiṁ saggaṁ lokaṁ upapannāti, iti dibbena cakkhunā visuddhena atikkantamānusakena satte passeyyaṁ cavamāne upapajjamāne hīne paṇīte suvaṇṇe dubbaṇṇe sugate duggate yathākammūpage satte pajāneyyan'ti,

A mendicant might wish: 'With clairvoyance that is purified and superhuman, may I see sentient beings passing away and being reborn—inferior and superior, beautiful and ugly, in a good place or a bad place—and understand how sentient beings are reborn according to their deeds: "These dear beings did bad things by way of body, speech, and mind. They spoke ill of the noble ones; they had wrong view; and they chose to act out of that wrong view. When their body breaks up, after death, they're reborn in a place of loss, a bad place, the underworld, hell. These dear beings, however, did good things by way of body, speech, and mind. They never spoke ill of the noble ones; they had right view; and they chose to act out of that right view. When their body breaks up, after death, they're reborn in a good place, a heavenly realm." And so, with clairvoyance that is purified and superhuman, may I see sentient beings passing away and being reborn— inferior and superior, beautiful and ugly, in a good place or a bad place. And may I understand how sentient beings are reborn according to their deeds.'

sīlesvevassa paripūrakārī ajjhattaṁ cetosamathamanuyutto anirākatajjhāno vipassanāya samannāgato brūhetā suññāgārānaṁ.

So let them fulfill their precepts ...

Ākaṅkheyya ce, bhikkhave, bhikkhu: 'āsavānaṁ khayā anāsavaṁ cetovimuttiṁ paññāvimuttiṁ diṭṭheva dhamme sayaṁ abhiññā sacchikatvā upasampajja vihareyyan'ti,

A mendicant might wish: 'May I realize the undefiled freedom of heart and freedom by wisdom in this very life, and live having realized it with my own insight due to the ending of defilements.'

sīlesvevassa paripūrakārī ajjhattaṁ cetosamathamanuyutto anirākatajjhāno vipassanāya samannāgato brūhetā suññāgārānaṁ.

So let them fulfill their precepts, be committed to inner serenity of the heart, not neglect absorption, be endowed with discernment, and frequent empty huts.

'Sampannasīlā, bhikkhave, viharatha sampannapātimokkhā; pātimokkhasaṁvarasaṁvutā viharatha ācāragocarasampannā aṇumattesu vajjesu bhayadassāvino; samādāya sikkhatha sikkhāpadesū'ti—

'Mendicants, live by the ethical precepts and the monastic code. Live restrained in the monastic code, conducting yourselves well and seeking alms in suitable places. Seeing danger in the slightest fault, keep the rules you've undertaken.'

iti yaṁ taṁ vuttaṁ idametaṁ paṭicca vuttan"ti.

That's what I said, and this is why I said it."

Idamavoca bhagavā.

That is what the Buddha said.

Attamanā te bhikkhū bhagavato bhāsitaṁ abhinandunti.

Satisfied, the mendicants were happy with what the Buddha said.

Ākaṅkheyyasuttaṁ niṭṭhitaṁ chaṭṭhaṁ.

7 Vatthasutta:

The Simile of the Cloth

Evaṁ me sutaṁ—

So I have heard.

ekaṁ samayaṁ bhagavā sāvatthiyaṁ viharati jetavane anāthapiṇḍikassa ārāme.

At one time the Buddha was staying near Sāvatthī in Jeta's Grove, Anāthapiṇḍika's monastery.

Tatra kho bhagavā bhikkhū āmantesi:

There the Buddha addressed the mendicants,

"bhikkhavo"ti.

"Mendicants!"

"Bhadante"ti te bhikkhū bhagavato paccassosuṁ.

"Venerable sir," they replied.

Bhagavā etadavoca:

The Buddha said this:

"Seyyathāpi, bhikkhave, vatthaṁ saṅkiliṭṭhaṁ malaggahitaṁ;

"Suppose, mendicants, there was a cloth that was dirty and soiled.

tamenaṁ rajako yasmiṁ yasmiṁ raṅgajāte upasaṁhareyya—yadi nīlakāya yadi pītakāya yadi lohitakāya yadi mañjiṭṭhakāya durattavaṇṇamevassa aparisuddhavaṇṇamevassa.

No matter what dye the dyer applied—whether blue or yellow or red or magenta—it would look poorly dyed and impure in color.

Taṁ kissa hetu?

Why is that?

Aparisuddhattā, bhikkhave, vatthassa.

Because of the impurity of the cloth.

Evameva kho, bhikkhave, citte saṅkiliṭṭhe, duggati pāṭikaṅkhā.

In the same way, when the mind is corrupt, a bad destiny is to be expected.

Seyyathāpi, bhikkhave, vatthaṁ parisuddhaṁ pariyodātaṁ;

Suppose there was a cloth that was pure and clean.

tamenaṁ rajako yasmiṁ yasmiṁ raṅgajāte upasaṁhareyya—yadi nīlakāya yadi pītakāya yadi lohitakāya yadi mañjiṭṭhakāya—surattavaṇṇamevassa parisuddhavaṇṇamevassa.

No matter what dye the dyer applied—whether blue or yellow or red or magenta—it would look well dyed and pure in color.

Taṁ kissa hetu?

Why is that?

Parisuddhattā, bhikkhave, vatthassa.

Because of the purity of the cloth.

Evameva kho, bhikkhave, citte asaṅkiliṭṭhe, sugati pāṭikaṅkhā.

In the same way, when the mind isn't corrupt, a good destiny is to be expected.

Katame ca, bhikkhave, cittassa upakkilesā?

And what are the corruptions of the mind?

Abhijjhāvisamalobho cittassa upakkileso, byāpādo cittassa upakkileso, kodho cittassa upakkileso, upanāho cittassa upakkileso, makkho cittassa upakkileso, palāso cittassa upakkileso, issā cittassa upakkileso, macchariyaṁ cittassa upakkileso, māyā cittassa upakkileso, sāṭheyyaṁ cittassa upakkileso, thambho cittassa upakkileso, sārambho cittassa upakkileso, māno cittassa upakkileso, atimāno cittassa upakkileso, mado cittassa upakkileso, pamādo cittassa upakkileso.

Covetousness and immoral greed, ill will, anger, hostility, disdain, contempt, jealousy, stinginess, deceit, deviousness, obstinacy, aggression, conceit, arrogance, vanity, and negligence are corruptions of the mind.

Sa kho so, bhikkhave, bhikkhu 'abhijjhāvisamalobho cittassa upakkileso'ti—iti viditvā abhijjhāvisamalobhaṁ cittassa upakkilesaṁ pajahati;

A mendicant who understands that covetousness and immoral greed are corruptions of the mind gives them up.

'byāpādo cittassa upakkileso'ti—

A mendicant who understands that ill will ...

iti viditvā byāpādaṁ cittassa upakkilesaṁ pajahati;

'kodho cittassa upakkileso'ti—

iti viditvā kodhaṁ cittassa upakkilesaṁ pajahati;

'upanāho cittassa upakkileso'ti—

iti viditvā upanāhaṁ cittassa upakkilesaṁ pajahati;

'makkho cittassa upakkileso'ti—

iti viditvā makkhaṁ cittassa upakkilesaṁ pajahati;

'palāso cittassa upakkileso'ti—

iti viditvā palāsaṁ cittassa upakkilesaṁ pajahati;

'issā cittassa upakkileso'ti—

iti viditvā issaṁ cittassa upakkilesaṁ pajahati;

'macchariyaṁ cittassa upakkileso'ti—

iti viditvā macchariyaṁ cittassa upakkilesaṁ pajahati;

'māyā cittassa upakkileso'ti—

iti viditvā māyaṁ cittassa upakkilesaṁ pajahati;

'sāṭheyyaṁ cittassa upakkileso'ti—

iti viditvā sāṭheyyaṁ cittassa upakkilesaṁ pajahati;

'thambho cittassa upakkileso'ti—

iti viditvā thambhaṁ cittassa upakkilesaṁ pajahati;

'sārambho cittassa upakkileso'ti—

iti viditvā sārambhaṁ cittassa upakkilesaṁ pajahati;

'māno cittassa upakkileso'ti—

iti viditvā mānaṁ cittassa upakkilesaṁ pajahati;

'atimāno cittassa upakkileso'ti—

iti viditvā atimānaṁ cittassa upakkilesaṁ pajahati;

'mado cittassa upakkileso'ti—

iti viditvā madaṁ cittassa upakkilesaṁ pajahati;

'pamādo cittassa upakkileso'ti—

negligence is a corruption of the mind gives it up.

iti viditvā pamādaṁ cittassa upakkilesaṁ pajahati.

Yato kho, bhikkhave, bhikkhuno 'abhijjhāvisamalobho cittassa upakkileso'ti—iti viditvā abhijjhāvisamalobho cittassa upakkileso pahīno hoti,

When they have understood these corruptions of the mind

'byāpādo cittassa upakkileso'ti—

for what they are, and have given them up,

iti viditvā byāpādo cittassa upakkileso pahīno hoti;

'kodho cittassa upakkileso'ti—

iti viditvā kodho cittassa upakkileso pahīno hoti;

'upanāho cittassa upakkileso'ti—

iti viditvā upanāho cittassa upakkileso pahīno hoti;

'makkho cittassa upakkileso'ti—

iti viditvā makkho cittassa upakkileso pahīno hoti;

'paḷāso cittassa upakkileso'ti—

iti viditvā paḷāso cittassa upakkileso pahīno hoti;

'issā cittassa upakkileso'ti—

iti viditvā issā cittassa upakkileso pahīno hoti;

'macchariyaṁ cittassa upakkileso'ti—

iti viditvā macchariyaṁ cittassa upakkileso pahīno hoti;

'māyā cittassa upakkileso'ti—

iti viditvā māyā cittassa upakkileso pahīno hoti;

'sāṭheyyaṁ cittassa upakkileso'ti—

iti viditvā sāṭheyyaṁ cittassa upakkileso pahīno hoti;

'thambho cittassa upakkileso'ti—

iti viditvā thambho cittassa upakkileso pahīno hoti;

'sārambho cittassa upakkileso'ti—

iti viditvā sārambho cittassa upakkileso pahīno hoti;

'māno cittassa upakkileso'ti—

iti viditvā māno cittassa upakkileso pahīno hoti;

'atimāno cittassa upakkileso'ti—

iti viditvā atimāno cittassa upakkileso pahīno hoti;

'mado cittassa upakkileso'ti—

iti viditvā mado cittassa upakkileso pahīno hoti;

'pamādo cittassa upakkileso'ti—

iti viditvā pamādo cittassa upakkileso pahīno hoti.

So buddhe aveccappasādena samannāgato hoti:

they have experiential confidence in the Buddha:

'itipi so bhagavā arahaṁ sammāsambuddho vijjācaraṇasampanno sugato lokavidū anuttaro purisadammasārathi satthā devamanussānaṁ buddho bhagavā'ti;

'That Blessed One is perfected, a fully awakened Buddha, accomplished in knowledge and conduct, holy, knower of the world, supreme guide for those who wish to train, teacher of gods and humans, awakened, blessed.'

dhamme aveccappasādena samannāgato hoti:

They have experiential confidence in the teaching:

'svākkhāto bhagavatā dhammo sandiṭṭhiko akāliko ehipassiko opaneyyiko paccattaṁ veditabbo viññūhī'ti;

'The teaching is well explained by the Buddha—apparent in the present life, immediately effective, inviting inspection, relevant, so that sensible people can know it for themselves.'

saṅghe aveccappasādena samannāgato hoti:

They have experiential confidence in the Saṅgha:

'suppaṭipanno bhagavato sāvakasaṅgho, ujuppaṭipanno bhagavato sāvakasaṅgho, ñāyappaṭipanno bhagavato sāvakasaṅgho, sāmīcippaṭipanno bhagavato sāvakasaṅgho, yadidaṁ cattāri purisayugāni, aṭṭha purisapuggalā. Esa bhagavato sāvakasaṅgho āhuneyyo pāhuneyyo dakkhiṇeyyo añjalikaraṇīyo, anuttaraṁ puññakkhettaṁ lokassā'ti.

'The Saṅgha of the Buddha's disciples is practicing the way that's good, direct, methodical, and proper. It consists of the four pairs, the eight individuals. This is the Saṅgha of the Buddha's disciples that is worthy of offerings dedicated to the gods, worthy of hospitality, worthy of a religious donation, worthy of greeting with joined palms, and is the supreme field of merit for the world.'

Yathodhi kho panassa cattaṁ hoti vantaṁ muttaṁ pahīnaṁ paṭinissaṭṭhaṁ, so 'buddhe aveccappasādena samannāgatomhī'ti labhati atthavedaṁ, labhati dhammavedaṁ, labhati dhammūpasaṁhitaṁ pāmojjaṁ.

When a mendicant has discarded, eliminated, released, given up, and relinquished to this extent, thinking, 'I have experiential confidence in the Buddha …

Pamuditassa pīti jāyati, pītimanassa kāyo passambhati, passaddhakāyo sukhaṁ vedeti, sukhino cittaṁ samādhiyati;

'dhamme …pe…

the teaching …

saṅghe aveccappasādena samannāgatomhī'ti labhati atthavedaṁ, labhati dhammavedaṁ, labhati dhammūpasaṁhitaṁ pāmojjaṁ;

the Saṅgha,' they find inspiration in the meaning and the teaching, and find joy connected with the teaching.

pamuditassa pīti jāyati, pītimanassa kāyo passambhati, passaddhakāyo sukhaṁ vedeti, sukhino cittaṁ samādhiyati.

'Yathodhi kho pana me cattaṁ vantaṁ muttaṁ pahīnaṁ paṭinissaṭṭhan'ti labhati atthavedaṁ, labhati dhammavedaṁ, labhati dhammūpasaṁhitaṁ pāmojjaṁ;

Thinking: 'I have discarded, eliminated, released, given up, and relinquished to this extent,' they find inspiration in the meaning and the teaching, and find joy connected with the teaching.

pamuditassa pīti jāyati, pītimanassa kāyo passambhati, passaddhakāyo sukhaṁ vedeti, sukhino cittaṁ samādhiyati.

When they're joyful, rapture springs up. When the mind is full of rapture, the body becomes tranquil. When the body is tranquil, they feel bliss. And when they're blissful, the mind becomes immersed in samādhi.

Sa kho so, bhikkhave, bhikkhu evaṁsīlo evaṁdhammo evampañño sālīnañcepi piṇḍapātaṁ bhuñjati vicitakāḷakaṁ anekasūpaṁ anekabyañjanaṁ, nevassa taṁ hoti antarāyāya.

When a mendicant of such ethics, such qualities, and such wisdom eats boiled fine rice with the dark grains picked out and served with many soups and sauces, that is no obstacle for them.

Seyyathāpi, bhikkhave, vatthaṁ saṅkiliṭṭhaṁ malaggahitaṁ acchodakaṁ āgamma parisuddhaṁ hoti pariyodātaṁ, ukkāmukhaṁ vā panāgamma jātarūpaṁ parisuddhaṁ hoti pariyodātaṁ;

Compare with cloth that is dirty and soiled; it can be made pure and clean by pure water. Or unrefined gold, which can be made pure and bright by a forge.

evameva kho, bhikkhave, bhikkhu evaṁsīlo evaṁdhammo evampañño sālīnañcepi piṇḍapātaṁ bhuñjati vicitakāḷakaṁ anekasūpaṁ anekabyañjanaṁ, nevassa taṁ hoti antarāyāya.

In the same way, when a mendicant of such ethics, such qualities, and such wisdom eats boiled fine rice with the dark grains picked out and served with many soups and sauces, that is no obstacle for them.

So mettāsahagatena cetasā ekaṁ disaṁ pharitvā viharati, tathā dutiyaṁ, tathā tatiyaṁ, tathā catutthaṁ. Iti uddhamadho tiriyaṁ sabbadhi sabbattatāya sabbāvantaṁ lokaṁ mettāsahagatena cetasā vipulena mahaggatena appamāṇena averena abyāpajjena pharitvā viharati;

They meditate spreading a heart full of love to one direction, and to the second, and to the third, and to the fourth. In the same way above, below, across, everywhere, all around, they spread a heart full of love to the whole world—abundant, expansive, limitless, free of enmity and ill will.

karuṇāsahagatena cetasā …pe…

They meditate spreading a heart full of compassion to one direction, and to the second, and to the third, and to the fourth. In the same way above, below, across, everywhere, all around, they spread a heart full of compassion to the whole world—abundant, expansive, limitless, free of enmity and ill will.

muditāsahagatena cetasā ...pe...

They meditate spreading a heart full of rejoicing to one direction, and to the second, and to the third, and to the fourth. In the same way above, below, across, everywhere, all around, they spread a heart full of rejoicing to the whole world—abundant, expansive, limitless, free of enmity and ill will.

upekkhāsahagatena cetasā ekaṁ disaṁ pharitvā viharati, tathā dutiyaṁ, tathā tatiyaṁ, tathā catutthaṁ. Iti uddhamadho tiriyaṁ sabbadhi sabbattatāya sabbāvantaṁ lokaṁ upekkhāsahagatena cetasā vipulena mahaggatena appamāṇena averena abyāpajjena pharitvā viharati.

They meditate spreading a heart full of equanimity to one direction, and to the second, and to the third, and to the fourth. In the same way above, below, across, everywhere, all around, they spread a heart full of equanimity to the whole world—abundant, expansive, limitless, free of enmity and ill will.

So 'atthi idaṁ, atthi hīnaṁ, atthi paṇītaṁ, atthi imassa saññāgatassa uttari nissaraṇan'ti pajānāti.

They understand: 'There is this, there is what is worse than this, there is what is better than this, and there is an escape beyond the scope of perception.'

Tassa evaṁ jānato evaṁ passato kāmāsavāpi cittaṁ vimuccati, bhavāsavāpi cittaṁ vimuccati, avijjāsavāpi cittaṁ vimuccati.

Knowing and seeing like this, their mind is freed from the defilements of sensuality, desire to be reborn, and ignorance.

Vimuttasmiṁ vimuttamiti ñāṇaṁ hoti.

When they're freed, they know they're freed.

'Khīṇā jāti, vusitaṁ brahmacariyaṁ, kataṁ karaṇīyaṁ, nāparaṁ itthattāyā'ti pajānāti.

They understand: 'Rebirth is ended, the spiritual journey has been completed, what had to be done has been done, there is no return to any state of existence.'

Ayaṁ vuccati, bhikkhave:

This is called

'bhikkhu sināto antarena sinānenā'"ti.

a mendicant who is bathed with the inner bathing."

Tena kho pana samayena sundarikabhāradvājo brāhmaṇo bhagavato avidūre nisinno hoti.

Now at that time the brahmin Sundarikabhāradvāja was sitting not far from the Buddha.

Atha kho sundarikabhāradvājo brāhmaṇo bhagavantaṁ etadavoca:

He said to the Buddha,

"gacchati pana bhavaṁ gotamo bāhukaṁ nadiṁ sināyitun"ti?

"But does Master Gotama go to the river Bāhuka to bathe?"

"Kiṁ, brāhmaṇa, bāhukāya nadiyā?

"Brahmin, why go to the river Bāhuka?

Kiṁ bāhukā nadī karissatī"ti?

What can the river Bāhuka do?"

"Lokkhasammatā hi, bho gotama, bāhukā nadī bahujanassa, puññasammatā hi, bho gotama, bāhukā nadī bahujanassa, bāhukāya pana nadiyā bahujano pāpakammaṁ kataṁ pavāhetī"ti.

"Many people agree that the river Bāhuka bestows cleanliness and merit. And many people wash off their bad deeds in the river Bāhuka."

Atha kho bhagavā sundarikabhāradvājaṁ brāhmaṇaṁ gāthāhi ajjhabhāsi:

Then the Buddha addressed Sundarikabhāradvāja in verse:

"Bāhukaṁ adhikakkañca,

gayaṁ sundarikaṁ mapi;

Sarassatiṁ payāgañca,

atho bāhumatiṁ nadiṁ;

Niccampi bālo pakkhando,

kaṇhakammo na sujjhati.

"The Bāhuka and the Adhikakka,

the Gayā and the Sundarikā too,

Sarasvatī and Payāga,

and the river Bāhumati:

a fool can constantly plunge into them

but it won't purify their dark deeds.

Kiṁ sundarikā karissati,

Kiṁ payāgā kiṁ bāhukā nadī;

Veriṁ katakibbisaṁ naraṁ,

Na hi naṁ sodhaye pāpakamminaṁ.

What can the Sundarikā do?

What the Payāga or the Bāhuka?

They can't cleanse a cruel and criminal person

from their bad deeds.

Suddhassa ve sadā phaggu,

Suddhassuposatho sadā;

Suddhassa sucikammassa,

Sadā sampajjate vataṁ;

Idheva sināhi brāhmaṇa,

Sabbabhūtesu karohi khemataṁ.

For the pure in heart it's always

the spring festival or the sabbath.

For the pure in heart and clean of deed,

their vows will always be fulfilled.

It's here alone that you should bathe, brahmin,

making yourself a sanctuary for all creatures.

Sace musā na bhaṇasi,

sace pāṇaṁ na hiṁsasi;

Sace adinnaṁ nādiyasi,

saddahāno amaccharī;

Kiṁ kāhasi gayaṁ gantvā,

udapānopi te gayā"ti.

And if you speak no lies,

nor harm any living creature,

nor steal anything not given,

and you're faithful and not stingy:

what's the point of going to Gayā?

For any well may be your Gayā!"

Evaṁ vutte, sundarikabhāradvājo brāhmaṇo bhagavantaṁ etadavoca:

When he had spoken, the brahmin Sundarikabhāradvāja said to the Buddha,

"abhikkantaṁ, bho gotama, abhikkantaṁ, bho gotama.

"Excellent, Master Gotama! Excellent!

Seyyathāpi, bho gotama, nikkujjitaṁ vā ukkujjeyya, paṭicchannaṁ vā vivareyya, mūḷhassa vā maggaṁ ācikkheyya, andhakāre vā telapajjotaṁ dhāreyya— cakkhumanto rūpāni dakkhantīti; evamevaṁ bhotā gotamena anekapariyāyena dhammo pakāsito.

As if he were righting the overturned, or revealing the hidden, or pointing out the path to the lost, or lighting a lamp in the dark so people with good eyes can see what's there, Master Gotama has made the teaching clear in many ways.

Esāhaṁ bhavantaṁ gotamaṁ saraṇaṁ gacchāmi dhammañca bhikkhusaṅghañca.

I go for refuge to Master Gotama, to the teaching, and to the mendicant Saṅgha.

Labheyyāhaṁ bhoto gotamassa santike pabbajjaṁ, labheyyaṁ upasampadan"ti.

May I receive the going forth, the ordination in the ascetic Gotama's presence?"

Alattha kho sundarikabhāradvājo brāhmaṇo bhagavato santike pabbajjaṁ, alattha upasampadaṁ.

And the brahmin Sundarikabhāradvāja received the going forth, the ordination in the Buddha's presence.

Acirūpasampanno kho panāyasmā bhāradvājo eko vūpakaṭṭho appamatto ātāpī pahitatto viharanto nacirasseva—yassatthāya kulaputtā sammadeva agārasmā anagāriyaṁ pabbajanti, tadanuttaraṁ—brahmacariyapariyosānaṁ diṭṭheva dhamme sayaṁ abhiññā sacchikatvā upasampajja vihāsi.

Not long after his ordination, Venerable Bhāradvāja, living alone, withdrawn, diligent, keen, and resolute, soon realized the supreme end of the spiritual path in this very life. He lived having achieved with his own insight the goal for which gentlemen rightly go forth from the lay life to homelessness.

"Khīṇā jāti, vusitaṁ brahmacariyaṁ, kataṁ karaṇīyaṁ, nāparaṁ itthattāyā"ti abbhaññāsi.

He understood: "Rebirth is ended; the spiritual journey has been completed; what had to be done has been done; there is no return to any state of existence."

Aññataro kho panāyasmā bhāradvājo arahataṁ ahosīti.

And Venerable Bhāradvāja became one of the perfected.

Vatthasuttaṁ niṭṭhitaṁ sattamaṁ.

8 Sallekhasutta:

Self-Effacement

Evaṁ me sutaṁ—

So I have heard.

ekaṁ samayaṁ bhagavā sāvatthiyaṁ viharati jetavane anāthapiṇḍikassa ārāme.

At one time the Buddha was staying near Sāvatthī in Jeta's Grove, Anāthapiṇḍika's monastery.

Atha kho āyasmā mahācundo sāyanhasamayaṁ paṭisallānā vuṭṭhito yena bhagavā tenupasaṅkami; upasaṅkamitvā bhagavantaṁ abhivādetvā ekamantaṁ nisīdi. Ekamantaṁ nisinno kho āyasmā mahācundo bhagavantaṁ etadavoca:

Then in the late afternoon, Venerable Mahācunda came out of retreat and went to the Buddha. He bowed, sat down to one side, and said to the Buddha:

"yā imā, bhante, anekavihitā diṭṭhiyo loke uppajjanti—

"Sir, there are many different views that arise in the world

attavādapaṭisaṁyuttā vā lokavādapaṭisaṁyuttā vā—

connected with doctrines of the self or with doctrines of the cosmos.

ādimeva nu kho, bhante, bhikkhuno manasikaroto evametāsaṁ diṭṭhīnaṁ pahānaṁ hoti, evametāsaṁ diṭṭhīnaṁ paṭinissaggo hotī"ti?

How does a mendicant who is focusing on the starting point give up and let go of these views?"

"Yā imā, cunda, anekavihitā diṭṭhiyo loke uppajjanti—

"Cunda, there are many different views that arise in the world attavādapaṭisaṁyuttā vā lokavādapaṭisaṁyuttā vā—

connected with doctrines of the self or with doctrines of the cosmos.

yattha cetā diṭṭhiyo uppajjanti yattha ca anusenti yattha ca samudācaranti taṁ 'netaṁ mama, nesohamasmi, na me so attā'ti—evametaṁ yathābhūtaṁ sammappaññā passato evametāsaṁ diṭṭhīnaṁ pahānaṁ hoti, evametāsaṁ diṭṭhīnaṁ paṭinissaggo hoti.

A mendicant gives up and lets go of these views by truly seeing with right wisdom where they arise, where they settle in, and where they operate as: 'This is not mine, I am not this, this is not my self.'

Ṭhānaṁ kho panetaṁ, cunda, vijjati yaṁ idhekacco bhikkhu vivicceva kāmehi vivicca akusalehi dhammehi savitakkaṁ savicāraṁ vivekajaṁ pītisukhaṁ paṭhamaṁ jhānaṁ upasampajja vihareyya.

It's possible that a certain mendicant, quite secluded from sensual pleasures, secluded from unskillful qualities, might enter and remain in the first absorption, which has the rapture and bliss born of seclusion, while placing the mind and keeping it connected.

Tassa evamassa:

They might think

'sallekhena viharāmī'ti.

they're practicing self-effacement.

Na kho panete, cunda, ariyassa vinaye sallekhā vuccanti.

But in the training of the Noble One these are not called 'self-effacement';

Diṭṭhadhammasukhavihārā ete ariyassa vinaye vuccanti.

they're called 'blissful meditations in the present life'.

Ṭhānaṁ kho panetaṁ, cunda, vijjati yaṁ idhekacco bhikkhu vitakkavicārānaṁ vūpasamā ajjhattaṁ sampasādanaṁ cetaso ekodibhāvaṁ avitakkaṁ avicāraṁ samādhijaṁ pītisukhaṁ dutiyaṁ jhānaṁ upasampajja vihareyya.

It's possible that some mendicant, as the placing of the mind and keeping it connected are stilled, might enter and remain in the second absorption, which has the rapture and bliss born of immersion, with internal clarity and confidence, and unified mind, without placing the mind and keeping it connected.

Tassa evamassa:

They might think

'sallekhena viharāmī'ti.

they're practicing self-effacement.

Na kho panete, cunda, ariyassa vinaye sallekhā vuccanti.

But in the training of the Noble One these are not called 'self-effacement';

Diṭṭhadhammasukhavihārā ete ariyassa vinaye vuccanti.

they're called 'blissful meditations in the present life'.

Ṭhānaṃ kho panetaṃ, cunda, vijjati yaṃ idhekacco bhikkhu pītiyā ca virāgā upekkhako ca vihareyya, sato ca sampajāno sukhañca kāyena paṭisaṃvedeyya, yaṃ taṃ ariyā ācikkhanti: 'upekkhako satimā sukhavihārī'ti tatiyaṃ jhānaṃ upasampajja vihareyya.

It's possible that some mendicant, with the fading away of rapture, might enter and remain in the third absorption, where they meditate with equanimity, mindful and aware, personally experiencing the bliss of which the noble ones declare, 'Equanimous and mindful, one meditates in bliss.'

Tassa evamassa:

They might think

'sallekhena viharāmī'ti.

they're practicing self-effacement.

Na kho panete, cunda, ariyassa vinaye sallekhā vuccanti.

But in the training of the Noble One these are not called 'self-effacement';

Diṭṭhadhammasukhavihārā ete ariyassa vinaye vuccanti.

they're called 'blissful meditations in the present life'.

Ṭhānaṃ kho panetaṃ, cunda, vijjati yaṃ idhekacco bhikkhu sukhassa ca pahānā dukkhassa ca pahānā pubbeva somanassadomanassānaṃ atthaṅgamā adukkhamasukhaṃ upekkhāsatipārisuddhiṃ catutthaṃ jhānaṃ upasampajja vihareyya.

It's possible that some mendicant, with the giving up of pleasure and pain, and the ending of former happiness and sadness, might enter and remain in the fourth absorption, without pleasure or pain, with pure equanimity and mindfulness.

Tassa evamassa:

They might think

'sallekhena viharāmī'ti.

they're practicing self-effacement.

Na kho panete, cunda, ariyassa vinaye sallekhā vuccanti.

But in the training of the Noble One these are not called 'self-effacement';

Diṭṭhadhammasukhavihārā ete ariyassa vinaye vuccanti.

they're called 'blissful meditations in the present life'.

Ṭhānaṁ kho panetaṁ, cunda, vijjati yaṁ idhekacco bhikkhu sabbaso rūpasaññānaṁ samatikkamā, paṭighasaññānaṁ atthaṅgamā, nānattasaññānaṁ amanasikārā, 'ananto ākāso'ti ākāsānañcāyatanaṁ upasampajja vihareyya.

It's possible that some mendicant, going totally beyond perceptions of form, with the ending of perceptions of impingement, not focusing on perceptions of diversity, aware that 'space is infinite', might enter and remain in the dimension of infinite space.

Tassa evamassa:

They might think

'sallekhena viharāmī'ti.

they're practicing self-effacement.

Na kho panete, cunda, ariyassa vinaye sallekhā vuccanti.

But in the training of the Noble One these are not called 'self-effacement';

Santā ete vihārā ariyassa vinaye vuccanti.

they're called 'peaceful meditations'.

Ṭhānaṁ kho panetaṁ, cunda, vijjati yaṁ idhekacco bhikkhu sabbaso ākāsānañcāyatanaṁ samatikkamma 'anantaṁ viññāṇan'ti viññāṇañcāyatanaṁ upasampajja vihareyya.

It's possible that some mendicant, going totally beyond the dimension of infinite space, aware that 'consciousness is infinite', might enter and remain in the dimension of infinite consciousness.

Tassa evamassa:

They might think

'sallekhena viharāmī'ti.

they're practicing self-effacement.

Na kho panete, cunda, ariyassa vinaye sallekhā vuccanti.

But in the training of the Noble One these are not called 'self-effacement';

Santā ete vihārā ariyassa vinaye vuccanti.

they're called 'peaceful meditations'.

Ṭhānaṁ kho panetaṁ, cunda, vijjati yaṁ idhekacco bhikkhu sabbaso viññāṇañcāyatanaṁ samatikkamma 'natthi kiñcī'ti ākiñcaññāyatanaṁ upasampajja vihareyya.

It's possible that some mendicant, going totally beyond the dimension of infinite consciousness, aware that 'there is nothing at all', might enter and remain in the dimension of nothingness.

Tassa evamassa:

They might think

'sallekhena viharāmī'ti.

they're practicing self-effacement.

Na kho panete, cunda, ariyassa vinaye sallekhā vuccanti.

But in the training of the Noble One these are not called 'self-effacement';

Santā ete vihārā ariyassa vinaye vuccanti.

they're called 'peaceful meditations'.

Ṭhānaṁ kho panetaṁ, cunda, vijjati yaṁ idhekacco bhikkhu sabbaso ākiñcaññāyatanaṁ samatikkamma nevasaññānāsaññāyatanaṁ upasampajja vihareyya.

It's possible that some mendicant, going totally beyond the dimension of nothingness, might enter and remain in the dimension of neither perception nor non-perception.

Tassa evamassa:

They might think

'sallekhena viharāmī'ti.

they're practicing self-effacement.

Na kho panete, cunda, ariyassa vinaye sallekhā vuccanti.

But in the training of the Noble One these are not called 'self-effacement';

Santā ete vihārā ariyassa vinaye vuccanti.

they're called 'peaceful meditations'.

1. Sallekhapariyaya

1. The Exposition of Self-Effacement

Idha kho pana vo, cunda, sallekho karaṇīyo.

Now, Cunda, you should work on self-effacement in each of the following ways.

'Pare vihiṁsakā bhavissanti, mayamettha avihiṁsakā bhavissāmā'ti sallekho karaṇīyo.

'Others will be cruel, but here we will not be cruel.'

'Pare pāṇātipātī bhavissanti, mayamettha pāṇātipātā paṭiviratā bhavissāmā'ti sallekho karaṇīyo.

'Others will kill living creatures, but here we will not kill living creatures.'

'Pare adinnādāyī bhavissanti, mayamettha adinnādānā paṭiviratā bhavissāmā'ti sallekho karaṇīyo.

'Others will steal, but here we will not steal.'

'Pare abrahmacārī bhavissanti, mayamettha brahmacārī bhavissāmā'ti sallekho karaṇīyo.

'Others will be unchaste, but here we will not be unchaste.'

'Pare musāvādī bhavissanti, mayamettha musāvādā paṭiviratā bhavissāmā'ti sallekho karaṇīyo.

'Others will lie, but here we will not lie.'

'Pare pisuṇavācā bhavissanti, mayamettha pisuṇāya vācāya paṭiviratā bhavissāmā'ti sallekho karaṇīyo.

'Others will speak divisively, but here we will not speak divisively.'

'Pare pharusavācā bhavissanti, mayamettha pharusāya vācāya paṭiviratā bhavissāmā'ti sallekho karaṇīyo.

'Others will speak harshly, but here we will not speak harshly.'

'Pare samphappalāpī bhavissanti, mayamettha samphappalāpā paṭiviratā bhavissāmā'ti sallekho karaṇīyo.

'Others will talk nonsense, but here we will not talk nonsense.'

'Pare abhijjhālū bhavissanti, mayamettha anabhijjhālū bhavissāmā'ti sallekho karaṇīyo.

'Others will be covetous, but here we will not be covetous.'

'Pare byāpannacittā bhavissanti, mayamettha abyāpannacittā bhavissāmā'ti sallekho karaṇīyo.

'Others will have ill will, but here we will not have ill will.'

'Pare micchādiṭṭhī bhavissanti, mayamettha sammādiṭṭhī bhavissāmā'ti sallekho karaṇīyo.

'Others will have wrong view, but here we will have right view.'

'Pare micchāsaṅkappā bhavissanti, mayamettha sammāsaṅkappā bhavissāmā'ti sallekho karaṇīyo.

'Others will have wrong thought, but here we will have right thought.'

'Pare micchāvācā bhavissanti, mayamettha sammāvācā bhavissāmā'ti sallekho karaṇīyo.

'Others will have wrong speech, but here we will have right speech.'

'Pare micchākammantā bhavissanti, mayamettha sammākammantā bhavissāmā'ti sallekho karaṇīyo.

'Others will have wrong action, but here we will have right action.'

'Pare micchāājīvā bhavissanti, mayamettha sammāājīvā bhavissāmā'ti sallekho karaṇīyo.

'Others will have wrong livelihood, but here we will have right livelihood.'

'Pare micchāvāyāmā bhavissanti, mayamettha sammāvāyāmā bhavissāmā'ti sallekho karaṇīyo.

'Others will have wrong effort, but here we will have right effort.'

'Pare micchāsatī bhavissanti, mayamettha sammāsatī bhavissāmā'ti sallekho karaṇīyo.

'Others will have wrong mindfulness, but here we will have right mindfulness.'

'Pare micchāsamādhi bhavissanti, mayamettha sammāsamādhī bhavissāmā'ti sallekho karaṇīyo.

'Others will have wrong immersion, but here we will have right immersion.'

'Pare micchāñāṇī bhavissanti, mayamettha sammāñāṇī bhavissāmā'ti sallekho karaṇīyo.

'Others will have wrong knowledge, but here we will have right knowledge.'

'Pare micchāvimuttī bhavissanti, mayamettha sammāvimuttī bhavissāmā'ti sallekho karaṇīyo.

'Others will have wrong freedom, but here we will have right freedom.'

'Pare thinamiddhapariyuṭṭhitā bhavissanti, mayamettha vigatathinamiddhā bhavissāmā'ti sallekho karaṇīyo.

'Others will be overcome with dullness and drowsiness, but here we will be rid of dullness and drowsiness.'

'Pare uddhatā bhavissanti, mayamettha anuddhatā bhavissāmā'ti sallekho karaṇīyo.

'Others will be restless, but here we will not be restless.'

'Pare vicikicchī bhavissanti, mayamettha tiṇṇavicikicchā bhavissāmā'ti sallekho karaṇīyo.

'Others will have doubts, but here we will have gone beyond doubt.'

'Pare kodhanā bhavissanti, mayamettha akkodhanā bhavissāmā'ti sallekho karaṇīyo.

'Others will be irritable, but here we will be without anger.'

'Pare upanāhī bhavissanti, mayamettha anupanāhī bhavissāmā'ti sallekho karaṇīyo.

'Others will be hostile, but here we will be without hostility.'

'Pare makkhī bhavissanti, mayamettha amakkhī bhavissāmā'ti sallekho karaṇīyo.

'Others will be offensive, but here we will be inoffensive.'

'Pare paḷāsī bhavissanti, mayamettha apaḷāsī bhavissāmā'ti sallekho karaṇīyo.

'Others will be contemptuous, but here we will be without contempt.'

'Pare issukī bhavissanti, mayamettha anissukī bhavissāmā'ti sallekho karaṇīyo.

'Others will be jealous, but here we will be without jealousy.'

'Pare maccharī bhavissanti, mayamettha amaccharī bhavissāmā'ti sallekho karaṇīyo.

'Others will be stingy, but here we will be without stinginess.'

'Pare saṭhā bhavissanti, mayamettha asaṭhā bhavissāmā'ti sallekho karaṇīyo.

'Others will be devious, but here we will not be devious.'

'Pare māyāvī bhavissanti, mayamettha amāyāvī bhavissāmā'ti sallekho karaṇīyo.

'Others will be deceitful, but here we will not be deceitful.'

'Pare thaddhā bhavissanti, mayamettha atthaddhā bhavissāmā'ti sallekho karaṇīyo.

'Others will be pompous, but here we will not be pompous.'

'Pare atimānī bhavissanti, mayamettha anatimānī bhavissāmā'ti sallekho karaṇīyo.

'Others will be arrogant, but here we will not be arrogant.'

'Pare dubbacā bhavissanti, mayamettha suvacā bhavissāmā'ti sallekho karaṇīyo.

'Others will be hard to admonish, but here we will not be hard to admonish.'

'Pare pāpamittā bhavissanti, mayamettha kalyāṇamittā bhavissāmā'ti sallekho karaṇīyo.

'Others will have bad friends, but here we will have good friends.'

'Pare pamattā bhavissanti, mayamettha appamattā bhavissāmā'ti sallekho karaṇīyo.

'Others will be negligent, but here we will be diligent.'

'Pare assaddhā bhavissanti, mayamettha saddhā bhavissāmā'ti sallekho karaṇīyo.

'Others will be faithless, but here we will have faith.'

'Pare ahirikā bhavissanti, mayamettha hirimanā bhavissāmā'ti sallekho karaṇīyo.

'Others will be conscienceless, but here we will have a sense of conscience.'

'Pare anottāpī bhavissanti, mayamettha ottāpī bhavissāmā'ti sallekho karaṇīyo.

'Others will be imprudent, but here we will be prudent.'

'Pare appassutā bhavissanti, mayamettha bahussutā bhavissāmā'ti sallekho karaṇīyo.

'Others will be unlearned, but here we will be well learned.'

'Pare kusītā bhavissanti, mayamettha āraddhavīriyā bhavissāmā'ti sallekho karaṇīyo.

'Others will be lazy, but here we will be energetic.'

'Pare muṭṭhassatī bhavissanti, mayamettha upaṭṭhitassatī bhavissāmā'ti sallekho karaṇīyo.

'Others will be unmindful, but here we will be mindful.'

'Pare duppaññā bhavissanti, mayamettha paññāsampannā bhavissāmā'ti sallekho karaṇīyo.

'Others will be witless, but here we will be accomplished in wisdom.'

'Pare sandiṭṭhiparāmāsī ādhānaggāhī duppaṭinissaggī bhavissanti, mayamettha asandiṭṭhiparāmāsī anādhānaggāhī suppaṭinissaggī bhavissāmā'ti sallekho karaṇīyo.

'Others will be attached to their own views, holding them tight, and refusing to let go, but here we will not be attached to our own views, not holding them tight, but will let them go easily.'

2. Cittupapadapariyaya

2. Giving Rise to the Thought

Cittuppādampi kho ahaṁ, cunda, kusalesu dhammesu bahukāraṁ vadāmi, ko pana vādo kāyena vācāya anuvidhīyanāsu.

Cunda, I say that even giving rise to the thought of skillful qualities is very helpful, let alone following that path in body and speech.

Tasmātiha, cunda, 'pare vihiṁsakā bhavissanti, mayamettha avihiṁsakā bhavissāmā'ti cittaṁ uppādetabbaṁ.

That's why you should give rise to the following thoughts. 'Others will be cruel, but here we will not be cruel.'

'Pare pāṇātipātī bhavissanti, mayamettha pāṇātipātā paṭiviratā bhavissāmā'ti cittaṁ uppādetabbaṁ ...pe...

'Others will kill living creatures, but here we will not kill living creatures.' ...

'pare sandiṭṭhiparāmāsī ādhānaggāhī duppaṭinissaggī bhavissanti, mayamettha asandiṭṭhiparāmāsī anādhānaggāhī suppaṭinissaggī bhavissāmā'ti cittaṁ uppādetabbaṁ.

'Others will be attached to their own views, holding them tight, and refusing to let go, but here we will not be attached to our own views, not holding them tight, but will let them go easily.'

3. Parikkamanapariyaya

3. A Way Around

Seyyathāpi, cunda, visamo maggo assa, tassa añño samo maggo parikkamanāya;

Cunda, suppose there was a rough path and another smooth path to get around it.

seyyathā vā pana, cunda, visamaṁ titthaṁ assa, tassa aññaṁ samaṁ titthaṁ parikkamanāya;

Or suppose there was a rough ford and another smooth ford to get around it.

evameva kho, cunda, vihiṁsakassa purisapuggalassa avihiṁsā hoti parikkamanāya, pāṇātipātissa purisapuggalassa pāṇātipātā veramaṇī hoti parikkamanāya, adinnādāyissa purisapuggalassa adinnādānā veramaṇī hoti parikkamanāya, abrahmacārissa purisapuggalassa abrahmacariyā veramaṇī hoti parikkamanāya, musāvādissa purisapuggalassa musāvādā veramaṇī hoti parikkamanāya, pisuṇavācassa purisapuggalassa pisuṇāya vācāya veramaṇī hoti parikkamanāya, pharusavācassa purisapuggalassa pharusāya vācāya veramaṇī hoti parikkamanāya, samphappalāpissa purisapuggalassa samphappalāpā veramaṇī hoti parikkamanāya, abhijjhālussa purisapuggalassa anabhijjhā hoti parikkamanāya, byāpannacittassa purisapuggalassa abyāpādo hoti parikkamanāya.

In the same way, a cruel individual gets around it by not being cruel. An individual who kills gets around it by not killing. ...

Micchādiṭṭhissa purisapuggalassa sammādiṭṭhi hoti parikkamanāya, micchāsaṅkappassa purisapuggalassa sammāsaṅkappo hoti parikkamanāya, micchāvācassa purisapuggalassa sammāvācā hoti parikkamanāya, micchākammantassa purisapuggalassa sammākammanto hoti parikkamanāya, micchāājīvassa purisapuggalassa sammāājīvo hoti parikkamanāya, micchāvāyāmassa purisapuggalassa sammāvāyāmo hoti parikkamanāya, micchāsatissa purisapuggalassa sammāsati hoti parikkamanāya, micchāsamādhissa purisapuggalassa sammāsamādhi hoti parikkamanāya, micchāñāṇissa purisapuggalassa sammāñāṇaṁ hoti parikkamanāya, micchāvimuttissa purisapuggalassa sammāvimutti hoti parikkamanāya.

Thinamiddhapariyuṭṭhitassa purisapuggalassa vigatathinamiddhatā hoti parikkamanāya, uddhatassa purisapuggalassa anuddhaccaṁ hoti parikkamanāya, vicikicchissa purisapuggalassa tiṇṇavicikicchatā hoti parikkamanāya, kodhanassa purisapuggalassa akkodho hoti parikkamanāya, upanāhissa purisapuggalassa anupanāho hoti parikkamanāya, makkhissa purisapuggalassa amakkho hoti parikkamanāya, paḷāsissa purisapuggalassa apaḷāso hoti parikkamanāya, issukissa purisapuggalassa anissukitā hoti parikkamanāya, maccharissa purisapuggalassa amacchariyaṁ hoti parikkamanāya, saṭhassa purisapuggalassa asāṭheyyaṁ hoti parikkamanāya, māyāvissa purisapuggalassa amāyā hoti parikkamanāya, thaddhassa purisapuggalassa atthaddhiyaṁ hoti parikkamanāya, atimānissa purisapuggalassa anatimāno hoti parikkamanāya, dubbacassa purisapuggalassa sovacassatā hoti parikkamanāya, pāpamittassa purisapuggalassa kalyāṇamittatā hoti parikkamanāya, pamattassa purisapuggalassa appamādo hoti parikkamanāya, assaddhassa purisapuggalassa saddhā hoti parikkamanāya, ahirikassa purisapuggalassa hirī hoti parikkamanāya, anottāpissa purisapuggalassa ottappaṁ hoti parikkamanāya, appassutassa purisapuggalassa bāhusaccaṁ hoti parikkamanāya, kusītassa purisapuggalassa vīriyārambho hoti parikkamanāya, muṭṭhassatissa purisapuggalassa upaṭṭhitassatitā hoti parikkamanāya, duppaññassa purisapuggalassa paññāsampadā hoti parikkamanāya, sandiṭṭhiparāmāsiādhānaggāhiduppaṭinissaggissa purisapuggalassa asandiṭṭhiparāmāsianādhānaggāhisuppaṭinissaggitā hoti parikkamanāya.

An individual who is attached to their own views, holding them tight, and refusing to let go, gets around it by not being attached to their own views, not holding them tight, but letting them go easily.

4. Uparibhagapariyaya

4. Going Up

Seyyathāpi, cunda, ye keci akusalā dhammā sabbe te adhobhāgaṅgamanīyā, ye keci kusalā dhammā sabbe te uparibhāgaṅgamanīyā;

Cunda, all unskillful qualities lead downwards, while all skillful qualities lead upwards.

evameva kho, cunda, vihiṁsakassa purisapuggalassa avihiṁsā hoti uparibhāgāya, pāṇātipātissa purisapuggalassa pāṇātipātā veramaṇī hoti uparibhāgāya ...pe...

In the same way, a cruel individual is led upwards by not being cruel. An individual who kills is led upwards by not killing ...

sandiṭṭhiparāmāsiādhānaggāhiduppaṭinissaggissa   purisapuggalassa asandiṭṭhiparāmāsianādhānaggāhisuppaṭinissaggitā hoti uparibhāgāya.

An individual who is attached to their own views, holding them tight, and refusing to let go, is led upwards by not being attached to their own views, not holding them tight, but letting them go easily.

5. Parinibbanapariyaya

5. The Exposition by Extinguishment

So vata, cunda, attanā palipapalipanno paraṁ palipapalipannaṁ uddharissatīti netaṁ ṭhānaṁ vijjati.

Truly, Cunda, if you're sinking down in the mud you can't pull out someone else who is also sinking down in the mud.

So vata, cunda, attanā apalipapalipanno paraṁ palipapalipannaṁ uddharissatīti ṭhānametaṁ vijjati.

But if you're not sinking down in the mud you can pull out someone else who is sinking down in the mud.

So vata, cunda, attanā adanto avinīto aparinibbuto paraṁ damessati vinessati parinibbāpessatīti netaṁ ṭhānaṁ vijjati.

Truly, if you're not tamed, trained, and extinguished you can't tame, train, and extinguish someone else.

So vata, cunda, attanā danto vinīto parinibbuto paraṁ damessati vinessati parinibbāpessatīti ṭhānametaṁ vijjati.

But if you're tamed, trained, and extinguished you can tame, train, and extinguish someone else.

Evameva kho, cunda, vihiṁsakassa purisapuggalassa avihiṁsā hoti parinibbānāya, pāṇātipātissa purisapuggalassa pāṇātipātā veramaṇī hoti parinibbānāya.

In the same way, a cruel individual extinguishes it by not being cruel. An individual who kills extinguishes it by not killing. …

Adinnādāyissa purisapuggalassa adinnādānā veramaṇī hoti parinibbānāya.

Abrahmacārissa purisapuggalassa abrahmacariyā veramaṇī hoti parinibbānāya.

Musāvādissa purisapuggalassa musāvādā veramaṇī hoti parinibbānāya.

Pisuṇavācassa purisapuggalassa pisuṇāya vācāya veramaṇī hoti parinibbānāya.

Pharusavācassa purisapuggalassa pharusāya vācāya veramaṇī hoti parinibbānāya.

Samphappalāpissa purisapuggalassa samphappalāpā veramaṇī hoti parinibbānāya.

Abhijjhālussa purisapuggalassa anabhijjhā hoti parinibbānāya.

Byāpannacittassa purisapuggalassa abyāpādo hoti parinibbānāya.

Micchādiṭṭhissa purisapuggalassa sammādiṭṭhi hoti parinibbānāya.

Micchāsaṅkappassa purisapuggalassa sammāsaṅkappo hoti parinibbānāya.

Micchāvācassa purisapuggalassa sammāvācā hoti parinibbānāya.

Micchākammantassa purisapuggalassa sammākammanto hoti parinibbānāya.

Micchāājīvassa purisapuggalassa sammāājīvo hoti parinibbānāya.

Micchāvāyāmassa purisapuggalassa sammāvāyāmo hoti parinibbānāya.

Micchāsatissa purisapuggalassa sammāsati hoti parinibbānāya.

Micchāsamādhissa purisapuggalassa sammāsamādhi hoti parinibbānāya.

Micchāñāṇissa purisapuggalassa sammāñāṇaṁ hoti parinibbānāya.

Micchāvimuttissa purisapuggalassa sammāvimutti hoti parinibbānāya.

Thinamiddhapariyuṭṭhitassa purisapuggalassa vigatathinamiddhatā hoti parinibbānāya.

Uddhatassa purisapuggalassa anuddhaccaṁ hoti parinibbānāya.

Vicikicchissa purisapuggalassa tiṇṇavicikicchatā hoti parinibbānāya.

Kodhanassa purisapuggalassa akkodho hoti parinibbānāya.

Upanāhissa purisapuggalassa anupanāho hoti parinibbānāya.

Makkhissa purisapuggalassa amakkho hoti parinibbānāya.

Paḷāsissa purisapuggalassa apaḷāso hoti parinibbānāya.

Issukissa purisapuggalassa anissukitā hoti parinibbānāya.

Maccharissa purisapuggalassa amacchariyaṁ hoti parinibbānāya.

Saṭhassa purisapuggalassa asāṭheyyaṁ hoti parinibbānāya.

Māyāvissa purisapuggalassa amāyā hoti parinibbānāya.

Thaddhassa purisapuggalassa atthaddhiyaṁ hoti parinibbānāya.

Atimānissa purisapuggalassa anatimāno hoti parinibbānāya.

Dubbacassa purisapuggalassa sovacassatā hoti parinibbānāya.

Pāpamittassa purisapuggalassa kalyāṇamittatā hoti parinibbānāya.

Pamattassa purisapuggalassa appamādo hoti parinibbānāya.

Assaddhassa purisapuggalassa saddhā hoti parinibbānāya.

Ahirikassa purisapuggalassa hirī hoti parinibbānāya.

Anottāpissa purisapuggalassa ottappaṁ hoti parinibbānāya.

Appassutassa purisapuggalassa bāhusaccaṁ hoti parinibbānāya.

Kusītassa purisapuggalassa vīriyārambho hoti parinibbānāya.

Muṭṭhassatissa purisapuggalassa upaṭṭhitassatitā hoti parinibbānāya.

Duppaññassa purisapuggalassa paññāsampadā hoti parinibbānāya.

Sandiṭṭhiparāmāsiādhānaggāhiduppaṭinissaggissa purisapuggalassa asandiṭṭhiparāmāsianādhānaggāhisuppaṭinissaggitā hoti parinibbānāya.

An individual who is attached to their own views, holding them tight, and refusing to let go, extinguishes it by not being attached to their own views, not holding them tight, but letting them go easily.

Iti kho, cunda, desito mayā sallekhapariyāyo, desito cittuppādapariyāyo, desito parikkamanapariyāyo, desito uparibhāgapariyāyo, desito parinibbānapariyāyo.

So, Cunda, I've taught the expositions by way of self-effacement, giving rise to thought, the way around, going up, and extinguishing.

Yaṁ kho, cunda, satthārā karaṇīyaṁ sāvakānaṁ hitesinā anukampakena anukampaṁ upādāya, kataṁ vo taṁ mayā.

Out of compassion, I've done what a teacher should do who wants what's best for their disciples.

Etāni, cunda, rukkhamūlāni, etāni suññāgārāni, jhāyatha, cunda, mā pamādattha, mā pacchāvippaṭisārino ahuvattha—ayaṁ kho amhākaṁ anusāsanī"ti.

Here are these roots of trees, and here are these empty huts. Practice absorption, Cunda! Don't be negligent! Don't regret it later! This is my instruction."

Idamavoca bhagavā.

That is what the Buddha said.

Attamano āyasmā mahācundo bhagavato bhāsitaṁ abhinandīti.

Satisfied, Venerable Mahācunda was happy with what the Buddha said.

Catuttālīsapadā vuttā,

sandhayo pañca desitā;

Sallekho nāma suttanto,

gambhīro sāgarūpamoti.

Forty-four items have been stated,

organized into five sections.

"Effacement" is the name of this discourse,

which is deep as the ocean.

Sallekhasuttaṁ niṭṭhitaṁ aṭṭhamaṁ.

9 Sammaditthisutta:

Right View

Evaṁ me sutaṁ—

So I have heard.

ekaṁ samayaṁ bhagavā sāvatthiyaṁ viharati jetavane anāthapiṇḍikassa ārāme.

At one time the Buddha was staying near Sāvatthī in Jeta's Grove, Anāthapiṇḍika's monastery.

Tatra kho āyasmā sāriputto bhikkhū āmantesi:

There Sāriputta addressed the mendicants:

"āvuso bhikkhave"ti.

"Reverends, mendicants!"

"Āvuso"ti kho te bhikkhū āyasmato sāriputtassa paccassosuṁ.

"Reverend," they replied.

Āyasmā sāriputto etadavoca:

Sāriputta said this:

"'Sammādiṭṭhi sammādiṭṭhī'ti, āvuso, vuccati.

"Reverends, they speak of this thing called 'right view'.

Kittāvatā nu kho, āvuso, ariyasāvako sammādiṭṭhi hoti, ujugatāssa diṭṭhi, dhamme aveccappasādena samannāgato, āgato imaṁ saddhamman"ti?

How do you define a noble disciple who has right view, whose view is correct, who has experiential confidence in the teaching, and has come to the true teaching?"

"Dūratopi kho mayaṁ, āvuso, āgaccheyyāma āyasmato sāriputtassa santike etassa bhāsitassa atthamaññātuṁ.

"Reverend, we would travel a long way to learn the meaning of this statement in the presence of Venerable Sāriputta.

Sādhu vatāyasmantaṁyeva sāriputtaṁ paṭibhātu etassa bhāsitassa attho.

May Venerable Sāriputta himself please clarify the meaning of this.

Āyasmato sāriputtassa sutvā bhikkhū dhāressantī"ti.

The mendicants will listen and remember it."

"Tena hi, āvuso, suṇātha, sādhukaṁ manasi karotha, bhāsissāmī"ti.

"Well then, reverends, listen and pay close attention, I will speak."

"Evamāvuso"ti kho te bhikkhū āyasmato sāriputtassa paccassosuṁ.

"Yes, reverend," they replied.

Āyasmā sāriputto etadavoca:

Sāriputta said this:

"Yato kho, āvuso, ariyasāvako akusalañca pajānāti, akusalamūlañca pajānāti, kusalañca pajānāti, kusalamūlañca pajānāti—

"A noble disciple understands the unskillful and its root, and the skillful and its root.

ettāvatāpi kho, āvuso, ariyasāvako sammādiṭṭhi hoti, ujugatāssa diṭṭhi, dhamme aveccappasādena samannāgato, āgato imaṁ saddhammaṁ.

When they've done this, they're defined as a noble disciple who has right view, whose view is correct, who has experiential confidence in the teaching, and has come to the true teaching.

Katamaṁ panāvuso, akusalaṁ, katamaṁ akusalamūlaṁ, katamaṁ kusalaṁ, katamaṁ kusalamūlaṁ?

But what is the unskillful and what is its root? And what is the skillful and what is its root?

Pāṇātipāto kho, āvuso, akusalaṁ, adinnādānaṁ akusalaṁ, kāmesumicchācāro akusalaṁ, musāvādo akusalaṁ, pisuṇā vācā akusalaṁ, pharusā vācā akusalaṁ, samphappalāpo akusalaṁ, abhijjhā akusalaṁ, byāpādo akusalaṁ, micchādiṭṭhi akusalaṁ—

Killing living creatures, stealing, and sexual misconduct; speech that's false, divisive, harsh, or nonsensical; and covetousness, ill will, and wrong view.

idaṁ vuccatāvuso akusalaṁ.

This is called the unskillful.

Katamañcāvuso, akusalamūlaṁ?

And what is the root of the unskillful?

Lobho akusalamūlaṁ, doso akusalamūlaṁ, moho akusalamūlaṁ—

Greed, hate, and delusion.

idaṁ vuccatāvuso, akusalamūlaṁ.

This is called the root of the unskillful.

Katamañcāvuso, kusalaṁ?

And what is the skillful?

Pāṇātipātā veramaṇī kusalaṁ, adinnādānā veramaṇī kusalaṁ, kāmesumicchācārā veramaṇī kusalaṁ, musāvādā veramaṇī kusalaṁ, pisuṇāya vācāya veramaṇī kusalaṁ, pharusāya vācāya veramaṇī kusalaṁ, samphappalāpā veramaṇī kusalaṁ, anabhijjhā kusalaṁ, abyāpādo kusalaṁ, sammādiṭṭhi kusalaṁ—

Avoiding killing living creatures, stealing, and sexual misconduct; avoiding speech that's false, divisive, harsh, or nonsensical; contentment, good will, and right view.

idaṁ vuccatāvuso, kusalaṁ.

This is called the skillful.

Katamañcāvuso, kusalamūlaṁ?

And what is the root of the skillful?

Alobho kusalamūlaṁ, adoso kusalamūlaṁ, amoho kusalamūlaṁ—

Contentment, love, and understanding.

idaṁ vuccatāvuso, kusalamūlaṁ.

This is called the root of the skillful.

Yato kho, āvuso, ariyasāvako evaṁ akusalaṁ pajānāti, evaṁ akusalamūlaṁ pajānāti, evaṁ kusalaṁ pajānāti, evaṁ kusalamūlaṁ pajānāti, so sabbaso rāgānusayaṁ pahāya, paṭighānusayaṁ paṭivinodetvā, 'asmī'ti diṭṭhimānānusayaṁ samūhanitvā, avijjaṁ pahāya vijjaṁ uppādetvā, diṭṭheva dhamme dukkhassantakaro hoti—

A noble disciple understands in this way the unskillful and its root, and the skillful and its root. They've completely given up the underlying tendency to greed, got rid of the underlying tendency to repulsion, and eradicated the underlying tendency to the view and conceit 'I am'. They've given up ignorance and given rise to knowledge, and make an end of suffering in this very life.

ettāvatāpi kho, āvuso, ariyasāvako sammādiṭṭhi hoti, ujugatāssa diṭṭhi, dhamme aveccappasādena samannāgato, āgato imaṁ saddhamman"ti.

When they've done this, they're defined as a noble disciple who has right view, whose view is correct, who has experiential confidence in the teaching, and has come to the true teaching."

"Sādhāvuso"ti kho te bhikkhū āyasmato sāriputtassa bhāsitaṁ abhinanditvā anumoditvā āyasmantaṁ sāriputtaṁ uttari pañhaṁ apucchuṁ:

Saying "Good, sir," those mendicants approved and agreed with what Sāriputta said. Then they asked another question:

"siyā panāvuso, aññopi pariyāyo yathā ariyasāvako sammādiṭṭhi hoti, ujugatāssa diṭṭhi, dhamme aveccappasādena samannāgato, āgato imaṁ saddhamman"ti?

"But reverend, might there be another way to describe a noble disciple who has right view, whose view is correct, who has experiential confidence in the teaching, and has come to the true teaching?"

"Siyā, āvuso.

"There might, reverends.

Yato kho, āvuso, ariyasāvako āhārañca pajānāti, āhārasamudayañca pajānāti, āhāranirodhañca pajānāti, āhāranirodhagāminiṁ paṭipadañca pajānāti—

A noble disciple understands fuel, its origin, its cessation, and the practice that leads to its cessation.

ettāvatāpi kho, āvuso, ariyasāvako sammādiṭṭhi hoti, ujugatāssa diṭṭhi, dhamme aveccappasādena samannāgato, āgato imaṁ saddhammaṁ.

When they've done this, they're defined as a noble disciple who has right view, whose view is correct, who has experiential confidence in the teaching, and has come to the true teaching.

Katamo panāvuso, āhāro, katamo āhārasamudayo, katamo āhāranirodho, katamā āhāranirodhagāminī paṭipadā?

But what is fuel? What is its origin, its cessation, and the practice that leads to its cessation?

Cattārome, āvuso, āhārā bhūtānaṁ vā sattānaṁ ṭhitiyā, sambhavesīnaṁ vā anuggahāya.

There are these four fuels. They maintain sentient beings that have been born and help those that are about to be born.

Katame cattāro?

What four?

Kabaḷīkāro āhāro oḷāriko vā sukhumo vā, phasso dutiyo, manosañcetanā tatiyā, viññāṇaṁ catutthaṁ.

Solid food, whether coarse or fine; contact is the second, mental intention the third, and consciousness the fourth.

Taṇhāsamudayā āhārasamudayo, taṇhānirodhā āhāranirodho, ayameva ariyo aṭṭhaṅgiko maggo āhāranirodhagāminī paṭipadā, seyyathidaṁ—

Fuel originates from craving. Fuel ceases when craving ceases. The practice that leads to the cessation of fuel is simply this noble eightfold path, that is:

sammādiṭṭhi sammāsaṅkappo sammāvācā sammākammanto, sammāājīvo sammāvāyāmo sammāsati sammāsamādhi.

right view, right thought, right speech, right action, right livelihood, right effort, right mindfulness, and right immersion.

Yato kho, āvuso, ariyasāvako evaṁ āhāraṁ pajānāti, evaṁ āhārasamudayaṁ pajānāti, evaṁ āhāranirodhaṁ pajānāti, evaṁ āhāranirodhagāminiṁ paṭipadaṁ pajānāti, so sabbaso rāgānusayaṁ pahāya, paṭighānusayaṁ paṭivinodetvā, 'asmī'ti diṭṭhimānānusayaṁ samūhanitvā, avijjaṁ pahāya vijjaṁ uppādetvā, diṭṭheva dhamme dukkhassantakaro hoti—

A noble disciple understands in this way fuel, its origin, its cessation, and the practice that leads to its cessation. They've completely given up the underlying tendency to greed, got rid of the underlying tendency to repulsion, and eradicated the underlying tendency to the view and conceit 'I am'. They've given up ignorance and given rise to knowledge, and make an end of suffering in this very life.

ettāvatāpi kho, āvuso, ariyasāvako sammādiṭṭhi hoti, ujugatassa diṭṭhi, dhamme aveccappasādena samannāgato, āgato imaṁ saddhamman"ti.

When they've done this, they're defined as a noble disciple who has right view, whose view is correct, who has experiential confidence in the teaching, and has come to the true teaching."

"Sādhāvuso"ti kho te bhikkhū āyasmato sāriputtassa bhāsitaṁ abhinanditvā anumoditvā āyasmantaṁ sāriputtaṁ uttari pañhaṁ apucchuṁ:

Saying "Good, sir," those mendicants … asked another question:

"siyā panāvuso, aññopi pariyāyo yathā ariyasāvako sammādiṭṭhi hoti, ujugatassa diṭṭhi, dhamme aveccappasādena samannāgato, āgato imaṁ saddhamman"ti?

"But reverend, might there be another way to describe a noble disciple who … has come to the true teaching?"

"Siyā, āvuso.

"There might, reverends.

Yato kho, āvuso, ariyasāvako dukkhañca pajānāti, dukkhasamudayañca pajānāti, dukkhanirodhañca pajānāti, dukkhanirodhagāminiṁ paṭipadañca pajānāti—

A noble disciple understands suffering, its origin, its cessation, and the practice that leads to its cessation.

ettāvatāpi kho, āvuso, ariyasāvako sammādiṭṭhi hoti, ujugatassa diṭṭhi, dhamme aveccappasādena samannāgato, āgato imaṁ saddhammaṁ.

When they've done this, they're defined as a noble disciple who … has come to the true teaching.

Katamaṁ panāvuso, dukkhaṁ, katamo dukkhasamudayo, katamo dukkhanirodho, katamā dukkhanirodhagāminī paṭipadā?

But what is suffering? What is its origin, its cessation, and the practice that leads to its cessation?

Jātipi dukkhā, jarāpi dukkhā, maraṇampi dukkhaṁ, sokaparidevadukkhadomanassupāyāsāpi dukkhā, appiyehi sampayogopi dukkho, piyehi vippayogopi dukkho, yampiccham na labhati tampi dukkhaṁ, saṅkhittena pañcupādānakkhandhā dukkhā—

Rebirth is suffering; old age is suffering; death is suffering; sorrow, lamentation, pain, sadness, and distress are suffering; association with the disliked is suffering; separation from the liked is suffering; not getting what you wish for is suffering. In brief, the five grasping aggregates are suffering.

idaṁ vuccatāvuso, dukkhaṁ.

This is called suffering.

Katamo cāvuso, dukkhasamudayo?

And what is the origin of suffering?

Yāyaṁ taṇhā ponobbhavikā nandīrāgasahagatā tatratatrābhinandinī, seyyathidaṁ—

It's the craving that leads to future lives, mixed up with relishing and greed, chasing pleasure in various realms. That is,

kāmataṇhā bhavataṇhā vibhavataṇhā—

craving for sensual pleasures, craving for continued existence, and craving to end existence.

ayaṁ vuccatāvuso, dukkhasamudayo.

This is called the origin of suffering.

Katamo cāvuso, dukkhanirodho?

And what is the cessation of suffering?

Yo tassāyeva taṇhāya asesavirāganirodho cāgo paṭinissaggo mutti anālayo—

It's the fading away and cessation of that very same craving with nothing left over; giving it away, letting it go, releasing it, and not adhering to it.

ayaṁ vuccatāvuso, dukkhanirodho.

This is called the cessation of suffering.

Katamā cāvuso, dukkhanirodhagāminī paṭipadā?

And what is the practice that leads to the cessation of suffering?

Ayameva ariyo aṭṭhaṅgiko maggo, seyyathidaṁ—

It is simply this noble eightfold path, that is:

sammādiṭṭhi ...pe... sammāsamādhi—

right view ... right immersion.

ayaṁ vuccatāvuso, dukkhanirodhagāminī paṭipadā.

This is called the practice that leads to the cessation of suffering.

Yato kho, āvuso, ariyasāvako evaṁ dukkhaṁ pajānāti, evaṁ dukkhasamudayaṁ pajānāti, evaṁ dukkhanirodhaṁ pajānāti, evaṁ dukkhanirodhagāminiṁ paṭipadaṁ pajānāti, so sabbaso rāgānusayaṁ pahāya, paṭighānusayaṁ paṭivinodetvā, 'asmī'ti diṭṭhimānānusayaṁ samūhanitvā, avijjaṁ pahāya vijjaṁ uppādetvā, diṭṭheva dhamme dukkhassantakaro hoti—

A noble disciple understands in this way suffering, its origin, its cessation, and the practice that leads to its cessation. They've completely given up the underlying tendency to greed, got rid of the underlying tendency to repulsion, and eradicated the underlying tendency to the view and conceit 'I am'. They've given up ignorance and given rise to knowledge, and make an end of suffering in this very life.

ettāvatāpi kho, āvuso, ariyasāvako sammādiṭṭhi hoti, ujugatassa diṭṭhi, dhamme aveccappasādena samannāgato, āgato imaṁ saddhamman"ti.

When they've done this, they're defined as a noble disciple who has right view, whose view is correct, who has experiential confidence in the teaching, and has come to the true teaching."

"Sādhāvuso"ti kho te bhikkhū āyasmato sāriputtassa bhāsitaṁ abhinanditvā anumoditvā āyasmantaṁ sāriputtaṁ uttari pañhaṁ apucchuṁ:

Saying "Good, sir," those mendicants … asked another question:

"siyā panāvuso, aññopi pariyāyo yathā ariyasāvako sammādiṭṭhi hoti, ujugatassa diṭṭhi, dhamme aveccappasādena samannāgato, āgato imaṁ saddhamman"ti?

"But reverend, might there be another way to describe a noble disciple who … has come to the true teaching?"

"Siyā, āvuso.

"There might, reverends.

Yato kho, āvuso, ariyasāvako jarāmaraṇañca pajānāti, jarāmaraṇasamudayañca pajānāti, jarāmaraṇanirodhañca pajānāti, jarāmaraṇanirodhagāminiṁ paṭipadañca pajānāti—

A noble disciple understands old age and death, their origin, their cessation, and the practice that leads to their cessation …

ettāvatāpi kho, āvuso, ariyasāvako sammādiṭṭhi hoti, ujugatassa diṭṭhi, dhamme aveccappasādena samannāgato, āgato imaṁ saddhammaṁ.

Katamaṁ panāvuso, jarāmaraṇaṁ, katamo jarāmaraṇasamudayo, katamo jarāmaraṇanirodho, katamā jarāmaraṇanirodhagāminī paṭipadā?

But what are old age and death? What is their origin, their cessation, and the practice that leads to their cessation?

Yā tesaṁ tesaṁ sattānaṁ tamhi tamhi sattanikāye jarā jīraṇatā khaṇḍiccaṁ pāliccaṁ valittacatā āyuno saṁhāni indriyānaṁ paripāko—

The old age, decrepitude, broken teeth, gray hair, wrinkly skin, diminished vitality, and failing faculties of the various sentient beings in the various orders of sentient beings.

ayaṁ vuccatāvuso, jarā.

This is called old age.

Katamañcāvuso, maraṇaṁ?

And what is death?

Yā tesaṁ tesaṁ sattānaṁ tamhā tamhā sattanikāyā cuti cavanatā bhedo antaradhānaṁ maccu maraṇaṁ kālaṅkiriyā khandhānaṁ bhedo, kaḷevarassa nikkhepo, jīvitindriyassupacchedo—

The passing away, perishing, disintegration, demise, mortality, death, decease, breaking up of the aggregates, laying to rest of the corpse, and cutting off of the life faculty of the various sentient beings in the various orders of sentient beings.

idaṁ vuccatāvuso, maraṇaṁ.

This is called death.

Iti ayañca jarā idañca maraṇaṁ—

Such is old age, and such is death.

idaṁ vuccatāvuso, jarāmaraṇaṁ.

This is called old age and death.

Jātisamudayā jarāmaraṇasamudayo, jātinirodhā jarāmaraṇanirodho, ayameva ariyo aṭṭhaṅgiko maggo jarāmaraṇanirodhagāminī paṭipadā, seyyathidaṁ—

Old age and death originate from rebirth. Old age and death cease when rebirth ceases. The practice that leads to the cessation of old age and death is simply this noble eightfold path ...”

sammādiṭṭhi ...pe... sammāsamādhi.

Yato kho, āvuso, ariyasāvako evaṁ jarāmaraṇaṁ pajānāti, evaṁ jarāmaraṇasamudayaṁ pajānāti, evaṁ jarāmaraṇanirodhaṁ pajānāti, evaṁ jarāmaraṇanirodhagāminiṁ paṭipadaṁ pajānāti, so sabbaso rāgānusayaṁ pahāya ...pe... dukkhassantakaro hoti—

ettāvatāpi kho, āvuso, ariyasāvako sammādiṭṭhi hoti, ujugatāssa diṭṭhi, dhamme aveccappasādena samannāgato, āgato imaṁ saddhamman”ti.

"Sādhāvuso"ti kho ...pe... apucchuṁ—

siyā panāvuso ...pe...

"Might there be another way to describe a noble disciple?"

"siyā, āvuso.

"There might, reverends.

Yato kho, āvuso, ariyasāvako jātiñca pajānāti, jātisamudayañca pajānāti, jātinirodhañca pajānāti, jātinirodhagāminiṁ paṭipadañca pajānāti—

A noble disciple understands rebirth, its origin, its cessation, and the practice that leads to its cessation ...

ettāvatāpi kho, āvuso, ariyasāvako sammādiṭṭhi hoti, ujugatāssa diṭṭhi, dhamme aveccappasādena samannāgato, āgato imaṁ saddhammaṁ.

Katamā panāvuso, jāti, katamo jātisamudayo, katamo jātinirodho, katamā jātinirodhagāminī paṭipadā?

But what is rebirth? What is its origin, its cessation, and the practice that leads to its cessation?

Yā tesaṁ tesaṁ sattānaṁ tamhi tamhi sattanikāye jāti sañjāti okkanti abhinibbatti khandhānaṁ pātubhāvo, āyatanānaṁ paṭilābho—

The rebirth, inception, conception, reincarnation, manifestation of the aggregates, and acquisition of the sense fields of the various sentient beings in the various orders of sentient beings.

ayaṁ vuccatāvuso, jāti.

This is called rebirth.

Bhavasamudayā jātisamudayo, bhavanirodhā jātinirodho, ayameva ariyo aṭṭhaṅgiko maggo jātinirodhagāminī paṭipadā, seyyathidaṁ—

Rebirth originates from continued existence. Rebirth ceases when continued existence ceases. The practice that leads to the cessation of rebirth is simply this noble eightfold path ..."

sammādiṭṭhi ...pe... sammāsamādhi.

Yato kho, āvuso, ariyasāvako evaṁ jātiṁ pajānāti, evaṁ jātisamudayaṁ pajānāti, evaṁ jātinirodhaṁ pajānāti, evaṁ jātinirodhagāminiṁ paṭipadaṁ pajānāti, so sabbaso rāgānusayaṁ pahāya ...pe... dukkhassantakaro hoti—

ettāvatāpi kho, āvuso, ariyasāvako sammādiṭṭhi hoti, ujugatāssa diṭṭhi, dhamme aveccappasādena samannāgato, āgato imaṁ saddhamman"ti.

"Sādhāvuso"ti kho ...pe... apucchuṁ—

siyā panāvuso ...pe...

"Might there be another way to describe a noble disciple?"

"siyā, āvuso.

"There might, reverends.

Yato kho, āvuso, ariyasāvako bhavañca pajānāti, bhavasamudayañca pajānāti, bhavanirodhañca pajānāti, bhavanirodhagāminiṁ paṭipadañca pajānāti—

A noble disciple understands continued existence, its origin, its cessation, and the practice that leads to its cessation.

ettāvatāpi kho, āvuso, ariyasāvako sammādiṭṭhi hoti, ujugatāssa diṭṭhi, dhamme aveccappasādena samannāgato, āgato imaṁ saddhammaṁ.

Katamo panāvuso, bhavo, katamo bhavasamudayo, katamo bhavanirodho, katamā bhavanirodhagāminī paṭipadā?

But what is continued existence? What is its origin, its cessation, and the practice that leads to its cessation?

Tayome, āvuso, bhavā—

There are these three states of continued existence.

kāmabhavo, rūpabhavo, arūpabhavo.

Existence in the sensual realm, the realm of luminous form, and the formless realm.

Upādānasamudayā bhavasamudayo, upādānanirodhā bhavanirodho, ayameva ariyo aṭṭhaṅgiko maggo bhavanirodhagāminī paṭipadā, seyyathidaṁ—

Continued existence originates from grasping. Continued existence ceases when grasping ceases. The practice that leads to the cessation of continued existence is simply this noble eightfold path ..."

sammādiṭṭhi ...pe... sammāsamādhi.

Yato kho, āvuso, ariyasāvako evaṁ bhavaṁ pajānāti, evaṁ bhavasamudayaṁ pajānāti, evaṁ bhavanirodhaṁ pajānāti, evaṁ bhavanirodhagāminiṁ paṭipadaṁ pajānāti, so sabbaso rāgānusayaṁ pahāya ...pe... dukkhassantakaro hoti.

Ettāvatāpi kho, āvuso, ariyasāvako sammādiṭṭhi hoti, ujugatāssa diṭṭhi, dhamme aveccappasādena samannāgato, āgato imaṁ saddhamman"ti.

"Sādhāvuso"ti kho ...pe... apucchuṁ—

siyā panāvuso ...pe...

"Might there be another way to describe a noble disciple?"

"siyā, āvuso.

"There might, reverends.

Yato kho, āvuso, ariyasāvako upādānañca pajānāti, upādānasamudayañca pajānāti, upādānanirodhañca pajānāti, upādānanirodhagāminiṁ paṭipadañca pajānāti—

A noble disciple understands grasping, its origin, its cessation, and the practice that leads to its cessation ...

ettāvatāpi kho, āvuso, ariyasāvako sammādiṭṭhi hoti, ujugatassa diṭṭhi, dhamme aveccappasādena samannāgato, āgato imaṁ saddhammaṁ.

Katamaṁ panāvuso, upādānaṁ, katamo upādānasamudayo, katamo upādānanirodho, katamā upādānanirodhagāminī paṭipadā?

But what is grasping? What is its origin, its cessation, and the practice that leads to its cessation?

Cattārimāni, āvuso, upādānāni—

There are these four kinds of grasping.

kāmupādānaṁ, diṭṭhupādānaṁ, sīlabbatupādānaṁ, attavādupādānaṁ.

Grasping at sensual pleasures, views, precepts and observances, and theories of a self.

Taṇhāsamudayā upādānasamudayo, taṇhānirodhā upādānanirodho, ayameva ariyo aṭṭhaṅgiko maggo upādānanirodhagāminī paṭipadā, seyyathidaṁ—

Grasping originates from craving. Grasping ceases when craving ceases. The practice that leads to the cessation of grasping is simply this noble eightfold path ..."

sammādiṭṭhi ...pe... sammāsamādhi.

Yato kho, āvuso, ariyasāvako evaṁ upādānaṁ pajānāti, evaṁ upādānasamudayaṁ pajānāti, evaṁ upādānanirodhaṁ pajānāti, evaṁ upādānanirodhagāminiṁ paṭipadaṁ pajānāti, so sabbaso rāgānusayaṁ pahāya ...pe... dukkhassantakaro hoti—

ettāvatāpi kho, āvuso, ariyasāvako sammādiṭṭhi hoti, ujugatassa diṭṭhi, dhamme aveccappasādena samannāgato, āgato imaṁ saddhamman"ti.

"Sādhāvuso"ti kho ...pe... apucchuṁ—

siyā panāvuso ...pe...

"Might there be another way to describe a noble disciple?"

"siyā, āvuso.

"There might, reverends.

Yato kho, āvuso, ariyasāvako taṇhañca pajānāti, taṇhāsamudayañca pajānāti, taṇhānirodhañca pajānāti, taṇhānirodhagāminiṁ paṭipadañca pajānāti—

A noble disciple understands craving, its origin, its cessation, and the practice that leads to its cessation ...

ettāvatāpi kho, āvuso, ariyasāvako sammādiṭṭhi hoti, ujugatāssa diṭṭhi, dhamme aveccappasādena samannāgato, āgato imaṁ saddhammaṁ.

Katamā panāvuso, taṇhā, katamo taṇhāsamudayo, katamo taṇhānirodho, katamā taṇhānirodhagāminī paṭipadā?

But what is craving? What is its origin, its cessation, and the practice that leads to its cessation?

Chayime, āvuso, taṇhākāyā—

There are these six classes of craving.

rūpataṇhā, saddataṇhā, gandhataṇhā, rasataṇhā, phoṭṭhabbataṇhā, dhammataṇhā.

Craving for sights, sounds, smells, tastes, touches, and thoughts.

Vedanāsamudayā taṇhāsamudayo, vedanānirodhā taṇhānirodho, ayameva ariyo aṭṭhaṅgiko maggo taṇhānirodhagāminī paṭipadā, seyyathidaṁ—

Craving originates from feeling. Craving ceases when feeling ceases. The practice that leads to the cessation of craving is simply this noble eightfold path ...”

sammādiṭṭhi ...pe... sammāsamādhi.

Yato kho, āvuso, ariyasāvako evaṁ taṇhaṁ pajānāti, evaṁ taṇhāsamudayaṁ pajānāti, evaṁ taṇhānirodhaṁ pajānāti, evaṁ taṇhānirodhagāminiṁ paṭipadaṁ pajānāti, so sabbaso rāgānusayam pahāya ...pe... dukkhassantakaro hoti—

ettāvatāpi kho, āvuso, ariyasāvako sammādiṭṭhi hoti, ujugatāssa diṭṭhi, dhamme aveccappasādena samannāgato, āgato imaṁ saddhamman”ti.

“Sādhāvuso”ti kho ...pe... apucchuṁ—

siyā panāvuso ...pe...

“Might there be another way to describe a noble disciple?"

"siyā, āvuso.

"There might, reverends.

Yato kho, āvuso, ariyasāvako vedanañca pajānāti, vedanāsamudayañca pajānāti, vedanānirodhañca pajānāti, vedanānirodhagāminiṁ paṭipadañca pajānāti—

A noble disciple understands feeling, its origin, its cessation, and the practice that leads to its cessation …

ettāvatāpi kho, āvuso, ariyasāvako sammādiṭṭhi hoti, ujugatāssa diṭṭhi, dhamme aveccappasādena samannāgato, āgato imaṁ saddhammaṁ.

Katamā panāvuso, vedanā, katamo vedanāsamudayo, katamo vedanānirodho, katamā vedanānirodhagāminī paṭipadā?

But what is feeling? What is its origin, its cessation, and the practice that leads to its cessation?

Chayime, āvuso, vedanākāyā—

There are these six classes of feeling.

cakkhusamphassajā vedanā, sotasamphassajā vedanā, ghānasamphassajā vedanā, jivhāsamphassajā vedanā, kāyasamphassajā vedanā, manosamphassajā vedanā.

Feeling born of contact through the eye, ear, nose, tongue, body, and mind.

Phassasamudayā vedanāsamudayo, phassanirodhā vedanānirodho, ayameva ariyo aṭṭhaṅgiko maggo vedanānirodhagāminī paṭipadā, seyyathidaṁ—

Feeling originates from contact. Feeling ceases when contact ceases. The practice that leads to the cessation of feeling is simply this noble eightfold path …"

sammādiṭṭhi …pe… sammāsamādhi.

Yato kho, āvuso, ariyasāvako evaṁ vedanaṁ pajānāti, evaṁ vedanāsamudayaṁ pajānāti, evaṁ vedanānirodhaṁ pajānāti, evaṁ vedanānirodhagāminiṁ paṭipadaṁ pajānāti, so sabbaso rāgānusayaṁ pahāya …pe… dukkhassantakaro hoti—

ettāvatāpi kho, āvuso, ariyasāvako sammādiṭṭhi hoti, ujugatāssa diṭṭhi, dhamme aveccappasādena samannāgato, āgato imaṁ saddhamman"ti.

"Sādhāvuso"ti kho …pe… apucchuṁ—

siyā panāvuso …pe…

"Might there be another way to describe a noble disciple?"

"siyā, āvuso.

"There might, reverends.

Yato kho, āvuso, ariyasāvako phassañca pajānāti, phassasamudayañca pajānāti, phassanirodhañca pajānāti, phassanirodhagāminiṁ paṭipadañca pajānāti—

A noble disciple understands contact, its origin, its cessation, and the practice that leads to its cessation …

ettāvatāpi kho, āvuso, ariyasāvako sammādiṭṭhi hoti, ujugatāssa diṭṭhi, dhamme aveccappasādena samannāgato, āgato imaṁ saddhammaṁ.

Katamo panāvuso, phasso, katamo phassasamudayo, katamo phassanirodho, katamā phassanirodhagāminī paṭipadā?

But what is contact? What is its origin, its cessation, and the practice that leads to its cessation?

Chayime, āvuso, phassakāyā—

There are these six classes of contact.

cakkhusamphasso, sotasamphasso, ghānasamphasso, jivhāsamphasso, kāyasamphasso, manosamphasso.

Contact through the eye, ear, nose, tongue, body, and mind.

Saḷāyatanasamudayā phassasamudayo, saḷāyatananirodhā phassanirodho, ayameva ariyo aṭṭhaṅgiko maggo phassanirodhagāminī paṭipadā, seyyathidaṁ—

Contact originates from the six sense fields. Contact ceases when the six sense fields cease. The practice that leads to the cessation of contact is simply this noble eightfold path …"

sammādiṭṭhi …pe… sammāsamādhi.

Yato kho, āvuso, ariyasāvako evaṁ phassaṁ pajānāti, evaṁ phassasamudayaṁ pajānāti, evaṁ phassanirodhaṁ pajānāti, evaṁ phassanirodhagāminiṁ paṭipadaṁ pajānāti, so sabbaso rāgānusayaṁ pahāya …pe… dukkhassantakaro hoti—

ettāvatāpi kho, āvuso, ariyasāvako sammādiṭṭhi hoti, ujugatāssa diṭṭhi, dhamme aveccappasādena samannāgato, āgato imaṁ saddhamman"ti.

"Sādhāvuso"ti kho …pe… apucchuṁ—

siyā panāvuso …pe…

"Might there be another way to describe a noble disciple?"

"siyā, āvuso.

"There might, reverends.

Yato kho, āvuso, ariyasāvako saḷāyatanañca pajānāti, saḷāyatanasamudayañca pajānāti, saḷāyatananirodhañca pajānāti, saḷāyatananirodhagāminiṁ paṭipadañca pajānāti—

A noble disciple understands the six sense fields, their origin, their cessation, and the practice that leads to their cessation …

ettāvatāpi kho, āvuso, ariyasāvako sammādiṭṭhi hoti, ujugatāssa diṭṭhi, dhamme aveccappasādena samannāgato, āgato imaṁ saddhammaṁ.

Katamaṁ panāvuso, saḷāyatanaṁ, katamo saḷāyatanasamudayo, katamo saḷāyatananirodho, katamā saḷāyatananirodhagāminī paṭipadā?

But what are the six sense fields? What is their origin, their cessation, and the practice that leads to their cessation?

Chayimāni, āvuso, āyatanāni—

There are these six sense fields.

cakkhāyatanaṁ, sotāyatanaṁ, ghānāyatanaṁ, jivhāyatanaṁ, kāyāyatanaṁ, manāyatanaṁ.

The sense fields of the eye, ear, nose, tongue, body, and mind.

Nāmarūpasamudayā saḷāyatanasamudayo, nāmarūpanirodhā saḷāyatananirodho, ayameva ariyo aṭṭhaṅgiko maggo saḷāyatananirodhagāminī paṭipadā, seyyathidaṁ—

The six sense fields originate from name and form. The six sense fields cease when name and form cease. The practice that leads to the cessation of the six sense fields is simply this noble eightfold path …"

sammādiṭṭhi …pe… sammāsamādhi.

Yato kho, āvuso, ariyasāvako evaṁ saḷāyatanaṁ pajānāti, evaṁ saḷāyatanasamudayaṁ pajānāti, evaṁ saḷāyatananirodhaṁ pajānāti, evaṁ saḷāyatananirodhagāminiṁ paṭipadaṁ pajānāti, so sabbaso rāgānusayaṁ pahāya …pe… dukkhassantakaro hoti—

ettāvatāpi kho, āvuso, ariyasāvako sammādiṭṭhi hoti, ujugatāssa diṭṭhi, dhamme aveccappasādena samannāgato, āgato imaṁ saddhamman"ti.

"Sādhāvuso"ti kho …pe… apucchuṁ—

siyā panāvuso …pe…

"Might there be another way to describe a noble disciple?"

"siyā, āvuso.

"There might, reverends.

Yato kho, āvuso, ariyasāvako nāmarūpañca pajānāti, nāmarūpasamudayañca pajānāti, nāmarūpanirodhañca pajānāti, nāmarūpanirodhagāminiṁ paṭipadañca pajānāti—

A noble disciple understands name and form, their origin, their cessation, and the practice that leads to their cessation ...

ettāvatāpi kho, āvuso, ariyasāvako sammādiṭṭhi hoti, ujugatassa diṭṭhi, dhamme aveccappasādena samannāgato, āgato imaṁ saddhammaṁ.

Katamaṁ panāvuso, nāmarūpaṁ, katamo nāmarūpasamudayo, katamo nāmarūpanirodho, katamā nāmarūpanirodhagāminī paṭipadā?

But what are name and form? What is their origin, their cessation, and the practice that leads to their cessation?

Vedanā, saññā, cetanā, phasso, manasikāro—

Feeling, perception, intention, contact, and attention—

idaṁ vuccatāvuso, nāmaṁ;

this is called name.

cattāri ca mahābhūtāni, catunnañca mahābhūtānaṁ upādāyarūpaṁ—

The four primary elements, and form derived from the four primary elements—

idaṁ vuccatāvuso, rūpaṁ.

this is called form.

Iti idañca nāmaṁ idañca rūpaṁ—

Such is name and such is form.

idaṁ vuccatāvuso, nāmarūpaṁ.

This is called name and form.

Viññāṇasamudayā nāmarūpasamudayo, viññāṇanirodhā nāmarūpanirodho, ayameva ariyo aṭṭhaṅgiko maggo nāmarūpanirodhagāminī paṭipadā, seyyathidaṁ—

Name and form originate from consciousness. Name and form cease when consciousness ceases. The practice that leads to the cessation of name and form is simply this noble eightfold path ...”

sammādiṭṭhi ...pe... sammāsamādhi.

Yato kho, āvuso, ariyasāvako evaṁ nāmarūpaṁ pajānāti, evaṁ nāmarūpasamudayaṁ pajānāti, evaṁ nāmarūpanirodhaṁ pajānāti, evaṁ nāmarūpanirodhagāminiṁ paṭipadaṁ pajānāti, so sabbaso rāgānusayaṁ pahāya ...pe... dukkhassantakaro hoti—

ettāvatāpi kho, āvuso, ariyasāvako sammādiṭṭhi hoti, ujugatassa diṭṭhi, dhamme aveccappasādena samannāgato, āgato imaṁ saddhamman"ti.

"Sādhāvuso"ti kho ...pe... apucchuṁ—

siyā panāvuso ...pe...

"Might there be another way to describe a noble disciple?"

"siyā, āvuso.

"There might, reverends.

Yato kho, āvuso, ariyasāvako viññāṇañca pajānāti, viññāṇasamudayañca pajānāti, viññāṇanirodhañca pajānāti, viññāṇanirodhagāminiṁ paṭipadañca pajānāti—

A noble disciple understands consciousness, its origin, its cessation, and the practice that leads to its cessation ...

ettāvatāpi kho, āvuso, ariyasāvako sammādiṭṭhi hoti, ujugatāssa diṭṭhi, dhamme aveccappasādena samannāgato, āgato imaṁ saddhammaṁ.

Katamaṁ panāvuso, viññāṇaṁ, katamo viññāṇasamudayo, katamo viññāṇanirodho, katamā viññāṇanirodhagāminī paṭipadā?

But what is consciousness? What is its origin, its cessation, and the practice that leads to its cessation?

Chayime, āvuso, viññāṇakāyā—

There are these six classes of consciousness.

cakkhuviññāṇaṁ, sotaviññāṇaṁ, ghānaviññāṇaṁ, jivhāviññāṇaṁ, kāyaviññāṇaṁ, manoviññāṇaṁ.

Eye, ear, nose, tongue, body, and mind consciousness.

Saṅkhārasamudayā viññāṇasamudayo, saṅkhāranirodhā viññāṇanirodho, ayameva ariyo aṭṭhaṅgiko maggo viññāṇanirodhagāminī paṭipadā, seyyathidaṁ—

Consciousness originates from choices. Consciousness ceases when choices cease. The practice that leads to the cessation of consciousness is simply this noble eightfold path ..."

sammādiṭṭhi ...pe... sammāsamādhi.

Yato kho, āvuso, ariyasāvako evaṁ viññāṇaṁ pajānāti, evaṁ viññāṇasamudayaṁ pajānāti, evaṁ viññāṇanirodhaṁ pajānāti, evaṁ viññāṇanirodhagāminiṁ paṭipadaṁ pajānāti, so sabbaso rāgānusayaṁ pahāya ...pe... dukkhassantakaro hoti—

ettāvatāpi kho, āvuso, ariyasāvako sammādiṭṭhi hoti, ujugatāssa diṭṭhi, dhamme aveccappasādena samannāgato, āgato imaṁ saddhamman"ti.

"Sādhāvuso"ti kho …pe… apucchuṁ—

siyā panāvuso …pe…

"Might there be another way to describe a noble disciple?"

"siyā, āvuso.

"There might, reverends.

Yato kho, āvuso, ariyasāvako saṅkhāre ca pajānāti, saṅkhārasamudayañca pajānāti, saṅkhāranirodhañca pajānāti, saṅkhāranirodhagāminiṁ paṭipadañca pajānāti—

A noble disciple understands choices, their origin, their cessation, and the practice that leads to their cessation …

ettāvatāpi kho, āvuso, ariyasāvako sammādiṭṭhi hoti, ujugatāssa diṭṭhi, dhamme aveccappasādena samannāgato, āgato imaṁ saddhammaṁ.

Katame panāvuso, saṅkhārā, katamo saṅkhārasamudayo, katamo saṅkhāranirodho, katamā saṅkhāranirodhagāminī paṭipadā?

But what are choices? What is their origin, their cessation, and the practice that leads to their cessation?

Tayome, āvuso, saṅkhārā—

There are these three kinds of choice.

kāyasaṅkhāro, vacīsaṅkhāro, cittasaṅkhāro.

Choices by way of body, speech, and mind.

Avijjāsamudayā saṅkhārasamudayo, avijjānirodhā saṅkhāranirodho, ayameva ariyo aṭṭhaṅgiko maggo saṅkhāranirodhagāminī paṭipadā, seyyathidaṁ—

Choices originate from ignorance. Choices cease when ignorance ceases. The practice that leads to the cessation of choices is simply this noble eightfold path …"

sammādiṭṭhi …pe… sammāsamādhi.

Yato kho, āvuso, ariyasāvako evaṁ saṅkhāre pajānāti, evaṁ saṅkhārasamudayaṁ pajānāti, evaṁ saṅkhāranirodhaṁ pajānāti, evaṁ saṅkhāranirodhagāminiṁ paṭipadaṁ pajānāti, so sabbaso rāgānusayaṁ pahāya, paṭighānusayaṁ paṭivinodetvā, 'asmī'ti diṭṭhimānānusayaṁ samūhanitvā, avijjaṁ pahāya vijjaṁ uppādetvā, diṭṭheva dhamme dukkhassantakaro hoti—

ettāvatāpi kho, āvuso, ariyasāvako sammādiṭṭhi hoti, ujugatāssa diṭṭhi, dhamme aveccappasādena samannāgato, āgato imaṁ saddhamman"ti.

"Sādhāvuso"ti kho …pe… apucchuṁ—

siyā panāvuso …pe…

"Might there be another way to describe a noble disciple?"

"siyā, āvuso.

"There might, reverends.

Yato kho, āvuso, ariyasāvako avijjañca pajānāti, avijjāsamudayañca pajānāti, avijjānirodhañca pajānāti, avijjānirodhagāminiṁ paṭipadañca pajānāti—

A noble disciple understands ignorance, its origin, its cessation, and the practice that leads to its cessation …

ettāvatāpi kho, āvuso, ariyasāvako sammādiṭṭhi hoti, ujugatāssa diṭṭhi, dhamme aveccappasādena samannāgato, āgato imaṁ saddhammaṁ.

Katamā panāvuso, avijjā, katamo avijjāsamudayo, katamo avijjānirodho, katamā avijjānirodhagāminī paṭipadā?

But what is ignorance? What is its origin, its cessation, and the practice that leads to its cessation?

Yaṁ kho, āvuso, dukkhe aññāṇaṁ, dukkhasamudaye aññāṇaṁ, dukkhanirodhe aññāṇaṁ, dukkhanirodhagāminiyā paṭipadāya aññāṇaṁ—

Not knowing about suffering, the origin of suffering, the cessation of suffering, and the practice that leads to the cessation of suffering.

ayaṁ vuccatāvuso, avijjā.

This is called ignorance.

Āsavasamudayā avijjāsamudayo, āsavanirodhā avijjānirodho, ayameva ariyo aṭṭhaṅgiko maggo avijjānirodhagāminī paṭipadā, seyyathidaṁ—

Ignorance originates from defilement. Ignorance ceases when defilement ceases. The practice that leads to the cessation of ignorance is simply this noble eightfold path …"

sammādiṭṭhi …pe… sammāsamādhi.

Yato kho, āvuso, ariyasāvako evaṁ avijjaṁ pajānāti, evaṁ avijjāsamudayaṁ pajānāti, evaṁ avijjānirodhaṁ pajānāti, evaṁ avijjānirodhagāminiṁ paṭipadaṁ pajānāti, so sabbaso rāgānusayaṁ pahāya, paṭighānusayaṁ paṭivinodetvā, 'asmī'ti diṭṭhimānānusayaṁ samūhanitvā, avijjaṁ pahāya vijjaṁ uppādetvā, diṭṭheva dhamme dukkhassantakaro hoti—

ettāvatāpi kho, āvuso, ariyasāvako sammādiṭṭhi hoti, ujugatāssa diṭṭhi, dhamme aveccappasādena samannāgato, āgato imaṁ saddhamman"ti.

"Sādhāvuso"ti kho te bhikkhū āyasmato sāriputtassa bhāsitaṁ abhinanditvā anumoditvā āyasmantaṁ sāriputtaṁ uttari pañhaṁ apucchuṁ:

Saying "Good, sir," those mendicants approved and agreed with what Sāriputta said. Then they asked another question:

"siyā panāvuso, aññopi pariyāyo yathā ariyasāvako sammādiṭṭhi hoti, ujugatāssa diṭṭhi, dhamme aveccappasādena samannāgato, āgato imaṁ saddhamman"ti?

"But reverend, might there be another way to describe a noble disciple who has right view, whose view is correct, who has experiential confidence in the teaching, and has come to the true teaching?"

"Siyā, āvuso.

"There might, reverends.

Yato kho, āvuso, ariyasāvako āsavañca pajānāti, āsavasamudayañca pajānāti, āsavanirodhañca pajānāti, āsavanirodhagāminiṁ paṭipadañca pajānāti—

A noble disciple understands defilement, its origin, its cessation, and the practice that leads to its cessation.

ettāvatāpi kho, āvuso, ariyasāvako sammādiṭṭhi hoti, ujugatāssa diṭṭhi, dhamme aveccappasādena samannāgato, āgato imaṁ saddhammaṁ.

When they've done this, they're defined as a noble disciple who has right view, whose view is correct, who has experiential confidence in the teaching, and has come to the true teaching.

Katamo panāvuso, āsavo, katamo āsavasamudayo, katamo āsavanirodho, katamā āsavanirodhagāminī paṭipadāti?

But what is defilement? What is its origin, its cessation, and the practice that leads to its cessation?

Tayome, āvuso, āsavā—

There are these three defilements.

kāmāsavo, bhavāsavo, avijjāsavo.

The defilements of sensuality, desire to be reborn, and ignorance.

Avijjāsamudayā āsavasamudayo, avijjānirodhā āsavanirodho, ayameva ariyo aṭṭhaṅgiko maggo āsavanirodhagāminī paṭipadā, seyyathidaṁ—

Defilement originates from ignorance. Defilement ceases when ignorance ceases. The practice that leads to the cessation of defilement is simply this noble eightfold path, that is:

sammādiṭṭhi ...pe... sammāsamādhi.

right view, right thought, right speech, right action, right livelihood, right effort, right mindfulness, and right immersion.

Yato kho, āvuso, ariyasāvako evaṁ āsavaṁ pajānāti, evaṁ āsavasamudayaṁ pajānāti, evaṁ āsavanirodhaṁ pajānāti, evaṁ āsavanirodhagāminiṁ paṭipadaṁ pajānāti, so sabbaso rāgānusayaṁ pahāya, paṭighānusayaṁ paṭivinodetvā, 'asmī'ti diṭṭhimānānusayaṁ samūhanitvā, avijjaṁ pahāya vijjaṁ uppādetvā, diṭṭheva dhamme dukkhassantakaro hoti—

A noble disciple understands in this way defilement, its origin, its cessation, and the practice that leads to its cessation. They've completely given up the underlying tendency to greed, got rid of the underlying tendency to repulsion, and eradicated the underlying tendency to the view and conceit 'I am'. They've given up ignorance and given rise to knowledge, and make an end of suffering in this very life.

ettāvatāpi kho, āvuso, ariyasāvako sammādiṭṭhi hoti, ujugatāssa diṭṭhi, dhamme aveccappasādena samannāgato, āgato imaṁ saddhamman"ti.

When they've done this, they're defined as a noble disciple who has right view, whose view is correct, who has experiential confidence in the teaching, and has come to the true teaching."

Idamavocāyasmā sāriputto.

This is what Venerable Sāriputta said.

Attamanā te bhikkhū āyasmato sāriputtassa bhāsitaṁ abhinandunti.

Satisfied, the mendicants were happy with what Sāriputta said.

Sammādiṭṭhisuttaṁ niṭṭhitaṁ navamaṁ.

10 Satipatthanasutta:

Mindfulness Meditation

Evaṁ me sutaṁ—

So I have heard.

ekaṁ samayaṁ bhagavā kurūsu viharati kammāsadhammaṁ nāma kurūnaṁ nigamo.

At one time the Buddha was staying in the land of the Kurus, near the Kuru town named Kammāsadamma.

Tatra kho bhagavā bhikkhū āmantesi:

There the Buddha addressed the mendicants,

"bhikkhavo"ti.

"Mendicants!"

"Bhadante"ti te bhikkhū bhagavato paccassosuṁ.

"Venerable sir," they replied.

Bhagavā etadavoca:

The Buddha said this:

"Ekāyano ayaṁ, bhikkhave, maggo sattānaṁ visuddhiyā, sokaparidevānaṁ samatikkamāya, dukkhadomanassānaṁ atthaṅgamāya, ñāyassa adhigamāya, nibbānassa sacchikiriyāya, yadidaṁ cattāro satipaṭṭhānā.

"Mendicants, the four kinds of mindfulness meditation are the path to convergence. They are in order to purify sentient beings, to get past sorrow and crying, to make an end of pain and sadness, to end the cycle of suffering, and to realize extinguishment.

Katame cattāro?

What four?

Idha, bhikkhave, bhikkhu kāye kāyānupassī viharati ātāpī sampajāno satimā, vineyya loke abhijjhādomanassaṁ;

It's when a mendicant meditates by observing an aspect of the body—keen, aware, and mindful, rid of desire and aversion for the world.

vedanāsu vedanānupassī viharati ātāpī sampajāno satimā, vineyya loke abhijjhādomanassaṁ;

They meditate observing an aspect of feelings—keen, aware, and mindful, rid of desire and aversion for the world.

citte cittānupassī viharati ātāpī sampajāno satimā, vineyya loke abhijjhādomanassaṁ;

They meditate observing an aspect of the mind—keen, aware, and mindful, rid of desire and aversion for the world.

dhammesu dhammānupassī viharati ātāpī sampajāno satimā, vineyya loke abhijjhādomanassaṁ.

They meditate observing an aspect of principles—keen, aware, and mindful, rid of desire and aversion for the world.

Uddeso niṭṭhito.

1. Kayanupassana

1. Observing the Body

1.1. Kāyānupassanāānāpānapabba

1.1. Mindfulness of Breathing

Kathañca, bhikkhave, bhikkhu kāye kāyānupassī viharati?

And how does a mendicant meditate observing an aspect of the body?

Idha, bhikkhave, bhikkhu araññagato vā rukkhamūlagato vā suññāgāragato vā nisīdati, pallaṅkaṁ ābhujitvā, ujuṁ kāyaṁ paṇidhāya, parimukhaṁ satiṁ upaṭṭhapetvā.

It's when a mendicant—gone to a wilderness, or to the root of a tree, or to an empty hut—sits down cross-legged, sets their body straight, and establishes mindfulness in front of them.

So satova assasati, satova passasati.

Just mindful, they breathe in. Mindful, they breathe out.

Dīghaṁ vā assasanto 'dīghaṁ assasāmī'ti pajānāti, dīghaṁ vā passasanto 'dīghaṁ passasāmī'ti pajānāti,

Breathing in heavily they know: 'I'm breathing in heavily.' Breathing out heavily they know: 'I'm breathing out heavily.'

rassaṁ vā assasanto 'rassaṁ assasāmī'ti pajānāti, rassaṁ vā passasanto 'rassaṁ passasāmī'ti pajānāti.

When breathing in lightly they know: 'I'm breathing in lightly.' Breathing out lightly they know: 'I'm breathing out lightly.'

'Sabbakāyapaṭisaṁvedī assasissāmī'ti sikkhati, 'sabbakāyapaṭisaṁvedī passasissāmī'ti sikkhati.

They practice like this: 'I'll breathe in experiencing the whole body.' They practice like this: 'I'll breathe out experiencing the whole body.'

'Passambhayaṁ kāyasaṅkhāraṁ assasissāmī'ti sikkhati, 'passambhayaṁ kāyasaṅkhāraṁ passasissāmī'ti sikkhati.

They practice like this: 'I'll breathe in stilling the physical process.' They practice like this: 'I'll breathe out stilling the physical process.'

Seyyathāpi, bhikkhave, dakkho bhamakāro vā bhamakārantevāsī vā dīghaṁ vā añchanto 'dīghaṁ añchāmī'ti pajānāti, rassaṁ vā añchanto 'rassaṁ añchāmī'ti pajānāti;

It's like a deft carpenter or carpenter's apprentice. When making a deep cut they know: 'I'm making a deep cut,' and when making a shallow cut they know: 'I'm making a shallow cut.'

evameva kho, bhikkhave, bhikkhu dīghaṁ vā assasanto 'dīghaṁ assasāmī'ti pajānāti, dīghaṁ vā passasanto 'dīghaṁ passasāmī'ti pajānāti, rassaṁ vā assasanto 'rassaṁ assasāmī'ti pajānāti, rassaṁ vā passasanto 'rassaṁ passasāmī'ti pajānāti;

'sabbakāyapaṭisaṁvedī assasissāmī'ti sikkhati, 'sabbakāyapaṭisaṁvedī passasissāmī'ti sikkhati;

'passambhayaṁ kāyasaṅkhāraṁ assasissāmī'ti sikkhati, 'passambhayaṁ kāyasaṅkhāraṁ passasissāmī'ti sikkhati.

Iti ajjhattaṁ vā kāye kāyānupassī viharati, bahiddhā vā kāye kāyānupassī viharati, ajjhattabahiddhā vā kāye kāyānupassī viharati;

And so they meditate observing an aspect of the body internally, externally, and both internally and externally.

samudayadhammānupassī vā kāyasmiṁ viharati, vayadhammānupassī vā kāyasmiṁ viharati, samudayavayadhammānupassī vā kāyasmiṁ viharati.

They meditate observing the body as liable to originate, as liable to vanish, and as liable to both originate and vanish.

'Atthi kāyo'ti vā panassa sati paccupaṭṭhitā hoti. Yāvadeva ñāṇamattāya paṭissatimattāya anissito ca viharati, na ca kiñci loke upādiyati.

Or mindfulness is established that the body exists, to the extent necessary for knowledge and mindfulness. They meditate independent, not grasping at anything in the world.

Evampi kho, bhikkhave, bhikkhu kāye kāyānupassī viharati.

That's how a mendicant meditates by observing an aspect of the body.

Ānāpānapabbaṁ niṭṭhitaṁ.

1.2. Kāyānupassanāiriyāpathapabba

1.2. The Postures

Puna caparaṁ, bhikkhave, bhikkhu gacchanto vā 'gacchāmī'ti pajānāti, ṭhito vā 'ṭhitomhī'ti pajānāti, nisinno vā 'nisinnomhī'ti pajānāti, sayāno vā 'sayānomhī'ti pajānāti.

Furthermore, when a mendicant is walking they know: 'I am walking.' When standing they know: 'I am standing.' When sitting they know: 'I am sitting.' And when lying down they know: 'I am lying down.'

Yathā yathā vā panassa kāyo paṇihito hoti tathā tathā naṁ pajānāti.

Whatever posture their body is in, they know it.

Iti ajjhattaṁ vā kāye kāyānupassī viharati, bahiddhā vā kāye kāyānupassī viharati, ajjhattabahiddhā vā kāye kāyānupassī viharati;

And so they meditate observing an aspect of the body internally, externally, and both internally and externally.

samudayadhammānupassī vā kāyasmiṁ viharati, vayadhammānupassī vā kāyasmiṁ viharati, samudayavayadhammānupassī vā kāyasmiṁ viharati.

They meditate observing the body as liable to originate, as liable to vanish, and as liable to both originate and vanish.

'Atthi kāyo'ti vā panassa sati paccupaṭṭhitā hoti. Yāvadeva ñāṇamattāya paṭissatimattāya anissito ca viharati, na ca kiñci loke upādiyati.

Or mindfulness is established that the body exists, to the extent necessary for knowledge and mindfulness. They meditate independent, not grasping at anything in the world.

Evampi kho, bhikkhave, bhikkhu kāye kāyānupassī viharati.

That too is how a mendicant meditates by observing an aspect of the body.

Iriyāpathapabbaṁ niṭṭhitaṁ.

1.3. Kāyānupassanāsampajānapabba

1.3. Situational Awareness

Puna caparaṁ, bhikkhave, bhikkhu abhikkante paṭikkante sampajānakārī hoti, ālokite vilokite sampajānakārī hoti, samiñjite pasārite sampajānakārī hoti, saṅghāṭipattacīvaradhāraṇe sampajānakārī hoti, asite pīte khāyite sāyite sampajānakārī hoti, uccārapassāvakamme sampajānakārī hoti, gate ṭhite nisinne sutte jāgarite bhāsite tuṇhībhāve sampajānakārī hoti.

Furthermore, a mendicant acts with situational awareness when going out and coming back; when looking ahead and aside; when bending and extending the limbs; when bearing the outer robe, bowl and robes; when eating, drinking, chewing, and tasting; when urinating and defecating; when walking, standing, sitting, sleeping, waking, speaking, and keeping silent.

Iti ajjhattaṁ vā kāye kāyānupassī viharati …pe…

And so they meditate observing an aspect of the body internally …

evampi kho, bhikkhave, bhikkhu kāye kāyānupassī viharati.

That too is how a mendicant meditates by observing an aspect of the body.

Sampajānapabbaṁ niṭṭhitaṁ.

1.4. Kāyānupassanāpaṭikūlamanasikārapabba

1.4. Focusing on the Repulsive

Puna caparaṁ, bhikkhave, bhikkhu imameva kāyaṁ uddhaṁ pādatalā, adho kesamatthakā, tacapariyantaṁ pūraṁ nānappakārassa asucino paccavekkhati:

Furthermore, a mendicant examines their own body, up from the soles of the feet and down from the tips of the hairs, wrapped in skin and full of many kinds of filth.

'atthi imasmiṁ kāye kesā lomā nakhā dantā taco maṁsaṁ nhāru aṭṭhi aṭṭhimiñjaṁ vakkaṁ hadayaṁ yakanaṁ kilomakaṁ pihakaṁ papphāsaṁ antaṁ antaguṇaṁ udariyaṁ karīsaṁ pittaṁ semhaṁ pubbo lohitaṁ sedo medo assu vasā kheḷo siṅghāṇikā lasikā muttan'ti.

'In this body there is head hair, body hair, nails, teeth, skin, flesh, sinews, bones, bone marrow, kidneys, heart, liver, diaphragm, spleen, lungs, intestines, mesentery, undigested food, feces, bile, phlegm, pus, blood, sweat, fat, tears, grease, saliva, snot, synovial fluid, urine.'

Seyyathāpi, bhikkhave, ubhatomukhā putoḷi pūrā nānāvihitassa dhaññassa, seyyathidaṁ—sālīnaṁ vīhīnaṁ muggānaṁ māsānaṁ tilānaṁ taṇḍulānaṁ. Tamenaṁ cakkhumā puriso muñcitvā paccavekkheyya: 'ime sālī ime vīhī ime muggā ime māsā ime tilā ime taṇḍulā'ti.

It's as if there were a bag with openings at both ends, filled with various kinds of grains, such as fine rice, wheat, mung beans, peas, sesame, and ordinary rice. And someone with good eyesight were to open it and examine the contents: 'These grains are fine rice, these are wheat, these are mung beans, these are peas, these are sesame, and these are ordinary rice.'

Evameva kho, bhikkhave, bhikkhu imameva kāyaṁ uddhaṁ pādatalā, adho kesamatthakā, tacapariyantaṁ pūraṁ nānappakārassa asucino paccavekkhati:

'atthi imasmiṁ kāye kesā lomā …pe… muttan'ti.

Iti ajjhattaṁ vā kāye kāyānupassī viharati …pe…

And so they meditate observing an aspect of the body internally …

evampi kho, bhikkhave, bhikkhu kāye kāyānupassī viharati.

That too is how a mendicant meditates by observing an aspect of the body.

Paṭikūlamanasikārapabbaṁ niṭṭhitaṁ.

1.5. Kāyānupassanādhātumanasikārapabba

1.5. Focusing on the Elements

Puna caparaṁ, bhikkhave, bhikkhu imameva kāyaṁ yathāṭhitaṁ yathāpaṇihitaṁ dhātuso paccavekkhati:

Furthermore, a mendicant examines their own body, whatever its placement or posture, according to the elements:

'atthi imasmiṁ kāye pathavīdhātu āpodhātu tejodhātu vāyodhātū'ti.

'In this body there is the earth element, the water element, the fire element, and the air element.'

Seyyathāpi, bhikkhave, dakkho goghātako vā goghātakantevāsī vā gāviṁ vadhitvā catumahāpathe bilaso vibhajitvā nisinno assa.

It's as if a deft butcher or butcher's apprentice were to kill a cow and sit down at the crossroads with the meat cut into portions.

Evameva kho, bhikkhave, bhikkhu imameva kāyaṁ yathāṭhitaṁ yathāpaṇihitaṁ dhātuso paccavekkhati:

'atthi imasmiṁ kāye pathavīdhātu āpodhātu tejodhātu vāyodhātū'ti.

Iti ajjhattaṁ vā kāye kāyānupassī viharati …pe…

And so they meditate observing an aspect of the body internally …

evampi kho, bhikkhave, bhikkhu kāye kāyānupassī viharati.

That too is how a mendicant meditates by observing an aspect of the body.

Dhātumanasikārapabbaṁ niṭṭhitaṁ.

1.6. Kāyānupassanānavasivathikapabba

1.6. The Charnel Ground Contemplations

Puna caparaṁ, bhikkhave, bhikkhu seyyathāpi passeyya sarīraṁ sivathikāya chaḍḍitaṁ ekāhamataṁ vā dvīhamataṁ vā tīhamataṁ vā uddhumātakaṁ vinīlakaṁ vipubbakajātaṁ.

Furthermore, suppose a mendicant were to see a corpse discarded in a charnel ground. And it had been dead for one, two, or three days, bloated, livid, and festering.

So imameva kāyaṁ upasaṁharati:

They'd compare it with their own body:

'ayampi kho kāyo evaṁdhammo evaṁbhāvī evamanatīto'ti.

'This body is also of that same nature, that same kind, and cannot go beyond that.'

Iti ajjhattaṁ vā kāye kāyānupassī viharati …pe…

And so they meditate observing an aspect of the body internally …

evampi kho, bhikkhave, bhikkhu kāye kāyānupassī viharati.

That too is how a mendicant meditates by observing an aspect of the body.

Puna caparaṁ, bhikkhave, bhikkhu seyyathāpi passeyya sarīraṁ sivathikāya chaḍḍitaṁ kākehi vā khajjamānaṁ kulalehi vā khajjamānaṁ gijjhehi vā khajjamānaṁ kaṅkehi vā khajjamānaṁ sunakhehi vā khajjamānaṁ byagghehi vā khajjamānaṁ dīpīhi vā khajjamānaṁ siṅgālehi vā khajjamānaṁ vividhehi vā pāṇakajātehi khajjamānaṁ.

Furthermore, suppose they were to see a corpse discarded in a charnel ground being devoured by crows, hawks, vultures, herons, dogs, tigers, leopards, jackals, and many kinds of little creatures.

So imameva kāyaṁ upasaṁharati:

They'd compare it with their own body:

'ayampi kho kāyo evaṁdhammo evaṁbhāvī evamanatīto'ti.

'This body is also of that same nature, that same kind, and cannot go beyond that.'

Iti ajjhattaṁ vā kāye kāyānupassī viharati …pe…

And so they meditate observing an aspect of the body internally …

evampi kho, bhikkhave, bhikkhu kāye kāyānupassī viharati.

That too is how a mendicant meditates by observing an aspect of the body.

Puna caparaṁ, bhikkhave, bhikkhu seyyathāpi passeyya sarīraṁ sivathikāya chaḍḍitaṁ aṭṭhikasaṅkhalikaṁ samaṁsalohitaṁ nhārusambandhaṁ …pe…

Furthermore, suppose they were to see a corpse discarded in a charnel ground, a skeleton with flesh and blood, held together by sinews …

Aṭṭhikasaṅkhalikaṁ nimaṁsalohitamakkhitaṁ nhārusambandhaṁ …pe…

A skeleton without flesh but smeared with blood, and held together by sinews …

Aṭṭhikasaṅkhalikaṁ apagatamaṁsalohitaṁ nhārusambandhaṁ …pe…

A skeleton rid of flesh and blood, held together by sinews …

Aṭṭhikāni apagatasambandhāni disā vidisā vikkhittāni, aññena hatthaṭṭhikaṁ aññena pādaṭṭhikaṁ aññena gopphakaṭṭhikaṁ aññena jaṅghaṭṭhikaṁ aññena ūruṭṭhikaṁ aññena kaṭiṭṭhikaṁ aññena phāsukaṭṭhikaṁ aññena piṭṭhiṭṭhikaṁ aññena khandhaṭṭhikaṁ aññena gīvaṭṭhikaṁ aññena hanukaṭṭhikaṁ aññena dantaṭṭhikaṁ aññena sīsakaṭāhaṁ.

Bones rid of sinews scattered in every direction. Here a hand-bone, there a foot-bone, here a shin-bone, there a thigh-bone, here a hip-bone, there a rib-bone, here a back-bone, there an arm-bone, here a neck-bone, there a jaw-bone, here a tooth, there the skull …

So imameva kāyaṁ upasaṁharati:

'ayampi kho kāyo evaṁdhammo evaṁbhāvī evaṁanatīto'ti.

Iti ajjhattaṁ vā kāye kāyānupassī viharati …pe…

evampi kho, bhikkhave, bhikkhu kāye kāyānupassī viharati.

Puna caparaṁ, bhikkhave, bhikkhu seyyathāpi passeyya sarīraṁ sivathikāya chaḍḍitaṁ, aṭṭhikāni setāni saṅkhavaṇṇapaṭibhāgāni …pe…

White bones, the color of shells …

Aṭṭhikāni puñjakitāni terovassikāni …pe…

Decrepit bones, heaped in a pile …

Aṭṭhikāni pūtīni cuṇṇakajātāni.

Bones rotted and crumbled to powder.

So imameva kāyaṁ upasaṁharati:

They'd compare it with their own body:

'ayampi kho kāyo evaṁdhammo evaṁbhāvī evaṁanatīto'ti.

'This body is also of that same nature, that same kind, and cannot go beyond that.'

Iti ajjhattaṁ vā kāye kāyānupassī viharati, bahiddhā vā kāye kāyānupassī viharati, ajjhattabahiddhā vā kāye kāyānupassī viharati;

And so they meditate observing an aspect of the body internally, externally, and both internally and externally.

samudayadhammānupassī vā kāyasmiṁ viharati, vayadhammānupassī vā kāyasmiṁ viharati, samudayavayadhammānupassī vā kāyasmiṁ viharati.

They meditate observing the body as liable to originate, as liable to vanish, and as liable to both originate and vanish.

'Atthi kāyo'ti vā panassa sati paccupaṭṭhitā hoti. Yāvadeva ñāṇamattāya paṭissatimattāya anissito ca viharati, na ca kiñci loke upādiyati.

Or mindfulness is established that the body exists, to the extent necessary for knowledge and mindfulness. They meditate independent, not grasping at anything in the world.

Evampi kho, bhikkhave, bhikkhu kāye kāyānupassī viharati.

That too is how a mendicant meditates by observing an aspect of the body.

Navasivathikapabbaṁ niṭṭhitaṁ.

Cuddasakāyānupassanā niṭṭhitā.

2. Vedananupassana

2. Observing the Feelings

Kathañca, bhikkhave, bhikkhu vedanāsu vedanānupassī viharati?

And how does a mendicant meditate observing an aspect of feelings?

Idha, bhikkhave, bhikkhu sukhaṁ vā vedanaṁ vedayamāno 'sukhaṁ vedanaṁ vedayāmī'ti pajānāti.

It's when a mendicant who feels a pleasant feeling knows: 'I feel a pleasant feeling.'

Dukkhaṁ vā vedanaṁ vedayamāno 'dukkhaṁ vedanaṁ vedayāmī'ti pajānāti.

When they feel a painful feeling, they know: 'I feel a painful feeling.'

Adukkhamasukhaṁ vā vedanaṁ vedayamāno 'adukkhamasukhaṁ vedanaṁ vedayāmī'ti pajānāti.

When they feel a neutral feeling, they know: 'I feel a neutral feeling.'

Sāmisaṁ vā sukhaṁ vedanaṁ vedayamāno 'sāmisaṁ sukhaṁ vedanaṁ vedayāmī'ti pajānāti.

When they feel a material pleasant feeling, they know: 'I feel a material pleasant feeling.'

Nirāmisaṁ vā sukhaṁ vedanaṁ vedayamāno 'nirāmisaṁ sukhaṁ vedanaṁ vedayāmī'ti pajānāti.

When they feel a spiritual pleasant feeling, they know: 'I feel a spiritual pleasant feeling.'

Sāmisaṁ vā dukkhaṁ vedanaṁ vedayamāno 'sāmisaṁ dukkhaṁ vedanaṁ vedayāmī'ti pajānāti.

When they feel a material painful feeling, they know: 'I feel a material painful feeling.'

Nirāmisaṁ vā dukkhaṁ vedanaṁ vedayamāno 'nirāmisaṁ dukkhaṁ vedanaṁ vedayāmī'ti pajānāti.

When they feel a spiritual painful feeling, they know: 'I feel a spiritual painful feeling.'

Sāmisaṁ vā adukkhamasukhaṁ vedanaṁ vedayamāno 'sāmisaṁ adukkhamasukhaṁ vedanaṁ vedayāmī'ti pajānāti.

When they feel a material neutral feeling, they know: 'I feel a material neutral feeling.'

Nirāmisaṁ vā adukkhamasukhaṁ vedanaṁ vedayamāno 'nirāmisaṁ adukkhamasukhaṁ vedanaṁ vedayāmī'ti pajānāti.

When they feel a spiritual neutral feeling, they know: 'I feel a spiritual neutral feeling.'

Iti ajjhattaṁ vā vedanāsu vedanānupassī viharati, bahiddhā vā vedanāsu vedanānupassī viharati, ajjhattabahiddhā vā vedanāsu vedanānupassī viharati;

And so they meditate observing an aspect of feelings internally, externally, and both internally and externally.

samudayadhammānupassī vā vedanāsu viharati, vayadhammānupassī vā vedanāsu viharati, samudayavayadhammānupassī vā vedanāsu viharati.

They meditate observing feelings as liable to originate, as liable to vanish, and as liable to both originate and vanish.

'Atthi vedanā'ti vā panassa sati paccupaṭṭhitā hoti. Yāvadeva ñāṇamattāya paṭissatimattāya anissito ca viharati, na ca kiñci loke upādiyati.

Or mindfulness is established that feelings exist, to the extent necessary for knowledge and mindfulness. They meditate independent, not grasping at anything in the world.

Evampi kho, bhikkhave, bhikkhu vedanāsu vedanānupassī viharati.

That's how a mendicant meditates by observing an aspect of feelings.

Vedanānupassanā niṭṭhitā.

3. Cittanupassana

3. Observing the Mind

Kathañca, bhikkhave, bhikkhu citte cittānupassī viharati?

And how does a mendicant meditate observing an aspect of the mind?

Idha, bhikkhave, bhikkhu sarāgaṁ vā cittaṁ 'sarāgaṁ cittan'ti pajānāti.

It's when a mendicant understands mind with greed as 'mind with greed,'

Vītarāgaṁ vā cittaṁ 'vītarāgaṁ cittan'ti pajānāti.

and mind without greed as 'mind without greed.'

Sadosaṁ vā cittaṁ 'sadosaṁ cittan'ti pajānāti.

They understand mind with hate as 'mind with hate,'

Vītadosaṁ vā cittaṁ 'vītadosaṁ cittan'ti pajānāti.

and mind without hate as 'mind without hate.'

Samohaṁ vā cittaṁ 'samohaṁ cittan'ti pajānāti.

They understand mind with delusion as 'mind with delusion,'

Vītamohaṁ vā cittaṁ 'vītamohaṁ cittan'ti pajānāti.

and mind without delusion as 'mind without delusion.'

Saṅkhittaṁ vā cittaṁ 'saṅkhittaṁ cittan'ti pajānāti.

They know constricted mind as 'constricted mind,'

Vikkhittaṁ vā cittaṁ 'vikkhittaṁ cittan'ti pajānāti.

and scattered mind as 'scattered mind.'

Mahaggataṁ vā cittaṁ 'mahaggataṁ cittan'ti pajānāti.

They know expansive mind as 'expansive mind,'

Amahaggataṁ vā cittaṁ 'amahaggataṁ cittan'ti pajānāti.

and unexpansive mind as 'unexpansive mind.'

Sauttaraṁ vā cittaṁ 'sauttaraṁ cittan'ti pajānāti.

They know mind that is not supreme as 'mind that is not supreme,'

Anuttaraṁ vā cittaṁ 'anuttaraṁ cittan'ti pajānāti.

and mind that is supreme as 'mind that is supreme.'

Samāhitaṁ vā cittaṁ 'samāhitaṁ cittan'ti pajānāti.

They know mind immersed in samādhi as 'mind immersed in samādhi,'

Asamāhitaṁ vā cittaṁ 'asamāhitaṁ cittan'ti pajānāti.

and mind not immersed in samādhi as 'mind not immersed in samādhi.'

Vimuttaṁ vā cittaṁ 'vimuttaṁ cittan'ti pajānāti.

They know freed mind as 'freed mind,'

Avimuttaṁ vā cittaṁ 'avimuttaṁ cittan'ti pajānāti.

and unfreed mind as 'unfreed mind.'

Iti ajjhattaṁ vā citte cittānupassī viharati, bahiddhā vā citte cittānupassī viharati, ajjhattabahiddhā vā citte cittānupassī viharati;

And so they meditate observing an aspect of the mind internally, externally, and both internally and externally.

samudayadhammānupassī vā cittasmiṁ viharati, vayadhammānupassī vā cittasmiṁ viharati, samudayavayadhammānupassī vā cittasmiṁ viharati.

They meditate observing the mind as liable to originate, as liable to vanish, and as liable to both originate and vanish.

'Atthi cittan'ti vā panassa sati paccupaṭṭhitā hoti. Yāvadeva ñāṇamattāya paṭissatimattāya anissito ca viharati, na ca kiñci loke upādiyati.

Or mindfulness is established that the mind exists, to the extent necessary for knowledge and mindfulness. They meditate independent, not grasping at anything in the world.

Evampi kho, bhikkhave, bhikkhu citte cittānupassī viharati.

That's how a mendicant meditates by observing an aspect of the mind.

Cittānupassanā niṭṭhitā.

4. Dhammanupassana

4. Observing Principles

4.1. Dhammānupassanānīvaraṇapabba

4.1. The Hindrances

Kathañca, bhikkhave, bhikkhu dhammesu dhammānupassī viharati?

And how does a mendicant meditate observing an aspect of principles?

Idha, bhikkhave, bhikkhu dhammesu dhammānupassī viharati pañcasu nīvaraṇesu.

It's when a mendicant meditates by observing an aspect of principles with respect to the five hindrances.

Kathañca pana, bhikkhave, bhikkhu dhammesu dhammānupassī viharati pañcasu nīvaraṇesu?

And how does a mendicant meditate observing an aspect of principles with respect to the five hindrances?

Idha, bhikkhave, bhikkhu santaṁ vā ajjhattaṁ kāmacchandaṁ 'atthi me ajjhattaṁ kāmacchando'ti pajānāti, asantaṁ vā ajjhattaṁ kāmacchandaṁ 'natthi me ajjhattaṁ kāmacchando'ti pajānāti; yathā ca anuppannassa kāmacchandassa uppādo hoti tañca pajānāti, yathā ca uppannassa kāmacchandassa pahānaṁ hoti tañca pajānāti, yathā ca pahīnassa kāmacchandassa āyatiṁ anuppādo hoti tañca pajānāti.

It's when a mendicant who has sensual desire in them understands: 'I have sensual desire in me.' When they don't have sensual desire in them, they understand: 'I don't have sensual desire in me.' They understand how sensual desire arises; how, when it's already arisen, it's given up; and how, once it's given up, it doesn't arise again in the future.

Santaṁ vā ajjhattaṁ byāpādaṁ 'atthi me ajjhattaṁ byāpādo'ti pajānāti, asantaṁ vā ajjhattaṁ byāpādaṁ 'natthi me ajjhattaṁ byāpādo'ti pajānāti; yathā ca anuppannassa byāpādassa uppādo hoti tañca pajānāti, yathā ca uppannassa byāpādassa pahānaṁ hoti tañca pajānāti, yathā ca pahīnassa byāpādassa āyatiṁ anuppādo hoti tañca pajānāti.

When they have ill will in them, they understand: 'I have ill will in me.' When they don't have ill will in them, they understand: 'I don't have ill will in me.' They understand how ill will arises; how, when it's already arisen, it's given up; and how, once it's given up, it doesn't arise again in the future.

Santaṁ vā ajjhattaṁ thinamiddhaṁ 'atthi me ajjhattaṁ thinamiddhan'ti pajānāti, asantaṁ vā ajjhattaṁ thinamiddhaṁ 'natthi me ajjhattaṁ thinamiddhan'ti pajānāti, yathā ca anuppannassa thinamiddhassa uppādo hoti tañca pajānāti, yathā ca uppannassa thinamiddhassa pahānaṁ hoti tañca pajānāti, yathā ca pahīnassa thinamiddhassa āyatiṁ anuppādo hoti tañca pajānāti.

When they have dullness and drowsiness in them, they understand: 'I have dullness and drowsiness in me.' When they don't have dullness and drowsiness in them, they understand: 'I don't have dullness and drowsiness in me.' They understand how dullness and drowsiness arise; how, when they've already arisen, they're given up; and how, once they're given up, they don't arise again in the future.

Santaṁ vā ajjhattaṁ uddhaccakukkuccaṁ 'atthi me ajjhattaṁ uddhaccakukkuccan'ti pajānāti, asantaṁ vā ajjhattaṁ uddhaccakukkuccaṁ 'natthi me ajjhattaṁ uddhaccakukkuccan'ti pajānāti; yathā ca anuppannassa uddhaccakukkuccassa uppādo hoti tañca pajānāti, yathā ca uppannassa uddhaccakukkuccassa pahānaṁ hoti tañca pajānāti, yathā ca pahīnassa uddhaccakukkuccassa āyatiṁ anuppādo hoti tañca pajānāti.

When they have restlessness and remorse in them, they understand: 'I have restlessness and remorse in me.' When they don't have restlessness and remorse in them, they understand: 'I don't have restlessness and remorse in me.' They understand how restlessness and remorse arise; how, when they've already arisen, they're given up; and how, once they're given up, they don't arise again in the future.

Santaṁ vā ajjhattaṁ vicikicchaṁ 'atthi me ajjhattaṁ vicikicchā'ti pajānāti, asantaṁ vā ajjhattaṁ vicikicchaṁ 'natthi me ajjhattaṁ vicikicchā'ti pajānāti; yathā ca anuppannāya vicikicchāya uppādo hoti tañca pajānāti, yathā ca uppannāya vicikicchāya pahānaṁ hoti tañca pajānāti, yathā ca pahīnāya vicikicchāya āyatiṁ anuppādo hoti tañca pajānāti.

When they have doubt in them, they understand: 'I have doubt in me.' When they don't have doubt in them, they understand: 'I don't have doubt in me.' They understand how doubt arises; how, when it's already arisen, it's given up; and how, once it's given up, it doesn't arise again in the future.

Iti ajjhattaṁ vā dhammesu dhammānupassī viharati, bahiddhā vā dhammesu dhammānupassī viharati, ajjhattabahiddhā vā dhammesu dhammānupassī viharati;

And so they meditate observing an aspect of principles internally, externally, and both internally and externally.

samudayadhammānupassī vā dhammesu viharati, vayadhammānupassī vā dhammesu viharati, samudayavayadhammānupassī vā dhammesu viharati.

They meditate observing the principles as liable to originate, as liable to vanish, and as liable to both originate and vanish.

'Atthi dhammā'ti vā panassa sati paccupaṭṭhitā hoti. Yāvadeva ñāṇamattāya paṭissatimattāya anissito ca viharati, na ca kiñci loke upādiyati.

Or mindfulness is established that principles exist, to the extent necessary for knowledge and mindfulness. They meditate independent, not grasping at anything in the world.

Evampi kho, bhikkhave, bhikkhu dhammesu dhammānupassī viharati pañcasu nīvaraṇesu.

That's how a mendicant meditates by observing an aspect of principles with respect to the five hindrances.

Nīvaraṇapabbaṁ niṭṭhitaṁ.

4.2. Dhammānupassanākhandhapabba

4.2. The Aggregates

Puna caparaṁ, bhikkhave, bhikkhu dhammesu dhammānupassī viharati pañcasu upādānakkhandhesu.

Furthermore, a mendicant meditates by observing an aspect of principles with respect to the five grasping aggregates.

Kathañca pana, bhikkhave, bhikkhu dhammesu dhammānupassī viharati pañcasu upādānakkhandhesu?

And how does a mendicant meditate observing an aspect of principles with respect to the five grasping aggregates?

Idha, bhikkhave, bhikkhu:

It's when a mendicant contemplates:

'iti rūpaṁ, iti rūpassa samudayo, iti rūpassa atthaṅgamo;

'Such is form, such is the origin of form, such is the ending of form.

iti vedanā, iti vedanāya samudayo, iti vedanāya atthaṅgamo;

Such is feeling, such is the origin of feeling, such is the ending of feeling.

iti saññā, iti saññāya samudayo, iti saññāya atthaṅgamo;

Such is perception, such is the origin of perception, such is the ending of perception.

iti saṅkhārā, iti saṅkhārānaṁ samudayo, iti saṅkhārānaṁ atthaṅgamo;

Such are choices, such is the origin of choices, such is the ending of choices.

iti viññāṇaṁ, iti viññāṇassa samudayo, iti viññāṇassa atthaṅgamo'ti;

Such is consciousness, such is the origin of consciousness, such is the ending of consciousness.'

iti ajjhattaṁ vā dhammesu dhammānupassī viharati, bahiddhā vā dhammesu dhammānupassī viharati, ajjhattabahiddhā vā dhammesu dhammānupassī viharati;

And so they meditate observing an aspect of principles internally …

samudayadhammānupassī vā dhammesu viharati, vayadhammānupassī vā dhammesu viharati, samudayavayadhammānupassī vā dhammesu viharati.

'Atthi dhammā'ti vā panassa sati paccupaṭṭhitā hoti. Yāvadeva ñāṇamattāya paṭissatimattāya anissito ca viharati, na ca kiñci loke upādiyati.

Evampi kho, bhikkhave, bhikkhu dhammesu dhammānupassī viharati pañcasu upādānakkhandhesu.

That's how a mendicant meditates by observing an aspect of principles with respect to the five grasping aggregates.

Khandhapabbaṁ niṭṭhitaṁ.

4.3. Dhammānupassanāāyatanapabba

4.3. The Sense Fields

Puna caparaṁ, bhikkhave, bhikkhu dhammesu dhammānupassī viharati chasu ajjhattikabāhiresu āyatanesu.

Furthermore, a mendicant meditates by observing an aspect of principles with respect to the six interior and exterior sense fields.

Kathañca pana, bhikkhave, bhikkhu dhammesu dhammānupassī viharati chasu ajjhattikabāhiresu āyatanesu?

And how does a mendicant meditate observing an aspect of principles with respect to the six interior and exterior sense fields?

Idha, bhikkhave, bhikkhu cakkhuñca pajānāti, rūpe ca pajānāti, yañca tadubhayaṁ paṭicca uppajjati samyojanaṁ tañca pajānāti, yathā ca anuppannassa samyojanassa uppādo hoti tañca pajānāti, yathā ca uppannassa samyojanassa pahānaṁ hoti tañca pajānāti, yathā ca pahīnassa samyojanassa āyatiṁ anuppādo hoti tañca pajānāti.

It's when a mendicant understands the eye, sights, and the fetter that arises dependent on both of these. They understand how the fetter that has not arisen comes to arise; how the arisen fetter comes to be abandoned; and how the abandoned fetter comes to not rise again in the future.

Sotañca pajānāti, sadde ca pajānāti, yañca tadubhayaṁ paṭicca uppajjati samyojanaṁ tañca pajānāti, yathā ca anuppannassa samyojanassa uppādo hoti tañca pajānāti, yathā ca uppannassa samyojanassa pahānaṁ hoti tañca pajānāti, yathā ca pahīnassa samyojanassa āyatiṁ anuppādo hoti tañca pajānāti.

They understand the ear, sounds, and the fetter …

Ghānañca pajānāti, gandhe ca pajānāti, yañca tadubhayaṁ paṭicca uppajjati samyojanaṁ tañca pajānāti, yathā ca anuppannassa samyojanassa uppādo hoti tañca pajānāti, yathā ca uppannassa samyojanassa pahānaṁ hoti tañca pajānāti, yathā ca pahīnassa samyojanassa āyatiṁ anuppādo hoti tañca pajānāti.

They understand the nose, smells, and the fetter …

Jivhañca pajānāti, rase ca pajānāti, yañca tadubhayaṁ paṭicca uppajjati samyojanaṁ tañca pajānāti, yathā ca anuppannassa samyojanassa uppādo hoti tañca pajānāti, yathā ca uppannassa samyojanassa pahānaṁ hoti tañca pajānāti, yathā ca pahīnassa samyojanassa āyatiṁ anuppādo hoti tañca pajānāti.

They understand the tongue, tastes, and the fetter …

Kāyañca pajānāti, phoṭṭhabbe ca pajānāti, yañca tadubhayaṁ paṭicca uppajjati samyojanaṁ tañca pajānāti, yathā ca anuppannassa samyojanassa uppādo hoti tañca pajānāti, yathā ca uppannassa samyojanassa pahānaṁ hoti tañca pajānāti, yathā ca pahīnassa samyojanassa āyatiṁ anuppādo hoti tañca pajānāti.

They understand the body, touches, and the fetter …

Manañca pajānāti, dhamme ca pajānāti, yañca tadubhayaṁ paṭicca uppajjati saṁyojanaṁ tañca pajānāti, yathā ca anuppannassa saṁyojanassa uppādo hoti tañca pajānāti, yathā ca uppannassa saṁyojanassa pahānaṁ hoti tañca pajānāti, yathā ca pahīnassa saṁyojanassa āyatiṁ anuppādo hoti tañca pajānāti.

They understand the mind, thoughts, and the fetter that arises dependent on both of these. They understand how the fetter that has not arisen comes to arise; how the arisen fetter comes to be abandoned; and how the abandoned fetter comes to not rise again in the future.

Iti ajjhattaṁ vā dhammesu dhammānupassī viharati, bahiddhā vā dhammesu dhammānupassī viharati, ajjhattabahiddhā vā dhammesu dhammānupassī viharati;

And so they meditate observing an aspect of principles internally ...

samudayadhammānupassī vā dhammesu viharati, vayadhammānupassī vā dhammesu viharati, samudayavayadhammānupassī vā dhammesu viharati.

'Atthi dhammā'ti vā panassa sati paccupaṭṭhitā hoti. Yāvadeva ñāṇamattāya paṭissatimattāya anissito ca viharati na ca kiñci loke upādiyati.

Evampi kho, bhikkhave, bhikkhu dhammesu dhammānupassī viharati chasu ajjhattikabāhiresu āyatanesu.

That's how a mendicant meditates by observing an aspect of principles with respect to the six internal and external sense fields.

Āyatanapabbaṁ niṭṭhitaṁ.

4.4. Dhammānupassanābojjhaṅgapabba

4.4. The Awakening Factors

Puna caparaṁ, bhikkhave, bhikkhu dhammesu dhammānupassī viharati sattasu bojjhaṅgesu.

Furthermore, a mendicant meditates by observing an aspect of principles with respect to the seven awakening factors.

Kathañca pana, bhikkhave, bhikkhu dhammesu dhammānupassī viharati sattasu bojjhaṅgesu?

And how does a mendicant meditate observing an aspect of principles with respect to the seven awakening factors?

Idha, bhikkhave, bhikkhu santaṁ vā ajjhattaṁ satisambojjhaṅgaṁ 'atthi me ajjhattaṁ satisambojjhaṅgo'ti pajānāti, asantaṁ vā ajjhattaṁ satisambojjhaṅgaṁ 'natthi me ajjhattaṁ satisambojjhaṅgo'ti pajānāti, yathā ca anuppannassa satisambojjhaṅgassa uppādo hoti tañca pajānāti, yathā ca uppannassa satisambojjhaṅgassa bhāvanāya pāripūrī hoti tañca pajānāti.

It's when a mendicant who has the awakening factor of mindfulness in them understands: 'I have the awakening factor of mindfulness in me.' When they don't have the awakening factor of mindfulness in them, they understand: 'I don't have the awakening factor of mindfulness in me.' They understand how the awakening factor of mindfulness that has not arisen comes to arise; and how the awakening factor of mindfulness that has arisen becomes fulfilled by development.

Santaṁ vā ajjhattaṁ dhammavicayasambojjhaṅgaṁ 'atthi me ajjhattaṁ dhammavicayasambojjhaṅgo'ti pajānāti, asantaṁ vā ajjhattaṁ dhammavicayasambojjhaṅgaṁ 'natthi me ajjhattaṁ dhammavicayasambojjhaṅgo'ti pajānāti, yathā ca anuppannassa dhammavicayasambojjhaṅgassa uppādo hoti tañca pajānāti, yathā ca uppannassa dhammavicayasambojjhaṅgassa bhāvanāya pāripūrī hoti tañca pajānāti.

When they have the awakening factor of investigation of principles …

Santaṁ vā ajjhattaṁ vīriyasambojjhaṅgaṁ 'atthi me ajjhattaṁ vīriyasambojjhaṅgo'ti pajānāti, asantaṁ vā ajjhattaṁ vīriyasambojjhaṅgaṁ 'natthi me ajjhattaṁ vīriyasambojjhaṅgo'ti pajānāti, yathā ca anuppannassa vīriyasambojjhaṅgassa uppādo hoti tañca pajānāti, yathā ca uppannassa vīriyasambojjhaṅgassa bhāvanāya pāripūrī hoti tañca pajānāti.

energy …

Santaṁ vā ajjhattaṁ pītisambojjhaṅgaṁ 'atthi me ajjhattaṁ pītisambojjhaṅgo'ti pajānāti, asantaṁ vā ajjhattaṁ pītisambojjhaṅgaṁ 'natthi me ajjhattaṁ pītisambojjhaṅgo'ti pajānāti, yathā ca anuppannassa pītisambojjhaṅgassa uppādo hoti tañca pajānāti, yathā ca uppannassa pītisambojjhaṅgassa bhāvanāya pāripūrī hoti tañca pajānāti.

rapture …

Santaṁ vā ajjhattaṁ passaddhisambojjhaṅgaṁ 'atthi me ajjhattaṁ passaddhisambojjhaṅgo'ti pajānāti, asantaṁ vā ajjhattaṁ passaddhisambojjhaṅgaṁ 'natthi me ajjhattaṁ passaddhisambojjhaṅgo'ti pajānāti, yathā ca anuppannassa passaddhisambojjhaṅgassa uppādo hoti tañca pajānāti, yathā ca uppannassa passaddhisambojjhaṅgassa bhāvanāya pāripūrī hoti tañca pajānāti.

tranquility …

Santaṁ vā ajjhattaṁ samādhisambojjhaṅgaṁ 'atthi me ajjhattaṁ samādhisambojjhaṅgo'ti pajānāti, asantaṁ vā ajjhattaṁ samādhisambojjhaṅgaṁ 'natthi me ajjhattaṁ samādhisambojjhaṅgo'ti pajānāti, yathā ca anuppannassa samādhisambojjhaṅgassa uppādo hoti tañca pajānāti, yathā ca uppannassa samādhisambojjhaṅgassa bhāvanāya pāripūrī hoti tañca pajānāti.

immersion …

Santaṁ vā ajjhattaṁ upekkhāsambojjhaṅgaṁ 'atthi me ajjhattaṁ upekkhāsambojjhaṅgo'ti pajānāti, asantaṁ vā ajjhattaṁ upekkhāsambojjhaṅgaṁ 'natthi me ajjhattaṁ upekkhāsambojjhaṅgo'ti pajānāti, yathā ca anuppannassa upekkhāsambojjhaṅgassa uppādo hoti tañca pajānāti, yathā ca uppannassa upekkhāsambojjhaṅgassa bhāvanāya pāripūrī hoti tañca pajānāti.

equanimity in them, they understand: 'I have the awakening factor of equanimity in me.' When they don't have the awakening factor of equanimity in them, they understand: 'I don't have the awakening factor of equanimity in me.' They understand how the awakening factor of equanimity that has not arisen comes to arise; and how the awakening factor of equanimity that has arisen becomes fulfilled by development.

Iti ajjhattaṁ vā dhammesu dhammānupassī viharati, bahiddhā vā dhammesu dhammānupassī viharati, ajjhattabahiddhā vā dhammesu dhammānupassī viharati;

And so they meditate observing an aspect of principles internally, externally, and both internally and externally.

samudayadhammānupassī vā dhammesu viharati, vayadhammānupassī vā dhammesu viharati, samudayavayadhammānupassī vā dhammesu viharati.

They meditate observing the principles as liable to originate, as liable to vanish, and as liable to both originate and vanish.

'Atthi dhammā'ti vā panassa sati paccupaṭṭhitā hoti. Yāvadeva ñāṇamattāya paṭissatimattāya anissito ca viharati, na ca kiñci loke upādiyati.

Or mindfulness is established that principles exist, to the extent necessary for knowledge and mindfulness. They meditate independent, not grasping at anything in the world.

Evampi kho, bhikkhave, bhikkhu dhammesu dhammānupassī viharati sattasu bojjhaṅgesu.

That's how a mendicant meditates by observing an aspect of principles with respect to the seven awakening factors.

Bojjhaṅgapabbaṁ niṭṭhitaṁ.

4.5. Dhammānupassanāsaccapabba

4.5. The Truths

Puna caparaṁ, bhikkhave, bhikkhu dhammesu dhammānupassī viharati catūsu ariyasaccesu.

Furthermore, a mendicant meditates by observing an aspect of principles with respect to the four noble truths.

Kathañca pana, bhikkhave, bhikkhu dhammesu dhammānupassī viharati catūsu ariyasaccesu?

And how does a mendicant meditate observing an aspect of principles with respect to the four noble truths?

Idha, bhikkhave, bhikkhu 'idaṁ dukkhan'ti yathābhūtaṁ pajānāti, 'ayaṁ dukkhasamudayo'ti yathābhūtaṁ pajānāti, 'ayaṁ dukkhanirodho'ti yathābhūtaṁ pajānāti, 'ayaṁ dukkhanirodhagāminī paṭipadā'ti yathābhūtaṁ pajānāti.

It's when a mendicant truly understands: 'This is suffering' ... 'This is the origin of suffering' ... 'This is the cessation of suffering' ... 'This is the practice that leads to the cessation of suffering.'

Iti ajjhattaṁ vā dhammesu dhammānupassī viharati, bahiddhā vā dhammesu dhammānupassī viharati, ajjhattabahiddhā vā dhammesu dhammānupassī viharati;

And so they meditate observing an aspect of principles internally, externally, and both internally and externally.

samudayadhammānupassī vā dhammesu viharati, vayadhammānupassī vā dhammesu viharati, samudayavayadhammānupassī vā dhammesu viharati.

They meditate observing the principles as liable to originate, as liable to vanish, and as liable to both originate and vanish.

'Atthi dhammā'ti vā panassa sati paccupaṭṭhitā hoti. Yāvadeva ñāṇamattāya paṭissatimattāya anissito ca viharati, na ca kiñci loke upādiyati.

Or mindfulness is established that principles exist, to the extent necessary for knowledge and mindfulness. They meditate independent, not grasping at anything in the world.

Evampi kho, bhikkhave, bhikkhu dhammesu dhammānupassī viharati catūsu ariyasaccesu.

That's how a mendicant meditates by observing an aspect of principles with respect to the four noble truths.

Saccapabbaṁ niṭṭhitaṁ.

Dhammānupassanā niṭṭhitā.

Yo hi koci, bhikkhave, ime cattāro satipaṭṭhāne evaṁ bhāveyya satta vassāni, tassa dvinnaṁ phalānaṁ aññataraṁ phalaṁ pāṭikaṅkhaṁ

Anyone who develops these four kinds of mindfulness meditation in this way for seven years can expect one of two results:

diṭṭheva dhamme aññā; sati vā upādisese anāgāmitā.

enlightenment in the present life, or if there's something left over, non-return.

Tiṭṭhantu, bhikkhave, satta vassāni.

Let alone seven years,

Yo hi koci, bhikkhave, ime cattāro satipaṭṭhāne evaṁ bhāveyya cha vassāni ... pe...

anyone who develops these four kinds of mindfulness meditation in this way for six years ...

pañca vassāni ...

five years ...

cattāri vassāni ...

four years ...

tīṇi vassāni ...

three years ...

dve vassāni ...

two years ...

ekaṁ vassaṁ ...

one year ...

tiṭṭhatu, bhikkhave, ekaṁ vassaṁ.

Yo hi koci, bhikkhave, ime cattāro satipaṭṭhāne evaṁ bhāveyya satta māsāni, tassa dvinnaṁ phalānaṁ aññataraṁ phalaṁ pāṭikaṅkhaṁ

seven months ...

diṭṭheva dhamme aññā; sati vā upādisese anāgāmitā.

Tiṭṭhantu, bhikkhave, satta māsāni.

Yo hi koci, bhikkhave, ime cattāro satipaṭṭhāne evaṁ bhāveyya cha māsāni ... pe...

six months ...

pañca māsāni ...

five months ...

cattāri māsāni ...

four months ...

tīṇi māsāni ...

three months …

dve māsāni …

two months …

ekaṁ māsaṁ …

one month …

aḍḍhamāsaṁ …

a fortnight …

tiṭṭhatu, bhikkhave, aḍḍhamāso.

Let alone a fortnight,

Yo hi koci, bhikkhave, ime cattāro satipaṭṭhāne evaṁ bhāveyya sattāhaṁ, tassa dvinnaṁ phalānaṁ aññataraṁ phalaṁ pāṭikaṅkhaṁ

anyone who develops these four kinds of mindfulness meditation in this way for seven days can expect one of two results:

diṭṭheva dhamme aññā sati vā upādisese anāgāmitāti.

enlightenment in the present life, or if there's something left over, non-return.

'Ekāyano ayaṁ, bhikkhave, maggo sattānaṁ visuddhiyā sokaparidevānaṁ samatikkamāya dukkhadomanassānaṁ atthaṅgamāya ñāyassa adhigamāya nibbānassa sacchikiriyāya yadidaṁ cattāro satipaṭṭhānā'ti.

'The four kinds of mindfulness meditation are the path to convergence. They are in order to purify sentient beings, to get past sorrow and crying, to make an end of pain and sadness, to end the cycle of suffering, and to realize extinguishment.'

Iti yaṁ taṁ vuttaṁ, idametaṁ paṭicca vuttan"ti.

That's what I said, and this is why I said it."

Idamavoca bhagavā.

That is what the Buddha said.

Attamanā te bhikkhū bhagavato bhāsitaṁ abhinandunti.

Satisfied, the mendicants were happy with what the Buddha said.

Satipaṭṭhānasuttaṁ niṭṭhitaṁ dasamaṁ.

Mūlapariyāyavaggo niṭṭhito paṭhamo.

Tassuddānaṁ

Mūlasusaṁvaradhammadāyādā,

Bheravānaṅgaṇākaṅkheyyavatthaṁ;

Sallekhasammādiṭṭhisatipaṭṭhaṁ,

Vaggavaro asamo susamatto.

SIHANADAVAGGA

THE DIVISION OF THE LION'S ROAR

11 Culasihanadasutta:

The Shorter Discourse on the Lion's Roar

Evaṁ me sutaṁ—

So I have heard.

ekaṁ samayaṁ bhagavā sāvatthiyaṁ viharati jetavane anāthapiṇḍikassa ārāme.

At one time the Buddha was staying near Sāvatthī in Jeta's Grove, Anāthapiṇḍika's monastery.

Tatra kho bhagavā bhikkhū āmantesi:

There the Buddha addressed the mendicants,

"bhikkhavo"ti.

"Mendicants!"

"Bhadante"ti te bhikkhū bhagavato paccassosuṁ.

"Venerable sir," they replied.

Bhagavā etadavoca:

The Buddha said this:

"Idheva, bhikkhave, samaṇo, idha dutiyo samaṇo, idha tatiyo samaṇo, idha catuttho samaṇo;

"'Only here is there a true ascetic, here a second ascetic, here a third ascetic, and here a fourth ascetic.

suññā parappavādā samaṇebhi aññehīti.

Other sects are empty of ascetics.'

Evametaṁ, bhikkhave, sammā sīhanādaṁ nadatha.

This, mendicants, is how you should rightly roar your lion's roar.

Ṭhānaṁ kho panetaṁ, bhikkhave, vijjati yaṁ aññatitthiyā paribbājakā evaṁ vadeyyuṁ:

It's possible that wanderers of other religions might say:

'ko panāyasmantānaṁ assāso, kiṁ balaṁ, yena tumhe āyasmanto evaṁ vadetha—

'But what is the source of the venerables' self-confidence and forcefulness that they say this?'

idheva samaṇo, idha dutiyo samaṇo, idha tatiyo samaṇo, idha catuttho samaṇo;

suññā parappavādā samaṇebhi aññehī'ti?

Evaṁvādino, bhikkhave, aññatitthiyā paribbājakā evamassu vacanīyā:

You should say to them:

'atthi kho no, āvuso, tena bhagavatā jānatā passatā arahatā sammāsambuddhena cattāro dhammā akkhātā ye mayaṁ attani sampassamānā evaṁ vadema—

'There are four things explained by the Blessed One, who knows and sees, the perfected one, the fully awakened Buddha. Seeing these things in ourselves we say that:

idheva samaṇo, idha dutiyo samaṇo, idha tatiyo samaṇo, idha catuttho samaṇo;

"Only here is there a true ascetic, here a second ascetic, here a third ascetic, and here a fourth ascetic.

suññā parappavādā samaṇebhi aññehīti.

Other sects are empty of ascetics."

Katame cattāro?

What four?

Atthi kho no, āvuso, satthari pasādo, atthi dhamme pasādo, atthi sīlesu paripūrakāritā;

We have confidence in the Teacher, we have confidence in the teaching, and we have fulfilled the precepts.

sahadhammikā kho pana piyā manāpā—

And we have love and affection for those who share our path,

gahaṭṭhā ceva pabbajitā ca.

both laypeople and renunciates.

Ime kho no, āvuso, tena bhagavatā jānatā passatā arahatā sammāsambuddhena cattāro dhammā akkhātā ye mayaṁ attani sampassamānā evaṁ vadema—

These are the four things.'

idheva samaṇo, idha dutiyo samaṇo, idha tatiyo samaṇo, idha catuttho samaṇo;

suññā parappavādā samaṇebhi aññehī'ti.

Ṭhānaṁ kho panetaṁ, bhikkhave, vijjati yaṁ aññatitthiyā paribbājakā evaṁ vadeyyuṁ:

It's possible that wanderers of other religions might say:

'amhākampi kho, āvuso, atthi satthari pasādo yo amhākaṁ satthā, amhākampi atthi dhamme pasādo yo amhākaṁ dhammo, mayampi sīlesu paripūrakārino yāni amhākaṁ sīlāni,

'We too have confidence in the Teacher—our Teacher; we have confidence in the teaching—our teaching; and we have fulfilled the precepts—our precepts.

amhākampi sahadhammikā piyā manāpā—

And we have love and affection for those who share our path,

gahaṭṭhā ceva pabbajitā ca.

both laypeople and renunciates.

Idha no, āvuso, ko viseso ko adhippayāso kiṁ nānākaraṇaṁ yadidaṁ tumhākañceva amhākañcā'ti?

What, then, is the difference between you and us?'

Evaṁvādino, bhikkhave, aññatitthiyā paribbājakā evamassu vacanīyā:

You should say to them:

'kiṁ panāvuso, ekā niṭṭhā, udāhu puthu niṭṭhā'ti?

'Well, reverends, is the goal one or many?'

Sammā byākaramānā, bhikkhave, aññatitthiyā paribbājakā evaṁ byākareyyuṁ:

Answering rightly, the wanderers would say:

'ekāvuso, niṭṭhā, na puthu niṭṭhā'ti.

'The goal is one, reverends, not many.'

'Sā panāvuso, niṭṭhā sarāgassa udāhu vītarāgassā'ti?

'But is that goal for the greedy or for those free of greed?'

Sammā byākaramānā, bhikkhave, aññatitthiyā paribbājakā evaṁ byākareyyuṁ:

Answering rightly, the wanderers would say:

'vītarāgassāvuso, sā niṭṭhā, na sā niṭṭhā sarāgassā'ti.

'That goal is for those free of greed, not for the greedy.'

'Sā panāvuso, niṭṭhā sadosassa udāhu vītadosassā'ti?

'Is it for the hateful or those free of hate?'

Sammā byākaramānā, bhikkhave, aññatitthiyā paribbājakā evaṁ byākareyyuṁ:

'vītadosassāvuso, sā niṭṭhā, na sā niṭṭhā sadosassā'ti.

'It's for those free of hate.'

'Sā panāvuso, niṭṭhā samohassa udāhu vītamohassā'ti?

'Is it for the delusional or those free of delusion?'

Sammā byākaramānā, bhikkhave, aññatitthiyā paribbājakā evaṁ byākareyyuṁ:

'vītamohassāvuso, sā niṭṭhā, na sā niṭṭhā samohassā'ti.

'It's for those free of delusion.'

'Sā panāvuso, niṭṭhā sataṇhassa udāhu vītataṇhassā'ti?

'Is it for those who crave or those rid of craving?'

Sammā byākaramānā, bhikkhave, aññatitthiyā paribbājakā evaṁ byākareyyuṁ:

'vītataṇhassāvuso, sā niṭṭhā, na sā niṭṭhā sataṇhassā'ti.

'It's for those rid of craving.'

'Sā panāvuso, niṭṭhā saupādānassa udāhu anupādānassā'ti?

'Is it for those who grasp or those who don't grasp?'

Sammā byākaramānā, bhikkhave, aññatitthiyā paribbājakā evaṁ byākareyyuṁ:

'anupādānassāvuso, sā niṭṭhā, na sā niṭṭhā saupādānassā'ti.

'It's for those who don't grasp.'

'Sā panāvuso, niṭṭhā viddasuno udāhu aviddasuno'ti?

'Is it for the knowledgeable or the ignorant?'

Sammā byākaramānā, bhikkhave, aññatitthiyā paribbājakā evaṁ byākareyyuṁ:

'viddasuno, āvuso, sā niṭṭhā, na sā niṭṭhā aviddasuno'ti.

'It's for the knowledgeable.'

'Sā panāvuso, niṭṭhā anuruddhappaṭiviruddhassa udāhu ananuruddhaappaṭiviruddhassā'ti?

'Is it for those who favor and oppose or for those who don't favor and oppose?'

Sammā byākaramānā, bhikkhave, aññatitthiyā paribbājakā evaṁ byākareyyuṁ:

'ananuruddhaappaṭiviruddhassāvuso, sā niṭṭhā, na sā niṭṭhā anuruddhappaṭiviruddhassā'ti.

'It's for those who don't favor and oppose.'

'Sā panāvuso, niṭṭhā papañcārāmassa papañcaratino udāhu nippapañcārāmassa nippapañcaratino'ti?

'But is that goal for those who enjoy proliferation or for those who enjoy non-proliferation?'

Sammā byākaramānā, bhikkhave, aññatitthiyā paribbājakā evaṁ byākareyyuṁ:

Answering rightly, the wanderers would say:

'nippapañcārāmassāvuso, sā niṭṭhā nippapañcaratino, na sā niṭṭhā papañcārāmassa papañcaratino'ti.

'It's for those who enjoy non-proliferation, not for those who enjoy proliferation.'

Dvemā, bhikkhave, diṭṭhiyo—

Mendicants, there are these two views:

bhavadiṭṭhi ca vibhavadiṭṭhi ca.

views favoring continued existence and views favoring ending existence.

Ye hi keci, bhikkhave, samaṇā vā brāhmaṇā vā bhavadiṭṭhiṁ allīnā bhavadiṭṭhiṁ upagatā bhavadiṭṭhiṁ ajjhositā, vibhavadiṭṭhiyā te paṭiviruddhā.

Any ascetics or brahmins who cling, hold, and attach to a view favoring continued existence will oppose a view favoring ending existence.

Ye hi keci, bhikkhave, samaṇā vā brāhmaṇā vā vibhavadiṭṭhiṁ allīnā vibhavadiṭṭhiṁ upagatā vibhavadiṭṭhiṁ ajjhositā, bhavadiṭṭhiyā te paṭiviruddhā.

Any ascetics or brahmins who cling, hold, and attach to a view favoring ending existence will oppose a view favoring continued existence.

Ye hi keci, bhikkhave, samaṇā vā brāhmaṇā vā imāsaṁ dvinnaṁ diṭṭhīnaṁ samudayañca atthaṅgamañca assādañca ādīnavañca nissaraṇañca yathābhūtaṁ nappajānanti, 'te sarāgā te sadosā te samohā te sataṇhā te saupādānā te aviddasuno te anuruddhappaṭiviruddhā te papañcārāmā papañcaratino;

There are some ascetics and brahmins who don't truly understand these two views' origin, ending, gratification, drawback, and escape. They're greedy, hateful, delusional, craving, grasping, and ignorant. They favor and oppose, and they enjoy proliferation.

te na parimuccanti jātiyā jarāya maraṇena sokehi paridevehi dukkhehi domanassehi upāyāsehi;

They're not freed from rebirth, old age, and death, from sorrow, lamentation, pain, sadness, and distress.

na parimuccanti dukkhasmā'ti vadāmi.

They're not freed from suffering, I say.

Ye ca kho keci, bhikkhave, samaṇā vā brāhmaṇā vā imāsaṁ dvinnaṁ diṭṭhīnaṁ samudayañca atthaṅgamañca assādañca ādīnavañca nissaraṇañca yathābhūtaṁ pajānanti, 'te vītarāgā te vītadosā te vītamohā te vītataṇhā te anupādānā te viddasuno te ananuruddhaappaṭiviruddhā te nippapañcārāmā nippapañcaratino;

There are some ascetics and brahmins who do truly understand these two views' origin, ending, gratification, drawback, and escape. They're rid of greed, hate, delusion, craving, grasping, and ignorance. They don't favor and oppose, and they enjoy non-proliferation.

te parimuccanti jātiyā jarāya maraṇena sokehi paridevehi dukkhehi domanassehi upāyāsehi;

They're freed from rebirth, old age, and death, from sorrow, lamentation, pain, sadness, and distress.

parimuccanti dukkhasmā'ti vadāmi.

They're freed from suffering, I say.

Cattārimāni, bhikkhave, upādānāni.

There are these four kinds of grasping.

Katamāni cattāri?

What four?

Kāmupādānaṁ, diṭṭhupādānaṁ, sīlabbatupādānaṁ, attavādupādānaṁ.

Grasping at sensual pleasures, views, precepts and observances, and theories of a self.

Santi, bhikkhave, eke samaṇabrāhmaṇā sabbupādānapariññāvādā paṭijānamānā.

There are some ascetics and brahmins who claim to propound the complete understanding of all kinds of grasping.

Te na sammā sabbupādānapariññaṁ paññapenti—

But they don't correctly describe the complete understanding of all kinds of grasping.

kāmupādānassa pariññaṁ paññapenti, na diṭṭhupādānassa pariññaṁ paññapenti, na sīlabbatupādānassa pariññaṁ paññapenti, na attavādupādānassa pariññaṁ paññapenti.

They describe the complete understanding of grasping at sensual pleasures, but not views, precepts and observances, and theories of a self.

Taṁ kissa hetu?

Why is that?

Imāni hi te bhonto samaṇabrāhmaṇā tīṇi ṭhānāni yathābhūtaṁ nappajānanti.

Because those gentlemen don't truly understand these three things.

Tasmā te bhonto samaṇabrāhmaṇā sabbupādānapariññāvādā paṭijānamānā;

That's why they claim to propound the complete understanding of all kinds of grasping,

te na sammā sabbupādānapariññaṁ paññapenti—

but they don't really.

kāmupādānassa pariññaṁ paññapenti, na diṭṭhupādānassa pariññaṁ paññapenti, na sīlabbatupādānassa pariññaṁ paññapenti, na attavādupādānassa pariññaṁ paññapenti.

Santi, bhikkhave, eke samaṇabrāhmaṇā sabbupādānapariññāvādā paṭijānamānā.

There are some other ascetics and brahmins who claim to propound the complete understanding of all kinds of grasping,

Te na sammā sabbupādānapariññaṁ paññapenti—

but they don't really.

kāmupādānassa pariññaṁ paññapenti, diṭṭhupādānassa pariññaṁ paññapenti, na sīlabbatupādānassa pariññaṁ paññapenti, na attavādupādānassa pariññaṁ paññapenti.

They describe the complete understanding of grasping at sensual pleasures and views, but not precepts and observances, and theories of a self.

Taṁ kissa hetu?

Why is that?

Imāni hi te bhonto samaṇabrāhmaṇā dve ṭhānāni yathābhūtaṁ nappajānanti.

Because those gentlemen don't truly understand these two things.

Tasmā te bhonto samaṇabrāhmaṇā sabbupādānapariññāvādā paṭijānamānā;

That's why they claim to propound the complete understanding of all kinds of grasping,

te na sammā sabbupādānapariññaṁ paññapenti—

but they don't really.

kāmupādānassa pariññaṁ paññapenti, diṭṭhupādānassa pariññaṁ paññapenti, na sīlabbatupādānassa pariññaṁ paññapenti, na attavādupādānassa pariññaṁ paññapenti.

Santi, bhikkhave, eke samaṇabrāhmaṇā sabbupādānapariññāvādā paṭijānamānā.

There are some other ascetics and brahmins who claim to propound the complete understanding of all kinds of grasping,

Te na sammā sabbupādānapariññaṁ paññapenti—

but they don't really.

kāmupādānassa pariññaṁ paññapenti, diṭṭhupādānassa pariññaṁ paññapenti, sīlabbatupādānassa pariññaṁ paññapenti, na attavādupādānassa pariññaṁ paññapenti.

They describe the complete understanding of grasping at sensual pleasures, views, and precepts and observances, but not theories of a self.

Taṁ kissa hetu?

Why is that?

Imañhi te bhonto samaṇabrāhmaṇā ekaṁ ṭhānaṁ yathābhūtaṁ nappajānanti.

Because those gentlemen don't truly understand this one thing.

Tasmā te bhonto samaṇabrāhmaṇā sabbupādānapariññāvādā paṭijānamānā;

That's why they claim to propound the complete understanding of all kinds of grasping, te na sammā sabbupādānapariññaṁ paññapenti—

but they don't really.

kāmupādānassa pariññaṁ paññapenti, diṭṭhupādānassa pariññaṁ paññapenti, sīlabbatupādānassa pariññaṁ paññapenti, na attavādupādānassa pariññaṁ paññapenti.

Evarūpe kho, bhikkhave, dhammavinaye yo satthari pasādo so na sammaggato akkhāyati;

In such a teaching and training, confidence in the Teacher is said to be far from ideal.

yo dhamme pasādo so na sammaggato akkhāyati;

Likewise, confidence in the teaching,

yā sīlesu paripūrakāritā sā na sammaggatā akkhāyati;

fulfillment of the precepts,

yā sahadhammikesu piyamanāpatā sā na sammaggatā akkhāyati.

and love and affection for those sharing the same path are said to be far from ideal.

Taṁ kissa hetu?

Why is that?

Evañhetaṁ, bhikkhave, hoti yathā taṁ durakkhāte dhammavinaye duppavedite aniyyānike anupasamasaṁvattanike asammāsambuddhappavedite.

It's because that teaching and training is poorly explained and poorly propounded, not emancipating, not leading to peace, proclaimed by someone who is not a fully awakened Buddha.

Tathāgato ca kho, bhikkhave, arahaṁ sammāsambuddho sabbupādānapariññāvādo paṭijānamāno sammā sabbupādānapariññaṁ paññapeti—

The Realized One, the perfected one, the fully awakened Buddha claims to propound the complete understanding of all kinds of grasping.

kāmupādānassa pariññaṁ paññapeti, diṭṭhupādānassa pariññaṁ paññapeti, sīlabbatupādānassa pariññaṁ paññapeti, attavādupādānassa pariññaṁ paññapeti.

He describes the complete understanding of grasping at sensual pleasures, views, precepts and observances, and theories of a self.

Evarūpe kho, bhikkhave, dhammavinaye yo satthari pasādo so sammaggato akkhāyati;

In such a teaching and training, confidence in the Teacher is said to be ideal.

yo dhamme pasādo so sammaggato akkhāyati;

Likewise, confidence in the teaching,

yā sīlesu paripūrakāritā sā sammaggatā akkhāyati;

fulfillment of the precepts,

yā sahadhammikesu piyamanāpatā sā sammaggatā akkhāyati.

and love and affection for those sharing the same path are said to be ideal.

Taṁ kissa hetu?

Why is that?

Evañhetaṁ, bhikkhave, hoti yathā taṁ svākkhāte dhammavinaye suppavedite niyyānike upasamasaṁvattanike sammāsambuddhappavedite.

It's because that teaching and training is well explained and well propounded, emancipating, leading to peace, proclaimed by a fully awakened Buddha.

Ime ca, bhikkhave, cattāro upādānā. Kiṁnidānā kiṁsamudayā kiṁjātikā kiṁpabhavā?

What is the source, origin, birthplace, and inception of these four kinds of grasping?

Ime cattāro upādānā taṇhānidānā taṇhāsamudayā taṇhājātikā taṇhāpabhavā.

Craving.

Taṇhā cāyaṁ, bhikkhave, kiṁnidānā kiṁsamudayā kiṁjātikā kiṁpabhavā?

And what is the source, origin, birthplace, and inception of craving?

Taṇhā vedanānidānā vedanāsamudayā vedanājātikā vedanāpabhavā.

Feeling.

Vedanā cāyaṁ, bhikkhave, kiṁnidānā kiṁsamudayā kiṁjātikā kiṁpabhavā?

And what is the source of feeling?

Vedanā phassanidānā phassasamudayā phassajātikā phassapabhavā.

Contact.

Phasso cāyaṁ, bhikkhave, kiṁnidāno kiṁsamudayo kiṁjātiko kiṁpabhavo?

And what is the source of contact?

Phasso saḷāyatananidāno saḷāyatanasamudayo saḷāyatanajātiko saḷāyatanapabhavo.

The six sense fields.

Saḷāyatanañcidaṁ, bhikkhave, kiṁnidānaṁ kiṁsamudayaṁ kiṁjātikaṁ kiṁpabhavaṁ?

And what is the source of the six sense fields?

Saḷāyatanaṁ nāmarūpanidānaṁ nāmarūpasamudayaṁ nāmarūpajātikaṁ nāmarūpapabhavaṁ.

Name and form.

Nāmarūpañcidaṁ, bhikkhave, kiṁnidānaṁ kiṁsamudayaṁ kiṁjātikaṁ kiṁpabhavaṁ?

And what is the source of name and form?

Nāmarūpaṁ viññāṇanidānaṁ viññāṇasamudayaṁ viññāṇajātikaṁ viññāṇapabhavaṁ.

Consciousness.

Viññāṇañcidaṁ, bhikkhave, kiṁnidānaṁ kiṁsamudayaṁ kiṁjātikaṁ kiṁpabhavaṁ?

And what is the source of consciousness?

Viññāṇaṁ saṅkhāranidānaṁ saṅkhārasamudayaṁ saṅkhārajātikaṁ saṅkhārapabhavaṁ.

Choices.

Saṅkhārā cime, bhikkhave, kiṁnidānā kiṁsamudayā kiṁjātikā kiṁpabhavā?

And what is the source of choices?

Saṅkhārā avijjānidānā avijjāsamudayā avijjājātikā avijjāpabhavā.

Ignorance.

Yato ca kho, bhikkhave, bhikkhuno avijjā pahīnā hoti vijjā uppannā, so avijjāvirāgā vijjuppādā neva kāmupādānaṁ upādiyati, na diṭṭhupādānaṁ upādiyati, na sīlabbatupādānaṁ upādiyati, na attavādupādānaṁ upādiyati.

When that mendicant has given up ignorance and given rise to knowledge, they don't grasp at sensual pleasures, views, precepts and observances, or theories of a self.

Anupādiyaṁ na paritassati, aparitassaṁ paccattaññeva parinibbāyati.

Not grasping, they're not anxious. Not being anxious, they personally become extinguished.

'Khīṇā jāti, vusitaṃ brahmacariyaṃ, kataṃ karaṇīyaṃ, nāparaṃ itthattāyā'ti pajānātī'ti.

They understand: 'Rebirth is ended, the spiritual journey has been completed, what had to be done has been done, there is no return to any state of existence.'"

Idamavoca bhagavā.

That is what the Buddha said.

Attamanā te bhikkhū bhagavato bhāsitaṃ abhinandunti.

Satisfied, the mendicants were happy with what the Buddha said.

Cūḷasīhanādasuttaṃ niṭṭhitaṃ paṭhamaṃ.

12 Mahasihanadasutta:

The Longer Discourse on the Lion's Roar

Evaṃ me sutaṃ—

So I have heard.

ekaṃ samayaṃ bhagavā vesāliyaṃ viharati bahinagare aparapure vanasaṇḍe.

At one time the Buddha was staying near Vesālī in a woodland grove behind the town.

Tena kho pana samayena sunakkhatto licchaviputto acirapakkanto hoti imasmā dhammavinayā.

Now at that time Sunakkhatta the Licchavi had recently left this teaching and training.

So vesāliyaṃ parisati evaṃ vācaṃ bhāsati:

He was telling a crowd in Vesālī:

"natthi samaṇassa gotamassa uttari manussadhammā alamariyañāṇadassanaviseso.

"The ascetic Gotama has no superhuman distinction in knowledge and vision worthy of the noble ones.

Takkapariyāhataṃ samaṇo gotamo dhammaṃ deseti vīmaṃsānucaritaṃ sayampaṭibhānaṁ.

He teaches what he's worked out by logic, following a line of inquiry, expressing his own perspective.

Yassa ca khvāssa atthāya dhammo desito so niyyāti takkarassa sammā dukkhakkhayāyā"ti.

And his teaching leads those who practice it to the complete ending of suffering, the goal for which it's taught."

Atha kho āyasmā sāriputto pubbaṇhasamayaṁ nivāsetvā pattacīvaramādāya vesāliṁ piṇḍāya pāvisi.

Then Venerable Sāriputta robed up in the morning and, taking his bowl and robe, entered Vesālī for alms.

Assosi kho āyasmā sāriputto sunakkhattassa licchaviputtassa vesāliyaṁ parisati evaṁ vācaṁ bhāsamānassa:

He heard what Sunakkhatta was saying.

"natthi samaṇassa gotamassa uttari manussadhammā alamariyañāṇadassanaviseso.

Takkapariyāhataṁ samaṇo gotamo dhammaṁ deseti vīmaṁsānucaritaṁ sayampaṭibhānaṁ.

Yassa ca khvāssa atthāya dhammo desito so niyyāti takkarassa sammā dukkhakkhayāyā"ti.

Atha kho āyasmā sāriputto vesāliyaṁ piṇḍāya caritvā pacchābhattaṁ piṇḍapātapaṭikkanto yena bhagavā tenupasaṅkami; upasaṅkamitvā bhagavantaṁ abhivādetvā ekamantaṁ nisīdi. Ekamantaṁ nisinno kho āyasmā sāriputto bhagavantaṁ etadavoca:

Then he wandered for alms in Vesālī. After the meal, on his return from almsround, he went to the Buddha, bowed, sat down to one side, and told him what had happened.

"sunakkhatto, bhante, licchaviputto acirapakkanto imasmā dhammavinayā.

So vesāliyaṁ parisati evaṁ vācaṁ bhāsati:

'natthi samaṇassa gotamassa uttari manussadhammā alamariyañāṇadassanaviseso.

Takkapariyāhataṁ samaṇo gotamo dhammaṁ deseti vīmaṁsānucaritaṁ sayampaṭibhānaṁ.

Yassa ca khvāssa atthāya dhammo desito so niyyāti takkarassa sammā dukkhakkhayāyā'"ti.

"Kodhano heso, sāriputta, sunakkhatto moghapuriso.

"Sāriputta, Sunakkhatta, that silly man, is angry.

Kodhā ca panassa esā vācā bhāsitā.

His words are spoken out of anger.

'Avaṇṇaṁ bhāsissāmī'ti kho, sāriputta, sunakkhatto moghapuriso vaṇṇaṁyeva tathāgatassa bhāsati.

Thinking he criticizes the Realized One, in fact he just praises him.

Vaṇṇo heso, sāriputta, tathāgatassa yo evaṁ vadeyya:

For it is praise of the Realized One to say:

'yassa ca khvāssa atthāya dhammo desito so niyyāti takkarassa sammā dukkhakkhayāyā'ti.

'His teaching leads those who practice it to the complete ending of suffering, the goal for which it's taught.'

Ayampi hi nāma, sāriputta, sunakkhattassa moghapurisassa mayi dhammanvayo na bhavissati:

But there's no way Sunakkhatta will infer about me from the teaching:

'itipi so bhagavā arahaṁ sammāsambuddho vijjācaraṇasampanno sugato lokavidū anuttaro purisadammasārathi, satthā devamanussānaṁ, buddho bhagavā'ti.

'That Blessed One is perfected, a fully awakened Buddha, accomplished in knowledge and conduct, holy, knower of the world, supreme guide for those who wish to train, teacher of gods and humans, awakened, blessed.'

Ayampi hi nāma, sāriputta, sunakkhattassa moghapurisassa mayi dhammanvayo na bhavissati:

And there's no way Sunakkhatta will infer about me from the teaching:

'itipi so bhagavā anekavihitaṁ iddhividhaṁ paccanubhoti—ekopi hutvā bahudhā hoti, bahudhāpi hutvā eko hoti; āvibhāvaṁ, tirobhāvaṁ; tirokuṭṭaṁ tiropākāraṁ tiropabbataṁ asajjamāno gacchati, seyyathāpi ākāse; pathaviyāpi ummujjanimujjaṁ karoti, seyyathāpi udake; udakepi abhijjamāne gacchati, seyyathāpi pathaviyaṁ; ākāsepi pallaṅkena kamati, seyyathāpi pakkhī sakuṇo; imepi candimasūriye evaṁmahiddhike evaṁmahānubhāve pāṇinā parimasati parimajjati; yāva brahmalokāpi kāyena vasaṁ vattetī'ti.

'That Blessed One wields the many kinds of psychic power: multiplying himself and becoming one again; appearing and disappearing; going unimpeded through a wall, a rampart, or a mountain as if through space; diving in and out of the earth as if it were water; walking on water as if it were earth; flying cross-legged through the sky like a bird; touching and stroking with the hand the sun and moon, so mighty and powerful; controlling the body as far as the Brahmā realm.'

Ayampi hi nāma, sāriputta, sunakkhattassa moghapurisassa mayi dhammanvayo na bhavissati:

And there's no way Sunakkhatta will infer about me from the teaching:

'itipi so bhagavā dibbāya sotadhātuyā visuddhāya atikkantamānusikāya ubho sadde suṇāti—dibbe ca mānuse ca, ye dūre santike cā'ti.

'That Blessed One, with clairaudience that is purified and superhuman, hears both kinds of sounds, human and divine, whether near or far.'

Ayampi hi nāma, sāriputta, sunakkhattassa moghapurisassa mayi dhammanvayo na bhavissati:

And there's no way Sunakkhatta will infer about me from the teaching:

'itipi so bhagavā parasattānaṁ parapuggalānaṁ cetasā ceto paricca pajānāti—

'That Blessed One understands the minds of other beings and individuals, having comprehended them with his own mind.

sarāgaṁ vā cittaṁ sarāgaṁ cittanti pajānāti,

He understands mind with greed as "mind with greed,"

vītarāgaṁ vā cittaṁ vītarāgaṁ cittanti pajānāti;

and mind without greed as "mind without greed."

sadosaṁ vā cittaṁ sadosaṁ cittanti pajānāti,

He understands mind with hate …

vītadosaṁ vā cittaṁ vītadosaṁ cittanti pajānāti;

mind without hate …

samohaṁ vā cittaṁ samohaṁ cittanti pajānāti,

mind with delusion …

vītamohaṁ vā cittaṁ vītamohaṁ cittanti pajānāti;

mind without delusion …

saṅkhittaṁ vā cittaṁ saṅkhittaṁ cittanti pajānāti,

constricted mind …

vikkhittaṁ vā cittaṁ vikkhittaṁ cittanti pajānāti;

scattered mind …

mahaggataṁ vā cittaṁ mahaggataṁ cittanti pajānāti,

expansive mind …

amahaggataṁ vā cittaṁ amahaggataṁ cittanti pajānāti;

unexpansive mind …

sauttaraṁ vā cittaṁ sauttaraṁ cittanti pajānāti,

mind that is supreme …

anuttaraṁ vā cittaṁ anuttaraṁ cittanti pajānāti;

mind that is not supreme …

samāhitaṁ vā cittaṁ samāhitaṁ cittanti pajānāti,

mind immersed in samādhi …

asamāhitaṁ vā cittaṁ asamāhitaṁ cittanti pajānāti;

mind not immersed in samādhi …

vimuttaṁ vā cittaṁ vimuttaṁ cittanti pajānāti,

freed mind as "freed mind,"

avimuttaṁ vā cittaṁ avimuttaṁ cittanti pajānātī'ti.

and unfreed mind as "unfreed mind."'

Dasa kho panimāni, sāriputta, tathāgatassa tathāgatabalāni yehi balehi samannāgato tathāgato āsabhaṁ ṭhānaṁ paṭijānāti, parisāsu sīhanādaṁ nadati, brahmacakkaṁ pavatteti.

The Realized One possesses ten powers of a Realized One. With these he claims the bull's place, roars his lion's roar in the assemblies, and turns the holy wheel.

Katamāni dasa?

What ten?

Idha, sāriputta, tathāgato ṭhānañca ṭhānato aṭṭhānañca aṭṭhānato yathābhūtaṁ pajānāti.

Firstly, the Realized One truly understands the possible as possible, and the impossible as impossible.

Yampi, sāriputta, tathāgato ṭhānañca ṭhānato aṭṭhānañca aṭṭhānato yathābhūtaṁ pajānāti, idampi, sāriputta, tathāgatassa tathāgatabalaṁ hoti yaṁ balaṁ āgamma tathāgato āsabhaṁ ṭhānaṁ paṭijānāti, parisāsu sīhanādaṁ nadati, brahmacakkaṁ pavatteti.

Since he truly understands this, this is a power of the Realized One. Relying on this he claims the bull's place, roars his lion's roar in the assemblies, and turns the holy wheel.

Puna caparaṁ, sāriputta, tathāgato atītānāgatapaccuppannānaṁ kammasamādānānaṁ ṭhānaso hetuso vipākaṁ yathābhūtaṁ pajānāti.

Furthermore, the Realized One truly understands the result of deeds undertaken in the past, future, and present in terms of causes and reasons.

Yampi, sāriputta, tathāgato atītānāgatapaccuppannānaṁ kammasamādānānaṁ ṭhānaso hetuso vipākaṁ yathābhūtaṁ pajānāti, idampi, sāriputta, tathāgatassa tathāgatabalaṁ hoti yaṁ balaṁ āgamma tathāgato āsabhaṁ ṭhānaṁ paṭijānāti, parisāsu sīhanādaṁ nadati, brahmacakkaṁ pavatteti.

Since he truly understands this, this is a power of the Realized One. ...

Puna caparaṁ, sāriputta, tathāgato sabbatthagāminiṁ paṭipadaṁ yathābhūtaṁ pajānāti.

Furthermore, the Realized One truly understands where all paths of practice lead.

Yampi, sāriputta, tathāgato sabbatthagāminiṁ paṭipadaṁ yathābhūtaṁ pajānāti, idampi, sāriputta, tathāgatassa tathāgatabalaṁ hoti yaṁ balaṁ āgamma tathāgato āsabhaṁ ṭhānaṁ paṭijānāti, parisāsu sīhanādaṁ nadati, brahmacakkaṁ pavatteti.

Since he truly understands this, this is a power of the Realized One. ...

Puna caparaṁ, sāriputta, tathāgato anekadhātunānādhātulokaṁ yathābhūtaṁ pajānāti.

Furthermore, the Realized One truly understands the world with its many and diverse elements.

Yampi, sāriputta, tathāgato anekadhātunānādhātulokaṁ yathābhūtaṁ pajānāti, idampi, sāriputta, tathāgatassa tathāgatabalaṁ hoti yaṁ balaṁ āgamma tathāgato āsabhaṁ ṭhānaṁ paṭijānāti, parisāsu sīhanādaṁ nadati, brahmacakkaṁ pavatteti.

Since he truly understands this, this is a power of the Realized One. ...

Puna caparaṁ, sāriputta, tathāgato sattānaṁ nānādhimuttikataṁ yathābhūtaṁ pajānāti.

Furthermore, the Realized One truly understands the diverse convictions of sentient beings.

Yampi, sāriputta, tathāgato sattānam nānādhimuttikataṁ yathābhūtaṁ pajānāti, idampi, sāriputta, tathāgatassa tathāgatabalaṁ hoti yaṁ balaṁ āgamma tathāgato āsabham ṭhānam paṭijānāti, parisāsu sīhanādam nadati, brahmacakkam pavatteti.

Since he truly understands this, this is a power of the Realized One. ...

Puna caparam, sāriputta, tathāgato parasattānam parapuggalānam indriyaparopariyattam yathābhūtam pajānāti.

Furthermore, the Realized One truly understands the faculties of other sentient beings and other individuals after comprehending them with his mind.

Yampi, sāriputta, tathāgato parasattānam parapuggalānam indriyaparopariyattam yathābhūtam pajānāti, idampi, sāriputta, tathāgatassa tathāgatabalam hoti yam balam āgamma tathāgato āsabham ṭhānam paṭijānāti, parisāsu sīhanādam nadati, brahmacakkam pavatteti.

Since he truly understands this, this is a power of the Realized One. ...

Puna caparam, sāriputta, tathāgato jhānavimokkhasamādhisamāpattīnam saṅkilesam vodānam vuṭṭhānam yathābhūtam pajānāti.

Furthermore, the Realized One truly understands corruption, cleansing, and emergence regarding the absorptions, liberations, immersions, and attainments.

Yampi, sāriputta, tathāgato jhānavimokkhasamādhisamāpattīnam saṅkilesam vodānam vuṭṭhānam yathābhūtam pajānāti, idampi, sāriputta, tathāgatassa tathāgatabalam hoti yam balam āgamma tathāgato āsabham ṭhānam paṭijānāti, parisāsu sīhanādam nadati, brahmacakkam pavatteti.

Since he truly understands this, this is a power of the Realized One. ...

Puna caparam, sāriputta, tathāgato anekavihitam pubbenivāsam anussarati, seyyathidam—ekampi jātim dvepi jātiyo tissopi jātiyo catassopi jātiyo pañcapi jātiyo dasapi jātiyo vīsampi jātiyo timsampi jātiyo cattālīsampi jātiyo paññāsampi jātiyo jātisatampi jātisahassampi jātisatasahassampi anekepi samvaṭṭakappe anekepi vivaṭṭakappe anekepi samvaṭṭavivaṭṭakappe: 'amutrāsim evamnāmo evaṅgotto evamvaṇṇo evamāhāro evamsukhadukkhappaṭisamvedī evamāyupariyanto, so tato cuto amutra udapādim; tatrāpāsim evamnāmo evaṅgotto evamvaṇṇo evamāhāro evamsukhadukkhappaṭisamvedī evamāyupariyanto, so tato cuto idhūpapanno'ti. Iti sākāram sauddesam anekavihitam pubbenivāsam anussarati.

Furthermore, the Realized One recollects many kinds of past lives. That is: one, two, three, four, five, ten, twenty, thirty, forty, fifty, a hundred, a thousand, a hundred thousand rebirths; many eons of the world contracting, many eons of the world expanding, many eons of the world contracting and expanding. He remembers: 'There, I was named this, my clan was that, I looked like this, and that was my food. This was how I felt pleasure and pain, and that was how my life ended. When I passed away from that place I was reborn somewhere else. There, too, I was named this, my clan was that, I looked like this, and that was my food. This was how I felt pleasure and pain, and that was how my life ended. When I passed away from that place I was reborn here.' And so he recollects his many kinds of past lives, with features and details.

Yampi, sāriputta, tathāgato anekavihitaṁ pubbenivāsaṁ anussarati, seyyathidaṁ—
ekampi jātiṁ dvepi jātiyo ...pe... iti sākāraṁ sauddesaṁ anekavihitaṁ
pubbenivāsaṁ anussarati, idampi, sāriputta, tathāgatassa tathāgatabalaṁ hoti yaṁ
balaṁ āgamma tathāgato āsabhaṁ ṭhānaṁ paṭijānāti, parisāsu sīhanādaṁ nadati,
brahmacakkaṁ pavatteti.

Since he truly understands this, this is a power of the Realized One. ...

Puna caparaṁ, sāriputta, tathāgato dibbena cakkhunā visuddhena
atikkantamānusakena satte passati cavamāne upapajjamāne hīne paṇīte suvaṇṇe
dubbaṇṇe sugate duggate yathākammūpage satte pajānāti: 'ime vata bhonto sattā
kāyaduccaritena samannāgatā vacīduccaritena samannāgatā manoduccaritena
samannāgatā ariyānaṁ upavādakā micchādiṭṭhikā micchādiṭṭhikammasamādānā,
te kāyassa bhedā paraṁ maraṇā apāyaṁ duggatiṁ vinipātaṁ nirayaṁ
upapannā. Ime vā pana bhonto sattā kāyasucaritena samannāgatā vacīsucaritena
samannāgatā manosucaritena samannāgatā ariyānaṁ anupavādakā sammādiṭṭhikā
sammādiṭṭhikammasamādānā, te kāyassa bhedā paraṁ maraṇā sugatiṁ saggaṁ
lokaṁ upapannā'ti. Iti dibbena cakkhunā visuddhena atikkantamānusakena satte
passati cavamāne upapajjamāne hīne paṇīte suvaṇṇe dubbaṇṇe sugate duggate
yathākammūpage satte pajānāti.

Furthermore, with clairvoyance that is purified and superhuman, the Realized
One sees sentient beings passing away and being reborn—inferior and superior,
beautiful and ugly, in a good place or a bad place. He understands how sentient
beings are reborn according to their deeds. 'These dear beings did bad things by
way of body, speech, and mind. They spoke ill of the noble ones; they had wrong
view; and they chose to act out of that wrong view. When their body breaks up,
after death, they're reborn in a place of loss, a bad place, the underworld, hell.
These dear beings, however, did good things by way of body, speech, and mind.
They never spoke ill of the noble ones; they had right view; and they chose to act
out of that right view. When their body breaks up, after death, they're reborn in
a good place, a heavenly realm.' And so, with clairvoyance that is purified and
superhuman, he sees sentient beings passing away and being reborn—inferior and
superior, beautiful and ugly, in a good place or a bad place. He understands how
sentient beings are reborn according to their deeds.

Yampi, sāriputta, tathāgato dibbena cakkhunā visuddhena atikkantamānusakena
satte passati cavamāne upapajjamāne hīne paṇīte suvaṇṇe dubbaṇṇe sugate
duggate yathākammūpage satte pajānāti: 'ime vata bhonto sattā kāyaduccaritena
samannāgatā vacīduccaritena samannāgatā manoduccaritena samannāgatā
ariyānaṁ upavādakā micchādiṭṭhikā micchādiṭṭhikammasamādānā, te kāyassa
bhedā paraṁ maraṇā apāyaṁ duggatiṁ vinipātaṁ nirayaṁ upapannā. Ime vā
pana bhonto sattā kāyasucaritena samannāgatā vacīsucaritena samannāgatā
manosucaritena samannāgatā ariyānaṁ anupavādakā sammādiṭṭhikā
sammādiṭṭhikammasamādānā, te kāyassa bhedā paraṁ maraṇā sugatiṁ saggaṁ
lokaṁ upapannā'ti. Iti dibbena cakkhunā visuddhena atikkantamānusakena satte
passati cavamāne upapajjamāne hīne paṇīte suvaṇṇe dubbaṇṇe sugate duggate

yathākammūpage satte pajānāti. Idampi, sāriputta, tathāgatassa tathāgatabalaṁ hoti yaṁ balaṁ āgamma tathāgato āsabhaṁ ṭhānaṁ paṭijānāti, parisāsu sīhanādaṁ nadati, brahmacakkaṁ pavatteti.

Since he truly understands this, this is a power of the Realized One. …

Puna caparaṁ, sāriputta, tathāgato āsavānaṁ khayā anāsavaṁ cetovimuttiṁ paññāvimuttiṁ diṭṭheva dhamme sayaṁ abhiññā sacchikatvā upasampajja viharati.

Furthermore, the Realized One has realized the undefiled freedom of heart and freedom by wisdom in this very life, and lives having realized it with his own insight due to the ending of defilements.

Yampi, sāriputta, tathāgato āsavānaṁ khayā anāsavaṁ cetovimuttiṁ paññāvimuttiṁ diṭṭheva dhamme sayaṁ abhiññā sacchikatvā upasampajja viharati, idampi, sāriputta, tathāgatassa tathāgatabalaṁ hoti yaṁ balaṁ āgamma tathāgato āsabhaṁ ṭhānaṁ paṭijānāti, parisāsu sīhanādaṁ nadati, brahmacakkaṁ pavatteti.

Since he truly understands this, this is a power of the Realized One. Relying on this he claims the bull's place, roars his lion's roar in the assemblies, and turns the holy wheel.

Imāni kho, sāriputta, dasa tathāgatassa tathāgatabalāni yehi balehi samannāgato tathāgato āsabhaṁ ṭhānaṁ paṭijānāti, parisāsu sīhanādaṁ nadati, brahmacakkaṁ pavatteti.

A Realized One possesses these ten powers of a Realized One. With these he claims the bull's place, roars his lion's roar in the assemblies, and turns the holy wheel.

Yo kho maṁ, sāriputta, evaṁ jānantaṁ evaṁ passantaṁ evaṁ vadeyya:

When I know and see in this way, suppose someone were to say this:

'natthi samaṇassa gotamassa uttari manussadhammā alamariyañāṇadassanaviseso;

'The ascetic Gotama has no superhuman distinction in knowledge and vision worthy of the noble ones.

takkapariyāhataṁ samaṇo gotamo dhammaṁ deseti vīmaṁsānucaritaṁ sayampaṭibhānan'ti,

He teaches what he's worked out by logic, following a line of inquiry, expressing his own perspective.'

taṁ, sāriputta, vācaṁ appahāya taṁ cittaṁ appahāya taṁ diṭṭhiṁ appaṭinissajjitvā yathābhataṁ nikkhitto evaṁ niraye.

Unless they give up that speech and that thought, and let go of that view, they will be cast down to hell.

Seyyathāpi, sāriputta, bhikkhu sīlasampanno samādhisampanno paññāsampanno diṭṭheva dhamme aññaṁ ārādheyya, evaṁ sampadamidaṁ, sāriputta, vadāmi.

Just as a mendicant accomplished in ethics, immersion, and wisdom would reach enlightenment in this very life, such is the consequence, I say.

Taṁ vācaṁ appahāya, taṁ cittaṁ appahāya taṁ diṭṭhiṁ appaṭinissajjitvā yathābhataṁ nikkhitto evaṁ niraye.

Unless they give up that speech and thought, and let go of that view, they will be cast down to hell.

Cattārimāni, sāriputta, tathāgatassa vesārajjāni yehi vesārajjehi samannāgato tathāgato āsabhaṁ ṭhānaṁ paṭijānāti, parisāsu sīhanādaṁ nadati, brahmacakkaṁ pavatteti.

Sāriputta, a Realized One has four kinds of self-assurance. With these he claims the bull's place, roars his lion's roar in the assemblies, and turns the holy wheel.

Katamāni cattāri?

What four?

'Sammāsambuddhassa te paṭijānato ime dhammā anabhisambuddhā'ti. Tatra vata maṁ samaṇo vā brāhmaṇo vā devo vā māro vā brahmā vā koci vā lokasmiṁ sahadhammena paṭicodessatīti nimittametaṁ, sāriputta, na samanupassāmi.

I see no reason for anyone—whether ascetic, brahmin, god, Māra, or Brahmā, or anyone else in the world—to legitimately scold me, saying: 'You claim to be fully awakened, but you don't understand these things.'

Etamahaṁ, sāriputta, nimittaṁ asamanupassanto khemappatto abhayappatto vesārajjappatto viharāmi.

Since I see no such reason, I live secure, fearless, and assured.

'Khīṇāsavassa te paṭijānato ime āsavā aparikkhīṇā'ti. Tatra vata maṁ samaṇo vā brāhmaṇo vā devo vā māro vā brahmā vā koci vā lokasmiṁ sahadhammena paṭicodessatīti nimittametaṁ, sāriputta, na samanupassāmi.

I see no reason for anyone—whether ascetic, brahmin, god, Māra, or Brahmā, or anyone else in the world—to legitimately scold me, saying: 'You claim to have ended all defilements, but these defilements have not ended.'

Etamahaṁ, sāriputta, nimittaṁ asamanupassanto khemappatto abhayappatto vesārajjappatto viharāmi.

Since I see no such reason, I live secure, fearless, and assured.

'Ye kho pana te antarāyikā dhamma vuttā, te paṭisevato nālaṁ antarāyāyā'ti. Tatra vata maṁ samaṇo vā brāhmaṇo vā devo vā māro vā brahmā vā koci vā lokasmiṁ sahadhammena paṭicodessatīti nimittametaṁ, sāriputta, na samanupassāmi.

I see no reason for anyone—whether ascetic, brahmin, god, Māra, or Brahmā, or anyone else in the world—to legitimately scold me, saying: 'The acts that you say are obstructions are not really obstructions for the one who performs them.'

Etamahaṁ, sāriputta, nimittaṁ asamanupassanto khemappatto abhayappatto vesārajjappatto viharāmi.

Since I see no such reason, I live secure, fearless, and assured.

'Yassa kho pana te atthāya dhammo desito, so na niyyāti takkarassa sammā dukkhakkhayāyā'ti. Tatra vata maṁ samaṇo vā brāhmaṇo vā devo vā māro vā brahmā vā koci vā lokasmiṁ sahadhammena paṭicodessatīti nimittametaṁ, sāriputta, na samanupassāmi.

I see no reason for anyone—whether ascetic, brahmin, god, Māra, or Brahmā, or anyone else in the world—to legitimately scold me, saying: 'The teaching doesn't lead those who practice it to the complete ending of suffering, the goal for which you taught it.'

Etamahaṁ, sāriputta, nimittaṁ asamanupassanto khemappatto abhayappatto vesārajjappatto viharāmi.

Since I see no such reason, I live secure, fearless, and assured.

Imāni kho, sāriputta, cattāri tathāgatassa vesārajjāni yehi vesārajjehi samannāgato tathāgato āsabhaṁ ṭhānaṁ paṭijānāti, parisāsu sīhanādaṁ nadati, brahmacakkaṁ pavatteti.

A Realized One has these four kinds of self-assurance. With these he claims the bull's place, roars his lion's roar in the assemblies, and turns the holy wheel.

Yo kho maṁ, sāriputta, evaṁ jānantaṁ evaṁ passantaṁ evaṁ vadeyya:

When I know and see in this way, suppose someone were to say this:

'natthi samaṇassa gotamassa uttari manussadhammā alamariyañāṇadassanaviseso, takkapariyāhataṁ samaṇo gotamo dhammaṁ deseti vīmaṁsānucaritaṁ sayampaṭibhānan'ti,

'The ascetic Gotama has no superhuman distinction in knowledge and vision worthy of the noble ones …'

taṁ, sāriputta, vācaṁ appahāya taṁ cittaṁ appahāya taṁ diṭṭhiṁ appaṭinissajjitvā yathābhataṁ nikkhitto evaṁ niraye.

Unless they give up that speech and that thought, and let go of that view, they will be cast down to hell.

Seyyathāpi, sāriputta, bhikkhu sīlasampanno samādhisampanno paññāsampanno diṭṭheva dhamme aññaṁ ārādheyya, evaṁ sampadamidaṁ, sāriputta, vadāmi.

Taṁ vācaṁ appahāya taṁ cittaṁ appahāya taṁ diṭṭhiṁ appaṭinissajjitvā yathābhataṁ nikkhitto evaṁ niraye.

Aṭṭha kho imā, sāriputta, parisā.

Sāriputta, there are these eight assemblies.

Katamā aṭṭha?

What eight?

Khattiyaparisā, brāhmaṇaparisā, gahapatiparisā, samaṇaparisā, cātumahārājikaparisā, tāvatiṁsaparisā, māraparisā, brahmaparisā—

The assemblies of aristocrats, brahmins, householders, and ascetics. An assembly of the gods under the Four Great Kings. An assembly of the gods under the Thirty-Three. An assembly of Māras. An assembly of Brahmās.

imā kho, sāriputta, aṭṭha parisā.

These are the eight assemblies.

Imehi kho, sāriputta, catūhi vesārajjehi samannāgato tathāgato imā aṭṭha parisā upasaṅkamati ajjhogāhati.

Possessing these four kinds of self-assurance, the Realized One approaches and enters right into these eight assemblies.

Abhijānāmi kho panāhaṁ, sāriputta, anekasataṁ khattiyaparisaṁ upasaṅkamitā.

I recall having approached an assembly of hundreds of aristocrats.

Tatrapi mayā sannisinnapubbañceva, sallapitapubbañca, sākacchā ca samāpajjitapubbā.

There I used to sit with them, converse, and engage in discussion.

Tatra vata maṁ bhayaṁ vā sārajjaṁ vā okkamissatīti nimittametaṁ, sāriputta, na samanupassāmi.

But I don't see any reason to feel afraid or insecure.

Etamahaṁ, sāriputta, nimittaṁ asamanupassanto khemappatto abhayappatto vesārajjappatto viharāmi.

Since I see no such reason, I live secure, fearless, and assured.

Abhijānāmi kho panāhaṁ, sāriputta, anekasataṁ brāhmaṇaparisaṁ …pe…

I recall having approached an assembly of hundreds of brahmins …

gahapatiparisaṁ ...

householders ...

samaṇaparisaṁ ...

ascetics ...

cātumahārājikaparisaṁ ...

the gods under the Four Great Kings ...

tāvatiṁsaparisaṁ ...

the gods under the Thirty-Three ...

māraparisaṁ ...

Māras ...

brahmaparisaṁ upasaṅkamitā.

Brahmās.

Tatrapi mayā sannisinnapubbañceva, sallapitapubbañca, sākacchā ca samāpajjitapubbā.

There too I used to sit with them, converse, and engage in discussion.

Tatra vata maṁ bhayaṁ vā sārajjaṁ vā okkamissatīti nimittametaṁ, sāriputta, na samanupassāmi.

But I don't see any reason to feel afraid or insecure.

Etamahaṁ, sāriputta, nimittaṁ asamanupassanto khemappatto abhayappatto vesārajjappatto viharāmi.

Since I see no such reason, I live secure, fearless, and assured.

Yo kho maṁ, sāriputta, evaṁ jānantaṁ evaṁ passantaṁ evaṁ vadeyya:

When I know and see in this way, suppose someone were to say this:

'natthi samaṇassa gotamassa uttari manussadhammā alamariyañāṇadassanaviseso, takkapariyāhataṁ samaṇo gotamo dhammaṁ deseti vīmaṁsānucaritaṁ sayampaṭibhānan'ti,

'The ascetic Gotama has no superhuman distinction in knowledge and vision worthy of the noble ones ...'

taṁ, sāriputta, vācaṁ appahāya taṁ cittaṁ appahāya taṁ diṭṭhiṁ appaṭinissajjitvā yathābhataṁ nikkhitto evaṁ niraye.

Unless they give up that speech and that thought, and let go of that view, they will be cast down to hell.

Seyyathāpi, sāriputta, bhikkhu sīlasampanno samādhisampanno paññāsampanno diṭṭheva dhamme aññaṃ ārādheyya, evaṃ sampadamidaṃ, sāriputta, vadāmi.

Taṃ vācaṃ appahāya taṃ cittaṃ appahāya taṃ diṭṭhiṃ appaṭinissajjitvā yathābhataṃ nikkhitto evaṃ niraye.

Catasso kho imā, sāriputta, yoniyo.

Sāriputta, there are these four kinds of reproduction.

Katamā catasso?

What four?

Aṇḍajā yoni, jalābujā yoni, saṃsedajā yoni, opapātikā yoni.

Reproduction for creatures born from an egg, from a womb, from moisture, or spontaneously.

Katamā ca, sāriputta, aṇḍajā yoni?

And what is reproduction from an egg?

Ye kho te, sāriputta, sattā aṇḍakosaṃ abhinibbhijja jāyanti—

There are beings who are born by breaking out of an eggshell.

ayaṃ vuccati, sāriputta, aṇḍajā yoni.

This is called reproduction from an egg.

Katamā ca, sāriputta, jalābujā yoni?

And what is reproduction from a womb?

Ye kho te, sāriputta, sattā vatthikosaṃ abhinibbhijja jāyanti—

There are beings who are born by breaking out of the amniotic sac.

ayaṃ vuccati, sāriputta, jalābujā yoni.

This is called reproduction from a womb.

Katamā ca, sāriputta, saṃsedajā yoni?

And what is reproduction from moisture?

Ye kho te, sāriputta, sattā pūtimacche vā jāyanti pūtikuṇape vā pūtikummāse vā candanikāye vā oḷigalle vā jāyanti—

There are beings who are born in a rotten fish, in a rotten carcass, in rotten dough, in a cesspool or a sump.

ayaṁ vuccati, sāriputta, saṁsedajā yoni.

This is called reproduction from moisture.

Katamā ca, sāriputta, opapātikā yoni?

And what is spontaneous reproduction?

Devā, nerayikā, ekacce ca manussā, ekacce ca vinipātikā—

Gods, hell-beings, certain humans, and certain beings in the lower realms.

ayaṁ vuccati, sāriputta, opapātikā yoni.

This is called spontaneous reproduction.

Imā kho, sāriputta, catasso yoniyo.

These are the four kinds of reproduction.

Yo kho maṁ, sāriputta, evaṁ jānantaṁ evaṁ passantaṁ evaṁ vadeyya:

When I know and see in this way, suppose someone were to say this:

'natthi samaṇassa gotamassa uttari manussadhammā alamariyañāṇadassanaviseso, takkapariyāhataṁ samaṇo gotamo dhammaṁ deseti vīmaṁsānucaritaṁ sayampaṭibhānan'ti,

'The ascetic Gotama has no superhuman distinction in knowledge and vision worthy of the noble ones …'

taṁ, sāriputta, vācaṁ appahāya taṁ cittaṁ appahāya taṁ diṭṭhiṁ appaṭinissajjitvā yathābhataṁ nikkhitto evaṁ niraye.

Unless they give up that speech and that thought, and let go of that view, they will be cast down to hell.

Seyyathāpi, sāriputta, bhikkhu sīlasampanno samādhisampanno paññāsampanno diṭṭheva dhamme aññaṁ ārādheyya, evaṁ sampadamidaṁ, sāriputta, vadāmi.

Taṁ vācaṁ appahāya taṁ cittaṁ appahāya taṁ diṭṭhiṁ appaṭinissajjitvā yathābhataṁ nikkhitto evaṁ niraye.

Pañca kho imā, sāriputta, gatiyo.

There are these five destinations.

Katamā pañca?

What five?

Nirayo, tiracchānayoni, pettivisayo, manussā, devā.

Hell, the animal realm, the ghost realm, humanity, and the gods.

Nirayañcāhaṁ, sāriputta, pajānāmi, nirayagāmiñca maggaṁ, nirayagāminiñca paṭipadaṁ;

I understand hell, and the path and practice that leads to hell.

yathā paṭipanno ca kāyassa bhedā paraṁ maraṇā apāyaṁ duggatiṁ vinipātaṁ nirayaṁ upapajjati tañca pajānāmi.

And I understand how someone practicing that way, when their body breaks up, after death, is reborn in a place of loss, a bad place, the underworld, hell.

Tiracchānayoniñcāhaṁ, sāriputta, pajānāmi, tiracchānayonigāmiñca maggaṁ, tiracchānayonigāminiñca paṭipadaṁ;

I understand the animal realm …

yathā paṭipanno ca kāyassa bhedā paraṁ maraṇā tiracchānayoniṁ upapajjati tañca pajānāmi.

Pettivisayañcāhaṁ, sāriputta, pajānāmi, pettivisayagāmiñca maggaṁ, pettivisayagāminiñca paṭipadaṁ;

yathā paṭipanno ca kāyassa bhedā paraṁ maraṇā pettivisayaṁ upapajjati tañca pajānāmi.

the ghost realm …

Manusse cāhaṁ, sāriputta, pajānāmi, manussalokagāmiñca maggaṁ, manussalokagāminiñca paṭipadaṁ;

humanity …

yathā paṭipanno ca kāyassa bhedā paraṁ maraṇā manussesu upapajjati tañca pajānāmi.

Deve cāhaṁ, sāriputta, pajānāmi, devalokagāmiñca maggaṁ, devalokagāminiñca paṭipadaṁ;

gods, and the path and practice that leads to the world of the gods.

yathā paṭipanno ca kāyassa bhedā paraṁ maraṇā sugatiṁ saggaṁ lokaṁ upapajjati tañca pajānāmi.

And I understand how someone practicing that way, when their body breaks up, after death, is reborn in a good place, a heavenly realm.

Nibbānañcāham, sāriputta, pajānāmi, nibbānagāmiñca maggam, nibbānagāminiñca paṭipadam;

And I understand extinguishment, and the path and practice that leads to extinguishment.

yathā paṭipanno ca āsavānam khayā anāsavam cetovimuttim paññāvimuttim diṭṭheva dhamme sayam abhiññā sacchikatvā upasampajja viharati tañca pajānāmi.

And I understand how someone practicing that way realizes the undefiled freedom of heart and freedom by wisdom in this very life, and lives having realized it with their own insight due to the ending of defilements.

Idhāham, sāriputta, ekaccam puggalam evam cetasā ceto paricca pajānāmi—

When I've comprehended the mind of a certain person, I understand:

tathāyam puggalo paṭipanno tathā ca iriyati tañca maggam samārūḷho, yathā kāyassa bhedā param maraṇā apāyam duggatim vinipātam nirayam upapajjissatīti.

'This person is practicing in such a way and has entered such a path that when their body breaks up, after death, they will be reborn in a place of loss, a bad place, the underworld, hell.'

Tamenam passāmi aparena samayena dibbena cakkhunā visuddhena atikkantamānusakena kāyassa bhedā param maraṇā apāyam duggatim vinipātam nirayam upapannam, ekantadukkhā tibbā kaṭukā vedanā vedayamānam.

Then some time later I see that they have indeed been reborn in hell, where they experience exclusively painful feelings, sharp and severe.

Seyyathāpi, sāriputta, aṅgārakāsu sādhikaporisā pūrā aṅgārānam vītaccikānam vītadhūmānam.

Suppose there was a pit of glowing coals deeper than a man's height, full of glowing coals that neither flamed nor smoked.

Atha puriso āgaccheyya ghammābhitatto ghammapareto kilanto tasito pipāsito ekāyanena maggena tameva aṅgārakāsum paṇidhāya.

Then along comes a person struggling in the oppressive heat, weary, thirsty, and parched. And they have set out on a path that meets with that same pit of coals.

Tamenam cakkhumā puriso disvā evam vadeyya:

If a person with good eyesight saw them, they'd say:

'tathāyam bhavam puriso paṭipanno tathā ca iriyati tañca maggam samārūḷho, yathā imamyeva aṅgārakāsum āgamissatī'ti.

'This person is proceeding in such a way and has entered such a path that they will arrive at that very pit of coals.'

Tamenaṁ passeyya aparena samayena tassā aṅgārakāsuyā patitaṁ, ekantadukkhā tibbā kaṭukā vedanā vedayamānaṁ.

Then some time later they see that they have indeed fallen into that pit of coals, where they experience exclusively painful feelings, sharp and severe. ...

Evameva kho ahaṁ, sāriputta, idhekaccaṁ puggalaṁ evaṁ cetasā ceto paricca pajānāmi—

tathāyaṁ puggalo paṭipanno tathā ca iriyati tañca maggaṁ samārūḷho yathā kāyassa bhedā paraṁ maraṇā apāyaṁ duggatiṁ vinipātaṁ nirayaṁ upapajjissatīti.

Tamenaṁ passāmi aparena samayena dibbena cakkhunā visuddhena atikkantamānusakena kāyassa bhedā paraṁ maraṇā apāyaṁ duggatiṁ vinipātaṁ nirayaṁ upapannaṁ, ekantadukkhā tibbā kaṭukā vedanā vedayamānaṁ.

Idha panāhaṁ, sāriputta, ekaccaṁ puggalaṁ evaṁ cetasā ceto paricca pajānāmi—

When I've comprehended the mind of a certain person, I understand:

tathāyaṁ puggalo paṭipanno tathā ca iriyati tañca maggaṁ samārūḷho, yathā kāyassa bhedā paraṁ maraṇā tiracchānayoniṁ upapajjissatīti.

'This person ... will be reborn in the animal realm.'

Tamenaṁ passāmi aparena samayena dibbena cakkhunā visuddhena atikkantamānusakena kāyassa bhedā paraṁ maraṇā tiracchānayoniṁ upapannaṁ, dukkhā tibbā kaṭukā vedanā vedayamānaṁ.

Then some time later I see that they have indeed been reborn in the animal realm, where they suffer painful feelings, sharp and severe.

Seyyathāpi, sāriputta, gūthakūpo sādhikaporiso, pūro gūthassa.

Suppose there was a sewer deeper than a man's height, full to the brim with feces.

Atha puriso āgaccheyya ghammābhitatto ghammapareto kilanto tasito pipāsito ekāyanena maggena tameva gūthakūpaṁ paṇidhāya.

Then along comes a person struggling in the oppressive heat, weary, thirsty, and parched. And they have set out on a path that meets with that same sewer.

Tamenaṁ cakkhumā puriso disvā evaṁ vadeyya:

If a person with good eyesight saw them, they'd say:

'tathāyaṁ bhavaṁ puriso paṭipanno tathā ca iriyati tañca maggaṁ samārūḷho yathā imaṁyeva gūthakūpaṁ āgamissatī'ti.

'This person is proceeding in such a way and has entered such a path that they will arrive at that very sewer.'

Tamenaṁ passeyya aparena samayena tasmiṁ gūthakūpe patitaṁ, dukkhā tibbā kaṭukā vedanā vedayamānaṁ.

Then some time later they see that they have indeed fallen into that sewer, where they suffer painful feelings, sharp and severe. …

Evameva kho ahaṁ, sāriputta, idhekaccaṁ puggalaṁ evaṁ cetasā ceto paricca pajānāmi—

tathāyaṁ puggalo paṭipanno tathā ca iriyati tañca maggaṁ samārūḷho, yathā kāyassa bhedā paraṁ maraṇā tiracchānayoniṁ upapajjissatīti.

Tamenaṁ passāmi aparena samayena dibbena cakkhunā visuddhena atikkantamānusakena kāyassa bhedā paraṁ maraṇā tiracchānayoniṁ upapannaṁ, dukkhā tibbā kaṭukā vedanā vedayamānaṁ.

Idha panāhaṁ, sāriputta, ekaccaṁ puggalaṁ evaṁ cetasā ceto paricca pajānāmi—

When I've comprehended the mind of a certain person, I understand:

tathāyaṁ puggalo paṭipanno tathā ca iriyati tañca maggaṁ samārūḷho, yathā kāyassa bhedā paraṁ maraṇā pettivisayaṁ upapajjissatīti.

'This person … will be reborn in the ghost realm.'

Tamenaṁ passāmi aparena samayena dibbena cakkhunā visuddhena atikkantamānusakena kāyassa bhedā paraṁ maraṇā pettivisayaṁ upapannaṁ, dukkhabahulā vedanā vedayamānaṁ.

Then some time later I see that they have indeed been reborn in the ghost realm, where they experience many painful feelings.

Seyyathāpi, sāriputta, rukkho visame bhūmibhāge jāto tanupattapalāso kabaracchāyo.

Suppose there was a tree growing on rugged ground, with thin foliage casting dappled shade.

Atha puriso āgaccheyya ghammābhitatto ghammapareto kilanto tasito pipāsito ekāyanena maggena tameva rukkhaṁ paṇidhāya.

Then along comes a person struggling in the oppressive heat, weary, thirsty, and parched. And they have set out on a path that meets with that same tree.

Tamenaṁ cakkhumā puriso disvā evaṁ vadeyya:

If a person with good eyesight saw them, they'd say:

'tathāyaṁ bhavaṁ puriso paṭipanno tathā ca iriyati tañca maggaṁ samārūḷho, yathā imaṁyeva rukkhaṁ āgamissatī'ti.

'This person is proceeding in such a way and has entered such a path that they will arrive at that very tree.'

Tamenaṁ passeyya, aparena samayena tassa rukkhassa chāyāya nisinnaṁ vā nipannaṁ vā dukkhabahulā vedanā vedayamānaṁ.

Then some time later they see them sitting or lying under that tree, where they experience many painful feelings. …

Evameva kho ahaṁ, sāriputta, idhekaccaṁ puggalaṁ evaṁ cetasā ceto paricca pajānāmi—

tathāyaṁ puggalo paṭipanno tathā ca iriyati tañca maggaṁ samārūḷho, yathā kāyassa bhedā paraṁ maraṇā pettivisayaṁ upapajjissatīti.

Tamenaṁ passāmi aparena samayena dibbena cakkhunā visuddhena atikkantamānusakena kāyassa bhedā paraṁ maraṇā pettivisayaṁ upapannaṁ, dukkhabahulā vedanā vedayamānaṁ.

Idha panāhaṁ, sāriputta, ekaccaṁ puggalaṁ evaṁ cetasā ceto paricca pajānāmi—

When I've comprehended the mind of a certain person, I understand:

tathāyaṁ puggalo paṭipanno tathā ca iriyati tañca maggaṁ samārūḷho yathā kāyassa bhedā paraṁ maraṇā manussesu upapajjissatīti.

'This person … will be reborn among human beings.'

Tamenaṁ passāmi aparena samayena dibbena cakkhunā visuddhena atikkantamānusakena kāyassa bhedā paraṁ maraṇā manussesu upapannaṁ, sukhabahulā vedanā vedayamānaṁ.

Then some time later I see that they have indeed been reborn among human beings, where they experience many pleasant feelings.

Seyyathāpi, sāriputta, rukkho same bhūmibhāge jāto bahalapattapalāso sandacchāyo.

Suppose there was a tree growing on smooth ground, with abundant foliage casting dense shade.

Atha puriso āgaccheyya ghammābhitatto ghammapareto kilanto tasito pipāsito ekāyanena maggena tameva rukkhaṁ paṇidhāya.

Then along comes a person struggling in the oppressive heat, weary, thirsty, and parched. And they have set out on a path that meets with that same tree.

Tamenaṁ cakkhumā puriso disvā evaṁ vadeyya:

If a person with good eyesight saw them, they'd say:

'tathāyaṁ bhavaṁ puriso paṭipanno tathā ca iriyati tañca maggaṁ samārūḷho, yathā imameva rukkhaṁ āgamissatī'ti.

'This person is proceeding in such a way and has entered such a path that they will arrive at that very tree.'

Tamenaṁ passeyya aparena samayena tassa rukkhassa chāyāya nisinnaṁ vā nipannaṁ vā sukhabahulā vedanā vedayamānaṁ.

Then some time later they see them sitting or lying under that tree, where they experience many pleasant feelings. …

Evameva kho ahaṁ, sāriputta, idhekaccaṁ puggalaṁ evaṁ cetasā ceto paricca pajānāmi—

tathāyaṁ puggalo paṭipanno tathā ca iriyati tañca maggaṁ samārūḷho yathā kāyassa bhedā paraṁ maraṇā manussesu upapajjissatīti.

Tamenaṁ passāmi aparena samayena dibbena cakkhunā visuddhena atikkantamānusakena kāyassa bhedā paraṁ maraṇā manussesu upapannaṁ, sukhabahulā vedanā vedayamānaṁ.

Idha panāhaṁ, sāriputta, ekaccaṁ puggalaṁ evaṁ cetasā ceto paricca pajānāmi:

When I've comprehended the mind of a certain person, I understand:

'tathāyaṁ puggalo paṭipanno tathā ca iriyati tañca maggaṁ samārūḷho, yathā kāyassa bhedā paraṁ maraṇā sugatiṁ saggaṁ lokaṁ upapajjissatī'ti.

'This person … will be reborn in a good place, a heavenly realm.'

Tamenaṁ passāmi aparena samayena dibbena cakkhunā visuddhena atikkantamānusakena kāyassa bhedā paraṁ maraṇā sugatiṁ saggaṁ lokaṁ upapannaṁ, ekantasukhā vedanā vedayamānaṁ.

Then some time later I see that they have indeed been reborn in a heavenly realm, where they experience exclusively pleasant feelings.

Seyyathāpi, sāriputta, pāsādo, tatrāssa kūṭāgāraṁ ullittāvalittaṁ nivātaṁ phusitaggaḷaṁ pihitavātapānaṁ.

Suppose there was a stilt longhouse with a peaked roof, plastered inside and out, draft-free, with latches fastened and windows shuttered.

Tatrāssa pallaṅko gonakatthato paṭikatthato paṭalikatthato kadalimigapavarapaccattharaṇo sauttaracchado ubhatolohitakūpadhāno.

And it had a couch spread with woolen covers—shag-piled, pure white, or embroidered with flowers—and spread with a fine deer hide, with a canopy above and red pillows at both ends.

Atha puriso āgaccheyya ghammābhitatto ghammapareto kilanto tasito pipāsito ekāyanena maggena tameva pāsādaṁ paṇidhāya.

Then along comes a person struggling in the oppressive heat, weary, thirsty, and parched. And they have set out on a path that meets with that same stilt longhouse.

Tamenaṁ cakkhumā puriso disvā evaṁ vadeyya:

If a person with good eyesight saw them, they'd say:

'tathāyaṁ bhavaṁ puriso paṭipanno tathā ca iriyati tañca maggaṁ samārūḷho, yathā imaṁyeva pāsādaṁ āgamissatī'ti.

'This person is proceeding in such a way and has entered such a path that they will arrive at that very stilt longhouse.'

Tamenaṁ passeyya aparena samayena tasmiṁ pāsāde tasmiṁ kūṭāgāre tasmiṁ pallaṅke nisinnaṁ vā nipannaṁ vā ekantasukhā vedanā vedayamānaṁ.

Then some time later they see them sitting or lying in that stilt longhouse, where they experience exclusively pleasant feelings. …

Evameva kho ahaṁ, sāriputta, idhekaccaṁ puggalaṁ evaṁ cetasā ceto paricca pajānāmi—

tathāyaṁ puggalo paṭipanno tathā ca iriyati tañca maggaṁ samārūḷho yathā kāyassa bhedā paraṁ maraṇā sugatiṁ saggaṁ lokaṁ upapajjissatīti.

Tamenaṁ passāmi aparena samayena dibbena cakkhunā visuddhena atikkantamānusakena kāyassa bhedā paraṁ maraṇā sugatiṁ saggaṁ lokaṁ upapannaṁ, ekantasukhā vedanā vedayamānaṁ.

Idha panāhaṁ, sāriputta, ekaccaṁ puggalaṁ cetasā ceto paricca pajānāmi—

When I've comprehended the mind of a certain person, I understand:

tathāyaṁ puggalo paṭipanno tathā ca iriyati tañca maggaṁ samārūḷho, yathā āsavānaṁ khayā anāsavaṁ cetovimuttiṁ paññāvimuttiṁ diṭṭheva dhamme sayaṁ abhiññā sacchikatvā upasampajja viharissatīti.

'This person is practicing in such a way and has entered such a path that they will realize the undefiled freedom of heart and freedom by wisdom in this very life, and live having realized it with their own insight due to the ending of defilements.'

Tamenaṁ passāmi aparena samayena āsavānaṁ khayā anāsavaṁ cetovimuttiṁ paññāvimuttiṁ diṭṭheva dhamme sayaṁ abhiññā sacchikatvā upasampajja viharantaṁ, ekantasukhā vedanā vedayamānaṁ.

Then some time later I see that they have indeed realized the undefiled freedom of heart and freedom by wisdom in this very life, and live having realized it with their own insight due to the ending of defilements, experiencing exclusively pleasant feelings.

Seyyathāpi, sāriputta, pokkharaṇī acchodakā sātodakā sītodakā setakā supatitthā ramaṇīyā.

Suppose there was a lotus pond with clear, sweet, cool water, clean, with smooth banks, delightful.

Avidūre cassā tibbo vanasaṇḍo.

And nearby was a dark forest grove.

Atha puriso āgaccheyya ghammābhitatto ghammapareto kilanto tasito pipāsito ekāyanena maggena tameva pokkharaṇiṃ paṇidhāya.

Then along comes a person struggling in the oppressive heat, weary, thirsty, and parched. And they have set out on a path that meets with that same lotus pond.

Tamenaṃ cakkhumā puriso disvā evaṃ vadeyya:

If a person with good eyesight saw them, they'd say:

'tathā bhavaṃ puriso paṭipanno tathā ca iriyati tañca maggaṃ samārūḷho, yathā imaṃyeva pokkharaṇiṃ āgamissatī'ti.

'This person is proceeding in such a way and has entered such a path that they will arrive at that very lotus pond.'

Tamenaṃ passeyya aparena samayena taṃ pokkharaṇiṃ ogāhetvā nhāyitvā ca pivitvā ca sabbadarathakilamathapariḷāhaṃ paṭippassambhetvā paccuttaritvā tasmiṃ vanasaṇḍe nisinnaṃ vā nipannaṃ vā, ekantasukhā vedanā vedayamānaṃ.

Then some time later they would see that person after they had plunged into that lotus pond, bathed and drunk. When all their stress, weariness, and heat exhaustion had faded away, they emerged and sat or lay down in that woodland thicket, where they experienced exclusively pleasant feelings.

Evameva kho ahaṃ, sāriputta, idhekaccaṃ puggalaṃ evaṃ cetasā ceto paricca pajānāmi:

In the same way, when I've comprehended the mind of a person, I understand:

'tathāyaṃ puggalo paṭipanno tathā ca iriyati tañca maggaṃ samārūḷho, yathā āsavānaṃ khayā anāsavaṃ cetovimuttiṃ paññāvimuttiṃ diṭṭheva dhamme sayaṃ abhiññā sacchikatvā upasampajja viharissatī'ti.

'This person is practicing in such a way and has entered such a path that they will realize the undefiled freedom of heart and freedom by wisdom in this very life, and live having realized it with their own insight due to the ending of defilements.'

Tamenaṃ passāmi aparena samayena āsavānaṃ khayā anāsavaṃ cetovimuttiṃ paññāvimuttiṃ diṭṭheva dhamme sayaṃ abhiññā sacchikatvā upasampajja viharantaṃ, ekantasukhā vedanā vedayamānaṃ.

Then some time later I see that they have indeed realized the undefiled freedom of heart and freedom by wisdom in this very life, and live having realized it with their own insight due to the ending of defilements, experiencing exclusively pleasant feelings.

Imā kho, sāriputta, pañca gatiyo.

These are the five destinations.

Yo kho maṁ, sāriputta, evaṁ jānantaṁ evaṁ passantaṁ evaṁ vadeyya:

When I know and see in this way, suppose someone were to say this:

'natthi samaṇassa gotamassa uttari manussadhammā alamariyañāṇadassanaviseso;

'The ascetic Gotama has no superhuman distinction in knowledge and vision worthy of the noble ones.

takkapariyāhataṁ samaṇo gotamo dhammaṁ deseti vīmaṁsānucaritaṁ sayampaṭibhānan'ti

He teaches what he's worked out by logic, following a line of inquiry, expressing his own perspective.'

taṁ, sāriputta, vācaṁ appahāya taṁ cittaṁ appahāya taṁ diṭṭhiṁ appaṭinissajjitvā yathābhataṁ nikkhitto evaṁ niraye.

Unless they give up that speech and that thought, and let go of that view, they will be cast down to hell.

Seyyathāpi, sāriputta, bhikkhu sīlasampanno samādhisampanno paññāsampanno diṭṭheva dhamme aññaṁ ārādheyya; evaṁ sampadamidaṁ, sāriputta, vadāmi

Just as a mendicant accomplished in ethics, immersion, and wisdom would reach enlightenment in this very life, such is the consequence, I say.

taṁ vācaṁ appahāya taṁ cittaṁ appahāya taṁ diṭṭhiṁ appaṭinissajjitvā yathābhataṁ nikkhitto evaṁ niraye.

Unless they give up that speech and thought, and let go of that view, they will be cast down to hell.

Abhijānāmi kho panāhaṁ, sāriputta, caturaṅgasamannāgataṁ brahmacariyaṁ caritā—

Sāriputta, I recall having practiced a spiritual path consisting of four factors.

tapassī sudaṁ homi paramatapassī, lūkho sudaṁ homi paramalūkho, jegucchī sudaṁ homi paramajegucchī, pavivitto sudaṁ homi paramapavivitto.

I used to be a self-mortifier, the ultimate self-mortifier. I used to live rough, the ultimate rough-liver. I used to live in disgust at sin, the ultimate one living in disgust at sin. I used to be secluded, in ultimate seclusion.

Tatrāssu me idaṁ, sāriputta, tapassitāya hoti—acelako homi muttācāro hatthāpalekhano, naehibhaddantiko natiṭṭhabhaddantiko; nābhihaṭaṁ na uddissakataṁ na nimantanaṁ sādiyāmi.

And this is what my self-mortification was like. I went naked, ignoring conventions. I licked my hands, and didn't come or stop when asked. I didn't consent to food brought to me, or food prepared specially for me, or an invitation for a meal.

So na kumbhimukhā paṭiggaṇhāmi, na kaḷopimukhā paṭiggaṇhāmi, na eḷakamantaraṁ, na daṇḍamantaraṁ, na musalamantaraṁ, na dvinnaṁ bhuñjamānānaṁ, na gabbhiniyā, na pāyamānāya, na purisantaragatāya, na saṅkittīsu, na yattha sā upaṭṭhito hoti, na yattha makkhikā saṇḍasaṇḍacārinī; na macchaṁ na maṁsaṁ na suraṁ na merayaṁ na thusodakaṁ pivāmi;

I didn't receive anything from a pot or bowl; or from someone who keeps sheep, or who has a weapon or a shovel in their home; or where a couple is eating; or where there is a woman who is pregnant, breastfeeding, or who has a man in her home; or where food for distribution is advertised; or where there's a dog waiting or flies buzzing. I accepted no fish or meat or liquor or wine, and drank no beer.

so ekāgāriko vā homi ekālopiko, dvāgāriko vā homi dvālopiko ...pe... sattāgāriko vā homi sattālopiko;

I went to just one house for alms, taking just one mouthful, or two houses and two mouthfuls, up to seven houses and seven mouthfuls.

ekissāpi dattiyā yāpemi, dvīhipi dattīhi yāpemi ...pe... sattahipi dattīhi yāpemi;

I fed on one saucer a day, two saucers a day, up to seven saucers a day.

ekāhikampi āhāraṁ āhāremi, dvīhikampi āhāraṁ āhāremi ... pe... sattāhikampi āhāraṁ āhāremi; iti evarūpaṁ addhamāsikampi pariyāyabhattabhojanānuyogamanuyutto viharāmi.

I ate once a day, once every second day, up to once a week, and so on, even up to once a fortnight. I lived committed to the practice of eating food at set intervals.

So sākabhakkho vā homi, sāmākabhakkho vā homi, nīvārabhakkho vā homi, daddulabhakkho vā homi, haṭabhakkho vā homi, kaṇabhakkho vā homi, ācāmabhakkho vā homi, piññākabhakkho vā homi, tiṇabhakkho vā homi, gomayabhakkho vā homi, vanamūlaphalāhāro yāpemi pavattaphalabhojī.

I ate herbs, millet, wild rice, poor rice, water lettuce, rice bran, scum from boiling rice, sesame flour, grass, or cow dung. I survived on forest roots and fruits, or eating fallen fruit.

So sāṇānipi dhāremi, masāṇānipi dhāremi, chavadussānipi dhāremi, paṁsukūlānipi dhāremi, tirīṭānipi dhāremi, ajinampi dhāremi, ajinakkhipampi dhāremi, kusacīrampi dhāremi, vākacīrampi dhāremi, phalakacīrampi dhāremi, kesakambalampi dhāremi, vāḷakambalampi dhāremi, ulūkapakkhampi dhāremi;

I wore robes of sunn hemp, mixed hemp, corpse-wrapping cloth, rags, lodh tree bark, antelope hide (whole or in strips), kusa grass, bark, wood-chips, human hair, horse-tail hair, or owls' wings.

kesamassulocakopi homi kesamassulocanānuyogamanuyutto;

I tore out hair and beard, committed to this practice.

ubbhaṭṭhakopi homi āsanapaṭikkhitto;

I constantly stood, refusing seats.

ukkuṭikopi homi ukkuṭikappadhānamanuyutto;

I squatted, committed to the endeavor of squatting.

kaṇṭakāpassayikopi homi kaṇṭakāpassaye seyyaṁ kappemi;

I lay on a mat of thorns, making a mat of thorns my bed.

sāyatatiyakampi udakorohanānuyogamanuyutto viharāmi—

I was committed to the practice of immersion in water three times a day, including the evening.

iti evarūpaṁ anekavihitaṁ kāyassa ātāpanaparitāpanānuyogamanuyutto viharāmi.

And so I lived committed to practicing these various ways of mortifying and tormenting the body.

Idaṁsu me, sāriputta, tapassitāya hoti.

Such was my practice of self-mortification.

Tatrāssu me idaṁ, sāriputta, lūkhasmiṁ hoti—

And this is what my rough living was like.

nekavassagaṇikaṁ rajojallaṁ kāye sannicitaṁ hoti papaṭikajātaṁ.

The dust and dirt built up on my body over many years until it started flaking off.

Seyyathāpi, sāriputta, tindukakhāṇu nekavassagaṇiko sannicito hoti papaṭikajāto, evamevāssu me, sāriputta, nekavassagaṇikaṁ rajojallaṁ kāye sannicitaṁ hoti papaṭikajātaṁ.

It's like the trunk of a pale-moon ebony tree, which builds up bark over many years until it starts flaking off.

Tassa mayhaṁ, sāriputta, na evaṁ hoti:

But it didn't occur to me:

'aho vatāhaṁ imaṁ rajojallaṁ pāṇinā parimajjeyyaṁ, aññe vā pana me imaṁ rajojallaṁ pāṇinā parimajjeyyun'ti.

'Oh, this dust and dirt must be rubbed off by my hand or another's.'

Evampi me, sāriputta, na hoti.

That didn't occur to me.

Idaṁsu me, sāriputta, lūkhasmiṁ hoti.

Such was my rough living.

Tatrāssu me idaṁ, sāriputta, jegucchismiṁ hoti—

And this is what my living in disgust of sin was like.

so kho ahaṁ, sāriputta, satova abhikkamāmi, satova paṭikkamāmi, yāva udakabindumhipi me dayā paccupaṭṭhitā hoti:

I'd step forward or back ever so mindfully. I was full of pity even regarding a drop of water, thinking:

'māhaṁ khuddake pāṇe visamagate saṅghātaṁ āpādesin'ti.

'May I not accidentally injure any little creatures that happen to be in the wrong place.'

Idaṁsu me, sāriputta, jegucchismiṁ hoti.

Such was my living in disgust of sin.

Tatrāssu me idaṁ, sāriputta, pavivittasmiṁ hoti—

And this is what my seclusion was like.

so kho ahaṁ, sāriputta, aññataraṁ araññāyatanaṁ ajjhogāhetvā viharāmi.

I would plunge deep into a wilderness region and stay there.

Yadā passāmi gopālakaṁ vā pasupālakaṁ vā tiṇahārakaṁ vā kaṭṭhahārakaṁ vā vanakammikaṁ vā, vanena vanaṁ gahanena gahanaṁ ninnena ninnaṁ thalena thalaṁ sampatāmi.

When I saw a cowherd or a shepherd, or someone gathering grass or sticks, or a lumberjack, I'd flee from forest to forest, from thicket to thicket, from valley to valley, from uplands to uplands.

Taṁ kissa hetu?

Why is that?

Mā maṁ te addasaṁsu ahañca mā te addasanti.

So that I wouldn't see them, nor they me.

Seyyathāpi, sāriputta, āraññako mago manusse disvā vanena vanaṁ gahanena gahanaṁ ninnena ninnaṁ thalena thalaṁ sampatati;

I fled like a wild deer seeing a human being.

evameva kho ahaṁ, sāriputta, yadā passāmi gopālakaṁ vā pasupālakaṁ vā tiṇahārakaṁ vā kaṭṭhahārakaṁ vā vanakammikaṁ vā vanena vanaṁ gahanena gahanaṁ ninnena ninnaṁ thalena thalaṁ sampatāmi.

Taṁ kissa hetu?

Mā maṁ te addasaṁsu ahañca mā te addasanti.

Idaṁsu me, sāriputta, pavivittasmiṁ hoti.

Such was my practice of seclusion.

So kho ahaṁ, sāriputta, ye te goṭṭhā paṭṭhitagāvo apagatagopālakā, tattha catukkuṇḍiko upasaṅkamitvā yāni tāni vacchakānaṁ taruṇakānaṁ dhenupakānaṁ gomayāni tāni sudaṁ āhāremi.

I would go on all fours into the cow-pens after the cattle had left and eat the dung of the young suckling calves.

Yāvakīvañca me, sāriputta, sakaṁ muttakarīsaṁ apariyādinnaṁ hoti, sakaṁyeva sudaṁ muttakarīsaṁ āhāremi.

As long as my own urine and excrement lasted, I would even eat that.

Idaṁsu me, sāriputta, mahāvikaṭabhojanasmiṁ hoti.

Such was my eating of most unnatural things.

So kho ahaṁ, sāriputta, aññataraṁ bhiṁsanakaṁ vanasaṇḍaṁ ajjhogāhetvā viharāmi.

I would plunge deep into an awe-inspiring forest grove and stay there.

Tatrāssudaṁ, sāriputta, bhiṁsanakassa vanasaṇḍassa bhiṁsanakatasmiṁ hoti—

It was so awe-inspiring that

yo koci avītarāgo taṁ vanasaṇḍaṁ pavisati, yebhuyyena lomāni haṁsanti.

normally it would make your hair stand on end if you weren't free of greed.

So kho ahaṁ, sāriputta, yā tā rattiyo sītā hemantikā antaraṭṭhakā himapātasamayā tathārūpāsu rattīsu rattiṁ abbhokāse viharāmi, divā vanasaṇḍe;

And on days such as the cold spell when the snow falls in the dead of winter, I stayed in the open by night and in the forest by day.

gimhānaṁ pacchime māse divā abbhokāse viharāmi, rattiṁ vanasaṇḍe.

But in the last month of summer I'd stay in the open by day and in the forest by night.

Apissu maṁ, sāriputta, ayaṁ anacchariyagāthā paṭibhāsi pubbe assutapubbā:

And then these verses, which were neither supernaturally inspired, nor learned before in the past, occurred to me:

'Sotatto sosinno ceva,

eko bhiṁsanake vane;

Naggo na caggimāsīno,

esanāpasuto munī'ti.

'Scorched and frozen,

alone in the awe-inspiring forest.

Naked, no fire to sit beside,

the sage still pursues his quest.'

So kho ahaṁ, sāriputta, susāne seyyaṁ kappemi chavaṭṭhikāni upadhāya.

I would make my bed in a charnel ground, with the bones of the dead for a pillow.

Apissu maṁ, sāriputta, gāmaṇḍalā upasaṅkamitvā oṭṭhubhantipi, omuttentipi, paṁsukenapi okiranti, kaṇṇasotesupi salākaṁ pavesenti.

Then the cowboys would come up to me. They'd spit and piss on me, throw mud on me, even poke sticks in my ears.

Na kho panāhaṁ, sāriputta, abhijānāmi tesu pāpakaṁ cittaṁ uppādetā.

But I don't recall ever having a bad thought about them.

Idaṁsu me, sāriputta, upekkhāvihārasmiṁ hoti.

Such was my abiding in equanimity.

Santi kho pana, sāriputta, eke samaṇabrāhmaṇā evaṁvādino evaṁdiṭṭhino:

There are some ascetics and brahmins who have this doctrine and view:

'āhārena suddhī'ti.

'Purity comes from food.'

Te evamāhaṁsu:

They say:

'kolehi yāpemā'ti.

'Let's live on jujubes.'

Te kolampi khādanti, kolacuṇṇampi khādanti, kolodakampi pivanti—

So they eat jujubes and jujube powder, and drink jujube juice.

anekavihitampi kolavikatiṁ paribhuñjanti.

And they enjoy many jujube concoctions.

Abhijānāmi kho panāhaṁ, sāriputta, ekaṁyeva kolaṁ āhāraṁ āhāritā.

I recall eating just a single jujube.

Siyā kho pana te, sāriputta, evamassa:

You might think that

'mahā nūna tena samayena kolo ahosī'ti.

at that time the jujubes must have been very big.

Na kho panetaṁ, sāriputta, evaṁ daṭṭhabbaṁ.

But you should not see it like this.

Tadāpi etaparamoyeva kolo ahosi seyyathāpi etarahi.

The jujubes then were at most the same size as today.

Tassa mayhaṁ, sāriputta, ekaṁyeva kolaṁ āhāraṁ āhārayato adhimattakasimānaṁ patto kāyo hoti.

Eating so very little, my body became extremely emaciated.

Seyyathāpi nāma āsītikapabbāni vā kāḷapabbāni vā; evamevassu me aṅgapaccaṅgāni bhavanti tāyevappāhāratāya.

Due to eating so little, my limbs became like the joints of an eighty-year-old or a corpse,

Seyyathāpi nāma oṭṭhapadaṁ; evamevassu me ānisadaṁ hoti tāyevappāhāratāya.

my bottom became like a camel's hoof,

Seyyathāpi nāma vaṭṭanāvaḷī; evamevassu me piṭṭhikaṇṭako unnatāvanato hoti tāyevappāhāratāya.

my vertebrae stuck out like beads on a string,

Seyyathāpi nāma jarasālāya gopānasiyo oluggaviluggā bhavanti; evamevassu me phāsuḷiyo oluggaviluggā bhavanti tāyevappāhāratāya.

and my ribs were as gaunt as the broken-down rafters on an old barn.

Seyyathāpi nāma gambhīre udapāne udakatārakā gambhīragatā okkhāyikā dissanti; evamevassu me akkhikūpesu akkhitārakā gambhīragatā okkhāyikā dissanti tāyevappāhāratāya.

Due to eating so little, the gleam of my eyes sank deep in their sockets, like the gleam of water sunk deep down a well.

Seyyathāpi nāma tittakālābu āmakacchinno vātātapena samphuṭito hoti sammilāto; evamevassu me sīsacchavi samphuṭitā hoti sammilātā tāyevappāhāratāya.

Due to eating so little, my scalp shriveled and withered like a green bitter-gourd in the wind and sun.

So kho ahaṃ, sāriputta, 'udaracchaviṃ parimasissāmī'ti piṭṭhikaṇṭakamyeva pariggaṇhāmi, 'piṭṭhikaṇṭakaṃ parimasissāmī'ti udaracchavimyeva pariggaṇhāmi, yāvassu me, sāriputta, udaracchavi piṭṭhikaṇṭakaṃ allīnā hoti tāyevappāhāratāya.

Due to eating so little, the skin of my belly stuck to my backbone, so that when I tried to rub the skin of my belly I grabbed my backbone, and when I tried to rub my backbone I rubbed the skin of my belly.

So kho ahaṃ, sāriputta, 'vaccaṃ vā muttaṃ vā karissāmī'ti tattheva avakujjo papatāmi tāyevappāhāratāya.

Due to eating so little, when I tried to urinate or defecate I fell face down right there.

So kho ahaṃ, sāriputta, tameva kāyaṃ assāsento pāṇinā gattāni anomajjāmi. Tassa mayhaṃ, sāriputta, pāṇinā gattāni anomajjato pūtimūlāni lomāni kāyasmā patanti tāyevappāhāratāya.

Due to eating so little, when I tried to relieve my body by rubbing my limbs with my hands, the hair, rotted at its roots, fell out.

Santi kho pana, sāriputta, eke samaṇabrāhmaṇā evaṃvādino evaṃdiṭṭhino:

There are some ascetics and brahmins who have this doctrine and view:

'āhārena suddhī'ti.

'Purity comes from food.'

Te evamāhaṁsu:

They say:

'muggehi yāpema …pe…

'Let's live on mung beans.' …

tilehi yāpema …pe…

'Let's live on sesame.' …

taṇḍulehi yāpemā'ti.

'Let's live on ordinary rice.' …

Te taṇḍulampi khādanti, taṇḍulacuṇṇampi khādanti, taṇḍulodakampi pivanti—

anekavihitampi taṇḍulavikatiṁ paribhuñjanti.

Abhijānāmi kho panāhaṁ, sāriputta, ekaṁyeva taṇḍulaṁ āhāraṁ āhāritā.

Siyā kho pana te, sāriputta, evamassa:

'mahā nūna tena samayena taṇḍulo ahosī'ti.

Na kho panetaṁ, sāriputta, evaṁ daṭṭhabbaṁ.

Tadāpi etaparamoyeva taṇḍulo ahosi, seyyathāpi etarahi.

Tassa mayhaṁ, sāriputta, ekaṁyeva taṇḍulaṁ āhāraṁ āhārayato adhimattakasimānaṁ patto kāyo hoti.

Seyyathāpi nāma āsītikapabbāni vā kāḷapabbāni vā; evamevassu me aṅgapaccaṅgāni bhavanti tāyevappāhāratāya.

Seyyathāpi nāma oṭṭhapadaṁ; evamevassu me ānisadaṁ hoti tāyevappāhāratāya.

Seyyathāpi nāma vaṭṭanāvaḷī; evamevassu me piṭṭhikaṇṭako unnatāvanato hoti tāyevappāhāratāya.

Seyyathāpi nāma jarasālāya gopānasiyo oluggaviluggā bhavanti; evamevassu me phāsuḷiyo oluggaviluggā bhavanti tāyevappāhāratāya.

Seyyathāpi nāma gambhīre udapāne udakatārakā gambhīragatā okkhāyikā dissanti; evamevassu me akkhikūpesu akkhitārakā gambhīragatā okkhāyikā dissanti tāyevappāhāratāya.

Seyyathāpi nāma tittakālābu amakacchinno vātātapena samphuṭito hoti sammilāto; evamevassu me sīsacchavi samphuṭitā hoti sammilātā tāyevappāhāratāya.

So kho ahaṁ, sāriputta, 'udaracchaviṁ parimasissāmī'ti piṭṭhikaṇṭakaṁyeva pariggaṇhāmi, 'piṭṭhikaṇṭakaṁ parimasissāmī'ti udaracchaviṁyeva pariggaṇhāmi. Yāvassu me, sāriputta, udaracchavi piṭṭhikaṇṭakaṁ allīnā hoti tāyevappāhāratāya.

So kho ahaṁ, sāriputta, 'vaccaṁ vā muttaṁ vā karissāmī'ti tattheva avakujjo papatāmi tāyevappāhāratāya.

So kho ahaṁ, sāriputta, tameva kāyaṁ assāsento pāṇinā gattāni anomajjāmi. Tassa mayhaṁ, sāriputta, pāṇinā gattāni anomajjato pūtimūlāni lomāni kāyasmā patanti tāyevappāhāratāya.

Due to eating so little, when I tried to relieve my body by rubbing my limbs with my hands, the hair, rotted at its roots, fell out.

Tāyapi kho ahaṁ, sāriputta, iriyāya tāya paṭipadāya tāya dukkarakārikāya nājjhagamaṁ uttariṁ manussadhammā alamariyañāṇadassanavisesaṁ.

But Sāriputta, I did not achieve any superhuman distinction in knowledge and vision worthy of the noble ones by that conduct, that practice, that grueling work.

Taṁ kissa hetu?

Why is that?

Imissāyeva ariyāya paññāya anadhigamā, yāyaṁ ariyā paññā adhigatā ariyā niyyānikā, niyyāti takkarassa sammā dukkhakkhayāya.

Because I didn't achieve that noble wisdom that's noble and emancipating, and which leads someone who practices it to the complete ending of suffering.

Santi kho pana, sāriputta, eke samaṇabrāhmaṇā evaṁvādino evaṁdiṭṭhino:

There are some ascetics and brahmins who have this doctrine and view:

'saṁsārena suddhī'ti.

'Purity comes from transmigration.'

Na kho pana so, sāriputta, saṁsāro sulabharūpo yo mayā asaṁsaritapubbo iminā dīghena addhunā, aññatra suddhāvāsehi devehi.

But it's not easy to find a realm that I haven't previously transmigrated to in all this long time, except for the gods of the pure abodes.

Suddhāvāse cāhaṁ, sāriputta, deve saṁsareyyaṁ, nayimaṁ lokaṁ punarāgaccheyyaṁ.

For if I had transmigrated to the gods of the pure abodes I would not have returned to this realm again.

Santi kho pana, sāriputta, eke samaṇabrāhmaṇā evaṁvādino evaṁdiṭṭhino:

There are some ascetics and brahmins who have this doctrine and view:

'upapattiyā suddhī'ti.

'Purity comes from rebirth.'

Na kho pana sā, sāriputta, upapatti sulabharūpā yā mayā anupapannapubbā iminā dīghena addhunā, aññatra suddhāvāsehi devehi.

But it's not easy to find any rebirth that I haven't previously been reborn in …

Suddhāvāse cāhaṁ, sāriputta, deve upapajjeyyaṁ, nayimaṁ lokaṁ punarāgaccheyyaṁ.

Santi kho pana, sāriputta, eke samaṇabrāhmaṇā evaṁvādino evaṁdiṭṭhino:

There are some ascetics and brahmins who have this doctrine and view:

'āvāsena suddhī'ti.

'Purity comes from abode of rebirth.'

Na kho pana so, sāriputta, āvāso sulabharūpo yo mayā anāvutthapubbo iminā dīghena addhunā, aññatra suddhāvāsehi devehi.

But it's not easy to find an abode where I haven't previously abided …

Suddhāvāse cāhaṁ, sāriputta, deve āvaseyyaṁ, nayimaṁ lokaṁ punarāgaccheyyaṁ.

Santi kho pana, sāriputta, eke samaṇabrāhmaṇā evaṁvādino evaṁdiṭṭhino:

There are some ascetics and brahmins who have this doctrine and view:

'yaññena suddhī'ti.

'Purity comes from sacrifice.'

Na kho pana so, sāriputta, yañño sulabharūpo yo mayā ayiṭṭhapubbo iminā dīghena addhunā, tañca kho raññā vā satā khattiyena muddhāvasittena brāhmaṇena vā mahāsālena.

But it's not easy to find a sacrifice that I haven't previously offered in all this long time, when I was an anointed aristocratic king or a well-to-do brahmin.

Santi kho pana, sāriputta, eke samaṇabrāhmaṇā evaṁvādino evaṁdiṭṭhino:

There are some ascetics and brahmins who have this doctrine and view:

'aggiparicariyāya suddhī'ti.

'Purity comes from serving the sacred flame.'

Na kho pana so, sāriputta, aggi sulabharūpo yo mayā aparicinnapubbo iminā dīghena addhunā, tañca kho raññā vā satā khattiyena muddhāvasittena brāhmaṇena vā mahāsālena.

But it's not easy to find a fire that I haven't previously served in all this long time, when I was an anointed aristocratic king or a well-to-do brahmin.

Santi kho pana, sāriputta, eke samaṇabrāhmaṇā evaṁvādino evaṁdiṭṭhino:

There are some ascetics and brahmins who have this doctrine and view:

'yāvadevāyaṁ bhavaṁ puriso daharo hoti yuvā susukāḷakeso bhadrena yobbanena samannāgato paṭhamena vayasā tāvadeva paramena paññāveyyattiyena samannāgato hoti.

'So long as this gentleman is youthful, young, black-haired, blessed with youth, in the prime of life he will be endowed with perfect lucidity of wisdom.

Yato ca kho ayaṁ bhavaṁ puriso jiṇṇo hoti vuddho mahallako addhagato vayoanuppatto, āsītiko vā nāvutiko vā vassasatiko vā jātiyā, atha tamhā paññāveyyattiyā, parihāyatī'ti.

But when he's old, elderly, and senior, advanced in years, and has reached the final stage of life—eighty, ninety, or a hundred years old—he will lose his lucidity of wisdom.'

Na kho panetaṁ, sāriputta, evaṁ daṭṭhabbaṁ.

But you should not see it like this.

Ahaṁ kho pana, sāriputta, etarahi jiṇṇo vuddho mahallako addhagato vayoanuppatto, āsītiko me vayo vattati.

For now I am old, elderly, and senior, I'm advanced in years, and have reached the final stage of life. I am eighty years old.

Idha me assu, sāriputta, cattāro sāvakā vassasatāyukā vassasatajīvino, paramāya satiyā ca gatiyā ca dhitiyā ca samannāgatā paramena ca paññāveyyattiyena.

Suppose I had four disciples with a lifespan of a hundred years. And they each were perfect in memory, range, retention, and perfect lucidity of wisdom.

Seyyathāpi, sāriputta, daḷhadhammā dhanuggaho sikkhito katahattho katūpāsano lahukena asanena appakasireneva tiriyaṁ tālacchāyaṁ atipāteyya,

Imagine how easily a well-trained expert archer with a strong bow would shoot a light arrow across the shadow of a palm tree.

evaṁ adhimattasatimanto evaṁ adhimattagatimanto evaṁ adhimattadhitimanto evaṁ paramena paññāveyyattiyena samannāgatā.

That's how extraordinary they were in memory, range, retention, and perfect lucidity of wisdom.

Te maṁ catunnaṁ satipaṭṭhānānaṁ upādāyupādāya pañhaṁ puccheyyuṁ, puṭṭho puṭṭho cāhaṁ tesaṁ byākareyyaṁ, byākatañca me byākatato dhāreyyuṁ, na ca maṁ dutiyakaṁ uttari paṭipuccheyyuṁ.

They'd bring up questions about the four kinds of mindfulness meditation again and again, and I would answer each question. They'd remember the answers and not ask the same question twice.

Aññatra asitapītakhāyitasāyitā aññatra uccārapassāvakammā, aññatra niddākilamathapaṭivinodanā apariyādinnāyevassa, sāriputta, tathāgatassa dhammadesanā, apariyādinnaṁyevassa tathāgatassa dhammapadabyañjanaṁ, apariyādinnaṁyevassa tathāgatassa pañhapaṭibhānaṁ.

And they'd pause only to eat and drink, go to the toilet, and sleep to dispel weariness. But the Realized One would not run out of Dhamma teachings, words and phrases of the teachings, or spontaneous answers.

Atha me te cattāro sāvakā vassasatāyukā vassasatajīvino vassasatassa accayena kālaṁ kareyyuṁ.

And at the end of a hundred years my four disciples would pass away.

Mañcakena cepi maṁ, sāriputta, pariharissatha, nevatthi tathāgatassa paññāveyyattiyassa aññathattaṁ.

Even if you have to carry me around on a stretcher, there will never be any deterioration in the Realized One's lucidity of wisdom.

Yaṁ kho taṁ, sāriputta, sammā vadamāno vadeyya:

And if there's anyone of whom it may be rightly said that

'asammohadhammo satto loke uppanno bahujanahitāya bahujanasukhāya lokānukampāya atthāya hitāya sukhāya devamanussānan'ti, mameva taṁ sammā vadamāno vadeyya

a being not liable to delusion has arisen in the world for the welfare and happiness of the people, out of compassion for the world, for the benefit, welfare, and happiness of gods and humans, it's of me that this should be said."

'asammohadhammo satto loke uppanno bahujanahitāya bahujanasukhāya lokānukampāya atthāya hitāya sukhāya devamanussānan'"ti.

Tena kho pana samayena āyasmā nāgasamālo bhagavato piṭṭhito ṭhito hoti bhagavantaṁ bījayamāno.

Now at that time Venerable Nāgasamāla was standing behind the Buddha fanning him.

Atha kho āyasmā nāgasamālo bhagavantaṁ etadavoca:

Then he said to the Buddha:

"acchariyaṁ, bhante, abbhutaṁ, bhante.

"It's incredible, sir, it's amazing!

Api hi me, bhante, imaṁ dhammapariyāyaṁ sutvā lomāni haṭṭhāni.

While I was listening to this exposition of the teaching my hair stood up!

Konāmo ayaṁ, bhante, dhammapariyāyo"ti?

What is the name of this exposition of the teaching?"

"Tasmātiha tvaṁ, nāgasamāla, imaṁ dhammapariyāyaṁ lomahaṁsanapariyāyotveva naṁ dhārehī"ti.

"Well, Nāgasamāla, you may remember this exposition of the teaching as 'The Hair-raising Discourse'."

Idamavoca bhagavā.

That is what the Buddha said.

Attamano āyasmā nāgasamālo bhagavato bhāsitaṁ abhinandīti.

Satisfied, Venerable Nāgasamāla was happy with what the Buddha said.

Mahāsīhanādasuttaṁ niṭṭhitaṁ dutiyaṁ.

13 Mahadukkhakkhandhasutta:

The Longer Discourse on the Mass of Suffering

Evaṁ me sutaṁ—

So I have heard.

ekaṁ samayaṁ bhagavā sāvatthiyaṁ viharati jetavane anāthapiṇḍikassa ārāme.

At one time the Buddha was staying near Sāvatthī in Jeta's Grove, Anāthapiṇḍika's monastery.

Atha kho sambahulā bhikkhū pubbaṇhasamayaṁ nivāsetvā pattacīvaramādāya sāvatthiṁ piṇḍāya pāvisiṁsu.

Then several mendicants robed up in the morning and, taking their bowls and robes, entered Sāvatthī for alms.

Atha kho tesaṁ bhikkhūnaṁ etadahosi:

Then it occurred to them,

"atippago kho tāva sāvatthiyaṁ piṇḍāya carituṁ,

"It's too early to wander for alms in Sāvatthī.

yaṁ nūna mayaṁ yena aññatitthiyānaṁ paribbājakānaṁ ārāmo tenupasaṅkameyyāmā"ti.

Why don't we go to the monastery of the wanderers of other religions?"

Atha kho te bhikkhū yena aññatitthiyānaṁ paribbājakānaṁ ārāmo tenupasaṅkamiṁsu; upasaṅkamitvā tehi aññatitthiyehi paribbājakehi saddhiṁ sammodiṁsu;

Then they went to the monastery of the wanderers of other religions, and exchanged greetings with the wanderers there.

sammodanīyaṁ kathaṁ sāraṇīyaṁ vītisāretvā ekamantaṁ nisīdiṁsu. Ekamantaṁ nisinne kho te bhikkhū te aññatitthiyā paribbājakā etadavocuṁ:

When the greetings and polite conversation were over, they sat down to one side. The wanderers said to them:

"samaṇo, āvuso, gotamo kāmānaṁ pariññaṁ paññapeti, mayampi kāmānaṁ pariññaṁ paññapema;

"Reverends, the ascetic Gotama advocates the complete understanding of sensual pleasures, and so do we.

samaṇo, āvuso, gotamo rūpānaṁ pariññaṁ paññapeti, mayampi rūpānaṁ pariññaṁ paññapema;

The ascetic Gotama advocates the complete understanding of sights, and so do we.

samaṇo, āvuso, gotamo vedanānaṁ pariññaṁ paññapeti, mayampi vedanānaṁ pariññaṁ paññapema;

The ascetic Gotama advocates the complete understanding of feelings, and so do we.

idha no, āvuso, ko viseso, ko adhippayāso, kiṁ nānākaraṇaṁ samaṇassa vā gotamassa amhākaṁ vā—

What, then, is the difference between the ascetic Gotama's teaching and instruction and ours?"

yadidaṁ dhammadesanāya vā dhammadesanaṁ, anusāsaniyā vā anusāsanin"ti?

Atha kho te bhikkhū tesaṁ aññatitthiyānaṁ paribbājakānaṁ bhāsitaṁ neva abhinandiṁsu, nappaṭikkosiṁsu;

Those mendicants neither approved nor dismissed that statement of the wanderers of other religions.

anabhinanditvā appaṭikkositvā uṭṭhāyāsanā pakkamiṁsu:

They got up from their seat, thinking,

"bhagavato santike etassa bhāsitassa atthaṁ ājānissāmā"ti.

"We will learn the meaning of this statement from the Buddha himself."

Atha kho te bhikkhū sāvatthiyaṁ piṇḍāya caritvā pacchābhattaṁ piṇḍapātapaṭikkantā yena bhagavā tenupasaṅkamiṁsu; upasaṅkamitvā bhagavantaṁ abhivādetvā ekamantaṁ nisīdiṁsu. Ekamantaṁ nisinnā kho te bhikkhū bhagavantaṁ etadavocuṁ:

Then, after the meal, when they returned from almsround, they went up to the Buddha, bowed, sat down to one side, and told him what had happened. The Buddha said:

"idha mayaṁ, bhante, pubbaṇhasamayaṁ nivāsetvā pattacīvaramādāya sāvatthiṁ piṇḍāya pāvisimha.

Tesaṁ no, bhante, amhākaṁ etadahosi:

'atippago kho tāva sāvatthiyaṁ piṇḍāya carituṁ,

yaṁ nūna mayaṁ yena aññatitthiyānaṁ paribbājakānaṁ ārāmo tenupasaṅkameyyāmā'ti.

Atha kho mayaṁ, bhante, yena aññatitthiyānaṁ paribbājakānaṁ ārāmo tenupasaṅkamimha; upasaṅkamitvā tehi aññatitthiyehi paribbājakehi saddhiṁ sammodimha;

sammodanīyaṁ kathaṁ sāraṇīyaṁ vītisāretvā ekamantaṁ nisīdimha. Ekamantaṁ nisinne kho amhe, bhante, te aññatitthiyā paribbājakā etadavocuṁ:

'samaṇo, āvuso, gotamo kāmānaṁ pariññaṁ paññapeti, mayampi kāmānaṁ pariññaṁ paññapema.

Samaṇo, āvuso, gotamo rūpānaṁ pariññaṁ paññapeti, mayampi rūpānaṁ pariññaṁ paññapema.

Samaṇo, āvuso, gotamo vedanānaṁ pariññaṁ paññapeti, mayampi vedanānaṁ pariññaṁ paññapema.

Idha no, āvuso, ko viseso, ko adhippayāso, kiṁ nānākaraṇaṁ samaṇassa vā gotamassa amhākaṁ vā, yadidaṁ dhammadesanāya vā dhammadesanaṁ anusāsaniyā vā anusāsanin'ti.

Atha kho mayaṁ, bhante, tesaṁ aññatitthiyānaṁ paribbājakānaṁ bhāsitaṁ neva abhinandimha, nappaṭikkosimha;

anabhinanditvā appaṭikkositvā uṭṭhāyāsanā pakkamimha:

'bhagavato santike etassa bhāsitassa atthaṁ ājānissāmā'"ti.

"Evaṁvādino, bhikkhave, aññatitthiyā paribbājakā evamassu vacanīyā:

"Mendicants, when wanderers of other religions say this, you should say to them:

'ko panāvuso, kāmānaṁ assādo, ko ādīnavo, kiṁ nissaraṇaṁ?

'But reverends, what's the gratification, the drawback, and the escape when it comes to sensual pleasures?

Ko rūpānaṁ assādo, ko ādīnavo, kiṁ nissaraṇaṁ?

What's the gratification, the drawback, and the escape when it comes to sights?

Ko vedanānaṁ assādo, ko ādīnavo, kiṁ nissaraṇan'ti?

What's the gratification, the drawback, and the escape when it comes to feelings?'

Evaṁ puṭṭhā, bhikkhave, aññatitthiyā paribbājakā na ceva sampāyissanti, uttariñca vighātaṁ āpajjissanti.

Questioned like this, the wanderers of other religions would be stumped, and, in addition, would get frustrated.

Taṁ kissa hetu?

Why is that?

Yathā taṁ, bhikkhave, avisayasmiṁ.

Because they're out of their element.

Nāhaṁ taṁ, bhikkhave, passāmi sadevake loke samārake sabrahmake sassamaṇabrāhmaṇiyā pajāya sadevamanussāya yo imesaṁ pañhānaṁ veyyākaraṇena cittaṁ ārādheyya, aññatra tathāgatena vā tathāgatasāvakena vā, ito vā pana sutvā.

I don't see anyone in this world—with its gods, Māras, and Brahmās, this population with its ascetics and brahmins, its gods and humans—who could provide a satisfying answer to these questions except for the Realized One or his disciple or someone who has heard it from them.

Ko ca, bhikkhave, kāmānaṁ assādo?

And what is the gratification of sensual pleasures?

Pañcime, bhikkhave, kāmaguṇā.

There are these five kinds of sensual stimulation.

Katame pañca?

What five?

Cakkhuviññeyyā rūpā iṭṭhā kantā manāpā piyarūpā kāmūpasaṁhitā rajanīyā,

Sights known by the eye that are likable, desirable, agreeable, pleasant, sensual, and arousing.

sotaviññeyyā saddā …pe…

Sounds known by the ear …

ghānaviññeyyā gandhā …

Smells known by the nose …

jivhāviññeyyā rasā …

Tastes known by the tongue …

kāyaviññeyyā phoṭṭhabbā iṭṭhā kantā manāpā piyarūpā kāmūpasaṁhitā rajanīyā—

Touches known by the body that are likable, desirable, agreeable, pleasant, sensual, and arousing.

ime kho, bhikkhave, pañca kāmaguṇā.

These are the five kinds of sensual stimulation.

Yaṁ kho, bhikkhave, ime pañca kāmaguṇe paṭicca uppajjati sukhaṁ somanassaṁ—ayaṁ kāmānaṁ assādo.

The pleasure and happiness that arise from these five kinds of sensual stimulation: this is the gratification of sensual pleasures.

Ko ca, bhikkhave, kāmānaṁ ādīnavo?

And what is the drawback of sensual pleasures?

Idha, bhikkhave, kulaputto yena sippaṭṭhānena jīvikaṁ kappeti—

It's when a gentleman earns a living by means such as

yadi muddāya yadi gaṇanāya yadi saṅkhānena yadi kasiyā yadi vaṇijjāya yadi gorakkhena yadi issatthena yadi rājaporisena yadi sippaññatarena—

computing, accounting, calculating, farming, trade, raising cattle, archery, government service, or one of the professions.

sītassa purakkhato uṇhassa purakkhato ḍaṁsamakasavātātapasarīsapasamphassehi rissamāno khuppipāsāya mīyamāno;

But they must face cold and heat, being hurt by the touch of flies, mosquitoes, wind, sun, and reptiles, and risking death from hunger and thirst.

ayampi, bhikkhave, kāmānaṁ ādīnavo sandiṭṭhiko, dukkhakkhandho kāmahetu kāmanidānaṁ kāmādhikaraṇaṁ kāmānameva hetu.

This is a drawback of sensual pleasures apparent in this very life, a mass of suffering caused by sensual pleasures.

Tassa ce, bhikkhave, kulaputtassa evaṁ uṭṭhahato ghaṭato vāyamato te bhogā nābhinipphajjanti.

That gentleman might try hard, strive, and make an effort, but fail to earn any money.

So socati kilamati paridevati urattāḷiṁ kandati, sammohaṁ āpajjati:

If this happens, they sorrow and wail and lament, beating their breast and falling into confusion, saying:

'moghaṁ vata me uṭṭhānaṁ, aphalo vata me vāyāmo'ti.

'Oh, my hard work is wasted. My efforts are fruitless!'

Ayampi, bhikkhave, kāmānaṁ ādīnavo sandiṭṭhiko dukkhakkhandho kāmahetu kāmanidānaṁ kāmādhikaraṇaṁ kāmānameva hetu.

This too is a drawback of sensual pleasures apparent in this very life, a mass of suffering caused by sensual pleasures.

Tassa ce, bhikkhave, kulaputtassa evaṁ uṭṭhahato ghaṭato vāyamato te bhogā abhinipphajjanti.

That gentleman might try hard, strive, and make an effort, and succeed in earning money.

So tesaṁ bhogānaṁ ārakkhādhikaraṇaṁ dukkhaṁ domanassaṁ paṭisaṁvedeti:

But they experience pain and sadness when they try to protect it, thinking:

'kinti me bhoge neva rājāno hareyyuṁ, na corā hareyyuṁ, na aggi daheyya, na udakaṁ vaheyya, na appiyā dāyādā hareyyun'ti.

'How can I prevent my wealth from being taken by rulers or bandits, consumed by fire, swept away by flood, or taken by unloved heirs?'

Tassa evaṁ ārakkhato gopayato te bhoge rājāno vā haranti, corā vā haranti, aggi vā dahati, udakaṁ vā vahati, appiyā vā dāyādā haranti.

And even though they protect it and ward it, rulers or bandits take it, or fire consumes it, or flood sweeps it away, or unloved heirs take it.

So socati kilamati paridevati urattāḷiṁ kandati, sammohaṁ āpajjati:

They sorrow and wail and lament, beating their breast and falling into confusion:

'yampi me ahosi tampi no natthī'ti.

'What used to be mine is gone.'

Ayampi, bhikkhave, kāmānaṁ ādīnavo sandiṭṭhiko, dukkhakkhandho kāmahetu kāmanidānaṁ kāmādhikaraṇaṁ kāmānameva hetu.

This too is a drawback of sensual pleasures apparent in this very life, a mass of suffering caused by sensual pleasures.

Puna caparaṁ, bhikkhave, kāmahetu kāmanidānaṁ kāmādhikaraṇaṁ kāmānameva hetu rājānopi rājūhi vivadanti, khattiyāpi khattiyehi vivadanti, brāhmaṇāpi brāhmaṇehi vivadanti, gahapatīpi gahapatīhi vivadanti, mātāpi puttena vivadati, puttopi mātarā vivadati, pitāpi puttena vivadati, puttopi pitarā vivadati, bhātāpi bhātarā vivadati, bhātāpi bhaginiyā vivadati, bhaginīpi bhātarā vivadati, sahāyopi sahāyena vivadati.

Furthermore, for the sake of sensual pleasures kings fight with kings, aristocrats fight with aristocrats, brahmins fight with brahmins, and householders fight with householders. A mother fights with her child, child with mother, father with child, and child with father. Brother fights with brother, brother with sister, sister with brother, and friend fights with friend.

Te tattha kalahaviggahavivādāpannā aññamaññaṁ pāṇīhipi upakkamanti, leḍḍūhipi upakkamanti, daṇḍehipi upakkamanti, satthehipi upakkamanti.

Once they've started quarreling, arguing, and disputing, they attack each other with fists, stones, rods, and swords,

Te tattha maraṇampi nigacchanti, maraṇamattampi dukkhaṁ.

resulting in death and deadly pain.

Ayampi, bhikkhave, kāmānaṁ ādīnavo sandiṭṭhiko, dukkhakkhandho kāmahetu kāmanidānaṁ kāmādhikaraṇaṁ kāmānameva hetu.

This too is a drawback of sensual pleasures apparent in this very life, a mass of suffering caused by sensual pleasures.

Puna caparaṁ, bhikkhave, kāmahetu kāmanidānaṁ kāmādhikaraṇaṁ kāmānameva hetu asicammaṁ gahetvā, dhanukalāpaṁ sannayhitvā, ubhatobyūḷhaṁ saṅgāmaṁ pakkhandanti usūsupi khippamānesu, sattīsupi khippamānāsu, asīsupi vijjotalantesu.

Furthermore, for the sake of sensual pleasures they don their sword and shield, fasten their bow and arrows, and plunge into a battle massed on both sides, with arrows and spears flying and swords flashing.

Te tattha usūhipi vijjhanti, sattiyāpi vijjhanti, asināpi sīsaṁ chindanti.

There they are struck with arrows and spears, and their heads are chopped off,

Te tattha maraṇampi nigacchanti, maraṇamattampi dukkhaṁ.

resulting in death and deadly pain.

Ayampi, bhikkhave, kāmānaṁ ādīnavo sandiṭṭhiko, dukkhakkhandho kāmahetu kāmanidānaṁ kāmādhikaraṇaṁ kāmānameva hetu.

This too is a drawback of sensual pleasures apparent in this very life, a mass of suffering caused by sensual pleasures.

Puna caparaṁ, bhikkhave, kāmahetu kāmanidānaṁ kāmādhikaraṇaṁ kāmānameva hetu asicammaṁ gahetvā, dhanukalāpaṁ sannayhitvā, addāvalepanā upakāriyo pakkhandanti usūsupi khippamānesu, sattīsupi khippamānāsu, asīsupi vijjotalantesu.

Furthermore, for the sake of sensual pleasures they don their sword and shield, fasten their bow and arrows, and charge wetly plastered bastions, with arrows and spears flying and swords flashing.

Te tattha usūhipi vijjhanti, sattiyāpi vijjhanti, chakaṇakāyapi osiñcanti, abhivaggenapi omaddanti, asināpi sīsaṁ chindanti.

There they are struck with arrows and spears, splashed with dung, crushed with spiked blocks, and their heads are chopped off,

Te tattha maraṇampi nigacchanti, maraṇamattampi dukkhaṁ.

resulting in death and deadly pain.

Ayampi, bhikkhave, kāmānaṁ ādīnavo sandiṭṭhiko, dukkhakkhandho kāmahetu kāmanidānaṁ kāmādhikaraṇaṁ kāmānameva hetu.

This too is a drawback of sensual pleasures apparent in this very life, a mass of suffering caused by sensual pleasures.

Puna caparaṁ, bhikkhave, kāmahetu kāmanidānaṁ kāmādhikaraṇaṁ kāmānameva hetu sandhimpi chindanti, nillopampi haranti, ekāgārikampi karonti, paripanthepi tiṭṭhanti, paradārampi gacchanti.

Furthermore, for the sake of sensual pleasures they break into houses, plunder wealth, steal from isolated buildings, commit highway robbery, and commit adultery.

Tamenaṁ rājāno gahetvā vividhā kammakāraṇā kārenti—

The rulers would arrest them and subject them to various punishments—

kasāhipi tāḷenti, vettehipi tāḷenti, aḍḍhadaṇḍakehipi tāḷenti; hatthampi chindanti, pādampi chindanti, hatthapādampi chindanti, kaṇṇampi chindanti, nāsampi chindanti, kaṇṇanāsampi chindanti; bilaṅgathālikampi karonti, saṅkhamuṇḍikampi karonti, rāhumukhampi karonti, jotimālikampi karonti, hatthapajjotikampi karonti, erakavattikampi karonti, cīrakavāsikampi karonti, eṇeyyakampi karonti, baḷisamaṁsikampi karonti, kahāpaṇikampi karonti, khārāpatacchikampi karonti, palighaparivattikampi karonti, palālapīṭhakampi karonti, tattenapi telena osiñcanti, sunakhehipi khādāpenti, jīvantampi sūle uttāsenti, asināpi sīsaṁ chindanti.

whipping, caning, and clubbing; cutting off hands or feet, or both; cutting off ears or nose, or both; the 'porridge pot', the 'shell-shave', the 'demon's mouth', the 'garland of fire', the 'burning hand', the 'grass blades', the 'bark dress', the 'antelope', the 'meat hook', the 'coins', the 'caustic pickle', the 'twisting bar', the 'straw mat'; being splashed with hot oil, being fed to the dogs, being impaled alive, and being beheaded.

Te tattha maraṇampi nigacchanti, maraṇamattampi dukkhaṁ.

These result in death and deadly pain.

Ayampi, bhikkhave, kāmānaṁ ādīnavo sandiṭṭhiko, dukkhakkhandho kāmahetu kāmanidānaṁ kāmādhikaraṇaṁ kāmānameva hetu.

This too is a drawback of sensual pleasures apparent in this very life, a mass of suffering caused by sensual pleasures.

Puna caparaṁ, bhikkhave, kāmahetu kāmanidānaṁ kāmādhikaraṇaṁ kāmānameva hetu kāyena duccaritaṁ caranti, vācāya duccaritaṁ caranti, manasā duccaritaṁ caranti.

Furthermore, for the sake of sensual pleasures, they conduct themselves badly by way of body, speech, and mind.

Te kāyena duccaritaṁ caritvā, vācāya duccaritaṁ caritvā, manasā duccaritaṁ caritvā, kāyassa bhedā paraṁ maraṇā apāyaṁ duggatiṁ vinipātaṁ nirayaṁ upapajjanti.

When their body breaks up, after death, they're reborn in a place of loss, a bad place, the underworld, hell.

Ayampi, bhikkhave, kāmānaṁ ādīnavo samparāyiko, dukkhakkhandho kāmahetu kāmanidānaṁ kāmādhikaraṇaṁ kāmānameva hetu.

This is a drawback of sensual pleasures to do with lives to come, a mass of suffering caused by sensual pleasures.

Kiñca, bhikkhave, kāmānaṁ nissaraṇaṁ?

And what is the escape from sensual pleasures?

Yo kho, bhikkhave, kāmesu chandarāgavinayo chandarāgappahānaṁ—idaṁ kāmānaṁ nissaraṇaṁ.

Removing and giving up desire and greed for sensual pleasures: this is the escape from sensual pleasures.

Ye hi keci, bhikkhave, samaṇā vā brāhmaṇā vā evaṁ kāmānaṁ assādañca assādato ādīnavañca ādīnavato nissaraṇañca nissaraṇato yathābhūtaṁ nappajānanti te vata sāmaṁ vā kāme parijānissanti, paraṁ vā tathattāya samādapessanti yathā paṭipanno kāme parijānissatīti—netaṁ ṭhānaṁ vijjati.

There are ascetics and brahmins who don't truly understand sensual pleasures' gratification, drawback, and escape in this way for what they are. It's impossible for them to completely understand sensual pleasures themselves, or to instruct another so that, practicing accordingly, they will completely understand sensual pleasures.

Ye ca kho keci, bhikkhave, samaṇā vā brāhmaṇā vā evaṁ kāmānaṁ assādañca assādato ādīnavañca ādīnavato nissaraṇañca nissaraṇato yathābhūtaṁ pajānanti, te vata sāmaṁ vā kāme parijānissanti paraṁ vā tathattāya samādapessanti yathā paṭipanno kāme parijānissatīti—ṭhānametaṁ vijjati.

There are ascetics and brahmins who do truly understand sensual pleasures' gratification, drawback, and escape in this way for what they are. It is possible for them to completely understand sensual pleasures themselves, or to instruct another so that, practicing accordingly, they will completely understand sensual pleasures.

Ko ca, bhikkhave, rūpānaṁ assādo?

And what is the gratification of sights?

Seyyathāpi, bhikkhave, khattiyakaññā vā brāhmaṇakaññā vā gahapatikaññā vā pannarasavassuddesikā vā soḷasavassuddesikā vā, nātidīghā nātirassā nātikisā nātithūlā nātikāḷī naccodātā paramā sā, bhikkhave, tasmiṁ samaye subhā vaṇṇanibhāti?

Suppose there was a girl of the brahmins, aristocrats, or householders in her fifteenth or sixteenth year, neither too tall nor too short, neither too thin nor too fat, neither too dark nor too fair. Is she not at the height of her beauty and prettiness?"

'Evaṁ, bhante'.

"Yes, sir."

Yaṁ kho, bhikkhave, subhaṁ vaṇṇanibhaṁ paṭicca uppajjati sukhaṁ somanassaṁ—

"The pleasure and happiness that arise from this beauty and prettiness

ayaṁ rūpānaṁ assādo.

is the gratification of sights.

Ko ca, bhikkhave, rūpānaṁ ādīnavo?

And what is the drawback of sights?

Idha, bhikkhave, tameva bhaginiṁ passeyya aparena samayena āsītikaṁ vā nāvutikaṁ vā vassasatikaṁ vā jātiyā, jiṇṇaṁ gopānasivaṅkaṁ bhoggaṁ daṇḍaparāyanaṁ pavedhamānaṁ gacchantiṁ āturaṁ gatayobbanaṁ khaṇḍadantaṁ palitakesaṁ, vilūnaṁ khalitasiraṁ valinaṁ tilakāhatagattaṁ.

Suppose that some time later you were to see that same sister—eighty, ninety, or a hundred years old—bent double, crooked, leaning on a staff, trembling as they walk, ailing, past their prime, with teeth broken, hair grey and scanty or bald, skin wrinkled, and limbs blotchy.

Taṁ kiṁ maññatha, bhikkhave,

What do you think, mendicants?

yā purimā subhā vaṇṇanibhā sā antarahitā, ādīnavo pātubhūtoti?

Has not that former beauty vanished and the drawback become clear?"

'Evaṁ, bhante'.

"Yes, sir."

Ayampi, bhikkhave, rūpānaṁ ādīnavo.

"This is the drawback of sights.

Puna caparaṁ, bhikkhave, tameva bhaginiṁ passeyya ābādhikaṁ dukkhitaṁ bāḷhagilānaṁ, sake muttakarīse palipannaṁ semānaṁ, aññehi vuṭṭhāpiyamānaṁ, aññehi saṁvesiyamānaṁ.

Furthermore, suppose that you were to see that same sister sick, suffering, gravely ill, collapsed in her own urine and feces, being picked up by some and put down by others.

Taṁ kiṁ maññatha, bhikkhave,

What do you think, mendicants?

yā purimā subhā vaṇṇanibhā sā antarahitā, ādīnavo pātubhūtoti?

Has not that former beauty vanished and the drawback become clear?"

'Evaṁ, bhante'.

"Yes, sir."

Ayampi, bhikkhave, rūpānaṁ ādīnavo.

"This too is the drawback of sights.

Puna caparaṁ, bhikkhave, tameva bhaginiṁ passeyya sarīraṁ sivathikāya chaḍḍitaṁ—

Furthermore, suppose that you were to see that same sister as a corpse discarded in a charnel ground. And she had been dead for one, two, or three days, bloated, livid, and festering.

ekāhamataṁ vā dvīhamataṁ vā tīhamataṁ vā, uddhumātakaṁ vinīlakaṁ vipubbakajātaṁ.

Taṁ kiṁ maññatha, bhikkhave,

What do you think, mendicants?

yā purimā subhā vaṇṇanibhā sā antarahitā, ādīnavo pātubhūtoti?

Has not that former beauty vanished and the drawback become clear?"

'Evaṁ, bhante'.

"Yes, sir."

Ayampi, bhikkhave, rūpānaṁ ādīnavo.

"This too is the drawback of sights.

Puna caparaṁ, bhikkhave, tameva bhaginiṁ passeyya sarīraṁ sivathikāya chaḍḍitaṁ—

Furthermore, suppose that you were to see that same sister as a corpse discarded in a charnel ground. And she was being devoured by crows, hawks, vultures, herons, dogs, tigers, leopards, jackals, and many kinds of little creatures …

kākehi vā khajjamānaṁ, kulalehi vā khajjamānaṁ, gijjhehi vā khajjamānaṁ, kaṅkehi vā khajjamānaṁ, sunakhehi vā khajjamānaṁ, byagghehi vā khajjamānaṁ, dīpīhi vā khajjamānaṁ, siṅgālehi vā khajjamānaṁ, vividhehi vā pāṇakajātehi khajjamānaṁ.

Taṁ kiṁ maññatha, bhikkhave, yā purimā subhā vaṇṇanibhā sā antarahitā, ādīnavo pātubhūtoti?

'Evaṁ, bhante'.

Ayampi, bhikkhave, rūpānam ādīnavo.

Puna caparam, bhikkhave, tameva bhaginim passeyya sarīram sivathikāya chaḍḍitam—

Furthermore, suppose that you were to see that same sister as a corpse discarded in a charnel ground.

aṭṭhikasaṅkhalikam samamsalohitam nhārusambandham, aṭṭhikasaṅkhalikam nimamsalohitamakkhitam nhārusambandham, aṭṭhikasaṅkhalikam apagatamamsalohitam nhārusambandham, aṭṭhikāni apagatasambandhāni disāvidisāvikkhittāni—

And she had been reduced to a skeleton with flesh and blood, held together by sinews ... a skeleton rid of flesh but smeared with blood, and held together by sinews ... a skeleton rid of flesh and blood, held together by sinews ...

aññena hatthaṭṭhikam, aññena pādaṭṭhikam, aññena gopphakaṭṭhikam, aññena jaṅghaṭṭhikam, aññena ūruṭṭhikam, aññena kaṭiṭṭhikam, aññena phāsukaṭṭhikam, aññena piṭṭhiṭṭhikam, aññena khandhaṭṭhikam, aññena gīvaṭṭhikam, aññena hanukaṭṭhikam, aññena dantaṭṭhikam, aññena sīsakaṭāham.

bones rid of sinews scattered in every direction. Here a hand-bone, there a foot-bone, here a shin-bone, there a thigh-bone, here a hip-bone, there a rib-bone, here a back-bone, there an arm-bone, here a neck-bone, there a jaw-bone, here a tooth, there the skull. ...

Tam kim maññatha, bhikkhave, yā purimā subhā vaṇṇanibhā sā antarahitā, ādīnavo pātubhūtoti?

'Evam, bhante'.

Ayampi, bhikkhave, rūpānam ādīnavo.

Puna caparam, bhikkhave, tameva bhaginim passeyya sarīram sivathikāya chaḍḍitam—

Furthermore, suppose that you were to see that same sister as a corpse discarded in a charnel ground.

aṭṭhikāni setāni saṅkhavaṇṇapaṭibhāgāni, aṭṭhikāni puñjakitāni terovassikāni, aṭṭhikāni pūtīni cuṇṇakajātāni.

And she had been reduced to white bones, the color of shells ... decrepit bones, heaped in a pile ... bones rotted and crumbled to powder.

Tam kim maññatha, bhikkhave,

What do you think, mendicants?

yā purimā subhā vaṇṇanibhā sā antarahitā, ādīnavo pātubhūtoti?

Has not that former beauty vanished and the drawback become clear?"

'Evaṁ, bhante'.

"Yes, sir."

Ayampi, bhikkhave, rūpānaṁ ādīnavo.

"This too is the drawback of sights.

Kiñca, bhikkhave, rūpānaṁ nissaraṇaṁ?

And what is the escape from sights?

Yo, bhikkhave, rūpesu chandarāgavinayo chandarāgappahānaṁ—idaṁ rūpānaṁ nissaraṇaṁ.

Removing and giving up desire and greed for sights: this is the escape from sights.

Ye hi keci, bhikkhave, samaṇā vā brāhmaṇā vā evaṁ rūpānaṁ assādañca assādato ādīnavañca ādīnavato nissaraṇañca nissaraṇato yathābhūtaṁ nappajānanti te vata sāmaṁ vā rūpe parijānissanti, paraṁ vā tathattāya samādapessanti yathā paṭipanno rūpe parijānissatīti—netaṁ ṭhānaṁ vijjati.

There are ascetics and brahmins who don't truly understand sights' gratification, drawback, and escape in this way for what they are. It's impossible for them to completely understand sights themselves, or to instruct another so that, practicing accordingly, they will completely understand sights.

Ye ca kho keci, bhikkhave, samaṇā vā brāhmaṇā vā evaṁ rūpānaṁ assādañca assādato ādīnavañca ādīnavato nissaraṇañca nissaraṇato yathābhūtaṁ pajānanti te vata sāmaṁ vā rūpe parijānissanti paraṁ vā tathattāya samādapessanti yathā paṭipanno rūpe parijānissatīti—ṭhānametaṁ vijjati.

There are ascetics and brahmins who do truly understand sights' gratification, drawback, and escape in this way for what they are. It is possible for them to completely understand sights themselves, or to instruct another so that, practicing accordingly, they will completely understand sights.

Ko ca, bhikkhave, vedanānaṁ assādo?

And what is the gratification of feelings?

Idha, bhikkhave, bhikkhu vivicceva kāmehi vivicca akusalehi dhammehi savitakkaṁ savicāraṁ vivekajaṁ pītisukhaṁ paṭhamaṁ jhānaṁ upasampajja viharati.

It's when a mendicant, quite secluded from sensual pleasures, secluded from unskillful qualities, enters and remains in the first absorption, which has the rapture and bliss born of seclusion, while placing the mind and keeping it connected.

Yasmiṁ samaye, bhikkhave, bhikkhu vivicceva kāmehi vivicca akusalehi dhammehi savitakkaṁ savicāraṁ vivekajaṁ pītisukhaṁ paṭhamaṁ jhānaṁ upasampajja viharati, neva tasmiṁ samaye attabyābādhāyapi ceteti, na parabyābādhāyapi ceteti, na ubhayabyābādhāyapi ceteti;

At that time a mendicant doesn't intend to hurt themselves, hurt others, or hurt both;

abyābajjhaṁyeva tasmiṁ samaye vedanaṁ vedeti.

they feel only feelings that are not hurtful.

Abyābajjhaparamāhaṁ, bhikkhave, vedanānaṁ assādaṁ vadāmi.

Freedom from being hurt is the ultimate gratification of feelings, I say.

Puna caparaṁ, bhikkhave, bhikkhu vitakkavicārānaṁ vūpasamā ajjhattaṁ sampasādanaṁ cetaso ekodibhāvaṁ avitakkaṁ avicāraṁ samādhijaṁ pītisukhaṁ dutiyaṁ jhānaṁ upasampajja viharati …pe…

Furthermore, a mendicant enters and remains in the second absorption …

yasmiṁ samaye, bhikkhave, bhikkhu pītiyā ca virāgā, upekkhako ca viharati, sato ca sampajāno sukhañca kāyena paṭisaṁvedeti yaṁ taṁ ariyā ācikkhanti: 'upekkhako satimā sukhavihārī'ti tatiyaṁ jhānaṁ upasampajja viharati …pe…

third absorption …

yasmiṁ samaye, bhikkhave, bhikkhu sukhassa ca pahānā dukkhassa ca pahānā pubbeva somanassadomanassānaṁ atthaṅgamā adukkhamasukhaṁ upekkhāsatipārisuddhiṁ catutthaṁ jhānaṁ upasampajja viharati, neva tasmiṁ samaye attabyābādhāyapi ceteti, na parabyābādhāyapi ceteti, na ubhayabyābādhāyapi ceteti;

fourth absorption. At that time a mendicant doesn't intend to hurt themselves, hurt others, or hurt both;

abyābajjhaṁyeva tasmiṁ samaye vedanaṁ vedeti.

they feel only feelings that are not hurtful.

Abyābajjhaparamāhaṁ, bhikkhave, vedanānaṁ assādaṁ vadāmi.

Freedom from being hurt is the ultimate gratification of feelings, I say.

Ko ca, bhikkhave, vedanānaṁ ādīnavo?

And what is the drawback of feelings?

Yaṁ, bhikkhave, vedanā aniccā dukkhā vipariṇāmadhammā—ayaṁ vedanānaṁ ādīnavo.

That feelings are impermanent, suffering, and perishable: this is their drawback.

Kiñca, bhikkhave, vedanānaṁ nissaraṇaṁ?

And what is the escape from feelings?

Yo, bhikkhave, vedanāsu chandarāgavinayo, chandarāgappahānaṁ—idaṁ vedanānaṁ nissaraṇaṁ.

Removing and giving up desire and greed for feelings: this is the escape from feelings.

Ye hi keci, bhikkhave, samaṇā vā brāhmaṇā vā evaṁ vedanānaṁ assādañca assādato ādīnavañca ādīnavato nissaraṇañca nissaraṇato yathābhūtaṁ nappajānanti, te vata sāmaṁ vā vedanaṁ parijānissanti, paraṁ vā tathattāya samādapessanti yathā paṭipanno vedanaṁ parijānissatīti—netaṁ ṭhānaṁ vijjati.

There are ascetics and brahmins who don't truly understand feelings' gratification, drawback, and escape in this way for what they are. It's impossible for them to completely understand feelings themselves, or to instruct another so that, practicing accordingly, they will completely understand feelings.

Ye ca kho keci, bhikkhave, samaṇā vā brāhmaṇā vā evaṁ vedanānaṁ assādañca assādato ādīnavañca ādīnavato nissaraṇañca nissaraṇato yathābhūtaṁ pajānanti te vata sāmaṁ vā vedanaṁ parijānissanti, paraṁ vā tathattāya samādapessanti yathā paṭipanno vedanaṁ parijānissatīti—ṭhānametaṁ vijjatī'ti.

There are ascetics and brahmins who do truly understand feelings' gratification, drawback, and escape in this way for what they are. It is possible for them to completely understand feelings themselves, or to instruct another so that, practicing accordingly, they will completely understand feelings."

Idamavoca bhagavā.

That is what the Buddha said.

Attamanā te bhikkhū bhagavato bhāsitaṁ abhinandunti.

Satisfied, the mendicants were happy with what the Buddha said.

Mahādukkhakkhandhasuttaṁ niṭṭhitaṁ tatiyaṁ.

14 Cūḷadukkhakkhandhasutta:

The Shorter Discourse on the Mass of Suffering

Evaṁ me sutaṁ—

So I have heard.

ekaṁ samayaṁ bhagavā sakkesu viharati kapilavatthusmiṁ nigrodhārāme.

At one time the Buddha was staying in the land of the Sakyans, near Kapilavatthu in the Banyan Tree Monastery.

Atha kho mahānāmo sakko yena bhagavā tenupasaṅkami; upasaṅkamitvā bhagavantaṁ abhivādetvā ekamantaṁ nisīdi. Ekamantaṁ nisinno kho mahānāmo sakko bhagavantaṁ etadavoca:

Then Mahānāma the Sakyan went up to the Buddha, bowed, sat down to one side, and said to him,

"dīgharattāhaṁ, bhante, bhagavatā evaṁ dhammaṁ desitaṁ ājānāmi:

"For a long time, sir, I have understood your teaching like this:

'lobho cittassa upakkileso, doso cittassa upakkileso, moho cittassa upakkileso'ti.

'Greed, hate, and delusion are corruptions of the mind.'

Evañcāhaṁ, bhante, bhagavatā dhammaṁ desitaṁ ājānāmi:

'lobho cittassa upakkileso, doso cittassa upakkileso, moho cittassa upakkileso'ti.

Atha ca pana me ekadā lobhadhammāpi cittaṁ pariyādāya tiṭṭhanti, dosadhammāpi cittaṁ pariyādāya tiṭṭhanti, mohadhammāpi cittaṁ pariyādāya tiṭṭhanti.

Despite understanding this, sometimes my mind is occupied by thoughts of greed, hate, and delusion.

Tassa mayhaṁ, bhante, evaṁ hoti:

'kosu nāma me dhammo ajjhattaṁ appahīno yena me ekadā lobhadhammāpi cittaṁ pariyādāya tiṭṭhanti, dosadhammāpi cittaṁ pariyādāya tiṭṭhanti, mohadhammāpi cittaṁ pariyādāya tiṭṭhantī'"ti.

I wonder what qualities remain in me that I have such thoughts?"

"So eva kho te, mahānāma, dhammo ajjhattaṁ appahīno yena te ekadā lobhadhammāpi cittaṁ pariyādāya tiṭṭhanti, dosadhammāpi cittaṁ pariyādāya tiṭṭhanti, mohadhammāpi cittaṁ pariyādāya tiṭṭhanti.

"Mahānāma, there is a quality that remains in you that makes you have such thoughts.

So ca hi te, mahānāma, dhammo ajjhattaṁ pahīno abhavissa, na tvaṁ agāraṁ ajjhāvaseyyāsi, na kāme paribhuñjeyyāsi.

For if you had given up that quality you would not still be living at home and enjoying sensual pleasures.

Yasmā ca kho te, mahānāma, so eva dhammo ajjhattaṁ appahīno tasmā tvaṁ agāraṁ ajjhāvasasi, kāme paribhuñjasi.

But because you haven't given up that quality you are still living at home and enjoying sensual pleasures.

'Appassādā kāmā bahudukkhā bahupāyāsā, ādīnavo ettha bhiyyo'ti—

Sensual pleasures give little gratification and much suffering and distress, and they are all the more full of drawbacks.

iti cepi, mahānāma, ariyasāvakassa yathābhūtaṁ sammappaññāya sudiṭṭhaṁ hoti, so ca aññatreva kāmehi aññatra akusalehi dhammehi pītisukhaṁ nādhigacchati, aññaṁ vā tato santataraṁ;

Even though a noble disciple has clearly seen this with right wisdom, so long as they don't achieve the rapture and bliss that are apart from sensual pleasures and unskillful qualities, or something even more peaceful than that,

atha kho so neva tāva anāvaṭṭī kāmesu hoti.

they might still return to sensual pleasures.

Yato ca kho, mahānāma, ariyasāvakassa 'appassādā kāmā bahudukkhā bahupāyāsā, ādīnavo ettha bhiyyo'ti—evametaṁ yathābhūtaṁ sammappaññāya sudiṭṭhaṁ hoti, so ca aññatreva kāmehi aññatra akusalehi dhammehi pītisukhaṁ adhigacchati aññaṁ vā tato santataraṁ;

But when they do achieve that rapture and bliss, or something more peaceful than that,

atha kho so anāvaṭṭī kāmesu hoti.

they will not return to sensual pleasures.

Mayhampi kho, mahānāma, pubbeva sambodhā, anabhisambuddhassa bodhisattasseva sato,

Before my awakening—when I was still unawakened but intent on awakening—I too clearly saw with right wisdom that:

'appassādā kāmā bahudukkhā bahupāyāsā, ādīnavo ettha bhiyyo'ti—evametaṁ yathābhūtaṁ sammappaññāya sudiṭṭhaṁ hoti,

'Sensual pleasures give little gratification and much suffering and distress, and they are all the more full of drawbacks.'

so ca aññatreva kāmehi aññatra akusalehi dhammehi pītisukhaṁ nājjhagamaṁ, aññaṁ vā tato santataraṁ;

But so long as I didn't achieve the rapture and bliss that are apart from sensual pleasures and unskillful qualities, or something even more peaceful than that,

atha khvāhaṁ neva tāva anāvattī kāmesu paccaññāsiṁ.

I didn't announce that I would not return to sensual pleasures.

Yato ca kho me, mahānāma, 'appassādā kāmā bahudukkhā bahupāyāsā, ādīnavo ettha bhiyyo'ti—evametaṁ yathābhūtaṁ sammappaññāya sudiṭṭhaṁ ahosi, so ca aññatreva kāmehi aññatra akusalehi dhammehi pītisukhaṁ ajjhagamaṁ, aññaṁ vā tato santataraṁ;

But when I did achieve that rapture and bliss, or something more peaceful than that,

athāhaṁ anāvattī kāmesu paccaññāsiṁ.

I announced that I would not return to sensual pleasures.

Ko ca, mahānāma, kāmānaṁ assādo?

And what is the gratification of sensual pleasures?

Pañcime, mahānāma, kāmaguṇā.

There are these five kinds of sensual stimulation.

Katame pañca?

What five?

Cakkhuviññeyyā rūpā iṭṭhā kantā manāpā piyarūpā kāmūpasaṁhitā rajanīyā;

Sights known by the eye that are likable, desirable, agreeable, pleasant, sensual, and arousing.

sotaviññeyyā saddā …pe…

Sounds known by the ear …

ghānaviññeyyā gandhā …

Smells known by the nose …

jivhāviññeyyā rasā …

Tastes known by the tongue …

kāyaviññeyyā phoṭṭhabbā iṭṭhā kantā manāpā piyarūpā kāmūpasaṁhitā rajanīyā—

Touches known by the body that are likable, desirable, agreeable, pleasant, sensual, and arousing.

ime kho, mahānāma, pañca kāmaguṇā.

These are the five kinds of sensual stimulation.

Yaṁ kho, mahānāma, ime pañca kāmaguṇe paṭicca uppajjati sukhaṁ somanassaṁ—

The pleasure and happiness that arise from these five kinds of sensual stimulation: this is the gratification of sensual pleasures.

ayaṁ kāmānaṁ assādo.

Ko ca, mahānāma, kāmānaṁ ādīnavo?

And what is the drawback of sensual pleasures?

Idha, mahānāma, kulaputto yena sippaṭṭhānena jīvikaṁ kappeti—

It's when a gentleman earns a living by means such as

yadi muddāya yadi gaṇanāya yadi saṅkhānena yadi kasiyā yadi vaṇijjāya yadi gorakkhena yadi issatthena yadi rājaporisena yadi sippaññatarena,

computing, accounting, calculating, farming, trade, raising cattle, archery, government service, or one of the professions.

sītassa purakkhato uṇhassa purakkhato ḍaṁsamakasavātātapasarīsapasamphassehi rissamāno khuppipāsāya mīyamāno;

But they must face cold and heat, being hurt by the touch of flies, mosquitoes, wind, sun, and reptiles, and risking death from hunger and thirst.

ayampi, mahānāma, kāmānaṁ ādīnavo sandiṭṭhiko dukkhakkhandho kāmahetu kāmanidānaṁ kāmādhikaraṇaṁ kāmānameva hetu.

This is a drawback of sensual pleasures apparent in this very life, a mass of suffering caused by sensual pleasures.

Tassa ce, mahānāma, kulaputtassa evaṁ uṭṭhahato ghaṭato vāyamato te bhogā nābhinipphajjanti,

That gentleman might try hard, strive, and make an effort, but fail to earn any money.

so socati kilamati paridevati urattāḷiṁ kandati sammohaṁ āpajjati 'moghaṁ vata me uṭṭhānaṁ, aphalo vata me vāyāmo'ti.

If this happens, they sorrow and wail and lament, beating their breast and falling into confusion, saying: 'Oh, my hard work is wasted. My efforts are fruitless!'

Ayampi, mahānāma, kāmānaṁ ādīnavo sandiṭṭhiko dukkhakkhandho kāmahetu kāmanidānaṁ kāmādhikaraṇaṁ kāmānameva hetu.

This too is a drawback of sensual pleasures apparent in this very life, a mass of suffering caused by sensual pleasures.

Tassa ce, mahānāma, kulaputtassa evaṁ uṭṭhahato ghaṭato vāyamato te bhogā abhinipphajjanti.

That gentleman might try hard, strive, and make an effort, and succeed in earning money.

So tesaṁ bhogānaṁ ārakkhādhikaraṇaṁ dukkhaṁ domanassaṁ paṭisaṁvedeti:

But they experience pain and sadness when they try to protect it, thinking:

'kinti me bhoge neva rājāno hareyyuṁ, na corā hareyyuṁ, na aggi daheyya, na udakaṁ vaheyya, na appiyā vā dāyādā hareyyun'ti.

'How can I prevent my wealth from being taken by rulers or bandits, consumed by fire, swept away by flood, or taken by unloved heirs?'

Tassa evaṁ ārakkhato gopayato te bhoge rājāno vā haranti, corā vā haranti, aggi vā dahati, udakaṁ vā vahati, appiyā vā dāyādā haranti.

And even though they protect it and ward it, rulers or bandits take it, or fire consumes it, or flood sweeps it away, or unloved heirs take it.

So socati kilamati paridevati urattāḷiṁ kandati sammohaṁ āpajjati:

They sorrow and wail and lament, beating their breast and falling into confusion:

'yampi me ahosi tampi no natthī'ti.

'What used to be mine is gone.'

Ayampi, mahānāma, kāmānaṁ ādīnavo sandiṭṭhiko dukkhakkhandho kāmahetu kāmanidānaṁ kāmādhikaraṇaṁ kāmānameva hetu.

This too is a drawback of sensual pleasures apparent in this very life, a mass of suffering caused by sensual pleasures.

Puna caparaṁ, mahānāma, kāmahetu kāmanidānaṁ kāmādhikaraṇaṁ kāmānameva hetu rājānopi rājūhi vivadanti, khattiyāpi khattiyehi vivadanti, brāhmaṇāpi brāhmaṇehi vivadanti, gahapatīpi gahapatīhi vivadanti, mātāpi puttena vivadati, puttopi mātarā vivadati, pitāpi puttena vivadati, puttopi pitarā vivadati, bhātāpi bhātarā vivadati, bhātāpi bhaginiyā vivadati, bhaginīpi bhātarā vivadati, sahāyopi sahāyena vivadati.

Furthermore, for the sake of sensual pleasures kings fight with kings, aristocrats fight with aristocrats, brahmins fight with brahmins, and householders fight with householders. A mother fights with her child, child with mother, father with child, and child with father. Brother fights with brother, brother with sister, sister with brother, and friend fights with friend.

Te tattha kalahaviggahavivādāpannā aññamaññaṁ pāṇīhipi upakkamanti, leḍḍūhipi upakkamanti, daṇḍehipi upakkamanti, satthehipi upakkamanti.

Once they've started quarreling, arguing, and disputing, they attack each other with fists, stones, rods, and swords,

Te tattha maraṇampi nigacchanti, maraṇamattampi dukkhaṁ.

resulting in death and deadly pain.

Ayampi, mahānāma, kāmānaṁ ādīnavo sandiṭṭhiko dukkhakkhandho kāmahetu kāmanidānaṁ kāmādhikaraṇaṁ kāmānameva hetu.

This too is a drawback of sensual pleasures apparent in this very life, a mass of suffering caused by sensual pleasures.

Puna caparaṁ, mahānāma, kāmahetu kāmanidānaṁ kāmādhikaraṇaṁ kāmānameva hetu asicammaṁ gahetvā, dhanukalāpaṁ sannayhitvā, ubhatobyūḷhaṁ saṅgāmaṁ pakkhandanti usūsupi khippamānesu, sattīsupi khippamānāsu, asīsupi vijjotalantesu.

Furthermore, for the sake of sensual pleasures they don their sword and shield, fasten their bow and arrows, and plunge into a battle massed on both sides, with arrows and spears flying and swords flashing.

Te tattha usūhipi vijjhanti, sattiyāpi vijjhanti, asināpi sīsaṁ chindanti.

There they are struck with arrows and spears, and their heads are chopped off,

Te tattha maraṇampi nigacchanti, maraṇamattampi dukkhaṁ.

resulting in death and deadly pain.

Ayampi, mahānāma, kāmānaṁ ādīnavo sandiṭṭhiko dukkhakkhandho kāmahetu kāmanidānaṁ kāmādhikaraṇaṁ kāmānameva hetu.

This too is a drawback of sensual pleasures apparent in this very life, a mass of suffering caused by sensual pleasures.

Puna caparaṁ, mahānāma, kāmahetu kāmanidānaṁ kāmādhikaraṇaṁ kāmānameva hetu asicammaṁ gahetvā, dhanukalāpaṁ sannayhitvā, addāvalepanā upakāriyo pakkhandanti usūsupi khippamānesu, sattīsupi khippamānāsu, asīsupi vijjotalantesu.

Furthermore, for the sake of sensual pleasures they don their sword and shield, fasten their bow and arrows, and charge wetly plastered bastions, with arrows and spears flying and swords flashing.

Te tattha usūhipi vijjhanti, sattiyāpi vijjhanti, chakaṇakāyapi osiñcanti, abhivaggenapi omaddanti, asināpi sīsaṁ chindanti.

There they are struck with arrows and spears, splashed with dung, crushed with spiked blocks, and their heads are chopped off,

Te tattha maraṇampi nigacchanti, maraṇamattampi dukkhaṁ.

resulting in death and deadly pain.

Ayampi, mahānāma, kāmānaṁ ādīnavo sandiṭṭhiko dukkhakkhandho kāmahetu kāmanidānaṁ kāmādhikaraṇaṁ kāmānameva hetu.

This too is a drawback of sensual pleasures apparent in this very life, a mass of suffering caused by sensual pleasures.

Puna caparaṁ, mahānāma, kāmahetu kāmanidānaṁ kāmādhikaraṇaṁ kāmānameva hetu sandhimpi chindanti, nillopampi haranti, ekāgārikampi karonti, paripanthepi tiṭṭhanti, paradārampi gacchanti.

Furthermore, for the sake of sensual pleasures they break into houses, plunder wealth, steal from isolated buildings, commit highway robbery, and commit adultery.

Tamenaṁ rājāno gahetvā vividhā kammakāraṇā kārenti—

The rulers would arrest them and subject them to various punishments—

kasāhipi tāḷenti, vettehipi tāḷenti, aḍḍhadaṇḍakehipi tāḷenti; hatthampi chindanti, pādampi chindanti, hatthapādampi chindanti, kaṇṇampi chindanti, nāsampi chindanti, kaṇṇanāsampi chindanti; bilaṅgathālikampi karonti, saṅkhamuṇḍikampi karonti, rāhumukhampi karonti, jotimālikampi karonti, hatthapajjotikampi karonti, erakavattikampi karonti, cīrakavāsikampi karonti, eṇeyyakampi karonti, baḷisamaṁsikampi karonti, kahāpaṇikampi karonti, khārāpatacchikampi karonti, palighaparivattikampi karonti, palālapīṭhakampi karonti, tattenapi telena osiñcanti, sunakhehipi khādāpenti, jīvantampi sūle uttāsenti, asināpi sīsaṁ chindanti.

whipping, caning, and clubbing; cutting off hands or feet, or both; cutting off ears or nose, or both; the 'porridge pot', the 'shell-shave', the 'demon's mouth', the 'garland of fire', the 'burning hand', the 'grass blades', the 'bark dress', the 'antelope', the 'meat hook', the 'coins', the 'caustic pickle', the 'twisting bar', the 'straw mat'; being splashed with hot oil, being fed to the dogs, being impaled alive, and being beheaded.

Te tattha maraṇampi nigacchanti, maraṇamattampi dukkhaṁ.

These result in death and deadly pain.

Ayampi, mahānāma, kāmānaṁ ādīnavo sandiṭṭhiko dukkhakkhandho kāmahetu kāmanidānaṁ kāmādhikaraṇaṁ kāmānameva hetu.

This too is a drawback of sensual pleasures apparent in this very life, a mass of suffering caused by sensual pleasures.

Puna caparaṁ, mahānāma, kāmahetu kāmanidānaṁ kāmādhikaraṇaṁ kāmānameva hetu kāyena duccaritaṁ caranti, vācāya duccaritaṁ caranti, manasā duccaritaṁ caranti.

Furthermore, for the sake of sensual pleasures, they conduct themselves badly by way of body, speech, and mind.

Te kāyena duccaritaṁ caritvā, vācāya duccaritaṁ caritvā, manasā duccaritaṁ caritvā, kāyassa bhedā paraṁ maraṇā, apāyaṁ duggatiṁ vinipātaṁ nirayaṁ upapajjanti.

When their body breaks up, after death, they're reborn in a place of loss, a bad place, the underworld, hell.

Ayampi, mahānāma, kāmānaṁ ādīnavo samparāyiko, dukkhakkhandho kāmahetu kāmanidānaṁ kāmādhikaraṇaṁ kāmānameva hetu.

This is a drawback of sensual pleasures to do with lives to come, a mass of suffering caused by sensual pleasures.

Ekamidāhaṁ, mahānāma, samayaṁ rājagahe viharāmi gijjhakūṭe pabbate.

Mahānāma, this one time I was staying near Rājagaha, on the Vulture's Peak Mountain.

Tena kho pana samayena sambahulā nigaṇṭhā isigilipasse kāḷasilāyaṁ ubbhaṭṭhakā honti āsanapaṭikkhittā, opakkamikā dukkhā tibbā kharā kaṭukā vedanā vedayanti.

Now at that time several Jain ascetics on the slopes of Isigili at the Black Rock were constantly standing, refusing seats. And they felt painful, sharp, severe, acute feelings due to overexertion.

Atha khvāhaṁ, mahānāma, sāyanhasamayaṁ paṭisallānā vuṭṭhito yena isigilipasse kāḷasilā yena te nigaṇṭhā tenupasaṅkamiṁ; upasaṅkamitvā te nigaṇṭhe etadavocaṁ:

Then in the late afternoon, I came out of retreat and went to the Black Rock to visit those Jain ascetics. I said to them,

'kiṁ nu tumhe, āvuso nigaṇṭhā, ubbhaṭṭhakā āsanapaṭikkhittā, opakkamikā dukkhā tibbā kharā kaṭukā vedanā vedayathā'ti?

'Reverends, why are you constantly standing, refusing seats, so that you suffer painful, sharp, severe, acute feelings due to overexertion?'

Evaṁ vutte, mahānāma, te nigaṇṭhā maṁ etadavocuṁ:

When I said this, those Jain ascetics said to me,

'nigaṇṭho, āvuso, nāṭaputto sabbaññū sabbadassāvī aparisesaṁ ñāṇadassanaṁ paṭijānāti:

'Reverend, the Jain ascetic of the Ñātika clan claims to be all-knowing and all-seeing, to know and see everything without exception, thus:

"carato ca me tiṭṭhato ca suttassa ca jāgarassa ca satataṁ samitaṁ ñāṇadassanaṁ paccupaṭṭhitan"ti.

"Knowledge and vision are constantly and continually present to me, while walking, standing, sleeping, and waking."

So evamāha:

He says,

"atthi kho vo, niganṭhā, pubbe pāpakammaṁ kataṁ, taṁ imāya kaṭukāya dukkarakārikāya nijjīretha;

"O Jain ascetics, you have done bad deeds in a past life. Wear them away with these severe and grueling austerities.

yaṁ panettha etarahi kāyena saṁvutā vācāya saṁvutā manasā saṁvutā taṁ āyatiṁ pāpassa kammassa akaraṇaṁ;

And when you refrain from such deeds in the present by way of body, speech, and mind, you're not doing any bad deeds for the future.

iti purāṇānaṁ kammānaṁ tapasā byantibhāvā, navānaṁ kammānaṁ akaraṇā, āyatiṁ anavassavo;

So, due to eliminating past deeds by mortification, and not doing any new deeds, there's nothing to come up in the future.

āyatiṁ anavassavā kammakkhayo, kammakkhayā dukkhakkhayo, dukkhakkhayā vedanākkhayo, vedanākkhayā sabbaṁ dukkhaṁ nijjiṇṇaṁ bhavissatī"ti.

With nothing to come up in the future, deeds end. With the ending of deeds, suffering ends. With the ending of suffering, feeling ends. And with the ending of feeling, all suffering will have been worn away."

Tañca panamhākaṁ ruccati ceva khamati ca, tena camha attamanā'ti.

We like and accept this, and we are satisfied with it.'

Evaṁ vutte, ahaṁ, mahānāma, te niganṭhe etadavocaṁ:

When they said this, I said to them,

'kiṁ pana tumhe, āvuso niganṭhā, jānātha—

'But reverends, do you know

ahuvamheva mayaṁ pubbe na nāhuvamhā'ti?

for sure that you existed in the past, and it is not the case that you didn't exist?'

'No hidaṁ, āvuso'.

'No we don't, reverend.'

'Kiṁ pana tumhe, āvuso nigaṇṭhā, jānātha—

'But reverends, do you know

akaramheva mayaṁ pubbe pāpakammaṁ na nākaramhā'ti?

for sure that you did bad deeds in the past?'

'No hidaṁ, āvuso'.

'No we don't, reverend.'

'Kiṁ pana tumhe, āvuso nigaṇṭhā, jānātha—

'But reverends, do you know

evarūpaṁ vā evarūpaṁ vā pāpakammaṁ akaramhā'ti?

that you did such and such bad deeds?'

'No hidaṁ, āvuso'.

'No we don't, reverend.'

'Kiṁ pana tumhe, āvuso nigaṇṭhā, jānātha—

'But reverends, do you know

ettakaṁ vā dukkhaṁ nijjiṇṇaṁ, ettakaṁ vā dukkhaṁ nijjīretabbaṁ, ettakamhi vā dukkhe nijjiṇṇe sabbaṁ dukkhaṁ nijjiṇṇaṁ bhavissatī'ti?

that so much suffering has already been worn away? Or that so much suffering still remains to be worn away? Or that when so much suffering is worn away all suffering will have been worn away?'

'No hidaṁ, āvuso'.

'No we don't, reverend.'

'Kiṁ pana tumhe, āvuso nigaṇṭhā, jānātha—

'But reverends, do you know

diṭṭheva dhamme akusalānaṁ dhammānaṁ pahānaṁ, kusalānaṁ dhammānaṁ upasampadan'ti?

about giving up unskillful qualities in the present life and embracing skillful qualities?'

'No hidaṁ, āvuso'.

'No we don't, reverend.'

'Iti kira tumhe, āvuso nigaṇṭhā, na jānātha—

'So it seems that you don't know any of these things.

ahuvamheva mayaṁ pubbe na nāhuvamhāti, na jānātha—

akaramheva mayaṁ pubbe pāpakammaṁ na nākaramhāti, na jānātha—

evarūpaṁ vā evarūpaṁ vā pāpakammaṁ akaramhāti, na jānātha—

ettakaṁ vā dukkhaṁ nijjiṇṇaṁ, ettakaṁ vā dukkhaṁ nijjīretabbaṁ, ettakamhi vā dukkhe nijjiṇṇe sabbaṁ dukkhaṁ nijjiṇṇaṁ bhavissatīti.

Na jānātha—

diṭṭheva dhamme akusalānaṁ dhammānaṁ pahānaṁ, kusalānaṁ dhammānaṁ upasampadaṁ.

Evaṁ sante, āvuso nigaṇṭhā, ye loke luddā lohitapāṇino kurūrakammantā manussesu paccājātā te nigaṇṭhesu pabbajantī'ti?

That being so, when those in the world who are violent and bloody-handed and make their living by cruelty are reborn among humans they go forth as Jain ascetics.'

'Na kho, āvuso gotama, sukhena sukhaṁ adhigantabbaṁ, dukkhena kho sukhaṁ adhigantabbaṁ;

'Reverend Gotama, pleasure is not gained through pleasure; pleasure is gained through pain.

sukhena cāvuso gotama, sukhaṁ adhigantabbaṁ abhavissa, rājā māgadho seniyo bimbisāro sukhaṁ adhigaccheyya, rājā māgadho seniyo bimbisāro sukhavihāritaro āyasmatā gotamenā'ti.

For if pleasure were to be gained through pleasure, King Seniya Bimbisāra of Magadha would gain pleasure, since he lives in greater pleasure than Venerable Gotama.'

'Addhāyasmantehi nigaṇṭhehi sahasā appaṭisaṅkhā vācā bhāsitā:

'Clearly the venerables have spoken rashly, without reflection.

"na kho, āvuso gotama, sukhena sukhaṁ adhigantabbaṁ, dukkhena kho sukhaṁ adhigantabbaṁ;

sukhena cāvuso gotama, sukhaṁ adhigantabbaṁ abhavissa, rājā māgadho seniyo bimbisāro sukhaṁ adhigaccheyya, rājā māgadho seniyo bimbisāro sukhavihāritaro āyasmatā gotamenā"ti.

Api ca ahameva tattha paṭipucchitabbo:

Rather, I'm the one who should be asked about

"ko nu kho āyasmantānaṁ sukhavihāritaro rājā vā māgadho seniyo bimbisāro āyasmā vā gotamo"ti?

who lives in greater pleasure, King Bimbisāra or Venerable Gotama?'

Addhāvuso gotama, amhehi sahasā appaṭisaṅkhā vācā bhāsitā, na kho, āvuso gotama, sukhena sukhaṁ adhigantabbaṁ, dukkhena kho sukhaṁ adhigantabbaṁ;

'Clearly we spoke rashly and without reflection.

sukhena cāvuso gotama, sukhaṁ adhigantabbaṁ abhavissa, rājā māgadho seniyo bimbisāro sukhaṁ adhigaccheyya, rājā māgadho seniyo bimbisāro sukhavihāritaro āyasmatā gotamenāti.

Api ca tiṭṭhatetaṁ, idānipi mayaṁ āyasmantaṁ gotamaṁ pucchāma:

But forget about that. Now we ask Venerable Gotama:

"ko nu kho āyasmantānaṁ sukhavihāritaro rājā vā māgadho seniyo bimbisāro āyasmā vā gotamo"ti?

"Who lives in greater pleasure, King Bimbisāra or Venerable Gotama?"'

Tena hāvuso nigaṇṭhā, tumheva tattha paṭipucchissāmi, yathā vo khameyya tathā naṁ byākareyyātha.

'Well then, reverends, I'll ask you about this in return, and you can answer as you like.

Taṁ kiṁ maññathāvuso nigaṇṭhā, pahoti rājā māgadho seniyo bimbisāro,

What do you think, reverends?

aniñjamāno kāyena, abhāsamāno vācaṁ, satta rattindivāni ekantasukhaṁ paṭisaṁvedī viharitun'ti?

Is King Bimbisāra capable of experiencing perfect happiness for seven days and nights without moving his body or speaking?'

'No hidaṁ, āvuso'.

'No he is not, reverend.'

'Taṁ kiṁ maññathāvuso nigaṇṭhā, pahoti rājā māgadho seniyo bimbisāro,

'What do you think, reverends?

aniñjamāno kāyena, abhāsamāno vācaṁ, cha rattindivāni …pe…

Is King Bimbisāra capable of experiencing perfect happiness for six days …

pañca rattindivāni …

five days …

cattāri rattindivāni …

four days …

tīṇi rattindivāni …

three days …

dve rattindivāni …

two days …

ekaṁ rattindivaṁ ekantasukhaṁ paṭisaṁvedī viharitun'ti?

one day?'

'No hidaṁ, āvuso'.

'No he is not, reverend.'

'Ahaṁ kho, āvuso nigaṇṭhā, pahomi aniñjamāno kāyena, abhāsamāno vācaṁ, ekaṁ rattindivaṁ ekantasukhaṁ paṭisaṁvedī viharituṁ.

'But I am capable of experiencing perfect happiness for one day and night without moving my body or speaking.

Ahaṁ kho, āvuso nigaṇṭhā, pahomi aniñjamāno kāyena, abhāsamāno vācaṁ, dve rattindivāni …

I am capable of experiencing perfect happiness for two days …

tīṇi rattindivāni …

three days …

cattāri rattindivāni …

four days …

pañca rattindivāni …

five days …

cha rattindivāni …

six days …

satta rattindivāni ekantasukham paṭisamvedī viharitum.

seven days.

Tam kim maññathāvuso nigaṇṭhā, evam sante ko sukhavihāritaro rājā vā māgadho seniyo bimbisāro aham vā'ti?

What do you think, reverends? This being so, who lives in greater pleasure, King Bimbisāra or I?'

'Evam sante āyasmāva gotamo sukhavihāritaro raññā māgadhena seniyena bimbisārenā'"ti.

'This being so, Venerable Gotama lives in greater pleasure than King Bimbisāra.'"

Idamavoca bhagavā.

That is what the Buddha said.

Attamano mahānāmo sakko bhagavato bhāsitam abhinandīti.

Satisfied, Mahānāma the Sakyan was happy with what the Buddha said.

Cūḷadukkhakkhandhasuttam niṭṭhitam catuttham.

15 Anumanasutta:

Measuring Up

Evam me sutam—

So I have heard.

ekam samayam āyasmā mahāmoggallāno bhaggesu viharati susumāragire bhesakaḷāvane migadāye.

At one time Venerable Mahāmoggallāna was staying in the land of the Bhaggas on Crocodile Hill, in the deer park at Bhesakaḷā's Wood.

Tatra kho āyasmā mahāmoggallāno bhikkhū āmantesi:

There Venerable Mahāmoggallāna addressed the mendicants:

"āvuso bhikkhavo"ti.

"Reverends, mendicants!"

"Āvuso"ti kho te bhikkhū āyasmato mahāmoggallānassa paccassosuṁ.

"Reverend," they replied.

Āyasmā mahāmoggallāno etadavoca:

Venerable Mahāmoggallāna said this:

"Pavāreti cepi, āvuso, bhikkhu:

"Suppose a mendicant invites

'vadantu maṁ āyasmanto, vacanīyomhi āyasmantehī'ti, so ca hoti dubbaco, dovacassakaraṇehi dhammehi samannāgato, akkhamo appadakkhiṇaggāhī anusāsaniṁ, atha kho naṁ sabrahmacārī na ceva vattabbaṁ maññanti, na ca anusāsitabbaṁ maññanti, na ca tasmiṁ puggale vissāsaṁ āpajjitabbaṁ maññanti.

other mendicants to admonish them. But they're hard to admonish, having qualities that make them hard to admonish. They're impatient, and don't take instruction respectfully. So their spiritual companions don't think it's worth advising and instructing them, and that person doesn't gain their trust.

Katame cāvuso, dovacassakaraṇā dhammā?

And what are the qualities that make them hard to admonish?

Idhāvuso, bhikkhu pāpiccho hoti, pāpikānaṁ icchānaṁ vasaṁ gato.

Firstly, a mendicant has corrupt wishes, having fallen under the sway of corrupt wishes.

Yampāvuso, bhikkhu pāpiccho hoti, pāpikānaṁ icchānaṁ vasaṁ gato—

ayampi dhammo dovacassakaraṇo.

This is a quality that makes them difficult to admonish.

Puna caparaṁ, āvuso, bhikkhu attukkaṁsako hoti paravambhī.

Furthermore, a mendicant glorifies themselves and puts others down. …

Yampāvuso, bhikkhu attukkaṁsako hoti paravambhī—

ayampi dhammo dovacassakaraṇo.

Puna caparaṁ, āvuso, bhikkhu kodhano hoti kodhābhibhūto.

They're irritable, overcome by anger …

Yampāvuso, bhikkhu kodhano hoti kodhābhibhūto—

ayampi dhammo dovacassakaraṇo.

Puna caparaṁ, āvuso, bhikkhu kodhano hoti kodhahetu upanāhī.

They're irritable, and hostile due to anger …

Yampāvuso, bhikkhu kodhano hoti kodhahetu upanāhī—

ayampi dhammo dovacassakaraṇo.

Puna caparaṁ, āvuso, bhikkhu kodhano hoti kodhahetu abhisaṅgī.

They're irritable, and stubborn due to anger …

Yampāvuso, bhikkhu kodhano hoti kodhahetu abhisaṅgī—

ayampi dhammo dovacassakaraṇo.

Puna caparaṁ, āvuso, bhikkhu kodhano hoti kodhasāmantā vācaṁ nicchāretā.

They're irritable, and blurt out words bordering on anger …

Yampāvuso, bhikkhu kodhano hoti kodhasāmantā vācaṁ nicchāretā—

ayampi dhammo dovacassakaraṇo.

Puna caparaṁ, āvuso, bhikkhu codito codakena codakaṁ paṭippharati.

When accused, they object to the accuser …

Yampāvuso, bhikkhu codito codakena codakaṁ paṭippharati—

ayampi dhammo dovacassakaraṇo.

Puna caparaṁ, āvuso, bhikkhu codito codakena codakaṁ apasādeti.

When accused, they rebuke the accuser …

Yampāvuso, bhikkhu codito codakena codakaṁ apasādeti—

ayampi dhammo dovacassakaraṇo.

Puna caparaṁ, āvuso, bhikkhu codito codakena codakassa paccāropeti.

When accused, they retort to the accuser …

Yampāvuso, bhikkhu codito codakena codakassa paccāropeti—

ayampi dhammo dovacassakaraṇo.

Puna caparaṁ, āvuso, bhikkhu codito codakena aññenaññaṁ paṭicarati, bahiddhā kathaṁ apanāmeti, kopañca dosañca appaccayañca pātukaroti.

When accused, they dodge the issue, distract the discussion with irrelevant points, and display annoyance, hate, and bitterness …

Yampāvuso, bhikkhu codito codakena aññenaññaṁ paṭicarati, bahiddhā kathaṁ apanāmeti, kopañca dosañca appaccayañca pātukaroti—

ayampi dhammo dovacassakaraṇo.

Puna caparaṁ, āvuso, bhikkhu codito codakena apadāne na sampāyati.

When accused, they are unable to account for the evidence …

Yampāvuso, bhikkhu codito codakena apadāne na sampāyati—

ayampi dhammo dovacassakaraṇo.

Puna caparaṁ, āvuso, bhikkhu makkhī hoti paḷāsī.

They are offensive and contemptuous …

Yampāvuso, bhikkhu makkhī hoti paḷāsī—

ayampi dhammo dovacassakaraṇo.

Puna caparaṁ, āvuso, bhikkhu issukī hoti macchari.

They're jealous and stingy …

Yampāvuso, bhikkhu issukī hoti macchari—

ayampi dhammo dovacassakaraṇo.

Puna caparaṁ, āvuso, bhikkhu saṭho hoti māyāvī.

They're devious and deceitful …

Yampāvuso, bhikkhu saṭho hoti māyāvī—

ayampi dhammo dovacassakaraṇo.

Puna caparaṁ, āvuso, bhikkhu thaddho hoti atimānī.

They're obstinate and vain …

Yampāvuso, bhikkhu thaddho hoti atimānī—

ayampi dhammo dovacassakaraṇo.

Puna caparaṁ, āvuso, bhikkhu sandiṭṭhiparāmāsī hoti ādhānaggāhī duppaṭinissaggī.

Furthermore, a mendicant is attached to their own views, holding them tight, and refusing to let go.

Yampāvuso, bhikkhu sandiṭṭhiparāmāsī hoti ādhānaggāhī duppaṭinissaggī—

ayampi dhammo dovacassakaraṇo.

This too is a quality that makes them difficult to admonish.

Ime vuccantāvuso, dovacassakaraṇā dhammā.

These are the qualities that make them hard to admonish.

No cepi, āvuso, bhikkhu pavāreti:

Suppose a mendicant doesn't invite

'vadantu maṁ āyasmanto, vacanīyomhi āyasmantehī'ti, so ca hoti suvaco, sovacassakaraṇehi dhammehi samannāgato, khamo padakkhiṇaggāhī anusāsaniṁ, atha kho naṁ sabrahmacārī vattabbañceva maññanti, anusāsitabbañca maññanti, tasmiñca puggale vissāsaṁ āpajjitabbaṁ maññanti.

other mendicants to admonish them. But they're easy to admonish, having qualities that make them easy to admonish. They're accepting, and take instruction respectfully. So their spiritual companions think it's worth advising and instructing them, and that person gains their trust.

Katame cāvuso, sovacassakaraṇā dhammā?

And what are the qualities that make them easy to admonish?

Idhāvuso, bhikkhu na pāpiccho hoti, na pāpikānaṁ icchānaṁ vasaṁ gato.

Firstly, a mendicant doesn't have corrupt wishes …

Yampāvuso, bhikkhu na pāpiccho hoti na pāpikānaṁ icchānaṁ vasaṁ gato—

ayampi dhammo sovacassakaraṇo.

Puna caparaṁ, āvuso, bhikkhu anattukkaṁsako hoti aparavambhī.

Yampāvuso, bhikkhu anattukkaṁsako hoti aparavambhī—

ayampi dhammo sovacassakaraṇo.

Puna caparaṁ, āvuso, bhikkhu na kodhano hoti na kodhābhibhūto.

Yampāvuso, bhikkhu na kodhano hoti na kodhābhibhūto—

ayampi dhammo sovacassakaraṇo.

Puna caparaṁ, āvuso, bhikkhu na kodhano hoti na kodhahetu upanāhī.

Yampāvuso, bhikkhu na kodhano hoti na kodhahetu upanāhī—

ayampi dhammo sovacassakaraṇo.

Puna caparaṁ, āvuso, bhikkhu na kodhano hoti na kodhahetu abhisaṅgī.

Yampāvuso, bhikkhu na kodhano hoti na kodhahetu abhisaṅgī—

ayampi dhammo sovacassakaraṇo.

Puna caparaṁ, āvuso, bhikkhu na kodhano hoti na kodhasāmantā vācaṁ nicchāretā.

Yampāvuso, bhikkhu na kodhano hoti na kodhasāmantā vācaṁ nicchāretā—

ayampi dhammo sovacassakaraṇo.

Puna caparaṁ, āvuso, bhikkhu codito codakena codakaṁ nappaṭippharati.

Yampāvuso, bhikkhu codito codakena codakaṁ nappaṭippharati—

ayampi dhammo sovacassakaraṇo.

Puna caparaṁ, āvuso, bhikkhu codito codakena codakaṁ na apasādeti.

Yampāvuso, bhikkhu codito codakena codakaṁ na apasādeti—

ayampi dhammo sovacassakaraṇo.

Puna caparaṁ, āvuso, bhikkhu codito codakena codakassa na paccāropeti.

Yampāvuso, bhikkhu codito codakena codakassa na paccāropeti—

ayampi dhammo sovacassakaraṇo.

Puna caparaṁ, āvuso, bhikkhu codito codakena na aññenaññaṁ paṭicarati, na bahiddhā kathaṁ apanāmeti, na kopañca dosañca appaccayañca pātukaroti.

Yampāvuso, bhikkhu codito codakena na aññenaññaṁ paṭicarati, na bahiddhā kathaṁ apanāmeti, na kopañca dosañca appaccayañca pātukaroti—

ayampi dhammo sovacassakaraṇo.

Puna caparaṁ, āvuso, bhikkhu codito codakena apadāne sampāyati.

Yampāvuso, bhikkhu codito codakena apadāne sampāyati—

ayampi dhammo sovacassakaraṇo.

Puna caparaṁ, āvuso, bhikkhu amakkhī hoti apaḷāsī.

Yampāvuso, bhikkhu amakkhī hoti apaḷāsī—

ayampi dhammo sovacassakaraṇo.

Puna caparaṁ, āvuso, bhikkhu anissukī hoti amaccharī.

Yampāvuso, bhikkhu anissukī hoti amaccharī—

ayampi dhammo sovacassakaraṇo.

Puna caparaṁ, āvuso, bhikkhu asaṭho hoti amāyāvī.

Yampāvuso, bhikkhu asaṭho hoti amāyāvī—

ayampi dhammo sovacassakaraṇo.

Puna caparaṁ, āvuso, bhikkhu atthaddho hoti anatimānī.

Yampāvuso, bhikkhu atthaddho hoti anatimānī—

ayampi dhammo sovacassakaraṇo.

Puna caparaṁ, āvuso, bhikkhu asandiṭṭhiparāmāsī hoti anādhānaggāhī suppaṭinissaggī.

Furthermore, a mendicant isn't attached to their own views, not holding them tight, but letting them go easily.

Yampāvuso, bhikkhu asandiṭṭhiparāmāsī hoti, anādhānaggāhī suppaṭinissaggī—

ayampi dhammo sovacassakaraṇo.

Ime vuccantāvuso, sovacassakaraṇā dhammā.

These are the qualities that make them easy to admonish.

Tatrāvuso, bhikkhunā attanāva attānaṁ evaṁ anuminitabbaṁ:

In such a case, a mendicant should measure themselves against another like this.

'yo khvāyaṁ puggalo pāpiccho, pāpikānaṁ icchānaṁ vasaṁ gato, ayaṁ me puggalo appiyo amanāpo;

'This person has corrupt wishes, having fallen under the sway of corrupt wishes. And I don't like or approve of this person.

ahañceva kho panassaṁ pāpiccho pāpikānaṁ icchānaṁ vasaṁ gato, ahampāssaṁ paresaṁ appiyo amanāpo'ti.

And if I were to fall under the sway of corrupt wishes, others wouldn't like or approve of me.'

Evaṁ jānantenāvuso, bhikkhunā 'na pāpiccho bhavissāmi, na pāpikānaṁ icchānaṁ vasaṁ gato'ti cittaṁ uppādetabbaṁ.

A mendicant who knows this should give rise to the thought: 'I will not fall under the sway of corrupt wishes.' …

'Yo khvāyaṁ puggalo attukkaṁsako paravambhī, ayaṁ me puggalo appiyo amanāpo;

ahañceva kho panassaṁ attukkaṁsako paravambhī, ahampāssaṁ paresaṁ appiyo amanāpo'ti.

Evaṁ jānantenāvuso, bhikkhunā 'anattukkaṁsako bhavissāmi aparavambhī'ti cittaṁ uppādetabbaṁ.

'Yo khvāyaṁ puggalo kodhano kodhābhibhūto, ayaṁ me puggalo appiyo amanāpo.

Ahañceva kho panassaṁ kodhano kodhābhibhūto, ahampāssaṁ paresaṁ appiyo amanāpo'ti.

Evaṁ jānantenāvuso, bhikkhunā 'na kodhano bhavissāmi na kodhābhibhūto'ti cittaṁ uppādetabbaṁ.

'Yo khvāyaṁ puggalo kodhano kodhahetu upanāhī, ayaṁ me puggalo appiyo amanāpo;

ahañceva kho panassaṁ kodhano kodhahetu upanāhī, ahampāssaṁ paresaṁ appiyo amanāpo'ti.

Evaṁ jānantenāvuso, bhikkhunā 'na kodhano bhavissāmi na kodhahetu upanāhī'ti cittaṁ uppādetabbaṁ.

'Yo khvāyaṁ puggalo kodhano kodhahetu abhisaṅgī, ayaṁ me puggalo appiyo amanāpo;

ahañceva kho panassaṁ kodhano kodhahetu abhisaṅgī, ahampāssaṁ paresaṁ appiyo amanāpo'ti.

Evaṁ jānantenāvuso, bhikkhunā 'na kodhano bhavissāmi na kodhahetu abhisaṅgī'ti cittaṁ uppādetabbaṁ.

'Yo khvāyaṁ puggalo kodhano kodhasāmantā vācaṁ nicchāretā, ayaṁ me puggalo appiyo amanāpo;

ahañceva kho panassaṁ kodhano kodhasāmantā vācaṁ nicchāretā, ahampāssaṁ paresaṁ appiyo amanāpo'ti.

Evaṁ jānantenāvuso, bhikkhunā 'na kodhano bhavissāmi na kodhasāmantā vācaṁ nicchāressāmī'ti cittaṁ uppādetabbaṁ.

'Yo khvāyaṁ puggalo codito codakena codakaṁ paṭippharati, ayaṁ me puggalo appiyo amanāpo;

ahañceva kho pana codito codakena codakaṁ paṭipphareyyaṁ, ahampāssaṁ paresaṁ appiyo amanāpo'ti.

Evaṁ jānantenāvuso, bhikkhunā 'codito codakena codakaṁ nappaṭippharissāmī'ti cittaṁ uppādetabbaṁ.

'Yo khvāyaṁ puggalo codito codakena codakaṁ apasādeti, ayaṁ me puggalo appiyo amanāpo;

ahañceva kho pana codito codakena codakaṁ apasādeyyaṁ, ahampāssaṁ paresaṁ appiyo amanāpo'ti.

Evaṁ jānantenāvuso, bhikkhunā 'codito codakena codakaṁ na apasādessāmī'ti cittaṁ uppādetabbaṁ.

'Yo khvāyaṁ puggalo codito codakena codakassa paccāropeti, ayaṁ me puggalo appiyo amanāpo;

ahañceva kho pana codito codakena codakassa paccāropeyyaṁ, ahampāssaṁ paresaṁ appiyo amanāpo'ti.

Evaṁ jānantenāvuso, bhikkhunā 'codito codakena codakassa na paccāropessāmī'ti cittaṁ uppādetabbaṁ.

'Yo khvāyaṁ puggalo codito codakena aññenaññaṁ paṭicarati, bahiddhā kathaṁ apanāmeti, kopañca dosañca appaccayañca pātukaroti, ayaṁ me puggalo appiyo amanāpo;

ahañceva kho pana codito codakena aññenaññaṁ paṭicareyyaṁ, bahiddhā kathaṁ apanāmeyyaṁ, kopañca dosañca appaccayañca pātukareyyaṁ, ahampāssaṁ paresaṁ appiyo amanāpo'ti.

Evaṁ jānantenāvuso, bhikkhunā 'codito codakena na aññenaññaṁ paṭicarissāmi, na bahiddhā kathaṁ apanāmessāmi, na kopañca dosañca appaccayañca pātukarissāmī'ti cittaṁ uppādetabbaṁ.

'Yo khvāyaṁ puggalo codito codakena apadāne na sampāyati, ayaṁ me puggalo appiyo amanāpo;

ahañceva kho pana codito codakena apadāne na sampāyeyyaṁ, ahampāssaṁ paresaṁ appiyo amanāpo'ti.

Evaṁ jānantenāvuso, bhikkhunā 'codito codakena apadāne sampāyissāmī'ti cittaṁ uppādetabbaṁ.

'Yo khvāyaṁ puggalo makkhī paḷāsī, ayaṁ me puggalo appiyo amanāpo;

ahañceva kho panassaṁ makkhī paḷāsī, ahampāssaṁ paresaṁ appiyo amanāpo'ti.

Evaṁ jānantenāvuso, bhikkhunā 'amakkhī bhavissāmi apaḷāsī'ti cittaṁ uppādetabbaṁ.

'Yo khvāyaṁ puggalo issukī maccharī, ayaṁ me puggalo appiyo amanāpo;

ahañceva kho panassaṁ issukī maccharī, ahampāssaṁ paresaṁ appiyo amanāpo'ti.

Evaṁ jānantenāvuso, bhikkhunā 'anissukī bhavissāmi amaccharī'ti cittaṁ uppādetabbaṁ.

'Yo khvāyaṁ puggalo saṭho māyāvī, ayaṁ me puggalo appiyo amanāpo;

ahañceva kho panassaṁ saṭho māyāvī, ahampāssaṁ paresaṁ appiyo amanāpo'ti.

Evaṁ jānantenāvuso, bhikkhunā 'asaṭho bhavissāmi amāyāvī'ti cittaṁ uppādetabbaṁ.

'Yo khvāyaṁ puggalo thaddho atimānī, ayaṁ me puggalo appiyo amanāpo;

ahañceva kho panassaṁ thaddho atimānī, ahampāssaṁ paresaṁ appiyo amanāpo'ti.

Evaṁ jānantenāvuso, bhikkhunā 'atthaddho bhavissāmi anatimānī'ti cittaṁ uppādetabbaṁ.

'Yo khvāyaṁ puggalo sandiṭṭhiparāmāsī ādhānaggāhī duppaṭinissaggī, ayaṁ me puggalo appiyo amanāpo;

'This person is attached to their own views, holding them tight and refusing to let go. And I don't like or approve of this person.

ahañceva kho panassaṁ sandiṭṭhiparāmāsī ādhānaggāhī duppaṭinissaggī, ahampāssaṁ paresaṁ appiyo amanāpo'ti.

And if I were to be attached to my own views, holding them tight and refusing to let go, others wouldn't like or approve of me.'

Evaṁ jānantenāvuso, bhikkhunā 'asandiṭṭhiparāmāsī bhavissāmi anādhānaggāhī suppaṭinissaggī'ti cittaṁ uppādetabbaṁ.

A mendicant who knows this should give rise to the thought: 'I will not be attached to my own views, holding them tight, but will let them go easily.'

Tatrāvuso, bhikkhunā attanāva attānaṁ evaṁ paccavekkhitabbaṁ:

In such a case, a mendicant should check themselves like this:

'kiṁ nu khomhi pāpiccho, pāpikānaṁ icchānaṁ vasaṁ gato'ti?

'Do I have corrupt wishes? Have I fallen under the sway of corrupt wishes?'

Sace, āvuso, bhikkhu paccavekkhamāno evaṁ jānāti:

Suppose that, upon checking, a mendicant knows that

'pāpiccho khomhi, pāpikānaṁ icchānaṁ vasaṁ gato'ti, tenāvuso, bhikkhunā tesaṁyeva pāpakānaṁ akusalānaṁ dhammānaṁ pahānāya vāyamitabbaṁ.

they have fallen under the sway of corrupt wishes. Then they should make an effort to give up those bad, unskillful qualities.

Sace panāvuso, bhikkhu paccavekkhamāno evaṁ jānāti:

But suppose that, upon checking, a mendicant knows that

'na khomhi pāpiccho, na pāpikānaṁ icchānaṁ vasaṁ gato'ti, tenāvuso, bhikkhunā teneva pītipāmojjena vihātabbaṁ ahorattānusikkhinā kusalesu dhammesu.

they haven't fallen under the sway of corrupt wishes. Then they should meditate with rapture and joy, training day and night in skillful qualities. ...

Puna caparaṁ, āvuso, bhikkhunā attanāva attānaṁ evaṁ paccavekkhitabbaṁ:

'kiṁ nu khomhi attukkaṁsako paravambhī'ti?

Sace, āvuso, bhikkhu paccavekkhamāno evaṁ jānāti:

'attukkaṁsako khomhi paravambhī'ti, tenāvuso, bhikkhunā tesaṁyeva pāpakānaṁ akusalānaṁ dhammānaṁ pahānāya vāyamitabbaṁ.

Sace panāvuso, bhikkhu paccavekkhamāno evaṁ jānāti:

'anattukkaṁsako khomhi aparavambhī'ti, tenāvuso, bhikkhunā teneva pītipāmojjena vihātabbaṁ ahorattānusikkhinā kusalesu dhammesu.

Puna caparaṁ, āvuso, bhikkhunā attanāva attānaṁ evaṁ paccavekkhitabbaṁ:

'kiṁ nu khomhi kodhano kodhābhibhūto'ti?

Sace, āvuso, bhikkhu paccavekkhamāno evaṁ jānāti:

'kodhano khomhi kodhābhibhūto'ti, tenāvuso, bhikkhunā tesaṁyeva pāpakānaṁ akusalānaṁ dhammānaṁ pahānāya vāyamitabbaṁ.

Sace panāvuso, bhikkhu paccavekkhamāno evaṁ jānāti:

'na khomhi kodhano kodhābhibhūto'ti, tenāvuso, bhikkhunā teneva pītipāmojjena vihātabbaṁ ahorattānusikkhinā kusalesu dhammesu.

Puna caparaṁ, āvuso, bhikkhunā attanāva attānaṁ evaṁ paccavekkhitabbaṁ:

'kiṁ nu khomhi kodhano kodhahetu upanāhī'ti?

Sace, āvuso, bhikkhu paccavekkhamāno evaṁ jānāti 'kodhano khomhi kodhahetu upanāhī'ti, tenāvuso, bhikkhunā tesaṁyeva pāpakānaṁ akusalānaṁ dhammānaṁ pahānāya vāyamitabbaṁ.

Sace panāvuso, bhikkhu paccavekkhamāno evaṁ jānāti 'na khomhi kodhano kodhahetu upanāhī'ti, tenāvuso, bhikkhunā teneva pītipāmojjena vihātabbaṁ ahorattānusikkhinā kusalesu dhammesu.

Puna caparaṁ, āvuso, bhikkhunā attanāva attānaṁ evaṁ paccavekkhitabbaṁ:

'kiṁ nu khomhi kodhano kodhahetu abhisaṅgī'ti?

Sace, āvuso, bhikkhu paccavekkhamāno evaṁ jānāti:

'kodhano khomhi kodhahetu abhisaṅgī'ti, tenāvuso, bhikkhunā tesaṁyeva pāpakānaṁ akusalānaṁ dhammānaṁ pahānāya vāyamitabbaṁ.

Sace panāvuso, bhikkhu paccavekkhamāno evaṁ jānāti:

'na khomhi kodhano kodhahetu abhisaṅgī'ti, tenāvuso, bhikkhunā teneva pītipāmojjena vihātabbaṁ ahorattānusikkhinā kusalesu dhammesu.

Puna caparaṁ, āvuso, bhikkhunā attanāva attānaṁ evaṁ paccavekkhitabbaṁ:

'kiṁ nu khomhi kodhano kodhasāmantā vācaṁ nicchāretā'ti?

Sace, āvuso, bhikkhu paccavekkhamāno evaṁ jānāti:

'kodhano khomhi kodhasāmantā vācaṁ nicchāretā'ti, tenāvuso, bhikkhunā tesaṁyeva pāpakānaṁ akusalānaṁ dhammānaṁ pahānāya vāyamitabbaṁ.

Sace panāvuso, bhikkhu paccavekkhamāno evaṁ jānāti:

'na khomhi kodhano kodhasāmantā vācaṁ nicchāretā'ti, tenāvuso, bhikkhunā teneva pītipāmojjena vihātabbaṁ ahorattānusikkhinā kusalesu dhammesu.

Puna caparaṁ, āvuso, bhikkhunā attanāva attānaṁ evaṁ paccavekkhitabbaṁ:

'kiṁ nu khomhi codito codakena codakaṁ paṭippharāmī'ti?

Sace, āvuso, bhikkhu paccavekkhamāno evaṁ jānāti 'codito khomhi codakena codakaṁ paṭippharāmī'ti, tenāvuso, bhikkhunā tesaṁyeva pāpakānaṁ akusalānaṁ dhammānaṁ pahānāya vāyamitabbaṁ.

Sace panāvuso, bhikkhu paccavekkhamāno evaṁ jānāti:

'codito khomhi codakena codakaṁ nappaṭippharāmī'ti, tenāvuso, bhikkhunā teneva pītipāmojjena vihātabbaṁ ahorattānusikkhinā kusalesu dhammesu.

Puna caparaṁ, āvuso, bhikkhunā attanāva attānaṁ evaṁ paccavekkhitabbaṁ:

'kiṁ nu khomhi codito codakena codakaṁ apasādemī'ti?

Sace, āvuso, bhikkhu paccavekkhamāno evaṁ jānāti 'codito khomhi codakena codakaṁ apasādemī'ti, tenāvuso, bhikkhunā tesaṁyeva pāpakānaṁ akusalānaṁ dhammānaṁ pahānāya vāyamitabbaṁ.

Sace panāvuso, bhikkhu paccavekkhamāno evaṁ jānāti:

'codito khomhi codakena codakaṁ na apasādemī'ti, tenāvuso, bhikkhunā teneva pītipāmojjena vihātabbaṁ ahorattānusikkhinā kusalesu dhammesu.

Puna caparaṁ, āvuso, bhikkhunā attanāva attānaṁ evaṁ paccavekkhitabbaṁ:

'kiṁ nu khomhi codito codakena codakassa paccāropemī'ti?

Sace, āvuso, bhikkhu paccavekkhamāno evaṁ jānāti:

'codito khomhi codakena codakassa paccāropemī'ti, tenāvuso, bhikkhunā tesaṁyeva pāpakānaṁ akusalānaṁ dhammānaṁ pahānāya vāyamitabbaṁ.

Sace panāvuso, bhikkhu paccavekkhamāno evaṁ jānāti:

'codito khomhi codakena codakassa na paccāropemī'ti, tenāvuso, bhikkhunā teneva pītipāmojjena vihātabbaṁ ahorattānusikkhinā kusalesu dhammesu.

Puna caparaṁ, āvuso, bhikkhunā attanāva attānaṁ evaṁ paccavekkhitabbaṁ:

'kiṁ nu khomhi codito codakena aññenaññaṁ paṭicarāmi, bahiddhā kathaṁ apanāmemi, kopañca dosañca appaccayañca pātukaromī'ti?

Sace, āvuso, bhikkhu paccavekkhamāno evaṁ jānāti:

'codito khomhi codakena aññenaññaṁ paṭicarāmi, bahiddhā kathaṁ apanāmemi, kopañca dosañca appaccayañca pātukaromī'ti, tenāvuso, bhikkhunā tesaṁyeva pāpakānaṁ akusalānaṁ dhammānaṁ pahānāya vāyamitabbaṁ.

Sace panāvuso, bhikkhu paccavekkhamāno evaṁ jānāti:

'codito khomhi codakena na aññenaññaṁ paṭicarāmi, na bahiddhā kathaṁ apanāmemi, na kopañca dosañca appaccayañca pātukaromī'ti, tenāvuso, bhikkhunā teneva pītipāmojjena vihātabbaṁ ahorattānusikkhinā kusalesu dhammesu.

Puna caparaṁ, āvuso, bhikkhunā attanāva attānaṁ evaṁ paccavekkhitabbaṁ:

'kiṁ nu khomhi codito codakena apadāne na sampāyāmī'ti?

Sace, āvuso, bhikkhu paccavekkhamāno evaṁ jānāti:

'codito khomhi codakena apadāne na sampāyāmī'ti, tenāvuso, bhikkhunā tesaṁyeva pāpakānaṁ akusalānaṁ dhammānaṁ pahānāya vāyamitabbaṁ.

Sace panāvuso, bhikkhu paccavekkhamāno evaṁ jānāti:

'codito khomhi codakena apadāne sampāyāmī'ti, tenāvuso, bhikkhunā teneva pītipāmojjena vihātabbaṁ ahorattānusikkhinā kusalesu dhammesu.

Puna caparaṁ, āvuso, bhikkhunā attanāva attānaṁ evaṁ paccavekkhitabbaṁ:

'kiṁ nu khomhi makkhī paḷāsī'ti?

Sace, āvuso, bhikkhu paccavekkhamāno evaṁ jānāti:

'makkhī khomhi paḷāsī'ti, tenāvuso, bhikkhunā tesaṁyeva pāpakānaṁ akusalānaṁ dhammānaṁ pahānāya vāyamitabbaṁ.

Sace panāvuso, bhikkhu paccavekkhamāno evaṁ jānāti:

'amakkhī khomhi apaḷāsī'ti, tenāvuso, bhikkhunā teneva pītipāmojjena vihātabbaṁ ahorattānusikkhinā kusalesu dhammesu.

Puna caparaṁ, āvuso, bhikkhunā attanāva attānaṁ evaṁ paccavekkhitabbaṁ:

'kiṁ nu khomhi issukī macchari'ti?

Sace, āvuso, bhikkhu paccavekkhamāno evaṁ jānāti:

'issukī khomhi macchari'ti, tenāvuso, bhikkhunā tesaṁyeva pāpakānaṁ akusalānaṁ dhammānaṁ pahānāya vāyamitabbaṁ.

Sace panāvuso, bhikkhu paccavekkhamāno evaṁ jānāti:

'anissukī khomhi amacchari'ti, tenāvuso, bhikkhunā teneva pītipāmojjena vihātabbaṁ ahorattānusikkhinā kusalesu dhammesu.

Puna caparaṁ, āvuso, bhikkhunā attanāva attānaṁ evaṁ paccavekkhitabbaṁ:

'kiṁ nu khomhi saṭho māyāvī'ti?

Sace, āvuso, bhikkhu paccavekkhamāno evaṁ jānāti:

'saṭho khomhi māyāvī'ti, tenāvuso, bhikkhunā tesaṁyeva pāpakānaṁ akusalānaṁ dhammānaṁ pahānāya vāyamitabbaṁ.

Sace panāvuso, bhikkhu paccavekkhamāno evaṁ jānāti:

'asaṭho khomhi amāyāvī'ti, tenāvuso, bhikkhunā teneva pītipāmojjena vihātabbaṁ ahorattānusikkhinā kusalesu dhammesu.

Puna caparaṁ, āvuso, bhikkhunā attanāva attānaṁ evaṁ paccavekkhitabbaṁ:

'kiṁ nu khomhi thaddho atimānī'ti?

Sace, āvuso, bhikkhu paccavekkhamāno evaṁ jānāti:

'thaddho khomhi atimānī'ti, tenāvuso, bhikkhunā tesaṁyeva pāpakānaṁ akusalānaṁ dhammānaṁ pahānāya vāyamitabbaṁ.

Sace panāvuso, bhikkhu paccavekkhamāno evaṁ jānāti:

'atthaddho khomhi anatimānī'ti, tenāvuso, bhikkhunā teneva pītipāmojjena vihātabbaṁ ahorattānusikkhinā kusalesu dhammesu.

Puna caparaṁ, āvuso, bhikkhunā attanāva attānaṁ evaṁ paccavekkhitabbaṁ:

'kiṁ nu khomhi sandiṭṭhiparāmāsī ādhānaggāhī duppaṭinissaggī'ti?

Sace, āvuso, bhikkhu paccavekkhamāno evaṁ jānāti:

Suppose that, upon checking, a mendicant knows that

'sandiṭṭhiparāmāsī khomhi ādhānaggāhī duppaṭinissaggī'ti, tenāvuso, bhikkhunā tesaṁyeva pāpakānaṁ akusalānaṁ dhammānaṁ pahānāya vāyamitabbaṁ.

they are attached to their own views, holding them tight, and refusing to let go. Then they should make an effort to give up those bad, unskillful qualities.

Sace panāvuso, bhikkhu paccavekkhamāno evaṁ jānāti:

Suppose that, upon checking, a mendicant knows that

'asandiṭṭhiparāmāsī khomhi anādhānaggāhī suppaṭinissaggī'ti, tenāvuso, bhikkhunā teneva pītipāmojjena vihātabbaṁ ahorattānusikkhinā kusalesu dhammesu.

they're not attached to their own views, holding them tight, but let them go easily. Then they should meditate with rapture and joy, training day and night in skillful qualities.

Sace, āvuso, bhikkhu paccavekkhamāno sabbepime pāpake akusale dhamme appahīne attani samanupassati, tenāvuso, bhikkhunā sabbesaṁyeva imesaṁ pāpakānaṁ akusalānaṁ dhammānaṁ pahānāya vāyamitabbaṁ.

Suppose that, upon checking, a mendicant sees that they haven't given up all these bad, unskillful qualities. Then they should make an effort to give them all up.

Sace panāvuso, bhikkhu paccavekkhamāno sabbepime pāpake akusale dhamme pahīne attani samanupassati, tenāvuso, bhikkhunā teneva pītipāmojjena vihātabbaṁ, ahorattānusikkhinā kusalesu dhammesu.

But suppose that, upon checking, a mendicant sees that they have given up all these bad, unskillful qualities. Then they should meditate with rapture and joy, training day and night in skillful qualities.

Seyyathāpi, āvuso, itthī vā puriso vā, daharo yuvā maṇḍanajātiko, ādāse vā parisuddhe pariyodāte, acche vā udakapatte, sakaṁ mukhanimittaṁ paccavekkhamāno, sace tattha passati rajaṁ vā aṅgaṇaṁ vā, tasseva rajassa vā aṅgaṇassa vā pahānāya vāyamati;

Suppose there was a woman or man who was young, youthful, and fond of adornments, and they check their own reflection in a clean bright mirror or a clear bowl of water. If they see any dirt or blemish there, they'd try to remove it.

no ce tattha passati rajaṁ vā aṅgaṇaṁ vā, teneva attamano hoti:

But if they don't see any dirt or blemish there, they're happy, thinking:

'lābhā vata me, parisuddhaṁ vata me'ti.

'How fortunate that I'm clean!'

Evameva kho, āvuso, sace bhikkhu paccavekkhamāno sabbepime pāpake akusale dhamme appahīne attani samanupassati, tenāvuso, bhikkhunā sabbesaṁyeva imesaṁ pāpakānaṁ akusalānaṁ dhammānaṁ pahānāya vāyamitabbaṁ.

In the same way, suppose that, upon checking, a mendicant sees that they haven't given up all these bad, unskillful qualities. Then they should make an effort to give them all up.

Sace panāvuso, bhikkhu paccavekkhamāno sabbepime pāpake akusale dhamme pahīne attani samanupassati, tenāvuso, bhikkhunā teneva pītipāmojjena vihātabbaṁ, ahorattānusikkhinā kusalesu dhammesū"ti.

But suppose that, upon checking, a mendicant sees that they have given up all these bad, unskillful qualities. Then they should meditate with rapture and joy, training day and night in skillful qualities."

Idamavocāyasmā mahāmoggallāno.

This is what Venerable Mahāmoggallāna said.

Attamanā te bhikkhū āyasmato mahāmoggallānassa bhāsitaṁ abhinandunti.

Satisfied, the mendicants were happy with what Venerable Mahāmoggallāna said.

Anumānasuttaṁ niṭṭhitaṁ pañcamaṁ.

16 Cetokhilasutta:

Emotional Barrenness

Evaṁ me sutaṁ—

So I have heard.

ekaṁ samayaṁ bhagavā sāvatthiyaṁ viharati jetavane anāthapiṇḍikassa ārāme.

At one time the Buddha was staying near Sāvatthī in Jeta's Grove, Anāthapiṇḍika's monastery.

Tatra kho bhagavā bhikkhū āmantesi:

There the Buddha addressed the mendicants,

"bhikkhavo"ti.

"Mendicants!"

"Bhadante"ti te bhikkhū bhagavato paccassosuṁ.

"Venerable sir," they replied.

Bhagavā etadavoca:

The Buddha said this:

"Yassa kassaci, bhikkhave, bhikkhuno pañca cetokhilā appahīnā, pañca cetasovinibandhā asamucchinnā, so vatimasmiṁ dhammavinaye vuddhiṁ virūḷhiṁ vepullaṁ āpajjissatīti—netaṁ ṭhānaṁ vijjati.

"Mendicants, when a mendicant has not given up five kinds of emotional barrenness and cut off five emotional shackles, it's not possible for them to achieve growth, improvement, or maturity in this teaching and training.

Katamāssa pañca cetokhilā appahīnā honti?

What are the five kinds of emotional barrenness they haven't given up?

Idha, bhikkhave, bhikkhu satthari kaṅkhati vicikicchati nādhimuccati na sampasīdati.

Firstly, a mendicant has doubts about the Teacher. They're uncertain, undecided, and lacking confidence.

Yo so, bhikkhave, bhikkhu satthari kaṅkhati vicikicchati nādhimuccati na sampasīdati tassa cittaṁ na namati ātappāya anuyogāya sātaccāya padhānāya.

This being so, their mind doesn't incline toward keenness, commitment, persistence, and striving.

Yassa cittaṁ na namati ātappāya anuyogāya sātaccāya padhānāya, evamassāyaṁ paṭhamo cetokhilo appahīno hoti.

This is the first kind of emotional barrenness they haven't given up.

Puna caparaṁ, bhikkhave, bhikkhu dhamme kaṅkhati vicikicchati nādhimuccati na sampasīdati ...pe...

Furthermore, a mendicant has doubts about the teaching ...

evamassāyaṁ dutiyo cetokhilo appahīno hoti.

This is the second kind of emotional barrenness.

Puna caparaṁ, bhikkhave, bhikkhu saṅghe kaṅkhati vicikicchati nādhimuccati na sampasīdati ...pe...

They have doubts about the Saṅgha ...

evamassāyaṁ tatiyo cetokhilo appahīno hoti.

This is the third kind of emotional barrenness.

Puna caparaṁ, bhikkhave, bhikkhu sikkhāya kaṅkhati vicikicchati nādhimuccati na sampasīdati.

They have doubts about the training …

Yo so, bhikkhave, bhikkhu sikkhāya kaṅkhati vicikicchati nādhimuccati na sampasīdati, tassa cittaṁ na namati ātappāya anuyogāya sātaccāya padhānāya.

Yassa cittaṁ na namati ātappāya anuyogāya sātaccāya padhānāya, evamassāyaṁ catuttho cetokhilo appahīno hoti.

This is the fourth kind of emotional barrenness.

Puna caparaṁ, bhikkhave, bhikkhu sabrahmacārīsu kupito hoti anattamano āhatacitto khilajāto.

Furthermore, a mendicant is angry and upset with their spiritual companions, resentful and closed off.

Yo so, bhikkhave, bhikkhu sabrahmacārīsu kupito hoti anattamano āhatacitto khilajāto, tassa cittaṁ na namati ātappāya anuyogāya sātaccāya padhānāya.

This being so, their mind doesn't incline toward keenness, commitment, persistence, and striving.

Yassa cittaṁ na namati ātappāya anuyogāya sātaccāya padhānāya, evamassāyaṁ pañcamo cetokhilo appahīno hoti.

This is the fifth kind of emotional barrenness they haven't given up.

Imāssa pañca cetokhilā appahīnā honti.

These are the five kinds of emotional barrenness they haven't given up.

Katamāssa pañca cetasovinibandhā asamucchinnā honti?

What are the five emotional shackles they haven't cut off?

Idha, bhikkhave, bhikkhu kāme avītarāgo hoti avigatacchando avigatapemo avigatapipāso avigatapariḷāho avigatataṇho.

Firstly, a mendicant isn't free of greed, desire, fondness, thirst, passion, and craving for sensual pleasures.

Yo so, bhikkhave, bhikkhu kāme avītarāgo hoti avigatacchando avigatapemo avigatapipāso avigatapariḷāho avigatataṇho, tassa cittaṁ na namati ātappāya anuyogāya sātaccāya padhānāya.

This being so, their mind doesn't incline toward keenness, commitment, persistence, and striving.

Yassa cittaṁ na namati ātappāya anuyogāya sātaccāya padhānāya, evamassāyaṁ paṭhamo cetasovinibandho asamucchinno hoti.

This is the first emotional shackle they haven't cut off.

Puna caparaṁ, bhikkhave, bhikkhu kāye avītarāgo hoti …pe…

Furthermore, a mendicant isn't free of greed for the body …

evamassāyaṁ dutiyo cetasovinibandho asamucchinno hoti.

This is the second emotional shackle.

Puna caparaṁ, bhikkhave, bhikkhu rūpe avītarāgo hoti …pe…

Furthermore, a mendicant isn't free of greed for form …

evamassāyaṁ tatiyo cetasovinibandho asamucchinno hoti.

This is the third emotional shackle.

Puna caparaṁ, bhikkhave, bhikkhu yāvadatthaṁ udarāvadehakaṁ bhuñjitvā seyyasukhaṁ passasukhaṁ middhasukhaṁ anuyutto viharati.

They eat as much as they like until their belly is full, then indulge in the pleasures of sleeping, lying down, and drowsing …

Yo so, bhikkhave, bhikkhu yāvadatthaṁ udarāvadehakaṁ bhuñjitvā seyyasukhaṁ passasukhaṁ middhasukhaṁ anuyutto viharati, tassa cittaṁ na namati ātappāya anuyogāya sātaccāya padhānāya.

Yassa cittaṁ na namati ātappāya anuyogāya sātaccāya padhānāya, evamassāyaṁ catuttho cetasovinibandho asamucchinno hoti.

This is the fourth emotional shackle.

Puna caparaṁ, bhikkhave, bhikkhu aññataraṁ devanikāyaṁ paṇidhāya brahmacariyaṁ carati: 'imināhaṁ sīlena vā vatena vā tapena vā brahmacariyena vā devo vā bhavissāmi devaññataro vā'ti.

They lead the spiritual life hoping to be reborn in one of the orders of gods, thinking: 'By this precept or observance or mortification or spiritual life, may I become one of the gods!'

Yo so, bhikkhave, bhikkhu aññataraṁ devanikāyaṁ paṇidhāya brahmacariyaṁ carati: 'imināhaṁ sīlena vā vatena vā tapena vā brahmacariyena vā devo vā bhavissāmi devaññataro vā'ti, tassa cittaṁ na namati ātappāya anuyogāya sātaccāya padhānāya.

This being so, their mind doesn't incline toward keenness, commitment, persistence, and striving.

Yassa cittaṁ na namati ātappāya anuyogāya sātaccāya padhānāya, evamassāyaṁ pañcamo cetasovinibandho asamucchinno hoti.

This is the fifth emotional shackle they haven't cut off.

Imāssa pañca cetasovinibandhā asamucchinnā honti.

These are the five emotional shackles they haven't cut off.

Yassa kassaci, bhikkhave, bhikkhuno ime pañca cetokhilā appahīnā, ime pañca cetasovinibandhā asamucchinnā, so vatimasmiṁ dhammavinaye vuddhiṁ virūḷhiṁ vepullaṁ āpajjissatīti—netaṁ ṭhānaṁ vijjati.

When a mendicant has not given up these five kinds of emotional barrenness and cut off these five emotional shackles, it's not possible for them to achieve growth, improvement, or maturity in this teaching and training.

Yassa kassaci, bhikkhave, bhikkhuno pañca cetokhilā pahīnā, pañca cetasovinibandhā susamucchinnā, so vatimasmiṁ dhammavinaye vuddhiṁ virūḷhiṁ vepullaṁ āpajjissatīti—ṭhānametaṁ vijjati.

When a mendicant has given up these five kinds of emotional barrenness and cut off these five emotional shackles, it is possible for them to achieve growth, improvement, and maturity in this teaching and training.

Katamāssa pañca cetokhilā pahīnā honti?

What are the five kinds of emotional barrenness they've given up?

Idha, bhikkhave, bhikkhu satthari na kaṅkhati na vicikicchati adhimuccati sampasīdati.

Firstly, a mendicant has no doubts about the Teacher. They're not uncertain, undecided, or lacking confidence.

Yo so, bhikkhave, bhikkhu satthari na kaṅkhati na vicikicchati adhimuccati sampasīdati, tassa cittaṁ namati ātappāya anuyogāya sātaccāya padhānāya.

This being so, their mind inclines toward keenness, commitment, persistence, and striving.

Yassa cittaṁ namati ātappāya anuyogāya sātaccāya padhānāya, evamassāyaṁ paṭhamo cetokhilo pahīno hoti.

This is the first kind of emotional barrenness they've given up.

Puna caparaṁ, bhikkhave, bhikkhu dhamme na kaṅkhati na vicikicchati adhimuccati sampasīdati ...pe...

Furthermore, a mendicant has no doubts about the teaching ...

evamassāyaṁ dutiyo cetokhilo pahīno hoti.

Puna caparaṁ, bhikkhave, bhikkhu saṅghe na kaṅkhati na vicikicchati adhimuccati sampasīdati ...pe...

They have no doubts about the Saṅgha ...

evamassāyaṁ tatiyo cetokhilo pahīno hoti.

Puna caparaṁ, bhikkhave, bhikkhu sikkhāya na kaṅkhati na vicikicchati adhimuccati sampasīdati ...pe...

They have no doubts about the training ...

evamassāyaṁ catuttho cetokhilo pahīno hoti.

Puna caparaṁ, bhikkhave, bhikkhu sabrahmacārīsu na kupito hoti na anattamano anāhatacitto akhilajāto.

They're not angry and upset with their spiritual companions, not resentful or closed off.

Yo so, bhikkhave, bhikkhu sabrahmacārīsu na kupito hoti na anattamano anāhatacitto akhilajāto, tassa cittaṁ namati ātappāya anuyogāya sātaccāya padhānāya.

This being so, their mind inclines toward keenness, commitment, persistence, and striving.

Yassa cittaṁ namati ātappāya anuyogāya sātaccāya padhānāya, evamassāyaṁ pañcamo cetokhilo pahīno hoti.

This is the fifth kind of emotional barrenness they've given up.

Imāssa pañca cetokhilā pahīnā honti.

These are the five kinds of emotional barrenness they've given up.

Katamāssa pañca cetasovinibandhā susamucchinnā honti?

What are the five emotional shackles they've cut off?

Idha, bhikkhave, bhikkhu kāme vītarāgo hoti vigatacchando vigatapemo vigatapipāso vigatapariḷāho vigatataṇho.

Firstly, a mendicant is rid of greed, desire, fondness, thirst, passion, and craving for sensual pleasures.

Yo so, bhikkhave, bhikkhu kāme vītarāgo hoti vigatacchando vigatapemo vigatapipāso vigatapariḷāho vigatataṇho, tassa cittaṁ namati ātappāya anuyogāya sātaccāya padhānāya.

This being so, their mind inclines toward keenness, commitment, persistence, and striving.

Yassa cittaṁ namati ātappāya anuyogāya sātaccāya padhānāya, evamassāyaṁ paṭhamo cetasovinibandho susamucchinno hoti.

This is the first emotional shackle they've cut off.

Puna caparaṁ, bhikkhave, bhikkhu kāye vītarāgo hoti …pe…

Furthermore, a mendicant is rid of greed for the body …

rūpe vītarāgo hoti …pe…

They're rid of greed for form …

na yāvadatthaṁ udarāvadehakaṁ bhuñjitvā seyyasukhaṁ passasukhaṁ middhasukhaṁ anuyutto viharati.

They don't eat as much as they like until their belly is full, then indulge in the pleasures of sleeping, lying down, and drowsing …

Yo so, bhikkhave, bhikkhu na yāvadatthaṁ udarāvadehakaṁ bhuñjitvā seyyasukhaṁ passasukhaṁ middhasukhaṁ anuyutto viharati, tassa cittaṁ namati ātappāya anuyogāya sātaccāya padhānāya.

Yassa cittaṁ namati ātappāya anuyogāya sātaccāya padhānāya, evamassāyaṁ catuttho cetasovinibandho susamucchinno hoti.

Puna caparaṁ, bhikkhave, bhikkhu na aññataraṁ devanikāyaṁ paṇidhāya brahmacariyaṁ carati: 'imināhaṁ sīlena vā vatena vā tapena vā brahmacariyena vā devo vā bhavissāmi devaññataro vā'ti.

They don't lead the spiritual life hoping to be reborn in one of the orders of gods, thinking: 'By this precept or observance or mortification or spiritual life, may I become one of the gods!'

Yo so, bhikkhave, bhikkhu na aññataraṁ devanikāyaṁ paṇidhāya brahmacariyaṁ carati: 'imināhaṁ sīlena vā vatena vā tapena vā brahmacariyena vā devo vā bhavissāmi devaññataro vā'ti, tassa cittaṁ namati ātappāya anuyogāya sātaccāya padhānāya.

This being so, their mind inclines toward keenness, commitment, persistence, and striving.

Yassa cittaṁ namati ātappāya anuyogāya sātaccāya padhānāya, evamassāyaṁ pañcamo cetasovinibandho susamucchinno hoti.

This is the fifth emotional shackle they've cut off.

Imāssa pañca cetasovinibandhā susamucchinnā honti.

These are the five emotional shackles they've cut off.

Yassa kassaci, bhikkhave, bhikkhuno ime pañca cetokhilā pahīnā, ime pañca cetasovinibandhā susamucchinnā, so vatimasmiṁ dhammavinaye vuddhiṁ virūḷhiṁ vepullaṁ āpajjissatīti—ṭhānametaṁ vijjati.

When a mendicant has given up these five kinds of emotional barrenness and cut off these five emotional shackles, it is possible for them to achieve growth, improvement, or maturity in this teaching and training.

So chandasamādhipadhānasaṅkhārasamannāgataṁ iddhipādaṁ bhāveti,

They develop the basis of psychic power that has immersion due to enthusiasm, and active effort …

vīriyasamādhipadhānasaṅkhārasamannāgataṁ iddhipādaṁ bhāveti,

the basis of psychic power that has immersion due to energy, and active effort …

cittasamādhipadhānasaṅkhārasamannāgataṁ iddhipādaṁ bhāveti,

the basis of psychic power that has immersion due to mental development, and active effort …

vīmaṁsāsamādhipadhānasaṅkhārasamannāgataṁ iddhipādaṁ bhāveti, ussoḷhīyeva pañcamī.

the basis of psychic power that has immersion due to inquiry, and active effort. And the fifth is sheer vigor.

Sa kho so, bhikkhave, evaṁ ussoḷhipannarasaṅgasamannāgato bhikkhu bhabbo abhinibbidāya, bhabbo sambodhāya, bhabbo anuttarassa yogakkhemassa adhigamāya.

A mendicant who possesses these fifteen factors, including vigor, is capable of breaking out, becoming awakened, and reaching the supreme sanctuary.

Seyyathāpi, bhikkhave, kukkuṭiyā aṇḍāni aṭṭha vā dasa vā dvādasa vā.

Suppose there was a chicken with eight or ten or twelve eggs.

Tānassu kukkuṭiyā sammā adhisayitāni sammā pariseditāni sammā paribhāvitāni.

And she properly sat on them to keep them warm and incubated.

Kiñcāpi tassā kukkuṭiyā na evaṁ icchā uppajjeyya:

Even if that chicken doesn't wish:

'aho vatime kukkuṭapotakā pādanakhasikhāya vā mukhatuṇḍakena vā aṇḍakosaṁ padāletvā sotthinā abhinibbhijjeyyun'ti.

'If only my chicks could break out of the eggshell with their claws and beak and hatch safely!'

Atha kho bhabbāva te kukkuṭapotakā pādanakhasikhāya vā mukhatuṇḍakena vā aṇḍakosaṁ padāletvā sotthinā abhinibbhijjituṁ.

Still they can break out and hatch safely.

Evameva kho, bhikkhave, evaṁ ussoḷhipannarasaṅgasamannāgato bhikkhu bhabbo abhinibbidāya, bhabbo sambodhāya, bhabbo anuttarassa yogakkhemassa adhigamāyā"ti.

In the same way, a mendicant who possesses these fifteen factors, including vigor, is capable of breaking out, becoming awakened, and reaching the supreme sanctuary."

Idamavoca bhagavā.

That is what the Buddha said.

Attamanā te bhikkhū bhagavato bhāsitaṁ abhinandunti.

Satisfied, the mendicants were happy with what the Buddha said.

Cetokhilasuttaṁ niṭṭhitaṁ chaṭṭhaṁ.

17 Vanapatthasutta:

Jungle Thickets

Evaṁ me sutaṁ—

So I have heard.

ekaṁ samayaṁ bhagavā sāvatthiyaṁ viharati jetavane anāthapiṇḍikassa ārāme.

At one time the Buddha was staying near Sāvatthī in Jeta's Grove, Anāthapiṇḍika's monastery.

Tatra kho bhagavā bhikkhū āmantesi:

There the Buddha addressed the mendicants,

"bhikkhavo"ti.

"Mendicants!"

"Bhadante"ti te bhikkhū bhagavato paccassosuṁ.

"Venerable sir," they replied.

Bhagavā etadavoca:

The Buddha said this:

"vanapatthapariyāyaṁ vo, bhikkhave, desessāmi,

"Mendicants, I will teach you an exposition about jungle thickets.

taṁ suṇātha, sādhukaṁ manasikarotha, bhāsissāmī"ti.

Listen and pay close attention, I will speak."

"Evaṁ, bhante"ti kho te bhikkhū bhagavato paccassosuṁ.

"Yes, sir," they replied.

Bhagavā etadavoca:

The Buddha said this:

"Idha, bhikkhave, bhikkhu aññataraṁ vanapatthaṁ upanissāya viharati.

"Mendicants, take the case of a mendicant who lives close by a jungle thicket.

Tassa taṁ vanapatthaṁ upanissāya viharato anupaṭṭhitā ceva sati na upaṭṭhāti, asamāhitañca cittaṁ na samādhiyati, aparikkhīṇā ca āsavā na parikkhayaṁ gacchanti, ananuppattañca anuttaraṁ yogakkhemaṁ nānupāpuṇāti.

As they do so, their mindfulness does not become established, their mind does not become immersed in samādhi, their defilements do not come to an end, and they do not arrive at the supreme sanctuary.

Ye ca kho ime pabbajitena jīvitaparikkhārā samudānetabbā—cīvarapiṇḍapātasenāsanagilānappaccayabhesajjaparikkhārā—te kasirena samudāgacchanti.

And the necessities of life that a renunciate requires—robes, almsfood, lodgings, and medicines and supplies for the sick—are hard to come by.

Tena, bhikkhave, bhikkhunā iti paṭisañcikkhitabbaṁ:

That mendicant should reflect:

'ahaṁ kho imaṁ vanapatthaṁ upanissāya viharāmi, tassa me imaṁ vanapatthaṁ upanissāya viharato anupaṭṭhitā ceva sati na upaṭṭhāti, asamāhitañca cittaṁ na samādhiyati, aparikkhīṇā ca āsavā na parikkhayaṁ gacchanti, ananuppattañca anuttaraṁ yogakkhemaṁ nānupāpuṇāmi.

'While living close by this jungle thicket, my mindfulness does not become established, my mind does not become immersed in samādhi, my defilements do not come to an end, and I do not arrive at the supreme sanctuary.

Ye ca kho ime pabbajitena jīvitaparikkhārā samudānetabbā—cīvarapiṇḍapātasenāsanagilānappaccayabhesajjaparikkhārā—te kasirena samudāgacchantī'ti.

And the necessities of life that a renunciate requires—robes, almsfood, lodgings, and medicines and supplies for the sick—are hard to come by.'

Tena, bhikkhave, bhikkhunā rattibhāgaṁ vā divasabhāgaṁ vā tamhā vanapatthā pakkamitabbaṁ, na vatthabbaṁ.

That mendicant should leave that jungle thicket that very time of night or day; they shouldn't stay there.

Idha pana, bhikkhave, bhikkhu aññataraṁ vanapatthaṁ upanissāya viharati.

Take another case of a mendicant who lives close by a jungle thicket.

Tassa taṁ vanapatthaṁ upanissāya viharato anupaṭṭhitā ceva sati na upaṭṭhāti, asamāhitañca cittaṁ na samādhiyati, aparikkhīṇā ca āsavā na parikkhayaṁ gacchanti, ananuppattañca anuttaraṁ yogakkhemaṁ nānupāpuṇāti.

Their mindfulness does not become established …

Ye ca kho ime pabbajitena jīvitaparikkhārā samudānetabbā—cīvarapiṇḍapātasenāsanagilānappaccayabhesajjaparikkhārā—te appakasirena samudāgacchanti.

But the necessities of life are easy to come by.

Tena, bhikkhave, bhikkhunā iti paṭisañcikkhitabbaṁ:

That mendicant should reflect:

'ahaṁ kho imaṁ vanapatthaṁ upanissāya viharāmi. Tassa me imaṁ vanapatthaṁ upanissāya viharato anupaṭṭhitā ceva sati na upaṭṭhāti asamāhitañca cittaṁ na samādhiyati, aparikkhīṇā ca āsavā na parikkhayaṁ gacchanti, ananuppattañca anuttaraṁ yogakkhemaṁ nānupāpuṇāmi.

'While living close by this jungle thicket, my mindfulness does not become established …

Ye ca kho ime pabbajitena jīvitaparikkhārā samudānetabbā—cīvarapiṇḍapātasenāsanagilānappaccayabhesajjaparikkhārā—te appakasirena samudāgacchanti.

But the necessities of life are easy to come by.

Na kho panāhaṁ cīvarahetu agārasmā anagāriyaṁ pabbajito na piṇḍapātahetu …pe… na senāsanahetu …pe… na gilānappaccayabhesajjaparikkhārahetu agārasmā anagāriyaṁ pabbajito.

But I didn't go forth from the lay life to homelessness for the sake of a robe, almsfood, lodgings, or medicines and supplies for the sick.

Atha ca pana me imaṁ vanapatthaṁ upanissāya viharato anupaṭṭhitā ceva sati na upaṭṭhāti, asamāhitañca cittaṁ na samādhiyati, aparikkhīṇā ca āsavā na parikkhayaṁ gacchanti, ananuppattañca anuttaraṁ yogakkhemaṁ nānupāpuṇāmī'ti.

Moreover, while living close by this jungle thicket, my mindfulness does not become established …'

Tena, bhikkhave, bhikkhunā saṅkhāpi tamhā vanapatthā pakkamitabbaṁ, na vatthabbaṁ.

After appraisal, that mendicant should leave that jungle thicket; they shouldn't stay there.

Idha pana, bhikkhave, bhikkhu aññataraṁ vanapatthaṁ upanissāya viharati.

Take another case of a mendicant who lives close by a jungle thicket.

Tassa taṁ vanapatthaṁ upanissāya viharato anupaṭṭhitā ceva sati upaṭṭhāti, asamāhitañca cittaṁ samādhiyati, aparikkhīṇā ca āsavā parikkhayaṁ gacchanti, ananuppattañca anuttaraṁ yogakkhemaṁ anupāpuṇāti.

As they do so, their mindfulness becomes established, their mind becomes immersed in samādhi, their defilements come to an end, and they arrive at the supreme sanctuary.

Ye ca kho ime pabbajitena jīvitaparikkhārā samudānetabbā—cīvarapiṇḍapātasenāsanagilānappaccayabhesajjaparikkhārā, te kasirena samudāgacchanti. Tena, bhikkhave, bhikkhunā iti paṭisañcikkhitabbaṁ:

But the necessities of life that a renunciate requires—robes, almsfood, lodgings, and medicines and supplies for the sick—are hard to come by. That mendicant should reflect:

'ahaṁ kho imaṁ vanapatthaṁ upanissāya viharāmi.

Tassa me imaṁ vanapatthaṁ upanissāya viharato anupaṭṭhitā ceva sati upaṭṭhāti asamāhitañca cittaṁ samādhiyati, aparikkhīṇā ca āsavā parikkhayaṁ gacchanti, ananuppattañca anuttaraṁ yogakkhemaṁ anupāpuṇāmi.

'While living close by this jungle thicket, my mindfulness becomes established …

Ye ca kho ime pabbajitena jīvitaparikkhārā samudānetabbā—cīvarapiṇḍapātasenāsanagilānappaccayabhesajjaparikkhārā—te kasirena samudāgacchanti.

But the necessities of life are hard to come by.

Na kho panāhaṁ cīvarahetu agārasmā anagāriyaṁ pabbajito, na piṇḍapātahetu … pe… na senāsanahetu …pe… na gilānappaccayabhesajjaparikkhārahetu agārasmā anagāriyaṁ pabbajito.

But I didn't go forth from the lay life to homelessness for the sake of a robe, almsfood, lodgings, or medicines and supplies for the sick.

Atha ca pana me imaṁ vanapatthaṁ upanissāya viharato anupaṭṭhitā ceva sati upaṭṭhāti, asamāhitañca cittaṁ samādhiyati, aparikkhīṇā ca āsavā parikkhayaṁ gacchanti, ananuppattañca anuttaraṁ yogakkhemaṁ anupāpuṇāmī'ti.

Moreover, while living close by this jungle thicket, my mindfulness becomes established …'

Tena, bhikkhave, bhikkhunā saṅkhāpi tasmiṁ vanapatthe vatthabbaṁ, na pakkamitabbaṁ.

After appraisal, that mendicant should stay in that jungle thicket; they shouldn't leave.

Idha pana, bhikkhave, bhikkhu aññataraṁ vanapatthaṁ upanissāya viharati.

Take another case of a mendicant who lives close by a jungle thicket.

Tassa taṁ vanapatthaṁ upanissāya viharato anupaṭṭhitā ceva sati upaṭṭhāti, asamāhitañca cittaṁ samādhiyati, aparikkhīṇā ca āsavā parikkhayaṁ gacchanti, ananuppattañca anuttaraṁ yogakkhemaṁ anupāpuṇāti.

Their mindfulness becomes established …

Ye ca kho ime pabbajitena jīvitaparikkhārā samudānetabbā—cīvarapiṇḍapātasenāsanagilānappaccayabhesajjaparikkhārā—te appakasirena samudāgacchanti.

And the necessities of life are easy to come by.

Tena, bhikkhave, bhikkhunā iti paṭisañcikkhitabbaṁ:

That mendicant should reflect:

'ahaṁ kho imaṁ vanapatthaṁ upanissāya viharāmi. Tassa me imaṁ vanapatthaṁ upanissāya viharato anupaṭṭhitā ceva sati upaṭṭhāti asamāhitañca cittaṁ samādhiyati, aparikkhīṇā ca āsavā parikkhayaṁ gacchanti, ananuppattañca anuttaraṁ yogakkhemaṁ anupāpuṇāmi.

'While living close by this jungle thicket, my mindfulness becomes established …

Ye ca kho ime pabbajitena jīvitaparikkhārā samudānetabbā—cīvarapiṇḍapātasenāsanagilānappaccayabhesajjaparikkhārā—te appakasirena samudāgacchantī'ti.

And the necessities of life are easy to come by.'

Tena, bhikkhave, bhikkhunā yāvajīvampi tasmiṁ vanapatthe vatthabbaṁ, na pakkamitabbaṁ.

That mendicant should stay in that jungle thicket for the rest of their life; they shouldn't leave.

Idha, bhikkhave, bhikkhu aññataraṁ gāmaṁ upanissāya viharati …pe…

Take the case of a mendicant who lives supported by a village …

aññataraṁ nigamaṁ upanissāya viharati …pe…

town …

aññataraṁ nagaraṁ upanissāya viharati …pe…

city …

aññataraṁ janapadaṁ upanissāya viharati …pe…

country …

aññataraṁ puggalaṁ upanissāya viharati.

an individual.

Tassa taṁ puggalaṁ upanissāya viharato anupaṭṭhitā ceva sati na upaṭṭhāti, asamāhitañca cittaṁ na samādhiyati, aparikkhīṇā ca āsavā na parikkhayaṁ gacchanti, ananuppattañca anuttaraṁ yogakkhemaṁ nānupāpuṇāti.

As they do so, their mindfulness does not become established, their mind does not become immersed in samādhi, their defilements do not come to an end, and they do not arrive at the supreme sanctuary.

Ye ca kho ime pabbajitena jīvitaparikkhārā samudānetabbā—cīvarapiṇḍapātasenāsanagilānappaccayabhesajjaparikkhārā—te kasirena samudāgacchanti.

And the necessities of life that a renunciate requires—robes, almsfood, lodgings, and medicines and supplies for the sick—are hard to come by….

Tena, bhikkhave, bhikkhunā iti paṭisañcikkhitabbaṁ:

'ahaṁ kho imaṁ puggalaṁ upanissāya viharāmi. Tassa me imaṁ puggalaṁ upanissāya viharato anupaṭṭhitā ceva sati na upaṭṭhāti, asamāhitañca cittaṁ na samādhiyati, aparikkhīṇā ca āsavā na parikkhayaṁ gacchanti, ananuppattañca anuttaraṁ yogakkhemaṁ nānupāpuṇāmi.

Ye ca kho ime pabbajitena jīvitaparikkhārā samudānetabbā—cīvarapiṇḍapātasenāsanagilānappaccayabhesajjaparikkhārā—te kasirena samudāgacchantī'ti.

Tena, bhikkhave, bhikkhunā rattibhāgaṁ vā divasabhāgaṁ vā so puggalo anāpucchā pakkamitabbaṁ, nānubandhitabbo.

That mendicant should leave that person at any time of the day or night, without asking. They shouldn't follow them. ...

Idha pana, bhikkhave, bhikkhu aññataraṁ puggalaṁ upanissāya viharati.

Tassa taṁ puggalaṁ upanissāya viharato anupaṭṭhitā ceva sati na upaṭṭhāti, asamāhitañca cittaṁ na samādhiyati, aparikkhīṇā ca āsavā na parikkhayaṁ gacchanti, ananuppattañca anuttaraṁ yogakkhemaṁ nānupāpuṇāti.

Ye ca kho ime pabbajitena jīvitaparikkhārā samudānetabbā—cīvarapiṇḍapātasenāsanagilānappaccayabhesajjaparikkhārā, te appakasirena samudāgacchanti.

Tena, bhikkhave, bhikkhunā iti paṭisañcikkhitabbaṁ:

'ahaṁ kho imaṁ puggalaṁ upanissāya viharāmi. Tassa me imaṁ puggalaṁ upanissāya viharato anupaṭṭhitā ceva sati na upaṭṭhāti, asamāhitañca cittaṁ na samādhiyati, aparikkhīṇā ca āsavā na parikkhayaṁ gacchanti, ananuppattañca anuttaraṁ yogakkhemaṁ nānupāpuṇāmi.

Ye ca kho ime pabbajitena jīvitaparikkhārā samudānetabbā—cīvarapiṇḍapātasenāsanagilānappaccayabhesajjaparikkhārā—te appakasirena samudāgacchanti.

Na kho panāhaṁ cīvarahetu agārasmā anagāriyaṁ pabbajito, na piṇḍapātahetu ... pe... na senāsanahetu ...pe... na gilānappaccayabhesajjaparikkhārahetu agārasmā anagāriyaṁ pabbajito.

Atha ca pana me imaṁ puggalaṁ upanissāya viharato anupaṭṭhitā ceva sati na upaṭṭhāti, asamāhitañca cittaṁ na samādhiyati, aparikkhīṇā ca āsavā na parikkhayaṁ gacchanti, ananuppattañca anuttaraṁ yogakkhemaṁ nānupāpuṇāmī'ti.

Tena, bhikkhave, bhikkhunā saṅkhāpi so puggalo āpucchā pakkamitabbaṁ, nānubandhitabbo.

Idha pana, bhikkhave, bhikkhu aññataraṁ puggalaṁ upanissāya viharati.

Tassa taṁ puggalaṁ upanissāya viharato anupaṭṭhitā ceva sati upaṭṭhāti, asamāhitañca cittaṁ samādhiyati, aparikkhīṇā ca āsavā parikkhayaṁ gacchanti, ananuppattañca anuttaraṁ yogakkhemaṁ anupāpuṇāti.

Ye ca kho ime pabbajitena jīvitaparikkhārā samudānetabbā—cīvarapiṇḍapātasenāsanagilānappaccayabhesajjaparikkhārā—te kasirena samudāgacchanti.

Tena, bhikkhave, bhikkhunā iti paṭisañcikkhitabbaṁ:

'ahaṁ kho imaṁ puggalaṁ upanissāya viharāmi. Tassa me imaṁ puggalaṁ upanissāya viharato anupaṭṭhitā ceva sati upaṭṭhāti, asamāhitañca cittaṁ samādhiyati, aparikkhīṇā ca āsavā parikkhayaṁ gacchanti, ananuppattañca anuttaraṁ yogakkhemaṁ anupāpuṇāmi.

Ye ca kho ime pabbajitena jīvitaparikkhārā samudānetabbā—cīvarapiṇḍapātasenāsanagilānappaccayabhesajjaparikkhārā—te kasirena samudāgacchanti.

Na kho panāhaṃ cīvarahetu agārasmā anagāriyaṃ pabbajito, na piṇḍapātahetu … pe… na senāsanahetu …pe… na gilānappaccayabhesajjaparikkhārahetu agārasmā anagāriyaṃ pabbajito.

Atha ca pana me imaṃ puggalaṃ upanissāya viharato anupaṭṭhitā ceva sati upaṭṭhāti, asamāhitañca cittaṃ samādhiyati, aparikkhīṇā ca āsavā parikkhayaṃ gacchanti, ananuppattañca anuttaraṃ yogakkhemaṃ anupāpuṇāmī'ti.

Tena, bhikkhave, bhikkhunā saṅkhāpi so puggalo anubandhitabbo, na pakkamitabbaṃ.

Idha pana, bhikkhave, bhikkhu aññataraṃ puggalaṃ upanissāya viharati.

Take another case of a mendicant who lives supported by an individual.

Tassa taṃ puggalaṃ upanissāya viharato anupaṭṭhitā ceva sati upaṭṭhāti, asamāhitañca cittaṃ samādhiyati, aparikkhīṇā ca āsavā parikkhayaṃ gacchanti, ananuppattañca anuttaraṃ yogakkhemaṃ anupāpuṇāti.

As they do so, their mindfulness becomes established, their mind becomes immersed in samādhi, their defilements come to an end, and they arrive at the supreme sanctuary.

Ye ca kho ime pabbajitena jīvitaparikkhārā samudānetabbā—cīvarapiṇḍapātasenāsanagilānappaccayabhesajjaparikkhārā—te appakasirena samudāgacchanti.

And the necessities of life that a renunciate requires—robes, almsfood, lodgings, and medicines and supplies for the sick—are easy to come by.

Tena, bhikkhave, bhikkhunā iti paṭisañcikkhitabbaṃ:

That mendicant should reflect:

'ahaṃ kho imaṃ puggalaṃ upanissāya viharāmi. Tassa me imaṃ puggalaṃ upanissāya viharato anupaṭṭhitā ceva sati upaṭṭhāti, asamāhitañca cittaṃ samādhiyati, aparikkhīṇā ca āsavā parikkhayaṃ gacchanti, ananuppattañca anuttaraṃ yogakkhemaṃ anupāpuṇāmi.

'While living supported by this person, my mindfulness becomes established …

Ye ca kho ime pabbajitena jīvitaparikkhārā samudānetabbā—cīvarapiṇḍapātasenāsanagilānappaccayabhesajjaparikkhārā—te appakasirena samudāgacchantī'ti.

And the necessities of life are easy to come by.'

Tena, bhikkhave, bhikkhunā yāvajīvampi so puggalo anubandhitabbo, na pakkamitabbaṁ, api panujjamānenapī"ti.

That mendicant should follow that person for the rest of their life. They shouldn't leave them, even if sent away."

Idamavoca bhagavā.

That is what the Buddha said.

Attamanā te bhikkhū bhagavato bhāsitaṁ abhinandunti.

Satisfied, the mendicants were happy with what the Buddha said.

Vanapatthasuttaṁ niṭṭhitaṁ sattamaṁ.

18 Madhupindikasutta:

The Honey-Cake

Evaṁ me sutaṁ—

So I have heard.

ekaṁ samayaṁ bhagavā sakkesu viharati kapilavatthusmiṁ nigrodhārāme.

At one time the Buddha was staying in the land of the Sakyans, near Kapilavatthu in the Banyan Tree Monastery.

Atha kho bhagavā pubbaṇhasamayaṁ nivāsetvā pattacīvaramādāya kapilavatthuṁ piṇḍāya pāvisi.

Then the Buddha robed up in the morning and, taking his bowl and robe, entered Kapilavatthu for alms.

Kapilavatthusmiṁ piṇḍāya caritvā pacchābhattaṁ piṇḍapātapaṭikkanto yena mahāvanaṁ tenupasaṅkami divāvihārāya.

He wandered for alms in Kapilavatthu. After the meal, on his return from almsround, he went to the Great Wood,

Mahāvanaṁ ajjhogāhetvā beluvalaṭṭhikāya mūle divāvihāraṁ nisīdi.

plunged deep into it, and sat at the root of a young wood apple tree for the day's meditation.

Daṇḍapāṇipi kho sakko jaṅghāvihāraṁ anucaṅkamamāno anuvicaramāno yena mahāvanaṁ tenupasaṅkami.

Daṇḍapāṇi the Sakyan, while going for a walk,

Mahāvanaṁ ajjhogāhetvā yena beluvalaṭṭhikā yena bhagavā tenupasaṅkami; upasaṅkamitvā bhagavatā saddhiṁ sammodi.

plunged deep into the Great Wood. He approached the Buddha and exchanged greetings with him.

Sammodanīyaṁ kathaṁ sāraṇīyaṁ vītisāretvā daṇḍamolubbha ekamantaṁ aṭṭhāsi. Ekamantaṁ ṭhito kho daṇḍapāṇi sakko bhagavantaṁ etadavoca:

When the greetings and polite conversation were over, he stood to one side leaning on his staff, and said to the Buddha,

"kiṁvādī samaṇo kimakkhāyī"ti?

"What does the ascetic teach? What does he explain?"

"Yathāvādī kho, āvuso, sadevake loke samārake sabrahmake sassamaṇabrāhmaṇiyā pajāya sadevamanussāya na kenaci loke viggayha tiṭṭhati, yathā ca pana kāmehi visaṁyuttaṁ viharantaṁ taṁ brāhmaṇaṁ akathaṅkathiṁ chinnakukkuccaṁ bhavābhave vītataṇhaṁ saññā nānusenti—

"Sir, my teaching is such that one does not conflict with anyone in this world with its gods, Māras, and Brahmās, this population with its ascetics and brahmins, its gods and humans. And it is such that perceptions do not underlie the brahmin who lives detached from sensual pleasures, without doubting, stripped of worry, and rid of craving for rebirth in this or that state.

evaṁvādī kho ahaṁ, āvuso, evamakkhāyī"ti.

That's what I teach, and that's what I explain."

Evaṁ vutte, daṇḍapāṇi sakko sīsaṁ okampetvā, jivhaṁ nillāḷetvā, tivisākhaṁ nalāṭikaṁ nalāṭe vuṭṭhāpetvā daṇḍamolubbha pakkāmi.

When he had spoken, Daṇḍapāṇi shook his head, waggled his tongue, raised his eyebrows until his brow puckered in three furrows, and he departed leaning on his staff.

Atha kho bhagavā sāyanhasamayaṁ paṭisallānā vuṭṭhito yena nigrodhārāmo tenupasaṅkami; upasaṅkamitvā paññatte āsane nisīdi.

Then in the late afternoon, the Buddha came out of retreat and went to the Banyan Tree Monastery, sat down on the seat spread out,

Nisajja kho bhagavā bhikkhū āmantesi:

and told the mendicants what had happened.

"idhāhaṁ, bhikkhave, pubbaṇhasamayaṁ nivāsetvā pattacīvaramādāya kapilavatthuṁ piṇḍāya pāvisiṁ.

Kapilavatthusmiṁ piṇḍāya caritvā pacchābhattaṁ piṇḍapātapaṭikkanto yena mahāvanaṁ tenupasaṅkamiṁ divāvihārāya.

Mahāvanaṁ ajjhogāhetvā beluvalaṭṭhikāya mūle divāvihāraṁ nisīdiṁ.

Daṇḍapāṇipi kho, bhikkhave, sakko jaṅghāvihāraṁ anucaṅkamamāno anuvicaramāno yena mahāvanaṁ tenupasaṅkami.

Mahāvanaṁ ajjhogāhetvā yena beluvalaṭṭhikā yenāhaṁ tenupasaṅkami; upasaṅkamitvā mayā saddhiṁ sammodi.

Sammodanīyaṁ kathaṁ sāraṇīyaṁ vītisāretvā daṇḍamolubbha ekamantaṁ aṭṭhāsi. Ekamantaṁ ṭhito kho, bhikkhave, daṇḍapāṇi sakko maṁ etadavoca:

'kiṁvādī samaṇo kimakkhāyī'ti?

Evaṁ vutte, ahaṁ, bhikkhave, daṇḍapāṇiṁ sakkaṁ etadavocaṁ:

'yathāvādī kho, āvuso, sadevake loke samārake sabrahmake sassamaṇabrāhmaṇiyā pajāya sadevamanussāya na kenaci loke viggayha tiṭṭhati, yathā ca pana kāmehi visaṁyuttaṁ viharantaṁ taṁ brāhmaṇaṁ akathaṅkathiṁ chinnakukkuccaṁ bhavābhave vītataṇhaṁ saññā nānusenti—

evaṁvādī kho ahaṁ, āvuso, evamakkhāyī'ti.

Evaṁ vutte, bhikkhave, daṇḍapāṇi sakko sīsaṁ okampetvā, jivhaṁ nillāḷetvā, tivisākhaṁ nalāṭikaṁ nalāṭe vuṭṭhāpetvā daṇḍamolubbha pakkāmī'ti.

Evaṁ vutte, aññataro bhikkhu bhagavantaṁ etadavoca:

When he had spoken, one of the mendicants said to him,

"kiṁvādī pana, bhante, bhagavā sadevake loke samārake sabrahmake sassamaṇabrāhmaṇiyā pajāya sadevamanussāya na kenaci loke viggayha tiṭṭhati?

"But sir, what is the teaching such that the Buddha does not conflict with anyone in this world with its gods, Māras, and Brahmās, this population with its ascetics and brahmins, its gods and humans?

Kathañca pana, bhante, bhagavantaṁ kāmehi visaṁyuttaṁ viharantaṁ taṁ brāhmaṇaṁ akathaṅkathiṁ chinnakukkuccaṁ bhavābhave vītataṇhaṁ saññā nānusentī"ti?

And how is it that perceptions do not underlie the Buddha, the brahmin who lives detached from sensual pleasures, without indecision, stripped of worry, and rid of craving for rebirth in this or that state?"

"Yatonidānaṁ, bhikkhu, purisaṁ papañcasaññāsaṅkhā samudācaranti.

"Mendicant, a person is beset by concepts of identity that emerge from the proliferation of perceptions.

Ettha ce natthi abhinanditabbaṁ abhivaditabbaṁ ajjhositabbaṁ.

If they don't find anything worth approving, welcoming, or getting attached to in the source from which these arise,

Esevanto rāgānusayānaṁ, esevanto paṭighānusayānaṁ, esevanto diṭṭhānusayānaṁ, esevanto vicikicchānusayānaṁ, esevanto mānānusayānaṁ, esevanto bhavarāgānusayānaṁ, esevanto avijjānusayānaṁ, esevanto daṇḍādānasatthādānakalahaviggahavivādatuvaṁtuvaṁpesuññamusāvādānaṁ.

just this is the end of the underlying tendencies to desire, repulsion, views, doubt, conceit, the desire to be reborn, and ignorance. This is the end of taking up the rod and the sword, the end of quarrels, arguments, and disputes, of accusations, divisive speech, and lies.

Etthete pāpakā akusalā dhammā aparisesā nirujjhantī"ti.

This is where these bad, unskillful qualities cease without anything left over."

Idamavoca bhagavā.

That is what the Buddha said.

Idaṁ vatvāna sugato utthāyāsanā vihāraṁ pāvisi.

When he had spoken, the Holy One got up from his seat and entered his dwelling.

Atha kho tesaṁ bhikkhūnaṁ acirapakkantassa bhagavato etadahosi:

Soon after the Buddha left, those mendicants considered,

"idaṁ kho no, āvuso, bhagavā saṅkhittena uddesaṁ uddisitvā, vitthārena atthaṁ avibhajitvā, utthāyāsanā vihāraṁ paviṭṭho:

"The Buddha gave this brief passage for recitation, then entered his dwelling without explaining the meaning in detail.

'yatonidānaṁ, bhikkhu, purisaṁ papañcasaññāsaṅkhā samudācaranti.

Ettha ce natthi abhinanditabbaṁ abhivaditabbaṁ ajjhositabbaṁ.

Esevanto rāgānusayānaṁ ...pe...

etthete pāpakā akusalā dhammā aparisesā nirujjhantī'ti.

Ko nu kho imassa bhagavatā saṅkhittena uddesassa udditṭhassa vitthārena atthaṁ avibhattassa vitthārena atthaṁ vibhajeyyā"ti?

Who can explain in detail the meaning of this brief passage for recitation given by the Buddha?"

Atha kho tesaṁ bhikkhūnaṁ etadahosi:

Then those mendicants thought,

"ayaṁ kho āyasmā mahākaccāno satthu ceva saṁvaṇṇito sambhāvito ca viññūnaṁ sabrahmacārīnaṁ.

"This Venerable Mahākaccāna is praised by the Buddha and esteemed by his sensible spiritual companions.

Pahoti cāyasmā mahākaccāno imassa bhagavatā saṅkhittena uddesassa udditṭhassa vitthārena atthaṁ avibhattassa vitthārena atthaṁ vibhajituṁ.

He is capable of explaining in detail the meaning of this brief passage for recitation given by the Buddha.

Yannūna mayaṁ yenāyasmā mahākaccāno tenupasaṅkameyyāma; upasaṅkamitvā āyasmantaṁ mahākaccānaṁ etamatthaṁ paṭipuccheyyāmā"ti.

Let's go to him, and ask him about this matter."

Atha kho te bhikkhū yenāyasmā mahākaccāno tenupasaṅkamiṁsu; upasaṅkamitvā āyasmatā mahākaccānena saddhiṁ sammodiṁsu.

Then those mendicants went to Mahākaccāna, and exchanged greetings with him.

Sammodanīyaṁ kathaṁ sāraṇīyaṁ vītisāretvā ekamantaṁ nisīdiṁsu. Ekamantaṁ nisinnā kho te bhikkhū āyasmantaṁ mahākaccānaṁ etadavocuṁ:

When the greetings and polite conversation were over, they sat down to one side. They told him what had happened, and said:

"idaṁ kho no, āvuso kaccāna, bhagavā saṅkhittena uddesaṁ uddisitvā vitthārena atthaṁ avibhajitvā utṭhāyāsanā vihāraṁ paviṭṭho:

'yatonidānaṁ, bhikkhu, purisaṁ papañcasaññāsaṅkhā samudācaranti.

Ettha ce natthi abhinanditabbaṁ abhivaditabbaṁ ajjhositabbaṁ.

Esevanto rāgānusayānaṁ …pe…

etthete pāpakā akusalā dhammā aparisesā nirujjhantī'ti.

Tesaṁ no, āvuso kaccāna, amhākaṁ acirapakkantassa bhagavato etadahosi:

'idaṁ kho no, āvuso, bhagavā saṅkhittena uddesaṁ uddisitvā vitthārena atthaṁ avibhajitvā utṭhāyāsanā vihāraṁ paviṭṭho:

"yatonidānaṁ, bhikkhu, purisaṁ papañcasaññāsaṅkhā samudācaranti.

Ettha ce natthi abhinanditabbaṁ abhivaditabbaṁ ajjhositabbaṁ.

Esevanto rāgānusayānaṁ …pe…

etthete pāpakā akusalā dhammā aparisesā nirujjhantī"'ti.

Ko nu kho imassa bhagavatā saṅkhittena uddesassa udditṭhassa vitthārena atthaṁ avibhattassa vitthārena atthaṁ vibhajeyyāti?

Tesaṁ no, āvuso kaccāna, amhākaṁ etadahosi:

'ayaṁ kho āyasmā mahākaccāno satthu ceva saṁvaṇṇito sambhāvito ca viññūnaṁ sabrahmacārīnaṁ, pahoti cāyasmā mahākaccāno imassa bhagavatā saṅkhittena uddesassa udditṭhassa vitthārena atthaṁ avibhattassa vitthārena atthaṁ vibhajituṁ.

Yannūna mayaṁ yenāyasmā mahākaccāno tenupasaṅkameyyāma; upasaṅkamitvā āyasmantaṁ mahākaccānaṁ etamatthaṁ paṭipuccheyyāmā'ti.

Vibhajatāyasmā mahākaccāno"ti.

"May Venerable Mahākaccāna please explain this."

"Seyyathāpi, āvuso, puriso sāratthiko sāragavesī sārapariyesanaṁ caramāno mahato rukkhassa tiṭṭhato sāravato atikkammeva mūlaṁ, atikkamma khandhaṁ, sākhāpalāse sāraṁ pariyesitabbaṁ maññeyya;

"Reverends, suppose there was a person in need of heartwood. And while wandering in search of heartwood he'd come across a large tree standing with heartwood. But he'd pass over the roots and trunk, imagining that the heartwood should be sought in the branches and leaves.

evaṁsampadamidaṁ āyasmantānaṁ satthari sammukhībhūte, taṁ bhagavantaṁ atisitvā, amhe etamatthaṁ paṭipucchitabbaṁ maññatha.

Such is the consequence for the venerables. Though you were face to face with the Buddha, you overlooked him, imagining that you should ask me about this matter.

So hāvuso, bhagavā jānaṁ jānāti, passaṁ passati, cakkhubhūto ñāṇabhūto dhammabhūto brahmabhūto, vattā pavattā, atthassa ninnetā, amatassa dātā, dhammassāmī tathāgato.

For he is the Buddha, who knows and sees. He is vision, he is knowledge, he is the truth, he is holiness. He is the teacher, the proclaimer, the elucidator of meaning, the bestower of the deathless, the lord of truth, the Realized One.

So ceva panetassa kālo ahosi, yaṁ bhagavantaṁyeva etamatthaṁ paṭipuccheyyātha.

That was the time to approach the Buddha and ask about this matter.

Yathā vo bhagavā byākareyya tathā naṁ dhāreyyāthā"ti.

You should have remembered it in line with the Buddha's answer."

"Addhāvuso kaccāna, bhagavā jānaṁ jānāti, passaṁ passati, cakkhubhūto ñāṇabhūto dhammabhūto brahmabhūto, vattā pavattā, atthassa ninnetā, amatassa dātā, dhammassāmī tathāgato.

"Certainly he is the Buddha, who knows and sees. He is vision, he is knowledge, he is the truth, he is holiness. He is the teacher, the proclaimer, the elucidator of meaning, the bestower of the deathless, the lord of truth, the Realized One.

So ceva panetassa kālo ahosi, yaṁ bhagavantaṁyeva etamatthaṁ paṭipuccheyyāma.

That was the time to approach the Buddha and ask about this matter.

Yathā no bhagavā byākareyya tathā naṁ dhāreyyāma.

We should have remembered it in line with the Buddha's answer.

Api cāyasmā mahākaccāno satthu ceva saṁvaṇṇito sambhāvito ca viññūnaṁ sabrahmacārīnaṁ,

Still, Mahākaccāna is praised by the Buddha and esteemed by his sensible spiritual companions.

pahoti cāyasmā mahākaccāno imassa bhagavatā saṅkhittena uddesassa udditthassa vitthārena atthaṁ avibhattassa vitthārena atthaṁ vibhajituṁ.

You are capable of explaining in detail the meaning of this brief passage for recitation given by the Buddha.

Vibhajatāyasmā mahākaccāno agaruṁ katvā"ti.

Please explain this, if it's no trouble."

"Tena hāvuso, suṇātha, sādhukaṁ manasikarotha, bhāsissāmī"ti.

"Well then, reverends, listen and pay close attention, I will speak."

"Evamāvuso"ti kho te bhikkhū āyasmato mahākaccānassa paccassosuṁ.

"Yes, reverend," they replied.

Āyasmā mahākaccāno etadavoca:

Venerable Mahākaccāna said this:

"Yaṁ kho no, āvuso, bhagavā saṅkhittena uddesaṁ uddisitvā vitthārena atthaṁ avibhajitvā utthāyāsanā vihāraṁ paviṭṭho:

"Reverends, the Buddha gave this brief passage for recitation, then entered his dwelling without explaining the meaning in detail:

'yatonidānaṁ, bhikkhu, purisaṁ papañcasaññāsaṅkhā samudācaranti.

'A person is beset by concepts of identity that emerge from the proliferation of perceptions.

Ettha ce natthi abhinanditabbaṁ abhivaditabbaṁ ajjhositabbaṁ, esevanto rāgānusayānaṁ …pe…

If they don't find anything worth approving, welcoming, or getting attached to in the source from which these arise …

etthete pāpakā akusalā dhammā aparisesā nirujjhantī'ti, imassa kho ahaṁ, āvuso, bhagavatā saṅkhittena uddesassa udditthassa vitthārena atthaṁ avibhattassa evaṁ vitthārena atthaṁ ājānāmi—

This is where these bad, unskillful qualities cease without anything left over.' This is how I understand the detailed meaning of this passage for recitation.

Cakkhuñcāvuso, paṭicca rūpe ca uppajjati cakkhuviññāṇaṁ, tiṇṇaṁ saṅgati phasso, phassapaccayā vedanā, yaṁ vedeti taṁ sañjānāti, yaṁ sañjānāti taṁ vitakketi, yaṁ vitakketi taṁ papañceti, yaṁ papañceti tatonidānaṁ purisaṁ papañcasaññāsaṅkhā samudācaranti atītānāgatapaccuppannesu cakkhuviññeyyesu rūpesu.

Eye consciousness arises dependent on the eye and sights. The meeting of the three is contact. Contact is a condition for feeling. What you feel, you perceive. What you perceive, you think about. What you think about, you proliferate. What you proliferate about is the source from which a person is beset by concepts of identity that emerge from the proliferation of perceptions. This occurs with respect to sights known by the eye in the past, future, and present.

Sotañcāvuso, paṭicca sadde ca uppajjati sotaviññāṇaṁ …pe…

Ear consciousness arises dependent on the ear and sounds. …

ghānañcāvuso, paṭicca gandhe ca uppajjati ghānaviññāṇaṁ …pe…

Nose consciousness arises dependent on the nose and smells. …

jivhañcāvuso, paṭicca rase ca uppajjati jivhāviññāṇaṁ …pe…

Tongue consciousness arises dependent on the tongue and tastes. …

kāyañcāvuso, paṭicca phoṭṭhabbe ca uppajjati kāyaviññāṇaṁ …pe…

Body consciousness arises dependent on the body and touches. …

manañcāvuso, paṭicca dhamme ca uppajjati manoviññāṇaṁ, tiṇṇaṁ saṅgati phasso, phassapaccayā vedanā, yaṁ vedeti taṁ sañjānāti, yaṁ sañjānāti taṁ vitakketi, yaṁ vitakketi taṁ papañceti, yaṁ papañceti tatonidānaṁ purisaṁ papañcasaññāsaṅkhā samudācaranti atītānāgatapaccuppannesu manoviññeyyesu dhammesu.

Mind consciousness arises dependent on the mind and thoughts. The meeting of the three is contact. Contact is a condition for feeling. What you feel, you perceive.

What you perceive, you think about. What you think about, you proliferate. What you proliferate about is the source from which a person is beset by concepts of identity that emerge from the proliferation of perceptions. This occurs with respect to thoughts known by the mind in the past, future, and present.

So vatāvuso, cakkhusmiṁ sati rūpe sati cakkhuviññāṇe sati phassapaññattiṁ paññāpessatīti—ṭhānametaṁ vijjati.

When there is the eye, sights, and eye consciousness, it's possible to point out what's known as 'contact'.

Phassapaññattiyā sati vedanāpaññattiṁ paññāpessatīti—ṭhānametaṁ vijjati.

When there is what's known as contact, it's possible to point out what's known as 'feeling'.

Vedanāpaññattiyā sati saññāpaññattiṁ paññāpessatīti—ṭhānametaṁ vijjati.

When there is what's known as feeling, it's possible to point out what's known as 'perception'.

Saññāpaññattiyā sati vitakkapaññattiṁ paññāpessatīti—ṭhānametaṁ vijjati.

When there is what's known as perception, it's possible to point out what's known as 'thought'.

Vitakkapaññattiyā sati papañcasaññāsaṅkhāsamudācaraṇapaññattiṁ paññāpessatīti—ṭhānametaṁ vijjati.

When there is what's known as thought, it's possible to point out what's known as 'being beset by concepts of identity that emerge from the proliferation of perceptions'.

So vatāvuso, sotasmiṁ sati sadde sati …pe…

When there is the ear …

ghānasmiṁ sati gandhe sati …pe…

nose …

jivhāya sati rase sati …pe…

tongue …

kāyasmiṁ sati phoṭṭhabbe sati …pe…

body …

manasmiṁ sati dhamme sati manoviññāṇe sati phassapaññattiṁ paññāpessatīti—ṭhānametaṁ vijjati.

mind, thoughts, and mind consciousness, it's possible to point out what's known as 'contact'. …

Phassapaññattiyā sati vedanāpaññattiṁ paññāpessatīti—ṭhānametaṁ vijjati.

Vedanāpaññattiyā sati saññāpaññattiṁ paññāpessatīti—ṭhānametaṁ vijjati.

Saññāpaññattiyā sati vitakkapaññattiṁ paññāpessatīti—ṭhānametaṁ vijjati.

Vitakkapaññattiyā sati papañcasaññāsaṅkhāsamudācaraṇapaññattiṁ paññāpessatīti—ṭhānametaṁ vijjati.

When there is what's known as thought, it's possible to point out what's known as 'being beset by concepts of identity that emerge from the proliferation of perceptions'.

So vatāvuso, cakkhusmiṁ asati rūpe asati cakkhuviññāṇe asati phassapaññattiṁ paññāpessatīti—netaṁ ṭhānaṁ vijjati.

When there is no eye, no sights, and no eye consciousness, it's not possible to point out what's known as 'contact'.

Phassapaññattiyā asati vedanāpaññattiṁ paññāpessatīti—netaṁ ṭhānaṁ vijjati.

When there isn't what's known as contact, it's not possible to point out what's known as 'feeling'.

Vedanāpaññattiyā asati saññāpaññattiṁ paññāpessatīti—netaṁ ṭhānaṁ vijjati.

When there isn't what's known as feeling, it's not possible to point out what's known as 'perception'.

Saññāpaññattiyā asati vitakkapaññattiṁ paññāpessatīti—netaṁ ṭhānaṁ vijjati.

When there isn't what's known as perception, it's not possible to point out what's known as 'thought'.

Vitakkapaññattiyā asati papañcasaññāsaṅkhāsamudācaraṇapaññattiṁ paññāpessatīti—netaṁ ṭhānaṁ vijjati.

When there isn't what's known as thought, it's not possible to point out what's known as 'being beset by concepts of identity that emerge from the proliferation of perceptions'.

So vatāvuso, sotasmiṁ asati sadde asati …pe…

When there is no ear …

ghānasmiṁ asati gandhe asati …pe…

nose …

jivhāya asati rase asati ...pe...

tongue ...

kāyasmiṁ asati phoṭṭhabbe asati ...pe...

body ...

manasmiṁ asati dhamme asati manoviññāṇe asati phassapaññattiṁ paññāpessatīti—netaṁ ṭhānaṁ vijjati.

mind, no thoughts, and no mind consciousness, it's not possible to point out what's known as 'contact'. ...

Phassapaññattiyā asati vedanāpaññattiṁ paññāpessatīti—netaṁ ṭhānaṁ vijjati.

Vedanāpaññattiyā asati saññāpaññattiṁ paññāpessatīti—netaṁ ṭhānaṁ vijjati.

Saññāpaññattiyā asati vitakkapaññattiṁ paññāpessatīti—netaṁ ṭhānaṁ vijjati.

Vitakkapaññattiyā asati papañcasaññāsaṅkhāsamudācaraṇapaññattiṁ paññāpessatīti—netaṁ ṭhānaṁ vijjati.

When there isn't what's known as thought, it's not possible to point out what's known as 'being beset by concepts of identity that emerge from the proliferation of perceptions'.

Yaṁ kho no, āvuso, bhagavā saṅkhittena uddesaṁ uddisitvā vitthārena atthaṁ avibhajitvā uṭṭhāyāsanā vihāraṁ paviṭṭho:

This is how I understand the detailed meaning of that brief passage for recitation given by the Buddha.

'yatonidānaṁ, bhikkhu, purisaṁ papañcasaññāsaṅkhā samudācaranti ettha ce natthi abhinanditabbaṁ abhivaditabbaṁ ajjhositabbaṁ esevanto rāgānusayānaṁ ...pe...

etthete pāpakā akusalā dhammā aparisesā nirujjhantī'ti, imassa kho ahaṁ, āvuso, bhagavatā saṅkhittena uddesassa uddiṭṭhassa vitthārena atthaṁ avibhattassa evaṁ vitthārena atthaṁ ājānāmi.

Ākaṅkhamānā ca pana tumhe āyasmanto bhagavantaṁyeva upasaṅkamitvā etamatthaṁ paṭipuccheyyātha.

If you wish, you may go to the Buddha and ask him about this.

Yathā vo bhagavā byākaroti tathā naṁ dhāreyyāthā"ti.

You should remember it in line with the Buddha's answer."

Atha kho te bhikkhū āyasmato mahākaccānassa bhāsitaṁ abhinanditvā anumoditvā uṭṭhāyāsanā yena bhagavā tenupasaṅkamiṁsu; upasaṅkamitvā bhagavantaṁ abhivādetvā ekamantaṁ nisīdiṁsu. Ekamantaṁ nisinnā kho te bhikkhū bhagavantaṁ etadavocuṁ:

"Yes, reverend," said those mendicants, approving and agreeing with what Mahākaccāna said. Then they rose from their seats and went to the Buddha, bowed, sat down to one side, and told him what had happened. Then they said:

"yaṁ kho no, bhante, bhagavā saṅkhittena uddesaṁ uddisitvā vitthārena atthaṁ avibhajitvā uṭṭhāyāsanā vihāraṁ paviṭṭho:

'yatonidānaṁ, bhikkhu, purisaṁ papañcasaññāsaṅkhā samudācaranti.

Ettha ce natthi abhinanditabbaṁ abhivaditabbaṁ ajjhositabbaṁ.

Esevanto rāgānusayānaṁ …pe…

etthete pāpakā akusalā dhammā aparisesā nirujjhantī'ti.

Tesaṁ no, bhante, amhākaṁ acirapakkantassa bhagavato etadahosi:

'idaṁ kho no, āvuso, bhagavā saṅkhittena uddesaṁ uddisitvā vitthārena atthaṁ avibhajitvā uṭṭhāyāsanā vihāraṁ paviṭṭho:

"yatonidānaṁ, bhikkhu, purisaṁ papañcasaññāsaṅkhā samudācaranti.

Ettha ce natthi abhinanditabbaṁ abhivaditabbaṁ ajjhositabbaṁ.

Esevanto rāgānusayānaṁ, esevanto paṭighānusayānaṁ, esevanto diṭṭhānusayānaṁ, esevanto vicikicchānusayānaṁ, esevanto mānānusayānaṁ, esevanto bhavarāgānusayānaṁ, esevanto avijjānusayānaṁ, esevanto daṇḍādānasatthādānakalahaviggahavivādatuvaṁtuvaṁpesuññamusāvādānaṁ.

Etthete pāpakā akusalā dhammā aparisesā nirujjhantī'ti.

Ko nu kho imassa bhagavatā saṅkhittena uddesassa uddiṭṭhassa vitthārena atthaṁ avibhattassa vitthārena atthaṁ vibhajeyyā'ti?

Tesaṁ no, bhante, amhākaṁ etadahosi:

'ayaṁ kho āyasmā mahākaccāno satthu ceva saṁvaṇṇito sambhāvito ca viññūnaṁ sabrahmacārīnaṁ, pahoti cāyasmā mahākaccāno imassa bhagavatā saṅkhittena uddesassa uddiṭṭhassa vitthārena atthaṁ avibhattassa vitthārena atthaṁ vibhajituṁ, yannūna mayaṁ yenāyasmā mahākaccāno tenupasaṅkameyyāma; upasaṅkamitvā āyasmantaṁ mahākaccānaṁ etamatthaṁ paṭipuccheyyāmā'ti.

Atha kho mayaṁ, bhante, yenāyasmā mahākaccāno tenupasaṅkamimha; upasaṅkamitvā āyasmantaṁ mahākaccānaṁ etamatthaṁ paṭipucchimha.

Tesaṁ no, bhante, āyasmatā mahākaccānena imehi ākārehi imehi padehi imehi byañjanehi attho vibhatto"ti.

"Mahākaccāna clearly explained the meaning to us in this manner, with these words and phrases."

"Paṇḍito, bhikkhave, mahākaccāno; mahāpañño, bhikkhave, mahākaccāno.

"Mahākaccāna is astute, mendicants, he has great wisdom.

Mañcepi tumhe, bhikkhave, etamatthaṁ paṭipuccheyyātha, ahampi taṁ evamevaṁ byākareyyaṁ yathā taṁ mahākaccānena byākataṁ.

If you came to me and asked this question, I would answer it in exactly the same way as Mahākaccāna.

Eso cevetassa attho. Evañca naṁ dhārethā"ti.

That is what it means, and that's how you should remember it."

Evaṁ vutte, āyasmā ānando bhagavantaṁ etadavoca:

When he said this, Venerable Ānanda said to the Buddha,

"seyyathāpi, bhante, puriso jighacchādubbalyapareto madhupiṇḍikaṁ adhigaccheyya, so yato yato sāyeyya, labhetheva sādurasaṁ asecanakaṁ.

"Sir, suppose a person who was weak with hunger was to obtain a honey-cake. Wherever they taste it, they would enjoy a sweet, delicious flavor.

Evameva kho, bhante, cetaso bhikkhu dabbajātiko, yato yato imassa dhammapariyāyassa paññāya atthaṁ upaparikkheyya, labhetheva attamanataṁ, labhetheva cetaso pasādaṁ.

In the same way, wherever a sincere, capable mendicant might examine with wisdom the meaning of this exposition of the teaching they would only gain joy and clarity.

Ko nāmo ayaṁ, bhante, dhammapariyāyo"ti?

Sir, what is the name of this exposition of the teaching?"

"Tasmātiha tvaṁ, ānanda, imaṁ dhammapariyāyaṁ madhupiṇḍikapariyāyotveva naṁ dhārehī"ti.

"Well, Ānanda, you may remember this exposition of the teaching as 'The Honey-Cake Discourse'."

Idamavoca bhagavā.

That is what the Buddha said.

Attamano āyasmā ānando bhagavato bhāsitaṁ abhinandīti.

Satisfied, Venerable Ānanda was happy with what the Buddha said.

Madhupiṇḍikasuttaṁ niṭṭhitaṁ aṭṭhamaṁ.

19 Dvedhavitakkasutta:

Two Kinds of Thought

Evaṁ me sutaṁ—

So I have heard.

ekaṁ samayaṁ bhagavā sāvatthiyaṁ viharati jetavane anāthapiṇḍikassa ārāme.

At one time the Buddha was staying near Sāvatthī in Jeta's Grove, Anāthapiṇḍika's monastery.

Tatra kho bhagavā bhikkhū āmantesi:

There the Buddha addressed the mendicants,

"bhikkhavo"ti.

"Mendicants!"

"Bhadante"ti te bhikkhū bhagavato paccassosuṁ.

"Venerable sir," they replied.

Bhagavā etadavoca:

The Buddha said this:

"Pubbeva me, bhikkhave, sambodhā anabhisambuddhassa bodhisattasseva sato etadahosi:

"Mendicants, before my awakening—when I was still unawakened but intent on awakening—I thought:

'yannūnāhaṁ dvidhā katvā dvidhā katvā vitakke vihareyyan'ti.

'Why don't I meditate by continually dividing my thoughts into two classes?'

So kho ahaṁ, bhikkhave, yo cāyaṁ kāmavitakko yo ca byāpādavitakko yo ca vihiṁsāvitakko—

So I assigned sensual, malicious, and cruel thoughts

imaṁ ekaṁ bhāgamakāsiṁ;

to one class.

yo cāyaṁ nekkhammavitakko yo ca abyāpādavitakko yo ca avihiṁsāvitakko—

And I assigned thoughts of renunciation, good will, and harmlessness

imaṁ dutiyaṁ bhāgamakāsiṁ.

to the second class.

Tassa mayhaṁ, bhikkhave, evaṁ appamattassa ātāpino pahitattassa viharato uppajjati kāmavitakko.

Then, as I meditated—diligent, keen, and resolute—a sensual thought arose.

So evaṁ pajānāmi:

I understood:

'uppanno kho me ayaṁ kāmavitakko.

'This sensual thought has arisen in me.

So ca kho attabyābādhāyapi saṁvattati, parabyābādhāyapi saṁvattati, ubhayabyābādhāyapi saṁvattati, paññānirodhiko vighātapakkhiko anibbānasaṁvattaniko'.

It leads to hurting myself, hurting others, and hurting both. It blocks wisdom, it's on the side of anguish, and it doesn't lead to extinguishment.'

'Attabyābādhāya saṁvattatī'tipi me, bhikkhave, paṭisañcikkhato abbhatthaṁ gacchati;

When I reflected that it leads to hurting myself, it went away.

'parabyābādhāya saṁvattatī'tipi me, bhikkhave, paṭisañcikkhato abbhatthaṁ gacchati;

When I reflected that it leads to hurting others, it went away.

'ubhayabyābādhāya saṁvattatī'tipi me, bhikkhave, paṭisañcikkhato abbhatthaṁ gacchati;

When I reflected that it leads to hurting both, it went away.

'paññānirodhiko vighātapakkhiko anibbānasaṁvattaniko'tipi me, bhikkhave, paṭisañcikkhato abbhatthaṁ gacchati.

When I reflected that it blocks wisdom, it's on the side of anguish, and it doesn't lead to extinguishment, it went away.

So kho ahaṁ, bhikkhave, uppannuppannaṁ kāmavitakkaṁ pajahameva vinodameva byantameva naṁ akāsiṁ.

So I gave up, got rid of, and eliminated any sensual thoughts that arose.

Tassa mayhaṁ, bhikkhave, evaṁ appamattassa ātāpino pahitattassa viharato uppajjati byāpādavitakko …pe…

Then, as I meditated—diligent, keen, and resolute—a malicious thought arose …

uppajjati vihiṁsāvitakko.

a cruel thought arose.

So evaṁ pajānāmi:

I understood:

'uppanno kho me ayaṁ vihiṁsāvitakko.

'This cruel thought has arisen in me.

So ca kho attabyābādhāyapi saṁvattati, parabyābādhāyapi saṁvattati, ubhayabyābādhāyapi saṁvattati, paññānirodhiko vighātapakkhiko anibbānasaṁvattaniko'.

It leads to hurting myself, hurting others, and hurting both. It blocks wisdom, it's on the side of anguish, and it doesn't lead to extinguishment.'

'Attabyābādhāya saṁvattatī'tipi me, bhikkhave, paṭisañcikkhato abbhatthaṁ gacchati;

When I reflected that it leads to hurting myself …

'parabyābādhāya saṁvattatī'tipi me, bhikkhave, paṭisañcikkhato abbhatthaṁ gacchati;

hurting others …

'ubhayabyābādhāya saṁvattatī'tipi me, bhikkhave, paṭisañcikkhato abbhatthaṁ gacchati;

hurting both, it went away.

'paññānirodhiko vighātapakkhiko anibbānasaṁvattaniko'tipi me, bhikkhave, paṭisañcikkhato abbhatthaṁ gacchati.

When I reflected that it blocks wisdom, it's on the side of anguish, and it doesn't lead to extinguishment, it went away.

So kho ahaṁ, bhikkhave, uppannuppannaṁ vihiṁsāvitakkaṁ pajahameva vinodameva byantameva naṁ akāsiṁ.

So I gave up, got rid of, and eliminated any cruel thoughts that arose.

Yaññadeva, bhikkhave, bhikkhu bahulamanuvitakketi anuvicāreti, tathā tathā nati hoti cetaso.

Whatever a mendicant frequently thinks about and considers becomes their heart's inclination.

Kāmavitakkañce, bhikkhave, bhikkhu bahulamanuvitakketi anuvicāreti, pahāsi nekkhammavitakkaṁ, kāmavitakkaṁ bahulamakāsi, tassa taṁ kāmavitakkāya cittaṁ namati.

If they often think about and consider sensual thoughts, they've given up the thought of renunciation to cultivate sensual thought. Their mind inclines to sensual thoughts.

Byāpādavitakkañce, bhikkhave ...pe...

If they often think about and consider malicious thoughts ... their mind inclines to malicious thoughts.

vihiṁsāvitakkañce, bhikkhave, bhikkhu bahulamanuvitakketi anuvicāreti, pahāsi avihiṁsāvitakkaṁ, vihiṁsāvitakkaṁ bahulamakāsi, tassa taṁ vihiṁsāvitakkāya cittaṁ namati.

If they often think about and consider cruel thoughts ... their mind inclines to cruel thoughts.

Seyyathāpi, bhikkhave, vassānaṁ pacchime māse saradasamaye kiṭṭhasambādhe gopālako gāvo rakkheyya.

Suppose it's the last month of the rainy season, when the crops grow closely together, and a cowherd must take care of the cattle.

So tā gāvo tato tato daṇḍena ākoṭeyya paṭikoṭeyya sannirundheyya sannivāreyya.

He'd tap and poke them with his staff on this side and that to keep them in check.

Taṁ kissa hetu?

Why is that?

Passati hi so, bhikkhave, gopālako tatonidānaṁ vadhaṁ vā bandhanaṁ vā jāniṁ vā garahaṁ vā.

For he sees that if they wander into the crops he could be executed, imprisoned, fined, or condemned.

Evameva kho ahaṁ, bhikkhave, addasaṁ akusalānaṁ dhammānaṁ ādīnavaṁ okāraṁ saṅkilesaṁ, kusalānaṁ dhammānaṁ nekkhamme ānisaṁsaṁ vodānapakkhaṁ.

In the same way, I saw that unskillful qualities have the drawbacks of sordidness and corruption, and that skillful qualities have the benefit and cleansing power of renunciation.

Tassa mayhaṁ, bhikkhave, evaṁ appamattassa ātāpino pahitattassa viharato uppajjati nekkhammavitakko.

Then, as I meditated—diligent, keen, and resolute—a thought of renunciation arose.

So evaṁ pajānāmi:

I understood:

'uppanno kho me ayaṁ nekkhammavitakko.

'This thought of renunciation has arisen in me.

So ca kho nevattabyābādhāya saṁvattati, na parabyābādhāya saṁvattati, na ubhayabyābādhāya saṁvattati, paññāvuddhiko avighātapakkhiko nibbānasaṁvattaniko'.

It doesn't lead to hurting myself, hurting others, or hurting both. It nourishes wisdom, it's on the side of freedom from anguish, and it leads to extinguishment.'

Rattiñcepi naṁ, bhikkhave, anuvitakkeyyaṁ anuvicāreyyaṁ, neva tatonidānaṁ bhayaṁ samanupassāmi.

If I were to keep on thinking and considering this all night …

Divasañcepi naṁ, bhikkhave, anuvitakkeyyaṁ anuvicāreyyaṁ, neva tatonidānaṁ bhayaṁ samanupassāmi.

all day …

Rattindivañcepi naṁ, bhikkhave, anuvitakkeyyaṁ anuvicāreyyaṁ, neva tatonidānaṁ bhayaṁ samanupassāmi.

all night and day, I see no danger that would come from that.

Api ca kho me aticiraṁ anuvitakkayato anuvicārayato kāyo kilameyya.

Still, thinking and considering for too long would tire my body.

Kāye kilante cittaṁ ūhaññeyya.

And when the body is tired, the mind is stressed.

Ūhate citte ārā cittaṁ samādhimhāti.

And when the mind is stressed, it's far from immersion.

So kho ahaṁ, bhikkhave, ajjhattameva cittaṁ saṇṭhapemi sannisādemi ekodiṁ karomi samādahāmi.

So I stilled, settled, unified, and immersed my mind internally.

Taṁ kissa hetu?

Why is that?

'Mā me cittaṁ ūhaññī'ti.

So that my mind would not be stressed.

Tassa mayhaṁ, bhikkhave, evaṁ appamattassa ātāpino pahitattassa viharato uppajjati abyāpādavitakko ...pe...

Then, as I meditated—diligent, keen, and resolute—a thought of good will arose …

uppajjati avihiṁsāvitakko.

a thought of harmlessness arose.

So evaṁ pajānāmi:

I understood:

'uppanno kho me ayaṁ avihiṁsāvitakko.

'This thought of harmlessness has arisen in me.

So ca kho nevattabyābādhāya saṁvattati, na parabyābādhāya saṁvattati, na ubhayabyābādhāya saṁvattati, paññāvuddhiko avighātapakkhiko nibbānasaṁvattaniko'.

It doesn't lead to hurting myself, hurting others, or hurting both. It nourishes wisdom, it's on the side of freedom from anguish, and it leads to extinguishment.'

Rattiñcepi naṁ, bhikkhave, anuvitakkeyyaṁ anuvicāreyyaṁ, neva tatonidānaṁ bhayaṁ samanupassāmi.

If I were to keep on thinking and considering this all night …

Divasañcepi naṁ, bhikkhave, anuvitakkeyyaṁ anuvicāreyyaṁ, neva tatonidānaṁ bhayaṁ samanupassāmi.

all day …

Rattindivañcepi naṁ, bhikkhave, anuvitakkeyyaṁ anuvicāreyyaṁ, neva tatonidānaṁ bhayaṁ samanupassāmi.

all night and day, I see no danger that would come from that.

Api ca kho me aticiraṁ anuvitakkayato anuvicārayato kāyo kilameyya.

Still, thinking and considering for too long would tire my body.

Kāye kilante cittaṁ ūhaññeyya.

And when the body is tired, the mind is stressed.

Ūhate citte ārā cittaṁ samādhimhāti.

And when the mind is stressed, it's far from immersion.

So kho ahaṁ, bhikkhave, ajjhattameva cittaṁ saṇṭhapemi, sannisādemi, ekodiṁ karomi samādahāmi.

So I stilled, settled, unified, and immersed my mind internally.

Taṁ kissa hetu?

Why is that?

'Mā me cittaṁ ūhaññī'ti.

So that my mind would not be stressed.

Yaññadeva, bhikkhave, bhikkhu bahulamanuvitakketi anuvicāreti, tathā tathā nati hoti cetaso.

Whatever a mendicant frequently thinks about and considers becomes their heart's inclination.

Nekkhammavitakkañce, bhikkhave, bhikkhu bahulamanuvitakketi anuvicāreti, pahāsi kāmavitakkaṁ, nekkhammavitakkaṁ bahulamakāsi, tassaṁ taṁ nekkhammavitakkāya cittaṁ namati.

If they often think about and consider thoughts of renunciation, they've given up sensual thought to cultivate the thought of renunciation. Their mind inclines to thoughts of renunciation.

Abyāpādavitakkañce, bhikkhave …pe…

If they often think about and consider thoughts of good will … their mind inclines to thoughts of good will.

avihiṁsāvitakkañce, bhikkhave, bhikkhu bahulamanuvitakketi anuvicāreti, pahāsi vihiṁsāvitakkaṁ, avihiṁsāvitakkaṁ bahulamakāsi, tassa taṁ avihiṁsāvitakkāya cittaṁ namati.

If they often think about and consider thoughts of harmlessness … their mind inclines to thoughts of harmlessness.

Seyyathāpi, bhikkhave, gimhānaṁ pacchime māse sabbasassesu

gāmantasambhatesu gopālako gāvo rakkheyya, tassa rukkhamūlagatassa vā abbhokāsagatassa vā satikaraṇīyameva hoti:

Suppose it's the last month of summer, when all the crops have been gathered within a village, and a cowherd must take care of the cattle. While at the root of a tree or in the open he need only be mindful that

'etā gāvo'ti.

the cattle are there.

Evamevaṁ kho, bhikkhave, satikaraṇīyameva ahosi:

In the same way I needed only to be mindful that

'ete dhammā'ti.

those things were there.

Āraddhaṁ kho pana me, bhikkhave, vīriyaṁ ahosi asallīnaṁ, upaṭṭhitā sati asammuṭṭhā, passaddho kāyo asāraddho, samāhitaṁ cittaṁ ekaggaṁ.

My energy was roused up and unflagging, my mindfulness was established and lucid, my body was tranquil and undisturbed, and my mind was immersed in samādhi.

So kho ahaṁ, bhikkhave, vivicceva kāmehi vivicca akusalehi dhammehi savitakkaṁ savicāraṁ vivekajaṁ pītisukhaṁ paṭhamaṁ jhānaṁ upasampajja vihāsiṁ.

Quite secluded from sensual pleasures, secluded from unskillful qualities, I entered and remained in the first absorption, which has the rapture and bliss born of seclusion, while placing the mind and keeping it connected.

Vitakkavicārānaṁ vūpasamā ajjhattaṁ sampasādanaṁ cetaso ekodibhāvaṁ avitakkaṁ avicāraṁ samādhijaṁ pītisukhaṁ dutiyaṁ jhānaṁ upasampajja vihāsiṁ.

As the placing of the mind and keeping it connected were stilled, I entered and remained in the second absorption, which has the rapture and bliss born of immersion, with internal clarity and confidence, and unified mind, without placing the mind and keeping it connected.

Pītiyā ca virāgā upekkhako ca vihāsiṁ sato ca sampajāno, sukhañca kāyena paṭisaṁvedesiṁ, yaṁ taṁ ariyā ācikkhanti 'upekkhako satimā sukhavihārī'ti, tatiyaṁ jhānaṁ upasampajja vihāsiṁ.

And with the fading away of rapture, I entered and remained in the third absorption, where I meditated with equanimity, mindful and aware, personally experiencing the bliss of which the noble ones declare, 'Equanimous and mindful, one meditates in bliss.'

Sukhassa ca pahānā dukkhassa ca pahānā pubbeva somanassadomanassānaṁ atthaṅgamā adukkhamasukhaṁ upekkhāsatipārisuddhiṁ catutthaṁ jhānaṁ upasampajja vihāsiṁ.

With the giving up of pleasure and pain, and the ending of former happiness and sadness, I entered and remained in the fourth absorption, without pleasure or pain, with pure equanimity and mindfulness.

So evaṁ samāhite citte parisuddhe pariyodāte anaṅgaṇe vigatūpakkilese mudubhūte kammaniye ṭhite āneñjappatte pubbenivāsānussatiñāṇāya cittaṁ abhininnāmesiṁ.

When my mind had immersed in samādhi like this—purified, bright, flawless, rid of corruptions, pliable, workable, steady, and imperturbable—I extended it toward recollection of past lives.

So anekavihitaṁ pubbenivāsaṁ anussarāmi. Seyyathidaṁ—ekampi jātiṁ …pe… iti sākāraṁ sauddesaṁ anekavihitaṁ pubbenivāsaṁ anussarāmi.

I recollected many kinds of past lives, with features and details.

Ayaṁ kho me, bhikkhave, rattiyā paṭhame yāme paṭhamā vijjā adhigatā;

This was the first knowledge, which I achieved in the first watch of the night.

avijjā vihatā vijjā uppannā; tamo vihato āloko uppanno; yathā taṁ appamattassa ātāpino pahitattassa viharato.

Ignorance was destroyed and knowledge arose; darkness was destroyed and light arose, as happens for a meditator who is diligent, keen, and resolute.

So evaṁ samāhite citte parisuddhe pariyodāte anaṅgaṇe vigatūpakkilese mudubhūte kammaniye ṭhite āneñjappatte sattānaṁ cutūpapātañāṇāya cittaṁ abhininnāmesiṁ.

When my mind had become immersed in samādhi like this, I extended it toward knowledge of the death and rebirth of sentient beings.

So dibbena cakkhunā visuddhena atikkantamānusakena satte passāmi cavamāne upapajjamāne …pe… ime vata bhonto sattā kāyaduccaritena samannāgatā …pe… iti dibbena cakkhunā visuddhena atikkantamānusakena satte passāmi cavamāne upapajjamāne hīne paṇīte suvaṇṇe dubbaṇṇe sugate duggate, yathākammūpage satte pajānāmi.

With clairvoyance that is purified and superhuman, I saw sentient beings passing away and being reborn—inferior and superior, beautiful and ugly, in a good place or a bad place. I understood how sentient beings are reborn according to their deeds.

Ayaṁ kho me, bhikkhave, rattiyā majjhime yāme dutiyā vijjā adhigatā;

This was the second knowledge, which I achieved in the middle watch of the night.

avijjā vihatā vijjā uppannā; tamo vihato āloko uppanno; yathā taṁ appamattassa ātāpino pahitattassa viharato.

Ignorance was destroyed and knowledge arose; darkness was destroyed and light arose, as happens for a meditator who is diligent, keen, and resolute.

So evaṁ samāhite citte parisuddhe pariyodāte anaṅgaṇe vigatūpakkilese mudubhūte kammaniye ṭhite āneñjappatte āsavānaṁ khayañāṇāya cittaṁ abhininnāmesiṁ.

When my mind had become immersed in samādhi like this, I extended it toward knowledge of the ending of defilements.

So 'idaṁ dukkhan'ti yathābhūtaṁ abbhaññāsiṁ, 'ayaṁ dukkhasamudayo'ti yathābhūtaṁ abbhaññāsiṁ, 'ayaṁ dukkhanirodho'ti yathābhūtaṁ abbhaññāsiṁ, 'ayaṁ dukkhanirodhagāminī paṭipadā'ti yathābhūtaṁ abbhaññāsiṁ.

I truly understood: 'This is suffering' ... 'This is the origin of suffering' ... 'This is the cessation of suffering' ... 'This is the practice that leads to the cessation of suffering.'

'Ime āsavā'ti yathābhūtaṁ abbhaññāsiṁ, 'ayaṁ āsavasamudayo'ti yathābhūtaṁ abbhaññāsiṁ, 'ayaṁ āsavanirodho'ti yathābhūtaṁ abbhaññāsiṁ, 'ayaṁ āsavanirodhagāminī paṭipadā'ti yathābhūtaṁ abbhaññāsiṁ.

I truly understood: 'These are defilements' ... 'This is the origin of defilements' ... 'This is the cessation of defilements' ... 'This is the practice that leads to the cessation of defilements.'

Tassa me evaṁ jānato evaṁ passato kāmāsavāpi cittaṁ vimuccittha, bhavāsavāpi cittaṁ vimuccittha, avijjāsavāpi cittaṁ vimuccittha, vimuttasmiṁ vimuttamiti ñāṇaṁ ahosi:

Knowing and seeing like this, my mind was freed from the defilements of sensuality, desire to be reborn, and ignorance.

'khīṇā jāti, vusitaṁ brahmacariyaṁ, kataṁ karaṇīyaṁ, nāparaṁ itthattāyā'ti abbhaññāsiṁ.

I understood: 'Rebirth is ended; the spiritual journey has been completed; what had to be done has been done; there is no return to any state of existence.'

Ayaṁ kho me, bhikkhave, rattiyā pacchime yāme tatiyā vijjā adhigatā;

This was the third knowledge, which I achieved in the last watch of the night.

avijjā vihatā vijjā uppannā; tamo vihato āloko uppanno; yathā taṁ appamattassa ātāpino pahitattassa viharato.

Ignorance was destroyed and knowledge arose; darkness was destroyed and light

arose, as happens for a meditator who is diligent, keen, and resolute.

Seyyathāpi, bhikkhave, araññe pavane mahantaṁ ninnaṁ pallalaṁ.

Suppose that in a forested wilderness there was an expanse of low-lying marshes,

Tamenaṁ mahāmigasaṅgho upanissāya vihareyya.

and a large herd of deer lived nearby.

Tassa kocideva puriso uppajjeyya anatthakāmo ahitakāmo ayogakkhemakāmo.

Then along comes a person who wants to harm, injure, and threaten them.

So yvāssa maggo khemo sovatthiko pītigamanīyo taṁ maggaṁ pidaheyya, vivareyya kummaggaṁ, odaheyya okacaraṁ, ṭhapeyya okacārikaṁ.

They close off the safe, secure path that leads to happiness, and open the wrong path. There they plant domesticated male and female deer as decoys

Evañhi so, bhikkhave, mahāmigasaṅgho aparena samayena anayabyasanaṁ āpajjeyya.

so that, in due course, that herd of deer would fall to ruin and disaster.

Tasseva kho pana, bhikkhave, mahato migasaṅghassa kocideva puriso uppajjeyya atthakāmo hitakāmo yogakkhemakāmo.

Then along comes a person who wants to help keep the herd of deer safe.

So yvāssa maggo khemo sovatthiko pītigamanīyo taṁ maggaṁ vivareyya, pidaheyya kummaggaṁ, ūhaneyya okacaraṁ, nāseyya okacārikaṁ.

They open up the safe, secure path that leads to happiness, and close off the wrong path. They get rid of the decoys

Evañhi so, bhikkhave, mahāmigasaṅgho aparena samayena vuddhiṁ virūḷhiṁ vepullaṁ āpajjeyya.

so that, in due course, that herd of deer would grow, increase, and mature.

Upamā kho me ayaṁ, bhikkhave, katā atthassa viññāpanāya.

I've made up this simile to make a point.

Ayaṁ cevettha attho—

And this is what it means.

mahantaṁ ninnaṁ pallalanti kho, bhikkhave, kāmānametaṁ adhivacanaṁ.

'An expanse of low-lying marshes' is a term for sensual pleasures.

Mahāmigasaṅghoti kho, bhikkhave, sattānametaṁ adhivacanaṁ.

'A large herd of deer' is a term for sentient beings.

Puriso anatthakāmo ahitakāmo ayogakkhemakāmoti kho, bhikkhave, mārassetaṁ pāpimato adhivacanaṁ.

'A person who wants to harm, injure, and threaten them' is a term for Māra the Wicked.

Kummaggoti kho, bhikkhave, aṭṭhaṅgikassetaṁ micchāmaggassa adhivacanaṁ, seyyathidaṁ—

'The wrong path' is a term for the wrong eightfold path, that is,

micchādiṭṭhiyā micchāsaṅkappassa micchāvācāya micchākammantassa micchāājīvassa micchāvāyāmassa micchāsatiyā micchāsamādhissa.

wrong view, wrong thought, wrong speech, wrong action, wrong livelihood, wrong effort, wrong mindfulness, and wrong immersion.

Okacaroti kho, bhikkhave, nandīrāgassetaṁ adhivacanaṁ.

'A domesticated male deer' is a term for greed and relishing.

Okacārikāti kho, bhikkhave, avijjāyetaṁ adhivacanaṁ.

'A domesticated female deer' is a term for ignorance.

Puriso atthakāmo hitakāmo yogakkhemakāmoti kho, bhikkhave, tathāgatassetaṁ adhivacanaṁ arahato sammāsambuddhassa.

'A person who wants to help keep the herd of deer safe' is a term for the Realized One, the perfected one, the fully awakened Buddha.

Khemo maggo sovatthiko pītigamanīyoti kho, bhikkhave, ariyassetaṁ aṭṭhaṅgikassa maggassa adhivacanaṁ, seyyathidaṁ—

'The safe, secure path that leads to happiness' is a term for the noble eightfold path, that is:

sammādiṭṭhiyā sammāsaṅkappassa sammāvācāya sammākammantassa sammāājīvassa sammāvāyāmassa sammāsatiyā sammāsamādhissa.

right view, right thought, right speech, right action, right livelihood, right effort, right mindfulness, and right immersion.

Iti kho, bhikkhave, vivaṭo mayā khemo maggo sovatthiko pītigamanīyo, pihito kummaggo, ūhato okacaro, nāsitā okacārikā.

So, mendicants, I have opened up the safe, secure path to happiness and closed off the wrong path. And I have got rid of the male and female decoys.

Yaṁ, bhikkhave, satthārā karaṇīyaṁ sāvakānaṁ hitesinā anukampakena anukampaṁ upādāya, kataṁ vo taṁ mayā.

Out of compassion, I've done what a teacher should do who wants what's best for their disciples.

Etāni, bhikkhave, rukkhamūlāni, etāni suññāgārāni; jhāyatha, bhikkhave, mā pamādattha; mā pacchā vippaṭisārino ahuvattha. Ayaṁ vo amhākaṁ anusāsanī"ti.

Here are these roots of trees, and here are these empty huts. Practice absorption, mendicants! Don't be negligent! Don't regret it later! This is my instruction to you."

Idamavoca bhagavā.

That is what the Buddha said.

Attamanā te bhikkhū bhagavato bhāsitaṁ abhinandunti.

Satisfied, the mendicants were happy with what the Buddha said.

Dvedhāvitakkasuttaṁ niṭṭhitaṁ navamaṁ.

20 Vitakkasanthanasutta:

How to Stop Thinking

Evaṁ me sutaṁ—

So I have heard.

ekaṁ samayaṁ bhagavā sāvatthiyaṁ viharati jetavane anāthapiṇḍikassa ārāme.

At one time the Buddha was staying near Sāvatthī in Jeta's Grove, Anāthapiṇḍika's monastery.

Tatra kho bhagavā bhikkhū āmantesi:

There the Buddha addressed the mendicants,

"bhikkhavo"ti.

"Mendicants!"

"Bhadante"ti te bhikkhū bhagavato paccassosuṁ.

"Venerable sir," they replied.

Bhagavā etadavoca:

The Buddha said this:

"Adhicittamanuyuttena, bhikkhave, bhikkhunā pañca nimittāni kālena kālaṁ manasi kātabbāni.

"Mendicants, a mendicant committed to the higher mind should focus on five foundations of meditation from time to time.

Katamāni pañca?

What five?

Idha, bhikkhave, bhikkhuno yaṁ nimittaṁ āgamma yaṁ nimittaṁ manasikaroto uppajjanti pāpakā akusalā vitakkā chandūpasaṁhitāpi dosūpasaṁhitāpi mohūpasaṁhitāpi, tena, bhikkhave, bhikkhunā tamhā nimittā aññaṁ nimittaṁ manasi kātabbaṁ kusalūpasaṁhitaṁ.

Take a mendicant who is focusing on some foundation of meditation that gives rise to bad, unskillful thoughts connected with desire, hate, and delusion. That mendicant should focus on some other foundation of meditation connected with the skillful.

Tassa tamhā nimittā aññaṁ nimittaṁ manasikaroto kusalūpasaṁhitaṁ ye pāpakā akusalā vitakkā chandūpasaṁhitāpi dosūpasaṁhitāpi mohūpasaṁhitāpi te pahīyanti te abbhatthaṁ gacchanti.

As they do so, those bad thoughts are given up and come to an end.

Tesaṁ pahānā ajjhattameva cittaṁ santiṭṭhati sannisīdati ekodi hoti samādhiyati.

Their mind becomes stilled internally; it settles, unifies, and becomes immersed in samādhi.

Seyyathāpi, bhikkhave, dakkho palagaṇḍo vā palagaṇḍantevāsī vā sukhumāya āṇiyā oḷārikaṁ āṇiṁ abhinihaneyya abhinīhareyya abhinivatteyya;

It's like a deft carpenter or their apprentice who'd knock out or extract a large peg with a finer peg.

evameva kho, bhikkhave, bhikkhuno yaṁ nimittaṁ āgamma yaṁ nimittaṁ manasikaroto uppajjanti pāpakā akusalā vitakkā chandūpasaṁhitāpi dosūpasaṁhitāpi mohūpasaṁhitāpi, tena, bhikkhave, bhikkhunā tamhā nimittā aññaṁ nimittaṁ manasi kātabbaṁ kusalūpasaṁhitaṁ.

In the same way, a mendicant ... should focus on some other foundation of meditation connected with the skillful ...

Tassa tamhā nimittā aññaṁ nimittaṁ manasikaroto kusalūpasaṁhitaṁ ye pāpakā akusalā vitakkā chandūpasaṁhitāpi dosūpasaṁhitāpi mohūpasaṁhitāpi te pahīyanti te abbhatthaṁ gacchanti.

Tesaṁ pahānā ajjhattameva cittaṁ santiṭṭhati sannisīdati ekodi hoti samādhiyati.

Tassa ce, bhikkhave, bhikkhuno tamhā nimittā aññaṁ nimittaṁ manasikaroto kusalūpasaṁhitaṁ uppajjanteva pāpakā akusalā vitakkā chandūpasaṁhitāpi dosūpasaṁhitāpi mohūpasaṁhitāpi, tena, bhikkhave, bhikkhunā tesaṁ vitakkānaṁ ādīnavo upaparikkhitabbo:

Now, suppose that mendicant is focusing on some other foundation of meditation connected with the skillful, but bad, unskillful thoughts connected with desire, hate, and delusion keep coming up. They should examine the drawbacks of those thoughts:

'itipime vitakkā akusalā, itipime vitakkā sāvajjā, itipime vitakkā dukkhavipākā'ti.

'So these thoughts are unskillful, they're blameworthy, and they result in suffering.'

Tassa tesaṁ vitakkānaṁ ādīnavaṁ upaparikkhato ye pāpakā akusalā vitakkā chandūpasaṁhitāpi dosūpasaṁhitāpi mohūpasaṁhitāpi te pahīyanti te abbhatthaṁ gacchanti.

As they do so, those bad thoughts are given up and come to an end.

Tesaṁ pahānā ajjhattameva cittaṁ santiṭṭhati sannisīdati ekodi hoti samādhiyati.

Their mind becomes stilled internally; it settles, unifies, and becomes immersed in samādhi.

Seyyathāpi, bhikkhave, itthī vā puriso vā daharo yuvā maṇḍanakajātiko ahikuṇapena vā kukkurakuṇapena vā manussakuṇapena vā kaṇṭhe āsattena aṭṭiyeyya harāyeyya jiguccheyya;

Suppose there was a woman or man who was young, youthful, and fond of adornments. If the carcass of a snake or a dog or a human were hung around their neck, they'd be horrified, repelled, and disgusted.

evameva kho, bhikkhave, tassa ce bhikkhuno tamhāpi nimittā aññaṁ nimittaṁ manasikaroto kusalūpasaṁhitaṁ uppajjanteva pāpakā akusalā vitakkā chandūpasaṁhitāpi dosūpasaṁhitāpi mohūpasaṁhitāpi, tena, bhikkhave, bhikkhunā tesaṁ vitakkānaṁ ādīnavo upaparikkhitabbo:

In the same way, a mendicant ... should examine the drawbacks of those thoughts ...

'itipime vitakkā akusalā, itipime vitakkā sāvajjā, itipime vitakkā dukkhavipākā'ti.

Tassa tesaṁ vitakkānaṁ ādīnavaṁ upaparikkhato ye pāpakā akusalā vitakkā chandūpasaṁhitāpi dosūpasaṁhitāpi mohūpasaṁhitāpi te pahīyanti te abbhatthaṁ gacchanti.

Tesaṁ pahānā ajjhattameva cittaṁ santiṭṭhati sannisīdati ekodi hoti samādhiyati.

Tassa ce, bhikkhave, bhikkhuno tesampi vitakkānaṁ ādīnavaṁ upaparikkhato uppajjanteva pāpakā akusalā vitakkā chandūpasaṁhitāpi dosūpasaṁhitāpi mohūpasaṁhitāpi, tena, bhikkhave, bhikkhunā tesaṁ vitakkānaṁ asatiamanasikāro āpajjitabbo.

Now, suppose that mendicant is examining the drawbacks of those thoughts, but bad, unskillful thoughts connected with desire, hate, and delusion keep coming up. They should try to ignore and forget about them.

Tassa tesaṁ vitakkānaṁ asatiamanasikāraṁ āpajjato ye pāpakā akusalā vitakkā chandūpasaṁhitāpi dosūpasaṁhitāpi mohūpasaṁhitāpi te pahīyanti te abbhatthaṁ gacchanti.

As they do so, those bad thoughts are given up and come to an end.

Tesaṁ pahānā ajjhattameva cittaṁ santiṭṭhati sannisīdati ekodi hoti samādhiyati.

Their mind becomes stilled internally; it settles, unifies, and becomes immersed in samādhi.

Seyyathāpi, bhikkhave, cakkhumā puriso āpāthagatānaṁ rūpānaṁ adassanakāmo assa;

Suppose there was a person with good eyesight, and some undesirable sights came into their range of vision.

so nimīleyya vā aññena vā apalokeyya;

They'd just close their eyes or look away.

evameva kho, bhikkhave, tassa ce bhikkhuno tesampi vitakkānaṁ ādīnavaṁ upaparikkhato uppajjanteva pāpakā akusalā vitakkā chandūpasaṁhitāpi dosūpasaṁhitāpi mohūpasaṁhitāpi, te pahīyanti te abbhatthaṁ gacchanti.

In the same way, a mendicant ... those bad thoughts are given up and come to an end ...

Tesaṁ pahānā ajjhattameva cittaṁ santiṭṭhati sannisīdati ekodi hoti samādhiyati.

Tassa ce, bhikkhave, bhikkhuno tesampi vitakkānaṁ asatiamanasikāraṁ āpajjato uppajjanteva pāpakā akusalā vitakkā chandūpasaṁhitāpi dosūpasaṁhitāpi mohūpasaṁhitāpi, tena, bhikkhave, bhikkhunā tesaṁ vitakkānaṁ vitakkasaṅkhārasanṭhānaṁ manasikātabbaṁ.

Now, suppose that mendicant is ignoring and forgetting about those thoughts, but bad, unskillful thoughts connected with desire, hate, and delusion keep coming up. They should focus on stopping the formation of thoughts.

Tassa tesaṁ vitakkānaṁ vitakkasaṅkhārasanṭhānaṁ manasikaroto ye pāpakā akusalā vitakkā chandūpasaṁhitāpi dosūpasaṁhitāpi mohūpasaṁhitāpi te pahīyanti te abbhatthaṁ gacchanti.

As they do so, those bad thoughts are given up and come to an end.

Tesaṁ pahānā ajjhattameva cittaṁ santiṭṭhati sannisīdati ekodi hoti samādhiyati.

Their mind becomes stilled internally; it settles, unifies, and becomes immersed in samādhi.

Seyyathāpi, bhikkhave, puriso sīghaṁ gaccheyya.

Suppose there was a person walking quickly.

Tassa evamassa:

They'd think:

'kiṁ nu kho ahaṁ sīghaṁ gacchāmi?

'Why am I walking so quickly?

Yannūnāhaṁ saṇikaṁ gaccheyyan'ti.

Why don't I slow down?'

So saṇikaṁ gaccheyya.

So they'd slow down.

Tassa evamassa:

They'd think:

'kiṁ nu kho ahaṁ saṇikaṁ gacchāmi?

'Why am I walking slowly?

Yannūnāhaṁ tiṭṭheyyan'ti.

Why don't I stand still?'

So tiṭṭheyya.

So they'd stand still.

Tassa evamassa:

They'd think:

'kiṁ nu kho ahaṁ ṭhito?

'Why am I standing still?

Yannūnāhaṁ nisīdeyyan'ti.

Why don't I sit down?'

So nisīdeyya.

So they'd sit down.

Tassa evamassa:

They'd think:

'kiṁ nu kho ahaṁ nisinno?

'Why am I sitting?

Yannūnāhaṁ nipajjeyyan'ti.

Why don't I lie down?'

So nipajjeyya.

So they'd lie down.

Evañhi so, bhikkhave, puriso oḷārikaṁ oḷārikaṁ iriyāpathaṁ abhinivajjetvā sukhumaṁ sukhumaṁ iriyāpathaṁ kappeyya.

And so that person would reject successively coarser postures and adopt more subtle ones.

Evamevakho, bhikkhave, tassace bhikkhuno tesampi vitakkānaṁ asatiamanasikāraṁ āpajjato uppajjanteva pāpakā akusalā vitakkā chandūpasaṁhitāpi dosūpasaṁhitāpi mohūpasaṁhitāpi te pahīyanti te abbhatthaṁ gacchanti.

In the same way, a mendicant … those thoughts are given up and come to an end …

Tesaṁ pahānā ajjhattameva cittaṁ santiṭṭhati sannisīdati ekodi hoti samādhiyati.

Tassa ce, bhikkhave, bhikkhuno tesampi vitakkānaṁ vitakkasaṅkhārasaṇṭhānaṁ manasikaroto uppajjanteva pāpakā akusalā vitakkā chandūpasaṁhitāpi dosūpasaṁhitāpi mohūpasaṁhitāpi.

Now, suppose that mendicant is focusing on stopping the formation of thoughts, but bad, unskillful thoughts connected with desire, hate, and delusion keep coming up.

Tena, bhikkhave, bhikkhunā dantebhidantamādhāya jivhāya tāluṁ āhacca cetasā cittaṁ abhiniggaṇhitabbaṁ abhinippīḷetabbaṁ abhisantāpetabbaṁ.

With teeth clenched and tongue pressed against the roof of the mouth, they should squeeze, squash, and torture mind with mind.

Tassa dantebhidantamādhāya jivhāya tāluṁ āhacca cetasā cittaṁ abhiniggaṇhato abhinippīḷayato abhisantāpayato ye pāpakā akusalā vitakkā chandūpasaṁhitāpi dosūpasaṁhitāpi mohūpasaṁhitāpi te pahīyanti te abbhatthaṁ gacchanti.

As they do so, those bad thoughts are given up and come to an end.

Tesaṁ pahānā ajjhattameva cittaṁ santiṭṭhati sannisīdati ekodi hoti samādhiyati.

Their mind becomes stilled internally; it settles, unifies, and becomes immersed in samādhi.

Seyyathāpi, bhikkhave, balavā puriso dubbalataraṁ purisaṁ sīse vā gale vā khandhe vā gahetvā abhiniggaṇheyya abhinippīḷeyya abhisantāpeyya;

It's like a strong man who grabs a weaker man by the head or throat or shoulder and squeezes, squashes, and tortures them.

evameva kho, bhikkhave, tassa ce bhikkhuno tesampi vitakkānaṁ vitakkasaṅkhārasaṇṭhānaṁ manasikaroto uppajjanteva pāpakā akusalā vitakkā chandūpasaṁhitāpi dosūpasaṁhitāpi mohūpasaṁhitāpi.

In the same way, a mendicant …

Tena, bhikkhave, bhikkhunā dantebhidantamādhāya jivhāya tāluṁ āhacca cetasā cittaṁ abhiniggaṇhitabbaṁ abhinippīḷetabbaṁ abhisantāpetabbaṁ.

with teeth clenched and tongue pressed against the roof of the mouth, should squeeze, squash, and torture mind with mind.

Tassa dantebhidantamādhāya jivhāya tāluṁ āhacca cetasā cittaṁ abhiniggaṇhato abhinippīḷayato abhisantāpayato ye pāpakā akusalā vitakkā chandūpasaṁhitāpi dosūpasaṁhitāpi mohūpasaṁhitāpi te pahīyanti te abbhatthaṁ gacchanti.

As they do so, those bad thoughts are given up and come to an end.

Tesaṁ pahānā ajjhattameva cittaṁ santiṭṭhati sannisīdati ekodi hoti samādhiyati.

Their mind becomes stilled internally; it settles, unifies, and becomes immersed in samādhi.

Yato kho, bhikkhave, bhikkhuno yaṁ nimittaṁ āgamma yaṁ nimittaṁ manasikaroto uppajjanti pāpakā akusalā vitakkā chandūpasaṁhitāpi dosūpasaṁhitāpi mohūpasaṁhitāpi, tassa tamhā nimittā aññaṁ nimittaṁ manasikaroto kusalūpasaṁhitaṁ ye pāpakā akusalā vitakkā chandūpasaṁhitāpi dosūpasaṁhitāpi mohūpasaṁhitāpi te pahīyanti te abbhatthaṁ gacchanti.

Now, take the mendicant who is focusing on some foundation of meditation that gives rise to bad, unskillful thoughts connected with desire, hate, and delusion. They focus on some other foundation of meditation connected with the skillful …

Tesaṁ pahānā ajjhattameva cittaṁ santiṭṭhati sannisīdati ekodi hoti samādhiyati.

Tesampi vitakkānaṁ ādīnavaṁ upaparikkhato ye pāpakā akusalā vitakkā chandūpasaṁhitāpi dosūpasaṁhitāpi mohūpasaṁhitāpi te pahīyanti te abbhatthaṁ gacchanti.

They examine the drawbacks of those thoughts …

Tesaṁ pahānā ajjhattameva cittaṁ santiṭṭhati sannisīdati ekodi hoti samādhiyati.

Tesampi vitakkānaṁ asatiamanasikāraṁ āpajjato ye pāpakā akusalā vitakkā chandūpasaṁhitāpi dosūpasaṁhitāpi mohūpasaṁhitāpi te pahīyanti te abbhatthaṁ gacchanti.

They try to ignore and forget about those thoughts …

Tesaṁ pahānā ajjhattameva cittaṁ santiṭṭhati sannisīdati ekodi hoti samādhiyati.

Tesampi vitakkānaṁ vitakkasaṅkhārasanthānaṁ manasikaroto ye pāpakā akusalā vitakkā chandūpasaṁhitāpi dosūpasaṁhitāpi mohūpasaṁhitāpi te pahīyanti te abbhatthaṁ gacchanti.

They focus on stopping the formation of thoughts …

Tesaṁ pahānā ajjhattameva cittaṁ santiṭṭhati sannisīdati ekodi hoti samādhiyati.

Dantebhidantamādhāya jivhāya tāluṁ āhacca cetasā cittaṁ abhinigganhato abhinippīḷayato abhisantāpayato ye pāpakā akusalā vitakkā chandūpasaṁhitāpi dosūpasaṁhitāpi mohūpasaṁhitāpi te pahīyanti te abbhatthaṁ gacchanti.

With teeth clenched and tongue pressed against the roof of the mouth, they squeeze, squash, and torture mind with mind. When they succeed in each of these things, those bad thoughts are given up and come to an end.

Tesaṁ pahānā ajjhattameva cittaṁ santiṭṭhati sannisīdati ekodi hoti samādhiyati.

Their mind becomes stilled internally; it settles, unifies, and becomes immersed in samādhi.

Ayaṁ vuccati, bhikkhave, bhikkhu vasī vitakkapariyāyapathesu.

This is called a mendicant who is a master of the ways of thought.

Yaṁ vitakkaṁ ākaṅkhissati taṁ vitakkaṁ vitakkessati, yaṁ vitakkaṁ nākaṅkhissati na taṁ vitakkaṁ vitakkessati.

They'll think what they want to think, and they won't think what they don't want to think.

Acchecchi taṇhaṁ, vivattayi saṁyojanaṁ, sammā mānābhisamayā antamakāsi dukkhassā"ti.

They've cut off craving, untied the fetters, and by rightly comprehending conceit have made an end of suffering."

Idamavoca bhagavā.

That is what the Buddha said.

Attamanā te bhikkhū bhagavato bhāsitaṁ abhinandunti.

Satisfied, the mendicants were happy with what the Buddha said.

Vitakkasaṇṭhānasuttaṁ niṭṭhitaṁ dasamaṁ.

Sīhanādavaggo niṭṭhito dutiyo.

Tassuddānaṁ

Cūḷasīhanādalomahaṁsavaro,

Mahācūḷadukkhakkhandhaanumānikasuttaṁ;

Khilapatthamadhupiṇḍikadvidhāvitakka,

Pañcanimittakathā puna vaggo.

OPAMMAVAGGA

THE DIVISION OF SIMILES

21 Kakacupamasutta:

The Simile of the Saw

Evaṁ me sutaṁ—

So I have heard.

ekaṁ samayaṁ bhagavā sāvatthiyaṁ viharati jetavane anāthapiṇḍikassa ārāme.

At one time the Buddha was staying near Sāvatthī in Jeta's Grove, Anāthapiṇḍika's monastery.

Tena kho pana samayena āyasmā moḷiyaphagguno bhikkhunīhi saddhiṁ ativelaṁ saṁsaṭṭho viharati.

Now at that time, Venerable Phagguna of the Top-Knot was mixing too closely together with the nuns.

Evaṁ saṁsaṭṭho āyasmā moḷiyaphagguno bhikkhunīhi saddhiṁ viharati—

So much so that

sace koci bhikkhu āyasmato moḷiyaphaggunassa sammukhā tāsaṁ bhikkhunīnaṁ avaṇṇaṁ bhāsati, tenāyasmā moḷiyaphagguno kupito anattamano adhikaraṇampi karoti.

if any mendicant criticized those nuns in his presence, Phagguna of the Top-Knot got angry and upset, and even instigated disciplinary proceedings.

Sace pana koci bhikkhu tāsaṁ bhikkhunīnaṁ sammukhā āyasmato moḷiyaphaggunassa avaṇṇaṁ bhāsati, tena tā bhikkhuniyo kupitā anattamanā adhikaraṇampi karonti.

And if any mendicant criticized Phagguna of the Top-Knot in their presence, those nuns got angry and upset, and even instigated disciplinary proceedings.

Evaṁ saṁsaṭṭho āyasmā moḷiyaphagguno bhikkhunīhi saddhiṁ viharati.

That's how much Phagguna of the Top-Knot was mixing too closely together with the nuns.

Atha kho aññataro bhikkhu yena bhagavā tenupasaṅkami; upasaṅkamitvā bhagavantaṁ abhivādetvā ekamantaṁ nisīdi. Ekamantaṁ nisinno kho so bhikkhu bhagavantaṁ etadavoca:

Then a mendicant went up to the Buddha, bowed, sat down to one side, and told him what was going on.

"āyasmā, bhante, moḷiyaphagguno bhikkhunīhi saddhiṁ ativelaṁ saṁsaṭṭho viharati.

Evaṁ saṁsaṭṭho, bhante, āyasmā moḷiyaphagguno bhikkhunīhi saddhiṁ viharati—

sace koci bhikkhu āyasmato moḷiyaphaggunassa sammukhā tāsaṁ bhikkhunīnaṁ avaṇṇaṁ bhāsati, tenāyasmā moḷiyaphagguno kupito anattamano adhikaraṇampi karoti.

Sace pana koci bhikkhu tāsaṁ bhikkhunīnaṁ sammukhā āyasmato moḷiyaphaggunassa avaṇṇaṁ bhāsati, tena tā bhikkhuniyo kupitā anattamanā adhikaraṇampi karonti.

Evaṁ saṁsaṭṭho, bhante, āyasmā moḷiyaphagguno bhikkhunīhi saddhiṁ viharatī"ti.

Atha kho bhagavā aññataraṁ bhikkhuṁ āmantesi:

So the Buddha addressed a certain monk,

"ehi tvaṁ, bhikkhu, mama vacanena moḷiyaphaggunaṁ bhikkhuṁ āmantehi:

"Please, monk, in my name tell the mendicant Phagguna of the Top-Knot that

'satthā taṁ, āvuso phagguna, āmantetī'"ti.

the teacher summons him."

"Evaṁ, bhante"ti kho so bhikkhu bhagavato paṭissutvā yenāyasmā moḷiyaphagguno tenupasaṅkami; upasaṅkamitvā āyasmantaṁ moḷiyaphaggunaṁ etadavoca:

"Yes, sir," that monk replied. He went to Phagguna of the Top-Knot and said to him,

"satthā taṁ, āvuso phagguna, āmantetī"ti.

"Reverend Phagguna, the teacher summons you."

"Evamāvuso"ti kho āyasmā moḷiyaphagguno tassa bhikkhuno paṭissutvā yena bhagavā tenupasaṅkami; upasaṅkamitvā bhagavantaṁ abhivādetvā ekamantaṁ nisīdi. Ekamantaṁ nisinnaṁ kho āyasmantaṁ moḷiyaphaggunaṁ bhagavā etadavoca:

"Yes, reverend," Phagguna replied. He went to the Buddha, bowed, and sat down to one side. The Buddha said to him:

"Saccaṁ kira tvaṁ, phagguna, bhikkhunīhi saddhiṁ ativelaṁ saṁsaṭṭho viharasi?

"Is it really true, Phagguna, that you've been mixing overly closely together with the nuns?

Evaṁ saṁsaṭṭho kira tvaṁ, phagguna, bhikkhunīhi saddhiṁ viharasi—

So much so that

sace koci bhikkhu tuyhaṁ sammukhā tāsaṁ bhikkhunīnaṁ avaṇṇaṁ bhāsati, tena tvaṁ kupito anattamano adhikaraṇampi karosi.

if any mendicant criticizes those nuns in your presence, you get angry and upset, and even instigate disciplinary proceedings?

Sace pana koci bhikkhu tāsaṁ bhikkhunīnaṁ sammukhā tuyhaṁ avaṇṇaṁ bhāsati, tena tā bhikkhuniyo kupitā anattamanā adhikaraṇampi karonti.

And if any mendicant criticizes you in those nuns' presence, they get angry and upset, and even instigate disciplinary proceedings?

Evaṁ saṁsaṭṭho kira tvaṁ, phagguna, bhikkhunīhi saddhiṁ viharasī"ti?

Is that how much you're mixing overly closely together with the nuns?"

"Evaṁ, bhante"ti.

"Yes, sir."

"Nanu tvaṁ, phagguna, kulaputto saddhā agārasmā anagāriyaṁ pabbajito"ti?

"Phagguna, are you not a gentleman who has gone forth from the lay life to homelessness?"

"Evaṁ, bhante"ti.

"Yes, sir."

"Na kho te etaṁ, phagguna, patirūpaṁ kulaputtassa saddhā agārasmā anagāriyaṁ pabbajitassa, yaṁ tvaṁ bhikkhunīhi saddhiṁ ativelaṁ saṁsaṭṭho vihareyyāsi.

"As such, it's not appropriate for you to mix so closely with the nuns.

Tasmātiha, phagguna, tava cepi koci sammukhā tāsaṁ bhikkhunīnaṁ avaṇṇaṁ bhāseyya, tatrāpi tvaṁ, phagguna, ye gehasitā chandā ye gehasitā vitakkā te pajaheyyāsi.

So if anyone criticizes those nuns in your presence, you should give up any desires or thoughts of the lay life.

Tatrāpi te, phagguna, evaṁ sikkhitabbaṁ:

If that happens, you should train like this:

'na ceva me cittaṁ vipariṇataṁ bhavissati, na ca pāpikaṁ vācaṁ nicchāressāmi, hitānukampī ca viharissāmi mettacitto, na dosantaro'ti.

'My mind will be unaffected. I will blurt out no bad words. I will remain full of compassion, with a heart of love and no secret hate.'

Evañhi te, phagguna, sikkhitabbaṁ.

That's how you should train.

Tasmātiha, phagguna, tava cepi koci sammukhā tāsaṁ bhikkhunīnaṁ pāṇinā pahāraṁ dadeyya, leḍḍunā pahāraṁ dadeyya, daṇḍena pahāraṁ dadeyya, satthena pahāraṁ dadeyya. Tatrāpi tvaṁ, phagguna, ye gehasitā chandā ye gehasitā vitakkā te pajaheyyāsi.

So even if someone strikes those nuns with fists, stones, rods, and swords in your presence, you should give up any desires or thoughts of the lay life.

Tatrāpi te, phagguna, evaṁ sikkhitabbaṁ

If that happens, you should train like this:

'na ceva me cittaṁ vipariṇataṁ bhavissati, na ca pāpikaṁ vācaṁ nicchāressāmi, hitānukampī ca viharissāmi mettacitto, na dosantaro'ti.

'My mind will be unaffected. I will blurt out no bad words. I will remain full of compassion, with a heart of love and no secret hate.'

Evañhi te, phagguna, sikkhitabbaṁ.

That's how you should train.

Tasmātiha, phagguna, tava cepi koci sammukhā avaṇṇaṁ bhāseyya, tatrāpi tvaṁ, phagguna, ye gehasitā chandā ye gehasitā vitakkā te pajaheyyāsi.

So if anyone criticizes you in your presence, you should give up any desires or thoughts of the lay life.

Tatrāpi te, phagguna, evaṁ sikkhitabbaṁ 'na ceva me cittaṁ vipariṇataṁ bhavissati, na ca pāpikaṁ vācaṁ nicchāressāmi, hitānukampī ca viharissāmi mettacitto, na dosantaro'ti.

If that happens, you should train like this: 'My mind will be unaffected. I will blurt out no bad words. I will remain full of compassion, with a heart of love and no secret hate.'

Evañhi te, phagguna, sikkhitabbaṁ.

That's how you should train.

Tasmātiha, phagguna, tava cepi koci pāṇinā pahāraṁ dadeyya, leḍḍunā pahāraṁ dadeyya, daṇḍena pahāraṁ dadeyya, satthena pahāraṁ dadeyya, tatrāpi tvaṁ, phagguna, ye gehasitā chandā ye gehasitā vitakkā te pajaheyyāsi.

So Phagguna, even if someone strikes you with fists, stones, rods, and swords, you should give up any desires or thoughts of the lay life.

Tatrāpi te, phagguna, evaṁ sikkhitabbaṁ 'na ceva me cittaṁ vipariṇataṁ bhavissati, na ca pāpikaṁ vācaṁ nicchāressāmi, hitānukampī ca viharissāmi mettacitto, na dosantaro'ti.

If that happens, you should train like this: 'My mind will be unaffected. I will blurt out no bad words. I will remain full of compassion, with a heart of love and no secret hate.'

Evañhi te, phagguna, sikkhitabban"ti.

That's how you should train."

Atha kho bhagavā bhikkhū āmantesi:

Then the Buddha said to the mendicants:

"ārādhayiṁsu vata me, bhikkhave, bhikkhū ekaṁ samayaṁ cittaṁ.

"Mendicants, I used to be satisfied with the mendicants.

Idhāhaṁ, bhikkhave, bhikkhū āmantesiṁ—

Once, I addressed them:

ahaṁ kho, bhikkhave, ekāsanabhojanaṁ bhuñjāmi.

'I eat my food in one sitting per day.

Ekāsanabhojanaṁ kho ahaṁ, bhikkhave, bhuñjamāno appābādhatañca sañjānāmi appātaṅkatañca lahuṭṭhānañca balañca phāsuvihārañca.

Doing so, I find that I'm healthy and well, nimble, strong, and living comfortably.

Etha tumhepi, bhikkhave, ekāsanabhojanaṁ bhuñjatha.

You too should eat your food in one sitting per day.

Ekāsanabhojanaṁ kho, bhikkhave, tumhepi bhuñjamānā appābādhatañca sañjānissatha appātaṅkatañca lahuṭṭhānañca balañca phāsuvihārañcāti.

Doing so, you'll find that you're healthy and well, nimble, strong, and living comfortably.'

Na me, bhikkhave, tesu bhikkhūsu anusāsanī karaṇīyā ahosi;

I didn't have to keep on instructing those mendicants;

satuppādakaraṇīyameva me, bhikkhave, tesu bhikkhūsu ahosi.

I just had to prompt their mindfulness.

Seyyathāpi, bhikkhave, subhūmiyaṁ catumahāpathe ājaññaratho yutto assa ṭhito odhastapatodo.

Suppose a chariot stood harnessed to thoroughbreds at a level crossroads, with a goad ready.

Tamenaṁ dakkho yoggācariyo assadammasārathi abhiruhitvā, vāmena hatthena rasmiyo gahetvā, dakkhiṇena hatthena patodaṁ gahetvā, yenicchakaṁ yadicchakaṁ sāreyyapi paccāsāreyyapi.

Then a deft horse trainer, a master charioteer, might mount the chariot, taking the reins in his right hand and goad in the left. He'd drive out and back wherever he wishes, whenever he wishes.

Evameva kho, bhikkhave, na me tesu bhikkhūsu anusāsanī karaṇīyā ahosi,

In the same way, I didn't have to keep on instructing those mendicants;

satuppādakaraṇīyameva me, bhikkhave, tesu bhikkhūsu ahosi.

I just had to prompt their mindfulness.

Tasmātiha, bhikkhave, tumhepi akusalaṁ pajahatha, kusalesu dhammesu āyogaṁ karotha.

So, mendicants, you too should give up what's unskillful and devote yourselves to skillful qualities.

Evañhi tumhepi imasmiṁ dhammavinaye vuddhiṁ virūḷhiṁ vepullaṁ āpajjissatha.

In this way you'll achieve growth, improvement, and maturity in this teaching and training.

Seyyathāpi, bhikkhave, gāmassa vā nigamassa vā avidūre mahantaṁ sālavanaṁ.

Suppose that not far from a town or village there was a large grove of sal trees

Tañcassa eḷaṇḍehi sañchannaṁ.

that was choked with castor-oil weeds.

Tassa kocideva puriso uppajjeyya atthakāmo hitakāmo yogakkhemakāmo.

Then along comes a person who wants to help protect and nurture that grove.

So yā tā sālalaṭṭhiyo kuṭilā ojāpaharaṇiyo tā chetvā bahiddhā nīhareyya, antovanaṁ suvisodhitaṁ visodheyya.

They'd cut down the crooked sal saplings that were robbing the sap, and throw them out. They'd clean up the interior of the grove,

Yā pana tā sālalaṭṭhiyo ujukā sujātā tā sammā parihareyya.

and properly care for the straight, well-formed sal saplings.

Evañhetaṁ, bhikkhave, sālavanaṁ aparena samayena vuddhiṁ virūḷhiṁ vepullaṁ āpajjeyya.

In this way, in due course, that sal grove would grow, increase, and mature.

Evameva kho, bhikkhave, tumhepi akusalaṁ pajahatha, kusalesu dhammesu āyogaṁ karotha.

In the same way, mendicants, you too should give up what's unskillful and devote yourselves to skillful qualities.

Evañhi tumhepi imasmiṁ dhammavinaye vuddhiṁ virūḷhiṁ vepullaṁ āpajjissatha.

In this way you'll achieve growth, improvement, and maturity in this teaching and training.

Bhūtapubbaṁ, bhikkhave, imissāyeva sāvatthiyā vedehikā nāma gahapatānī ahosi.

Once upon a time, mendicants, right here in Sāvatthī there was a housewife named Vedehikā.

Vedehikāya, bhikkhave, gahapatāniyā evaṁ kalyāṇo kittisaddo abbhuggato:

She had this good reputation:

'soratā vedehikā gahapatānī, nivātā vedehikā gahapatānī, upasantā vedehikā gahapatānī'ti.

'The housewife Vedehikā is sweet, even-tempered, and calm.'

Vedehikāya kho pana, bhikkhave, gahapatāniyā kāḷī nāma dāsī ahosi dakkhā analasā susaṁvihitakammantā.

Now, Vedehikā had a bonded maid named Kāḷī who was deft, tireless, and well-organized in her work.

Atha kho, bhikkhave, kāḷiyā dāsiyā etadahosi:

Then Kāḷī thought,

'mayhaṁ kho ayyāya evaṁ kalyāṇo kittisaddo abbhuggato:

'My mistress has a good reputation as being

"soratā vedehikā gahapatānī, nivātā vedehikā gahapatānī, upasantā vedehikā gahapatānī"ti.

sweet, even-tempered, and calm.

Kiṁ nu kho me ayyā santaṁyeva nu kho ajjhattaṁ kopaṁ na pātukaroti udāhu asantaṁ

But does she actually have anger in her and just not show it? Or does she have no anger?

udāhu mayhamevete kammantā susaṁvihitā yena me ayyā santaṁyeva ajjhattaṁ kopaṁ na pātukaroti, no asantaṁ?

Or is it just because my work is well-organized that she doesn't show anger, even though she still has it inside?

Yannūnāhaṁ ayyaṁ vīmaṁseyyan'ti.

Why don't I test my mistress?'

Atha kho, bhikkhave, kāḷī dāsī divā uṭṭhāsi.

So Kāḷī got up during the day.

Atha kho, bhikkhave, vedehikā gahapatānī kāḷiṁ dāsiṁ etadavoca:

Vedehikā said to her,

'he je kāḷī'ti.

'Oi wench, Kāḷī!'

'Kiṁ, ayye'ti?

'What is it, madam?'

'Kiṁ, je, divā uṭṭhāsī'ti?

'You're getting up in the day—what's up with you, wench?'

'Na khvayye, kiñcī'ti.

'Nothing, madam.'

'No vata re kiñci, pāpi dāsi, divā uṭṭhāsī'ti kupitā anattamanā bhākuṭiṁ akāsi.

'Oh, so nothing's up, you naughty maid, but you get up in the day!' Angry and upset, she scowled.

Atha kho, bhikkhave, kāḷiyā dāsiyā etadahosi:

Then Kāḷī thought,

'santaṁyeva kho me ayyā ajjhattaṁ kopaṁ na pātukaroti, no asantaṁ;

'My mistress actually has anger in her and just doesn't show it; it's not that she has no anger.

mayhamevete kammantā susaṁvihitā, yena me ayyā santaṁyeva ajjhattaṁ kopaṁ na pātukaroti, no asantaṁ.

It's just because my work is well-organized that she doesn't show anger, even though she still has it inside.

Yannūnāhaṁ bhiyyoso mattāya ayyaṁ vīmaṁseyyan'ti.

Why don't I test my mistress further?'

Atha kho, bhikkhave, kāḷī dāsī divātaraṁyeva uṭṭhāsi.

So Kāḷī got up later in the day.

Atha kho, bhikkhave, vedehikā gahapatānī kāḷiṁ dāsiṁ etadavoca:

Vedehikā said to her,

'he je kāḷī'ti.

'Oi wench, Kāḷī!'

'Kiṁ, ayye'ti?

'What is it, madam?'

'Kiṁ, je, divātaraṁ uṭṭhāsī'ti?

'You're getting up even later in the day—what's up with you, wench?'

'Na khvayye, kiñcī'ti.

'Nothing, madam.'

'No vata re kiñci, pāpi dāsi, divātaraṁ uṭṭhāsī'ti kupitā anattamanā anattamanavācaṁ nicchāresi.

'Oh, so nothing's up, you naughty maid, but you get up later in the day!' Angry and upset, she blurted out angry words.

Atha kho, bhikkhave, kāḷiyā dāsiyā etadahosi:

Then Kāḷī thought,

'santaṁyeva kho me ayyā ajjhattaṁ kopaṁ na pātukaroti, no asantaṁ.

'My mistress actually has anger in her and just doesn't show it; it's not that she has no anger.

Mayhamevete kammantā susaṁvihitā, yena me ayyā santaṁyeva ajjhattaṁ kopaṁ na pātukaroti, no asantaṁ.

It's just because my work is well-organized that she doesn't show anger, even though she still has it inside.

Yannūnāhaṁ bhiyyoso mattāya ayyaṁ vīmaṁseyyan'ti.

Why don't I test my mistress further?'

Atha kho, bhikkhave, kāḷī dāsī divātaraṁyeva uṭṭhāsi.

So Kāḷī got up even later in the day.

Atha kho, bhikkhave, vedehikā gahapatānī kāḷiṁ dāsiṁ etadavoca:

Vedehikā said to her,

'he je kāḷī'ti.

'Oi wench, Kāḷī!'

'Kiṁ, ayye'ti?

'What is it, madam?'

'Kiṁ, je, divā uṭṭhāsī'ti?

'You're getting up even later in the day—what's up with you, wench?'

'Na khvayye, kiñcī'ti.

'Nothing, madam.'

'No vata re kiñci, pāpi dāsi, divā uṭṭhāsī'ti kupitā anattamanā aggaḷasūciṁ gahetvā sīse pahāraṁ adāsi, sīsaṁ vobhindi.

'Oh, so nothing's up, you naughty maid, but you get up even later in the day!' Angry and upset, she grabbed a rolling-pin and hit Kāḷī on the head, cracking it open.

Atha kho, bhikkhave, kāḷī dāsī bhinnena sīsena lohitena galantena paṭivissakānaṁ ujjhāpesi:

Then Kāḷī, with blood pouring from her cracked skull, denounced her mistress to the neighbors,

'passathayye, soratāya kammaṁ;

'See, ladies, what the sweet one did!

passathayye, nivātāya kammaṁ, passathayye, upasantāya kammaṁ.

See what the even-tempered one did! See what the calm one did!

Kathañhi nāma ekadāsikāya divā uṭṭhāsīti kupitā anattamanā aggaḷasūciṁ gahetvā sīse pahāraṁ dassati, sīsaṁ vobhindissatī'ti.

How on earth can she grab a rolling-pin and hit her only maid on the head, cracking it open, just for getting up late?'

Atha kho, bhikkhave, vedehikāya gahapatāniyā aparena samayena evaṁ pāpako kittisaddo abbhuggacchi:

Then after some time the housewife Vedehikā got this bad reputation:

'caṇḍī vedehikā gahapatānī, anivātā vedehikā gahapatānī, anupasantā vedehikā gahapatānī'ti.

'The housewife Vedehikā is fierce, ill-tempered, and not calm at all.'

Evameva kho, bhikkhave, idhekacco bhikkhu tāvadeva soratasorato hoti nivātanivāto hoti upasantūpasanto hoti yāva na amanāpā vacanapathā phusanti.

In the same way, a mendicant may be the sweetest of the sweet, the most even-tempered of the even-tempered, the calmest of the calm, so long as they don't encounter any disagreeable criticism.

Yato ca, bhikkhave, bhikkhuṁ amanāpā vacanapathā phusanti, atha bhikkhu 'sorato'ti veditabbo, 'nivāto'ti veditabbo, 'upasanto'ti veditabbo.

But it's when they encounter disagreeable criticism that you'll know whether they're really sweet, even-tempered, and calm.

Nāhaṁ taṁ, bhikkhave, bhikkhuṁ 'suvaco'ti vadāmi yo cīvarapiṇḍapātasenāsanagilānappaccayabhesajjaparikkhārahetu suvaco hoti, sovacassataṁ āpajjati.

I don't say that a mendicant is easy to admonish if they make themselves easy to admonish only for the sake of robes, almsfood, lodgings, and medicines and supplies for the sick.

Taṁ kissa hetu?

Why is that?

Tañhi so, bhikkhave, bhikkhu cīvarapiṇḍapātasenāsanagilānappaccayabhesajjaparikkhāraṁ alabhamāno na suvaco hoti, na sovacassataṁ āpajjati.

Because when they don't get robes, almsfood, lodgings, and medicines and supplies for the sick, they're no longer easy to admonish.

Yo ca kho, bhikkhave, bhikkhu dhammaṁyeva sakkaronto, dhammaṁ garuṁ karonto, dhammaṁ mānento, dhammaṁ pūjento, dhammaṁ apacāyamāno suvaco hoti, sovacassataṁ āpajjati, tamahaṁ 'suvaco'ti vadāmi.

But when a mendicant is easy to admonish purely because they honor, respect, revere, worship, and venerate the teaching, then I say that they're easy to admonish.

Tasmātiha, bhikkhave, 'dhammaṁyeva sakkarontā, dhammaṁ garuṁ karontā, dhammaṁ mānentā, dhammaṁ pūjentā, dhammaṁ apacāyamānā suvacā bhavissāma, sovacassataṁ āpajjissāmā'ti.

So, mendicants, you should train yourselves: 'We will be easy to admonish purely because we honor, respect, revere, worship, and venerate the teaching.'

Evañhi vo, bhikkhave, sikkhitabbaṁ.

That's how you should train.

Pañcime, bhikkhave, vacanapathā yehi vo pare vadamānā vadeyyuṁ—

Mendicants, there are these five ways in which others might criticize you.

kālena vā akālena vā;

Their speech may be timely or untimely,

bhūtena vā abhūtena vā;

true or false,

saṇhena vā pharusena vā;

gentle or harsh,

atthasaṁhitena vā anatthasaṁhitena vā;

beneficial or harmful,

mettacittā vā dosantarā vā.

from a heart of love or from secret hate.

Kālena vā, bhikkhave, pare vadamānā vadeyyuṁ akālena vā;

When others criticize you, they may do so in any of these ways.

bhūtena vā, bhikkhave, pare vadamānā vadeyyuṁ abhūtena vā;

saṇhena vā, bhikkhave, pare vadamānā vadeyyuṁ pharusena vā;

atthasaṁhitena vā, bhikkhave, pare vadamānā vadeyyuṁ anatthasaṁhitena vā;

mettacittā vā, bhikkhave, pare vadamānā vadeyyuṁ dosantarā vā.

Tatrāpi vo, bhikkhave, evaṁ sikkhitabbaṁ:

If that happens, you should train like this:

'na ceva no cittaṁ vipariṇataṁ bhavissati, na ca pāpikaṁ vācaṁ nicchāressāma, hitānukampī ca viharissāma mettacittā, na dosantarā.

'Our minds will remain unaffected. We will blurt out no bad words. We will remain full of compassion, with a heart of love and no secret hate.

Tañca puggalaṁ mettāsahagatena cetasā pharitvā viharissāma, tadārammaṇañca sabbāvantaṁ lokaṁ mettāsahagatena cittena vipulena mahaggatena appamāṇena averena abyābajjhena pharitvā viharissāmā'ti.

We will meditate spreading a heart of love to that person. And with them as a basis, we will meditate spreading a heart full of love to everyone in the world— abundant, expansive, limitless, free of enmity and ill will.'

Evañhi vo, bhikkhave, sikkhitabbaṁ.

That's how you should train.

Seyyathāpi, bhikkhave, puriso āgaccheyya kudālapiṭakaṁ ādāya.

Suppose a person was to come along carrying a spade and basket

So evaṁ vadeyya:

and say,

'ahaṁ imaṁ mahāpathaviṁ apathaviṁ karissāmī'ti.

'I shall make this great earth be without earth!'

So tatra tatra vikhaṇeyya, tatra tatra vikireyya, tatra tatra oṭṭhubheyya, tatra tatra omutteyya:

And they'd dig all over, scatter all over, spit all over, and urinate all over, saying,

'apathavī bhavasi, apathavī bhavasī'ti.

'Be without earth! Be without earth!'

Taṁ kiṁ maññatha, bhikkhave,

What do you think, mendicants?

api nu so puriso imaṁ mahāpathaviṁ apathaviṁ kareyyā"ti?

Could that person make this great earth be without earth?"

"No hetaṁ, bhante".

"No, sir.

"Taṁ kissa hetu"?

Why is that?

"Ayañhi, bhante, mahāpathavī gambhīrā appameyyā.

Because this great earth is deep and limitless.

Sā na sukarā apathavī kātuṁ;

It's not easy to make it be without earth.

yāvadeva ca pana so puriso kilamathassa vighātassa bhāgī assā"ti.

That person will eventually get weary and frustrated."

"Evameva kho, bhikkhave, pañcime vacanapathā yehi vo pare vadamānā vadeyyuṁ—

"In the same way, there are these five ways in which others might criticize you.

kālena vā akālena vā;

Their speech may be timely or untimely,

bhūtena vā abhūtena vā;

true or false,

saṇhena vā pharusena vā;

gentle or harsh,

atthasaṁhitena vā anatthasaṁhitena vā;

beneficial or harmful,

mettacittā vā dosantarā vā.

from a heart of love or from secret hate.

Kālena vā, bhikkhave, pare vadamānā vadeyyuṁ akālena vā;

When others criticize you, they may do so in any of these ways.

bhūtena vā bhikkhave, pare vadamānā vadeyyuṁ abhūtena vā;

saṇhena vā, bhikkhave, pare vadamānā vadeyyuṁ pharusena vā;

atthasaṁhitena vā, bhikkhave, pare vadamānā vadeyyuṁ anatthasaṁhitena vā;

mettacittā vā, bhikkhave, pare vadamānā vadeyyuṁ dosantarā vā.

Tatrāpi vo, bhikkhave, evaṁ sikkhitabbaṁ:

If that happens, you should train like this:

'na ceva no cittaṁ vipariṇataṁ bhavissati, na ca pāpikaṁ vācaṁ niccharessāma, hitānukampī ca viharissāma mettacittā na dosantarā.

'Our minds will remain unaffected. We will blurt out no bad words. We will remain full of compassion, with a heart of love and no secret hate.

Tañca puggalaṁ mettāsahagatena cetasā pharitvā viharissāma, tadārammaṇañca sabbāvantaṁ lokaṁ pathavisamena cetasā vipulena mahaggatena appamāṇena averena abyābajjhena pharitvā viharissāmā'ti.

We will meditate spreading a heart of love to that person. And with them as a basis, we will meditate spreading a heart like the earth to everyone in the world— abundant, expansive, limitless, free of enmity and ill will.'

Evañhi vo, bhikkhave, sikkhitabbaṁ.

That's how you should train.

Seyyathāpi, bhikkhave, puriso āgaccheyya lākhaṁ vā haliddiṁ vā nīlaṁ vā mañjiṭṭhaṁ vā ādāya.

Suppose a person was to come along with dye such as red lac, turmeric, indigo, or rose madder,

So evaṁ vadeyya:

and say,

'ahaṁ imasmiṁ ākāse rūpaṁ likhissāmi, rūpapātubhāvaṁ karissāmī'ti.

'I shall draw pictures on the sky, making pictures appear there.'

Taṁ kiṁ maññatha, bhikkhave,

What do you think, mendicants?

api nu so puriso imasmiṁ ākāse rūpaṁ likheyya, rūpapātubhāvaṁ kareyyā"ti?

Could that person draw pictures on the sky?"

"No hetaṁ, bhante".

"No, sir.

"Taṁ kissa hetu"?

Why is that?

"Ayañhi, bhante, ākāso arūpī anidassano.

Because the sky is formless and invisible.

Tattha na sukaraṁ rūpaṁ likhituṁ, rūpapātubhāvaṁ kātuṁ;

It's not easy to draw pictures there.

yāvadeva ca pana so puriso kilamathassa vighātassa bhāgī assā"ti.

That person will eventually get weary and frustrated."

"Evameva kho, bhikkhave, pañcime vacanapathā yehi vo pare vadamānā vadeyyuṁ kālena vā akālena vā …pe…

"In the same way, there are these five ways in which others might criticize you …

tadārammaṇañca sabbāvantaṁ lokaṁ ākāsasamena cetasā vipulena mahaggatena appamāṇena averena abyābajjhena pharitvā viharissāmā'ti.

Evañhi vo, bhikkhave, sikkhitabbaṁ.

Seyyathāpi, bhikkhave, puriso āgaccheyya ādittaṁ tiṇukkaṁ ādāya.

Suppose a person was to come along carrying a blazing grass torch,

So evaṁ vadeyya:

and say,

'ahaṁ imāya ādittāya tiṇukkāya gaṅgaṁ nadiṁ santāpessāmi samparitāpessāmī'ti.

'I shall burn and scorch the river Ganges with this blazing grass torch.'

Taṁ kiṁ maññatha, bhikkhave,

What do you think, mendicants?

api nu so puriso ādittāya tiṇukkāya gaṅgaṁ nadiṁ santāpeyya samparitāpeyyā"ti?

Could that person burn and scorch the river Ganges with a blazing grass torch?"

"No hetaṁ, bhante".

"No, sir.

"Taṁ kissa hetu"?

Why is that?

"Gaṅgā hi, bhante, nadī gambhīrā appameyyā.

Because the river Ganges is deep and limitless.

Sā na sukarā ādittāya tiṇukkāya santāpetuṁ samparitāpetuṁ;

It's not easy to burn and scorch it with a blazing grass torch.

yāvadeva ca pana so puriso kilamathassa vighātassa bhāgī assā"ti.

That person will eventually get weary and frustrated."

"Evameva kho, bhikkhave, pañcime vacanapathā yehi vo pare vadamānā vadeyyuṁ kālena vā akālena vā …pe…

"In the same way, there are these five ways in which others might criticize you …

tadārammaṇañca sabbāvantaṁ lokaṁ gaṅgāsamena cetasā vipulena mahaggatena appamāṇena averena abyābajjhena pharitvā viharissāmā'ti.

Evañhi vo, bhikkhave, sikkhitabbaṁ.

Seyyathāpi, bhikkhave, biḷārabhastā madditā sumadditā suparimadditā, mudukā tūlinī chinnasassarā chinnabhabbharā.

Suppose there was a catskin bag that was rubbed, well-rubbed, very well-rubbed, soft, silky, rid of rustling and crackling.

Atha puriso āgaccheyya kaṭṭhaṁ vā kathalaṁ vā ādāya.

Then a person comes along carrying a stick or a stone,

So evaṁ vadeyya:

and says,

'ahaṁ imaṁ biḷārabhastaṁ madditaṁ sumadditaṁ suparimadditaṁ, mudukaṁ tūliniṁ, chinnasassaraṁ chinnabhabbharaṁ kaṭṭhena vā kathalena vā sarasaraṁ karissāmi bharabharaṁ karissāmī'ti.

'I shall make this soft catskin bag rustle and crackle with this stick or stone.'

Taṁ kiṁ maññatha, bhikkhave,

What do you think, mendicants?

api nu so puriso amuṁ biḷārabhastaṁ madditaṁ sumadditaṁ suparimadditaṁ, mudukaṁ tūliniṁ, chinnasassaraṁ chinnabhabbharaṁ kaṭṭhena vā kathalena vā sarasaraṁ kareyya, bharabharaṁ kareyyā"ti?

Could that person make that soft catskin bag rustle and crackle with that stick or stone?"

"No hetaṁ, bhante".

"No, sir.

"Taṁ kissa hetu"?

Why is that?

"Amu hi, bhante, biḷārabhastā madditā sumadditā suparimadditā, mudukā tūlinī, chinnasassarā chinnabhabbharā.

Because that catskin bag is rubbed, well-rubbed, very well-rubbed, soft, silky, rid of rustling and crackling.

Sā na sukarā kaṭṭhena vā kathalena vā sarasaraṁ kātuṁ bharabharaṁ kātuṁ;

It's not easy to make it rustle or crackle with a stick or stone.

yāvadeva ca pana so puriso kilamathassa vighātassa bhāgī assā"ti.

That person will eventually get weary and frustrated."

"Evameva kho, bhikkhave, pañcime vacanapathā yehi vo pare vadamānā vadeyyuṁ

"In the same way, there are these five ways in which others might criticize you.

kālena vā akālena vā;

Their speech may be timely or untimely,

bhūtena vā abhūtena vā;

true or false,

saṇhena vā pharusena vā;

gentle or harsh,

atthasaṁhitena vā anatthasaṁhitena vā;

beneficial or harmful,

mettacittā vā dosantarā vā.

from a heart of love or from secret hate.

Kālena vā, bhikkhave, pare vadamānā vadeyyuṁ akālena vā;

When others criticize you, they may do so in any of these ways.

bhūtena vā, bhikkhave, pare vadamānā vadeyyuṁ abhūtena vā;

saṇhena vā, bhikkhave, pare vadamānā vadeyyuṁ pharusena vā;

atthasaṁhitena vā, bhikkhave, pare vadamānā vadeyyuṁ anatthasaṁhitena vā;

mettacittā vā, bhikkhave, pare vadamānā vadeyyuṁ dosantarā vā.

Tatrāpi vo, bhikkhave, evaṁ sikkhitabbaṁ:

If that happens, you should train like this:

'na ceva no cittaṁ vipariṇataṁ bhavissati, na ca pāpikaṁ vācaṁ nicchāressāma hitānukampī ca viharissāma mettacittā na dosantarā.

'Our minds will remain unaffected. We will blurt out no bad words. We will remain full of compassion, with a heart of love and no secret hate.

Tañca puggalaṁ mettāsahagatena cetasā pharitvā viharissāma, tadārammaṇañca sabbāvantaṁ lokaṁ biḷārabhastāsamena cetasā vipulena mahaggatena appamāṇena averena abyābajjhena pharitvā viharissāmā'ti.

We will meditate spreading a heart of love to that person. And with them as a basis, we will meditate spreading a heart like a catskin bag to everyone in the world—abundant, expansive, limitless, free of enmity and ill will.'

Evañhi vo, bhikkhave, sikkhitabbaṁ.

That's how you should train.

Ubhatodaṇḍakena cepi, bhikkhave, kakacena corā ocarakā aṅgamaṅgāni okanteyyuṁ, tatrāpi yo mano padūseyya, na me so tena sāsanakaro.

Even if low-down bandits were to sever you limb from limb with a two-handled saw, anyone who had a malevolent thought on that account would not be following my instructions.

Tatrāpi vo, bhikkhave, evaṁ sikkhitabbaṁ:

If that happens, you should train like this:

'na ceva no cittaṁ vipariṇataṁ bhavissati, na ca pāpikaṁ vācaṁ nicchāressāma, hitānukampī ca viharissāma mettacittā na dosantarā.

'Our minds will remain unaffected. We will blurt out no bad words. We will remain full of compassion, with a heart of love and no secret hate.

Tañca puggalaṁ mettāsahagatena cetasā pharitvā viharissāma tadārammaṇañca sabbāvantaṁ lokaṁ mettāsahagatena cetasā vipulena mahaggatena appamāṇena averena abyābajjhena pharitvā viharissāmā'ti.

We will meditate spreading a heart of love to that person. And with them as a basis, we will meditate spreading a heart full of love to everyone in the world—abundant, expansive, limitless, free of enmity and ill will.'

Evañhi vo, bhikkhave, sikkhitabbaṁ.

That's how you should train.

Imañca tumhe, bhikkhave, kakacūpamaṁ ovādaṁ abhikkhaṇaṁ manasi kareyyātha.

If you frequently reflect on this advice—the simile of the saw—

Passatha no tumhe, bhikkhave, taṁ vacanapathaṁ, aṇuṁ vā thūlaṁ vā, yaṁ tumhe nādhivāseyyāthā"ti?

do you see any criticism, large or small, that you could not endure?"

"No hetaṁ, bhante".

"No, sir."

"Tasmātiha, bhikkhave, imaṁ kakacūpamaṁ ovādaṁ abhikkhaṇaṁ manasikarotha.

"So, mendicants, you should frequently reflect on this advice, the simile of the saw.

Taṁ vo bhavissati dīgharattaṁ hitāya sukhāyā"ti.

This will be for your lasting welfare and happiness."

Idamavoca bhagavā.

That is what the Buddha said.

Attamanā te bhikkhū bhagavato bhāsitaṁ abhinandunti.

Satisfied, the mendicants were happy with what the Buddha said.

Kakacūpamasuttaṁ niṭṭhitaṁ paṭhamaṁ.

22 Alagaddupamasutta:

The Simile of the Snake

Evaṁ me sutaṁ—

So I have heard.

ekaṁ samayaṁ bhagavā sāvatthiyaṁ viharati jetavane anāthapiṇḍikassa ārāme.

At one time the Buddha was staying near Sāvatthī in Jeta's Grove, Anāthapiṇḍika's monastery.

Tena kho pana samayena ariṭṭhassa nāma bhikkhuno gaddhabādhipubbassa evarūpaṁ pāpakaṁ diṭṭhigataṁ uppannaṁ hoti:

Now at that time a mendicant called Ariṭṭha, who had previously been a vulture trapper, had the following harmful misconception:

"tathāhaṁ bhagavatā dhammaṁ desitaṁ ājānāmi yathā yeme antarāyikā dhammā vuttā bhagavatā te paṭisevato nālaṁ antarāyāyā"ti.

"As I understand the Buddha's teachings, the acts that he says are obstructions are not really obstructions for the one who performs them."

Assosuṁ kho sambahulā bhikkhū:

Several mendicants heard about this.

"ariṭṭhassa kira nāma bhikkhuno gaddhabādhipubbassa evarūpaṁ pāpakaṁ diṭṭhigataṁ uppannaṁ:

'tathāhaṁ bhagavatā dhammaṁ desitaṁ ājānāmi yathā yeme antarāyikā dhammā vuttā bhagavatā te paṭisevato nālaṁ antarāyāyā'"ti.

Atha kho te bhikkhū yena ariṭṭho bhikkhu gaddhabādhipubbo tenupasaṅkamiṁsu; upasaṅkamitvā ariṭṭhaṁ bhikkhuṁ gaddhabādhipubbaṁ etadavocuṁ:

They went up to Ariṭṭha and said to him,

"saccaṁ kira te, āvuso ariṭṭha, evarūpaṁ pāpakaṁ diṭṭhigataṁ uppannaṁ:

"Is it really true, Reverend Ariṭṭha, that you have such a harmful misconception:

'tathāhaṁ bhagavatā dhammaṁ desitaṁ ājānāmi yathā yeme antarāyikā dhammā vuttā bhagavatā te paṭisevato nālaṁ antarāyāyā'"ti.

'As I understand the Buddha's teachings, the acts that he says are obstructions are not really obstructions for the one who performs them'?"

"Evaṁ byā kho ahaṁ, āvuso, bhagavatā dhammaṁ desitaṁ ājānāmi yathā yeme antarāyikā dhammā vuttā bhagavatā te paṭisevato nālaṁ antarāyāyā"ti.

"Absolutely, reverends. As I understand the Buddha's teachings, the acts that he says are obstructions are not really obstructions for the one who performs them."

Atha kho tepi bhikkhū ariṭṭhaṁ bhikkhuṁ gaddhabādhipubbaṁ etasmā pāpakā diṭṭhigatā vivecetukāmā samanuyuñjanti samanugāhanti samanubhāsanti:

Then, wishing to dissuade Ariṭṭha from his view, the mendicants pursued, pressed, and grilled him,

"mā hevaṁ, āvuso ariṭṭha, avaca, mā bhagavantaṁ abbhācikkhi; na hi sādhu bhagavato abbhakkhānaṁ, na hi bhagavā evaṁ vadeyya.

"Don't say that, Ariṭṭha! Don't misrepresent the Buddha, for misrepresentation of the Buddha is not good. And the Buddha would not say that.

Anekapariyāyenāvuso ariṭṭha, antarāyikā dhammā antarāyikā vuttā bhagavatā, alañca pana te paṭisevato antarāyāya.

In many ways the Buddha has said that obstructive acts are obstructive, and that they really do obstruct the one who performs them.

Appassādā kāmā vuttā bhagavatā bahudukkhā bahupāyāsā, ādīnavo ettha bhiyyo.

The Buddha says that sensual pleasures give little gratification and much suffering and distress, and they are all the more full of drawbacks.

Aṭṭhikaṅkalūpamā kāmā vuttā bhagavatā …

With the similes of a skeleton …

maṁsapesūpamā kāmā vuttā bhagavatā …

a lump of meat …

tiṇukkūpamā kāmā vuttā bhagavatā …

a grass torch …

aṅgārakāsūpamā kāmā vuttā bhagavatā …

a pit of glowing coals …

supinakūpamā kāmā vuttā bhagavatā …

a dream …

yācitakūpamā kāmā vuttā bhagavatā …

borrowed goods …

rukkhaphalūpamā kāmā vuttā bhagavatā …

fruit on a tree …

asisūnūpamā kāmā vuttā bhagavatā …

a butcher's knife and chopping block …

sattisūlūpamā kāmā vuttā bhagavatā …

a staking sword …

sappasirūpamā kāmā vuttā bhagavatā bahudukkhā bahupāyāsā, ādīnavo ettha bhiyyo"ti.

a snake's head, the Buddha says that sensual pleasures give little gratification and much suffering and distress, and they are all the more full of drawbacks."

Evampi kho ariṭṭho bhikkhu gaddhabādhipubbo tehi bhikkhūhi samanuyuñjiyamāno samanugāhiyamāno samanubhāsiyamāno tadeva pāpakaṃ diṭṭhigataṃ thāmasā parāmāsā abhinivissa voharati:

But even though the mendicants pursued, pressed, and grilled him in this way, Ariṭṭha obstinately stuck to his misconception and insisted on stating it.

"evaṃ byā kho ahaṃ, āvuso, bhagavatā dhammaṃ desitaṃ ājānāmi yathā yeme antarāyikā dhammā vuttā bhagavatā te paṭisevato nālaṃ antarāyāyā"ti.

Yato kho te bhikkhū nāsakkhiṃsu ariṭṭhaṃ bhikkhuṃ gaddhabādhipubbaṃ etasmā pāpakā diṭṭhigatā vivecetuṃ, atha kho te bhikkhū yena bhagavā tenupasaṅkamiṃsu; upasaṅkamitvā bhagavantaṃ abhivādetvā ekamantaṃ nisīdiṃsu. Ekamantaṃ nisinnā kho te bhikkhū bhagavantaṃ etadavocuṃ:

When they weren't able to dissuade Ariṭṭha from his view, the mendicants went to the Buddha, bowed, sat down to one side, and told him what had happened.

"ariṭṭhassa nāma, bhante, bhikkhuno gaddhabādhipubbassa evarūpaṃ pāpakaṃ diṭṭhigataṃ uppannaṃ:

'tathāhaṃ bhagavatā dhammaṃ desitaṃ ājānāmi yathā yeme antarāyikā dhammā vuttā bhagavatā te paṭisevato nālaṃ antarāyāyā'ti.

Assumha kho mayaṃ, bhante:

'ariṭṭhassa kira nāma bhikkhuno gaddhabādhipubbassa evarūpaṃ pāpakaṃ diṭṭhigataṃ uppannaṃ—

tathāhaṃ bhagavatā dhammaṃ desitaṃ ājānāmi yathā yeme antarāyikā dhammā vuttā bhagavatā te paṭisevato nālaṃ antarāyāyā'ti.

Atha kho mayaṃ, bhante, yena ariṭṭho bhikkhu gaddhabādhipubbo tenupasaṅkamimha; upasaṅkamitvā ariṭṭhaṃ bhikkhuṃ gaddhabādhipubbaṃ etadavocumha:

'saccaṃ kira te, āvuso ariṭṭha, evarūpaṃ pāpakaṃ diṭṭhigataṃ uppannaṃ—

tathāhaṃ bhagavatā dhammaṃ desitaṃ ājānāmi yathā yeme antarāyikā dhammā vuttā bhagavatā te paṭisevato nālaṃ antarāyāyā'ti?

Evaṃ vutte, bhante, ariṭṭho bhikkhu gaddhabādhipubbo amhe etadavoca:

'evaṃ byā kho ahaṃ, āvuso, bhagavatā dhammaṃ desitaṃ ājānāmi yathā yeme antarāyikā dhammā vuttā bhagavatā te paṭisevato nālaṃ antarāyāyā'ti.

Atha kho mayaṃ, bhante, ariṭṭhaṃ bhikkhuṃ gaddhabādhipubbaṃ etasmā pāpakā diṭṭhigatā vivecetukāmā samanuyuñjimha samanugāhimha samanubhāsimha:

'mā hevaṁ, āvuso ariṭṭha, avaca, mā bhagavantaṁ abbhācikkhi; na hi sādhu bhagavato abbhakkhānaṁ, na hi bhagavā evaṁ vadeyya.

Anekapariyāyenāvuso ariṭṭha, antarāyikā dhammā antarāyikā vuttā bhagavatā, alañca pana te paṭisevato antarāyāya.

Appassādā kāmā vuttā bhagavatā bahudukkhā bahupāyāsā, ādīnavo ettha bhiyyo.

Aṭṭhikaṅkalūpamā kāmā vuttā bhagavatā …pe…

sappasirūpamā kāmā vuttā bhagavatā bahudukkhā bahupāyāsā, ādīnavo ettha bhiyyo'ti.

Evampi kho, bhante, ariṭṭho bhikkhu gaddhabādhipubbo amhehi samanuyuñjiyamāno samanugāhiyamāno samanubhāsiyamāno tadeva pāpakaṁ diṭṭhigataṁ thāmasā parāmāsā abhinivissa voharati:

'evaṁ byā kho ahaṁ, āvuso, bhagavatā dhammaṁ desitaṁ ājānāmi yathā yeme antarāyikā dhammā vuttā bhagavatā te paṭisevato nālaṁ antarāyāyā'ti.

Yato kho mayaṁ, bhante, nāsakkhimha ariṭṭhaṁ bhikkhuṁ gaddhabādhipubbaṁ etasmā pāpakā diṭṭhigatā vivecetuṁ, atha mayaṁ etamatthaṁ bhagavato ārocemā"ti.

Atha kho bhagavā aññataraṁ bhikkhuṁ āmantesi:

So the Buddha addressed a certain monk,

"ehi tvaṁ, bhikkhu, mama vacanena ariṭṭhaṁ bhikkhuṁ gaddhabādhipubbaṁ āmantehi:

"Please, monk, in my name tell the mendicant Ariṭṭha, formerly a vulture trapper, that

'satthā taṁ, āvuso ariṭṭha, āmantetī'"ti.

the teacher summons him."

"Evaṁ, bhante"ti kho so bhikkhu bhagavato paṭissutvā, yena ariṭṭho bhikkhu gaddhabādhipubbo tenupasaṅkami; upasaṅkamitvā ariṭṭhaṁ bhikkhuṁ gaddhabādhipubbaṁ etadavoca:

"Yes, sir," that monk replied. He went to Ariṭṭha and said to him,

"satthā taṁ, āvuso ariṭṭha, āmantetī"ti.

"Reverend Ariṭṭha, the teacher summons you."

"Evamāvuso"ti kho ariṭṭho bhikkhu gaddhabādhipubbo tassa bhikkhuno paṭissutvā yena bhagavā tenupasaṅkami; upasaṅkamitvā bhagavantaṁ abhivādetvā ekamantaṁ nisīdi. Ekamantaṁ nisinnaṁ kho ariṭṭhaṁ bhikkhuṁ gaddhabādhipubbaṁ bhagavā etadavoca:

"Yes, reverend," Ariṭṭha replied. He went to the Buddha, bowed, and sat down to one side. The Buddha said to him,

"saccaṁ kira te, ariṭṭha, evarūpaṁ pāpakaṁ diṭṭhigataṁ uppannaṁ:

"Is it really true, Ariṭṭha, that you have such a harmful misconception:

'tathāhaṁ bhagavatā dhammaṁ desitaṁ ājānāmi yathā yeme antarāyikā dhammā vuttā bhagavatā te paṭisevato nālaṁ antarāyāyā'"ti?

'As I understand the Buddha's teachings, the acts that he says are obstructions are not really obstructions for the one who performs them'?"

"Evaṁ byā kho ahaṁ, bhante, bhagavatā dhammaṁ desitaṁ ājānāmi: 'yathā yeme antarāyikā dhammā vuttā bhagavatā te paṭisevato nālaṁ antarāyāyā'"ti.

"Absolutely, sir. As I understand the Buddha's teachings, the acts that he says are obstructions are not really obstructions for the one who performs them."

"Kassa kho nāma tvaṁ, moghapurisa, mayā evaṁ dhammaṁ desitaṁ ājānāsi?

"Silly man, who on earth have you ever known me to teach in that way?

Nanu mayā, moghapurisa, anekapariyāyena antarāyikā dhammā antarāyikā vuttā? Alañca pana te paṭisevato antarāyāya.

Haven't I said in many ways that obstructive acts are obstructive, and that they really do obstruct the one who performs them?

Appassādā kāmā vuttā mayā, bahudukkhā bahupāyāsā, ādīnavo ettha bhiyyo.

I've said that sensual pleasures give little gratification and much suffering and distress, and they are all the more full of drawbacks.

Aṭṭhikaṅkalūpamā kāmā vuttā mayā ...

With the similes of a skeleton ...

maṁsapesūpamā kāmā vuttā mayā ...

a lump of meat ...

tiṇukkūpamā kāmā vuttā mayā ...

a grass torch ...

aṅgārakāsūpamā kāmā vuttā mayā ...

a pit of glowing coals ...

supinakūpamā kāmā vuttā mayā ...

a dream …

yācitakūpamā kāmā vuttā mayā …

borrowed goods …

rukkhaphalūpamā kāmā vuttā mayā …

fruit on a tree …

asisūnūpamā kāmā vuttā mayā …

a butcher's knife and chopping block …

sattisūlūpamā kāmā vuttā mayā …

a staking sword …

sappasirūpamā kāmā vuttā mayā, bahudukkhā bahupāyāsā, ādīnavo ettha bhiyyo.

a snake's head, I've said that sensual pleasures give little gratification and much suffering and distress, and they are all the more full of drawbacks.

Atha ca pana tvaṁ, moghapurisa, attanā duggahitena amhe ceva abbhācikkhasi, attānañca khanasi, bahuñca apuññaṁ pasavasi.

But still you misrepresent me by your wrong grasp, harm yourself, and make much bad karma.

Tañhi te, moghapurisa, bhavissati dīgharattaṁ ahitāya dukkhāyā"ti.

This will be for your lasting harm and suffering."

Atha kho bhagavā bhikkhū āmantesi:

Then the Buddha said to the mendicants,

"Taṁ kiṁ maññatha, bhikkhave,

"What do you think, mendicants?

api nāyaṁ ariṭṭho bhikkhu gaddhabādhipubbo usmīkatopi imasmiṁ dhammavinaye"ti?

Has this mendicant Ariṭṭha kindled even a spark of wisdom in this teaching and training?"

"Kiñhi siyā, bhante;

"How could that be, sir?

no hetaṁ, bhante"ti.

No, sir."

Evaṁ vutte, ariṭṭho bhikkhu gaddhabādhipubbo tuṇhībhūto maṅkubhūto pattakkhandho adhomukho pajjhāyanto appaṭibhāno nisīdi.

When this was said, Ariṭṭha sat silent, dismayed, shoulders drooping, downcast, depressed, with nothing to say.

Atha kho bhagavā ariṭṭhaṁ bhikkhuṁ gaddhabādhipubbaṁ tuṇhībhūtaṁ maṅkubhūtaṁ pattakkhandhaṁ adhomukhaṁ pajjhāyantaṁ appaṭibhānaṁ viditvā ariṭṭhaṁ bhikkhuṁ gaddhabādhipubbaṁ etadavoca:

Knowing this, the Buddha said,

"paññāyissasi kho tvaṁ, moghapurisa, etena sakena pāpakena diṭṭhigatena.

"Silly man, you will be known by your own harmful misconception.

Idhāhaṁ bhikkhū paṭipucchissāmī"ti.

I'll question the mendicants about this."

Atha kho bhagavā bhikkhū āmantesi:

Then the Buddha said to the mendicants,

"tumhepi me, bhikkhave, evaṁ dhammaṁ desitaṁ ājānātha yathāyaṁ ariṭṭho bhikkhu gaddhabādhipubbo attanā duggahitena amhe ceva abbhācikkhati, attānañca khanati, bahuñca apuññaṁ pasavatī"ti?

"Mendicants, do you understand my teachings as Ariṭṭha does, when he misrepresents me by his wrong grasp, harms himself, and makes much bad karma?"

"No hetaṁ, bhante.

"No, sir.

Anekapariyāyena hi no, bhante, antarāyikā dhammā antarāyikā vuttā bhagavatā;

For in many ways the Buddha has said that obstructive acts are obstructive, and that they really do obstruct the one who performs them.

alañca pana te paṭisevato antarāyāya.

Appassādā kāmā vuttā bhagavatā bahudukkhā bahupāyāsā, ādīnavo ettha bhiyyo.

The Buddha has said that sensual pleasures give little gratification and much suffering and distress, and they are all the more full of drawbacks.

Aṭṭhikaṅkalūpamā kāmā vuttā bhagavatā …pe…

With the similes of a skeleton …

sappasirūpamā kāmā vuttā bhagavatā bahudukkhā bahupāyāsā, ādīnavo ettha bhiyyo"ti.

a snake's head, the Buddha has said that sensual pleasures give little gratification and much suffering and distress, and they are all the more full of drawbacks."

"Sādhu sādhu, bhikkhave, sādhu, kho me tumhe, bhikkhave, evaṁ dhammaṁ desitaṁ ājānātha.

"Good, good, mendicants! It's good that you understand my teaching like this.

Anekapariyāyena hi kho, bhikkhave, antarāyikā dhammā vuttā mayā, alañca pana te paṭisevato antarāyāya.

For in many ways I have said that obstructive acts are obstructive …

Appassādā kāmā vuttā mayā, bahudukkhā bahupāyāsā, ādīnavo ettha bhiyyo.

Aṭṭhikaṅkalūpamā kāmā vuttā mayā …pe…

sappasirūpamā kāmā vuttā mayā, bahudukkhā bahupāyāsā, ādīnavo ettha bhiyyo.

I've said that sensual pleasures give little gratification and much suffering and distress, and they are all the more full of drawbacks.

Atha ca panāyaṁ ariṭṭho bhikkhu gaddhabādhipubbo attanā duggahitena amhe ceva abbhācikkhati, attānañca khanati, bahuñca apuññaṁ pasavati.

But still this Ariṭṭha misrepresents me by his wrong grasp, harms himself, and makes much bad karma.

Tañhi tassa moghapurisassa bhavissati dīgharattaṁ ahitāya dukkhāya.

This will be for his lasting harm and suffering.

So vata, bhikkhave, aññatreva kāmehi aññatra kāmasaññāya aññatra kāmavitakkehi kāme paṭisevissatīti—netaṁ ṭhānaṁ vijjati.

Truly, mendicants, it's not possible to perform sensual acts without sensual pleasures, sensual perceptions, and sensual thoughts.

Idha, bhikkhave, ekacce moghapurisā dhammaṁ pariyāpuṇanti—

Take a foolish person who memorizes the teaching—

suttaṁ, geyyaṁ, veyyākaraṇaṁ, gāthaṁ, udānaṁ, itivuttakaṁ, jātakaṁ, abbhutadhammaṁ, vedallaṁ.

statements, songs, discussions, verses, inspired exclamations, legends, stories of past lives, amazing stories, and classifications.

Te taṁ dhammaṁ pariyāpuṇitvā tesaṁ dhammānaṁ paññāya atthaṁ na upaparikkhanti.

But they don't examine the meaning of those teachings with wisdom,

Tesaṁ te dhammā paññāya atthaṁ anupaparikkhataṁ na nijjhānaṁ khamanti.

and so don't come to a considered acceptance of them.

Te upārambhānisaṁsā ceva dhammaṁ pariyāpuṇanti itivādappamokkhānisaṁsā ca.

They just memorize the teaching for the sake of finding fault and winning debates.

Yassa catthāya dhammaṁ pariyāpuṇanti tañcassa atthaṁ nānubhonti.

They don't realize the goal for which they memorized them.

Tesaṁ te dhammā duggahitā dīgharattaṁ ahitāya dukkhāya saṁvattanti.

Because they're wrongly grasped, those teachings lead to their lasting harm and suffering.

Taṁ kissa hetu?

Why is that?

Duggahitattā, bhikkhave, dhammānaṁ.

Because of their wrong grasp of the teachings.

Seyyathāpi, bhikkhave, puriso alagaddatthiko alagaddagavesī alagaddapariyesanaṁ caramāno.

Suppose there was a person in need of a snake. And while wandering in search of a snake

So passeyya mahantaṁ alagaddaṁ.

they'd see a big snake,

Tamenaṁ bhoge vā naṅguṭṭhe vā gaṇheyya.

and grasp it by the coil or the tail.

Tassa so alagaddo paṭiparivattitvā hatthe vā bāhāya vā aññatarasmiṁ vā aṅgapaccaṅge ḍaṁseyya.

But that snake would twist back and bite them on the hand or the arm or limb,

So tatonidānaṁ maraṇaṁ vā nigaccheyya maraṇamattaṁ vā dukkhaṁ.

resulting in death or deadly pain.

Taṁ kissa hetu?

Why is that?

Duggahitattā, bhikkhave, alagaddassa.

Because of their wrong grasp of the snake.

Evameva kho, bhikkhave, idhekacce moghapurisā dhammaṁ pariyāpuṇanti—

In the same way, a foolish person memorizes the teaching ...

suttaṁ, geyyaṁ, veyyākaraṇaṁ, gāthaṁ, udānaṁ, itivuttakaṁ, jātakaṁ, abbhutadhammaṁ, vedallaṁ.

Te taṁ dhammaṁ pariyāpuṇitvā tesaṁ dhammānaṁ paññāya atthaṁ na upaparikkhanti.

Tesaṁ te dhammā paññāya atthaṁ anupaparikkhataṁ na nijjhānaṁ khamanti.

Te upārambhānisaṁsā ceva dhammaṁ pariyāpuṇanti itivādappamokkhānisaṁsā ca.

Yassa catthāya dhammaṁ pariyāpuṇanti tañcassa atthaṁ nānubhonti.

Tesaṁ te dhammā duggahitā dīgharattaṁ ahitāya dukkhāya saṁvattanti.

and those teachings lead to their lasting harm and suffering.

Taṁ kissa hetu?

Why is that?

Duggahitattā, bhikkhave, dhammānaṁ.

Because of their wrong grasp of the teachings.

Idha pana, bhikkhave, ekacce kulaputtā dhammaṁ pariyāpuṇanti—

Now, take a gentleman who memorizes the teaching—

suttaṁ, geyyaṁ, veyyākaraṇaṁ, gāthaṁ, udānaṁ, itivuttakaṁ, jātakaṁ, abbhutadhammaṁ, vedallaṁ.

statements, songs, discussions, verses, inspired exclamations, legends, stories of past lives, amazing stories, and classifications.

Te taṁ dhammaṁ pariyāpuṇitvā tesaṁ dhammānaṁ paññāya atthaṁ upaparikkhanti.

And once he's memorized them, he examines their meaning with wisdom,

Tesaṁ te dhammā paññāya atthaṁ upaparikkhataṁ nijjhānaṁ khamanti.

and comes to a considered acceptance of them.

Te na ceva upārambhānisamsā dhammam pariyāpuṇanti na itivādappamokkhānisamsā ca.

He doesn't memorize the teaching for the sake of finding fault and winning debates.

Yassa catthāya dhammam pariyāpuṇanti tañcassa attham anubhonti.

He realizes the goal for which he memorized them.

Tesam te dhammā suggahitā dīgharattam hitāya sukhāya samvattanti.

Because they're correctly grasped, those teachings lead to his lasting welfare and happiness.

Tam kissa hetu?

Why is that?

Suggahitattā bhikkhave dhammānam.

Because of his correct grasp of the teachings.

Seyyathāpi, bhikkhave, puriso alagaddatthiko alagaddagavesī alagaddapariyesanam caramāno.

Suppose there was a person in need of a snake. And while wandering in search of a snake

So passeyya mahantam alagaddam.

they'd see a big snake,

Tamenam ajapadena daṇḍena suniggahitam nigganheyya.

and hold it down carefully with a cleft stick.

Ajapadena daṇḍena suniggahitam niggahitvā, gīvāya suggahitam ganheyya.

Only then would they correctly grasp it by the neck.

Kiñcāpi so, bhikkhave, alagaddo tassa purisassa hattham vā bāham vā aññataram vā angapaccangam bhogehi paliveṭheyya, atha kho so neva tatonidānam maranam vā nigaccheyya maranamattam vā dukkham.

And even though that snake might wrap its coils around that person's hand or arm or some other limb, that wouldn't result in death or deadly pain.

Tam kissa hetu?

Why is that?

Suggahitattā, bhikkhave, alagaddassa.

Because of their correct grasp of the snake.

Evameva kho, bhikkhave, idhekacce kulaputtā dhammam pariyāpuṇanti—

In the same way, a gentleman memorizes the teaching …

suttam, geyyam, veyyākaraṇam, gātham, udānam, itivuttakam, jātakam, abbhutadhammam, vedallam.

Te tam dhammam pariyāpuṇitvā tesam dhammānam paññāya attham upaparikkhanti.

Tesam te dhammā paññāya attham upaparikkhatam nijjhānam khamanti.

Te na ceva upārambhānisamsā dhammam pariyāpuṇanti, na itivādappamokkhānisamsā ca.

Yassa catthāya dhammam pariyāpuṇanti, tañcassa attham anubhonti.

Tesam te dhammā suggahitā dīgharattam atthāya hitāya sukhāya samvattanti.

and those teachings lead to his lasting welfare and happiness.

Tam kissa hetu?

Why is that?

Suggahitattā, bhikkhave, dhammānam.

Because of his correct grasp of the teachings.

Tasmātiha, bhikkhave, yassa me bhāsitassa attham ājāneyyātha, tathā nam dhāreyyātha.

So, mendicants, when you understand what I've said, you should remember it accordingly.

Yassa ca pana me bhāsitassa attham na ājāneyyātha, aham vo tattha paṭipucchitabbo, ye vā panāssu viyattā bhikkhū.

But if I've said anything that you don't understand, you should ask me about it, or some competent mendicants.

Kullūpamam vo, bhikkhave, dhammam desessāmi nittharaṇatthāya, no gahaṇatthāya.

Mendicants, I will teach you how the Dhamma is similar to a raft: it's for crossing over, not for holding on.

Taṁ suṇātha, sādhukaṁ manasikarotha, bhāsissāmī”ti.

Listen and pay close attention, I will speak.”

“Evaṁ, bhante”ti kho te bhikkhū bhagavato paccassosuṁ.

“Yes, sir,” they replied.

Bhagavā etadavoca:

The Buddha said this:

“Seyyathāpi, bhikkhave, puriso addhānamaggappaṭipanno.

“Suppose there was a person traveling along the road.

So passeyya mahantaṁ udakaṇṇavam, orimaṁ tīraṁ sāsaṅkaṁ sappaṭibhayaṁ, pārimaṁ tīraṁ khemaṁ appaṭibhayaṁ;

They’d see a large deluge, whose near shore was dubious and perilous, while the far shore was a sanctuary free of peril.

na cassa nāvā santāraṇī uttarasetu vā apārā pāraṁ gamanāya.

But there was no ferryboat or bridge for crossing over.

Tassa evamassa:

They’d think,

‘ayaṁ kho mahāudakaṇṇavo, orimaṁ tīraṁ sāsaṅkaṁ sappaṭibhayaṁ, pārimaṁ tīraṁ khemaṁ appaṭibhayaṁ;

natthi ca nāvā santāraṇī uttarasetu vā apārā pāraṁ gamanāya.

Yannūnāhaṁ tiṇakaṭṭhasākhāpalāsaṁ saṅkaḍḍhitvā, kullaṁ bandhitvā, taṁ kullaṁ nissāya hatthehi ca pādehi ca vāyamamāno sotthinā pāraṁ uttareyyan’ti.

‘Why don’t I gather grass, sticks, branches, and leaves and make a raft? Riding on the raft, and paddling with my hands and feet, I can safely reach the far shore.’

Atha kho so, bhikkhave, puriso tiṇakaṭṭhasākhāpalāsaṁ saṅkaḍḍhitvā, kullaṁ bandhitvā taṁ kullaṁ nissāya hatthehi ca pādehi ca vāyamamāno sotthinā pāraṁ uttareyya.

And so they’d do exactly that.

Tassa purisassa uttiṇṇassa pāraṅgatassa evamassa:

And when they’d crossed over to the far shore, they’d think,

‘bahukāro kho me ayaṁ kullo;

'This raft has been very helpful to me.

imāhaṁ kullaṁ nissāya hatthehi ca pādehi ca vāyamamāno sotthinā pāraṁ uttiṇṇo.

Riding on the raft, and paddling with my hands and feet, I have safely crossed over to the far shore.

Yannūnāhaṁ imaṁ kullaṁ sīse vā āropetvā khandhe vā uccāretvā yena kāmaṁ pakkameyyan'ti.

Why don't I hoist it on my head or pick it up on my shoulder and go wherever I want?'

Taṁ kiṁ maññatha, bhikkhave,

What do you think, mendicants?

api nu so puriso evaṅkārī tasmiṁ kulle kiccakārī assā"ti?

Would that person be doing what should be done with that raft?"

"No hetaṁ, bhante".

"No, sir."

"Kathaṅkārī ca so, bhikkhave, puriso tasmiṁ kulle kiccakārī assa?

"And what, mendicants, should that person do with the raft?

Idha, bhikkhave, tassa purisassa uttiṇṇassa pāraṅgatassa evamassa:

When they'd crossed over they should think,

'bahukāro kho me ayaṁ kullo;

'This raft has been very helpful to me. …

imāhaṁ kullaṁ nissāya hatthehi ca pādehi ca vāyamamāno sotthinā pāraṁ uttiṇṇo.

Yannūnāhaṁ imaṁ kullaṁ thale vā ussādetvā udake vā opilāpetvā yena kāmaṁ pakkameyyan'ti.

Why don't I beach it on dry land or set it adrift on the water and go wherever I want?'

Evaṅkārī kho so, bhikkhave, puriso tasmiṁ kulle kiccakārī assa.

That's what that person should do with the raft.

Evameva kho, bhikkhave, kullūpamo mayā dhammo desito nittharaṇatthāya, no gahaṇatthāya.

In the same way, I have taught how the teaching is similar to a raft: it's for crossing over, not for holding on.

Kullūpamaṁ vo, bhikkhave, dhammaṁ desitaṁ, ājānantehi dhammāpi vo pahātabbā pageva adhammā.

By understanding the simile of the raft, you will even give up the teachings, let alone what is against the teachings.

Chayimāni, bhikkhave, diṭṭhiṭṭhānāni.

Mendicants, there are these six grounds for views.

Katamāni cha?

What six?

Idha, bhikkhave, assutavā puthujjano ariyānaṁ adassāvī ariyadhammassa akovido ariyadhamme avinīto, sappurisānaṁ adassāvī sappurisadhammassa akovido sappurisadhamme avinīto,

Take an unlearned ordinary person who has not seen the noble ones, and is neither skilled nor trained in the teaching of the noble ones. They've not seen good persons, and are neither skilled nor trained in the teaching of the good persons.

rūpaṁ 'etaṁ mama, esohamasmi, eso me attā'ti samanupassati;

They regard form like this: 'This is mine, I am this, this is my self.'

vedanaṁ 'etaṁ mama, esohamasmi, eso me attā'ti samanupassati;

They also regard feeling …

saññaṁ 'etaṁ mama, esohamasmi, eso me attā'ti samanupassati;

perception …

saṅkhāre 'etaṁ mama, esohamasmi, eso me attā'ti samanupassati;

choices …

yampi taṁ diṭṭhaṁ sutaṁ mutaṁ viññātaṁ pattaṁ pariyesitaṁ, anuvicaritaṁ manasā tampi 'etaṁ mama, esohamasmi, eso me attā'ti samanupassati;

whatever is seen, heard, thought, known, attained, sought, and explored by the mind like this: 'This is mine, I am this, this is my self.'

yampi taṁ diṭṭhiṭṭhānaṁ—

And the same for this ground for views:

so loko so attā, so pecca bhavissāmi nicco dhuvo sassato avipariṇāmadhammo, sassatisamaṁ tatheva ṭhassāmīti—

'The self and the cosmos are one and the same. After death I will be permanent, everlasting, eternal, imperishable, and will last forever and ever.'

tampi 'etaṁ mama, esohamasmi, eso me attā'ti samanupassati.

They also regard this: 'This is mine, I am this, this is my self.'

Sutavā ca kho, bhikkhave, ariyasāvako ariyānaṁ dassāvī ariyadhammassa kovido ariyadhamme suvinīto, sappurisānaṁ dassāvī sappurisadhammassa kovido sappurisadhamme suvinīto,

But a learned noble disciple has seen the noble ones, and is skilled and trained in the teaching of the noble ones. They've seen good persons, and are skilled and trained in the teaching of the good persons.

rūpaṁ 'netaṁ mama, nesohamasmi, na meso attā'ti samanupassati;

They regard form like this: 'This is not mine, I am not this, this is not my self.'

vedanaṁ 'netaṁ mama, nesohamasmi, na meso attā'ti samanupassati;

They also regard feeling …

saññaṁ 'netaṁ mama, nesohamasmi, na meso attā'ti samanupassati;

perception …

saṅkhāre 'netaṁ mama, nesohamasmi, na meso attā'ti samanupassati;

choices …

yampi taṁ diṭṭhaṁ sutaṁ mutaṁ viññātaṁ pattaṁ pariyesitaṁ, anuvicaritaṁ manasā, tampi 'netaṁ mama, nesohamasmi, na meso attā'ti samanupassati;

whatever is seen, heard, thought, known, attained, sought, and explored by the mind like this: 'This is not mine, I am not this, this is not my self.'

yampi taṁ diṭṭhiṭṭhānaṁ—

And the same for this ground for views:

so loko so attā, so pecca bhavissāmi nicco dhuvo sassato avipariṇāmadhammo, sassatisamaṁ tatheva ṭhassāmīti—

'The self and the cosmos are one and the same. After death I will be permanent, everlasting, eternal, imperishable, and will last forever and ever.'

tampi 'netaṁ mama, nesohamasmi, na meso attā'ti samanupassati.

They also regard this: 'This is not mine, I am not this, this is not my self.'

So evaṁ samanupassanto asati na paritassatī"ti.

Seeing in this way they're not anxious about what doesn't exist."

Evaṁ vutte, aññataro bhikkhu bhagavantaṁ etadavoca:

When he said this, one of the mendicants asked the Buddha,

"siyā nu kho, bhante, bahiddhā asati paritassanā"ti?

"Sir, can there be anxiety about what doesn't exist externally?"

"Siyā, bhikkhū"ti—bhagavā avoca.

"There can, mendicant," said the Buddha.

"Idha bhikkhu ekaccassa evaṁ hoti:

"It's when someone thinks,

'ahu vata me, taṁ vata me natthi;

'Oh, but it used to be mine, and it is mine no more.

siyā vata me, taṁ vatāhaṁ na labhāmī'ti.

Oh, but it could be mine, and I will get it no more.'

So socati kilamati paridevati urattāḷiṁ kandati sammohaṁ āpajjati.

They sorrow and wail and lament, beating their breast and falling into confusion.

Evaṁ kho, bhikkhu, bahiddhā asati paritassanā hotī"ti.

That's how there is anxiety about what doesn't exist externally."

"Siyā pana, bhante, bahiddhā asati aparitassanā"ti?

"But can there be no anxiety about what doesn't exist externally?"

"Siyā, bhikkhū"ti—bhagavā avoca.

"There can, mendicant," said the Buddha.

"Idha bhikkhu ekaccassa na evaṁ hoti:

"It's when someone doesn't think,

'ahu vata me, taṁ vata me natthi;

'Oh, but it used to be mine, and it is mine no more.

siyā vata me, taṁ vatāhaṁ na labhāmī'ti.

Oh, but it could be mine, and I will get it no more.'

So na socati na kilamati na paridevati na urattāḷiṁ kandati na sammohaṁ āpajjati.

They don't sorrow and wail and lament, beating their breast and falling into confusion.

Evaṁ kho, bhikkhu, bahiddhā asati aparitassanā hotī"ti.

That's how there is no anxiety about what doesn't exist externally."

"Siyā nu kho, bhante, ajjhattaṁ asati paritassanā"ti?

"But can there be anxiety about what doesn't exist internally?"

"Siyā, bhikkhū"ti—bhagavā avoca.

"There can, mendicant," said the Buddha.

"Idha, bhikkhu, ekaccassa evaṁ diṭṭhi hoti:

"It's when someone has such a view:

'so loko so attā, so pecca bhavissāmi nicco dhuvo sassato avipariṇāmadhammo, sassatisamaṁ tatheva ṭhassāmī'ti.

'The self and the cosmos are one and the same. After death I will be permanent, everlasting, eternal, imperishable, and will last forever and ever.'

So suṇāti tathāgatassa vā tathāgatasāvakassa vā sabbesaṁ diṭṭhiṭṭhānādhiṭṭhānapariyuṭṭhānābhinivesānusayānaṁ samugghātāya sabbasaṅkhārasamathāya sabbūpadhipaṭinissaggāya taṇhākkhayāya virāgāya nirodhāya nibbānāya dhammaṁ desentassa.

They hear the Realized One or their disciple teaching Dhamma for the uprooting of all grounds, fixations, obsessions, insistences, and underlying tendencies regarding views; for the stilling of all activities, the letting go of all attachments, the ending of craving, fading away, cessation, extinguishment.

Tassa evaṁ hoti:

They think,

'ucchijjissāmi nāmassu, vinassissāmi nāmassu, nassu nāma bhavissāmī'ti.

'Whoa, I'm going to be annihilated and destroyed! I won't exist any more!'

So socati kilamati paridevati urattāḷiṁ kandati sammohaṁ āpajjati.

They sorrow and wail and lament, beating their breast and falling into confusion.

Evaṁ kho, bhikkhu, ajjhattaṁ asati paritassanā hotī"ti.

That's how there is anxiety about what doesn't exist internally."

"Siyā pana, bhante, ajjhattaṁ asati aparitassanā"ti?

"But can there be no anxiety about what doesn't exist internally?"

"Siyā, bhikkhū"ti bhagavā avoca.

"There can," said the Buddha.

"Idha, bhikkhu, ekaccassa na evaṁ diṭṭhi hoti:

"It's when someone doesn't have such a view:

'so loko so attā, so pecca bhavissāmi nicco dhuvo sassato avipariṇāmadhammo, sassatisamaṁ tatheva ṭhassāmī'ti.

'The self and the cosmos are one and the same. After death I will be permanent, everlasting, eternal, imperishable, and will last forever and ever.'

So suṇāti tathāgatassa vā tathāgatasāvakassa vā sabbesaṁ diṭṭhiṭṭhānādhiṭṭhānapariyuṭṭhānābhinivesānusayānaṁ samugghātāya sabbasaṅkhārasamathāya sabbūpadhipaṭinissaggāya taṇhākkhayāya virāgāya nirodhāya nibbānāya dhammaṁ desentassa.

They hear the Realized One or their disciple teaching Dhamma for the uprooting of all grounds, fixations, obsessions, insistences, and underlying tendencies regarding views; for the stilling of all activities, the letting go of all attachments, the ending of craving, fading away, cessation, extinguishment.

Tassa na evaṁ hoti:

It never occurs to them,

'ucchijjissāmi nāmassu, vinassissāmi nāmassu, nassu nāma bhavissāmī'ti.

'Whoa, I'm going to be annihilated and destroyed! I won't exist any more!'

So na socati na kilamati na paridevati na urattāḷiṁ kandati na sammohaṁ āpajjati.

They don't sorrow and wail and lament, beating their breast and falling into confusion.

Evaṁ kho, bhikkhu, ajjhattaṁ asati aparitassanā hoti.

That's how there is no anxiety about what doesn't exist internally.

Taṁ, bhikkhave, pariggahaṁ pariggaṇheyyātha, yvāssa pariggaho nicco dhuvo sassato avipariṇāmadhammo, sassatisamaṁ tatheva tiṭṭheyya.

Mendicants, it would make sense to be possessive about something that's permanent, everlasting, eternal, imperishable, and will last forever and ever.

Passatha no tumhe, bhikkhave, taṁ pariggahaṁ yvāssa pariggaho nicco dhuvo sassato avipariṇāmadhammo, sassatisamaṁ tatheva tiṭṭheyyā"ti?

But do you see any such possession?"

"No hetaṁ, bhante".

"No, sir."

"Sādhu, bhikkhave.

"Good, mendicants!

Ahampi kho taṁ, bhikkhave, pariggahaṁ na samanupassāmi yvāssa pariggaho nicco dhuvo sassato avipariṇāmadhammo sassatisamaṁ tatheva tiṭṭheyya.

I also can't see any such possession.

Taṁ, bhikkhave, attavādupādānaṁ upādiyetha, yaṁsa attavādupādānaṁ upādiyato na uppajjeyyuṁ sokaparidevadukkhadomanassupāyāsā.

It would make sense to grasp at a doctrine of self that didn't give rise to sorrow, lamentation, pain, sadness, and distress.

Passatha no tumhe, bhikkhave, taṁ attavādupādānaṁ yaṁsa attavādupādānaṁ upādiyato na uppajjeyyuṁ sokaparidevadukkhadomanassupāyāsā"ti?

But do you see any such doctrine of self?"

"No hetaṁ, bhante".

"No, sir."

"Sādhu, bhikkhave.

"Good, mendicants!

Ahampi kho taṁ, bhikkhave, attavādupādānaṁ na samanupassāmi yaṁsa attavādupādānaṁ upādiyato na uppajjeyyuṁ sokaparidevadukkhadomanassupāyāsā.

I also can't see any such doctrine of self.

Taṁ, bhikkhave, diṭṭhinissayaṁ nissayetha yaṁsa diṭṭhinissayaṁ nissayato na uppajjeyyuṁ sokaparidevadukkhadomanassupāyāsā.

It would make sense to rely on a view that didn't give rise to sorrow, lamentation, pain, sadness, and distress.

Passatha no tumhe, bhikkhave, taṁ diṭṭhinissayaṁ yaṁsa diṭṭhinissayaṁ nissayato na uppajjeyyuṁ sokaparidevadukkhadomanassupāyāsā"ti?

But do you see any such view to rely on?"

"No hetaṁ, bhante".

"No, sir."

"Sādhu, bhikkhave.

"Good, mendicants!

Ahampi kho taṁ, bhikkhave, diṭṭhinissayaṁ na samanupassāmi yaṁsa ditṭhinissayaṁ nissayato na uppajjeyyuṁ sokaparidevadukkhadomanassupāyāsā".

I also can't see any such view to rely on.

"Attani vā, bhikkhave, sati 'attaniyaṁ me'ti assā"ti?

Mendicants, were a self to exist, would there be the thought, 'Belonging to my self'?"

"Evaṁ, bhante".

"Yes, sir."

"Attaniye vā, bhikkhave, sati 'attā me'ti assā"ti?

"Were what belongs to a self to exist, would there be the thought, 'My self'?"

"Evaṁ, bhante".

"Yes, sir."

"Attani ca, bhikkhave, attaniye ca saccato thetato anupalabbhamāne, yampi taṁ diṭṭhiṭṭhānaṁ:

"But self and what belongs to a self are not acknowledged as a genuine fact. This being so, is not the following a totally foolish teaching:

'so loko so attā, so pecca bhavissāmi nicco dhuvo sassato aviparināmadhammo, sassatisamaṁ tatheva ṭhassāmī'ti—

'The self and the cosmos are one and the same. After death I will be permanent, everlasting, eternal, imperishable, and will last forever and ever'?"

nanāyaṁ, bhikkhave, kevalo paripūro bāladhammo"ti?

"Kiñhi no siyā, bhante, kevalo hi, bhante, paripūro bāladhammo"ti.

"What else could it be, sir? It's a totally foolish teaching."

"Taṁ kiṁ maññatha, bhikkhave,

"What do you think, mendicants?

rūpaṁ niccaṁ vā aniccaṁ vā"ti?

Is form permanent or impermanent?”

“Aniccaṁ, bhante”.

“Impermanent, sir.”

“Yaṁ panāniccaṁ dukkhaṁ vā taṁ sukhaṁ vā”ti?

“But if it’s impermanent, is it suffering or happiness?”

“Dukkhaṁ, bhante”.

“Suffering, sir.”

“Yaṁ panāniccaṁ dukkhaṁ vipariṇāmadhammaṁ, kallaṁ nu taṁ samanupassituṁ—

“But if it’s impermanent, suffering, and perishable, is it fit to be regarded thus:

etaṁ mama, esohamasmi, eso me attā”ti?

‘This is mine, I am this, this is my self’?”

“No hetaṁ, bhante”.

“No, sir.”

“Taṁ kiṁ maññatha, bhikkhave,

“What do you think, mendicants?

vedanā …pe…

Is feeling …

saññā …

perception …

saṅkhārā …

choices …

viññāṇaṁ niccaṁ vā aniccaṁ vā”ti?

consciousness permanent or impermanent?”

“Aniccaṁ, bhante”.

“Impermanent, sir.”

“Yaṁ panāniccaṁ dukkhaṁ vā taṁ sukhaṁ vā”ti?

"But if it's impermanent, is it suffering or happiness?"

"Dukkhaṁ, bhante".

"Suffering, sir."

"Yaṁ panāniccaṁ dukkhaṁ vipariṇāmadhammaṁ, kallaṁ nu taṁ samanupassituṁ—

"But if it's impermanent, suffering, and perishable, is it fit to be regarded thus:

etaṁ mama, esohamasmi, eso me attā"ti?

'This is mine, I am this, this is my self'?"

"No hetaṁ, bhante".

"No, sir."

"Tasmātiha, bhikkhave, yaṁ kiñci rūpaṁ atītānāgatapaccuppannaṁ, ajjhattaṁ vā bahiddhā vā, oḷārikaṁ vā sukhumaṁ vā, hīnaṁ vā paṇītaṁ vā, yaṁ dūre santike vā, sabbaṁ rūpaṁ 'netaṁ mama, nesohamasmi, na meso attā'ti—evametaṁ yathābhūtaṁ sammappaññāya daṭṭhabbaṁ.

"So, mendicants, you should truly see any kind of form at all—past, future, or present; internal or external; coarse or fine; inferior or superior; far or near: all form—with right understanding: 'This is not mine, I am not this, this is not my self.'

Yā kāci vedanā …pe…

You should truly see any kind of feeling …

yā kāci saññā …

perception …

ye keci saṅkhārā …

choices …

yaṁ kiñci viññāṇaṁ atītānāgatapaccuppannaṁ, ajjhattaṁ vā bahiddhā vā, oḷārikaṁ vā sukhumaṁ vā, hīnaṁ vā paṇītaṁ vā, yaṁ dūre santike vā, sabbaṁ viññāṇaṁ 'netaṁ mama, nesohamasmi, na meso attā'ti—evametaṁ yathābhūtaṁ sammappaññāya daṭṭhabbaṁ.

consciousness at all—past, future, or present; internal or external; coarse or fine; inferior or superior; far or near: all consciousness—with right understanding: 'This is not mine, I am not this, this is not my self.'

Evaṁ passaṁ, bhikkhave, sutavā ariyasāvako rūpasmiṁ nibbindati, vedanāya nibbindati, saññāya nibbindati, saṅkhāresu nibbindati, viññāṇasmiṁ nibbindati,

Seeing this, a learned noble disciple grows disillusioned with form, feeling, perception, choices, and consciousness.

nibbidā virajjati, virāgā vimuccati, vimuttasmiṁ vimuttamiti ñāṇaṁ hoti.

Being disillusioned, desire fades away. When desire fades away they're freed. When they're freed, they know they're freed.

'Khīṇā jāti, vusitaṁ brahmacariyaṁ, kataṁ karaṇīyaṁ, nāparaṁ itthattāyā'ti pajānāti.

They understand: 'Rebirth is ended, the spiritual journey has been completed, what had to be done has been done, there is no return to any state of existence.'

Ayaṁ vuccati, bhikkhave, bhikkhu ukkhittapaligho itipi, saṅkiṇṇaparikkho itipi, abbūḷhesiko itipi, niraggaḷo itipi, ariyo pannaddhajo pannabhāro visaṁyutto itipi.

This is called a mendicant who has lifted up the cross-bar, filled in the trench, and pulled up the pillar; who is unbarred, a noble one with banner and burden put down, detached.

Kathañca, bhikkhave, bhikkhu ukkhittapaligho hoti?

And how has a mendicant lifted the cross-bar?

Idha, bhikkhave, bhikkhuno avijjā pahīnā hoti, ucchinnamūlā tālāvatthukatā anabhāvaṅkatā, āyatiṁ anuppādadhammā.

It's when a mendicant has given up ignorance, cut it off at the root, made it like a palm stump, obliterated it, so it's unable to arise in the future.

Evaṁ kho, bhikkhave, bhikkhu ukkhittapaligho hoti.

That's how a mendicant has lifted the cross-bar.

Kathañca, bhikkhave, bhikkhu saṅkiṇṇaparikkho hoti?

And how has a mendicant filled in the trench?

Idha, bhikkhave, bhikkhuno ponobbhaviko jātisaṁsāro pahīno hoti, ucchinnamūlo tālāvatthukato anabhāvaṅkato, āyatiṁ anuppādadhammo.

It's when a mendicant has given up transmigrating through births in future lives, cut it off at the root, made it like a palm stump, obliterated it, so it's unable to arise in the future.

Evaṁ kho, bhikkhave, bhikkhu saṅkiṇṇaparikkho hoti.

That's how a mendicant has filled in the trench.

Kathañca, bhikkhave, bhikkhu abbūḷhesiko hoti?

And how has a mendicant pulled up the pillar?

Idha, bhikkhave, bhikkhuno taṇhā pahīnā hoti, ucchinnamūlā tālāvatthukatā anabhāvaṅkatā, āyatiṁ anuppādadhammā.

It's when a mendicant has given up craving, cut it off at the root, made it like a palm stump, obliterated it, so it's unable to arise in the future.

Evaṁ kho, bhikkhave, bhikkhu abbūḷhesiko hoti.

That's how a mendicant has pulled up the pillar.

Kathañca, bhikkhave, bhikkhu niraggaḷo hoti?

And how is a mendicant unbarred?

Idha, bhikkhave, bhikkhuno pañca orambhāgiyāni saṁyojanāni pahīnāni honti, ucchinnamūlāni tālāvatthukatāni anabhāvaṅkatāni, āyatiṁ anuppādadhammāni.

It's when a mendicant has given up the five lower fetters, cut them off at the root, made them like a palm stump, obliterated them, so they're unable to arise in the future.

Evaṁ kho, bhikkhave, bhikkhu niraggaḷo hoti.

That's how a mendicant is unbarred.

Kathañca, bhikkhave, bhikkhu ariyo pannaddhajo pannabhāro visaṁyutto hoti?

And how is a mendicant a noble one with banner and burden put down, detached?

Idha, bhikkhave, bhikkhuno asmimāno pahīno hoti, ucchinnamūlo tālāvatthukato anabhāvaṅkato, āyatiṁ anuppādadhammo.

It's when a mendicant has given up the conceit 'I am', cut it off at the root, made it like a palm stump, obliterated it, so it's unable to arise in the future.

Evaṁ kho, bhikkhave, bhikkhu ariyo pannaddhajo pannabhāro visaṁyutto hoti.

That's how a mendicant is a noble one with banner and burden put down, detached.

Evaṁ vimuttacittaṁ kho, bhikkhave, bhikkhuṁ saindā devā sabrahmakā sapajāpatikā anvesaṁ nādhigacchanti:

When a mendicant's mind was freed like this, the gods together with Indra, Brahmā, and Pajāpati, search as they may, will not discover:

'idaṁ nissitaṁ tathāgatassa viññāṇan'ti.

'This is what the Realized One's consciousness depends on.'

Taṁ kissa hetu?

Why is that?

Diṭṭhevāhaṁ, bhikkhave, dhamme tathāgataṁ ananuvijjoti vadāmi.

Because even in the present life the Realized One is not found, I say.

Evaṁvādiṁ kho maṁ, bhikkhave, evamakkhāyiṁ eke samaṇabrāhmaṇā asatā tucchā musā abhūtena abbhācikkhanti:

Though I speak and explain like this, certain ascetics and brahmins misrepresent me with the false, hollow, lying, untruthful claim:

'venayiko samaṇo gotamo, sato sattassa ucchedaṁ vināsaṁ vibhavaṁ paññāpetī'ti.

'The ascetic Gotama is an exterminator. He advocates the annihilation, eradication, and obliteration of an existing being.'

Yathā cāhaṁ na, bhikkhave, yathā cāhaṁ na vadāmi, tathā maṁ te bhonto samaṇabrāhmaṇā asatā tucchā musā abhūtena abbhācikkhanti:

I have been falsely misrepresented as being what I am not, and saying what I do not say.

'venayiko samaṇo gotamo, sato sattassa ucchedaṁ vināsaṁ vibhavaṁ paññāpetī'ti.

Pubbe cāhaṁ, bhikkhave, etarahi ca dukkhañceva paññāpemi, dukkhassa ca nirodhaṁ.

In the past, as today, what I describe is suffering and the cessation of suffering.

Tatra ce, bhikkhave, pare tathāgataṁ akkosanti paribhāsanti rosenti vihesenti, tatra, bhikkhave, tathāgatassa na hoti āghāto na appaccayo na cetaso anabhiraddhi.

This being so, if others abuse, attack, harass, and trouble the Realized One, he doesn't get resentful, bitter, and emotionally exasperated.

Tatra ce, bhikkhave, pare tathāgataṁ sakkaronti garuṁ karonti mānenti pūjenti, tatra, bhikkhave, tathāgatassa na hoti ānando na somanassaṁ na cetaso uppilāvitattaṁ.

Or if others honor, respect, revere, or venerate him, he doesn't get thrilled, elated, and emotionally excited.

Tatra ce, bhikkhave, pare vā tathāgataṁ sakkaronti garuṁ karonti mānenti pūjenti, tatra, bhikkhave, tathāgatassa evaṁ hoti:

He just thinks,

'yaṁ kho idaṁ pubbe pariññātaṁ tattha me evarūpā kārā karīyantī'ti.

'They do such things for what has already been completely understood.'

Tasmātiha, bhikkhave, tumhe cepi pare akkoseyyuṁ paribhāseyyuṁ roseyyuṁ viheseyyuṁ, tatra tumhe hi na āghāto na appaccayo na cetaso anabhiraddhi karaṇīyā.

So, mendicants, if others abuse, attack, harass, and trouble you, don't make yourselves resentful, bitter, and emotionally exasperated.

Tasmātiha, bhikkhave, tumhe cepi pare sakkareyyuṁ garuṁ kareyyuṁ māneyyuṁ pūjeyyuṁ, tatra tumhehi na ānando na somanassaṁ na cetaso uppilāvitattaṁ karaṇīyaṁ.

Or if others honor, respect, revere, or venerate you, don't make yourselves thrilled, elated, and emotionally excited.

Tasmātiha, bhikkhave, tumhe cepi pare sakkareyyuṁ garuṁ kareyyuṁ māneyyuṁ pūjeyyuṁ, tatra tumhākaṁ evamassa:

Just think,

'yaṁ kho idaṁ pubbe pariññātaṁ, tatthame evarūpā kārā karīyantī'ti.

'They do such things for what has already been completely understood.'

Tasmātiha, bhikkhave, yaṁ na tumhākaṁ taṁ pajahatha;

So, mendicants, give up what isn't yours.

taṁ vo pahīnaṁ dīgharattaṁ hitāya sukhāya bhavissati.

Giving it up will be for your lasting welfare and happiness.

Kiñca, bhikkhave, na tumhākaṁ?

And what isn't yours?

Rūpaṁ, bhikkhave, na tumhākaṁ, taṁ pajahatha;

Form isn't yours: give it up.

taṁ vo pahīnaṁ dīgharattaṁ hitāya sukhāya bhavissati.

Giving it up will be for your lasting welfare and happiness.

Vedanā, bhikkhave, na tumhākaṁ, taṁ pajahatha;

Feeling …

sā vo pahīnā dīgharattaṁ hitāya sukhāya bhavissati.

Saññā, bhikkhave, na tumhākaṁ, taṁ pajahatha;

perception …

sā vo pahīnā dīgharattaṁ hitāya sukhāya bhavissati.

Saṅkhārā, bhikkhave, na tumhākaṁ, te pajahatha;

choices …

te vo pahīnā dīgharattaṁ hitāya sukhāya bhavissanti.

Viññāṇaṁ, bhikkhave, na tumhākaṁ, taṁ pajahatha;

consciousness isn't yours: give it up.

taṁ vo pahīnaṁ dīgharattaṁ hitāya sukhāya bhavissati.

Giving it up will be for your lasting welfare and happiness.

Taṁ kiṁ maññatha, bhikkhave,

What do you think, mendicants?

yaṁ imasmiṁ jetavane tiṇakaṭṭhasākhāpalāsaṁ, taṁ jano hareyya vā daheyya vā yathāpaccayaṁ vā kareyya.

Suppose a person was to carry off the grass, sticks, branches, and leaves in this Jeta's Grove, or burn them, or do what they want with them.

Api nu tumhākaṁ evamassa:

Would you think,

'amhe jano harati vā dahati vā yathāpaccayaṁ vā karotī'''ti?

'This person is carrying us off, burning us, or doing what they want with us'?"

"No hetaṁ, bhante".

"No, sir.

"Taṁ kissa hetu"?

Why is that?

"Na hi no etaṁ, bhante, attā vā attaniyaṁ vā"ti.

Because that's neither self nor belonging to self."

"Evameva kho, bhikkhave, yaṁ na tumhākaṁ taṁ pajahatha;

"In the same way, mendicants, give up what isn't yours.

taṁ vo pahīnaṁ dīgharattaṁ hitāya sukhāya bhavissati.

Giving it up will be for your lasting welfare and happiness.

Kiñca, bhikkhave, na tumhākaṁ?

And what isn't yours?

Rūpaṁ, bhikkhave, na tumhākaṁ, taṁ pajahatha;

Form …

taṁ vo pahīnaṁ dīgharattaṁ hitāya sukhāya bhavissati.

Vedanā, bhikkhave …pe…

feeling …

saññā, bhikkhave …

perception …

saṅkhārā, bhikkhave …pe…

choices …

viññāṇaṁ, bhikkhave, na tumhākaṁ, taṁ pajahatha;

consciousness isn't yours: give it up.

taṁ vo pahīnaṁ dīgharattaṁ hitāya sukhāya bhavissati.

Giving it up will be for your lasting welfare and happiness.

Evaṁ svākkhāto, bhikkhave, mayā dhammo uttāno vivaṭo pakāsito chinnapilotiko.

Thus the teaching has been well explained by me, made clear, opened, illuminated, and stripped of patchwork.

Evaṁ svākkhāte, bhikkhave, mayā dhamme uttāne vivaṭe pakāsite chinnapilotike ye te bhikkhū arahanto khīṇāsavā vusitavanto katakaraṇīyā ohitabhārā anuppattasadatthā parikkhīṇabhavasaṁyojanā sammadaññāvimuttā, vaṭṭaṁ tesaṁ natthi paññāpanāya.

In this teaching there are mendicants who are perfected, who have ended the defilements, completed the spiritual journey, done what had to be done, laid down the burden, achieved their own goal, utterly ended the fetters of rebirth, and are rightly freed through enlightenment. For them, there is no cycle of rebirths to be found. …

Evaṁ svākkhāto, bhikkhave, mayā dhammo uttāno vivaṭo pakāsito chinnapilotiko.

Evaṁ svākkhāte, bhikkhave, mayā dhamme uttāne vivaṭe pakāsite chinnapilotike yesaṁ bhikkhūnaṁ pañcorambhāgiyāni saṁyojanāni pahīnāni, sabbe te opapātikā, tattha parinibbāyino, anāvattidhammā tasmā lokā.

In this teaching there are mendicants who have given up the five lower fetters. All of them are reborn spontaneously. They are extinguished there, and are not liable to return from that world. ...

Evaṁ svākkhāto, bhikkhave, mayā dhammo uttāno vivaṭo pakāsito chinnapilotiko.

Evaṁ svākkhāte, bhikkhave, mayā dhamme uttāne vivaṭe pakāsite chinnapilotike yesaṁ bhikkhūnaṁ tīṇi saṁyojanāni pahīnāni, rāgadosamohā tanubhūtā, sabbe te sakadāgāmino, sakideva imaṁ lokaṁ āgantvā dukkhassantaṁ karissanti.

In this teaching there are mendicants who, having given up three fetters, and weakened greed, hate, and delusion, are once-returners. All of them come back to this world once only, then make an end of suffering. ...

Evaṁ svākkhāto, bhikkhave, mayā dhammo uttāno vivaṭo pakāsito chinnapilotiko.

Evaṁ svākkhāte, bhikkhave, mayā dhamme uttāne vivaṭe pakāsite chinnapilotike yesaṁ bhikkhūnaṁ tīṇi saṁyojanāni pahīnāni, sabbe te sotāpannā, avinipātadhammā, niyatā sambodhiparāyanā.

In this teaching there are mendicants who have ended three fetters. All of them are stream-enterers, not liable to be reborn in the underworld, bound for awakening. ...

Evaṁ svākkhāto, bhikkhave, mayā dhammo uttāno vivaṭo pakāsito chinnapilotiko.

Evaṁ svākkhāte, bhikkhave, mayā dhamme uttāne vivaṭe pakāsite chinnapilotike ye te bhikkhū dhammānusārino saddhānusārino sabbe te sambodhiparāyanā.

In this teaching there are mendicants who are followers of principles, or followers by faith. All of them are bound for awakening.

Evaṁ svākkhāto, bhikkhave, mayā dhammo uttāno vivaṭo pakāsito chinnapilotiko.

Thus the teaching has been well explained by me, made clear, opened, illuminated, and stripped of patchwork.

Evaṁ svākkhāte, bhikkhave, mayā dhamme uttāne vivaṭe pakāsite chinnapilotike yesaṁ mayi saddhāmattaṁ pemamattaṁ sabbe te saggaparāyanā”ti.

In this teaching there are those who have a degree of faith and love for me. All of them are bound for heaven.”

Idamavoca bhagavā.

That is what the Buddha said.

Attamanā te bhikkhū bhagavato bhāsitaṁ abhinandunti.

Satisfied, the mendicants were happy with what the Buddha said.

Alagaddūpamasuttaṁ niṭṭhitaṁ dutiyaṁ.

23 Vammikasutta:

The Ant-Hill

Evaṁ me sutaṁ—

So I have heard.

ekaṁ samayaṁ bhagavā sāvatthiyaṁ viharati jetavane anāthapiṇḍikassa ārāme.

At one time the Buddha was staying near Sāvatthī in Jeta's Grove, Anāthapiṇḍika's monastery.

Tena kho pana samayena āyasmā kumārakassapo andhavane viharati.

Now at that time Venerable Kassapa the Prince was staying in the Dark Forest.

Atha kho aññatarā devatā abhikkantāya rattiyā abhikkantavaṇṇā kevalakappaṁ andhavanaṁ obhāsetvā yenāyasmā kumārakassapo tenupasaṅkami; upasaṅkamitvā ekamantaṁ aṭṭhāsi. Ekamantaṁ ṭhitā kho sā devatā āyasmantaṁ kumārakassapaṁ etadavoca:

Then, late at night, a glorious deity, lighting up the entire Dark Forest, went up to Kassapa the Prince, stood to one side, and said:

"Bhikkhu bhikkhu, ayaṁ vammiko rattiṁ dhūmāyati, divā pajjalati.

"Monk, monk! This ant-hill fumes by night and flames by day.

Brāhmaṇo evamāha:

The brahmin said,

'abhikkhaṇa, sumedha, satthaṁ ādāyā'ti.

'Take up the sword and dig, O sage!'

Abhikkhaṇanto sumedho satthaṁ ādāya addasa laṅgiṁ

Taking up the sword and digging, the sage saw a bar:

'laṅgī, bhadante'ti.

'A bar, sir!'

Brāhmaṇo evamāha:

The brahmin said,

'ukkhipa laṅgiṁ;

'Throw out the bar!

abhikkhaṇa, sumedha, satthaṁ ādāyā'ti.

Take up the sword and dig, O sage!'

Abhikkhaṇanto sumedho satthaṁ ādāya addasa uddhumāyikaṁ.

Taking up the sword and digging, the sage saw a bullfrog:

'Uddhumāyikā, bhadante'ti.

'A bullfrog, sir!'

Brāhmaṇo evamāha:

The brahmin said,

'ukkhipa uddhumāyikaṁ;

'Throw out the bullfrog!

abhikkhaṇa, sumedha, satthaṁ ādāyā'ti.

Take up the sword and dig, O sage!'

Abhikkhaṇanto sumedho satthaṁ ādāya addasa dvidhāpathaṁ.

Taking up the sword and digging, the sage saw a forked path:

'Dvidhāpatho, bhadante'ti.

'A forked path, sir!'

Brāhmaṇo evamāha:

The brahmin said,

'ukkhipa dvidhāpathaṁ;

'Throw out the forked path!

abhikkhaṇa, sumedha, satthaṁ ādāyā'ti.

Take up the sword and dig, O sage!'

Abhikkhaṇanto sumedho satthaṁ ādāya addasa caṅgavāraṁ.

Taking up the sword and digging, the sage saw a box:

'Caṅgavāro, bhadante'ti.

'A box, sir!'

Brāhmaṇo evamāha:

The brahmin said,

'ukkhipa caṅgavāraṁ;

'Throw out the box!

abhikkhaṇa, sumedha, satthaṁ ādāyā'ti.

Take up the sword and dig, O sage!'

Abhikkhaṇanto sumedho satthaṁ ādāya addasa kummaṁ.

Taking up the sword and digging, the sage saw a tortoise:

'Kummo, bhadante'ti.

'A tortoise, sir!'

Brāhmaṇo evamāha:

The brahmin said,

'ukkhipa kummaṁ;

'Throw out the tortoise!

abhikkhaṇa, sumedha, satthaṁ ādāyā'ti.

Take up the sword and dig, O sage!'

Abhikkhaṇanto sumedho satthaṁ ādāya addasa asisūnaṁ.

Taking up the sword and digging, the sage saw an axe and block:

'Asisūnā, bhadante'ti.

'An axe and block, sir!'

Brāhmaṇo evamāha:

The brahmin said,

'ukkhipa asisūnaṁ;

'Throw out the axe and block!

abhikkhaṇa, sumedha, satthaṁ ādāyā'ti.

Take up the sword and dig, O sage!'

Abhikkhaṇanto sumedho satthaṁ ādāya addasa maṁsapesiṁ.

Taking up the sword and digging, the sage saw a lump of meat:

'Maṁsapesi, bhadante'ti.

'A lump of meat, sir!'

Brāhmaṇo evamāha:

The brahmin said,

'ukkhipa maṁsapesiṁ;

'Throw out the lump of meat!

abhikkhaṇa, sumedha, satthaṁ ādāyā'ti.

Take up the sword and dig, O sage!'

Abhikkhaṇanto sumedho satthaṁ ādāya addasa nāgaṁ.

Taking up the sword and digging, the sage saw a dragon:

'Nāgo, bhadante'ti.

'A dragon, sir!'

Brāhmaṇo evamāha:

The brahmin said,

'tiṭṭhatu nāgo, mā nāgaṁ ghaṭṭesi; namo karohi nāgassā'ti.

'Leave the dragon! Do not disturb the dragon! Worship the dragon!'

Ime kho tvaṁ, bhikkhu, pañhe bhagavantaṁ upasaṅkamitvā puccheyyāsi, yathā ca te bhagavā byākaroti tathā naṁ dhāreyyāsi.

Mendicant, go to the Buddha and ask him about this riddle. You should remember it in line with his answer.

Nāhaṁ taṁ, bhikkhu, passāmi sadevake loke samārake sabrahmake sassamaṇabrāhmaṇiyā pajāya sadevamanussāya, yo imesaṁ pañhānaṁ veyyākaraṇena cittaṁ ārādheyya aññatra tathāgatena vā, tathāgatasāvakena vā, ito vā pana sutvā"ti—

I don't see anyone in this world—with its gods, Māras, and Brahmās, this population with its ascetics and brahmins, its gods and humans—who could provide a satisfying answer to this riddle except for the Realized One or his disciple or someone who has heard it from them."

Idamavoca sā devatā.

That is what that deity said

Idaṁ vatvā tatthevantaradhāyi.

before vanishing right there.

Atha kho āyasmā kumārakassapo tassā rattiyā accayena yena bhagavā tenupasaṅkami; upasaṅkamitvā bhagavantaṁ abhivādetvā ekamantaṁ nisīdi. Ekamantaṁ nisinno kho āyasmā kumārakassapo bhagavantaṁ etadavoca:

Then, when the night had passed, Kassapa the Prince went to the Buddha, bowed, sat down to one side, and told him what had happened. Then he asked:

"imaṁ, bhante, rattiṁ aññatarā devatā abhikkantāya rattiyā abhikkantavaṇṇā kevalakappaṁ andhavanaṁ obhāsetvā yenāhaṁ tenupasaṅkami; upasaṅkamitvā ekamantaṁ aṭṭhāsi. Ekamantaṁ ṭhitā kho, bhante, sā devatā maṁ etadavoca:

'bhikkhu bhikkhu, ayaṁ vammiko rattiṁ dhūmāyati, divā pajjalati.

Brāhmaṇo evamāha:

"abhikkhaṇa, sumedha, satthaṁ ādāyā"ti.

Abhikkhaṇanto sumedho satthaṁ ādāya …pe…

ito vā pana sutvā'ti.

Idamavoca, bhante, sā devatā.

Idaṁ vatvā tatthevantaradhāyi.

Ko nu kho, bhante, vammiko, kā rattiṁ dhūmāyanā, kā divā pajjalanā, ko brāhmaṇo, ko sumedho, kiṁ satthaṁ, kiṁ abhikkhaṇaṁ, kā laṅgī, kā uddhumāyikā, ko dvidhāpatho, kiṁ caṅgavāraṁ, ko kummo, kā asisūnā, kā maṁsapesi, ko nāgo"ti?

"Sir, what is the ant-hill? What is the fuming by night and flaming by day? Who is the brahmin, and who the sage? What are the sword, the digging, the bar, the bullfrog, the forked path, the box, the tortoise, the axe and block, and the lump of meat? And what is the dragon?"

"'Vammiko'ti kho, bhikkhu, imassetaṁ cātumahābhūtikassa kāyassa adhivacanaṁ, mātāpettikasambhavassa odanakummāsūpacayassa aniccucchādanaparimaddanabhedanaviddhaṁsanadhammassa.

"Mendicant, 'ant-hill' is a term for this body made up of the four primary elements, produced by mother and father, built up from rice and porridge, liable to impermanence, to wearing away and erosion, to breaking up and destruction.

Yaṁ kho, bhikkhu, divā kammante ārabbha rattiṁ anuvitakketi anuvicāreti—

Thinking and considering all night about what you did during the day—

ayaṁ rattiṁ dhūmāyanā.

this is the fuming at night.

Yaṁ kho, bhikkhu, rattiṁ anuvitakketvā anuvicāretvā divā kammante payojeti kāyena vācāya 'manasā'—

The work you apply yourself to during the day by body, speech, and mind after thinking about it all night—

ayaṁ divā pajjalanā.

this is the flaming by day.

'Brāhmaṇo'ti kho, bhikkhu, tathāgatassetaṁ adhivacanaṁ arahato sammāsambuddhassa.

'Brahmin' is a term for the Realized One, the perfected one, the fully awakened Buddha.

'Sumedho'ti kho, bhikkhu, sekkhassetaṁ bhikkhuno adhivacanaṁ.

'Sage' is a term for the trainee mendicant.

'Satthan'ti kho, bhikkhu, ariyāyetaṁ paññāya adhivacanaṁ.

'Sword' is a term for noble wisdom.

'Abhikkhaṇan'ti kho, bhikkhu, vīriyārambhassetaṁ adhivacanaṁ.

'Digging' is a term for being energetic.

'Laṅgī'ti kho, bhikkhu, avijjāyetaṁ adhivacanaṁ.

'Bar' is a term for ignorance.

Ukkhipa laṅgiṁ, pajaha avijjaṁ;

'Throw out the bar' means 'give up ignorance,

abhikkhaṇa, sumedha, satthaṁ ādāyāti ayametassa attho.

take up the sword, sage, and dig.'

'Uddhumāyikā'ti kho, bhikkhu, kodhūpāyāsassetaṁ adhivacanaṁ.

'Bullfrog' is a term for anger and distress.

Ukkhipa uddhumāyikaṁ, pajaha kodhūpāyāsaṁ;

'Throw out the bullfrog' means 'give up anger and distress' …

abhikkhaṇa, sumedha, satthaṁ ādāyāti ayametassa attho.

'Dvidhāpatho'ti kho, bhikkhu, vicikicchāyetaṁ adhivacanaṁ.

'A forked path' is a term for doubt.

Ukkhipa dvidhāpathaṁ, pajaha vicikicchaṁ;

'Throw out the forked path' means 'give up doubt' …

abhikkhaṇa, sumedha, satthaṁ ādāyāti ayametassa attho.

'Caṅgavāran'ti kho, bhikkhu, pañcannetaṁ nīvaraṇānaṁ adhivacanaṁ, seyyathidaṁ—

'Box' is a term for the five hindrances, that is:

kāmacchandanīvaraṇassa, byāpādanīvaraṇassa, thinamiddhanīvaraṇassa, uddhaccakukkuccanīvaraṇassa, vicikicchānīvaraṇassa.

the hindrances of sensual desire, ill will, dullness and drowsiness, restlessness and remorse, and doubt.

Ukkhipa caṅgavāraṁ, pajaha pañca nīvaraṇe;

'Throw out the box' means 'give up the five hindrances' …

abhikkhaṇa, sumedha, satthaṁ ādāyāti ayametassa attho.

'Kummo'ti kho, bhikkhu, pañcannetaṁ upādānakkhandhānaṁ adhivacanaṁ, seyyathidaṁ—

'Tortoise' is a term for the five grasping aggregates, that is:

rūpupādānakkhandhassa, vedanupādānakkhandhassa, saññupādānakkhandhassa, saṅkhārupādānakkhandhassa, viññāṇupādānakkhandhassa.

form, feeling, perception, choices, and consciousness.

Ukkhipa kummaṁ, pajaha pañcupādānakkhandhe;

'Throw out the tortoise' means 'give up the five grasping aggregates' …

abhikkhaṇa, sumedha, satthaṁ ādāyāti ayametassa attho.

'Asisūnā'ti kho, bhikkhu, pañcannetaṁ kāmaguṇānaṁ adhivacanaṁ—

'Axe and block' is a term for the five kinds of sensual stimulation.

cakkhuviññeyyānaṁ rūpānaṁ iṭṭhānaṁ kantānaṁ manāpānaṁ piyarūpānaṁ kāmūpasaṁhitānaṁ rajanīyānaṁ,

Sights known by the eye that are likable, desirable, agreeable, pleasant, sensual, and arousing.

sotaviññeyyānaṁ saddānaṁ …pe…

Sounds known by the ear …

ghānaviññeyyānaṁ gandhānaṁ …pe…

Smells known by the nose …

jivhāviññeyyānaṁ rasānaṁ …pe…

Tastes known by the tongue …

kāyaviññeyyānaṁ phoṭṭhabbānaṁ iṭṭhānaṁ kantānaṁ manāpānaṁ piyarūpānaṁ kāmūpasaṁhitānaṁ rajanīyānaṁ.

Touches known by the body that are likable, desirable, agreeable, pleasant, sensual, and arousing.

Ukkhipa asisūnaṁ, pajaha pañca kāmaguṇe;

'Throw out the axe and block' means 'give up the five kinds of sensual stimulation' …

abhikkhaṇa, sumedha, satthaṁ ādāyāti ayametassa attho.

'Maṁsapesī'ti kho, bhikkhu, nandīrāgassetaṁ adhivacanaṁ.

'Lump of meat' is a term for greed and relishing.

Ukkhipa maṁsapesiṁ, pajaha nandīrāgaṁ;

'Throw out the lump of meat' means 'give up greed and relishing' …

abhikkhaṇa, sumedha, satthaṁ ādāyāti ayametassa attho.

'Nāgo'ti kho, bhikkhu, khīṇāsavassetaṁ bhikkhuno adhivacanaṁ.

'Dragon' is a term for a mendicant who has ended the defilements.

Tiṭṭhatu nāgo, mā nāgaṁ ghaṭṭesi; namo karohi nāgassāti ayametassa attho"ti.

This is the meaning of: 'Leave the dragon! Do not disturb the dragon! Worship the dragon.'"

Idamavoca bhagavā.

That is what the Buddha said.

Attamano āyasmā kumārakassapo bhagavato bhāsitaṁ abhinandīti.

Satisfied, Venerable Kassapa the Prince was happy with what the Buddha said.

Vammikasuttaṁ niṭṭhitaṁ tatiyaṁ.

24 Rathavinitasutta:

Prepared Chariots

Evaṁ me sutaṁ—

So I have heard.

ekaṁ samayaṁ bhagavā rājagahe viharati veḷuvane kalandakanivāpe.

At one time the Buddha was staying near Rājagaha, in the Bamboo Grove, the squirrels' feeding ground.

Atha kho sambahulā jātibhūmakā bhikkhū jātibhūmiyaṁ vassaṁvutthā yena bhagavā tenupasaṅkamiṁsu; upasaṅkamitvā bhagavantaṁ abhivādetvā ekamantaṁ nisīdiṁsu. Ekamantaṁ nisinne kho te bhikkhū bhagavā etadavoca:

Then several mendicants who had completed the rainy season residence in their native land went to the Buddha, bowed, and sat down to one side. The Buddha said to them:

"Ko nu kho, bhikkhave, jātibhūmiyaṁ jātibhūmakānaṁ bhikkhūnaṁ sabrahmacārīnaṁ evaṁ sambhāvito:

"In your native land, mendicants, which of the native mendicants is esteemed in this way:

'attanā ca appiccho appicchakathañca bhikkhūnaṁ kattā, attanā ca santuṭṭho santuṭṭhikathañca bhikkhūnaṁ kattā, attanā ca pavivitto pavivekakathañca bhikkhūnaṁ kattā, attanā ca asaṁsaṭṭho asaṁsaggakathañca bhikkhūnaṁ kattā, attanā ca āraddhavīriyo vīriyārambhakathañca bhikkhūnaṁ kattā, attanā ca sīlasampanno sīlasampadākathañca bhikkhūnaṁ kattā, attanā ca samādhisampanno samādhisampadākathañca bhikkhūnaṁ kattā, attanā ca paññāsampanno paññāsampadākathañca bhikkhūnaṁ kattā, attanā ca vimuttisampanno vimuttisampadākathañca bhikkhūnaṁ kattā, attanā ca vimuttiñāṇadassanasampanno vimuttiñāṇadassanasampadākathañca bhikkhūnaṁ kattā, ovādako viññāpako sandassako samādapako samuttejako sampahaṁsako sabrahmacārīnan'"ti?

'Personally having few wishes, they speak to the mendicants on having few wishes. Personally having contentment, seclusion, aloofness, energy, ethics, immersion, wisdom, freedom, and the knowledge and vision of freedom, they speak to the mendicants on all these things. They're an adviser and instructor, one who educates, encourages, fires up, and inspires their spiritual companions.'"

"Puṇṇo nāma, ·bhante, āyasmā mantāṇiputto jātibhūmiyaṁ jātibhūmakānaṁ bhikkhūnaṁ sabrahmacārīnam evaṁ sambhāvito:

"Puṇṇa son of Mantāṇī, sir, is esteemed in this way in our native land."

'attanā ca appiccho appicchakathañca bhikkhūnaṁ kattā, attanā ca santuṭṭho … pe… ovādako viññāpako sandassako samādapako samuttejako sampahaṁsako sabrahmacārīnan'"ti.

Tena kho pana samayena āyasmā sāriputto bhagavato avidūre nisinno hoti.

Now at that time Venerable Sāriputta was meditating not far from the Buddha.

Atha kho āyasmato sāriputtassa etadahosi:

Then he thought:

"lābhā āyasmato puṇṇassa mantāṇiputtassa, suladdhalābhā āyasmato puṇṇassa mantāṇiputtassa,

"Puṇṇa son of Mantāṇī is fortunate, so very fortunate,

yassa viññū sabrahmacārī satthu sammukhā anumassa anumassa vaṇṇaṁ bhāsanti, tañca satthā abbhanumodati.

in that his sensible spiritual companions praise him point by point in the presence of the Teacher, and that the Teacher seconds that appreciation.

Appeva nāma mayampi kadāci karahaci āyasmatā puṇṇena mantāṇiputtena saddhiṁ samāgaccheyyāma, appeva nāma siyā kocideva kathāsallāpo"ti.

Hopefully, some time or other I'll get to meet Venerable Puṇṇa, and we can have a discussion."

Atha kho bhagavā rājagahe yathābhirantaṁ viharitvā yena sāvatthi tena cārikaṁ pakkāmi.

When the Buddha had stayed in Rājagaha as long as he pleased, he set out for Sāvatthī.

Anupubbena cārikaṁ caramāno yena sāvatthi tadavasari.

Traveling stage by stage, he arrived at Sāvatthī,

Tatra sudaṁ bhagavā sāvatthiyaṁ viharati jetavane anāthapiṇḍikassa ārāme.

where he stayed in Jeta's Grove, Anāthapiṇḍika's monastery.

Assosi kho āyasmā puṇṇo mantāṇiputto: "bhagavā kira sāvatthiṁ anuppatto; sāvatthiyaṁ viharati jetavane anāthapiṇḍikassa ārāme"ti.

Puṇṇa heard that the Buddha had arrived at Sāvatthī.

Atha kho āyasmā puṇṇo mantāṇiputto senāsanaṁ saṁsāmetvā pattacīvaramādāya yena sāvatthi tena cārikaṁ pakkāmi.

Then he set his lodgings in order and, taking his bowl and robe, set out for Sāvatthī.

Anupubbena cārikaṁ caramāno yena sāvatthi jetavanaṁ anāthapiṇḍikassa ārāmo yena bhagavā tenupasaṅkami; upasaṅkamitvā bhagavantaṁ abhivādetvā ekamantaṁ nisīdi.

Eventually he came to Sāvatthī and Jeta's Grove. He went up to the Buddha, bowed, and sat down to one side.

Ekamantaṁ nisinnaṁ kho āyasmantaṁ puṇṇaṁ mantāṇiputtaṁ bhagavā dhammiyā kathāya sandassesi samādapesi samuttejesi sampahaṁsesi.

The Buddha educated, encouraged, fired up, and inspired him with a Dhamma talk.

Atha kho āyasmā puṇṇo mantāṇiputto bhagavatā dhammiyā kathāya sandassito samādapito samuttejito sampahaṁsito bhagavato bhāsitaṁ abhinanditvā anumoditvā uṭṭhāyāsanā bhagavantaṁ abhivādetvā padakkhiṇaṁ katvā yena andhavanaṁ tenupasaṅkami divāvihārāya.

Then, having approved and agreed with what the Buddha said, Puṇṇa got up from his seat, bowed, and respectfully circled the Buddha, keeping him on his right. Then he went to the Dark Forest for the day's meditation.

Atha kho aññataro bhikkhu yenāyasmā sāriputto tenupasaṅkami; upasaṅkamitvā āyasmantaṁ sāriputtaṁ etadavoca:

Then a certain mendicant went up to Venerable Sāriputta, and said to him,

"yassa kho tvaṁ, āvuso sāriputta, puṇṇassa nāma bhikkhuno mantāṇiputtassa abhiṇhaṁ kittayamāno ahosi, so bhagavatā dhammiyā kathāya sandassito samādapito samuttejito sampahaṁsito bhagavato bhāsitaṁ abhinanditvā anumoditvā uṭṭhāyāsanā bhagavantaṁ abhivādetvā padakkhiṇaṁ katvā yena andhavanaṁ tena pakkanto divāvihārāyā"ti.

"Reverend Sāriputta, the mendicant named Puṇṇa, of whom you have often spoken so highly, after being inspired by a talk of the Buddha's, left for the Dark Forest for the day's meditation."

Atha kho āyasmā sāriputto taramānarūpo nisīdanaṁ ādāya āyasmantaṁ puṇṇaṁ mantāṇiputtaṁ piṭṭhito piṭṭhito anubandhi sīsānulokī.

Sāriputta quickly grabbed his sitting cloth and followed behind Puṇṇa, keeping sight of his head.

Atha kho āyasmā puṇṇo mantāṇiputto andhavanaṁ ajjhogāhetvā aññatarasmiṁ rukkhamūle divāvihāraṁ nisīdi.

Puṇṇa plunged deep into the Dark Forest and sat at the root of a tree for the day's meditation.

Āyasmāpi kho sāriputto andhavanaṁ ajjhogāhetvā aññatarasmiṁ rukkhamūle divāvihāraṁ nisīdi.

And Sāriputta did likewise.

Atha kho āyasmā sāriputto sāyanhasamayaṁ paṭisallānā vuṭṭhito yenāyasmā puṇṇo mantāniputto tenupasaṅkami; upasaṅkamitvā āyasmatā puṇṇena mantāniputtena saddhiṁ sammodi.

Then in the late afternoon, Sāriputta came out of retreat, went to Puṇṇa, and exchanged greetings with him.

Sammodanīyaṁ kathaṁ sāraṇīyaṁ vītisāretvā ekamantaṁ nisīdi. Ekamantaṁ nisinno kho āyasmā sāriputto āyasmantaṁ puṇṇaṁ mantāniputtaṁ etadavoca:

When the greetings and polite conversation were over, he sat down to one side and said to Puṇṇa:

"Bhagavati no, āvuso, brahmacariyaṁ vussatī"ti?

"Reverend, is our spiritual life lived under the Buddha?"

"Evamāvuso"ti.

"Yes, reverend."

"Kiṁ nu kho, āvuso, sīlavisuddhatthaṁ bhagavati brahmacariyaṁ vussatī"ti?

"Is the spiritual life lived under the Buddha for the sake of purification of ethics?"

"No hidaṁ, āvuso".

"Certainly not."

"Kiṁ panāvuso, cittavisuddhatthaṁ bhagavati brahmacariyaṁ vussatī"ti?

"Then is the spiritual life lived under the Buddha for the sake of purification of mind?"

"No hidaṁ, āvuso".

"Certainly not."

"Kiṁ nu kho, āvuso, diṭṭhivisuddhatthaṁ bhagavati brahmacariyaṁ vussatī"ti?

"Is the spiritual life lived under the Buddha for the sake of purification of view?"

"No hidaṁ, āvuso".

"Certainly not."

"Kiṁ panāvuso, kaṅkhāvitaraṇavisuddhatthaṁ bhagavati brahmacariyaṁ vussatī"ti?

"Then is the spiritual life lived under the Buddha for the sake of purification through overcoming doubt?"

"No hidaṁ, āvuso".

"Certainly not."

"Kiṁ nu kho, āvuso, maggāmaggañāṇadassanavisuddhatthaṁ bhagavati brahmacariyaṁ vussatī"ti?

"Is the spiritual life lived under the Buddha for the sake of purification of knowledge and vision of the variety of paths?"

"No hidaṁ, āvuso".

"Certainly not."

"Kiṁ panāvuso, paṭipadāñāṇadassanavisuddhatthaṁ bhagavati brahmacariyaṁ vussatī"ti?

"Then is the spiritual life lived under the Buddha for the sake of purification of knowledge and vision of the practice?"

"No hidaṁ, āvuso".

"Certainly not."

"Kiṁ nu kho, āvuso, ñāṇadassanavisuddhatthaṁ bhagavati brahmacariyaṁ vussatī"ti?

"Is the spiritual life lived under the Buddha for the sake of purification of knowledge and vision?"

"No hidaṁ, āvuso".

"Certainly not."

"'Kiṁ nu kho, āvuso, sīlavisuddhatthaṁ bhagavati brahmacariyaṁ vussatī'ti iti puṭṭho samāno 'no hidaṁ, āvuso'ti vadesi.

"When asked each of these questions, you answered, 'Certainly not.'

'Kiṁ panāvuso, cittavisuddhatthaṁ bhagavati brahmacariyaṁ vussatī'ti iti puṭṭho samāno 'no hidaṁ, āvuso'ti vadesi.

'Kiṁ nu kho, āvuso, diṭṭhivisuddhatthaṁ ...pe...

kaṅkhāvitaraṇavisuddhatthaṁ …pe…

maggāmaggañāṇadassanavisuddhatthaṁ …pe…

paṭipadāñāṇadassanavisuddhatthaṁ …pe…

kiṁ nu kho, āvuso, ñāṇadassanavisuddhatthaṁ bhagavati brahmacariyaṁ vussatī'ti iti puṭṭho samāno 'no hidaṁ āvuso'ti vadesi.

Kimatthaṁ carahāvuso, bhagavati brahmacariyaṁ vussatī'ti?

Then what exactly is the purpose of leading the spiritual life under the Buddha?"

"Anupādāparinibbānatthaṁ kho, āvuso, bhagavati brahmacariyaṁ vussatī'ti.

"The purpose of leading the spiritual life under the Buddha is extinguishment by not grasping."

"Kiṁ nu kho, āvuso, sīlavisuddhi anupādāparinibbānan"ti?

"Reverend, is purification of ethics extinguishment by not grasping?"

"No hidaṁ, āvuso".

"Certainly not."

"Kiṁ panāvuso, cittavisuddhi anupādāparinibbānan"ti?

"No hidaṁ, āvuso".

"Kiṁ nu kho, āvuso, diṭṭhivisuddhi anupādāparinibbānan"ti?

"No hidaṁ, āvuso".

"Kiṁ panāvuso, kaṅkhāvitaraṇavisuddhi anupādāparinibbānan"ti?

"No hidaṁ, āvuso".

"Kiṁ nu kho, āvuso, maggāmaggañāṇadassanavisuddhi anupādāparinibbānan"ti?

"No hidaṁ, āvuso".

"Kiṁ panāvuso, paṭipadāñāṇadassanavisuddhi anupādāparinibbānan"ti?

"No hidaṁ, āvuso".

"Kiṁ nu kho, āvuso, ñāṇadassanavisuddhi anupādāparinibbānan"ti?

"Is purification of knowledge and vision extinguishment by not grasping?"

"No hidaṁ, āvuso".

"Certainly not."

"Kiṁ panāvuso, aññatra imehi dhammehi anupādāparinibbānan"ti?

"Then is extinguishment by not grasping something apart from these things?"

"No hidaṁ, āvuso".

"Certainly not."

"'Kiṁ nu kho, āvuso, sīlavisuddhi anupādāparinibbānan'ti iti puṭṭho samāno 'no hidaṁ, āvuso'ti vadesi.

"When asked each of these questions, you answered, 'Certainly not.'

'Kiṁ panāvuso, cittavisuddhi anupādāparinibbānan'ti iti puṭṭho samāno 'no hidaṁ, āvuso'ti vadesi.

'Kiṁ nu kho, āvuso, diṭṭhivisuddhi anupādāparinibbānan'ti …pe…

kaṅkhāvitaraṇavisuddhi …

maggāmaggañāṇadassanavisuddhi …

paṭipadāñāṇadassanavisuddhi …

'kiṁ nu kho, āvuso, ñāṇadassanavisuddhi anupādāparinibbānan'ti iti puṭṭho samāno 'no hidaṁ, āvuso'ti vadesi.

'Kiṁ panāvuso, aññatra imehi dhammehi anupādāparinibbānan'ti iti puṭṭho samāno 'no hidaṁ, āvuso'ti vadesi.

Yathākathaṁ panāvuso, imassa bhāsitassa attho daṭṭhabbo"ti?

How then should we see the meaning of this statement?"

"Sīlavisuddhiñce, āvuso, bhagavā anupādāparinibbānaṁ paññapeyya, saupādānaṁyeva samānaṁ anupādāparinibbānaṁ paññapeyya.

"If the Buddha had declared purification of ethics to be extinguishment by not grasping, he would have declared that which has grasping to be extinguishment by not grasping. …

Cittavisuddhiñce, āvuso, bhagavā anupādāparinibbānaṁ paññapeyya, saupādānaṁyeva samānaṁ anupādāparinibbānaṁ paññapeyya.

Diṭṭhivisuddhiñce, āvuso, bhagavā anupādāparinibbānaṁ paññapeyya, saupādānaṁyeva samānaṁ anupādāparinibbānaṁ paññapeyya.

Kaṅkhāvitaraṇavisuddhiñce, āvuso, bhagavā anupādāparinibbānaṁ paññapeyya, saupādānaṁyeva samānaṁ anupādāparinibbānaṁ paññapeyya.

Maggāmaggañāṇadassanavisuddhiñce, āvuso, bhagavā anupādāparinibbānaṁ paññapeyya, saupādānaṁyeva samānaṁ anupādāparinibbānaṁ paññapeyya.

Paṭipadāñāṇadassanavisuddhiñce, āvuso, bhagavā anupādāparinibbānaṃ paññapeyya, saupādānaṃyeva samānaṃ anupādāparinibbānaṃ paññapeyya.

Ñāṇadassanavisuddhiñce, āvuso, bhagavā anupādāparinibbānaṃ paññapeyya, saupādānaṃyeva samānaṃ anupādāparinibbānaṃ paññapeyya.

If the Buddha had declared purification of knowledge and vision to be extinguishment by not grasping, he would have declared that which has grasping to be extinguishment by not grasping.

Aññatra ce, āvuso, imehi dhammehi anupādāparinibbānaṃ abhavissa, puthujjano parinibbāyeyya.

But if extinguishment by not grasping was something apart from these things, an ordinary person would become extinguished.

Puthujjano hi, āvuso, aññatra imehi dhammehi.

For an ordinary person lacks these things.

Tena hāvuso, upamaṃ te karissāmi;

Well then, reverend, I shall give you a simile.

upamāyapidhekacce viññū purisā bhāsitassa atthaṃ ājānanti.

For by means of a simile some sensible people understand the meaning of what is said.

Seyyathāpi, āvuso, rañño pasenadissa kosalassa sāvatthiyaṃ paṭivasantassa sākete kiñcideva accāyikaṃ karaṇīyaṃ uppajjeyya.

Suppose that, while staying in Sāvatthī, King Pasenadi of Kosala had some urgent business come up in Sāketa.

Tassa antarā ca sāvatthiṃ antarā ca sāketaṃ satta rathavinītāni upaṭṭhapeyyuṃ.

Now, between Sāvatthī and Sāketa seven prepared chariots were stationed ready for him.

Atha kho, āvuso, rājā pasenadi kosalo sāvatthiyā nikkhamitvā antepuradvārā paṭhamaṃ rathavinītaṃ abhiruheyya, paṭhamena rathavinītena dutiyaṃ rathavinītaṃ pāpuṇeyya, paṭhamaṃ rathavinītaṃ vissajjeyya dutiyaṃ rathavinītaṃ abhiruheyya.

Then Pasenadi, having departed Sāvatthī, mounted the first prepared chariot by the gate of the royal compound. The first prepared chariot would bring him to the second, where he'd dismount and mount the second chariot.

Dutiyena rathavinītena tatiyaṃ rathavinītaṃ pāpuṇeyya, dutiyaṃ rathavinītaṃ vissajjeyya, tatiyaṃ rathavinītaṃ abhiruheyya.

The second prepared chariot would bring him to the third ...

Tatiyena rathavinītena catutthaṁ rathavinītaṁ pāpuṇeyya, tatiyaṁ rathavinītaṁ vissajjeyya, catutthaṁ rathavinītaṁ abhiruheyya.

The third prepared chariot would bring him to the fourth ...

Catutthena rathavinītena pañcamaṁ rathavinītaṁ pāpuṇeyya, catutthaṁ rathavinītaṁ vissajjeyya, pañcamaṁ rathavinītaṁ abhiruheyya.

The fourth prepared chariot would bring him to the fifth ...

Pañcamena rathavinītena chaṭṭhaṁ rathavinītaṁ pāpuṇeyya, pañcamaṁ rathavinītaṁ vissajjeyya, chaṭṭhaṁ rathavinītaṁ abhiruheyya.

The fifth prepared chariot would bring him to the sixth ...

Chaṭṭhena rathavinītena sattamaṁ rathavinītaṁ pāpuṇeyya, chaṭṭhaṁ rathavinītaṁ vissajjeyya, sattamaṁ rathavinītaṁ abhiruheyya.

The sixth prepared chariot would bring him to the seventh, where he'd dismount and mount the seventh chariot.

Sattamena rathavinītena sāketaṁ anupāpuṇeyya antepuradvāraṁ.

The seventh prepared chariot would bring him to the gate of the royal compound of Sāketa.

Tamenaṁ antepuradvāragataṁ samānaṁ mittāmaccā ñātisālohitā evaṁ puccheyyuṁ:

And when he was at the gate, friends and colleagues, relatives and kin would ask him:

'iminā tvaṁ, mahārāja, rathavinītena sāvatthiyā sāketaṁ anuppatto antepuradvāran'ti?

'Great king, did you come to Sāketa from Sāvatthī by this prepared chariot?'

Kathaṁ byākaramāno nu kho, āvuso, rājā pasenadi kosalo sammā byākaramāno byākareyyā"ti?

If asked this, how should King Pasenadi rightly reply?"

"Evaṁ byākaramāno kho, āvuso, rājā pasenadi kosalo sammā byākaramāno byākareyya:

"The king should reply:

'idha me sāvatthiyaṁ paṭivasantassa sākete kiñcideva accāyikaṁ karaṇīyaṁ uppajji.

'Well, while staying in Sāvatthī, I had some urgent business come up in Sāketa.

Tassa me antarā ca sāvatthiṁ antarā ca sāketaṁ satta rathavinītāni upaṭṭhapesuṁ.

Now, between Sāvatthī and Sāketa seven prepared chariots were stationed ready for me.

Atha khvāhaṁ sāvatthiyā nikkhamitvā antepuradvārā paṭhamaṁ rathavinītaṁ abhiruhiṁ.

Then, having departed Sāvatthī, I mounted the first prepared chariot by the gate of the royal compound.

Paṭhamena rathavinītena dutiyaṁ rathavinītaṁ pāpuṇiṁ, paṭhamaṁ rathavinītaṁ vissajjiṁ dutiyaṁ rathavinītaṁ abhiruhiṁ.

The first prepared chariot brought me to the second, where I dismounted and mounted the second chariot. ...

Dutiyena rathavinītena tatiyaṁ rathavinītaṁ pāpuṇiṁ, dutiyaṁ rathavinītaṁ vissajjiṁ, tatiyaṁ rathavinītaṁ abhiruhiṁ.

Tatiyena rathavinītena catutthaṁ rathavinītaṁ pāpuṇiṁ, tatiyaṁ rathavinītaṁ vissajjiṁ, catutthaṁ rathavinītaṁ abhiruhiṁ.

Catutthena rathavinītena pañcamaṁ rathavinītaṁ pāpuṇiṁ, catutthaṁ rathavinītaṁ vissajjiṁ, pañcamaṁ rathavinītaṁ abhiruhiṁ.

Pañcamena rathavinītena chaṭṭhaṁ rathavinītaṁ pāpuṇiṁ, pañcamaṁ rathavinītaṁ vissajjiṁ, chaṭṭhaṁ rathavinītaṁ abhiruhiṁ.

Chaṭṭhena rathavinītena sattamaṁ rathavinītaṁ pāpuṇiṁ, chaṭṭhaṁ rathavinītaṁ vissajjiṁ, sattamaṁ rathavinītaṁ abhiruhiṁ.

The sixth prepared chariot brought me to the seventh, where I dismounted and mounted the seventh chariot.

Sattamena rathavinītena sāketaṁ anuppatto antepuradvāran'ti.

The seventh prepared chariot brought me to the gate of the royal compound of Sāketa.'

Evaṁ byākaramāno kho, āvuso, rājā pasenadi kosalo sammā byākaramāno byākareyyā"ti.

That's how King Pasenadi should rightly reply."

"Evameva kho, āvuso, sīlavisuddhi yāvadeva cittavisuddhatthā, cittavisuddhi yāvadeva diṭṭhivisuddhatthā, diṭṭhivisuddhi yāvadeva kaṅkhāvitaraṇavisuddhatthā, kaṅkhāvitaraṇavisuddhi yāvadeva maggāmaggañāṇadassanavisuddhatthā, maggāmaggañāṇadassanavisuddhi yāvadeva paṭipadāñāṇadassanavisuddhatthā, paṭipadāñāṇadassanavisuddhi yāvadeva ñāṇadassanavisuddhatthā, ñāṇadassanavisuddhi yāvadeva anupādāparinibbānatthā.

"In the same way, reverend, purification of ethics is only for the sake of purification of mind. Purification of mind is only for the sake of purification of view. Purification of view is only for the sake of purification through overcoming doubt. Purification through overcoming doubt is only for the sake of purification of knowledge and vision of the variety of paths. Purification of knowledge and vision of the variety of paths is only for the sake of purification of knowledge and vision of the practice. Purification of knowledge and vision of the practice is only for the sake of purification of knowledge and vision. Purification of knowledge and vision is only for the sake of extinguishment by not grasping.

Anupādāparinibbānatthaṁ kho, āvuso, bhagavati brahmacariyaṁ vussatī"ti.

The spiritual life is lived under the Buddha for the sake of extinguishment by not grasping."

Evaṁ vutte, āyasmā sāriputto āyasmantaṁ puṇṇaṁ mantāṇiputtaṁ etadavoca:

When he said this, Sāriputta said to Puṇṇa,

"konāmo āyasmā, kathañca panāyasmantaṁ sabrahmacārī jānantī"ti?

"What is the venerable's name? And how are you known among your spiritual companions?"

"Puṇṇoti kho me, āvuso, nāmaṁ;

"Reverend, my name is Puṇṇa.

mantāṇiputtoti ca pana maṁ sabrahmacārī jānantī"ti.

And I am known as Mantāṇiputta among my spiritual companions."

"Acchariyaṁ, āvuso, abbhutaṁ, āvuso.

"It's incredible, reverend, it's amazing!

Yathā taṁ sutavatā sāvakena sammadeva satthusāsanaṁ ājānantena, evameva āyasmatā puṇṇena mantāṇiputtena gambhīrā gambhīrapañhā anumassa anumassa byākatā.

Venerable Puṇṇa son of Mantāṇī has answered each deep question point by point, as a learned disciple who rightly understands the teacher's instructions.

Lābhā sabrahmacārīnaṁ, suladdhalābhā sabrahmacārīnaṁ,

It is fortunate for his spiritual companions, so very fortunate,

ye āyasmantaṁ puṇṇaṁ mantāṇiputtaṁ labhanti dassanāya, labhanti payirūpāsanāya.

that they get to see Venerable Puṇṇa son of Mantāṇī and pay homage to him.

Celaṇḍukena cepi sabrahmacārī āyasmantaṁ puṇṇaṁ mantāṇiputtaṁ muddhanā pariharantā labheyyuṁ dassanāya, labheyyuṁ payirupāsanāya, tesampi lābhā tesampi suladdhaṁ, amhākampi lābhā amhākampi suladdhaṁ, ye mayaṁ āyasmantaṁ puṇṇaṁ mantāṇiputtaṁ labhāma dassanāya, labhāma payirupāsanāyā"ti.

Even if they only got to see him and pay respects to him by carrying him around on their heads on a roll of cloth, it would still be very fortunate for them! And it's fortunate for me, so very fortunate, that I get to see the venerable and pay homage to him."

Evaṁ vutte, āyasmā puṇṇo mantāṇiputto āyasmantaṁ sāriputtaṁ etadavoca:

When he said this, Puṇṇa said to Sāriputta,

"ko nāmo āyasmā, kathañca panāyasmantaṁ sabrahmacārī jānantī"ti?

"What is the venerable's name? And how are you known among your spiritual companions?"

"Upatissoti kho me, āvuso, nāmaṁ;

"Reverend, my name is Upatissa.

sāriputtoti ca pana maṁ sabrahmacārī jānantī"ti.

And I am known as Sāriputta among my spiritual companions."

"Satthukappena vata kira, bho, sāvakena saddhiṁ mantayamānā na jānimha:

"Goodness! I had no idea I was consulting with the Venerable Sāriputta, the disciple who is fit to be compared with the Teacher himself!

'āyasmā sāriputto'ti.

Sace hi mayaṁ jāneyyāma 'āyasmā sāriputto'ti, ettakampi no nappaṭibhāseyya.

If I'd known, I wouldn't have said so much.

Acchariyaṁ, āvuso, abbhutaṁ, āvuso.

It's incredible, reverend, it's amazing!

Yathā taṁ sutavatā sāvakena sammadeva satthusāsanaṁ ājānantena, evameva āyasmatā sāriputtena gambhīrā gambhīrapañhā anumassa anumassa pucchitā.

Venerable Sāriputta has asked each deep question point by point, as a learned disciple who rightly understands the teacher's instructions.

Lābhā sabrahmacārīnaṁ suladdhalābhā sabrahmacārīnaṁ,

It is fortunate for his spiritual companions, so very fortunate,

ye āyasmantaṁ sāriputtaṁ labhanti dassanāya, labhanti payirūpāsanāya.

that they get to see Venerable Sāriputta and pay homage to him.

Celaṇḍukena cepi sabrahmacārī āyasmantaṁ sāriputtaṁ muddhanā pariharantā labheyyuṁ dassanāya, labheyyuṁ payirūpāsanāya, tesampi lābhā tesampi suladdhaṁ, amhākampi lābhā amhākampi suladdhaṁ, ye mayaṁ āyasmantaṁ sāriputtaṁ labhāma dassanāya, labhāma payirūpāsanāyā"ti.

Even if they only got to see him and pay respects to him by carrying him around on their heads on a roll of cloth, it would still be very fortunate for them! And it's fortunate for me, so very fortunate, that I get to see the venerable and pay homage to him."

Itiha te ubhopi mahānāgā aññamaññassa subhāsitaṁ samanumodiṁsūti.

And so these two spiritual giants agreed with each others' fine words.

Rathavinītasuttaṁ niṭṭhitaṁ catutthaṁ.

25 Nivapasutta:

Fodder

Evaṁ me sutaṁ—

So I have heard.

ekaṁ samayaṁ bhagavā sāvatthiyaṁ viharati jetavane anāthapiṇḍikassa ārāme.

At one time the Buddha was staying near Sāvatthī in Jeta's Grove, Anāthapiṇḍika's monastery.

Tatra kho bhagavā bhikkhū āmantesi:

There the Buddha addressed the mendicants,

"bhikkhavo"ti.

"Mendicants!"

"Bhadante"ti te bhikkhū bhagavato paccassosuṁ.

"Venerable sir," they replied.

Bhagavā etadavoca:

The Buddha said this:

"Na, bhikkhave, nevāpiko nivāpaṁ nivapati migajātānaṁ:

"Mendicants, a trapper doesn't cast bait for deer thinking,

'imaṁ me nivāpaṁ nivuttaṁ migajātā paribhuñjantā dīghāyukā vaṇṇavanto ciraṁ dīghamaddhānaṁ yāpentū'ti.

'May the deer, enjoying this bait, be healthy and in good condition. May they live long and prosper!'

Evañca kho, bhikkhave, nevāpiko nivāpaṁ nivapati migajātānaṁ:

A trapper casts bait for deer thinking,

'imaṁ me nivāpaṁ nivuttaṁ migajātā anupakhajja mucchitā bhojanāni bhuñjissanti, anupakhajja mucchitā bhojanāni bhuñjamānā madaṁ āpajjissanti, mattā samānā pamādaṁ āpajjissanti, pamattā samānā yathākāmakaraṇīyā bhavissanti imasmiṁ nivāpe'ti.

'When these deer intrude on where I cast the bait, they'll recklessly enjoy eating it. They'll become indulgent, then they'll become negligent, and then I'll be able to do what I want with them on account of this bait.'

Tatra, bhikkhave, paṭhamā migajātā amuṁ nivāpaṁ nivuttaṁ nevāpikassa anupakhajja mucchitā bhojanāni bhuñjiṁsu, te tattha anupakhajja mucchitā bhojanāni bhuñjamānā madaṁ āpajjiṁsu, mattā samānā pamādaṁ āpajjiṁsu, pamattā samānā yathākāmakaraṇīyā ahesuṁ nevāpikassa amusmiṁ nivāpe.

And indeed, the first herd of deer intruded on where the trapper cast the bait and recklessly enjoyed eating it. They became indulgent, then they became negligent, and then the trapper was able to do what he wanted with them on account of that bait.

Evañhi te, bhikkhave, paṭhamā migajātā na parimucciṁsu nevāpikassa iddhānubhāvā.

And that's how the first herd of deer failed to get free from the trapper's power.

Tatra, bhikkhave, dutiyā migajātā evaṁ samacintesuṁ:

So then a second herd of deer thought up a plan,

'ye kho te paṭhamā migajātā amuṁ nivāpaṁ nivuttaṁ nevāpikassa anupakhajja mucchitā bhojanāni bhuñjiṁsu.

'The first herd of deer became indulgent …

Te tattha anupakhajja mucchitā bhojanāni bhuñjamānā madaṁ āpajjiṁsu, mattā samānā pamādaṁ āpajjiṁsu, pamattā samānā yathākāmakaraṇīyā ahesuṁ nevāpikassa amusmiṁ nivāpe.

Evañhi te paṭhamā migajātā na parimucciṁsu nevāpikassa iddhānubhāvā.

and failed to get free of the trapper's power.

Yannūna mayaṁ sabbaso nivāpabhojanā paṭivirameyyāma, bhayabhogā paṭiviratā araññāyatanāni ajjhogāhetvā vihareyyāmā'ti.

Why don't we avoid eating the bait altogether? Avoiding dangerous food, we can venture deep into a wilderness region and live there.'

Te sabbaso nivāpabhojanā paṭiviramiṁsu, bhayabhogā paṭiviratā araññāyatanāni ajjhogāhetvā vihariṁsu.

And that's just what they did.

Tesaṁ gimhānaṁ pacchime māse, tiṇodakasaṅkhaye, adhimattakasimānaṁ patto kāyo hoti.

But when it came to the last month of summer, the grass and water ran out. Their bodies became much too thin,

Tesaṁ adhimattakasimānaṁ pattakāyānaṁ balavīriyaṁ parihāyi.

and they lost their strength and energy.

Balavīriye parihīne tameva nivāpaṁ nivuttaṁ nevāpikassa paccāgamiṁsu.

So they went back to that same place where the trapper had cast bait.

Te tattha anupakhajja mucchitā bhojanāni bhuñjiṁsu.

Intruding on that place, they recklessly enjoyed eating it …

Te tattha anupakhajja mucchitā bhojanāni bhuñjamānā madaṁ āpajjiṁsu, mattā samānā pamādaṁ āpajjiṁsu, pamattā samānā yathākāmakaraṇīyā ahesuṁ nevāpikassa amusmiṁ nivāpe.

Evañhi te, bhikkhave, dutiyāpi migajātā na parimucciṁsu nevāpikassa iddhānubhāvā.

And that's how the second herd failed to get free from the trapper's power.

Tatra, bhikkhave, tatiyā migajātā evaṁ samacintesuṁ:

So then a third herd of deer thought up a plan,

'ye kho te paṭhamā migajātā amuṁ nivāpaṁ nivuttaṁ nevāpikassa …pe…

'The first …

evañhi te paṭhamā migajātā na parimucciṁsu nevāpikassa iddhānubhāvā.

Yepi te dutiyā migajātā evaṁ samacintesuṁ:

and second herds of deer ...

"ye kho te paṭhamā migajātā amuṁ nivāpaṁ nivuttaṁ nevāpikassa ...pe...

evañhi te paṭhamā migajātā na parimucciṁsu nevāpikassa iddhānubhāvā.

Yannūna mayaṁ sabbaso nivāpabhojanā paṭivirameyyāma, bhayabhogā paṭiviratā araññāyatanāni ajjhogāhetvā vihareyyāmā"ti.

Te sabbaso nivāpabhojanā paṭiviramiṁsu, bhayabhogā paṭiviratā araññāyatanāni ajjhogāhetvā vihariṁsu.

Tesaṁ gimhānaṁ pacchime māse tiṇodakasaṅkhaye adhimattakasimānaṁ patto kāyo hoti.

Tesaṁ adhimattakasimānaṁ pattakāyānaṁ balavīriyaṁ parihāyi.

Balavīriye parihīne tameva nivāpaṁ nivuttaṁ nevāpikassa paccāgamiṁsu.

Te tattha anupakhajja mucchitā bhojanāni bhuñjiṁsu.

Te tattha anupakhajja mucchitā bhojanāni bhuñjamānā madaṁ āpajjiṁsu, mattā samānā pamādaṁ āpajjiṁsu, pamattā samānā yathākāmakaraṇīyā ahesuṁ nevāpikassa amusmiṁ nivāpe.

Evañhi te dutiyāpi migajātā na parimucciṁsu nevāpikassa iddhānubhāvā.

failed to get free of the trapper's power.

Yannūna mayaṁ amuṁ nivāpaṁ nivuttaṁ nevāpikassa upanissāya āsayaṁ kappeyyāma.

Why don't we set up our lair close by the place where the trapper has cast the bait?

Tatrāsayaṁ kappetvā amuṁ nivāpaṁ nivuttaṁ nevāpikassa ananupakhajja amucchitā bhojanāni bhuñjissāma, ananupakhajja amucchitā bhojanāni bhuñjamānā na madaṁ āpajjissāma, amattā samānā na pamādaṁ āpajjissāma, appamattā samānā na yathākāmakaraṇīyā bhavissāma nevāpikassa amusmiṁ nivāpe'ti.

Then we can intrude on it and enjoy eating without being reckless. We won't become indulgent, then we won't become negligent, and then the trapper won't be able to do what he wants with us on account of that bait.'

Te amuṁ nivāpaṁ nivuttaṁ nevāpikassa upanissāya āsayaṁ kappayiṁsu.

And that's just what they did.

Tatrāsayaṁ kappetvā amuṁ nivāpaṁ nivuttaṁ nevāpikassa ananupakhajja amucchitā bhojanāni bhuñjiṁsu, te tattha ananupakhajja amucchitā bhojanāni bhuñjamānā na madaṁ āpajjiṁsu, amattā samānā na pamādaṁ āpajjiṁsu, appamattā samānā na yathākāmakaraṇīyā ahesuṁ nevāpikassa amusmiṁ nivāpe.

Tatra, bhikkhave, nevāpikassa ca nevāpikaparisāya ca etadahosi:

So the trapper and his companions thought,

'saṭhāssunāmime tatiyā migajātā ketabino, iddhimantāssunāmime tatiyā migajātā parajanā;

'Wow, this third herd of deer is so sneaky and devious, they must be some kind of unnatural spirits with psychic power!

imañca nāma nivāpaṁ nivuttaṁ paribhuñjanti, na ca nesaṁ jānāma āgatiṁ vā gatiṁ vā.

For they eat the bait we've cast without us knowing how they come and go.

Yannūna mayaṁ imaṁ nivāpaṁ nivuttaṁ mahatīhi daṇḍavākarāhi samantā sappadesaṁ anuparivāreyyāma, appeva nāma tatiyānaṁ migajātānaṁ āsayaṁ passeyyāma, yattha te gāhaṁ gaccheyyun'ti.

Why don't we surround the bait on all sides by staking out high nets? Hopefully we might get to see their lair, where they go to hide out.'

Te amuṁ nivāpaṁ nivuttaṁ mahatīhi daṇḍavākarāhi samantā sappadesaṁ anuparivāresuṁ.

And that's just what they did.

Addasaṁsu kho, bhikkhave, nevāpiko ca nevāpikaparisā ca tatiyānaṁ migajātānaṁ āsayaṁ, yattha te gāhaṁ agamaṁsu.

And they saw where the third herd of deer had their lair, where they went to hide out.

Evañhi te, bhikkhave, tatiyāpi migajātā na parimucciṁsu nevāpikassa iddhānubhāvā.

And that's how the third herd failed to get free from the trapper's power.

Tatra, bhikkhave, catutthā migajātā evaṁ samacintesuṁ:

So then a fourth herd of deer thought up a plan,

'ye kho te paṭhamā migajātā ...pe...

'The first ...

evañhi te paṭhamā migajātā na parimucciṁsu nevāpikassa iddhānubhāvā.

Yepi te dutiyā migajātā evaṁ samacintesuṁ:

second ...

"ye kho te paṭhamā migajātā ...pe...

evañhi te paṭhamā migajātā na parimucciṁsu nevāpikassa iddhānubhāvā.

Yannūna mayaṁ sabbaso nivāpabhojanā paṭivirameyyāma, bhayabhogā paṭiviratā araññāyatanāni ajjhogāhetvā vihareyyāmā"ti.

Te sabbaso nivāpabhojanā paṭiviramiṁsu ...pe...

evañhi te dutiyāpi migajātā na parimucciṁsu nevāpikassa iddhānubhāvā.

Yepi te tatiyā migajātā evaṁ samacintesuṁ:

and third herds of deer ...

"ye kho te paṭhamā migajātā ...pe...

evañhi te paṭhamā migajātā na parimucciṁsu nevāpikassa iddhānubhāvā.

Yepi te dutiyā migajātā evaṁ samacintesuṁ:

'ye kho te paṭhamā migajātā ...pe...

evañhi te paṭhamā migajātā na parimucciṁsu nevāpikassa iddhānubhāvā.

Yannūna mayaṁ sabbaso nivāpabhojanā paṭivirameyyāma, bhayabhogā paṭiviratā araññāyatanāni ajjhogāhetvā vihareyyāmā'ti.

Te sabbaso nivāpabhojanā paṭiviramiṁsu ...pe...

evañhi te dutiyāpi migajātā na parimucciṁsu nevāpikassa iddhānubhāvā.

Yannūna mayaṁ amuṁ nivāpaṁ nivuttaṁ nevāpikassa upanissāya āsayaṁ kappeyyāma, tatrāsayaṁ kappetvā amuṁ nivāpaṁ nivuttaṁ nevāpikassa ananupakhajja amucchitā bhojanāni bhuñjissāma, ananupakhajja amucchitā bhojanāni bhuñjamānā na madaṁ āpajjissāma, amattā samānā na pamādaṁ āpajjissāma, appamattā samānā na yathākāmakaraṇīyā bhavissāma nevāpikassa amusmiṁ nivāpe"ti.

Te amuṁ nivāpaṁ nivuttaṁ nevāpikassa upanissāya āsayaṁ kappayiṁsu, tatrāsayaṁ kappetvā amuṁ nivāpaṁ nivuttaṁ nevāpikassa ananupakhajja amucchitā bhojanāni bhuñjiṁsu, te tattha ananupakhajja amucchitā bhojanāni bhuñjamānā na madaṁ āpajjiṁsu, amattā samānā na pamādaṁ āpajjiṁsu, appamattā samānā na yathākāmakaraṇīyā ahesuṁ nevāpikassa amusmiṁ nivāpe.

Tatra nevāpikassa ca nevāpikaparisāya ca etadahosi:

"saṭhāssunāmime tatiyā migajātā ketabino, iddhimantāssunāmime tatiyā migajātā parajanā, imañca nāma nivāpam nivuttam paribhuñjanti.

Na ca nesam jānāma āgatim vā gatim vā.

Yannūna mayam imam nivāpam nivuttam mahatīhi daṇḍavākarāhi samantā sappadesam anuparivāreyyāma, appeva nāma tatiyānam migajātānam āsayam passeyyāma, yattha te gāham gaccheyyun"ti.

Te amum nivāpam nivuttam mahatīhi daṇḍavākarāhi samantā sappadesam anuparivāresum.

Addasamsu kho nevāpiko ca nevāpikaparisā ca tatiyānam migajātānam āsayam, yattha te gāham agamamsu.

Evañhi te tatiyāpi migajātā na parimuccimsu nevāpikassa iddhānubhāvā.

failed to get free of the trapper's power.

Yannūna mayam yattha agati nevāpikassa ca nevāpikaparisāya ca tatrāsayam kappeyyāma, tatrāsayam kappetvā amum nivāpam nivuttam nevāpikassa ananupakhajja amucchitā bhojanāni bhuñjissāma, ananupakhajja amucchitā bhojanāni bhuñjamānā na madam āpajjissāma, amattā samānā na pamādam āpajjissāma, appamattā samānā na yathākāmakaraṇīyā bhavissāma nevāpikassa amusmim nivāpe'ti.

Why don't we set up our lair somewhere the trapper and his companions can't go? Then we can intrude on where the trapper has cast the bait and enjoy eating it without being reckless. We won't become indulgent, then we won't become negligent, and then the trapper won't be able to do with them what he wants on account of that bait.'

Te yattha agati nevāpikassa ca nevāpikaparisāya ca tatrāsayam kappayimsu.

And that's just what they did.

Tatrāsayam kappetvā amum nivāpam nivuttam nevāpikassa ananupakhajja amucchitā bhojanāni bhuñjimsu, te tattha ananupakhajja amucchitā bhojanāni bhuñjamānā na madam āpajjimsu, amattā samānā na pamādam āpajjimsu, appamattā samānā na yathākāmakaraṇīyā ahesum nevāpikassa amusmim nivāpe.

Tatra, bhikkhave, nevāpikassa ca nevāpikaparisāya ca etadahosi:

So the trapper and his companions thought,

'saṭhāssunāmime catutthā migajātā ketabino, iddhimantāssunāmime catutthā migajātā parajanā.

'Wow, this fourth herd of deer is so sneaky and devious, they must be some kind of unnatural spirits with psychic power!

Imañca nāma nivāpam nivuttam paribhuñjanti, na ca nesam jānāma āgatim vā gatiṁ vā.

For they eat the bait we've cast without us knowing how they come and go.

Yannūna mayaṁ imaṁ nivāpaṁ nivuttaṁ mahatīhi daṇḍavākarāhi samantā sappadesaṁ anuparivāreyyāma, appeva nāma catutthānaṁ migajātānaṁ āsayaṁ passeyyāma yattha te gāhaṁ gaccheyyun'ti.

Why don't we surround the bait on all sides by staking out high nets? Hopefully we might get to see their lair, where they go to hide out.'

Te amuṁ nivāpaṁ nivuttaṁ mahatīhi daṇḍavākarāhi samantā sappadesaṁ anuparivāresuṁ.

And that's just what they did.

Neva kho, bhikkhave, addasaṁsu nevāpiko ca nevāpikaparisā ca catutthānaṁ migajātānaṁ āsayaṁ, yattha te gāhaṁ gaccheyyuṁ.

But they couldn't see where the fourth herd of deer had their lair, where they went to hide out.

Tatra, bhikkhave, nevāpikassa ca nevāpikaparisāya ca etadahosi:

So the trapper and his companions thought,

'sace kho mayaṁ catutthe migajāte ghaṭṭessāma, te ghaṭṭitā aññe ghaṭṭissanti te ghaṭṭitā aññe ghaṭṭissanti.

'If we disturb this fourth herd of deer, they'll disturb others, who in turn will disturb even more.

Evaṁ imaṁ nivāpaṁ nivuttaṁ sabbaso migajātā parimuñcissanti.

Then all of the deer will be free from this bait we've cast.

Yannūna mayaṁ catutthe migajāte ajjhupekkheyyāmā'ti.

Why don't we just keep an eye on that fourth herd?'

Ajjhupekkhiṁsu kho, bhikkhave, nevāpiko ca nevāpikaparisā ca catutthe migajāte.

And that's just what they did.

Evañhi te, bhikkhave, catutthā migajātā parimucciṁsu nevāpikassa iddhānubhāvā.

And that's how the fourth herd of deer got free from the trapper's power.

Upamā kho me ayaṁ, bhikkhave, katā atthassa viññāpanāya.

I've made up this simile to make a point.

Ayaṁ cevettha attho—

And this is what it means.

nivāpoti kho, bhikkhave, pañcannetaṁ kāmaguṇānaṁ adhivacanaṁ.

'Bait' is a term for the five kinds of sensual stimulation.

Nevāpikoti kho, bhikkhave, mārassetaṁ pāpimato adhivacanaṁ.

'Trapper' is a term for Māra the Wicked.

Nevāpikaparisāti kho, bhikkhave, māraparisāyetaṁ adhivacanaṁ.

'Trapper's companions' is a term for Māra's assembly.

Migajātāti kho, bhikkhave, samaṇabrāhmaṇānametaṁ adhivacanaṁ.

'Deer' is a term for ascetics and brahmins.

Tatra, bhikkhave, paṭhamā samaṇabrāhmaṇā amuṁ nivāpaṁ nivuttaṁ mārassa amūni ca lokāmisāni anupakhajja mucchitā bhojanāni bhuñjiṁsu.

Now, the first group of ascetics and brahmins intruded on where the bait and the material delights of the world were cast by Māra and recklessly enjoyed eating it.

Te tattha anupakhajja mucchitā bhojanāni bhuñjamānā madaṁ āpajjiṁsu, mattā samānā pamādaṁ āpajjiṁsu, pamattā samānā yathākāmakaraṇīyā ahesuṁ mārassa amusmiṁ nivāpe amusmiñca lokāmise.

They became indulgent, then they became negligent, and then Māra was able to do what he wanted with them on account of that bait and the material delights of the world.

Evañhi te, bhikkhave, paṭhamā samaṇabrāhmaṇā na parimucciṁsu mārassa iddhānubhāvā.

And that's how the first group of ascetics and brahmins failed to get free from Māra's power.

Seyyathāpi te, bhikkhave, paṭhamā migajātā tathūpame ahaṁ ime paṭhame samaṇabrāhmaṇe vadāmi.

This first group of ascetics and brahmins is just like the first herd of deer, I say.

Tatra, bhikkhave, dutiyā samaṇabrāhmaṇā evaṁ samacintesuṁ:

So then a second group of ascetics and brahmins thought up a plan,

'ye kho te paṭhamā samaṇabrāhmaṇā amuṁ nivāpaṁ nivuttaṁ mārassa amūni ca lokāmisāni anupakhajja mucchitā bhojanāni bhuñjiṁsu.

'The first group of ascetics and brahmins became indulgent ...

Te tattha anupakhajja mucchitā bhojanāni bhuñjamānā madaṁ āpajjiṁsu, mattā samānā pamādaṁ āpajjiṁsu, pamattā samānā yathākāmakaraṇīyā ahesuṁ mārassa amusmiṁ nivāpe amusmiñca lokāmise.

Evañhi te paṭhamā samaṇabrāhmaṇā na parimucciṁsu mārassa iddhānubhāvā.

and failed to get free of Māra's power.

Yannūna mayaṁ sabbaso nivāpabhojanā lokāmisā paṭivirameyyāma, bhayabhogā paṭiviratā araññāyatanāni ajjhogāhetvā vihareyyāmā'ti.

Why don't we avoid eating the bait and the world's material delights altogether? Avoiding dangerous food, we can venture deep into a wilderness region and live there.'

Te sabbaso nivāpabhojanā lokāmisā paṭiviramiṁsu, bhayabhogā paṭiviratā araññāyatanāni ajjhogāhetvā vihareyyāmāti.

Te sabbaso nivāpabhojanā lokāmisā paṭiviramiṁsu, bhayabhogā paṭiviratā araññāyatanāni ajjhogāhetvā vihariṁsu.

And that's just what they did.

Te tattha sākabhakkhāpi ahesuṁ, sāmākabhakkhāpi ahesuṁ, nīvārabhakkhāpi ahesuṁ, daddulabhakkhāpi ahesuṁ, haṭabhakkhāpi ahesuṁ, kaṇabhakkhāpi ahesuṁ, ācāmabhakkhāpi ahesuṁ, piññākabhakkhāpi ahesuṁ, tiṇabhakkhāpi ahesuṁ, gomayabhakkhāpi ahesuṁ, vanamūlaphalāhārā yāpesuṁ pavattaphalabhojī.

They ate herbs, millet, wild rice, poor rice, water lettuce, rice bran, scum from boiling rice, sesame flour, grass, or cow dung. They survived on forest roots and fruits, or eating fallen fruit.

Tesaṁ gimhānaṁ pacchime māse, tiṇodakasaṅkhaye, adhimattakasimānaṁ patto kāyo hoti.

But when it came to the last month of summer, the grass and water ran out. Their bodies became much too thin,

Tesaṁ adhimattakasimānaṁ pattakāyānaṁ balavīriyaṁ parihāyi.

and they lost their strength and energy.

Balavīriye parihīne cetovimutti parihāyi.

Because of this, they lost their heart's release,

Cetovimuttiyā parihīnāya tameva nivāpaṁ nivuttaṁ mārassa paccāgamiṁsu tāni ca lokāmisāni.

so they went back to that same place where Mära had cast the bait and the material delights of the world.

Te tattha anupakhajja mucchitā bhojanāni bhuñjiṁsu.

Intruding on that place, they recklessly enjoyed eating them …

Te tattha anupakhajja mucchitā bhojanāni bhuñjamānā madaṁ āpajjiṁsu, mattā samānā pamādaṁ āpajjiṁsu, pamattā samānā yathākāmakaraṇīyā ahesuṁ mārassa amusmiṁ nivāpe amusmiñca lokāmise.

Evañhi te, bhikkhave, dutiyāpi samaṇabrāhmaṇā na parimucciṁsu mārassa iddhānubhāvā.

And that's how the second group of ascetics and brahmins failed to get free from Māra's power.

Seyyathāpi te, bhikkhave, dutiyā migajātā tathūpame ahaṁ ime dutiye samaṇabrāhmaṇe vadāmi.

This second group of ascetics and brahmins is just like the second herd of deer, I say.

Tatra, bhikkhave, tatiyā samaṇabrāhmaṇā evaṁ samacintesuṁ:

So then a third group of ascetics and brahmins thought up a plan,

'ye kho te paṭhamā samaṇabrāhmaṇā amuṁ nivāpaṁ nivuttaṁ mārassa amūni ca lokāmisāni …pe….

'The first …

Evañhi te paṭhamā samaṇabrāhmaṇā na parimucciṁsu mārassa iddhānubhāvā.

Yepi te dutiyā samaṇabrāhmaṇā evaṁ samacintesuṁ:

and second groups of ascetics and brahmins …

"ye kho te paṭhamā samaṇabrāhmaṇā amuṁ nivāpaṁ nivuttaṁ mārassa amūni ca lokāmisāni …pe….

Evañhi te paṭhamā samaṇabrāhmaṇā na parimucciṁsu mārassa iddhānubhāvā.

Yannūna mayaṁ sabbaso nivāpabhojanā lokāmisā paṭivirameyyāma, bhayabhogā paṭiviratā araññāyatanāni ajjhogāhetvā vihareyyāmā"ti.

Te sabbaso nivāpabhojanā lokāmisā paṭiviramiṁsu.

Bhayabhogā paṭiviratā araññāyatanāni ajjhogāhetvā vihariṁsu.

Te tattha sākabhakkhāpi ahesuṁ …pe… pavattaphalabhojī.

Tesaṁ gimhānaṁ pacchime māse tiṇodakasaṅkhaye adhimattakasimānaṁ patto kāyo hoti.

Tesaṁ adhimattakasimānaṁ pattakāyānaṁ balavīriyaṁ parihāyi, balavīriye parihīne cetovimutti parihāyi, cetovimuttiyā parihīnāya tameva nivāpaṁ nivuttaṁ mārassa paccāgamiṁsu tāni ca lokāmisāni.

Te tattha anupakhajja mucchitā bhojanāni bhuñjiṁsu.

Te tattha anupakhajja mucchitā bhojanāni bhuñjamānā madaṁ āpajjiṁsu, mattā samānā pamādaṁ āpajjiṁsu, pamattā samānā yathākāmakaraṇīyā ahesuṁ mārassa amusmiṁ nivāpe amusmiñca lokāmise.

Evañhi te dutiyāpi samaṇabrāhmaṇā na parimucciṁsu mārassa iddhānubhāvā.

failed to get free of Māra's power.

Yannūna mayaṁ amuṁ nivāpaṁ nivuttaṁ mārassa amūni ca lokāmisāni upanissāya āsayaṁ kappeyyāma, tatrāsayaṁ kappetvā amuṁ nivāpaṁ nivuttaṁ mārassa amūni ca lokāmisāni ananupakhajja amucchitā bhojanāni bhuñjissāma, ananupakhajja amucchitā bhojanāni bhuñjamānā na madaṁ āpajjissāma, amattā samānā na pamādaṁ āpajjissāma, appamattā samānā na yathākāmakaraṇīyā bhavissāma mārassa amusmiṁ nivāpe amusmiñca lokāmise'ti.

Why don't we set up our lair close by the place where Māra has cast the bait and those material delights of the world? Then we can intrude on it and enjoy eating without being reckless. We won't become indulgent, then we won't become negligent, and then Māra won't be able to do what he wants with us on account of that bait and those material delights of the world.'

Te amuṁ nivāpaṁ nivuttaṁ mārassa amūni ca lokāmisāni upanissāya āsayaṁ kappayiṁsu.

And that's just what they did.

Tatrāsayaṁ kappetvā amuṁ nivāpaṁ nivuttaṁ mārassa amūni ca lokāmisāni ananupakhajja amucchitā bhojanāni bhuñjiṁsu.

Te tattha ananupakhajja amucchitā bhojanāni bhuñjamānā na madaṁ āpajjiṁsu, amattā samānā na pamādaṁ āpajjiṁsu, appamattā samānā na yathākāmakaraṇīyā ahesuṁ mārassa amusmiṁ nivāpe amusmiñca lokāmise.

Api ca kho evaṁdiṭṭhikā ahesuṁ—

Still, they had such views as these:

sassato loko itipi, asassato loko itipi;

'The cosmos is eternal' or 'The cosmos is not eternal';

antavā loko itipi, anantavā loko itipi;

'The world is finite' or 'The world is infinite';

taṁ jīvaṁ taṁ sarīraṁ itipi, aññaṁ jīvaṁ aññaṁ sarīraṁ itipi;

'The soul and the body are the same thing' or 'The soul and the body are different things';

hoti tathāgato paraṁ maraṇā itipi, na hoti tathāgato paraṁ maraṇā itipi, hoti ca na ca hoti tathāgato paraṁ maraṇā itipi, neva hoti na na hoti tathāgato paraṁ maraṇā itipi.

or that after death, a Realized One exists, or doesn't exist, or both exists and doesn't exist, or neither exists nor doesn't exist.

Evañhi te, bhikkhave, tatiyāpi samaṇabrāhmaṇā na parimucciṁsu mārassa iddhānubhāvā.

And that's how the third group of ascetics and brahmins failed to get free from Māra's power.

Seyyathāpi te, bhikkhave, tatiyā migajātā tathūpame ahaṁ ime tatiye samaṇabrāhmaṇe vadāmi.

This third group of ascetics and brahmins is just like the third herd of deer, I say.

Tatra, bhikkhave, catutthā samaṇabrāhmaṇā evaṁ samacintesuṁ:

So then a fourth group of ascetics and brahmins thought up a plan,

'ye kho te paṭhamā samaṇabrāhmaṇā amuṁ nivāpaṁ nivuttaṁ mārassa ...pe....

'The first ...

Evañhi te paṭhamā samaṇabrāhmaṇā na parimucciṁsu mārassa iddhānubhāvā.

Yepi te dutiyā samaṇabrāhmaṇā evaṁ samacintesuṁ:

second ...

'ye kho te paṭhamā samaṇabrāhmaṇā ...pe....

Evañhi te paṭhamā samaṇabrāhmaṇā na parimucciṁsu mārassa iddhānubhāvā.

Yannūna mayaṁ sabbaso nivāpabhojanā lokāmisā paṭivirameyyāma bhayabhogā paṭiviratā araññāyatanāni ajjhogāhetvā vihareyyāmā'ti.

Te sabbaso nivāpabhojanā lokāmisā paṭiviramiṁsu ...pe....

Evañhi te dutiyāpi samaṇabrāhmaṇā na parimucciṁsu mārassa iddhānubhāvā.

Yepi te tatiyā samaṇabrāhmaṇā evaṁ samacintesuṁ ye kho te paṭhamā samaṇabrāhmaṇā ...pe....

and third groups of ascetics and brahmins ...

Evañhi te paṭhamā samaṇabrāhmaṇā na parimucciṁsu mārassa iddhānubhāvā.

Yepi te dutiyā samaṇabrāhmaṇā evaṁ samacintesuṁ ye kho te paṭhamā samaṇabrāhmaṇā ...pe....

Evañhi te paṭhamā samaṇabrāhmaṇā na parimucciṁsu mārassa iddhānubhāvā.

Yannūna mayaṁ sabbaso nivāpabhojanā lokāmisā paṭivirameyyāma, bhayabhogā paṭiviratā araññāyatanāni ajjhogāhetvā vihareyyāmā’ti.

Te sabbaso nivāpabhojanā lokāmisā paṭiviramiṁsu ...pe....

Evañhi te dutiyāpi samaṇabrāhmaṇā na parimucciṁsu mārassa iddhānubhāvā.

Yannūna mayaṁ amuṁ nivāpaṁ nivuttaṁ mārassa amūni ca lokāmisāni upanissāya āsayaṁ kappeyyāma.

Tatrāsayaṁ kappetvā amuṁ nivāpaṁ nivuttaṁ mārassa amūni ca lokāmisāni ananupakhajja amucchitā bhojanāni bhuñjissāma, ananupakhajja amucchitā bhojanāni bhuñjamānā na madaṁ āpajjissāma, amattā samānā na pamādaṁ āpajjissāma, appamattā samānā na yathākāmakaraṇīyā bhavissāma mārassa amusmiṁ nivāpe amusmiñca lokāmiseti.

Te amuṁ nivāpaṁ nivuttaṁ mārassa amūni ca lokāmisāni upanissāya āsayaṁ kappayiṁsu.

Tatrāsayaṁ kappetvā amuṁ nivāpaṁ nivuttaṁ mārassa amūni ca lokāmisāni ananupakhajja amucchitā bhojanāni bhuñjiṁsu.

Te tattha ananupakhajja amucchitā bhojanāni bhuñjamānā na madaṁ āpajjiṁsu.

Amattā samānā na pamādaṁ āpajjiṁsu.

Appamattā samānā na yathākāmakaraṇīyā ahesuṁ mārassa amusmiṁ nivāpe amusmiñca lokāmise.

Api ca kho evaṁdiṭṭhikā ahesuṁ sassato loko itipi ...pe...

neva hoti na na hoti tathāgato paraṁ maraṇā itipi.

Evañhi te tatiyāpi samaṇabrāhmaṇā na parimucciṁsu mārassa iddhānubhāvā.

failed to get free of Māra's power.

Yannūna mayaṁ yattha agati mārassa ca māraparisāya ca tatrāsayaṁ kappeyyāma.

Why don't we set up our lair somewhere Māra and his assembly can't go?

Tatrāsayaṁ kappetvā amuṁ nivāpaṁ nivuttaṁ mārassa amūni ca lokāmisāni ananupakhajja amucchitā bhojanāni bhuñjissāma, ananupakhajja amucchitā bhojanāni bhuñjamānā na madaṁ āpajjissāma, amattā samānā na pamādaṁ āpajjissāma, appamattā samānā na yathākāmakaraṇīyā bhavissāma mārassa amusmiṁ nivāpe amusmiñca lokāmiseti.

Then we can intrude on where Māra has cast the bait and those material delights of the world, and enjoy eating without being reckless. We won't become indulgent, then we won't become negligent, and then Māra won't be able to do what he wants with us on account of that bait and those material delights of the world.'

Te yattha agati mārassa ca māraparisāya ca tatrāsayaṁ kappayiṁsu.

And that's just what they did.

Tatrāsayaṁ kappetvā amuṁ nivāpaṁ nivuttaṁ mārassa amūni ca lokāmisāni ananupakhajja amucchitā bhojanāni bhuñjiṁsu, te tattha ananupakhajja amucchitā bhojanāni bhuñjamānā na madaṁ āpajjiṁsu, amattā samānā na pamādaṁ āpajjiṁsu, appamattā samānā na yathākāmakaraṇīyā ahesuṁ mārassa amusmiṁ nivāpe amusmiñca lokāmise.

Evañhi te, bhikkhave, catutthā samaṇabrāhmaṇā parimucciṁsu mārassa iddhānubhāvā.

And that's how the fourth group of ascetics and brahmins got free from Māra's power.

Seyyathāpi te, bhikkhave, catutthā migajātā tathūpame ahaṁ ime catutthe samaṇabrāhmaṇe vadāmi.

This fourth group of ascetics and brahmins is just like the fourth herd of deer, I say.

Kathañca, bhikkhave, agati mārassa ca māraparisāya ca?

And where is it that Māra and his assembly can't go?

Idha, bhikkhave, bhikkhu vivicceva kāmehi vivicca akusalehi dhammehi savitakkaṁ savicāraṁ vivekajaṁ pītisukhaṁ paṭhamaṁ jhānaṁ upasampajja viharati.

It's when a mendicant, quite secluded from sensual pleasures, secluded from unskillful qualities, enters and remains in the first absorption, which has the rapture and bliss born of seclusion, while placing the mind and keeping it connected.

Ayaṁ vuccati, bhikkhave, bhikkhu andhamakāsi māraṁ, apadaṁ vadhitvā māracakkhuṁ adassanaṁ gato pāpimato.

This is called a mendicant who has blinded Māra, put out his eyes without a trace, and gone where the Wicked One cannot see.

Puna caparaṁ, bhikkhave, bhikkhu vitakkavicārānaṁ vūpasamā ajjhattaṁ sampasādanaṁ cetaso ekodibhāvaṁ avitakkaṁ avicāraṁ samādhijaṁ pītisukhaṁ dutiyaṁ jhānaṁ upasampajja viharati.

Furthermore, as the placing of the mind and keeping it connected are stilled, a mendicant enters and remains in the second absorption, which has the rapture and bliss born of immersion, with internal clarity and confidence, and unified mind, without placing the mind and keeping it connected.

Ayaṁ vuccati, bhikkhave …pe… pāpimato.

This is called a mendicant who has blinded Māra …

Puna caparaṁ, bhikkhave, bhikkhu pītiyā ca virāgā upekkhako ca viharati sato ca sampajāno, sukhañca kāyena paṭisaṁvedeti yaṁ taṁ ariyā ācikkhanti 'upekkhako satimā sukhavihārī'ti tatiyaṁ jhānaṁ upasampajja viharati.

Furthermore, with the fading away of rapture, a mendicant enters and remains in the third absorption, where they meditate with equanimity, mindful and aware, personally experiencing the bliss of which the noble ones declare, 'Equanimous and mindful, one meditates in bliss.'

Ayaṁ vuccati, bhikkhave …pe… pāpimato.

This is called a mendicant who has blinded Māra …

Puna caparaṁ, bhikkhave, bhikkhu sukhassa ca pahānā dukkhassa ca pahānā, pubbeva somanassadomanassānaṁ atthaṅgamā, adukkhamasukhaṁ upekkhāsatipārisuddhiṁ catutthaṁ jhānaṁ upasampajja viharati.

Furthermore, giving up pleasure and pain, and ending former happiness and sadness, a mendicant enters and remains in the fourth absorption, without pleasure or pain, with pure equanimity and mindfulness.

Ayaṁ vuccati, bhikkhave …pe… pāpimato.

This is called a mendicant who has blinded Māra …

Puna caparaṁ, bhikkhave, bhikkhu sabbaso rūpasaññānaṁ samatikkamā paṭighasaññānaṁ atthaṅgamā nānattasaññānaṁ amanasikārā 'ananto ākāso'ti ākāsānañcāyatanaṁ upasampajja viharati.

Furthermore, a mendicant, going totally beyond perceptions of form, with the ending of perceptions of impingement, not focusing on perceptions of diversity, aware that 'space is infinite', enters and remains in the dimension of infinite space.

Ayaṁ vuccati, bhikkhave …pe… pāpimato.

This is called a mendicant who has blinded Māra …

Puna caparaṁ, bhikkhave, bhikkhu sabbaso ākāsānañcāyatanaṁ samatikkamma 'anantaṁ viññāṇan'ti viññāṇañcāyatanaṁ upasampajja viharati.

Furthermore, a mendicant, going totally beyond the dimension of infinite space, aware that 'consciousness is infinite', enters and remains in the dimension of infinite consciousness.

Ayaṁ vuccati, bhikkhave …pe… pāpimato.

This is called a mendicant who has blinded Māra …

Puna caparaṁ, bhikkhave, bhikkhu sabbaso viññāṇañcāyatanaṁ samatikkamma 'natthi kiñcī'ti ākiñcaññāyatanaṁ upasampajja viharati.

Furthermore, a mendicant, going totally beyond the dimension of infinite consciousness, aware that 'there is nothing at all', enters and remains in the dimension of nothingness.

Ayaṁ vuccati, bhikkhave …pe… pāpimato.

This is called a mendicant who has blinded Māra …

Puna caparaṁ, bhikkhave, bhikkhu sabbaso ākiñcaññāyatanaṁ samatikkamma nevasaññānāsaññāyatanaṁ upasampajja viharati.

Furthermore, a mendicant, going totally beyond the dimension of nothingness, enters and remains in the dimension of neither perception nor non-perception.

Ayaṁ vuccati, bhikkhave …pe… pāpimato.

This is called a mendicant who has blinded Māra …

Puna caparaṁ, bhikkhave, bhikkhu sabbaso nevasaññānāsaññāyatanaṁ samatikkamma saññāvedayitanirodhaṁ upasampajja viharati. Paññāya cassa disvā āsavā parikkhīṇā honti.

Furthermore, a mendicant, going totally beyond the dimension of neither perception nor non-perception, enters and remains in the cessation of perception and feeling. And, having seen with wisdom, their defilements come to an end.

Ayaṁ vuccati, bhikkhave, bhikkhu andhamakāsi māraṁ, apadaṁ vadhitvā māracakkhuṁ adassanaṁ gato pāpimato tiṇṇo loke visattikan"ti.

This is called a mendicant who has blinded Māra, put out his eyes without a trace, and gone where the Wicked One cannot see. And they've crossed over clinging to the world."

Idamavoca bhagavā.

That is what the Buddha said.

Attamanā te bhikkhū bhagavato bhāsitaṁ abhinandunti.

Satisfied, the mendicants were happy with what the Buddha said.

Nivāpasuttaṁ niṭṭhitaṁ pañcamaṁ.

26 Pasarasisutta:

The Noble Search

Evaṁ me sutaṁ—

So I have heard.

ekaṁ samayaṁ bhagavā sāvatthiyaṁ viharati jetavane anāthapiṇḍikassa ārāme.

At one time the Buddha was staying near Sāvatthī in Jeta's Grove, Anāthapiṇḍika's monastery.

Atha kho bhagavā pubbaṇhasamayaṁ nivāsetvā pattacīvaramādāya sāvatthiṁ piṇḍāya pāvisi.

Then the Buddha robed up in the morning and, taking his bowl and robe, entered Sāvatthī for alms.

Atha kho sambahulā bhikkhū yenāyasmā ānando tenupasaṅkamiṁsu; upasaṅkamitvā āyasmantaṁ ānandaṁ etadavocuṁ:

Then several mendicants went up to Venerable Ānanda and said to him,

"cirassutā no, āvuso ānanda, bhagavato sammukhā dhammī kathā.

"Reverend, it's been a long time since we've heard a Dhamma talk from the Buddha.

Sādhu mayaṁ, āvuso ānanda, labheyyāma bhagavato sammukhā dhammiṁ kathaṁ savanāyā"ti.

It would be good if we got to hear a Dhamma talk from the Buddha."

"Tena hāyasmanto yena rammakassa brāhmaṇassa assamo tenupasaṅkamatha;

"Well then, reverends, go to the brahmin Rammaka's hermitage.

appeva nāma labheyyātha bhagavato sammukhā dhammiṁ kathaṁ savanāyā"ti.

Hopefully you'll get to hear a Dhamma talk from the Buddha."

"Evamāvuso"ti kho te bhikkhū āyasmato ānandassa paccassosuṁ.

"Yes, reverend," they replied.

Atha kho bhagavā sāvatthiyaṁ piṇḍāya caritvā pacchābhattaṁ piṇḍapātapaṭikkanto āyasmantaṁ ānandaṁ āmantesi:

Then, after the meal, on his return from almsround, the Buddha addressed Ānanda,

"āyāmānanda, yena pubbārāmo migāramātupāsādo tenupasaṅkamissāma divāvihārāyā"ti.

"Come, Ānanda, let's go to the Eastern Monastery, the stilt longhouse of Migāra's mother for the day's meditation."

"Evaṁ, bhante"ti kho āyasmā ānando bhagavato paccassosi.

"Yes, sir," Ānanda replied.

Atha kho bhagavā āyasmatā ānandena saddhiṁ yena pubbārāmo migāramātupāsādo tenupasaṅkami divāvihāraya.

So the Buddha went with Ānanda to the Eastern Monastery.

Atha kho bhagavā sāyanhasamayaṁ paṭisallānā vuṭṭhito āyasmantaṁ ānandaṁ āmantesi:

In the late afternoon the Buddha came out of retreat and addressed Ānanda,

"āyāmānanda, yena pubbakoṭṭhako tenupasaṅkamissāma gattāni parisiñcitun"ti.

"Come, Ānanda, let's go to the eastern gate to bathe."

"Evaṁ, bhante"ti kho āyasmā ānando bhagavato paccassosi.

"Yes, sir," Ānanda replied.

Atha kho bhagavā āyasmatā ānandena saddhiṁ yena pubbakoṭṭhako tenupasaṅkami gattāni parisiñcituṁ.

So the Buddha went with Ānanda to the eastern gate to bathe.

Pubbakoṭṭhake gattāni parisiñcitvā paccuttaritvā ekacīvaro aṭṭhāsi gattāni pubbāpayamāno.

When he had bathed and emerged from the water he stood in one robe drying himself.

Atha kho āyasmā ānando bhagavantaṁ etadavoca:

Then Ānanda said to the Buddha,

"ayaṁ, bhante, rammakassa brāhmaṇassa assamo avidūre.

"Sir, the hermitage of the brahmin Rammaka is nearby.

Ramaṇīyo, bhante, rammakassa brāhmaṇassa assamo;

It's so delightful,

pāsādiko, bhante, rammakassa brāhmaṇassa assamo.

so lovely.

Sādhu, bhante, bhagavā yena rammakassa brāhmaṇassa assamo tenupasaṅkamatu anukampaṁ upādāyā"ti.

Please visit it out of compassion."

Adhivāsesi bhagavā tuṇhībhāvena.

The Buddha consented with silence.

Atha kho bhagavā yena rammakassa brāhmaṇassa assamo tenupasaṅkami.

He went to the brahmin Rammaka's hermitage.

Tena kho pana samayena sambahulā bhikkhū rammakassa brāhmaṇassa assame dhammiyā kathāya sannisinnā honti.

Now at that time several mendicants were sitting together in the hermitage talking about the teaching.

Atha kho bhagavā bahidvārakoṭṭhake aṭṭhāsi kathāpariyosānaṁ āgamayamāno.

The Buddha stood outside the door waiting for the talk to end.

Atha kho bhagavā kathāpariyosānaṁ viditvā ukkāsitvā aggaḷaṁ ākoṭesi.

When he knew the talk had ended he cleared his throat and knocked with the latch.

Vivariṁsu kho te bhikkhū bhagavato dvāraṁ.

The mendicants opened the door for the Buddha,

Atha kho bhagavā rammakassa brāhmaṇassa assamaṁ pavisitvā paññatte āsane nisīdi.

and he entered the hermitage, where he sat on the seat spread out

Nisajja kho bhagavā bhikkhū āmantesi:

and addressed the mendicants,

"kāya nuttha, bhikkhave, etarahi kathāya sannisinnā? Kā ca pana vo antarākathā vippakatā"ti?

"Mendicants, what were you sitting talking about just now? What conversation was left unfinished?"

"Bhagavantameva kho no, bhante, ārabbha dhammī kathā vippakatā, atha bhagavā anuppatto"ti.

"Sir, our unfinished discussion on the teaching was about the Buddha himself when the Buddha arrived."

"Sādhu, bhikkhave.

"Good, mendicants!

Etaṁ kho, bhikkhave, tumhākaṁ patirūpaṁ kulaputtānaṁ saddhā agārasmā anagāriyaṁ pabbajitānaṁ yaṁ tumhe dhammiyā kathāya sannisīdeyyātha.

It's appropriate for gentlemen like you, who have gone forth in faith from the lay life to homelessness, to sit together and talk about the teaching.

Sannipatitānaṁ vo, bhikkhave, dvayaṁ karaṇīyaṁ—

When you're sitting together you should do one of two things:

dhammī vā kathā, ariyo vā tuṇhībhāvo.

discuss the teachings or keep noble silence.

Dvemā, bhikkhave, pariyesanā—

Mendicants, there are these two searches:

ariyā ca pariyesanā, anariyā ca pariyesanā.

the noble search and the ignoble search.

Katamā ca, bhikkhave, anariyā pariyesanā?

And what is the ignoble search?

Idha, bhikkhave, ekacco attanā jātidhammo samāno jātidhammaṁyeva pariyesati, attanā jarādhammo samāno jarādhammaṁyeva pariyesati, attanā byādhidhammo samāno byādhidhammaṁyeva pariyesati, attanā maraṇadhammo samāno maraṇadhammaṁyeva pariyesati, attanā sokadhammo samāno sokadhammaṁyeva pariyesati, attanā saṅkilesadhammo samāno saṅkilesadhammaṁyeva pariyesati.

It's when someone who is themselves liable to be reborn seeks what is also liable to be reborn. Themselves liable to grow old, fall sick, die, sorrow, and become corrupted, they seek what is also liable to these things.

Kiñca, bhikkhave, jātidhammaṁ vadetha?

And what should be described as liable to be reborn?

Puttabhariyaṁ, bhikkhave, jātidhammaṁ, dāsidāsaṁ jātidhammaṁ, ajeḷakaṁ jātidhammaṁ, kukkuṭasūkaraṁ jātidhammaṁ, hatthigavāssavaḷavaṁ jātidhammaṁ, jātarūparajataṁ jātidhammaṁ.

Partners and children, male and female bondservants, goats and sheep, chickens and pigs, and elephants and cattle are liable to be reborn.

Jātidhammā hete, bhikkhave, upadhayo.

These attachments are liable to be reborn.

Etthāyaṁ gathito mucchito ajjhāpanno attanā jātidhammo samāno jātidhammaṁyeva pariyesati.

Someone who is tied, infatuated, and attached to such things, themselves liable to being reborn, seeks what is also liable to be reborn.

Kiñca, bhikkhave, jarādhammaṁ vadetha?

And what should be described as liable to grow old?

Puttabhariyaṁ, bhikkhave, jarādhammaṁ, dāsidāsaṁ jarādhammaṁ, ajeḷakaṁ jarādhammaṁ, kukkuṭasūkaraṁ jarādhammaṁ, hatthigavāssavaḷavaṁ jarādhammaṁ, jātarūparajataṁ jarādhammaṁ.

Partners and children, male and female bondservants, goats and sheep, chickens and pigs, and elephants and cattle are liable to grow old.

Jarādhammā hete, bhikkhave, upadhayo.

These attachments are liable to grow old.

Etthāyaṁ gathito mucchito ajjhāpanno attanā jarādhammo samāno jarādhammaṁyeva pariyesati.

Someone who is tied, infatuated, and attached to such things, themselves liable to grow old, seeks what is also liable to grow old.

Kiñca, bhikkhave, byādhidhammaṁ vadetha?

And what should be described as liable to fall sick?

Puttabhariyaṁ, bhikkhave, byādhidhammaṁ, dāsidāsaṁ byādhidhammaṁ, ajeḷakaṁ byādhidhammaṁ, kukkuṭasūkaraṁ byādhidhammaṁ, hatthigavāssavaḷavaṁ byādhidhammaṁ.

Partners and children, male and female bondservants, goats and sheep, chickens and pigs, and elephants and cattle are liable to fall sick.

Byādhidhammā hete, bhikkhave, upadhayo.

These attachments are liable to fall sick.

Etthāyaṁ gathito mucchito ajjhāpanno attanā byādhidhammo samāno byādhidhammaṁyeva pariyesati.

Someone who is tied, infatuated, and attached to such things, themselves liable to falling sick, seeks what is also liable to fall sick.

Kiñca, bhikkhave, maraṇadhammaṁ vadetha?

And what should be described as liable to die?

Puttabhariyaṁ, bhikkhave, maraṇadhammaṁ, dāsidāsaṁ maraṇadhammaṁ, ajeḷakaṁ maraṇadhammaṁ, kukkuṭasūkaraṁ maraṇadhammaṁ, hatthigavāssavaḷavaṁ maraṇadhammaṁ.

Partners and children, male and female bondservants, goats and sheep, chickens and pigs, and elephants and cattle are liable to die.

Maraṇadhammā hete, bhikkhave, upadhayo.

These attachments are liable to die.

Etthāyaṁ gathito mucchito ajjhāpanno attanā maraṇadhammo samāno maraṇadhammaṁyeva pariyesati.

Someone who is tied, infatuated, and attached to such things, themselves liable to die, seeks what is also liable to die.

Kiñca, bhikkhave, sokadhammaṁ vadetha?

And what should be described as liable to sorrow?

Puttabhariyaṁ, bhikkhave, sokadhammaṁ, dāsidāsaṁ sokadhammaṁ, ajeḷakaṁ sokadhammaṁ, kukkuṭasūkaraṁ sokadhammaṁ, hatthigavāssavaḷavaṁ sokadhammaṁ.

Partners and children, male and female bondservants, goats and sheep, chickens and pigs, and elephants and cattle are liable to sorrow.

Sokadhammā hete, bhikkhave, upadhayo.

These attachments are liable to sorrow.

Etthāyaṁ gathito mucchito ajjhāpanno attanā sokadhammo samāno sokadhammaṁyeva pariyesati.

Someone who is tied, infatuated, and attached to such things, themselves liable to sorrow, seeks what is also liable to sorrow.

Kiñca, bhikkhave, saṅkilesadhammaṁ vadetha?

And what should be described as liable to corruption?

Puttabhariyaṁ, bhikkhave, saṅkilesadhammaṁ, dāsidāsaṁ saṅkilesadhammaṁ, ajeḷakaṁ saṅkilesadhammaṁ, kukkuṭasūkaraṁ saṅkilesadhammaṁ, hatthigavāssavaḷavaṁ saṅkilesadhammaṁ, jātarūparajataṁ saṅkilesadhammaṁ.

Partners and children, male and female bondservants, goats and sheep, chickens and pigs, elephants and cattle, and gold and money are liable to corruption.

Saṅkilesadhammā hete, bhikkhave, upadhayo.

These attachments are liable to corruption.

Etthāyaṁ gathito mucchito ajjhāpanno attanā saṅkilesadhammo samāno saṅkilesadhammaṁyeva pariyesati.

Someone who is tied, infatuated, and attached to such things, themselves liable to corruption, seeks what is also liable to corruption.

Ayaṁ, bhikkhave, anariyā pariyesanā.

This is the ignoble search.

Katamā ca, bhikkhave, ariyā pariyesanā?

And what is the noble search?

Idha, bhikkhave, ekacco attanā jātidhammo samāno jātidhamme ādīnavaṁ viditvā ajātaṁ anuttaraṁ yogakkhemaṁ nibbānaṁ pariyesati, attanā jarādhammo samāno jarādhamme ādīnavaṁ viditvā ajaraṁ anuttaraṁ yogakkhemaṁ nibbānaṁ pariyesati, attanā byādhidhammo samāno byādhidhamme ādīnavaṁ viditvā abyādhiṁ anuttaraṁ yogakkhemaṁ nibbānaṁ pariyesati, attanā maraṇadhammo samāno maraṇadhamme ādīnavaṁ viditvā amataṁ anuttaraṁ yogakkhemaṁ nibbānaṁ pariyesati, attanā sokadhammo samāno sokadhamme ādīnavaṁ viditvā asokaṁ anuttaraṁ yogakkhemaṁ nibbānaṁ pariyesati, attanā saṅkilesadhammo samāno saṅkilesadhamme ādīnavaṁ viditvā asaṅkiliṭṭhaṁ anuttaraṁ yogakkhemaṁ nibbānaṁ pariyesati.

It's when someone who is themselves liable to be reborn, understanding the drawbacks in being liable to be reborn, seeks the unborn supreme sanctuary, extinguishment. Themselves liable to grow old, fall sick, die, sorrow, and become corrupted, understanding the drawbacks in these things, they seek the unaging, unailing, undying, sorrowless, uncorrupted supreme sanctuary, extinguishment.

Ayaṁ, bhikkhave, ariyā pariyesanā.

This is the noble search.

Ahampi sudaṁ, bhikkhave, pubbeva sambodhā anabhisambuddho bodhisattova samāno attanā jātidhammo samāno jātidhammaṁyeva pariyesāmi, attanā jarādhammo samāno jarādhammaṁyeva pariyesāmi, attanā byādhidhammo samāno byādhidhammaṁyeva pariyesāmi, attanā maraṇadhammo samāno maraṇadhammaṁyevapariyesāmi, attanāsokadhammosamānosokadhammaṁyeva pariyesāmi, attanā saṅkilesadhammo samāno saṅkilesadhammaṁyeva pariyesāmi.

Mendicants, before my awakening—when I was still unawakened but intent on awakening—I too, being liable to be reborn, sought what is also liable to be reborn. Myself liable to grow old, fall sick, die, sorrow, and become corrupted, I sought what is also liable to these things.

Tassa mayhaṁ, bhikkhave, etadahosi:

Then it occurred to me:

'kiṁ nu kho ahaṁ attanā jātidhammo samāno jātidhammaṁyeva pariyesāmi, attanā jarādhammo samāno ...pe... byādhidhammo samāno ... maraṇadhammo samāno ... sokadhammo samāno ... attanā saṅkilesadhammo samāno saṅkilesadhammaṁyeva pariyesāmi?

'Why do I, being liable to be reborn, grow old, fall sick, sorrow, die, and become corrupted, seek things that have the same nature?

Yannūnāhaṁ attanā jātidhammo samāno jātidhamme ādīnavaṁ viditvā ajātaṁ anuttaraṁ yogakkhemaṁ nibbānaṁ pariyeseyyaṁ, attanā jarādhammo samāno jarādhamme ādīnavaṁ viditvā ajaraṁ anuttaraṁ yogakkhemaṁ nibbānaṁ pariyeseyyaṁ, attanā byādhidhammo samāno byādhidhamme ādīnavaṁ viditvā abyādhiṁ anuttaraṁ yogakkhemaṁ nibbānaṁ pariyeseyyaṁ, attanā maraṇadhammo samāno maraṇadhamme ādīnavaṁ viditvā amataṁ anuttaraṁ yogakkhemaṁ nibbānaṁ pariyeseyyaṁ, attanā sokadhammo samāno sokadhamme ādīnavaṁ viditvā asokaṁ anuttaraṁ yogakkhemaṁ nibbānaṁ pariyeseyyaṁ, attanā saṅkilesadhammo samāno saṅkilesadhamme ādīnavaṁ viditvā asaṅkiliṭṭhaṁ anuttaraṁ yogakkhemaṁ nibbānaṁ pariyeseyyan'ti.

Why don't I seek the unborn, unaging, unailing, undying, sorrowless, uncorrupted supreme sanctuary, extinguishment?'

So kho ahaṁ, bhikkhave, aparena samayena daharova samāno susukāḷakeso, bhadrena yobbanena samannāgato paṭhamena vayasā akāmakānaṁ mātāpitūnaṁ assumukhānaṁ rudantānaṁ kesamassuṁ ohāretvā kāsāyāni vatthāni acchādetvā agārasmā anagāriyaṁ pabbajiṁ.

Some time later, while still black-haired, blessed with youth, in the prime of life—though my mother and father wished otherwise, weeping with tearful faces—I shaved off my hair and beard, dressed in ocher robes, and went forth from the lay life to homelessness.

So evaṁ pabbajito samāno kiṅkusalagavesī anuttaraṁ santivarapadaṁ pariyesamāno yena āḷāro kālāmo tenupasaṅkamiṁ. upasaṅkamitvā āḷāraṁ kālāmaṁ etadavocam:

Once I had gone forth I set out to discover what is skillful, seeking the supreme state of sublime peace. I approached Āḷāra Kālāma and said to him,

'icchāmahaṁ, āvuso kālāma, imasmiṁ dhammavinaye brahmacariyaṁ caritun'ti.

'Reverend Kālāma, I wish to lead the spiritual life in this teaching and training.'

Evaṁ vutte, bhikkhave, āḷāro kālāmo maṁ etadavoca:

Āḷāra Kālāma replied,

'viharatāyasmā;

'Stay, venerable.

tādiso ayaṁ dhammo yattha viññū puriso nacirasseva sakaṁ ācariyakaṁ sayaṁ abhiññā sacchikatvā upasampajja vihareyyā'ti.

This teaching is such that a sensible person can soon realize their own tradition with their own insight and live having achieved it.'

So kho ahaṁ, bhikkhave, nacirasseva khippameva taṁ dhammaṁ pariyāpuṇiṁ.

I quickly memorized that teaching.

So kho ahaṁ, bhikkhave, tāvatakeneva oṭṭhapahatamattena lapitalāpanamattena ñāṇavādañca vadāmi theravādañca, 'jānāmi passāmī'ti ca paṭijānāmi ahañceva aññe ca.

So far as lip-recital and oral recitation were concerned, I spoke with knowledge and the authority of the elders. I claimed to know and see, and so did others.

Tassa mayhaṁ, bhikkhave, etadahosi:

Then it occurred to me,

'na kho āḷāro kālāmo imaṁ dhammaṁ kevalaṁ saddhāmattakena sayaṁ abhiññā sacchikatvā upasampajja viharāmīti pavedeti;

'It is not solely by mere faith that Āḷāra Kālāma declares: "I realize this teaching with my own insight, and live having achieved it."

addhā āḷāro kālāmo imaṁ dhammaṁ jānaṁ passaṁ viharatī'ti.

Surely he meditates knowing and seeing this teaching.'

Atha khvāhaṁ, bhikkhave, yena āḷāro kālāmo tenupasaṅkamiṁ; upasaṅkamitvā āḷāraṁ kālāmaṁ etadavocaṁ:

So I approached Āḷāra Kālāma and said to him,

'kittāvatā no, āvuso kālāma, imaṁ dhammaṁ sayaṁ abhiññā sacchikatvā upasampajja viharāmīti pavedesī'ti?

'Reverend Kālāma, to what extent do you say you've realized this teaching with your own insight?'

Evaṁ vutte, bhikkhave, āḷāro kālāmo ākiñcaññāyatanaṁ pavedesi.

When I said this, he declared the dimension of nothingness.

Tassa mayhaṁ, bhikkhave, etadahosi:

Then it occurred to me,

'na kho āḷārasseva kālāmassa atthi saddhā, mayhampatthi saddhā;

'It's not just Āḷāra Kālāma who has faith,

na kho āḷārasseva kālāmassa atthi vīriyaṁ, mayhampatthi vīriyaṁ;

energy,

na kho āḷārasseva kālāmassa atthi sati, mayhampatthi sati;

mindfulness,

na kho āḷārasseva kālāmassa atthi samādhi, mayhampatthi samādhi;

immersion,

na kho āḷārasseva kālāmassa atthi paññā, mayhampatthi paññā.

and wisdom; I too have these things.

Yannūnāhaṁ yaṁ dhammaṁ āḷāro kālāmo sayaṁ abhiññā sacchikatvā upasampajja viharāmīti pavedeti, tassa dhammassa sacchikiriyāya padaheyyan'ti.

Why don't I make an effort to realize the same teaching that Āḷāra Kālāma says he has realized with his own insight?'

So kho ahaṁ, bhikkhave, nacirasseva khippameva taṁ dhammaṁ sayaṁ abhiññā sacchikatvā upasampajja vihāsiṁ.

I quickly realized that teaching with my own insight, and lived having achieved it.

Atha khvāhaṁ, bhikkhave, yena āḷāro kālāmo tenupasaṅkamiṁ; upasaṅkamitvā āḷāraṁ kālāmaṁ etadavocaṁ:

So I approached Āḷāra Kālāma and said to him,

'Ettāvatā no, āvuso kālāma, imaṁ dhammaṁ sayaṁ abhiññā sacchikatvā upasampajja pavedesī'ti?

'Reverend Kālāma, have you realized this teaching with your own insight up to this point, and declare having achieved it?'

'Ettāvatā kho ahaṁ, āvuso, imaṁ dhammaṁ sayaṁ abhiññā sacchikatvā upasampajja pavedemī'ti.

'I have, reverend.'

'Ahampi kho, āvuso, ettāvatā imaṁ dhammaṁ sayaṁ abhiññā sacchikatvā upasampajja viharāmī'ti.

'I too, reverend, have realized this teaching with my own insight up to this point, and live having achieved it.'

'Lābhā no, āvuso, suladdhaṁ no, āvuso,

'We are fortunate, reverend, so very fortunate

ye mayaṁ āyasmantaṁ tādisaṁ sabrahmacāriṁ passāma.

to see a venerable such as yourself as one of our spiritual companions!

Iti yāhaṁ dhammaṁ sayaṁ abhiññā sacchikatvā upasampajja pavedemi taṁ tvaṁ dhammaṁ sayaṁ abhiññā sacchikatvā upasampajja viharasi.

So the teaching that I've realized with my own insight, and declare having achieved it, you've realized with your own insight, and live having achieved it.

Yaṁ tvaṁ dhammaṁ sayaṁ abhiññā sacchikatvā upasampajja viharasi tamahaṁ dhammaṁ sayaṁ abhiññā sacchikatvā upasampajja pavedemi.

The teaching that you've realized with your own insight, and live having achieved it, I've realized with my own insight, and declare having achieved it.

Iti yāhaṁ dhammaṁ jānāmi taṁ tvaṁ dhammaṁ jānāsi, yaṁ tvaṁ dhammaṁ jānāsi tamahaṁ dhammaṁ jānāmi.

So the teaching that I know, you know, and the teaching that you know, I know.

Iti yādiso ahaṁ tādiso tuvaṁ, yādiso tuvaṁ tādiso ahaṁ.

I am like you and you are like me.

Ehi dāni, āvuso, ubhova santā imaṁ gaṇaṁ pariharāmā'ti.

Come now, reverend! We should both lead this community together.'

Iti kho, bhikkhave, āḷāro kālāmo ācariyo me samāno attano antevāsiṁ maṁ samānaṁ attanā samasamaṁ ṭhapesi, uḷārāya ca maṁ pūjāya pūjesi.

And that is how my teacher Āḷāra Kālāma placed me, his student, on the same position as him, and honored me with lofty praise.

Tassa mayhaṁ, bhikkhave, etadahosi:

Then it occurred to me,

'nāyaṁ dhammo nibbidāya na virāgāya na nirodhāya na upasamāya na abhiññāya na sambodhāya na nibbānāya saṁvattati, yāvadeva ākiñcaññāyatanūpapattiyā'ti.

'This teaching doesn't lead to disillusionment, dispassion, cessation, peace, insight, awakening, and extinguishment. It only leads as far as rebirth in the dimension of nothingness.'

So kho ahaṁ, bhikkhave, taṁ dhammaṁ analaṅkaritvā tasmā dhammā nibbijja apakkamiṁ.

Realizing that this teaching was inadequate, I left disappointed.

So kho ahaṁ, bhikkhave, kiṁ kusalagavesī anuttaraṁ santivarapadaṁ pariyesamāno yena udako rāmaputto tenupasaṅkamiṁ; upasaṅkamitvā udakaṁ rāmaputtaṁ etadavocaṁ:

I set out to discover what is skillful, seeking the supreme state of sublime peace. I approached Uddaka, son of Rāma, and said to him,

'icchāmahaṁ, āvuso, imasmiṁ dhammavinaye brahmacariyaṁ caritun'ti.

'Reverend, I wish to lead the spiritual life in this teaching and training.'

Evaṁ vutte, bhikkhave, udako rāmaputto maṁ etadavoca:

Uddaka replied,

'viharatāyasmā;

'Stay, venerable.

tādiso ayaṁ dhammo yattha viññū puriso nacirasseva sakaṁ ācariyakaṁ sayaṁ abhiññā sacchikatvā upasampajja vihareyyā'ti.

This teaching is such that a sensible person can soon realize their own tradition with their own insight and live having achieved it.'

So kho ahaṁ, bhikkhave, nacirasseva khippameva taṁ dhammaṁ pariyāpuṇiṁ.

I quickly memorized that teaching.

So kho ahaṁ, bhikkhave, tāvatakeneva oṭṭhapahatamattena lapitalāpanamattena ñāṇavādañca vadāmi theravādañca, 'jānāmi passāmī'ti ca paṭijānāmi ahañceva aññe ca.

So far as lip-recital and oral recitation were concerned, I spoke with knowledge and the authority of the elders. I claimed to know and see, and so did others.

Tassa mayhaṁ, bhikkhave, etadahosi:

Then it occurred to me,

'na kho rāmo imaṁ dhammaṁ kevalaṁ saddhāmattakena sayaṁ abhiññā sacchikatvā upasampajja viharāmīti pavedesi;

'It is not solely by mere faith that Rāma declared: "I realize this teaching with my own insight, and live having achieved it."

addhā rāmo imaṁ dhammaṁ jānaṁ passaṁ vihāsī'ti.

Surely he meditated knowing and seeing this teaching.'

Atha khvāhaṁ, bhikkhave, yena udako rāmaputto tenupasaṅkamiṁ; upasaṅkamitvā udakaṁ rāmaputtaṁ etadavocaṁ:

So I approached Uddaka, son of Rāma, and said to him,

'kittāvatā no, āvuso, rāmo imaṁ dhammaṁ sayaṁ abhiññā sacchikatvā upasampajja viharāmīti pavedesī'ti?

'Reverend, to what extent did Rāma say he'd realized this teaching with his own insight?'

Evaṁ vutte, bhikkhave, udako rāmaputto nevasaññānāsaññāyatanaṁ pavedesi.

When I said this, Uddaka, son of Rāma, declared the dimension of neither perception nor non-perception.

Tassa mayhaṁ, bhikkhave, etadahosi:

Then it occurred to me,

'na kho rāmasseva ahosi saddhā, mayhampatthi saddhā;

'It's not just Rāma who had faith,

na kho rāmasseva ahosi vīriyaṁ, mayhampatthi vīriyaṁ;

energy,

na kho rāmasseva ahosi sati, mayhampatthi sati;

mindfulness,

na kho rāmasseva ahosi samādhi, mayhampatthi samādhi,

immersion,

na kho rāmasseva ahosi paññā, mayhampatthi paññā.

and wisdom; I too have these things.

Yannūnāhaṁ yaṁ dhammaṁ rāmo sayaṁ abhiññā sacchikatvā upasampajja viharāmīti pavedesi, tassa dhammassa sacchikiriyāya padaheyyan'ti.

Why don't I make an effort to realize the same teaching that Rāma said he had realized with his own insight?'

So kho ahaṁ, bhikkhave, nacirasseva khippameva taṁ dhammaṁ sayaṁ abhiññā sacchikatvā upasampajja vihāsiṁ.

I quickly realized that teaching with my own insight, and lived having achieved it.

Atha khvāhaṁ, bhikkhave, yena udako rāmaputto tenupasaṅkamiṁ; upasaṅkamitvā udakaṁ rāmaputtaṁ etadavocaṁ:

So I approached Uddaka, son of Rāma, and said to him,

'Ettāvatā no, āvuso, rāmo imaṁ dhammaṁ sayaṁ abhiññā sacchikatvā upasampajja pavedesī'ti?

'Reverend, had Rāma realized this teaching with his own insight up to this point, and declared having achieved it?'

'Ettāvatā kho, āvuso, rāmo imaṁ dhammaṁ sayaṁ abhiññā sacchikatvā upasampajja pavedesī'ti.

'He had, reverend.'

'Ahampi kho, āvuso, ettāvatā imaṁ dhammaṁ sayaṁ abhiññā sacchikatvā upasampajja viharāmī'ti.

'I too have realized this teaching with my own insight up to this point, and live having achieved it.'

'Lābhā no, āvuso, suladdhaṁ no, āvuso,

'We are fortunate, reverend, so very fortunate

ye mayaṁ āyasmantaṁ tādisaṁ sabrahmacāriṁ passāma.

to see a venerable such as yourself as one of our spiritual companions!

Iti yaṁ dhammaṁ rāmo sayaṁ abhiññā sacchikatvā upasampajja pavedesi, taṁ tvaṁ dhammaṁ sayaṁ abhiññā sacchikatvā upasampajja viharasi.

So the teaching that Rāma had realized with his own insight, and declared having achieved it, you've realized with your own insight, and live having achieved it.

Yaṁ tvaṁ dhammaṁ sayaṁ abhiññā sacchikatvā upasampajja viharasi, taṁ dhammaṁ rāmo sayaṁ abhiññā sacchikatvā upasampajja pavedesi.

The teaching that you've realized with your own insight, and live having achieved it, Rāma had realized with his own insight, and declared having achieved it.

Iti yaṁ dhammaṁ rāmo abhiññāsi taṁ tvaṁ dhammaṁ jānāsi, yaṁ tvaṁ dhammaṁ jānāsi, taṁ dhammaṁ rāmo abhiññāsi.

So the teaching that Rāma directly knew, you know, and the teaching you know, Rāma directly knew.

Iti yādiso rāmo ahosi tādiso tuvaṁ, yādiso tuvaṁ tādiso rāmo ahosi.

Rāma was like you and you are like Rāma.

Ehi dāni, āvuso, tuvaṁ imaṁ gaṇaṁ pariharā'ti.

Come now, reverend! You should lead this community.'

Iti kho, bhikkhave, udako rāmaputto sabrahmacārī me samāno ācariyaṭṭhāne maṁ ṭhapesi, uḷārāya ca maṁ pūjāya pūjesi.

And that is how my spiritual companion Uddaka, son of Rāma, placed me in the position of a teacher, and honored me with lofty praise.

Tassa mayhaṁ, bhikkhave, etadahosi:

Then it occurred to me,

'nāyaṁ dhammo nibbidāya na virāgāya na nirodhāya na upasamāya na abhiññāya na sambodhāya na nibbānāya saṁvattati, yāvadeva nevasaññānāsaññāyatanūpapattiyā'ti.

'This teaching doesn't lead to disillusionment, dispassion, cessation, peace, insight, awakening, and extinguishment. It only leads as far as rebirth in the dimension of neither perception nor non-perception.'

So kho ahaṁ, bhikkhave, taṁ dhammaṁ analaṅkaritvā tasmā dhammā nibbijja apakkamiṁ.

Realizing that this teaching was inadequate, I left disappointed.

So kho ahaṁ, bhikkhave, kiṁ kusalagavesī anuttaraṁ santivarapadaṁ pariyesamāno magadhesu anupubbena cārikaṁ caramāno yena uruvelā senānigamo tadavasariṁ.

I set out to discover what is skillful, seeking the supreme state of sublime peace. Traveling stage by stage in the Magadhan lands, I arrived at Senanigama near Uruvelā.

Tatthaddasaṁ ramaṇīyaṁ bhūmibhāgaṁ, pāsādikañca vanasaṇḍaṁ, nadiñca sandantiṁ setakaṁ supatitthaṁ ramaṇīyaṁ, samantā ca gocaragāmaṁ.

There I saw a delightful park, a lovely grove with a flowing river that was clean and charming, with smooth banks. And nearby was a village for alms.

Tassa mayhaṁ, bhikkhave, etadahosi:

Then it occurred to me,

'ramaṇīyo vata bho bhūmibhāgo, pāsādiko ca vanasaṇḍo, nadī ca sandati setakā supatitthā ramaṇīyā, samantā ca gocaragāmo.

'This park is truly delightful, a lovely grove with a flowing river that's clean and charming, with smooth banks. And nearby there's a village to go for alms.

Alaṁ vatidaṁ kulaputtassa padhānatthikassa padhānāyā'ti.

This is good enough for a gentleman who wishes to put forth effort in meditation.'

So kho ahaṁ, bhikkhave, tattheva nisīdiṁ—

So I sat down right there, thinking,

alamidaṁ padhānāyāti.

'This is good enough for meditation.'

So kho ahaṁ, bhikkhave, attanā jātidhammo samāno jātidhamme ādīnavaṁ viditvā ajātaṁ anuttaraṁ yogakkhemaṁ nibbānaṁ pariyesamāno ajātaṁ anuttaraṁ yogakkhemaṁ nibbānaṁ ajjhagamaṁ, attanā jarādhammo samāno jarādhamme ādīnavaṁ viditvā ajaraṁ anuttaraṁ yogakkhemaṁ nibbānaṁ pariyesamāno ajaraṁ anuttaraṁ yogakkhemaṁ nibbānaṁ ajjhagamaṁ, attanā byādhidhammo samāno byādhidhamme ādīnavaṁ viditvā abyādhiṁ anuttaraṁ yogakkhemaṁ nibbānaṁ pariyesamāno abyādhiṁ anuttaraṁ yogakkhemaṁ nibbānaṁ ajjhagamaṁ, attanā maraṇadhammo samāno maraṇadhamme ādīnavaṁ viditvā amataṁ anuttaraṁ yogakkhemaṁ nibbānaṁ ajjhagamaṁ, attanā sokadhammo samāno sokadhamme ādīnavaṁ viditvā asokaṁ anuttaraṁ yogakkhemaṁ nibbānaṁ ajjhagamaṁ, attanā saṅkilesadhammo samāno saṅkilesadhamme ādīnavaṁ viditvā asaṅkiliṭṭhaṁ anuttaraṁ yogakkhemaṁ nibbānaṁ pariyesamāno asaṅkiliṭṭhaṁ anuttaraṁ yogakkhemaṁ nibbānaṁ ajjhagamaṁ.

And so, being myself liable to be reborn, understanding the drawbacks in being liable to be reborn, I sought the unborn supreme sanctuary, extinguishment—and I found it. Being myself liable to grow old, fall sick, die, sorrow, and become corrupted, understanding the drawbacks in these things, I sought the unaging, unailing, undying, sorrowless, uncorrupted supreme sanctuary, extinguishment—and I found it.

Ñāṇañca pana me dassanaṁ udapādi:

Knowledge and vision arose in me:

'akuppā me vimutti, ayamantimā jāti, natthi dāni punabbhavo'ti.

'My freedom is unshakable; this is my last rebirth; now there are no more future lives.'

Tassa mayhaṁ, bhikkhave, etadahosi:

Then it occurred to me,

'adhigato kho myāyaṁ dhammo gambhīro duddaso duranubodho santo paṇīto atakkāvacaro nipuṇo paṇḍitavedanīyo.

'This principle I have discovered is deep, hard to see, hard to understand, peaceful, sublime, beyond the scope of logic, subtle, comprehensible to the astute.

Ālayarāmā kho panāyaṁ pajā ālayaratā ālayasammuditā.

But people like attachment, they love it and enjoy it.

Ālayarāmāya kho pana pajāya ālayaratāya ālayasammuditāya duddasaṁ idaṁ ṭhānaṁ yadidaṁ—idappaccayatā paṭiccasamuppādo.

It's hard for them to see this thing; that is, specific conditionality, dependent origination.

Idampi kho ṭhānaṁ duddasaṁ yadidaṁ—sabbasaṅkhārasamatho sabbūpadhipaṭinissaggo taṇhākkhayo virāgo nirodho nibbānaṁ.

It's also hard for them to see this thing; that is, the stilling of all activities, the letting go of all attachments, the ending of craving, fading away, cessation, extinguishment.

Ahañceva kho pana dhammaṁ deseyyaṁ, pare ca me na ājāneyyuṁ, so mamassa kilamatho, sā mamassa vihesā'ti.

And if I were to teach the Dhamma, others might not understand me, which would be wearying and troublesome for me.'

Apissu maṁ, bhikkhave, imā anacchariyā gāthāyo paṭibhaṁsu pubbe assutapubbā:

And then these verses, which were neither supernaturally inspired, nor learned before in the past, occurred to me:

'Kicchena me adhigataṁ,

halaṁ dāni pakāsituṁ;

Rāgadosaparetehi,

nāyaṁ dhammo susambudho.

'I've struggled hard to realize this,

enough with trying to explain it!

This teaching is not easily understood

by those mired in greed and hate.

Paṭisotagāmiṁ nipuṇaṁ,

gambhīraṁ duddasaṁ aṇuṁ;

Rāgarattā na dakkhanti,

tamokhandhena āvuṭā'ti.

Those besotted by greed can't see

what's subtle, going against the stream,

deep, hard to see, and very fine,

for they're shrouded in a mass of darkness.'

Itiha me, bhikkhave, paṭisañcikkhato appossukkatāya cittaṁ namati, no dhammadesanāya.

So, as I reflected like this, my mind inclined to remaining passive, not to teaching the Dhamma.

Athakho, bhikkhave, brahmuno sahampatissa mama cetasā cetoparivitakkamaññāya etadahosi:

Then Brahmā Sahampati, knowing what I was thinking, thought,

'nassati vata bho loko, vinassati vata bho loko, yatra hi nāma tathāgatassa arahato sammāsambuddhassa appossukkatāya cittaṁ namati, no dhammadesanāyā'ti.

'Oh my goodness! The world will be lost, the world will perish! For the mind of the Realized One, the perfected one, the fully awakened Buddha, inclines to remaining passive, not to teaching the Dhamma.'

Atha kho, bhikkhave, brahmā sahampati—seyyathāpi nāma balavā puriso samiñjitaṁ vā bāhaṁ pasāreyya, pasāritaṁ vā bāhaṁ samiñjeyya; evameva— brahmaloke antarahito mama purato pāturahosi.

Then, as easily as a strong person would extend or contract their arm, he vanished from the Brahmā realm and reappeared in front of the Buddha.

Atha kho, bhikkhave, brahmā sahampati ekaṁsaṁ uttarāsaṅgaṁ karitvā yenāhaṁ tenañjaliṁ paṇāmetvā maṁ etadavoca:

He arranged his robe over one shoulder, raised his joined palms toward the Buddha, and said,

'desetu, bhante, bhagavā dhammaṁ, desetu sugato dhammaṁ.

'Sir, let the Blessed One teach the Dhamma! Let the Holy One teach the Dhamma!

Santi sattā apparajakkhajātikā, assavanatā dhammassa parihāyanti.

There are beings with little dust in their eyes. They're in decline because they haven't heard the teaching.

Bhavissanti dhammassa aññātāro'ti.

There will be those who understand the teaching!'

Idamavoca, bhikkhave, brahmā sahampati.

That's what Brahmā Sahampati said.

Idaṁ vatvā athāparaṁ etadavoca:

Then he went on to say:

'Pāturahosi magadhesu pubbe,

Dhammo asuddho samalehi cintito;

Apāpuretaṁ amatassa dvāraṁ,

Suṇantu dhammaṁ vimalenānubuddhaṁ.

'Among the Magadhans there appeared in the past

an impure teaching thought up by those still stained.

Fling open the door to the deathless!

Let them hear the teaching

the immaculate one discovered.

Sele yathā pabbatamuddhaniṭṭhito,

Yathāpi passe janataṁ samantato;

Tathūpamaṁ dhammamayaṁ sumedha,

Pāsādamāruyha samantacakkhu;

Sokāvatiṇṇaṁ janatamapetasoko,

Avekkhassu jātijarābhibhūtaṁ.

Standing high on a rocky mountain,

you can see the people all around.

In just the same way, all-seer, wise one,

having ascended the Temple of Truth,

rid of sorrow, look upon the people

swamped with sorrow,

oppressed by rebirth and old age.

Uṭṭhehi vīra vijitasaṅgāma,

Satthavāha aṇaṇa vicara loke;

Desassu bhagavā dhammaṁ,

Aññātāro bhavissantī'ti.

Rise, hero! Victor in battle, leader of the caravan,

wander the world without obligation.

Let the Blessed One teach the Dhamma!

There will be those who understand!'

Atha kho ahaṁ, bhikkhave, brahmuno ca ajjhesanaṁ viditvā sattesu ca kāruññataṁ paṭicca buddhacakkhunā lokaṁ volokesiṁ.

Then, understanding Brahmā's invitation, I surveyed the world with the eye of a Buddha, because of my compassion for sentient beings.

Addasaṁ kho ahaṁ, bhikkhave, buddhacakkhunā lokaṁ volokento satte apparajakkhe mahārajakkhe, tikkhindriye mudindriye, svākāre dvākāre, suviññāpaye duviññāpaye, appekacce paralokavajjabhayadassāvine viharante, appekacce na paralokavajjabhayadassāvine viharante.

And I saw sentient beings with little dust in their eyes, and some with much dust in their eyes; with keen faculties and with weak faculties, with good qualities and with bad qualities, easy to teach and hard to teach. And some of them lived seeing the danger in the fault to do with the next world, while others did not.

Seyyathāpi nāma uppaliniyaṁ vā paduminiyaṁ vā puṇḍarīkiniyaṁ vā appekaccāni uppalāni vā padumāni vā puṇḍarīkāni vā udake jātāni udake saṁvaḍḍhāni udakānuggatāni antonimuggaposīni, appekaccāni uppalāni vā padumāni vā puṇḍarīkāni vā udake jātāni udake saṁvaḍḍhāni udakānuggatāni samodakaṁ ṭhitāni, appekaccāni uppalāni vā padumāni vā puṇḍarīkāni vā udake jātāni udake saṁvaḍḍhāni udakaṁ accuggamma ṭhitāni anupalittāni udakena;

It's like a pool with blue water lilies, or pink or white lotuses. Some of them sprout and grow in the water without rising above it, thriving underwater. Some of them sprout and grow in the water reaching the water's surface. And some of them sprout and grow in the water but rise up above the water and stand with no water clinging to them.

evameva kho ahaṁ, bhikkhave, buddhacakkhunā lokaṁ volokento addasaṁ satte apparajakkhe mahārajakkhe, tikkhindriye mudindriye, svākāre dvākāre, suviññāpaye duviññāpaye, appekacce paralokavajjabhayadassāvine viharante, appekacce na paralokavajjabhayadassāvine viharante.

In the same way, I saw sentient beings with little dust in their eyes, and some with much dust in their eyes.

Atha khvāhaṁ, bhikkhave, brahmānaṁ sahampatiṁ gāthāya paccabhāsiṁ:

Then I replied in verse to Brahmā Sahampati:

'Apārutā tesaṁ amatassa dvārā,

Ye sotavanto pamuñcantu saddhaṁ;

Vihiṁsasaññī paguṇaṁ na bhāsiṁ,

Dhammaṁ paṇītaṁ manujesu brahme'ti.

'Flung open are the doors to the deathless!

Let those with ears to hear commit to faith.

Thinking it would be troublesome, Brahmā,

I did not teach

the sophisticated, sublime Dhamma among humans.'

Atha kho, bhikkhave, brahmā sahampati 'katāvakāso khomhi bhagavatā dhammadesanāyā'ti maṁ abhivādetvā padakkhiṇaṁ katvā tatthevantaradhāyi.

Then Brahmā Sahampati, knowing that his request for me to teach the Dhamma had been granted, bowed and respectfully circled me, keeping me on his right, before vanishing right there.

Tassa mayhaṁ, bhikkhave, etadahosi:

Then I thought,

'kassa nu kho ahaṁ paṭhamaṁ dhammaṁ deseyyaṁ;

'Who should I teach first of all?

ko imaṁ dhammaṁ khippameva ājānissatī'ti?

Who will quickly understand this teaching?'

Tassa mayhaṁ, bhikkhave, etadahosi:

Then it occurred to me,

'ayaṁ kho āḷāro kālāmo paṇḍito viyatto medhāvī dīgharattaṁ apparajakkhajātiko.

'That Āḷāra Kālāma is astute, competent, clever, and has long had little dust in his eyes.

Yannūnāhaṁ āḷārassa kālāmassa paṭhamaṁ dhammaṁ deseyyaṁ.

Why don't I teach him first of all?

So imaṁ dhammaṁ khippameva ājānissatī'ti.

He'll quickly understand the teaching.'

Atha kho maṁ, bhikkhave, devatā upasaṅkamitvā etadavoca:

But a deity came to me and said,

'sattāhakālaṅkato, bhante, āḷāro kālāmo'ti.

'Sir, Āḷāra Kālāma passed away seven days ago.'

Ñāṇañca pana me dassanaṁ udapādi:

And knowledge and vision arose in me,

'sattāhakālaṅkato āḷāro kālāmo'ti.

'Āḷāra Kālāma passed away seven days ago.'

Tassa mayhaṁ, bhikkhave, etadahosi:

I thought,

'mahājāniyo kho āḷāro kālāmo.

'This is a great loss for Āḷāra Kālāma.

Sace hi so imaṁ dhammaṁ suṇeyya, khippameva ājāneyyā'ti.

If he had heard the teaching, he would have understood it quickly.'

Tassa mayhaṁ, bhikkhave, etadahosi:

Then I thought,

'kassa nu kho ahaṁ paṭhamaṁ dhammaṁ deseyyaṁ;

'Who should I teach first of all?

ko imaṁ dhammaṁ khippameva ājānissatī'ti?

Who will quickly understand this teaching?'

Tassa mayhaṁ, bhikkhave, etadahosi:

Then it occurred to me,

'ayaṁ kho udako rāmaputto paṇḍito viyatto medhāvī dīgharattaṁ apparajakkhajātiko.

'That Uddaka, son of Rāma, is astute, competent, clever, and has long had little dust in his eyes.

Yannūnāhaṁ udakassa rāmaputtassa paṭhamaṁ dhammaṁ deseyyaṁ.

Why don't I teach him first of all?

So imaṁ dhammaṁ khippameva ājānissatī'ti.

He'll quickly understand the teaching.'

Atha kho maṁ, bhikkhave, devatā upasaṅkamitvā etadavoca:

But a deity came to me and said,

'abhidosakālaṅkato, bhante, udako rāmaputto'ti.

'Sir, Uddaka, son of Rāma, passed away just last night.'

Ñāṇañca pana me dassanaṁ udapādi:

And knowledge and vision arose in me,

'abhidosakālaṅkato udako rāmaputto'ti.

'Uddaka, son of Rāma, passed away just last night.'

Tassa mayhaṁ, bhikkhave, etadahosi:

I thought,

'mahājāniyo kho udako rāmaputto.

'This is a great loss for Uddaka.

Sace hi so imaṁ dhammaṁ suṇeyya, khippameva ājāneyyā'ti.

If he had heard the teaching, he would have understood it quickly.'

Tassa mayhaṁ, bhikkhave, etadahosi:

Then I thought,

'kassa nu kho ahaṁ paṭhamaṁ dhammaṁ deseyyaṁ;

'Who should I teach first of all?

ko imaṁ dhammaṁ khippameva ājānissatī'ti?

Who will quickly understand this teaching?'

Tassa mayhaṁ, bhikkhave, etadahosi:

Then it occurred to me,

'bahukārā kho me pañcavaggiyā bhikkhū, ye maṁ padhānapahitattaṁ upaṭṭhahiṁsu.

'The group of five mendicants were very helpful to me. They looked after me during my time of resolute striving.

Yannūnāhaṁ pañcavaggiyānaṁ bhikkhūnaṁ paṭhamaṁ dhammaṁ deseyyan'ti.

Why don't I teach them first of all?'

Tassa mayhaṁ, bhikkhave, etadahosi:

Then I thought,

'kahaṁ nu kho etarahi pañcavaggiyā bhikkhū viharantī'ti?

'Where are the group of five mendicants staying these days?'

Addasaṁ kho ahaṁ, bhikkhave, dibbena cakkhunā visuddhena atikkantamānusakena pañcavaggiye bhikkhū bārāṇasiyaṁ viharante isipatane migadāye.

With clairvoyance that is purified and superhuman I saw that the group of five mendicants were staying near Benares, in the deer park at Isipatana.

Atha khvāhaṁ, bhikkhave, uruvelāyaṁ yathābhirantaṁ viharitvā yena bārāṇasī tena cārikaṁ pakkamiṁ.

So, when I had stayed in Uruvelā as long as I pleased, I set out for Benares.

Addasā kho maṁ, bhikkhave, upako ājīvako antarā ca gayaṁ antarā ca bodhiṁ addhānamaggappaṭipannaṁ.

While I was traveling along the road between Gayā and Bodhgaya, the Ājīvaka ascetic Upaka saw me

Disvāna maṁ etadavoca:

and said,

'vippasannāni kho te, āvuso, indriyāni, parisuddho chavivaṇṇo pariyodāto.

'Reverend, your faculties are so very clear, and your complexion is pure and bright.

Kaṁsi tvaṁ, āvuso, uddissa pabbajito, ko vā te satthā, kassa vā tvaṁ dhammaṁ rocesī'ti?

In whose name have you gone forth, reverend? Who is your Teacher? Whose teaching do you believe in?'

Evaṁ vutte, ahaṁ, bhikkhave, upakaṁ ājīvakaṁ gāthāhi ajjhabhāsiṁ:

I replied to Upaka in verse:

'Sabbābhibhū sabbaviduhamasmi,

Sabbesu dhammesu anūpalitto;

Sabbañjaho taṇhākkhaye vimutto,

Sayaṁ abhiññāya kamuddiseyyaṁ.

'I am the champion, the knower of all,

unsullied in the midst of all things.

I've given up all, freed through the ending of craving.

Since I know for myself, whose follower should I be?

Na me ācariyo atthi,

sadiso me na vijjati;

Sadevakasmiṁ lokasmiṁ,

natthi me paṭipuggalo.

I have no teacher.

There is no-one like me.

In the world with its gods,

I have no counterpart.

Ahañhi arahā loke,

ahaṁ satthā anuttaro;

Ekomhi sammāsambuddho,

sītibhūtosmi nibbuto.

For in this world, I am the perfected one;

I am the supreme Teacher.

I alone am fully awakened,

cooled, extinguished.

Dhammacakkaṁ pavattetuṁ,

Gacchāmi kāsinaṁ puraṁ;

Andhībhūtasmiṁ lokasmiṁ,

Āhañchaṁ amatadundubhin'ti.

I am going to the city of Kāsi

to roll forth the Wheel of Dhamma.

In this world that is so blind,

I'll beat the deathless drum!'

'Yathā kho tvaṁ, āvuso, paṭijānāsi, arahasi anantajino'ti.

'According to what you claim, reverend, you ought to be the Infinite Victor.'

'Mādisā ve jinā honti,

ye pattā āsavakkhayaṁ;

Jitā me pāpakā dhammā,

tasmāhamupaka jino'ti.

'The victors are those who, like me,

have reached the ending of defilements.

I have conquered bad qualities, Upaka—

that's why I'm a victor.'

Evaṁ vutte, bhikkhave, upako ājīvako 'hupeyyapāvuso'ti vatvā sīsaṁ okampetvā ummaggaṁ gahetvā pakkāmi.

When I had spoken, Upaka said: 'If you say so, reverend.' Shaking his head, he took a wrong turn and left.

Atha khvāhaṁ, bhikkhave, anupubbena cārikaṁ caramāno yena bārāṇasī isipatanaṁ migadāyo yena pañcavaggiyā bhikkhū tenupasaṅkamiṁ.

Traveling stage by stage, I arrived at Benares, and went to see the group of five mendicants in the deer park at Isipatana.

Addasaṁsu kho maṁ, bhikkhave, pañcavaggiyā bhikkhū dūrato āgacchantaṁ.

The group of five mendicants saw me coming off in the distance

Disvāna aññamaññaṁ saṇṭhapesuṁ:

and stopped each other, saying,

'ayaṁ kho, āvuso, samaṇo gotamo āgacchati bāhulliko padhānavibbhanto āvatto bāhullāya.

'Here comes the ascetic Gotama. He's so indulgent; he strayed from the struggle and returned to indulgence.

So neva abhivādetabbo, na paccuṭṭhātabbo; nāssa pattacīvaraṁ paṭiggahetabbaṁ.

We shouldn't bow to him or rise for him or receive his bowl and robe.

Api ca kho āsanaṁ ṭhapetabbaṁ, sace ākaṅkhissati nisīdissatī'ti.

But we can set out a seat; he can sit if he likes.'

Yathā yathā kho ahaṁ, bhikkhave, upasaṅkamiṁ tathā tathā pañcavaggiyā bhikkhū nāsakkhiṁsu sakāya katikāya saṇṭhātuṁ.

Yet as I drew closer, the group of five mendicants were unable to stop themselves as they had agreed.

Appekacce maṁ paccuggantvā pattacīvaraṁ paṭiggahesuṁ, appekacce āsanaṁ paññapesuṁ, appekacce pādodakaṁ upaṭṭhapesuṁ.

Some came out to greet me and receive my bowl and robe, some spread out a seat, while others set out water for washing my feet.

Api ca kho maṁ nāmena ca āvusovādena ca samudācaranti.

But they still addressed me by name and as 'reverend'.

Evaṁ vutte, ahaṁ, bhikkhave, pañcavaggiye bhikkhū etadavocaṁ:

So I said to them,

'mā, bhikkhave, tathāgataṁ nāmena ca āvusovādena ca samudācaratha.

'Mendicants, don't address me by name and as 'reverend'.

Arahaṁ, bhikkhave, tathāgato sammāsambuddho.

The Realized One is perfected, a fully awakened Buddha.

Odahatha, bhikkhave, sotaṁ, amatamadhigataṁ, ahamanusāsāmi, ahaṁ dhammaṁ desemi.

Listen up, mendicants: I have achieved the Deathless! I shall instruct you, I will teach you the Dhamma.

Yathānusiṭṭhaṁ tathāpaṭipajjamānānacirasseva—yassatthāyakulaputtāsammadeva agārasmā anagāriyaṁ pabbajanti, tadanuttaraṁ—brahmacariyapariyosānaṁ diṭṭheva dhamme sayaṁ abhiññā sacchikatvā upasampajja viharissathā'ti.

By practicing as instructed you will soon realize the supreme end of the spiritual path in this very life. You will live having achieved with your own insight the goal for which gentlemen rightly go forth from the lay life to homelessness.'

Evaṁ vutte, bhikkhave, pañcavaggiyā bhikkhū maṁ etadavocuṁ:

But they said to me,

'tāyapi kho tvaṁ, āvuso gotama, iriyāya tāya paṭipadāya tāya dukkarakārikāya nājjhagamā uttari manussadhammā alamariyañāṇadassanavisesaṁ, kiṁ pana tvaṁ etarahi bāhulliko padhānavibbhanto āvatto bāhullāya adhigamissasi uttari manussadhammā alamariyañāṇadassanavisesan'ti?

'Reverend Gotama, even by that conduct, that practice, that grueling work you did not achieve any superhuman distinction in knowledge and vision worthy of the noble ones. How could you have achieved such a state now that you've become indulgent, strayed from the struggle and returned to indulgence?'

Evaṁ vutte, ahaṁ, bhikkhave, pañcavaggiye bhikkhū etadavocaṁ:

So I said to them,

'na, bhikkhave, tathāgato bāhulliko, na padhānavibbhanto, na āvatto bāhullāya.

'The Realized One has not become indulgent, strayed from the struggle and returned to indulgence.

Arahaṁ, bhikkhave, tathāgato sammāsambuddho.

The Realized One is perfected, a fully awakened Buddha.

Odahatha, bhikkhave, sotaṁ, amatamadhigataṁ, ahamanusāsāmi, ahaṁ dhammaṁ desemi.

Listen up, mendicants: I have achieved the Deathless! I shall instruct you, I will teach you the Dhamma.

Yathānusiṭṭhaṁ tathāpaṭipajjamānānacirasseva—yassatthāyakulaputtāsammadeva agārasmā anagāriyaṁ pabbajanti, tadanuttaraṁ—brahmacariyapariyosānaṁ diṭṭheva dhamme sayaṁ abhiññā sacchikatvā upasampajja viharissathā'ti.

By practicing as instructed you will soon realize the supreme end of the spiritual path in this very life.'

Dutiyampi kho, bhikkhave, pañcavaggiyā bhikkhū maṁ etadavocuṁ:

But for a second time they said to me,

'tāyapi kho tvaṁ, āvuso gotama, iriyāya tāya paṭipadāya tāya dukkarakārikāya nājjhagamā uttari manussadhammā alamariyañāṇadassanavisesaṁ, kiṁ pana tvaṁ etarahi bāhulliko padhānavibbhanto āvatto bāhullāya adhigamissasi uttari manussadhammā alamariyañāṇadassanavisesan'ti?

'Reverend Gotama … you've returned to indulgence.'

Dutiyampi kho ahaṁ, bhikkhave, pañcavaggiye bhikkhū etadavocaṁ:

So for a second time I said to them,

'na, bhikkhave, tathāgato bāhulliko …pe…

'The Realized One has not become indulgent …'

upasampajja viharissathā'ti.

Tatiyampi kho, bhikkhave, pañcavaggiyā bhikkhū maṁ etadavocuṁ:

But for a third time they said to me,

'tāyapi kho tvaṁ, āvuso gotama, iriyāya tāya paṭipadāya tāya dukkarakārikāya nājjhagamā uttari manussadhammā alamariyañāṇadassanavisesaṁ, kiṁ pana tvaṁ etarahi bāhulliko padhānavibbhanto āvatto bāhullāya adhigamissasi uttari manussadhammā alamariyañāṇadassanavisesan'ti?

'Reverend Gotama, even by that conduct, that practice, that grueling work you did not achieve any superhuman distinction in knowledge and vision worthy of the noble ones. How could you have achieved such a state now that you've become indulgent, strayed from the struggle and returned to indulgence?'

Evaṁ vutte, ahaṁ, bhikkhave, pañcavaggiye bhikkhū etadavocaṁ:

So I said to them,

'abhijānātha me no tumhe, bhikkhave, ito pubbe evarūpaṁ pabhāvitametan'ti?

'Mendicants, have you ever known me to speak like this before?'

'No hetaṁ, bhante'.

'No sir, we have not.'

'Arahaṁ, bhikkhave, tathāgato sammāsambuddho.

'The Realized One is perfected, a fully awakened Buddha.

Odahatha, bhikkhave, sotaṁ, amatamadhigataṁ, ahamanusāsāmi, ahaṁ dhammaṁ desemi.

Listen up, mendicants: I have achieved the Deathless! I shall instruct you, I will teach you the Dhamma.

Yathānusiṭṭhaṁ tathāpaṭipajjamānānacirasseva—yassatthāyakulaputtāsammadeva agārasmā anagāriyaṁ pabbajanti, tadanuttaraṁ—brahmacariyapariyosānaṁ diṭṭheva dhamme sayaṁ abhiññā sacchikatvā upasampajja viharissathā'ti.

By practicing as instructed you will soon realize the supreme end of the spiritual path in this very life. You will live having achieved with your own insight the goal for which gentlemen rightly go forth from the lay life to homelessness.'

Asakkhiṁ kho ahaṁ, bhikkhave, pañcavaggiye bhikkhū saññāpetuṁ.

I was able to persuade the group of five mendicants.

Dvepi sudaṁ, bhikkhave, bhikkhū ovadāmi, tayo bhikkhū piṇḍāya caranti.

Then sometimes I advised two mendicants, while the other three went for alms.

Yaṁ tayo bhikkhū piṇḍāya caritvā āharanti tena chabbaggiyā yāpema.

Then those three would feed all six of us with what they brought back.

Tayopi sudaṁ, bhikkhave, bhikkhū ovadāmi, dve bhikkhū piṇḍāya caranti.

Sometimes I advised three mendicants, while the other two went for alms.

Yaṁ dve bhikkhū piṇḍāya caritvā āharanti tena chabbaggiyā yāpema.

Then those two would feed all six of us with what they brought back.

Atha kho, bhikkhave, pañcavaggiyā bhikkhū mayā evaṁ ovadiyamānā evaṁ anusāsiyamānā attanā jātidhammā samānā jātidhamme ādīnavaṁ viditvā ajātaṁ anuttaraṁ yogakkhemaṁ nibbānaṁ pariyesamānā ajātaṁ anuttaraṁ yogakkhemaṁ nibbānaṁ ajjhagamaṁsu, attanā jarādhammā samānā jarādhamme ādīnavaṁ viditvā ajaraṁ anuttaraṁ yogakkhemaṁ nibbānaṁ pariyesamānā ajaraṁ anuttaraṁ yogakkhemaṁ nibbānaṁ ajjhagamaṁsu, attanā byādhidhammā samānā ...pe... attanā maraṇadhammā samānā ... attanā sokadhammā samānā ... attanā saṅkilesadhammā samānā saṅkilesadhamme ādīnavaṁ viditvā asaṅkiliṭṭhaṁ anuttaraṁ yogakkhemaṁ nibbānaṁ pariyesamānā asaṅkiliṭṭhaṁ anuttaraṁ yogakkhemaṁ nibbānaṁ ajjhagamaṁsu.

As the group of five mendicants were being advised and instructed by me like this, being themselves liable to be reborn, understanding the drawbacks in being liable to be reborn, they sought the unborn supreme sanctuary, extinguishment—and they found it. Being themselves liable to grow old, fall sick, die, sorrow, and become corrupted, understanding the drawbacks in these things, they sought the unaging, unailing, undying, sorrowless, uncorrupted supreme sanctuary, extinguishment—and they found it.

Ñāṇañca pana nesaṁ dassanaṁ udapādi:

Knowledge and vision arose in them:

'akuppā no vimutti, ayamantimā jāti, natthi dāni punabbhavo'ti.

'Our freedom is unshakable; this is our last rebirth; now there are no more future lives.'

Pañcime, bhikkhave, kāmaguṇā.

Mendicants, there are these five kinds of sensual stimulation.

Katame pañca?

What five?

Cakkhuviññeyyā rūpā iṭṭhā kantā manāpā piyarūpā kāmūpasaṁhitā rajanīyā,

Sights known by the eye that are likable, desirable, agreeable, pleasant, sensual, and arousing.

sotaviññeyyā saddā ...pe...

Sounds known by the ear ...

ghānaviññeyyā gandhā ...

Smells known by the nose ...

jivhāviññeyyā rasā ...

Tastes known by the tongue ...

kāyaviññeyyā phoṭṭhabbā iṭṭhā kantā manāpā piyarūpā kāmūpasaṁhitā rajanīyā.

Touches known by the body that are likable, desirable, agreeable, pleasant, sensual, and arousing.

Ime kho, bhikkhave, pañca kāmaguṇā.

These are the five kinds of sensual stimulation.

Ye hi keci, bhikkhave, samaṇā vā brāhmaṇā vā ime pañca kāmaguṇe gathitā mucchitā ajjhopannā anādīnavadassāvino anissaraṇapaññā paribhuñjanti, te evamassu veditabbā:

There are ascetics and brahmins who enjoy these five kinds of sensual stimulation tied, infatuated, attached, blind to the drawbacks, and not understanding the escape. You should understand that they

'anayamāpannā byasanamāpannā yathākāmakaraṇīyā pāpimato'.

have met with calamity and disaster, and the Wicked One can do with them what he wants.

Seyyathāpi, bhikkhave, āraññako mago baddho pāsarāsiṁ adhisayeyya.

Suppose a deer in the wilderness was lying caught on a pile of snares.

So evamassa veditabbo:

You'd know that it

'anayamāpanno byasanamāpanno yathākāmakaraṇīyo luddassa.

has met with calamity and disaster, and the hunter can do with them what he wants.

Āgacchante ca pana ludde yena kāmaṁ na pakkamissatī'ti.

And when the hunter comes, it cannot flee where it wants.

Evameva kho, bhikkhave, ye hi keci samaṇā vā brāhmaṇā vā ime pañca kāmaguṇe gathitā mucchitā ajjhopannā anādīnavadassāvino anissaraṇapaññā paribhuñjanti, te evamassu veditabbā:

In the same way, there are ascetics and brahmins who enjoy these five kinds of sensual stimulation tied, infatuated, attached, blind to the drawbacks, and not understanding the escape. You should understand that they

'anayamāpannā byasanamāpannā yathākāmakaraṇīyā pāpimato'.

have met with calamity and disaster, and the Wicked One can do with them what he wants.

Ye ca kho keci, bhikkhave, samaṇā vā brāhmaṇā vā ime pañca kāmaguṇe agathitā amucchitā anajjhopannā ādīnavadassāvino nissaraṇapaññā paribhuñjanti, te evamassu veditabbā:

There are ascetics and brahmins who enjoy these five kinds of sensual stimulation without being tied, infatuated, or attached, seeing the drawbacks, and understanding the escape. You should understand that they

'na anayamāpannā na byasanamāpannā na yathākāmakaraṇīyā pāpimato'.

haven't met with calamity and disaster, and the Wicked One cannot do what he wants with them.

Seyyathāpi, bhikkhave, āraññako mago abaddho pāsarāsiṁ adhisayeyya.

Suppose a deer in the wilderness was lying on a pile of snares without being caught.

So evamassa veditabbo:

You'd know that it

'na anayamāpanno na byasanamāpanno na yathākāmakaraṇīyo luddassa.

hasn't met with calamity and disaster, and the hunter cannot do what he wants with them.

Āgacchante ca pana ludde yena kāmaṁ pakkamissatī'ti.

And when the hunter comes, it can flee where it wants.

Evameva kho, bhikkhave, ye hi keci samaṇā vā brāhmaṇā vā ime pañca kāmaguṇe agathitā amucchitā anajjhopannā ādīnavadassāvino nissaraṇapaññā paribhuñjanti, te evamassu veditabbā:

In the same way, there are ascetics and brahmins who enjoy these five kinds of sensual stimulation without being tied, infatuated, or attached, seeing the drawbacks, and understanding the escape. You should understand that they

'na anayamāpannā na byasanamāpannā na yathākāmakaraṇīyā pāpimato'.

haven't met with calamity and disaster, and the Wicked One cannot do what he wants with them.

Seyyathāpi, bhikkhave, āraññako mago araññe pavane caramāno vissattho gacchati, vissattho tiṭṭhati, vissattho nisīdati, vissattho seyyaṁ kappeti.

Suppose there was a wild deer wandering in the forest that walked, stood, sat, and laid down in confidence.

Taṁ kissa hetu?

Why is that?

Anāpāthagato, bhikkhave, luddassa.

Because it's out of the hunter's range.

Evameva kho, bhikkhave, bhikkhu vivicceva kāmehi vivicca akusalehi dhammehi savitakkaṁ savicāraṁ vivekajaṁ pītisukhaṁ paṭhamaṁ jhānaṁ upasampajja viharati.

In the same way, a mendicant, quite secluded from sensual pleasures, secluded from unskillful qualities, enters and remains in the first absorption, which has the rapture and bliss born of seclusion, while placing the mind and keeping it connected.

Ayaṁ vuccati, bhikkhave, bhikkhu andhamakāsi māraṁ apadaṁ, vadhitvā māracakkhuṁ adassanaṁ gato pāpimato.

This is called a mendicant who has blinded Māra, put out his eyes without a trace, and gone where the Wicked One cannot see.

Puna caparaṁ, bhikkhave, bhikkhu vitakkavicārānaṁ vūpasamā ajjhattaṁ sampasādanaṁ cetaso ekodibhāvaṁ avitakkaṁ avicāraṁ samādhijaṁ pītisukhaṁ dutiyaṃ jhānaṃ upasampajja viharati.

Furthermore, as the placing of the mind and keeping it connected are stilled, a mendicant enters and remains in the second absorption, which has the rapture and bliss born of immersion, with internal clarity and confidence, and unified mind, without placing the mind and keeping it connected.

Ayaṃ vuccati, bhikkhave …pe… pāpimato.

This is called a mendicant who has blinded Māra …

Puna caparaṃ, bhikkhave, bhikkhu pītiyā ca virāgā upekkhako ca viharati, sato ca sampajāno, sukhañca kāyena paṭisaṃvedeti yaṃ taṃ ariyā ācikkhanti 'upekkhako satimā sukhavihārī'ti tatiyaṃ jhānaṃ upasampajja viharati.

Furthermore, with the fading away of rapture, a mendicant enters and remains in the third absorption, where they meditate with equanimity, mindful and aware, personally experiencing the bliss of which the noble ones declare, 'Equanimous and mindful, one meditates in bliss.'

Ayaṃ vuccati, bhikkhave …pe… pāpimato.

This is called a mendicant who has blinded Māra …

Puna caparaṃ, bhikkhave, bhikkhu sukhassa ca pahānā dukkhassa ca pahānā pubbeva somanassadomanassānaṃ atthaṅgamā adukkhamasukhaṃ upekkhāsatipārisuddhiṃ catutthaṃ jhānaṃ upasampajja viharati.

Furthermore, giving up pleasure and pain, and ending former happiness and sadness, a mendicant enters and remains in the fourth absorption, without pleasure or pain, with pure equanimity and mindfulness.

Ayaṃ vuccati, bhikkhave …pe… pāpimato.

This is called a mendicant who has blinded Māra …

Puna caparaṃ, bhikkhave, bhikkhu sabbaso rūpasaññānaṃ samatikkamā paṭighasaññānaṃ atthaṅgamā nānattasaññānaṃ amanasikārā 'ananto ākāso'ti ākāsānañcāyatanaṃ upasampajja viharati.

Furthermore, a mendicant, going totally beyond perceptions of form, with the ending of perceptions of impingement, not focusing on perceptions of diversity, aware that 'space is infinite', enters and remains in the dimension of infinite space.

Ayaṃ vuccati, bhikkhave …pe… pāpimato.

This is called a mendicant who has blinded Māra …

Puna caparaṃ, bhikkhave, bhikkhu sabbaso ākāsānañcāyatanaṃ samatikkamma 'anantaṃ viññāṇan'ti viññāṇañcāyatanaṃ upasampajja viharati.

Furthermore, a mendicant, going totally beyond the dimension of infinite space, aware that 'consciousness is infinite', enters and remains in the dimension of infinite consciousness.

Ayaṁ vuccati, bhikkhave …pe… pāpimato.

This is called a mendicant who has blinded Māra …

Puna caparaṁ, bhikkhave, bhikkhu sabbaso viññāṇañcāyatanaṁ samatikkamma 'natthi kiñcī'ti ākiñcaññāyatanaṁ upasampajja viharati.

Furthermore, a mendicant, going totally beyond the dimension of infinite consciousness, aware that 'there is nothing at all', enters and remains in the dimension of nothingness.

Ayaṁ vuccati, bhikkhave …pe… pāpimato.

This is called a mendicant who has blinded Māra …

Puna caparaṁ, bhikkhave, bhikkhu sabbaso ākiñcaññāyatanaṁ samatikkamma nevasaññānāsaññāyatanaṁ upasampajja viharati.

Furthermore, a mendicant, going totally beyond the dimension of nothingness, enters and remains in the dimension of neither perception nor non-perception.

Ayaṁ vuccati, bhikkhave …pe… pāpimato.

This is called a mendicant who has blinded Māra …

Puna caparaṁ, bhikkhave, bhikkhu sabbaso nevasaññānāsaññāyatanaṁ samatikkamma saññāvedayitanirodhaṁ upasampajja viharati, paññāya cassa disvā āsavā parikkhīṇā honti.

Furthermore, a mendicant, going totally beyond the dimension of neither perception nor non-perception, enters and remains in the cessation of perception and feeling. And, having seen with wisdom, their defilements come to an end.

Ayaṁ vuccati, bhikkhave, bhikkhu andhamakāsi māraṁ apadaṁ, vadhitvā māracakkhuṁ adassanaṁ gato pāpimato.

This is called a mendicant who has blinded Māra, put out his eyes without a trace, and gone where the Wicked One cannot see.

Tiṇṇo loke visattikaṁ vissattho gacchati, vissattho tiṭṭhati, vissattho nisīdati, vissattho seyyaṁ kappeti.

They've crossed over clinging to the world. And they walk, stand, sit, and lie down in confidence.

Taṁ kissa hetu?

Why is that?

Anāpāthagato, bhikkhave, pāpimato”ti.

Because they're out of the Wicked One's range.”

Idamavoca bhagavā.

That is what the Buddha said.

Attamanā te bhikkhū bhagavato bhāsitaṁ abhinandunti.

Satisfied, the mendicants were happy with what the Buddha said.

Pāsarāsisuttaṁ niṭṭhitaṁ chaṭṭhaṁ.

27 Culahatthipadopamasutta:

The Shorter Simile of the Elephant's Footprint

Evaṁ me sutaṁ—

So I have heard.

ekaṁ samayaṁ bhagavā sāvatthiyaṁ viharati jetavane anāthapiṇḍikassa ārāme.

At one time the Buddha was staying near Sāvatthī in Jeta's Grove, Anāthapiṇḍika's monastery.

Tena kho pana samayena jāṇussoṇi brāhmaṇo sabbasetena vaḷavābhirathena sāvatthiyā niyyāti divādivassa.

Now at that time the brahmin Jāṇussoṇi drove out from Sāvatthī in the middle of the day in an all-white chariot drawn by mares.

Addasā kho jāṇussoṇi brāhmaṇo pilotikaṁ paribbājakaṁ dūratova āgacchantaṁ.

He saw the wanderer Pilotika coming off in the distance,

Disvāna pilotikaṁ paribbājakaṁ etadavoca:

and said to him,

“Handa kuto nu bhavaṁ vacchāyano āgacchati divādivassā”ti?

“So, Master Vacchāyana, where are you coming from in the middle of the day?”

“Ito hi kho ahaṁ, bho, āgacchāmi samaṇassa gotamassa santikā”ti.

“Just now, good sir, I've come from the presence of the ascetic Gotama.”

"Taṁ kiṁ maññati bhavaṁ vacchāyano samaṇassa gotamassa paññāveyyattiyaṁ paṇḍito maññe"ti.

"What do you think of the ascetic Gotama's lucidity of wisdom? Do you think he's astute?"

"Ko cāhaṁ, bho, ko ca samaṇassa gotamassa paññāveyyattiyaṁ jānissāmi.

"My good man, who am I to judge the ascetic Gotama's lucidity of wisdom?

Sopi nūnassa tādisova yo samaṇassa gotamassa paññāveyyattiyaṁ jāneyyā"ti.

You'd really have to be on the same level to judge his lucidity of wisdom."

"Uḷārāya khalu bhavaṁ vacchāyano samaṇaṁ gotamaṁ pasaṁsāya pasaṁsatī"ti.

"Master Vacchāyana praises the ascetic Gotama with lofty praise indeed."

"Ko cāhaṁ, bho, ko ca samaṇaṁ gotamaṁ pasaṁsissāmi,

"Who am I to praise the ascetic Gotama?

pasatthapasatthova so bhavaṁ gotamo seṭṭho devamanussānan"ti.

He is praised by the praised as the first among gods and humans."

"Kaṁ pana bhavaṁ vacchāyano atthavasaṁ sampassamāno samaṇe gotame evaṁ abhippasanno"ti?

"But for what reason are you so devoted to the ascetic Gotama?"

"Seyyathāpi, bho, kusalo nāgavaniko nāgavanaṁ paviseyya.

"Suppose that a skilled elephant tracker were to enter an elephant wood.

So passeyya nāgavane mahantaṁ hatthipadaṁ, dīghato ca āyataṁ, tiriyañca vitthataṁ.

There he'd see a large elephant's footprint, long and broad.

So niṭṭhaṁ gaccheyya:

He'd draw the conclusion,

'mahā vata bho nāgo'ti.

'This must be a big bull elephant.'

Evameva kho ahaṁ, bho, yato addasaṁ samaṇe gotame cattāri padāni athāhaṁ niṭṭhamagamaṁ:

In the same way, because I saw four footprints of the ascetic Gotama I drew the conclusion, 'sammāsambuddho bhagavā, svākkhāto bhagavatā dhammo, suppaṭipanno bhagavato sāvakasaṅgho'ti.

'The Blessed One is a fully awakened Buddha. The teaching is well explained. The Saṅgha is practicing well.'

Katamāni cattāri?

What four?

Idhāhaṁ, bho, passāmi ekacce khattiyapaṇḍite nipuṇe kataparappavāde vālavedhirūpe, te bhindantā maññe caranti paññāgatena diṭṭhigatāni.

Firstly, I see some clever aristocrats who are subtle, accomplished in the doctrines of others, hair-splitters. You'd think they live to demolish convictions with their intellect.

Te suṇanti:

They hear,

'samaṇo khalu, bho, gotamo amukaṁ nāma gāmaṁ vā nigamaṁ vā osarissatī'ti.

'So, gentlemen, that ascetic Gotama will come down to such and such village or town.'

Te pañhaṁ abhisaṅkharonti:

They formulate a question, thinking,

'imaṁ mayaṁ pañhaṁ samaṇaṁ gotamaṁ upasaṅkamitvā pucchissāma.

'We'll approach the ascetic Gotama and ask him this question.

Evañce no puṭṭho evaṁ byākarissati, evamassa mayaṁ vādaṁ āropessāma.

If he answers like this, we'll refute him like that;

Evañcepi no puṭṭho evaṁ byākarissati, evampissa mayaṁ vādaṁ āropessāmā'ti.

and if he answers like that, we'll refute him like this.'

Te suṇanti:

When they hear that

'samaṇo khalu, bho, gotamo amukaṁ nāma gāmaṁ vā nigamaṁ vā osaṭo'ti.

he has come down

Te yena samaṇo gotamo tenupasaṅkamanti.

they approach him.

Te samaṇo gotamo dhammiyā kathāya sandasseti samādapeti samuttejeti sampahaṁseti.

The ascetic Gotama educates, encourages, fires up, and inspires them with a Dhamma talk.

Te samaṇena gotamena dhammiyā kathāya sandassitā samādapitā samuttejitā sampahaṁsitā na ceva samaṇaṁ gotamaṁ pañhaṁ pucchanti, kutossa vādaṁ āropessanti?

They don't even get around to asking their question to the ascetic Gotama, so how could they refute his answer?

Aññadatthu samaṇasseva gotamassa sāvakā sampajjanti.

Invariably, they become his disciples.

Yadāhaṁ, bho, samaṇe gotame imaṁ paṭhamaṁ padaṁ addasaṁ athāhaṁ niṭṭhamagamaṁ:

When I saw this first footprint of the ascetic Gotama, I drew the conclusion,

'sammāsambuddho bhagavā, svākkhāto bhagavatā dhammo, suppaṭipanno bhagavato sāvakasaṅgho'ti.

'The Blessed One is a fully awakened Buddha. The teaching is well explained. The Saṅgha is practicing well.'

Puna caparāhaṁ, bho, passāmi idhekacce brāhmaṇapaṇḍite …pe…

Furthermore, I see some clever brahmins …

gahapatipaṇḍite …

some clever householders …

pe…

they become his disciples.

samaṇapaṇḍite nipuṇe kataparappavāde vālavedhirūpe te bhindantā maññe caranti paññāgatena diṭṭhigatāni.

Furthermore, I see some clever ascetics who are subtle, accomplished in the doctrines of others, hair-splitters. …

Te suṇanti:

'samaṇo khalu bho gotamo amukaṁ nāma gāmaṁ vā nigamaṁ vā osarissatī'ti.

Te pañhaṁ abhisaṅkharonti 'imaṁ mayaṁ pañhaṁ samaṇaṁ gotamaṁ upasaṅkamitvā pucchissāma.

Evañce no puṭṭho evaṁ byākarissati, evamassa mayaṁ vādaṁ āropessāma.

Evañcepi no puṭṭho evaṁ byākarissati, evampissa mayaṁ vādaṁ āropessāmā'ti.

Te suṇanti 'samaṇo khalu bho gotamo amukaṁ nāma gāmaṁ vā nigamaṁ vā osaṭo'ti.

Te yena samaṇo gotamo tenupasaṅkamanti.

Te samaṇo gotamo dhammiyā kathāya sandasseti samādapeti samuttejeti sampahaṁseti.

Te samaṇena gotamena dhammiyā kathāya sandassitā samādapitā samuttejitā sampahaṁsitā na ceva samaṇaṁ gotamaṁ pañhaṁ pucchanti, kutossa vādaṁ āropessanti?

They don't even get around to asking their question to the ascetic Gotama, so how could they refute his answer?

Aññadatthu samaṇaṁyeva gotamaṁ okāsaṁ yācanti agārasmā anagāriyaṁ pabbajjāya.

Invariably, they ask the ascetic Gotama for the chance to go forth.

Te samaṇo gotamo pabbājeti.

And he gives them the going-forth.

Te tattha pabbajitā samānā vūpakaṭṭhā appamattā ātāpino pahitattā viharantā nacirasseva—yassatthāya kulaputtā sammadeva agārasmā anagāriyaṁ pabbajanti, tadanuttaraṁ—brahmacariyapariyosānaṁ diṭṭheva dhamme sayaṁ abhiññā sacchikatvā upasampajja viharanti.

Soon after going forth, living withdrawn, diligent, keen, and resolute, they realize the supreme end of the spiritual path in this very life. They live having achieved with their own insight the goal for which gentlemen rightly go forth from the lay life to homelessness.

Te evamāhaṁsu:

They say,

'manaṁ vata, bho, anassāma, manaṁ vata, bho, panassāma;

'We were almost lost! We almost perished!

mayañhi pubbe assamaṇāva samānā samaṇamhāti paṭijānimha, abrāhmaṇāva samānā brāhmaṇamhāti paṭijānimha, anarahantova samānā arahantamhāti paṭijānimha.

For we used to claim that we were ascetics, brahmins, and perfected ones, but we were none of these things.

Idāni khomha samaṇā, idāni khomha brāhmaṇā, idāni khomha arahanto'ti.

But now we really are ascetics, brahmins, and perfected ones!'

Yadāhaṁ, bho, samaṇe gotame imaṁ catutthaṁ padaṁ addasaṁ athāhaṁ niṭṭhamagamaṁ:

When I saw this fourth footprint of the ascetic Gotama, I drew the conclusion,

'sammāsambuddho bhagavā, svākkhāto bhagavatā dhammo, suppaṭipanno bhagavato sāvakasaṅgho'ti.

'The Blessed One is a fully awakened Buddha. The teaching is well explained. The Saṅgha is practicing well.'

Yato kho ahaṁ, bho, samaṇe gotame imāni cattāri padāni addasaṁ athāhaṁ niṭṭhamagamaṁ:

It's because I saw these four footprints of the ascetic Gotama that I drew the conclusion,

'sammāsambuddho bhagavā, svākkhāto bhagavatā dhammo, suppaṭipanno bhagavato sāvakasaṅgho'"ti.

'The Blessed One is a fully awakened Buddha. The teaching is well explained. The Saṅgha is practicing well.'"

Evaṁ vutte, jāṇussoṇi brāhmaṇo sabbasetā vaḷavābhirathā orohitvā ekaṁsaṁ uttarāsaṅgaṁ karitvā yena bhagavā tenañjaliṁ paṇāmetvā tikkhattuṁ udānaṁ udānesi:

When he had spoken, Jāṇussoṇi got down from his chariot, arranged his robe over one shoulder, raised his joined palms toward the Buddha, and expressed this heartfelt sentiment three times:

"Namo tassa bhagavato arahato sammāsambuddhassa;

"Homage to that Blessed One, the perfected one, the fully awakened Buddha!

namo tassa bhagavato arahato sammāsambuddhassa;

Homage to that Blessed One, the perfected one, the fully awakened Buddha!

namo tassa bhagavato arahato sammāsambuddhassāti.

Homage to that Blessed One, the perfected one, the fully awakened Buddha!

Appeva nāma mayampi kadāci karahaci tena bhotā gotamena saddhiṁ samāgaccheyyāma, appeva nāma siyā kocideva kathāsallāpo"ti.

Hopefully, some time or other I'll get to meet Master Gotama, and we can have a discussion."

Atha kho jāṇussoṇi brāhmaṇo yena bhagavā tenupasaṅkami; upasaṅkamitvā bhagavatā saddhiṁ sammodi.

Then the brahmin Jāṇussoṇi went up to the Buddha, and exchanged greetings with him.

Sammodanīyaṁ kathaṁ sāraṇīyaṁ vītisāretvā ekamantaṁ nisīdi.

When the greetings and polite conversation were over, he sat down to one side,

Ekamantaṁ nisinno kho jāṇussoṇi brāhmaṇo yāvatako ahosi pilotikena paribbājakena saddhiṁ kathāsallāpo taṁ sabbaṁ bhagavato ārocesi.

and informed the Buddha of all they had discussed.

Evaṁ vutte, bhagavā jāṇussoṇiṁ brāhmaṇaṁ etadavoca:

When he had spoken, the Buddha said to him,

"na kho, brāhmaṇa, ettāvatā hatthipadopamo vitthārena paripūro hoti.

"Brahmin, the simile of the elephant's footprint is not yet completed in detail.

Api ca, brāhmaṇa, yathā hatthipadopamo vitthārena paripūro hoti

As to how it is completed in detail,

taṁ suṇāhi, sādhukaṁ manasi karohi, bhāsissāmī"ti.

listen and pay close attention, I will speak."

"Evaṁ, bho"ti kho jāṇussoṇi brāhmaṇo bhagavato paccassosi.

"Yes sir," Jāṇussoṇi replied.

Bhagavā etadavoca:

The Buddha said this:

"Seyyathāpi, brāhmaṇa, nāgavaniko nāgavanaṁ paviseyya.

"Suppose that an elephant tracker were to enter an elephant wood.

So passeyya nāgavane mahantaṁ hatthipadaṁ, dīghato ca āyataṁ, tiriyañca vitthataṁ.

There they'd see a large elephant's footprint, long and broad.

Yo hoti kusalo nāgavaniko neva tāva niṭṭhaṁ gacchati:

A skilled elephant tracker wouldn't yet come to the conclusion,

'mahā vata bho nāgo'ti.

'This must be a big bull elephant.'

Taṁ kissa hetu?

Why not?

Santi hi, brāhmaṇa, nāgavane vāmanikā nāma hatthiniyo mahāpadā, tāsaṁ petaṁ padaṁ assāti.

Because in an elephant wood there are dwarf she-elephants with big footprints, and this footprint might be one of theirs.

So tamanugacchati.

Tamanugacchanto passati nāgavane mahantaṁ hatthipadaṁ, dīghato ca āyataṁ, tiriyañca vitthataṁ, uccā ca nisevitaṁ.

They keep following the track until they see a big footprint, long and broad, and, high up, signs of usage.

Yo hoti kusalo nāgavaniko neva tāva niṭṭhaṁ gacchati:

A skilled elephant tracker wouldn't yet come to the conclusion,

'mahā vata bho nāgo'ti.

'This must be a big bull elephant.'

Taṁ kissa hetu?

Why not?

Santi hi, brāhmaṇa, nāgavane uccā kāḷārikā nāma hatthiniyo mahāpadā, tāsaṁ petaṁ padaṁ assāti.

Because in an elephant wood there are tall she-elephants with long trunks and big footprints, and this footprint might be one of theirs.

So tamanugacchati.

Tamanugacchanto passati nāgavane mahantaṁ hatthipadaṁ, dīghato ca āyataṁ, tiriyañca vitthataṁ, uccā ca nisevitaṁ, uccā ca dantehi ārañjitāni.

They keep following the track until they see a big footprint, long and broad, and, high up, signs of usage and tusk-marks.

Yo hoti kusalo nāgavaniko neva tāva niṭṭhaṁ gacchati:

A skilled elephant tracker wouldn't yet come to the conclusion,

'mahā vata bho nāgo'ti.

'This must be a big bull elephant.'

Tam kissa hetu?

Why not?

Santi hi, brāhmaṇa, nāgavane uccā kaṇerukā nāma hatthiniyo mahāpadā, tāsam petam padam assāti.

Because in an elephant wood there are tall and fully-grown she-elephants with big footprints, and this footprint might be one of theirs.

So tamanugacchati.

Tamanugacchanto passati nāgavane mahantam hatthipadam, dīghato ca āyatam, tiriyañca vitthatam, uccā ca nisevitam, uccā ca dantehi ārañjitāni, uccā ca sākhābhaṅgam.

They keep following the track until they see a big footprint, long and broad, and, high up, signs of usage, tusk-marks, and broken branches.

Tañca nāgam passati rukkhamūlagatam vā abbhokāsagatam vā gacchantam vā tiṭṭhantam vā nisinnam vā nipannam vā.

And they see that bull elephant walking, standing, sitting, or lying down at the root of a tree or in the open.

So niṭṭham gacchati:

Then they'd come to the conclusion,

'ayameva so mahānāgo'ti.

'This is that big bull elephant.'

Evameva kho, brāhmaṇa, idha tathāgato loke uppajjati araham sammāsambuddho vijjācaraṇasampanno sugato lokavidū anuttaro purisadammasārathi satthā devamanussānam buddho bhagavā.

In the same way, brahmin, a Realized One arises in the world, perfected, a fully awakened Buddha, accomplished in knowledge and conduct, holy, knower of the world, supreme guide for those who wish to train, teacher of gods and humans, awakened, blessed.

So imam lokam sadevakam samārakam sabrahmakam sassamaṇabrāhmaṇim pajam sadevamanussam sayam abhiññā sacchikatvā pavedeti.

He realizes with his own insight this world—with its gods, Māras and Brahmās, this population with its ascetics and brahmins, gods and humans—and he makes it known to others.

So dhammam deseti ādikalyāṇam majjhekalyāṇam pariyosānakalyāṇam sāttham sabyañjanaṁ; kevalaparipuṇṇaṁ parisuddhaṁ brahmacariyaṁ pakāseti.

He teaches Dhamma that's good in the beginning, good in the middle, and good in the end, meaningful and well-phrased. And he reveals a spiritual practice that's entirely complete and pure.

Taṁ dhammaṁ suṇāti gahapati vā gahapatiputto vā aññatarasmiṁ vā kule paccājāto.

A householder hears that teaching, or a householder's child, or someone reborn in some good family.

So taṁ dhammaṁ sutvā tathāgate saddhaṁ paṭilabhati.

They gain faith in the Realized One,

So tena saddhāpaṭilābhena samannāgato iti paṭisañcikkhati:

and reflect,

'sambādho gharāvāso rajopatho, abbhokāso pabbajjā.

'Living in a house is cramped and dirty, but the life of one gone forth is wide open.

Nayidaṁ sukaraṁ agāraṁ ajjhāvasatā ekantaparipuṇṇaṁ ekantaparisuddhaṁ saṅkhalikhitaṁ brahmacariyaṁ carituṁ.

It's not easy for someone living at home to lead the spiritual life utterly full and pure, like a polished shell.

Yannūnāhaṁ kesamassuṁ ohāretvā kāsāyāni vatthāni acchādetvā agārasmā anagāriyaṁ pabbajeyyan'ti.

Why don't I shave off my hair and beard, dress in ocher robes, and go forth from the lay life to homelessness?'

So aparena samayena appaṁ vā bhogakkhandhaṁ pahāya mahantaṁ vā bhogakkhandhaṁ pahāya appaṁ vā ñātiparivaṭṭaṁ pahāya mahantaṁ vā ñātiparivaṭṭaṁ pahāya kesamassuṁ ohāretvā kāsāyāni vatthāni acchādetvā agārasmā anagāriyaṁ pabbajati.

After some time they give up a large or small fortune, and a large or small family circle. They shave off hair and beard, dress in ocher robes, and go forth from the lay life to homelessness.

So evaṁ pabbajito samāno bhikkhūnaṁ sikkhāsājīvasamāpanno pāṇātipātaṁ pahāya pāṇātipātā paṭivirato hoti, nihitadaṇḍo nihitasattho lajjī dayāpanno sabbapāṇabhūtahitānukampī viharati.

Once they've gone forth, they take up the training and livelihood of the mendicants. They give up killing living creatures, renouncing the rod and the sword. They're scrupulous and kind, living full of compassion for all living beings.

Adinnādānaṁ pahāya adinnādānā paṭivirato hoti dinnādāyī dinnapāṭikaṅkhī. Athenena sucibhūtena attanā viharati.

They give up stealing. They take only what's given, and expect only what's given. They keep themselves clean by not thieving.

Abrahmacariyaṁ pahāya brahmacārī hoti ārācārī virato methunā gāmadhammā.

They give up unchastity. They are celibate, set apart, avoiding the vulgar act of sex.

Musāvādaṁ pahāya musāvādā paṭivirato hoti saccavādī saccasandho theto paccayiko avisaṁvādako lokassa.

They give up lying. They speak the truth and stick to the truth. They're honest and trustworthy, and don't trick the world with their words.

Pisuṇaṁ vācaṁ pahāya pisuṇāya vācāya paṭivirato hoti, ito sutvā na amutra akkhātā imesaṁ bhedāya, amutra vā sutvā na imesaṁ akkhātā amūsaṁ bhedāya. Iti bhinnānaṁ vā sandhātā sahitānaṁ vā anuppadātā, samaggārāmo samaggarato samagganandī samaggakaraṇiṁ vācaṁ bhāsitā hoti.

They give up divisive speech. They don't repeat in one place what they heard in another so as to divide people against each other. Instead, they reconcile those who are divided, supporting unity, delighting in harmony, loving harmony, speaking words that promote harmony.

Pharusaṁ vācaṁ pahāya pharusāya vācāya paṭivirato hoti. Yā sā vācā nelā kaṇṇasukhā pemanīyā hadayaṅgamā porī bahujanakantā bahujanamanāpā tathārūpiṁ vācaṁ bhāsitā hoti.

They give up harsh speech. They speak in a way that's mellow, pleasing to the ear, lovely, going to the heart, polite, likable, and agreeable to the people.

Samphappalāpaṁ pahāya samphappalāpā paṭivirato hoti kālavādī bhūtavādī atthavādī dhammavādī vinayavādī, nidhānavatiṁ vācaṁ bhāsitā kālena sāpadesaṁ pariyantavatiṁ atthasaṁhitaṁ.

They give up talking nonsense. Their words are timely, true, and meaningful, in line with the teaching and training. They say things at the right time which are valuable, reasonable, succinct, and beneficial.

So bījagāmabhūtagāmasamārambhā paṭivirato hoti,

They avoid injuring plants and seeds.

ekabhattiko hoti rattūparato, virato vikālabhojanā,

They eat in one part of the day, abstaining from eating at night and at the wrong time.

naccagītavāditavisūkadassanā paṭivirato hoti,

They avoid dancing, singing, music, and seeing shows.

mālāgandhavilepanadhāraṇamaṇḍanavibhūsanaṭṭhānā paṭivirato hoti,

They avoid beautifying and adorning themselves with garlands, perfumes, and makeup.

uccāsayanamahāsayanā paṭivirato hoti,

They avoid high and luxurious beds.

jātarūparajatapaṭiggahaṇā paṭivirato hoti,

They avoid receiving gold and money,

āmakadhaññapaṭiggahaṇā paṭivirato hoti,

raw grains,

āmakamaṁsapaṭiggahaṇā paṭivirato hoti,

raw meat,

itthikumārikapaṭiggahaṇā paṭivirato hoti,

women and girls,

dāsidāsapaṭiggahaṇā paṭivirato hoti,

male and female bondservants,

ajeḷakapaṭiggahaṇā paṭivirato hoti,

goats and sheep,

kukkuṭasūkarapaṭiggahaṇā paṭivirato hoti,

chickens and pigs,

hatthigavāssavaḷavapaṭiggahaṇā paṭivirato hoti,

elephants, cows, horses, and mares,

khettavatthupaṭiggahaṇā paṭivirato hoti,

and fields and land.

dūteyyapahiṇagamanānuyogā paṭivirato hoti,

They avoid running errands and messages;

kayavikkayā paṭivirato hoti,

buying and selling;

tulākūṭakaṁsakūṭamānakūṭā paṭivirato hoti,

falsifying weights, metals, or measures;

ukkoṭanavañcananikatisāciyogā paṭivirato hoti,

bribery, fraud, cheating, and duplicity;

chedanavadhabandhanaviparāmosaālopasahasākārā paṭivirato hoti.

mutilation, murder, abduction, banditry, plunder, and violence.

So santuṭṭho hoti kāyaparihārikena cīvarena kucchiparihārikena piṇḍapātena. So yena yeneva pakkamati samādāyeva pakkamati.

They're content with robes to look after the body and almsfood to look after the belly. Wherever they go, they set out taking only these things.

Seyyathāpi nāma pakkhī sakuṇo yena yeneva ḍeti sapattabhārova ḍeti;

They're like a bird: wherever it flies, wings are its only burden.

evameva bhikkhu santuṭṭho hoti kāyaparihārikena cīvarena kucchiparihārikena piṇḍapātena. So yena yeneva pakkamati samādāyeva pakkamati.

In the same way, a mendicant is content with robes to look after the body and almsfood to look after the belly. Wherever they go, they set out taking only these things.

So iminā ariyena sīlakkhandhena samannāgato ajjhattaṁ anavajjasukhaṁ paṭisaṁvedeti.

When they have this entire spectrum of noble ethics, they experience a blameless happiness inside themselves.

So cakkhunā rūpaṁ disvā na nimittaggāhī hoti nānubyañjanaggāhī.

When they see a sight with their eyes, they don't get caught up in the features and details.

Yatvādhikaraṇamenaṁ cakkhundriyaṁ asaṁvutaṁ viharantaṁ abhijjhādomanassā pāpakā akusalā dhammā anvāssaveyyuṁ tassa saṁvarāya paṭipajjati, rakkhati cakkhundriyaṁ, cakkhundriye saṁvaraṁ āpajjati.

If the faculty of sight were left unrestrained, bad unskillful qualities of desire and aversion would become overwhelming. For this reason, they practice restraint, protecting the faculty of sight, and achieving its restraint.

Sotena saddaṁ sutvā ...pe...

When they hear a sound with their ears ...

ghānena gandhaṁ ghāyitvā ...

When they smell an odor with their nose ...

jivhāya rasaṁ sāyitvā ...

When they taste a flavor with their tongue ...

kāyena phoṭṭhabbaṁ phusitvā ...

When they feel a touch with their body ...

manasā dhammaṁ viññāya na nimittaggāhī hoti nānubyañjanaggāhī.

When they know a thought with their mind, they don't get caught up in the features and details.

Yatvādhikaraṇamenaṁ manindriyaṁ asaṁvutaṁ viharantaṁ abhijjhādomanassā pāpakā akusalā dhammā anvāssaveyyuṁ tassa saṁvarāya paṭipajjati, rakkhati manindriyaṁ, manindriye saṁvaraṁ āpajjati.

If the faculty of mind were left unrestrained, bad unskillful qualities of desire and aversion would become overwhelming. For this reason, they practice restraint, protecting the faculty of mind, and achieving its restraint.

So iminā ariyena indriyasaṁvarena samannāgato ajjhattaṁ abyāsekasukhaṁ paṭisaṁvedeti.

When they have this noble sense restraint, they experience an unsullied bliss inside themselves.

So abhikkante paṭikkante sampajānakārī hoti, ālokite vilokite sampajānakārī hoti, samiñjite pasārite sampajānakārī hoti, saṅghāṭipattacīvaradhāraṇe sampajānakārī hoti, asite pīte khāyite sāyite sampajānakārī hoti, uccārapassāvakamme sampajānakārī hoti, gate ṭhite nisinne sutte jāgarite bhāsite tuṇhībhāve sampajānakārī hoti.

They act with situational awareness when going out and coming back; when looking ahead and aside; when bending and extending the limbs; when bearing the outer robe, bowl and robes; when eating, drinking, chewing, and tasting; when urinating and defecating; when walking, standing, sitting, sleeping, waking, speaking, and keeping silent.

So iminā ca ariyena sīlakkhandhena samannāgato, imāya ca ariyāya santuṭṭhiyā samannāgato iminā ca ariyena indriyasaṁvarena samannāgato, iminā ca ariyena satisampajaññena samannāgato

When they have this noble spectrum of ethics, this noble contentment, this noble sense restraint, and this noble mindfulness and situational awareness,

vivittaṁ senāsanaṁ bhajati araññaṁ rukkhamūlaṁ pabbataṁ kandaraṁ giriguhaṁ susānaṁ vanapatthaṁ abbhokāsaṁ palālapuñjaṁ.

they frequent a secluded lodging—a wilderness, the root of a tree, a hill, a ravine, a mountain cave, a charnel ground, a forest, the open air, a heap of straw.

So pacchābhattaṁ piṇḍapātapaṭikkanto nisīdati pallaṅkaṁ ābhujitvā, ujuṁ kāyaṁ paṇidhāya, parimukhaṁ satiṁ upaṭṭhapetvā.

After the meal, they return from almsround, sit down cross-legged, set their body straight, and establish mindfulness in front of them.

So abhijjhaṁ loke pahāya vigatābhijjhena cetasā viharati, abhijjhāya cittaṁ parisodheti.

Giving up desire for the world, they meditate with a heart rid of desire, cleansing the mind of desire.

Byāpādapadosaṁ pahāya abyāpannacitto viharati, sabbapāṇabhūtahitānukampī byāpādapadosā cittaṁ parisodheti.

Giving up ill will and malevolence, they meditate with a mind rid of ill will, full of compassion for all living beings, cleansing the mind of ill will.

Thinamiddhaṁ pahāya vigatathinamiddho viharati ālokasaññī sato sampajāno, thinamiddhā cittaṁ parisodheti.

Giving up dullness and drowsiness, they meditate with a mind rid of dullness and drowsiness, perceiving light, mindful and aware, cleansing the mind of dullness and drowsiness.

Uddhaccakukkuccaṁ pahāya anuddhato viharati, ajjhattaṁ vūpasantacitto uddhaccakukkuccā cittaṁ parisodheti.

Giving up restlessness and remorse, they meditate without restlessness, their mind peaceful inside, cleansing the mind of restlessness and remorse.

Vicikicchaṁ pahāya tiṇṇavicikiccho viharati akathaṅkathī kusalesu dhammesu, vicikicchāya cittaṁ parisodheti.

Giving up doubt, they meditate having gone beyond doubt, not undecided about skillful qualities, cleansing the mind of doubt.

So ime pañca nīvaraṇe pahāya cetaso upakkilese paññāya dubbalīkaraṇe,

They give up these five hindrances, corruptions of the heart that weaken wisdom.

vivicceva kāmehi vivicca akusalehi dhammehi savitakkaṁ savicāraṁ vivekajaṁ pītisukhaṁ paṭhamaṁ jhānaṁ upasampajja viharati.

Then, quite secluded from sensual pleasures, secluded from unskillful qualities, they enter and remain in the first absorption, which has the rapture and bliss born of seclusion, while placing the mind and keeping it connected.

Idampi vuccati, brāhmaṇa, tathāgatapadaṁ itipi, tathāgatanisevitaṁ itipi, tathāgatārañjitaṁ itipi.

This, brahmin, is called 'a footprint of the Realized One' and also 'used by the Realized One' and also 'marked by the Realized One'.

Na tveva tāva ariyasāvako niṭṭhaṁ gacchati:

But a noble disciple wouldn't yet come to the conclusion,

'sammāsambuddho bhagavā, svākkhāto bhagavatā dhammo, suppaṭipanno bhagavato sāvakasaṅgho'ti.

'The Blessed One is a fully awakened Buddha. The teaching is well explained. The Saṅgha is practicing well.'

Puna caparaṁ, brāhmaṇa, bhikkhu vitakkavicārānaṁ vūpasamā ajjhattaṁ sampasādanaṁ cetaso ekodibhāvaṁ avitakkaṁ avicāraṁ samādhijaṁ pītisukhaṁ dutiyaṁ jhānaṁ upasampajja viharati.

Furthermore, as the placing of the mind and keeping it connected are stilled, a mendicant enters and remains in the second absorption, which has the rapture and bliss born of immersion, with internal clarity and confidence, and unified mind, without placing the mind and keeping it connected.

Idampi vuccati, brāhmaṇa …pe…

This too is called 'a footprint of the Realized One' …

suppaṭipanno bhagavato sāvakasaṅgho'ti.

Puna caparaṁ, brāhmaṇa, bhikkhu pītiyā ca virāgā upekkhako ca viharati sato ca sampajāno, sukhañca kāyena paṭisaṁvedeti, yaṁ taṁ ariyā ācikkhanti 'upekkhako satimā sukhavihārī'ti tatiyaṁ jhānaṁ upasampajja viharati.

Furthermore, with the fading away of rapture, a mendicant enters and remains in the third absorption, where they meditate with equanimity, mindful and aware, personally experiencing the bliss of which the noble ones declare, 'Equanimous and mindful, one meditates in bliss.'

Idampi vuccati, brāhmaṇa …pe…

This too is called 'a footprint of the Realized One' …

suppaṭipanno bhagavato sāvakasaṅgho'ti.

Puna caparaṁ, brāhmaṇa, bhikkhu sukhassa ca pahānā dukkhassa ca pahānā, pubbeva somanassadomanassānaṁ atthaṅgamā, adukkhamasukhaṁ upekkhāsatipārisuddhiṁ catutthaṁ jhānaṁ upasampajja viharati.

Furthermore, giving up pleasure and pain, and ending former happiness and sadness, a mendicant enters and remains in the fourth absorption, without pleasure or pain, with pure equanimity and mindfulness.

Idampi vuccati, brāhmaṇa, tathāgatapadaṁ itipi, tathāgatanisevitaṁ itipi, tathāgatārañjitaṁ itipi.

This too is called 'a footprint of the Realized One' ...

Na tveva tāva ariyasāvako niṭṭhaṁ gacchati:

'sammāsambuddho bhagavā, svākkhāto bhagavatā dhammo, suppaṭipanno bhagavato sāvakasaṅgho'ti.

So evaṁ samāhite citte parisuddhe pariyodāte anaṅgaṇe vigatūpakkilese mudubhūte kammaniye ṭhite āneñjappatte pubbenivāsānussatiñāṇāya cittaṁ abhininnāmeti.

When their mind has become immersed in samādhi like this—purified, bright, flawless, rid of corruptions, pliable, workable, steady, and imperturbable—they extend it toward recollection of past lives.

So anekavihitaṁ pubbenivāsaṁ anussarati, seyyathidaṁ—ekampi jātiṁ, dvepi jātiyo ...pe... iti sākāraṁ sauddesaṁ anekavihitaṁ pubbenivāsaṁ anussarati.

They recollect many kinds of past lives, that is, one, two, three, four, five, ten, twenty, thirty, forty, fifty, a hundred, a thousand, a hundred thousand rebirths; many eons of the world contracting, many eons of the world expanding, many eons of the world contracting and expanding. ... They recollect their many kinds of past lives, with features and details.

Idampi vuccati, brāhmaṇa, tathāgatapadaṁ itipi, tathāgatanisevitaṁ itipi, tathāgatārañjitaṁ itipi.

This too is called 'a footprint of the Realized One' ...

Na tveva tāva ariyasāvako niṭṭhaṁ gacchati:

'sammāsambuddho bhagavā, svākkhāto bhagavatā dhammo, suppaṭipanno bhagavato sāvakasaṅgho'ti.

So evaṁ samāhite citte parisuddhe pariyodāte anaṅgaṇe vigatūpakkilese mudubhūte kammaniye ṭhite āneñjappatte sattānaṁ cutūpapātañāṇāya cittaṁ abhininnāmeti.

When their mind has become immersed in samādhi like this—purified, bright, flawless, rid of corruptions, pliable, workable, steady, and imperturbable—they extend it toward knowledge of the death and rebirth of sentient beings.

So dibbena cakkhunā visuddhena atikkantamānusakena …pe… yathākammūpage satte pajānāti.

With clairvoyance that is purified and surpasses the human, they understand how sentient beings are reborn according to their deeds.

Idampi vuccati, brāhmaṇa, tathāgatapadaṁ itipi, tathāgatanisevitaṁ itipi, tathāgatārañjitaṁ itipi.

This too is called 'a footprint of the Realized One' …

Na tveva tāva ariyasāvako niṭṭhaṁ gacchati:

'sammāsambuddho bhagavā, svākkhāto bhagavatā dhammo, suppaṭipanno bhagavato sāvakasaṅgho'ti.

So evaṁ samāhite citte parisuddhe pariyodāte anaṅgaṇe vigatūpakkilese mudubhūte kammaniye ṭhite āneñjappatte āsavānaṁ khayañāṇāya cittaṁ abhininnāmeti.

When their mind has become immersed in samādhi like this—purified, bright, flawless, rid of corruptions, pliable, workable, steady, and imperturbable—they extend it toward knowledge of the ending of defilements.

So 'idaṁ dukkhan'ti yathābhūtaṁ pajānāti, 'ayaṁ dukkhasamudayo'ti yathābhūtaṁ pajānāti, 'ayaṁ dukkhanirodho'ti yathābhūtaṁ pajānāti, 'ayaṁ dukkhanirodhagāminī paṭipadā'ti yathābhūtaṁ pajānāti.

They truly understand: 'This is suffering' … 'This is the origin of suffering' … 'This is the cessation of suffering' … 'This is the practice that leads to the cessation of suffering.'

'Ime āsavā'ti yathābhūtaṁ pajānāti, 'ayaṁ āsavasamudayo'ti yathābhūtaṁ pajānāti, 'ayaṁ āsavanirodho'ti yathābhūtaṁ pajānāti, 'ayaṁ āsavanirodhagāminī paṭipadā'ti yathābhūtaṁ pajānāti.

They truly understand: 'These are defilements' … 'This is the origin of defilements' … 'This is the cessation of defilements' … 'This is the practice that leads to the cessation of defilements.'

Idampi vuccati, brāhmaṇa, tathāgatapadaṁ itipi, tathāgatanisevitaṁ itipi, tathāgatārañjitaṁ itipi.

This, brahmin, is called 'a footprint of the Realized One' and also 'used by the Realized One' and also 'marked by the Realized One'.

Na tveva tāva ariyasāvako niṭṭhaṁ gato hoti, api ca kho niṭṭhaṁ gacchati:

At this point a noble disciple has not yet come to a conclusion, but they are coming to the conclusion,

'sammāsambuddho bhagavā, svākkhāto bhagavatā dhammo, suppaṭipanno bhagavato sāvakasaṅgho'ti.

'The Blessed One is a fully awakened Buddha. The teaching is well explained. The Saṅgha is practicing well.'

Tassa evaṁ jānato evaṁ passato kāmāsavāpi cittaṁ vimuccati, bhavāsavāpi cittaṁ vimuccati, avijjāsavāpi cittaṁ vimuccati.

Knowing and seeing like this, their mind is freed from the defilements of sensuality, desire to be reborn, and ignorance.

Vimuttasmiṁ vimuttamiti ñāṇaṁ hoti.

When they're freed, they know they're freed.

'Khīṇā jāti, vusitaṁ brahmacariyaṁ, kataṁ karaṇīyaṁ, nāparaṁ itthattāyā'ti pajānāti.

They understand: 'Rebirth is ended, the spiritual journey has been completed, what had to be done has been done, there is no return to any state of existence.'

Idampi vuccati, brāhmaṇa, tathāgatapadaṁ itipi, tathāgatanisevitaṁ itipi, tathāgatārañjitaṁ itipi.

This, brahmin, is called 'a footprint of the Realized One' and also 'used by the Realized One' and also 'marked by the Realized One'.

Ettāvatā kho, brāhmaṇa, ariyasāvako niṭṭhaṁ gato hoti:

At this point a noble disciple has come to the conclusion,

'sammāsambuddho bhagavā, svākkhāto bhagavatā dhammo, suppaṭipanno bhagavato sāvakasaṅgho'ti.

'The Blessed One is a fully awakened Buddha. The teaching is well explained. The Saṅgha is practicing well.'

Ettāvatā kho, brāhmaṇa, hatthipadopamo vitthārena paripūro hotī'ti.

And it is at this point that the simile of the elephant's footprint has been completed in detail."

Evaṁ vutte, jāṇussoṇi brāhmaṇo bhagavantaṁ etadavoca:

When he had spoken, the brahmin Jāṇussoṇi said to the Buddha,

"abhikkantaṁ, bho gotama, abhikkantaṁ, bho gotama.

"Excellent, Master Gotama! Excellent!

Seyyathāpi, bho gotama, nikkujjitaṁ vā ukkujjeyya, paṭicchannaṁ vā vivareyya, mūḷhassa vā maggaṁ ācikkheyya, andhakāre vā telapajjotaṁ dhāreyya: 'cakkhumanto rūpāni dakkhantī'ti; evamevaṁ bhotā gotamena anekapariyāyena dhammo pakāsito.

As if he were righting the overturned, or revealing the hidden, or pointing out the path to the lost, or lighting a lamp in the dark so people with good eyes can see what's there, Master Gotama has made the teaching clear in many ways.

Esāhaṁ bhavantaṁ gotamaṁ saraṇaṁ gacchāmi, dhammañca, bhikkhusaṅghañca.

I go for refuge to Master Gotama, to the teaching, and to the mendicant Saṅgha.

Upāsakaṁ maṁ bhavaṁ gotamo dhāretu ajjatagge pāṇupetaṁ saraṇaṁ gatan"ti.

From this day forth, may Master Gotama remember me as a lay follower who has gone for refuge for life."

Cūḷahatthipadopamasuttaṁ niṭṭhitaṁ sattamaṁ.

28 Mahahatthipadopamasutta:

The Longer Simile of the Elephant's Footprint

Evaṁ me sutaṁ—

So I have heard.

ekaṁ samayaṁ bhagavā sāvatthiyaṁ viharati jetavane anāthapiṇḍikassa ārāme.

At one time the Buddha was staying near Sāvatthī in Jeta's Grove, Anāthapiṇḍika's monastery.

Tatra kho āyasmā sāriputto bhikkhū āmantesi:

There Sāriputta addressed the mendicants,

"āvuso bhikkhave"ti.

"Reverends, mendicants!"

"Āvuso"ti kho te bhikkhū āyasmato sāriputtassa paccassosuṁ.

"Reverend," they replied.

Āyasmā sāriputto etadavoca:

Sāriputta said this:

"Seyyathāpi, āvuso, yāni kānici jaṅgalānaṁ pāṇanaṁ padajātāni sabbāni tāni hatthipade samodhānaṁ gacchanti, hatthipadaṁ tesaṁ aggamakkhāyati yadidaṁ mahantattena;

"The footprints of all creatures that walk can fit inside an elephant's footprint, so an elephant's footprint is said to be the biggest of them all.

evameva kho, āvuso, ye keci kusalā dhammā sabbete catūsu ariyasaccesu saṅgahaṁ gacchanti.

In the same way, all skillful qualities can be included in the four noble truths.

Katamesu catūsu?

What four?

Dukkhe ariyasacce, dukkhasamudaye ariyasacce, dukkhanirodhe ariyasacce, dukkhanirodhagāminiyā paṭipadāya ariyasacce.

The noble truths of suffering, the origin of suffering, the cessation of suffering, and the practice that leads to the cessation of suffering.

Katamañcāvuso, dukkhaṁ ariyasaccaṁ?

And what is the noble truth of suffering?

Jātipi dukkhā, jarāpi dukkhā, maraṇampi dukkhaṁ, sokaparidevadukkhadomanassupāyāsāpi dukkhā, yampicchaṁ na labhati tampi dukkhaṁ; saṅkhittena, pañcupādānakkhandhā dukkhā.

Rebirth is suffering; old age is suffering; death is suffering; sorrow, lamentation, pain, sadness, and distress are suffering; not getting what you wish for is suffering. In brief, the five grasping aggregates are suffering.

Katame cāvuso, pañcupādānakkhandhā?

And what are the five grasping aggregates?

Seyyathidaṁ—rūpupādānakkhandho, vedanupādānakkhandho, saññupādānakkhandho, saṅkhārupādānakkhandho, viññāṇupādānakkhandho.

They are as follows: the grasping aggregates of form, feeling, perception, choices, and consciousness.

Katamo cāvuso, rūpupādānakkhandho?

And what is the grasping aggregate of form?

Cattāri ca mahābhūtāni, catunnañca mahābhūtānaṁ upādāya rūpaṁ.

The four primary elements, and form derived from the four primary elements.

Katamā cāvuso, cattāro mahābhūtā?

And what are the four primary elements?

Pathavīdhātu, āpodhātu, tejodhātu, vāyodhātu.

The elements of earth, water, fire, and air.

Katamā cāvuso, pathavīdhātu?

And what is the earth element?

Pathavīdhātu siyā ajjhattikā, siyā bāhirā.

The earth element may be interior or exterior.

Katamā cāvuso, ajjhattikā pathavīdhātu?

And what is the interior earth element?

Yaṁ ajjhattaṁ paccattaṁ kakkhaḷaṁ kharigataṁ upādinnaṁ, seyyathidaṁ—

Anything hard, solid, and appropriated that's internal, pertaining to an individual. This includes:

kesā lomā nakhā dantā taco maṁsaṁ nhāru aṭṭhi aṭṭhimiñjaṁ vakkaṁ hadayaṁ yakanaṁ kilomakaṁ pihakaṁ papphāsaṁ antaṁ antaguṇaṁ udariyaṁ karīsaṁ, yaṁ vā panaññampi kiñci ajjhattaṁ paccattaṁ kakkhaḷaṁ kharigataṁ upādinnaṁ.

head hair, body hair, nails, teeth, skin, flesh, sinews, bones, bone marrow, kidneys, heart, liver, diaphragm, spleen, lungs, intestines, mesentery, undigested food, feces, or anything else hard, solid, and appropriated that's internal, pertaining to an individual.

Ayaṁ vuccatāvuso, ajjhattikā pathavīdhātu.

This is called the interior earth element.

Yā ceva kho pana ajjhattikā pathavīdhātu, yā ca bāhirā pathavīdhātu, pathavīdhāturevesā.

The interior earth element and the exterior earth element are just the earth element.

'Taṁ netaṁ mama, nesohamasmi, na meso attā'ti—evametaṁ yathābhūtaṁ sammappaññāya daṭṭhabbaṁ.

This should be truly seen with right understanding like this: 'This is not mine, I am not this, this is not my self.'

Evametaṁ yathābhūtaṁ sammappaññāya disvā pathavīdhātuyā nibbindati, pathavīdhātuyā cittaṃ virājeti.

When you truly see with right understanding, you grow disillusioned with the earth element, detaching the mind from the earth element.

Hoti kho so, āvuso, samayo yaṃ bāhirā āpodhātu pakuppati.

There comes a time when the exterior water element flares up.

Antarahitā tasmiṃ samaye bāhirā pathavīdhātu hoti.

At that time the exterior earth element vanishes.

Tassā hi nāma, āvuso, bāhirāya pathavīdhātuyā tāva mahallikāya aniccatā paññāyissati, khayadhammatā paññāyissati, vayadhammatā paññāyissati, vipariṇāmadhammatā paññāyissati.

So for all its great age, the earth element will be revealed as impermanent, liable to end, vanish, and perish.

Kiṃ panimassa mattaṭṭhakassa kāyassa taṇhupādinnassa 'ahanti vā mamanti vā asmī'ti vā? Atha khvāssa notevettha hoti.

What then of this ephemeral body appropriated by craving? Rather than take it to be 'I' or 'mine' or 'I am', they still just consider it to be none of these things.

Tañce, āvuso, bhikkhuṃ pare akkosanti paribhāsanti rosenti vihesenti, so evaṃ pajānāti:

If others abuse, attack, harass, and trouble that mendicant, they understand:

'uppannā kho me ayaṃ sotasamphassajā dukkhavedanā.

'This painful feeling born of ear contact has arisen in me.

Sā ca kho paṭicca, no apaṭicca.

That's dependent, not independent.

Kiṃ paṭicca?

Dependent on what?

Phassaṃ paṭicca'.

Dependent on contact.'

So phasso aniccoti passati, vedanā aniccāti passati, saññā aniccāti passati, saṅkhārā aniccāti passati, viññāṇaṃ aniccanti passati.

They see that contact, feeling, perception, choices, and consciousness are impermanent.

Tassa dhātārammaṇameva cittaṁ pakkhandati pasīdati santiṭṭhati adhimuccati.

Based on that element alone, their mind becomes eager, confident, settled, and decided.

Tañce, āvuso, bhikkhuṁ pare aniṭṭhehi akantehi amanāpehi samudācaranti—

Others might treat that mendicant with disliking, loathing, and detestation,

pāṇisamphassenapi   leḍḍusamphassenapi   daṇḍasamphassenapi satthasamphassenapi.

striking them with fists, stones, sticks, and swords.

So evaṁ pajānāti:

They understand:

'tathābhūto kho ayaṁ kāyo yathābhūtasmiṁ kāye pāṇisamphassāpi kamanti, leḍḍusamphassāpi kamanti, daṇḍasamphassāpi kamanti, satthasamphassāpi kamanti.

'This body is such that fists, stones, sticks, and swords strike it.

Vuttaṁ kho panetaṁ bhagavatā kakacūpamovāde:

But the Buddha has said in the Simile of the Saw:

"ubhatodaṇḍakena cepi, bhikkhave, kakacena corā ocarakā aṅgamaṅgāni okanteyyuṁ, tatrāpi yo mano padūseyya na me so tena sāsanakaro"ti.

"Even if low-down bandits were to sever you limb from limb, anyone who had a malevolent thought on that account would not be following my instructions."

Āraddhaṁ kho pana me vīriyaṁ bhavissati asallīnaṁ, upaṭṭhitā sati asammuṭṭhā, passaddho kāyo asāraddho, samāhitaṁ cittaṁ ekaggaṁ.

My energy shall be roused up and unflagging, my mindfulness established and lucid, my body tranquil and undisturbed, and my mind immersed in samādhi.

Kāmaṁ dāni imasmiṁ kāye pāṇisamphassāpi kamantu, leḍḍusamphassāpi kamantu, daṇḍasamphassāpi kamantu, satthasamphassāpi kamantu, karīyati hidaṁ buddhānaṁ sāsanan'ti.

Gladly now, let fists, stones, sticks, and swords strike this body! For this is how the instructions of the Buddhas are followed.'

Tassa ce, āvuso, bhikkhuno evaṁ buddhaṁ anussarato evaṁ dhammaṁ anussarato evaṁ saṅghaṁ anussarato upekkhā kusalanissitā na saṇṭhāti.

While recollecting the Buddha, the teaching, and the Saṅgha in this way, equanimity based on the skillful may not become stabilized in them.

So tena saṁvijjati saṁvegaṁ āpajjati:

In that case they stir up a sense of urgency:

'alābhā vata me, na vata me lābhā; dulladdhaṁ vata me, na vata me suladdhaṁ,

'It's my loss, my misfortune,

yassa me evaṁ buddhaṁ anussarato, evaṁ dhammaṁ anussarato, evaṁ saṅghaṁ anussarato, upekkhā kusalanissitā na saṇṭhātī'ti.

that while recollecting the Buddha, the teaching, and the Saṅgha in this way, equanimity based on the skillful does not become stabilized in me.'

Seyyathāpi, āvuso, suṇisā sasuraṁ disvā saṁvijjati saṁvegaṁ āpajjati;

They're like a daughter-in-law who stirs up a sense of urgency when they see their father-in-law.

evameva kho, āvuso, tassa ce bhikkhuno evaṁ buddhaṁ anussarato, evaṁ dhammaṁ anussarato, evaṁ saṅghaṁ anussarato, upekkhā kusalanissitā na saṇṭhāti, so tena saṁvijjati saṁvegaṁ āpajjati:

'alābhā vata me, na vata me lābhā; dulladdhaṁ vata me, na vata me suladdhaṁ, yassa me evaṁ buddhaṁ anussarato evaṁ dhammaṁ anussarato, evaṁ saṅghaṁ anussarato, upekkhā kusalanissitā na saṇṭhātī'ti.

Tassa ce, āvuso, bhikkhuno evaṁ buddhaṁ anussarato, evaṁ dhammaṁ anussarato, evaṁ saṅghaṁ anussarato upekkhā kusalanissitā saṇṭhāti, so tena attamano hoti.

But if, while recollecting the Buddha, the teaching, and the Saṅgha in this way, equanimity based on the skillful does become stabilized in them, they're happy with that.

Ettāvatāpi kho, āvuso, bhikkhuno bahukataṁ hoti.

At this point, much has been done by that mendicant.

Katamā cāvuso, āpodhātu?

And what is the water element?

Āpodhātu siyā ajjhattikā, siyā bāhirā.

The water element may be interior or exterior.

Katamā cāvuso, ajjhattikā āpodhātu?

And what is the interior water element?

Yaṁ ajjhattaṁ paccattaṁ āpo āpogataṁ upādinnaṁ, seyyathidaṁ—

Anything that's water, watery, and appropriated that's internal, pertaining to an individual. This includes:

pittaṁ semhaṁ pubbo lohitaṁ sedo medo assu vasā kheḷo siṅghāṇikā lasikā muttaṁ, yaṁ vā panaññampi kiñci ajjhattaṁ paccattaṁ āpo āpogataṁ upādinnaṁ—

bile, phlegm, pus, blood, sweat, fat, tears, grease, saliva, snot, synovial fluid, urine, or anything else that's water, watery, and appropriated that's internal, pertaining to an individual.

ayaṁ vuccatāvuso, ajjhattikā āpodhātu.

This is called the interior water element.

Yā ceva kho pana ajjhattikā āpodhātu yā ca bāhirā āpodhātu, āpodhāturevesā.

The interior water element and the exterior water element are just the water element.

'Taṁ netaṁ mama, nesohamasmi, na meso attā'ti evametaṁ yathābhūtaṁ sammappaññāya daṭṭhabbaṁ.

This should be truly seen with right understanding like this: 'This is not mine, I am not this, this is not my self.'

Evametaṁ yathābhūtaṁ sammappaññāya disvā āpodhātuyā nibbindati, āpodhātuyā cittaṁ virājeti.

When you truly see with right understanding, you grow disillusioned with the water element, detaching the mind from the water element.

Hoti kho so, āvuso, samayo yaṁ bāhirā āpodhātu pakuppati.

There comes a time when the exterior water element flares up.

Sā gāmampi vahati, nigamampi vahati, nagarampi vahati, janapadampi vahati, janapadapadesampi vahati.

It sweeps away villages, towns, cities, countries, and regions.

Hoti kho so, āvuso, samayo yaṁ mahāsamudde yojanasatikānipi udakāni ogacchanti, dviyojanasatikānipi udakāni ogacchanti, tiyojanasatikānipi udakāni ogacchanti, catuyojanasatikānipi udakāni ogacchanti, pañcayojanasatikānipi udakāni ogacchanti, chayojanasatikānipi udakāni ogacchanti, sattayojanasatikānipi udakāni ogacchanti.

There comes a time when the water in the ocean sinks down a hundred leagues, or two, three, four, five, six, up to seven hundred leagues.

Hoti kho so, āvuso, samayo yaṁ mahāsamudde sattatālampi udakaṁ saṇṭhāti, chattālampi udakaṁ saṇṭhāti, pañcatālampi udakaṁ saṇṭhāti, catuttālampi udakaṁ santhati, titālampi udakam santhāti, dvitālampi udakam santhāti, tālamattampi udakam santhāti.

There comes a time when the water in the ocean stands just seven palm trees deep, or six, five, four, three, two, or even just one palm tree deep.

Hoti kho so, āvuso, samayo yam mahāsamudde sattaporisampi udakam santhāti, chapporisampi udakam santhāti, pañcaporisampi udakam santhāti, catupporisampi udakam santhāti, tiporisampi udakam santhāti, dviporisampi udakam santhāti, porisamattampi udakam santhāti.

There comes a time when the water in the ocean stands just seven fathoms deep, or six, five, four, three, two, or even just one fathom deep.

Hoti kho so, āvuso, samayo yam mahāsamudde aḍḍhaporisampi udakam santhāti, katimattampi udakam santhāti, jāṇukamattampi udakam santhāti, gopphakamattampi udakam santhāti.

There comes a time when the water in the ocean stands just half a fathom deep, or waist deep, or knee deep, or even just ankle deep.

Hoti kho so, āvuso, samayo, yam mahāsamudde aṅgulipabbatemanamattampi udakam na hoti.

There comes a time when there isn't enough water in the ocean even to wet the tip of your finger.

Tassā hi nāma, āvuso, bāhirāya āpodhātuyā tāva mahallikāya aniccatā paññāyissati, khayadhammatā paññāyissati, vayadhammatā paññāyissati, vipariṇāmadhammatā paññāyissati.

So for all its great age, the water element will be revealed as impermanent, liable to end, vanish, and perish.

Kim panimassa mattaṭṭhakassa kāyassa taṇhupādinnassa 'ahanti vā mamanti vā asmī'ti vā? Atha khvāssa notevettha hoti …pe…

What then of this ephemeral body appropriated by craving? Rather than take it to be 'I' or 'mine' or 'I am', they still just consider it to be none of these things. …

tassa ce, āvuso, bhikkhuno evam buddham anussarato, evam dhammam anussarato, evam sangham anussarato upekkhā kusalanissitā santhāti. So tena attamano hoti.

If, while recollecting the Buddha, the teaching, and the Saṅgha in this way, equanimity based on the skillful does become stabilized in them, they're happy with that.

Ettāvatāpi kho, āvuso, bhikkhuno bahukatam hoti.

At this point, much has been done by that mendicant.

Katamā cāvuso, tejodhātu?

And what is the fire element?

Tejodhātu siyā ajjhattikā, siyā bāhirā.

The fire element may be interior or exterior.

Katamā cāvuso, ajjhattikā tejodhātu?

And what is the interior fire element?

Yaṁ ajjhattaṁ paccattaṁ tejo tejogataṁ upādinnaṁ, seyyathidaṁ—

Anything that's fire, fiery, and appropriated that's internal, pertaining to an individual. This includes:

yena ca santappati, yena ca jīrīyati, yena ca pariḍayhati, yena ca asitapītakhāyitasāyitaṁ sammā pariṇāmaṁ gacchati, yaṁ vā panaññampi kiñci ajjhattaṁ paccattaṁ tejo tejogataṁ upādinnaṁ—

that which warms, that which ages, that which heats you up when feverish, that which properly digests food and drink, or anything else that's fire, fiery, and appropriated that's internal, pertaining to an individual.

ayaṁ vuccatāvuso, ajjhattikā tejodhātu.

This is called the interior fire element.

Yā ceva kho pana ajjhattikā tejodhātu yā ca bāhirā tejodhātu, tejodhāturevesā.

The interior fire element and the exterior fire element are just the fire element.

'Taṁ netaṁ mama, nesohamasmi, na meso attā'ti evametaṁ yathābhūtaṁ sammappaññāya daṭṭhabbaṁ.

This should be truly seen with right understanding like this: 'This is not mine, I am not this, this is not my self.'

Evametaṁ yathābhūtaṁ sammappaññāya disvā tejodhātuyā nibbindati, tejodhātuyā cittaṁ virājeti.

When you truly see with right understanding, you grow disillusioned with the fire element, detaching the mind from the fire element.

Hoti kho so, āvuso, samayo yaṁ bāhirā tejodhātu pakuppati.

There comes a time when the exterior fire element flares up.

Sā gāmampi dahati, nigamampi dahati, nagarampi dahati, janapadampi dahati, janapadapadesampi dahati.

It burns up villages, towns, cities, countries, and regions until

Sā haritantaṁ vā panthantaṁ vā selantaṁ vā udakantaṁ vā ramaṇīyaṁ vā bhūmibhāgaṁ āgamma anāhārā nibbāyati.

it reaches a green field, a roadside, a cliff's edge, a body of water, or cleared parkland, where it's extinguished for lack of fuel.

Hoti kho so, āvuso, samayo yaṁ kukkuṭapattenapi nhārudaddulenapi aggiṁ gavesanti.

There comes a time when they go looking for a fire, taking just a chicken feather or a scrap of sinew as kindling.

Tassā hi nāma, āvuso, bāhirāya tejodhātuyā tāva mahallikāya aniccatā paññāyissati, khayadhammatā paññāyissati, vayadhammatā paññāyissati, vipariṇāmadhammatā paññāyissati.

So for all its great age, the fire element will be revealed as impermanent, liable to end, vanish, and perish.

Kiṁ panimassa mattaṭṭhakassa kāyassa taṇhupādinnassa 'ahanti vā mamanti vā asmī'ti vā?

What then of this ephemeral body appropriated by craving? Rather than take it to be 'I' or 'mine' or 'I am', they still just consider it to be none of these things. …

Atha khvāssa notevettha hoti …pe… tassa ce, āvuso, bhikkhuno evaṁ buddhaṁ anussarato evaṁ dhammaṁ anussarato evaṁ saṅghaṁ anussarato upekkhā kusalanissitā saṇṭhāti, so tena attamano hoti.

If, while recollecting the Buddha, the teaching, and the Saṅgha in this way, equanimity based on the skillful does become stabilized in them, they're happy with that.

Ettāvatāpi kho, āvuso, bhikkhuno bahukataṁ hoti.

At this point, much has been done by that mendicant.

Katamā cāvuso, vāyodhātu?

And what is the air element?

Vāyodhātu siyā ajjhattikā, siyā bāhirā.

The air element may be interior or exterior.

Katamā cāvuso, ajjhattikā vāyodhātu?

And what is the interior air element?

Yaṁ ajjhattaṁ paccattaṁ vāyo vāyogataṁ upādinnaṁ, seyyathidaṁ—

Anything that's wind, windy, and appropriated that's internal, pertaining to an individual. This includes:

uddhaṅgamā vātā, adhogamā vātā, kucchisayā vātā, koṭṭhāsayā vātā, aṅgamaṅgānusārino vātā, assāso passāso iti, yaṁ vā panaññampi kiñci ajjhattaṁ paccattaṁ vāyo vāyogataṁ upādinnaṁ—

winds that go up or down, winds in the belly or the bowels, winds that flow through the limbs, in-breaths and out-breaths, or anything else that's wind, windy, and appropriated that's internal, pertaining to an individual.

ayaṁ vuccatāvuso, ajjhattikā vāyodhātu.

This is called the interior air element.

Yā ceva kho pana ajjhattikā vāyodhātu, yā ca bāhirā vāyodhātu, vāyodhāturevesā.

The interior air element and the exterior air element are just the air element.

'Taṁ netaṁ mama nesohamasmi na meso attā'ti evametaṁ yathābhūtaṁ sammappaññāya daṭṭhabbaṁ.

This should be truly seen with right understanding like this: 'This is not mine, I am not this, this is not my self.'

Evametaṁ yathābhūtaṁ sammappaññāya disvā vāyodhātuyā nibbindati vāyodhātuyā cittaṁ virājeti.

When you truly see with right understanding, you reject the air element, detaching the mind from the air element.

Hoti kho so, āvuso, samayo yaṁ bāhirā vāyodhātu pakuppati.

There comes a time when the exterior air element flares up.

Sā gāmampi vahati, nigamampi vahati, nagarampi vahati, janapadampi vahati, janapadapadesampi vahati.

It sweeps away villages, towns, cities, countries, and regions.

Hoti kho so, āvuso, samayo yaṁ gimhānaṁ pacchime māse tālavaṇṭenapi vidhūpanenapi vātaṁ pariyesanti, ossavanepi tiṇāni na icchanti.

There comes a time, in the last month of summer, when they look for wind by using a palm-leaf or fan, and even the grasses in the drip-fringe of a thatch roof don't stir.

Tassā hi nāma, āvuso, bāhirāya vāyodhātuyā tāva mahallikāya aniccatā paññāyissati, khayadhammatā paññāyissati, vayadhammatā paññāyissati, vipariṇāmadhammatā paññāyissati.

So for all its great age, the air element will be revealed as impermanent, liable to end, vanish, and perish.

Kiṁ panimassa mattaṭṭhakassa kāyassa taṇhupādinnassa 'ahanti vā mamanti vā asmī'ti vā? Atha khvāssa notevettha hoti.

What then of this ephemeral body appropriated by craving? Rather than take it to be 'I' or 'mine' or 'I am', they still just consider it to be none of these things. ...

Tañce, āvuso, bhikkhuṁ pare akkosanti paribhāsanti rosenti vihesenti.

If others abuse, attack, harass, and trouble that mendicant, they understand:

So evaṁ pajānāti, uppannā kho me ayaṁ sotasamphassajā dukkhā vedanā.

'This painful feeling born of ear contact has arisen in me.

Sā ca kho paṭicca, no apaṭicca.

That's dependent, not independent.

Kiṁ paṭicca?

Dependent on what?

Phassaṁ paṭicca.

Dependent on contact.

Sopi phasso aniccoti passati, vedanā aniccāti passati, saññā aniccāti passati, saṅkhārā aniccāti passati, viññāṇaṁ aniccanti passati.

They see that contact, feeling, perception, choices, and consciousness are impermanent.

Tassa dhātārammaṇameva cittaṁ pakkhandati pasīdati santiṭṭhati adhimuccati.

Based on that element alone, their mind becomes eager, confident, settled, and decided.

Tañce, āvuso, bhikkhuṁ pare aniṭṭhehi akantehi amanāpehi samudācaranti, pāṇisamphassenapi leḍḍusamphassenapi daṇḍasamphassenapi satthasamphassenapi.

Others might treat that mendicant with disliking, loathing, and detestation, striking them with fists, stones, sticks, and swords.

So evaṁ pajānāti 'tathābhūto kho ayaṁ kāyo yathābhūtasmiṁ kāye pāṇisamphassāpi kamanti, leḍḍusamphassāpi kamanti, daṇḍasamphassāpi kamanti, satthasamphassāpi kamanti.

They understand: 'This body is such that fists, stones, sticks, and swords strike it.

Vuttaṁ kho panetaṁ bhagavatā kakacūpamovāde "ubhatodaṇḍakena cepi, bhikkhave, kakacena corā ocarakā aṅgamaṅgāni okanteyyuṁ. Tatrāpi yo mano padūseyya, na me so tena sāsanakaro"ti.

But the Buddha has said in the Simile of the Saw: "Even if low-down bandits were to sever you limb from limb, anyone who had a thought of hate on that account would not be following my instructions."

Āraddhaṁ kho pana me vīriyaṁ bhavissati asallīnaṁ, upaṭṭhitā sati asammuṭṭhā, passaddho kāyo asāraddho, samāhitaṁ cittaṁ ekaggaṁ.

My energy shall be roused up and unflagging, my mindfulness established and lucid, my body tranquil and undisturbed, and my mind immersed in samādhi.

Kāmaṁ dāni imasmiṁ kāye pāṇisamphassāpi kamantu, leḍḍusamphassāpi kamantu, daṇḍasamphassāpi kamantu, satthasamphassāpi kamantu. Karīyati hidaṁ buddhānaṁ sāsanan'ti.

Gladly now, let fists, stones, sticks, and swords strike this body! For this is how the instructions of the Buddhas are followed.'

Tassa ce, āvuso, bhikkhuno evaṁ buddhaṁ anussarato, evaṁ dhammaṁ anussarato, evaṁ saṅghaṁ anussarato upekkhā kusalanissitā na saṇṭhāti.

While recollecting the Buddha, the teaching, and the Saṅgha in this way, equanimity based on the skillful may not become stabilized in them.

So tena saṁvijjati saṁvegaṁ āpajjati:

In that case they stir up a sense of urgency:

'alābhā vata me, na vata me lābhā; dulladdhaṁ vata me, na vata me suladdhaṁ.

'It's my loss, my misfortune,

Yassa me evaṁ buddhaṁ anussarato, evaṁ dhammaṁ anussarato, evaṁ saṅghaṁ anussarato upekkhā kusalanissitā na saṇṭhātī'ti.

that while recollecting the Buddha, the teaching, and the Saṅgha in this way, equanimity based on the skillful does not become stabilized in me.'

Seyyathāpi, āvuso, suṇisā sasuraṁ disvā saṁvijjati saṁvegaṁ āpajjati;

They're like a daughter-in-law who stirs up a sense of urgency when they see their father-in-law.

evameva kho, āvuso, tassa ce bhikkhuno evaṁ buddhaṁ anussarato, evaṁ dhammaṁ anussarato, evaṁ saṅghaṁ anussarato, upekkhā kusalanissitā na saṇṭhāti.

So tena saṁvijjati saṁvegaṁ āpajjati:

'alābhā vata me, na vata me lābhā; dulladdhaṁ vata me, na vata me suladdhaṁ.

Yassa me evaṁ buddhaṁ anussarato, evaṁ dhammaṁ anussarato, evaṁ saṅghaṁ anussarato, upekkhā kusalanissitā na saṇṭhātī'ti.

Tassa ce, āvuso, bhikkhuno evaṁ buddhaṁ anussarato, evaṁ dhammaṁ anussarato, evaṁ saṅghaṁ anussarato, upekkhā kusalanissitā saṇṭhāti, so tena attamano hoti.

But if, while recollecting the Buddha, the teaching, and the Saṅgha in this way, equanimity based on the skillful does become stabilized in them, they're happy with that.

Ettāvatāpi kho, āvuso, bhikkhuno bahukataṁ hoti.

At this point, much has been done by that mendicant.

Seyyathāpi, āvuso, kaṭṭhañca paṭicca valliñca paṭicca tiṇañca paṭicca mattikañca paṭicca ākāso parivārito agārantveva saṅkhaṁ gacchati;

When a space is enclosed by sticks, creepers, grass, and mud it becomes known as a 'building'.

evameva kho, āvuso, aṭṭhiñca paṭicca nhāruñca paṭicca maṁsañca paṭicca cammañca paṭicca ākāso parivārito rūpantveva saṅkhaṁ gacchati.

In the same way, when a space is enclosed by bones, sinews, flesh, and skin it becomes known as a 'form'.

Ajjhattikañceva, āvuso, cakkhuṁ aparibhinnaṁ hoti, bāhirā ca rūpā na āpāthaṁ āgacchanti, no ca tajjo samannāhāro hoti, neva tāva tajjassa viññāṇabhāgassa pātubhāvo hoti.

Reverends, though the eye is intact internally, so long as exterior sights don't come into range and there's no corresponding engagement, there's no manifestation of the corresponding type of consciousness.

Ajjhattikañceva, āvuso, cakkhuṁ aparibhinnaṁ hoti bāhirā ca rūpā āpāthaṁ āgacchanti, no ca tajjo samannāhāro hoti, neva tāva tajjassa viññāṇabhāgassa pātubhāvo hoti.

Though the eye is intact internally and exterior sights come into range, so long as there's no corresponding engagement, there's no manifestation of the corresponding type of consciousness.

Yato ca kho, āvuso, ajjhattikañceva cakkhuṁ aparibhinnaṁ hoti, bāhirā ca rūpā āpāthaṁ āgacchanti, tajjo ca samannāhāro hoti. Evaṁ tajjassa viññāṇabhāgassa pātubhāvo hoti.

But when the eye is intact internally and exterior sights come into range and there is corresponding engagement, there is the manifestation of the corresponding type of consciousness.

Yaṁ tathābhūtassa rūpaṁ taṁ rūpupādānakkhandhe saṅgahaṁ gacchati, yā tathābhūtassa vedanā sā vedanupādānakkhandhe saṅgahaṁ gacchati, yā tathābhūtassa saññā sā saññupādānakkhandhe saṅgahaṁ gacchati, ye tathābhūtassa saṅkhārā te saṅkhārupādānakkhandhe saṅgahaṁ gacchanti, yaṁ tathābhūtassa viññāṇaṁ taṁ viññāṇupādānakkhandhe saṅgahaṁ gacchati.

The form produced in this way is included in the grasping aggregate of form. The feeling, perception, choices, and consciousness produced in this way are each included in the corresponding grasping aggregate.

So evaṁ pajānāti:

They understand:

'evañhi kira imesaṁ pañcannaṁ upādānakkhandhānaṁ saṅgaho sannipāto samavāyo hoti.

'So this is how there comes to be inclusion, gathering together, and joining together into these five grasping aggregates.

Vuttaṁ kho panetaṁ bhagavatā:

But the Buddha has said:

"yo paṭiccasamuppādaṁ passati so dhammaṁ passati;

"One who sees dependent origination sees the teaching.

yo dhammaṁ passati so paṭiccasamuppādaṁ passatī"ti.

One who sees the teaching sees dependent origination."

Paṭiccasamuppannā kho panime yadidaṁ pañcupādānakkhandhā.

And these five grasping aggregates are indeed dependently originated.

Yo imesu pañcasu upādānakkhandhesu chando ālayo anunayo ajjhosānaṁ so dukkhasamudayo.

The desire, adherence, attraction, and attachment for these five grasping aggregates is the origin of suffering.

Yo imesu pañcasu upādānakkhandhesu chandarāgavinayo chandarāgappahānaṁ, so dukkhanirodho'ti.

Giving up and getting rid of desire and greed for these five grasping aggregates is the cessation of suffering.'

Ettāvatāpi kho, āvuso, bhikkhuno bahukataṁ hoti.

At this point, much has been done by that mendicant.

Ajjhattikañceva, āvuso, sotaṁ aparibhinnaṁ hoti …pe…

Though the ear …

ghānaṁ aparibhinnaṁ hoti …

nose …

jivhā aparibhinnā hoti …

tongue …

kāyo aparibhinno hoti …

body …

mano aparibhinno hoti, bāhirā ca dhammā na āpāthaṁ āgacchanti no ca tajjo samannāhāro hoti, neva tāva tajjassa viññāṇabhāgassa pātubhāvo hoti.

mind is intact internally, so long as exterior thoughts don't come into range and there's no corresponding engagement, there's no manifestation of the corresponding type of consciousness.

Ajjhattiko ceva, āvuso, mano aparibhinno hoti, bāhirā ca dhammā āpāthaṁ āgacchanti, no ca tajjo samannāhāro hoti, neva tāva tajjassa viññāṇabhāgassa pātubhāvo hoti.

Though the mind is intact internally and exterior thoughts come into range, so long as there's no corresponding engagement, there's no manifestation of the corresponding type of consciousness.

Yato ca kho, āvuso, ajjhattiko ceva mano aparibhinno hoti, bāhirā ca dhammā āpāthaṁ āgacchanti, tajjo ca samannāhāro hoti, evaṁ tajjassa viññāṇabhāgassa pātubhāvo hoti.

But when the mind is intact internally and exterior thoughts come into range and there is corresponding engagement, there is the manifestation of the corresponding type of consciousness.

Yaṁ tathābhūtassa rūpaṁ taṁ rūpupādānakkhandhe saṅgahaṁ gacchati, yā tathābhūtassa vedanā sā vedanupādānakkhandhe saṅgahaṁ gacchati, yā tathābhūtassa saññā sā saññupādānakkhandhe saṅgahaṁ gacchati, ye tathābhūtassa saṅkhārā te saṅkhārupādānakkhandhe saṅgahaṁ gacchanti, yaṁ tathābhūtassa viññāṇaṁ taṁ viññāṇupādānakkhandhe saṅgahaṁ gacchati.

The form produced in this way is included in the grasping aggregate of form. The feeling, perception, choices, and consciousness produced in this way are each included in the corresponding grasping aggregate.

So evaṁ pajānāti:

They understand:

'evañhi kira imesaṁ pañcannaṁ upādānakkhandhānaṁ saṅgaho sannipāto samavāyo hoti.

'So this is how there comes to be inclusion, gathering together, and joining together into these five grasping aggregates.

Vuttaṁ kho panetaṁ bhagavatā:

But the Buddha has also said:

"yo paṭiccasamuppādaṁ passati so dhammaṁ passati;

"One who sees dependent origination sees the teaching.

yo dhammaṁ passati so paṭiccasamuppādaṁ passatī"ti.

One who sees the teaching sees dependent origination."

Paṭiccasamuppannā kho panime yadidaṁ pañcupādānakkhandhā.

And these five grasping aggregates are indeed dependently originated.

Yo imesu pañcasu upādānakkhandhesu chando ālayo anunayo ajjhosānaṁ so dukkhasamudayo.

The desire, adherence, attraction, and attachment for these five grasping aggregates is the origin of suffering.

Yo imesu pañcasu upādānakkhandhesu chandarāgavinayo chandarāgappahānaṁ so dukkhanirodho'ti.

Giving up and getting rid of desire and greed for these five grasping aggregates is the cessation of suffering.'

Ettāvatāpi kho, āvuso, bhikkhuno bahukataṁ hotī"ti.

At this point, much has been done by that mendicant."

Idamavoca āyasmā sāriputto.

That's what Venerable Sāriputta said.

Attamanā te bhikkhū āyasmato sāriputtassa bhāsitaṁ abhinandunti.

Satisfied, the mendicants were happy with what Sāriputta said.

Mahāhatthipadopamasuttaṁ niṭṭhitaṁ aṭṭhamaṁ.

29 Mahasaropamasutta:

The Longer Simile of the Heartwood

Evaṁ me sutaṁ—

So I have heard.

ekaṁ samayaṁ bhagavā rājagahe viharati gijjhakūṭe pabbate acirapakkante devadatte.

At one time the Buddha was staying near Rājagaha, on the Vulture's Peak Mountain, not long after Devadatta had left.

Tatra kho bhagavā devadattaṁ ārabbha bhikkhū āmantesi:

There the Buddha spoke to the mendicants about Devadatta:

"Idha, bhikkhave, ekacco kulaputto saddhā agārasmā anagāriyaṁ pabbajito hoti:

"Mendicants, take the case of a gentleman who has gone forth from the lay life to homelessness, thinking,

'otiṇṇomhi jātiyā jarāya maraṇena sokehi paridevehi dukkhehi domanassehi upāyāsehi, dukkhotiṇṇo dukkhapareto,

'I'm swamped by rebirth, old age, and death; by sorrow, lamentation, pain, sadness, and distress. I'm swamped by suffering, mired in suffering.

appeva nāma imassa kevalassa dukkhakkhandhassa antakiriyā paññāyethā'ti.

Hopefully I can find an end to this entire mass of suffering.'

So evaṁ pabbajito samāno lābhasakkārasilokaṁ abhinibbatteti.

When they've gone forth they generate possessions, honor, and popularity.

So tena lābhasakkārasilokena attamano hoti paripuṇṇasaṅkappo.

They're happy with that, and they've got all they wished for.

So tena lābhasakkārasilokena attānukkaṁseti paraṁ vambheti:

And they glorify themselves and put others down because of that:

'ahamasmi lābhasakkārasilokavā, ime panaññe bhikkhū appaññātā appesakkhā'ti.

'I'm the one with possessions, honor, and popularity. These other mendicants are obscure and insignificant.'

So tena lābhasakkārasilokena majjati pamajjati pamādaṁ āpajjati, pamatto samāno dukkhaṁ viharati.

And so they become indulgent and fall into negligence regarding those possessions, honor, and popularity. And being negligent they live in suffering.

Seyyathāpi, bhikkhave, puriso sāratthiko sāragavesī sārapariyesanaṁ caramāno mahato rukkhassa tiṭṭhato sāravato atikkammeva sāraṁ atikkamma pheggguṁ atikkamma tacaṁ atikkamma papaṭikaṁ, sākhāpalāsaṁ chetvā ādāya pakkameyya 'sāran'ti maññamāno.

Suppose there was a person in need of heartwood. And while wandering in search of heartwood he'd come across a large tree standing with heartwood. But, passing over the heartwood, softwood, bark, and shoots, he'd cut off the branches and leaves and depart imagining they were heartwood.

Tamenaṁ cakkhumā puriso disvā evaṁ vadeyya:

If a person with good eyesight saw him they'd say,

'na vatāyaṁ bhavaṁ puriso aññāsi sāraṁ, na aññāsi pheggguṁ, na aññāsi tacaṁ, na aññāsi papaṭikaṁ, na aññāsi sākhāpalāsaṁ.

'This gentleman doesn't know what heartwood, softwood, bark, shoots, or branches and leaves are.

Tathā hayaṁ bhavaṁ puriso sāratthiko sāragavesī sārapariyesanaṁ caramāno mahato rukkhassa tiṭṭhato sāravato atikkammeva sāraṁ atikkamma pheggguṁ atikkamma tacaṁ atikkamma papaṭikaṁ, sākhāpalāsaṁ chetvā ādāya pakkanto "sāran"ti maññamāno.

That's why he passed them over, cut off the branches and leaves, and departed imagining they were heartwood.

Yañcassa sārena sārakaraṇīyaṁ tañcassa atthaṁ nānubhavissatī'ti.

Whatever he needs to make from heartwood, he won't succeed.' …

Evameva kho, bhikkhave, idhekacco kulaputto saddhā agārasmā anagāriyaṁ pabbajito hoti:

'otiṇṇomhi jātiyā jarāya maraṇena sokehi paridevehi dukkhehi domanassehi upāyāsehi, dukkhotiṇṇo dukkhapareto,

appeva nāma imassa kevalassa dukkhakkhandhassa antakiriyā paññāyethā'ti.

So evaṁ pabbajito samāno lābhasakkārasilokaṁ abhinibbatteti.

So tena lābhasakkārasilokena attamano hoti paripuṇṇasaṅkappo.

So tena lābhasakkārasilokena attānukkaṁseti, paraṁ vambheti 'ahamasmi lābhasakkārasilokavā, ime panaññe bhikkhū appaññātā appesakkhā'ti.

So tena lābhasakkārasilokena majjati pamajjati pamādaṁ āpajjati, pamatto samāno dukkhaṁ viharati.

Ayaṁ vuccati, bhikkhave, bhikkhu sākhāpalāsaṁ aggahesi brahmacariyassa;

This is called a mendicant who has grabbed the branches and leaves of the spiritual life

tena ca vosānaṁ āpādi.

and stopped short with that.

Idha pana, bhikkhave, ekacco kulaputto saddhā agārasmā anagāriyaṁ pabbajito hoti:

Next, take a gentleman who has gone forth from the lay life to homelessness …

'otiṇṇomhi jātiyā jarāya maraṇena sokehi paridevehi dukkhehi domanassehi upāyāsehi, dukkhotiṇṇo dukkhapareto,

appeva nāma imassa kevalassa dukkhakkhandhassa antakiriyā paññāyethā'ti.

So evaṁ pabbajito samāno lābhasakkārasilokaṁ abhinibbatteti.

When they've gone forth they generate possessions, honor, and popularity.

So tena lābhasakkārasilokena na attamano hoti na paripuṇṇasaṅkappo.

They're not happy with that, and haven't got all they wished for.

So tena lābhasakkārasilokena na attānukkaṁseti, na paraṁ vambheti.

They don't glorify themselves and put others down on account of that.

So tena lābhasakkārasilokena na majjati nappamajjati na pamādaṁ āpajjati.

Nor do they become indulgent and fall into negligence regarding those possessions, honor, and popularity.

Appamatto samāno sīlasampadaṁ ārādheti.

Being diligent, they become accomplished in ethics.

So tāya sīlasampadāya attamano hoti paripuṇṇasaṅkappo.

They're happy with that, and they've got all they wished for.

So tāya sīlasampadāya attānukkaṁseti, paraṁ vambheti:

And they glorify themselves and put others down on account of that:

'ahamasmi sīlavā kalyāṇadhammo, ime panaññe bhikkhū dussīlā pāpadhammā'ti.

'I'm the one who is ethical, of good character. These other mendicants are unethical, of bad character.'

So tāya sīlasampadāya majjati pamajjati pamādaṁ āpajjati, pamatto samāno dukkhaṁ viharati.

And so they become indulgent and fall into negligence regarding their accomplishment in ethics. And being negligent they live in suffering.

Seyyathāpi, bhikkhave, puriso sāratthiko sāragavesī sārapariyesanaṁ caramāno mahato rukkhassa tiṭṭhato sāravato atikkammeva sāraṁ atikkamma phegguṁ atikkamma tacaṁ, papaṭikaṁ chetvā ādāya pakkameyya 'saran'ti maññamāno.

Suppose there was a person in need of heartwood. And while wandering in search of heartwood he'd come across a large tree standing with heartwood. But, passing over the heartwood, softwood, and bark, he'd cut off the shoots and depart imagining they were heartwood.

Tamenaṁ cakkhumā puriso disvā evaṁ vadeyya:

If a person with good eyesight saw him they'd say,

'na vatāyaṁ bhavaṁ puriso aññāsi sāraṁ, na aññāsi phegguṁ, na aññāsi tacaṁ, na aññāsi papaṭikaṁ, na aññāsi sākhāpalāsaṁ.

'This gentleman doesn't know what heartwood, softwood, bark, shoots, or branches and leaves are.

Tathā hayaṁ bhavaṁ puriso sāratthiko sāragavesī sārapariyesanaṁ caramāno mahato rukkhassa tiṭṭhato sāravato atikkammeva sāraṁ atikkamma phegguṁ atikkamma tacaṁ, papaṭikaṁ chetvā ādāya pakkanto "saran"ti maññamāno;

That's why he passed them over, cut off the shoots, and departed imagining they were heartwood.

yañcassa sārena sārakaraṇīyaṁ tañcassa atthaṁ nānubhavissatī'ti.

Whatever he needs to make from heartwood, he won't succeed.' …

Evameva kho, bhikkhave, idhekacco kulaputto saddhā agārasmā anagāriyaṁ pabbajito hoti:

'otiṇṇomhi jātiyā jarāya maraṇena sokehi paridevehi dukkhehi domanassehi upāyāsehi, dukkhotiṇṇo dukkhapareto,

appeva nāma imassa kevalassa dukkhakkhandhassa antakiriyā paññāyethā'ti.

So evaṁ pabbajito samāno lābhasakkārasilokaṁ abhinibbatteti.

So tena lābhasakkārasilokena na attamano hoti na paripuṇṇasaṅkappo.

So tena lābhasakkārasilokena na attānukkaṁseti, na paraṁ vambheti.

So tena lābhasakkārasilokena na majjati nappamajjati na pamādam āpajjati.

Appamatto samāno sīlasampadam ārādheti.

So tāya sīlasampadāya attamano hoti paripuṇṇasaṅkappo.

So tāya sīlasampadāya attānukkamseti, param vambheti:

'ahamasmi sīlavā kalyāṇadhammo, ime panaññe bhikkhū dussīlā pāpadhammā'ti.

So tāya sīlasampadāya majjati pamajjati pamādam āpajjati, pamatto samāno dukkham viharati.

Ayam vuccati, bhikkhave, bhikkhu papaṭikam aggahesi brahmacariyassa;

This is called a mendicant who has grabbed the shoots of the spiritual life

tena ca vosānam āpādi.

and stopped short with that.

Idha pana, bhikkhave, ekacco kulaputto saddhā agārasmā anagāriyam pabbajito hoti:

Next, take a gentleman who has gone forth from the lay life to homelessness …

'otiṇṇomhi jātiyā jarāya maraṇena sokehi paridevehi dukkhehi domanassehi upāyāsehi, dukkhotiṇṇo dukkhapareto,

appeva nāma imassa kevalassa dukkhakkhandhassa antakiriyā paññāyethā'ti.

So evam pabbajito samāno lābhasakkārasilokam abhinibbatteti.

When they've gone forth they generate possessions, honor, and popularity. …

So tena lābhasakkārasilokena na attamano hoti na paripuṇṇasaṅkappo.

So tena lābhasakkārasilokena na attānukkamseti, na param vambheti.

So tena lābhasakkārasilokena na majjati nappamajjati na pamādam āpajjati, appamatto samāno sīlasampadam ārādheti.

So tāya sīlasampadāya attamano hoti no ca kho paripuṇṇasaṅkappo.

So tāya sīlasampadāya na attānukkamseti, na param vambheti.

So tāya sīlasampadāya na majjati nappamajjati na pamādam āpajjati.

Appamatto samāno samādhisampadam ārādheti.

Being diligent, they achieve immersion.

So tāya samādhisampadāya attamano hoti paripuṇṇasaṅkappo.

They're happy with that, and they've got all they wished for.

So tāya samādhisampadāya attānukkaṁseti, paraṁ vambheti:

And they glorify themselves and put others down on account of that:

'ahamasmi samāhito ekaggacitto, ime panaññe bhikkhū asamāhitā vibbhantacittā'ti.

'I'm the one with immersion and unified mind. These other mendicants lack immersion, they have straying minds.'

So tāya samādhisampadāya majjati pamajjati pamādaṁ āpajjati, pamatto samāno dukkhaṁ viharati.

And so they become indulgent and fall into negligence regarding that accomplishment in immersion. And being negligent they live in suffering.

Seyyathāpi, bhikkhave, puriso sāratthiko sāragavesī sārapariyesanaṁ caramāno mahato rukkhassa tiṭṭhato sāravato atikkammeva sāraṁ atikkamma phegguṁ tacaṁ chetvā ādāya pakkameyya 'sāran'ti maññamāno.

Suppose there was a person in need of heartwood. And while wandering in search of heartwood he'd come across a large tree standing with heartwood. But, passing over the heartwood and softwood, he'd cut off the bark and depart imagining it was heartwood.

Tamenaṁ cakkhumā puriso disvā evaṁ vadeyya 'na vatāyaṁ bhavaṁ puriso aññāsi sāraṁ, na aññāsi phegguṁ, na aññāsi tacaṁ, na aññāsi papaṭikaṁ, na aññāsi sākhāpalāsaṁ.

If a person with good eyesight saw him they'd say: 'This gentleman doesn't know what heartwood, softwood, bark, shoots, or branches and leaves are.

Tathā hayaṁ bhavaṁ puriso sāratthiko sāragavesī sārapariyesanaṁ caramāno mahato rukkhassa tiṭṭhato sāravato atikkammeva sāraṁ atikkamma phegguṁ tacaṁ chetvā ādāya pakkanto "sāran"ti maññamāno.

That's why he passed them over, cut off the bark, and departed imagining it was heartwood.

Yañcassa sārena sārakaraṇīyaṁ tañcassa atthaṁ nānubhavissatī'ti.

Whatever he needs to make from heartwood, he won't succeed.' ...

Evameva kho, bhikkhave, idhekacco kulaputto saddhā agārasmā anagāriyaṁ pabbajito hoti:

'otiṇṇomhi jātiyā jarāya maraṇena sokehi paridevehi dukkhehi domanassehi upāyāsehi, dukkhotiṇṇo dukkhapareto,

appeva nāma imassa kevalassa dukkhakkhandhassa antakiriyā paññāyethā'ti.

So evaṁ pabbajito samāno lābhasakkārasilokaṁ abhinibbatteti.

So tena lābhasakkārasilokena na attamano hoti na paripuṇṇasaṅkappo.

So tena lābhasakkārasilokena na attānukkaṁseti, na paraṁ vambheti.

So tena lābhasakkārasilokena na majjati nappamajjati na pamādaṁ āpajjati, appamatto samāno sīlasampadaṁ ārādheti.

So tāya sīlasampadāya attamano hoti no ca kho paripuṇṇasaṅkappo.

So tāya sīlasampadāya na attānukkaṁseti, na paraṁ vambheti.

So tāya sīlasampadāya na majjati nappamajjati na pamādaṁ āpajjati, appamatto samāno samādhisampadaṁ ārādheti.

So tāya samādhisampadāya attamano hoti paripuṇṇasaṅkappo.

So tāya samādhisampadāya attānukkaṁseti, paraṁ vambheti:

'ahamasmi samāhito ekaggacitto, ime panaññe bhikkhū asamāhitā vibbhantacittā'ti.

So tāya samādhisampadāya majjati pamajjati pamādaṁ āpajjati, pamatto samāno dukkhaṁ viharati.

Ayaṁ vuccati, bhikkhave, bhikkhu tacaṁ aggahesi brahmacariyassa;

This is called a mendicant who has grabbed the bark of the spiritual life

tena ca vosānaṁ āpādi.

and stopped short with that.

Idha pana, bhikkhave, ekacco kulaputto saddhā agārasmā anagāriyaṁ pabbajito hoti:

Next, take a gentleman who has gone forth from the lay life to homelessness …

'otiṇṇomhi jātiyā jarāya maraṇena sokehi paridevehi dukkhehi domanassehi upāyāsehi, dukkhotiṇṇo dukkhapareto,

appeva nāma imassa kevalassa dukkhakkhandhassa antakiriyā paññāyethā'ti.

So evaṁ pabbajito samāno lābhasakkārasilokaṁ abhinibbatteti.

When they've gone forth they generate possessions, honor, and popularity. …

So tena lābhasakkārasilokena na attamano hoti na paripuṇṇasaṅkappo.

So tena lābhasakkārasilokena na attānukkaṁseti, na paraṁ vambheti.

So tena lābhasakkārasilokena na majjati nappamajjati na pamādaṁ āpajjati.

Appamatto samāno sīlasampadaṁ ārādheti.

So tāya sīlasampadāya attamano hoti, no ca kho paripuṇṇasaṅkappo.

So tāya sīlasampadāya na attānukkaṁseti, na paraṁ vambheti.

So tāya sīlasampadāya na majjati nappamajjati na pamādaṁ āpajjati, appamatto samāno samādhisampadaṁ ārādheti.

So tāya samādhisampadāya attamano hoti, no ca kho paripuṇṇasaṅkappo.

So tāya samādhisampadāya na attānukkaṁseti, na paraṁ vambheti.

So tāya samādhisampadāya na majjati nappamajjati na pamādaṁ āpajjati appamatto samāno ñāṇadassanaṁ ārādheti.

Being diligent, they achieve knowledge and vision.

So tena ñāṇadassanena attamano hoti paripuṇṇasaṅkappo.

They're happy with that, and they've got all they wished for.

So tena ñāṇadassanena attānukkaṁseti, paraṁ vambheti:

And they glorify themselves and put others down on account of that,

'ahamasmi jānaṁ passaṁ viharāmi.

'I'm the one who meditates knowing and seeing.

Ime panaññe bhikkhū ajānaṁ apassaṁ viharantī'ti.

These other mendicants meditate without knowing and seeing.'

So tena ñāṇadassanena majjati pamajjati pamādaṁ āpajjati, pamatto samāno dukkhaṁ viharati.

And so they become indulgent and fall into negligence regarding that knowledge and vision. And being negligent they live in suffering.

Seyyathāpi, bhikkhave, puriso sāratthiko sāragavesī sārapariyesanaṁ caramāno mahato rukkhassa tiṭṭhato sāravato atikkammeva sāraṁ pheggum chetvā ādāya pakkameyya 'sāran'ti maññamāno.

Suppose there was a person in need of heartwood. And while wandering in search of heartwood he'd come across a large tree standing with heartwood. But, passing over the heartwood, he'd cut out the softwood and depart imagining it was heartwood.

Tamenaṁ cakkhumā puriso disvā evaṁ vadeyya:

If a person with good eyesight saw him they'd say,

'na vatāyaṁ bhavaṁ puriso aññāsi sāraṁ na aññāsi pheggūṁ na aññāsi tacaṁ na aññāsi papaṭikaṁ na aññāsi sākhāpalāsaṁ.

'This gentleman doesn't know what heartwood, softwood, bark, shoots, or branches and leaves are.

Tathā hayaṁ bhavaṁ puriso sāratthiko sāragavesī sārapariyesanaṁ caramāno mahato rukkhassa tiṭṭhato sāravato atikkammeva sāraṁ pheggūṁ chetvā ādāya pakkanto "sāran"ti maññamāno.

That's why he passed them over, cut out the softwood, and departed imagining it was heartwood.

Yañcassa sārena sārakaraṇīyaṁ tañcassa atthaṁ nānubhavissatī'ti.

Whatever he needs to make from heartwood, he won't succeed.' …

Evameva kho, bhikkhave, idhekacco kulaputto saddhā agārasmā anagāriyaṁ pabbajito hoti:

'otiṇṇomhi jātiyā jarāya maraṇena sokehi paridevehi dukkhehi domanassehi upāyāsehi, dukkhotiṇṇo dukkhapareto,

appeva nāma imassa kevalassa dukkhakkhandhassa antakiriyā paññāyethā'ti.

So evaṁ pabbajito samāno lābhasakkārasilokaṁ abhinibbatteti.

So tena lābhasakkārasilokena na attamano hoti na paripuṇṇasaṅkappo.

So tena lābhasakkārasilokena na attānukkaṁseti, na paraṁ vambheti.

So tena lābhasakkārasilokena na majjati nappamajjati na pamādaṁ āpajjati, appamatto samāno sīlasampadaṁ ārādheti.

So tāya sīlasampadāya attamano hoti, no ca kho paripuṇṇasaṅkappo.

So tāya sīlasampadāya na attānukkaṁseti, na paraṁ vambheti.

So tāya sīlasampadāya na majjati nappamajjati na pamādaṁ āpajjati, appamatto samāno samādhisampadaṁ ārādheti.

So tāya samādhisampadāya attamano hoti, no ca kho paripuṇṇasaṅkappo.

So tāya samādhisampadāya na attānukkaṁseti, na paraṁ vambheti.

So tāya samādhisampadāya na majjati nappamajjati na pamādaṁ āpajjati, appamatto samāno ñāṇadassanaṁ ārādheti.

So tena ñāṇadassanena attamano hoti paripuṇṇasaṅkappo.

So tena ñāṇadassanena attānukkaṁseti, paraṁ vambheti:

'ahamasmi jānaṁ passaṁ viharāmi, ime panaññe bhikkhū ajānaṁ apassaṁ viharantī'ti.

So tena ñāṇadassanena majjati pamajjati pamādaṁ āpajjati, pamatto samāno dukkhaṁ viharati.

Ayaṁ vuccati, bhikkhave, bhikkhu pheggum aggahesi brahmacariyassa;

This is called a mendicant who has grabbed the softwood of the spiritual life

tena ca vosānaṁ āpādi.

and stopped short with that.

Idha pana, bhikkhave, ekacco kulaputto saddhā agārasmā anagāriyaṁ pabbajito hoti:

Next, take a gentleman who has gone forth from the lay life to homelessness, thinking,

'otiṇṇomhi jātiyā jarāya maraṇena sokehi paridevehi dukkhehi domanassehi upāyāsehi, dukkhotiṇṇo dukkhapareto,

'I'm swamped by rebirth, old age, and death; by sorrow, lamentation, pain, sadness, and distress. I'm swamped by suffering, mired in suffering.

appeva nāma imassa kevalassa dukkhakkhandhassa antakiriyā paññāyethā'ti.

Hopefully I can find an end to this entire mass of suffering.'

So evaṁ pabbajito samāno lābhasakkārasilokaṁ abhinibbatteti.

When they've gone forth they generate possessions, honor, and popularity.

So tena lābhasakkārasilokena na attamano hoti, na paripuṇṇasaṅkappo.

They're not happy with that, and haven't got all they wished for.

So tena lābhasakkārasilokena na attānukkaṁseti, na paraṁ vambheti.

They don't glorify themselves and put others down on account of that.

So tena lābhasakkārasilokena na majjati nappamajjati na pamādaṁ āpajjati, appamatto samāno sīlasampadaṁ ārādheti.

Nor do they become indulgent and fall into negligence regarding those possessions, honor, and popularity. Being diligent, they become accomplished in ethics.

So tāya sīlasampadāya attamano hoti, no ca kho paripuṇṇasaṅkappo.

They're happy with that, but they haven't got all they wished for.

So tāya sīlasampadāya na attānukkaṁseti, na paraṁ vambheti.

They don't glorify themselves and put others down on account of that.

So tāya sīlasampadāya na majjati nappamajjati na pamādaṁ āpajjati, appamatto samāno samādhisampadaṁ ārādheti.

Nor do they become indulgent and fall into negligence regarding that accomplishment in ethics. Being diligent, they achieve immersion.

So tāya samādhisampadāya attamano hoti, no ca kho paripuṇṇasaṅkappo.

They're happy with that, but they haven't got all they wished for.

So tāya samādhisampadāya na attānukkaṁseti, na paraṁ vambheti.

They don't glorify themselves and put others down on account of that.

So tāya samādhisampadāya na majjati nappamajjati na pamādaṁ āpajjati, appamatto samāno ñāṇadassanaṁ ārādheti.

Nor do they become indulgent and fall into negligence regarding that accomplishment in immersion. Being diligent, they achieve knowledge and vision.

So tena ñāṇadassanena attamano hoti, no ca kho paripuṇṇasaṅkappo.

They're happy with that, but they haven't got all they wished for.

So tena ñāṇadassanena na attānukkaṁseti, na paraṁ vambheti.

They don't glorify themselves and put others down on account of that.

So tena ñāṇadassanena na majjati nappamajjati na pamādaṁ āpajjati, appamatto samāno asamayavimokkhaṁ ārādheti.

Nor do they become indulgent and fall into negligence regarding that knowledge and vision. Being diligent, they achieve permanent liberation.

Aṭṭhānametaṁ, bhikkhave, anavakāso yaṁ so bhikkhu tāya asamayavimuttiyā parihāyetha.

And it's impossible for that mendicant to fall away from that irreversible liberation.

Seyyathāpi, bhikkhave, puriso sāratthiko sāragavesī sārapariyesanaṁ caramāno mahato rukkhassa tiṭṭhato sāravato sāraññeva chetvā ādāya pakkameyya 'sāran'ti jānamāno.

Suppose there was a person in need of heartwood. And while wandering in search of heartwood he'd come across a large tree standing with heartwood. He'd cut out just the heartwood and depart knowing it was heartwood.

Tamenaṁ cakkhumā puriso disvā evaṁ vadeyya:

If a person with good eyesight saw him they'd say,

'aññāsi vatāyaṁ bhavaṁ puriso sāraṁ, aññāsi phegguṁ, aññāsi tacaṁ, aññāsi papaṭikaṁ, aññāsi sākhāpalāsaṁ.

'This gentleman knows what heartwood, softwood, bark, shoots, and branches and leaves are.

Tathā hayaṁ bhavaṁ puriso sāratthiko sāragavesī sārapariyesanaṁ caramāno mahato rukkhassa tiṭṭhato sāravato sāraññeva chetvā ādāya pakkanto "saran"ti jānamāno.

That's why he cut out just the heartwood and departed knowing it was heartwood.

Yañcassa sārena sārakaraṇīyaṁ tañcassa atthaṁ anubhavissatī'ti.

Whatever he needs to make from heartwood, he will succeed.' ...

Evameva kho, bhikkhave, idhekacco kulaputto saddhā agārasmā anagāriyaṁ pabbajito hoti:

'otiṇṇomhi jātiyā jarāya maraṇena sokehi paridevehi dukkhehi domanassehi upāyāsehi, dukkhotiṇṇo dukkhapareto,

appeva nāma imassa kevalassa dukkhakkhandhassa antakiriyā paññāyethā'ti.

So evaṁ pabbajito samāno lābhasakkārasilokaṁ abhinibbatteti.

So tena lābhasakkārasilokena na attamano hoti, na paripuṇṇasaṅkappo.

So tena lābhasakkārasilokena na attānukkaṁseti, na paraṁ vambheti.

So tena lābhasakkārasilokena na majjati nappamajjati na pamādaṁ āpajjati, appamatto samāno sīlasampadaṁ ārādheti.

So tāya sīlasampadāya attamano hoti, no ca kho paripuṇṇasaṅkappo.

So tāya sīlasampadāya na attānukkaṁseti, na paraṁ vambheti.

So tāya sīlasampadāya na majjati nappamajjati na pamādaṁ āpajjati, appamatto samāno samādhisampadaṁ ārādheti.

So tāya samādhisampadāya attamano hoti, no ca kho paripuṇṇasaṅkappo.

So tāya samādhisampadāya na attānukkaṁseti, na paraṁ vambheti.

So tāya samādhisampadāya na majjati nappamajjati na pamādaṁ āpajjati, appamatto samāno ñāṇadassanaṁ ārādheti.

So tena ñāṇadassanena attamano hoti, no ca kho paripuṇṇasaṅkappo.

So tena ñāṇadassanena na attānukkaṁseti, na paraṁ vambheti.

So tena ñāṇadassanena na majjati nappamajjati na pamādaṁ āpajjati, appamatto samāno asamayavimokkhaṁ ārādheti.

Aṭṭhānametaṁ, bhikkhave, anavakāso yaṁ so bhikkhu tāya asamayavimuttiyā parihāyetha.

It's impossible for that mendicant to fall away from that irreversible liberation.

Iti kho, bhikkhave, nayidaṁ brahmacariyaṁ lābhasakkārasilokānisaṁsaṁ, na sīlasampadānisaṁsaṁ, na samādhisampadānisaṁsaṁ, na ñāṇadassanānisaṁsaṁ.

And so, mendicants, this spiritual life is not lived for the sake of possessions, honor, and popularity, or for accomplishment in ethics, or for accomplishment in immersion, or for knowledge and vision.

Yā ca kho ayaṁ, bhikkhave, akuppā cetovimutti—

Rather, the goal, heartwood, and final end of the spiritual life is the unshakable freedom of heart."

etadatthamidaṁ, bhikkhave, brahmacariyaṁ, etaṁ sāraṁ etaṁ pariyosānan"ti.

Idamavoca bhagavā.

That is what the Buddha said.

Attamanā te bhikkhū bhagavato bhāsitaṁ abhinandunti.

Satisfied, the mendicants were happy with what the Buddha said.

Mahāsāropamasuttaṁ niṭṭhitaṁ navamaṁ.

30 Culasaropamasutta:

The Shorter Simile of the Heartwood

Evaṁ me sutaṁ—

So I have heard.

ekaṁ samayaṁ bhagavā sāvatthiyaṁ viharati jetavane anāthapiṇḍikassa ārāme.

At one time the Buddha was staying near Sāvatthī in Jeta's Grove, Anāthapiṇḍika's monastery.

Atha kho piṅgalakoccho brāhmaṇo yena bhagavā tenupasaṅkami; upasaṅkamitvā bhagavatā saddhiṁ sammodi.

Then the brahmin Piṅgalakoccha went up to the Buddha, and exchanged greetings with him.

Sammodanīyaṁ kathaṁ sāraṇīyaṁ vītisāretvā ekamantaṁ nisīdi. Ekamantaṁ nisinno kho piṅgalakoccho brāhmaṇo bhagavantaṁ etadavoca:

When the greetings and polite conversation were over, he sat down to one side and said to the Buddha:

"yeme, bho gotama, samaṇabrāhmaṇā saṅghino gaṇino gaṇācariyā ñātā yasassino titthakarā sādhusammatā, bahujanassa,

"Master Gotama, there are those ascetics and brahmins who lead an order and a community, and teach a community. They're well-known and famous religious founders, regarded as holy by many people.

seyyathidaṁ—pūraṇo kassapo, makkhali gosālo, ajito kesakambalo, pakudho kaccāyano, sañcayo belaṭṭhaputto, nigaṇṭho nāṭaputto,

Namely: Pūraṇa Kassapa, Makkhali Gosāla, Ajita of the hair blanket, Pakudha Kaccāyana, Sañjaya Belaṭṭhiputta, and the Jain ascetic of the Ñātika clan.

sabbete sakāya paṭiññāya abbhaññaṁsu sabbeva nābbhaññaṁsu, udāhu ekacce abbhaññaṁsu ekacce nābbhaññaṁsū"ti?

According to their own claims, did all of them have direct knowledge, or none of them, or only some?"

"Alaṁ, brāhmaṇa, tiṭṭhatetaṁ—

"Enough, brahmin, let this be:

sabbete sakāya paṭiññāya abbhaññaṁsu sabbeva nābbhaññaṁsu, udāhu ekacce abbhaññaṁsu ekacce nābbhaññaṁsūti.

'According to their own claims, did all of them have direct knowledge, or none of them, or only some?'

Dhammaṁ te, brāhmaṇa, desessāmi,

I will teach you the Dhamma.

taṁ suṇāhi, sādhukaṁ manasi karohi, bhāsissāmī"ti.

Listen and pay close attention, I will speak."

"Evaṁ, bho"ti kho piṅgalakoccho brāhmaṇo bhagavato paccassosi.

"Yes sir," Piṅgalakoccha replied.

Bhagavā etadavoca:

The Buddha said this:

"Seyyathāpi, brāhmaṇa, puriso sāratthiko sāragavesī sārapariyesanaṁ caramāno mahato rukkhassa tiṭṭhato sāravato atikkammeva sāraṁ atikkamma phegguṁ atikkamma tacaṁ atikkamma papaṭikaṁ, sākhāpalāsaṁ chetvā ādāya pakkameyya 'sāran'ti maññamāno.

"Suppose there was a person in need of heartwood. And while wandering in search of heartwood he'd come across a large tree standing with heartwood. But, passing over the heartwood, softwood, bark, and shoots, he'd cut off the branches and leaves and depart imagining they were heartwood.

Tamenaṁ cakkhumā puriso disvā evaṁ vadeyya:

If a person with good eyesight saw him they'd say:

'na vatāyaṁ bhavaṁ puriso aññāsi sāraṁ, na aññāsi phegguṁ, na aññāsi tacaṁ, na aññāsi papaṭikaṁ, na aññāsi sākhāpalāsaṁ.

'This gentleman doesn't know what heartwood, softwood, bark, shoots, or branches and leaves are.

Tathā hayaṁ bhavaṁ puriso sāratthiko sāragavesī sārapariyesanaṁ caramāno mahato rukkhassa tiṭṭhato sāravato atikkammeva sāraṁ atikkamma phegguṁ atikkamma tacaṁ atikkamma papaṭikaṁ, sākhāpalāsaṁ chetvā ādāya pakkanto "sāran"ti maññamāno.

That's why he passed them over, cut off the branches and leaves, and departed imagining they were heartwood.

Yañcassa sārena sārakaraṇīyaṁ tañcassa atthaṁ nānubhavissatī'ti.

Whatever he needs to make from heartwood, he won't succeed.'

Seyyathāpi vā pana, brāhmaṇa, puriso sāratthiko sāragavesī sārapariyesanaṁ caramāno mahato rukkhassa tiṭṭhato sāravato atikkammeva sāraṁ atikkamma phegguṁ atikkamma tacaṁ, papaṭikaṁ chetvā ādāya pakkameyya 'sāran'ti maññamāno.

Suppose there was another person in need of heartwood … he'd cut off the shoots and depart imagining they were heartwood …

Tamenaṁ cakkhumā puriso disvā evaṁ vadeyya:

'na vatāyaṁ bhavaṁ puriso aññāsi sāraṁ, na aññāsi phegguṁ, na aññāsi tacaṁ, na aññāsi papaṭikaṁ, na aññāsi sākhāpalāsaṁ.

Tathā hayaṁ bhavaṁ puriso sāratthiko sāragavesī sārapariyesanaṁ caramāno mahato rukkhassa tiṭṭhato sāravato atikkammeva sāraṁ atikkamma phegguṁ atikkamma tacaṁ papaṭikaṁ chetvā ādāya pakkanto "sāran"ti maññamāno.

Yañcassa sārena sārakaraṇīyaṁ tañcassa atthaṁ nānubhavissatī'ti.

Seyyathāpi vā pana, brāhmaṇa, puriso sāratthiko sāragavesī sārapariyesanaṁ caramāno mahato rukkhassa tiṭṭhato sāravato atikkammeva sāraṁ atikkamma phegguṁ, tacaṁ chetvā ādāya pakkameyya 'sāran'ti maññamāno.

Suppose there was another person in need of heartwood ... he'd cut off the bark and depart imagining it was heartwood ...

Tamenaṁ cakkhumā puriso disvā evaṁ vadeyya:

'na vatāyaṁ bhavaṁ puriso aññāsi sāraṁ, na aññāsi phegguṁ, na aññāsi tacaṁ, na aññāsi papaṭikaṁ, na aññāsi sākhāpalāsaṁ.

Tathā hayaṁ bhavaṁ puriso sāratthiko sāragavesī sārapariyesanaṁ caramāno mahato rukkhassa tiṭṭhato sāravato atikkammeva sāraṁ atikkamma phegguṁ, tacaṁ chetvā ādāya pakkanto "sāran"ti maññamāno.

Yañcassa sārena sārakaraṇīyaṁ tañcassa atthaṁ nānubhavissatī'ti.

Seyyathāpi vā pana, brāhmaṇa, puriso sāratthiko sāragavesī sārapariyesanaṁ caramāno mahato rukkhassa tiṭṭhato sāravato atikkammeva sāraṁ, phegguṁ chetvā ādāya pakkameyya 'sāran'ti maññamāno.

Suppose there was another person in need of heartwood ... he'd cut out the softwood and depart imagining it was heartwood ...

Tamenaṁ cakkhumā puriso disvā evaṁ vadeyya:

'na vatāyaṁ bhavaṁ puriso aññāsi sāraṁ, na aññāsi phegguṁ, na aññāsi tacaṁ, na aññāsi papaṭikaṁ, na aññāsi sākhāpalāsaṁ.

Tathā hayaṁ bhavaṁ puriso sāratthiko sāragavesī sārapariyesanaṁ caramāno mahato rukkhassa tiṭṭhato sāravato atikkammeva sāraṁ, phegguṁ chetvā ādāya pakkanto "sāran"ti maññamāno.

Yañcassa sārena sārakaraṇīyaṁ tañcassa atthaṁ nānubhavissatī'ti.

Seyyathāpi vā pana, brāhmaṇa, puriso sāratthiko sāragavesī sārapariyesanaṁ caramāno mahato rukkhassa tiṭṭhato sāravato sāraññeva chetvā ādāya pakkameyya 'sāran'ti jānamāno.

Suppose there was another person in need of heartwood. And while wandering in search of heartwood he'd come across a large tree standing with heartwood. He'd cut out just the heartwood and depart knowing it was heartwood.

Tamenaṁ cakkhumā puriso disvā evaṁ vadeyya:

If a person with good eyesight saw him they'd say:

'aññāsi vatāyaṁ bhavaṁ puriso sāraṁ, aññāsi phegguṁ, aññāsi tacaṁ, aññāsi papaṭikaṁ, aññāsi sākhāpalāsaṁ.

'This gentleman knows what heartwood, softwood, bark, shoots, or branches and leaves are.

Tathā hayaṁ bhavaṁ puriso sāratthiko sāragavesī sārapariyesanaṁ caramāno mahato rukkhassa tiṭṭhato sāravato sāraññeva chetvā ādāya pakkanto "saran"ti jānamāno.

That's why he cut out just the heartwood and departed knowing it was heartwood.

Yañcassa sārena sārakaraṇīyaṁ tañcassa atthaṁ anubhavissatī'ti.

Whatever he needs to make from heartwood, he will succeed.'

Evameva kho, brāhmaṇa, idhekacco puggalo saddhā agārasmā anagāriyaṁ pabbajito hoti:

In the same way, take a certain person who goes forth from the lay life to homelessness, thinking:

'otiṇṇomhi jātiyā jarāya maraṇena sokehi paridevehi dukkhehi domanassehi upāyāsehi, dukkhotiṇṇo dukkhapareto,

'I'm swamped by rebirth, old age, and death; by sorrow, lamentation, pain, sadness, and distress. I'm swamped by suffering, mired in suffering.

appeva nāma imassa kevalassa dukkhakkhandhassa antakiriyā paññāyethā'ti.

Hopefully I can find an end to this entire mass of suffering.'

So evaṁ pabbajito samāno lābhasakkārasilokaṁ abhinibbatteti.

When they've gone forth they generate possessions, honor, and popularity.

So tena lābhasakkārasilokena attamano hoti paripuṇṇasaṅkappo.

They're happy with that, and they've got all they wished for.

So tena lābhasakkārasilokena attānukkaṁseti, paraṁ vambheti:

And they glorify themselves and put others down on account of that:

'ahamasmi lābhasakkārasilokavā, ime panaññe bhikkhū appaññātā appesakkhā'ti.

'I'm the one with possessions, honor, and popularity. These other mendicants are obscure and insignificant.'

Lābhasakkārasilokena ca ye aññe dhammā uttaritarā ca paṇītatarā ca tesaṁ dhammānaṁ sacchikiriyāya na chandaṁ janeti, na vāyamati, olīnavuttiko ca hoti sāthaliko.

They become lazy and slack regarding their possessions, honor, and popularity, not generating enthusiasm or trying to realize those things that are better and finer. …

Seyyathāpi so, brāhmaṇa, puriso sāratthiko sāragavesī sārapariyesanaṁ caramāno mahato rukkhassa tiṭṭhato sāravato atikkammeva sāraṁ atikkamma pheggaṁ atikkamma tacaṁ atikkamma papaṭikaṁ, sākhāpalāsaṁ chetvā ādāya pakkanto 'saran'ti maññamāno.

Yañcassa sārena sārakaraṇīyaṁ tañcassa atthaṁ nānubhavissati.

Tathūpamāhaṁ, brāhmaṇa, imaṁ puggalaṁ vadāmi.

They're like the person who mistakes branches and leaves for heartwood, I say.

Idha pana, brāhmaṇa, ekacco puggalo saddhā agārasmā anagāriyaṁ pabbajito hoti:

Next, take a gentleman who has gone forth from the lay life to homelessness …

'otiṇṇomhi jātiyā jarāya maraṇena sokehi paridevehi dukkhehi domanassehi upāyāsehi, dukkhotiṇṇo dukkhapareto,

appeva nāma imassa kevalassa dukkhakkhandhassa antakiriyā paññāyethā'ti.

So evaṁ pabbajito samāno lābhasakkārasilokaṁ abhinibbatteti.

So tena lābhasakkārasilokena na attamano hoti na paripuṇṇasaṅkappo.

So tena lābhasakkārasilokena na attānukkaṁseti, na paraṁ vambheti.

Lābhasakkārasilokena ca ye aññe dhammā uttaritarā ca paṇītatarā ca tesaṁ dhammānaṁ sacchikiriyāya chandaṁ janeti, vāyamati, anolīnavuttiko ca hoti asāthaliko.

So sīlasampadaṁ ārādheti.

So tāya sīlasampadāya attamano hoti, paripuṇṇasaṅkappo.

So tāya sīlasampadāya attānukkaṁseti, paraṁ vambheti:

'ahamasmi sīlavā kalyāṇadhammo, ime panaññe bhikkhū dussīlā pāpadhammā'ti.

Sīlasampadāya ca ye aññe dhammā uttaritarā ca paṇītatarā ca tesaṁ dhammānaṁ sacchikiriyāya na chandaṁ janeti, na vāyamati, olīnavuttiko ca hoti sāthaliko.

They become lazy and slack regarding their accomplishment in ethics, not generating enthusiasm or trying to realize those things that are better and finer. …

Seyyathāpi so, brāhmaṇa, puriso sāratthiko sāragavesī sārapariyesanaṁ caramāno mahato rukkhassa tiṭṭhato sāravato atikkammeva sāraṁ atikkamma pheggaṁ atikkamma tacaṁ, papaṭikaṁ chetvā ādāya pakkanto 'saran'ti maññamāno.

Yañcassa sārena sārakaraṇīyaṁ, tañcassa atthaṁ nānubhavissati.

Tathūpamāhaṁ, brāhmaṇa, imaṁ puggalaṁ vadāmi.

They're like the person who mistakes shoots for heartwood, I say.

Idha pana, brāhmaṇa, ekacco puggalo saddhā agārasmā anagāriyaṁ pabbajito hoti:

Next, take a gentleman who has gone forth from the lay life to homelessness …

'otiṇṇomhi jātiyā jarāya maraṇena sokehi paridevehi dukkhehi domanassehi upāyāsehi, dukkhotiṇṇo dukkhapareto,

appeva nāma imassa kevalassa dukkhakkhandhassa antakiriyā paññāyethā'ti.

So evaṁ pabbajito samāno lābhasakkārasilokaṁ abhinibbatteti.

So tena lābhasakkārasilokena na attamano hoti, na paripuṇṇasaṅkappo.

So tena lābhasakkārasilokena na attānukkaṁseti, na paraṁ vambheti.

Lābhasakkārasilokena ca ye aññe dhammā uttaritarā ca paṇītatarā ca tesaṁ dhammānaṁ sacchikiriyāya chandaṁ janeti, vāyamati, anolīnavuttiko ca hoti asāthaliko.

So sīlasampadaṁ ārādheti.

So tāya sīlasampadāya attamano hoti no ca kho paripuṇṇasaṅkappo.

So tāya sīlasampadāya na attānukkaṁseti, na paraṁ vambheti.

Sīlasampadāya ca ye aññe dhammā uttaritarā ca paṇītatarā ca tesaṁ dhammānaṁ sacchikiriyāya chandaṁ janeti, vāyamati, anolīnavuttiko ca hoti asāthaliko.

So samādhisampadaṁ ārādheti.

So tāya samādhisampadāya attamano hoti, paripuṇṇasaṅkappo.

So tāya samādhisampadāya attānukkaṁseti, paraṁ vambheti:

'ahamasmi samāhito ekaggacitto, ime panaññe bhikkhū asamāhitā vibbhantacittā'ti.

Samādhisampadāya ca ye aññe dhammā uttaritarā ca paṇītatarā ca, tesaṁ dhammānaṁ sacchikiriyāya na chandaṁ janeti, na vāyamati, olīnavuttiko ca hoti sāthaliko.

They become lazy and slack regarding their accomplishment in immersion, not generating enthusiasm or trying to realize those things that are better and finer. …

Seyyathāpi so, brāhmaṇa, puriso sāratthiko sāragavesī sārapariyesanaṁ caramāno mahato rukkhassa tiṭṭhato sāravato atikkammeva sāraṁ atikkamma phegguṁ, tacaṁ chetvā ādāya pakkanto 'sāran'ti maññamāno.

Yañcassa sārena sārakaraṇīyaṁ tañcassa atthaṁ nānubhavissati.

Tathūpamāhaṁ, brāhmaṇa, imaṁ puggalaṁ vadāmi.

They're like the person who mistakes bark for heartwood, I say.

Idha pana, brāhmaṇa, ekacco puggalo saddhā agārasmā anagāriyaṁ pabbajito hoti:

Next, take a gentleman who has gone forth from the lay life to homelessness …

'otiṇṇomhi jātiyā jarāya maraṇena …pe…

antakiriyā paññāyethā'ti.

So evaṁ pabbajito samāno lābhasakkārasilokaṁ abhinibbatteti.

So tena lābhasakkārasilokena na attamano hoti na paripuṇṇasaṅkappo.

So tena lābhasakkārasilokena na attānukkaṁseti, na paraṁ vambheti.

Lābhasakkārasilokena ca ye aññe dhammā uttaritarā ca paṇītatarā ca tesaṁ dhammānaṁ sacchikiriyāya chandaṁ janeti, vāyamati, anolīnavuttiko ca hoti asāthaliko.

So sīlasampadaṁ ārādheti.

So tāya sīlasampadāya attamano hoti, no ca kho paripuṇṇasaṅkappo.

So tāya sīlasampadāya na attānukkaṁseti, na paraṁ vambheti.

Sīlasampadāya ca ye aññe dhammā uttaritarā ca paṇītatarā ca tesaṁ dhammānaṁ sacchikiriyāya chandaṁ janeti, vāyamati, anolīnavuttiko ca hoti asāthaliko.

So samādhisampadaṁ ārādheti.

So tāya samādhisampadāya attamano hoti, no ca kho paripuṇṇasaṅkappo.

So tāya samādhisampadāya na attānukkaṁseti, na paraṁ vambheti.

Samādhisampadāya ca ye aññe dhammā uttaritarā ca paṇītatarā ca tesaṁ dhammānaṁ sacchikiriyāya chandaṁ janeti, vāyamati, anolīnavuttiko ca hoti asāthaliko.

So ñāṇadassanaṁ ārādheti.

So tena ñāṇadassanena attamano hoti, paripuṇṇasaṅkappo.

So tena ñāṇadassanena attānukkaṁseti, paraṁ vambheti:

'ahamasmi jānaṁ passaṁ viharāmi, ime panaññe bhikkhū ajānaṁ apassaṁ viharantī'ti.

Ñāṇadassanena ca ye aññe dhammā uttaritarā ca paṇītatarā ca tesaṁ dhammānaṁ sacchikiriyāya na chandaṁ janeti, na vāyamati, olīnavuttiko ca hoti sāthaliko.

They become lazy and slack regarding their knowledge and vision, not generating enthusiasm or trying to realize those things that are better and finer. …

Seyyathāpi so, brāhmaṇa, puriso sāratthiko sāragavesī sārapariyesanaṁ caramāno mahato rukkhassa tiṭṭhato sāravato atikkammeva sāraṁ, phegguṁ chetvā ādāya pakkanto 'saran'ti maññamāno.

Yañcassa sārena sārakaraṇīyaṁ tañcassa atthaṁ nānubhavissati.

Tathūpamāhaṁ, brāhmaṇa, imaṁ puggalaṁ vadāmi.

They're like the person who mistakes softwood for heartwood, I say.

Idha pana, brāhmaṇa, ekacco puggalo saddhā agārasmā anagāriyaṁ pabbajito hoti:

Next, take a gentleman who has gone forth from the lay life to homelessness, thinking:

'otiṇṇomhi jātiyā jarāya maraṇena sokehi paridevehi dukkhehi domanassehi upāyāsehi, dukkhotiṇṇo dukkhapareto,

'I'm swamped by rebirth, old age, and death; by sorrow, lamentation, pain, sadness, and distress. I'm swamped by suffering, mired in suffering.

appeva nāma imassa kevalassa dukkhakkhandhassa antakiriyā paññāyethā'ti.

Hopefully I can find an end to this entire mass of suffering.'

So evaṁ pabbajito samāno lābhasakkārasilokaṁ abhinibbatteti.

When they've gone forth they generate possessions, honor, and popularity.

So tena lābhasakkārasilokena na attamano hoti, na paripuṇṇasaṅkappo.

They're not happy with that, and haven't got all they wished for.

So tena lābhasakkārasilokena na attānukkaṁseti, na paraṁ vambheti.

They don't glorify themselves and put others down on account of that.

Lābhasakkārasilokena ca ye aññe dhammā uttaritarā ca paṇītatarā ca tesaṁ dhammānaṁ sacchikiriyāya chandaṁ janeti, vāyamati, anolīnavuttiko ca hoti asāthaliko.

They don't become lazy and slack regarding their possessions, honor, and popularity, but generate enthusiasm and try to realize those things that are better and finer.

So sīlasampadaṁ ārādheti.

They become accomplished in ethics.

So tāya sīlasampadāya attamano hoti, no ca kho paripuṇṇasaṅkappo.

They're happy with that, but they haven't got all they wished for.

So tāya sīlasampadāya na attānukkaṁseti, na paraṁ vambheti.

They don't glorify themselves and put others down on account of that.

Sīlasampadāya ca ye aññe dhammā uttaritarā ca paṇītatarā ca tesaṁ dhammānaṁ sacchikiriyāya chandaṁ janeti, vāyamati, anolīnavuttiko ca hoti asāthaliko.

They don't become lazy and slack regarding their accomplishment in ethics, but generate enthusiasm and try to realize those things that are better and finer.

So samādhisampadaṁ ārādheti.

They become accomplished in immersion.

So tāya samādhisampadāya attamano hoti, no ca kho paripuṇṇasaṅkappo.

They're happy with that, but they haven't got all they wished for.

So tāya samādhisampadāya na attānukkaṁseti, na paraṁ vambheti.

They don't glorify themselves and put others down on account of that.

Samādhisampadāya ca ye aññe dhammā uttaritarā ca paṇītatarā ca tesaṁ dhammānaṁ sacchikiriyāya chandaṁ janeti, vāyamati, anolīnavuttiko ca hoti asāthaliko.

They don't become lazy and slack regarding their accomplishment in immersion, but generate enthusiasm and try to realize those things that are better and finer.

So ñāṇadassanaṁ ārādheti.

They achieve knowledge and vision.

So tena ñāṇadassanena attamano hoti, no ca kho paripuṇṇasaṅkappo.

They're happy with that, but they haven't got all they wished for.

So tena ñāṇadassanena na attānukkaṁseti, na paraṁ vambheti.

They don't glorify themselves and put others down on account of that.

Ñāṇadassanena ca ye aññe dhammā uttaritarā ca paṇītatarā ca tesaṁ dhammānaṁ sacchikiriyāya chandaṁ janeti, vāyamati, anolīnavuttiko ca hoti asāthaliko.

They don't become lazy and slack regarding their knowledge and vision, but generate enthusiasm and try to realize those things that are better and finer.

Katame ca, brāhmaṇa, dhammā ñāṇadassanena uttaritarā ca paṇītatarā ca?

And what are those things that are better and finer than knowledge and vision?

Idha, brāhmaṇa, bhikkhu viviceva kāmehi vivicca akusalehi dhammehi savitakkaṁ savicāraṁ vivekajaṁ pītisukhaṁ paṭhamaṁ jhānaṁ upasampajja viharati.

Take a mendicant who, quite secluded from sensual pleasures, secluded from unskillful qualities, enters and remains in the first absorption, which has the rapture and bliss born of seclusion, while placing the mind and keeping it connected.

Ayampi kho, brāhmaṇa, dhammo ñāṇadassanena uttaritaro ca paṇītataro ca.

This is something better and finer than knowledge and vision.

Puna caparaṁ, brāhmaṇa, bhikkhu vitakkavicārānaṁ vūpasamā ajjhattaṁ sampasādanaṁ cetaso ekodibhāvaṁ avitakkaṁ avicāraṁ samādhijaṁ pītisukhaṁ dutiyaṁ jhānaṁ upasampajja viharati.

Furthermore, as the placing of the mind and keeping it connected are stilled, a mendicant enters and remains in the second absorption, which has the rapture and bliss born of immersion, with internal clarity and confidence, and unified mind, without placing the mind and keeping it connected.

Ayampi kho, brāhmaṇa, dhammo ñāṇadassanena uttaritaro ca paṇītataro ca.

This too is something better and finer than knowledge and vision.

Puna caparaṁ, brāhmaṇa, bhikkhu pītiyā ca virāgā upekkhako ca viharati, sato ca sampajāno sukhañca kāyena paṭisaṁvedeti, yaṁ taṁ ariyā ācikkhanti: 'upekkhako satimā sukhavihārī'ti tatiyaṁ jhānaṁ upasampajja viharati.

Furthermore, with the fading away of rapture, a mendicant enters and remains in the third absorption, where they meditate with equanimity, mindful and aware, personally experiencing the bliss of which the noble ones declare, 'Equanimous and mindful, one meditates in bliss.'

Ayampi kho, brāhmaṇa, dhammo ñāṇadassanena uttaritaro ca paṇītataro ca.

This too is something better and finer than knowledge and vision.

Puna caparaṁ, brāhmaṇa, bhikkhu sukhassa ca pahānā dukkhassa ca pahānā pubbeva somanassadomanassānaṁ atthaṅgamā adukkhamasukhaṁ upekkhāsatipārisuddhiṁ catutthaṁ jhānaṁ upasampajja viharati.

Furthermore, giving up pleasure and pain, and ending former happiness and sadness, a mendicant enters and remains in the fourth absorption, without pleasure or pain, with pure equanimity and mindfulness.

Ayampi kho, brāhmaṇa, dhammo ñāṇadassanena uttaritaro ca paṇītataro ca.

This too is something better and finer than knowledge and vision.

Puna caparaṁ, brāhmaṇa, bhikkhu sabbaso rūpasaññānaṁ samatikkamā paṭighasaññānaṁ atthaṅgamā nānattasaññānaṁ amanasikārā 'ananto ākāso'ti ākāsānañcāyatanaṁ upasampajja viharati.

Furthermore, a mendicant, going totally beyond perceptions of form, with the ending of perceptions of impingement, not focusing on perceptions of diversity, aware that 'space is infinite', enters and remains in the dimension of infinite space.

Ayampi kho, brāhmaṇa, dhammo ñāṇadassanena uttaritaro ca paṇītataro ca.

This too is something better and finer than knowledge and vision.

Puna caparaṁ, brāhmaṇa, bhikkhu sabbaso ākāsānañcāyatanaṁ samatikkamma 'anantaṁ viññāṇan'ti viññāṇañcāyatanaṁ upasampajja viharati.

Furthermore, a mendicant, going totally beyond the dimension of infinite space, aware that 'consciousness is infinite', enters and remains in the dimension of infinite consciousness.

Ayampi kho, brāhmaṇa, dhammo ñāṇadassanena uttaritaro ca paṇītataro ca.

This too is something better and finer than knowledge and vision.

Puna caparaṁ, brāhmaṇa, bhikkhu sabbaso viññāṇañcāyatanaṁ samatikkamma 'natthi kiñcī'ti ākiñcaññāyatanaṁ upasampajja viharati.

Furthermore, a mendicant, going totally beyond the dimension of infinite consciousness, aware that 'there is nothing at all', enters and remains in the dimension of nothingness.

Ayampi kho, brāhmaṇa, dhammo ñāṇadassanena uttaritaro ca paṇītataro ca.

This too is something better and finer than knowledge and vision.

Puna caparaṁ, brāhmaṇa, bhikkhu sabbaso ākiñcaññāyatanaṁ samatikkamma nevasaññānāsaññāyatanaṁ upasampajja viharati.

Furthermore, take a mendicant who, going totally beyond the dimension of nothingness, enters and remains in the dimension of neither perception nor non-perception.

Ayampi kho, brāhmaṇa, dhammo ñāṇadassanena uttaritaro ca paṇītataro ca.

This too is something better and finer than knowledge and vision.

Puna caparaṁ, brāhmaṇa, bhikkhu sabbaso nevasaññānāsaññāyatanaṁ samatikkamma saññāvedayitanirodhaṁ upasampajja viharati, paññāya cassa disvā āsavā parikkhīṇā honti.

Furthermore, take a mendicant who, going totally beyond the dimension of neither perception nor non-perception, enters and remains in the cessation of perception and feeling. And, having seen with wisdom, their defilements come to an end.

Ayampi kho, brāhmaṇa, dhammo ñāṇadassanena uttaritaro ca paṇītataro ca.

This too is something better and finer than knowledge and vision.

Ime kho, brāhmaṇa, dhammā ñāṇadassanena uttaritarā ca paṇītatarā ca.

These are the things that are better and finer than knowledge and vision.

Seyyathāpi so, brāhmaṇa, puriso sāratthiko sāragavesī sārapariyesanaṃ caramāno mahato rukkhassa tiṭṭhato sāravato sāraṃyeva chetvā ādāya pakkanto 'sāran'ti jānamāno.

Suppose there was a person in need of heartwood. And while wandering in search of heartwood he'd come across a large tree standing with heartwood. He'd cut out just the heartwood and depart knowing it was heartwood.

Yañcassa sārena sārakaraṇīyaṃ tañcassa atthaṃ anubhavissati.

Whatever he needs to make from heartwood, he will succeed.

Tathūpamāhaṃ, brāhmaṇa, imaṃ puggalaṃ vadāmi.

That's what this person is like, I say.

Iti kho, brāhmaṇa, nayidaṃ brahmacariyaṃ lābhasakkārasilokānisaṃsaṃ, na sīlasampadānisaṃsaṃ, na samādhisampadānisaṃsaṃ, na ñāṇadassanānisaṃsaṃ.

And so, brahmin, this spiritual life is not lived for the sake of possessions, honor, and popularity, or for accomplishment in ethics, or for accomplishment in immersion, or for knowledge and vision.

Yā ca kho ayaṃ, brāhmaṇa, akuppā cetovimutti—

Rather, the goal, heartwood, and final end of the spiritual life is the unshakable freedom of heart."

etadatthamidaṃ, brāhmaṇa, brahmacariyaṃ, etaṃ sāraṃ etaṃ pariyosānan"ti.

Evaṃ vutte, piṅgalakoccho brāhmaṇo bhagavantaṃ etadavoca:

When he had spoken, the brahmin Piṅgalakoccha said to the Buddha,

"abhikkantaṃ, bho gotama, abhikkantaṃ, bho gotama …pe…

"Excellent, Master Gotama! Excellent! …

upāsakaṃ maṃ bhavaṃ gotamo dhāretu ajjatagge pāṇupetaṃ saraṇaṃ gatan"ti.

From this day forth, may Master Gotama remember me as a lay follower who has gone for refuge for life."

Cūḷasāropamasuttaṁ niṭṭhitaṁ dasamaṁ.

Opammavaggo niṭṭhito tatiyo.

Tassuddānaṁ

Moḷiyaphaggunariṭṭhañca nāmo,

Andhavane kathipuṇṇaṁ nivāpo;

Rāsikaṇerumahāgajanāmo,

Sārūpamo puna piṅgalakoccho.

MAHAYAMAKAVAGGA

THE GREAT DIVISION OF PAIRS

31 Culagosingasutta:

The Shorter Discourse at Gosinga

Evaṁ me sutaṁ—

So I have heard.

ekaṁ samayaṁ bhagavā nātike viharati giñjakāvasathe.

At one time the Buddha was staying at Ñātika in the brick house.

Tena kho pana samayena āyasmā ca anuruddho āyasmā ca nandiyo āyasmā ca kimilo gosiṅgasālavanadāye viharanti.

Now at that time the venerables Anuruddha, Nandiya, and Kimbila were staying in the sal forest park at Gosiṅga.

Atha kho bhagavā sāyanhasamayaṁ paṭisallānā vuṭṭhito yena gosiṅgasālavanadāyo tenupasaṅkami.

Then in the late afternoon, the Buddha came out of retreat and went to that park.

Addasā kho dāyapālo bhagavantaṁ dūratova āgacchantaṁ.

The park keeper saw the Buddha coming off in the distance

Disvāna bhagavantaṁ etadavoca:

and said to him,

"mā, samaṇa, etaṁ dāyaṁ pāvisi.

"Don't come into this park, ascetic.

Santettha tayo kulaputtā attakāmarūpā viharanti.

There are three gentlemen who love themselves staying here.

Mā tesaṁ aphāsumakāsī"ti.

Don't disturb them."

Assosi kho āyasmā anuruddho dāyapālassa bhagavatā saddhiṁ mantayamānassa.

Anuruddha heard the park keeper conversing with the Buddha,

Sutvāna dāyapālaṁ etadavoca:

and said to him,

"mā, āvuso dāyapāla, bhagavantaṁ vāresi.

"Don't keep the Buddha out, good park keeper!

Satthā no bhagavā anuppatto"ti.

Our Teacher, the Blessed One, has arrived."

Atha kho āyasmā anuruddho yenāyasmā ca nandiyo āyasmā ca kimilo tenupasaṅkami; upasaṅkamitvā āyasmantañca nandiyaṁ āyasmantañca kimilaṁ etadavoca:

Then Anuruddha went to Nandiya and Kimbila, and said to them,

"abhikkamathāyasmanto, abhikkamathāyasmanto, satthā no bhagavā anuppatto"ti.

"Come forth, venerables, come forth! Our Teacher, the Blessed One, has arrived!"

Atha kho āyasmā ca anuruddho āyasmā ca nandiyo āyasmā ca kimilo bhagavantaṁ paccuggantvā—

Then Anuruddha, Nandiya, and Kimbila came out to greet the Buddha.

eko bhagavato pattacīvaraṁ paṭiggahesi, eko āsanaṁ paññapesi, eko pādodakaṁ upaṭṭhāpesi.

One received his bowl and robe, one spread out a seat, and one set out water for washing his feet.

Nisīdi bhagavā paññatte āsane.

He sat on the seat spread out

Nisajja kho bhagavā pāde pakkhālesi.

and washed his feet.

Tepi kho āyasmanto bhagavantaṁ abhivādetvā ekamantaṁ nisīdiṁsu.

Those venerables bowed and sat down to one side.

Ekamantaṁ nisinnaṁ kho āyasmantaṁ anuruddhaṁ bhagavā etadavoca:

The Buddha said to Anuruddha,

"Kacci vo, anuruddhā, khamanīyaṁ, kacci yāpanīyaṁ, kacci piṇḍakena na kilamathā"ti?

"I hope you're keeping well, Anuruddha and friends; I hope you're alright. And I hope you're having no trouble getting almsfood."

"Khamanīyaṁ, bhagavā, yāpanīyaṁ, bhagavā; na ca mayaṁ, bhante, piṇḍakena kilamāmā"ti.

"We're alright, Blessed One, we're getting by. And we have no trouble getting almsfood."

"Kacci pana vo, anuruddhā, samaggā sammodamānā avivadamānā khīrodakībhūtā aññamaññaṁ piyacakkhūhi sampassantā viharathā"ti?

"I hope you're living in harmony, appreciating each other, without quarreling, blending like milk and water, and regarding each other with kindly eyes?"

"Taggha mayaṁ, bhante, samaggā sammodamānā avivadamānā khīrodakībhūtā aññamaññaṁ piyacakkhūhi sampassantā viharāmā"ti.

"Indeed, sir, we live in harmony like this."

"Yathā kathaṁ pana tumhe, anuruddhā, samaggā sammodamānā avivadamānā khīrodakībhūtā aññamaññaṁ piyacakkhūhi sampassantā viharathā"ti?

"But how do you live this way?"

"Idha mayhaṁ, bhante, evaṁ hoti:

"In this case, sir, I think,

'lābhā vata me, suladdhaṁ vata me,

'I'm fortunate, so very fortunate,

yohaṁ evarūpehi sabrahmacārīhi saddhiṁ viharāmī'ti.

to live together with spiritual companions such as these.'

Tassa mayhaṁ, bhante, imesu āyasmantesu mettaṁ kāyakammaṁ paccupaṭṭhitaṁ āvi ceva raho ca;

I consistently treat these venerables with kindness by way of body, speech, and mind, both in public and in private.

mettaṁ vacīkammaṁ paccupaṭṭhitaṁ āvi ceva raho ca;

mettaṁ manokammaṁ paccupaṭṭhitaṁ āvi ceva raho ca.

Tassa mayhaṁ, bhante, evaṁ hoti:

I think,

'yannūnāhaṁ sakaṁ cittaṁ nikkhipitvā imesaṁyeva āyasmantānaṁ cittassa vasena vatteyyan'ti.

'Why don't I set aside my own ideas and just go along with these venerables' ideas?'

So kho ahaṁ, bhante, sakaṁ cittaṁ nikkhipitvā imesaṁyeva āyasmantānaṁ cittassa vasena vattāmi.

And that's what I do.

Nānā hi kho no, bhante, kāyā ekañca pana maññe cittan"ti.

Though we're different in body, sir, we're one in mind, it seems to me."

Āyasmāpi kho nandiyo …pe…

And the venerables Nandiya and Kimbila spoke likewise, and they added:

āyasmāpi kho kimilo bhagavantaṁ etadavoca:

"mayhampi, bhante, evaṁ hoti:

'lābhā vata me, suladdhaṁ vata me,

yohaṁ evarūpehi sabrahmacārīhi saddhiṁ viharāmī'ti.

Tassa mayhaṁ, bhante, imesu āyasmantesu mettaṁ kāyakammaṁ paccupaṭṭhitaṁ āvi ceva raho ca,

mettaṁ vacīkammaṁ paccupaṭṭhitaṁ āvi ceva raho ca,

mettaṁ manokammaṁ paccupaṭṭhitaṁ āvi ceva raho ca.

Tassa mayhaṁ, bhante, evaṁ hoti:

'yannūnāhaṁ sakaṁ cittaṁ nikkhipitvā imesaṁyeva āyasmantānaṁ cittassa vasena vatteyyan'ti.

So kho ahaṁ, bhante, sakaṁ cittaṁ nikkhipitvā imesaṁyeva āyasmantānaṁ cittassa vasena vattāmi.

Nānā hi kho no, bhante, kāyā ekañca pana maññe cittan"ti.

"Evaṁ kho mayaṁ, bhante, samaggā sammodamānā avivadamānā khīrodakībhūtā aññamaññaṁ piyacakkhūhi sampassantā viharāmā"ti.

"That's how we live in harmony, appreciating each other, without quarreling, blending like milk and water, and regarding each other with kindly eyes."

"Sādhu sādhu, anuruddhā.

"Good, good, Anuruddha and friends!

Kacci pana vo, anuruddhā, appamattā ātāpino pahitattā viharathā"ti?

But I hope you're living diligently, keen, and resolute?"

"Taggha mayaṁ, bhante, appamattā ātāpino pahitattā viharāmā"ti.

"Indeed, sir, we live diligently."

"Yathā kathaṁ pana tumhe, anuruddhā, appamattā ātāpino pahitattā viharathā"ti?

"But how do you live this way?"

"Idha, bhante, amhākaṁ yo paṭhamaṁ gāmato piṇḍāya paṭikkamati so āsanāni paññapeti, pānīyaṁ paribhojanīyaṁ upaṭṭhāpeti, avakkārapātiṁ upaṭṭhāpeti.

"In this case, sir, whoever returns first from almsround prepares the seats, and puts out the drinking water and the rubbish bin.

Yo pacchā gāmato piṇḍāya paṭikkamati, sace hoti bhuttāvaseso sace ākaṅkhati bhuñjati, no ce ākaṅkhati appaharite vā chaḍḍeti, appāṇake vā udake opilāpeti.

If there's anything left over, whoever returns last eats it if they like. Otherwise they throw it out where there is little that grows, or drop it into water that has no living creatures.

So āsanāni paṭisāmeti, pānīyaṁ paribhojanīyaṁ paṭisāmeti, avakkārapātiṁ paṭisāmeti, bhattaggaṁ sammajjati.

Then they put away the seats, drinking water, and rubbish bin, and sweep the refectory.

Yo passati pānīyaghaṭaṁ vā paribhojanīyaghaṭaṁ vā vaccaghaṭaṁ vā rittaṁ tucchaṁ so upaṭṭhāpeti.

If someone sees that the pot of water for washing, drinking, or the toilet is empty they set it up.

Sacassa hoti avisayhaṁ, hatthavikārena dutiyaṁ āmantetvā hatthavilaṅghakena upaṭṭhāpema, na tveva mayaṁ, bhante, tappaccayā vācaṁ bhindāma.

If he can't do it, he summons another with a wave of the hand, and they set it up by lifting it with their hands. But we don't break into speech for that reason.

Pañcāhikaṁ kho pana mayaṁ, bhante, sabbarattikaṁ dhammiyā kathāya sannisīdāma.

And every five days we sit together for the whole night and discuss the teachings.

Evaṁ kho mayaṁ, bhante, appamattā ātāpino pahitattā viharāmā"ti.

That's how we live diligently, keen, and resolute."

"Sādhu sādhu, anuruddhā.

"Good, good, Anuruddha and friends!

Atthi pana vo, anuruddhā, evaṁ appamattānaṁ ātāpīnaṁ pahitattānaṁ viharantānaṁ uttari manussadhammā alamariyañāṇadassanaviseso adhigato phāsuvihāro"ti?

But as you live diligently like this, have you achieved any superhuman distinction in knowledge and vision worthy of the noble ones, a meditation at ease?"

"Kiñhi no siyā, bhante.

"How could we not, sir?

Idha mayaṁ, bhante, yāvadeva ākaṅkhāma vivicceva kāmehi vivicca akusalehi dhammehi savitakkaṁ savicāraṁ vivekajaṁ pītisukhaṁ paṭhamaṁ jhānaṁ upasampajja viharāma.

Whenever we want, quite secluded from sensual pleasures, secluded from unskillful qualities, we enter and remain in the first absorption, which has the rapture and bliss born of seclusion, while placing the mind and keeping it connected.

Ayaṁ kho no, bhante, amhākaṁ appamattānaṁ ātāpīnaṁ pahitattānaṁ viharantānaṁ uttari manussadhammā alamariyañāṇadassanaviseso adhigato phāsuvihāro"ti.

This is a superhuman distinction in knowledge and vision worthy of the noble ones, a meditation at ease, that we have achieved while living diligent, keen, and resolute."

"Sādhu sādhu, anuruddhā.

"Good, good!

Etassa pana vo, anuruddhā, vihārassa samatikkamāya etassa vihārassa paṭippassaddhiyā atthañño uttari manussadhammā alamariyañāṇadassanaviseso adhigato phāsuvihāro"ti?

But have you achieved any other superhuman distinction for going beyond and stilling that meditation?"

"Kiñhi no siyā, bhante.

"How could we not, sir?

Idha mayaṁ, bhante, yāvadeva ākaṅkhāma vitakkavicārānaṁ vūpasamā ajjhattaṁ sampasādanaṁ cetaso ekodibhāvaṁ avitakkaṁ avicāraṁ samādhijaṁ pītisukhaṁ dutiyaṁ jhānaṁ upasampajja viharāma.

Whenever we want, as the placing of the mind and keeping it connected are stilled, we enter and remain in the second absorption, which has the rapture and bliss born of immersion, with internal clarity and confidence, and unified mind, without placing the mind and keeping it connected.

Etassa, bhante, vihārassa samatikkamāya etassa vihārassa paṭippassaddhiyā ayamañño uttari manussadhammā alamariyañāṇadassanaviseso adhigato phāsuvihāro”ti.

This is another superhuman distinction that we have achieved for going beyond and stilling that meditation.”

“Sādhu sādhu, anuruddhā.

“Good, good!

Etassa pana vo, anuruddhā, vihārassa samatikkamāya etassa vihārassa paṭippassaddhiyā atthañño uttari manussadhammā alamariyañāṇadassanaviseso adhigato phāsuvihāro”ti?

But have you achieved any other superhuman distinction for going beyond and stilling that meditation?”

“Kiñhi no siyā, bhante.

“How could we not, sir?

Idha mayaṁ, bhante, yāvadeva ākaṅkhāma pītiyā ca virāgā upekkhakā ca viharāma, satā ca sampajānā, sukhañca kāyena paṭisaṁvedema, yaṁ taṁ ariyā ācikkhanti: ‘upekkhako satimā sukhavihārī’ti tatiyaṁ jhānaṁ upasampajja viharāma.

Whenever we want, with the fading away of rapture, we enter and remain in the third absorption, where we meditate with equanimity, mindful and aware, personally experiencing the bliss of which the noble ones declare, ‘Equanimous and mindful, one meditates in bliss.’

Etassa, bhante, vihārassa samatikkamāya etassa vihārassa paṭippassaddhiyā ayamañño uttari manussadhammā alamariyañāṇadassanaviseso adhigato phāsuvihāro”ti.

This is another superhuman distinction that we have achieved for going beyond and stilling that meditation.”

“Sādhu sādhu, anuruddhā.

“Good, good!

Etassa pana vo, anuruddhā, vihārassa samatikkamāya etassa vihārassa paṭippassaddhiyā atthañño uttari manussadhammā alamariyañāṇadassanaviseso adhigato phāsuvihāro"ti?

But have you achieved any other superhuman distinction for going beyond and stilling that meditation?"

"Kiñhi no siyā, bhante.

"How could we not, sir?

Idha mayaṁ, bhante, yāvadeva ākaṅkhāma sukhassa ca pahānā dukkhassa ca pahānā, pubbeva somanassadomanassānaṁ atthaṅgamā, adukkhamasukhaṁ upekkhāsatipārisuddhiṁ catutthaṁ jhānaṁ upasampajja viharāma.

Whenever we want, with the giving up of pleasure and pain, and the ending of former happiness and sadness, we enter and remain in the fourth absorption, without pleasure or pain, with pure equanimity and mindfulness.

Etassa, bhante, vihārassa samatikkamāya etassa vihārassa paṭippassaddhiyā ayamañño uttari manussadhammā alamariyañāṇadassanaviseso adhigato phāsuvihāro"ti.

This is another superhuman distinction that we have achieved for going beyond and stilling that meditation."

"Sādhu sādhu, anuruddhā.

"Good, good!

Etassa pana vo, anuruddhā, vihārassa samatikkamāya etassa vihārassa paṭippassaddhiyā atthañño uttari manussadhammā alamariyañāṇadassanaviseso adhigato phāsuvihāro"ti?

But have you achieved any other superhuman distinction for going beyond and stilling that meditation?"

"Kiñhi no siyā, bhante.

"How could we not, sir?

Idha mayaṁ, bhante, yāvadeva ākaṅkhāma sabbaso rūpasaññānaṁ samatikkamā paṭighasaññānaṁ atthaṅgamā nānattasaññānaṁ amanasikārā 'ananto ākāso'ti ākāsānañcāyatanaṁ upasampajja viharāma.

Whenever we want, going totally beyond perceptions of form, with the ending of perceptions of impingement, not focusing on perceptions of diversity, aware that 'space is infinite', we enter and remain in the dimension of infinite space.

Etassa, bhante, vihārassa samatikkamāya etassa vihārassa paṭippassaddhiyā ayamañño uttari manussadhammā alamariyañāṇadassanaviseso adhigato phāsuvihāro"ti.

This is another superhuman distinction that we have achieved for going beyond and stilling that meditation."

"Sādhu sādhu, anuruddhā.

"Good, good!

Etassa pana vo, anuruddhā, vihārassa samatikkamāya etassa vihārassa paṭippassaddhiyā atthañño uttari manussadhammā alamariyañāṇadassanaviseso adhigato phāsuvihāro"ti?

But have you achieved any other superhuman distinction for going beyond and stilling that meditation?"

"Kiñhi no siyā, bhante.

"How could we not, sir?

Idha mayaṁ, bhante, yāvadeva ākaṅkhāma sabbaso ākāsānañcāyatanaṁ samatikkamma 'anantaṁ viññāṇan'ti viññāṇañcāyatanaṁ upasampajja viharāma …pe…

Whenever we want, going totally beyond the dimension of infinite space, aware that 'consciousness is infinite', we enter and remain in the dimension of infinite consciousness. …

sabbaso viññāṇañcāyatanaṁ samatikkamma 'natthi kiñcī'ti ākiñcaññāyatanaṁ upasampajja viharāma …pe…

going totally beyond the dimension of infinite consciousness, aware that 'there is nothing at all', we enter and remain in the dimension of nothingness. …

sabbaso ākiñcaññāyatanaṁ samatikkamma nevasaññānāsaññāyatanaṁ upasampajja viharāma.

going totally beyond the dimension of nothingness, we enter and remain in the dimension of neither perception nor non-perception.

Etassa, bhante, vihārassa samatikkamāya etassa vihārassa paṭippassaddhiyā ayamañño uttari manussadhammā alamariyañāṇadassanaviseso adhigato phāsuvihāro"ti.

This is another superhuman distinction that we have achieved for going beyond and stilling that meditation."

"Sādhu sādhu, anuruddhā.

"Good, good!

Etassa pana vo, anuruddhā, vihārassa samatikkamāya etassa vihārassa paṭippassaddhiyā atthañño uttari manussadhammā alamariyañāṇadassanaviseso adhigato phāsuvihāro”ti?

But have you achieved any other superhuman distinction for going beyond and stilling that meditation?”

“Kiñhi no siyā, bhante.

“How could we not, sir?

Idha mayaṁ, bhante, yāvadeva ākaṅkhāma sabbaso nevasaññānāsaññāyatanaṁ samatikkamma saññāvedayitanirodhaṁ upasampajja viharāma, paññāya ca no disvā āsavā parikkhīṇā.

Whenever we want, going totally beyond the dimension of neither perception nor non-perception, we enter and remain in the cessation of perception and feeling. And, having seen with wisdom, our defilements have come to an end.

Etassa, bhante, vihārassa samatikkamāya etassa vihārassa paṭippassaddhiyā ayamañño uttari manussadhammā alamariyañāṇadassanaviseso adhigato phāsuvihāro.

This is another superhuman distinction in knowledge and vision worthy of the noble ones, a meditation at ease, that we have achieved for going beyond and stilling that meditation.

Imamhā ca mayaṁ, bhante, phāsuvihārā aññaṁ phāsuvihāraṁ uttaritaraṁ vā paṇītataraṁ vā na samanupassāmā”ti.

And we don’t see any better or finer way of meditating at ease than this.”

“Sādhu sādhu, anuruddhā.

“Good, good!

Imamhā phāsuvihārā uttaritaro vā paṇītataro vā phāsuvihāro natthī”ti.

There is no better or finer way of meditating at ease than this.”

Atha kho bhagavā āyasmantañca anuruddhaṁ āyasmantañca nandiyaṁ āyasmantañca kimilaṁ dhammiyā kathāya sandassetvā samādapetvā samuttejetvā sampahaṁsetvā uṭṭhāyāsanā pakkāmi.

Then the Buddha educated, encouraged, fired up, and inspired the venerables Anuruddha, Nandiya, and Kimbila with a Dhamma talk, after which he got up from his seat and left.

Atha kho āyasmā ca anuruddho āyasmā ca nandiyo āyasmā ca kimilo bhagavantaṁ anusaṁyāyitvā tato paṭinivattitvā āyasmā ca nandiyo āyasmā ca kimilo āyasmantaṁ anuruddhaṁ etadavocuṁ:

The venerables then accompanied the Buddha for a little way before turning back.

Nandiya and Kimbila said to Anuruddha,

"kiṁ nu kho mayaṁ āyasmato anuruddhassa evamārocimha:

"Did we ever tell you that we had

'imāsañca imāsañca vihārasamāpattīnaṁ mayaṁ lābhino'ti, yaṁ no āyasmā anuruddho bhagavato sammukhā yāva āsavānaṁ khayā pakāsetī"ti?

gained such and such meditations and attainments, up to the ending of defilements, as you revealed to the Buddha?"

"Na kho me āyasmanto evamārocesuṁ:

"The venerables did not tell me that they had

'imāsañca imāsañca vihārasamāpattīnaṁ mayaṁ lābhino'ti, api ca me āyasmantānaṁ cetasā ceto paricca vidito:

gained such meditations and attainments. But I discovered it by comprehending your minds,

'imāsañca imāsañca vihārasamāpattīnaṁ ime āyasmanto lābhino'ti.

Devatāpi me etamatthaṁ ārocesuṁ:

and deities also told me.

'imāsañca imāsañca vihārasamāpattīnaṁ ime āyasmanto lābhino'ti.

Tamenaṁ bhagavatā pañhābhiputṭhena byākatan"ti.

I answered when the Buddha directly asked about it."

Atha kho dīgho parajano yakkho yena bhagavā tenupasaṅkami; upasaṅkamitvā bhagavantaṁ abhivādetvā ekamantaṁ aṭṭhāsi. Ekamantaṁ ṭhito kho dīgho parajano yakkho bhagavantaṁ etadavoca:

Then the native spirit Dīgha Parajana went up to the Buddha, bowed, stood to one side, and said to him,

"lābhā vata, bhante, vajjīnaṁ, suladdhalābhā vajjipajāya,

"The Vajjis are lucky! The Vajjian people are so very lucky

yattha tathāgato viharati arahaṁ sammāsambuddho, ime ca tayo kulaputtā—

that the Realized One, the perfected one, the fully awakened Buddha stays there, as well as these three gentlemen,

āyasmā ca anuruddho, āyasmā ca nandiyo, āyasmā ca kimilo"ti.

the venerables Anuruddha, Nandiya, and Kimbila.”

Dīghassa parajanassa yakkhassa saddaṁ sutvā bhummā devā saddamanussāvesuṁ:

Hearing the cry of Dīgha Parajana, the Earth Gods raised the cry …

“lābhā vata, bho, vajjīnaṁ, suladdhalābhā vajjipajāya,

yattha tathāgato viharati arahaṁ sammāsambuddho, ime ca tayo kulaputtā—

āyasmā ca anuruddho, āyasmā ca nandiyo, āyasmā ca kimilo”ti.

Bhummānaṁ devānaṁ saddaṁ sutvā cātumahārājikā devā …pe…

Hearing the cry of the Earth Gods, the Gods of the Four Great Kings …

tāvatiṁsā devā …pe…

the Gods of the Thirty-Three …

yāmā devā …pe…

the Gods of Yama …

tusitā devā …pe…

the Joyful Gods …

nimmānaratī devā …pe…

the Gods Who Love to Create …

paranimmitavasavattī devā …pe…

the Gods Who Control the Creations of Others …

brahmakāyikā devā saddamanussāvesuṁ:

the Gods of Brahmā’s Host raised the cry,

“lābhā vata, bho, vajjīnaṁ, suladdhalābhā vajjipajāya,

“The Vajjis are lucky! The Vajjian people are so very lucky

yattha tathāgato viharati arahaṁ sammāsambuddho, ime ca tayo kulaputtā—

that the Realized One, the perfected one, the fully awakened Buddha stays there,
as well as these three gentlemen,

āyasmā ca anuruddho, āyasmā ca nandiyo, āyasmā ca kimilo”ti.

the venerables Anuruddha, Nandiya, and Kimbila.”

Itiha te āyasmanto tena khaṇena tena layena tena muhuttena yāva brahmalokā viditā ahesuṁ.

And so at that moment, in that instant, those venerables were known as far as the Brahmā realm.

"Evametaṁ, dīgha, evametaṁ, dīgha.

"That's so true, Dīgha! That's so true!

Yasmāpi, dīgha, kulā ete tayo kulaputtā agārasmā anagāriyaṁ pabbajitā, tañcepi kulaṁ ete tayo kulaputte pasannacittaṁ anussareyya, tassapāssa kulassa dīgharattaṁ hitāya sukhāya.

If the family from which those three gentlemen went forth from the lay life to homelessness were to recollect those venerables with confident heart, that would be for that family's lasting welfare and happiness.

Yasmāpi, dīgha, kulaparivaṭṭā ete tayo kulaputtā agārasmā anagāriyaṁ pabbajitā, so cepi kulaparivaṭṭo ete tayo kulaputte pasannacitto anussareyya, tassapāssa kulaparivaṭṭassa dīgharattaṁ hitāya sukhāya.

If the family circle …

Yasmāpi, dīgha, gāmā ete tayo kulaputtā agārasmā anagāriyaṁ pabbajitā, so cepi gāmo ete tayo kulaputte pasannacitto anussareyya, tassapāssa gāmassa dīgharattaṁ hitāya sukhāya.

village …

Yasmāpi, dīgha, nigamā ete tayo kulaputtā agārasmā anagāriyaṁ pabbajitā, so cepi nigamo ete tayo kulaputte pasannacitto anussareyya, tassapāssa nigamassa dīgharattaṁ hitāya sukhāya.

town …

Yasmāpi, dīgha, nagarā ete tayo kulaputtā agārasmā anagāriyaṁ pabbajitā, tañcepi nagaraṁ ete tayo kulaputte pasannacittaṁ anussareyya, tassapāssa nagarassa dīgharattaṁ hitāya sukhāya.

city …

Yasmāpi, dīgha, janapadā ete tayo kulaputtā agārasmā anagāriyaṁ pabbajitā, so cepi janapado ete tayo kulaputte pasannacitto anussareyya, tassapāssa janapadassa dīgharattaṁ hitāya sukhāya.

country …

Sabbe cepi, dīgha, khattiyā ete tayo kulaputte pasannacittā anussareyyuṁ, sabbesānampāssa khattiyānaṁ dīgharattaṁ hitāya sukhāya.

all the aristocrats …

Sabbe cepi, dīgha, brāhmaṇā …pe…

all the brahmins …

sabbe cepi, dīgha, vessā …pe…

all the merchants …

sabbe cepi, dīgha, suddā ete tayo kulaputte pasannacittā anussareyyuṁ, sabbesānampāssa suddānaṁ dīgharattaṁ hitāya sukhāya.

all the workers were to recollect those venerables with confident heart, that would be for all those workers' lasting welfare and happiness.

Sadevako cepi, dīgha, loko samārako sabrahmako sassamaṇabrāhmaṇī pajā sadevamanussā ete tayo kulaputte pasannacittā anussareyya, sadevakassapāssa lokassa samārakassa sabrahmakassa sassamaṇabrāhmaṇiyā pajāya sadevamanussāya dīgharattaṁ hitāya sukhāya.

If the whole world—with its gods, Māras and Brahmās, this population with its ascetics and brahmins, gods and humans—were to recollect those venerables with confident heart, that would be for the whole world's lasting welfare and happiness.

Passa, dīgha, yāva ete tayo kulaputtā bahujanahitāya paṭipannā bahujanasukhāya lokānukampāya, atthāya hitāya sukhāya devamanussānan"ti.

See, Dīgha, how those three gentlemen are practicing for the welfare and happiness of the people, out of compassion for the world, for the benefit, welfare, and happiness of gods and humans!"

Idamavoca bhagavā.

That is what the Buddha said.

Attamano dīgho parajano yakkho bhagavato bhāsitaṁ abhinandīti.

Satisfied, the native spirit Dīgha Parajana was happy with what the Buddha said.

Cūḷagosiṅgasuttaṁ niṭṭhitaṁ paṭhamaṁ.

32 Mahagosingasutta:

The Longer Discourse at Gosinga

Evaṁ me sutaṁ—

So I have heard.

ekaṁ samayaṁ bhagavā gosiṅgasālavanadāye viharati sambahulehi abhiññātehi abhiññātehi therehi sāvakehi saddhiṁ—

At one time the Buddha was staying in the sal forest park at Gosiṅga, together with several well-known senior disciples, such as

āyasmatā ca sāriputtena āyasmatā ca mahāmoggallānena āyasmatā ca mahākassapena āyasmatā ca anuruddhena āyasmatā ca revatena āyasmatā ca ānandena, aññehi ca abhiññātehi abhiññātehi therehi sāvakehi saddhiṁ.

the venerables Sāriputta, Mahāmoggallāna, Mahākassapa, Anuruddha, Revata, Ānanda, and others.

Atha kho āyasmā mahāmoggallāno sāyanhasamayaṁ paṭisallānā vuṭṭhito yenāyasmā mahākassapo tenupasaṅkami; upasaṅkamitvā āyasmantaṁ mahākassapaṁ etadavoca:

Then in the late afternoon, Venerable Mahāmoggallāna came out of retreat, went to Venerable Mahākassapa, and said,

"āyāmāvuso, kassapa, yenāyasmā sāriputto tenupasaṅkamissāma dhammassavanāyā"ti.

"Come, Reverend Kassapa, let's go to Venerable Sāriputta to hear the teaching."

"Evamāvuso"ti kho āyasmā mahākassapo āyasmato mahāmoggallānassa paccassosi.

"Yes, reverend," Mahākassapa replied.

Atha kho āyasmā ca mahāmoggallāno āyasmā ca mahākassapo āyasmā ca anuruddho yenāyasmā sāriputto tenupasaṅkamiṁsu dhammassavanāya.

Then, together with Venerable Anuruddha, they went to Sāriputta to hear the teaching.

Addasā kho āyasmā ānando āyasmantañca mahāmoggallānaṁ āyasmantañca mahākassapaṁ āyasmantañca anuruddhaṁ yenāyasmā sāriputto tenupasaṅkamante dhammassavanāya.

Seeing them, Venerable Ānanda

Disvāna yenāyasmā revato tenupasaṅkami; upasaṅkamitvā āyasmantaṁ revataṁ etadavoca:

went to Venerable Revata, told him what was happening,

"upasaṅkamantā kho amū, āvuso revata, sappurisā yenāyasmā sāriputto tena dhammassavanāya.

and invited him also.

Āyāmāvuso revata, yenāyasmā sāriputto tenupasaṅkamissāma dhammassavanāyā"ti.

"Evamāvuso"ti kho āyasmā revato āyasmato ānandassa paccassosi.

Atha kho āyasmā ca revato āyasmā ca ānando yenāyasmā sāriputto tenupasaṅkamiṁsu dhammassavanāya.

Addasā kho āyasmā sāriputto āyasmantañca revataṁ āyasmantañca ānandaṁ dūratova āgacchante.

Sāriputta saw them coming off in the distance

Disvāna āyasmantaṁ ānandaṁ etadavoca:

and said to Ānanda,

"etu kho āyasmā ānando.

"Come, Venerable Ānanda.

Svāgataṁ āyasmato ānandassa bhagavato upaṭṭhākassa bhagavato santikāvacarassa.

Welcome to Ānanda, the Buddha's attendant, who is so close to the Buddha.

Ramaṇīyaṁ, āvuso ānanda, gosiṅgasālavanaṁ, dosinā ratti, sabbaphāliphullā sālā, dibbā, maññe, gandhā sampavanti;

Ānanda, the sal forest park at Gosiṅga is lovely, the night is bright, the sal trees are in full blossom, and divine scents seem to float on the air.

kathaṁrūpena, āvuso ānanda, bhikkhunā gosiṅgasālavanaṁ sobheyyā"ti?

What kind of mendicant would beautify this park?"

"Idhāvuso sāriputta, bhikkhu bahussuto hoti sutadharo sutasannicayo. Ye te dhammā ādikalyāṇā majjhekalyāṇā pariyosānakalyāṇā sātthā sabyañjanā; kevalaparipuṇṇaṁ parisuddhaṁ brahmacariyaṁ abhivadanti, tathārūpāssa dhammā bahussutā honti, dhātā, vacasā paricitā, manasānupekkhitā, diṭṭhiyā suppaṭividdhā.

"Reverend Sāriputta, it's a mendicant who is very learned, remembering and keeping what they've learned. These teachings are good in the beginning, good in the middle, and good in the end, meaningful and well-phrased, describing a spiritual practice that's entirely full and pure. They are very learned in such teachings, remembering them, reinforcing them by recitation, mentally scrutinizing them, and comprehending them theoretically.

So catassannaṁ parisānaṁ dhammaṁ deseti parimaṇḍalehi padabyañjanehi anuppabandhehi anusayasamugghātāya.

And they teach the four assemblies in order to uproot the underlying tendencies with well-rounded and systematic words and phrases.

Evarūpena kho, āvuso sāriputta, bhikkhunā gosiṅgasālavanaṁ sobheyyā"ti.

That's the kind of mendicant who would beautify this park."

Evaṁ vutte, āyasmā sāriputto āyasmantaṁ revataṁ etadavoca:

When he had spoken, Sāriputta said to Revata,

"byākataṁ kho, āvuso revata, āyasmatā ānandena yathāsakaṁ paṭibhānaṁ.

"Reverend Revata, Ānanda has answered by speaking from his heart.

Tattha dāni mayaṁ āyasmantaṁ revataṁ pucchāma:

And now we ask you the same question."

'ramaṇīyaṁ, āvuso revata, gosiṅgasālavanaṁ, dosinā ratti, sabbaphāliphullā sālā, dibbā, maññe, gandhā sampavanti;

kathaṁrūpena, āvuso revata, bhikkhunā gosiṅgasālavanaṁ sobheyyā'"ti?

"Idhāvuso sāriputta, bhikkhu paṭisallānārāmo hoti paṭisallānarato, ajjhattaṁ cetosamathamanuyutto anirākatajjhāno, vipassanāya samannāgato, brūhetā suññāgārānaṁ.

"Reverend Sāriputta, it's a mendicant who enjoys retreat and loves retreat. They're committed to inner serenity of the heart, they don't neglect absorption, they're endowed with discernment, and they frequent empty huts.

Evarūpena kho, āvuso sāriputta, bhikkhunā gosiṅgasālavanaṁ sobheyyā"ti.

That's the kind of mendicant who would beautify this park."

Evaṁ vutte, āyasmā sāriputto āyasmantaṁ anuruddhaṁ etadavoca:

When he had spoken, Sāriputta said to Anuruddha,

"byākataṁ kho, āvuso anuruddha, āyasmatā revatena yathāsakaṁ paṭibhānaṁ.

"Reverend Anuruddha, Revata has answered by speaking from his heart.

Tattha dāni mayaṁ āyasmantaṁ anuruddhaṁ pucchāma:

And now we ask you the same question."

'ramaṇīyaṁ, āvuso anuruddha, gosiṅgasālavanaṁ, dosinā ratti, sabbaphāliphullā sālā, dibbā, maññe, gandhā sampavanti;

kathaṁrūpena, āvuso anuruddha, bhikkhunā gosiṅgasālavanaṁ sobheyyā'"ti?

"Idhāvuso sāriputta, bhikkhu dibbena cakkhunā visuddhena atikkantamānusakena sahassaṁ lokānaṁ voloketi.

"Reverend Sāriputta, it's a mendicant who surveys the entire galaxy with clairvoyance that is purified and surpasses the human,

Seyyathāpi, āvuso sāriputta, cakkhumā puriso uparipāsādavaragato sahassaṁ nemimaṇḍalānaṁ volokeyya;

just as a person with good sight could survey a thousand wheel rims from the upper floor of a stilt longhouse.

evameva kho, āvuso sāriputta, bhikkhu dibbena cakkhunā visuddhena atikkantamānusakena sahassaṁ lokānaṁ voloketi.

Evarūpena kho, āvuso sāriputta, bhikkhunā gosiṅgasālavanaṁ sobheyyā"ti.

That's the kind of mendicant who would beautify this park."

Evaṁ vutte, āyasmā sāriputto āyasmantaṁ mahākassapaṁ etadavoca:

When he had spoken, Sāriputta said to Mahākassapa,

"byākataṁ kho, āvuso kassapa, āyasmatā anuruddhena yathāsakaṁ paṭibhānaṁ.

"Reverend Kassapa, Anuruddha has answered by speaking from his heart.

Tattha dāni mayaṁ āyasmantaṁ mahākassapaṁ pucchāma:

And now we ask you the same question."

'ramaṇīyaṁ, āvuso kassapa, gosiṅgasālavanaṁ, dosinā ratti, sabbaphāliphullā sālā, dibbā, maññe, gandhā sampavanti;

kathaṁrūpena, āvuso kassapa, bhikkhunā gosiṅgasālavanaṁ sobheyyā'"ti?

"Idhāvuso sāriputta, bhikkhu attanā ca āraññiko hoti āraññikattassa ca vaṇṇavādī, attanā ca piṇḍapātiko hoti piṇḍapātikattassa ca vaṇṇavādī, attanā ca paṁsukūliko hoti paṁsukūlikattassa ca vaṇṇavādī, attanā ca tecīvariko hoti tecīvarikattassa ca vaṇṇavādī, attanā ca appiccho hoti appicchatāya ca vaṇṇavādī, attanā ca santuṭṭho hoti santuṭṭhiyā ca vaṇṇavādī, attanā ca pavivitto hoti pavivekassa ca vaṇṇavādī, attanā ca asaṁsaṭṭho hoti asaṁsaggassa ca vaṇṇavādī, attanā ca āraddhavīriyo hoti vīriyārambhassa ca vaṇṇavādī, attanā ca sīlasampanno hoti sīlasampadāya ca vaṇṇavādī, attanā ca samādhisampanno hoti samādhisampadāya ca vaṇṇavādī, attanā ca paññāsampanno hoti paññāsampadāya ca vaṇṇavādī, attanā ca vimuttisampanno hoti vimuttisampadāya ca vaṇṇavādī, attanā ca vimuttiñāṇadassanasampanno hoti vimuttiñāṇadassanasampadāya ca vaṇṇavādī.

"Reverend Sāriputta, it's a mendicant who lives in the wilderness, eats only almsfood, wears rag robes, and owns just three robes; and they praise these things. They are of few wishes, content, secluded, aloof, and energetic; and they praise these things. They are accomplished in ethics, immersion, wisdom, freedom, and the knowledge and vision of freedom; and they praise these things.

Evarūpena kho, āvuso sāriputta, bhikkhunā gosingasālavanaṁ sobheyyā”ti.

That's the kind of mendicant who would beautify this park."

Evaṁ vutte, āyasmā sāriputto āyasmantaṁ mahāmoggallānaṁ etadavoca:

When he had spoken, Sāriputta said to Mahāmoggallāna,

“byākataṁ kho, āvuso moggallāna, āyasmatā mahākassapena yathāsakaṁ paṭibhānaṁ.

“Reverend Moggallāna, Mahākassapa has answered by speaking from his heart.

Tattha dāni mayaṁ āyasmantaṁ mahāmoggallānaṁ pucchāma:

And now we ask you the same question."

‘ramaṇīyaṁ, āvuso moggallāna, gosingasālavanaṁ, dosinā ratti, sabbaphāliphullā sālā, dibbā, maññe, gandhā sampavanti;

kathaṁrūpena, āvuso moggallāna, bhikkhunā gosingasālavanaṁ sobheyyā’”ti?

“Idhāvuso sāriputta, dve bhikkhū abhidhammakathaṁ kathenti, te aññamaññaṁ pañhaṁ pucchanti, aññamaññassa pañhaṁ puṭṭhā vissajjenti, no ca saṁsādenti, dhammī ca nesaṁ kathā pavattinī hoti.

“Reverend Sāriputta, it's when two mendicants engage in discussion about the teaching. They question each other and answer each other's questions without faltering, and their discussion on the teaching flows on.

Evarūpena kho, āvuso sāriputta, bhikkhunā gosingasālavanaṁ sobheyyā”ti.

That's the kind of mendicant who would beautify this park."

Atha kho āyasmā mahāmoggallāno āyasmantaṁ sāriputtaṁ etadavoca:

Then Mahāmoggallāna said to Sāriputta,

“byākataṁ kho, āvuso sāriputta, amhehi sabbeheva yathāsakaṁ paṭibhānaṁ.

“Each of us has spoken from our heart.

Tattha dāni mayaṁ āyasmantaṁ sāriputtaṁ pucchāma:

And now we ask you:

‘ramaṇīyaṁ, āvuso sāriputta, gosingasālavanaṁ, dosinā ratti, sabbaphāliphullā sālā, dibbā, maññe, gandhā sampavanti;

Sāriputta, the sal forest park at Gosiṅga is lovely, the night is bright, the sal trees are in full blossom, and divine scents seem to float on the air.

kathaṁrūpena, āvuso sāriputta, bhikkhunā gosiṅgasālavanaṁ sobheyyā'"ti?

What kind of mendicant would beautify this park?"

"Idhāvuso moggallāna, bhikkhu cittaṁ vasaṁ vatteti, no ca bhikkhu cittassa vasena vattati.

"Reverend Moggallāna, it's when a mendicant masters their mind and is not mastered by it.

So yāya vihārasamāpattiyā ākaṅkhati pubbaṇhasamayaṁ viharituṁ, tāya vihārasamāpattiyā pubbaṇhasamayaṁ viharati;

In the morning, they abide in whatever meditation or attainment they want.

yāya vihārasamāpattiyā ākaṅkhati majjhanhikasamayaṁ viharituṁ, tāya vihārasamāpattiyā majjhanhikasamayaṁ viharati;

At midday,

yāya vihārasamāpattiyā ākaṅkhati sāyanhasamayaṁ viharituṁ, tāya vihārasamāpattiyā sāyanhasamayaṁ viharati.

and in the evening, they abide in whatever meditation or attainment they want.

Seyyathāpi, āvuso moggallāna, rañño vā rājamahāmattassa vā nānārattānaṁ dussānaṁ dussakaraṇḍako pūro assa.

Suppose that a ruler or their minister had a chest full of garments of different colors.

So yaññadeva dussayugaṁ ākaṅkheyya pubbaṇhasamayaṁ pārupituṁ, taṁ tadeva dussayugaṁ pubbaṇhasamayaṁ pārupeyya;

In the morning, they'd don whatever pair of garments they wanted.

yaññadeva dussayugaṁ ākaṅkheyya majjhanhikasamayaṁ pārupituṁ, taṁ tadeva dussayugaṁ majjhanhikasamayaṁ pārupeyya;

At midday,

yaññadeva dussayugaṁ ākaṅkheyya sāyanhasamayaṁ pārupituṁ, taṁ tadeva dussayugaṁ sāyanhasamayaṁ pārupeyya.

and in the evening, they'd don whatever pair of garments they wanted.

Evameva kho, āvuso moggallāna, bhikkhu cittaṁ vasaṁ vatteti, no ca bhikkhu cittassa vasena vattati.

In the same way, a mendicant masters their mind and is not mastered by it.

So yāya vihārasamāpattiyā ākaṅkhati pubbaṇhasamayaṃ viharituṃ, tāya vihārasamāpattiyā pubbaṇhasamayaṃ viharati;

In the morning, they abide in whatever meditation or attainment they want.

yāya vihārasamāpattiyā ākaṅkhati majjhanhikasamayaṃ viharituṃ, tāya vihārasamāpattiyā majjhanhikasamayaṃ viharati;

At midday,

yāya vihārasamāpattiyā ākaṅkhati sāyanhasamayaṃ viharituṃ, tāya vihārasamāpattiyā sāyanhasamayaṃ viharati.

and in the evening, they abide in whatever meditation or attainment they want.

Evarūpena kho, āvuso moggallāna, bhikkhunā gosiṅgasālavanaṃ sobheyyā”ti.

That's the kind of mendicant who would beautify this park.”

Atha kho āyasmā sāriputto te āyasmante etadavoca:

Then Sāriputta said to those venerables,

“byākataṃ kho, āvuso, amhehi sabbeheva yathāsakaṃ paṭibhānaṃ.

“Each of us has spoken from the heart.

Āyāmāvuso, yena bhagavā tenupasaṅkamissāma; upasaṅkamitvā etamatthaṃ bhagavato ārocessāma.

Come, reverends, let's go to the Buddha, and inform him about this.

Yathā no bhagavā byākarissati tathā naṃ dhāressāmā”ti.

As he answers, so we'll remember it.”

“Evamāvuso”ti kho te āyasmanto āyasmato sāriputtassa paccassosuṃ.

“Yes, reverend,” they replied.

Atha kho te āyasmanto yena bhagavā tenupasaṅkamiṃsu; upasaṅkamitvā bhagavantaṃ abhivādetvā ekamantaṃ nisīdiṃsu. Ekamantaṃ nisinno kho āyasmā sāriputto bhagavantaṃ etadavoca:

Then those venerables went to the Buddha, bowed, and sat down to one side. Venerable Sāriputta told the Buddha of how the mendicants had come to see him, and how he had asked Ānanda:

“idha, bhante, āyasmā ca revato āyasmā ca ānando yenāhaṃ tenupasaṅkamiṃsu dhammassavanāya.

Addasaṁ kho ahaṁ, bhante, āyasmantañca revataṁ āyasmantañca ānandaṁ dūratova āgacchante.

Disvāna āyasmantaṁ ānandaṁ etadavocaṁ:

'etu kho āyasmā ānando.

Svāgataṁ āyasmato ānandassa bhagavato upaṭṭhākassa bhagavato santikāvacarassa.

Ramaṇīyaṁ, āvuso ānanda, gosiṅgasālavanaṁ, dosinā ratti, sabbaphāliphullā sālā, dibbā, maññe, gandhā sampavanti;

"'Ānanda, the sal forest park at Gosiṅga is lovely, the night is bright, the sal trees are in full blossom, and divine scents seem to float on the air.

kathaṁrūpena, āvuso ānanda, bhikkhunā gosiṅgasālavanaṁ sobheyyā'ti?

What kind of mendicant would beautify this park?'

Evaṁ vutte, bhante, āyasmā ānando maṁ etadavoca:

When I had spoken, Ānanda said to me:

'idhāvuso, sāriputta, bhikkhu bahussuto hoti sutadharo …pe…

'Reverend Sāriputta, it's a mendicant who is very learned …

anusayasamugghātāya.

Evarūpena kho, āvuso sāriputta, bhikkhunā gosiṅgasālavanaṁ sobheyyā'"ti.

That's the kind of mendicant who would beautify this park.'"

"Sādhu sādhu, sāriputta.

"Good, good, Sāriputta!

Yathā taṁ ānandova sammā byākaramāno byākareyya.

Ānanda answered in the right way for him.

Ānando hi, sāriputta, bahussuto sutadharo sutasannicayo. Ye te dhammā ādikalyāṇā majjhekalyāṇā pariyosānakalyāṇā sātthā sabyañjanā; kevalaparipuṇṇaṁ parisuddhaṁ brahmacariyaṁ abhivadanti, tathārūpāssa dhammā bahussutā honti, dhātā, vacasā paricitā, manasānupekkhitā, diṭṭhiyā suppaṭividdhā.

For Ānanda is very learned …"

So catassannaṁ parisānaṁ dhammaṁ deseti parimaṇḍalehi padabyañjanehi anuppabandhehi anusayasamugghātāyā"ti.

"Evaṁ vutte, ahaṁ, bhante, āyasmantaṁ revataṁ etadavocaṁ:

"Next I asked Revata the same question.

'byākataṁ kho, āvuso revata, āyasmatā ānandena yathāsakaṁ paṭibhānaṁ.

Tattha dāni mayaṁ āyasmantaṁ revataṁ pucchāma—

ramaṇīyaṁ, āvuso revata, gosiṅgasālavanaṁ, dosinā ratti, sabbaphāliphullā sālā, dibbā maññe gandhā sampavanti.

Kathaṁrūpena, āvuso revata, bhikkhunā gosiṅgasālavanaṁ sobheyyā'ti?

Evaṁ vutte, bhante, āyasmā revato maṁ etadavoca:

He said:

'idhāvuso sāriputta, bhikkhu paṭisallānārāmo hoti paṭisallānarato, ajjhattaṁ cetosamathamanuyutto, anirākatajjhāno, vipassanāya samannāgato, brūhetā suññāgārānaṁ.

'It's a mendicant who enjoys retreat …

Evarūpena kho, āvuso sāriputta, bhikkhunā gosiṅgasālavanaṁ sobheyyā'"ti.

That's the kind of mendicant who would beautify this park.'"

"Sādhu sādhu, sāriputta.

"Good, good, Sāriputta!

Yathā taṁ revatova sammā byākaramāno byākareyya.

Revata answered in the right way for him.

Revato hi, sāriputta, paṭisallānārāmo paṭisallānarato, ajjhattaṁ cetosamathamanuyutto anirākatajjhāno, vipassanāya samannāgato brūhetā suññāgārānan"ti.

For Revata enjoys retreat …"

"Evaṁ vutte, ahaṁ, bhante, āyasmantaṁ anuruddhaṁ etadavocaṁ:

"Next I asked Anuruddha the same question.

'byākataṁ kho, āvuso anuruddha, āyasmatā revatena …pe…

kathaṁrūpena, āvuso anuruddha, bhikkhunā gosiṅgasālavanaṁ sobheyyā'ti.

Evaṁ vutte, bhante, āyasmā anuruddho maṁ etadavoca:

He said:

'idhāvuso sāriputta, bhikkhu dibbena cakkhunā visuddhena atikkantamānusakena sahassaṁ lokānaṁ voloketi.

'It's a mendicant who surveys the entire galaxy with clairvoyance that is purified and surpasses the human …

Seyyathāpi, āvuso sāriputta, cakkhumā puriso …pe…

evarūpena kho, āvuso sāriputta, bhikkhunā gosiṅgasālavanaṃ sobheyyā'"ti.

That's the kind of mendicant who would beautify this park.'"

"Sādhu sādhu, sāriputta, yathā taṃ anuruddhova sammā byākaramāno byākareyya.

"Good, good, Sāriputta! Anuruddha answered in the right way for him.

Anuruddho hi, sāriputta, dibbena cakkhunā visuddhena atikkantamānusakena sahassaṃ lokānaṃ voloketī'"ti.

For Anuruddha surveys the entire galaxy with clairvoyance that is purified and surpasses the human."

"Evaṃ vutte, ahaṃ, bhante, āyasmantaṃ mahākassapaṃ etadavocaṃ:

"Next I asked Mahākassapa the same question.

'byākataṃ kho, āvuso kassapa, āyasmatā anuruddhena yathāsakaṃ paṭibhānaṃ.

Tattha dāni mayaṃ āyasmantaṃ mahākassapaṃ pucchāma …pe…

kathaṃrūpena kho, āvuso kassapa, bhikkhunā gosiṅgasālavanaṃ sobheyyā'ti?

Evaṃ vutte, bhante, āyasmā mahākassapo maṃ etadavoca:

He said:

'idhāvuso sāriputta, bhikkhu attanā ca āraññiko hoti āraññikattassa ca vaṇṇavādī, attanā ca piṇḍapātiko hoti …pe… attanā ca paṃsukūliko hoti …pe… attanā ca tecīvariko hoti …pe… attanā ca appiccho hoti …pe… attanā ca santuṭṭho hoti …pe… attanā ca pavivitto hoti …pe… attanā ca asaṃsaṭṭho hoti … pe… attanā ca āraddhavīriyo hoti …pe… attanā ca sīlasampanno hoti …pe… attanā ca samādhisampanno hoti …pe… attanā ca paññāsampanno hoti … attanā ca vimuttisampanno hoti … attanā ca vimuttiñāṇadassanasampanno hoti vimuttiñāṇadassanasampadāya ca vaṇṇavādī.

'It's a mendicant who lives in the wilderness … and is accomplished in the knowledge and vision of freedom; and they praise these things.

Evarūpena kho, āvuso sāriputta, bhikkhunā gosiṅgasālavanaṃ sobheyyā'"ti.

That's the kind of mendicant who would beautify this park.'"

"Sādhu sādhu, sāriputta.

"Good, good, Sāriputta!

Yathā taṁ kassapova sammā byākaramāno byākareyya.

Kassapa answered in the right way for him.

Kassapo hi, sāriputta, attanā ca āraññiko āraññikattassa ca vaṇṇavādī, attanā ca piṇḍapātiko piṇḍapātikattassa ca vaṇṇavādī, attanā ca paṁsukūliko paṁsukūlikattassa ca vaṇṇavādī, attanā ca tecīvariko tecīvarikattassa ca vaṇṇavādī, attanā ca appiccho appicchatāya ca vaṇṇavādī, attanā ca santuṭṭho santuṭṭhiyā ca vaṇṇavādī, attanā ca pavivitto pavivekassa ca vaṇṇavādī, attanā ca asaṁsaṭṭho asaṁsaggassa ca vaṇṇavādī, attanā ca āraddhavīriyo vīriyārambhassa ca vaṇṇavādī, attanā ca sīlasampanno sīlasampadāya ca vaṇṇavādī, attanā ca samādhisampanno samādhisampadāya ca vaṇṇavādī, attanā ca paññāsampanno paññāsampadāya ca vaṇṇavādī, attanā ca vimuttisampanno vimuttisampadāya ca vaṇṇavādī, attanā ca vimuttiñāṇadassanasampanno vimuttiñāṇadassanasampadāya ca vaṇṇavādī”ti.

For Kassapa lives in the wilderness … and is accomplished in the knowledge and vision of freedom; and he praises these things.”

“Evaṁ vutte, ahaṁ bhante āyasmantaṁ mahāmoggallānaṁ etadavocaṁ:

“Next I asked Mahāmoggallāna the same question.

‘byākataṁ kho, āvuso moggallāna, āyasmatā mahākassapena yathāsakaṁ paṭibhānaṁ.

Tattha dāni mayaṁ āyasmantaṁ mahāmoggallānaṁ pucchāma …pe…

kathaṁrūpena, āvuso moggallāna, bhikkhunā gosiṅgasālavanaṁ sobheyyā’ti?

Evaṁ vutte, bhante, āyasmā mahāmoggallāno maṁ etadavoca:

He said:

‘idhāvuso sāriputta, dve bhikkhū abhidhammakathaṁ kathenti. Te aññamaññaṁ pañhaṁ pucchanti, aññamaññassa pañhaṁ puṭṭhā vissajjenti, no ca saṁsādenti, dhammī ca nesaṁ kathā pavattinī hoti.

‘It’s when two mendicants engage in discussion about the teaching …

Evarūpena kho, āvuso sāriputta, bhikkhunā gosiṅgasālavanaṁ sobheyyā’”ti.

That’s the kind of mendicant who would beautify this park.’”

“Sādhu sādhu, sāriputta, yathā taṁ moggallānova sammā byākaramāno byākareyya.

“Good, good, Sāriputta! Moggallāna answered in the right way for him.

Moggallāno hi, sāriputta, dhammakathiko”ti.

For Moggallāna is a Dhamma speaker.”

Evaṁ vutte, āyasmā mahāmoggallāno bhagavantaṁ etadavoca:

When he had spoken, Moggallāna said to the Buddha,

"atha khvāhaṁ, bhante, āyasmantaṁ sāriputtaṁ etadavocaṁ:

"Next, I asked Sāriputta:

'byākataṁ kho, āvuso sāriputta, amhehi sabbeheva yathāsakaṁ paṭibhānaṁ.

'Each of us has spoken from our heart.

Tattha dāni mayaṁ āyasmantaṁ sāriputtaṁ pucchāma—

And now we ask you:

ramaṇīyaṁ, āvuso sāriputta, gosiṅgasālavanaṁ, dosinā ratti, sabbaphāliphullā sālā, dibbā, maññe, gandhā sampavanti.

Sāriputta, the sal forest park at Gosiṅga is lovely, the night is bright, the sal trees are in full blossom, and divine scents seem to float on the air.

Kathaṁrūpena, āvuso sāriputta, bhikkhunā gosiṅgasālavanaṁ sobheyyā'ti?

What kind of mendicant would beautify this park?'

Evaṁ vutte, bhante, āyasmā sāriputto maṁ etadavoca:

When I had spoken, Sāriputta said to me:

'idhāvuso moggallāna, bhikkhu cittaṁ vasaṁ vatteti no ca bhikkhu cittassa vasena vattati.

'Reverend Moggallāna, it's when a mendicant masters their mind and is not mastered by it …

So yāya vihārasamāpattiyā ākaṅkhati pubbaṇhasamayaṁ viharituṁ, tāya vihārasamāpattiyā pubbaṇhasamayaṁ viharati;

yāya vihārasamāpattiyā ākaṅkhati majjhanhikasamayaṁ viharituṁ, tāya vihārasamāpattiyā majjhanhikasamayaṁ viharati;

yāya vihārasamāpattiyā ākaṅkhati sāyanhasamayaṁ viharituṁ, tāya vihārasamāpattiyā sāyanhasamayaṁ viharati.

Seyyathāpi, āvuso moggallāna, rañño vā rājamahāmattassa vā nānārattānaṁ dussānaṁ dussakaraṇḍako pūro assa.

So yaññadeva dussayugaṁ ākaṅkheyya pubbaṇhasamayaṁ pārupituṁ, taṁ tadeva dussayugaṁ pubbaṇhasamayaṁ pārupeyya;

yaññadeva dussayugaṁ ākaṅkheyya majjhanhikasamayaṁ pārupituṁ, taṁ tadeva dussayugaṃ majjhanhikasamayaṃ pārupeyya;

yaññadeva dussayugaṃ ākaṅkheyya sāyanhasamayaṃ pārupituṃ, taṃ tadeva dussayugaṃ sāyanhasamayaṃ pārupeyya.

Evameva kho, āvuso moggallāna, bhikkhu cittaṃ vasaṃ vatteti, no ca bhikkhu cittassa vasena vattati.

So yāya vihārasamāpattiyā ākaṅkhati pubbaṇhasamayaṃ viharituṃ, tāya vihārasamāpattiyā pubbaṇhasamayaṃ viharati;

yāya vihārasamāpattiyā ākaṅkhati majjhanhikasamayaṃ viharituṃ, tāya vihārasamāpattiyā majjhanhikasamayaṃ viharati;

yāya vihārasamāpattiyā ākaṅkhati sāyanhasamayaṃ viharituṃ, tāya vihārasamāpattiyā sāyanhasamayaṃ viharati.

Evarūpena kho, āvuso moggallāna, bhikkhunā gosiṅgasālavanaṃ sobheyyā’”ti.

That's the kind of mendicant who would beautify this park.'"

"Sādhu sādhu, moggallāna.

"Good, good, Moggallāna!

Yathā taṃ sāriputtova sammā byākaramāno byākareyya.

Sāriputta answered in the right way for him.

Sāriputto hi, moggallāna, cittaṃ vasaṃ vatteti no ca sāriputto cittassa vasena vattati.

For Sāriputta masters his mind and is not mastered by it …"

So yāya vihārasamāpattiyā ākaṅkhati pubbaṇhasamayaṃ viharituṃ, tāya vihārasamāpattiyā pubbaṇhasamayaṃ viharati;

yāya vihārasamāpattiyā ākaṅkhati majjhanhikasamayaṃ viharituṃ, tāya vihārasamāpattiyā majjhanhikasamayaṃ viharati;

yāya vihārasamāpattiyā ākaṅkhati sāyanhasamayaṃ viharituṃ, tāya vihārasamāpattiyā sāyanhasamayaṃ viharatī”ti.

Evaṃ vutte, āyasmā sāriputto bhagavantaṃ etadavoca:

When he had spoken, Sāriputta asked the Buddha,

"kassa nu kho, bhante, subhāsitan”ti?

"Sir, who has spoken well?"

"Sabbesaṃ vo, sāriputta, subhāsitaṃ pariyāyena.

"You've all spoken well in your own way.

Api ca mamapi suṇātha yathārūpena bhikkhunā gosiṅgasālavanaṁ sobheyya.

However, listen to me also as to what kind of mendicant would beautify this sal forest park at Gosiṅga.

Idha, sāriputta, bhikkhu pacchābhattaṁ piṇḍapātapaṭikkanto nisīdati pallaṅkaṁ ābhujitvā ujuṁ kāyaṁ paṇidhāya parimukhaṁ satiṁ upaṭṭhapetvā:

It's a mendicant who, after the meal, returns from almsround, sits down cross-legged, sets their body straight, and establishes mindfulness in front of them, thinking:

'na tāvāhaṁ imaṁ pallaṅkaṁ bhindissāmi yāva me nānupādāya āsavehi cittaṁ vimuccissatī'ti.

'I will not break this sitting posture until my mind is freed from the defilements by not grasping!'

Evarūpena kho, sāriputta, bhikkhunā gosiṅgasālavanaṁ sobheyyā"ti.

That's the kind of mendicant who would beautify this park."

Idamavoca bhagavā.

That is what the Buddha said.

Attamanā te āyasmanto bhagavato bhāsitaṁ abhinandunti.

Satisfied, those venerables were happy with what the Buddha said.

Mahāgosiṅgasuttaṁ niṭṭhitaṁ dutiyaṁ.

33 Mahagopalakasutta:

The Longer Discourse on the Cowherd

Evaṁ me sutaṁ—

So I have heard.

ekaṁ samayaṁ bhagavā sāvatthiyaṁ viharati jetavane anāthapiṇḍikassa ārāme.

At one time the Buddha was staying near Sāvatthī in Jeta's Grove, Anāthapiṇḍika's monastery.

Tatra kho bhagavā bhikkhū āmantesi:

There the Buddha addressed the mendicants,

"bhikkhavo"ti.

"Mendicants!"

"Bhadante"ti te bhikkhū bhagavato paccassosuṁ.

"Venerable sir," they replied.

Bhagavā etadavoca:

The Buddha said this:

"Ekādasahi, bhikkhave, aṅgehi samannāgato gopālako abhabbo gogaṇaṁ pariharituṁ phātiṁ kātuṁ.

"Mendicants, a cowherd with eleven factors can't maintain and expand a herd of cattle.

Katamehi ekādasahi?

What eleven?

Idha, bhikkhave, gopālako na rūpaññū hoti, na lakkhaṇakusalo hoti, na āsāṭikaṁ hāretā hoti, na vaṇaṁ paṭicchādetā hoti, na dhūmaṁ kattā hoti, na titthaṁ jānāti, na pītaṁ jānāti, na vīthiṁ jānāti, na gocarakusalo hoti anavasesadohī ca hoti. Ye te usabhā gopitaro gopariṇāyakā te na atirekapūjāya pūjetā hoti.

It's when a cowherd doesn't know form, is unskilled in characteristics, doesn't pick out flies' eggs, doesn't dress wounds, doesn't smoke out pests, doesn't know the ford, doesn't know satisfaction, doesn't know the trail, is not skilled in pastures, milks dry, and doesn't show extra respect to the bulls who are fathers and leaders of the herd.

Imehi kho, bhikkhave, ekādasahi aṅgehi samannāgato gopālako abhabbo gogaṇaṁ pariharituṁ phātiṁ kātuṁ.

A cowherd with these eleven factors can't maintain and expand a herd of cattle.

Evameva kho, bhikkhave, ekādasahi dhammehi samannāgato bhikkhu abhabbo imasmiṁ dhammavinaye vuddhiṁ virūḷhiṁ vepullaṁ āpajjituṁ.

In the same way, a mendicant with eleven qualities can't achieve growth, improvement, or maturity in this teaching and training.

Katamehi ekādasahi?

What eleven?

Idha, bhikkhave, bhikkhu na rūpaññū hoti, na lakkhaṇakusalo hoti, na āsāṭikaṁ hāretā hoti, na vaṇaṁ paṭicchādetā hoti, na dhūmaṁ kattā hoti, na titthaṁ jānāti, na pītaṁ jānāti, na vīthiṁ jānāti, na gocarakusalo hoti, anavasesadohī ca hoti. Ye te bhikkhū therā rattaññū cirapabbajitā saṅghapitaro saṅghapariṇāyakā te na atirekapūjāya pūjetā hoti.

It's when a mendicant doesn't know form, is unskilled in characteristics, doesn't pick out flies' eggs, doesn't dress wounds, doesn't smoke out pests, doesn't know the ford, doesn't know satisfaction, doesn't know the trail, is not skilled in pastures, milks dry, and doesn't show extra respect to senior mendicants of long standing, long gone forth, fathers and leaders of the Saṅgha.

Kathañca, bhikkhave, bhikkhu na rūpaññū hoti?

And how does a mendicant not know form?

Idha, bhikkhave, bhikkhu yaṁ kiñci rūpaṁ sabbaṁ rūpaṁ 'cattāri mahābhūtāni, catunnañca mahābhūtānaṁ upādāyarūpan'ti yathābhūtaṁ nappajānāti.

It's when a mendicant doesn't truly understand that all form is the four primary elements, or form derived from the four primary elements.

Evaṁ kho, bhikkhave, bhikkhu na rūpaññū hoti.

That's how a mendicant doesn't know form.

Kathañca, bhikkhave, bhikkhu na lakkhaṇakusalo hoti?

And how is a mendicant not skilled in characteristics?

Idha, bhikkhave, bhikkhu 'kammalakkhaṇo bālo, kammalakkhaṇo paṇḍito'ti yathābhūtaṁ nappajānāti.

It's when a mendicant doesn't understand that a fool is characterized by their deeds, and an astute person is characterized by their deeds.

Evaṁ kho, bhikkhave, bhikkhu na lakkhaṇakusalo hoti.

That's how a mendicant isn't skilled in characteristics.

Kathañca, bhikkhave, bhikkhu na āsāṭikaṁ hāretā hoti?

And how does a mendicant not pick out flies' eggs?

Idha, bhikkhave, bhikkhu uppannaṁ kāmavitakkaṁ adhivāseti, nappajahati na vinodeti na byantī karoti na anabhāvaṁ gameti. Uppannaṁ byāpādavitakkaṁ ...pe... uppannaṁ vihiṁsāvitakkaṁ ...pe... uppannuppanne pāpake akusale dhamme adhivāseti, nappajahati na vinodeti na byantī karoti na anabhāvaṁ gameti.

It's when a mendicant tolerates a sensual, malicious, or cruel thought that has arisen. They tolerate any bad, unskillful qualities that have arisen. They don't give them up, get rid of them, eliminate them, and obliterate them.

Evaṁ kho, bhikkhave, bhikkhu na āsāṭikaṁ hāretā hoti.

That's how a mendicant doesn't pick out flies' eggs.

Kathañca, bhikkhave, bhikkhu na vaṇaṁ paṭicchādetā hoti?

And how does a mendicant not dress wounds?

Idha, bhikkhave, bhikkhu cakkhunā rūpaṁ disvā nimittaggāhī hoti anubyañjanaggāhī.

When a mendicant sees a sight with their eyes, they get caught up in the features and details.

Yatvādhikaraṇamenaṁ cakkhundriyaṁ asaṁvutaṁ viharantaṁ abhijjhādomanassā pāpakā akusalā dhammā anvāssaveyyuṁ, tassa saṁvarāya na paṭipajjati, na rakkhati cakkhundriyaṁ, cakkhundriye na saṁvaraṁ āpajjati.

Since the faculty of sight is left unrestrained, bad unskillful qualities of desire and aversion become overwhelming. They don't practice restraint, they don't protect the faculty of sight, and they don't achieve its restraint.

Sotena saddaṁ sutvā ...pe...

When they hear a sound with their ears ...

ghānena gandhaṁ ghāyitvā ...pe...

smell an odor with their nose ...

jivhāya rasaṁ sāyitvā ...pe...

taste a flavor with their tongue ...

kāyena phoṭṭhabbaṁ phusitvā ...pe...

feel a touch with their body ...

manasā dhammaṁ viññāya nimittaggāhī hoti anubyañjanaggāhī.

know a thought with their mind, they get caught up in the features and details.

Yatvādhikaraṇamenaṁ manindriyaṁ asaṁvutaṁ viharantaṁ abhijjhādomanassā pāpakā akusalā dhammā anvāssaveyyuṁ, tassa saṁvarāya na paṭipajjati, na rakkhati manindriyaṁ, manindriye na saṁvaraṁ āpajjati.

Since the faculty of the mind is left unrestrained, bad unskillful qualities of desire and aversion become overwhelming. They don't practice restraint, they don't protect the faculty of the mind, and they don't achieve its restraint.

Evaṁ kho, bhikkhave, bhikkhu na vaṇaṁ paṭicchādetā hoti.

That's how a mendicant doesn't dress wounds.

Kathañca, bhikkhave, bhikkhu na dhūmaṁ kattā hoti?

And how does a mendicant not smoke out pests?

Idha, bhikkhave, bhikkhu yathāsutaṁ yathāpariyattaṁ dhammaṁ na vitthārena paresaṁ desetā hoti.

It's when a mendicant doesn't teach others the Dhamma in detail as they learned and memorized it.

Evaṁ kho, bhikkhave, bhikkhu na dhūmaṁ kattā hoti.

That's how a mendicant doesn't smoke out pests.

Kathañca, bhikkhave, bhikkhu na titthaṁ jānāti?

And how does a mendicant not know the ford?

Idha, bhikkhave, bhikkhu ye te bhikkhū bahussutā āgatāgamā dhammadharā vinayadharā mātikādharā, te kālena kālaṁ upasaṅkamitvā na paripucchati, na paripañhati:

It's when a mendicant doesn't from time to time go up to those mendicants who are very learned—inheritors of the heritage, who have memorized the teachings, the monastic law, and the outlines—and ask them questions:

'idaṁ, bhante, kathaṁ?

'Why, sir, does it say this?

Imassa ko attho'ti?

What does that mean?'

Tassa te āyasmanto avivaṭañceva na vivaranti, anuttānīkatañca na uttānīkaronti, anekavihitesu ca kaṅkhāṭhānīyesu dhammesu kaṅkhaṁ na paṭivinodenti.

Those venerables don't clarify what is unclear, reveal what is obscure, and dispel doubt regarding the many doubtful matters.

Evaṁ kho, bhikkhave, bhikkhu na titthaṁ jānāti.

That's how a mendicant doesn't know the ford.

Kathañca, bhikkhave, bhikkhu na pītaṁ jānāti?

And how does a mendicant not know satisfaction?

Idha, bhikkhave, bhikkhu tathāgatappavedite dhammavinaye desiyamāne na labhati atthavedaṁ, na labhati dhammavedaṁ, na labhati dhammūpasaṁhitaṁ pāmojjaṁ.

It's when a mendicant, when the teaching and training proclaimed by the Realized One are being taught, finds no inspiration in the meaning and the teaching, and finds no joy connected with the teaching.

Evaṁ kho, bhikkhave, bhikkhu na pītaṁ jānāti.

That's how a mendicant doesn't know satisfaction.

Kathañca, bhikkhave, bhikkhu na vīthiṁ jānāti?

And how does a mendicant not know the trail?

Idha, bhikkhave, bhikkhu ariyaṁ aṭṭhaṅgikaṁ maggaṁ yathābhūtaṁ nappajānāti.

It's when a mendicant doesn't truly understand the noble eightfold path.

Evaṁ kho, bhikkhave, bhikkhu na vīthiṁ jānāti.

That's how a mendicant doesn't know the trail.

Kathañca, bhikkhave, bhikkhu na gocarakusalo hoti?

And how is a mendicant not skilled in pastures?

Idha, bhikkhave, bhikkhu cattāro satipaṭṭhāne yathābhūtaṁ nappajānāti.

It's when a mendicant doesn't truly understand the four kinds of mindfulness meditation.

Evaṁ kho, bhikkhave, bhikkhu na gocarakusalo hoti.

That's how a mendicant is not skilled in pastures.

Kathañca, bhikkhave, bhikkhu anavasesadohī hoti?

And how does a mendicant milk dry?

Idha, bhikkhave, bhikkhuṁ saddhā gahapatikā abhihaṭṭhuṁ pavārenti cīvarapiṇḍapātasenāsanagilānappaccayabhesajjaparikkhārehi, tatra bhikkhu mattaṁ na jānāti paṭiggahaṇāya.

It's when a mendicant is invited by a householder to accept robes, almsfood, lodgings, and medicines and supplies for the sick, and that mendicant doesn't know moderation in accepting.

Evaṁ kho, bhikkhave, bhikkhu anavasesadohī hoti.

That's how a mendicant milks dry.

Kathañca, bhikkhave, bhikkhu ye te bhikkhū therā rattaññū cirapabbajitā saṅghapitaro saṅghapariṇāyakā te na atirekapūjāya pūjetā hoti?

And how does a mendicant not show extra respect to senior mendicants of long standing, long gone forth, fathers and leaders of the Saṅgha?

Idha, bhikkhave, bhikkhu ye te bhikkhū therā rattaññū cirapabbajitā saṅghapitaro saṅghapariṇāyakā, tesu na mettaṁ kāyakammaṁ paccupaṭṭhāpeti āvi ceva raho ca;

It's when a mendicant doesn't consistently treat senior mendicants of long standing, long gone forth, fathers and leaders of the Saṅgha with kindness by way of body, speech, and mind, both in public and in private.

na mettaṁ vacīkammaṁ paccupaṭṭhāpeti āvi ceva raho ca;

na mettaṁ manokammaṁ paccupaṭṭhāpeti āvi ceva raho ca.

Evaṁ kho, bhikkhave, bhikkhu ye te bhikkhū therā rattaññū cirapabbajitā saṅghapitaro saṅghapariṇāyakā te na atirekapūjāya pūjetā hoti.

That's how a mendicant doesn't show extra respect to senior mendicants of long standing, long gone forth, fathers and leaders of the Saṅgha.

Imehi kho, bhikkhave, ekādasahi dhammehi samannāgato bhikkhu abhabbo imasmiṁ dhammavinaye vuddhiṁ virūḷhiṁ vepullaṁ āpajjituṁ.

A mendicant with these eleven qualities can't achieve growth, improvement, or maturity in this teaching and training.

Ekādasahi, bhikkhave, aṅgehi samannāgato gopālako bhabbo gogaṇaṁ pariharituṁ phātiṁ kātuṁ.

A cowherd with eleven factors can maintain and expand a herd of cattle.

Katamehi ekādasahi?

What eleven?

Idha, bhikkhave, gopālako rūpaññū hoti, lakkhaṇakusalo hoti, āsāṭikaṁ hāretā hoti, vaṇaṁ paṭicchādetā hoti, dhūmaṁ kattā hoti, titthaṁ jānāti, pītaṁ jānāti, vīthiṁ jānāti, gocarakusalo hoti, sāvasesadohī ca hoti. Ye te usabhā gopitaro gopariṇāyakā te atirekapūjāya pūjetā hoti.

It's when a cowherd knows form, is skilled in characteristics, picks out flies' eggs, dresses wounds, smokes out pests, knows the ford, knows satisfaction, knows the trail, is skilled in pastures, doesn't milk dry, and shows extra respect to the bulls who are fathers and leaders of the herd.

Imehi kho, bhikkhave, ekādasahi aṅgehi samannāgato gopālako bhabbo gogaṇaṁ pariharituṁ phātiṁ kātuṁ.

A cowherd with these eleven factors can maintain and expand a herd of cattle.

Evameva kho, bhikkhave, ekādasahi dhammehi samannāgato bhikkhu bhabbo imasmiṁ dhammavinaye vuddhiṁ virūḷhiṁ vepullaṁ āpajjituṁ.

In the same way, a mendicant with eleven qualities can achieve growth, improvement, and maturity in this teaching and training.

Katamehi ekādasahi?

What eleven?

Idha, bhikkhave, bhikkhu rūpaññū hoti, lakkhaṇakusalo hoti, āsāṭikaṁ hāretā hoti, vaṇaṁ paṭicchādetā hoti, dhūmaṁ kattā hoti, titthaṁ jānāti, pītaṁ jānāti, vīthiṁ jānāti, gocarakusalo hoti, sāvasesadohī ca hoti. Ye te bhikkhū therā rattaññū cirapabbajitā saṅghapitaro saṅghapariṇāyakā te atirekapūjāya pūjetā hoti.

It's when a mendicant knows form, is skilled in characteristics, picks out flies' eggs, dresses wounds, smokes out pests, knows the ford, knows satisfaction, knows the trail, is skilled in pastures, doesn't milk dry, and shows extra respect to senior mendicants of long standing, long gone forth, fathers and leaders of the Saṅgha.

Kathañca, bhikkhave, bhikkhu rūpaññū hoti?

And how does a mendicant know form?

Idha, bhikkhave, bhikkhu yaṁ kiñci rūpaṁ sabbaṁ rūpaṁ 'cattāri mahābhūtāni, catunnañca mahābhūtānaṁ upādāyarūpan'ti yathābhūtaṁ pajānāti.

It's when a mendicant truly understands that all form is the four primary elements, or form derived from the four primary elements.

Evaṁ kho, bhikkhave, bhikkhu rūpaññū hoti.

That's how a mendicant knows form.

Kathañca, bhikkhave, bhikkhu lakkhaṇakusalo hoti?

And how is a mendicant skilled in characteristics?

Idha, bhikkhave, bhikkhu kammalakkhaṇo bālo, kammalakkhaṇo paṇḍitoti yathābhūtaṁ pajānāti.

It's when a mendicant understands that a fool is characterized by their deeds, and an astute person is characterized by their deeds.

Evaṁ kho, bhikkhave, bhikkhu lakkhaṇakusalo hoti.

That's how a mendicant is skilled in characteristics.

Kathañca, bhikkhave, bhikkhu āsāṭikaṁ hāretā hoti?

And how does a mendicant pick out flies' eggs?

Idha, bhikkhave, bhikkhu uppannaṁ kāmavitakkaṁ nādhivāseti, pajahati vinodeti byantī karoti anabhāvaṁ gameti. Uppannaṁ byāpādavitakkaṁ …pe… uppannaṁ vihiṁsāvitakkaṁ …pe… uppannuppanne pāpake akusale dhamme nādhivāseti, pajahati vinodeti byantī karoti anabhāvaṁ gameti.

It's when a mendicant doesn't tolerate a sensual, malicious, or cruel thought that has arisen. They don't tolerate any bad, unskillful qualities that have arisen, but give them up, get rid of them, eliminate them, and obliterate them.

Evaṁ kho, bhikkhave, bhikkhu āsāṭikaṁ hāretā hoti.

That's how a mendicant picks out flies' eggs.

Kathañca, bhikkhave, bhikkhu vaṇaṁ paṭicchādetā hoti?

And how does a mendicant dress wounds?

Idha, bhikkhave, bhikkhu cakkhunā rūpaṁ disvā na nimittaggāhī hoti nānubyañjanaggāhī.

When a mendicant sees a sight with their eyes, they don't get caught up in the features and details.

Yatvādhikaraṇamenaṁ cakkhundriyaṁ asaṁvutaṁ viharantaṁ abhijjhādomanassā pāpakā akusalā dhammā anvāssaveyyuṁ tassa saṁvarāya paṭipajjati, rakkhati cakkhundriyaṁ, cakkhundriye saṁvaraṁ āpajjati.

If the faculty of sight were left unrestrained, bad unskillful qualities of desire and aversion would become overwhelming. For this reason, they practice restraint, protecting the faculty of sight, and achieving its restraint.

Sotena saddaṁ sutvā …pe…

When they hear a sound with their ears …

ghānena gandhaṁ ghāyitvā …pe…

smell an odor with their nose …

jivhāya rasaṁ sāyitvā …pe…

taste a flavor with their tongue …

kāyena phoṭṭhabbaṁ phusitvā …pe…

feel a touch with their body …

manasā dhammaṁ viññāya na nimittaggāhī hoti nānubyañjanaggāhī.

know a thought with their mind, they don't get caught up in the features and details.

Yatvādhikaraṇamenaṁ manindriyaṁ asaṁvutaṁ viharantaṁ abhijjhādomanassā pāpakā akusalā dhammā anvāssaveyyuṁ tassa saṁvarāya paṭipajjati, rakkhati manindriyaṁ, manindriye saṁvaraṁ āpajjati.

If the faculty of mind were left unrestrained, bad unskillful qualities of desire and aversion would become overwhelming. For this reason, they practice restraint, protecting the faculty of mind, and achieving its restraint.

Evaṁ kho, bhikkhave, bhikkhu vaṇaṁ paṭicchādetā hoti.

That's how a mendicant dresses wounds.

Kathañca, bhikkhave, bhikkhu dhūmaṁ kattā hoti?

And how does a mendicant smoke out pests?

Idha, bhikkhave, bhikkhu yathāsutaṁ yathāpariyattaṁ dhammaṁ vitthārena paresaṁ desetā hoti.

It's when a mendicant teaches others the Dhamma in detail as they learned and memorized it.

Evaṁ kho, bhikkhave, bhikkhu dhūmaṁ kattā hoti.

That's how a mendicant smokes out pests.

Kathañca, bhikkhave, bhikkhu titthaṁ jānāti?

And how does a mendicant know the ford?

Idha, bhikkhave, bhikkhu ye te bhikkhū bahussutā āgatāgamā dhammadharā vinayadharā mātikādharā te kālena kālaṁ upasankamitvā paripucchati, paripañhati:

It's when from time to time a mendicant goes up to those mendicants who are very learned—inheritors of the heritage, who have memorized the teachings, the monastic law, and the outlines—and asks them questions:

'idaṁ, bhante, kathaṁ?

'Why, sir, does it say this?

Imassa ko attho'ti?

What does that mean?'

Tassa te āyasmanto avivaṭañceva vivaranti, anuttānīkatañca uttānīkaronti, anekavihitesu ca kankhāṭhānīyesu dhammesu kankhaṁ paṭivinodenti.

Those venerables clarify what is unclear, reveal what is obscure, and dispel doubt regarding the many doubtful matters.

Evaṁ kho, bhikkhave, bhikkhu titthaṁ jānāti.

That's how a mendicant knows the ford.

Kathañca bhikkhave, bhikkhu pītaṁ jānāti?

And how does a mendicant know satisfaction?

Idha, bhikkhave, bhikkhu tathāgatappavedite dhammavinaye desiyamāne labhati atthavedaṁ, labhati dhammavedaṁ, labhati dhammūpasaṁhitaṁ pāmojjaṁ.

It's when a mendicant, when the teaching and training proclaimed by the Realized One are being taught, finds inspiration in the meaning and the teaching, and finds joy connected with the teaching.

Evaṁ kho, bhikkhave, bhikkhu pītaṁ jānāti.

That's how a mendicant knows satisfaction.

Kathañca, bhikkhave, bhikkhu vīthiṁ jānāti?

And how does a mendicant know the trail?

Idha, bhikkhave, bhikkhu ariyaṁ aṭṭhaṅgikaṁ maggaṁ yathābhūtaṁ pajānāti.

It's when a mendicant truly understands the noble eightfold path.

Evaṁ kho, bhikkhave, bhikkhu vīthiṁ jānāti.

That's how a mendicant knows the trail.

Kathañca, bhikkhave, bhikkhu gocarakusalo hoti?

And how is a mendicant skilled in pastures?

Idha, bhikkhave, bhikkhu cattāro satipaṭṭhāne yathābhūtaṁ pajānāti.

It's when a mendicant truly understands the four kinds of mindfulness meditation.

Evaṁ kho, bhikkhave, bhikkhu gocarakusalo hoti.

That's how a mendicant is skilled in pastures.

Kathañca, bhikkhave, bhikkhu sāvasesadohī hoti?

And how does a mendicant not milk dry?

Idha, bhikkhave, bhikkhuṁ saddhā gahapatikā abhihaṭṭhuṁ pavārenti cīvarapiṇḍapātasenāsanagilānappaccayabhesajjaparikkhārehi.

It's when a mendicant is invited by a householder to accept robes, almsfood, lodgings, and medicines and supplies for the sick,

Tatra bhikkhu mattaṁ jānāti paṭiggahaṇāya.

and that mendicant knows moderation in accepting.

Evaṁ kho, bhikkhave, bhikkhu sāvasesadohī hoti.

That's how a mendicant doesn't milk dry.

Kathañca, bhikkhave, bhikkhu ye te bhikkhū therā rattaññū cirapabbajitā saṅghapitaro saṅghapariṇāyakā, te atirekapūjāya pūjetā hoti?

And how does a mendicant show extra respect to senior mendicants of long standing, long gone forth, fathers and leaders of the Saṅgha?

Idha, bhikkhave, bhikkhu ye te bhikkhū therā rattaññū cirapabbajitā saṅghapitaro saṅghapariṇāyakā tesu mettaṁ kāyakammaṁ paccupaṭṭhāpeti āvi ceva raho ca;

It's when a mendicant consistently treats senior mendicants of long standing, long gone forth, fathers and leaders of the Saṅgha with kindness by way of body, speech, and mind, both in public and in private.

mettaṁ vacīkammaṁ paccupaṭṭhāpeti āvi ceva raho ca;

mettaṁ manokammaṁ paccupaṭṭhāpeti āvi ceva raho ca.

Evaṁ kho, bhikkhave, bhikkhu ye te bhikkhū therā rattaññū cirapabbajitā saṅghapitaro saṅghapariṇāyakā te atirekapūjāya pūjetā hoti.

That's how a mendicant shows extra respect to senior mendicants of long standing, long gone forth, fathers and leaders of the Saṅgha.

Imehi kho, bhikkhave, ekādasahi dhammehi samannāgato bhikkhu bhabbo imasmiṁ dhammavinaye vuddhiṁ virūḷhiṁ vepullaṁ āpajjitun"ti.

A mendicant with these eleven qualities can achieve growth, improvement, and maturity in this teaching and training."

Idamavoca bhagavā.

That is what the Buddha said.

Attamanā te bhikkhū bhagavato bhāsitaṁ abhinandunti.

Satisfied, the mendicants were happy with what the Buddha said.

Mahāgopālakasuttaṁ niṭṭhitaṁ tatiyaṁ.

34 Culagopalakasutta:

The Shorter Discourse on the Cowherd

Evaṁ me sutaṁ—

So I have heard.

ekaṁ samayaṁ bhagavā vajjīsu viharati ukkacelāyaṁ gaṅgāya nadiyā tīre.

At one time the Buddha was staying in the land of the Vajjis near Ukkacelā on the bank of the Ganges river.

Tatra kho bhagavā bhikkhū āmantesi:

There the Buddha addressed the mendicants,

"bhikkhavo"ti.

"Mendicants!"

"Bhadante"ti te bhikkhū bhagavato paccassosuṁ.

"Venerable sir," they replied.

Bhagavā etadavoca:

The Buddha said this:

"Bhūtapubbaṁ, bhikkhave, māgadhako gopālako duppaññajātiko, vassānaṁ pacchime māse saradasamaye, asamavekkhitvā gaṅgāya nadiyā orimaṁ tīraṁ, asamavekkhitvā pārimaṁ tīraṁ, atittheneva gāvo patāresi uttaraṁ tīraṁ suvidehānaṁ.

"Once upon a time, mendicants, there was an unintelligent Magadhan cowherd. In the last month of the rainy season, without inspecting the near shore or the far shore, he drove his cattle across a place with no ford on the Ganges river to the land of the Suvidehans on the northern shore.

Atha kho, bhikkhave, gāvo majjhegaṅgāya nadiyā sote āmaṇḍaliyaṁ karitvā tattheva anayabyasanaṁ āpajjiṁsu.

But the cattle bunched up in mid-stream and came to ruin right there.

Taṁ kissa hetu?

Why is that?

Tathā hi so, bhikkhave, māgadhako gopālako duppaññajātiko, vassānaṁ pacchime māse saradasamaye, asamavekkhitvā gaṅgāya nadiyā orimaṁ tīraṁ, asamavekkhitvā pārimaṁ tīraṁ, atittheneva gāvo patāresi uttaraṁ tīraṁ suvidehānaṁ.

Because the unintelligent cowherd failed to inspect the shores before driving the cattle across at a place with no ford.

Evameva kho, bhikkhave, ye hi keci samaṇā vā brāhmaṇā vā akusalā imassa lokassa akusalā parassa lokassa, akusalā māradheyyassa akusalā amāradheyyassa, akusalā maccudheyyassa akusalā amaccudheyyassa, tesaṁ ye sotabbaṁ saddahātabbaṁ maññissanti, tesaṁ taṁ bhavissati dīgharattaṁ ahitāya dukkhāya.

In the same way, there are ascetics and brahmins who are unskilled in this world and the other world, unskilled in Māra's domain and its opposite, and unskilled in Death's domain and its opposite. If anyone thinks they are worth listening to and trusting, it will be for their lasting harm and suffering.

Bhūtapubbaṁ, bhikkhave, māgadhako gopālako sappaññajātiko, vassānaṁ pacchime māse saradasamaye, samavekkhitvā gaṅgāya nadiyā orimaṁ tīraṁ, samavekkhitvā pārimaṁ tīraṁ, tittheneva gāvo patāresi uttaraṁ tīraṁ suvidehānaṁ.

Once upon a time, mendicants, there was an intelligent Magadhan cowherd. In the last month of the rainy season, after inspecting the near shore and the far shore, he drove his cattle across a ford on the Ganges river to the land of the Suvidehans on the northern shore.

So paṭhamaṁ patāresi ye te usabhā gopitaro gopariṇāyakā.

First he drove across the bulls, the fathers and leaders of the herd.

Te tiriyaṁ gaṅgāya sotaṁ chetvā sotthinā pāraṁ agamaṁsu.

They breasted the stream of the Ganges and safely reached the far shore.

Athāpare patāresi balavagāvo dammagāvo.

Then he drove across the strong and tractable cattle.

Tepi tiriyaṁ gaṅgāya sotaṁ chetvā sotthinā pāraṁ agamaṁsu.

They too breasted the stream of the Ganges and safely reached the far shore.

Athāpare patāresi vacchatare vacchatariyo.

Then he drove across the bullocks and heifers.

Tepi tiriyaṁ gaṅgāya sotaṁ chetvā sotthinā pāraṁ agamaṁsu.

They too breasted the stream of the Ganges and safely reached the far shore.

Athāpare patāresi vacchake kisābalake.

Then he drove across the calves and weak cattle.

Tepi tiriyaṁ gaṅgāya sotaṁ chetvā sotthinā pāraṁ agamaṁsu.

They too breasted the stream of the Ganges and safely reached the far shore.

Bhūtapubbaṁ, bhikkhave, vacchako taruṇako tāvadeva jātako mātugoravakena vuyhamāno, sopi tiriyaṁ gaṅgāya sotaṁ chetvā sotthinā pāraṁ agamāsi.

Once it happened that a baby calf had just been born. Urged on by its mother's lowing, even it managed to breast the stream of the Ganges and safely reach the far shore.

Taṁ kissa hetu?

Why is that?

Tathā hi so, bhikkhave, māgadhako gopālako sappaññajātiko, vassānaṁ pacchime māse saradasamaye, samavekkhitvā gaṅgāya nadiyā orimaṁ tīraṁ, samavekkhitvā pārimaṁ tīraṁ, tittheneva gāvo patāresi uttaraṁ tīraṁ suvidehānaṁ.

Because the intelligent cowherd inspected both shores before driving the cattle across at a ford.

Evameva kho, bhikkhave, ye hi keci samaṇā vā brāhmaṇā vā kusalā imassa lokassa kusalā parassa lokassa, kusalā māradheyyassa kusalā amāradheyyassa, kusalā maccudheyyassa kusalā amaccudheyyassa, tesaṁ ye sotabbaṁ saddahātabbaṁ maññissanti, tesaṁ taṁ bhavissati dīgharattaṁ hitāya sukhāya.

In the same way, there are ascetics and brahmins who are skilled in this world and the other world, skilled in Māra's domain and its opposite, and skilled in Death's domain and its opposite. If anyone thinks they are worth listening to and trusting, it will be for their lasting welfare and happiness.

Seyyathāpi, bhikkhave, ye te usabhā gopitaro gopariṇāyakā te tiriyaṁ gaṅgāya sotaṁ chetvā sotthinā pāraṁ agamaṁsu;

Just like the bulls, fathers and leaders of the herd, who crossed the Ganges to safety

evameva kho, bhikkhave, ye te bhikkhū arahanto khīṇāsavā vusitavanto katakaraṇīyā ohitabhārā anuppattasadatthā parikkhīṇabhavasaṁyojanā sammadaññāvimuttā, te tiriyaṁ mārassa sotaṁ chetvā sotthinā pāraṅgatā.

are the mendicants who are perfected, who have ended the defilements, completed the spiritual journey, done what had to be done, laid down the burden, achieved their own goal, utterly ended the fetters of rebirth, and are rightly freed through enlightenment. Having breasted Māra's stream, they have safely crossed over to the far shore.

Seyyathāpi te, bhikkhave, balavagāvo dammagāvo tiriyaṁ gaṅgāya sotaṁ chetvā sotthinā pāraṁ agamaṁsu;

Just like the strong and tractable cattle who crossed the Ganges to safety

evameva kho, bhikkhave, ye te bhikkhū pañcannaṁ orambhāgiyānaṁ saṁyojanānaṁ parikkhayā opapātikā tattha parinibbāyino anāvattidhammā tasmā lokā, tepi tiriyam mārassa sotam chetvā sotthinā pāram gamissanti.

are the mendicants who, with the ending of the five lower fetters, are reborn spontaneously. They're extinguished there, and are not liable to return from that world. They too, having breasted Māra's stream, will safely cross over to the far shore.

Seyyathāpi te, bhikkhave, vacchatarā vacchatariyo tiriyam gangāya sotam chetvā sotthinā pāram agamamsu;

Just like the bullocks and heifers who crossed the Ganges to safety

evameva kho, bhikkhave, ye te bhikkhū tinnam samyojanānam parikkhayā rāgadosamohānam tanuttā sakadāgāmino sakideva imam lokam āgantvā dukkhassantam karissanti, tepi tiriyam mārassa sotam chetvā sotthinā pāram gamissanti.

are the mendicants who, with the ending of three fetters, and the weakening of greed, hate, and delusion, are once-returners. They come back to this world once only, then make an end of suffering. They too, having breasted Māra's stream, will safely cross over to the far shore.

Seyyathāpi te, bhikkhave, vacchakā kisābalakā tiriyam gangāya sotam chetvā sotthinā pāram agamamsu;

Just like the calves and weak cattle who crossed the Ganges to safety

evameva kho, bhikkhave, ye te bhikkhū tinnam samyojanānam parikkhayā sotāpannā avinipātadhammā niyatā sambodhiparāyanā, tepi tiriyam mārassa sotam chetvā sotthinā pāram gamissanti.

are the mendicants who, with the ending of three fetters are stream-enterers, not liable to be reborn in the underworld, bound for awakening. They too, having breasted Māra's stream, will safely cross over to the far shore.

Seyyathāpi so, bhikkhave, vacchako tarunako tāvadeva jātako mātugoravakena vuyhamāno tiriyam gangāya sotam chetvā sotthinā pāram agamāsi;

Just like the baby calf who had just been born, but, urged on by its mother's lowing, still managed to cross the Ganges to safety

evameva kho, bhikkhave, ye te bhikkhū dhammānusārino saddhānusārino, tepi tiriyam mārassa sotam chetvā sotthinā pāram gamissanti.

are the mendicants who are followers of principles, followers by faith. They too, having breasted Māra's stream, will safely cross over to the far shore.

Aham kho pana, bhikkhave, kusalo imassa lokassa kusalo parassa lokassa, kusalo māradheyyassa kusalo amāradheyyassa, kusalo maccudheyyassa kusalo amaccudheyyassa. Tassa mayham, bhikkhave, ye sotabbam saddahātabbam maññissanti, tesam tam bhavissati dīgharattam hitāya sukhāyā"ti.

Mendicants, I am skilled in this world and the other world, skilled in Māra's domain and its opposite, and skilled in Death's domain and its opposite. If anyone thinks I am worth listening to and trusting, it will be for their lasting welfare and happiness."

Idamavoca bhagavā.

That is what the Buddha said.

Idaṁ vatvā sugato athāparaṁ etadavoca satthā:

Then the Holy One, the Teacher, went on to say:

"Ayaṁ loko paro loko,

jānatā suppakāsito;

Yañca mārena sampattaṁ,

appattaṁ yañca maccunā.

"This world and the other world

have been clearly explained by one who knows;

as well as Māra's reach,

and what's out of Death's reach.

Sabbaṁ lokaṁ abhiññāya,

sambuddhena pajānatā;

Vivaṭaṁ amatadvāraṁ,

khemaṁ nibbānapattiyā.

Directly knowing the whole world,

the Buddha who understands

has flung open the door of the deathless,

for realizing the sanctuary, extinguishment.

Chinnaṁ pāpimato sotaṁ,

Viddhastaṁ vinaḷīkataṁ;

Pāmojjabahulā hotha,

Khemaṁ pattattha bhikkhavo"ti.

The Wicked One's stream has been cut,

it's blown away and mown down.

Be full of joy, mendicants,

set your heart on the sanctuary!"

Cūḷagopālakasuttaṁ niṭṭhitaṁ catutthaṁ.

35 Culasaccakasutta:

The Shorter Discourse With Saccaka

Evaṁ me sutaṁ—

So I have heard.

ekaṁ samayaṁ bhagavā vesāliyaṁ viharati mahāvane kūṭāgārasālāyaṁ.

At one time the Buddha was staying near Vesālī, at the Great Wood, in the hall with the peaked roof.

Tena kho pana samayena saccako nigaṇṭhaputto vesāliyaṁ paṭivasati bhassappavādako paṇḍitavādo sādhusammato bahujanassa.

Now at that time Saccaka, the son of Jain parents, was staying in Vesālī. He was a debater and clever speaker regarded as holy by many people.

So vesāliyaṁ parisati evaṁ vācaṁ bhāsati:

He was telling a crowd in Vesālī,

"nāhaṁ taṁ passāmi samaṇaṁ vā brāhmaṇaṁ vā, saṅghiṁ gaṇiṁ gaṇācariyaṁ, api arahantaṁ sammāsambuddhaṁ paṭijānamānaṁ, yo mayā vādena vādaṁ samāraddho na saṅkampeyya na sampakampeyya na sampavedheyya, yassa na kacchehi sedā mucceyyuṁ.

"If I was to take them on in debate, I don't see any ascetic or brahmin—leader of an order or a community, or the teacher of a community, even one who claims to be a perfected one, a fully awakened Buddha—who would not shake and rock and tremble, sweating from the armpits.

Thūṇaṁ cepāhaṁ acetanaṁ vādena vādaṁ samārabheyyaṁ, sāpi mayā vādena vādaṁ samāraddhā saṅkampeyya sampakampeyya sampavedheyya.

Even if I took on an insentient post in debate, it would shake and rock and tremble.

Ko pana vādo manussabhūtassā"ti?

How much more then a human being!"

Atha kho āyasmā assaji pubbaṇhasamayaṁ nivāsetvā pattacīvaramādāya vesāliṁ piṇḍāya pāvisi.

Then Venerable Assaji robed up in the morning and, taking his bowl and robe, entered Vesālī for alms.

Addasā kho saccako nigaṇṭhaputto vesāliyaṁ jaṅghāvihāraṁ anucaṅkamamāno anuvicaramāno āyasmantaṁ assajiṁ dūratova āgacchantaṁ.

As Saccaka was going for a walk he saw Assaji coming off in the distance.

Disvāna yenāyasmā assaji tenupasaṅkami; upasaṅkamitvā āyasmatā assajinā saddhiṁ sammodi.

He approached him and exchanged greetings with him.

Sammodanīyaṁ kathaṁ sāraṇīyaṁ vītisāretvā ekamantaṁ aṭṭhāsi. Ekamantaṁ ṭhito kho saccako nigaṇṭhaputto āyasmantaṁ assajiṁ etadavoca:

When the greetings and polite conversation were over, Saccaka stood to one side and said to Assaji,

"kathaṁ pana, bho assaji, samaṇo gotamo sāvake vineti, kathaṁbhāgā ca pana samaṇassa gotamassa sāvakesu anusāsanī bahulā pavattatī"ti?

"Master Assaji, how does the ascetic Gotama guide his disciples? And how does instruction to his disciples generally proceed?"

"Evaṁ kho, aggivessana, bhagavā sāvake vineti, evaṁbhāgā ca pana bhagavato sāvakesu anusāsanī bahulā pavattati:

"Aggivessana, this is how the ascetic Gotama guides his disciples, and how instruction to his disciples generally proceeds:

'rūpaṁ, bhikkhave, aniccaṁ, vedanā aniccā, saññā aniccā, saṅkhārā aniccā, viññāṇaṁ aniccaṁ.

'Form, feeling, perception, choices, and consciousness are impermanent.

Rūpaṁ, bhikkhave, anattā, vedanā anattā, saññā anattā, saṅkhārā anattā, viññāṇaṁ anattā.

Form, feeling, perception, choices, and consciousness are not-self.

Sabbe saṅkhārā aniccā, sabbe dhammā anattā'ti.

All conditions are impermanent. All things are not-self.'

Evaṁ kho, aggivessana, bhagavā sāvake vineti, evaṁbhāgā ca pana bhagavato sāvakesu anusāsanī bahulā pavattatī"ti.

This is how the ascetic Gotama guides his disciples, and how instruction to his disciples generally proceeds."

"Dussutaṁ vata, bho assaji, assumha ye mayaṁ evaṁvādiṁ samaṇaṁ gotamaṁ assumha.

"It's sad to hear, Master Assaji, that the ascetic Gotama has such a doctrine.

Appeva nāma mayaṁ kadāci karahaci tena bhotā gotamena saddhiṁ samāgaccheyyāma, appeva nāma siyā kocideva kathāsallāpo, appeva nāma tasmā pāpakā diṭṭhigatā viveceyyāmā"ti.

Hopefully, some time or other I'll get to meet Master Gotama, and we can have a discussion. And hopefully I can dissuade him from this harmful misconception."

Tena kho pana samayena pañcamattāni licchavisatāni santhāgāre sannipatitāni honti kenacideva karaṇīyena.

Now at that time around five hundred Licchavis were sitting together at the town hall on some business.

Atha kho saccako nigaṇṭhaputto yena te licchavī tenupasaṅkami; upasaṅkamitvā te licchavī etadavoca:

Then Saccaka went up to them and said,

"abhikkamantu bhonto licchavī, abhikkamantu bhonto licchavī, ajja me samaṇena gotamena saddhiṁ kathāsallāpo bhavissati.

"Come forth, good Licchavīs, come forth! Today I am going to have a discussion with the ascetic Gotama.

Sace me samaṇo gotamo tathā patiṭṭhissati yathā ca me ñātaññatarena sāvakena assajinā nāma bhikkhunā patiṭṭhitaṁ, seyyathāpi nāma balavā puriso dīghalomikaṁ eḷakaṁ lomesu gahetvā ākaḍḍheyya parikaḍḍheyya samparikaḍḍheyya;

If he stands by the position stated to me by one of his well-known disciples—a mendicant named Assaji—I'll take him on in debate and drag him to and fro and round about, like a strong man would drag a fleecy sheep to and fro and round about!

evamevāhaṁ samaṇaṁ gotamaṁ vādena vādaṁ ākaḍḍhissāmi parikaḍḍhissāmi samparikaḍḍhissāmi.

Seyyathāpi nāma balavā soṇḍikākammakāro mahantaṁ soṇḍikākiḷañjaṁ gambhīre udakarahade pakkhipitvā kaṇṇe gahetvā ākaḍḍheyya parikaḍḍheyya samparikaḍḍheyya;

Taking him on in debate, I'll drag him to and fro and round about, like a strong brewer's worker would toss a large brewer's sieve into a deep lake, grab it by the corners, and drag it to and fro and round about!

evamevāhaṁ samaṇaṁ gotamaṁ vādena vādaṁ ākaḍḍhissāmi parikaḍḍhissāmi samparikaḍḍhissāmi.

Seyyathāpi nāma balavā soṇḍikādhutto vālaṁ kaṇṇe gahetvā odhuneyya niddhuneyya nipphoṭeyya;

Taking him on in debate, I'll shake him down and about, and give him a beating, like a strong brewer's mixer would grab a strainer by the corners and shake it down and about, and give it a beating!

evamevāhaṁ samaṇaṁ gotamaṁ vādena vādaṁ odhunissāmi niddhunissāmi nipphoṭessāmi.

Seyyathāpi nāma kuñjaro saṭṭhihāyano gambhīraṁ pokkharaṇiṁ ogāhetvā sāṇadhovikaṁ nāma kīḷitajātaṁ kīḷati;

I'll play a game of ear-washing with the ascetic Gotama, like a sixty-year-old elephant would plunge into a deep lotus pond and play a game of ear-washing!

evamevāhaṁ samaṇaṁ gotamaṁ sāṇadhovikaṁ maññe kīḷitajātaṁ kīḷissāmi.

Abhikkamantu bhonto licchavī, abhikkamantu bhonto licchavī, ajja me samaṇena gotamena saddhiṁ kathāsallāpo bhavissatī"ti.

Come forth, good Licchavīs, come forth! Today I am going to have a discussion with the ascetic Gotama."

Tatrekacce licchavī evamāhaṁsu:

At that, some of the Licchavis said,

"kiṁ samaṇo gotamo saccakassa niganṭhaputtassa vādaṁ āropessati, atha kho saccako niganṭhaputto samaṇassa gotamassa vādaṁ āropessatī"ti?

"How can the ascetic Gotama refute Saccaka's doctrine, when it is Saccaka who will refute Gotama's doctrine?"

Ekacce licchavī evamāhaṁsu:

But some of the Licchavis said,

"kiṁ so bhavamāno saccako niganṭhaputto yo bhagavato vādaṁ āropessati, atha kho bhagavā saccakassa niganṭhaputtassa vādaṁ āropessatī"ti?

"Who is Saccaka to refute the Buddha's doctrine, when it is the Buddha who will refute Saccaka's doctrine?"

Atha kho saccako niganṭhaputto pañcamattehi licchavisatehi parivuto yena mahāvanaṁ kūṭāgārasālā tenupasaṅkami.

Then Saccaka, escorted by the five hundred Licchavis, went to the hall with the peaked roof in the Great Wood.

Tena kho pana samayena sambahulā bhikkhū abbhokāse caṅkamanti.

At that time several mendicants were walking mindfully in the open air.

Atha kho saccako niganṭhaputto yena te bhikkhū tenupasaṅkami; upasaṅkamitvā te bhikkhū etadavoca:

Then Saccaka went up to them and said,

"kahaṁ nu kho, bho, etarahi so bhavaṁ gotamo viharati?

"Good sirs, where is Master Gotama at present?

Dassanakāmā hi mayaṁ taṁ bhavantaṁ gotaman"ti.

For we want to see him."

"Esa, aggivessana, bhagavā mahāvanaṁ ajjhogāhetvā aññatarasmiṁ rukkhamūle divāvihāraṁ nisinno"ti.

"Aggivessana, the Buddha has plunged deep into the Great Wood and is sitting at the root of a tree for the day's meditation."

Atha kho saccako niganṭhaputto mahatiyā licchaviparisāya saddhiṁ mahāvanaṁ ajjhogāhetvā yena bhagavā tenupasaṅkami; upasaṅkamitvā bhagavatā saddhiṁ sammodi.

Then Saccaka, together with a large group of Licchavis, went to see the Buddha in the Great Wood, and exchanged greetings with him.

Sammodanīyaṁ kathaṁ sāraṇīyaṁ vītisāretvā ekamantaṁ nisīdi.

When the greetings and polite conversation were over, he sat down to one side.

Tepi kho licchavī appekacce bhagavantaṁ abhivādetvā ekamantaṁ nisīdiṁsu, appekacce bhagavatā saddhiṁ sammodiṁsu, sammodanīyaṁ kathaṁ sāraṇīyaṁ vītisāretvā ekamantaṁ nisīdiṁsu. Appekacce yena bhagavā tenañjaliṁ paṇāmetvā ekamantaṁ nisīdiṁsu, appekacce bhagavato santike nāmagottaṁ sāvetvā ekamantaṁ nisīdiṁsu, appekacce tuṇhībhūtā ekamantaṁ nisīdiṁsu.

Before sitting down to one side, some of the Licchavīs bowed, some exchanged greetings and polite conversation, some held up their joined palms toward the Buddha, some announced their name and clan, while some kept silent.

Ekamantaṁ nisinno kho saccako niganṭhaputto bhagavantaṁ etadavoca:

Then Saccaka said to the Buddha,

"puccheyyāhaṁ bhavantaṁ gotamaṁ kiñcideva desaṁ, sace me bhavaṁ gotamo okāsaṁ karoti pañhassa veyyākaraṇāyā"ti.

"I'd like to ask Master Gotama about a certain point, if you'd take the time to answer."

"Puccha, aggivessana, yadākaṅkhasī"ti.

"Ask what you wish, Aggivessana."

"Kathaṁ pana bhavaṁ gotamo sāvake vineti, kathambhāgā ca pana bhoto gotamassa sāvakesu anusāsanī bahulā pavattatī"ti?

"How does the ascetic Gotama guide his disciples? And how does instruction to his disciples generally proceed?"

"Evaṁ kho ahaṁ, aggivessana, sāvake vinemi, evambhāgā ca pana me sāvakesu anusāsanī bahulā pavattati:

"This is how I guide my disciples, and how instruction to my disciples generally proceeds:

'rūpaṁ, bhikkhave, aniccaṁ, vedanā aniccā, saññā aniccā, saṅkhārā aniccā, viññāṇaṁ aniccaṁ.

'Form, feeling, perception, choices, and consciousness are impermanent.

Rūpaṁ, bhikkhave, anattā, vedanā anattā, saññā anattā, saṅkhārā anattā, viññāṇaṁ anattā.

Form, feeling, perception, choices, and consciousness are not-self.

Sabbe saṅkhārā aniccā, sabbe dhammā anattā'ti.

All conditions are impermanent. All things are not-self.'

Evaṁ kho ahaṁ, aggivessana, sāvake vinemi, evambhāgā ca pana me sāvakesu anusāsanī bahulā pavattatī"ti.

This is how I guide my disciples, and how instruction to my disciples generally proceeds."

"Upamā maṁ, bho gotama, paṭibhātī"ti.

"A simile strikes me, Master Gotama."

"Paṭibhātu taṁ, aggivessanā"ti bhagavā avoca.

"Then speak as you feel inspired," said the Buddha.

"Seyyathāpi, bho gotama, ye kecime bījagāmabhūtagāmā vuddhiṁ virūḷhiṁ vepullaṁ āpajjanti, sabbe te pathaviṁ nissāya pathaviyaṁ patiṭṭhāya.

"All the plants and seeds that achieve growth, increase, and maturity do so depending on the earth and grounded on the earth.

Evamete bījagāmabhūtagāmā vuddhiṁ virūḷhiṁ vepullaṁ āpajjanti.

Seyyathāpi vā pana, bho gotama, ye kecime balakaraṇīyā kammantā karīyanti, sabbe te pathaviṁ nissāya pathaviyaṁ patiṭṭhāya.

All the hard work that gets done depends on the earth and is grounded on the earth.

Evamete balakaraṇīyā kammantā karīyanti.

Evameva kho, bho gotama, rūpattāyaṁ purisapuggalo rūpe patiṭṭhāya puññaṁ vā apuññaṁ vā pasavati, vedanattāyaṁ purisapuggalo vedanāyaṁ patiṭṭhāya puññaṁ vā apuññaṁ vā pasavati, saññattāyaṁ purisapuggalo saññāyaṁ patiṭṭhāya puññaṁ vā apuññaṁ vā pasavati, saṅkhārattāyaṁ purisapuggalo saṅkhāresu patiṭṭhāya puññaṁ vā apuññaṁ vā pasavati, viññāṇattāyaṁ purisapuggalo viññāṇe patiṭṭhāya puññaṁ vā apuññaṁ vā pasavatī"ti.

In the same way, an individual's self is form. Grounded on form they make good and bad choices. An individual's self is feeling ... perception ... choices ... consciousness. Grounded on consciousness they make good and bad choices."

"Nanu tvaṁ, aggivessana, evaṁ vadesi:

"Aggivessana, are you not saying this:

'rūpaṁ me attā, vedanā me attā, saññā me attā, saṅkhārā me attā, viññāṇaṁ me attā'"ti?

'Form is my self, feeling is my self, perception is my self, choices are my self, consciousness is my self'?"

"Ahañhi, bho gotama, evaṁ vadāmi:

"Indeed, Master Gotama, that is what I am saying.

'rūpaṁ me attā, vedanā me attā, saññā me attā, saṅkhārā me attā, viññāṇaṁ me attā'ti, ayañca mahatī janatā"ti.

And this big crowd agrees with me!"

"Kiñhi te, aggivessana, mahatī janatā karissati?

"What has this big crowd to do with you?

Iṅgha tvaṁ, aggivessana, sakaññeva vādaṁ nibbeṭhehī"ti.

Please just explain your own statement."

"Ahañhi, bho gotama, evaṁ vadāmi:

"Then, Master Gotama, what I am saying is this:

'rūpaṁ me attā, vedanā me attā, saññā me attā, saṅkhārā me attā, viññāṇaṁ me attā'"ti.

'Form is my self, feeling is my self, perception is my self, choices are my self, consciousness is my self'."

"Tena hi, aggivessana, taññevettha paṭipucchissāmi, yathā te khameyya tathā naṁ byākareyyāsi.

"Well then, Aggivessana, I'll ask you about this in return, and you can answer as you like.

Taṁ kiṁ maññasi, aggivessana,

What do you think, Aggivessana?

vatteyya rañño khattiyassa muddhāvasittassa sakasmiṁ vijite vaso—

Consider an anointed aristocratic king such as Pasenadi of Kosala or Ajātasattu of Magadha, son of the princess of Videha.

ghātetāyaṁ vā ghātetuṁ, jāpetāyaṁ vā jāpetuṁ, pabbājetāyaṁ vā pabbājetuṁ, seyyathāpi rañño pasenadissa kosalassa, seyyathāpi vā pana rañño māgadhassa ajātasattussa vedehiputtassā"ti?

Would they have the power in their own realm to execute, fine, or banish those who are guilty?"

"Vatteyya, bho gotama, rañño khattiyassa muddhāvasittassa sakasmiṁ vijite vaso—

"An anointed king would have such power, Master Gotama.

ghātetāyaṁ vā ghātetuṁ, jāpetāyaṁ vā jāpetuṁ, pabbājetāyaṁ vā pabbājetuṁ, seyyathāpi rañño pasenadissa kosalassa, seyyathāpi vā pana rañño māgadhassa ajātasattussa vedehiputtassa.

Imesampi hi, bho gotama, saṅghānaṁ gaṇānaṁ—

Even federations such as the

Seyyathidaṁ—vajjīnaṁ mallānaṁ—

Vajjis and Mallas

vattati sakasmiṁ vijite vaso—

have such power in their own realm.

ghātetāyaṁ vā ghātetuṁ, jāpetāyaṁ vā jāpetuṁ, pabbājetāyaṁ vā pabbājetuṁ.

Kiṁ pana rañño khattiyassa muddhāvasittassa, seyyathāpi rañño pasenadissa kosalassa, seyyathāpi vā pana rañño māgadhassa ajātasattussa vedehiputtassa?

So of course an anointed king such as Pasenadi or Ajātasattu

Vatteyya, bho gotama, vattituñca marahatī"ti.

would wield such power, as is their right."

"Taṁ kiṁ maññasi, aggivessana,

"What do you think, Aggivessana?

yaṁ tvaṁ evaṁ vadesi:

When you say,

'rūpaṁ me attā'ti, vattati te tasmiṁ rūpe vaso—

'Form is my self,' do you have power over that form to say:

evaṁ me rūpaṁ hotu, evaṁ me rūpaṁ mā ahosī"ti?

'May my form be like this! May it not be like that'?"

Evaṁ vutte, saccako niganṭhaputto tuṇhī ahosi.

When he said this, Saccaka kept silent.

Dutiyampi kho bhagavā saccakaṁ niganṭhaputtaṁ etadavoca:

The Buddha asked the question a second time,

"taṁ kiṁ maññasi, aggivessana, yaṁ tvaṁ evaṁ vadesi:

'rūpaṁ me attā'ti, vattati te tasmiṁ rūpe vaso—

evaṁ me rūpaṁ hotu, evaṁ me rūpaṁ mā ahosī"ti?

Dutiyampi kho saccako niganṭhaputto tuṇhī ahosi.

but Saccaka still kept silent.

Atha kho bhagavā saccakaṁ niganṭhaputtaṁ etadavoca:

So the Buddha said to Saccaka,

"byākarohi dāni, aggivessana, na dāni te tuṇhībhāvassa kālo.

"Answer now, Aggivessana. Now is not the time for silence.

Yo koci, aggivessana tathāgatena yāvatatiyaṁ sahadhammikaṁ pañhaṁ puṭṭho na byākaroti, etthevassa sattadhā muddhā phalatī"ti.

If someone fails to answer a legitimate question when asked three times by the Buddha, their head explodes into seven pieces there and then."

Tena kho pana samayena vajirapāṇi yakkho āyasaṁ vajiraṁ ādāya ādittaṁ sampajjalitaṁ sajotibhūtaṁ saccakassa niganthaputtassa uparivehāsaṁ ṭhito hoti:

Now at that time the spirit Vajirapāṇī, taking up a burning iron thunderbolt, blazing and glowing, stood in the sky above Saccaka, thinking,

"sacāyaṁ saccako niganthaputto bhagavatā yāvatatiyaṁ sahadhammikaṁ pañhaṁ puṭṭho na byākarissati etthevassa sattadhā muddhaṁ phālessāmī"ti.

"If this Saccaka doesn't answer when asked a third time, I'll blow his head into seven pieces there and then!"

Taṁ kho pana vajirapāṇiṁ yakkhaṁ bhagavā ceva passati saccako ca niganthaputto.

And both the Buddha and Saccaka could see Vajirapāṇī.

Atha kho saccako niganthaputto bhīto saṁviggo lomahaṭṭhajāto bhagavantaṁyeva tāṇaṁ gavesī bhagavantaṁyeva leṇaṁ gavesī bhagavantaṁyeva saraṇaṁ gavesī bhagavantaṁ etadavoca:

Saccaka was terrified, shocked, and awestruck. Looking to the Buddha for shelter, protection, and refuge, he said,

"pucchatu maṁ bhavaṁ gotamo, byākarissāmī"ti.

"Ask me, Master Gotama. I will answer."

"Taṁ kiṁ maññasi, aggivessana,

"What do you think, Aggivessana?

yaṁ tvaṁ evaṁ vadesi:

When you say,

'rūpaṁ me attā'ti, vattati te tasmiṁ rūpe vaso—

'Form is my self,' do you have power over that form to say:

evaṁ me rūpaṁ hotu, evaṁ me rūpaṁ mā ahosī"ti?

'May my form be like this! May it not be like that'?"

"No hidaṁ, bho gotama".

"No, Master Gotama."

"Manasi karohi, aggivessana;

"Think about it, Aggivessana!

manasi karitvā kho, aggivessana, byākarohi.

You should think before answering.

Na kho te sandhiyati purimena vā pacchimaṁ pacchimena vā purimaṁ.

What you said before and what you said after don't match up.

Taṁ kiṁ maññasi, aggivessana,

What do you think, Aggivessana?

yaṁ tvaṁ evaṁ vadesi:

When you say,

'vedanā me attā'ti, vattati te tissaṁ vedanāyaṁ vaso—

'Feeling is my self,' do you have power over that feeling to say:

evaṁ me vedanā hotu, evaṁ me vedanā mā ahosī"ti?

'May my feeling be like this! May it not be like that'?"

"No hidaṁ, bho gotama".

"No, Master Gotama."

"Manasi karohi, aggivessana;

"Think about it, Aggivessana!

manasi karitvā kho, aggivessana, byākarohi.

You should think before answering.

Na kho te sandhiyati purimena vā pacchimaṁ, pacchimena vā purimaṁ.

What you said before and what you said after don't match up.

Taṁ kiṁ maññasi, aggivessana,

What do you think, Aggivessana?

yaṁ tvaṁ evaṁ vadesi:

When you say,

'saññā me attā'ti, vattati te tissaṁ saññāyaṁ vaso—

'Perception is my self,' do you have power over that perception to say:

evaṁ me saññā hotu, evaṁ me saññā mā ahosī'ti?

'May my perception be like this! May it not be like that'?"

"No hidaṁ, bho gotama".

"No, Master Gotama."

"Manasi karohi, aggivessana;

"Think about it, Aggivessana!

manasi karitvā kho, aggivessana, byākarohi.

You should think before answering.

Na kho te sandhiyati purimena vā pacchimaṁ, pacchimena vā purimaṁ.

What you said before and what you said after don't match up.

Taṁ kiṁ maññasi, aggivessana,

What do you think, Aggivessana?

yaṁ tvaṁ evaṁ vadesi:

When you say,

'saṅkhārā me attā'ti, vattati te tesu saṅkhāresu vaso—

'Choices are my self,' do you have power over those choices to say:

evaṁ me saṅkhārā hontu, evaṁ me saṅkhārā mā ahesun"ti?

'May my choices be like this! May they not be like that'?"

"No hidaṁ, bho gotama".

"No, Master Gotama."

"Manasi karohi, aggivessana;

"Think about it, Aggivessana!

manasi karitvā kho, aggivessana, byākarohi.

You should think before answering.

Na kho te sandhiyati purimena vā pacchimaṁ, pacchimena vā purimaṁ.

What you said before and what you said after don't match up.

Taṁ kiṁ maññasi, aggivessana,

What do you think, Aggivessana?

yaṁ tvaṁ evaṁ vadesi:

When you say,

'viññāṇaṁ me attā'ti, vattati te tasmiṁ viññāṇe vaso—

'Consciousness is my self,' do you have power over that consciousness to say:

evaṁ me viññāṇaṁ hotu, evaṁ me viññāṇaṁ mā ahosī"ti?

'May my consciousness be like this! May it not be like that'?"

"No hidaṁ, bho gotama".

"No, Master Gotama."

"Manasi karohi, aggivessana;

"Think about it, Aggivessana!

manasi karitvā kho, aggivessana, byākarohi.

You should think before answering.

Na kho te sandhiyati purimena vā pacchimaṁ, pacchimena vā purimaṁ.

What you said before and what you said after don't match up.

Taṁ kiṁ maññasi, aggivessana,

What do you think, Aggivessana?

rūpaṁ niccaṁ vā aniccaṁ vā"ti?

Is form permanent or impermanent?"

"Aniccaṁ, bho gotama".

"Impermanent."

"Yaṁ panāniccaṁ dukkhaṁ vā taṁ sukhaṁ vā"ti?

"But if it's impermanent, is it suffering or happiness?"

"Dukkhaṁ, bho gotama".

"Suffering."

"Yaṁ panāniccaṁ dukkhaṁ vipariṇāmadhammaṁ, kallaṁ nu taṁ samanupassituṁ:

"But if it's impermanent, suffering, and perishable, is it fit to be regarded thus:

'etaṁ mama, esohamasmi, eso me attā'"ti?

'This is mine, I am this, this is my self'?"

"No hidaṁ, bho gotama".

"No, Master Gotama."

"Taṁ kiṁ maññasi, aggivessana,

"What do you think, Aggivessana?

vedanā …pe…

Is feeling …

saññā …pe…

perception …

saṅkhārā …pe…

choices …

taṁ kiṁ maññasi, aggivessana, viññāṇaṁ niccaṁ vā aniccaṁ vā"ti?

consciousness permanent or impermanent?"

"Aniccaṁ, bho gotama".

"Impermanent."

"Yaṁ panāniccaṁ dukkhaṁ vā taṁ sukhaṁ vā"ti?

"But if it's impermanent, is it suffering or happiness?"

"Dukkhaṁ, bho gotama".

"Suffering."

"Yaṁ panāniccaṁ dukkhaṁ vipariṇāmadhammaṁ, kallaṁ nu taṁ samanupassituṁ:

"But if it's impermanent, suffering, and perishable, is it fit to be regarded thus:

'etaṁ mama, esohamasmi, eso me attā'"ti?

'This is mine, I am this, this is my self'?"

"No hidaṁ, bho gotama".

"No, Master Gotama."

"Taṁ kiṁ maññasi, aggivessana,

"What do you think, Aggivessana?

yo nu kho dukkhaṁ allīno dukkhaṁ upagato dukkhaṁ ajjhosito, dukkhaṁ 'etaṁ mama, esohamasmi, eso me attā'ti samanupassati, api nu kho so sāmaṁ vā dukkhaṁ parijāneyya, dukkhaṁ vā parikkhepetvā vihareyyā"ti?

Consider someone who clings, holds, and attaches to suffering, regarding it thus: 'This is mine, I am this, this is my self.' Would such a person be able to completely understand suffering themselves, or live having wiped out suffering?"

"Kiñhi siyā, bho gotama?

"How could they?

No hidaṁ, bho gotamā"ti.

No, Master Gotama."

"Taṁ kiṁ maññasi, aggivessana,

"What do you think, Aggivessana?

nanu tvaṁ evaṁ sante dukkhaṁ allīno dukkhaṁ upagato dukkhaṁ ajjhosito, dukkhaṁ:

This being so, aren't you someone who clings, holds, and attaches to suffering, regarding it thus: 'This is mine, I am this, this is my self'?"

'etaṁ mama, esohamasmi, eso me attā'ti samanupassasī'ti?

"Kiñhi no siyā, bho gotama?

"How could I not?

Evametaṁ, bho gotamā"ti.

Yes, Master Gotama."

"Seyyathāpi, aggivessana, puriso sāratthiko sāragavesī sārapariyesanaṁ caramāno tiṇhaṁ kuṭhāriṁ ādāya vanaṁ paviseyya.

"Suppose, Aggivessana, there was a person in need of heartwood. Wandering in search of heartwood, they'd take a sharp axe and enter a forest.

So tattha passeyya mahantaṁ kadalikkhandhaṁ ujuṁ navaṁ akukkukajātaṁ.

There they'd see a big banana tree, straight and young and grown free of defects.

Tamenaṁ mūle chindeyya, mūle chetvā agge chindeyya, agge chetvā pattavaṭṭiṁ vinibbhujeyya.

They'd cut it down at the base, cut off the top, and unroll the coiled sheaths.

So tattha pattavaṭṭiṁ vinibbhujanto pheggumpi nādhigaccheyya, kuto sāraṁ?

But they wouldn't even find sapwood, much less heartwood.

Evameva kho tvaṁ, aggivessana, mayā sakasmiṁ vāde samanuyuñjiyamāno samanugāhiyamāno samanubhāsiyamāno ritto tuccho aparaddho.

In the same way, when pursued, pressed, and grilled by me on your own doctrine, you turn out to be void, hollow, and mistaken.

Bhāsitā kho pana te esā, aggivessana, vesāliyaṁ parisati vācā:

But it was you who stated before the assembly of Vesālī:

'nāhaṁ taṁ passāmi samaṇaṁ vā brāhmaṇaṁ vā, saṅghiṁ gaṇiṁ gaṇācariyaṁ, api arahantaṁ sammāsambuddhaṁ paṭijānamānaṁ, yo mayā vādena vādaṁ samāraddho na saṅkampeyya na sampakampeyya na sampavedheyya, yassa na kacchehi sedā mucceyyuṁ.

'If I was to take them on in debate, I don't see any ascetic or brahmin—leader of an order or a community, or the teacher of a community, even one who claims to be a perfected one, a fully awakened Buddha—who would not shake and rock and tremble, sweating from the armpits.

Thūṇaṁ cepāhaṁ acetanaṁ vādena vādaṁ samārabheyyaṁ sāpi mayā vādena vādaṁ samāraddhā saṅkampeyya sampakampeyya sampavedheyya.

Even if I took on an insentient post in debate, it would shake and rock and tremble.

Ko pana vādo manussabhūtassā'ti?

How much more then a human being!'

Tuyhaṁ kho pana, aggivessana, appekaccāni sedaphusitāni nalāṭā muttāni, uttarāsaṅgaṁ vinibhinditvā bhūmiyaṁ patiṭṭhitāni.

But sweat is pouring from your forehead; it's soaked through your robe and drips on the ground.

Mayhaṁ kho pana, aggivessana, natthi etarahi kāyasmiṁ sedo"ti.

While I now have no sweat on my body."

Iti bhagavā tasmiṁ parisati suvaṇṇavaṇṇaṁ kāyaṁ vivari.

So the Buddha revealed his golden body to the assembly.

Evaṃ vutte, saccako niganṭhaputto tuṇhībhūto maṅkubhūto pattakkhandho adhomukho pajjhāyanto appaṭibhāno nisīdi.

When this was said, Saccaka sat silent, dismayed, shoulders drooping, downcast, depressed, with nothing to say.

Atha kho dummukho licchaviputto saccakaṃ niganṭhaputtaṃ tuṇhībhūtaṃ maṅkubhūtaṃ pattakkhandhaṃ adhomukhaṃ pajjhāyantaṃ appaṭibhānaṃ viditvā bhagavantaṃ etadavoca:

Knowing this, the Licchavi Dummukha said to the Buddha,

"upamā maṃ, bhagavā, paṭibhātī"ti.

"A simile strikes me, Blessed One."

"Paṭibhātu taṃ, dummukhā"ti bhagavā avoca.

"Then speak as you feel inspired," said the Buddha.

"Seyyathāpi, bhante, gāmassa vā nigamassa vā avidūre pokkharaṇī.

"Sir, suppose there was a lotus pond not far from a town or village,

Tatrāssa kakkaṭako.

and a crab lived there.

Atha kho, bhante, sambahulā kumārakā vā kumārikā vā tamhā gāmā vā nigamā vā nikkhamitvā yena sā pokkharaṇī tenupasaṅkameyyuṃ; upasaṅkamitvā taṃ pokkharaṇiṃ ogāhetvā taṃ kakkaṭakaṃ udakā uddharitvā thale patiṭṭhāpeyyuṃ.

Then several boys or girls would leave the town or village and go to the pond, where they'd pull out the crab and put it on dry land.

Yaññadeva hi so, bhante, kakkaṭako alaṃ abhininnāmeyya taṃ tadeva te kumārakā vā kumārikā vā kaṭṭhena vā kathalena vā sañchindeyyuṃ sambhañjeyyuṃ sampalibhañjeyyuṃ.

Whenever that crab extended a claw, those boys or girls would snap, crack, and break it off with a stick or a stone.

Evañhi so, bhante, kakkaṭako sabbehi aḷehi sañchinnehi sambhaggehi sampalibhaggehi abhabbo taṃ pokkharaṇiṃ puna otarituṃ, seyyathāpi pubbe.

And when that crab's claws had all been snapped, cracked, and broken off it wouldn't be able to return down into that lotus pond.

Evameva kho, bhante, yāni saccakassa niganṭhaputtassa visūkāyitāni visevitāni vipphanditāni tānipi sabbāni bhagavatā sañchinnāni sambhaggāni sampalibhaggāni;

In the same way, sir, the Buddha has snapped, cracked, and broken off all Saccaka's tricks, dodges, and evasions.

abhabbo ca dāni, bhante, saccako niganthaputto puna bhagavantaṁ upasaṅkamituṁ yadidaṁ vādādhippāyo"ti.

Now he can't get near the Buddha again looking for a debate."

Evaṁ vutte, saccako niganthaputto dummukhaṁ licchaviputtaṁ etadavoca:

But Saccaka said to him,

"āgamehi tvaṁ, dummukha, āgamehi tvaṁ, dummukha, (...) na mayaṁ tayā saddhiṁ mantema, idha mayaṁ bhotā gotamena saddhiṁ mantema.

"Hold on, Dummukha, hold on! I wasn't talking with you, I was talking with Master Gotama.

Tiṭṭhatesā, bho gotama, amhākañceva aññesañca puthusamaṇabrāhmaṇānaṁ vācā.

Master Gotama, leave aside that statement I made—as did various other ascetics and brahmins—

Vilāpaṁ vilapitaṁ maññe.

it was, like, just a bit of nonsense.

Kittāvatā ca nu kho bhoto gotamassa sāvako sāsanakaro hoti ovādapatikaro tiṇṇavicikiccho vigatakathaṅkatho vesārajjappatto aparappaccayo satthusāsane viharatī'ti?

How do you define a disciple of Master Gotama who follows instructions and responds to advice; who has gone beyond doubt, got rid of indecision, gained assurance, and is independent of others in the Teacher's instructions?"

"Idha, aggivessana, mama sāvako yaṁ kiñci rūpaṁ atītānāgatapaccuppannaṁ ajjhattaṁ vā bahiddhā vā oḷārikaṁ vā sukhumaṁ vā hīnaṁ vā paṇītaṁ vā yaṁ dūre santike vā, sabbaṁ rūpaṁ 'netaṁ mama, nesohamasmi, na meso attā'ti evametaṁ yathābhūtaṁ sammappaññāya passati;

"It's when one of my disciples truly sees any kind of form at all—past, future, or present; internal or external; coarse or fine; inferior or superior; far or near: all form—with right understanding: 'This is not mine, I am not this, this is not my self.'

yā kāci vedanā ...pe...

They truly see any kind of feeling ...

yā kāci saññā ...pe...

perception ...

ye keci saṅkhārā ...pe...

choices ...

yaṁ kiñci viññāṇaṁ atītānāgatapaccuppannaṁ ajjhattaṁ vā bahiddhā vā oḷārikaṁ vā sukhumaṁ vā hīnaṁ vā paṇītaṁ vā, yaṁ dūre santike vā, sabbaṁ viññāṇaṁ 'netaṁ mama, nesohamasmi, na meso attā'ti evametaṁ yathābhūtaṁ sammappaññāya passati.

consciousness at all—past, future, or present; internal or external; coarse or fine; inferior or superior; far or near: all consciousness—with right understanding: 'This is not mine, I am not this, this is not my self.'

Ettāvatā kho, aggivessana, mama sāvako sāsanakaro hoti ovādapatikaro tiṇṇavicikiccho vigatakathaṅkatho vesārajjappatto aparappaccayo satthusāsane viharatī'ti.

That's how to define one of my disciples who follows instructions and responds to advice; who has gone beyond doubt, got rid of indecision, gained assurance, and is independent of others in the Teacher's instructions."

"Kittāvatā pana, bho gotama, bhikkhu arahaṁ hoti khīṇāsavo vusitavā katakaraṇīyo ohitabhāro anuppattasadattho parikkhīṇabhavasaṁyojano sammadaññāvimutto"ti?

"But how do you define a mendicant who is a perfected one, with defilements ended, who has completed the spiritual journey, done what had to be done, laid down the burden, achieved their own true goal, utterly ended the fetters of rebirth, and is rightly freed through enlightenment?"

"Idha, aggivessana, bhikkhu yaṁ kiñci rūpaṁ atītānāgatapaccuppannaṁ ajjhattaṁ vā bahiddhā vā oḷārikaṁ vā sukhumaṁ vā hīnaṁ vā paṇītaṁ vā yaṁ dūre santike vā sabbaṁ rūpaṁ 'netaṁ mama, nesohamasmi, na meso attā'ti evametaṁ yathābhūtaṁ sammappaññāya disvā anupādā vimutto hoti;

"It's when one of my disciples truly sees any kind of form at all—past, future, or present; internal or external; coarse or fine; inferior or superior; far or near: all form—with right understanding: 'This is not mine, I am not this, this is not my self.' And having seen this with right understanding they're freed by not grasping.

yā kāci vedanā ...pe...

They truly see any kind of feeling ...

yā kāci saññā ...pe...

perception ...

ye keci saṅkhārā ...pe...

choices ...

yaṁ kiñci viññāṇaṁ atītānāgatapaccuppannaṁ ajjhattaṁ vā bahiddhā vā oḷārikaṁ vā sukhumaṁ vā hīnaṁ vā paṇītaṁ vā yaṁ dūre santike vā sabbaṁ viññāṇaṁ 'netaṁ mama, nesohamasmi, na meso attā'ti evametaṁ yathābhūtaṁ sammappaññāya disvā anupādā vimutto hoti.

consciousness at all—past, future, or present; internal or external; coarse or fine; inferior or superior; far or near: all consciousness—with right understanding: 'This is not mine, I am not this, this is not my self.' And having seen this with right understanding they're freed by not grasping.

Ettāvatā kho, aggivessana, bhikkhu arahaṁ hoti khīṇāsavo vusitavā katakaraṇīyo ohitabhāro anuppattasadattho parikkhīṇabhavasaṁyojano sammadaññāvimutto.

That's how to define a mendicant who is a perfected one, with defilements ended, who has completed the spiritual journey, done what had to be done, laid down the burden, achieved their own true goal, utterly ended the fetters of rebirth, and is rightly freed through enlightenment.

Evaṁ vimuttacitto kho, aggivessana, bhikkhu tīhi anuttariyehi samannāgato hoti—

A mendicant whose mind is freed like this has three unsurpassable qualities:

dassanānuttariyena, paṭipadānuttariyena, vimuttānuttariyena.

unsurpassable vision, practice, and freedom.

Evaṁ vimuttacitto kho, aggivessana, bhikkhu tathāgataññeva sakkaroti garuṁ karoti māneti pūjeti—

They honor, respect, esteem, and venerate only the Realized One:

buddho so bhagavā bodhāya dhammaṁ deseti, danto so bhagavā damathāya dhammaṁ deseti, santo so bhagavā samathāya dhammaṁ deseti, tiṇṇo so bhagavā taraṇāya dhammaṁ deseti, parinibbuto so bhagavā parinibbānāya dhammaṁ desetī"ti.

'The Blessed One is awakened, tamed, serene, crossed over, and extinguished. And he teaches Dhamma for awakening, self-control, serenity, crossing over, and extinguishment.'"

Evaṁ vutte, saccako nigaṇṭhaputto bhagavantaṁ etadavoca:

When he had spoken, Saccaka said to him,

"mayameva, bho gotama, dhaṁsī, mayaṁ pagabbā, ye mayaṁ bhavantaṁ gotamaṁ vādena vādaṁ āsādetabbaṁ amaññimha.

"Master Gotama, it was rude and impudent of me to imagine I could attack you in debate.

Siyā hi, bho gotama, hatthiṁ pabhinnaṁ āsajja purisassa sotthibhāvo, na tveva bhavantaṁ gotamaṁ āsajja siyā purisassa sotthibhāvo.

For a person might find safety after attacking a rutting elephant, but not after attacking Master Gotama.

Siyā hi, bho gotama, pajjalitaṁ aggikkhandhaṁ āsajja purisassa sotthibhāvo, na tveva bhavantaṁ gotamaṁ āsajja siyā purisassa sotthibhāvo.

A person might find safety after attacking a blazing mass of fire, but not after attacking Master Gotama.

Siyā hi, bho gotama, āsīvisaṁ ghoravisaṁ āsajja purisassa sotthibhāvo, na tveva bhavantaṁ gotamaṁ āsajja siyā purisassa sotthibhāvo.

They might find safety after attacking a poisonous viper, but not after attacking Master Gotama.

Mayameva, bho gotama, dhaṁsī, mayaṁ pagabbā, ye mayaṁ bhavantaṁ gotamaṁ vādena vādaṁ āsādetabbaṁ amaññimha.

It was rude and impudent of me to imagine I could attack you in debate.

Adhivāsetu me bhavaṁ gotamo svātanāya bhattaṁ saddhiṁ bhikkhusaṅghenā”ti.

Would Master Gotama together with the mendicant Saṅgha please accept tomorrow's meal from me?”

Adhivāsesi bhagavā tuṇhībhāvena.

The Buddha consented with silence.

Atha kho saccako nigaṇṭhaputto bhagavato adhivāsanaṁ viditvā te licchavī āmantesi:

Then, knowing that the Buddha had consented, Saccaka addressed those Licchavis,

“suṇantu me bhonto licchavī, samaṇo me gotamo nimantito svātanāya saddhiṁ bhikkhusaṅghena.

“Listen, gentlemen. I have invited the ascetic Gotama together with the Saṅgha of mendicants for tomorrow's meal.

Tena me abhihareyyātha yamassa patirūpaṁ maññeyyāthā”ti.

You may all bring me what you think is suitable.”

Atha kho te licchavī tassā rattiyā accayena saccakassa nigaṇṭhaputtassa pañcamattāni thālipākasatāni bhattābhihāraṁ abhihariṁsu.

Then, when the night had passed, those Licchavis presented Saccaka with an offering of five hundred servings of food.

Atha kho niganthaputto sake ārāme paṇītaṁ khādanīyaṁ bhojanīyaṁ paṭiyādāpetvā bhagavato kālaṁ ārocāpesi:

And Saccaka had delicious fresh and cooked foods prepared in his own home. Then he had the Buddha informed of the time, saying,

"kālo, bho gotama, niṭṭhitaṁ bhattan"ti.

"It's time, Master Gotama, the meal is ready."

Atha kho bhagavā pubbaṇhasamayaṁ nivāsetvā pattacīvaramādāya yena saccakassa niganthaputtassa ārāmo tenupasaṅkami; upasaṅkamitvā paññatte āsane nisīdi saddhiṁ bhikkhusaṅghena.

Then the Buddha robed up in the morning and, taking his bowl and robe, went to Saccaka's park, where he sat on the seat spread out, together with the Saṅgha of mendicants.

Atha kho saccako niganthaputto buddhappamukhaṁ bhikkhusaṅghaṁ paṇītena khādanīyena bhojanīyena sahatthā santappesi sampavāresi.

Then Saccaka served and satisfied the mendicant Saṅgha headed by the Buddha with his own hands with delicious fresh and cooked foods.

Atha kho saccako niganthaputto bhagavantaṁ bhuttāviṁ onītapattapāṇiṁ aññataraṁ nīcaṁ āsanaṁ gahetvā ekamantaṁ nisīdi.

When the Buddha had eaten and washed his hand and bowl, Saccaka took a low seat and sat to one side.

Ekamantaṁ nisinno kho saccako niganthaputto bhagavantaṁ etadavoca:

Then Saccaka said to the Buddha,

"yamidaṁ, bho gotama, dāne puññañca puññamahī ca taṁ dāyakānaṁ sukhāya hotū"ti.

"Master Gotama, may the merit and the growth of merit in this gift be for the happiness of the donors."

"Yaṁ kho, aggivessana, tādisaṁ dakkhiṇeyyaṁ āgamma avītarāgaṁ avītadosaṁ avītamohaṁ, taṁ dāyakānaṁ bhavissati.

"Aggivessana, whatever comes from giving to a recipient of a religious donation such as yourself—who is not free of greed, hate, and delusion—will accrue to the donors.

Yaṁ kho, aggivessana, mādisaṁ dakkhiṇeyyaṁ āgamma vītarāgaṁ vītadosaṁ vītamohaṁ, taṁ tuyhaṁ bhavissatī"ti.

Whatever comes from giving to a recipient of a religious donation such as myself—who is free of greed, hate, and delusion—will accrue to you.”

Cūḷasaccakasuttaṁ niṭṭhitaṁ pañcamaṁ.

36 Mahasaccakasutta:

The Longer Discourse With Saccaka

Evaṁ me sutaṁ—

So I have heard.

ekaṁ samayaṁ bhagavā vesāliyaṁ viharati mahāvane kūṭāgārasālāyaṁ.

At one time the Buddha was staying near Vesālī, at the Great Wood, in the hall with the peaked roof.

Tena kho pana samayena bhagavā pubbaṇhasamayaṁ sunivattho hoti pattacīvaramādāya vesāliṁ piṇḍāya pavisitukāmo.

Now at that time in the morning the Buddha, being properly dressed, took his bowl and robe, wishing to enter Vesālī for alms.

Atha kho saccako niganṭhaputto janghāvihāraṁ anucankamamāno anuvicaramāno yena mahāvanaṁ kūṭāgārasālā tenupasankami.

Then as Saccaka, the son of Jain parents, was going for a walk he approached the hall with the peaked roof in the Great Wood.

Addasā kho āyasmā ānando saccakaṁ niganṭhaputtaṁ dūratova āgacchantaṁ.

Venerable Ānanda saw him coming off in the distance,

Disvāna bhagavantaṁ etadavoca:

and said to the Buddha,

“ayaṁ, bhante, saccako niganṭhaputto āgacchati bhassappavādako paṇḍitavādo sādhusammato bahujanassa.

“Sir, Saccaka, the son of Jain parents, is coming. He’s a debater and clever speaker regarded as holy by many people.

Eso kho, bhante, avaṇṇakāmo buddhassa, avaṇṇakāmo dhammassa, avaṇṇakāmo sanghassa.

He wants to discredit the Buddha, the teaching, and the Sangha.

Sādhu, bhante, bhagavā muhuttaṁ nisīdatu anukampaṁ upādāyā"ti.

Please, sir, sit for a moment out of compassion."

Nisīdi bhagavā paññatte āsane.

The Buddha sat on the seat spread out.

Atha kho saccako niganthaputto yena bhagavā tenupasaṅkami; upasaṅkamitvā bhagavatā saddhiṁ sammodi, sammodanīyaṁ kathaṁ sāraṇīyaṁ vītisāretvā ekamantaṁ nisīdi. Ekamantaṁ nisinno kho saccako niganthaputto bhagavantaṁ etadavoca:

Then Saccaka went up to the Buddha, and exchanged greetings with him. When the greetings and polite conversation were over, he sat down to one side and said to the Buddha,

"Santi, bho gotama, eke samaṇabrāhmaṇā kāyabhāvanānuyogamanuyuttā viharanti, no cittabhāvanaṁ.

"Master Gotama, there are some ascetics and brahmins who live committed to the practice of developing physical endurance, without developing the mind.

Phusanti hi te, bho gotama, sārīrikaṁ dukkhaṁ vedanaṁ.

They suffer painful physical feelings.

Bhūtapubbaṁ, bho gotama, sārīrikāya dukkhāya vedanāya phuṭṭhassa sato ūrukkhambhopi nāma bhavissati, hadayampi nāma phalissati, uṇhampi lohitaṁ mukhato uggamissati, ummādampi pāpuṇissati cittakkhepaṁ.

This happened to someone once. Their thighs became paralyzed, their heart burst, hot blood gushed from their mouth, and they went mad and lost their mind.

Tassa kho etaṁ, bho gotama, kāyanvayaṁ cittaṁ hoti, kāyassa vasena vattati.

Their mind was subject to the body, and the body had power over it.

Taṁ kissa hetu?

Why is that?

Abhāvitattā cittassa.

Because their mind was not developed.

Santi pana, bho gotama, eke samaṇabrāhmaṇā cittabhāvanānuyogamanuyuttā viharanti, no kāyabhāvanaṁ.

There are some ascetics and brahmins who live committed to the practice of developing the mind, without developing physical endurance.

Phusanti hi te, bho gotama, cetasikaṁ dukkhaṁ vedanaṁ.

They suffer painful mental feelings.

Bhūtapubbaṁ, bho gotama, cetasikāya dukkhāya vedanāya phuṭṭhassa sato ūrukkhambhopi nāma bhavissati, hadayampi nāma phalissati, uṇhampi lohitaṁ mukhato uggamissati, ummādampi pāpuṇissati cittakkhepaṁ.

This happened to someone once. Their thighs became paralyzed, their heart burst, hot blood gushed from their mouth, and they went mad and lost their mind.

Tassa kho eso, bho gotama, cittanvayo kāyo hoti, cittassa vasena vattati.

Their body was subject to the mind, and the mind had power over it.

Taṁ kissa hetu?

Why is that?

Abhāvitattā kāyassa.

Because their physical endurance was not developed.

Tassa mayhaṁ, bho gotama, evaṁ hoti:

It occurs to me that

'addhā bhoto gotamassa sāvakā cittabhāvanānuyogamanuyuttā viharanti, no kāyabhāvanan'"ti.

Master Gotama's disciples must live committed to the practice of developing the mind, without developing physical endurance."

"Kinti pana te, aggivessana, kāyabhāvanā sutā"ti?

"But Aggivessana, what have you heard about the development of physical endurance?"

"Seyyathidaṁ—

"Take, for example,

nando vaccho, kiso saṅkicco, makkhali gosālo—

Nanda Vaccha, Kisa Saṅkicca, and Makkhali Gosāla.

etehi, bho gotama, acelakā muttācārā hatthāpalekhanā naehibhaddantikā natiṭṭhabhaddantikā na abhihaṭaṁ na uddissakataṁ na nimantanaṁ sādiyanti,

They go naked, ignoring conventions. They lick their hands, and don't come or wait when called. They don't consent to food brought to them, or food prepared on purpose for them, or an invitation for a meal.

te na kumbhimukhā paṭiggaṇhanti na kaḷopimukhā paṭiggaṇhanti na eḷakamantaraṁ na daṇḍamantaraṁ na musalamantaraṁ na dvinnaṁ bhuñjamānānaṁ na gabbhiniyā na pāyamānāya na purisantaragatāya na saṅkittīsu na yattha sā upaṭṭhito hoti na yattha makkhikā saṇḍasaṇḍacārinī, na macchaṁ na maṁsaṁ na suraṁ na merayaṁ na thusodakaṁ pivanti.

They don't receive anything from a pot or bowl; or from someone who keeps sheep, or who has a weapon or a shovel in their home; or where a couple is eating; or where there is a woman who is pregnant, breastfeeding, or who has a man in her home; or where there's a dog waiting or flies buzzing. They accept no fish or meat or liquor or wine, and drink no beer.

Te ekāgārikā vā honti ekālopikā, dvāgārikā vā honti dvālopikā …pe… sattāgārikā vā honti sattālopikā.

They go to just one house for alms, taking just one mouthful, or two houses and two mouthfuls, up to seven houses and seven mouthfuls.

Ekissāpi dattiyā yāpenti, dvīhipi dattīhi yāpenti …pe… sattahipi dattīhi yāpenti.

They feed on one saucer a day, two saucers a day, up to seven saucers a day.

Ekāhikampi āhāraṁ āhārenti, dvīhikampi āhāraṁ āhārenti … pe… sattāhikampi āhāraṁ āhārenti. Iti evarūpaṁ addhamāsikampi pariyāyabhattabhojanānuyogamanuyuttā viharantī"ti.

They eat once a day, once every second day, up to once a week, and so on, even up to once a fortnight. They live committed to the practice of eating food at set intervals."

"Kiṁ pana te, aggivessana, tāvatakeneva yāpentī"ti?

"But Aggivessana, do they get by on so little?"

"No hidaṁ, bho gotama.

"No, Master Gotama.

Appekadā, bho gotama, uḷārāni uḷārāni khādanīyāni khādanti, uḷārāni uḷārāni bhojanāni bhuñjanti, uḷārāni uḷārāni sāyanīyāni sāyanti, uḷārāni uḷārāni pānāni pivanti.

Sometimes they eat luxury fresh and cooked foods and drink a variety of luxury beverages.

Te imaṁ kāyaṁ balaṁ gāhenti nāma, brūhenti nāma, medenti nāmā"ti.

They gather their body's strength, build it up, and get fat."

"Yaṁ kho te, aggivessana, purimaṁ pahāya pacchā upacinanti, evaṁ imassa kāyassa ācayāpacayo hoti.

"What they earlier gave up, they later got back. That is how there is the increase and decrease of this body.

Kinti pana te, aggivessana, cittabhāvanā sutā"ti?

But Aggivessana, what have you heard about development of the mind?"

Cittabhāvanāya kho saccako niganthaputto bhagavatā puttho samāno na sampāyāsi.

When Saccaka was questioned by the Buddha about development of the mind, he was stumped.

Atha kho bhagavā saccakam niganthaputtam etadavoca:

So the Buddha said to Saccaka,

"yāpi kho te esā, aggivessana, purimā kāyabhāvanā bhāsitā sāpi ariyassa vinaye no dhammikā kāyabhāvanā.

"The development of physical endurance that you have described is not the legitimate development of physical endurance in the noble one's training.

Kāyabhāvanampi kho tvam, aggivessana, na aññāsi, kuto pana tvam cittabhāvanam jānissasi?

And since you don't even understand the development of physical endurance, how can you possibly understand the development of the mind?

Api ca, aggivessana, yathā abhāvitakāyo ca hoti abhāvitacitto ca, bhāvitakāyo ca hoti bhāvitacitto ca.

Still, as to how someone is undeveloped in physical endurance and mind, and how someone is developed in physical endurance and mind,

Tam sunāhi, sādhukam manasi karohi, bhāsissāmī"ti.

listen and pay close attention, I will speak."

"Evam, bho"ti kho saccako niganthaputto bhagavato paccassosi.

"Yes, sir," replied Saccaka.

Bhagavā etadavoca:

The Buddha said this:

"Kathañca, aggivessana, abhāvitakāyo ca hoti abhāvitacitto ca?

"And how is someone undeveloped in physical endurance and mind?

Idha, aggivessana, assutavato puthujjanassa uppajjati sukhā vedanā.

Take an unlearned ordinary person who has a pleasant feeling.

So sukhāya vedanāya phuṭṭho samāno sukhasārāgī ca hoti sukhasārāgitañca āpajjati.

When they experience pleasant feeling they become full of lust for it.

Tassa sā sukhā vedanā nirujjhati.

Then that pleasant feeling ceases.

Sukhāya vedanāya nirodhā uppajjati dukkhā vedanā.

And when it ceases, a painful feeling arises.

So dukkhāya vedanāya phuṭṭho samāno socati kilamati paridevati urattāḷiṃ kandati sammohaṃ āpajjati.

When they suffer painful feeling, they sorrow and wail and lament, beating their breast and falling into confusion.

Tassa kho esā, aggivessana, uppannāpi sukhā vedanā cittaṃ pariyādāya tiṭṭhati abhāvitattā kāyassa, uppannāpi dukkhā vedanā cittaṃ pariyādāya tiṭṭhati abhāvitattā cittassa.

Because their physical endurance is undeveloped, pleasant feelings occupy the mind. And because their mind is undeveloped, painful feelings occupy the mind.

Yassa kassaci, aggivessana, evaṃ ubhatopakkhaṃ uppannāpi sukhā vedanā cittaṃ pariyādāya tiṭṭhati abhāvitattā kāyassa, uppannāpi dukkhā vedanā cittaṃ pariyādāya tiṭṭhati abhāvitattā cittassa, evaṃ kho, aggivessana, abhāvitakāyo ca hoti abhāvitacitto ca.

Someone whose mind is occupied by both pleasant and painful feelings like this is undeveloped in physical endurance and in mind.

Kathañca, aggivessana, bhāvitakāyo ca hoti bhāvitacitto ca?

And how is someone developed in physical endurance and mind?

Idha, aggivessana, sutavato ariyasāvakassa uppajjati sukhā vedanā.

Take a learned noble disciple who has a pleasant feeling.

So sukhāya vedanāya phuṭṭho samāno na sukhasārāgī ca hoti, na sukhasārāgitañca āpajjati.

When they experience pleasant feeling they don't become full of lust for it.

Tassa sā sukhā vedanā nirujjhati.

Then that pleasant feeling ceases.

Sukhāya vedanāya nirodhā uppajjati dukkhā vedanā.

And when it ceases, painful feeling arises.

So dukkhāya vedanāya phuṭṭho samāno na socati na kilamati na paridevati na urattāḷiṁ kandati na sammohaṁ āpajjati.

When they suffer painful feelings they don't sorrow or wail or lament, beating their breast and falling into confusion.

Tassa kho esā, aggivessana, uppannāpi sukhā vedanā cittaṁ na pariyādāya tiṭṭhati bhāvitattā kāyassa, uppannāpi dukkhā vedanā cittaṁ na pariyādāya tiṭṭhati bhāvitattā cittassa.

Because their physical endurance is developed, pleasant feelings don't occupy the mind. And because their mind is developed, painful feelings don't occupy the mind.

Yassa kassaci, aggivessana, evaṁ ubhatopakkhaṁ uppannāpi sukhā vedanā cittaṁ na pariyādāya tiṭṭhati bhāvitattā kāyassa, uppannāpi dukkhā vedanā cittaṁ na pariyādāya tiṭṭhati bhāvitattā cittassa. Evaṁ kho, aggivessana, bhāvitakāyo ca hoti bhāvitacitto cā"ti.

Someone whose mind is not occupied by both pleasant and painful feelings like this is developed in physical endurance and in mind."

"Evaṁ pasanno ahaṁ bhoto gotamassa.

"I am quite confident that Master Gotama

Bhavañhi gotamo bhāvitakāyo ca hoti bhāvitacitto cā"ti.

is developed in physical endurance and in mind."

"Addhā kho te ayaṁ, aggivessana, āsajja upanīya vācā bhāsitā,

"Your words are clearly invasive and intrusive, Aggivessana.

api ca te ahaṁ byākarissāmi.

Nevertheless, I will answer you.

Yato kho ahaṁ, aggivessana, kesamassuṁ ohāretvā kāsāyāni vatthāni acchādetvā agārasmā anagāriyaṁ pabbajito, taṁ vata me uppannā vā sukhā vedanā cittaṁ pariyādāya ṭhassati, uppannā vā dukkhā vedanā cittaṁ pariyādāya ṭhassatīti netaṁ ṭhānaṁ vijjatī"ti.

Ever since I shaved off my hair and beard, dressed in ocher robes, and went forth from the lay life to homelessness, it has not been possible for any pleasant or painful feeling to occupy my mind."

"Na hi nūna bhoto gotamassa uppajjati tathārūpā sukhā vedanā yathārūpā uppannā sukhā vedanā cittaṁ pariyādāya tiṭṭheyya; na hi nūna bhoto gotamassa uppajjati tathārūpā dukkhā vedanā yathārūpā uppannā dukkhā vedanā cittaṁ pariyādāya tiṭṭheyyā"ti.

"Surely you must have had feelings so pleasant or so painful that they could occupy your mind?"

"Kiñhi no siyā, aggivessana?

"How could I not, Aggivessana?

Idha me, aggivessana, pubbeva sambodhā anabhisambuddhassa bodhisattasseva sato etadahosi:

Before my awakening—when I was still unawakened but intent on awakening—I thought:

'sambādho gharāvāso rajāpatho, abbhokāso pabbajjā.

'Living in a house is cramped and dirty, but the life of one gone forth is wide open.

Nayidaṁ sukaraṁ agāraṁ ajjhāvasatā ekantaparipuṇṇaṁ ekantaparisuddhaṁ saṅkhalikhitaṁ brahmacariyaṁ carituṁ.

It's not easy for someone living at home to lead the spiritual life utterly full and pure, like a polished shell.

Yannūnāhaṁ kesamassuṁ ohāretvā kāsāyāni vatthāni acchādetvā agārasmā anagāriyaṁ pabbajeyyan'ti.

Why don't I shave off my hair and beard, dress in ocher robes, and go forth from the lay life to homelessness?'

So kho ahaṁ, aggivessana, aparena samayena daharova samāno, susukāḷakeso bhadrena yobbanena samannāgato paṭhamena vayasā, akāmakānaṁ mātāpitūnaṁ assumukhānaṁ rudantānaṁ, kesamassuṁ ohāretvā kāsāyāni vatthāni acchādetvā agārasmā anagāriyaṁ pabbajiṁ.

Some time later, while still black-haired, blessed with youth, in the prime of life— though my mother and father wished otherwise, weeping with tearful faces—I shaved off my hair and beard, dressed in ocher robes, and went forth from the lay life to homelessness.

So evaṁ pabbajito samāno kiṅkusalagavesī anuttaraṁ santivarapadaṁ pariyesamāno yena āḷāro kālāmo tenupasaṅkamiṁ; upasaṅkamitvā āḷāraṁ kālāmaṁ etadavocaṁ:

Once I had gone forth I set out to discover what is skillful, seeking the supreme state of sublime peace. I approached Āḷāra Kālāma and said to him,

'icchāmahaṁ, āvuso kālāma, imasmiṁ dhammavinaye brahmacariyaṁ caritun'ti.

'Reverend Kālāma, I wish to lead the spiritual life in this teaching and training.'

Evaṁ vutte, aggivessana, āḷāro kālāmo maṁ etadavoca:

Āḷāra Kālāma replied,

'viharatāyasmā,

'Stay, venerable.

tādiso ayaṁ dhammo yattha viññū puriso nacirasseva sakaṁ ācariyakaṁ sayaṁ abhiññā sacchikatvā upasampajja vihareyyā'ti.

This teaching is such that a sensible person can soon realize their own tradition with their own insight and live having achieved it.'

So kho ahaṁ, aggivessana, nacirasseva khippameva taṁ dhammaṁ pariyāpuṇiṁ.

I quickly memorized that teaching.

So kho ahaṁ, aggivessana, tāvatakeneva oṭṭhapahatamattena lapitalāpanamattena ñāṇavādañca vadāmi theravādañca, 'jānāmi passāmī'ti ca paṭijānāmi, ahañceva aññe ca.

So far as lip-recital and oral recitation were concerned, I spoke with knowledge and the authority of the elders. I claimed to know and see, and so did others.

Tassa mayhaṁ, aggivessana, etadahosi:

Then it occurred to me,

'na kho āḷāro kālāmo imaṁ dhammaṁ kevalaṁ saddhāmattakena sayaṁ abhiññā sacchikatvā upasampajja viharāmīti pavedeti,

'It is not solely by mere faith that Āḷāra Kālāma declares: "I realize this teaching with my own insight, and live having achieved it."

addhā āḷāro kālāmo imaṁ dhammaṁ jānaṁ passaṁ viharatī'ti.

Surely he meditates knowing and seeing this teaching.'

Atha khvāhaṁ, aggivessana, yena āḷāro kālāmo tenupasaṅkamiṁ; upasaṅkamitvā āḷāraṁ kālāmaṁ etadavocaṁ:

So I approached Āḷāra Kālāma and said to him,

'kittāvatā no, āvuso kālāma, imaṁ dhammaṁ sayaṁ abhiññā sacchikatvā upasampajja viharāmīti pavedesī'ti?

'Reverend Kālāma, to what extent do you say you've realized this teaching with your own insight?'

Evaṁ vutte, aggivessana, āḷāro kālāmo ākiñcaññāyatanaṁ pavedesi.

When I said this, he declared the dimension of nothingness.

Tassa mayhaṁ, aggivessana, etadahosi:

Then it occurred to me,

'na kho āḷārasseva kālāmassa atthi saddhā, mayhampatthi saddhā;

'It's not just Āḷāra Kālāma who has faith,

na kho āḷārasseva kālāmassa atthi vīriyaṁ, mayhampatthi vīriyaṁ;

energy,

na kho āḷārasseva kālāmassa atthi sati, mayhampatthi sati;

mindfulness,

na kho āḷārasseva kālāmassa atthi samādhi, mayhampatthi samādhi;

immersion,

na kho āḷārasseva kālāmassa atthi paññā, mayhampatthi paññā;

and wisdom; I too have these things.

yannūnāhaṁ yaṁ dhammaṁ āḷāro kālāmo sayaṁ abhiññā sacchikatvā upasampajja viharāmīti pavedeti tassa dhammassa sacchikiriyāya padaheyyan'ti.

Why don't I make an effort to realize the same teaching that Āḷāra Kālāma says he has realized with his own insight?'

So kho ahaṁ, aggivessana, nacirasseva khippameva taṁ dhammaṁ sayaṁ abhiññā sacchikatvā upasampajja vihāsiṁ.

I quickly realized that teaching with my own insight, and lived having achieved it.

Atha khvāhaṁ, aggivessana, yena āḷāro kālāmo tenupasaṅkamiṁ; upasaṅkamitvā āḷāraṁ kālāmaṁ etadavocaṁ:

So I approached Āḷāra Kālāma and said to him,

'ettāvatā no, āvuso kālāma, imaṁ dhammaṁ sayaṁ abhiññā sacchikatvā upasampajja pavedesī'ti?

'Reverend Kālāma, have you realized this teaching with your own insight up to this point, and declare having achieved it?'

'Ettāvatā kho ahaṁ, āvuso, imaṁ dhammaṁ sayaṁ abhiññā sacchikatvā upasampajja pavedemī'ti.

'I have, reverend.'

'Ahampi kho, āvuso, ettāvatā imaṁ dhammaṁ sayaṁ abhiññā sacchikatvā upasampajja viharāmī'ti.

'I too have realized this teaching with my own insight up to this point, and live having achieved it.'

'Lābhā no, āvuso, suladdhaṁ no, āvuso,

'We are fortunate, reverend, so very fortunate

ye mayaṁ āyasmantaṁ tādisaṁ sabrahmacāriṁ passāma.

to see a venerable such as yourself as one of our spiritual companions!

Iti yāhaṁ dhammaṁ sayaṁ abhiññā sacchikatvā upasampajja pavedemi taṁ tvaṁ dhammaṁ sayaṁ abhiññā sacchikatvā upasampajja viharasi;

So the teaching that I've realized with my own insight, and declare having achieved it, you've realized with your own insight, and live having achieved it.

yaṁ tvaṁ dhammaṁ sayaṁ abhiññā sacchikatvā upasampajja viharasi tamahaṁ dhammaṁ sayaṁ abhiññā sacchikatvā upasampajja pavedemi.

The teaching that you've realized with your own insight, and live having achieved it, I've realized with my own insight, and declare having achieved it.

Iti yāhaṁ dhammaṁ jānāmi taṁ tvaṁ dhammaṁ jānāsi; yaṁ tvaṁ dhammaṁ jānāsi tamahaṁ dhammaṁ jānāmi.

So the teaching that I know, you know, and the teaching you know, I know.

Iti yādiso ahaṁ tādiso tuvaṁ, yādiso tuvaṁ tādiso ahaṁ.

I am like you and you are like me.

Ehi dāni, āvuso, ubhova santā imaṁ gaṇaṁ pariharāmā'ti.

Come now, reverend! We should both lead this community together.'

Iti kho, aggivessana, āḷāro kālāmo ācariyo me samāno attano antevāsiṁ maṁ samānaṁ attanā samasamaṁ ṭhapesi, uḷārāya ca maṁ pūjāya pūjesi.

And that is how my teacher Āḷāra Kālāma placed me, his student, on the same position as him, and honored me with lofty praise.

Tassa mayhaṁ, aggivessana, etadahosi:

Then it occurred to me,

'nāyaṁ dhammo nibbidāya na virāgāya na nirodhāya na upasamāya na abhiññāya na sambodhāya na nibbānāya saṁvattati, yāvadeva ākiñcaññāyatanūpapattiyā'ti.

'This teaching doesn't lead to disillusionment, dispassion, cessation, peace, insight, awakening, and extinguishment. It only leads as far as rebirth in the dimension of nothingness.'

So kho ahaṁ, aggivessana, taṁ dhammaṁ analaṅkaritvā tasmā dhammā nibbijja apakkamiṁ.

Realizing that this teaching was inadequate, I left disappointed.

So kho ahaṁ, aggivessana, kiṅkusalagavesī anuttaraṁ santivarapadaṁ pariyesamāno yena udako rāmaputto tenupasaṅkamiṁ; upasaṅkamitvā udakaṁ rāmaputtaṁ etadavocaṁ:

I set out to discover what is skillful, seeking the supreme state of sublime peace. I approached Uddaka, son of Rāma, and said to him,

'icchāmahaṁ, āvuso, imasmiṁ dhammavinaye brahmacariyaṁ caritun'ti.

'Reverend, I wish to lead the spiritual life in this teaching and training.'

Evaṁ vutte, aggivessana, udako rāmaputto maṁ etadavoca:

Uddaka replied,

'viharatāyasmā,

'Stay, venerable.

tādiso ayaṁ dhammo yattha viññū puriso nacirasseva sakaṁ ācariyakaṁ sayaṁ abhiññā sacchikatvā upasampajja vihareyyā'ti.

This teaching is such that a sensible person can soon realize their own tradition with their own insight and live having achieved it.'

So kho ahaṁ, aggivessana, nacirasseva khippameva taṁ dhammaṁ pariyāpuṇiṁ.

I quickly memorized that teaching.

So kho ahaṁ, aggivessana, tāvatakeneva oṭṭhapahatamattena lapitalāpanamattena ñāṇavādañca vadāmi theravādañca, 'jānāmi passāmī'ti ca paṭijānāmi, ahañceva aññe ca.

So far as lip-recital and oral recitation were concerned, I spoke with knowledge and the authority of the elders. I claimed to know and see, and so did others.

Tassa mayhaṁ, aggivessana, etadahosi:

Then it occurred to me,

'na kho rāmo imaṁ dhammaṁ kevalaṁ saddhāmattakena sayaṁ abhiññā sacchikatvā upasampajja viharāmīti pavedesi.

'It is not solely by mere faith that Rāma declared: "I realize this teaching with my own insight, and live having achieved it."

Addhā rāmo imaṁ dhammaṁ jānaṁ passaṁ vihāsī'ti.

Surely he meditated knowing and seeing this teaching.'

Atha khvāhaṁ, aggivessana, yena udako rāmaputto tenupasaṅkamiṁ; upasaṅkamitvā udakaṁ rāmaputtaṁ etadavocaṁ:

So I approached Uddaka, son of Rāma, and said to him,

'kittāvatā no āvuso rāmo imaṁ dhammaṁ sayaṁ abhiññā sacchikatvā upasampajja viharāmīti pavedesī'ti?

'Reverend, to what extent did Rāma say he'd realized this teaching with his own insight?'

Evaṁ vutte, aggivessana, udako rāmaputto nevasaññānāsaññāyatanaṁ pavedesi.

When I said this, Uddaka, son of Rāma, declared the dimension of neither perception nor non-perception.

Tassa mayhaṁ, aggivessana, etadahosi:

Then it occurred to me,

'na kho rāmasseva ahosi saddhā, mayhampatthi saddhā;

'It's not just Rāma who had faith,

na kho rāmasseva ahosi vīriyaṁ, mayhampatthi vīriyaṁ;

energy,

na kho rāmasseva ahosi sati, mayhampatthi sati;

mindfulness,

na kho rāmasseva ahosi samādhi, mayhampatthi samādhi;

immersion,

na kho rāmasseva ahosi paññā, mayhampatthi paññā;

and wisdom; I too have these things.

yannūnāhaṁ yaṁ dhammaṁ rāmo sayaṁ abhiññā sacchikatvā upasampajja viharāmīti pavedesi tassa dhammassa sacchikiriyāya padaheyyan'ti.

Why don't I make an effort to realize the same teaching that Rāma said he had realized with his own insight?'

So kho ahaṁ, aggivessana, nacirasseva khippameva taṁ dhammaṁ sayaṁ abhiññā sacchikatvā upasampajja vihāsiṁ.

I quickly realized that teaching with my own insight, and lived having achieved it.

Atha khvāhaṁ, aggivessana, yena udako rāmaputto tenupasaṅkamiṁ; upasaṅkamitvā udakaṁ rāmaputtaṁ etadavocaṁ:

So I approached Uddaka, son of Rāma, and said to him,

'ettāvatā no āvuso rāmo imaṁ dhammaṁ sayaṁ abhiññā sacchikatvā upasampajja pavedesī'ti?

'Reverend, had Rāma realized this teaching with his own insight up to this point, and declared having achieved it?'

'Ettāvatā kho āvuso rāmo imaṁ dhammaṁ sayaṁ abhiññā sacchikatvā upasampajja pavedesī'ti.

'He had, reverend.'

'Ahampi kho, āvuso, ettāvatā imaṁ dhammaṁ sayaṁ abhiññā sacchikatvā upasampajja viharāmī'ti.

'I too have realized this teaching with my own insight up to this point, and live having achieved it.'

'Lābhā no, āvuso, suladdhaṁ no, āvuso,

'We are fortunate, reverend, so very fortunate

ye mayaṁ āyasmantaṁ tādisaṁ sabrahmacāriṁ passāma.

to see a venerable such as yourself as one of our spiritual companions!

Iti yaṁ dhammaṁ rāmo sayaṁ abhiññā sacchikatvā upasampajja pavedesi, taṁ tvaṁ dhammaṁ sayaṁ abhiññā sacchikatvā upasampajja viharasi; yaṁ tvaṁ dhammaṁ sayaṁ abhiññā sacchikatvā upasampajja viharasi, taṁ dhammaṁ rāmo sayaṁ abhiññā sacchikatvā upasampajja pavedesi.

The teaching that Rāma had realized with his own insight, and declared having achieved it, you have realized with your own insight, and live having achieved it. The teaching that you've realized with your own insight, and live having achieved it, Rāma had realized with his own insight, and declared having achieved it.

Iti yaṁ dhammaṁ rāmo abhiññāsi taṁ tvaṁ dhammaṁ jānāsi; yaṁ tvaṁ dhammaṁ jānāsi taṁ dhammaṁ rāmo abhiññāsi.

So the teaching that Rāma directly knew, you know, and the teaching you know, Rāma directly knew.

Iti yādiso rāmo ahosi tādiso tuvaṁ; yādiso tuvaṁ tādiso rāmo ahosi.

Rāma was like you and you are like Rāma.

Ehi dāni, āvuso, tuvaṁ imaṁ gaṇaṁ pariharā'ti.

Come now, reverend! You should lead this community.'

Iti kho, aggivessana, udako rāmaputto sabrahmacārī me samāno ācariyaṭṭhāne ca mam ṭhapesi, uḷārāya ca mam pūjāya pūjesi.

And that is how my spiritual companion Uddaka, son of Rāma, placed me in the position of a teacher, and honored me with lofty praise.

Tassa mayham, aggivessana, etadahosi:

Then it occurred to me,

'nāyam dhammo nibbidāya na virāgāya na nirodhāya na upasamāya na abhiññāya na sambodhāya na nibbānāya samvattati, yāvadeva nevasaññānāsaññāyatanūpapattiyā'ti.

'This teaching doesn't lead to disillusionment, dispassion, cessation, peace, insight, awakening, and extinguishment. It only leads as far as rebirth in the dimension of neither perception nor non-perception.'

So kho aham, aggivessana, tam dhammam analankaritvā tasmā dhammā nibbijja apakkamim.

Realizing that this teaching was inadequate, I left disappointed.

So kho aham, aggivessana, kinkusalagavesī anuttaram santivarapadam pariyesamāno magadhesu anupubbena cārikam caramāno yena uruvelā senānigamo tadavasarim.

I set out to discover what is skillful, seeking the supreme state of sublime peace. Traveling stage by stage in the Magadhan lands, I arrived at Senanigama near Uruvelā.

Tatthaddasam ramaṇīyam bhūmibhāgam, pāsādikañca vanasaṇḍam, nadiñca sandantim setakam supatittham ramaṇīyam, samantā ca gocaragāmam.

There I saw a delightful park, a lovely grove with a flowing river that was clean and charming, with smooth banks. And nearby was a village to go for alms.

Tassa mayham, aggivessana, etadahosi:

Then it occurred to me,

'ramaṇīyo vata bho bhūmibhāgo, pāsādiko ca vanasaṇḍo, nadī ca sandati setakā supatitthā ramaṇīyā, samantā ca gocaragāmo.

'This park is truly delightful, a lovely grove with a flowing river that's clean and charming, with smooth banks. And nearby there's a village to go for alms.

Alaṁ vatidaṁ kulaputtassa padhānatthikassa padhānāyā'ti.

This is good enough for a gentleman who wishes to put forth effort in meditation.'

So kho ahaṁ, aggivessana, tattheva nisīdiṁ

So I sat down right there, thinking:

'alamidaṁ padhānāyā'ti.

'This is good enough for meditation.'

Apissumaṁ, aggivessana, tisso upamā paṭibhaṁsu anacchariyā pubbe assutapubbā.

And then these three examples, which were neither supernaturally inspired, nor learned before in the past, occurred to me.

Seyyathāpi, aggivessana, allaṁ kaṭṭhaṁ sasnehaṁ udake nikkhittaṁ.

Suppose there was a green, sappy log, and it was lying in water.

Atha puriso āgaccheyya uttarāraṇiṁ ādāya:

Then a person comes along with a drill-stick, thinking

'aggiṁ abhinibbattessāmi, tejo pātukarissāmī'ti.

to light a fire and produce heat.

Taṁ kiṁ maññasi, aggivessana,

What do you think, Aggivessana?

api nu so puriso amuṁ allaṁ kaṭṭhaṁ sasnehaṁ, udake nikkhittaṁ, uttarāraṇiṁ ādāya abhimanthento aggiṁ abhinibbatteyya, tejo pātukareyyā"ti?

By drilling the stick against that green, sappy log lying in the water, could they light a fire and produce heat?"

"No hidaṁ, bho gotama".

"No, Master Gotama.

"Taṁ kissa hetu"?

Why not?

"Aduñhi, bho gotama, allaṁ kaṭṭhaṁ sasnehaṁ, tañca pana udake nikkhittaṁ.

Because it's a green, sappy log, and it's lying in the water.

Yāvadeva ca pana so puriso kilamathassa vighātassa bhāgī assā"ti.

That person will eventually get weary and frustrated."

"Evameva kho, aggivessana, ye hi keci samaṇā vā brāhmaṇā vā kāyena ceva cittena ca kāmehi avūpakaṭṭhā viharanti, yo ca nesaṁ kāmesu kāmacchando kāmasneho kāmamucchā kāmapipāsā kāmapariḷāho, so ca ajjhattaṁ na suppahīno hoti, na suppaṭippassaddho, opakkamikā cepi te bhonto samaṇabrāhmaṇā dukkhā tibbā kharā kaṭukā vedanā vedayanti, abhabbāva te ñāṇāya dassanāya anuttarāya sambodhāya.

"In the same way, there are ascetics and brahmins who don't live withdrawn in body and mind from sensual pleasures. They haven't internally given up or stilled desire, affection, infatuation, thirst, and passion for sensual pleasures. Regardless of whether or not they feel painful, sharp, severe, acute feelings due to overexertion, they are incapable of knowledge and vision, of supreme awakening.

No cepi te bhonto samaṇabrāhmaṇā opakkamikā dukkhā tibbā kharā kaṭukā vedanā vedayanti, abhabbāva te ñāṇāya dassanāya anuttarāya sambodhāya.

Ayaṁ kho maṁ, aggivessana, paṭhamā upamā paṭibhāsi anacchariyā pubbe assutapubbā.

This was the first example that occurred to me.

Aparāpi kho maṁ, aggivessana, dutiyā upamā paṭibhāsi anacchariyā pubbe assutapubbā.

Then a second example occurred to me.

Seyyathāpi, aggivessana, allaṁ kaṭṭhaṁ sasnehaṁ, ārakā udakā thale nikkhittaṁ.

Suppose there was a green, sappy log, and it was lying on dry land far from the water.

Atha puriso āgaccheyya uttarāraṇiṁ ādāya:

Then a person comes along with a drill-stick, thinking

'aggiṁ abhinibbattessāmi, tejo pātukarissāmī'ti.

to light a fire and produce heat.

Taṁ kiṁ maññasi, aggivessana,

What do you think, Aggivessana?

api nu so puriso amuṁ allaṁ kaṭṭhaṁ sasnehaṁ, ārakā udakā thale nikkhittaṁ, uttarāraṇiṁ ādāya abhimanthento aggiṁ abhinibbatteyya tejo pātukareyyā"ti?

By drilling the stick against that green, sappy log on dry land far from water, could they light a fire and produce heat?"

"No hidaṁ, bho gotama".

"No, Master Gotama.

"Taṁ kissa hetu"?

Why not?

"Aduñhi, bho gotama, allaṁ kaṭṭhaṁ sasnehaṁ, kiñcāpi ārakā udakā thale nikkhittaṁ.

Because it's still a green, sappy log, despite the fact that it's lying on dry land far from water.

Yāvadeva ca pana so puriso kilamathassa vighātassa bhāgī assā"ti.

That person will eventually get weary and frustrated."

"Evameva kho, aggivessana, ye hi keci samaṇā vā brāhmaṇā vā kāyena ceva cittena ca kāmehi vūpakaṭṭhā viharanti, yo ca nesaṁ kāmesu kāmacchando kāmasneho kāmamucchā kāmapipāsā kāmapariḷāho so ca ajjhattaṁ na suppahīno hoti, na suppaṭippassaddho, opakkamikā cepi te bhonto samaṇabrāhmaṇā dukkhā tibbā kharā kaṭukā vedanā vedayanti, abhabbāva te ñāṇāya dassanāya anuttarāya sambodhāya. No cepi te bhonto samaṇabrāhmaṇā opakkamikā dukkhā tibbā kharā kaṭukā vedanā vedayanti, abhabbāva te ñāṇāya dassanāya anuttarāya sambodhāya.

"In the same way, there are ascetics and brahmins who live withdrawn in body and mind from sensual pleasures. But they haven't internally given up or stilled desire, affection, infatuation, thirst, and passion for sensual pleasures. Regardless of whether or not they suffer painful, sharp, severe, acute feelings due to overexertion, they are incapable of knowledge and vision, of supreme awakening.

Ayaṁ kho maṁ, aggivessana, dutiyā upamā paṭibhāsi anacchariyā pubbe assutapubbā

This was the second example that occurred to me.

Aparāpi kho maṁ, aggivessana, tatiyā upamā paṭibhāsi anacchariyā pubbe assutapubbā.

Then a third example occurred to me.

Seyyathāpi, aggivessana, sukkhaṁ kaṭṭhaṁ koḷāpaṁ, ārakā udakā thale nikkhittaṁ.

Suppose there was a dried up, withered log, and it was lying on dry land far from the water.

Atha puriso āgaccheyya uttarāraṇiṁ ādāya:

Then a person comes along with a drill-stick, thinking

'aggiṁ abhinibbattessāmi, tejo pātukarissāmī'ti.

to light a fire and produce heat.

Taṁ kiṁ maññasi, aggivessana,

What do you think, Aggivessana?

api nu so puriso amuṁ sukkhaṁ kaṭṭhaṁ koḷāpaṁ, ārakā udakā thale nikkhittaṁ, uttarāraṇiṁ ādāya abhimanthento aggiṁ abhinibbatteyya, tejo pātukareyyā"ti?

By drilling the stick against that dried up, withered log on dry land far from water, could they light a fire and produce heat?"

"Evaṁ, bho gotama".

"Yes, Master Gotama.

"Taṁ kissa hetu"?

Why is that?

"Aduñhi, bho gotama, sukkhaṁ kaṭṭhaṁ koḷāpaṁ, tañca pana ārakā udakā thale nikkhittan"ti.

Because it's a dried up, withered log, and it's lying on dry land far from water."

"Evameva kho, aggivessana, ye hi keci samaṇā vā brāhmaṇā vā kāyena ceva cittena ca kāmehi vūpakaṭṭhā viharanti, yo ca nesaṁ kāmesu kāmacchando kāmasneho kāmamucchā kāmapipāsā kāmapariḷāho, so ca ajjhattaṁ suppahīno hoti suppaṭippassaddho, opakkamikā cepi te bhonto samaṇabrāhmaṇā dukkhā tibbā kharā kaṭukā vedanā vedayanti, bhabbāva te ñāṇāya dassanāya anuttarāya sambodhāya. No cepi te bhonto samaṇabrāhmaṇā opakkamikā dukkhā tibbā kharā kaṭukā vedanā vedayanti, bhabbāva te ñāṇāya dassanāya anuttarāya sambodhāya.

"In the same way, there are ascetics and brahmins who live withdrawn in body and mind from sensual pleasures. And they have internally given up and stilled desire, affection, infatuation, thirst, and passion for sensual pleasures. Regardless of whether or not they suffer painful, sharp, severe, acute feelings due to overexertion, they are capable of knowledge and vision, of supreme awakening.

Ayaṁ kho maṁ, aggivessana, tatiyā upamā paṭibhāsi anacchariyā pubbe assutapubbā.

This was the third example that occurred to me.

Imā kho maṁ, aggivessana, tisso upamā paṭibhaṁsu anacchariyā pubbe assutapubbā.

These are the three examples, which were neither supernaturally inspired, nor learned before in the past, that occurred to me.

Tassa mayhaṁ, aggivessana, etadahosi:

Then it occurred to me,

'yannūnāhaṁ dantebhi dantamādhāya, jivhāya tāluṁ āhacca, cetasā cittaṁ abhinigganheyyaṁ abhinippīleyyaṁ abhisantāpeyyan'ti.

'Why don't I, with teeth clenched and tongue pressed against the roof of my mouth, squeeze, squash, and torture mind with mind.'

So kho ahaṁ, aggivessana, dantebhi dantamādhāya, jivhāya tāluṁ āhacca, cetasā cittaṁ abhinigganhāmi abhinippīlemi abhisantāpemi.

So that's what I did,

Tassa mayhaṁ, aggivessana, dantebhi dantamādhāya jivhāya tāluṁ āhacca cetasā cittaṁ abhinigganhato abhinippīlayato abhisantāpayato kacchehi sedā muccanti.

until sweat ran from my armpits.

Seyyathāpi, aggivessana, balavā puriso dubbalataraṁ purisaṁ sīse vā gahetvā khandhe vā gahetvā abhinigganheyya abhinippīleyya abhisantāpeyya;

It was like when a strong man grabs a weaker man by the head or throat or shoulder and squeezes, squashes, and tortures them.

evameva kho me, aggivessana, dantebhi dantamādhāya, jivhāya tāluṁ āhacca, cetasā cittaṁ abhinigganhato abhinippīlayato abhisantāpayato kacchehi sedā muccanti.

In the same way, with teeth clenched and tongue pressed against the roof of my mouth, I squeezed, squashed, and tortured mind with mind until sweat ran from my armpits.

Āraddhaṁ kho pana me, aggivessana, vīriyaṁ hoti asallīnaṁ, upaṭṭhitā sati asammuṭṭhā, sāraddho ca pana me kāyo hoti appaṭippassaddho teneva dukkhappadhānena padhānābhitunnassa sato.

My energy was roused up and unflagging, and my mindfulness was established and lucid, but my body was disturbed, not tranquil, because I'd pushed too hard with that painful striving.

Evarūpāpi kho me, aggivessana, uppannā dukkhā vedanā cittaṁ na pariyādāya tiṭṭhati.

But even such painful feeling did not occupy my mind.

Tassa mayhaṁ, aggivessana, etadahosi:

Then it occurred to me,

'yannūnāhaṁ appāṇakaṁyeva jhānaṁ jhāyeyyan'ti.

'Why don't I practice the breathless absorption?'

So kho ahaṁ, aggivessana, mukhato ca nāsato ca assāsapassāse uparundhiṁ.

So I cut off my breathing through my mouth and nose.

Tassa mayhaṁ, aggivessana, mukhato ca nāsato ca assāsapassāsesu uparuddhesu kaṇṇasotehi vātānaṁ nikkhamantānaṁ adhimatto saddo hoti.

But then winds came out my ears making a loud noise,

Seyyathāpi nāma kammāragaggariyā dhamamānāya adhimatto saddo hoti;

like the puffing of a blacksmith's bellows.

evameva kho me, aggivessana, mukhato ca nāsato ca assāsapassāsesu uparuddhesu kaṇṇasotehi vātānaṁ nikkhamantānaṁ adhimatto saddo hoti.

Āraddhaṁ kho pana me, aggivessana, vīriyaṁ hoti asallīnaṁ upaṭṭhitā sati asammuṭṭhā. Sāraddho ca pana me kāyo hoti appaṭippassaddho teneva dukkhappadhānena padhānābhitunnassa sato.

My energy was roused up and unflagging, and my mindfulness was established and lucid, but my body was disturbed, not tranquil, because I'd pushed too hard with that painful striving.

Evarūpāpi kho me, aggivessana, uppannā dukkhā vedanā cittaṁ na pariyādāya tiṭṭhati.

But even such painful feeling did not occupy my mind.

Tassa mayhaṁ, aggivessana, etadahosi:

Then it occurred to me,

'yannūnāhaṁ appāṇakaṁyeva jhānaṁ jhāyeyyan'ti.

'Why don't I keep practicing the breathless absorption?'

So kho ahaṁ, aggivessana, mukhato ca nāsato ca kaṇṇato ca assāsapassāse uparundhiṁ.

So I cut off my breathing through my mouth and nose and ears.

Tassa mayhaṁ, aggivessana, mukhato ca nāsato ca kaṇṇato ca assāsapassāsesu uparuddhesu adhimattā vātā muddhani ūhananti.

But then strong winds ground my head,

Seyyathāpi, aggivessana, balavā puriso tiṇhena sikharena muddhani abhimattheyya;

like a strong man was drilling into my head with a sharp point.

evameva kho me, aggivessana, mukhato ca nāsato ca kaṇṇato ca assāsapassāsesu uparuddhesu adhimattā vātā muddhani ūhananti.

Āraddhaṁ kho pana me, aggivessana, vīriyaṁ hoti asallīnaṁ upaṭṭhitā sati asammuṭṭhā. Sāraddho ca pana me kāyo hoti appaṭippassaddho teneva dukkhappadhānena padhānābhitunnassa sato.

My energy was roused up and unflagging, and my mindfulness was established and lucid, but my body was disturbed, not tranquil, because I'd pushed too hard with that painful striving.

Evarūpāpi kho me, aggivessana, uppannā dukkhā vedanā cittaṁ na pariyādāya tiṭṭhati.

But even such painful feeling did not occupy my mind.

Tassa mayhaṁ, aggivessana, etadahosi:

Then it occurred to me,

'yannūnāhaṁ appāṇakaṁyeva jhānaṁ jhāyeyyan'ti.

'Why don't I keep practicing the breathless absorption?'

So kho ahaṁ, aggivessana, mukhato ca nāsato ca kaṇṇato ca assāsapassāse uparundhiṁ.

So I cut off my breathing through my mouth and nose and ears.

Tassa mayhaṁ, aggivessana, mukhato ca nāsato ca kaṇṇato ca assāsapassāsesu uparuddhesu adhimattā sīse sīsavedanā honti.

But then I got a severe headache,

Seyyathāpi, aggivessana, balavā puriso daḷhena varattakkhaṇḍena sīse sīsaveṭhaṁ dadeyya;

like a strong man was tightening a tough leather strap around my head.

evameva kho me, aggivessana, mukhato ca nāsato ca kaṇṇato ca assāsapassāsesu uparuddhesu adhimattā sīse sīsavedanā honti.

Āraddhaṁ kho pana me, aggivessana, vīriyaṁ hoti asallīnaṁ upaṭṭhitā sati asammuṭṭhā. Sāraddho ca pana me kāyo hoti appaṭippassaddho teneva dukkhappadhānena padhānābhitunnassa sato.

My energy was roused up and unflagging, and my mindfulness was established and lucid, but my body was disturbed, not tranquil, because I'd pushed too hard with that painful striving.

Evarūpāpi kho me, aggivessana, uppannā dukkhā vedanā cittaṁ na pariyādāya tiṭṭhati.

But even such painful feeling did not occupy my mind.

Tassa mayhaṁ, aggivessana, etadahosi:

Then it occurred to me,

'yannūnāhaṁ appāṇakaṁyeva jhānaṁ jhāyeyyan'ti.

'Why don't I keep practicing the breathless absorption?'

So kho ahaṁ, aggivessana, mukhato ca nāsato ca kaṇṇato ca assāsapassāse uparundhiṁ.

So I cut off my breathing through my mouth and nose and ears.

Tassa mayhaṁ, aggivessana, mukhato ca nāsato ca kaṇṇato ca assāsapassāsesu uparuddhesu adhimattā vātā kucchiṁ parikantanti.

But then strong winds carved up my belly,

Seyyathāpi, aggivessana, dakkho goghātako vā goghātakantevāsī vā tiṇhena govikantanena kucchiṁ parikanteyya;

like a deft butcher or their apprentice was slicing my belly open with a meat cleaver.

evameva kho me, aggivessana, mukhato ca nāsato ca kaṇṇato ca assāsapassāsesu uparuddhesu adhimattā vātā kucchiṁ parikantanti.

Āraddhaṁ kho pana me, aggivessana, vīriyaṁ hoti asallīnaṁ upaṭṭhitā sati asammuṭṭhā. Sāraddho ca pana me kāyo hoti appaṭippassaddho teneva dukkhappadhānena padhānābhitunnassa sato.

My energy was roused up and unflagging, and my mindfulness was established and lucid, but my body was disturbed, not tranquil, because I'd pushed too hard with that painful striving.

Evarūpāpi kho me, aggivessana, uppannā dukkhā vedanā cittaṁ na pariyādāya tiṭṭhati.

But even such painful feeling did not occupy my mind.

Tassa mayhaṁ, aggivessana, etadahosi:

Then it occurred to me,

'yannūnāhaṁ appāṇakaṁyeva jhānaṁ jhāyeyyan'ti.

'Why don't I keep practicing the breathless absorption?'

So kho ahaṁ, aggivessana, mukhato ca nāsato ca kaṇṇato ca assāsapassāse uparundhiṁ.

So I cut off my breathing through my mouth and nose and ears.

Tassa mayhaṁ, aggivessana, mukhato ca nāsato ca kaṇṇato ca assāsapassāsesu uparuddhesu adhimatto kāyasmiṁ ḍāho hoti.

But then there was an intense burning in my body,

Seyyathāpi, aggivessana, dve balavanto purisā dubbalataraṁ purisaṁ nānābāhāsu gahetvā aṅgārakāsuyā santāpeyyuṁ samparitāpeyyuṁ;

like two strong men grabbing a weaker man by the arms to burn and scorch him on a pit of glowing coals.

evameva kho me, aggivessana, mukhato ca nāsato ca kaṇṇato ca assāsapassāsesu uparuddhesu adhimatto kāyasmiṁ ḍāho hoti.

Āraddhaṁ kho pana me, aggivessana, vīriyaṁ hoti asallīnaṁ upaṭṭhitā sati asammuṭṭhā. Sāraddho ca pana me kāyo hoti appaṭippassaddho teneva dukkhappadhānena padhānābhitunnassa sato.

My energy was roused up and unflagging, and my mindfulness was established and lucid, but my body was disturbed, not tranquil, because I'd pushed too hard with that painful striving.

Evarūpāpi kho me, aggivessana, uppannā dukkhā vedanā cittaṁ na pariyādāya tiṭṭhati.

But even such painful feeling did not occupy my mind.

Apissu maṁ, aggivessana, devatā disvā evamāhaṁsu:

Then some deities saw me and said,

'kālaṅkato samaṇo gotamo'ti.

'The ascetic Gotama is dead.'

Ekaccā devatā evamāhaṁsu:

Others said,

'na kālaṅkato samaṇo gotamo, api ca kālaṁ karotī'ti.

'He's not dead, but he's dying.'

Ekaccā devatā evamāhaṁsu:

Others said,

'na kālaṅkato samaṇo gotamo, napi kālaṁ karoti, arahaṁ samaṇo gotamo, vihāro tveva so arahato evarūpo hotī'ti.

'He's not dead or dying. The ascetic Gotama is a perfected one, for that is how the perfected ones live.'

Tassa mayhaṁ, aggivessana, etadahosi:

Then it occurred to me,

'yannūnāhaṁ sabbaso āhārupacchedāya paṭipajjeyyan'ti.

'Why don't I practice completely cutting off food?'

Atha kho maṁ, aggivessana, devatā upasaṅkamitvā etadavocuṁ:

But deities came to me and said,

'mā kho tvaṁ, mārisa, sabbaso āhārupacchedāya paṭipajji.

'Good sir, don't practice totally cutting off food.

Sace kho tvaṁ, mārisa, sabbaso āhārupacchedāya paṭipajjissasi, tassa te mayaṁ dibbaṁ ojaṁ lomakūpehi ajjhohāressāma, tāya tvaṁ yāpessasī'ti.

If you do, we'll infuse divine nectar into your pores and you will live on that.'

Tassa mayhaṁ, aggivessana, etadahosi:

Then I thought,

'ahañceva kho pana sabbaso ajajjitaṁ paṭijāneyyaṁ, imā ca me devatā dibbaṁ ojaṁ lomakūpehi ajjhohāreyyuṁ, tāya cāhaṁ yāpeyyaṁ, taṁ mamassa musā'ti.

'If I claim to be completely fasting while these deities are infusing divine nectar in my pores, that would be a lie on my part.'

So kho ahaṁ, aggivessana, tā devatā paccācikkhāmi, 'halan'ti vadāmi.

So I dismissed those deities, saying, 'There's no need.'

Tassa mayhaṁ, aggivessana, etadahosi:

Then it occurred to me,

'yannūnāhaṁ thokaṁ thokaṁ āhāraṁ āhāreyyaṁ, pasataṁ pasataṁ, yadi vā muggayūsaṁ, yadi vā kulatthayūsaṁ, yadi vā kaḷāyayūsaṁ, yadi vā hareṇukayūsan'ti.

'Why don't I just take a little bit of food each time, a cup of broth made from mung beans, horse gram, chickpeas, or green gram.'

So kho ahaṁ, aggivessana, thokaṁ thokaṁ āhāraṁ āhāresiṁ, pasataṁ pasataṁ, yadi vā muggayūsaṁ, yadi vā kulatthayūsaṁ, yadi vā kaḷāyayūsaṁ, yadi vā hareṇukayūsaṁ.

So that's what I did,

Tassa mayhaṁ, aggivessana, thokaṁ thokaṁ āhāraṁ āhārayato, pasataṁ pasataṁ, yadi vā muggayūsaṁ, yadi vā kulatthayūsaṁ, yadi vā kaḷāyayūsaṁ, yadi vā hareṇukayūsaṁ, adhimattakasimānaṁ patto kāyo hoti.

until my body became extremely emaciated.

Seyyathāpi nāma āsītikapabbāni vā kāḷapabbāni vā; evamevassu me aṅgapaccaṅgāni bhavanti tāyevappahāratāya.

Due to eating so little, my limbs became like the joints of an eighty-year-old or a corpse,

Seyyathāpi nāma oṭṭhapadaṁ; evamevassu me ānisadaṁ hoti tāyevappahāratāya.

my bottom became like a camel's hoof,

Seyyathāpi nāma vaṭṭanāvaḷī; evamevassu me piṭṭhikaṇṭako uṇṇatāvanato hoti tāyevappahāratāya.

my vertebrae stuck out like beads on a string,

Seyyathāpi nāma jarasālāya gopānasiyo oluggaviluggā bhavanti; evamevassu me phāsuḷiyo oluggaviluggā bhavanti tāyevappahāratāya.

and my ribs were as gaunt as the broken-down rafters on an old barn.

Seyyathāpi nāma gambhīre udapāne udakatārakā gambhīragatā okkhāyikā dissanti; evamevassu me akkhikūpesu akkhitārakā gambhīragatā okkhāyikā dissanti tāyevappahāratāya.

Due to eating so little, the gleam of my eyes sank deep in their sockets, like the gleam of water sunk deep down a well.

Seyyathāpi nāma tittakālābu āmakacchinno vātātapena samphuṭito hoti sammilāto; evamevassu me sīsacchavi samphuṭitā hoti sammilātā tāyevappahāratāya.

Due to eating so little, my scalp shriveled and withered like a green bitter-gourd in the wind and sun.

So kho ahaṁ, aggivessana, udaracchaviṁ parimasissāmīti piṭṭhikaṇṭakaṁyeva pariggaṇhāmi, piṭṭhikaṇṭakaṁ parimasissāmīti udaracchaviṁyeva pariggaṇhāmi, yāvassu me, aggivessana, udaracchavi piṭṭhikaṇṭakaṁ allīnā hoti tāyevappahāratāya.

Due to eating so little, the skin of my belly stuck to my backbone, so that when I tried to rub the skin of my belly I grabbed my backbone, and when I tried to rub my backbone I rubbed the skin of my belly.

So kho ahaṁ, aggivessana, vaccaṁ vā muttaṁ vā karissāmīti tattheva avakujjo papatāmi tāyevappāharatāya.

Due to eating so little, when I tried to urinate or defecate I fell face down right there.

So kho ahaṁ, aggivessana, imameva kāyaṁ assāsento pāṇinā gattāni anumajjāmi. Tassa mayhaṁ, aggivessana, pāṇinā gattāni anumajjato pūtimūlāni lomāni kāyasmā papatanti tāyevappāharatāya.

Due to eating so little, when I tried to relieve my body by rubbing my limbs with my hands, the hair, rotted at its roots, fell out.

Apissu maṁ, aggivessana, manussā disvā evamāhaṁsu: 'kāḷo samaṇo gotamo'ti.

Then some people saw me and said: 'The ascetic Gotama is black.'

Ekacce manussā evamāhaṁsu: 'na kāḷo samaṇo gotamo, sāmo samaṇo gotamo'ti.

Some said: 'He's not black, he's brown.'

Ekacce manussā evamāhaṁsu: 'na kāḷo samaṇo gotamo, napi sāmo, maṅguracchavi samaṇo gotamo'ti.

Some said: 'He's neither black nor brown. The ascetic Gotama has tawny skin.'

Yāvassu me, aggivessana, tāva parisuddho chavivaṇṇo pariyodāto upahato hoti tāyevappāharatāya.

That's how far the pure, bright complexion of my skin had been ruined by taking so little food.

Tassa mayhaṁ, aggivessana, etadahosi:

Then I thought,

'ye kho keci atītamaddhānaṁ samaṇā vā brāhmaṇā vā opakkamikā dukkhā tibbā kharā kaṭukā vedanā vedayiṁsu, etāvaparamaṁ, nayito bhiyyo.

'Whatever ascetics and brahmins have experienced painful, sharp, severe, acute feelings due to overexertion—whether in the past, future, or present—this is as far as it goes, no-one has done more than this.

Yepi hi keci anāgatamaddhānaṁ samaṇā vā brāhmaṇā vā opakkamikā dukkhā tibbā kharā kaṭukā vedanā vedayissanti, etāvaparamaṁ, nayito bhiyyo.

Yepi hi keci etarahi samaṇā vā brāhmaṇā vā opakkamikā dukkhā tibbā kharā kaṭukā vedanā vedayanti, etāvaparamaṁ, nayito bhiyyo.

Na kho panāhaṁ imāya kaṭukāya dukkarakārikāya adhigacchāmi uttari manussadhammā alamariyañāṇadassanavisesaṁ.

But I have not achieved any superhuman distinction in knowledge and vision worthy of the noble ones by this severe, grueling work.

Siyā nu kho añño maggo bodhāyā'ti?

Could there be another path to awakening?'

Tassa mayhaṁ, aggivessana, etadahosi:

Then it occurred to me,

'abhijānāmi kho panāhaṁ pitu sakkassa kammante sītāya jambucchāyāya nisinno vivicceva kāmehi vivicca akusalehi dhammehi savitakkaṁ savicāraṁ vivekajaṁ pītisukhaṁ paṭhamaṁ jhānaṁ upasampajja viharitā.

'I recall sitting in the cool shade of the rose-apple tree while my father the Sakyan was off working. Quite secluded from sensual pleasures, secluded from unskillful qualities, I entered and remained in the first absorption, which has the rapture and bliss born of seclusion, while placing the mind and keeping it connected.

Siyā nu kho eso maggo bodhāyā'ti?

Could that be the path to awakening?'

Tassa mayhaṁ, aggivessana, satānusāri viññāṇaṁ ahosi:

Stemming from that memory came the realization:

'eseva maggo bodhāyā'ti.

'That is the path to awakening!'

Tassa mayhaṁ, aggivessana, etadahosi:

Then it occurred to me,

'kiṁ nu kho ahaṁ tassa sukhassa bhāyāmi, yaṁ taṁ sukhaṁ aññatreva kāmehi aññatra akusalehi dhammehī'ti?

'Why am I afraid of that pleasure, for it has nothing to do with sensual pleasures or unskillful qualities?'

Tassa mayhaṁ, aggivessana, etadahosi:

Then I thought,

'na kho ahaṁ tassa sukhassa bhāyāmi, yaṁ taṁ sukhaṁ aññatreva kāmehi aññatra akusalehi dhammehī'ti.

'I'm not afraid of that pleasure, for it has nothing to do with sensual pleasures or unskillful qualities.'

Tassa mayhaṁ, aggivessana, etadahosi:

Then I thought,

'na kho taṁ sukaraṁ sukhaṁ adhigantuṁ evaṁ adhimattakasimānaṁ pattakāyena, yannūnāhaṁ oḷārikaṁ āhāraṁ āhāreyyaṁ odanakummāsan'ti.

'I can't achieve that pleasure with a body so excessively emaciated. Why don't I eat some solid food, some rice and porridge?'

So kho ahaṁ, aggivessana, oḷārikaṁ āhāraṁ āhāresiṁ odanakummāsaṁ.

So I ate some solid food.

Tena kho pana maṁ, aggivessana, samayena pañca bhikkhū paccupaṭṭhitā honti:

Now at that time the five mendicants were attending on me, thinking,

'yaṁ kho samaṇo gotamo dhammaṁ adhigamissati, taṁ no ārocessatī'ti.

'The ascetic Gotama will tell us of any truth that he realizes.'

Yato kho ahaṁ, aggivessana, oḷārikaṁ āhāraṁ āhāresiṁ odanakummāsaṁ, atha me te pañca bhikkhū nibbijja pakkamiṁsu:

But when I ate some solid food, they left disappointed in me, saying,

'bāhulliko samaṇo gotamo, padhānavibbhanto, āvatto bāhullāyā'ti.

'The ascetic Gotama has become indulgent; he has strayed from the struggle and returned to indulgence.'

So kho ahaṁ, aggivessana, oḷārikaṁ āhāraṁ āhāretvā, balaṁ gahetvā, vivicceva kāmehi vivicca akusalehi dhammehi savitakkaṁ savicāraṁ vivekajaṁ pītisukhaṁ paṭhamaṁ jhānaṁ upasampajja vihāsiṁ.

After eating solid food and gathering my strength, quite secluded from sensual pleasures, secluded from unskillful qualities, I entered and remained in the first absorption, which has the rapture and bliss born of seclusion, while placing the mind and keeping it connected.

Evarūpāpi kho me, aggivessana, uppannā sukhā vedanā cittaṁ na pariyādāya tiṭṭhati.

But even such pleasant feeling did not occupy my mind.

Vitakkavicārānaṁ vūpasamā ajjhattaṁ sampasādanaṁ cetaso ekodibhāvaṁ avitakkaṁ avicāraṁ samādhijaṁ pītisukhaṁ dutiyaṁ jhānaṁ upasampajja vihāsiṁ.

As the placing of the mind and keeping it connected were stilled, I entered and remained in the second absorption, which has the rapture and bliss born of immersion, with internal clarity and confidence, and unified mind, without placing the mind and keeping it connected.

Evarūpāpi kho me, aggivessana, uppannā sukhā vedanā cittaṁ na pariyādāya tiṭṭhati.

But even such pleasant feeling did not occupy my mind.

Pītiyā ca virāgā upekkhako ca vihāsiṁ, sato ca sampajāno. Sukhañca kāyena paṭisaṁvedesiṁ yaṁ taṁ ariyā ācikkhanti: 'upekkhako satimā sukhavihārī'ti tatiyaṁ jhānaṁ upasampajja vihāsiṁ.

And with the fading away of rapture, I entered and remained in the third absorption, where I meditated with equanimity, mindful and aware, personally experiencing the bliss of which the noble ones declare, 'Equanimous and mindful, one meditates in bliss.'

Evarūpāpi kho me, aggivessana, uppannā sukhā vedanā cittaṁ na pariyādāya tiṭṭhati.

But even such pleasant feeling did not occupy my mind.

Sukhassa ca pahānā dukkhassa ca pahānā, pubbeva somanassadomanassānaṁ atthaṅgamā, adukkhamasukhaṁ upekkhāsatipārisuddhiṁ catutthaṁ jhānaṁ upasampajja vihāsiṁ.

With the giving up of pleasure and pain, and the ending of former happiness and sadness, I entered and remained in the fourth absorption, without pleasure or pain, with pure equanimity and mindfulness.

Evarūpāpi kho me, aggivessana, uppannā sukhā vedanā cittaṁ na pariyādāya tiṭṭhati.

But even such pleasant feeling did not occupy my mind.

So evaṁ samāhite citte parisuddhe pariyodāte anaṅgaṇe vigatūpakkilese mudubhūte kammaniye ṭhite āneñjappatte pubbenivāsānussatiñāṇāya cittaṁ abhininnāmesiṁ.

When my mind had immersed in samādhi like this—purified, bright, flawless, rid of corruptions, pliable, workable, steady, and imperturbable—I extended it toward recollection of past lives.

So anekavihitaṁ pubbenivāsaṁ anussarāmi, seyyathidaṁ—ekampi jātiṁ …pe… iti sākāraṁ sauddesaṁ anekavihitaṁ pubbenivāsaṁ anussarāmi.

I recollected my many kinds of past lives, with features and details.

Ayaṁ kho me, aggivessana, rattiyā paṭhame yāme paṭhamā vijjā adhigatā;

This was the first knowledge, which I achieved in the first watch of the night.

avijjā vihatā, vijjā uppannā; tamo vihato, āloko uppanno; yathā taṁ appamattassa ātāpino pahitattassa viharato.

Ignorance was destroyed and knowledge arose; darkness was destroyed and light arose, as happens for a meditator who is diligent, keen, and resolute.

Evarūpāpi kho me, aggivessana, uppannā sukhā vedanā cittaṁ na pariyādāya tiṭṭhati.

But even such pleasant feeling did not occupy my mind.

So evaṁ samāhite citte parisuddhe pariyodāte anaṅgaṇe vigatūpakkilese mudubhūte kammaniye ṭhite āneñjappatte sattānaṁ cutūpapātañāṇāya cittaṁ abhininnāmesiṁ.

When my mind had immersed in samādhi like this—purified, bright, flawless, rid of corruptions, pliable, workable, steady, and imperturbable—I extended it toward knowledge of the death and rebirth of sentient beings.

So dibbena cakkhunā visuddhena atikkantamānusakena satte passāmi cavamāne upapajjamāne hīne paṇīte suvaṇṇe dubbaṇṇe sugate duggate yathākammūpage satte pajānāmi …pe…

With clairvoyance that is purified and superhuman, I saw sentient beings passing away and being reborn—inferior and superior, beautiful and ugly, in a good place or a bad place. I understood how sentient beings are reborn according to their deeds.

ayaṁ kho me, aggivessana, rattiyā majjhime yāme dutiyā vijjā adhigatā;

This was the second knowledge, which I achieved in the middle watch of the night.

avijjā vihatā, vijjā uppannā; tamo vihato, āloko uppanno; yathā taṁ appamattassa ātāpino pahitattassa viharato.

Ignorance was destroyed and knowledge arose; darkness was destroyed and light arose, as happens for a meditator who is diligent, keen, and resolute.

Evarūpāpi kho me, aggivessana, uppannā sukhā vedanā cittaṁ na pariyādāya tiṭṭhati.

But even such pleasant feeling did not occupy my mind.

So evaṁ samāhite citte parisuddhe pariyodāte anaṅgaṇe vigatūpakkilese mudubhūte kammaniye ṭhite āneñjappatte āsavānaṁ khayañāṇāya cittaṁ abhininnāmesiṁ.

When my mind had immersed in samādhi like this—purified, bright, flawless, rid of corruptions, pliable, workable, steady, and imperturbable—I extended it toward knowledge of the ending of defilements.

So 'idaṁ dukkhan'ti yathābhūtaṁ abbhaññāsiṁ, 'ayaṁ dukkhasamudayo'ti yathābhūtaṁ abbhaññāsiṁ, 'ayaṁ dukkhanirodho'ti yathābhūtaṁ abbhaññāsiṁ, 'ayaṁ dukkhanirodhagāminī paṭipadā'ti yathābhūtaṁ abbhaññāsiṁ.

I truly understood: 'This is suffering' ... 'This is the origin of suffering' ... 'This is the cessation of suffering' ... 'This is the practice that leads to the cessation of suffering.'

'Ime āsavā'ti yathābhūtaṁ abbhaññāsiṁ, 'ayaṁ āsavasamudayo'ti yathābhūtaṁ abbhaññāsiṁ, 'ayaṁ āsavanirodho'ti yathābhūtaṁ abbhaññāsiṁ, 'ayaṁ āsavanirodhagāminī paṭipadā'ti yathābhūtaṁ abbhaññāsiṁ.

I truly understood: 'These are defilements' ... 'This is the origin of defilements' ... 'This is the cessation of defilements' ... 'This is the practice that leads to the cessation of defilements.'

Tassa me evaṁ jānato evaṁ passato kāmāsavāpi cittaṁ vimuccittha, bhavāsavāpi cittaṁ vimuccittha, avijjāsavāpi cittaṁ vimuccittha.

Knowing and seeing like this, my mind was freed from the defilements of sensuality, desire to be reborn, and ignorance.

Vimuttasmiṁ vimuttamiti ñāṇaṁ ahosi.

When it was freed, I knew it was freed.

'Khīṇā jāti, vusitaṁ brahmacariyaṁ, kataṁ karaṇīyaṁ, nāparaṁ itthattāyā'ti abbhaññāsiṁ.

I understood: 'Rebirth is ended; the spiritual journey has been completed; what had to be done has been done; there is no return to any state of existence.'

Ayaṁ kho me, aggivessana, rattiyā pacchime yāme tatiyā vijjā adhigatā;

This was the third knowledge, which I achieved in the last watch of the night.

avijjā vihatā, vijjā uppannā; tamo vihato, āloko uppanno; yathā taṁ appamattassa ātāpino pahitattassa viharato.

Ignorance was destroyed and knowledge arose; darkness was destroyed and light arose, as happens for a meditator who is diligent, keen, and resolute.

Evarūpāpi kho me, aggivessana, uppannā sukhā vedanā cittaṁ na pariyādāya tiṭṭhati.

But even such pleasant feeling did not occupy my mind.

Abhijānāmi kho panāhaṁ, aggivessana, anekasatāya parisāya dhammaṁ desetā.

Aggivessana, I recall teaching the Dhamma to an assembly of many hundreds,

Apissu maṁ ekameko evaṁ maññati:

and each person thinks

'mamevārabbha samaṇo gotamo dhammaṁ desetī'ti.

that I am teaching the Dhamma especially for them.

Na kho panetaṁ, aggivessana, evaṁ daṭṭhabbaṁ;

But it should not be seen like this.

yāvadeva viññāpanatthāya tathāgato paresaṁ dhammaṁ deseti.

The Realized One teaches others only so that they can understand.

So kho ahaṁ, aggivessana, tassāyeva kathāya pariyosāne, tasmiṁyeva purimasmiṁ samādhinimitte ajjhattameva cittaṁ saṇṭhapemi sannisādemi ekodiṁ karomi samādahāmi, yena sudaṁ niccakappaṁ viharāmī"ti.

When that talk is finished, I still, settle, unify, and immerse my mind in samādhi internally, using the same meditation subject as a foundation of immersion that I used before, which is my usual meditation."

"Okappaniyametaṁ bhoto gotamassa yathā taṁ arahato sammāsambuddhassa.

"I'd believe that of Master Gotama, just like a perfected one, a fully awakened Buddha.

Abhijānāti kho pana bhavaṁ gotamo divā supitā"ti?

But do you ever recall sleeping during the day?"

"Abhijānāmahaṁ, aggivessana, gimhānaṁ pacchime māse pacchābhattaṁ piṇḍapātapaṭikkanto catuggunaṁ saṅghāṭiṁ paññapetvā dakkhiṇena passena sato sampajāno niddaṁ okkamitā"ti.

"I do recall that in the last month of the summer, I have spread out my outer robe folded in four and lain down in the lion's posture—on the right side, placing one foot on top of the other—mindful and aware."

"Etaṁ kho, bho gotama, eke samaṇabrāhmaṇā sammohavihārasmiṁ vadantī"ti?

"Some ascetics and brahmins call that a deluded abiding."

"Na kho, aggivessana, ettāvatā sammūḷho vā hoti asammūḷho vā.

"That's not how to define whether someone is deluded or not.

Api ca, aggivessana, yathā sammūḷho ca hoti asammūḷho ca,

But as to how to define whether someone is deluded or not,

taṁ suṇāhi, sādhukaṁ manasi karohi, bhāsissāmī"ti.

listen and pay close attention, I will speak."

"Evaṁ, bho"ti kho saccako nigaṇṭhaputto bhagavato paccassosi.

"Yes, sir," replied Saccaka.

Bhagavā etadavoca:

The Buddha said this:

"Yassa kassaci, aggivessana, ye āsavā saṅkilesikā ponobbhavikā sadarā dukkhavipākā āyatiṁ jātijarāmaraṇiyā appahīnā, tamahaṁ 'sammūḷho'ti vadāmi.

"Whoever has not given up the defilements that are corrupting, leading to future lives, hurtful, resulting in suffering and future rebirth, old age, and death is deluded, I say.

Āsavānañhi, aggivessana, appahānā sammūḷho hoti.

For it's not giving up the defilements that makes you deluded.

Yassa kassaci, aggivessana, ye āsavā saṅkilesikā ponobbhavikā sadarā dukkhavipākā āyatiṁ jātijarāmaraṇiyā pahīnā, tamahaṁ 'asammūḷho'ti vadāmi.

Whoever has given up the defilements that are corrupting, leading to future lives, hurtful, resulting in suffering and future rebirth, old age, and death—is not deluded, I say.

Āsavānañhi, aggivessana, pahānā asammūḷho hoti.

For it's giving up the defilements that makes you not deluded.

Tathāgatassa kho, aggivessana, ye āsavā saṅkilesikā ponobbhavikā sadarā dukkhavipākā āyatiṁ jātijarāmaraṇiyā pahīnā ucchinnamūlā tālāvatthukatā anabhāvaṅkatā āyatiṁ anuppādadhammā.

The Realized One has given up the defilements that are corrupting, leading to future lives, hurtful, resulting in suffering and future rebirth, old age, and death. He has cut them off at the root, made them like a palm stump, obliterated them so they are unable to arise in the future.

Seyyathāpi, aggivessana, tālo matthakacchinno abhabbo puna virūḷhiyā;

Just as a palm tree with its crown cut off is incapable of further growth,

evameva kho, aggivessana, tathāgatassa ye āsavā saṅkilesikā ponobbhavikā sadarā dukkhavipākā āyatiṁ jātijarāmaraṇiyā pahīnā ucchinnamūlā tālāvatthukatā anabhāvaṅkatā āyatiṁ anuppādadhammā"ti.

in the same way, the Realized One has given up the defilements so they are unable to arise in the future."

Evaṁ vutte, saccako nigaṇṭhaputto bhagavantaṁ etadavoca:

When he had spoken, Saccaka said to him,

"acchariyaṁ, bho gotama, abbhutaṁ, bho gotama.

"It's incredible, Master Gotama, it's amazing!

Yāvañcidaṁ bhoto gotamassa evaṁ āsajja āsajja vuccamānassa, upanītehi vacanappathehi samudācariyamānassa, chavivaṇṇo ceva pariyodāyati, mukhavaṇṇo ca vippasīdati, yathā taṁ arahato sammāsambuddhassa.

When Master Gotama is repeatedly attacked with inappropriate and intrusive criticism, the complexion of his skin brightens and the color of his face becomes clear, just like a perfected one, a fully awakened Buddha.

Abhijānāmahaṁ, bho gotama, pūraṇaṁ kassapaṁ vādena vādaṁ samārabhitā.

I recall taking on Pūraṇa Kassapa in debate.

Sopi mayā vādena vādaṁ samāraddho aññenaññaṁ paṭicari, bahiddhā kathaṁ apanāmesi, kopañca dosañca appaccayañca pātvākāsi.

He dodged the issue, distracting the discussion with irrelevant points, and displaying annoyance, hate, and bitterness.

Bhoto pana gotamassa evaṁ āsajja āsajja vuccamānassa, upanītehi vacanappathehi samudācariyamānassa, chavivaṇṇo ceva pariyodāyati, mukhavaṇṇo ca vippasīdati, yathā taṁ arahato sammāsambuddhassa.

But when Master Gotama is repeatedly attacked with inappropriate and intrusive criticism, the complexion of his skin brightens and the color of his face becomes clear, just like a perfected one, a fully awakened Buddha.

Abhijānāmahaṁ, bho gotama, makkhaliṁ gosālaṁ …pe…

I recall taking on Makkhali Gosāla,

ajitaṁ kesakambalaṁ …

Ajita of the hair blanket,

pakudhaṁ kaccāyanaṁ …

Pakudha Kaccāyana,

sañjayaṁ belaṭṭhaputtaṁ …

Sañjaya Belaṭṭhiputta,

nigaṇṭhaṁ nāṭaputtaṁ vādena vādaṁ samārabhitā.

and the Jain ascetic of the Ñātika clan in debate.

Sopi mayā vādena vādaṁ samāraddho aññenaññaṁ paṭicari, bahiddhā kathaṁ apanāmesi, kopañca dosañca appaccayañca pātvākāsi.

They all dodged the issue, distracting the discussion with irrelevant points, and displaying annoyance, hate, and bitterness.

Bhoto pana gotamassa evaṁ āsajja āsajja vuccamānassa, upanītehi vacanappathehi samudācariyamānassa, chavivaṇṇo ceva pariyodāyati, mukhavaṇṇo ca vippasīdati, yathā taṁ arahato sammāsambuddhassa.

But when Master Gotama is repeatedly attacked with inappropriate and intrusive criticism, the complexion of his skin brightens and the color of his face becomes clear, just like a perfected one, a fully awakened Buddha.

Handa ca dāni mayaṁ, bho gotama, gacchāma.

Well, now, Master Gotama, I must go.

Bahukiccā mayaṁ, bahukaraṇīyā”ti.

I have many duties, and much to do.”

“Yassadāni tvaṁ, aggivessana, kālaṁ maññasī”ti.

“Please, Aggivessana, go at your convenience.”

Atha kho saccako nigaṇṭhaputto bhagavato bhāsitaṁ abhinanditvā anumoditvā uṭṭhāyāsanā pakkāmīti.

Then Saccaka, the son of Jain parents, having approved and agreed with what the Buddha said, got up from his seat and left.

Mahāsaccakasuttaṁ niṭṭhitaṁ chaṭṭhaṁ.

37 Culatanhasankhayasutta:

The Shorter Discourse on the Ending of Craving

Evaṁ me sutaṁ—

So I have heard.

ekaṁ samayaṁ bhagavā sāvatthiyaṁ viharati pubbārāme migāramātupāsāde.

At one time the Buddha was staying near Sāvatthī in the Eastern Monastery, the stilt longhouse of Migāra’s mother.

Atha kho sakko devānamindo yena bhagavā tenupasaṅkami; upasaṅkamitvā bhagavantaṁ abhivādetvā ekamantaṁ aṭṭhāsi. Ekamantaṁ ṭhito kho sakko devānamindo bhagavantaṁ etadavoca:

And then Sakka, lord of gods, went up to the Buddha, bowed, stood to one side, and said to him:

"kittāvatā nu kho, bhante, bhikkhu saṅkhittena taṇhāsaṅkhayavimutto hoti accantaniṭṭho accantayogakkhemī accantabrahmacārī accantapariyosāno seṭṭho devamanussānan"ti?

"Sir, how do you briefly define a mendicant who is freed through the ending of craving, who has reached the ultimate end, the ultimate sanctuary, the ultimate spiritual life, the ultimate goal, and is best among gods and humans?"

"Idha, devānaminda, bhikkhuno sutaṁ hoti:

"Lord of Gods, it's when a mendicant has heard:

'sabbe dhammā nālaṁ abhinivesāyā'ti.

'Nothing is worth insisting on.'

Evañcetaṁ, devānaminda, bhikkhuno sutaṁ hoti:

When a mendicant has heard that

'sabbe dhammā nālaṁ abhinivesāyā'ti.

nothing is worth insisting on,

So sabbaṁ dhammaṁ abhijānāti; sabbaṁ dhammaṁ abhiññāya sabbaṁ dhammaṁ parijānāti; sabbaṁ dhammaṁ pariññāya yaṁ kiñci vedanaṁ vedeti—

they directly know all things. Directly knowing all things, they completely understand all things. Having completely understood all things, when they experience any kind of feeling—pleasant, unpleasant, or neutral—

sukhaṁ vā dukkhaṁ vā adukkhamasukhaṁ vā, so tāsu vedanāsu aniccānupassī viharati, virāgānupassī viharati, nirodhānupassī viharati, paṭinissaggānupassī viharati.

they meditate observing impermanence, dispassion, cessation, and letting go in those feelings.

So tāsu vedanāsu aniccānupassī viharanto, virāgānupassī viharanto, nirodhānupassī viharanto, paṭinissaggānupassī viharanto na kiñci loke upādiyati.

Meditating in this way, they don't grasp at anything in the world.

Anupādiyaṁ na paritassati, aparitassaṁ paccattaññeva parinibbāyati:

Not grasping, they're not anxious. Not being anxious, they personally become extinguished.

'khīṇā jāti, vusitaṁ brahmacariyaṁ, kataṁ karaṇīyaṁ, nāparaṁ itthattāyā'ti pajānāti.

They understand: 'Rebirth is ended, the spiritual journey has been completed, what had to be done has been done, there is no return to any state of existence.'

Ettāvatā kho, devānaminda, bhikkhu saṅkhittena taṇhāsaṅkhayavimutto hoti accantaniṭṭho accantayogakkhemī accantabrahmacārī accantapariyosāno seṭṭho devamanussānan"ti.

That's how I briefly define a mendicant who is freed through the ending of craving, who has reached the ultimate end, the ultimate sanctuary, the ultimate spiritual life, the ultimate goal, and is best among gods and humans."

Atha kho sakko devānamindo bhagavato bhāsitaṁ abhinanditvā anumoditvā bhagavantaṁ abhivādetvā padakkhiṇaṁ katvā tatthevantaradhāyi.

Then Sakka, lord of gods, having approved and agreed with what the Buddha said, bowed and respectfully circled the Buddha, keeping him on his right, before vanishing right there.

Tena kho pana samayena āyasmā mahāmoggallāno bhagavato avidūre nisinno hoti.

Now at that time Venerable Mahāmoggallāna was sitting not far from the Buddha.

Atha kho āyasmato mahāmoggallānassa etadahosi:

He thought,

"kiṁ nu kho so yakkho bhagavato bhāsitaṁ abhisamecca anumodi udāhu no;

"Did that spirit comprehend what the Buddha said when he agreed with him, or not?

yannūnāhaṁ taṁ yakkhaṁ jāneyyaṁ—

Why don't I find out?"

yadi vā so yakkho bhagavato bhāsitaṁ abhisamecca anumodi yadi vā no"ti?

Atha kho āyasmā mahāmoggallāno—seyyathāpi nāma balavā puriso samiñjitaṁ vā bāhaṁ pasāreyya, pasāritaṁ vā bāhaṁ samiñjeyya; evameva—pubbārāme migāramātupāsāde antarahito devesu tāvatiṁsesu pāturahosi.

And then Venerable Mahāmoggallāna, as easily as a strong person would extend or contract their arm, vanished from the Eastern Monastery and reappeared among the gods of the Thirty-Three.

Tena kho pana samayena sakko devānamindo ekapuṇḍarīke uyyāne dibbehi pañcahi tūriyasatehi samappito samaṅgībhūto paricāreti.

Now at that time Sakka was amusing himself in the Single Lotus Park, supplied and provided with a divine orchestra.

Addasā kho sakko devānamindo āyasmantaṁ mahāmoggallānaṁ dūratova āgacchantaṁ.

Seeing Mahāmoggallāna coming off in the distance,

Disvāna tāni dibbāni pañca tūriyasatāni paṭippaṇāmetvā yenāyasmā mahāmoggallāno tenupasaṅkami; upasaṅkamitvā āyasmantaṁ mahāmoggallānaṁ etadavoca:

he dismissed the orchestra, approached Mahāmoggallāna, and said,

"ehi kho, mārisa moggallāna, svāgataṁ, mārisa moggallāna.

"Come, my good Moggallāna! Welcome, good sir!

Cirassaṁ kho, mārisa moggallāna, imaṁ pariyāyaṁ akāsi yadidaṁ idhāgamanāya.

It's been a long time since you took the opportunity to come here.

Nisīda, mārisa moggallāna, idamāsanaṁ paññattan"ti.

Sit, my good Moggallāna, this seat is for you."

Nisīdi kho āyasmā mahāmoggallāno paññatte āsane.

Mahāmoggallāna sat down on the seat spread out,

Sakkopi kho devānamindo aññataraṁ nīcaṁ āsanaṁ gahetvā ekamantaṁ nisīdi.

while Sakka took a low seat and sat to one side.

Ekamantaṁ nisinnaṁ kho sakkaṁ devānamindaṁ āyasmā mahāmoggallāno etadavoca:

Mahāmoggallāna said to him,

"yathā kathaṁ pana kho, kosiya, bhagavā saṅkhittena taṇhāsaṅkhayavimuttiṁ abhāsi?

"Kosiya, how did the Buddha briefly explain freedom through the ending of craving?

Sādhu mayampi etissā kathāya bhāgino assāma savanāyā"ti.

Please share this talk with me so that I can also get to hear it."

"Mayaṁ kho, mārisa moggallāna, bahukiccā bahukaraṇīyā—

"My good Moggallāna, I have many duties, and much to do,

appeva sakena karaṇīyena, api ca devānaṁyeva tāvatiṁsānaṁ karaṇīyena.

not only for myself, but also for the Gods of the Thirty-Three.

Api ca, mārisa moggallāna, sussutaṁyeva hoti suggahitaṁ sumanasikataṁ sūpadhāritaṁ, yaṁ no khippameva antaradhāyati.

Besides, I quickly forget even things I've properly heard, learned, attended, and memorized.

Bhūtapubbaṁ, mārisa moggallāna, devāsurasaṅgāmo samupabyūḷho ahosi.

Once upon a time, a battle was fought between the gods and the demons.

Tasmiṁ kho pana, mārisa moggallāna, saṅgāme devā jiniṁsu, asurā parājiniṁsu.

In that battle the gods won and the demons lost.

So kho ahaṁ, mārisa moggallāna, taṁ saṅgāmaṁ abhivijinitvā vijitasaṅgāmo tato paṭinivattitvā vejayantaṁ nāma pāsādaṁ māpesiṁ.

When I returned from that battle as a conqueror, I created the Palace of Victory.

Vejayantassa kho, mārisa moggallāna, pāsādassa ekasataṁ niyyūhaṁ.

The Palace of Victory has a hundred towers.

Ekekasmiṁ niyyūhe satta satta kūṭāgārasatāni.

Each tower has seven hundred chambers.

Ekamekasmiṁ kūṭāgāre satta satta accharāyo.

Each chamber has seven nymphs.

Ekamekissā accharāya satta satta paricārikāyo.

Each nymph has seven maids.

Iccheyyāsi no tvaṁ, mārisa moggallāna, vejayantassa pāsādassa rāmaṇeyyakaṁ daṭṭhun"ti?

Would you like to see the lovely Palace of Victory?"

Adhivāsesi kho āyasmā mahāmoggallāno tuṇhībhāvena.

Mahāmoggallāna consented with silence.

Atha kho sakko ca devānamindo vessavaṇo ca mahārājā āyasmantaṁ mahāmoggallānaṁ purakkhatvā yena vejayanto pāsādo tenupasaṅkamiṁsu.

Then, putting Venerable Mahāmoggallāna in front, Sakka, lord of gods, and Vessavaṇa, the Great King, went to the Palace of Victory.

Addasaṁsu kho sakkassa devānamindassa paricārikāyo āyasmantaṁ mahāmoggallānaṁ dūratova āgacchantaṁ;

When they saw Moggallāna coming off in the distance, Sakka's maids,

disvā ottappamānā hirīyamānā sakaṁ sakaṁ ovarakaṁ pavisiṁsu.

being prudent and discreet, each went to her own bedroom.

Seyyathāpi nāma suṇisā sasuraṁ disvā ottappati hirīyati;

They were just like a daughter-in-law who is prudent and discreet when they see their father-in-law.

evameva sakkassa devānamindassa paricārikāyo āyasmantaṁ mahāmoggallānaṁ disvā ottappamānā hirīyamānā sakaṁ sakaṁ ovarakaṁ pavisiṁsu.

Atha kho sakko ca devānamindo vessavaṇo ca mahārājā āyasmantaṁ mahāmoggallānaṁ vejayante pāsāde anucaṅkamāpenti anuvicarāpenti:

Then Sakka and Vessavaṇa encouraged Moggallāna to wander and explore the palace, saying,

"idampi, mārisa moggallāna, passa vejayantassa pāsādassa rāmaṇeyyakaṁ;

"See, in the palace, my good Moggallāna, this lovely thing!

idampi, mārisa moggallāna, passa vejayantassa pāsādassa rāmaṇeyyakan"ti.

And that lovely thing!"

"Sobhati idaṁ āyasmato kosiyassa, yathā taṁ pubbe katapuññassa.

"That looks nice for Venerable Kosiya, just like for someone who has made merit in the past.

Manussāpi kiñcideva rāmaṇeyyakaṁ disvā evamāhaṁsu:

Humans, when they see something lovely, also say:

'sobhati vata bho yathā devānaṁ tāvatiṁsānan'ti.

'It looks nice enough for the Gods of the Thirty-Three!'

Tayidaṁ āyasmato kosiyassa sobhati, yathā taṁ pubbe katapuññassā"ti.

That looks nice for Venerable Kosiya, just like for someone who has made merit in the past."

Atha kho āyasmato mahāmoggallānassa etadahosi:

Then Moggallāna thought,

"atibāḷhaṁ kho ayaṁ yakkho pamatto viharati.

"This spirit lives much too negligently.

Yannūnāhaṁ imaṁ yakkhaṁ saṁvejeyyan"ti.

Why don't I stir up a sense of urgency in him?"

Atha kho āyasmā mahāmoggallāno tathārūpaṁ iddhābhisaṅkhāraṁ abhisaṅkhāsi yathā vejayantaṁ pāsādaṁ pādaṅguṭṭhakena saṅkampesi sampakampesi sampavedhesi.

Then Moggallāna used his psychic power to make the Palace of Victory shake and rock and tremble with his big toe.

Atha kho sakko ca devānamindo, vessavaṇo ca mahārājā, devā ca tāvatiṁsā acchariyabbhutacittajātā ahesuṁ:

Then Sakka, Vessavaṇa, and the Gods of the Thirty-Three, their minds full of wonder and amazement, thought,

"acchariyaṁ vata, bho, abbhutaṁ vata, bho.

"It's incredible, it's amazing!

Samaṇassa mahiddhikatā mahānubhāvatā, yatra hi nāma dibbabhavanaṁ pādaṅguṭṭhakena saṅkampessati sampakampessati sampavedhessatī"ti.

The ascetic has such power and might that he makes the god's home shake and rock and tremble with his big toe!"

Atha kho āyasmā mahāmoggallāno sakkaṁ devānamindaṁ saṁviggaṁ lomahaṭṭhajātaṁ viditvā sakkaṁ devānamindaṁ etadavoca:

Knowing that Sakka was shocked and awestruck, Moggallāna said to him,

"yathā kathaṁ pana kho, kosiya, bhagavā saṅkhittena taṇhāsaṅkhayavimuttiṁ abhāsi?

"Kosiya, how did the Buddha briefly explain freedom through the ending of craving?

Sādhu mayampi etissā kathāya bhāgino assāma savanāyā"ti.

Please share this talk with me so that I can also get to hear it."

"Idhāhaṁ, mārisa moggallāna, yena bhagavā tenupasaṅkamiṁ; upasaṅkamitvā bhagavantaṁ abhivādetvā ekamantaṁ aṭṭhāsiṁ. Ekamantaṁ ṭhito kho ahaṁ, mārisa moggallāna, bhagavantaṁ etadavocaṁ:

"My dear Moggallāna, I approached the Buddha, bowed, stood to one side, and said to him,

'kittāvatā nu kho, bhante, bhikkhu saṅkhittena taṇhāsaṅkhayavimutto hoti accantaniṭṭho accantayogakkhemī accantabrahmacārī accantapariyosāno seṭṭho devamanussānan'ti?

'Sir, how do you briefly define a mendicant who is freed with the ending of craving, who has reached the ultimate end, the ultimate sanctuary, the ultimate spiritual life, the ultimate goal, and is best among gods and humans?'

Evaṁ vutte, mārisa moggallāna, bhagavā maṁ etadavoca:

When I had spoken the Buddha said to me:

'idha, devānaminda, bhikkhuno sutaṁ hoti:

'Lord of Gods, it's when a mendicant has heard:

"sabbe dhammā nālaṁ abhinivesāyā"ti.

"Nothing is worth insisting on"

Evañcetaṁ, devānaminda, bhikkhuno sutaṁ hoti

When a mendicant has heard that

"sabbe dhammā nālaṁ abhinivesāyā"ti.

nothing is worth insisting on,

So sabbaṁ dhammaṁ abhijānāti, sabbaṁ dhammaṁ abhiññāya sabbaṁ dhammaṁ parijānāti, sabbaṁ dhammaṁ pariññāya yaṁ kiñci vedanaṁ vedeti sukhaṁ vā dukkhaṁ vā adukkhamasukhaṁ vā.

they directly know all things. Directly knowing all things, they completely understand all things. Having completely understood all things, when they experience any kind of feeling—pleasant, unpleasant, or neutral—

So tāsu vedanāsu aniccānupassī viharati, virāgānupassī viharati, nirodhānupassī viharati, paṭinissaggānupassī viharati.

they meditate observing impermanence, dispassion, cessation, and letting go in those feelings.

So tāsu vedanāsu aniccānupassī viharanto, virāgānupassī viharanto, nirodhānupassī viharanto, paṭinissaggānupassī viharanto na kiñci loke upādiyati,

Meditating in this way, they don't grasp at anything in the world.

anupādiyaṁ na paritassati, aparitassaṁ paccattaññeva parinibbāyati:

Not grasping, they're not anxious. Not being anxious, they personally become extinguished.

"khīṇā jāti, vusitaṁ brahmacariyaṁ, kataṁ karaṇīyaṁ, nāparaṁ itthattāyā"ti pajānāti.

They understand: "Rebirth is ended, the spiritual journey has been completed, what had to be done has been done, there is no return to any state of existence."

Ettāvatā kho, devānaminda, bhikkhu saṅkhittena taṇhāsaṅkhayavimutto hoti accantaniṭṭho accantayogakkhemī accantabrahmacārī accantapariyosāno seṭṭho devamanussānan'ti.

That's how I briefly define a mendicant who is freed through the ending of craving, who has reached the ultimate end, the ultimate sanctuary, the ultimate spiritual life, the ultimate goal, and is best among gods and humans.'

Evaṁ kho me, mārisa moggallāna, bhagavā saṅkhittena taṇhāsaṅkhayavimuttiṁ abhāsī"ti.

That's how the Buddha briefly explained freedom through the ending of craving to me."

Atha kho āyasmā mahāmoggallāno sakkassa devānamindassa bhāsitaṁ abhinanditvā anumoditvā—seyyathāpi nāma balavā puriso samiñjitaṁ vā bāhaṁ pasāreyya, pasāritaṁ vā bāhaṁ samiñjeyya; evameva—devesu tāvatiṁsesu antarahito pubbārāme migāramātupāsāde pāturahosi.

Moggallāna approved and agreed with what Sakka said. As easily as a strong person would extend or contract their arm, he vanished from among the Gods of the Thirty-Three and reappeared in the Eastern Monastery.

Atha kho sakkassa devānamindassa paricārikāyo acirapakkante āyasmante mahāmoggallāne sakkaṁ devānamindaṁ etadavocuṁ:

Soon after Moggallāna left, Sakka's maids said to him,

"eso nu te, mārisa, so bhagavā satthā"ti?

"Good sir, was that the Blessed One, your Teacher?"

"Na kho me, mārisa, so bhagavā satthā.

"No, it was not.

Sabrahmacārī me eso āyasmā mahāmoggallāno"ti.

That was my spiritual companion Venerable Mahāmoggallāna."

"Lābhā te, mārisa, suladdhaṁ te, mārisa

"You're fortunate, good sir, so very fortunate,

yassa te sabrahmacārī evaṁmahiddhiko evaṁmahānubhāvo.

to have a spiritual companion of such power and might!

Aho nūna te so bhagavā satthā"ti.

We can't believe that's not the Blessed One, your Teacher!"

Atha kho āyasmā mahāmoggallāno yena bhagavā tenupasaṅkami; upasaṅkamitvā bhagavantaṁ abhivādetvā ekamantaṁ nisīdi. Ekamantaṁ nisinno kho āyasmā mahāmoggallāno bhagavantaṁ etadavoca:

Then Mahāmoggallāna went up to the Buddha, bowed, sat down to one side, and said to him,

"abhijānāti no, bhante, bhagavā ahu ñātaññatarassa mahesakkhassa yakkhassa saṅkhittena taṇhāsaṅkhayavimuttiṁ bhāsitā"ti?

"Sir, do you recall briefly explaining freedom through the ending of craving to a certain well-known and illustrious spirit?"

"Abhijānāmahaṁ, moggallāna, idha sakko devānamindo yenāhaṁ tenupasaṅkami; upasaṅkamitvā maṁ abhivādetvā ekamantaṁ aṭṭhāsi. Ekamantaṁ ṭhito kho, moggallāna, sakko devānamindo maṁ etadavoca:

"I do, Moggallāna." And the Buddha retold all that happened when Sakka came to visit him, adding:

'kittāvatā nu kho, bhante, bhikkhu saṅkhittena taṇhāsaṅkhayavimutto hoti accantaniṭṭho accantayogakkhemī accantabrahmacārī accantapariyosāno seṭṭho devamanussānan'ti.

Evaṁ vutte, ahaṁ, moggallāna, sakkaṁ devānamindaṁ etadavocaṁ

'idha devānaminda, bhikkhuno sutaṁ hoti

"sabbe dhammā nālaṁ abhinivesāyā"ti.

Evaṁ cetaṁ, devānaminda, bhikkhuno sutaṁ hoti

"sabbe dhammā nālaṁ abhinivesāyā"ti.

So sabbaṁ dhammaṁ abhijānāti, sabbaṁ dhammaṁ abhiññāya sabbaṁ dhammaṁ parijānāti, sabbaṁ dhammaṁ pariññāya yaṁ kiñci vedanaṁ vedeti sukhaṁ vā dukkhaṁ vā adukkhamasukhaṁ vā.

So tāsu vedanāsu aniccānupassī viharati, virāgānupassī viharati, nirodhānupassī viharati, paṭinissaggānupassī viharati.

So tāsu vedanāsu aniccānupassī viharanto, virāgānupassī viharanto, nirodhānupassī viharanto,

paṭinissaggānupassī viharanto na kiñci loke upādiyati,

anupādiyaṁ na paritassati, aparitassaṁ paccattaññeva parinibbāyati:

"khīṇā jāti, vusitaṁ brahmacariyaṁ, kataṁ karaṇīyaṁ, nāparaṁ itthattāyā"ti pajānāti.

Ettāvatā kho, devānaminda, bhikkhu saṅkhittena taṇhāsaṅkhayavimutto hoti accantaniṭṭho accantayogakkhemī accantabrahmacārī accantapariyosāno seṭṭho devamanussānan'ti.

Evaṁ kho ahaṁ, moggallāna, abhijānāmi sakkassa devānamindassa saṅkhittena taṇhāsaṅkhayavimuttiṁ bhāsitā"ti.

"That's how I recall briefly explaining freedom through the ending of craving to Sakka, lord of gods."

Idamavoca bhagavā.

That is what the Buddha said.

Attamano āyasmā mahāmoggallāno bhagavato bhāsitaṁ abhinandīti.

Satisfied, Venerable Mahāmoggallāna was happy with what the Buddha said.

Cūḷataṇhāsaṅkhayasuttaṁ niṭṭhitaṁ sattamaṁ.

38 Mahatanhasankhayasutta:

The Longer Discourse on the Ending of Craving

Evaṁ me sutaṁ—

So I have heard.

ekaṁ samayaṁ bhagavā sāvatthiyaṁ viharati jetavane anāthapiṇḍikassa ārāme.

At one time the Buddha was staying near Sāvatthī in Jeta's Grove, Anāthapiṇḍika's monastery.

Tena kho pana samayena sātissa nāma bhikkhuno kevaṭṭaputtassa evarūpaṁ pāpakaṁ diṭṭhigataṁ uppannaṁ hoti:

Now at that time a mendicant called Sāti, the fisherman's son, had the following harmful misconception:

"tathāhaṁ bhagavatā dhammaṁ desitaṁ ājānāmi yathā tadevidaṁ viññāṇaṁ sandhāvati saṁsarati anaññan"ti.

"As I understand the Buddha's teachings, it is this very same consciousness that roams and transmigrates, not another."

Assosuṁ kho sambahulā bhikkhū:

Several mendicants heard about this.

"sātissa kira nāma bhikkhuno kevaṭṭaputtassa evarūpaṁ pāpakaṁ diṭṭhigataṁ uppannaṁ:

'tathāhaṁ bhagavatā dhammaṁ desitaṁ ājānāmi yathā tadevidaṁ viññāṇaṁ sandhāvati saṁsarati, anaññan'"ti.

Atha kho te bhikkhū yena sāti bhikkhu kevaṭṭaputto tenupasaṅkamiṁsu; upasaṅkamitvā sātiṁ bhikkhuṁ kevaṭṭaputtaṁ etadavocuṁ:

They went up to Sāti and said to him,

"saccaṁ kira te, āvuso sāti, evarūpaṁ pāpakaṁ diṭṭhigataṁ uppannaṁ:

"Is it really true, Reverend Sāti, that you have such a harmful misconception:

'tathāhaṁ bhagavatā dhammaṁ desitaṁ ājānāmi yathā tadevidaṁ viññāṇaṁ sandhāvati saṁsarati, anaññan'"ti?

'As I understand the Buddha's teachings, it is this very same consciousness that roams and transmigrates, not another'?"

"Evaṁ byā kho ahaṁ, āvuso, bhagavatā dhammaṁ desitaṁ ājānāmi yathā tadevidaṁ viññāṇaṁ sandhāvati saṁsarati, anaññan"ti.

"Absolutely, reverends. As I understand the Buddha's teachings, it is this very same consciousness that roams and transmigrates, not another."

Atha kho te bhikkhū sātiṁ bhikkhuṁ kevaṭṭaputtaṁ etasmā pāpakā diṭṭhigatā vivecetukāmā samanuyuñjanti samanugāhanti samanubhāsanti:

Then, wishing to dissuade Sāti from his view, the mendicants pursued, pressed, and grilled him,

"mā evaṁ, āvuso sāti, avaca, mā bhagavantaṁ abbhācikkhi, na hi sādhu bhagavato abbhakkhānaṁ, na hi bhagavā evaṁ vadeyya.

"Don't say that, Sāti! Don't misrepresent the Buddha, for misrepresentation of the Buddha is not good. And the Buddha would not say that.

Anekapariyāyenāvuso sāti, paṭiccasamuppannaṁ viññāṇaṁ vuttaṁ bhagavatā, aññatra paccayā natthi viññāṇassa sambhavo"ti.

In many ways the Buddha has said that consciousness is dependently originated, since without a cause, consciousness does not come to be."

Evampi kho sāti bhikkhu kevaṭṭaputto tehi bhikkhūhi samanuyuñjiyamāno samanugāhiyamāno samanubhāsiyamāno tadeva pāpakaṁ diṭṭhigataṁ thāmasā parāmāsā abhinivissa voharati:

But even though the mendicants pressed him in this way, Sāti obstinately stuck to his misconception and insisted on stating it.

"evaṁ byā kho ahaṁ, āvuso, bhagavatā dhammaṁ desitaṁ ājānāmi yathā tadevidaṁ viññāṇaṁ sandhāvati saṁsarati anaññan"ti.

Yato kho te bhikkhū nāsakkhiṁsu sātiṁ bhikkhuṁ kevaṭṭaputtaṁ etasmā pāpakā diṭṭhigatā vivecetuṁ, atha kho te bhikkhū yena bhagavā tenupasaṅkamiṁsu; upasaṅkamitvā bhagavantaṁ abhivādetvā ekamantaṁ nisīdiṁsu. Ekamantaṁ nisinnā kho te bhikkhū bhagavantaṁ etadavocuṁ:

When they weren't able to dissuade Sāti from his view, the mendicants went to the Buddha, bowed, sat down to one side, and told him what had happened.

"sātissa nāma, bhante, bhikkhuno kevaṭṭaputtassa evarūpaṁ pāpakaṁ diṭṭhigataṁ uppannaṁ:

'tathāhaṁ bhagavatā dhammaṁ desitaṁ ājānāmi yathā tadevidaṁ viññāṇaṁ sandhāvati saṁsarati, anaññan'ti.

Assumha kho mayaṁ, bhante, sātissa kira nāma bhikkhuno kevaṭṭaputtassa evarūpaṁ pāpakaṁ diṭṭhigataṁ uppannaṁ:

'tathāhaṁ bhagavatā dhammaṁ desitaṁ ājānāmi yathā tadevidaṁ viññāṇaṁ sandhāvati saṁsarati, anaññan'ti.

Atha kho mayaṁ, bhante, yena sāti bhikkhu kevaṭṭaputto tenupasaṅkamimha; upasaṅkamitvā sātiṁ bhikkhuṁ kevaṭṭaputtaṁ etadavocumha:

'saccaṁ kira te, āvuso sāti, evarūpaṁ pāpakaṁ diṭṭhigataṁ uppannaṁ:

"tathāhaṁ bhagavatā dhammaṁ desitaṁ ājānāmi yathā tadevidaṁ viññāṇaṁ sandhāvati saṁsarati, anaññan"'ti?

Evaṁ vutte, bhante, sāti bhikkhu kevaṭṭaputto amhe etadavoca:

'evaṁ byā kho ahaṁ, āvuso, bhagavatā dhammaṁ desitaṁ ājānāmi yathā tadevidaṁ viññāṇaṁ sandhāvati saṁsarati, anaññan'ti.

Atha kho mayaṁ, bhante, sātiṁ bhikkhuṁ kevaṭṭaputtaṁ etasmā pāpakā diṭṭhigatā vivecetukāmā samanuyuñjimha samanugāhimha samanubhāsimha:

'mā evaṁ, āvuso sāti, avaca, mā bhagavantaṁ abbhācikkhi, na hi sādhu bhagavato abbhakkhānaṁ, na hi bhagavā evaṁ vadeyya.

Anekapariyāyenāvuso sāti, paṭiccasamuppannaṁ viññāṇaṁ vuttaṁ bhagavatā, aññatra paccayā natthi viññāṇassa sambhavo'ti.

Evampi kho, bhante, sāti bhikkhu kevaṭṭaputto amhehi samanuyuñjiyamāno samanugāhiyamāno samanubhāsiyamāno tadeva pāpakaṁ diṭṭhigataṁ thāmasā parāmasā abhinivissa voharati:

'evaṁ byā kho ahaṁ, āvuso, bhagavatā dhammaṁ desitaṁ ājānāmi yathā tadevidaṁ viññāṇaṁ sandhāvati saṁsarati, anaññan'ti.

Yato kho mayaṁ, bhante, nāsakkhimha sātiṁ bhikkhuṁ kevaṭṭaputtaṁ etasmā pāpakā diṭṭhigatā vivecetuṁ, atha mayaṁ etamatthaṁ bhagavato ārocemā"ti.

Atha kho bhagavā aññataraṁ bhikkhuṁ āmantesi:

So the Buddha addressed a certain monk,

"ehi tvaṁ bhikkhu, mama vacanena sātiṁ bhikkhuṁ kevaṭṭaputtaṁ āmantehi:

"Please, monk, in my name tell the mendicant Sāti that

'satthā taṁ, āvuso sāti, āmantetī'"ti.

the teacher summons him."

"Evaṁ, bhante"ti kho so bhikkhu bhagavato paṭissutvā yena sāti bhikkhu kevaṭṭaputto tenupasaṅkami; upasaṅkamitvā sātiṁ bhikkhuṁ kevaṭṭaputtaṁ etadavoca:

"Yes, sir," that monk replied. He went to Sāti and said to him,

"satthā taṁ, āvuso sāti, āmantetī'"ti.

"Reverend Sāti, the teacher summons you."

"Evamāvuso"ti kho sāti bhikkhu kevaṭṭaputto tassa bhikkhuno paṭissutvā yena bhagavā tenupasaṅkami; upasaṅkamitvā bhagavantaṁ abhivādetvā ekamantaṁ nisīdi. Ekamantaṁ nisinnaṁ kho sātiṁ bhikkhuṁ kevaṭṭaputtaṁ bhagavā etadavoca:

"Yes, reverend," Sāti replied. He went to the Buddha, bowed, and sat down to one side. The Buddha said to him,

"saccaṁ kira te, sāti, evarūpaṁ pāpakaṁ diṭṭhigataṁ uppannaṁ:

"Is it really true, Sāti, that you have such a harmful misconception:

'tathāhaṁ bhagavatā dhammaṁ desitaṁ ājānāmi yathā tadevidaṁ viññāṇaṁ sandhāvati saṁsarati, anaññan'"ti?

'As I understand the Buddha's teachings, it is this very same consciousness that roams and transmigrates, not another'?"

"Evaṁ byā kho ahaṁ, bhante, bhagavatā dhammaṁ desitaṁ ājānāmi yathā tadevidaṁ viññāṇaṁ sandhāvati saṁsarati, anaññan"ti.

"Absolutely, sir. As I understand the Buddha's teachings, it is this very same consciousness that roams and transmigrates, not another."

"Katamaṁ taṁ, sāti, viññāṇan"ti?

"Sāti, what is that consciousness?"

"Yvāyaṁ, bhante, vado vedeyyo tatra tatra kalyāṇapāpakānaṁ kammānaṁ vipākaṁ paṭisaṁvedetī"ti.

"Sir, he is the speaker and feeler who experiences the results of good and bad deeds in all the different realms."

"Kassa nu kho nāma tvaṁ, moghapurisa, mayā evaṁ dhammaṁ desitaṁ ājānāsi?

"Silly man, who on earth have you ever known me to teach in that way?

Nanu mayā, moghapurisa, anekapariyāyena paṭiccasamuppannaṁ viññāṇaṁ vuttaṁ, aññatra paccayā natthi viññāṇassa sambhavoti?

Haven't I said in many ways that consciousness is dependently originated, since consciousness does not arise without a cause?

Atha ca pana tvaṁ, moghapurisa, attanā duggahitena amhe ceva abbhācikkhasi, attānañca khaṇasi, bahuñca apuññaṁ pasavasi.

But still you misrepresent me by your wrong grasp, harm yourself, and make much bad karma.

Tañhi te, moghapurisa, bhavissati dīgharattaṁ ahitāya dukkhāyā"ti.

This will be for your lasting harm and suffering."

Atha kho bhagavā bhikkhū āmantesi:

Then the Buddha said to the mendicants,

"Taṁ kiṁ maññatha, bhikkhave,

"What do you think, mendicants?

api nāyaṁ sāti bhikkhu kevaṭṭaputto usmīkatopi imasmiṁ dhammavinaye"ti?

Has this mendicant Sāti kindled even a spark of wisdom in this teaching and training?"

"Kiñhi siyā, bhante?

"How could that be, sir?

No hetaṁ, bhante"ti.

No, sir."

Evaṁ vutte, sāti bhikkhu kevaṭṭaputto tuṇhībhūto maṅkubhūto pattakkhandho adhomukho pajjhāyanto appaṭibhāno nisīdi.

When this was said, Sāti sat silent, dismayed, shoulders drooping, downcast, depressed, with nothing to say.

Atha kho bhagavā satiṁ bhikkhuṁ kevaṭṭaputtaṁ tuṇhībhūtaṁ maṅkubhūtaṁ pattakkhandhaṁ adhomukhaṁ pajjhāyantaṁ appaṭibhānaṁ viditvā satiṁ bhikkhuṁ kevaṭṭaputtaṁ etadavoca:

Knowing this, the Buddha said,

"paññāyissasi kho tvaṁ, moghapurisa, etena sakena pāpakena diṭṭhigatena.

"Silly man, you will be known by your own harmful misconception.

Idhāhaṁ bhikkhū paṭipucchissāmī"ti.

I'll question the mendicants about this."

Atha kho bhagavā bhikkhū āmantesi:

Then the Buddha said to the mendicants,

"tumhepi me, bhikkhave, evaṁ dhammaṁ desitaṁ ājānātha yathāyaṁ sāti bhikkhu kevaṭṭaputto attanā duggahitena amhe ceva abbhācikkhati, attānañca khaṇati, bahuñca apuññaṁ pasavatī"ti?

"Mendicants, do you understand my teachings as Sāti does, when he misrepresents me by his wrong grasp, harms himself, and makes much bad karma?"

"No hetaṁ, bhante.

"No, sir.

Anekapariyāyena hi no, bhante, paṭiccasamuppannaṁ viññāṇaṁ vuttaṁ bhagavatā, aññatra paccayā natthi viññāṇassa sambhavo"ti.

For in many ways the Buddha has told us that consciousness is dependently originated, since without a cause, consciousness does not come to be."

"Sādhu sādhu, bhikkhave.

"Good, good, mendicants!

Sādhu kho me tumhe, bhikkhave, evaṁ dhammaṁ desitaṁ ājānātha.

It's good that you understand my teaching like this.

Anekapariyāyena hi vo, bhikkhave, paṭiccasamuppannaṁ viññāṇaṁ vuttaṁ mayā, aññatra paccayā natthi viññāṇassa sambhavo"ti.

For in many ways I have told you that consciousness is dependently originated, since without a cause, consciousness does not come to be.

Atha ca panāyaṁ sāti bhikkhu kevaṭṭaputto attanā duggahitena amhe ceva abbhācikkhati, attānañca khaṇati, bahuñca apuññaṁ pasavati.

But still this Sāti misrepresents me by his wrong grasp, harms himself, and makes much bad karma.

Tañhi tassa moghapurisassa bhavissati dīgharattaṁ ahitāya dukkhāya.

This will be for his lasting harm and suffering.

"Yaṁ yadeva, bhikkhave, paccayaṁ paṭicca uppajjati viññāṇaṁ, tena teneva viññāṇantveva saṅkhyaṁ gacchati.

Consciousness is reckoned according to the specific conditions dependent upon which it arises.

Cakkhuñca paṭicca rūpe ca uppajjati viññāṇaṁ, cakkhuviññāṇantveva saṅkhyaṁ gacchati;

Consciousness that arises dependent on the eye and sights is reckoned as eye consciousness.

sotañca paṭicca sadde ca uppajjati viññāṇaṁ, sotaviññāṇantveva saṅkhyaṁ gacchati;

Consciousness that arises dependent on the ear and sounds is reckoned as ear consciousness.

ghānañca paṭicca gandhe ca uppajjati viññāṇaṁ, ghānaviññāṇantveva saṅkhyaṁ gacchati;

Consciousness that arises dependent on the nose and smells is reckoned as nose consciousness.

jivhañca paṭicca rase ca uppajjati viññāṇaṁ, jivhāviññāṇantveva saṅkhyaṁ gacchati;

Consciousness that arises dependent on the tongue and tastes is reckoned as tongue consciousness.

kāyañca paṭicca phoṭṭhabbe ca uppajjati viññāṇaṁ, kāyaviññāṇantveva saṅkhyaṁ gacchati;

Consciousness that arises dependent on the body and touches is reckoned as body consciousness.

manañca paṭicca dhamme ca uppajjati viññāṇaṁ, manoviññāṇantveva saṅkhyaṁ gacchati.

Consciousness that arises dependent on the mind and thoughts is reckoned as mind consciousness.

Seyyathāpi, bhikkhave, yaṁ yadeva paccayaṁ paṭicca aggi jalati tena teneva saṅkhyaṁ gacchati.

It's like fire, which is reckoned according to the specific conditions dependent upon which it burns.

Kaṭṭhañca paṭicca aggi jalati, kaṭṭhaggitveva saṅkhyaṁ gacchati;

A fire that burns dependent on logs is reckoned as a log fire.

sakalikañca paṭicca aggi jalati, sakalikaggitveva saṅkhyaṁ gacchati;

A fire that burns dependent on twigs is reckoned as a twig fire.

tiṇañca paṭicca aggi jalati, tiṇaggitveva saṅkhyaṁ gacchati;

A fire that burns dependent on grass is reckoned as a grass fire.

gomayañca paṭicca aggi jalati, gomayaggitveva saṅkhyaṁ gacchati;

A fire that burns dependent on cow-dung is reckoned as a cow-dung fire.

thusañca paṭicca aggi jalati, thusaggitveva saṅkhyaṁ gacchati;

A fire that burns dependent on husks is reckoned as a husk fire.

saṅkārañca paṭicca aggi jalati, saṅkāraggitveva saṅkhyaṁ gacchati.

A fire that burns dependent on rubbish is reckoned as a rubbish fire.

Evameva kho, bhikkhave, yaṁ yadeva paccayaṁ paṭicca uppajjati viññāṇaṁ, tena teneva saṅkhyaṁ gacchati.

In the same way, consciousness is reckoned according to the specific conditions dependent upon which it arises. ...

Cakkhuñca paṭicca rūpe ca uppajjati viññāṇaṁ, cakkhuviññāṇantveva saṅkhyaṁ gacchati;

sotañca paṭicca sadde ca uppajjati viññāṇaṁ, sotaviññāṇantveva saṅkhyaṁ gacchati,

ghānañca paṭicca gandhe ca uppajjati viññāṇaṁ, ghānaviññāṇantveva saṅkhyaṁ gacchati,

jivhañca paṭicca rase ca uppajjati viññāṇaṁ, jivhāviññāṇantveva saṅkhyaṁ gacchati.

Kāyañca paṭicca phoṭṭhabbe ca uppajjati viññāṇaṁ, kāyaviññāṇantveva saṅkhyaṁ gacchati.

Manañca paṭicca dhamme ca uppajjati viññāṇaṁ, manoviññāṇantveva saṅkhyaṁ gacchati.

Bhūtamidanti, bhikkhave, passathā"ti?

Mendicants, do you see that this has come to be?"

"Evaṁ, bhante".

"Yes, sir."

"Tadāhārasambhavanti, bhikkhave, passathā"ti?

"Do you see that it originated with that as fuel?"

"Evaṁ, bhante".

"Yes, sir."

"Tadāhāranirodhā yaṁ bhūtaṁ, taṁ nirodhadhammanti, bhikkhave, passathā"ti?

"Do you see that when that fuel ceases, what has come to be is liable to cease?"

"Evaṁ, bhante".

"Yes, sir."

"Bhūtamidaṁ nossūti, bhikkhave, kaṅkhato uppajjati vicikicchā"ti?

"Does doubt arise when you're uncertain whether or not this has come to be?"

"Evaṁ, bhante".

"Yes, sir."

"Tadāhārasambhavaṁ nossūti, bhikkhave, kaṅkhato uppajjati vicikicchā"ti?

"Does doubt arise when you're uncertain whether or not this has originated with that as fuel?"

"Evaṁ, bhante".

"Yes, sir."

"Tadāhāranirodhā yaṁ bhūtaṁ, taṁ nirodhadhammaṁ nossūti, bhikkhave, kaṅkhato uppajjati vicikicchā"ti?

"Does doubt arise when you're uncertain whether or not when that fuel ceases, what has come to be is liable to cease?"

"Evaṁ, bhante".

"Yes, sir."

"Bhūtamidanti, bhikkhave, yathābhūtaṁ sammappaññāya passato yā vicikicchā sā pahīyatī"ti?

"Is doubt given up in someone who truly sees with right understanding that this has come to be?"

"Evaṁ, bhante".

"Yes, sir."

"Tadāhārasambhavanti, bhikkhave, yathābhūtaṁ sammappaññāya passato yā vicikicchā sā pahīyatī"ti?

"Is doubt given up in someone who truly sees with right understanding that this has originated with that as fuel?"

"Evaṁ, bhante".

"Yes, sir."

"Tadāhāranirodhā yaṁ bhūtaṁ, taṁ nirodhadhammanti, bhikkhave, yathābhūtaṁ sammappaññāya passato yā vicikicchā sā pahīyatī"ti?

"Is doubt given up in someone who truly sees with right understanding that when that fuel ceases, what has come to be is liable to cease?"

"Evaṁ, bhante".

"Yes, sir."

"Bhūtamidanti, bhikkhave, itipi vo ettha nibbicikicchā"ti?

"Are you free of doubt as to whether this has come to be?"

"Evaṁ, bhante".

"Yes, sir."

"Tadāhārasambhavanti, bhikkhave, itipi vo ettha nibbicikicchā"ti?

"Are you free of doubt as to whether this has originated with that as fuel?"

"Evaṁ, bhante".

"Yes, sir."

"Tadāhāranirodhā yaṁ bhūtaṁ taṁ nirodhadhammanti, bhikkhave, itipi vo ettha nibbicikicchā"ti?

"Are you free of doubt as to whether when that fuel ceases, what has come to be is liable to cease?"

"Evaṁ, bhante".

"Yes, sir."

"Bhūtamidanti, bhikkhave, yathābhūtaṁ sammappaññāya suditṭhan"ti?

"Have you truly seen clearly with right understanding that this has come to be?"

"Evaṁ, bhante".

"Yes, sir."

"Tadāhārasambhavanti, bhikkhave, yathābhūtaṁ sammappaññāya suditṭhan"ti?

"Have you truly seen clearly with right understanding that this has originated with that as fuel?"

"Evaṁ, bhante".

"Yes, sir."

"Tadāhāranirodhā yaṁ bhūtaṁ taṁ nirodhadhammanti, bhikkhave, yathābhūtaṁ sammappaññāya suditṭhan"ti?

"Have you truly seen clearly with right understanding that when that fuel ceases, what has come to be is liable to cease?"

"Evaṁ, bhante".

"Yes, sir."

"Imañce tumhe, bhikkhave, diṭṭhiṁ evaṁ parisuddhaṁ evaṁ pariyodātaṁ allīyetha kelāyetha dhanāyetha mamāyetha, api nu me tumhe, bhikkhave, kullūpamaṁ dhammaṁ desitaṁ ājāneyyātha nittharaṇatthāya no gahaṇatthāyā"ti?

"Pure and bright as this view is, mendicants, if you cherish it, fancy it, treasure it, and treat it as your own, would you be understanding how the Dhamma is similar to a raft: for crossing over, not for holding on?"

"No hetaṁ, bhante".

"No, sir."

"Imañce tumhe, bhikkhave, diṭṭhiṁ evaṁ parisuddhaṁ evaṁ pariyodātaṁ na allīyetha na kelāyetha na dhanāyetha na mamāyetha, api nu me tumhe, bhikkhave, kullūpamaṁ dhammaṁ desitaṁ ājāneyyātha nittharaṇatthāya no gahaṇatthāyā"ti?

"Pure and bright as this view is, mendicants, if you don't cherish it, fancy it, treasure it, and treat it as your own, would you be understanding how the Dhamma is similar to a raft: for crossing over, not for holding on?"

"Evaṁ, bhante".

"Yes, sir."

"Cattārome, bhikkhave, āhārā bhūtānaṁ vā sattānaṁ ṭhitiyā, sambhavesīnaṁ vā anuggahāya.

"Mendicants, there are these four fuels. They maintain sentient beings that have been born and help those that are about to be born.

Katame cattāro?

What four?

Kabaḷīkāro āhāro oḷāriko vā sukhumo vā, phasso dutiyo, manosañcetanā tatiyā, viññāṇaṁ catutthaṁ.

Solid food, whether coarse or fine; contact is the second, mental intention the third, and consciousness the fourth.

Ime ca, bhikkhave, cattāro āhārā kiṁnidānā kiṁsamudayā kiṁjātikā kiṁpabhavā?

What is the source, origin, birthplace, and inception of these four fuels?

Ime cattāro āhārā taṇhānidānā taṇhāsamudayā taṇhājātikā taṇhāpabhavā.

Craving.

Taṇhā cāyaṁ, bhikkhave, kiṁnidānā kiṁsamudayā kiṁjātikā kiṁpabhavā?

And what is the source of craving?

Taṇhā vedanānidānā vedanāsamudayā vedanājātikā vedanāpabhavā.

Feeling.

Vedanā cāyaṁ, bhikkhave, kiṁnidānā kiṁsamudayā kiṁjātikā kiṁpabhavā?

And what is the source of feeling?

Vedanā phassanidānā phassasamudayā phassajātikā phassapabhavā.

Contact.

Phasso cāyaṁ, bhikkhave, kiṁnidāno kiṁsamudayo kiṁjātiko kiṁpabhavo?

And what is the source of contact?

Phasso saḷāyatananidāno saḷāyatanasamudayo saḷāyatanajātiko saḷāyatanapabhavo.

The six sense fields.

Saḷāyatanañcidaṁ, bhikkhave, kiṁnidānaṁ kiṁsamudayaṁ kiṁjātikaṁ kiṁpabhavaṁ?

And what is the source of the six sense fields?

Saḷāyatanaṁ nāmarūpanidānaṁ nāmarūpasamudayaṁ nāmarūpajātikaṁ nāmarūpapabhavaṁ.

Name and form.

Nāmarūpañcidaṁ, bhikkhave, kiṁnidānaṁ kiṁsamudayaṁ kiṁjātikaṁ kiṁpabhavaṁ?

And what is the source of name and form?

Nāmarūpaṁ viññāṇanidānaṁ viññāṇasamudayaṁ viññāṇajātikaṁ viññāṇapabhavaṁ.

Consciousness.

Viññāṇañcidaṁ, bhikkhave, kiṁnidānaṁ kiṁsamudayaṁ kiṁjātikaṁ kiṁpabhavaṁ?

And what is the source of consciousness?

Viññāṇaṁ saṅkhāranidānaṁ saṅkhārasamudayaṁ saṅkhārajātikaṁ saṅkhārapabhavaṁ.

Choices.

Saṅkhārā cime, bhikkhave, kiṁnidānā kiṁsamudayā kiṁjātikā kiṁpabhavā?

And what is the source of choices?

Saṅkhārā avijjānidānā avijjāsamudayā avijjājātikā avijjāpabhavā.

Ignorance.

Iti kho, bhikkhave, avijjāpaccayā saṅkhārā,

So, ignorance is a condition for choices.

saṅkhārapaccayā viññāṇaṁ,

Choices are a condition for consciousness.

viññāṇapaccayā nāmarūpaṁ,

Consciousness is a condition for name and form.

nāmarūpapaccayā saḷāyatanaṁ,

Name and form are conditions for the six sense fields.

saḷāyatanapaccayā phasso,

The six sense fields are conditions for contact.

phassapaccayā vedanā,

Contact is a condition for feeling.

vedanāpaccayā taṇhā,

Feeling is a condition for craving.

taṇhāpaccayā upādānaṁ,

Craving is a condition for grasping.

upādānapaccayā bhavo,

Grasping is a condition for continued existence.

bhavapaccayā jāti,

Continued existence is a condition for rebirth.

jātipaccayā jarāmaraṇaṁ sokaparidevadukkhadomanassupāyāsā sambhavanti.

Rebirth is a condition for old age and death, sorrow, lamentation, pain, sadness, and distress to come to be.

Evametassa kevalassa dukkhakkhandhassa samudayo hoti.

That is how this entire mass of suffering originates.

Jātipaccayā jarāmaraṇanti iti kho panetaṁ vuttaṁ;

'Rebirth is a condition for old age and death.' That's what I said.

jātipaccayā nu kho, bhikkhave, jarāmaraṇaṁ, no vā, kathaṁ vā ettha hotī"ti?

Is that how you see this or not?"

"Jātipaccayā, bhante, jarāmaraṇaṁ;

evaṁ no ettha hoti—

"That's how we see it."

jātipaccayā jarāmaraṇan"ti.

"Bhavapaccayā jātīti iti kho panetaṁ vuttaṁ;

"'Continued existence is a condition for rebirth.' …

bhavapaccayā nu kho, bhikkhave, jāti, no vā, kathaṁ vā ettha hotī"ti?

"Bhavapaccayā, bhante, jāti;

evaṁ no ettha hoti—

bhavapaccayā jātī"ti.

"Upādānapaccayā bhavoti iti kho panetaṁ vuttaṁ;

upādānapaccayā nu kho, bhikkhave, bhavo, no vā, kathaṁ vā ettha hotī"ti?

"Upādānapaccayā, bhante, bhavo;

evaṁ no ettha hoti—

upādānapaccayā bhavo"ti.

"Taṇhāpaccayā upādānanti iti kho panetaṁ vuttaṁ, taṇhāpaccayā nu kho, bhikkhave, upādānaṁ, no vā, kathaṁ vā ettha hotī"ti?

"Taṇhāpaccayā, bhante, upādānaṁ;

evaṁ no ettha hoti—

taṇhāpaccayā upādānan"ti.

"Vedanāpaccayā taṇhāti iti kho panetaṁ vuttaṁ;

vedanāpaccayā nu kho, bhikkhave, taṇhā, no vā, kathaṁ vā ettha hotī"ti?

"Vedanāpaccayā, bhante, taṇhā;

evaṁ no ettha hoti—

vedanāpaccayā taṇhā"ti.

"Phassapaccayā vedanāti iti kho panetaṁ vuttaṁ;

phassapaccayā nu kho, bhikkhave, vedanā, no vā, kathaṁ vā ettha hotī"ti?

"Phassapaccayā, bhante, vedanā;

evaṁ no ettha hoti—

phassapaccayā vedanā"ti.

"Saḷāyatanapaccayā phassoti iti kho panetaṁ vuttaṁ;

saḷāyatanapaccayā nu kho, bhikkhave, phasso, no vā, kathaṁ vā ettha hotī"ti?

"Saḷāyatanapaccayā, bhante, phasso;

evaṁ no ettha hoti—

saḷāyatanapaccayā phasso”ti.

“Nāmarūpapaccayā saḷāyatananti iti kho panetaṁ vuttaṁ;

nāmarūpapaccayā nu kho, bhikkhave, saḷāyatanaṁ, no vā, kathaṁ vā ettha hotī”ti?

“Nāmarūpapaccayā, bhante, saḷāyatanaṁ;

evaṁ no ettha hoti—

nāmarūpapaccayā saḷāyatanan”ti.

“Viññāṇapaccayā nāmarūpanti iti kho panetaṁ vuttaṁ;

viññāṇapaccayā nu kho, bhikkhave, nāmarūpaṁ, no vā, kathaṁ vā ettha hotī”ti?

“Viññāṇapaccayā, bhante, nāmarūpaṁ;

evaṁ no ettha hoti—

viññāṇapaccayā nāmarūpan”ti.

“Saṅkhārapaccayā viññāṇanti iti kho panetaṁ vuttaṁ;

saṅkhārapaccayā nu kho, bhikkhave, viññāṇaṁ, no vā, kathaṁ vā ettha hotī”ti?

“Saṅkhārapaccayā, bhante, viññāṇaṁ;

evaṁ no ettha hoti—

saṅkhārapaccayā viññāṇan”ti.

“Avijjāpaccayā saṅkhārāti iti kho panetaṁ vuttaṁ;

‘Ignorance is a condition for choices.’ That’s what I said.

avijjāpaccayā nu kho, bhikkhave, saṅkhārā, no vā, kathaṁ vā ettha hotī”ti?

Is that how you see this or not?”

“Avijjāpaccayā, bhante, saṅkhārā;

evaṁ no ettha hoti—

“That’s how we see it.”

avijjāpaccayā saṅkhārā”ti.

“Sādhu, bhikkhave.

“Good, mendicants!

Iti kho, bhikkhave, tumhepi evaṁ vadetha, ahampi evaṁ vadāmi—

So both you and I say this.

imasmiṁ sati idaṁ hoti, imassuppādā idaṁ uppajjati, yadidaṁ—

When this exists, that is; due to the arising of this, that arises. That is:

avijjāpaccayā saṅkhārā,

Ignorance is a condition for choices.

saṅkhārapaccayā viññāṇaṁ,

Choices are a condition for consciousness.

viññāṇapaccayā nāmarūpaṁ,

Consciousness is a condition for name and form.

nāmarūpapaccayā saḷāyatanaṁ,

Name and form are conditions for the six sense fields.

saḷāyatanapaccayā phasso,

The six sense fields are conditions for contact.

phassapaccayā vedanā,

Contact is a condition for feeling.

vedanāpaccayā taṇhā,

Feeling is a condition for craving.

taṇhāpaccayā upādānaṁ,

Craving is a condition for grasping.

upādānapaccayā bhavo,

Grasping is a condition for continued existence.

bhavapaccayā jāti,

Continued existence is a condition for rebirth.

jātipaccayā jarāmaraṇaṁ sokaparidevadukkhadomanassupāyāsā sambhavanti.

Rebirth is a condition for old age and death, sorrow, lamentation, pain, sadness, and distress to come to be.

Evametassa kevalassa dukkhakkhandhassa samudayo hoti.

That is how this entire mass of suffering originates.

Avijjāya tveva asesavirāganirodhā saṅkhāranirodho,

When ignorance fades away and ceases with nothing left over, choices cease.

saṅkhāranirodhā viññāṇanirodho,

When choices cease, consciousness ceases.

viññāṇanirodhā nāmarūpanirodho,

When consciousness ceases, name and form cease.

nāmarūpanirodhā saḷāyatananirodho,

When name and form cease, the six sense fields cease.

saḷāyatananirodhā phassanirodho,

When the six sense fields cease, contact ceases.

phassanirodhā vedanānirodho,

When contact ceases, feeling ceases.

vedanānirodhā taṇhānirodho,

When feeling ceases, craving ceases.

taṇhānirodhā upādānanirodho,

When craving ceases, grasping ceases.

upādānanirodhā bhavanirodho,

When grasping ceases, continued existence ceases.

bhavanirodhā jātinirodho,

When continued existence ceases, rebirth ceases.

jātinirodhā jarāmaraṇaṁ sokaparidevadukkhadomanassupāyāsā nirujjhanti.

When rebirth ceases, old age and death, sorrow, lamentation, pain, sadness, and distress cease.

Evametassa kevalassa dukkhakkhandhassa nirodho hoti.

That is how this entire mass of suffering ceases.

Jātinirodhā jarāmaraṇanirodhoti iti kho panetaṁ vuttaṁ;

'When rebirth ceases, old age and death cease.' That's what I said.

jātinirodhā nu kho, bhikkhave, jarāmaraṇanirodho, no vā, kathaṃ vā ettha hotī"ti?

Is that how you see this or not?"

"Jātinirodhā, bhante, jarāmaraṇanirodho;

evaṃ no ettha hoti—

"That's how we see it."

jātinirodhā jarāmaraṇanirodho"ti.

"Bhavanirodhā jātinirodhoti iti kho panetaṃ vuttaṃ;

'When continued existence ceases, rebirth ceases.' …

bhavanirodhā nu kho, bhikkhave, jātinirodho, no vā, kathaṃ vā ettha hotī"ti?

"Bhavanirodhā, bhante, jātinirodho;

evaṃ no ettha hoti—

bhavanirodhā jātinirodho"ti.

"Upādānanirodhā bhavanirodhoti iti kho panetaṃ vuttaṃ;

upādānanirodhā nu kho, bhikkhave, bhavanirodho, no vā, kathaṃ vā ettha hotī"ti?

"Upādānanirodhā, bhante, bhavanirodho;

evaṃ no ettha hoti—

upādānanirodhā bhavanirodho"ti.

"Taṇhānirodhā upādānanirodhoti iti kho panetaṃ vuttaṃ;

taṇhānirodhā nu kho, bhikkhave, upādānanirodho, no vā, kathaṃ vā ettha hotī"ti?

"Taṇhānirodhā, bhante, upādānanirodho;

evaṃ no ettha hoti—

taṇhānirodhā upādānanirodho"ti.

"Vedanānirodhā taṇhānirodhoti iti kho panetaṃ vuttaṃ;

vedanānirodhā nu kho, bhikkhave, taṇhānirodho, no vā, kathaṃ vā ettha hotī"ti?

"Vedanānirodhā, bhante, taṇhānirodho;

evaṃ no ettha hoti—

vedanānirodhā taṇhānirodho"ti.

"Phassanirodhā vedanānirodhoti iti kho panetaṁ vuttaṁ;

phassanirodhā nu kho, bhikkhave, vedanānirodho, no vā, kathaṁ vā ettha hotī"ti?

"Phassanirodhā, bhante, vedanānirodho;

evaṁ no ettha hoti—

phassanirodhā vedanānirodho"ti.

"Saḷāyatananirodhā phassanirodhoti iti kho panetaṁ vuttaṁ;

saḷāyatananirodhā nu kho, bhikkhave, phassanirodho, no vā, kathaṁ vā ettha hotīti?

Saḷāyatananirodhā, bhante, phassanirodho;

evaṁ no ettha hoti—

saḷāyatananirodhā phassanirodho"ti.

"Nāmarūpanirodhā saḷāyatananirodhoti iti kho panetaṁ vuttaṁ;

nāmarūpanirodhā nu kho, bhikkhave, saḷāyatananirodho, no vā, kathaṁ vā ettha hotī"ti?

"Nāmarūpanirodhā, bhante, saḷāyatananirodho;

evaṁ no ettha hoti—

nāmarūpanirodhā saḷāyatananirodho"ti.

"Viññāṇanirodhā nāmarūpanirodhoti iti kho panetaṁ vuttaṁ;

viññāṇanirodhā nu kho, bhikkhave, nāmarūpanirodho, no vā, kathaṁ vā ettha hotī"ti?

"Viññāṇanirodhā, bhante, nāmarūpanirodho;

evaṁ no ettha hoti—

viññāṇanirodhā nāmarūpanirodho"ti.

"Saṅkhāranirodhā viññāṇanirodhoti iti kho panetaṁ vuttaṁ;

saṅkhāranirodhā nu kho, bhikkhave, viññāṇanirodho, no vā, kathaṁ vā ettha hotī"ti?

"Saṅkhāranirodhā, bhante, viññāṇanirodho;

evaṁ no ettha hoti—

saṅkhāranirodhā viññāṇanirodho”ti.

“Avijjānirodhā saṅkhāranirodhoti iti kho panetaṁ vuttaṁ;

'When ignorance ceases, choices cease.' That's what I said.

avijjānirodhā nu kho, bhikkhave, saṅkhāranirodho, no vā, kathaṁ vā ettha hotī”ti?

Is that how you see this or not?”

“Avijjānirodhā, bhante, saṅkhāranirodho;

evaṁ no ettha hoti—

“That's how we see it.”

avijjānirodhā saṅkhāranirodho”ti.

“Sādhu, bhikkhave.

“Good, mendicants!

Iti kho, bhikkhave, tumhepi evaṁ vadetha, ahampi evaṁ vadāmi—

So both you and I say this.

imasmiṁ asati idaṁ na hoti, imassa nirodhā idaṁ nirujjhati, yadidaṁ—

When this doesn't exist, that is not; due to the cessation of this, that ceases. That is:

avijjānirodhā saṅkhāranirodho,

When ignorance ceases, choices cease.

saṅkhāranirodhā viññāṇanirodho,

When choices cease, consciousness ceases.

viññāṇanirodhā nāmarūpanirodho,

When consciousness ceases, name and form cease.

nāmarūpanirodhā saḷāyatananirodho,

When name and form cease, the six sense fields cease.

saḷāyatananirodhā phassanirodho,

When the six sense fields cease, contact ceases.

phassanirodhā vedanānirodho,

When contact ceases, feeling ceases.

vedanānirodhā taṇhānirodho,

When feeling ceases, craving ceases.

taṇhānirodhā upādānanirodho,

When craving ceases, grasping ceases.

upādānanirodhā bhavanirodho,

When grasping ceases, continued existence ceases.

bhavanirodhā jātinirodho,

When continued existence ceases, rebirth ceases.

jātinirodhā jarāmaraṇaṁ sokaparidevadukkhadomanassupāyāsā nirujjhanti.

When rebirth ceases, old age and death, sorrow, lamentation, pain, sadness, and distress cease.

Evametassa kevalassa dukkhakkhandhassa nirodho hoti.

That is how this entire mass of suffering ceases.

Api nu tumhe, bhikkhave, evaṁ jānantā evaṁ passantā pubbantaṁ vā paṭidhāveyyātha:

Knowing and seeing in this way, mendicants, would you turn back to the past, thinking,

'ahesumha nu kho mayaṁ atītamaddhānaṁ, nanu kho ahesumha atītamaddhānaṁ, kiṁ nu kho ahesumha atītamaddhānaṁ, kathaṁ nu kho ahesumha atītamaddhānaṁ, kiṁ hutvā kiṁ ahesumha nu kho mayaṁ atītamaddhānan'"ti?

'Did we exist in the past? Did we not exist in the past? What were we in the past? How were we in the past? After being what, what did we become in the past?'?"

"No hetaṁ, bhante".

"No, sir."

"Api nu tumhe, bhikkhave, evaṁ jānantā evaṁ passantā aparantaṁ vā paṭidhāveyyātha—

"Knowing and seeing in this way, mendicants, would you turn forward to the future, thinking,

bhavissāma nu kho mayaṁ anāgatamaddhānaṁ, nanu kho bhavissāma anāgatamaddhānaṁ, kiṁ nu kho bhavissāma anāgatamaddhānaṁ, kathaṁ nu kho bhavissāma anāgatamaddhānaṁ, kiṁ hutvā kiṁ bhavissāma nu kho mayaṁ anāgatamaddhānan"ti?

'Will we exist in the future? Will we not exist in the future? What will we be in the future? How will we be in the future? After being what, what will we become in the future?'?"

"No hetaṁ, bhante".

"No, sir."

"Api nu tumhe, bhikkhave, evaṁ jānantā evaṁ passantā etarahi vā paccuppannamaddhānaṁ ajjhattaṁ kathaṅkathī assatha—

"Knowing and seeing in this way, mendicants, would you be undecided about the present, thinking,

ahaṁ nu khosmi, no nu khosmi, kiṁ nu khosmi, kathaṁ nu khosmi, ayaṁ nu kho satto kuto āgato, so kuhiṁ gāmī bhavissatī"ti?

'Am I? Am I not? What am I? How am I? This sentient being—where did it come from? And where will it go?'?"

"No hetaṁ, bhante".

"No, sir."

"Api nu tumhe, bhikkhave, evaṁ jānantā evaṁ passantā evaṁ vadeyyātha—

"Knowing and seeing in this way, would you say,

satthā no garu, satthugāravena ca mayaṁ evaṁ vademā"ti?

'Our teacher is respected. We speak like this out of respect for our teacher.'?"

"No hetaṁ, bhante".

"No, sir."

"Api nu tumhe, bhikkhave, evaṁ jānantā evaṁ passantā evaṁ vadeyyātha—

"Knowing and seeing in this way, would you say,

samaṇo evamāha, samaṇā ca nāma mayaṁ evaṁ vademā"ti?

'Our ascetic says this. It's only because of him that we say this'?"

"No hetaṁ, bhante".

"No, sir."

"Api nu tumhe, bhikkhave, evaṁ jānantā evaṁ passantā aññaṁ satthāraṁ uddiseyyātha"ti?

"Knowing and seeing in this way, would you acknowledge another teacher?"

"No hetaṁ, bhante".

"No, sir."

"Api nu tumhe, bhikkhave, evaṁ jānantā evaṁ passantā yāni tāni puthusamaṇabrāhmaṇānaṁ vata kotūhalamaṅgalāni tāni sārato paccāgaccheyyāthā"ti?

"Knowing and seeing in this way, would you believe that the observances and noisy, superstitious rites of the various ascetics and brahmins are the most important things?"

"No hetaṁ, bhante".

"No, sir."

"Nanu, bhikkhave, yadeva tumhākaṁ sāmaṁ ñātaṁ sāmaṁ diṭṭhaṁ sāmaṁ viditaṁ, tadeva tumhe vadethā"ti.

"Aren't you speaking only of what you have known and seen and realized for yourselves?"

"Evaṁ, bhante".

"Yes, sir."

"Sādhu, bhikkhave, upanītā kho me tumhe, bhikkhave, iminā sandiṭṭhikena dhammena akālikena ehipassikena opaneyyikena paccattaṁ veditabbena viññūhi.

"Good, mendicants! You have been guided by me with this teaching that's apparent in the present life, immediately effective, inviting inspection, relevant, so that sensible people can know it for themselves.

Sandiṭṭhiko ayaṁ, bhikkhave, dhammo akāliko ehipassiko opaneyyiko paccattaṁ veditabbo viññūhi—

For when I said that this teaching is apparent in the present life, immediately effective, inviting inspection, relevant, so that sensible people can know it for themselves,

iti yantaṁ vuttaṁ, idametaṁ paṭicca vuttanti.

this is what I was referring to.

Tiṇṇaṁ kho pana, bhikkhave, sannipātā gabbhassāvakkanti hoti.

Mendicants, when three things come together an embryo is conceived.

Idha mātāpitaro ca sannipatitā honti, mātā ca na utunī hoti, gandhabbo ca na paccupaṭṭhito hoti, neva tāva gabbhassāvakkanti hoti.

In a case where the mother and father come together, but the mother is not in the fertile phase of her menstrual cycle, and the virile spirit is not potent, the embryo is not conceived.

Idha mātāpitaro ca sannipatitā honti, mātā ca utunī hoti, gandhabbo ca na paccupaṭṭhito hoti, neva tāva gabbhassāvakkanti hoti.

In a case where the mother and father come together, the mother is in the fertile phase of her menstrual cycle, but the virile spirit is not potent, the embryo is not conceived.

Yato ca kho, bhikkhave, mātāpitaro ca sannipatitā honti, mātā ca utunī hoti, gandhabbo ca paccupaṭṭhito hoti—evaṁ tiṇṇaṁ sannipātā gabbhassāvakkanti hoti.

But when these three things come together—the mother and father come together, the mother is in the fertile phase of her menstrual cycle, and the virile spirit is potent—an embryo is conceived.

Tamenaṁ, bhikkhave, mātā nava vā dasa vā māse gabbhaṁ kucchinā pariharati mahatā saṁsayena garubhāraṁ.

The mother nurtures the embryo in her womb for nine or ten months at great risk to her heavy burden.

Tamenaṁ, bhikkhave, mātā navannaṁ vā dasannaṁ vā māsānaṁ accayena vijāyati mahatā saṁsayena garubhāraṁ.

When nine or ten months have passed, the mother gives birth at great risk to her heavy burden.

Tamenaṁ jātaṁ samānaṁ sakena lohitena poseti.

When the infant is born she nourishes it with her own blood.

Lohitañhetaṁ, bhikkhave, ariyassa vinaye yadidaṁ mātuthaññaṁ.

For mother's milk is regarded as blood in the training of the Noble One.

Sa kho so, bhikkhave, kumāro vuddhimanvāya indriyānaṁ paripākamanvāya

That boy grows up and his faculties mature.

yāni tāni kumārakānaṁ kīḷāpanakāni tehi kīḷati, seyyathidaṁ—vaṅkakaṁ ghaṭikaṁ mokkhacikaṁ ciṅgulakaṁ pattāḷhakaṁ rathakaṁ dhanukaṁ.

He accordingly plays childish games such as toy plows, tipcat, somersaults, pinwheels, toy measures, toy carts, and toy bows.

Sa kho so, bhikkhave, kumāro vuddhimanvāya indriyānaṁ paripākamanvāya

That boy grows up and his faculties mature further.

pañcahi kāmaguṇehi samappito samaṅgībhūto paricāreti—

He accordingly amuses himself, supplied and provided with the five kinds of sensual stimulation.

cakkhuviññeyyehi rūpehi iṭṭhehi kantehi manāpehi piyarūpehi kāmūpasaṁhitehi rajanīyehi,

Sights known by the eye that are likable, desirable, agreeable, pleasant, sensual, and arousing.

sotaviññeyyehi saddehi ...

Sounds known by the ear ...

ghānaviññeyyehi gandhehi ...

Smells known by the nose ...

jivhāviññeyyehi rasehi ...

Tastes known by the tongue ...

kāyaviññeyyehi phoṭṭhabbehi iṭṭhehi kantehi manāpehi piyarūpehi kāmūpasaṁhitehi rajanīyehi.

Touches known by the body that are likable, desirable, agreeable, pleasant, sensual, and arousing.

So cakkhunā rūpaṁ disvā piyarūpe rūpe sārajjati, appiyarūpe rūpe byāpajjati, anupaṭṭhitakāyasati ca viharati parittacetaso.

When they see a sight with their eyes, if it's pleasant they desire it, but if it's unpleasant they dislike it. They live with mindfulness of the body unestablished and their heart restricted.

Tañca cetovimuttiṁ paññāvimuttiṁ yathābhūtaṁ nappajānāti yatthassa te pāpakā akusalā dhammā aparisesā nirujjhanti.

And they don't truly understand the freedom of heart and freedom by wisdom where those arisen bad, unskillful qualities cease without anything left over.

So evaṁ anurodhavirodhaṁ samāpanno yaṁ kiñci vedanaṁ vedeti sukhaṁ vā dukkhaṁ vā adukkhamasukhaṁ vā, so taṁ vedanaṁ abhinandati abhivadati ajjhosāya tiṭṭhati.

Being so full of favoring and opposing, when they experience any kind of feeling—pleasant, unpleasant, or neutral—they approve, welcome, and keep clinging to it.

Tassa taṁ vedanaṁ abhinandato abhivadato ajjhosāya tiṭṭhato uppajjati nandī.

This gives rise to relishing.

Yā vedanāsu nandī tadupādānaṁ, tassupādānapaccayā bhavo, bhavapaccayā jāti, jātipaccayā jarāmaraṇaṁ sokaparidevadukkhadomanassupāyāsā sambhavanti.

Relishing feelings is grasping. Their grasping is a condition for continued existence. Continued existence is a condition for rebirth. Rebirth is a condition for old age and death, sorrow, lamentation, pain, sadness, and distress to come to be.

Evametassa kevalassa dukkhakkhandhassa samudayo hoti.

That is how this entire mass of suffering originates.

Sotena saddaṁ sutvā …pe…

When they hear a sound with their ears …

ghānena gandhaṁ ghāyitvā …pe…

When they smell an odor with their nose …

jivhāya rasaṁ sāyitvā …pe…

When they taste a flavor with their tongue …

kāyena phoṭṭhabbaṁ phusitvā …pe…

When they feel a touch with their body …

manasā dhammaṁ viññāya piyarūpe dhamme sārajjati, appiyarūpe dhamme byāpajjati, anupaṭṭhitakāyasati ca viharati parittacetaso.

When they know a thought with their mind, if it's pleasant they desire it, but if it's unpleasant they dislike it. They live with mindfulness of the body unestablished and their heart restricted.

Tañca cetovimuttiṁ paññāvimuttiṁ yathābhūtaṁ nappajānāti yatthassa te pāpakā akusalā dhammā aparisesā nirujjhanti.

And they don't truly understand the freedom of heart and freedom by wisdom where those arisen bad, unskillful qualities cease without anything left over.

So evaṁ anurodhavirodhaṁ samāpanno yaṁ kiñci vedanaṁ vedeti sukhaṁ vā dukkhaṁ vā adukkhamasukhaṁ vā, so taṁ vedanaṁ abhinandati abhivadati ajjhosāya tiṭṭhati.

Being so full of favoring and opposing, when they experience any kind of feeling— pleasant, unpleasant, or neutral—they approve, welcome, and keep clinging to it.

Tassa taṁ vedanaṁ abhinandato abhivadato ajjhosāya tiṭṭhato uppajjati nandī.

This gives rise to relishing.

Yā vedanāsu nandī tadupādānaṁ, tassupādānapaccayā bhavo, bhavapaccayā jāti, jātipaccayā jarāmaraṇaṁ sokaparidevadukkhadomanassupāyāsā sambhavanti.

Relishing feelings is grasping. Their grasping is a condition for continued existence. Continued existence is a condition for rebirth. Rebirth is a condition for old age and death, sorrow, lamentation, pain, sadness, and distress to come to be.

Evametassa kevalassa dukkhakkhandhassa samudayo hoti.

That is how this entire mass of suffering originates.

Idha, bhikkhave, tathāgato loke uppajjati arahaṁ sammāsambuddho vijjācaraṇasampanno sugato lokavidū anuttaro purisadammasārathi satthā devamanussānaṁ buddho bhagavā.

But consider when a Realized One arises in the world, perfected, a fully awakened Buddha, accomplished in knowledge and conduct, holy, knower of the world, supreme guide for those who wish to train, teacher of gods and humans, awakened, blessed.

So imaṁ lokaṁ sadevakaṁ samārakaṁ sabrahmakaṁ sassamaṇabrāhmaṇiṁ pajaṁ sadevamanussaṁ sayaṁ abhiññā sacchikatvā pavedeti.

He has realized with his own insight this world—with its gods, Māras and Brahmās, this population with its ascetics and brahmins, gods and humans—and he makes it known to others.

So dhammaṁ deseti ādikalyāṇaṁ majjhekalyāṇaṁ pariyosānakalyāṇaṁ sātthaṁ sabyañjanaṁ;

He proclaims a teaching that is good in the beginning, good in the middle, and good in the end, with the right meaning and phrasing.

kevalaparipuṇṇaṁ parisuddhaṁ brahmacariyaṁ pakāseti.

He reveals an entirely full and pure spiritual life.

Taṁ dhammaṁ suṇāti gahapati vā gahapatiputto vā aññatarasmiṁ vā kule paccājāto.

A householder hears that teaching, or a householder's child, or someone reborn in some good family.

So taṁ dhammaṁ sutvā tathāgate saddhaṁ paṭilabhati.

They gain faith in the Realized One

So tena saddhāpaṭilābhena samannāgato iti paṭisañcikkhati:

and reflect,

'sambādho gharāvāso rajāpatho, abbhokāso pabbajjā.

'Living in a house is cramped and dirty, but the life of one gone forth is wide open.

Nayidaṁ sukaraṁ agāraṁ ajjhāvasatā ekantaparipuṇṇaṁ ekantaparisuddhaṁ saṅkhalikhitaṁ brahmacariyaṁ carituṁ.

It's not easy for someone living at home to lead the spiritual life utterly full and pure, like a polished shell.

Yannūnāhaṁ kesamassuṁ ohāretvā, kāsāyāni vatthāni acchādetvā, agārasmā anagāriyaṁ pabbajeyyan'"ti.

Why don't I shave off my hair and beard, dress in ocher robes, and go forth from lay life to homelessness?'

So aparena samayena appaṁ vā bhogakkhandhaṁ pahāya, mahantaṁ vā bhogakkhandhaṁ pahāya, appaṁ vā ñātiparivaṭṭaṁ pahāya, mahantaṁ vā ñātiparivaṭṭaṁ pahāya, kesamassuṁ ohāretvā, kāsāyāni vatthāni acchādetvā, agārasmā anagāriyaṁ pabbajati.

After some time they give up a large or small fortune, and a large or small family circle. They shave off hair and beard, dress in ocher robes, and go forth from the lay life to homelessness.

So evaṁ pabbajito samāno bhikkhūnaṁ sikkhāsājīvasamāpanno pāṇātipātaṁ pahāya pāṇātipātā paṭivirato hoti, nihitadaṇḍo nihitasattho lajjī dayāpanno sabbapāṇabhūtahitānukampī viharati.

Once they've gone forth, they take up the training and livelihood of the mendicants. They give up killing living creatures, renouncing the rod and the sword. They're scrupulous and kind, living full of compassion for all living beings.

Adinnādānaṁ pahāya adinnādānā paṭivirato hoti, dinnādāyī dinnapāṭikaṅkhī athenena sucibhūtena attanā viharati.

They give up stealing. They take only what's given, and expect only what's given. They keep themselves clean by not thieving.

Abrahmacariyaṁ pahāya brahmacārī hoti, ārācārī virato methunā gāmadhammā.

They give up unchastity. They are celibate, set apart, avoiding the vulgar act of sex.

Musāvādaṁ pahāya musāvādā paṭivirato hoti, saccavādī saccasandho theto paccayiko avisaṁvādako lokassa.

They give up lying. They speak the truth and stick to the truth. They're honest and trustworthy, and don't trick the world with their words.

Pisuṇaṁ vācaṁ pahāya pisuṇāya vācāya paṭivirato hoti—ito sutvā na amutra akkhātā imesaṁ bhedāya, amutra vā sutvā na imesaṁ akkhātā amūsaṁ bhedāya. Iti bhinnānaṁ vā sandhātā, sahitānaṁ vā anuppadātā samaggārāmo samaggarato samagganandī, samaggakaraṇiṁ vācaṁ bhāsitā hoti.

They give up divisive speech. They don't repeat in one place what they heard in another so as to divide people against each other. Instead, they reconcile those who are divided, supporting unity, delighting in harmony, loving harmony, speaking words that promote harmony.

Pharusaṁ vācaṁ pahāya pharusāya vācāya paṭivirato hoti—yā sā vācā nelā kaṇṇasukhā pemanīyā hadayaṅgamā porī bahujanakantā bahujanamanāpā tathārūpiṁ vācaṁ bhāsitā hoti.

They give up harsh speech. They speak in a way that's mellow, pleasing to the ear, lovely, going to the heart, polite, likable and agreeable to the people.

Samphappalāpaṁ pahāya samphappalāpā paṭivirato hoti, kālavādī bhūtavādī atthavādī dhammavādī vinayavādī, nidhānavatiṁ vācaṁ bhāsitā kālena, sāpadesaṁ pariyantavatiṁ atthasaṁhitaṁ.

They give up talking nonsense. Their words are timely, true, and meaningful, in line with the teaching and training. They say things at the right time which are valuable, reasonable, succinct, and beneficial.

So bījagāmabhūtagāmasamārambhā paṭivirato hoti,

They avoid injuring plants and seeds.

ekabhattiko hoti rattūparato, virato vikālabhojanā.

They eat in one part of the day, abstaining from eating at night and food at the wrong time.

Naccagītavāditavisūkadassanā paṭivirato hoti,

They avoid dancing, singing, music, and seeing shows.

mālāgandhavilepanadhāraṇamaṇḍanavibhūsanaṭṭhānā paṭivirato hoti,

They avoid beautifying and adorning themselves with garlands, perfumes, and makeup.

uccāsayanamahāsayanā paṭivirato hoti,

They avoid high and luxurious beds.

jātarūparajatapaṭiggahaṇā paṭivirato hoti,

They avoid receiving gold and money,

āmakadhaññapaṭiggahaṇā paṭivirato hoti,

raw grains,

āmakamaṁsapaṭiggahaṇā paṭivirato hoti,

raw meat,

itthikumārikapaṭiggahaṇā paṭivirato hoti,

women and girls,

dāsidāsapaṭiggahaṇā paṭivirato hoti,

male and female bondservants,

ajeḷakapaṭiggahaṇā paṭivirato hoti,

goats and sheep,

kukkuṭasūkarapaṭiggahaṇā paṭivirato hoti,

chickens and pigs,

hatthigavāssavaḷavapaṭiggahaṇā paṭivirato hoti,

elephants, cows, horses, and mares,

khettavatthupaṭiggahaṇā paṭivirato hoti,

and fields and land.

dūteyyapahiṇagamanānuyogā paṭivirato hoti,

They avoid running errands and messages;

kayavikkayā paṭivirato hoti,

buying and selling;

tulākūṭakaṁsakūṭamānakūṭā paṭivirato hoti,

falsifying weights, metals, or measures;

ukkoṭanavañcananikatisāciyogā paṭivirato hoti,

bribery, fraud, cheating, and duplicity;

chedanavadhabandhanaviparāmosaālopasahasākārā paṭivirato hoti.

mutilation, murder, abduction, banditry, plunder, and violence.

So santuṭṭho hoti kāyaparihārikena cīvarena kucchiparihārikena piṇḍapātena. So yena yeneva pakkamati samādāyeva pakkamati.

They're content with robes to look after the body and almsfood to look after the belly. Wherever they go, they set out taking only these things.

Seyyathāpi nāma pakkhī sakuṇo yena yeneva ḍeti sapattabhārova ḍeti;

They're like a bird: wherever it flies, wings are its only burden.

evameva bhikkhu santuṭṭho hoti kāyaparihārikena cīvarena, kucchiparihārikena piṇḍapātena. So yena yeneva pakkamati samādāyeva pakkamati.

In the same way, a mendicant is content with robes to look after the body and almsfood to look after the belly. Wherever they go, they set out taking only these things.

So iminā ariyena sīlakkhandhena samannāgato ajjhattaṁ anavajjasukhaṁ paṭisaṁvedeti.

When they have this entire spectrum of noble ethics, they experience a blameless happiness inside themselves.

So cakkhunā rūpaṁ disvā na nimittaggāhī hoti nānubyañjanaggāhī.

When they see a sight with their eyes, they don't get caught up in the features and details.

Yatvādhikaraṇamenaṁ cakkhundriyaṁ asaṁvutaṁ viharantaṁ abhijjhādomanassā pāpakā akusalā dhammā anvāssaveyyuṁ tassa saṁvarāya paṭipajjati, rakkhati cakkhundriyaṁ, cakkhundriye saṁvaraṁ āpajjati.

If the faculty of sight were left unrestrained, bad unskillful qualities of desire and aversion would become overwhelming. For this reason, they practice restraint, protecting the faculty of sight, and achieving its restraint.

Sotena saddaṁ sutvā ...pe...

When they hear a sound with their ears ...

ghānena gandhaṁ ghāyitvā ...pe...

When they smell an odor with their nose ...

jivhāya rasaṁ sāyitvā ...pe...

When they taste a flavor with their tongue ...

kāyena phoṭṭhabbaṁ phusitvā ...pe...

When they feel a touch with their body ...

manasā dhammaṁ viññāya na nimittaggāhī hoti nānubyañjanaggāhī.

When they know a thought with their mind, they don't get caught up in the features and details.

Yatvādhikaraṇamenaṁ manindriyaṁ asaṁvutaṁ viharantaṁ abhijjhādomanassā pāpakā akusalā dhammā anvāssaveyyuṁ tassa saṁvarāya paṭipajjati, rakkhati manindriyaṁ manindriye saṁvaraṁ āpajjati.

If the faculty of mind were left unrestrained, bad unskillful qualities of desire and aversion would become overwhelming. For this reason, they practice restraint, protecting the faculty of mind, and achieving its restraint.

So iminā ariyena indriyasaṁvarena samannāgato ajjhattaṁ abyāsekasukhaṁ paṭisaṁvedeti.

When they have this noble sense restraint, they experience an unsullied bliss inside themselves.

So abhikkante paṭikkante sampajānakārī hoti, ālokite vilokite sampajānakārī hoti, samiñjite pasārite sampajānakārī hoti, saṅghāṭipattacīvaradhāraṇe sampajānakārī hoti, asite pīte khāyite sāyite sampajānakārī hoti, uccārapassāvakamme sampajānakārī hoti, gate ṭhite nisinne sutte jāgarite bhāsite tuṇhībhāve sampajānakārī hoti.

They act with situational awareness when going out and coming back; when looking ahead and aside; when bending and extending the limbs; when bearing the outer robe, bowl and robes; when eating, drinking, chewing, and tasting; when urinating and defecating; when walking, standing, sitting, sleeping, waking, speaking, and keeping silent.

So iminā ca ariyena sīlakkhandhena samannāgato, imāya ca ariyāya santuṭṭhiyā samannāgato, iminā ca ariyena indriyasaṁvarena samannāgato, iminā ca ariyena satisampajaññena samannāgato,

When they have this noble spectrum of ethics, this noble sense restraint, and this noble mindfulness and situational awareness,

vivittaṁ senāsanaṁ bhajati—araññaṁ rukkhamūlaṁ pabbataṁ kandaraṁ giriguhaṁ susānaṁ vanapatthaṁ abbhokāsaṁ palālapuñjaṁ.

they frequent a secluded lodging—a wilderness, the root of a tree, a hill, a ravine, a mountain cave, a charnel ground, a forest, the open air, a heap of straw.

So pacchābhattaṁ piṇḍapātapaṭikkanto nisīdati pallaṅkaṁ ābhujitvā, ujuṁ kāyaṁ paṇidhāya, parimukhaṁ satiṁ upaṭṭhapetvā.

After the meal, they return from almsround, sit down cross-legged, set their body straight, and establish mindfulness in front of them.

So abhijjhaṁ loke pahāya vigatābhijjhena cetasā viharati, abhijjhāya cittaṁ parisodheti;

Giving up desire for the world, they meditate with a heart rid of desire, cleansing the mind of desire.

byāpādapadosaṁ pahāya abyāpannacitto viharati, sabbapāṇabhūtahitānukampī, byāpādapadosā cittaṁ parisodheti;

Giving up ill will and malevolence, they meditate with a mind rid of ill will, full of compassion for all living beings, cleansing the mind of ill will.

thinamiddhaṁ pahāya vigatathinamiddho viharati ālokasaññī, sato sampajāno, thinamiddhā cittaṁ parisodheti;

Giving up dullness and drowsiness, they meditate with a mind rid of dullness and drowsiness, perceiving light, mindful and aware, cleansing the mind of dullness and drowsiness.

uddhaccakukkuccaṁ pahāya anuddhato viharati ajjhattaṁ vūpasantacitto, uddhaccakukkuccā cittaṁ parisodheti;

Giving up restlessness and remorse, they meditate without restlessness, their mind peaceful inside, cleansing the mind of restlessness and remorse.

vicikicchaṁ pahāya tiṇṇavicikiccho viharati akathaṅkathī kusalesu dhammesu, vicikicchāya cittaṁ parisodheti.

Giving up doubt, they meditate having gone beyond doubt, not undecided about skillful qualities, cleansing the mind of doubt.

So ime pañca nīvaraṇe pahāya cetaso upakkilese paññāya dubbalīkaraṇe,

They give up these five hindrances, corruptions of the heart that weaken wisdom.

vivicceva kāmehi vivicca akusalehi dhammehi savitakkaṁ savicāraṁ vivekajaṁ pītisukhaṁ paṭhamaṁ jhānaṁ upasampajja viharati.

Then, quite secluded from sensual pleasures, secluded from unskillful qualities, they enter and remain in the first absorption, which has the rapture and bliss born of seclusion, while placing the mind and keeping it connected.

Puna caparaṁ, bhikkhave, bhikkhu vitakkavicārānaṁ vūpasamā ajjhattaṁ sampasādanaṁ cetaso ekodibhāvaṁ avitakkaṁ avicāraṁ samādhijaṁ pītisukhaṁ dutiyaṁ jhānaṁ …pe…

Furthermore, as the placing of the mind and keeping it connected are stilled, a mendicant enters and remains in the second absorption …

tatiyaṁ jhānaṁ …pe…

third absorption …

catutthaṁ jhānaṁ upasampajja viharati.

fourth absorption.

So cakkhunā rūpaṁ disvā piyarūpe rūpe na sārajjati, appiyarūpe rūpe na byāpajjati, upaṭṭhitakāyasati ca viharati appamāṇacetaso.

When they see a sight with their eyes, if it's pleasant they don't desire it, and if it's unpleasant they don't dislike it. They live with mindfulness of the body established and a limitless heart.

Tañca cetovimuttiṁ paññāvimuttiṁ yathābhūtaṁ pajānāti yatthassa te pāpakā akusalā dhammā aparisesā nirujjhanti.

And they truly understand the freedom of heart and freedom by wisdom where those arisen bad, unskillful qualities cease without anything left over.

So evaṁ anurodhavirodhavippahīno yaṁ kiñci vedanaṁ vedeti, sukhaṁ vā dukkhaṁ vā adukkhamasukhaṁ vā, so taṁ vedanaṁ nābhinandati nābhivadati nājjhosāya tiṭṭhati.

Having given up favoring and opposing, when they experience any kind of feeling—pleasant, unpleasant, or neutral—they don't approve, welcome, or keep clinging to it.

Tassa taṁ vedanaṁ anabhinandato anabhivadato anajjhosāya tiṭṭhato yā vedanāsu nandī sā nirujjhati.

As a result, relishing of feelings ceases.

Tassa nandīnirodhā upādānanirodho, upādānanirodhā bhavanirodho, bhavanirodhā jātinirodho, jātinirodhā jarāmaraṇaṁ sokaparidevadukkhadomanassupāyāsā nirujjhanti.

When their relishing ceases, grasping ceases. When grasping ceases, continued existence ceases. When continued existence ceases, rebirth ceases. When rebirth ceases, old age and death, sorrow, lamentation, pain, sadness, and distress cease.

Evametassa kevalassa dukkhakkhandhassa nirodho hoti.

That is how this entire mass of suffering ceases.

Sotena saddaṁ sutvā …pe…

When they hear a sound with their ears …

ghānena gandhaṁ ghāyitvā …pe…

When they smell an odor with their nose …

jivhāya rasaṁ sāyitvā …pe…

When they taste a flavor with their tongue …

kāyena phoṭṭhabbaṁ phusitvā …pe…

When they feel a touch with their body …

manasā dhammaṁ viññāya piyarūpe dhamme na sārajjati, appiyarūpe dhamme na byāpajjati, upaṭṭhitakāyasati ca viharati appamāṇacetaso,

When they know a thought with their mind, if it's pleasant they don't desire it, and if it's unpleasant they don't dislike it. They live with mindfulness of the body established and a limitless heart.

tañca cetovimuttiṁ paññāvimuttiṁ yathābhūtaṁ pajānāti yatthassa te pāpakā akusalā dhammā aparisesā nirujjhanti.

And they truly understand the freedom of heart and freedom by wisdom where those arisen bad, unskillful qualities cease without anything left over.

So evaṁ anurodhavirodhavippahīno yaṁ kiñci vedanaṁ vedeti, sukhaṁ vā dukkhaṁ vā adukkhamasukhaṁ vā, so taṁ vedanaṁ nābhinandati nābhivadati nājjhosāya tiṭṭhati.

Having given up favoring and opposing, when they experience any kind of feeling—pleasant, unpleasant, or neutral—they don't approve, welcome, or keep clinging to it.

Tassa taṁ vedanaṁ anabhinandato anabhivadato anajjhosāya tiṭṭhato yā vedanāsu nandī sā nirujjhati.

As a result, relishing of feelings ceases.

Tassa nandīnirodhā upādānanirodho, upādānanirodhā bhavanirodho, bhavanirodhā jātinirodho, jātinirodhā jarāmaraṇaṁ sokaparidevadukkhadomanassupāyāsā nirujjhanti.

When their relishing ceases, grasping ceases. When grasping ceases, continued existence ceases. When continued existence ceases, rebirth ceases. When rebirth ceases, old age and death, sorrow, lamentation, pain, sadness, and distress cease.

Evametassa kevalassa dukkhakkhandhassa nirodho hoti.

That is how this entire mass of suffering ceases.

Imaṁ kho me tumhe, bhikkhave, saṅkhittena taṇhāsaṅkhayavimuttiṁ dhāretha, sātiṁ pana bhikkhuṁ kevaṭṭaputtaṁ mahātaṇhājālataṇhāsaṅghāṭappaṭimukkan"ti.

Mendicants, you should memorize that brief statement on freedom through the ending of craving. But the mendicant Sāti, the fisherman's son, is caught in a vast net of craving, a tangle of craving."

Idamavoca bhagavā.

That is what the Buddha said.

Attamanā te bhikkhū bhagavato bhāsitaṁ abhinandunti.

Satisfied, the mendicants were happy with what the Buddha said.

Mahātaṇhāsaṅkhayasuttaṃ niṭṭhitaṃ aṭṭhamaṃ.

39 Mahaassapurasutta:

The Longer Discourse at Assapura

Evaṃ me sutaṃ—

So I have heard.

ekaṃ samayaṃ bhagavā aṅgesu viharati assapuraṃ nāma aṅgānaṃ nigamo.

At one time the Buddha was staying in the land of the Aṅgas, near the Aṅgan town named Assapura.

Tatra kho bhagavā bhikkhū āmantesi:

There the Buddha addressed the mendicants,

"bhikkhavo"ti.

"Mendicants!"

"Bhadante"ti te bhikkhū bhagavato paccassosuṃ.

"Venerable sir," they replied.

Bhagavā etadavoca:

The Buddha said this:

"Samaṇā samaṇāti vo, bhikkhave, jano sañjānāti.

"Mendicants, people label you as ascetics.

Tumhe ca pana 'ke tumhe'ti puṭṭhā samānā 'samaṇāmhā'ti paṭijānātha;

And when they ask you what you are, you claim to be ascetics.

tesaṃ vo, bhikkhave, evaṃsamaññānaṃ sataṃ evaṃpaṭiññānaṃ sataṃ 'ye dhammā samaṇakaraṇā ca brāhmaṇakaraṇā ca te dhamme samādāya vattissāma, evaṃ no ayaṃ amhākaṃ samaññā ca saccā bhavissati paṭiññā ca bhūtā.

Given this label and this claim, you should train like this: 'We will undertake and follow the things that make one an ascetic and a brahmin. That way our label will be accurate and our claim correct.

Yesañca mayaṃ cīvarapiṇḍapātasenāsanagilānappaccayabhesajjaparikkhāraṃ paribhuñjāma, tesaṃ te kārā amhesu mahapphalā bhavissanti mahānisaṃsā, amhākañcevāyaṁ pabbajjā avañjhā bhavissati saphalā saudrayā'ti.

Any robes, almsfood, lodgings, and medicines and supplies for the sick that we use will be very fruitful and beneficial for the donor. And our going forth will not be wasted, but will be fruitful and fertile.'

Evañhi vo, bhikkhave, sikkhitabbaṁ.

Katame ca, bhikkhave, dhammā samaṇakaraṇā ca brāhmaṇakaraṇā ca?

And what are the things that make one an ascetic and a brahmin?

'Hirottappena samannāgatā bhavissāmā'ti evañhi vo, bhikkhave, sikkhitabbaṁ.

You should train like this: 'We will have conscience and prudence.'

Siyā kho pana, bhikkhave, tumhākaṁ evamassa:

Now, mendicants, you might think,

'hirottappenamha samannāgatā, alamettāvatā katamettāvatā, anuppatto no sāmaññattho, natthi no kiñci uttariṁ karaṇīyan'ti tāvatakeneva tuṭṭhiṁ āpajjeyyātha.

'We have conscience and prudence. Just this much is enough. We have achieved the goal of life as an ascetic. There is nothing more to do.' And you might rest content with just that much.

Ārocayāmi vo, bhikkhave, paṭivedayāmi vo, bhikkhave:

I declare this to you, mendicants, I announce this to you:

'mā vo sāmaññatthikānaṁ sataṁ sāmaññattho parihāyi, sati uttariṁ karaṇīye'.

'You who seek to be true ascetics, do not lose sight of the goal of the ascetic life while there is still more to do.'

Kiñca, bhikkhave, uttariṁ karaṇīyaṁ?

What more is there to do?

'Parisuddho no kāyasamācāro bhavissati uttāno vivaṭo na ca chiddavā saṁvuto ca.

You should train like this: 'Our bodily behavior will be pure, clear, open, neither inconsistent nor secretive.

Tāya ca pana parisuddhakāyasamācāratāya nevattānukkaṁsessāma na paraṁ vambhessāmā'ti evañhi vo, bhikkhave, sikkhitabbaṁ.

And we won't glorify ourselves or put others down on account of our pure bodily behavior.'

Siyā kho pana, bhikkhave, tumhākaṁ evamassa:

Now, mendicants, you might think,

'hirottappenamha samannāgatā, parisuddho no kāyasamācāro;

'We have conscience and prudence, and our bodily behavior is pure.

alamettāvatā katamettāvatā, anuppatto no sāmaññattho, natthi no kiñci uttariṁ karaṇīyan'ti tāvatakeneva tuṭṭhiṁ āpajjeyyātha.

Just this much is enough …'

Ārocayāmi vo, bhikkhave, paṭivedayāmi vo, bhikkhave:

I declare this to you, mendicants, I announce this to you:

'mā vo sāmaññatthikānaṁ sataṁ sāmaññattho parihāyi, sati uttariṁ karaṇīye'.

'You who seek to be true ascetics, do not lose sight of the goal of the ascetic life while there is still more to do.'

Kiñca, bhikkhave, uttariṁ karaṇīyaṁ?

What more is there to do?

'Parisuddho no vacīsamācāro bhavissati uttāno vivaṭo na ca chiddavā saṁvuto ca.

You should train like this: 'Our verbal behavior …

Tāya ca pana parisuddhavacīsamācāratāya nevattānukkaṁsessāma na paraṁ vambhessāmā'ti evañhi vo, bhikkhave, sikkhitabbaṁ.

Siyā kho pana, bhikkhave, tumhākaṁ evamassa:

'hirottappenamha samannāgatā, parisuddho no kāyasamācāro, parisuddho vacīsamācāro;

alamettāvatā katamettāvatā, anuppatto no sāmaññattho, natthi no kiñci uttariṁ karaṇīyan'ti tāvatakeneva tuṭṭhiṁ āpajjeyyātha.

Ārocayāmi vo, bhikkhave, paṭivedayāmi vo, bhikkhave:

'mā vo sāmaññatthikānaṁ sataṁ sāmaññattho parihāyi, sati uttariṁ karaṇīye'.

Kiñca, bhikkhave, uttariṁ karaṇīyaṁ?

'Parisuddho no manosamācāro bhavissati uttāno vivaṭo na ca chiddavā saṁvuto ca.

mental behavior …

Tāya ca pana parisuddhamanosamācāratāya nevattānukkaṁsessāma na paraṁ vambhessāmā'ti evañhi vo, bhikkhave, sikkhitabbaṁ.

Siyā kho pana, bhikkhave, tumhākaṁ evamassa:

'hirottappenamha samannāgatā, parisuddho no kāyasamācāro, parisuddho vacīsamācāro, parisuddho manosamācāro;

alamettāvatā katamettāvatā, anuppatto no sāmaññattho, natthi no kiñci uttariṁ karaṇīyan'ti tāvatakeneva tuṭṭhiṁ āpajjeyyātha.

Ārocayāmi vo, bhikkhave, paṭivedayāmi vo, bhikkhave:

'mā vo sāmaññatthikānaṁ sataṁ sāmaññattho parihāyi, sati uttariṁ karaṇīye'.

Kiñca, bhikkhave, uttariṁ karaṇīyaṁ?

'Parisuddho no ājīvo bhavissati uttāno vivaṭo na ca chiddavā saṁvuto ca.

livelihood will be pure, clear, open, neither inconsistent nor secretive.

Tāya ca pana parisuddhājīvatāya nevattānukkaṁsessāma na paraṁ vambhessāmā'ti evañhi vo, bhikkhave, sikkhitabbaṁ.

And we won't glorify ourselves or put others down on account of our pure livelihood.'

Siyā kho pana, bhikkhave, tumhākaṁ evamassa:

Now, mendicants, you might think,

'hirottappenamha samannāgatā, parisuddho no kāyasamācāro, parisuddho vacīsamācāro, parisuddho manosamācāro, parisuddho ājīvo;

'We have conscience and prudence, our bodily, verbal, and mental behavior is pure, and our livelihood is pure.

alamettāvatā katamettāvatā, anuppatto no sāmaññattho, natthi no kiñci uttariṁ karaṇīyan'ti tāvatakeneva tuṭṭhiṁ āpajjeyyātha.

Just this much is enough. We have achieved the goal of life as an ascetic. There is nothing more to do.' And you might rest content with just that much.

Ārocayāmi vo, bhikkhave, paṭivedayāmi vo, bhikkhave:

I declare this to you, mendicants, I announce this to you:

'mā vo sāmaññatthikānaṁ sataṁ sāmaññattho parihāyi, sati uttariṁ karaṇīye'.

'You who seek to be true ascetics, do not lose sight of the goal of the ascetic life while there is still more to do.'

Kiñca, bhikkhave, uttariṁ karaṇīyaṁ?

What more is there to do?

'Indriyesu guttadvārā bhavissāma;

You should train yourselves like this: 'We will restrain our sense doors.

cakkhunā rūpaṃ disvā na nimittaggāhī nānubyañjanaggāhī.

When we see a sight with our eyes, we won't get caught up in the features and details.

Yatvādhikaraṇamenaṃ cakkhundriyaṃ asaṃvutaṃ viharantaṃ abhijjhādomanassā pāpakā akusalā dhammā anvāssaveyyuṃ, tassa saṃvarāya paṭipajjissāma, rakkhissāma cakkhundriyaṃ, cakkhundriye saṃvaraṃ āpajjissāma.

If the faculty of sight were left unrestrained, bad unskillful qualities of desire and aversion would become overwhelming. For this reason, we will practice restraint, we will protect the faculty of sight, and we will achieve its restraint.

Sotena saddaṃ sutvā ...pe...

When we hear a sound with our ears ...

ghānena gandhaṃ ghāyitvā ...pe...

When we smell an odor with our nose ...

jivhāya rasaṃ sāyitvā ...pe...

When we taste a flavor with our tongue ...

kāyena phoṭṭhabbaṃ phusitvā ...pe...

When we feel a touch with our body ...

manasā dhammaṃ viññāya na nimittaggāhī nānubyañjanaggāhī.

When we know a thought with our mind, we won't get caught up in the features and details.

Yatvādhikaraṇamenaṃ manindriyaṃ asaṃvutaṃ viharantaṃ abhijjhādomanassā pāpakā akusalā dhammā anvāssaveyyuṃ, tassa saṃvarāya paṭipajjissāma, rakkhissāma manindriyaṃ, manindriye saṃvaraṃ āpajjissāmā'ti evañhi vo, bhikkhave, sikkhitabbaṃ.

If the faculty of mind were left unrestrained, bad unskillful qualities of desire and aversion would become overwhelming. For this reason, we will practice restraint, we will protect the faculty of mind, and we will achieve its restraint.'

Siyā kho pana, bhikkhave, tumhākaṃ evamassa:

Now, mendicants, you might think,

'hirottappenamha samannāgatā, parisuddho no kāyasamācāro, parisuddho vacīsamācāro, parisuddho manosamācāro, parisuddho ājīvo, indriyesumha guttadvārā;

'We have conscience and prudence, our bodily, verbal, and mental behavior is pure, our livelihood is pure, and our sense doors are restrained.

alamettāvatā katamettāvatā, anuppatto no sāmaññattho, natthi no kiñci uttariṁ karaṇīyan'ti tāvatakeneva tutthiṁ āpajjeyyātha.

Just this much is enough …'

Ārocayāmi vo, bhikkhave, paṭivedayāmi vo, bhikkhave:

'mā vo sāmaññatthikānam satam sāmaññattho parihāyi, sati uttarim karaṇīye'.

Kiñca, bhikkhave, uttariṁ karaṇīyaṁ?

What more is there to do?

'Bhojane mattaññuno bhavissāma, paṭisankhā yoniso āhāraṁ āharissāma,

You should train yourselves like this: 'We will not eat too much. We will only eat after reflecting properly on our food.

neva davāya na madāya na maṇḍanāya na vibhūsanāya yāvadeva imassa kāyassa ṭhitiyā yāpanāya, vihiṁsūparatiyā, brahmacariyānuggahāya, iti purāṇañca vedanaṁ paṭihankhāma navañca vedanaṁ na uppādessāma, yātrā ca no bhavissati, anavajjatā ca, phāsu vihāro cā'ti evañhi vo, bhikkhave, sikkhitabbaṁ.

We will eat not for fun, indulgence, adornment, or decoration, but only to sustain this body, to avoid harm, and to support spiritual practice. In this way, we shall put an end to old discomfort and not give rise to new discomfort, and we will live blamelessly and at ease.'

Siyā kho pana, bhikkhave, tumhākaṁ evamassa:

Now, mendicants, you might think,

'hirottappenamha samannāgatā, parisuddho no kāyasamācāro, parisuddho vacīsamācāro, parisuddho manosamācāro, parisuddho ājīvo, indriyesumha guttadvārā, bhojane mattaññuno;

'We have conscience and prudence, our bodily, verbal, and mental behavior is pure, our livelihood is pure, our sense doors are restrained, and we don't eat too much.

alamettāvatā katamettāvatā, anuppatto no sāmaññattho, natthi no kiñci uttariṁ karaṇīyan'ti tāvatakeneva tutthiṁ āpajjeyyātha.

Just this much is enough …'

Ārocayāmi vo, bhikkhave, paṭivedayāmi vo, bhikkhave:

'mā vo, sāmaññatthikānaṁ sataṁ sāmaññattho parihāyi sati uttariṁ karaṇīye'.

Kiñca, bhikkhave, uttariṁ karaṇīyaṁ?

What more is there to do?

'Jāgariyaṁ anuyuttā bhavissāma, divasaṁ caṅkamena nisajjāya āvaraṇīyehi dhammehi cittaṁ parisodhessāma.

You should train yourselves like this: 'We will be dedicated to wakefulness. When practicing walking and sitting meditation by day, we will purify our mind from obstacles.

Rattiyā paṭhamaṁ yāmaṁ caṅkamena nisajjāya āvaraṇīyehi dhammehi cittaṁ parisodhessāma.

In the evening, we will continue to practice walking and sitting meditation.

Rattiyā majjhimaṁ yāmaṁ dakkhiṇena passena sīhaseyyaṁ kappessāma pāde pādaṁ accādhāya, sato sampajāno uṭṭhānasaññaṁ manasi karitvā.

In the middle of the night, we will lie down in the lion's posture—on the right side, placing one foot on top of the other—mindful and aware, and focused on the time of getting up.

Rattiyā pacchimaṁ yāmaṁ paccuṭṭhāya caṅkamena nisajjāya āvaraṇīyehi dhammehi cittaṁ parisodhessāmā'ti, evañhi vo, bhikkhave, sikkhitabbaṁ.

In the last part of the night, we will get up and continue to practice walking and sitting meditation, purifying our mind from obstacles.'

Siyā kho pana, bhikkhave, tumhākaṁ evamassa:

Now, mendicants, you might think,

'hirottappenamha samannāgatā, parisuddho no kāyasamācāro, parisuddho vacīsamācāro, parisuddho manosamācāro, parisuddho ājīvo, indriyesumha guttadvārā, bhojane mattaññuno, jāgariyaṁ anuyuttā;

'We have conscience and prudence, our bodily, verbal, and mental behavior is pure, our livelihood is pure, our sense doors are restrained, we don't eat too much, and we are dedicated to wakefulness.

alamettāvatā katamettāvatā, anuppatto no sāmaññattho, natthi no kiñci uttariṁ karaṇīyan'ti, tāvatakeneva tuṭṭhiṁ āpajjeyyātha.

Just this much is enough …'

Ārocayāmi vo, bhikkhave, paṭivedayāmi vo, bhikkhave:

'mā vo, sāmaññatthikānaṁ sataṁ sāmaññattho parihāyi sati uttariṁ karaṇīye'.

Kiñca, bhikkhave, uttariṁ karaṇīyaṁ?

What more is there to do?

'Satisampajaññena samannāgatā bhavissāma, abhikkante paṭikkante sampajānakārī, ālokite vilokite sampajānakārī, samiñjite pasārite sampajānakārī, saṅghāṭipattacīvaradhāraṇe sampajānakārī, asite pīte khāyite sāyite sampajānakārī, uccārapassāvakamme sampajānakārī, gate ṭhite nisinne sutte jāgarite bhāsite tuṇhībhāve sampajānakārī'ti, evañhi vo, bhikkhave, sikkhitabbaṁ.

You should train yourselves like this: 'We will have situational awareness and mindfulness. We will act with situational awareness when going out and coming back; when looking ahead and aside; when bending and extending the limbs; when bearing the outer robe, bowl and robes; when eating, drinking, chewing, and tasting; when urinating and defecating; when walking, standing, sitting, sleeping, waking, speaking, and keeping silent.'

Siyā kho pana, bhikkhave, tumhākaṁ evamassa:

Now, mendicants, you might think,

'hirottappenamha samannāgatā, parisuddho no kāyasamācāro, parisuddho vacīsamācāro, parisuddho manosamācāro, parisuddho ājīvo, indriyesumha guttadvārā, bhojane mattaññuno, jāgariyaṁ anuyuttā, satisampajaññena samannāgatā;

'We have conscience and prudence, our bodily, verbal, and mental behavior is pure, our livelihood is pure, our sense doors are restrained, we don't eat too much, we are dedicated to wakefulness, and we have mindfulness and situational awareness.

alamettāvatā katamettāvatā, anuppatto no sāmaññattho, natthi no kiñci uttariṁ karaṇīyan'ti tāvatakeneva tuṭṭhiṁ āpajjeyyātha.

Just this much is enough ...'

Ārocayāmi vo, bhikkhave, paṭivedayāmi vo, bhikkhave:

'mā vo, sāmaññatthikānaṁ sataṁ sāmaññattho parihāyi sati uttariṁ karaṇīye'.

Kiñca, bhikkhave, uttariṁ karaṇīyaṁ?

What more is there to do?

Idha, bhikkhave, bhikkhu vivittaṁ senāsanaṁ bhajati—araññaṁ rukkhamūlaṁ pabbataṁ kandaraṁ giriguhaṁ susānaṁ vanappatthaṁ abbhokāsaṁ palālapuñjaṁ.

Take a mendicant who frequents a secluded lodging—a wilderness, the root of a tree, a hill, a ravine, a mountain cave, a charnel ground, a forest, the open air, a heap of straw.

So pacchābhattaṁ piṇḍapātapaṭikkanto nisīdati pallaṅkaṁ ābhujitvā, ujuṁ kāyaṁ paṇidhāya parimukhaṁ satiṁ upaṭṭhapetvā.

After the meal, they return from almsround, sit down cross-legged, set their body straight, and establish mindfulness in front of them.

So abhijjhaṁ loke pahāya vigatābhijjhena cetasā viharati, abhijjhāya cittaṁ parisodheti;

Giving up desire for the world, they meditate with a heart rid of desire, cleansing the mind of desire.

byāpādapadosaṁ pahāya abyāpannacitto viharati, sabbapāṇabhūtahitānukampī, byāpādapadosā cittaṁ parisodheti;

Giving up ill will and malevolence, they meditate with a mind rid of ill will, full of compassion for all living beings, cleansing the mind of ill will.

thinamiddhaṁ pahāya vigatathinamiddho viharati, ālokasaññī sato sampajāno, thinamiddhā cittaṁ parisodheti;

Giving up dullness and drowsiness, they meditate with a mind rid of dullness and drowsiness, perceiving light, mindful and aware, cleansing the mind of dullness and drowsiness.

uddhaccakukkuccaṁ pahāya anuddhato viharati, ajjhattaṁ vūpasantacitto, uddhaccakukkuccā cittaṁ parisodheti;

Giving up restlessness and remorse, they meditate without restlessness, their mind peaceful inside, cleansing the mind of restlessness and remorse.

vicikicchaṁ pahāya tiṇṇavicikiccho viharati, akathaṅkathī kusalesu dhammesu, vicikicchāya cittaṁ parisodheti.

Giving up doubt, they meditate having gone beyond doubt, not undecided about skillful qualities, cleansing the mind of doubt.

Seyyathāpi, bhikkhave, puriso iṇaṁ ādāya kammante payojeyya.

Suppose a man who has gotten into debt were to apply himself to work,

Tassa te kammantā samijjheyyuṁ.

and his efforts proved successful.

So yāni ca porāṇāni iṇamūlāni tāni ca byantī kareyya, siyā cassa uttariṁ avasiṭṭhaṁ dārabharaṇāya.

He would pay off the original loan and have enough left over to support his partner.

Tassa evamassa:

Thinking about this,

'ahaṁ kho pubbe iṇaṁ ādāya kammante payojesiṁ, tassa me te kammantā samijjhiṁsu.

Sohaṁ yāni ca porāṇāni iṇamūlāni tāni ca byantī akāsiṁ, atthi ca me uttariṁ avasiṭṭhaṁ dārabharaṇāyā'ti.

So tatonidānaṁ labhetha pāmojjaṁ, adhigaccheyya somanassaṁ.

he'd be filled with joy and happiness.

Seyyathāpi, bhikkhave, puriso ābādhiko assa dukkhito bāḷhagilāno, bhattañcassa nacchādeyya, na cassa kāye balamattā.

Suppose a person was sick, suffering, and gravely ill. They'd lose their appetite and get physically weak.

So aparena samayena tamhā ābādhā mucceyya, bhattañcassa chādeyya, siyā cassa kāye balamattā.

But after some time they'd recover from that illness, and regain their appetite and their strength.

Tassa evamassa:

Thinking about this,

'ahaṁ kho pubbe ābādhiko ahosiṁ dukkhito bāḷhagilāno, bhattañca me nacchādesi, na ca me āsi kāye balamattā, somhi etarahi tamhā ābādhā mutto, bhattañca me chādeti, atthi ca me kāye balamattā'ti.

So tatonidānaṁ labhetha pāmojjaṁ, adhigaccheyya somanassaṁ.

they'd be filled with joy and happiness.

Seyyathāpi, bhikkhave, puriso bandhanāgāre baddho assa.

Suppose a person was imprisoned in a jail.

So aparena samayena tamhā bandhanā mucceyya sotthinā abbhayena, na cassa kiñci bhogānaṁ vayo.

But after some time they were released from jail, safe and sound, with no loss of wealth.

Tassa evamassa:

Thinking about this,

'ahaṁ kho pubbe bandhanāgāre baddho ahosiṁ, somhi etarahi tamhā bandhanā mutto, sotthinā abbhayena, natthi ca me kiñci bhogānaṁ vayo'ti.

So tatonidānaṁ labhetha pāmojjaṁ, adhigaccheyya somanassaṁ.

they'd be filled with joy and happiness.

Seyyathāpi, bhikkhave, puriso dāso assa anattādhīno parādhīno na yenakāmaṅgamo.

Suppose a person was a bondservant. They belonged to someone else and were unable to go where they wished.

So aparena samayena tamhā dāsabyā mucceyya attādhīno aparādhīno bhujisso yenakāmaṅgamo.

But after some time they'd be freed from servitude and become their own master, an emancipated individual able to go where they wished.

Tassa evamassa:

Thinking about this,

'ahaṁ kho pubbe dāso ahosiṁ anattādhīno parādhīno na yenakāmaṅgamo, somhi etarahi tamhā dāsabyā mutto attādhīno aparādhīno bhujisso yenakāmaṅgamo'ti.

So tatonidānaṁ labhetha pāmojjaṁ, adhigaccheyya somanassaṁ.

they'd be filled with joy and happiness.

Seyyathāpi, bhikkhave, puriso sadhano sabhogo kantāraddhānamaggaṁ paṭipajjeyya.

Suppose there was a person with wealth and property who was traveling along a desert road.

So aparena samayena tamhā kantārā nitthareyya sotthinā abbhayena, na cassa kiñci bhogānaṁ vayo.

But after some time they crossed over the desert, safe and sound, with no loss of wealth.

Tassa evamassa:

Thinking about this,

'ahaṁ kho pubbe sadhano sabhogo kantāraddhānamaggaṁ paṭipajjiṁ.

Somhi etarahi tamhā kantārā nitthiṇṇo sotthinā abbhayena, natthi ca me kiñci bhogānaṁ vayo'ti.

So tatonidānaṁ labhetha pāmojjaṁ, adhigaccheyya somanassaṁ.

they'd be filled with joy and happiness.

Evameva kho, bhikkhave, bhikkhu yathā iṇaṁ yathā rogaṁ yathā bandhanāgāraṁ yathā dāsabyaṁ yathā kantāraddhānamaggaṁ, ime pañca nīvaraṇe appahīne attani samanupassati.

In the same way, as long as these five hindrances are not given up inside themselves, a mendicant regards them as a debt, a disease, a prison, slavery, and a desert crossing.

Seyyathāpi, bhikkhave, āṇaṇyaṁ yathā ārogyaṁ yathā bandhanāmokkhaṁ yathā bhujissaṁ yathā khemantabhūmiṁ; evameva bhikkhu ime pañca nīvaraṇe pahīne attani samanupassati.

But when these five hindrances are given up inside themselves, a mendicant regards this as freedom from debt, good health, release from prison, emancipation, and sanctuary.

So ime pañca nīvaraṇe pahāya cetaso upakkilese paññāya dubbalīkaraṇe,

They give up these five hindrances, corruptions of the heart that weaken wisdom.

vivicceva kāmehi vivicca akusalehi dhammehi, savitakkaṁ savicāraṁ vivekajaṁ pītisukhaṁ paṭhamaṁ jhānaṁ upasampajja viharati.

Then, quite secluded from sensual pleasures, secluded from unskillful qualities, they enter and remain in the first absorption, which has the rapture and bliss born of seclusion, while placing the mind and keeping it connected.

So imameva kāyaṁ vivekajena pītisukhena abhisandeti parisandeti paripūreti parippharati, nāssa kiñci sabbāvato kāyassa vivekajena pītisukhena apphuṭaṁ hoti.

They drench, steep, fill, and spread their body with rapture and bliss born of seclusion. There's no part of the body that's not spread with rapture and bliss born of seclusion.

Seyyathāpi, bhikkhave, dakkho nhāpako vā nhāpakantevāsī vā kaṁsathāle nhānīyacuṇṇāni ākiritvā udakena paripphosakaṁ paripphosakaṁ sanneyya. Sāyaṁ nhānīyapiṇḍi snehānugatā snehaparetā santarabāhirā, phuṭā snehena na ca pagghariṇī.

It's like when a deft bathroom attendant or their apprentice pours bath powder into a bronze dish, sprinkling it little by little with water. They knead it until the ball of bath powder is soaked and saturated with moisture, spread through inside and out; yet no moisture oozes out.

Evameva kho, bhikkhave, bhikkhu imameva kāyaṁ vivekajena pītisukhena abhisandeti parisandeti paripūreti parippharati, nāssa kiñci sabbāvato kāyassa vivekajena pītisukhena apphuṭaṁ hoti.

In the same way, a mendicant drenches, steeps, fills, and spreads their body with rapture and bliss born of seclusion. There's no part of the body that's not spread with rapture and bliss born of seclusion.

Puna caparaṁ, bhikkhave, bhikkhu vitakkavicārānaṁ vūpasamā ajjhattaṁ sampasādanaṁ cetaso ekodibhāvaṁ avitakkaṁ avicāraṁ samādhijaṁ pītisukhaṁ dutiyaṁ jhānaṁ upasampajja viharati.

Furthermore, as the placing of the mind and keeping it connected are stilled, a mendicant enters and remains in the second absorption, which has the rapture and bliss born of immersion, with internal clarity and confidence, and unified mind, without placing the mind and keeping it connected.

So imameva kāyaṁ samādhijena pītisukhena abhisandeti parisandeti paripūreti parippharati, nāssa kiñci sabbāvato kāyassa samādhijena pītisukhena apphuṭaṁ hoti.

They drench, steep, fill, and spread their body with rapture and bliss born of immersion. There's no part of the body that's not spread with rapture and bliss born of immersion.

Seyyathāpi, bhikkhave, udakarahado ubbhidodako. Tassa nevassa puratthimāya disāya udakassa āyamukhaṁ, na pacchimāya disāya udakassa āyamukhaṁ, na uttarāya disāya udakassa āyamukhaṁ, na dakkhiṇāya disāya udakassa āyamukhaṁ, devo ca na kālena kālaṁ sammādhāraṁ anuppaveccheyya. Atha kho tamhāva udakarahadā sītā vāridhārā ubbhijjitvā tameva udakarahadaṁ sītena vārinā abhisandeyya parisandeyya paripūreyya paripphareyya, nāssa kiñci sabbāvato udakarahadassa sītena vārinā apphuṭaṁ assa.

It's like a deep lake fed by spring water. There's no inlet to the east, west, north, or south, and no rainfall to replenish it from time to time. But the stream of cool water welling up in the lake drenches, steeps, fills, and spreads throughout the lake. There's no part of the lake that's not spread through with cool water.

Evameva kho, bhikkhave, bhikkhu imameva kāyaṁ samādhijena pītisukhena abhisandeti parisandeti paripūreti parippharati, nāssa kiñci sabbāvato kāyassa samādhijena pītisukhena apphuṭaṁ hoti.

In the same way, a mendicant drenches, steeps, fills, and spreads their body with rapture and bliss born of immersion. There's no part of the body that's not spread with rapture and bliss born of immersion.

Puna caparaṁ, bhikkhave, bhikkhu pītiyā ca virāgā upekkhako ca viharati, sato ca sampajāno, sukhañca kāyena paṭisaṁvedeti, yaṁ taṁ ariyā ācikkhanti: 'upekkhako satimā sukhavihārī'ti tatiyaṁ jhānaṁ upasampajja viharati.

Furthermore, with the fading away of rapture, a mendicant enters and remains in the third absorption, where they meditate with equanimity, mindful and aware, personally experiencing the bliss of which the noble ones declare, 'Equanimous and mindful, one meditates in bliss.'

So imameva kāyaṁ nippītikena sukhena abhisandeti parisandeti paripūreti parippharati, nāssa kiñci sabbāvato kāyassa nippītikena sukhena apphuṭaṁ hoti.

They drench, steep, fill, and spread their body with bliss free of rapture. There's no part of the body that's not spread with bliss free of rapture.

Seyyathāpi, bhikkhave, uppaliniyaṁ vā paduminiyaṁ vā puṇḍarīkiniyaṁ vā appekaccāni uppalāni vā padumāni vā puṇḍarīkāni vā udake jātāni udake saṁvaḍḍhāni udakānuggatāni antonimuggaposīni, tāni yāva caggā yāva ca mūlā sītena vārinā abhisannāni parisannāni paripūrāni paripphuṭāni, nāssa kiñci sabbāvataṁ uppalānaṁ vā padumānaṁ vā puṇḍarīkānaṁ vā sītena vārinā apphuṭaṁ assa.

It's like a pool with blue water lilies, or pink or white lotuses. Some of them sprout and grow in the water without rising above it, thriving underwater. From the tip to the root they're drenched, steeped, filled, and soaked with cool water. There's no part of them that's not soaked with cool water.

Evameva kho, bhikkhave, bhikkhu imameva kāyaṁ nippītikena sukhena abhisandeti parisandeti paripūreti parippharati, nāssa kiñci sabbāvato kāyassa nippītikena sukhena apphuṭaṁ hoti.

In the same way, a mendicant drenches, steeps, fills, and spreads their body with bliss free of rapture. There's no part of the body that's not spread with bliss free of rapture.

Puna caparaṁ, bhikkhave, bhikkhu sukhassa ca pahānā dukkhassa ca pahānā, pubbeva somanassadomanassānaṁ atthaṅgamā, adukkhamasukhaṁ upekkhāsatipārisuddhiṁ catutthaṁ jhānaṁ upasampajja viharati.

Furthermore, giving up pleasure and pain, and ending former happiness and sadness, a mendicant enters and remains in the fourth absorption, without pleasure or pain, with pure equanimity and mindfulness.

So imameva kāyaṁ parisuddhena cetasā pariyodātena pharitvā nisinno hoti, nāssa kiñci sabbāvato kāyassa parisuddhena cetasā pariyodātena apphuṭaṁ hoti.

They sit spreading their body through with pure bright mind. There's no part of the body that's not spread with pure bright mind.

Seyyathāpi, bhikkhave, puriso odātena vatthena sasīsaṁ pārupetvā nisinno assa, nāssa kiñci sabbāvato kāyassa odātena vatthena apphuṭaṁ assa.

It's like someone sitting wrapped from head to foot with white cloth. There's no part of the body that's not spread over with white cloth.

Evameva kho, bhikkhave, bhikkhu imameva kāyaṁ parisuddhena cetasā pariyodātena pharitvā nisinno hoti, nāssa kiñci sabbāvato kāyassa parisuddhena cetasā pariyodātena apphuṭaṁ hoti.

In the same way, they sit spreading their body through with pure bright mind.

There's no part of the body that's not spread with pure bright mind.

So evaṁ samāhite citte parisuddhe pariyodāte anaṅgaṇe vigatūpakkilese mudubhūte kammaniye ṭhite āneñjappatte pubbenivāsānussatiñāṇāya cittaṁ abhininnāmeti.

When their mind has become immersed in samādhi like this—purified, bright, flawless, rid of corruptions, pliable, workable, steady, and imperturbable—they extend it toward recollection of past lives.

So anekavihitaṁ pubbenivāsaṁ anussarati, seyyathidaṁ—ekampi jātiṁ, dvepi jātiyo ...pe... iti sākāraṁ sauddesaṁ anekavihitaṁ pubbenivāsaṁ anussarati.

They recollect many kinds of past lives, with features and details.

Seyyathāpi, bhikkhave, puriso sakamhā gāmā aññaṁ gāmaṁ gaccheyya, tamhāpi gāmā aññaṁ gāmaṁ gaccheyya, so tamhā gāmā sakamyeva gāmaṁ paccāgaccheyya. Tassa evamassa: 'ahaṁ kho sakamhā gāmā amuṁ gāmaṁ agacchiṁ, tatrapi evaṁ aṭṭhāsiṁ evaṁ nisīdiṁ evaṁ abhāsiṁ evaṁ tuṇhī ahosiṁ; tamhāpi gāmā amuṁ gāmaṁ agacchiṁ, tatrapi evaṁ aṭṭhāsiṁ evaṁ nisīdiṁ evaṁ abhāsiṁ evaṁ tuṇhī ahosiṁ; somhi tamhā gāmā sakamyeva gāmaṁ paccāgato'ti.

Suppose a person was to leave their home village and go to another village. From that village they'd go to yet another village. And from that village they'd return to their home village. They'd think: 'I went from my home village to another village. There I stood like this, sat like that, spoke like this, or kept silent like that. From that village I went to yet another village. There too I stood like this, sat like that, spoke like this, or kept silent like that. And from that village I returned to my home village.'

Evameva kho, bhikkhave, bhikkhu anekavihitaṁ pubbenivāsaṁ anussarati, seyyathidaṁ—ekampi jātiṁ dvepi jātiyo ...pe... iti sākāraṁ sauddesaṁ anekavihitaṁ pubbenivāsaṁ anussarati.

In the same way, a mendicant recollects their many kinds of past lives, with features and details.

So evaṁ samāhite citte parisuddhe pariyodāte anaṅgaṇe vigatūpakkilese mudubhūte kammaniye ṭhite āneñjappatte sattānaṁ cutūpapātañāṇāya cittaṁ abhininnāmeti.

When their mind has become immersed in samādhi like this—purified, bright, flawless, rid of corruptions, pliable, workable, steady, and imperturbable—they extend it toward knowledge of the death and rebirth of sentient beings.

So dibbena cakkhunā visuddhena atikkantamānusakena satte passati cavamāne upapajjamāne hīne paṇīte suvaṇṇe dubbaṇṇe, sugate duggate, yathākammūpage satte pajānāti ...pe...

With clairvoyance that is purified and superhuman, they see sentient beings passing away and being reborn—inferior and superior, beautiful and ugly, in a good place or a bad place. They understand how sentient beings are reborn according to their deeds.

seyyathāpi, bhikkhave, dve agārā sadvārā. Tattha cakkhumā puriso majjhe ṭhito passeyya manusse gehaṁ pavisantepi nikkhamantepi, anucaṅkamantepi anuvicarantepi.

Suppose there were two houses with doors. A person with good eyesight standing in between them would see people entering and leaving a house and wandering to and fro.

Evameva kho, bhikkhave, bhikkhu dibbena cakkhunā visuddhena atikkantamānusakena satte passati cavamāne upapajjamāne hīne paṇīte suvaṇṇe dubbaṇṇe, sugate duggate yathākammūpage satte pajānāti ...pe....

In the same way, with clairvoyance that is purified and superhuman, they see sentient beings passing away and being reborn—inferior and superior, beautiful and ugly, in a good place or a bad place. They understand how sentient beings are reborn according to their deeds.

So evaṁ samāhite citte parisuddhe pariyodāte anaṅgaṇe vigatūpakkilese mudubhūte kammaniye ṭhite āneñjappatte āsavānaṁ khayañāṇāya cittaṁ abhininnāmeti.

When their mind has become immersed in samādhi like this—purified, bright, flawless, rid of corruptions, pliable, workable, steady, and imperturbable—they extend it toward knowledge of the ending of defilements.

So 'idaṁ dukkhan'ti yathābhūtaṁ pajānāti, 'ayaṁ dukkhasamudayo'ti yathābhūtaṁ pajānāti, 'ayaṁ dukkhanirodho'ti yathābhūtaṁ pajānāti, 'ayaṁ dukkhanirodhagāminī paṭipadā'ti yathābhūtaṁ pajānāti.

They truly understand: 'This is suffering' ... 'This is the origin of suffering' ... 'This is the cessation of suffering' ... 'This is the practice that leads to the cessation of suffering.'

'Ime āsavā'ti yathābhūtaṁ pajānāti, 'ayaṁ āsavasamudayo'ti yathābhūtaṁ pajānāti, 'ayaṁ āsavanirodho'ti yathābhūtaṁ pajānāti, 'ayaṁ āsavanirodhagāminī paṭipadā'ti yathābhūtaṁ pajānāti.

They truly understand: 'These are defilements' ... 'This is the origin of defilements' ... 'This is the cessation of defilements' ... 'This is the practice that leads to the cessation of defilements.'

Tassa evaṁ jānato evaṁ passato kāmāsavāpi cittaṁ vimuccati, bhavāsavāpi cittaṁ vimuccati, avijjāsavāpi cittaṁ vimuccati.

Knowing and seeing like this, their mind is freed from the defilements of sensuality, desire to be reborn, and ignorance.

Vimuttasmiṁ vimuttamiti ñāṇaṁ hoti:

When they're freed, they know they're freed.

'khīṇā jāti, vusitaṁ brahmacariyaṁ, kataṁ karaṇīyaṁ, nāparaṁ itthattāyā'ti pajānāti.

They understand: 'Rebirth is ended, the spiritual journey has been completed, what had to be done has been done, there is no return to any state of existence.'

Seyyathāpi, bhikkhave, pabbatasankhepe udakarahado accho vippasanno anāvilo.

Suppose that in a mountain glen there was a lake that was transparent, clear, and unclouded. A person with good eyesight standing on the bank would see the clams and mussels, and pebbles and gravel, and schools of fish swimming about or staying still.

Tattha cakkhumā puriso tīre ṭhito passeyya sippisambukampi sakkharakathalampi macchagumbampi, carantampi tiṭṭhantampi.

Tassa evamassa:

They'd think:

'ayaṁ kho udakarahado accho vippasanno anāvilo. Tatrime sippisambukāpi sakkharakathalāpi macchagumbāpi carantipi tiṭṭhantipī'ti'.

'This lake is transparent, clear, and unclouded. And here are the clams and mussels, and pebbles and gravel, and schools of fish swimming about or staying still.'

Evameva kho, bhikkhave, bhikkhu 'idaṁ dukkhan'ti yathābhūtaṁ pajānāti … pe…

In the same way, a mendicant truly understands: 'This is suffering' … 'This is the origin of suffering' … 'This is the cessation of suffering' … 'This is the practice that leads to the cessation of suffering.'

nāparaṁ itthattāyāti pajānāti.

They understand: '… there is no return to any state of existence.'

Ayaṁ vuccati, bhikkhave, bhikkhu 'samaṇo' itipi 'brāhmaṇo'itipi 'nhātako'itipi 'vedagū'itipi 'sottiyo'itipi 'ariyo'itipi 'arahaṁ'itipi.

This mendicant is called an 'ascetic', a 'brahmin', a 'bathed initiate', a 'knowledge master', a 'scholar', a 'noble one', and a 'perfected one'.

Kathañca, bhikkhave, bhikkhu samaṇo hoti?

And how is a mendicant an ascetic?

Samitāssa honti pāpakā akusalā dhammā, sankilesikā, ponobbhavikā, sadarā, dukkhavipākā, āyatiṁ, jātijarāmaraṇiyā.

They have quelled the bad, unskillful qualities that are corrupting, leading to future lives, hurtful, resulting in suffering and future rebirth, old age, and death.

Evaṁ kho, bhikkhave, bhikkhu samaṇo hoti.

That's how a mendicant is an ascetic.

Kathañca, bhikkhave, bhikkhu brāhmaṇo hoti?

And how is a mendicant a brahmin?

Bāhitassa honti pāpakā akusalā dhammā, saṅkilesikā, ponobbhavikā, sadarā, dukkhavipākā, āyatiṁ, jātijarāmaraṇiyā.

They have banished the bad, unskillful qualities.

Evaṁ kho, bhikkhave, bhikkhu brāhmaṇo hoti.

That's how a mendicant is a brahmin.

Kathañca, bhikkhave, bhikkhu nhātako hoti?

And how is a mendicant a bathed initiate?

Nhātassa honti pāpakā akusalā dhammā, saṅkilesikā, ponobbhavikā, sadarā, dukkhavipākā, āyatiṁ, jātijarāmaraṇiyā.

They have bathed off the bad, unskillful qualities.

Evaṁ kho, bhikkhave, bhikkhu nhātako hoti.

That's how a mendicant is a bathed initiate.

Kathañca, bhikkhave, bhikkhu vedagū hoti?

And how is a mendicant a knowledge master?

Viditassa honti pāpakā akusalā dhammā, saṅkilesikā, ponobbhavikā, sadarā, dukkhavipākā, āyatiṁ, jātijarāmaraṇiyā.

They have known the bad, unskillful qualities.

Evaṁ kho, bhikkhave, bhikkhu vedagū hoti.

That's how a mendicant is a knowledge master.

Kathañca, bhikkhave, bhikkhu sottiyo hoti?

And how is a mendicant a scholar?

Nissutassa honti pāpakā akusalā dhammā, saṅkilesikā, ponobbhavikā, sadarā, dukkhavipākā, āyatiṁ, jātijarāmaraṇiyā.

They have scoured off the bad, unskillful qualities.

Evaṁ kho, bhikkhave, bhikkhu sottiyo hoti.

That's how a mendicant is a scholar.

Kathañca, bhikkhave, bhikkhu ariyo hoti?

And how is a mendicant a noble one?

Ārakāssa honti pāpakā akusalā dhammā, saṅkilesikā, ponobbhavikā, sadarā, dukkhavipākā, āyatiṁ, jātijarāmaraṇiyā.

They are far away from the bad, unskillful qualities.

Evaṁ kho, bhikkhave, bhikkhu ariyo hoti.

That's how a mendicant is a noble one.

Kathañca, bhikkhave, bhikkhu arahaṁ hoti?

And how is a mendicant a perfected one?

Ārakāssa honti pāpakā akusalā dhammā, saṅkilesikā, ponobbhavikā, sadarā, dukkhavipākā, āyatiṁ, jātijarāmaraṇiyā.

They are far away from the bad, unskillful qualities that are corrupting, leading to future lives, hurtful, resulting in suffering and future rebirth, old age, and death.

Evaṁ kho, bhikkhave, bhikkhu arahaṁ hotī"ti.

That's how a mendicant is a perfected one."

Idamavoca bhagavā.

That is what the Buddha said.

Attamanā te bhikkhū bhagavato bhāsitaṁ abhinandunti.

Satisfied, the mendicants were happy with what the Buddha said.

Mahāassapurasuttaṁ niṭṭhitaṁ navamaṁ.

40 Culaassapurasutta:

The Shorter Discourse at Assapura

Evaṁ me sutaṁ—

So I have heard.

ekaṁ samayaṁ bhagavā aṅgesu viharati assapuraṁ nāma aṅgānaṁ nigamo.

At one time the Buddha was staying in the land of the Aṅgas, near the Aṅgan town named Assapura.

Tatra kho bhagavā bhikkhū āmantesi:

There the Buddha addressed the mendicants,

"bhikkhavo"ti.

"Mendicants!"

"Bhadante"ti te bhikkhū bhagavato paccassosuṁ.

"Venerable sir," they replied.

Bhagavā etadavoca:

The Buddha said this:

"Samaṇā samaṇāti vo, bhikkhave, jano sañjānāti.

"Mendicants, people label you as ascetics.

Tumhe ca pana 'ke tumhe'ti puṭṭhā samānā 'samaṇāmhā'ti paṭijānātha.

And when they ask you what you are, you claim to be ascetics.

Tesaṁ vo, bhikkhave, evaṁsamaññānaṁ sataṁ evampaṭiññānaṁ sataṁ:

Given this label and this claim, you should train like this: 'We will practice in the way that is proper for an ascetic. That way our label will be accurate and our claim correct.

'yā samaṇasāmīcippaṭipadā taṁ paṭipajjissāma;

evaṁ no ayaṁ amhākaṁ samaññā ca saccā bhavissati paṭiññā ca bhūtā;

yesañca mayaṁ cīvarapiṇḍapātasenāsanagilānappaccayabhesajjaparikkhāraṁ paribhuñjāma, tesaṁ te kārā amhesu mahapphalā bhavissanti mahānisaṁsā, amhākañcevāyaṁ pabbajjā avañjhā bhavissati saphalā saudrayā'ti.

Any robes, almsfood, lodgings, and medicines and supplies for the sick that we use will be very fruitful and beneficial for the donor. And our going forth will not be wasted, but will be fruitful and fertile.'

Evañhi vo, bhikkhave, sikkhitabbaṁ.

Kathañca, bhikkhave, bhikkhu na samaṇasāmīcippaṭipadaṁ paṭipanno hoti?

And how does a mendicant not practice in the way that is proper for an ascetic?

Yassa kassaci, bhikkhave, bhikkhuno abhijjhālussa abhijjhā appahīnā hoti, byāpannacittassa byāpādo appahīno hoti, kodhanassa kodho appahīno hoti, upanāhissa upanāho appahīno hoti, makkhissa makkho appahīno hoti, paḷāsissa paḷāso appahīno hoti, issukissa issā appahīnā hoti, maccharissa macchariyaṁ appahīnaṁ hoti, saṭhassa sāṭheyyaṁ appahīnaṁ hoti, māyāvissa māyā appahīnā hoti, pāpicchassa pāpikā icchā appahīnā hoti, micchādiṭṭhikassa micchādiṭṭhi appahīnā hoti—

There are some mendicants who have not given up covetousness, ill will, irritability, hostility, disdain, contempt, jealousy, stinginess, deviousness, deceit, corrupt wishes, and wrong view.

imesaṁ kho ahaṁ, bhikkhave, samaṇamalānaṁ samaṇadosānaṁ samaṇakasaṭānaṁ āpāyikānaṁ ṭhānānaṁ duggativedaniyānaṁ appahānā 'na samaṇasāmīcippaṭipadaṁ paṭipanno'ti vadāmi.

These stains, defects, and dregs of an ascetic are grounds for rebirth in places of loss, and are experienced in bad places. As long as they have not given these up, they do not practice in the way that is proper for an ascetic, I say.

Seyyathāpi, bhikkhave, matajaṁ nāma āvudhajātaṁ ubhatodhāraṁ pītanisitaṁ.

I say that such a mendicant's going forth may be compared to the kind of weapon called 'death-dealer'—double-edged, hardened, and keen—covered and wrapped in the outer robe.

Tadassa saṅghāṭiyā sampārutaṁ sampaliveṭhitaṁ.

Tathūpamāhaṁ, bhikkhave, imassa bhikkhuno pabbajjaṁ vadāmi.

Nāhaṁ, bhikkhave, saṅghāṭikassa saṅghāṭidhāraṇamattena sāmaññaṁ vadāmi.

I say that you don't deserve the label 'outer robe wearer' just because you wear an outer robe.

Nāhaṁ, bhikkhave, acelakassa acelakamattena sāmaññaṁ vadāmi.

You don't deserve the label 'naked ascetic' just because you go naked.

Nāhaṁ, bhikkhave, rajojallikassa rajojallikamattena sāmaññaṁ vadāmi.

You don't deserve the label 'dust and dirt wearer' just because you're caked in dust and dirt.

Nāhaṁ, bhikkhave, udakorohakassa udakorohaṇamattena sāmaññaṁ vadāmi.

You don't deserve the label 'water immerser' just because you immerse yourself in water.

Nāhaṁ, bhikkhave, rukkhamūlikassa rukkhamūlikamattena sāmaññaṁ vadāmi.

You don't deserve the label 'tree root dweller' just because you stay at the root of a tree.

Nāhaṁ, bhikkhave, abbhokāsikassa abbhokāsikamattena sāmaññaṁ vadāmi.

You don't deserve the label 'open air dweller' just because you stay in the open air.

Nāhaṁ, bhikkhave, ubbhaṭṭhakassa ubbhaṭṭhakamattena sāmaññaṁ vadāmi.

You don't deserve the label 'stander' just because you continually stand.

Nāhaṁ, bhikkhave, pariyāyabhattikassa pariyāyabhattikamattena sāmaññaṁ vadāmi.

You don't deserve the label 'interval eater' just because you eat food at set intervals.

Nāhaṁ, bhikkhave, mantajjhāyakassa mantajjhāyakamattena sāmaññaṁ vadāmi.

You don't deserve the label 'reciter' just because you recite scriptures.

Nāhaṁ, bhikkhave, jaṭilakassa jaṭādhāraṇamattena sāmaññaṁ vadāmi.

You don't deserve the label 'matted-hair ascetic' just because you have matted hair.

Saṅghāṭikassa ce, bhikkhave, saṅghāṭidhāraṇamattena abhijjhālussa abhijjhā pahīyetha, byāpannacittassa byāpādo pahīyetha, kodhanassa kodho pahīyetha, upanāhissa upanāho pahīyetha, makkhissa makkho pahīyetha, paḷāsissa paḷāso pahīyetha, issukissa issā pahīyetha, maccharissa macchariyaṁ pahīyetha, saṭhassa sāṭheyyaṁ pahīyetha, māyāvissa māyā pahīyetha, pāpicchassa pāpikā icchā pahīyetha, micchādiṭṭhikassa micchādiṭṭhi pahīyetha, tamenaṁ mittāmaccā ñātisālohitā jātameva naṁ saṅghāṭikaṁ kareyyuṁ, saṅghāṭikattameva samādapeyyuṁ:

Imagine that just by wearing an outer robe someone with covetousness, ill will, irritability, hostility, disdain, contempt, jealousy, stinginess, deviousness, deceit, corrupt wishes, and wrong view could give up these things. If that were the case, your friends and colleagues, relatives and kin would make you an outer robe wearer as soon as you were born. They'd encourage you:

'ehi tvaṁ, bhadramukha, saṅghāṭiko hohi, saṅghāṭikassa te sato saṅghāṭidhāraṇamattena abhijjhālussa abhijjhā pahīyissati, byāpannacittassa byāpādo pahīyissati, kodhanassa kodho pahīyissati, upanāhissa upanāho pahīyissati, makkhissa makkho pahīyissati, paḷāsissa paḷāso pahīyissati, issukissa issā pahīyissati, maccharissa macchariyaṁ pahīyissati, saṭhassa sāṭheyyaṁ pahīyissati, māyāvissa māyā pahīyissati, pāpicchassa pāpikā icchā pahīyissati, micchādiṭṭhikassa micchādiṭṭhi pahīyissatī'ti.

'Please, my dear, wear an outer robe! By doing so you will give up covetousness, ill will, irritability, hostility, disdain, contempt, jealousy, stinginess, deviousness, deceit, corrupt wishes, and wrong view.'

Yasmā ca kho ahaṁ, bhikkhave, saṅghāṭikampi idhekaccaṁ passāmi abhijjhāluṁ byāpannacittaṁ kodhanaṁ upanāhiṁ makkhiṁ paḷāsiṁ issukiṁ macchariṁ saṭhaṁ māyāviṁ pāpicchaṁ micchādiṭṭhikaṁ, tasmā na saṅghāṭikassa saṅghāṭidhāraṇamattena sāmaññaṁ vadāmi.

But sometimes I see someone with these bad qualities who is an outer robe wearer. That's why I say that you don't deserve the label 'outer robe wearer' just because you wear an outer robe.

Acelakassa ce, bhikkhave …pe…

Imagine that just by going naked …

rajojallikassa ce, bhikkhave …pe…

wearing dust and dirt …

udakorohakassa ce, bhikkhave …pe…

immersing in water …

rukkhamūlikassa ce, bhikkhave …pe…

staying at the root of a tree …

abbhokāsikassa ce, bhikkhave …pe…

staying in the open air …

ubbhaṭṭhakassa ce, bhikkhave …pe…

standing continually …

pariyāyabhattikassa ce, bhikkhave …pe…

eating at set intervals …

mantajjhāyakassa ce, bhikkhave …pe…

reciting scriptures …

jaṭilakassa ce, bhikkhave, jaṭādhāraṇamattena abhijjhālussa abhijjhā pahīyetha, byāpannacittassa byāpādo pahīyetha, kodhanassa kodho pahīyetha, upanāhissa upanāho pahīyetha, makkhissa makkho pahīyetha, paḷāsissa paḷāso pahīyetha, issukissa issā pahīyetha, maccharissa macchariyaṁ pahīyetha, saṭhassa sāṭheyyaṁ pahīyetha, māyāvissa māyā pahīyetha, pāpicchassa pāpikā icchā pahīyetha, micchādiṭṭhikassa micchādiṭṭhi pahīyetha, tamenaṁ mittāmaccā ñātisālohitā jātameva naṁ jaṭilakaṁ kareyyuṁ, jaṭilakattameva samādapeyyuṁ:

having matted hair someone with covetousness, ill will, irritability, hostility, disdain, contempt, jealousy, stinginess, deviousness, deceit, corrupt wishes, and wrong view could give up these things. If that were the case, your friends and colleagues, relatives and kin would make you a matted-hair ascetic as soon as you were born. They'd encourage you:

'ehi tvaṁ, bhadramukha, jaṭilako hohi, jaṭilakassa te sato jaṭādhāraṇamattena abhijjhālussa abhijjhā pahīyissati byāpannacittassa byāpādo pahīyissati, kodhanassa kodho pahīyissati ...pe... pāpicchassa pāpikā icchā pahīyissati micchādiṭṭhikassa micchādiṭṭhi pahīyissatī'ti.

'Please, my dear, become a matted-hair ascetic! By doing so you will give up covetousness, ill will, irritability, hostility, disdain, contempt, jealousy, stinginess, deviousness, deceit, corrupt wishes, and wrong view.'

Yasmā ca kho ahaṁ, bhikkhave, jaṭilakampi idhekaccaṁ passāmi abhijjhāluṁ byāpannacittaṁ kodhanaṁ upanāhiṁ makkhiṁ palāsiṁ issukiṁ maccharim saṭhaṁ māyāviṁ pāpicchaṁ micchādiṭṭhiṁ, tasmā na jaṭilakassa jaṭādhāraṇamattena sāmaññaṁ vadāmi.

But sometimes I see someone with these bad qualities who is a matted-hair ascetic. That's why I say that you don't deserve the label 'matted-hair ascetic' just because you have matted hair.

Kathañca, bhikkhave, bhikkhu samaṇasāmīcippaṭipadaṁ paṭipanno hoti?

And how does a mendicant practice in the way that is proper for an ascetic?

Yassa kassaci, bhikkhave, bhikkhuno abhijjhālussa abhijjhā pahīnā hoti, byāpannacittassa byāpādo pahīno hoti, kodhanassa kodho pahīno hoti, upanāhissa upanāho pahīno hoti, makkhissa makkho pahīno hoti, palāsissa palāso pahīno hoti, issukissa issā pahīnā hoti, maccharissa macchariyaṁ pahīnaṁ hoti, saṭhassa sāṭheyyaṁ pahīnaṁ hoti, māyāvissa māyā pahīnā hoti, pāpicchassa pāpikā icchā pahīnā hoti, micchādiṭṭhikassa micchādiṭṭhi pahīnā hoti—

There are some mendicants who have given up covetousness, ill will, irritability, hostility, disdain, contempt, jealousy, stinginess, deviousness, deceit, corrupt wishes, and wrong view.

imesaṁ kho ahaṁ, bhikkhave, samaṇamalānaṁ samaṇadosānaṁ samaṇakasaṭānaṁ āpāyikānaṁ ṭhānānaṁ duggativedaniyānaṁ pahānā 'samaṇasāmīcippaṭipadaṁ paṭipanno'ti vadāmi.

These stains, defects, and dregs of an ascetic are grounds for rebirth in places of loss, and are experienced in bad places. When they have given these up, they are practicing in the way that is proper for an ascetic, I say.

So sabbehi imehi pāpakehi akusalehi dhammehi visuddhamattānaṁ samanupassati (...).

They see themselves purified from all these bad, unskillful qualities.

Tassa sabbehi imehi pāpakehi akusalehi dhammehi visuddhamattānaṁ samanupassato (…) pāmojjaṁ jāyati, pamuditassa pīti jāyati, pītimanassa kāyo passambhati, passaddhakāyo sukhaṁ vedeti, sukhino cittaṁ samādhiyati.

Seeing this, joy springs up. Being joyful, rapture springs up. When the mind is full of rapture, the body becomes tranquil. When the body is tranquil, they feel bliss. And when blissful, the mind becomes immersed in samādhi.

So mettāsahagatena cetasā ekaṁ disaṁ pharitvā viharati, tathā dutiyaṁ, tathā tatiyaṁ, tathā catutthaṁ. Iti uddhamadho tiriyaṁ sabbadhi sabbattatāya sabbāvantaṁ lokaṁ mettāsahagatena cetasā vipulena mahaggatena appamāṇena averena abyābajjhena pharitvā viharati.

They meditate spreading a heart full of love to one direction, and to the second, and to the third, and to the fourth. In the same way above, below, across, everywhere, all around, they spread a heart full of love to the whole world—abundant, expansive, limitless, free of enmity and ill will.

Karuṇāsahagatena cetasā …pe…

They meditate spreading a heart full of compassion …

muditāsahagatena cetasā …pe…

They meditate spreading a heart full of rejoicing …

upekkhāsahagatena cetasā ekaṁ disam pharitvā viharati, tathā dutiyaṁ, tathā tatiyaṁ, tathā catutthaṁ. Iti uddhamadho tiriyaṁ sabbadhi sabbattatāya sabbāvantaṁ lokaṁ upekkhāsahagatena cetasā vipulena mahaggatena appamāṇena averena abyābajjhena pharitvā viharati.

They meditate spreading a heart full of equanimity to one direction, and to the second, and to the third, and to the fourth. In the same way above, below, across, everywhere, all around, they spread a heart full of equanimity to the whole world—abundant, expansive, limitless, free of enmity and ill will.

Seyyathāpi, bhikkhave, pokkharaṇī acchodakā sātodakā sītodakā setakā supatitthā ramaṇīyā.

Suppose there was a lotus pond with clear, sweet, cool water, clean, with smooth banks, delightful.

Puratthimāya cepi disāya puriso āgaccheyya ghammābhitatto ghammapareto kilanto tasito pipāsito.

Then along comes a person—whether from the east, west, north, or south—struggling in the oppressive heat, weary, thirsty, and parched.

So taṁ pokkharaṇiṁ āgamma vineyya udakapipāsaṁ vineyya ghammapariḷāhaṁ …pe… pacchimāya cepi disāya puriso āgaccheyya …pe… uttarāya cepi disāya puriso āgaccheyya …pe… dakkhiṇāya cepi disāya puriso āgaccheyya. Yato kuto cepi naṁ puriso āgaccheyya ghammābhitatto ghammapareto, kilanto tasito pipāsito. So taṁ pokkharaṇiṁ āgamma vineyya udakapipāsaṁ, vineyya ghammapariḷāhaṁ.

No matter what direction they come from, when they arrive at that lotus pond they would alleviate their thirst and heat exhaustion.

Evameva kho, bhikkhave, khattiyakulā cepi agārasmā anagāriyaṁ pabbajito hoti, so ca tathāgatappaveditaṁ dhammavinayaṁ āgamma, evaṁ mettaṁ karuṇaṁ muditaṁ upekkhaṁ bhāvetvā labhati ajjhattaṁ vūpasamaṁ. Ajjhattaṁ vūpasamā 'samaṇasāmīcippaṭipadaṁ paṭipanno'ti vadāmi. Brāhmaṇakulā cepi …pe… vessakulā cepi …pe… suddakulā cepi …pe… yasmā kasmā cepi kulā agārasmā anagāriyaṁ pabbajito hoti, so ca tathāgatappaveditaṁ dhammavinayaṁ āgamma, evaṁ mettaṁ karuṇaṁ muditaṁ upekkhaṁ bhāvetvā labhati ajjhattaṁ vūpasamaṁ.

In the same way, suppose someone has gone forth from the lay life to homelessness—whether from a family of aristocrats, brahmins, merchants, or workers—and has arrived at the teaching and training proclaimed by a Realized One. Having developed love, compassion, rejoicing, and equanimity in this way they gain inner peace.

Ajjhattaṁ vūpasamā 'samaṇasāmīcippaṭipadaṁ paṭipanno'ti vadāmi.

Because of that inner peace they are practicing the way proper for an ascetic, I say.

Khattiyakulā cepi agārasmā anagāriyaṁ pabbajito hoti.

And suppose someone has gone forth from the lay life to homelessness—whether from a family of aristocrats, brahmins, merchants, or workers—

So ca āsavānaṁ khayā anāsavaṁ cetovimuttiṁ paññāvimuttiṁ diṭṭheva dhamme sayaṁ abhiññā sacchikatvā upasampajja viharati.

and they realize the undefiled freedom of heart and freedom by wisdom in this very life. And they live having realized it with their own insight due to the ending of defilements.

Āsavānaṁ khayā samaṇo hoti. Brāhmaṇakulā cepi …pe… vessakulā cepi … suddakulā cepi … yasmā kasmā cepi kulā agārasmā anagāriyaṁ pabbajito hoti, so ca āsavānaṁ khayā anāsavaṁ cetovimuttiṁ paññāvimuttiṁ diṭṭheva dhamme sayaṁ abhiññā sacchikatvā upasampajja viharati. Āsavānaṁ khayā samaṇo hotī"ti.

They're an ascetic because of the ending of defilements."

Idamavoca bhagavā.

That is what the Buddha said.

Attamanā te bhikkhū bhagavato bhāsitaṁ abhinandunti.

Satisfied, the mendicants were happy with what the Buddha said.

Cūḷaassapurasuttaṁ niṭṭhitaṁ dasamaṁ.

Mahāyamakavaggo niṭṭhito catuttho.

Tassuddānaṁ

Giñjakasālavanaṁ pariharituṁ,

Paññavato puna saccakanisedho;

Mukhavaṇṇapasīdanatāpindo,

Kevaṭṭaassapurajaṭilena.

CUḶAYAMAKAVAGGA

THE SHORTER DIVISION OF PAIRS

41 Saleyyakasutta:

The People of Sala

Evaṁ me sutaṁ—

So I have heard.

ekaṁ samayaṁ bhagavā kosalesu cārikaṁ caramāno mahatā bhikkhusaṅghena saddhiṁ yena sālā nāma kosalānaṁ brāhmaṇagāmo tadavasari.

At one time the Buddha was wandering in the land of the Kosalans together with a large Saṅgha of mendicants when he arrived at a village of the Kosalan brahmins named Sālā.

Assosuṁ kho sāleyyakā brāhmaṇagahapatikā:

The brahmins and householders of Sālā heard,

"samaṇo khalu, bho, gotamo sakyaputto sakyakulā pabbajito kosalesu cārikaṁ caramāno mahatā bhikkhusaṅghena saddhiṁ sālaṁ anuppatto.

"It seems the ascetic Gotama—a Sakyan, gone forth from a Sakyan family—while wandering in the land of the Kosalans has arrived at Sālā, together with a large Saṅgha of mendicants.

Taṁ kho pana bhavantaṁ gotamaṁ evaṁ kalyāṇo kittisaddo abbhuggato:

He has this good reputation:

'itipi so bhagavā arahaṁ sammāsambuddho vijjācaraṇasampanno sugato lokavidū anuttaro purisadammasārathi satthā devamanussānaṁ buddho bhagavā'.

'That Blessed One is perfected, a fully awakened Buddha, accomplished in knowledge and conduct, holy, knower of the world, supreme guide for those who wish to train, teacher of gods and humans, awakened, blessed.'

So imaṁ lokaṁ sadevakaṁ samārakaṁ sabrahmakaṁ sassamaṇabrāhmaṇiṁ pajaṁ sadevamanussaṁ sayaṁ abhiññā sacchikatvā pavedeti.

He has realized with his own insight this world—with its gods, Māras and Brahmās, this population with its ascetics and brahmins, gods and humans—and he makes it known to others.

So dhammaṁ deseti ādikalyāṇaṁ majjhekalyāṇaṁ pariyosānakalyāṇaṁ sātthaṁ sabyañjanaṁ;

He proclaims a teaching that is good in the beginning, good in the middle, and good in the end, with the right meaning and phrasing.

kevalaparipuṇṇaṁ parisuddhaṁ brahmacariyaṁ pakāseti.

He reveals an entirely full and pure spiritual life.

Sādhu kho pana tathārūpānaṁ arahataṁ dassanaṁ hotī"ti.

It's good to see such perfected ones."

Atha kho sāleyyakā brāhmaṇagahapatikā yena bhagavā tenupasaṅkamiṁsu; upasaṅkamitvā appekacce bhagavantaṁ abhivādetvā ekamantaṁ nisīdiṁsu; appekacce bhagavatā saddhiṁ sammodiṁsu, sammodanīyaṁ kathaṁ sāraṇīyaṁ vītisāretvā ekamantaṁ nisīdiṁsu; appekacce yena bhagavā tenañjaliṁ paṇāmetvā ekamantaṁ nisīdiṁsu; appekacce bhagavato santike nāmagottaṁ sāvetvā ekamantaṁ nisīdiṁsu; appekacce tuṇhībhūtā ekamantaṁ nisīdiṁsu. Ekamantaṁ nisinnā kho sāleyyakā brāhmaṇagahapatikā bhagavantaṁ etadavocuṁ:

Then the brahmins and householders of Sālā went up to the Buddha. Before sitting down to one side, some bowed, some exchanged greetings and polite conversation, some held up their joined palms toward the Buddha, some announced their name and clan, while some kept silent. Seated to one side they said to the Buddha:

"ko nu kho, bho gotama, hetu, ko paccayo, yena m'idhekacce sattā kāyassa bhedā paraṁ maraṇā apāyaṁ duggatiṁ vinipātaṁ nirayaṁ upapajjanti?

"What is the cause, Master Gotama, what is the reason why some sentient beings, when their body breaks up, after death, are reborn in a place of loss, a bad place, the underworld, hell?

Ko pana, bho gotama, hetu, ko paccayo, yena m'idhekacce sattā kāyassa bhedā paraṁ maraṇā sugatiṁ saggaṁ lokaṁ upapajjantī"ti?

And what is the cause, Master Gotama, what is the reason why some sentient beings, when their body breaks up, after death, are reborn in a good place, a heavenly realm?"

"Adhammacariyāvisamacariyāhetu kho, gahapatayo, evam'idhekacce sattā kāyassa bhedā paraṁ maraṇā apāyaṁ duggatiṁ vinipātaṁ nirayaṁ upapajjanti.

"Unprincipled and immoral conduct is the reason why some sentient beings, when their body breaks up, after death, are reborn in a place of loss, a bad place, the underworld, hell.

Dhammacariyāsamacariyāhetu kho, gahapatayo, evam'idhekacce sattā kāyassa bhedā paraṁ maraṇā sugatiṁ saggaṁ lokaṁ upapajjantī"ti.

Principled and moral conduct is the reason why some sentient beings, when their body breaks up, after death, are reborn in a good place, a heavenly realm."

"Na kho mayaṁ imassa bhoto gotamassa saṅkhittena bhāsitassa, vitthārena atthaṁ avibhattassa, vitthārena atthaṁ ājānāma.

"We don't understand the detailed meaning of Master Gotama's brief statement.

Sādhu no bhavaṁ gotamo tathā dhammaṁ desetu, yathā mayaṁ imassa bhoto gotamassa saṅkhittena bhāsitassa, vitthārena atthaṁ avibhattassa, vitthārena atthaṁ ājāneyyāmā"ti.

Master Gotama, please teach us this matter in detail so we can understand the meaning."

"Tena hi, gahapatayo, suṇātha, sādhukaṁ manasi karotha, bhāsissāmī"ti.

"Well then, householders, listen and pay close attention, I will speak."

"Evaṁ, bho"ti kho sāleyyakā brāhmaṇagahapatikā bhagavato paccassosuṁ.

"Yes, sir," they replied.

Bhagavā etadavoca:

The Buddha said this:

"Tividhaṁ kho, gahapatayo, kāyena adhammacariyāvisamacariyā hoti, catubbidhaṁ vācāya adhammacariyāvisamacariyā hoti, tividhaṁ manasā adhammacariyāvisamacariyā hoti.

"Householders, unprincipled and immoral conduct is threefold by way of body, fourfold by way of speech, and threefold by way of mind.

Kathañca, gahapatayo, tividhaṁ kāyena adhammacariyāvisamacariyā hoti?

And how is unprincipled and immoral conduct threefold by way of body?

Idha, gahapatayo, ekacco pāṇātipātī hoti, luddo lohitapāṇi hatappahate niviṭṭho adayāpanno pāṇabhūtesu.

It's when a certain person kills living creatures. They're violent, bloody-handed, a hardened killer, merciless to living beings.

Adinnādāyī kho pana hoti. Yaṁ taṁ parassa paravittūpakaraṇaṁ, gāmagataṁ vā araññagataṁ vā, taṁ adinnaṁ theyyasaṅkhātaṁ ādātā hoti.

They steal. With the intention to commit theft, they take the wealth or belongings of others from village or wilderness.

Kāmesumicchācārī kho pana hoti. Yā tā māturakkhitā piturakkhitā mātāpiturakkhitā bhāturakkhitā bhaginirakkhitā ñātirakkhitā gottarakkhitā dhammarakkhitā sassāmikā saparidaṇḍā antamaso mālāguḷaparikkhittāpi, tathārūpāsu cārittaṃ āpajjitā hoti.

They commit sexual misconduct. They have sexual relations with women who have their mother, father, both mother and father, brother, sister, relatives, or clan as guardian. They have sexual relations with a woman who is protected on principle, or who has a husband, or whose violation is punishable by law, or even one who has been garlanded as a token of betrothal.

Evaṃ kho, gahapatayo, tividhaṃ kāyena adhammacariyāvisamacariyā hoti.

This is how unprincipled and immoral conduct is threefold by way of body.

Kathañca, gahapatayo, catubbidhaṃ vācāya adhammacariyāvisamacariyā hoti?

And how is unprincipled and immoral conduct fourfold by way of speech?

Idha, gahapatayo, ekacco musāvādī hoti. Sabhāgato vā parisāgato vā, ñātimajjhagato vā pūgamajjhagato vā rājakulamajjhagato vā, abhinīto sakkhipuṭṭho: 'ehambho purisa, yaṃ jānāsi taṃ vadehī'ti, so ajānaṃ vā āha: 'jānāmī'ti, jānaṃ vā āha: na jānāmī'ti, 'apassaṃ vā āha: 'passāmī'ti, passaṃ vā āha: 'na passāmī'ti. Iti attahetu vā parahetu vā āmisakiñcikkhahetu vā sampajānamusā bhāsitā hoti.

It's when a certain person lies. They're summoned to a council, an assembly, a family meeting, a guild, or to the royal court, and asked to bear witness: 'Please, mister, say what you know.' Not knowing, they say 'I know.' Knowing, they say 'I don't know.' Not seeing, they say 'I see.' And seeing, they say 'I don't see.' So they deliberately lie for the sake of themselves or another, or for some trivial worldly reason.

Pisuṇavāco kho pana hoti. Ito sutvā amutra akkhātā imesaṃ bhedāya, amutra vā sutvā imesaṃ akkhātā amūsaṃ bhedāya. Iti samaggānaṃ vā bhettā, bhinnānaṃ vā anuppadātā, vaggārāmo vaggarato vagganandī vaggakaraṇiṃ vācaṃ bhāsitā hoti.

They speak divisively. They repeat in one place what they heard in another so as to divide people against each other. And so they divide those who are harmonious, supporting division, delighting in division, loving division, speaking words that promote division.

Pharusavāco kho pana hoti. Yā sā vācā aṇḍakā kakkasā parakaṭukā parābhisajjanī kodhasāmantā asamādhisaṃvattanikā, tathārūpiṃ vācaṃ bhāsitā hoti.

They speak harshly. They use the kinds of words that are cruel, nasty, hurtful, offensive, bordering on anger, not leading to immersion.

Samphappalāpī kho pana hoti. Akālavādī abhūtavādī anatthavādī adhammavādī avinayavādī. Anidhānavatiṃ vācaṃ bhāsitā hoti akālena anapadesaṃ apariyantavatiṃ anatthasaṃhitaṃ.

They talk nonsense. Their speech is untimely, and is neither factual nor beneficial. It has nothing to do with the teaching or the training. Their words have no value, and are untimely, unreasonable, rambling, and pointless.

Evaṁ kho, gahapatayo, catubbidhaṁ vācāya adhammacariyāvisamacariyā hoti.

This is how unprincipled and immoral conduct is fourfold by way of speech.

Kathañca, gahapatayo, tividhaṁ manasā adhammacariyāvisamacariyā hoti?

And how is unprincipled and immoral conduct threefold by way of mind?

Idha, gahapatayo, ekacco abhijjhālu hoti, yaṁ taṁ parassa paravittūpakaraṇaṁ taṁ abhijjhātā hoti: 'aho vata yaṁ parassa taṁ mamassā'ti.

It's when a certain person is covetous. They covet the wealth and belongings of others: 'Oh, if only their belongings were mine!'

Byāpannacitto kho pana hoti paduṭṭhamanasaṅkappo: 'ime sattā haññantu vā vajjhantu vā ucchijjantu vā vinassantu vā mā vā ahesun'ti.

They have ill will and malicious intentions: 'May these sentient beings be killed, slaughtered, slain, destroyed, or annihilated!'

Micchādiṭṭhiko kho pana hoti viparītadassano:

They have wrong view. Their perspective is distorted:

'natthi dinnaṁ natthi yiṭṭhaṁ natthi hutaṁ, natthi sukatadukkaṭānaṁ kammānaṁ phalaṁ vipāko, natthi ayaṁ loko natthi paro loko, natthi mātā natthi pitā, natthi sattā opapātikā, natthi loke samaṇabrāhmaṇā sammaggatā sammāpaṭipannā ye imañca lokaṁ parañca lokaṁ sayaṁ abhiññā sacchikatvā pavedentī'ti.

'There's no meaning in giving, sacrifice, or offerings. There's no fruit or result of good and bad deeds. There's no afterlife. There's no such thing as mother and father, or beings that are reborn spontaneously. And there's no ascetic or brahmin who is well attained and practiced, and who describes the afterlife after realizing it with their own insight.'

Evaṁ kho, gahapatayo, tividhaṁ manasā adhammacariyāvisamacariyā hoti.

This is how unprincipled and immoral conduct is threefold by way of mind.

Evaṁ adhammacariyāvisamacariyāhetu kho, gahapatayo, evam'idhekacce sattā kāyassa bhedā paraṁ maraṇā apāyaṁ duggatiṁ vinipātaṁ nirayaṁ upapajjanti.

That's how unprincipled and immoral conduct is the reason why some sentient beings, when their body breaks up, after death, are reborn in a place of loss, a bad place, the underworld, hell.

Tividhaṁ kho, gahapatayo, kāyena dhammacariyāsamacariyā hoti, catubbidhaṁ vācāya dhammacariyāsamacariyā hoti, tividhaṁ manasā dhammacariyāsamacariyā hoti.

Householders, principled and moral conduct is threefold by way of body, fourfold by way of speech, and threefold by way of mind.

Kathañca, gahapatayo, tividhaṁ kāyena dhammacariyāsamacariyā hoti?

And how is principled and moral conduct threefold by way of body?

Idha, gahapatayo, ekacco pāṇātipātaṁ pahāya pāṇātipātā paṭivirato hoti, nihitadaṇḍo nihitasattho lajjī dayāpanno sabbapāṇabhūtahitānukampī viharati.

It's when a certain person gives up killing living creatures. They renounce the rod and the sword. They're scrupulous and kind, living full of compassion for all living beings.

Adinnādānaṁ pahāya adinnādānā paṭivirato hoti. Yaṁ taṁ parassa paravittūpakaraṇaṁ, gāmagataṁ vā araññagataṁ vā, taṁ nādinnaṁ theyyasaṅkhātaṁ ādātā hoti.

They give up stealing. They don't, with the intention to commit theft, take the wealth or belongings of others from village or wilderness.

Kāmesumicchācāraṁ pahāya kāmesumicchācārā paṭivirato hoti. Yā tā māturakkhitā piturakkhitā mātāpiturakkhitā bhāturakkhitā bhaginirakkhitā ñātirakkhitā gottarakkhitā dhammarakkhitā sassāmikā saparidaṇḍā antamaso mālāguḷaparikkhittāpi, tathārūpāsu na cārittaṁ āpajjitā hoti.

They give up sexual misconduct. They don't have sexual relations with women who have their mother, father, both mother and father, brother, sister, relatives, or clan as guardian. They don't have sexual relations with a woman who is protected on principle, or who has a husband, or whose violation is punishable by law, or even one who has been garlanded as a token of betrothal.

Evaṁ kho, gahapatayo, tividhaṁ kāyena dhammacariyāsamacariyā hoti.

This is how principled and moral conduct is threefold by way of body.

Kathañca, gahapatayo, catubbidhaṁ vācāya dhammacariyāsamacariyā hoti?

And how is principled and moral conduct fourfold by way of speech?

Idha, gahapatayo, ekacco musāvādaṁ pahāya musāvādā paṭivirato hoti. Sabhāgato vā parisāgato vā, ñātimajjhagato vā pūgamajjhagato vā rājakulamajjhagato vā, abhinīto sakkhipuṭṭho: 'ehambho purisa, yaṁ jānāsi taṁ vadehī'ti, so ajānaṁ vā āha: 'na jānāmī'ti, jānaṁ vā āha: 'jānāmī'ti, apassaṁ vā āha: 'na passāmī'ti, passaṁ vā āha: 'passāmī'ti. Iti attahetu vā parahetu vā āmisakiñcikkhahetu vā na sampajānamusā bhāsitā hoti.

It's when a certain person gives up lying. They're summoned to a council, an assembly, a family meeting, a guild, or to the royal court, and asked to bear witness: 'Please, mister, say what you know.' Not knowing, they say 'I don't know.' Knowing, they say 'I know.' Not seeing, they say 'I don't see.' And seeing, they say 'I see.' So they don't deliberately lie for the sake of themselves or another, or for some trivial worldly reason.

Pisuṇaṁ vācaṁ pahāya pisuṇāya vācāya paṭivirato hoti, ito sutvā na amutra akkhātā imesaṁ bhedāya, amutra vā sutvā na imesaṁ akkhātā amūsaṁ bhedāya. Iti bhinnānaṁ vā sandhātā, sahitānaṁ vā anuppadātā, samaggārāmo samaggarato samagganandī samaggakaraṇiṁ vācaṁ bhāsitā hoti.

They give up divisive speech. They don't repeat in one place what they heard in another so as to divide people against each other. Instead, they reconcile those who are divided, supporting unity, delighting in harmony, loving harmony, speaking words that promote harmony.

Pharusaṁ vācaṁ pahāya pharusāya vācāya paṭivirato hoti. Yā sā vācā nelā kaṇṇasukhā pemanīyā hadayaṅgamā porī bahujanakantā bahujanamanāpā—tathārūpiṁ vācaṁ bhāsitā hoti.

They give up harsh speech. They speak in a way that's mellow, pleasing to the ear, lovely, going to the heart, polite, likable, and agreeable to the people.

Samphappalāpaṁ pahāya samphappalāpā paṭivirato hoti. Kālavādī bhūtavādī atthavādī dhammavādī vinayavādī nidhānavatiṁ vācaṁ bhāsitā hoti kālena sāpadesaṁ pariyantavatiṁ atthasaṁhitaṁ.

They give up talking nonsense. Their words are timely, true, and meaningful, in line with the teaching and training. They say things at the right time which are valuable, reasonable, succinct, and beneficial.

Evaṁ kho, gahapatayo, catubbidhaṁ vācāya dhammacariyāsamacariyā hoti.

This is how principled and moral conduct is fourfold by way of speech.

Kathañca, gahapatayo, tividhaṁ manasā dhammacariyāsamacariyā hoti?

And how is principled and moral conduct threefold by way of mind?

Idha, gahapatayo, ekacco anabhijjhālu hoti, yaṁ taṁ parassa paravittūpakaraṇaṁ taṁ nābhijjhātā hoti: 'aho vata yaṁ parassa taṁ mamassā'ti.

It's when a certain person is not covetous. They don't covet the wealth and belongings of others: 'Oh, if only their belongings were mine!'

Abyāpannacitto kho pana hoti appaduṭṭhamanasaṅkappo: 'ime sattā averā abyābajjhā anīghā sukhī attānaṁ pariharantū'ti.

They have a kind heart and loving intentions: 'May these sentient beings live free of enmity and ill will, untroubled and happy!'

Sammādiṭṭhiko kho pana hoti aviparītadassano:

They have right view, an undistorted perspective:

'atthi dinnaṁ atthi yiṭṭhaṁ atthi hutaṁ, atthi sukatadukkaṭānaṁ kammānaṁ phalaṁ vipāko, atthi ayaṁ loko atthi paro loko, atthi mātā atthi pitā, atthi sattā opapātikā, atthi loke samaṇabrāhmaṇā sammaggatā sammāpaṭipannā ye imañca lokaṁ parañca lokaṁ sayaṁ abhiññā sacchikatvā pavedentī'ti.

'There is meaning in giving, sacrifice, and offerings. There are fruits and results of good and bad deeds. There is an afterlife. There are such things as mother and father, and beings that are reborn spontaneously. And there are ascetics and brahmins who are well attained and practiced, and who describe the afterlife after realizing it with their own insight.'

Evaṁ kho, gahapatayo, tividhaṁ manasā dhammacariyāsamacariyā hoti.

This is how principled and moral conduct is threefold by way of mind.

Evaṁ dhammacariyāsamacariyāhetu kho, gahapatayo, evam'idhekacce sattā kāyassa bhedā paraṁ maraṇā sugatiṁ saggaṁ lokaṁ upapajjanti.

This is how principled and moral conduct is the reason why some sentient beings, when their body breaks up, after death, are reborn in a good place, a heavenly realm.

Ākaṅkheyya ce, gahapatayo, dhammacārī samacārī:

A person of principled and moral conduct might wish:

'aho vatāhaṁ kāyassa bhedā paraṁ maraṇā khattiyamahāsālānaṁ sahabyataṁ upapajjeyyan'ti;

'If only, when my body breaks up, after death, I would be reborn in the company of well-to-do aristocrats!'

ṭhānaṁ kho panetaṁ vijjati, yaṁ so kāyassa bhedā paraṁ maraṇā khattiyamahāsālānaṁ sahabyataṁ upapajjeyya.

It's possible that this might happen.

Taṁ kissa hetu?

Why is that?

Tathā hi so dhammacārī samacārī.

Because they have principled and moral conduct.

Ākaṅkheyya ce, gahapatayo, dhammacārī samacārī:

A person of principled and moral conduct might wish:

'aho vatāhaṃ kāyassa bhedā paraṃ maraṇā brāhmaṇamahāsālānaṃ ...pe...

'If only, when my body breaks up, after death, I would be reborn in the company of well-to-do brahmins ...

gahapatimahāsālānaṃ sahabyataṃ upapajjeyyan'ti;

well-to-do householders ...

ṭhānaṃ kho panetaṃ vijjati, yaṃ so kāyassa bhedā paraṃ maraṇā gahapatimahāsālānaṃ sahabyataṃ upapajjeyya.

Taṃ kissa hetu?

Tathā hi so dhammacārī samacārī.

Ākaṅkheyya ce, gahapatayo, dhammacārī samacārī:

'aho vatāhaṃ kāyassa bhedā paraṃ maraṇā cātumahārājikānaṃ devānaṃ sahabyataṃ upapajjeyyan'ti;

the Gods of the Four Great Kings ...

ṭhānaṃ kho panetaṃ vijjati, yaṃ so kāyassa bhedā paraṃ maraṇā cātumahārājikānaṃ devānaṃ sahabyataṃ upapajjeyya.

Taṃ kissa hetu?

Tathā hi so dhammacārī samacārī.

Ākaṅkheyya ce, gahapatayo, dhammacārī samacārī:

'aho vatāhaṃ kāyassa bhedā paraṃ maraṇā tāvatiṃsānaṃ devānaṃ ...pe...

the Gods of the Thirty-Three ...

yāmānaṃ devānaṃ ...

the Gods of Yama ...

tusitānaṃ devānaṃ ...

the Joyful Gods ...

nimmānaratīnaṃ devānaṃ ...

the Gods Who Love to Create ...

paranimmitavasavattīnaṃ devānaṃ ...

the Gods Who Control the Creations of Others ...

brahmakāyikānaṃ devānaṃ sahabyataṃ upapajjeyyan'ti;

the Gods of Brahmā's Host …

ṭhānaṁ kho panetaṁ vijjati, yaṁ so kāyassa bhedā paraṁ maraṇā brahmakāyikānaṁ devānaṁ sahabyataṁ upapajjeyya.

Taṁ kissa hetu?

Tathā hi so dhammacārī samacārī.

Ākaṅkheyya ce, gahapatayo, dhammacārī samacārī:

'aho vatāhaṁ kāyassa bhedā paraṁ maraṇā ābhānaṁ devānaṁ sahabyataṁ upapajjeyyan'ti;

the Radiant Gods …

ṭhānaṁ kho panetaṁ vijjati, yaṁ so kāyassa bhedā paraṁ maraṇā ābhānaṁ devānaṁ sahabyataṁ upapajjeyya.

Taṁ kissa hetu?

Tathā hi so dhammacārī samacārī.

Ākaṅkheyya ce, gahapatayo, dhammacārī samacārī:

'aho vatāhaṁ kāyassa bhedā paraṁ maraṇā parittābhānaṁ devānaṁ …pe…

the Gods of Limited Radiance …

appamāṇābhānaṁ devānaṁ …

the Gods of Limitless Radiance …

ābhassarānaṁ devānaṁ …

the Gods of Streaming Radiance …

parittasubhānaṁ devānaṁ …

the Gods of Limited Glory …

appamāṇasubhānaṁ devānaṁ …

the Gods of Limitless Glory …

subhakiṇhānaṁ devānaṁ …

the Gods Replete with Glory …

vehapphalānaṁ devānaṁ …

the Gods of Abundant Fruit …

avihānaṁ devānaṁ …

the Gods of Aviha …

atappānaṁ devānaṁ …

the Gods of Atappa …

sudassānaṁ devānaṁ …

the Gods Fair to See …

sudassīnaṁ devānaṁ …

the Fair Seeing Gods …

akaniṭṭhānaṁ devānaṁ …

the Gods of Akaniṭṭha …

ākāsānañcāyatanūpagānaṁ devānaṁ …

the gods of the dimension of infinite space …

viññāṇañcāyatanūpagānaṁ devānaṁ …

the gods of the dimension of infinite consciousness …

ākiñcaññāyatanūpagānaṁ devānaṁ …

the gods of the dimension of nothingness …

nevasaññānāsaññāyatanūpagānaṁ devānaṁ sahabyataṁ upapajjeyyan'ti;

the gods of the dimension of neither perception nor non-perception.'

ṭhānaṁ kho panetaṁ vijjati, yaṁ so kāyassa bhedā paraṁ maraṇā nevasaññānāsaññāyatanūpagānaṁ devānaṁ sahabyataṁ upapajjeyya.

It's possible that this might happen.

Taṁ kissa hetu?

Why is that?

Tathā hi so dhammacārī samacārī.

Because they have principled and moral conduct.

Ākaṅkheyya ce, gahapatayo, dhammacārī samacārī:

A person of principled and moral conduct might wish:

'aho vatāhaṁ āsavānaṁ khayā anāsavaṁ cetovimuttiṁ paññāvimuttiṁ diṭṭheva dhamme sayaṁ abhiññā sacchikatvā upasampajja vihareyyan'ti;

'If only I might realize the undefiled freedom of heart and freedom by wisdom in this very life, and live having realized it with my own insight due to the ending of defilements.'

ṭhānaṁ kho panetaṁ vijjati, yaṁ so āsavānaṁ khayā anāsavaṁ cetovimuttiṁ paññāvimuttiṁ diṭṭheva dhamme sayaṁ abhiññā sacchikatvā upasampajja vihareyya.

It's possible that this might happen.

Taṁ kissa hetu?

Why is that?

Tathā hi so dhammacārī samacārī"ti.

Because they have principled and moral conduct."

Evaṁ vutte, sāleyyakā brāhmaṇagahapatikā bhagavantaṁ etadavocuṁ:

When he had spoken, the brahmins and householders of Sālā said to the Buddha,

"abhikkantaṁ, bho gotama, abhikkantaṁ, bho gotama.

"Excellent, Master Gotama! Excellent!

Seyyathāpi, bho gotama, nikkujjitaṁ vā ukkujjeyya, paṭicchannaṁ vā vivareyya, mūḷhassa vā maggaṁ ācikkheyya, andhakāre vā telapajjotaṁ dhāreyya: 'cakkhumanto rūpāni dakkhantī'ti; evamevaṁ bhotā gotamena anekapariyāyena dhammo pakāsito.

As if he were righting the overturned, or revealing the hidden, or pointing out the path to the lost, or lighting a lamp in the dark so people with good eyes can see what's there, Master Gotama has made the teaching clear in many ways.

Ete mayaṁ bhavantaṁ gotamaṁ saraṇaṁ gacchāma dhammañca bhikkhusaṅghañca.

We go for refuge to Master Gotama, to the teaching, and to the mendicant Saṅgha.

Upāsake no bhavaṁ gotamo dhāretu ajjatagge pāṇupete saraṇaṁ gate"ti.

From this day forth, may Master Gotama remember us as lay followers who have gone for refuge for life."

Sāleyyakasuttaṁ niṭṭhitaṁ paṭhamaṁ.

42 Veranjakasutta:

The People of Veranja

Evaṁ me sutaṁ—

So I have heard.

ekaṁ samayaṁ bhagavā sāvatthiyaṁ viharati jetavane anāthapiṇḍikassa ārāme.

At one time the Buddha was staying near Sāvatthī in Jeta's Grove, Anāthapiṇḍika's monastery.

Tena kho pana samayena verañjakā brāhmaṇagahapatikā sāvatthiyaṁ paṭivasanti kenacideva karaṇīyena.

Now at that time the brahmins and householders of Verañja were residing in Sāvatthī on some business.

Assosuṁ kho verañjakā brāhmaṇagahapatikā:

The brahmins and householders of Verañja heard:

"samaṇo khalu, bho, gotamo sakyaputto sakyakulā pabbajito sāvatthiyaṁ viharati jetavane anāthapiṇḍikassa ārāme.

"It seems the ascetic Gotama—a Sakyan, gone forth from a Sakyan family—is staying near Sāvatthī in Jeta's Grove, Anāthapiṇḍika's monastery.

Taṁ kho pana bhavantaṁ gotamaṁ evaṁ kalyāṇo kittisaddo abbhuggato:

He has this good reputation ..." ...

'itipi so bhagavā arahaṁ sammāsambuddho vijjācaraṇasampanno sugato lokavidū anuttaro purisadammasārathi satthā devamanussānaṁ buddho bhagavā'.

So imaṁ lokaṁ sadevakaṁ samārakaṁ sabrahmakaṁ sassamaṇabrāhmaṇiṁ pajaṁ sadevamanussaṁ sayaṁ abhiññā sacchikatvā pavedeti.

So dhammaṁ deseti ādikalyāṇaṁ majjhekalyāṇaṁ pariyosānakalyāṇaṁ sātthaṁ sabyañjanaṁ; kevalaparipuṇṇaṁ parisuddhaṁ brahmacariyaṁ pakāseti.

Sādhu kho pana tathārūpānaṁ arahataṁ dassanaṁ hotī"ti.

Atha kho verañjakā brāhmaṇagahapatikā yena bhagavā tenupasaṅkamiṁsu; upasaṅkamitvā appekacce bhagavantaṁ abhivādetvā ekamantaṁ nisīdiṁsu; appekacce bhagavatā saddhiṁ sammodiṁsu, sammodanīyaṁ kathaṁ sāraṇīyaṁ vītisāretvā ekamantaṁ nisīdiṁsu; appekacce yena bhagavā tenañjaliṁ paṇāmetvā ekamantaṁ nisīdiṁsu; appekacce bhagavato santike nāmagottaṁ sāvetvā ekamantaṁ nisīdiṁsu; appekacce tuṇhībhūtā ekamantaṁ nisīdiṁsu. Ekamantaṁ nisinnā kho verañjakā brāhmaṇagahapatikā bhagavantaṁ etadavocuṁ:

"ko nu kho, bho gotama, hetu, ko paccayo yena m'idhekacce sattā kāyassa bhedā paraṁ maraṇā apāyaṁ duggatiṁ vinipātaṁ nirayaṁ upapajjanti?

Ko pana, bho gotama, hetu, ko paccayo yena m'idhekacce sattā kāyassa bhedā paraṁ maraṇā sugatiṁ saggaṁ lokaṁ upapajjantī"ti?

"Adhammacariyāvisamacariyāhetu kho, gahapatayo, evam'idhekacce sattā kāyassa bhedā paraṁ maraṇā apāyaṁ duggatiṁ vinipātaṁ nirayaṁ upapajjanti.

Dhammacariyāsamacariyāhetu kho, gahapatayo, evam'idhekacce sattā kāyassa bhedā paraṁ maraṇā sugatiṁ saggaṁ lokaṁ upapajjantī"ti.

"Na kho mayaṁ imassa bhoto gotamassa saṅkhittena bhāsitassa, vitthārena atthaṁ avibhattassa, vitthārena atthaṁ ājānāma.

Sādhu no bhavaṁ gotamo tathā dhammaṁ desetu yathā mayaṁ imassa bhoto gotamassa saṅkhittena bhāsitassa, vitthārena atthaṁ avibhattassa, vitthārena atthaṁ ājāneyyāmā"ti.

"Tena hi, gahapatayo, suṇātha sādhukaṁ manasi karotha, bhāsissāmī"ti.

"Evaṁ, bho"ti kho verañjakā brāhmaṇagahapatikā bhagavato paccassosuṁ.

Bhagavā etadavoca:

"Tividhaṁ kho, gahapatayo, kāyena adhammacārī visamacārī hoti, catubbidhaṁ vācāya adhammacārī visamacārī hoti, tividhaṁ manasā adhammacārī visamacārī hoti.

"Householders, a person of unprincipled and immoral conduct is threefold by way of body, fourfold by way of speech, and threefold by way of mind. ..." ...

Kathañca, gahapatayo, tividhaṁ kāyena adhammacārī visamacārī hoti?

(The remainder of this discourse is identical with MN 41.)

Idha, gahapatayo, ekacco pāṇātipātī hoti. Luddo lohitapāṇi hatappahate niviṭṭho adayāpanno pāṇabhūtesu.

Adinnādāyī kho pana hoti. Yaṁ taṁ parassa paravittūpakaraṇaṁ ... taṁ adinnaṁ theyyasaṅkhātaṁ ādātā hoti.

Kāmesumicchācārī kho pana hoti. Yā tā māturakkhitā ... tathārūpāsu cārittaṁ āpajjitā hoti.

Evaṁ kho, gahapatayo, tividhaṁ kāyena adhammacārī visamacārī hoti.

Kathañca, gahapatayo, catubbidhaṁ vācāya adhammacārī visamacārī hoti?

Idha, gahapatayo, ekacco musāvādī hoti. Sabhāgato vā ... sampajānamusā bhāsitā hoti.

Pisuṇavāco kho pana hoti. Ito sutvā amutra akkhātā … vaggakaraṇiṁ vācaṁ bhāsitā hoti.

Pharusavāco kho pana hoti. Yā sā vācā aṇḍakā kakkasā … tathārūpiṁ vācaṁ bhāsitā hoti.

Samphappalāpī kho pana hoti. Akālavādī … apariyantavatiṁ anatthasaṁhitaṁ.

Evaṁ kho, gahapatayo, catubbidhaṁ vācāya adhammacārī visamacārī hoti.

Kathañca, gahapatayo, tividhaṁ manasā adhammacārī visamacārī hoti?

Idha, gahapatayo, ekacco abhijjhālu hoti …pe… taṁ mamassā'ti.

Byāpannacitto kho pana hoti paduṭṭhamanasaṅkappo: 'ime sattā haññantu vā … mā vā ahesun'ti.

Micchādiṭṭhiko kho pana hoti viparītadassano:

'natthi dinnaṁ, natthi yiṭṭhaṁ … sacchikatvā pavedentī'ti.

Evaṁ kho, gahapatayo, tividhaṁ manasā adhammacārī visamacārī hoti.

Evaṁ adhammacariyāvisamacariyāhetu kho, gahapatayo, evam'idhekacce sattā kāyassa bhedā paraṁ maraṇā apāyaṁ duggatiṁ vinipātaṁ nirayaṁ upapajjanti.

Tividhaṁ kho, gahapatayo, kāyena dhammacārī samacārī hoti, catubbidhaṁ vācāya dhammacārī samacārī hoti, tividhaṁ manasā dhammacārī samacārī hoti.

Kathañca, gahapatayo, tividhaṁ kāyena dhammacārī samacārī hoti?

Idha, gahapatayo, ekacco pāṇātipātaṁ pahāya pāṇātipātā paṭivirato hoti, nihitadaṇḍo nihitasattho lajjī dayāpanno sabbapāṇabhūtahitānukampī viharati.

Adinnādānaṁ pahāya adinnādānā paṭivirato hoti, yaṁ taṁ parassa … taṁ nādinnaṁ theyyasaṅkhātaṁ ādātā hoti.

Kāmesumicchācāraṁ pahāya … tathārūpāsu na cārittaṁ āpajjitā hoti.

Evaṁ kho, gahapatayo, tividhaṁ kāyena dhammacārī samacārī hoti.

Kathañca, gahapatayo, catubbidhaṁ vācāya dhammacārī samacārī hoti?

Idha, gahapatayo, ekacco musāvādaṁ pahāya musāvādā paṭivirato hoti. Sabhāgato vā …pe… na sampajānamusā bhāsitā hoti.

Pisuṇaṁ vācaṁ pahāya … samaggakaraṇiṁ vācaṁ bhāsitā hoti.

Pharusaṁ vācaṁ pahāya … tathārūpaṁ vācaṁ bhāsitā hoti.

Samphappalāpaṁ pahāya ... kālena sāpadesaṁ pariyantavatiṁ atthasaṁhitaṁ.

Evaṁ kho, gahapatayo, catubbidhaṁ vācāya dhammacārī samacārī hoti.

Kathañca, gahapatayo, tividhaṁ manasā dhammacārī samacārī hoti?

Idha, gahapatayo, ekacco anabhijjhālu hoti. Yaṁ taṁ parassa paravittūpakaraṇaṁ taṁ nābhijjhātā hoti: 'aho vata yaṁ parassa, taṁ mamassā'ti.

Abyāpannacitto kho pana hoti appaduṭṭhamanasaṅkappo: 'ime sattā averā abyābajjhā anīghā sukhī attānaṁ pariharantū'ti.

Sammādiṭṭhiko kho pana hoti aviparītadassano:

'atthi dinnaṁ, atthi yiṭṭhaṁ ... sayaṁ abhiññā sacchikatvā pavedentī'ti.

Evaṁ kho, gahapatayo, tividhaṁ manasā dhammacārī samacārī hoti.

Evaṁ dhammacariyāsamacariyāhetu kho, gahapatayo, evam'idhekacce sattā kāyassa bhedā paraṁ maraṇā sugatiṁ saggaṁ lokaṁ upapajjanti.

Ākaṅkheyya ce, gahapatayo, dhammacārī samacārī:

'aho vatāhaṁ kāyassa bhedā paraṁ maraṇā khattiyamahāsālānaṁ sahabyataṁ upapajjeyyan'ti;

ṭhānaṁ kho panetaṁ vijjati, yaṁ so kāyassa bhedā paraṁ maraṇā khattiyamahāsālānaṁ sahabyataṁ upapajjeyya.

Taṁ kissa hetu?

Tathā hi so dhammacārī samacārī.

Ākaṅkheyya ce, gahapatayo, dhammacārī samacārī:

'aho vatāhaṁ kāyassa bhedā paraṁ maraṇā brāhmaṇamahāsālānaṁ ...pe...

gahapatimahāsālānaṁ sahabyataṁ upapajjeyyan'ti;

ṭhānaṁ kho panetaṁ vijjati, yaṁ so kāyassa bhedā paraṁ maraṇā gahapatimahāsālānaṁ sahabyataṁ upapajjeyya.

Taṁ kissa hetu?

Tathā hi so dhammacārī samacārī.

Ākaṅkheyya ce, gahapatayo, dhammacārī samacārī:

'aho vatāhaṁ kāyassa bhedā paraṁ maraṇā cātumahārājikānaṁ devānaṁ sahabyataṁ upapajjeyyan'ti;

ṭhānaṁ kho panetaṁ vijjati, yaṁ so kāyassa bhedā paraṁ maraṇā catumahārājikānam devānam sahabyatam upapajjeyya.

Tam kissa hetu?

Tathā hi so dhammacārī samacārī.

Ākaṅkheyya ce, gahapatayo, dhammacārī samacārī:

'aho vatāham kāyassa bhedā param maraṇā tāvatimsānam devānam …

yāmānam devānam …

tusitānam devānam …

nimmānaratīnam devānam …

paranimmitavasavattīnam devānam …

brahmakāyikānam devānam sahabyatam upapajjeyyan'ti;

ṭhānam kho panetam vijjati, yam so kāyassa bhedā param maraṇā brahmakāyikānam devānam sahabyatam upapajjeyya.

Tam kissa hetu?

Tathā hi so dhammacārī samacārī.

Ākaṅkheyya ce, gahapatayo, dhammacārī samacārī:

'aho vatāham kāyassa bhedā param maraṇā ābhānam devānam sahabyatam upapajjeyyan'ti;

ṭhānam kho panetam vijjati, yam so kāyassa bhedā param maraṇā ābhānam devānam sahabyatam upapajjeyya.

Tam kissa hetu?

Tathā hi so dhammacārī samacārī.

Ākaṅkheyya ce, gahapatayo, dhammacārī samacārī:

'aho vatāham kāyassa bhedā param maraṇā parittābhānam devānam …pe…

appamāṇābhānam devānam …

ābhassarānam devānam …

parittasubhānam devānam …

appamāṇasubhānam devānam …

subhakiṇhānam devānam …

vehapphalānaṁ devānaṁ …

avihānaṁ devānaṁ …

atappānaṁ devānaṁ …

sudassānaṁ devānaṁ …

sudassīnaṁ devānaṁ …

akaniṭṭhānaṁ devānaṁ …

ākāsānañcāyatanūpagānaṁ devānaṁ …

viññāṇañcāyatanūpagānaṁ devānaṁ …

ākiñcaññāyatanūpagānaṁ devānaṁ …

nevasaññānāsaññāyatanūpagānaṁ devānaṁ sahabyataṁ upapajjeyyan’ti;

ṭhānaṁ kho panetaṁ vijjati, yaṁ so kāyassa bhedā paraṁ maraṇā nevasaññānāsaññāyatanūpagānaṁ devānaṁ sahabyataṁ upapajjeyya.

Taṁ kissa hetu?

Tathā hi so dhammacārī samacārī.

Ākaṅkheyya ce, gahapatayo, dhammacārī samacārī:

‘aho vatāhaṁ āsavānaṁ khayā anāsavaṁ cetovimuttiṁ paññāvimuttiṁ diṭṭheva dhamme sayaṁ abhiññā sacchikatvā upasampajja vihareyyan’ti;

ṭhānaṁ kho panetaṁ vijjati, ‘yaṁ so āsavānaṁ khayā anāsavaṁ cetovimuttiṁ paññāvimuttiṁ diṭṭheva dhamme sayaṁ abhiññā sacchikatvā upasampajja vihareyya.

Taṁ kissa hetu?

Tathā hi so dhammacārī samacārī’”ti.

Evaṁ vutte, verañjakā brāhmaṇagahapatikā bhagavantaṁ etadavocuṁ:

“abhikkantaṁ, bho gotama, abhikkantaṁ, bho gotama.

Seyyathāpi, bho gotama, nikkujjitaṁ vā ukkujjeyya, paṭicchannaṁ vā vivareyya, mūḷhassa vā maggaṁ ācikkheyya, andhakāre vā telapajjotaṁ dhāreyya: ‘cakkhumanto rūpāni dakkhantī’ti; evamevaṁ bhotā gotamena anekapariyāyena dhammo pakāsito.

Ete mayaṁ bhavantaṁ gotamaṁ saraṇaṁ gacchāma dhammañca bhikkhusaṅghañca.

Upāsake no bhavaṁ gotamo dhāretu ajjatagge pāṇupete saraṇaṁ gate"ti.

Verañjakasuttaṁ niṭṭhitaṁ dutiyaṁ.

43 Mahavedallasutta:

The Great Classification

Evaṁ me sutaṁ—

So I have heard.

ekaṁ samayaṁ bhagavā sāvatthiyaṁ viharati jetavane anāthapiṇḍikassa ārāme.

At one time the Buddha was staying near Sāvatthī in Jeta's Grove, Anāthapiṇḍika's monastery.

Atha kho āyasmā mahākoṭṭhiko sāyanhasamayaṁ paṭisallānā vuṭṭhito yenāyasmā sāriputto tenupasaṅkami; upasaṅkamitvā āyasmatā sāriputtena saddhiṁ sammodi.

Then in the late afternoon, Venerable Mahākoṭṭhita came out of retreat, went to Venerable Sāriputta, and exchanged greetings with him.

Sammodanīyaṁ kathaṁ sāraṇīyaṁ vītisāretvā ekamantaṁ nisīdi. Ekamantaṁ nisinno kho āyasmā mahākoṭṭhiko āyasmantaṁ sāriputtaṁ etadavoca:

When the greetings and polite conversation were over, he sat down to one side and said to Sāriputta:

"'Duppañño duppañño'ti, āvuso, vuccati.

"Reverend, they speak of 'a witless person'.

Kittāvatā nu kho, āvuso, duppaññoti vuccatī"ti?

How is a witless person defined?"

"'Nappajānāti nappajānātī'ti kho, āvuso, tasmā duppaññoti vuccati.

"Reverend, they're called witless because they don't understand.

Kiñca nappajānāti?

And what don't they understand?

'Idaṁ dukkhan'ti nappajānāti, 'ayaṁ dukkhasamudayo'ti nappajānāti, 'ayaṁ dukkhanirodho'ti nappajānāti, 'ayaṁ dukkhanirodhagāminī paṭipadā'ti nappajānāti.

They don't understand: 'This is suffering' … 'This is the origin of suffering' … 'This is the cessation of suffering' … 'This is the practice that leads to the cessation of suffering.'

'Nappajānāti nappajānātī'ti kho, āvuso, tasmā duppaññoti vuccatī''ti.

They're called witless because they don't understand."

"Sādhāvuso''ti kho āyasmā mahākoṭṭhiko āyasmato sāriputtassa bhāsitaṁ abhinanditvā anumoditvā āyasmantaṁ sāriputtaṁ uttariṁ pañhaṁ apucchi:

Saying "Good, reverend," Mahākoṭṭhita approved and agreed with what Sāriputta said. Then he asked another question:

"'Paññavā paññavā'ti, āvuso, vuccati.

"They speak of 'a wise person'.

Kittāvatā nu kho, āvuso, paññavāti vuccatī''ti?

How is a wise person defined?"

"'Pajānāti pajānātī'ti kho, āvuso, tasmā paññavāti vuccati.

"They're called wise because they understand.

Kiñca pajānāti?

And what do they understand?

'Idaṁ dukkhan'ti pajānāti, 'ayaṁ dukkhasamudayo'ti pajānāti, 'ayaṁ dukkhanirodho'ti pajānāti, 'ayaṁ dukkhanirodhagāminī paṭipadā'ti pajānāti.

They understand: 'This is suffering' … 'This is the origin of suffering' … 'This is the cessation of suffering' … 'This is the practice that leads to the cessation of suffering.'

'Pajānāti pajānātī'ti kho, āvuso, tasmā paññavāti vuccatī''ti.

They're called wise because they understand."

"'Viññāṇaṁ viññāṇan'ti, āvuso, vuccati.

"They speak of 'consciousness'.

Kittāvatā nu kho, āvuso, viññāṇanti vuccatī''ti?

How is consciousness defined?"

"'Vijānāti vijānātī'ti kho, āvuso, tasmā viññāṇanti vuccati.

"It's called consciousness because it cognizes.

Kiñca vijānāti?

And what does it cognize?

Sukhantipi vijānāti, dukkhantipi vijānāti, adukkhamasukhantipi vijānāti.

It cognizes 'pleasure' and 'pain' and 'neutral'.

'Vijānāti vijānātī'ti kho, āvuso, tasmā viññāṇanti vuccatī"ti.

It's called consciousness because it cognizes."

"Yā cāvuso, paññā yañca viññāṇaṁ—

"Wisdom and consciousness—

ime dhammā saṁsaṭṭhā udāhu visaṁsaṭṭhā?

are these things mixed or separate?

Labbhā ca panimesaṁ dhammānaṁ vinibbhujitvā vinibbhujitvā nānākaraṇaṁ paññāpetun"ti?

And can we completely dissect them so as to describe the difference between them?"

"Yā cāvuso, paññā yañca viññāṇaṁ—

"Wisdom and consciousness—

ime dhammā saṁsaṭṭhā, no visaṁsaṭṭhā.

these things are mixed, not separate.

Na ca labbhā imesaṁ dhammānaṁ vinibbhujitvā vinibbhujitvā nānākaraṇaṁ paññāpetuṁ.

And you can never completely dissect them so as to describe the difference between them.

Yaṁ hāvuso, pajānāti taṁ vijānāti, yaṁ vijānāti taṁ pajānāti.

For you understand what you cognize, and you cognize what you understand.

Tasmā ime dhammā saṁsaṭṭhā, no visaṁsaṭṭhā.

That's why these things are mixed, not separate.

Na ca labbhā imesaṁ dhammānaṁ vinibbhujitvā vinibbhujitvā nānākaraṇaṁ paññāpetun"ti.

And you can never completely dissect them so as to describe the difference between them."

"Yā cāvuso, paññā yañca viññāṇaṁ—

"Wisdom and consciousness—

imesaṁ dhammānaṁ saṁsaṭṭhānaṁ no visaṁsaṭṭhānaṁ kiṁ nānākaraṇan"ti?

what is the difference between these things that are mixed, not separate?"

"Yā cāvuso, paññā yañca viññāṇaṁ—

imesaṁ dhammānaṁ saṁsaṭṭhānaṁ no visaṁsaṭṭhānaṁ paññā bhāvetabbā, viññāṇaṁ pariññeyyaṁ.

"The difference between these things is that wisdom should be developed, while consciousness should be completely understood."

Idaṁ nesaṁ nānākaraṇan"ti.

"'Vedanā vedanā'ti, āvuso, vuccati.

"They speak of this thing called 'feeling'.

Kittāvatā nu kho, āvuso, vedanāti vuccatī"ti?

How is feeling defined?"

"'Vedeti vedetī'ti kho, āvuso, tasmā vedanāti vuccati.

"It's called feeling because it feels.

Kiñca vedeti?

And what does it feel?

Sukhampi vedeti, dukkhampi vedeti, adukkhamasukhampi vedeti.

It feels pleasure, pain, and neutral.

'Vedeti vedetī'ti kho, āvuso, tasmā vedanāti vuccatī"ti.

It's called feeling because it feels."

"'Saññā saññā'ti, āvuso, vuccati.

"They speak of this thing called 'perception'.

Kittāvatā nu kho, āvuso, saññāti vuccatī"ti?

How is perception defined?"

"'Sañjānāti sañjānātī'ti kho, āvuso, tasmā saññāti vuccati.

"It's called perception because it perceives.

Kiñca sañjānāti?

And what does it perceive?

Nīlakampi sañjānāti, pītakampi sañjānāti, lohitakampi sañjānāti, odātampi sañjānāti.

It perceives blue, yellow, red, and white.

'Sañjānāti sañjānātī'ti kho, āvuso, tasmā saññāti vuccatī'ti.

It's called perception because it perceives."

"Yā cāvuso, vedanā yā ca saññā yañca viññāṇaṁ—

"Feeling, perception, and consciousness—

ime dhammā saṁsaṭṭhā udāhu visaṁsaṭṭhā?

are these things mixed or separate?

Labbhā ca panimesaṁ dhammānaṁ vinibbhujitvā vinibbhujitvā nānākaraṇaṁ paññāpetun"ti?

And can we completely dissect them so as to describe the difference between them?"

"Yā cāvuso, vedanā yā ca saññā yañca viññāṇaṁ—

"Feeling, perception, and consciousness—

ime dhammā saṁsaṭṭhā, no visaṁsaṭṭhā.

these things are mixed, not separate.

Na ca labbhā imesaṁ dhammānaṁ vinibbhujitvā vinibbhujitvā nānākaraṇaṁ paññāpetuṁ.

And you can never completely dissect them so as to describe the difference between them.

Yaṁ hāvuso, vedeti taṁ sañjānāti, yaṁ sañjānāti taṁ vijānāti.

For you perceive what you feel, and you cognize what you perceive.

Tasmā ime dhammā saṁsaṭṭhā no visaṁsaṭṭhā.

That's why these things are mixed, not separate.

Na ca labbhā imesaṁ dhammānaṁ vinibbhujitvā vinibbhujitvā nānākaraṇaṁ paññāpetun"ti.

And you can never completely dissect them so as to describe the difference between them."

"Nissaṭṭhena hāvuso, pañcahi indriyehi parisuddhena manoviññāṇena kiṁ neyyan"ti?

"What can be known by purified mind consciousness released from the five senses?"

"Nissaṭṭhena, āvuso, pañcahi indriyehi parisuddhena manoviññāṇena 'ananto ākāso'ti ākāsānañcāyatanaṁ neyyaṁ, 'anantaṁ viññāṇan'ti viññāṇañcāyatanaṁ neyyaṁ, 'natthi kiñcī'ti ākiñcaññāyatanaṁ neyyan"ti.

"Aware that 'space is infinite' it can know the dimension of infinite space. Aware that 'consciousness is infinite' it can know the dimension of infinite consciousness. Aware that 'there is nothing at all' it can know the dimension of nothingness."

"Neyyaṁ panāvuso, dhammaṁ kena pajānātī"ti?

"How do you understand something that can be known?"

"Neyyaṁ kho, āvuso, dhammaṁ paññācakkhunā pajānātī"ti.

"You understand something that can be known with the eye of wisdom."

"Paññā panāvuso, kimatthiyā"ti?

"What is the purpose of wisdom?"

"Paññā kho, āvuso, abhiññatthā pariññatthā pahānatthā"ti.

"The purpose of wisdom is direct knowledge, complete understanding, and giving up."

"Kati panāvuso, paccayā sammādiṭṭhiyā uppādāyā"ti?

"How many conditions are there for the arising of right view?"

"Dve kho, āvuso, paccayā sammādiṭṭhiyā uppādāya—

"There are two conditions for the arising of right view:

parato ca ghoso, yoniso ca manasikāro.

the words of another and proper attention.

Ime kho, āvuso, dve paccayā sammādiṭṭhiyā uppādāyā"ti.

These are the two conditions for the arising of right view."

"Katihi panāvuso, aṅgehi anuggahitā sammādiṭṭhi cetovimuttiphalā ca hoti cetovimuttiphalānisaṁsā ca, paññāvimuttiphalā ca hoti paññāvimuttiphalānisaṁsā cā"ti?

"When right view is supported by how many factors does it have freedom of heart and freedom by wisdom as its fruit and benefit?"

"Pañcahi kho, āvuso, aṅgehi anuggahitā sammādiṭṭhi cetovimuttiphalā ca hoti cetovimuttiphalānisaṁsā ca, paññāvimuttiphalā ca hoti paññāvimuttiphalānisaṁsā ca.

"When right view is supported by five factors it has freedom of heart and freedom by wisdom as its fruit and benefit.

Idhāvuso, sammādiṭṭhi sīlānuggahitā ca hoti, sutānuggahitā ca hoti, sākacchānuggahitā ca hoti, samathānuggahitā ca hoti, vipassanānuggahitā ca hoti.

It's when right view is supported by ethics, learning, discussion, serenity, and discernment.

Imehi kho, āvuso, pañcahaṅgehi anuggahitā sammādiṭṭhi cetovimuttiphalā ca hoti cetovimuttiphalānisaṁsā ca, paññāvimuttiphalā ca hoti paññāvimuttiphalānisaṁsā cā"ti.

When right view is supported by these five factors it has freedom of heart and freedom by wisdom as its fruit and benefit."

"Kati panāvuso, bhavā"ti?

"How many states of existence are there?"

"Tayome, āvuso, bhavā—

"Reverend, there are these three states of existence.

kāmabhavo, rūpabhavo, arūpabhavo"ti.

Existence in the sensual realm, the realm of luminous form, and the formless realm."

"Kathaṁ panāvuso, āyatiṁ punabbhavābhinibbatti hotī"ti?

"But how is there rebirth into a new state of existence in the future?"

"Avijjānīvaraṇānaṁ kho, āvuso, sattānaṁ taṇhāsaṁyojanānaṁ tatratatrābhinandanā—

"It's because of sentient beings—shrouded by ignorance and fettered by craving—chasing pleasure in various realms.

evaṁ āyatiṁ punabbhavābhinibbatti hotī"ti.

That's how there is rebirth into a new state of existence in the future."

"Kathaṁ panāvuso, āyatiṁ punabbhavābhinibbatti na hotī"ti?

"But how is there no rebirth into a new state of existence in the future?"

"Avijjāvirāgā kho, āvuso, vijjuppādā taṇhānirodhā—

"It's when ignorance fades away, knowledge arises, and craving ceases.

evaṁ āyatiṁ punabbhavābhinibbatti na hotī"ti.

That's how there is no rebirth into a new state of existence in the future."

"Katamaṁ panāvuso, pathamaṁ jhānan"ti?

"But what, reverend, is the first absorption?"

"Idhāvuso, bhikkhu vivicceva kāmehi vivicca akusalehi dhammehi savitakkaṁ savicāraṁ vivekajaṁ pītisukhaṁ paṭhamaṁ jhānaṁ upasampajja viharati—

"Reverend, it's when a mendicant, quite secluded from sensual pleasures, secluded from unskillful qualities, enters and remains in the first absorption, which has the rapture and bliss born of seclusion, while placing the mind and keeping it connected.

idaṁ vuccati, āvuso, paṭhamaṁ jhānan"ti.

This is called the first absorption."

"Paṭhamaṁ panāvuso, jhānaṁ katiaṅgikan"ti?

"But how many factors does the first absorption have?"

"Paṭhamaṁ kho, āvuso, jhānaṁ pañcaṅgikaṁ.

"The first absorption has five factors.

Idhāvuso, paṭhamaṁ jhānaṁ samāpannassa bhikkhuno vitakko ca vattati, vicāro ca pīti ca sukhañca cittekaggatā ca.

When a mendicant has entered the first absorption, placing the mind, keeping it connected, rapture, bliss, and unification of mind are present.

Paṭhamaṁ kho, āvuso, jhānaṁ evaṁ pañcaṅgikan"ti.

That's how the first absorption has five factors."

"Paṭhamaṁ panāvuso, jhānaṁ kataṅgavippahīnaṁ kataṅgasamannāgatan"ti?

"But how many factors has the first absorption given up and how many does it possess?"

"Paṭhamaṁ kho, āvuso, jhānaṁ pañcaṅgavippahīnaṁ, pañcaṅgasamannāgataṁ.

"The first absorption has given up five factors and possesses five factors.

Idhāvuso, paṭhamaṃ jhānaṃ samāpannassa bhikkhuno kāmacchando pahīno hoti, byāpādo pahīno hoti, thinamiddhaṃ pahīnaṃ hoti, uddhaccakukkuccaṃ pahīnaṃ hoti, vicikicchā pahīnā hoti;

When a mendicant has entered the first absorption, sensual desire, ill will, dullness and drowsiness, restlessness and remorse, and doubt are given up.

vitakko ca vattati, vicāro ca pīti ca sukhañca cittekaggatā ca.

Placing the mind, keeping it connected, rapture, bliss, and unification of mind are present.

Paṭhamaṃ kho, āvuso, jhānaṃ evaṃ pañcaṅgavippahīnaṃ pañcaṅgasamannāgatan"ti.

That's how the first absorption has given up five factors and possesses five factors."

"Pañcimāni, āvuso, indriyāni nānāvisayāni nānāgocarāni, na aññamaññassa gocaravisayaṃ paccanubhonti, seyyathidaṃ—

"Reverend, these five faculties have different scopes and different ranges, and don't experience each others' scope and range. That is,

cakkhundriyaṃ, sotindriyaṃ, ghānindriyaṃ, jivhindriyaṃ, kāyindriyaṃ.

the faculties of the eye, ear, nose, tongue, and body.

Imesaṃ kho, āvuso, pañcannaṃ indriyānaṃ nānāvisayānaṃ nānāgocarānaṃ, na aññamaññassa gocaravisayaṃ paccanubhontānaṃ, kiṃ paṭisaraṇaṃ, ko ca nesaṃ gocaravisayaṃ paccanubhotī"ti?

What do these five faculties, with their different scopes and ranges, have recourse to? What experiences their scopes and ranges?"

"Pañcimāni, āvuso, indriyāni nānāvisayāni nānāgocarāni, na aññamaññassa gocaravisayaṃ paccanubhonti, seyyathidaṃ—

cakkhundriyaṃ, sotindriyaṃ, ghānindriyaṃ, jivhindriyaṃ, kāyindriyaṃ.

Imesaṃ kho, āvuso, pañcannaṃ indriyānaṃ nānāvisayānaṃ nānāgocarānaṃ, na aññamaññassa gocaravisayaṃ paccanubhontānaṃ, mano paṭisaraṇaṃ, mano ca nesaṃ gocaravisayaṃ paccanubhotī"ti.

"These five faculties, with their different scopes and ranges, have recourse to the mind. And the mind experiences their scopes and ranges."

"Pañcimāni, āvuso, indriyāni, seyyathidaṃ—

cakkhundriyaṃ, sotindriyaṃ, ghānindriyaṃ, jivhindriyaṃ, kāyindriyaṃ.

Imāni kho, āvuso, pañcindriyāni kiṃ paṭicca tiṭṭhantī"ti?

"These five faculties depend on what to continue?"

"Pañcimāni, āvuso, indriyāni, seyyathidaṁ—

cakkhundriyaṁ, sotindriyaṁ, ghānindriyaṁ, jivhindriyaṁ, kāyindriyaṁ.

Imāni kho, āvuso, pañcindriyāni āyuṁ paṭicca tiṭṭhantī"ti.

"These five faculties depend on life to continue."

"Āyu panāvuso, kiṁ paṭicca tiṭṭhatī"ti?

"But what does life depend on to continue?"

"Āyu usmaṁ paṭicca tiṭṭhatī"ti.

"Life depends on warmth to continue."

"Usmā panāvuso, kiṁ paṭicca tiṭṭhatī"ti?

"But what does warmth depend on to continue?"

"Usmā āyuṁ paṭicca tiṭṭhatī"ti.

"Warmth depends on life to continue."

"Idāneva kho mayaṁ, āvuso, āyasmato sāriputtassa bhāsitaṁ evaṁ ājānāma:

"Just now I understood you to say:

'āyu usmaṁ paṭicca tiṭṭhatī'ti.

'Life depends on warmth to continue.'

Idāneva pana mayaṁ, āvuso, āyasmato sāriputtassa bhāsitaṁ evaṁ ājānāma:

But I also understood you to say:

'usmā āyuṁ paṭicca tiṭṭhatī'ti.

'Warmth depends on life to continue.'

Yathā kathaṁ panāvuso, imassa bhāsitassa attho daṭṭhabbo"ti?

How then should we see the meaning of this statement?"

"Tena hāvuso, upamaṁ te karissāmi;

"Well then, reverend, I shall give you a simile.

upamāyapidhekacce viññū purisā bhāsitassa atthaṁ ājānanti.

For by means of a simile some sensible people understand the meaning of what is said.

Seyyathāpi, āvuso, telappadīpassa jhāyato acciṁ paṭicca ābhā paññāyati, ābhaṁ paṭicca acci paññāyati;

Suppose there was an oil lamp burning. The light appears dependent on the flame, and the flame appears dependent on the light.

evameva kho, āvuso, āyu usmaṁ paṭicca tiṭṭhati, usmā āyuṁ paṭicca tiṭṭhatī"ti.

In the same way, life depends on warmth to continue, and warmth depends on life to continue."

"Teva nu kho, āvuso, āyusaṅkhārā, te vedaniyā dhammā udāhu aññe āyusaṅkhārā aññe vedaniyā dhammā"ti?

"Are the life forces the same things as the phenomena that are felt? Or are they different things?"

"Na kho, āvuso, teva āyusaṅkhārā te vedaniyā dhammā.

"The life forces are not the same things as the phenomena that are felt.

Te ca hāvuso, āyusaṅkhārā abhaviṁsu te vedaniyā dhammā, na yidaṁ saññāvedayitanirodhaṁ samāpannassa bhikkhuno vuṭṭhānaṁ paññāyetha.

For if the life forces and the phenomena that are felt were the same things, a mendicant who had attained the cessation of perception and feeling would not emerge from it.

Yasmā ca kho, āvuso, aññe āyusaṅkhārā aññe vedaniyā dhammā, tasmā saññāvedayitanirodhaṁ samāpannassa bhikkhuno vuṭṭhānaṁ paññāyatī"ti.

But because the life forces and the phenomena that are felt are different things, a mendicant who has attained the cessation of perception and feeling can emerge from it."

"Yadā nu kho, āvuso, imaṁ kāyaṁ kati dhammā jahanti; athāyaṁ kāyo ujjhito avakkhitto seti, yathā kaṭṭhaṁ acetanan"ti?

"How many things must this body lose before it lies forsaken, tossed aside like an insentient log?"

"Yadā kho, āvuso, imaṁ kāyaṁ tayo dhammā jahanti—āyu usmā ca viññāṇaṁ; athāyaṁ kāyo ujjhito avakkhitto seti, yathā kaṭṭhaṁ acetanan"ti.

"This body must lose three things before it lies forsaken, tossed aside like an insentient log: vitality, warmth, and consciousness."

"Yvāyaṁ, āvuso, mato kālaṅkato, yo cāyaṁ bhikkhu saññāvedayitanirodhaṁ samāpanno—imesaṁ kiṁ nānākaraṇan"ti?

"What's the difference between someone who has passed away and a mendicant who has attained the cessation of perception and feeling?"

"Yvāyaṁ, āvuso, mato kālaṅkato tassa kāyasaṅkhārā niruddhā paṭippassaddhā, vacīsaṅkhārā niruddhā paṭippassaddhā, cittasaṅkhārā niruddhā paṭippassaddhā, āyu parikkhīṇo, usmā vūpasantā, indriyāni paribhinnāni.

"When someone dies, their physical, verbal, and mental processes have ceased and stilled; their vitality is spent; their warmth is dissipated; and their faculties have disintegrated.

Yo cāyaṁ bhikkhu saññāvedayitanirodhaṁ samāpanno tassapi kāyasaṅkhārā niruddhā paṭippassaddhā, vacīsaṅkhārā niruddhā paṭippassaddhā, cittasaṅkhārā niruddhā paṭippassaddhā, āyu na parikkhīṇo, usmā avūpasantā, indriyāni vippasannāni.

When a mendicant has attained the cessation of perception and feeling, their physical, verbal, and mental processes have ceased and stilled. But their vitality is not spent; their warmth is not dissipated; and their faculties are very clear.

Yvāyaṁ, āvuso, mato kālaṅkato, yo cāyaṁ bhikkhu saññāvedayitanirodhaṁ samāpanno—idaṁ nesaṁ nānākaraṇan"ti.

That's the difference between someone who has passed away and a mendicant who has attained the cessation of perception and feeling."

"Kati panāvuso, paccayā adukkhamasukhāya cetovimuttiyā samāpattiyā"ti?

"How many conditions are necessary to attain the neutral release of the heart?"

"Cattāro kho, āvuso, paccayā adukkhamasukhāya cetovimuttiyā samāpattiyā.

"Four conditions are necessary to attain the neutral release of the heart.

Idhāvuso, bhikkhu sukhassa ca pahānā dukkhassa ca pahānā pubbeva somanassadomanassānaṁ atthaṅgamā adukkhamasukhaṁ upekkhāsatipārisuddhiṁ catutthaṁ jhānaṁ upasampajja viharati.

Giving up pleasure and pain, and ending former happiness and sadness, a mendicant enters and remains in the fourth absorption, without pleasure or pain, with pure equanimity and mindfulness.

Ime kho, āvuso, cattāro paccayā adukkhamasukhāya cetovimuttiyā samāpattiyā"ti.

These four conditions are necessary to attain the neutral release of the heart."

"Kati panāvuso, paccayā animittāya cetovimuttiyā samāpattiyā"ti?

"How many conditions are necessary to attain the signless release of the heart?"

"Dve kho, āvuso, paccayā animittāya cetovimuttiyā samāpattiyā—

"Two conditions are necessary to attain the signless release of the heart:

sabbanimittānañca amanasikāro, animittāya ca dhātuyā manasikāro.

not focusing on any signs, and focusing on the signless.

Ime kho, āvuso, dve paccayā animittāya cetovimuttiyā samāpattiyā"ti.

These two conditions are necessary to attain the signless release of the heart."

"Kati panāvuso, paccayā animittāya cetovimuttiyā ṭhitiyā"ti?

"How many conditions are necessary to remain in the signless release of the heart?"

"Tayo kho, āvuso, paccayā animittāya cetovimuttiyā ṭhitiyā—

"Three conditions are necessary to remain in the signless release of the heart:

sabbanimittānañca amanasikāro, animittāya ca dhātuyā manasikāro, pubbe ca abhisaṅkhāro.

not focusing on any signs, focusing on the signless, and a previous determination.

Ime kho, āvuso, tayo paccayā animittāya cetovimuttiyā ṭhitiyā"ti.

These three conditions are necessary to remain in the signless release of the heart."

"Kati panāvuso, paccayā animittāya cetovimuttiyā vuṭṭhānāyā"ti?

"How many conditions are necessary to emerge from the signless release of the heart?"

"Dve kho, āvuso, paccayā animittāya cetovimuttiyā vuṭṭhānāya—

"Two conditions are necessary to emerge from the signless release of the heart:

sabbanimittānañca manasikāro, animittāya ca dhātuyā amanasikāro.

focusing on all signs, and not focusing on the signless.

Ime kho, āvuso, dve paccayā animittāya cetovimuttiyā vuṭṭhānāyā"ti.

These two conditions are necessary to emerge from the signless release of the heart."

"Yā cāyaṁ, āvuso, appamāṇā cetovimutti, yā ca ākiñcaññā cetovimutti, yā ca suññatā cetovimutti, yā ca animittā cetovimutti—ime dhammā nānātthā ceva nānābyañjanā ca udāhu ekatthā byañjanameva nānan"ti?

"The limitless release of the heart, and the release of the heart through nothingness, and the release of the heart through emptiness, and the signless release of the heart: do these things differ in both meaning and phrasing? Or do they mean the same thing, and differ only in the phrasing?"

"Yā cāyaṁ, āvuso, appamāṇā cetovimutti, yā ca ākiñcaññā cetovimutti, yā ca suññatā cetovimutti, yā ca animittā cetovimutti—atthi kho, āvuso, pariyāyo yaṁ pariyāyaṁ āgamma ime dhammā nānātthā ceva nānābyañjanā ca;

"There is a way in which these things differ in both meaning and phrasing.

atthi ca kho, āvuso, pariyāyo yaṁ pariyāyaṁ āgamma ime dhammā ekatthā, byañjanameva nānaṁ.

But there's also a way in which they mean the same thing, and differ only in the phrasing.

Katamo cāvuso, pariyāyo yaṁ pariyāyaṁ āgamma ime dhammā nānātthā ceva nānābyañjanā ca?

And what's the way in which these things differ in both meaning and phrasing?

Idhāvuso, bhikkhu mettāsahagatena cetasā ekaṁ disaṁ pharitvā viharati, tathā dutiyaṁ, tathā tatiyaṁ, tathā catutthaṁ. Iti uddhamadho tiriyaṁ sabbadhi sabbattatāya sabbāvantaṁ lokaṁ mettāsahagatena cetasā vipulena mahaggatena appamāṇena averena abyābajjhena pharitvā viharati.

Firstly, a mendicant meditates spreading a heart full of love to one direction, and to the second, and to the third, and to the fourth. In the same way above, below, across, everywhere, all around, they spread a heart full of love to the whole world—abundant, expansive, limitless, free of enmity and ill will.

Karuṇāsahagatena cetasā …pe…

They meditate spreading a heart full of compassion …

muditāsahagatena cetasā …

They meditate spreading a heart full of rejoicing …

upekkhāsahagatena cetasā ekaṁ disaṁ pharitvā viharati, tathā dutiyaṁ, tathā tatiyaṁ, tathā catutthaṁ. Iti uddhamadho tiriyaṁ sabbadhi sabbattatāya sabbāvantaṁ lokaṁ upekkhāsahagatena cetasā vipulena mahaggatena appamāṇena averena abyābajjhena pharitvā viharati.

They meditate spreading a heart full of equanimity to one direction, and to the second, and to the third, and to the fourth. In the same way above, below, across, everywhere, all around, they spread a heart full of equanimity to the whole world—abundant, expansive, limitless, free of enmity and ill will.

Ayaṁ vuccatāvuso, appamāṇā cetovimutti.

This is called the limitless release of the heart.

Katamā cāvuso, ākiñcaññā cetovimutti?

And what is the release of the heart through nothingness?

Idhāvuso, bhikkhu sabbaso viññāṇañcāyatanaṁ samatikkamma natthi kiñcīti ākiñcaññāyatanaṁ upasampajja viharati.

It's when a mendicant, going totally beyond the dimension of infinite consciousness, aware that 'there is nothing at all', enters and remains in the dimension of nothingness.

Ayaṁ vuccatāvuso, ākiñcaññā cetovimutti.

This is called the heart's release through nothingness.

Katamā cāvuso, suññatā cetovimutti?

And what is the release of the heart through emptiness?

Idhāvuso, bhikkhu araññagato vā rukkhamūlagato vā suññāgāragato vā iti paṭisañcikkhati:

It's when a mendicant has gone to a wilderness, or to the root of a tree, or to an empty hut, and reflects like this:

'suññamidaṁ attena vā attaniyena vā'ti.

'This is empty of a self or what belongs to a self.'

Ayaṁ vuccatāvuso, suññatā cetovimutti.

This is called the release of the heart through emptiness.

Katamā cāvuso, animittā cetovimutti?

And what is the signless release of the heart?

Idhāvuso, bhikkhu sabbanimittānaṁ amanasikārā animittaṁ cetosamādhiṁ upasampajja viharati.

It's when a mendicant, not focusing on any signs, enters and remains in the signless immersion of the heart.

Ayaṁ vuccatāvuso, animittā cetovimutti.

This is called the signless release of the heart.

Ayaṁ kho, āvuso, pariyāyo yaṁ pariyāyaṁ āgamma ime dhammā nānātthā ceva nānābyañjanā ca.

This is the way in which these things differ in both meaning and phrasing.

Katamo cāvuso, pariyāyo yaṁ pariyāyaṁ āgamma ime dhammā ekatthā byañjanameva nānaṁ?

And what's the way in which they mean the same thing, and differ only in the phrasing?

Rāgo kho, āvuso, pamāṇakaraṇo, doso pamāṇakaraṇo, moho pamāṇakaraṇo.

Greed, hate, and delusion are makers of limits.

Te khīṇāsavassa bhikkhuno pahīnā ucchinnamūlā tālāvatthukatā anabhāvaṅkatā āyatiṁ anuppādadhammā.

A mendicant who has ended the defilements has given these up, cut them off at the root, made them like a palm stump, and obliterated them, so they are unable to arise in the future.

Yāvatā kho, āvuso, appamāṇā cetovimuttiyo, akuppā tāsaṁ cetovimutti aggamakkhāyati.

The unshakable release of the heart is said to be the best kind of limitless release of the heart.

Sā kho panākuppā cetovimutti suññā rāgena, suññā dosena, suññā mohena.

That unshakable release of the heart is empty of greed, hate, and delusion.

Rāgo kho, āvuso, kiñcano, doso kiñcano, moho kiñcano.

Greed is something, hate is something, and delusion is something.

Te khīṇāsavassa bhikkhuno pahīnā ucchinnamūlā tālāvatthukatā anabhāvaṅkatā āyatiṁ anuppādadhammā.

A mendicant who has ended the defilements has given these up, cut them off at the root, made them like a palm stump, and obliterated them, so they are unable to arise in the future.

Yāvatā kho, āvuso, ākiñcaññā cetovimuttiyo, akuppā tāsaṁ cetovimutti aggamakkhāyati.

The unshakable release of the heart is said to be the best kind of release of the heart through nothingness.

Sā kho panākuppā cetovimutti suññā rāgena, suññā dosena, suññā mohena.

That unshakable release of the heart is empty of greed, hate, and delusion.

Rāgo kho, āvuso, nimittakaraṇo, doso nimittakaraṇo, moho nimittakaraṇo.

Greed, hate, and delusion are makers of signs.

Te khīṇāsavassa bhikkhuno pahīnā ucchinnamūlā tālāvatthukatā anabhāvaṅkatā āyatiṁ anuppādadhammā.

A mendicant who has ended the defilements has given these up, cut them off at the root, made them like a palm stump, and obliterated them, so they are unable to arise in the future.

Yāvatā kho, āvuso, animittā cetovimuttiyo, akuppā tāsaṁ cetovimutti aggamakkhāyati.

The unshakable release of the heart is said to be the best kind of signless release of the heart.

Sā kho panākuppā cetovimutti suññā rāgena, suññā dosena, suññā mohena.

That unshakable release of the heart is empty of greed, hate, and delusion.

Ayaṁ kho, āvuso, pariyāyo yaṁ pariyāyaṁ āgamma ime dhammā ekatthā byañjanameva nānan"ti.

This is the way in which they mean the same thing, and differ only in the phrasing."

Idamavocāyasmā sāriputto.

This is what Venerable Sāriputta said.

Attamano āyasmā mahākoṭṭhiko āyasmato sāriputtassa bhāsitaṁ abhinandīti.

Satisfied, Venerable Mahākoṭṭhita was happy with what Sāriputta said.

Mahāvedallasuttaṁ niṭṭhitaṁ tatiyaṁ.

44 Culavedallasutta:

The Shorter Classification

Evaṁ me sutaṁ—

So I have heard.

ekaṁ samayaṁ bhagavā rājagahe viharati veḷuvane kalandakanivāpe.

At one time the Buddha was staying near Rājagaha, in the Bamboo Grove, the squirrels' feeding ground.

Atha kho visākho upāsako yena dhammadinnā bhikkhunī tenupasaṅkami; upasaṅkamitvā dhammadinnaṁ bhikkhuniṁ abhivādetvā ekamantaṁ nisīdi. Ekamantaṁ nisinno kho visākho upāsako dhammadinnaṁ bhikkhuniṁ etadavoca:

Then the layman Visākha went to see the nun Dhammadinnā, bowed, sat down to one side, and said to her:

"'sakkāyo sakkāyo'ti, ayye, vuccati.

"Ma'am, they speak of this thing called 'identity'.

Katamo nu kho, ayye, sakkāyo vutto bhagavatā"ti?

What is this identity that the Buddha spoke of?"

"Pañca kho ime, āvuso visākha, upādānakkhandhā sakkāyo vutto bhagavatā,

"Visākha, the Buddha said that these five grasping aggregates are identity.

seyyathidaṁ—rūpupādānakkhandho, vedanupādānakkhandho, saññupādānakkhandho, saṅkhārupādānakkhandho, viññāṇupādānakkhandho.

That is: form, feeling, perception, choices, and consciousness.

Ime kho, āvuso visākha, pañcupādānakkhandhā sakkāyo vutto bhagavatā"ti.

The Buddha said that these five grasping aggregates are identity."

"Sādhayye"ti kho visākho upāsako dhammadinnāya bhikkhuniyā bhāsitaṁ abhinanditvā anumoditvā dhammadinnaṁ bhikkhuniṁ uttariṁ pañhaṁ apucchi:

Saying "Good, ma'am," Visākha approved and agreed with what Dhammadinnā said. Then he asked another question:

"'sakkāyasamudayo sakkāyasamudayo'ti, ayye, vuccati.

"Ma'am, they speak of this thing called 'the origin of identity'.

Katamo nu kho, ayye, sakkāyasamudayo vutto bhagavatā"ti?

What is the origin of identity that the Buddha spoke of?"

"Yāyaṁ, āvuso visākha, taṇhā ponobbhavikā nandīrāgasahagatā tatratatrābhinandinī, seyyathidaṁ—

"It's the craving that leads to future lives, mixed up with relishing and greed, chasing pleasure in various realms. That is,

kāmataṇhā bhavataṇhā vibhavataṇhā;

craving for sensual pleasures, craving to continue existence, and craving to end existence.

ayaṁ kho, āvuso visākha, sakkāyasamudayo vutto bhagavatā"ti.

The Buddha said that this is the origin of identity."

"'Sakkāyanirodho sakkāyanirodho'ti, ayye, vuccati.

"Ma'am, they speak of this thing called 'the cessation of identity'.

Katamo nu kho, ayye, sakkāyanirodho vutto bhagavatā"ti?

What is the cessation of identity that the Buddha spoke of?"

"Yo kho, āvuso visākha, tassāyeva taṇhāya asesavirāganirodho cāgo paṭinissaggo mutti anālayo;

"It's the fading away and cessation of that very same craving with nothing left over; giving it away, letting it go, releasing it, and not adhering to it.

ayaṁ kho, āvuso visākha, sakkāyanirodho vutto bhagavatā"ti.

The Buddha said that this is the cessation of identity."

"'Sakkāyanirodhagāminī paṭipadā sakkāyanirodhagāminī paṭipadā'ti, ayye, vuccati.

"Ma'am, they speak of the practice that leads to the cessation of identity.

Katamā nu kho, ayye, sakkāyanirodhagāminī paṭipadā vuttā bhagavatā"ti?

What is the practice that leads to the cessation of identity that the Buddha spoke of?"

"Ayameva kho, āvuso visākha, ariyo aṭṭhaṅgiko maggo sakkāyanirodhagāminī paṭipadā vuttā bhagavatā, seyyathidaṁ—

"The practice that leads to the cessation of identity that the Buddha spoke of is simply this noble eightfold path, that is:

sammādiṭṭhi sammāsaṅkappo sammāvācā sammākammanto sammāājīvo sammāvāyāmo sammāsati sammāsamādhī"ti.

right view, right thought, right speech, right action, right livelihood, right effort, right mindfulness, and right immersion."

"Taññeva nu kho, ayye, upādānaṁ te pañcupādānakkhandhā udāhu aññatra pañcahupādānakkhandhehi upādānan"ti?

"But ma'am, is that grasping the exact same thing as the five grasping aggregates? Or is grasping one thing and the five grasping aggregates another?"

"Na kho, āvuso visākha, taññeva upādānaṁ te pañcupādānakkhandhā, nāpi aññatra pañcahupādānakkhandhehi upādānaṁ.

"That grasping is not the exact same thing as the five grasping aggregates. Nor is grasping one thing and the five grasping aggregates another.

Yo kho, āvuso visākha, pañcasu upādānakkhandhesu chandarāgo taṁ tattha upādānan"ti.

The desire and greed for the five grasping aggregates is the grasping there."

"Kathaṁ panāyye, sakkāyadiṭṭhi hotī"ti?

"But ma'am, how does identity view come about?"

"Idhāvuso visākha, assutavā puthujjano, ariyānaṁ adassāvī ariyadhammassa akovido ariyadhamme avinīto, sappurisānaṁ adassāvī sappurisadhammassa akovido sappurisadhamme avinīto,

"It's when an unlearned ordinary person has not seen the noble ones, and is neither skilled nor trained in the teaching of the noble ones. They've not seen good persons, and are neither skilled nor trained in the teaching of the good persons.

rūpaṁ attato samanupassati, rūpavantaṁ vā attānaṁ, attani vā rūpaṁ, rūpasmiṁ vā attānaṁ.

They regard form as self, self as having form, form in self, or self in form.

Vedanaṁ …pe…

They regard feeling …

saññaṁ …

perception …

saṅkhāre …

choices …

viññāṇaṁ attato samanupassati, viññāṇavantaṁ vā attānaṁ, attani vā viññāṇaṁ, viññāṇasmiṁ vā attānaṁ.

consciousness as self, self as having consciousness, consciousness in self, or self in consciousness.

Evaṁ kho, āvuso visākha, sakkāyadiṭṭhi hotī"ti.

That's how identity view comes about."

"Kathaṁ panāyye, sakkāyadiṭṭhi na hotī"ti?

"But ma'am, how does identity view not come about?"

"Idhāvuso visākha, sutavā ariyasāvako, ariyānaṁ dassāvī ariyadhammassa kovido ariyadhamme suvinīto, sappurisānaṁ dassāvī sappurisadhammassa kovido sappurisadhamme suvinīto,

"It's when a learned noble disciple has seen the noble ones, and is skilled and trained in the teaching of the noble ones. They've seen good persons, and are skilled and trained in the teaching of the good persons.

na rūpaṁ attato samanupassati, na rūpavantaṁ vā attānaṁ, na attani vā rūpaṁ, na rūpasmiṁ vā attānaṁ.

They don't regard form as self, self as having form, form in self, or self in form.

Na vedanaṁ …pe…

They don't regard feeling …

na saññaṁ …

perception …

na saṅkhāre …pe…

choices …

na viññāṇaṁ attato samanupassati, na viññāṇavantaṁ vā attānaṁ, na attani vā viññāṇaṁ, na viññāṇasmiṁ vā attānaṁ.

consciousness as self, self as having consciousness, consciousness in self, or self in consciousness.

Evaṁ kho, āvuso visākha, sakkāyadiṭṭhi na hotī"ti.

That's how identity view does not come about."

"Katamo panāyye, ariyo aṭṭhaṅgiko maggo"ti?

"But ma'am, what is the noble eightfold path?"

"Ayameva kho, āvuso visākha, ariyo aṭṭhaṅgiko maggo, seyyathidaṁ—

"It is simply this noble eightfold path, that is:

sammādiṭṭhi sammāsaṅkappo sammāvācā sammākammanto sammāājīvo sammāvāyāmo sammāsati sammāsamādhī"ti.

right view, right thought, right speech, right action, right livelihood, right effort, right mindfulness, and right immersion."

"Ariyo panāyye, aṭṭhaṅgiko maggo saṅkhato udāhu asaṅkhato"ti?

"But ma'am, is the noble eightfold path conditioned or unconditioned?"

"Ariyo kho, āvuso visākha, aṭṭhaṅgiko maggo saṅkhato"ti.

"The noble eightfold path is conditioned."

"Ariyena nu kho, ayye, aṭṭhaṅgikena maggena tayo khandhā saṅgahitā udāhu tīhi khandhehi ariyo aṭṭhaṅgiko maggo saṅgahito"ti?

"Are the three practice categories included in the noble eightfold path? Or is the noble eightfold path included in the three practice categories?"

"Na kho, āvuso visākha, ariyena aṭṭhaṅgikena maggena tayo khandhā saṅgahitā; tīhi ca kho, āvuso visākha, khandhehi ariyo aṭṭhaṅgiko maggo saṅgahito.

"The three practice categories are not included in the noble eightfold path. Rather, the noble eightfold path is included in the three practice categories.

Yā cāvuso visākha, sammāvācā yo ca sammākammanto yo ca sammāājīvo ime dhammā sīlakkhandhe saṅgahitā.

Right speech, right action, and right livelihood: these things are included in the category of ethics.

Yo ca sammāvāyāmo yā ca sammāsati yo ca sammāsamādhi ime dhammā samādhikkhandhe saṅgahitā.

Right effort, right mindfulness, and right immersion: these things are included in the category of immersion.

Yā ca sammādiṭṭhi yo ca sammāsaṅkappo, ime dhammā paññākkhandhe saṅgahitā"ti.

Right view and right thought: these things are included in the category of wisdom."

"Katamo panāyye, samādhi, katame dhammā samādhinimittā, katame dhammā samādhiparikkhārā, katamā samādhibhāvanā"ti?

"But ma'am, what is immersion? What things are the foundations of immersion? What things are the prerequisites for immersion? What is the development of immersion?"

"Yā kho, āvuso visākha, cittassa ekaggatā ayaṁ samādhi;

"Unification of the mind is immersion.

cattāro satipaṭṭhānā samādhinimittā;

The four kinds of mindfulness meditation are the foundations of immersion.

cattāro sammappadhānā samādhiparikkhārā.

The four right efforts are the prerequisites for immersion.

Yā tesaṁyeva dhammānaṁ āsevanā bhāvanā bahulīkammaṁ, ayaṁ ettha samādhibhāvanā"ti.

The cultivation, development, and making much of these very same things is the development of immersion.”

“Kati panāyye, saṅkhārā”ti?

“How many processes are there?”

“Tayome, āvuso visākha, saṅkhārā—

“There are these three processes.

kāyasaṅkhāro, vacīsaṅkhāro, cittasaṅkhāro”ti.

Physical, verbal, and mental processes.”

“Katamo panāyye, kāyasaṅkhāro, katamo vacīsaṅkhāro, katamo cittasaṅkhāro”ti?

“But ma’am, what is the physical process? What’s the verbal process? What’s the mental process?”

“Assāsapassāsā kho, āvuso visākha, kāyasaṅkhāro, vitakkavicārā vacīsaṅkhāro, saññā ca vedanā ca cittasaṅkhāro”ti.

“Breathing is a physical process. Placing the mind and keeping it connected are verbal processes. Perception and feeling are mental processes.”

“Kasmā panāyye, assāsapassāsā kāyasaṅkhāro, kasmā vitakkavicārā vacīsaṅkhāro, kasmā saññā ca vedanā ca cittasaṅkhāro”ti?

“But ma’am, why is breathing a physical process? Why are placing the mind and keeping it connected verbal processes? Why are perception and feeling mental processes?”

“Assāsapassāsā kho, āvuso visākha, kāyikā ete dhammā kāyappaṭibaddhā, tasmā assāsapassāsā kāyasaṅkhāro.

“Breathing is physical. It’s tied up with the body, that’s why breathing is a physical process.

Pubbe kho, āvuso visākha, vitakketvā vicāretvā pacchā vācaṁ bhindati, tasmā vitakkavicārā vacīsaṅkhāro.

First you place the mind and keep it connected, then you break into speech. That’s why placing the mind and keeping it connected are verbal processes.

Saññā ca vedanā ca cetasikā ete dhammā cittappaṭibaddhā, tasmā saññā ca vedanā ca cittasaṅkhāro”ti.

Perception and feeling are mental. They’re tied up with the mind, that’s why perception and feeling are mental processes.”

“Kathaṁ panāyye, saññāvedayitanirodhasamāpatti hotī”ti?

"But ma'am, how does someone attain the cessation of perception and feeling?"

"Na kho, āvuso visākha, saññāvedayitanirodhaṁ samāpajjantassa bhikkhuno evaṁ hoti:

"A mendicant who is entering such an attainment does not think:

'ahaṁ saññāvedayitanirodhaṁ samāpajjissan'ti vā, 'ahaṁ saññāvedayitanirodhaṁ samāpajjāmī'ti vā, 'ahaṁ saññāvedayitanirodhaṁ samāpanno'ti vā.

'I will enter the cessation of perception and feeling' or 'I am entering the cessation of perception and feeling' or 'I have entered the cessation of perception and feeling.'

Atha khvāssa pubbeva tathā cittaṁ bhāvitaṁ hoti yaṁ taṁ tathattāya upanetī'ti.

Rather, their mind has been previously developed so as to lead to such a state."

"Saññāvedayitanirodhaṁ samāpajjantassa panāyye, bhikkhuno katame dhammā paṭhamaṁ nirujjhanti—yadi vā kāyasaṅkhāro, yadi vā vacīsaṅkhāro, yadi vā cittasaṅkhāro"ti?

"But ma'am, which cease first for a mendicant who is entering the cessation of perception and feeling: physical, verbal, or mental processes?"

"Saññāvedayitanirodhaṁ samāpajjantassa kho, āvuso visākha, bhikkhuno paṭhamaṁ nirujjhati vacīsaṅkhāro, tato kāyasaṅkhāro, tato cittasaṅkhāro"ti.

"Verbal processes cease first, then physical, then mental."

"Kathaṁ panāyye, saññāvedayitanirodhasamāpattiyā vuṭṭhānaṁ hotī"ti?

"But ma'am, how does someone emerge from the cessation of perception and feeling?"

"Na kho, āvuso visākha, saññāvedayitanirodhasamāpattiyā vuṭṭhahantassa bhikkhuno evaṁ hoti:

"A mendicant who is emerging from such an attainment does not think:

'ahaṁ saññāvedayitanirodhasamāpattiyā vuṭṭhahissan'ti vā, 'ahaṁ saññāvedayitanirodhasamāpattiyā vuṭṭhahāmī'ti vā, 'ahaṁ saññāvedayitanirodhasamāpattiyā vuṭṭhito'ti vā.

'I will emerge from the cessation of perception and feeling' or 'I am emerging from the cessation of perception and feeling' or 'I have emerged from the cessation of perception and feeling.'

Atha khvāssa pubbeva tathā cittaṁ bhāvitaṁ hoti yaṁ taṁ tathattāya upanetī'ti.

Rather, their mind has been previously developed so as to lead to such a state."

"Saññāvedayitanirodhasamāpattiyā vuṭṭhahantassa panāyye, bhikkhuno katame dhammā paṭhamaṁ uppajjanti—yadi vā kāyasaṅkhāro, yadi vā vacīsaṅkhāro, yadi vā cittasaṅkhāro"ti?

"But ma'am, which arise first for a mendicant who is emerging from the cessation of perception and feeling: physical, verbal, or mental processes?"

"Saññāvedayitanirodhasamāpattiyā vuṭṭhahantassa kho, āvuso visākha, bhikkhuno paṭhamaṁ uppajjati cittasaṅkhāro, tato kāyasaṅkhāro, tato vacīsaṅkhāro"ti.

"Mental processes arise first, then physical, then verbal."

"Saññāvedayitanirodhasamāpattiyā vuṭṭhitaṁ panāyye, bhikkhuṁ kati phassā phusantī"ti?

"But ma'am, when a mendicant has emerged from the attainment of the cessation of perception and feeling, how many kinds of contact do they experience?"

"Saññāvedayitanirodhasamāpattiyā vuṭṭhitaṁ kho, āvuso visākha, bhikkhuṁ tayo phassā phusanti—suññato phasso, animitto phasso, appaṇihito phasso"ti.

"They experience three kinds of contact: emptiness, signless, and undirected contacts."

"Saññāvedayitanirodhasamāpattiyā vuṭṭhitassa panāyye, bhikkhuno kiṁninnaṁ cittaṁ hoti kiṁpoṇaṁ kiṁpabbhāran"ti?

"But ma'am, when a mendicant has emerged from the attainment of the cessation of perception and feeling, what does their mind slant, slope, and incline to?"

"Saññāvedayitanirodhasamāpattiyā vuṭṭhitassa kho, āvuso visākha, bhikkhuno vivekaninnaṁ cittaṁ hoti, vivekapoṇaṁ vivekapabbhāran"ti.

"Their mind slants, slopes, and inclines to seclusion."

"Kati panāyye, vedanā"ti?

"But ma'am, how many feelings are there?"

"Tisso kho imā, āvuso visākha, vedanā—

"There are three feelings:

sukhā vedanā, dukkhā vedanā, adukkhamasukhā vedanā"ti.

pleasant, painful, and neutral feeling."

"Katamā panāyye, sukhā vedanā, katamā dukkhā vedanā, katamā adukkhamasukhā vedanā"ti?

"What are these three feelings?"

"Yaṁ kho, āvuso visākha, kāyikaṁ vā cetasikaṁ vā sukhaṁ sātaṁ vedayitaṁ—

"Anything felt physically or mentally as pleasant or enjoyable.

ayaṁ sukhā vedanā.

This is pleasant feeling.

Yaṁ kho, āvuso visākha, kāyikaṁ vā cetasikaṁ vā dukkhaṁ asātaṁ vedayitaṁ—

Anything felt physically or mentally as painful or unpleasant.

ayaṁ dukkhā vedanā.

This is painful feeling.

Yaṁ kho, āvuso visākha, kāyikaṁ vā cetasikaṁ vā neva sātaṁ nāsātaṁ vedayitaṁ—

Anything felt physically or mentally as neither pleasurable nor painful.

ayaṁ adukkhamasukhā vedanā"ti.

This is neutral feeling."

"Sukhā panāyye, vedanā kiṁsukhā kiṁdukkhā, dukkhā vedanā kiṁsukhā kiṁdukkhā, adukkhamasukhā vedanā kiṁsukhā kiṁdukkhā"ti?

"What is pleasant and what is painful in each of the three feelings?"

"Sukhā kho, āvuso visākha, vedanā ṭhitisukhā vipariṇāmadukkhā;

"Pleasant feeling is pleasant when it remains and painful when it perishes.

dukkhā vedanā ṭhitidukkhā vipariṇāmasukhā;

Painful feeling is painful when it remains and pleasant when it perishes.

adukkhamasukhā vedanā ñāṇasukhā aññāṇadukkhā"ti.

Neutral feeling is pleasant when there is knowledge, and painful when there is ignorance."

"Sukhāya panāyye, vedanāya kiṁ anusayo anuseti, dukkhāya vedanāya kiṁ anusayo anuseti, adukkhamasukhāya vedanāya kiṁ anusayo anusetī"ti?

"What underlying tendencies underlie each of the three feelings?"

"Sukhāya kho, āvuso visākha, vedanāya rāgānusayo anuseti, dukkhāya vedanāya paṭighānusayo anuseti, adukkhamasukhāya vedanāya avijjānusayo anusetī"ti.

"The underlying tendency for greed underlies pleasant feeling. The underlying tendency for repulsion underlies painful feeling. The underlying tendency for ignorance underlies neutral feeling."

"Sabbāya nu kho, ayye, sukhāya vedanāya rāgānusayo anuseti, sabbāya dukkhāya vedanāya paṭighānusayo anuseti, sabbāya adukkhamasukhāya vedanāya avijjānusayo anusetī"ti?

"Do these underlying tendencies always underlie these feelings?"

"Na kho, āvuso visākha, sabbāya sukhāya vedanāya rāgānusayo anuseti, na sabbāya dukkhāya vedanāya paṭighānusayo anuseti, na sabbāya adukkhamasukhāya vedanāya avijjānusayo anusetī"ti.

"No, they do not."

"Sukhāya panāyye, vedanāya kiṁ pahātabbaṁ, dukkhāya vedanāya kiṁ pahātabbaṁ, adukkhamasukhāya vedanāya kiṁ pahātabban"ti?

"What should be given up in regard to each of these three feelings?"

"Sukhāya kho, āvuso visākha, vedanāya rāgānusayo pahātabbo, dukkhāya vedanāya paṭighānusayo pahātabbo, adukkhamasukhāya vedanāya avijjānusayo pahātabbo"ti.

"The underlying tendency to greed should be given up when it comes to pleasant feeling. The underlying tendency to repulsion should be given up when it comes to painful feeling. The underlying tendency to ignorance should be given up when it comes to neutral feeling."

"Sabbāya nu kho, ayye, sukhāya vedanāya rāgānusayo pahātabbo, sabbāya dukkhāya vedanāya paṭighānusayo pahātabbo, sabbāya adukkhamasukhāya vedanāya avijjānusayo pahātabbo"ti?

"Should these underlying tendencies be given up regarding all instances of these feelings?"

"Na kho, āvuso visākha, sabbāya sukhāya vedanāya rāgānusayo pahātabbo, na sabbāya dukkhāya vedanāya paṭighānusayo pahātabbo, na sabbāya adukkhamasukhāya vedanāya avijjānusayo pahātabbo.

"No, not in all instances.

Idhāvuso visākha, bhikkhu vivicceva kāmehi vivicca akusalehi dhammehi savitakkaṁ savicāraṁ vivekajaṁ pītisukhaṁ paṭhamaṁ jhānaṁ upasampajja viharati.

Take a mendicant who, quite secluded from sensual pleasures, secluded from unskillful qualities, enters and remains in the first absorption, which has the rapture and bliss born of seclusion, while placing the mind and keeping it connected.

Rāgaṁ tena pajahati, na tattha rāgānusayo anuseti.

With this they give up greed, and the underlying tendency to greed does not lie within that.

Idhāvuso visākha, bhikkhu iti paṭisañcikkhati:

And take a mendicant who reflects:

'kudāssu nāmāhaṁ tadāyatanaṁ upasampajja viharissāmi yadariyā etarahi āyatanaṁ upasampajja viharantī'ti?

'Oh, when will I enter and remain in the same dimension that the noble ones enter and remain in today?'

Iti anuttaresu vimokkhesu pihaṁ upaṭṭhāpayato uppajjati pihāppaccayā domanassaṁ.

Nursing such a longing for the supreme liberations gives rise to sadness due to longing.

Paṭighaṁ tena pajahati, na tattha paṭighānusayo anuseti.

With this they give up repulsion, and the underlying tendency to repulsion does not lie within that.

Idhāvuso visākha, bhikkhu sukhassa ca pahānā, dukkhassa ca pahānā, pubbeva somanassadomanassānaṁ atthaṅgamā, adukkhamasukhaṁ upekkhāsatipārisuddhiṁ catutthaṁ jhānaṁ upasampajja viharati.

Take a mendicant who, giving up pleasure and pain, and ending former happiness and sadness, enters and remains in the fourth absorption, without pleasure or pain, with pure equanimity and mindfulness.

Avijjaṁ tena pajahati, na tattha avijjānusayo anusetī"ti.

With this they give up ignorance, and the underlying tendency to ignorance does not lie within that."

"Sukhāya panāyye, vedanāya kiṁ paṭibhāgo"ti?

"But ma'am, what is the counterpart of pleasant feeling?"

"Sukhāya kho, āvuso visākha, vedanāya dukkhā vedanā paṭibhāgo"ti.

"Painful feeling."

"Dukkhāya pannāyye, vedanāya kiṁ paṭibhāgo"ti?

"What is the counterpart of painful feeling?"

"Dukkhāya kho, āvuso visākha, vedanāya sukhā vedanā paṭibhāgo"ti.

"Pleasant feeling."

"Adukkhamasukhāya panāyye, vedanāya kiṁ paṭibhāgo"ti?

"What is the counterpart of neutral feeling?"

"Adukkhamasukhāya kho, āvuso visākha, vedanāya avijjā paṭibhāgo"ti.

"Ignorance."

"Avijjāya panāyye, kiṁ paṭibhāgo"ti?

"What is the counterpart of ignorance?"

"Avijjāya kho, āvuso visākha, vijjā paṭibhāgo"ti.

"Knowledge."

"Vijjāya panāyye, kiṁ paṭibhāgo"ti?

"What is the counterpart of knowledge?"

"Vijjāya kho, āvuso visākha, vimutti paṭibhāgo"ti.

"Freedom."

"Vimuttiyā panāyye, kiṁ paṭibhāgo"ti?

"What is the counterpart of freedom?"

"Vimuttiyā kho, āvuso visākha, nibbānaṁ paṭibhāgo"ti.

"Extinguishment."

"Nibbānassa panāyye, kiṁ paṭibhāgo"ti?

"What is the counterpart of extinguishment?"

"Accayāsi, āvuso visākha, pañhaṁ, nāsakkhi pañhānaṁ pariyantaṁ gahetuṁ.

"Your question goes too far, Visākha. You couldn't figure out the limit of questions.

Nibbānogadhañhi, āvuso visākha, brahmacariyaṁ, nibbānaparāyanaṁ nibbānapariyosānaṁ.

For extinguishment is the culmination, destination, and end of the spiritual life.

Ākaṅkhamāno ca tvaṁ, āvuso visākha, bhagavantaṁ upasaṅkamitvā etamatthaṁ puccheyyāsi, yathā ca te bhagavā byākaroti tathā naṁ dhāreyyāsī"ti.

If you wish, go to the Buddha and ask him this question. You should remember it in line with his answer."

Atha kho visākho upāsako dhammadinnāya bhikkhuniyā bhāsitaṁ abhinanditvā anumoditvā uṭṭhāyāsanā dhammadinnaṁ bhikkhuniṁ abhivādetvā padakkhiṇaṁ katvā yena bhagavā tenupasaṅkami; upasaṅkamitvā bhagavantaṁ abhivādetvā ekamantaṁ nisīdi.

And then the layman Visākha approved and agreed with what the nun Dhammadinnā said. He got up from his seat, bowed, and respectfully circled her, keeping her on his right. Then he went up to the Buddha, bowed, sat down to one side,

Ekamantaṁ nisinno kho visākho upāsako yāvatako ahosi dhammadinnāya bhikkhuniyā saddhiṁ kathāsallāpo taṁ sabbaṁ bhagavato ārocesi.

and informed the Buddha of all they had discussed.

Evaṁ vutte, bhagavā visākhaṁ upāsakaṁ etadavoca:

When he had spoken, the Buddha said to him,

"paṇḍitā, visākha, dhammadinnā bhikkhunī, mahāpaññā, visākha, dhammadinnā bhikkhunī.

"The nun Dhammadinnā is astute, Visākha, she has great wisdom.

Mañcepi tvaṁ, visākha, etamatthaṁ puccheyyāsi, ahampi taṁ evamevaṁ byākareyyaṁ, yathā taṁ dhammadinnāya bhikkhuniyā byākataṁ.

If you came to me and asked this question, I would answer it in exactly the same way as the nun Dhammadinnā.

Eso cevetassa attho. Evañca naṁ dhārehī"ti.

That is what it means, and that's how you should remember it."

Idamavoca bhagavā.

That is what the Buddha said.

Attamano visākho upāsako bhagavato bhāsitaṁ abhinandīti.

Satisfied, the layman Visākha was happy with what the Buddha said.

Cūḷavedallasuttaṁ niṭṭhitaṁ catutthaṁ.

45 Culadhammasamadanasutta:

The Shorter Discourse on Taking Up Practices

Evaṁ me sutaṁ—

So I have heard.

ekaṁ samayaṁ bhagavā sāvatthiyaṁ viharati jetavane anāthapiṇḍikassa ārāme.

At one time the Buddha was staying near Sāvatthī in Jeta's Grove, Anāthapiṇḍika's monastery.

Tatra kho bhagavā bhikkhū āmantesi:

There the Buddha addressed the mendicants,

"bhikkhavo"ti.

"Mendicants!"

"Bhadante"ti te bhikkhū bhagavato paccassosuṁ.

"Venerable sir," they replied.

Bhagavā etadavoca:

The Buddha said this:

"cattārimāni, bhikkhave, dhammasamādānāni.

"Mendicants, there are these four ways of taking up practices.

Katamāni cattāri?

What four?

Atthi, bhikkhave, dhammasamādānaṁ paccuppannasukhaṁ āyatiṁ dukkhavipākaṁ;

There is a way of taking up practices that is pleasant now but results in future pain.

atthi, bhikkhave, dhammasamādānaṁ paccuppannadukkhañceva āyatiñca dukkhavipākaṁ;

There is a way of taking up practices that is painful now and results in future pain.

atthi, bhikkhave, dhammasamādānaṁ paccuppannadukkhaṁ āyatiṁ sukhavipākaṁ;

There is a way of taking up practices that is painful now but results in future pleasure.

atthi, bhikkhave, dhammasamādānaṁ paccuppannasukhañceva āyatiñca sukhavipākaṁ.

There is a way of taking up practices that is pleasant now and results in future pleasure.

Katamañca, bhikkhave, dhammasamādānaṁ paccuppannasukhaṁ āyatiṁ dukkhavipākaṁ?

And what is the way of taking up practices that is pleasant now but results in future pain?

Santi, bhikkhave, eke samaṇabrāhmaṇā evaṁvādino evaṁdiṭṭhino:

There are some ascetics and brahmins who have this doctrine and view:

'natthi kāmesu doso'ti.

'There's nothing wrong with sensual pleasures.'

Te kāmesu pātabyataṁ āpajjanti.

They throw themselves into sensual pleasures,

Te kho moḷibaddhāhi paribbājikāhi paricārenti.

cavorting with female wanderers with fancy hair-dos.

Te evamāhaṁsu:

They say,

'kiṁsu nāma te bhonto samaṇabrāhmaṇā kāmesu anāgatabhayaṁ sampassamānā kāmānaṁ pahānamāhaṁsu, kāmānaṁ pariññaṁ paññapenti?

'What future danger do those ascetics and brahmins see in sensual pleasures that they speak of giving up sensual pleasures, and advocate the complete understanding of sensual pleasures?

Sukho imissā paribbājikāya taruṇāya mudukāya lomasāya bāhāya samphasso'ti te kāmesu pātabyataṁ āpajjanti.

Pleasant is the touch of this female wanderer's arm, tender, soft, and downy!' And they throw themselves into sensual pleasures.

Te kāmesu pātabyataṁ āpajjitvā kāyassa bhedā paraṁ maraṇā apāyaṁ duggatiṁ vinipātaṁ nirayaṁ upapajjanti.

When their body breaks up, after death, they're reborn in a place of loss, a bad place, the underworld, hell.

Te tattha dukkhā tibbā kharā kaṭukā vedanā vedayanti.

And there they feel painful, sharp, severe, acute feelings.

Te evamāhaṁsu:

They say,

'idaṁ kho te bhonto samaṇabrāhmaṇā kāmesu anāgatabhayaṁ sampassamānā kāmānaṁ pahānamāhaṁsu, kāmānaṁ pariññaṁ paññapenti, ime hi mayaṁ kāmahetu kāmanidānaṁ dukkhā tibbā kharā kaṭukā vedanā vedayāmā'ti.

'This is that future danger that those ascetics and brahmins saw. For it is because of sensual pleasures that I'm feeling painful, sharp, severe, acute feelings.'

Seyyathāpi, bhikkhave, gimhānaṁ pacchime māse māluvāsipāṭikā phaleyya.

Suppose that in the last month of summer a camel's foot creeper pod were to burst open

Atha kho taṁ, bhikkhave, māluvābījaṁ aññatarasmiṁ sālamūle nipateyya.

and a seed were to fall at the root of a sal tree.

Atha kho, bhikkhave, yā tasmiṁ sāle adhivatthā devatā sā bhītā saṁviggā santāsaṁ āpajjeyya.

Then the deity haunting that sal tree would become apprehensive and nervous.

Atha kho, bhikkhave, tasmiṁ sāle adhivatthāya devatāya mittāmaccā ñātisālohitā ārāmadevatā vanadevatā rukkhadevatā osadhitiṇavanappatīsu adhivatthā devatā saṅgamma samāgamma evaṁ samassāseyyuṁ:

But their friends and colleagues, relatives and kin—deities of the parks, forests, trees, and those who haunt the herbs, grass, and big trees—would come together to reassure them,

'mā bhavaṁ bhāyi, mā bhavaṁ bhāyi;

'Do not fear, sir, do not fear!

appeva nāmetaṁ māluvābījaṁ moro vā gileyya, mago vā khādeyya, davaḍāho vā ḍaheyya, vanakammikā vā uddhareyyuṁ, upacikā vā uṭṭhaheyyuṁ, abījaṁ vā panassā'ti.

Hopefully that seed will be swallowed by a peacock, or eaten by a deer, or burnt by a forest fire, or picked up by a lumberjack, or eaten by termites, or it may not even be fertile.'

Atha kho taṁ, bhikkhave, māluvābījaṁ neva moro gileyya, na mago khādeyya, na davaḍāho ḍaheyya, na vanakammikā uddhareyyuṁ, na upacikā uṭṭhaheyyuṁ, bījañca panassa taṁ pāvussakena meghena abhippavuṭṭhaṁ sammadeva viruheyya.

But none of these things happened. And the seed was fertile, so that when the clouds soaked it with rain, it sprouted.

Sāssa māluvālatā taruṇā mudukā lomasā vilambinī, sā taṁ sālaṁ upaniseveyya.

And the creeper wound its tender, soft, and downy tendrils around that sal tree.

Atha kho, bhikkhave, tasmiṁ sāle adhivatthāya devatāya evamassa:

Then the deity thought,

'kiṁsu nāma te bhonto mittāmaccā ñātisālohitā ārāmadevatā vanadevatā rukkhadevatā osadhitiṇavanappatīsu adhivatthā devatā māluvābīje anāgatabhayaṁ sampassamānā saṅgamma samāgamma evaṁ samassāsesuṁ:

'What future danger did my friends see when they said:

"mā bhavaṁ bhāyi mā bhavaṁ bhāyi,

'Do not fear, sir, do not fear!

appeva nāmetaṁ māluvābījaṁ moro vā gileyya, mago vā khādeyya, davaḍāho vā ḍaheyya, vanakammikā vā uddhareyyuṁ, upacikā vā uṭṭhaheyyuṁ, abījaṁ vā panassā"ti;

Hopefully that seed will be swallowed by a peacock, or eaten by a deer, or burnt by a forest fire, or picked up by a lumberjack, or eaten by termites, or it may not even be fertile.'

sukho imissā māluvālatāya taruṇāya mudukāya lomasāya vilambiniyā samphasso'ti.

Pleasant is the touch of this creeper's tender, soft, and downy tendrils.'

Sā taṁ sālaṁ anuparihareyya.

Then the creeper enfolded the sal tree,

Sā taṁ sālaṁ anupariharitvā upari viṭabhiṁ kareyya.

made a canopy over it,

Upari viṭabhiṁ karitvā oghanaṁ janeyya.

draped a curtain around it,

Oghanaṁ janetvā ye tassa sālassa mahantā mahantā khandhā te padāleyya.

and split apart all the main branches.

Atha kho, bhikkhave, tasmiṁ sāle adhivatthāya devatāya evamassa:

Then the deity thought,

'idaṁ kho te bhonto mittāmaccā ñātisālohitā ārāmadevatā vanadevatā rukkhadevatā osadhitiṇavanappatīsu adhivatthā devatā māluvābīje anāgatabhayaṁ sampassamānā saṅgamma samāgamma evaṁ samassāsesuṁ:

'This is the future danger that my friends saw!

"mā bhavaṁ bhāyi mā bhavaṁ bhāyi, appeva nāmetaṁ māluvābījaṁ moro vā gileyya, mago vā khādeyya, davaḍāho vā ḍaheyya, vanakammikā vā uddhareyyuṁ, upacikā vā uṭṭhaheyyuṁ abījaṁ vā panassā"ti.

Yañcāhaṁ māluvābījahetu dukkhā tibbā kharā kaṭukā vedanā vedayāmī'ti.

It's because of that camel's foot creeper seed that I'm feeling painful, sharp, severe, acute feelings.'

Evameva kho, bhikkhave, santi eke samaṇabrāhmaṇā evaṁvādino evaṁdiṭṭhino 'natthi kāmesu doso'ti.

In the same way, there are some ascetics and brahmins who have this doctrine and view: 'There's nothing wrong with sensual pleasures' …

Te kāmesu pātabyataṁ āpajjanti.

Te moḷibaddhāhi paribbājikāhi paricārenti.

Te evamāhaṁsu:

'kiṁsu nāma te bhonto samaṇabrāhmaṇā kāmesu anāgatabhayaṁ sampassamānā kāmānaṁ pahānamāhaṁsu, kāmānaṁ pariññaṁ paññapenti?

Sukho imissā paribbājikāya taruṇāya mudukāya lomasāya bāhāya samphasso'ti.

Te kāmesu pātabyataṁ āpajjanti.

Te kāmesu pātabyataṁ āpajjitvā kāyassa bhedā paraṁ maraṇā apāyaṁ duggatiṁ vinipātaṁ nirayaṁ upapajjanti.

Te tattha dukkhā tibbā kharā kaṭukā vedanā vedayanti.

Te evamāhaṁsu:

'idaṁ kho te bhonto samaṇabrāhmaṇā kāmesu anāgatabhayaṁ sampassamānā kāmānaṁ pahānamāhaṁsu, kāmānaṁ pariññaṁ paññapenti.

Ime hi mayaṁ kāmahetu kāmanidānaṁ dukkhā tibbā kharā kaṭukā vedanā vedayāmā'ti.

Idaṁ vuccati, bhikkhave, dhammasamādānaṁ paccuppannasukhaṁ āyatiṁ dukkhavipākaṁ.

This is called the way of taking up practices that is pleasant now but results in future pain.

Katamañca, bhikkhave, dhammasamādānaṁ paccuppannadukkhañceva āyatiñca dukkhavipākaṁ?

And what is the way of taking up practices that is painful now and results in future pain?

Idha, bhikkhave, ekacco acelako hoti muttācāro hatthāpalekhano, naehibhaddantiko, natiṭṭhabhaddantiko, nābhihaṭaṁ, na uddissakataṁ, na nimantanaṁ sādiyati,

It's when someone goes naked, ignoring conventions. They lick their hands, and don't come or wait when called. They don't consent to food brought to them, or food prepared on purpose for them, or an invitation for a meal.

so na kumbhimukhā paṭigganhāti, na kaḷopimukhā paṭigganhāti, na eḷakamantaraṁ, na daṇḍamantaraṁ, na musalamantaraṁ, na dvinnaṁ bhuñjamānānaṁ, na gabbhiniyā, na pāyamānāya, na purisantaragatāya, na saṅkittīsu, na yattha sā upaṭṭhito hoti, na yattha makkhikā saṇḍasaṇḍacārinī, na macchaṁ, na maṁsaṁ, na suraṁ, na merayaṁ, na thusodakaṁ pivati.

They don't receive anything from a pot or bowl; or from someone who keeps sheep, or who has a weapon or a shovel in their home; or where a couple is eating; or where there is a woman who is pregnant, breastfeeding, or who has a man in her home; or where there's a dog waiting or flies buzzing. They accept no fish or meat or liquor or wine, and drink no beer.

So ekāgāriko vā hoti ekālopiko, dvāgāriko vā hoti dvālopiko …pe… sattāgāriko vā hoti sattālopiko.

They go to just one house for alms, taking just one mouthful, or two houses and two mouthfuls, up to seven houses and seven mouthfuls.

Ekissāpi dattiyā yāpeti, dvīhipi dattīhi yāpeti … sattahipi dattīhi yāpeti.

They feed on one saucer a day, two saucers a day, up to seven saucers a day.

Ekāhikampi āhāraṁ āhāreti, dvīhikampi āhāraṁ āhāreti … sattāhikampi āhāraṁ āhāreti. Iti evarūpaṁ addhamāsikampi pariyāyabhattabhojanānuyogamanuyutto viharati.

They eat once a day, once every second day, up to once a week, and so on, even up to once a fortnight. They live committed to the practice of eating food at set intervals.

So sākabhakkho vā hoti, sāmākabhakkho vā hoti, nīvārabhakkho vā hoti, daddulabhakkho vā hoti, haṭabhakkho vā hoti, kaṇabhakkho vā hoti, ācāmabhakkho vā hoti, piññākabhakkho vā hoti, tiṇabhakkho vā hoti, gomayabhakkho vā hoti, vanamūlaphalāhāro yāpeti pavattaphalabhojī.

They eat herbs, millet, wild rice, poor rice, water lettuce, rice bran, scum from boiling rice, sesame flour, grass, or cow dung. They survive on forest roots and fruits, or eating fallen fruit.

So sāṇānipi dhāreti, masāṇānipi dhāreti, chavadussānipi dhāreti, paṁsukūlānipi dhāreti, tirīṭānipi dhāreti, ajinampi dhāreti, ajinakkhipampi dhāreti, kusacīrampi dhāreti, vākacīrampi dhāreti, phalakacīrampi dhāreti, kesakambalampi dhāreti, vāḷakambalampi dhāreti, ulūkapakkhampi dhāreti,

They wear robes of sunn hemp, mixed hemp, corpse-wrapping cloth, rags, lodh tree bark, antelope hide (whole or in strips), kusa grass, bark, wood-chips, human hair, horse-tail hair, or owls' wings.

kesamassulocakopi hoti, kesamassulocanānuyogamanuyutto,

They tear out their hair and beard, committed to this practice.

ubbhaṭṭhakopi hoti, āsanapaṭikkhitto,

They stand forever, refusing seats.

ukkuṭikopi hoti ukkuṭikappadhānamanuyutto,

They squat, committed to persisting in the squatting position.

kaṇṭakāpassayikopi hoti, kaṇṭakāpassaye seyyaṁ kappeti,

They lie on a mat of thorns, making a mat of thorns their bed.

sāyatatiyakampi udakorohanānuyogamanuyutto viharati.

They're committed to the practice of immersion in water three times a day, including the evening.

Iti evarūpaṁ anekavihitaṁ kāyassa ātāpanaparitāpanānuyogamanuyutto viharati.

And so they live committed to practicing these various ways of mortifying and tormenting the body.

So kāyassa bhedā paraṁ maraṇā apāyaṁ duggatiṁ vinipātaṁ nirayaṁ upapajjati.

When their body breaks up, after death, they're reborn in a place of loss, a bad place, the underworld, hell.

Idaṁ vuccati, bhikkhave, dhammasamādānaṁ paccuppannadukkhañceva āyatiñca dukkhavipākaṁ.

This is called the way of taking up practices that is painful now and results in future pain.

Katamañca, bhikkhave, dhammasamādānaṁ paccuppannadukkhaṁ āyatiṁ sukhavipākaṁ?

And what is the way of taking up practices that is painful now but results in future pleasure?

Idha, bhikkhave, ekacco pakatiyā tibbarāgajātiko hoti, so abhikkhaṇaṁ rāgajaṁ dukkhaṁ domanassaṁ paṭisaṁvedeti;

It's when someone is ordinarily full of acute greed, hate, and delusion. They often feel the pain and sadness that greed, hate, and delusion bring.

pakatiyā tibbadosajātiko hoti, so abhikkhaṇaṁ dosajaṁ dukkhaṁ domanassaṁ paṭisaṁvedeti;

pakatiyā tibbamohajātiko hoti, so abhikkhaṇaṁ mohajaṁ dukkhaṁ domanassaṁ paṭisaṁvedeti.

So sahāpi dukkhena, sahāpi domanassena, assumukhopi rudamāno paripuṇṇaṁ parisuddhaṁ brahmacariyaṁ carati.

They lead the full and pure spiritual life in pain and sadness, weeping, with tearful faces.

So kāyassa bhedā paraṁ maraṇā sugatiṁ saggaṁ lokaṁ upapajjati.

When their body breaks up, after death, they're reborn in a good place, a heavenly realm.

Idaṁ vuccati, bhikkhave, dhammasamādānaṁ paccuppannadukkhaṁ āyatiṁ sukhavipākaṁ.

This is called the way of taking up practices that is painful now but results in future pleasure.

Katamañca, bhikkhave, dhammasamādānaṁ paccuppannasukhañceva āyatiñca sukhavipākaṁ?

And what is the way of taking up practices that is pleasant now and results in future pleasure?

Idha, bhikkhave, ekacco pakatiyā na tibbarāgajātiko hoti, so na abhikkhaṇaṁ rāgajaṁ dukkhaṁ domanassaṁ paṭisaṁvedeti;

It's when someone is not ordinarily full of acute greed, hate, and delusion. They rarely feel the pain and sadness that greed, hate, and delusion bring.

pakatiyā na tibbadosajātiko hoti, so na abhikkhaṇaṁ dosajaṁ dukkhaṁ domanassaṁ paṭisaṁvedeti;

pakatiyā na tibbamohajātiko hoti, so na abhikkhaṇaṁ mohajaṁ dukkhaṁ domanassaṁ paṭisaṁvedeti.

So vivicceva kāmehi vivicca akusalehi dhammehi savitakkaṁ savicāraṁ vivekajaṁ pītisukhaṁ paṭhamaṁ jhānaṁ upasampajja viharati.

Quite secluded from sensual pleasures, secluded from unskillful qualities, they enter and remain in the first absorption …

Vitakkavicārānaṁ vūpasamā ajjhattaṁ sampasādanaṁ cetaso ekodibhāvaṁ avitakkaṁ avicāraṁ samādhijaṁ pītisukhaṁ dutiyaṁ jhānaṁ …pe…

second absorption …

tatiyaṁ jhānaṁ …

third absorption …

catutthaṁ jhānaṁ upasampajja viharati.

fourth absorption.

So kāyassa bhedā paraṁ maraṇā sugatiṁ saggaṁ lokaṁ upapajjati.

When their body breaks up, after death, they're reborn in a good place, a heavenly realm.

Idaṁ vuccati, bhikkhave, dhammasamādānaṁ paccuppannasukhañceva āyatiñca sukhavipākaṁ.

This is called the way of taking up practices that is pleasant now and results in future pleasure.

Imāni kho, bhikkhave, cattāri dhammasamādānānī"ti.

These are the four ways of taking up practices."

Idamavoca bhagavā.

That is what the Buddha said.

Attamanā te bhikkhū bhagavato bhāsitaṁ abhinandunti.

Satisfied, the mendicants were happy with what the Buddha said.

Cūḷadhammasamādānasuttaṁ niṭṭhitaṁ pañcamaṁ.

46 Mahadhammasamadanasutta:

The Great Discourse on Taking Up Practices

Evaṁ me sutaṁ—

So I have heard.

ekaṁ samayaṁ bhagavā sāvatthiyaṁ viharati jetavane anāthapiṇḍikassa ārāme.

At one time the Buddha was staying near Sāvatthī in Jeta's Grove, Anāthapiṇḍika's monastery.

Tatra kho bhagavā bhikkhū āmantesi:

There the Buddha addressed the mendicants,

"bhikkhavo"ti.

"Mendicants!"

"Bhadante"ti te bhikkhū bhagavato paccassosuṁ.

"Venerable sir," they replied.

Bhagavā etadavoca:

The Buddha said this:

"yebhuyyena, bhikkhave, sattā evaṅkāmā evaṁchandā evamadhippāyā:

"Mendicants, sentient beings typically have the wish, desire, and hope:

'aho vata aniṭṭhā akantā amanāpā dhammā parihāyeyyuṁ, iṭṭhā kantā manāpā dhammā abhivaḍḍheyyun'ti.

'Oh, if only unlikable, undesirable, and disagreeable things would decrease, and likable, desirable, and agreeable things would increase!'

Tesaṁ, bhikkhave, sattānaṁ evaṅkāmānaṁ evaṁchandānaṁ evamadhippāyānaṁ aniṭṭhā akantā amanāpā dhammā abhivaḍḍhanti, iṭṭhā kantā manāpā dhammā parihāyanti.

But exactly the opposite happens to them.

Tatra tumhe, bhikkhave, kaṁ hetuṁ paccethā"ti?

What do you take to be the reason for this?"

"Bhagavammūlakā no, bhante, dhammā, bhagavaṁnettikā, bhagavaṁpaṭisaraṇā. Sādhu vata, bhante, bhagavantaññeva paṭibhātu etassa bhāsitassa attho; bhagavato sutvā bhikkhū dhāressantī"ti.

"Our teachings are rooted in the Buddha. He is our guide and our refuge. Sir, may the Buddha himself please clarify the meaning of this. The mendicants will listen and remember it."

"Tena hi, bhikkhave, suṇātha, sādhukaṁ manasi karotha, bhāsissāmī"ti.

"Well then, mendicants, listen and pay close attention, I will speak."

"Evaṁ, bhante"ti kho te bhikkhū bhagavato paccassosuṁ.

"Yes, sir," they replied.

Bhagavā etadavoca:

The Buddha said this:

"Idha, bhikkhave, assutavā puthujjano, ariyānaṁ adassāvī ariyadhammassa akovido ariyadhamme avinīto, sappurisānaṁ adassāvī sappurisadhammassa akovido sappurisadhamme avinīto,

"Take an unlearned ordinary person who has not seen the noble ones, and is neither skilled nor trained in the teaching of the noble ones. They've not seen good persons, and are neither skilled nor trained in the teaching of the good persons.

sevitabbe dhamme na jānāti asevitabbe dhamme na jānāti, bhajitabbe dhamme na jānāti abhajitabbe dhamme na jānāti.

They don't know what practices they should cultivate and foster, and what practices they shouldn't cultivate and foster.

So sevitabbe dhamme ajānanto asevitabbe dhamme ajānanto, bhajitabbe dhamme ajānanto abhajitabbe dhamme ajānanto, asevitabbe dhamme sevati sevitabbe dhamme na sevati, abhajitabbe dhamme bhajati bhajitabbe dhamme na bhajati.

So they cultivate and foster practices they shouldn't, and don't cultivate and foster practices they should.

Tassa asevitabbe dhamme sevato sevitabbe dhamme asevato, abhajitabbe dhamme bhajato bhajitabbe dhamme abhajato aniṭṭhā akantā amanāpā dhammā abhivaḍḍhanti, iṭṭhā kantā manāpā dhammā parihāyanti.

When they do so, unlikable, undesirable, and disagreeable things increase, and likable, desirable, and agreeable things decrease.

Taṁ kissa hetu?

Why is that?

Evañhetaṁ, bhikkhave, hoti yathā taṁ aviddasuno.

Because that's what it's like for someone who doesn't know.

Sutavā ca kho, bhikkhave, ariyasāvako, ariyānaṁ dassāvī ariyadhammassa kovido ariyadhamme suvinīto, sappurisānaṁ dassāvī sappurisadhammassa kovido sappurisadhamme suvinīto,

But a learned noble disciple has seen the noble ones, and is skilled and trained in the teaching of the noble ones. They've seen good persons, and are skilled and trained in the teaching of the good persons.

sevitabbe dhamme jānāti asevitabbe dhamme jānāti, bhajitabbe dhamme jānāti abhajitabbe dhamme jānāti.

They know what practices they should cultivate and foster, and what practices they shouldn't cultivate and foster.

So sevitabbe dhamme jānanto asevitabbe dhamme jānanto, bhajitabbe dhamme jānanto abhajitabbe dhamme jānanto, asevitabbe dhamme na sevati sevitabbe dhamme sevati, abhajitabbe dhamme na bhajati bhajitabbe dhamme bhajati.

So they cultivate and foster practices they should, and don't cultivate and foster practices they shouldn't.

Tassa asevitabbe dhamme asevato sevitabbe dhamme sevato, abhajitabbe dhamme abhajato bhajitabbe dhamme bhajato, aniṭṭhā akantā amanāpā dhammā parihāyanti, iṭṭhā kantā manāpā dhammā abhivaḍḍhanti.

When they do so, unlikable, undesirable, and disagreeable things decrease, and likable, desirable, and agreeable things increase.

Taṁ kissa hetu?

Why is that?

Evañhetaṁ, bhikkhave, hoti yathā taṁ viddasuno.

Because that's what it's like for someone who knows.

Cattārimāni, bhikkhave, dhammasamādānāni.

Mendicants, there are these four ways of taking up practices.

Katamāni cattāri?

What four?

Atthi, bhikkhave, dhammasamādānaṁ paccuppannadukkhañceva āyatiñca dukkhavipākaṁ;

There is a way of taking up practices that is painful now and results in future pain.

atthi, bhikkhave, dhammasamādānaṁ paccuppannasukhaṁ āyatiṁ dukkhavipākaṁ;

There is a way of taking up practices that is pleasant now but results in future pain.

atthi, bhikkhave, dhammasamādānaṁ paccuppannadukkhaṁ āyatiṁ sukhavipākaṁ;

There is a way of taking up practices that is painful now but results in future pleasure.

atthi, bhikkhave, dhammasamādānaṁ paccuppannasukhañceva āyatiñca sukhavipākaṁ.

There is a way of taking up practices that is pleasant now and results in future pleasure.

Tatra, bhikkhave, yamidaṁ dhammasamādānaṁ paccuppannadukkhañceva āyatiñca dukkhavipākaṁ, taṁ avidvā avijjāgato yathābhūtaṁ nappajānāti:

When it comes to the way of taking up practices that is painful now and results in future pain, an ignoramus, without knowing this, doesn't truly understand:

'idaṁ kho dhammasamādānaṁ paccuppannadukkhañceva āyatiñca dukkhavipākan'ti.

'This is the way of taking up practices that is painful now and results in future pain.'

Taṁ avidvā avijjāgato yathābhūtaṁ appajānanto taṁ sevati, taṁ na parivajjeti.

So instead of avoiding that practice, they cultivate it.

Tassa taṁ sevato, taṁ aparivajjayato, aniṭṭhā akantā amanāpā dhammā abhivaḍḍhanti, iṭṭhā kantā manāpā dhammā parihāyanti.

When they do so, unlikable, undesirable, and disagreeable things increase, and likable, desirable, and agreeable things decrease.

Taṁ kissa hetu?

Why is that?

Evañhetaṁ, bhikkhave, hoti yathā taṁ aviddasuno.

Because that's what it's like for someone who doesn't know.

Tatra, bhikkhave, yamidaṁ dhammasamādānaṁ paccuppannasukhaṁ āyatiṁ dukkhavipākaṁ taṁ avidvā avijjāgato yathābhūtaṁ nappajānāti:

When it comes to the way of taking up practices that is pleasant now and results in future pain, an ignoramus …

'idaṁ kho dhammasamādānaṁ paccuppannasukhaṁ āyatiṁ dukkhavipākan'ti.

Taṁ avidvā avijjāgato yathābhūtaṁ appajānanto taṁ sevati, taṁ na parivajjeti.

cultivates it …

Tassa taṁ sevato, taṁ aparivajjayato, aniṭṭhā akantā amanāpā dhammā abhivaḍḍhanti, iṭṭhā kantā manāpā dhammā parihāyanti.

and disagreeable things increase …

Taṁ kissa hetu?

Evañhetaṁ, bhikkhave, hoti yathā taṁ aviddasuno.

Tatra, bhikkhave, yamidaṁ dhammasamādānaṁ paccuppannadukkhaṁ āyatiṁ sukhavipākaṁ, taṁ avidvā avijjāgato yathābhūtaṁ nappajānāti:

When it comes to the way of taking up practices that is painful now and results in future pleasure, an ignoramus …

'idaṁ kho dhammasamādānaṁ paccuppannadukkhaṁ āyatiṁ sukhavipākan'ti.

Taṁ avidvā avijjāgato yathābhūtaṁ appajānanto taṁ na sevati, taṁ parivajjeti.

doesn't cultivate it …

Tassa taṁ asevato, taṁ parivajjayato, aniṭṭhā akantā amanāpā dhammā abhivaḍḍhanti, iṭṭhā kantā manāpā dhammā parihāyanti.

and disagreeable things increase …

Taṁ kissa hetu?

Evañhetaṁ, bhikkhave, hoti yathā taṁ aviddasuno.

Tatra, bhikkhave, yamidaṁ dhammasamādānaṁ paccuppannasukhañceva āyatiñca sukhavipākaṁ, taṁ avidvā avijjāgato yathābhūtaṁ nappajānāti:

When it comes to the way of taking up practices that is pleasant now and results in future pleasure, an ignoramus …

'idaṁ kho dhammasamādānaṁ paccuppannasukhañceva āyatiñca sukhavipākan'ti.

Taṁ avidvā avijjāgato yathābhūtaṁ appajānanto taṁ na sevati, taṁ parivajjeti.

doesn't cultivate it …

Tassa taṁ asevato, taṁ parivajjayato, aniṭṭhā akantā amanāpā dhammā abhivaḍḍhanti, iṭṭhā kantā manāpā dhammā parihāyanti.

and disagreeable things increase …

Taṁ kissa hetu?

Why is that?

Evañhetaṁ, bhikkhave, hoti yathā taṁ aviddasuno.

Because that's what it's like for someone who doesn't know.

Tatra, bhikkhave, yamidaṁ dhammasamādānaṁ paccuppannadukkhañceva āyatiñca dukkhavipākaṁ taṁ vidvā vijjāgato yathābhūtaṁ pajānāti:

When it comes to the way of taking up practices that is painful now and results in future pain, a wise person, knowing this, truly understands:

'idaṁ kho dhammasamādānaṁ paccuppannadukkhañceva āyatiñca dukkhavipākan'ti.

'This is the way of taking up practices that is painful now and results in future pain.'

Taṁ vidvā vijjāgato yathābhūtaṁ pajānanto taṁ na sevati, taṁ parivajjeti.

So instead of cultivating that practice, they avoid it.

Tassa taṁ asevato, taṁ parivajjayato, aniṭṭhā akantā amanāpā dhammā parihāyanti, iṭṭhā kantā manāpā dhammā abhivaḍḍhanti.

When they do so, unlikable, undesirable, and disagreeable things decrease, and likable, desirable, and agreeable things increase.

Taṁ kissa hetu?

Why is that?

Evañhetaṁ, bhikkhave, hoti yathā taṁ viddasuno.

Because that's what it's like for someone who knows.

Tatra, bhikkhave, yamidaṁ dhammasamādānaṁ paccuppannasukhaṁ āyatiṁ dukkhavipākaṁ taṁ vidvā vijjāgato yathābhūtaṁ pajānāti:

When it comes to the way of taking up practices that is pleasant now and results in future pain, a wise person …

'idaṁ kho dhammasamādānaṁ paccuppannasukhaṁ āyatiṁ dukkhavipākan'ti.

Taṁ vidvā vijjāgato yathābhūtaṁ pajānanto taṁ na sevati, taṁ parivajjeti.

doesn't cultivate it …

Tassa taṁ asevato, taṁ parivajjayato, aniṭṭhā akantā amanāpā dhammā parihāyanti, iṭṭhā kantā manāpā dhammā abhivaḍḍhanti.

and agreeable things increase …

Taṁ kissa hetu?

Evañhetaṁ, bhikkhave, hoti yathā taṁ viddasuno.

Tatra, bhikkhave, yamidaṁ dhammasamādānaṁ paccuppannadukkhaṁ āyatiṁ sukhavipākaṁ taṁ vidvā vijjāgato yathābhūtaṁ pajānāti:

When it comes to the way of taking up practices that is painful now and results in future pleasure, a wise person …

'idaṁ kho dhammasamādānaṁ paccuppannadukkhaṁ āyatiṁ sukhavipākan'ti.

Taṁ vidvā vijjāgato yathābhūtaṁ pajānanto taṁ sevati, taṁ na parivajjeti.

cultivates it …

Tassa taṁ sevato, taṁ aparivajjayato, aniṭṭhā akantā amanāpā dhammā parihāyanti, iṭṭhā kantā manāpā dhammā abhivaḍḍhanti.

and agreeable things increase …

Taṁ kissa hetu?

Evañhetaṁ, bhikkhave, hoti yathā taṁ viddasuno.

Tatra, bhikkhave, yamidaṁ dhammasamādānaṁ paccuppannasukhañceva āyatiñca sukhavipākaṁ taṁ vidvā vijjāgato yathābhūtaṁ pajānāti:

When it comes to the way of taking up practices that is pleasant now and results in future pleasure, a wise person, knowing this, truly understands:

'idaṁ kho dhammasamādānaṁ paccuppannasukhañceva āyatiñca sukhavipākan'ti.

'This is the way of taking up practices that is pleasant now and results in future pleasure.'

Taṁ vidvā vijjāgato yathābhūtaṁ pajānanto taṁ sevati, taṁ na parivajjeti.

So instead of avoiding that practice, they cultivate it.

Tassa taṁ sevato, taṁ aparivajjayato, aniṭṭhā akantā amanāpā dhammā parihāyanti, iṭṭhā kantā manāpā dhammā abhivaḍḍhanti.

When they do so, unlikable, undesirable, and disagreeable things decrease, and likable, desirable, and agreeable things increase.

Taṁ kissa hetu?

Why is that?

Evañhetaṁ, bhikkhave, hoti yathā taṁ viddasuno.

Because that's what it's like for someone who knows.

Katamañca, bhikkhave, dhammasamādānaṁ paccuppannadukkhañceva āyatiñca dukkhavipākaṁ?

And what is the way of taking up practices that is painful now and results in future pain?

Idha, bhikkhave, ekacco sahāpi dukkhena sahāpi domanassena pāṇātipātī hoti, pāṇātipātapaccayā ca dukkhaṁ domanassaṁ paṭisaṁvedeti;

It's when someone in pain and sadness kills living creatures, steals, and commits sexual misconduct. They use speech that's false, divisive, harsh, or nonsensical. And they're covetous, malicious, with wrong view. Because of these things they experience pain and sadness.

sahāpi dukkhena sahāpi domanassena adinnādāyī hoti, adinnādānapaccayā ca dukkhaṁ domanassaṁ paṭisaṁvedeti;

sahāpi dukkhena sahāpi domanassena kāmesu micchācārī hoti, kāmesu micchācārapaccayā ca dukkhaṁ domanassaṁ paṭisaṁvedeti;

sahāpi dukkhena sahāpi domanassena musāvādī hoti, musāvādapaccayā ca dukkhaṁ domanassaṁ paṭisaṁvedeti;

sahāpi dukkhena sahāpi domanassena pisuṇavāco hoti, pisuṇavācāpaccayā ca dukkhaṁ domanassaṁ paṭisaṁvedeti;

sahāpi dukkhena sahāpi domanassena pharusavāco hoti, pharusavācāpaccayā ca dukkhaṁ domanassaṁ paṭisaṁvedeti;

sahāpi dukkhena sahāpi domanassena samphappalāpī hoti, samphappalāpapaccayā ca dukkhaṁ domanassaṁ paṭisaṁvedeti;

sahāpi dukkhena sahāpi domanassena abhijjhālu hoti, abhijjhāpaccayā ca dukkhaṁ domanassaṁ paṭisaṁvedeti;

sahāpi dukkhena sahāpi domanassena byāpannacitto hoti, byāpādapaccayā ca dukkhaṁ domanassaṁ paṭisaṁvedeti;

sahāpi dukkhena sahāpi domanassena micchādiṭṭhi hoti, micchādiṭṭhipaccayā ca dukkhaṁ domanassaṁ paṭisaṁvedeti.

So kāyassa bhedā paraṁ maraṇā apāyaṁ duggatiṁ vinipātaṁ nirayaṁ upapajjati.

And when their body breaks up, after death, they're reborn in a place of loss, a bad place, the underworld, hell.

Idaṁ vuccati, bhikkhave, dhammasamādānaṁ paccuppannadukkhañceva āyatiñca dukkhavipākaṁ.

This is called the way of taking up practices that is painful now and results in future pain.

Katamañca, bhikkhave, dhammasamādānaṁ paccuppannasukhaṁ āyatiṁ dukkhavipākaṁ?

And what is the way of taking up practices that is pleasant now but results in future pain?

Idha, bhikkhave, ekacco sahāpi sukhena sahāpi somanassena pāṇātipātī hoti, pāṇātipātapaccayā ca sukhaṁ somanassaṁ paṭisaṁvedeti;

It's when someone with pleasure and happiness kills living creatures, steals, and commits sexual misconduct. They use speech that's false, divisive, harsh, or nonsensical. And they're covetous, malicious, with wrong view. Because of these things they experience pleasure and happiness.

sahāpi sukhena sahāpi somanassena adinnādāyī hoti, adinnādānapaccayā ca sukhaṁ somanassaṁ paṭisaṁvedeti;

sahāpi sukhena sahāpi somanassena kāmesumicchācārī hoti, kāmesumicchācārapaccayā ca sukhaṁ somanassaṁ paṭisaṁvedeti;

sahāpi sukhena sahāpi somanassena musāvādī hoti, musāvādapaccayā ca sukhaṁ somanassaṁ paṭisaṁvedeti;

sahāpi sukhena sahāpi somanassena pisuṇavāco hoti, pisuṇavācāpaccayā ca sukhaṁ somanassaṁ paṭisaṁvedeti;

sahāpi sukhena sahāpi somanassena pharusavāco hoti, pharusavācāpaccayā ca sukhaṁ somanassaṁ paṭisaṁvedeti;

sahāpi sukhena sahāpi somanassena samphappalāpī hoti, samphappalāpapaccayā ca sukhaṁ somanassaṁ paṭisaṁvedeti;

sahāpi sukhena sahāpi somanassena abhijjhālu hoti, abhijjhāpaccayā ca sukhaṁ somanassaṁ paṭisaṁvedeti;

sahāpi sukhena sahāpi somanassena byāpannacitto hoti, byāpādapaccayā ca sukhaṁ somanassaṁ paṭisaṁvedeti;

sahāpi sukhena sahāpi somanassena micchādiṭṭhi hoti, micchādiṭṭhipaccayā ca sukhaṁ somanassaṁ paṭisaṁvedeti.

So kāyassa bhedā paraṁ maraṇā apāyaṁ duggatiṁ vinipātaṁ nirayaṁ upapajjati.

But when their body breaks up, after death, they're reborn in a place of loss, a bad place, the underworld, hell.

Idaṁ vuccati, bhikkhave, dhammasamādānaṁ paccuppannasukhaṁ āyatiṁ dukkhavipākaṁ.

This is called the way of taking up practices that is pleasant now but results in future pain.

Katamañca, bhikkhave, dhammasamādānaṁ paccuppannadukkhaṁ āyatiṁ sukhavipākaṁ?

And what is the way of taking up practices that is painful now but results in future pleasure?

Idha, bhikkhave, ekacco sahāpi dukkhena sahāpi domanassena pāṇātipātā paṭivirato hoti, pāṇātipātā veramaṇīpaccayā ca dukkhaṁ domanassaṁ paṭisaṁvedeti;

It's when someone in pain and sadness doesn't kill living creatures, steal, or commit sexual misconduct. They don't use speech that's false, divisive, harsh, or nonsensical. And they're contented, kind-hearted, with right view. Because of these things they experience pain and sadness.

sahāpi dukkhena sahāpi domanassena adinnādānā paṭivirato hoti, adinnādānā veramaṇīpaccayā ca dukkhaṁ domanassaṁ paṭisaṁvedeti;

sahāpi dukkhena sahāpi domanassena kāmesumicchācārā paṭivirato hoti, kāmesumicchācārā veramaṇīpaccayā ca dukkhaṁ domanassaṁ paṭisaṁvedeti;

sahāpi dukkhena sahāpi domanassena musāvādā paṭivirato hoti, musāvādā veramaṇīpaccayā ca dukkhaṁ domanassaṁ paṭisaṁvedeti;

sahāpi dukkhena sahāpi domanassena pisuṇāya vācāya paṭivirato hoti, pisuṇāya vācāya veramaṇīpaccayā ca dukkhaṁ domanassaṁ paṭisaṁvedeti;

sahāpi dukkhena sahāpi domanassena pharusāya vācāya paṭivirato hoti, pharusāya vācāya veramaṇīpaccayā ca dukkhaṁ domanassaṁ paṭisaṁvedeti;

sahāpi dukkhena sahāpi domanassena samphappalāpā paṭivirato hoti, samphappalāpā veramaṇīpaccayā ca dukkhaṁ domanassaṁ paṭisaṁvedeti;

sahāpi dukkhena sahāpi domanassena anabhijjhālu hoti, anabhijjhāpaccayā ca dukkhaṁ domanassaṁ paṭisaṁvedeti;

sahāpi dukkhena sahāpi domanassena abyāpannacitto hoti, abyāpādapaccayā ca dukkhaṁ domanassaṁ paṭisaṁvedeti;

sahāpi dukkhena sahāpi domanassena sammādiṭṭhi hoti, sammādiṭṭhipaccayā ca dukkhaṁ domanassaṁ paṭisaṁvedeti.

So kāyassa bhedā paraṁ maraṇā sugatiṁ saggaṁ lokaṁ upapajjati.

But when their body breaks up, after death, they're reborn in a good place, a heavenly realm.

Idaṁ vuccati, bhikkhave, dhammasamādānaṁ paccuppannadukkhaṁ āyatiṁ sukhavipākaṁ.

This is called the way of taking up practices that is painful now but results in future pleasure.

Katamañca, bhikkhave, dhammasamādānaṁ paccuppannasukhañceva āyatiñca sukhavipākaṁ?

And what is the way of taking up practices that is pleasant now and results in future pleasure?

Idha, bhikkhave, ekacco sahāpi sukhena sahāpi somanassena pāṇātipātā paṭivirato hoti, pāṇātipātā veramaṇīpaccayā ca sukhaṁ somanassaṁ paṭisaṁvedeti;

It's when someone with pleasure and happiness doesn't kill living creatures, steal, or commit sexual misconduct. They don't use speech that's false, divisive, harsh, or nonsensical. And they're contented, kind-hearted, with right view. Because of these things they experience pleasure and happiness.

sahāpi sukhena sahāpi somanassena adinnādānā paṭivirato hoti, adinnādānā veramaṇīpaccayā ca sukhaṁ somanassaṁ paṭisaṁvedeti;

sahāpi sukhena sahāpi somanassena kāmesumicchācārā paṭivirato hoti, kāmesumicchācārā veramaṇīpaccayā ca sukhaṁ somanassaṁ paṭisaṁvedeti;

sahāpi sukhena sahāpi somanassena musāvādā paṭivirato hoti, musāvādā veramaṇīpaccayā ca sukhaṁ somanassaṁ paṭisaṁvedeti;

sahāpi sukhena sahāpi somanassena pisuṇāya vācāya paṭivirato hoti, pisuṇāya vācāya veramaṇīpaccayā ca sukhaṁ somanassaṁ paṭisaṁvedeti;

sahāpi sukhena sahāpi somanassena pharusāya vācāya paṭivirato hoti, pharusāya vācāya veramaṇīpaccayā ca sukhaṁ somanassaṁ paṭisaṁvedeti;

sahāpi sukhena sahāpi somanassena samphappalāpā paṭivirato hoti, samphappalāpā veramaṇīpaccayā ca sukhaṁ somanassaṁ paṭisaṁvedeti;

sahāpi sukhena sahāpi somanassena anabhijjhālu hoti, anabhijjhāpaccayā ca sukhaṁ somanassaṁ paṭisaṁvedeti;

sahāpi sukhena sahāpi somanassena abyāpannacitto hoti, abyāpādapaccayā ca sukhaṁ somanassaṁ paṭisaṁvedeti;

sahāpi sukhena sahāpi somanassena sammādiṭṭhi hoti, sammādiṭṭhipaccayā ca sukhaṁ somanassaṁ paṭisaṁvedeti.

So kāyassa bhedā paraṁ maraṇā sugatiṁ saggaṁ lokaṁ upapajjati.

And when their body breaks up, after death, they're reborn in a good place, a heavenly realm.

Idaṁ, vuccati, bhikkhave, dhammasamādānaṁ paccuppannasukhañceva āyatiñca sukhavipākaṁ.

This is called the way of taking up practices that is pleasant now and results in future pleasure.

Imāni kho, bhikkhave, cattāri dhammasamādānāni.

These are the four ways of taking up practices.

Seyyathāpi, bhikkhave, tittakālābu visena saṁsaṭṭho.

Suppose there was some bitter gourd mixed with poison.

Atha puriso āgaccheyya jīvitukāmo amaritukāmo sukhakāmo dukkhappaṭikūlo.

Then a man would come along who wants to live and doesn't want to die, who wants to be happy and recoils from pain.

Tamenaṁ evaṁ vadeyyuṁ:

They'd say to him:

'ambho purisa, ayaṁ tittakālābu visena saṁsaṭṭho,

'Here, mister, this is bitter gourd mixed with poison.

sace ākaṅkhasi piva.

Drink it if you like.

Tassa te pivato ceva nacchādessati vaṇṇenapi gandhenapi rasenapi, pivitvā ca pana maraṇaṁ vā nigacchasi maraṇamattaṁ vā dukkhan'ti.

If you drink it, the color, aroma, and flavor will be unappetizing, and it will result in death or deadly pain.'

So taṁ appaṭisaṅkhāya piveyya, nappaṭinissajjeyya.

He wouldn't reject it. Without reflection, he'd drink it.

Tassa taṁ pivato ceva nacchādeyya vaṇṇenapi gandhenapi rasenapi, pivitvā ca pana maraṇaṁ vā nigaccheyya maraṇamattaṁ vā dukkham.

The color, aroma, and flavor would be unappetizing, and it would result in death or deadly pain.

Tathūpamāhaṁ, bhikkhave, imaṁ dhammasamādānaṁ vadāmi, yamidaṁ dhammasamādānaṁ paccuppannadukkhañceva āyatiñca dukkhavipākaṁ.

This is comparable to the way of taking up practices that is painful now and results in future pain, I say.

Seyyathāpi, bhikkhave, āpānīyakaṁso vaṇṇasampanno gandhasampanno rasasampanno.

Suppose there was a bronze cup of beverage that had a nice color, aroma, and flavor.

So ca kho visena saṁsaṭṭho.

But it was mixed with poison.

Atha puriso āgaccheyya jīvitukāmo amaritukāmo sukhakāmo dukkhappaṭikūlo.

Then a man would come along who wants to live and doesn't want to die, who wants to be happy and recoils from pain.

Tamenaṁ evaṁ vadeyyuṁ:

They'd say to him:

'ambho purisa, ayaṁ āpānīyakaṁso vaṇṇasampanno gandhasampanno rasasampanno.

'Here, mister, this bronze cup of beverage has a nice color, aroma, and flavor.

So ca kho visena saṁsaṭṭho,

But it's mixed with poison.

sace ākaṅkhasi piva.

Drink it if you like.

Tassa te pivatohi kho chādessati vaṇṇenapi gandhenapi rasenapi, pivitvā ca pana maraṇaṁ vā nigacchasi maraṇamattaṁ vā dukkhan'ti.

If you drink it, the color, aroma, and flavor will be appetizing, but it will result in death or deadly pain.'

So taṁ appaṭisaṅkhāya piveyya, nappaṭinissajjeyya.

He wouldn't reject it. Without reflection, he'd drink it.

Tassa taṁ pivatohi kho chādeyya vaṇṇenapi gandhenapi rasenapi, pivitvā ca pana maraṇaṁ vā nigaccheyya maraṇamattaṁ vā dukkhaṁ.

The color, aroma, and flavor would be appetizing, but it would result in death or deadly pain.

Tathūpamāhaṁ, bhikkhave, imaṁ dhammasamādānaṁ vadāmi, yamidaṁ dhammasamādānaṁ paccuppannasukhaṁ āyatiṁ dukkhavipākaṁ.

This is comparable to the way of taking up practices that is pleasant now and results in future pain, I say.

Seyyathāpi, bhikkhave, pūtimuttaṁ nānābhesajjehi saṁsaṭṭhaṁ.

Suppose there was some fermented urine mixed with different medicines.

Atha puriso āgaccheyya paṇḍukarogī.

Then a man with jaundice would come along.

Tamenaṁ evaṁ vadeyyuṁ:

They'd say to him:

'ambho purisa, idaṁ pūtimuttaṁ nānābhesajjehi saṁsaṭṭhaṁ, sace ākaṅkhasi piva.

'Here, mister, this is fermented urine mixed with different medicines. Drink it if you like.

Tassa te pivatohi kho nacchādessati vaṇṇenapi gandhenapi rasenapi, pivitvā ca pana sukhī bhavissasī'ti.

If you drink it, the color, aroma, and flavor will be unappetizing, but after drinking it you will be happy.'

So taṁ paṭisaṅkhāya piveyya, nappaṭinissajjeyya.

He wouldn't reject it. After appraisal, he'd drink it.

Tassa taṁ pivatohi kho nacchādeyya vaṇṇenapi gandhenapi rasenapi, pivitvā ca pana sukhī assa.

The color, aroma, and flavor would be unappetizing, but after drinking it he would be happy.

Tathūpamāhaṁ, bhikkhave, imaṁ dhammasamādānaṁ vadāmi, yamidaṁ dhammasamādānaṁ paccuppannadukkhaṁ āyatiṁ sukhavipākaṁ.

This is comparable to the way of taking up practices that is painful now and results in future pleasure, I say.

Seyyathāpi, bhikkhave, dadhi ca madhu ca sappi ca phāṇitañca ekajjhaṁ saṁsaṭṭhaṁ.

Suppose there was some curds, honey, ghee, and molasses all mixed together.

Atha puriso āgaccheyya lohitapakkhandiko.

Then a man with bloody dysentery would come along.

Tamenaṁ evaṁ vadeyyuṁ:

They'd say to him:

'ambho purisa, idaṁ dadhi ca madhu ca sappi ca phāṇitañca ekajjhaṁ saṁsaṭṭhaṁ, sace ākaṅkhasi piva.

'Here, mister, this is curds, honey, ghee, and molasses all mixed together. Drink it if you like.

Tassa te pivato ceva chādessati vaṇṇenapi gandhenapi rasenapi, pivitvā ca pana sukhī bhavissasī'ti.

If you drink it, the color, aroma, and flavor will be appetizing, and after drinking it you will be happy.'

So taṁ paṭisaṅkhāya piveyya, nappaṭinissajjeyya.

He wouldn't reject it. After appraisal, he'd drink it.

Tassa taṁ pivato ceva chādeyya vaṇṇenapi gandhenapi rasenapi, pivitvā ca pana sukhī assa.

The color, aroma, and flavor would be appetizing, and after drinking it he would be happy.

Tathūpamāhaṁ, bhikkhave, imaṁ dhammasamādānaṁ vadāmi, yamidaṁ dhammasamādānaṁ paccuppannasukhañceva āyatiñca sukhavipākaṁ.

This is comparable to the way of taking up practices that is pleasant now and results in future pleasure, I say.

Seyyathāpi, bhikkhave, vassānaṁ pacchime māse saradasamaye viddhe vigatavalāhake deve ādicco nabhaṁ abbhussakkamāno sabbaṁ ākāsagataṁ tamagataṁ abhivihacca bhāsate ca tapate ca virocate ca;

It's like the time after the rainy season when the sky is clear and cloudless. And when the sun rises, it dispels all the darkness from the sky as it shines and glows and radiates.

evameva kho, bhikkhave, yamidaṁ dhammasamādānaṁ paccuppannasukhañceva āyatiñca sukhavipākaṁ tadaññe puthusamaṇabrāhmaṇaparappavāde abhivihacca bhāsate ca tapate ca virocate cā"ti.

In the same way, this way of taking up practices that is pleasant now and results in future pleasure dispels the doctrines of the various other ascetics and brahmins as it shines and glows and radiates."

Idamavoca bhagavā.

That is what the Buddha said.

Attamanā te bhikkhū bhagavato bhāsitaṁ abhinandunti.

Satisfied, the mendicants were happy with what the Buddha said.

Mahādhammasamādānasuttaṁ niṭṭhitaṁ chaṭṭhaṁ.

47 Vimaṁsakasutta:

The Inquirer

Evaṁ me sutaṁ—

So I have heard.

ekaṁ samayaṁ bhagavā sāvatthiyaṁ viharati jetavane anāthapiṇḍikassa ārāme.

At one time the Buddha was staying near Sāvatthī in Jeta's Grove, Anāthapiṇḍika's monastery.

Tatra kho bhagavā bhikkhū āmantesi:

There the Buddha addressed the mendicants,

"bhikkhavo"ti.

"Mendicants!"

"Bhadante"ti te bhikkhū bhagavato paccassosuṁ.

"Venerable sir," they replied.

Bhagavā etadavoca:

The Buddha said this:

"vīmaṁsakena, bhikkhave, bhikkhunā parassa cetopariyāyaṁ ajānantena tathāgate samannesanā kātabbā 'sammāsambuddho vā no vā' iti viññāṇāyā"ti.

"Mendicants, a mendicant who is an inquirer, unable to comprehend another's mind, should scrutinize the Realized One to see whether he is a fully awakened Buddha or not."

"Bhagavaṁmūlakā no, bhante, dhammā, bhagavaṁnettikā bhagavaṁpaṭisaraṇā; sādhu vata, bhante, bhagavantaṁyeva paṭibhātu etassa bhāsitassa attho; bhagavato sutvā bhikkhū dhāressantī"ti.

"Our teachings are rooted in the Buddha. He is our guide and our refuge. Sir, may the Buddha himself please clarify the meaning of this. The mendicants will listen and remember it."

"Tena hi, bhikkhave, suṇātha, sādhukaṁ manasi karotha, bhāsissāmī"ti.

"Well then, mendicants, listen and pay close attention, I will speak."

"Evaṁ, bhante"ti kho te bhikkhū bhagavato paccassosuṁ.

"Yes, sir," they replied.

Bhagavā etadavoca:

The Buddha said this:

"Vīmaṁsakena, bhikkhave, bhikkhunā parassa cetopariyāyaṁ ajānantena dvīsu dhammesu tathāgato samannesitabbo cakkhusotaviññeyyesu dhammesu:

"Mendicants, a mendicant who is an inquirer, unable to comprehend another's mind, should scrutinize the Realized One for two things—things that can be seen and heard:

'ye saṅkiliṭṭhā cakkhusotaviññeyyā dhammā, saṁvijjanti vā te tathāgatassa no vā'ti?

'Can anything corrupt be seen or heard in the Realized One or not?'

Tamenaṁ samannesamāno evaṁ jānāti:

Scrutinizing him they find that

'ye saṅkiliṭṭhā cakkhusotaviññeyyā dhammā, na te tathāgatassa saṁvijjantī'ti.

nothing corrupt can be seen or heard in the Realized One.

Yato naṁ samannesamāno evaṁ jānāti:

'ye saṅkiliṭṭhā cakkhusotaviññeyyā dhammā, na te tathāgatassa saṁvijjantī'ti, tato naṁ uttariṁ samannesati:

They scrutinize further:

'ye vītimissā cakkhusotaviññeyyā dhammā, saṁvijjanti vā te tathāgatassa no vā'ti?

'Can anything mixed be seen or heard in the Realized One or not?'

Tamenaṁ samannesamāno evaṁ jānāti:

Scrutinizing him they find that

'ye vītimissā cakkhusotaviññeyyā dhammā, na te tathāgatassa saṁvijjantī'ti.

nothing mixed can be seen or heard in the Realized One.

Yato naṁ samannesamāno evaṁ jānāti:

'ye vītimissā cakkhusotaviññeyyā dhammā, na te tathāgatassa saṁvijjantī'ti, tato naṁ uttariṁ samannesati:

They scrutinize further:

'ye vodātā cakkhusotaviññeyyā dhammā, saṁvijjanti vā te tathāgatassa no vā'ti?

'Can anything clean be seen or heard in the Realized One or not?'

Tamenaṁ samannesamāno evaṁ jānāti:

Scrutinizing him they find that

'ye vodātā cakkhusotaviññeyyā dhammā, saṁvijjanti te tathāgatassā'ti.

clean things can be seen and heard in the Realized One.

Yato naṁ samannesamāno evaṁ jānāti:

'ye vodātā cakkhusotaviññeyyā dhammā, saṁvijjanti te tathāgatassā'ti, tato naṁ uttariṁ samannesati:

They scrutinize further:

'dīgharattaṁ samāpanno ayamāyasmā imaṁ kusalaṁ dhammaṁ, udāhu ittarasamāpanno'ti?

'Did the venerable attain this skillful state a long time ago, or just recently?'

Tamenaṁ samannesamāno evaṁ jānāti:

Scrutinizing him they find that

'dīgharattaṁ samāpanno ayamāyasmā imaṁ kusalaṁ dhammaṁ, nāyamāyasmā ittarasamāpanno'ti.

the venerable attained this skillful state a long time ago, not just recently.

Yato naṁ samannesamāno evaṁ jānāti:

'dīgharattaṁ samāpanno ayamāyasmā imaṁ kusalaṁ dhammaṁ, nāyamāyasmā ittarasamāpanno'ti, tato naṁ uttariṁ samannesati:

They scrutinize further:

'ñattajjhāpanno ayamāyasmā bhikkhu yasappatto, saṁvijjantassa idhekacce ādīnavā'ti?

'Are certain dangers found in that venerable mendicant who has achieved fame and renown?'

Na tāva, bhikkhave, bhikkhuno idhekacce ādīnavā saṁvijjanti yāva na ñattajjhāpanno hoti yasappatto.

For, mendicants, so long as a mendicant has not achieved fame and renown, certain dangers are not found in them.

Yato ca kho, bhikkhave, bhikkhu ñattajjhāpanno hoti yasappatto, athassa idhekacce ādīnavā saṁvijjanti.

But when they achieve fame and renown, those dangers appear.

Tamenaṁ samannesamāno evaṁ jānāti:

Scrutinizing him they find that

'ñattajjhāpanno ayamāyasmā bhikkhu yasappatto, nāssa idhekacce ādīnavā saṁvijjantī'ti.

those dangers are not found in that venerable mendicant who has achieved fame and renown.

Yato naṁ samannesamāno evaṁ jānāti:

'ñattajjhāpanno ayamāyasmā bhikkhu yasappatto, nāssa idhekacce ādīnavā saṁvijjantī'ti, tato naṁ uttariṁ samannesati:

They scrutinize further:

'abhayūparato ayamāyasmā, nāyamāyasmā bhayūparato;

'Is this venerable securely stopped or insecurely stopped?

vītarāgattā kāme na sevati khayā rāgassā'ti?

Is the reason they don't indulge in sensual pleasures that they're free of greed because greed has ended?'

Tamenaṁ samannesamāno evaṁ jānāti:

Scrutinizing him they find that

'abhayūparato ayamāyasmā, nāyamāyasmā bhayūparato;

that venerable is securely stopped, not insecurely stopped.

vītarāgattā kāme na sevati khayā rāgassā'ti.

The reason they don't indulge in sensual pleasures is that they're free of greed because greed has ended.

Tañce, bhikkhave, bhikkhuṁ pare evaṁ puccheyyuṁ:

If others should ask that mendicant,

'ke panāyasmato ākārā, ke anvayā, yenāyasmā evaṁ vadesi—

'But what reason and evidence does the venerable have for saying this?'

abhayūparato ayamāyasmā, nāyamāyasmā bhayūparato;

vītarāgattā kāme na sevati khayā rāgassā'ti.

Sammā byākaramāno, bhikkhave, bhikkhu evaṁ byākareyya:

Answering rightly, the mendicant should say,

'tathā hi pana ayamāyasmā saṅghe vā viharanto eko vā viharanto, ye ca tattha sugatā ye ca tattha duggatā, ye ca tattha gaṇamanusāsanti, ye ca idhekacce āmisesu sandissanti, ye ca idhekacce āmisena anupalittā, nāyamāyasmā taṁ tena avajānāti.

'Because, whether that venerable is staying in a community or alone, some people there are in a good state or a sorry state, some instruct a group, and some are seen among material pleasures, while others remain unsullied. Yet that venerable doesn't look down on them for that.

Sammukhā kho pana metaṁ bhagavato sutaṁ sammukhā paṭiggahitaṁ—

Also, I have heard and learned this in the presence of the Buddha:

abhayūparatohamasmi, nāhamasmi bhayūparato, vītarāgattā kāme na sevāmi khayā rāgassā'ti.

"I am securely stopped, not insecurely stopped. The reason I don't indulge in sensual pleasures is that I'm free of greed because greed has ended."'

Tatra, bhikkhave, tathāgatova uttariṁ paṭipucchitabbo:

Next, they should ask the Realized One himself about this,

'ye saṅkiliṭṭhā cakkhusotaviññeyyā dhammā, saṁvijjanti vā te tathāgatassa no vā'ti?

'Can anything corrupt be seen or heard in the Realized One or not?'

Byākaramāno, bhikkhave, tathāgato evaṁ byākareyya:

The Realized One would answer,

'ye saṅkiliṭṭhā cakkhusotaviññeyyā dhammā, na te tathāgatassa saṁvijjantī'ti.

'Nothing corrupt can be seen or heard in the Realized One.'

'Ye vītimissā cakkhusotaviññeyyā dhammā, saṁvijjanti vā te tathāgatassa no vā'ti?

'Can anything mixed be seen or heard in the Realized One or not?'

Byākaramāno, bhikkhave, tathāgato evaṁ byākareyya:

The Realized One would answer,

'ye vītimissā cakkhusotaviññeyyā dhammā, na te tathāgatassa saṁvijjantī'ti.

'Nothing mixed can be seen or heard in the Realized One.'

'Ye vodātā cakkhusotaviññeyyā dhammā, saṁvijjanti vā te tathāgatassa no vā'ti?

'Can anything clean be seen or heard in the Realized One or not?'

Byākaramāno, bhikkhave, tathāgato evaṁ byākareyya:

The Realized One would answer,

'ye vodātā cakkhusotaviññeyyā dhammā, saṁvijjanti te tathāgatassa;

'Clean things can be seen and heard in the Realized One.

etaṁ pathohamasmi, etaṁ gocaro, no ca tena tammayo'ti.

I am that range and that territory, but I do not identify with that.'

Evaṁvādiṁ kho, bhikkhave, satthāraṁ arahati sāvako upasaṅkamituṁ dhammassavanāya.

A disciple ought to approach a teacher who has such a doctrine in order to listen to the teaching.

Tassa satthā dhammaṁ deseti uttaruttariṁ paṇītapaṇītaṁ kaṇhasukkasappaṭibhāgaṁ.

The teacher explains Dhamma with its higher and higher stages, with its better and better stages, with its dark and bright sides.

Yathā yathā kho, bhikkhave, bhikkhuno satthā dhammaṁ deseti uttaruttariṁ paṇītapaṇītaṁ kaṇhasukkasappaṭibhāgaṁ tathā tathā so tasmiṁ dhamme abhiññāya idhekaccaṁ dhammaṁ dhammesu niṭṭhaṁ gacchati, satthari pasīdati:

When they directly know a certain principle of those teachings, in accordance with how they were taught, the mendicant comes to a conclusion about the teachings. They have confidence in the teacher:

'sammāsambuddho bhagavā, svākkhāto bhagavatā dhammo, suppaṭipanno saṅgho'ti.

'The Blessed One is a fully awakened Buddha! The teaching is well explained! The Saṅgha is practicing well!'

Tañce, bhikkhave, bhikkhuṁ pare evaṁ puccheyyuṁ:

If others should ask that mendicant,

'ke panāyasmato ākārā, ke anvayā, yenāyasmā evaṁ vadesi—

'But what reason and evidence does the venerable have for saying this?'

sammāsambuddho bhagavā, svākkhāto bhagavatā dhammo, suppaṭipanno saṅgho'ti?

Sammā byākaramāno, bhikkhave, bhikkhu evaṁ byākareyya:

Answering rightly, the mendicant should say,

'idhāhaṁ, āvuso, yena bhagavā tenupasaṅkamiṁ dhammassavanāya.

'Reverends, I approached the Buddha to listen to the teaching.

Tassa me bhagavā dhammaṁ deseti uttaruttariṁ paṇītapaṇītaṁ kaṇhasukkasappaṭibhāgaṁ.

He explained Dhamma with its higher and higher stages, with its better and better stages, with its dark and bright sides.

Yathā yathā me, āvuso, bhagavā dhammaṁ deseti uttaruttariṁ paṇītapaṇītaṁ kaṇhasukkasappaṭibhāgaṁ tathā tathāhaṁ tasmiṁ dhamme abhiññāya idhekaccaṁ dhammaṁ dhammesu niṭṭhamagamaṁ, satthari pasīdiṁ—

When I directly knew a certain principle of those teachings, in accordance with how I was taught, I came to a conclusion about the teachings. I had confidence in the Teacher:

sammāsambuddho bhagavā, svākkhāto bhagavatā, dhammo, suppaṭipanno saṅgho'ti.

"The Blessed One is a fully awakened Buddha! The teaching is well explained! The Saṅgha is practicing well!'"

Yassa kassaci, bhikkhave, imehi ākārehi imehi padehi imehi byañjanehi tathāgate saddhā niviṭṭhā hoti mūlajātā patiṭṭhitā, ayaṁ vuccati, bhikkhave, ākāravatī saddhā dassanamūlikā, daḷhā;

When someone's faith is settled, rooted, and planted in the Realized One in this manner, with these words and phrases, it's said to be grounded faith that's based on evidence.

asaṁhāriyā samaṇena vā brāhmaṇena vā devena vā mārena vā brahmunā vā kenaci vā lokasmiṁ.

It is firm, and cannot be shifted by any ascetic or brahmin or god or Māra or Brahmā or by anyone in the world.

Evaṁ kho, bhikkhave, tathāgate dhammasamannesanā hoti.

This is how to scrutinize the Realized One's qualities.

Evañca pana tathāgato dhammatāsusamanniṭṭho hotī"ti.

But the Realized One has already been properly searched in this way by nature."

Idamavoca bhagavā.

That is what the Buddha said.

Attamanā te bhikkhū bhagavato bhāsitaṁ abhinandunti.

Satisfied, the mendicants were happy with what the Buddha said.

Vīmaṁsakasuttaṁ niṭṭhitaṁ sattamaṁ.

48 Kosambiyasutta:

The Mendicants of Kosambi

Evaṁ me sutaṁ—

So I have heard.

ekaṁ samayaṁ bhagavā kosambiyaṁ viharati ghositārāme.

At one time the Buddha was staying near Kosambī, in Ghosita's Monastery.

Tena kho pana samayena kosambiyaṁ bhikkhū bhaṇḍanajātā kalahajātā vivādāpannā aññamaññaṁ mukhasattīhi vitudantā viharanti.

Now at that time the mendicants of Kosambī were arguing, quarreling, and disputing, continually wounding each other with barbed words.

Te na ceva aññamaññaṁ saññāpenti na ca saññattiṁ upenti, na ca aññamaññaṁ nijjhāpenti, na ca nijjhattiṁ upenti.

They couldn't persuade each other or be persuaded, nor could they convince each other or be convinced.

Atha kho aññataro bhikkhu yena bhagavā tenupasaṅkami; upasaṅkamitvā bhagavantaṁ abhivādetvā ekamantaṁ nisīdi. Ekamantaṁ nisinno kho so bhikkhu bhagavantaṁ etadavoca:

Then a mendicant went up to the Buddha, bowed, sat down to one side, and told him what was happening.

"idha, bhante, kosambiyaṁ bhikkhū bhaṇḍanajātā kalahajātā vivādāpannā aññamaññaṁ mukhasattīhi vitudantā viharanti, te na ceva aññamaññaṁ saññāpenti, na ca saññattiṁ upenti, na ca aññamaññaṁ nijjhāpenti, na ca nijjhattiṁ upentī"ti.

Atha kho bhagavā aññataraṁ bhikkhuṁ āmantesi:

So the Buddha addressed a certain monk,

"ehi tvaṁ, bhikkhu, mama vacanena te bhikkhū āmantehi:

"Please, monk, in my name tell those mendicants that

'satthā vo āyasmante āmantetī'"ti.

the teacher summons them.

"Evaṁ, bhante"ti kho so bhikkhu bhagavato paṭissutvā yena te bhikkhū tenupasaṅkami; upasaṅkamitvā te bhikkhū etadavoca:

"Yes, sir," that monk replied. He went to those monks and said,

"satthā āyasmante āmantetī"ti.

"Venerables, the teacher summons you."

"Evamāvuso"ti kho te bhikkhū tassa bhikkhuno paṭissutvā yena bhagavā tenupasaṅkamiṃsu; upasaṅkamitvā bhagavantaṃ abhivādetvā ekamantaṃ nisīdiṃsu. Ekamantaṃ nisinne kho te bhikkhū bhagavā etadavoca:

"Yes, reverend," those monks replied. They went to the Buddha, bowed, and sat down to one side. The Buddha said to them,

"saccaṃ kira tumhe, bhikkhave, bhaṇḍanajātā kalahajātā vivādāpannā aññamaññaṃ mukhasattīhi vitudantā viharatha,

"Is it really true, mendicants, that you have been arguing, quarreling, and disputing, continually wounding each other with barbed words?

te na ceva aññamaññaṃ saññāpetha, na ca saññattiṃ upetha, na ca aññamaññaṃ nijjhāpetha, na ca nijjhattiṃ upethā"ti?

And that you can't persuade each other or be persuaded, nor can you convince each other or be convinced?"

"Evaṃ, bhante".

"Yes, sir," they said.

"Taṃ kiṃ maññatha, bhikkhave,

"What do you think, mendicants?

yasmiṃ tumhe samaye bhaṇḍanajātā kalahajātā vivādāpannā aññamaññaṃ mukhasattīhi vitudantā viharatha, api nu tumhākaṃ tasmiṃ samaye mettaṃ kāyakammaṃ paccupaṭṭhitaṃ hoti sabrahmacārīsu āvi ceva raho ca, mettaṃ vacīkammaṃ …pe… mettaṃ manokammaṃ paccupaṭṭhitaṃ hoti sabrahmacārīsu āvi ceva raho cā"ti?

When you're arguing, quarreling, and disputing, continually wounding each other with barbed words, are you treating your spiritual companions with kindness by way of body, speech, and mind, both in public and in private?"

"No hetaṃ, bhante".

"No, sir."

"Iti kira, bhikkhave, yasmiṃ tumhe samaye bhaṇḍanajātā kalahajātā vivādāpannā aññamaññaṃ mukhasattīhi vitudantā viharatha, neva tumhākaṃ tasmiṃ samaye mettaṃ kāyakammaṃ paccupaṭṭhitaṃ hoti sabrahmacārīsu āvi ceva raho ca, na mettaṁ vacīkammaṁ ...pe... na mettaṁ manokammaṁ paccupaṭṭhitaṁ hoti sabrahmacārīsu āvi ceva raho ca.

"So it seems that when you're arguing you are not treating each other with kindness.

Atha kiñcarahi tumhe, moghapurisā, kiṁ jānantā kiṁ passantā bhaṇḍanajātā kalahajātā vivādāpannā aññamaññaṁ mukhasattīhi vitudantā viharatha, te na ceva aññamaññaṁ saññāpetha, na ca saññattiṁ upetha, na ca aññamaññaṁ nijjhāpetha, na ca nijjhattiṁ upetha?

So what exactly do you know and see, you foolish men, that you behave in such a way?

Tañhi tumhākaṁ, moghapurisā, bhavissati dīgharattaṁ ahitāya dukkhāyā"ti.

This will be for your lasting harm and suffering."

Atha kho bhagavā bhikkhū āmantesi:

Then the Buddha said to the mendicants:

"chayime, bhikkhave, dhammā sāraṇīyā piyakaraṇā garukaraṇā saṅgahāya avivādāya sāmaggiyā ekībhāvāya saṁvattanti.

"Mendicants, these six warm-hearted qualities make for fondness and respect, conducing to inclusion, harmony, and unity, without quarreling.

Katame cha?

What six?

Idha, bhikkhave, bhikkhuno mettaṁ kāyakammaṁ paccupaṭṭhitaṁ hoti sabrahmacārīsu āvi ceva raho ca.

Firstly, a mendicant consistently treats their spiritual companions with bodily kindness, both in public and in private.

Ayampi dhammo sāraṇīyo piyakaraṇo garukaraṇo saṅgahāya avivādāya sāmaggiyā ekībhāvāya saṁvattati.

This warm-hearted quality makes for fondness and respect, conducing to inclusion, harmony, and unity, without quarreling.

Puna caparaṁ, bhikkhave, bhikkhuno mettaṁ vacīkammaṁ paccupaṭṭhitaṁ hoti sabrahmacārīsu āvi ceva raho ca.

Furthermore, a mendicant consistently treats their spiritual companions with verbal kindness ...

Ayampi dhammo sāraṇīyo piyakaraṇo garukaraṇo saṅgahāya avivādāya sāmaggiyā ekībhāvāya saṁvattati.

Puna caparaṁ, bhikkhave, bhikkhuno mettaṁ manokammaṁ paccupaṭṭhitaṁ hoti sabrahmacārīsu āvi ceva raho ca.

Furthermore, a mendicant consistently treats their spiritual companions with mental kindness …

Ayampi dhammo sāraṇīyo piyakaraṇo garukaraṇo saṅgahāya avivādāya sāmaggiyā ekībhāvāya saṁvattati.

Puna caparaṁ, bhikkhave, bhikkhu ye te lābhā dhammikā dhammaladdhā antamaso pattapariyāpannamattampi, tathārūpehi lābhehi appaṭivibhattabhogī hoti sīlavantehi sabrahmacārīhi sādhāraṇabhogī.

Furthermore, a mendicant shares without reservation any material possessions they have gained by legitimate means, even the food placed in the alms-bowl, using them in common with their ethical spiritual companions …

Ayampi dhammo sāraṇīyo piyakaraṇo garukaraṇo saṅgahāya avivādāya sāmaggiyā ekībhāvāya saṁvattati.

Puna caparaṁ, bhikkhave, bhikkhu yāni tāni sīlāni akhaṇḍāni acchiddāni asabalāni akammāsāni bhujissāni viññuppasatthāni aparāmaṭṭhāni samādhisaṁvattanikāni tathārūpesu sīlesu sīlasāmaññagato viharati sabrahmacārīhi āvi ceva raho ca.

Furthermore, a mendicant lives according to the precepts shared with their spiritual companions, both in public and in private. Those precepts are unbroken, impeccable, spotless, and unmarred, liberating, praised by sensible people, not mistaken, and leading to immersion. …

Ayampi dhammo sāraṇīyo piyakaraṇo garukaraṇo saṅgahāya avivādāya sāmaggiyā ekībhāvāya saṁvattati.

Puna caparaṁ, bhikkhave, bhikkhu yāyaṁ diṭṭhi ariyā niyyānikā niyyāti takkarassa sammā dukkhakkhayāya tathārūpāya diṭṭhiyā diṭṭhisāmaññagato viharati sabrahmacārīhi āvi ceva raho ca.

Furthermore, a mendicant lives according to the view shared with their spiritual companions, both in public and in private. That view is noble and emancipating, and leads one who practices it to the complete ending of suffering.

Ayampi dhammo sāraṇīyo piyakaraṇo garukaraṇo saṅgahāya avivādāya sāmaggiyā ekībhāvāya saṁvattati.

This warm-hearted quality makes for fondness and respect, conducing to inclusion, harmony, and unity, without quarreling.

Ime kho, bhikkhave, cha sāraṇīyā dhammā piyakaraṇā garukaraṇā saṅgahāya avivādāya sāmaggiyā ekībhāvāya saṁvattanti.

These six warm-hearted qualities make for fondness and respect, conducing to inclusion, harmony, and unity, without quarreling.

Imesaṁ kho, bhikkhave, channaṁ sāraṇīyānaṁ dhammānaṁ etaṁ aggaṁ etaṁ saṅgāhikaṁ etaṁ saṅghāṭanikaṁ—yadidaṁ yāyaṁ diṭṭhi ariyā niyyānikā niyyāti takkarassa sammā dukkhakkhayāya.

Of these six warm-hearted qualities, the chief is the view that is noble and emancipating, and leads one who practices it to the complete ending of suffering. It holds and binds everything together.

Seyyathāpi, bhikkhave, kūṭāgārassa etaṁ aggaṁ etaṁ saṅgāhikaṁ etaṁ saṅghāṭanikaṁ yadidaṁ kūṭaṁ;

It's like a bungalow. The roof-peak is the chief point, which holds and binds everything together.

evameva kho, bhikkhave, imesaṁ channaṁ sāraṇīyānaṁ dhammānaṁ etaṁ aggaṁ etaṁ saṅgāhikaṁ etaṁ saṅghāṭanikaṁ yadidaṁ yāyaṁ diṭṭhi ariyā niyyānikā niyyāti takkarassa sammā dukkhakkhayāya.

In the same way, of these six warm-hearted qualities, the chief is the view that is noble and emancipating, and leads one who practices it to the complete ending of suffering. It holds and binds everything together.

Kathañca, bhikkhave, yāyaṁ diṭṭhi ariyā niyyānikā niyyāti takkarassa sammā dukkhakkhayāya?

And how does the view that is noble and emancipating lead one who practices it to the complete ending of suffering?

Idha, bhikkhave, bhikkhu araññagato vā rukkhamūlagato vā suññāgāragato vā iti paṭisañcikkhati:

It's when a mendicant has gone to a wilderness, or to the root of a tree, or to an empty hut, and reflects like this,

'atthi nu kho me taṁ pariyuṭṭhānaṁ ajjhattaṁ appahīnaṁ, yenāhaṁ pariyuṭṭhānena pariyuṭṭhitacitto yathābhūtaṁ nappajāneyyaṁ na passeyyan'ti?

'Is there anything that I'm overcome with internally and haven't given up, because of which I might not accurately know and see?'

Sace, bhikkhave, bhikkhu kāmarāgapariyuṭṭhito hoti, pariyuṭṭhitacittova hoti.

If a mendicant is overcome with sensual desire, it's their mind that's overcome.

Sace, bhikkhave, bhikkhu byāpādapariyuṭṭhito hoti, pariyuṭṭhitacittova hoti.

If a mendicant is overcome with ill will,

Sace, bhikkhave, bhikkhu thinamiddhapariyuṭṭhito hoti, pariyuṭṭhitacittova hoti.

dullness and drowsiness,

Sace, bhikkhave, bhikkhu uddhaccakukkuccapariyuṭṭhito hoti, pariyuṭṭhitacittova hoti.

restlessness and remorse,

Sace, bhikkhave, bhikkhu vicikicchāpariyuṭṭhito hoti, pariyuṭṭhitacittova hoti.

doubt,

Sace, bhikkhave, bhikkhu idhalokacintāya pasuto hoti, pariyuṭṭhitacittova hoti.

pursuing speculation about this world,

Sace, bhikkhave, bhikkhu paralokacintāya pasuto hoti, pariyuṭṭhitacittova hoti.

pursuing speculation about the next world,

Sace, bhikkhave, bhikkhu bhaṇḍanajāto kalahajāto vivādāpanno aññamaññaṁ mukhasattīhi vitudanto viharati, pariyuṭṭhitacittova hoti.

or arguing, quarreling, and disputing, continually wounding others with barbed words, it's their mind that's overcome.

So evaṁ pajānāti:

They understand,

'natthi kho me taṁ pariyuṭṭhānaṁ ajjhattaṁ appahīnaṁ, yenāhaṁ pariyuṭṭhānena pariyuṭṭhitacitto yathābhūtaṁ nappajāneyyaṁ na passeyyaṁ.

'There is nothing that I'm overcome with internally and haven't given up, because of which I might not accurately know and see.

Suppaṇihitaṁ me mānasaṁ saccānaṁ bodhāyā'ti.

My mind is properly disposed for awakening to the truths.'

Idamassa paṭhamaṁ ñāṇaṁ adhigataṁ hoti ariyaṁ lokuttaraṁ asādhāraṇaṁ puthujjanehi.

This is the first knowledge they have achieved that is noble and transcendent, and is not shared with ordinary people.

Puna caparaṁ, bhikkhave, ariyasāvako iti paṭisañcikkhati:

Furthermore, a noble disciple reflects,

'imaṁ nu kho ahaṁ diṭṭhiṁ āsevanto bhāvento bahulīkaronto labhāmi paccattaṁ samathaṁ, labhāmi paccattaṁ nibbutin'ti?

'When I develop, cultivate, and make much of this view, do I personally gain serenity and quenching?'

So evaṁ pajānāti:

They understand,

'imaṁ kho ahaṁ diṭṭhiṁ āsevanto bhāvento bahulīkaronto labhāmi paccattaṁ samathaṁ, labhāmi paccattaṁ nibbutin'ti.

'When I develop, cultivate, and make much of this view, I personally gain serenity and quenching.'

Idamassa dutiyaṁ ñāṇaṁ adhigataṁ hoti ariyaṁ lokuttaraṁ asādhāraṇaṁ puthujjanehi.

This is their second knowledge …

Puna caparaṁ, bhikkhave, ariyasāvako iti paṭisañcikkhati:

Furthermore, a noble disciple reflects,

'yathārūpāyāhaṁ diṭṭhiyā samannāgato, atthi nu kho ito bahiddhā añño samaṇo vā brāhmaṇo vā tathārūpāya diṭṭhiyā samannāgato'ti?

'Are there any ascetics or brahmins outside of the Buddhist community who have the same kind of view that I have?'

So evaṁ pajānāti:

They understand,

'yathārūpāyāhaṁ diṭṭhiyā samannāgato, natthi ito bahiddhā añño samaṇo vā brāhmaṇo vā tathārūpāya diṭṭhiyā samannāgato'ti.

'There are no ascetics or brahmins outside of the Buddhist community who have the same kind of view that I have.'

Idamassa tatiyaṁ ñāṇaṁ adhigataṁ hoti ariyaṁ lokuttaraṁ asādhāraṇaṁ puthujjanehi.

This is their third knowledge …

Puna caparaṁ, bhikkhave, ariyasāvako iti paṭisañcikkhati:

Furthermore, a noble disciple reflects,

'yathārūpāya dhammatāya diṭṭhisampanno puggalo samannāgato, ahampi tathārūpāya dhammatāya samannāgato'ti.

'Do I have the same nature as a person accomplished in view?'

Kathaṁrūpāya ca, bhikkhave, dhammatāya diṭṭhisampanno puggalo samannāgato?

And what, mendicants, is the nature of a person accomplished in view?

Dhammatā esā, bhikkhave, diṭṭhisampannassa puggalassa:

This is the nature of a person accomplished in view.

'kiñcāpi tathārūpiṃ āpattiṃ āpajjati, yathārūpāya āpattiyā vuṭṭhānaṃ paññāyati, atha kho naṃ khippameva satthari vā viññūsu vā sabrahmacārīsu deseti vivarati uttānīkaroti;

Though they may fall into a kind of offense for which rehabilitation has been laid down, they quickly disclose, clarify, and reveal it to the Teacher or a sensible spiritual companion.

desetvā vivaritvā uttānīkatvā āyatiṃ saṃvaraṃ āpajjati'.

And having revealed it they restrain themselves in the future.

Seyyathāpi, bhikkhave, daharo kumāro mando uttānaseyyako hatthena vā pādena vā aṅgāraṃ akkamitvā khippameva paṭisaṃharati;

Suppose there was a little baby boy. If he puts his hand or foot on a burning coal, he quickly pulls it back.

evameva kho, bhikkhave, dhammatā esā diṭṭhisampannassa puggalassa:

In the same way, this is the nature of a person accomplished in view.

'kiñcāpi tathārūpiṃ āpattiṃ āpajjati yathārūpāya āpattiyā vuṭṭhānaṃ paññāyati, atha kho naṃ khippameva satthari vā viññūsu vā sabrahmacārīsu deseti vivarati uttānīkaroti;

Though they may still fall into a kind of offense for which rehabilitation has been laid down, they quickly reveal it to the Teacher or a sensible spiritual companion.

desetvā vivaritvā uttānīkatvā āyatiṃ saṃvaraṃ āpajjati'.

And having revealed it they restrain themselves in the future.

So evaṃ pajānāti:

They understand,

'yathārūpāya dhammatāya diṭṭhisampanno puggalo samannāgato, ahampi tathārūpāya dhammatāya samannāgato'ti.

'I have the same nature as a person accomplished in view.'

Idamassa catutthaṃ ñāṇaṃ adhigataṃ hoti ariyaṃ lokuttaraṃ asādhāraṇaṃ puthujjanehi.

This is their fourth knowledge …

Puna caparaṃ, bhikkhave, ariyasāvako iti paṭisañcikkhati:

Furthermore, a noble disciple reflects,

'yathārūpāya dhammatāya diṭṭhisampanno puggalo samannāgato, ahampi tathārūpāya dhammatāya samannāgato'ti.

'Do I have the same nature as a person accomplished in view?'

Kathaṁrūpāya ca, bhikkhave, dhammatāya diṭṭhisampanno puggalo samannāgato?

And what, mendicants, is the nature of a person accomplished in view?

Dhammatā esā, bhikkhave, diṭṭhisampannassa puggalassa:

This is the nature of a person accomplished in view.

'kiñcāpi yāni tāni sabrahmacārīnaṁ uccāvacāni kiṅkaraṇīyāni tattha ussukkaṁ āpanno hoti, atha khvāssa tibbāpekkhā hoti adhisīlasikkhāya adhicittasikkhāya adhipaññāsikkhāya'.

Though they might manage a diverse spectrum of duties for their spiritual companions, they still feel a keen regard for the training in higher ethics, higher mind, and higher wisdom.

Seyyathāpi, bhikkhave, gāvī taruṇavacchā thambañca ālumpati vacchakañca apacinati;

Suppose there was a cow with a baby calf. She keeps the calf close as she grazes.

evameva kho, bhikkhave, dhammatā esā diṭṭhisampannassa puggalassa:

In the same way, this is the nature of a person accomplished in view.

'kiñcāpi yāni tāni sabrahmacārīnaṁ uccāvacāni kiṅkaraṇīyāni tattha ussukkaṁ āpanno hoti, atha khvāssa tibbāpekkhā hoti adhisīlasikkhāya adhicittasikkhāya adhipaññāsikkhāya'.

Though they might manage a diverse spectrum of duties for their spiritual companions, they still feel a keen regard for the training in higher ethics, higher mind, and higher wisdom.

So evaṁ pajānāti:

They understand,

'yathārūpāya dhammatāya diṭṭhisampanno puggalo samannāgato, ahampi tathārūpāya dhammatāya samannāgato'ti.

'I have the same nature as a person accomplished in view.'

Idamassa pañcamaṁ ñāṇaṁ adhigataṁ hoti ariyaṁ lokuttaraṁ asādhāraṇaṁ puthujjanehi.

This is their fifth knowledge …

Puna caparaṁ, bhikkhave, ariyasāvako iti paṭisañcikkhati:

Furthermore, a noble disciple reflects,

'yathārūpāya balatāya diṭṭhisampanno puggalo samannāgato, ahampi tathārūpāya balatāya samannāgato'ti.

'Do I have the same strength as a person accomplished in view?'

Kathaṁrūpāya ca, bhikkhave, balatāya diṭṭhisampanno puggalo samannāgato?

And what, mendicants, is the strength of a person accomplished in view?

Balatā esā, bhikkhave, diṭṭhisampannassa puggalassa yaṁ tathāgatappavedite dhammavinaye desiyamāne aṭṭhiṁ katvā manasikatvā sabbacetasā samannāharitvā ohitasoto dhammaṁ suṇāti.

The strength of a person accomplished in view is that, when the teaching and training proclaimed by the Realized One are being taught, they pay heed, pay attention, engage wholeheartedly, and lend an ear.

So evam pajānāti:

They understand,

'yathārūpāya balatāya diṭṭhisampanno puggalo samannāgato, ahampi tathārūpāya balatāya samannāgato'ti.

'I have the same strength as a person accomplished in view.'

Idamassa chaṭṭhaṁ ñāṇaṁ adhigataṁ hoti ariyaṁ lokuttaraṁ asādhāraṇaṁ puthujjanehi.

This is their sixth knowledge …

Puna caparaṁ, bhikkhave, ariyasāvako iti paṭisañcikkhati:

Furthermore, a noble disciple reflects,

'yathārūpāya balatāya diṭṭhisampanno puggalo samannāgato, ahampi tathārūpāya balatāya samannāgato'ti.

'Do I have the same strength as a person accomplished in view?'

Kathaṁrūpāya ca, bhikkhave, balatāya diṭṭhisampanno puggalo samannāgato?

And what, mendicants, is the strength of a person accomplished in view?

Balatā esā, bhikkhave, diṭṭhisampannassa puggalassa yaṁ tathāgatappavedite dhammavinaye desiyamāne labhati atthavedaṁ, labhati dhammavedaṁ, labhati dhammūpasaṁhitaṁ pāmojjaṁ.

The strength of a person accomplished in view is that, when the teaching and training proclaimed by the Realized One are being taught, they find inspiration in the meaning and the teaching, and find joy connected with the teaching.

So evaṁ pajānāti:

They understand,

'yathārūpāya balatāya diṭṭhisampanno puggalo samannāgato, ahampi tathārūpāya balatāya samannāgato'ti.

'I have the same strength as a person accomplished in view.'

Idamassa sattamaṁ ñāṇaṁ adhigataṁ hoti ariyaṁ lokuttaraṁ asādhāraṇaṁ puthujjanehi.

This is the seventh knowledge they have achieved that is noble and transcendent, and is not shared with ordinary people.

Evaṁ sattaṅgasamannāgatassa kho, bhikkhave, ariyasāvakassa dhammatā susamanniṭṭhā hoti sotāpattiphalasacchikiriyāya.

When a noble disciple has these seven factors, they have properly investigated their own nature with respect to the realization of the fruit of stream-entry.

Evaṁsattaṅgasamannāgatokho,bhikkhave,ariyasāvakosotāpattiphalasamannāgato hotī"ti.

A noble disciple with these seven factors has the fruit of stream-entry."

Idamavoca bhagavā.

That is what the Buddha said.

Attamanā te bhikkhū bhagavato bhāsitaṁ abhinandunti.

Satisfied, the mendicants were happy with what the Buddha said.

Kosambiyasuttaṁ niṭṭhitaṁ aṭṭhamaṁ.

49 Brahmanimantanikasutta:

On the Invitation of Brahma

Evaṁ me sutaṁ—

So I have heard.

ekaṁ samayaṁ bhagavā sāvatthiyaṁ viharati jetavane anāthapiṇḍikassa ārāme.

At one time the Buddha was staying near Sāvatthī in Jeta's Grove, Anāthapiṇḍika's monastery.

Tatra kho bhagavā bhikkhū āmantesi:

There the Buddha addressed the mendicants,

"bhikkhavo"ti.

"Mendicants!"

"Bhadante"ti te bhikkhū bhagavato paccassosuṁ.

"Venerable sir," they replied.

Bhagavā etadavoca:

The Buddha said this:

"Ekamidāhaṁ, bhikkhave, samayaṁ ukkaṭṭhāyaṁ viharāmi subhagavane sālarājamūle.

"At one time, mendicants, I was staying near Ukkaṭṭhā, in the Subhaga Forest at the root of a magnificent sal tree.

Tena kho pana, bhikkhave, samayena bakassa brahmuno evarūpaṁ pāpakaṁ diṭṭhigataṁ uppannaṁ hoti:

Now at that time Baka the Brahmā had the following harmful misconception:

'idaṁ niccaṁ, idaṁ dhuvaṁ, idaṁ sassataṁ, idaṁ kevalaṁ, idaṁ acavanadhammaṁ, idañhi na jāyati na jīyati na mīyati na cavati na upapajjati, ito ca panaññaṁ uttari nissaraṇaṁ natthī'ti.

'This is permanent, this is everlasting, this is eternal, this is whole, this is imperishable. For this is where there's no being born, growing old, dying, passing away, or being reborn. And there's no other escape beyond this.'

Atha khvāhaṁ, bhikkhave, bakassa brahmuno cetasā cetoparivitakkamaññāya—

Then I knew what Baka the Brahmā was thinking.

seyyathāpi nāma balavā puriso samiñjitaṁ vā bāhaṁ pasāreyya, pasāritaṁ vā bāhaṁ samiñjeyya; evameva—ukkaṭṭhāyaṁ subhagavane sālarājamūle antarahito tasmiṁ brahmaloke pāturahosiṁ.

As easily as a strong person would extend or contract their arm, I vanished from the Subhaga Forest and reappeared in that Brahmā realm.

Addasā kho maṁ, bhikkhave, bako brahmā dūratova āgacchantaṁ;

Baka saw me coming off in the distance

disvāna maṁ etadavoca:

and said,

'ehi kho, mārisa, svāgataṁ, mārisa.

'Come, good sir! Welcome, good sir!

Cirassaṁ kho, mārisa, imaṁ pariyāyamakāsi yadidaṁ idhāgamanāya.

It's been a long time since you took the opportunity to come here.

Idañhi, mārisa, niccaṁ, idaṁ dhuvaṁ, idaṁ sassataṁ, idaṁ kevalaṁ, idaṁ acavanadhammaṁ, idañhi na jāyati na jīyati na mīyati na cavati na upapajjati. Ito ca panaññaṁ uttari nissaraṇaṁ natthī'ti.

For this is permanent, this is everlasting, this is eternal, this is complete, this is imperishable. For this is where there's no being born, growing old, dying, passing away, or being reborn. And there's no other escape beyond this.'

Evaṁ vutte, ahaṁ, bhikkhave, bakaṁ brahmānaṁ etadavocaṁ:

When he had spoken, I said to him,

'avijjāgato vata bho bako brahmā, avijjāgato vata bho bako brahmā;

'Alas, Baka the Brahmā is lost in ignorance! Alas, Baka the Brahmā is lost in ignorance!

yatra hi nāma aniccaṁyeva samānaṁ niccanti vakkhati, addhuvaṁyeva samānaṁ dhuvanti vakkhati, asassataṁyeva samānaṁ sassatanti vakkhati, akevalaṁyeva samānaṁ kevalanti vakkhati, cavanadhammaṁyeva samānaṁ acavanadhammanti vakkhati;

Because what is actually impermanent, not lasting, transient, incomplete, and perishable, he says is permanent, everlasting, eternal, complete, and imperishable.

yattha ca pana jāyati jīyati mīyati cavati upapajjati tañca vakkhati:

And where there is being born, growing old, dying, passing away, and being reborn, he says that

"idañhi na jāyati na jīyati na mīyati na cavati na upapajjatī"ti;

there's no being born, growing old, dying, passing away, or being reborn.

santañca panaññaṁ uttari nissaraṇaṁ "natthaññaṁ uttari nissaraṇan"ti vakkhatī'ti.

And although there is another escape beyond this, he says that there's no other escape beyond this.'

Atha kho, bhikkhave, māro pāpimā aññataraṁ brahmapārisajjaṁ anvāvisitvā maṁ etadavoca:

Then Māra the Wicked took possession of a member of Brahmā's retinue and said this to me,

'bhikkhu bhikkhu, metamāsado metamāsado, eso hi, bhikkhu, brahmā mahābrahmā abhibhū anabhibhūto aññadatthudaso vasavattī issaro kattā nimmātā seṭṭho sajitā vasī pitā bhūtabhabyānaṁ.

'Mendicant, mendicant! Don't attack this one! Don't attack this one! For this is Brahmā, the Great Brahmā, the Undefeated, the Champion, the Universal Seer, the Wielder of Power, the Lord God, the Maker, the Author, the First, the Begetter, the Controller, the Father of those who have been born and those yet to be born.

Ahesuṁ kho ye, bhikkhu, tayā pubbe samaṇabrāhmaṇā lokasmiṁ pathavīgarahakā pathavījigucchakā, āpagarahakā āpajigucchakā, tejagarahakā tejajigucchakā, vāyagarahakā vāyajigucchakā, bhūtagarahakā bhūtajigucchakā, devagarahakā devajigucchakā, pajāpatigarahakā pajāpatijigucchakā, brahmagarahakā brahmajigucchakā—

There have been ascetics and brahmins before you, mendicant, who criticized and loathed earth, water, air, fire, creatures, gods, the Creator, and Brahmā.

te kāyassa bhedā pāṇupacchedā hīne kāye patiṭṭhitā ahesuṁ.

When their bodies broke up and their breath was cut off they were reborn in a lower realm.

Ye pana, bhikkhu, tayā pubbe samaṇabrāhmaṇā lokasmiṁ pathavīpasaṁsakā pathavābhinandino, āpapasaṁsakā āpābhinandino, tejapasaṁsakā tejābhinandino, vāyapasaṁsakā vāyābhinandino, bhūtapasaṁsakā bhūtābhinandino, devapasaṁsakā devābhinandino, pajāpatipasaṁsakā pajāpatābhinandino, brahmapasaṁsakā brahmābhinandino—

There have been ascetics and brahmins before you, mendicant, who praised and approved earth, water, air, fire, creatures, gods, the Creator, and Brahmā.

te kāyassa bhedā pāṇupacchedā paṇīte kāye patiṭṭhitā.

When their bodies broke up and their breath was cut off they were reborn in a higher realm.

Taṁ tāhaṁ, bhikkhu, evaṁ vadāmi:

So, mendicant, I tell you this:

"iṅgha tvaṁ, mārisa, yadeva te brahmā āha tadeva tvaṁ karohi, mā tvaṁ brahmuno vacanaṁ upātivattittho".

please, good sir, do exactly what Brahmā says. Don't go beyond the word of Brahmā.

Sace kho tvaṁ, bhikkhu, brahmuno vacanaṁ upātivattissasi, seyyathāpi nāma puriso siriṁ āgacchantiṁ daṇḍena paṭippaṇāmeyya, seyyathāpi vā pana, bhikkhu, puriso narakappapāte papatanto hatthehi ca pādehi ca pathaviṁ virādheyya, evaṁ sampadamidaṁ, bhikkhu, tuyhaṁ bhavissati.

If you do, then the consequence for you will be like that of a person who, when Lady Luck approaches, wards her off with a staff, or someone who shoves away the ground as they fall down the abyss into hell.

Iṅgha tvaṁ, mārisa, yadeva te brahmā āha tadeva tvaṁ karohi, mā tvaṁ brahmuno vacanaṁ upātivattittho.

Please, dear sir, do exactly what Brahmā says. Don't go beyond the word of Brahmā.

Nanu tvaṁ, bhikkhu, passasi brahmaparisaṁ sannipatitan'ti?

Do you not see the assembly of Brahmā gathered here?'

Iti kho maṁ, bhikkhave, māro pāpimā brahmaparisaṁ upanesi.

And that is how Māra the Wicked presented the assembly of Brahmā to me as an example.

Evaṁ vutte, ahaṁ, bhikkhave, māraṁ pāpimantaṁ etadavocaṁ:

When he had spoken, I said to Māra,

'jānāmi kho tāhaṁ, pāpima; mā tvaṁ maññittho:

'I know you, Wicked One. Do not think,

"na maṁ jānātī"ti.

"He does not know me."

Māro tvamasi, pāpima.

You are Māra the Wicked.

Yo ceva, pāpima, brahmā, yā ca brahmaparisā, ye ca brahmapārisajjā, sabbeva tava hatthagatā sabbeva tava vasaṅgatā.

And Brahmā, Brahmā's assembly, and Brahmā's retinue have all fallen into your hands; they're under your sway.

Tuyhañhi, pāpima, evaṁ hoti:

And you think,

"esopi me assa hatthagato, esopi me assa vasaṅgato"ti.

"Maybe this one, too, has fallen into my hands; maybe he's under my sway!"

Ahaṁ kho pana, pāpima, neva tava hatthagato neva tava vasaṅgato'ti.

But I haven't fallen into your hands; I'm not under your sway.'

Evaṁ vutte, bhikkhave, bako brahmā maṁ etadavoca:

When I had spoken, Baka the Brahmā said to me,

'ahañhi, mārisa, niccaṁyeva samānaṁ "niccan"ti vadāmi, dhuvaṁyeva samānaṁ "dhuvan"ti vadāmi, sassataṁyeva samānaṁ "sassatan"ti vadāmi, kevalaṁyeva samānaṁ "kevalan"ti vadāmi, acavanadhammaṁyeva samānaṁ "acavanadhamman"ti vadāmi, yattha ca pana na jāyati na jīyati na mīyati na cavati na upapajjati tadevāhaṁ vadāmi:

'But, good sir, what I say is permanent, everlasting, eternal, complete, and imperishable is in fact permanent, everlasting, eternal, complete, and imperishable. And where I say there's no being born, growing old, dying, passing away, or being reborn there is in fact

"idañhi na jāyati na jīyati na mīyati na cavati na upapajjatī"ti.

no being born, growing old, dying, passing away, or being reborn.

Asantañca panaññaṁ uttari nissaraṇaṁ "natthaññaṁ uttari nissaraṇan"ti vadāmi.

And when I say there's no other escape beyond this there is in fact no other escape beyond this.

Ahesuṁ kho, bhikkhu, tayā pubbe samaṇabrāhmaṇā lokasmiṁ yāvatakaṁ tuyhaṁ kasiṇaṁ āyu tāvatakaṁ tesaṁ tapokammameva ahosi.

There have been ascetics and brahmins in the world before you, mendicant, whose self-mortification lasted as long as your entire life.

Te kho evaṁ jāneyyuṁ santañca panaññaṁ uttari nissaraṇaṁ "atthaññaṁ uttari nissaraṇan"ti, asantaṁ vā aññaṁ uttari nissaraṇaṁ "natthaññaṁ uttari nissaraṇan"ti.

When there was another escape beyond this they knew it, and when there was no other escape beyond this, they knew it.

Taṁ tāhaṁ, bhikkhu, evaṁ vadāmi:

So, mendicant, I tell you this:

"na cevaññaṁ uttari nissaraṇaṁ dakkhissasi, yāvadeva ca pana kilamathassa vighātassa bhāgī bhavissasi.

you will never find another escape beyond this, and you will eventually get weary and frustrated.

Sace kho tvaṁ, bhikkhu, pathaviṁ ajjhosissasi, opasāyiko me bhavissasi vatthusāyiko, yathākāmakaraṇīyo bāhiteyyo.

If you attach to earth, you will lie close to me, in my domain, subject to my will, and expendable.

Sace āpaṁ …

If you attach to water …

tejaṁ …

fire …

vāyaṁ …

air …

bhūte …

creatures …

deve …

gods …

pajāpatiṁ …

the Creator …

brahmaṁ ajjhosissasi, opasāyiko me bhavissasi vatthusāyiko, yathākāmakaraṇīyo bāhiteyyo”’ti.

Brahmā, you will lie close to me, in my domain, subject to my will, and expendable.’

‘Ahampi kho evaṁ, brahme, jānāmi:

‘Brahmā, I too know that

“sace pathaviṁ ajjhosissāmi, opasāyiko te bhavissāmi vatthusāyiko, yathākāmakaraṇīyo bāhiteyyo.

if I attach to earth, I will lie close to you, in your domain, subject to your will, and expendable.

Sace āpaṁ …

If I attach to water …

tejaṁ …

fire …

vāyaṁ …

air …

bhūte …

creatures …

deve …

gods …

pajāpatiṁ …

the Creator …

brahmaṁ ajjhosissāmi, opasāyiko te bhavissāmi vatthusāyiko, yathākāmakaraṇīyo bāhiteyyo"ti api ca te ahaṁ, brahme, gatiñca pajānāmi, jutiñca pajānāmi:

Brahmā, I will lie close to you, in your domain, subject to your will, and expendable. And in addition, Brahmā, I understand your range and your light:

"evaṁ mahiddhiko bako brahmā, evaṁ mahānubhāvo bako brahmā, evaṁ mahesakkho bako brahmā"ti.

"That's how powerful is Baka the Brahmā, how illustrious and mighty."'

Yathākathaṁ pana me tvaṁ, mārisa, gatiñca pajānāsi, jutiñca pajānāsi:

'But in what way do you understand my range and my light?'

"evaṁ mahiddhiko bako brahmā, evaṁ mahānubhāvo bako brahmā, evaṁ mahesakkho bako brahmā"'ti?

'Yāvatā candimasūriyā,

Pariharanti disā bhanti virocanā;

Tāva sahassadhā loko,

Ettha te vattate vaso.

'A galaxy extends a thousand times as far

as the moon and sun revolve

and the shining ones light up the quarters.

And there you wield your power.

Paroparañca jānāsi,

atho rāgavirāginaṁ;

Itthabhāvaññathābhāvaṁ,

sattānaṁ āgatiṁ gatinti.

You know the high and low,

the passionate and dispassionate,

and the coming and going of sentient beings

from this realm to another.

Evaṁ kho te ahaṁ, brahme, gatiñca pajānāmi jutiñca pajānāmi:

That's how I understand your range and your light.

"evaṁ mahiddhiko bako brahmā, evaṁ mahānubhāvo bako brahmā, evaṁ mahesakkho bako brahmā"ti.

Atthi kho, brahme, añño kāyo, taṁ tvaṁ na jānāsi na passasi;

But there is another realm that you don't know or see.

tamahaṁ jānāmi passāmi.

But I know it and see it.

Atthi kho, brahme, ābhassarā nāma kāyo yato tvaṁ cuto idhūpapanno.

There is the realm named after the gods of streaming radiance. You passed away from there and were reborn here.

Tassa te aticiranivāsena sā sati pamuṭṭhā, tena taṁ tvaṁ na jānāsi na passasi;

You've dwelt here so long that you've forgotten about that, so you don't know it or see it.

tamahaṁ jānāmi passāmi.

But I know it and see it.

Evampi kho ahaṁ, brahme, neva te samasamo abhiññāya, kuto nīceyyaṁ?

So Brahmā, I am not your equal in knowledge, still less your inferior.

Atha kho ahameva tayā bhiyyo.

Rather, I know more than you.

Atthi kho, brahme, subhakiṇho nāma kāyo, vehapphalo nāma kāyo, abhibhū nāma kāyo, taṁ tvaṁ na jānāsi na passasi;

There is the realm named after the gods replete with glory … the realm named after the gods of abundant fruit … the realm named after the Overlord, which you don't know or see.

tamahaṁ jānāmi passāmi.

But I know it and see it.

Evampi kho ahaṁ, brahme, neva te samasamo abhiññāya, kuto nīceyyaṁ?

So Brahmā, I am not your equal in knowledge, still less your inferior.

Atha kho ahameva tayā bhiyyo.

Rather, I know more than you.

Pathaviṁ kho ahaṁ, brahme, pathavito abhiññāya yāvatā pathaviyā pathavattena ananubhūtaṁ tadabhiññāya pathaviṁ nāpahosiṁ, pathaviyā nāpahosiṁ, pathavito nāpahosiṁ, pathaviṁ meti nāpahosiṁ, pathaviṁ nābhivadiṁ.

Having directly known earth as earth, and having directly known that which does not fall within the scope of experience based on earth, I did not identify with earth, I did not identify regarding earth, I did not identify as earth, I did not identify 'earth is mine', I did not enjoy earth.

Evampi kho ahaṁ, brahme, neva te samasamo abhiññāya, kuto nīceyyaṁ?

So Brahmā, I am not your equal in knowledge, still less your inferior.

Atha kho ahameva tayā bhiyyo.

Rather, I know more than you.

Āpaṁ kho ahaṁ, brahme …pe…

Having directly known water …

tejaṁ kho ahaṁ, brahme …pe…

fire …

vāyaṁ kho ahaṁ, brahme …pe…

air …

bhūte kho ahaṁ, brahme …pe…

creatures …

deve kho ahaṁ, brahme …pe…

gods …

pajāpatiṁ kho ahaṁ, brahme …pe…

the Creator …

brahmaṁ kho ahaṁ, brahme …pe…

Brahmā …

ābhassare kho ahaṁ, brahme …pe…

the gods of streaming radiance …

subhakiṇhe kho ahaṁ, brahme …pe…

the gods replete with glory …

vehapphale kho ahaṁ, brahme …pe…

the gods of abundant fruit …

abhibhuṁ kho ahaṁ, brahme …pe…

the Overlord …

sabbaṁ kho ahaṁ, brahme, sabbato abhiññāya yāvatā sabbassa sabbattena ananubhūtaṁ tadabhiññāya sabbaṁ nāpahosiṁ sabbasmiṁ nāpahosiṁ sabbato nāpahosiṁ sabbaṁ meti nāpahosiṁ, sabbaṁ nābhivadiṁ.

Having directly known all as all, and having directly known that which does not fall within the scope of experience based on all, I did not identify with all, I did not identify regarding all, I did not identify as all, I did not identify 'all is mine', I did not enjoy all.

Evampi kho ahaṁ, brahme, neva te samasamo abhiññāya, kuto nīceyyaṁ?

So Brahmā, I am not your equal in knowledge, still less your inferior.

Atha kho ahameva tayā bhiyyo'ti.

Rather, I know more than you.'

'Sace kho, mārisa, sabbassa sabbattena ananubhūtaṁ, tadabhiññāya mā heva te rittakameva ahosi, tucchakameva ahosīti.

'Well, good sir, if you have directly known that which is not within the scope of experience based on all, may your words not turn out to be void and hollow!

Viññāṇaṁ anidassanaṁ anantaṁ sabbato pabhaṁ, taṁ pathaviyā pathavattena ananubhūtaṁ, āpassa āpattena ananubhūtaṁ, tejassa tejattena ananubhūtaṁ, vāyassa vāyattena ananubhūtaṁ, bhūtānaṁ bhūtattena ananubhūtaṁ, devānaṁ devattena ananubhūtaṁ, pajāpatissa pajāpatittena ananubhūtaṁ, brahmānaṁ brahmattena ananubhūtaṁ, ābhassarānaṁ ābhassarattena ananubhūtaṁ, subhakiṇhānaṁ subhakiṇhattena ananubhūtaṁ, vehapphalānaṁ vehapphalattena ananubhūtaṁ, abhibhussa abhibhuttena ananubhūtaṁ, sabbassa sabbattena ananubhūtaṁ.

Consciousness that is invisible, infinite, entirely given up—that's what is not within the scope of experience based on earth, water, fire, air, creatures, gods, the Creator, Brahmā, the gods of streaming radiance, the gods replete with glory, the gods of abundant fruit, the Overlord, and the all.

Handa carahi te, mārisa, passa antaradhāyāmī'ti.

Well look now, good sir, I will vanish from you!'

'Handa carahi me tvaṁ, brahme, antaradhāyassu, sace visahasī'ti.

'All right, then, Brahmā, vanish from me—if you can.'

Atha kho, bhikkhave, bako brahmā:

Then Baka the Brahmā said,

'antaradhāyissāmi samaṇassa gotamassa, antaradhāyissāmi samaṇassa gotamassā'ti nevassu me sakkoti antaradhāyituṁ.

'I will vanish from the ascetic Gotama! I will vanish from the ascetic Gotama!' But he was unable to vanish from me.

Evaṁ vutte, ahaṁ, bhikkhave, bakaṁ brahmānaṁ etadavocaṁ:

So I said to him,

'handa carahi te brahme antaradhāyāmī'ti.

'Well look now, Brahmā, I will vanish from you!'

'Handa carahi me tvaṁ, mārisa, antaradhāyassu sace visahasī'ti.

'All right, then, good sir, vanish from me—if you can.'

Atha kho ahaṁ, bhikkhave, tathārūpaṁ iddhābhisaṅkhāraṁ abhisaṅkhāsiṁ:

Then I used my psychic power to will that

'ettāvatā brahmā ca brahmaparisā ca brahmapārisajjā ca saddañca me sossanti, na ca maṁ dakkhantī'ti.

my voice would extend so that Brahmā, his assembly, and his retinue would hear me, but they would not see me.

Antarahito imaṁ gāthaṁ abhāsiṁ:

And while invisible I recited this verse:

'Bhavevāhaṁ bhayaṁ disvā,

bhavañca vibhavesinaṁ;

Bhavaṁ nābhivadiṁ kiñci,

nandiñca na upādiyin'ti.

'Seeing the danger in continued existence—

that life in any existence will cease to be—

I didn't welcome any kind of existence,

and didn't grasp at relishing.'

Atha kho, bhikkhave, brahmā ca brahmaparisā ca brahmapārisajjā ca acchariyabbhutacittajātā ahesuṁ:

Then Brahmā, his assembly, and his retinue, their minds full of wonder and amazement, thought,

'acchariyaṁ vata bho, abbhutaṁ vata bho.

'It's incredible, it's amazing!

Samaṇassa gotamassa mahiddhikatā mahānubhāvatā, na ca vata no ito pubbe diṭṭho vā, suto vā, añño samaṇo vā brāhmaṇo vā evaṁ mahiddhiko evaṁ mahānubhāvo yathāyaṁ samaṇo gotamo sakyaputto sakyakulā pabbajito.

The ascetic Gotama has such psychic power and might! We've never before seen or heard of any other ascetic or brahmin with psychic power and might like the ascetic Gotama, who has gone forth from the Sakyan clan.

Bhavarāmāya vata, bho, pajāya bhavaratāya bhavasammuditāya samūlaṁ bhavaṁ udabbahī'ti.

Though people enjoy continued existence, loving it so much, he has extracted it, root and all.'

Atha kho, bhikkhave, māro pāpimā aññataraṁ brahmapārisajjaṁ anvāvisitvā maṁ etadavoca:

Then Māra the Wicked took possession of a member of Brahmā's retinue and said this to me,

'sace kho tvaṁ, mārisa, evaṁ pajānāsi, sace tvaṁ evaṁ anubuddho, mā sāvake upanesi, mā pabbajite;

'If such is your understanding, good sir, do not present it to your disciples or those gone forth!

mā sāvakānaṁ dhammaṁ desesi, mā pabbajitānaṁ;

Do not teach this Dhamma to your disciples or those gone forth!

mā sāvakesu gedhimakāsi, mā pabbajitesu.

Do not wish this for your disciples or those gone forth!

Ahesuṁ kho, bhikkhu, tayā pubbe samaṇabrāhmaṇā lokasmiṁ arahanto sammāsambuddhā paṭijānamānā.

There have been ascetics and brahmins before you, mendicant, who claimed to be perfected ones, fully awakened Buddhas.

Te sāvake upanesuṁ pabbajite, sāvakānaṁ dhammaṁ desesuṁ pabbajitānaṁ, sāvakesu gedhimakaṁsu pabbajitesu, te sāvake upanetvā pabbajite, sāvakānaṁ dhammaṁ desetvā pabbajitānaṁ, sāvakesu gedhitacittā pabbajitesu,

They presented, taught, and wished this for their disciples and those gone forth.

kāyassa bhedā pāṇupacchedā hīne kāye patiṭṭhitā.

When their bodies broke up and their breath was cut off they were reborn in a lower realm.

Ahesuṁ ye pana, bhikkhu, tayā pubbe samaṇabrāhmaṇā lokasmiṁ arahanto sammāsambuddhā paṭijānamānā.

But there have also been other ascetics and brahmins before you, mendicant, who claimed to be perfected ones, fully awakened Buddhas.

Te na sāvake upanesuṁ na pabbajite, na sāvakānaṁ dhammaṁ desesuṁ na pabbajitānaṁ, na sāvakesu gedhimakaṁsu na pabbajitesu, te na sāvake upanetvā na pabbajite, na sāvakānaṁ dhammaṁ desetvā na pabbajitānaṁ, na sāvakesu gedhitacittā na pabbajitesu,

They did not present, teach, or wish this for their disciples and those gone forth.

kāyassa bhedā pāṇupacchedā paṇīte kāye patiṭṭhitā.

When their bodies broke up and their breath was cut off they were reborn in a higher realm.

Taṁ tāhaṁ, bhikkhu, evaṁ vadāmi—

So, mendicant, I tell you this:

iṅgha tvaṁ, mārisa, appossukko diṭṭhadhammasukhavihāramanuyutto viharassu, anakkhātaṁ kusalañhi, mārisa, mā paraṁ ovadāhī'ti.

please, good sir, remain passive, dwelling in blissful meditation in the present life, for this is better left unsaid. Good sir, do not instruct others.'

Evaṁ vutte, ahaṁ, bhikkhave, māraṁ pāpimantaṁ etadavocaṁ:

When he had spoken, I said to Māra,

'jānāmi kho tāhaṁ, pāpima, mā tvaṁ maññittho:

'I know you, Wicked One. Do not think,

"na maṁ jānātī"ti.

"He doesn't know me."

Māro tvamasi, pāpima.

You are Māra the Wicked.

Na maṁ tvaṁ, pāpima, hitānukampī evaṁ vadesi;

You don't speak to me like this out of compassion,

ahitānukampī maṁ tvaṁ, pāpima, evaṁ vadesi.

but with no compassion.

Tuyhañhi, pāpima, evaṁ hoti:

For you think,

"yesaṁ samaṇo gotamo dhammaṁ desessati, te me visayaṁ upātivattissantī"ti.

"Those who the ascetic Gotama teaches will go beyond my reach."

Asammāsambuddhāva pana te, pāpima, samānā sammāsambuddhāmhāti paṭijāniṁsu.

Those who formerly claimed to be fully awakened Buddhas were not in fact fully awakened Buddhas.

Ahaṁ kho pana, pāpima, sammāsambuddhova samāno sammāsambuddhomhīti paṭijānāmi.

But I am.

Desentopi hi, pāpima, tathāgato sāvakānaṁ dhammaṁ tādisova adesentopi hi, pāpima, tathāgato sāvakānaṁ dhammaṁ tādisova.

The Realized One remains as such whether or not he teaches disciples.

Upanentopi hi, pāpima, tathāgato sāvake tādisova, anupanentopi hi, pāpima, tathāgato sāvake tādisova.

The Realized One remains as such whether or not he presents the teaching to disciples.

Taṁ kissa hetu?

Why is that?

Tathāgatassa, pāpima, ye āsavā saṅkilesikā ponobbhavikā sadarā dukkhavipākā āyatiṁ jātijarāmaraṇiyā—

Because the Realized One has given up the defilements that are corrupting, leading to future lives, hurtful, resulting in suffering and future rebirth, old age, and death.

te pahīnā ucchinnamūlā tālāvatthukatā anabhāvaṅkatā āyatiṁ anuppādadhammā.

He has cut them off at the root, made them like a palm stump, obliterated them so they are unable to arise in the future.

Seyyathāpi, pāpima, tālo matthakacchinno abhabbo puna virūḷhiyā;

Just as a palm tree with its crown cut off is incapable of further growth,

evameva kho, pāpima, tathāgatassa ye āsavā saṅkilesikā ponobbhavikā sadarā dukkhavipākā āyatiṁ jātijarāmaraṇiyā—

the Realized One has given up the defilements that are corrupting, leading to future lives, hurtful, resulting in suffering and future rebirth, old age, and death.

te pahīnā ucchinnamūlā tālāvatthukatā anabhāvaṅkatā āyatiṁ anuppādadhammā'ti.

He has cut them off at the root, made them like a palm stump, obliterated them so they are unable to arise in the future.'"

Iti hidaṁ mārassa ca anālapanatāya brahmuno ca abhinimantanatāya, tasmā imassa veyyākaraṇassa brahmanimantanikantveva adhivacanan"ti.

And so, because of the silencing of Māra, and because of the invitation of Brahmā, the name of this discussion is "On the Invitation of Brahmā".

Brahmanimantanikasuttaṁ niṭṭhitaṁ navamaṁ.

50 Maratajjaniyasutta:

The Rebuke of Mara

Evaṁ me sutaṁ—

So I have heard.

ekaṁ samayaṁ āyasmā mahāmoggallāno bhaggesu viharati susumāragire bhesakaḷāvane migadāye.

At one time Venerable Mahāmoggallāna was staying in the land of the Bhaggas on Crocodile Hill, in the deer park at Bhesakaḷā's Wood.

Tena kho pana samayena āyasmā mahāmoggallāno abbhokāse caṅkamati.

At that time Moggallāna was walking mindfully in the open air.

Tena kho pana samayena māro pāpimā āyasmato mahāmoggallānassa kucchigato hoti koṭṭhamanupaviṭṭho.

Now at that time Māra the Wicked had got inside Moggallāna's belly.

Atha kho āyasmato mahāmoggallānassa etadahosi:

Moggallāna thought,

"kiṁ nu kho me kucchi garugaro viya?

"Why now is my belly so very heavy,

Māsācitaṁ maññe"ti.

like I've just eaten a load of beans?"

Atha kho āyasmā mahāmoggallāno caṅkamā orohitvā vihāraṁ pavisitvā paññatte āsane nisīdi.

Then he stepped down from the walking path, entered his dwelling, sat down on the seat spread out,

Nisajja kho āyasmā mahāmoggallāno paccattaṁ yoniso manasākāsi.

and investigated inside himself.

Addasā kho āyasmā mahāmoggallāno māraṁ pāpimantaṁ kucchigataṁ koṭṭhamanupaviṭṭhaṁ.

He saw that Māra the Wicked had got inside his belly.

Disvāna māraṁ pāpimantaṁ etadavoca:

So he said to Māra,

"nikkhama, pāpima;

"Come out, Wicked One,

nikkhama, pāpima.

come out!

Mā tathāgataṁ vihesesi, mā tathāgatasāvakaṁ.

Do not harass the Realized One or his disciple.

Mā te ahosi dīgharattaṁ ahitāya dukkhāyā”ti.

Don't create lasting harm and suffering for yourself!”

Atha kho mārassa pāpimato etadahosi:

Then Māra thought,

“ajānameva kho maṁ ayaṁ samaṇo apassaṁ evamāha:

“This ascetic doesn't really know me or see me when he tells me to come out.

‘nikkhama, pāpima;

nikkhama, pāpima.

Mā tathāgataṁ vihesesi, mā tathāgatasāvakaṁ.

Mā te ahosi dīgharattaṁ ahitāya dukkhāyā’ti.

Yopissa so satthā sopi maṁ neva khippaṁ jāneyya, kuto pana maṁ ayaṁ sāvako jānissatī”ti?

Not even the Teacher could recognize me so quickly, so how could a disciple?”

Atha kho āyasmā mahāmoggallāno māraṁ pāpimantaṁ etadavoca:

Then Moggallāna said to Māra,

“evampi kho tāhaṁ, pāpima, jānāmi, mā tvaṁ maññittho:

“I know you even when you're like this, Wicked One. Do not think,

‘na maṁ jānātī’ti.

‘He doesn't know me.’

Māro tvamasi, pāpima;

You are Māra the Wicked.

tuyhañhi, pāpima, evaṁ hoti:

And you think,

‘ajānameva kho maṁ ayaṁ samaṇo apassaṁ evamāha—

‘This ascetic doesn't really know me or see me when he tells me to come out.

nikkhama, pāpima;

nikkhama, pāpima.

Mā tathāgataṁ vihesesi, mā tathāgatasāvakaṁ.

Mā te ahosi dīgharattaṁ ahitāya dukkhāyāti.

Yopissa so satthā sopi maṁ neva khippaṁ jāneyya, kuto pana maṁ ayaṁ sāvako jānissatī'"ti?

Not even the Teacher could recognize me so quickly, so how could a disciple?'"

Atha kho mārassa pāpimato etadahosi:

Then Māra thought,

"jānameva kho maṁ ayaṁ samaṇo passaṁ evamāha:

"This ascetic really does know me and see me when he tells me to come out."

'nikkhama, pāpima;

nikkhama, pāpima.

Mā tathāgataṁ vihesesi, mā tathāgatasāvakaṁ.

Mā te ahosi dīgharattaṁ ahitāya dukkhāyā'"ti.

Atha kho māro pāpimā āyasmato mahāmoggallānassa mukhato uggantvā paccaggaḷe aṭṭhāsi.

Then Māra came up out of Moggallāna's mouth and stood against the door bar.

Addasā kho āyasmā mahāmoggallāno māraṁ pāpimantaṁ paccaggaḷe ṭhitaṁ;

Moggallāna saw him there

disvāna māraṁ pāpimantaṁ etadavoca:

and said,

"etthāpi kho tāhaṁ, pāpima, passāmi; mā tvaṁ maññittho

"I see you even there, Wicked One. Do not think,

'na maṁ passatī'ti.

'He doesn't see me.'

Eso tvaṁ, pāpima, paccaggaḷe ṭhito.

That's you, Wicked One, standing against the door bar.

Bhūtapubbāhaṁ, pāpima, dūsī nāma māro ahosiṁ, tassa me kāḷī nāma bhaginī.

Once upon a time, Wicked One, I was a Māra named Dūsī, and I had a sister named Kāḷī.

Tassā tvaṁ putto.

You were her son,

So me tvaṁ bhāgineyyo ahosi.

which made you my nephew.

Tena kho pana, pāpima, samayena kakusandho bhagavā arahaṁ sammāsambuddho loke uppanno hoti.

At that time Kakusandha, the Blessed One, the perfected one, the fully awakened Buddha arose in the world.

Kakusandhassa kho pana, pāpima, bhagavato arahato sammāsambuddhassa vidhurasañjīvaṁ nāma sāvakayugaṁ ahosi aggaṁ bhaddayugaṁ.

Kakusandha had a fine pair of chief disciples named Vidhura and Sañjīva.

Yāvatā kho pana, pāpima, kakusandhassa bhagavato arahato sammāsambuddhassa sāvakā.

Of all the disciples of the Buddha Kakusandha,

Tesu na ca koci āyasmatā vidhurena samasamo hoti yadidaṁ dhammadesanāya.

none were the equal of Venerable Vidhura in teaching Dhamma.

Iminā kho evaṁ, pāpima, pariyāyena āyasmato vidhurassa vidhuroteva samaññā udapādi.

And that's how he came to be known as Vidhura.

Āyasmā pana, pāpima, sañjīvo araññagatopi rukkhamūlagatopi suññāgāragatopi appakasireneva saññāvedayitanirodhaṁ samāpajjati.

But when Venerable Sañjīva had gone to a wilderness, or to the root of a tree, or to an empty hut, he easily attained the cessation of perception and feeling.

Bhūtapubbaṁ, pāpima, āyasmā sañjīvo aññatarasmiṁ rukkhamūle saññāvedayitanirodhaṁ samāpanno nisinno hoti.

Once upon a time, Sañjīva was sitting at the root of a certain tree having attained the cessation of perception and feeling.

Addasaṁsu kho, pāpima, gopālakā pasupālakā kassakā pathāvino āyasmantaṁ sañjīvaṁ aññatarasmiṁ rukkhamūle saññāvedayitanirodhaṁ samāpannaṁ nisinnaṁ;

Some cowherds, shepherds, farmers, and passers-by saw him sitting there

disvāna tesaṁ etadahosi:

and said,

'acchariyaṁ vata bho, abbhutaṁ vata, bho.

'It's incredible, it's amazing!

Ayaṁ samaṇo nisinnakova kālaṅkato.

This ascetic passed away while sitting.

Handa naṁ dahāmā'ti.

We should cremate him.'

Atha kho te, pāpima, gopālakā pasupālakā kassakā pathāvino tiṇañca kaṭṭhañca gomayañca saṅkaḍḍhitvā āyasmato sañjīvassa kāye upacinitvā aggiṁ datvā pakkamiṁsu.

They collected grass, wood, and cow-dung, heaped it all on Sañjīva's body, set it on fire, and left.

Atha kho, pāpima, āyasmā sañjīvo tassā rattiyā accayena tāya samāpattiyā vuṭṭhahitvā cīvarāni papphoṭetvā pubbaṇhasamayaṁ nivāsetvā pattacīvaramādāya gāmaṁ piṇḍāya pāvisi.

Then, when the night had passed, Sañjīva emerged from that attainment, shook out his robes, and, since it was morning, he robed up and entered the village for alms.

Addasaṁsu kho te, pāpima, gopālakā pasupālakā kassakā pathāvino āyasmantaṁ sañjīvaṁ piṇḍāya carantaṁ;

Those cowherds, shepherds, farmers, and passers-by saw him wandering for alms

disvāna nesaṁ etadahosi:

and said,

'acchariyaṁ vata bho, abbhutaṁ vata, bho.

'It's incredible, it's amazing!

Ayaṁ samaṇo nisinnakova kālaṅkato, svāyaṁ paṭisañjīvito'ti.

This ascetic passed away while sitting, and now he has come back to life!'

Iminā kho evaṁ, pāpima, pariyāyena āyasmato sañjīvassa sañjīvoteva samaññā udapādi.

And that's how he came to be known as Sañjīva.

Atha kho, pāpima, dūsissa mārassa etadahosi:

Then it occurred to Māra Dūsī,

'imesaṁ kho ahaṁ bhikkhūnaṁ sīlavantānaṁ kalyāṇadhammānaṁ neva jānāmi āgatiṁ vā gatiṁ vā.

'I don't know the course of rebirth of these ethical mendicants of good character.

Yannūnāhaṁ brāhmaṇagahapatike anvāviseyyaṁ—

Why don't I take possession of these brahmins and householders and say,

etha, tumhe bhikkhū sīlavante kalyāṇadhamme akkosatha paribhāsatha rosetha vihesetha.

"Come, all of you, abuse, attack, harass, and trouble the ethical mendicants of good character.

Appeva nāma tumhehi akkosiyamānānaṁ paribhāsiyamānānaṁ rosiyamānānaṁ vihesiyamānānaṁ siyā cittassa aññathattaṁ, yathā taṁ dūsī māro labhetha otāran'ti.

Hopefully by doing this we can upset their minds so that Māra Dūsī can find a vulnerability."'

Atha kho te, pāpima, dūsī māro brāhmaṇagahapatike anvāvisi:

And that's exactly what he did.

'etha, tumhe bhikkhū sīlavante kalyāṇadhamme akkosatha paribhāsatha rosetha vihesetha.

Appeva nāma tumhehi akkosiyamānānaṁ paribhāsiyamānānaṁ rosiyamānānaṁ vihesiyamānānaṁ siyā cittassa aññathattaṁ, yathā taṁ dūsī māro labhetha otāran'ti.

Atha kho te, pāpima, brāhmaṇagahapatikā anvāvisiṭṭhā dūsinā mārena bhikkhū sīlavante kalyāṇadhamme akkosanti paribhāsanti rosenti vihesenti:

Then those brahmins and householders abused, attacked, harassed, and troubled the ethical mendicants of good character:

'ime pana muṇḍakā samaṇakā ibbhā kiṇhā bandhupādāpaccā "jhāyinosmā jhāyinosmā"ti pattakkhandhā adhomukhā madhurakajātā jhāyanti pajjhāyanti nijjhāyanti apajjhāyanti.

'These shavelings, fake ascetics, primitives, black spawn from the feet of our kinsman, say, "We practice absorption meditation! We practice absorption meditation!" Slouching, downcast, and dopey, they meditate and concentrate and contemplate and ruminate.

Seyyathāpi nāma ulūko rukkhasākhāyaṁ mūsikaṁ maggayamāno jhāyati pajjhāyati nijjhāyati apajjhāyati;

They're just like an owl on a branch, which meditates and concentrates and contemplates and ruminates as it hunts a mouse.

evamevime muṇḍakā samaṇakā ibbhā kiṇhā bandhupādāpaccā "jhāyinosmā jhāyinosmā"ti pattakkhandhā adhomukhā madhurakajātā jhāyanti pajjhāyanti nijjhāyanti apajjhāyanti.

Seyyathāpi nāma kotthu nadītīre macche maggayamāno jhāyati pajjhāyati nijjhāyati apajjhāyati;

They're just like a jackal on a river-bank, which meditates and concentrates and contemplates and ruminates as it hunts a fish.

evamevime muṇḍakā samaṇakā ibbhā kiṇhā bandhupādāpaccā "jhāyinosmā jhāyinosmā"ti pattakkhandhā adhomukhā madhurakajātā jhāyanti pajjhāyanti nijjhāyanti apajjhāyanti.

Seyyathāpi nāma biḷāro sandhisamalasaṅkaṭīre mūsikaṁ maggayamāno jhāyati pajjhāyati nijjhāyati apajjhāyati;

They're just like a cat by an alley or a drain or a dustbin, which meditates and concentrates and contemplates and ruminates as it hunts a mouse.

evamevime muṇḍakā samaṇakā ibbhā kiṇhā bandhupādāpaccā "jhāyinosmā jhāyinosmā"ti pattakkhandhā adhomukhā madhurakajātā jhāyanti pajjhāyanti nijjhāyanti apajjhāyanti.

Seyyathāpi nāma gadrabho vahacchinno sandhisamalasaṅkaṭīre jhāyati pajjhāyati nijjhāyati apajjhāyati;

They're just like an unladen donkey by an alley or a drain or a dustbin, which meditates and concentrates and contemplates and ruminates.

evamevime muṇḍakā samaṇakā ibbhā kiṇhā bandhupādāpaccā "jhāyinosmā jhāyinosmā"ti pattakkhandhā adhomukhā madhurakajātā jhāyanti pajjhāyanti nijjhāyanti apajjhāyantī'ti.

In the same way, these shavelings, fake ascetics, primitives, black spawn from the feet of our kinsman, say, "We practice absorption meditation! We practice absorption meditation!" Slouching, downcast, and dopey, they meditate and concentrate and contemplate and ruminate.'

Ye kho pana, pāpima, tena samayena manussā kālaṁ karonti yebhuyyena kāyassa bhedā paraṁ maraṇā apāyaṁ duggatiṁ vinipātaṁ nirayaṁ upapajjanti.

Most of the people who died at that time—when their body broke up, after death—were reborn in a place of loss, a bad place, the underworld, hell.

Atha kho, pāpima, kakusandho bhagavā arahaṁ sammāsambuddho bhikkhū āmantesi:

Then Kakusandha the Blessed One, the perfected one, the fully awakened Buddha, addressed the mendicants:

'anvāviṭṭhā kho, bhikkhave, brāhmaṇagahapatikā dūsinā mārena—

'Mendicants, the brahmins and householders have been possessed by Māra Dūsī.

etha, tumhe bhikkhū sīlavante kalyāṇadhamme akkosatha paribhāsatha rosetha vihesetha, appeva nāma tumhehi akkosiyamānānaṁ paribhāsiyamānānaṁ rosiyamānānaṁ vihesiyamānānaṁ siyā cittassa aññathattaṁ, yathā taṁ dūsī māro labhetha otāran'ti.

He told them to abuse you in the hope of upsetting your minds so that he can find a vulnerability.

Etha, tumhe, bhikkhave, mettāsahagatena cetasā ekaṁ disaṁ pharitvā viharatha, tathā dutiyaṁ, tathā tatiyaṁ, tathā catutthaṁ. Iti uddhamadho tiriyaṁ sabbadhi sabbattatāya sabbāvantaṁ lokaṁ mettāsahagatena cetasā vipulena mahaggatena appamāṇena averena abyābajjhena pharitvā viharatha.

Come, all of you mendicants, meditate spreading a heart full of love to one direction, and to the second, and to the third, and to the fourth. In the same way above, below, across, everywhere, all around, spread a heart full of love to the whole world—abundant, expansive, limitless, free of enmity and ill will.

Karuṇāsahagatena cetasā …pe…

Meditate spreading a heart full of compassion …

muditāsahagatena cetasā …pe…

Meditate spreading a heart full of rejoicing …

upekkhāsahagatena cetasā ekaṁ disaṁ pharitvā viharatha, tathā dutiyaṁ, tathā tatiyaṁ, tathā catutthaṁ. Iti uddhamadho tiriyaṁ sabbadhi sabbattatāya sabbāvantaṁ lokaṁ upekkhāsahagatena cetasā vipulena mahaggatena appamāṇena averena abyābajjhena pharitvā viharathā'ti.

Meditate spreading a heart full of equanimity to one direction, and to the second, and to the third, and to the fourth. In the same way above, below, across, everywhere, all around, spread a heart full of equanimity to the whole world—abundant, expansive, limitless, free of enmity and ill will.'

Atha kho te, pāpima, bhikkhū kakusandhena bhagavatā arahatā sammāsambuddhena evaṁ ovadiyamānā evaṁ anusāsiyamānā araññagatāpi rukkhamūlagatāpi suññāgāragatāpi mettāsahagatena cetasā ekaṁ disaṁ pharitvā vihariṁsu, tathā dutiyaṁ, tathā tatiyaṁ, tathā catutthaṁ. Iti uddhamadho tiriyaṁ sabbadhi sabbattatāya sabbāvantaṁ lokaṁ mettāsahagatena cetasā vipulena mahaggatena appamāṇena averena abyābajjhena pharitvā vihariṁsu.

When those mendicants were instructed and advised by the Buddha Kakusandha in this way, they went to a wilderness, or to the root of a tree, or to an empty hut, where they meditated spreading a heart full of love …

Karuṇāsahagatena cetasā …pe…

compassion …

muditāsahagatena cetasā …pe…

rejoicing …

upekkhāsahagatena cetasā ekaṁ disaṁ pharitvā vihariṁsu, tathā dutiyaṁ, tathā tatiyaṁ, tathā catutthaṁ. Iti uddhamadho tiriyaṁ sabbadhi sabbattatāya sabbāvantaṁ lokaṁ upekkhāsahagatena cetasā vipulena mahaggatena appamāṇena averena abyābajjhena pharitvā vihariṁsu.

equanimity.

Atha kho, pāpima, dūsissa mārassa etadahosi:

Then it occurred to Māra Dūsī,

'evampi kho ahaṁ karonto imesaṁ bhikkhūnaṁ sīlavantānaṁ kalyāṇadhammānaṁ neva jānāmi āgatiṁ vā gatiṁ vā, yannūnāhaṁ brāhmaṇagahapatike anvāviseyyaṁ:

'Even when I do this I don't know the course of rebirth of these ethical mendicants of good character. Why don't I take possession of these brahmins and householders and say,

"etha, tumhe bhikkhū sīlavante kalyāṇadhamme sakkarotha garuṁ karotha mānetha pūjetha,

"Come, all of you, honor, respect, esteem, and venerate the ethical mendicants of good character.

appeva nāma tumhehi sakkariyamānānaṁ garukariyamānānaṁ māniyamānānaṁ pūjiyamānānaṁ siyā cittassa aññathattaṁ, yathā taṁ dūsī māro labhetha otāran"'ti.

Hopefully by doing this we can upset their minds so that Māra Dūsī can find a vulnerability."'

Atha kho te, pāpima, dūsī māro brāhmaṇagahapatike anvāvisi:

And that's exactly what he did.

'etha, tumhe bhikkhū sīlavante kalyāṇadhamme sakkarotha garuṁ karotha mānetha pūjetha,

appeva nāma tumhehi sakkariyamānānaṁ garukariyamānānaṁ māniyamānānaṁ pūjiyamānānaṁ siyā cittassa aññathattaṁ, yathā taṁ dūsī māro labhetha otāran'ti.

Atha kho te, pāpima, brāhmaṇagahapatikā anvāviṭṭhā dūsinā mārena bhikkhū sīlavante kalyāṇadhamme sakkaronti garuṁ karonti mānenti pūjenti.

Then those brahmins and householders honored, respected, esteemed, and venerated the ethical mendicants of good character.

Ye kho pana, pāpima, tena samayena manussā kālaṁ karonti yebhuyyena kāyassa bhedā paraṁ maraṇā sugatiṁ saggaṁ lokaṁ upapajjanti.

Most of the people who died at that time—when their body broke up, after death— were reborn in a good place, a heavenly realm.

Atha kho, pāpima, kakusandho bhagavā arahaṁ sammāsambuddho bhikkhū āmantesi:

Then Kakusandha the Blessed One, the perfected one, the fully awakened Buddha, addressed the mendicants:

'anvāviṭṭhā kho, bhikkhave, brāhmaṇagahapatikā dūsinā mārena:

'Mendicants, the brahmins and householders have been possessed by Māra Dūsī.

"etha, tumhe bhikkhū sīlavante kalyāṇadhamme sakkarotha garuṁ karotha mānetha pūjetha,

He told them to venerate you

appeva nāma tumhehi sakkariyamānānaṁ garukariyamānānaṁ māniyamānānaṁ pūjiyamānānaṁ siyā cittassa aññathattaṁ, yathā taṁ dūsī māro labhetha otāran"ti.

in the hope of upsetting your minds so that he can find a vulnerability.

Etha, tumhe, bhikkhave, asubhānupassino kāye viharatha, āhāre paṭikūlasaññino, sabbaloke anabhiratisaññino, sabbasaṅkhāresu aniccānupassino'ti.

Come, all you mendicants, meditate observing the ugliness of the body, perceiving the repulsiveness of food, perceiving dissatisfaction with the whole world, and observing the impermanence of all conditions.'

Atha kho te, pāpima, bhikkhū kakusandhena bhagavatā arahatā sammāsambuddhena evaṁ ovadiyamānā evaṁ anusāsiyamānā araññagatāpi rukkhamūlagatāpi suññāgāragatāpi asubhānupassino kāye vihariṁsu, āhāre paṭikūlasaññino, sabbaloke anabhiratisaññino, sabbasaṅkhāresu aniccānupassino.

When those mendicants were instructed and advised by the Buddha Kakusandha in this way, they went to a wilderness, or to the root of a tree, or to an empty hut, where they meditated observing the ugliness of the body, perceiving the repulsiveness of food, perceiving dissatisfaction with the whole world, and observing the impermanence of all conditions.

Atha kho, pāpima, kakusandho bhagavā arahaṁ sammāsambuddho pubbaṇhasamayaṁ nivāsetvā pattacīvaramādāya āyasmatā vidhurena pacchāsamaṇena gāmaṁ piṇḍāya pāvisi.

Then the Buddha Kakusandha robed up in the morning and, taking this bowl and robe, entered the village for alms with Venerable Vidhura as his second monk.

Atha kho, pāpima, dūsī māro aññataraṁ kumārakaṁ anvāvisitvā sakkharaṁ gahetvā āyasmato vidhurassa sīse pahāramadāsi; sīsaṁ vobhindi.

Then Māra Dūsī took possession of a certain boy, picked up a rock, and hit Vidhura on the head, cracking it open.

Atha kho, pāpima, āyasmā vidhuro bhinnena sīsena lohitena galantena kakusandhaṁyeva bhagavantaṁ arahantaṁ sammāsambuddhaṁ piṭṭhito piṭṭhito anubandhi.

Then Vidhura, with blood pouring from his cracked skull, still followed behind the Buddha Kakusandha.

Atha kho, pāpima, kakusandho bhagavā arahaṁ sammāsambuddho nāgāpalokitaṁ apalokesi:

Then the Buddha Kakusandha turned to gaze back, the way that elephants do, saying,

'na vāyaṁ dūsī māro mattamaññāsī'ti.

'This Māra Dūsī knows no bounds.'

Sahāpalokanāya ca pana, pāpima, dūsī māro tamhā ca ṭhānā cavi mahānirayañca upapajji.

And with that look Māra Dūsī fell from that place and was reborn in the Great Hell.

Tassa kho pana, pāpima, mahānirayassa tayo nāmadheyyā honti—

Now that Great Hell is known by three names:

chaphassāyataniko itipi, saṅkusamāhato itipi, paccattavedaniyo itipi.

'The Six Fields of Contact' and also 'The Impaling With Spikes' and also 'Individually Painful'.

Atha kho maṁ, pāpima, nirayapālā upasaṅkamitvā etadavocuṁ:

Then the wardens of hell came to me and said,

'yadā kho te, mārisa, saṅkunā saṅku hadaye samāgaccheyya.

'When spike meets spike in your heart,

Atha naṁ tvaṁ jāneyyāsi:

you will know that

"vassasahassaṁ me niraye paccamānassā"'ti.

you've been roasting in hell for a thousand years.'

So kho ahaṁ, pāpima, bahūni vassāni bahūni vassasatāni bahūni vassasahassāni tasmiṁ mahāniraye apacciṁ.

I roasted for many years, many centuries, many millennia in that Great Hell.

Dasavassasahassāni tasseva mahānirayassa ussade apacciṁ vuṭṭhānimaṁ nāma vedanaṁ vediyamāno.

For ten thousand years I roasted in the annex of that Great Hell, experiencing the pain called 'this is emergence'.

Tassa mayhaṁ, pāpima, evarūpo kāyo hoti, seyyathāpi manussassa.

My body was in human form,

Evarūpaṁ sīsaṁ hoti, seyyathāpi macchassa.

but I had the head of a fish.

Kīdiso nirayo āsi,

yattha dūsī apaccatha;

Vidhuraṁ sāvakamāsajja,

kakusandhañca brāhmaṇaṁ.

What kind of hell was that,

where Dūsī was roasted

after attacking the disciple Vidhura

along with the brahmin Kakusandha?

Sataṁ āsi ayosaṅkū,

sabbe paccattavedanā;

Īdiso nirayo āsi,

yattha dūsī apaccatha;

Vidhuraṁ sāvakamāsajja,

kakusandhañca brāhmaṇaṁ.

There were 100 iron spikes,

each one individually painful.

That's the kind of hell

where Dūsī was roasted

after attacking the disciple Vidhura

along with the brahmin Kakusandha.

Yo etamabhijānāti,

bhikkhu buddhassa sāvako;

Tādisaṁ bhikkhumāsajja,

kaṇha dukkhaṁ nigacchasi.

Dark One, if you attack

a mendicant who directly knows this,

a disciple of the Buddha,

you'll fall into suffering.

Majjhe sarassa tiṭṭhanti,

vimānā kappaṭṭhāyino;

Veḷuriyavaṇṇā rucirā,

accimanto pabhassarā;

Accharā tattha naccanti,

puthu nānattavaṇṇiyo.

There are mansions that last for an eon

standing in the middle of a lake.

Sapphire-colored, brilliant,

they sparkle and shine.

Dancing there are nymphs

shining in all different colors.

Yo etamabhijānāti,

bhikkhu buddhassa sāvako;

Tādisaṁ bhikkhumāsajja,

kaṇha dukkhaṁ nigacchasi.

Dark One, if you attack

a mendicant who directly knows this,

a disciple of the Buddha,

you'll fall into suffering.

Yo ve buddhena codito,

bhikkhu saṅghassa pekkhato;

Migāramātupāsādaṁ,

pādaṅgutthena kampayi.

I'm the one who, urged by the Buddha,

shook the stilt longhouse of Migāra's mother

with his big toe

as the Saṅgha of mendicants watched.

Yo etamabhijānāti,

bhikkhu buddhassa sāvako;

Tādisaṁ bhikkhumāsajja,

kaṇha dukkhaṁ nigacchasi.

Dark One, if you attack

a mendicant who directly knows this,

a disciple of the Buddha,

you'll fall into suffering.

Yo vejayantaṁ pāsādaṁ,

pādaṅgutthena kampayi;

Iddhibalenupatthaddho,

saṁvejesi ca devatā.

I'm the one who shook the Palace of Victory

with his big toe

owing to psychic power,

inspiring deities to awe.

Yo etamabhijānāti,

bhikkhu buddhassa sāvako;

Tādisaṁ bhikkhumāsajja,

kaṇha dukkhaṁ nigacchasi.

Dark One, if you attack

a mendicant who directly knows this,

a disciple of the Buddha,

you'll fall into suffering.

Yo vejayantapāsāde,

sakkaṁ so paripucchati;

Api vāsava jānāsi,

taṇhākkhayavimuttiyo;

Tassa sakko viyākāsi,

pañhaṁ puṭṭho yathātathaṁ.

I'm the one who asked Sakka

in the Palace of Victory:

'Vāsava, do you know the freedom

that comes with the ending of craving?'

And I'm the one to whom Sakka

admitted the truth when asked.

Yo etamabhijānāti,

bhikkhu buddhassa sāvako;

Tādisaṁ bhikkhumāsajja,

kaṇha dukkhaṁ nigacchasi.

Dark One, if you attack

a mendicant who directly knows this,

a disciple of the Buddha,

you'll fall into suffering.

Yo brahmaṁ paripucchati,

sudhammāyābhito sabhaṁ;

Ajjāpi tyāvuso diṭṭhi,

yā te diṭṭhi pure ahu;

Passasi vītivattantaṁ,

brahmaloke pabhassaraṁ.

I'm the one who asked Brahmā

in the Hall of Justice before the assembly:

'Friend, do you still have the same view

that you had in the past?

Or do you see the radiance

transcending the Brahmā realm?'

Tassa brahmā viyākāsi,

anupubbaṁ yathātathaṁ;

Na me mārisa sā diṭṭhi,

yā me diṭṭhi pure ahu.

And I'm the one to whom Brahmā

truthfully admitted his progress:

'Good sir, I don't have that view

that I had in the past.

Passāmi vītivattantaṁ,

brahmaloke pabhassaraṁ;

Sohaṁ ajja kathaṁ vajjaṁ,

ahaṁ niccomhi sassato.

I see the radiance

transcending the Brahmā realm.

So how could I say today

that I am permanent and eternal?'

Yo etamabhijānāti,

bhikkhu buddhassa sāvako;

Tādisaṁ bhikkhumāsajja,

kaṇha dukkhaṁ nigacchasi.

Dark One, if you attack

a mendicant who directly knows this,

a disciple of the Buddha,

you'll fall into suffering.

Yo mahāmeruno kūṭaṁ,

vimokkhena aphassayi;

Vanaṁ pubbavidehānaṁ,

ye ca bhūmisayā narā.

I'm the one who touched the peak of Mount Meru

using the power of meditative liberation.

I've visited the forests of the people

who dwell in the Eastern Continent.

Yo etamabhijānāti,

bhikkhu buddhassa sāvako;

Tādisaṁ bhikkhumāsajja,

kaṇha dukkhaṁ nigacchasi.

Dark One, if you attack

a mendicant who directly knows this,

a disciple of the Buddha,

you'll fall into suffering.

Na ve aggi cetayati,

'ahaṁ bālaṁ ḍahāmī'ti;

Bālo ca jalitaṁ aggiṁ,

āsajja naṁ sa ḍayhati.

Though a fire doesn't think,

'I'll burn the fool!'

Still the fool who attacks

the fire gets burnt.

Evameva tuvaṁ māra,

āsajja naṁ tathāgataṁ;

Sayaṁ ḍahissasi attānaṁ,

bālo aggiṁva samphusaṁ.

In the same way, Māra,

in attacking the Realized One,

you'll only burn yourself,

like a fool touching the flames.

Apuññaṁ pasavī māro,

āsajja naṁ tathāgataṁ;

Kiṁ nu maññasi pāpima,

na me pāpaṁ vipaccati.

Māra's done a bad thing

in attacking the Realized One.

Wicked One, do you imagine that

your wickedness won't bear fruit?

Karoto cīyati pāpaṁ,

cirarattāya antaka;

Māra nibbinda buddhamhā,

āsaṁ mākāsi bhikkhusu.

Your deeds heap up wickedness

that will last a long time, terminator!

Forget about the Buddha, Māra!

And give up your hopes for the mendicants!"

Iti māraṁ atajjesi,

bhikkhu bhesakaḷāvane;

Tato so dummano yakkho,

tatthevantaradhāyathā"ti.

That is how, in the Bhesekaḷā grove,

the mendicant rebuked Māra.

That spirit, downcast,

disappeared right there!

Māratajjanīyasuttaṁ niṭṭhitaṁ dasamaṁ.

Cūḷayamakavaggo niṭṭhito pañcamo.

Tassuddānaṁ

Sāleyya verañjaduve ca tuṭṭhi,

Cūḷamahādhammasamādānañca;

Vīmaṁsakā kosambi ca brāhmaṇo,

Dūsī ca māro dasamo ca vaggo.

Idaṁ vaggānamuddānaṁ

Mūlapariyāyo ceva,

sīhanādo ca uttamo;

Kakaco ceva gosiṅgo,

sāleyyo ca ime pañca.

Mūlapaṇṇāsakaṁ samattaṁ.

MAJJHIMAPAṆṆASAPĀḶI

PART TWO: THE MIDDLE FIFTY DISCOURSES

GAHAPATIVAGGA

THE DIVISION ON HOUSEHOLDERS

51 Kandarakasutta:

With Kandaraka

Evaṁ me sutaṁ—

So I have heard.

ekaṁ samayaṁ bhagavā campāyaṁ viharati gaggarāya pokkharaṇiyā tīre mahatā bhikkhusaṅghena saddhiṁ.

At one time the Buddha was staying near Campā on the banks of the Gaggarā Lotus Pond together with a large Saṅgha of mendicants.

Atha kho pesso ca hatthārohaputto kandarako ca paribbājako yena bhagavā tenupasaṅkamiṁsu; upasaṅkamitvā pesso hatthārohaputto bhagavantaṁ abhivādetvā ekamantaṁ nisīdi.

Then Pessa the elephant driver's son and Kandaraka the wanderer went to see the Buddha. When they had approached, Pessa bowed and sat down to one side.

Kandarako pana paribbājako bhagavatā saddhiṁ sammodi. Sammodanīyaṁ kathaṁ sāraṇīyaṁ vītisāretvā ekamantaṁ aṭṭhāsi.

But the wanderer Kandaraka exchanged greetings with the Buddha and stood to one side.

Ekamantaṁ ṭhito kho kandarako paribbājako tuṇhībhūtaṁ tuṇhībhūtaṁ bhikkhusaṅghaṁ anuviloketvā bhagavantaṁ etadavoca:

He looked around the mendicant Saṅgha, who were so very silent, and said to the Buddha:

"acchariyaṁ, bho gotama, abbhutaṁ, bho gotama.

"It's incredible, Master Gotama, it's amazing!

Yāvañcidaṁ bhotā gotamena sammā bhikkhusaṅgho paṭipādito.

How the mendicant Saṅgha has been led to practice properly by Master Gotama!

Yepi te, bho gotama, ahesuṁ atītamaddhānaṁ arahanto sammāsambuddhā tepi bhagavanto etaparamaṁyeva sammā bhikkhusaṅghaṁ paṭipādesuṁ—

All the perfected ones, the fully awakened Buddhas in the past or the future who lead the mendicant Saṅgha to practice properly will at best do so

seyyathāpi etarahi bhotā gotamena sammā bhikkhusaṅgho paṭipādito.

like Master Gotama does in the present."

Yepi te, bho gotama, bhavissanti anāgatamaddhānaṁ arahanto sammāsambuddhā tepi bhagavanto etaparamaṁyeva sammā bhikkhusaṅghaṁ paṭipādessanti—

seyyathāpi etarahi bhotā gotamena sammā bhikkhusaṅgho paṭipādito"ti.

"Evametaṁ, kandaraka, evametaṁ, kandaraka.

"That's so true, Kandaraka! That's so true!

Yepi te, kandaraka, ahesuṁ atītamaddhānaṁ arahanto sammāsambuddhā tepi bhagavanto etaparamaṁyeva sammā bhikkhusaṅghaṁ paṭipādesuṁ—

All the perfected ones, the fully awakened Buddhas in the past or the future who lead the mendicant Saṅgha to practice properly will at best do so

seyyathāpi etarahi mayā sammā bhikkhusaṅgho paṭipādito.

like I do in the present.

Yepi te, kandaraka, bhavissanti anāgatamaddhānaṁ arahanto sammāsambuddhā tepi bhagavanto etaparamaṁyeva sammā bhikkhusaṅghaṁ paṭipādessanti—

seyyathāpi etarahi mayā sammā bhikkhusaṅgho paṭipādito.

Santi hi, kandaraka, bhikkhū imasmiṁ bhikkhusaṅghe arahanto khīṇāsavā vusitavanto katakaraṇīyā ohitabhārā anuppattasadatthā parikkhīṇabhavasaṁyojanā sammadaññāvimuttā.

For in this mendicant Saṅgha there are perfected mendicants, who have ended the defilements, completed the spiritual journey, done what had to be done, laid down the burden, achieved their own goal, utterly ended the fetters of rebirth, and are rightly freed through enlightenment.

Santi hi, kandaraka, bhikkhū imasmiṁ bhikkhusaṅghe sekkhā santatasīlā santatavuttino nipakā nipakavuttino;

And in this mendicant Saṅgha there are trainee mendicants who are consistently ethical, living consistently, alert, living alertly.

te catūsu satipaṭṭhānesu suppatiṭṭhitacittā viharanti.

They meditate with their minds firmly established in the four kinds of mindfulness meditation.

Katamesu catūsu?

What four?

Idha, kandaraka, bhikkhu kāye kāyānupassī viharati ātāpī sampajāno satimā, vineyya loke abhijjhādomanassaṁ;

It's when a mendicant meditates by observing an aspect of the body—keen, aware, and mindful, rid of desire and aversion for the world.

vedanāsu vedanānupassī viharati ātāpī sampajāno satimā, vineyya loke abhijjhādomanassaṁ;

They meditate observing an aspect of feelings—keen, aware, and mindful, rid of desire and aversion for the world.

citte cittānupassī viharati ātāpī sampajāno satimā, vineyya loke abhijjhādomanassaṁ;

They meditate observing an aspect of the mind—keen, aware, and mindful, rid of desire and aversion for the world.

dhammesu dhammānupassī viharati ātāpī sampajāno satimā, vineyya loke abhijjhādomanassan"ti.

They meditate observing an aspect of principles—keen, aware, and mindful, rid of desire and aversion for the world."

Evaṁ vutte, pesso hatthārohaputto bhagavantaṁ etadavoca:

When he had spoken, Pessa said to the Buddha:

"acchariyaṁ, bhante, abbhutaṁ, bhante.

"It's incredible, sir, it's amazing,

Yāva supaññattā cime, bhante, bhagavatā cattāro satipaṭṭhānā sattānaṁ visuddhiyā sokaparidevānaṁ samatikkamāya dukkhadomanassānaṁ atthaṅgamāya ñāyassa adhigamāya nibbānassa sacchikiriyāya.

how much the Buddha has clearly described the four kinds of mindfulness meditation! They are in order to purify sentient beings, to get past sorrow and crying, to make an end of pain and sadness, to end the cycle of suffering, and to realize extinguishment.

Mayampi hi, bhante, gihī odātavasanā kālena kālaṁ imesu catūsu satipaṭṭhānesu suppatiṭṭhitacittā viharāma.

For we white-clothed laypeople also from time to time meditate with our minds well established in the four kinds of mindfulness meditation.

Idha mayaṁ, bhante, kāye kāyānupassino viharāma ātāpino sampajānā satimanto, vineyya loke abhijjhādomanassaṁ;

We meditate observing an aspect of the body ...

vedanāsu vedanānupassino viharāma ātāpino sampajānā satimanto, vineyya loke abhijjhādomanassaṁ;

feelings ...

citte cittānupassino viharāma ātāpino sampajānā satimanto, vineyya loke abhijjhādomanassaṁ;

mind ...

dhammesu dhammānupassino viharāma ātāpino sampajānā satimanto, vineyya loke abhijjhādomanassaṁ.

principles—keen, aware, and mindful, rid of desire and aversion for the world.

Acchariyaṁ, bhante, abbhutaṁ, bhante.

It's incredible, sir, it's amazing!

Yāvañcidaṁ, bhante, bhagavā evaṁ manussagahane evaṁ manussakasaṭe evaṁ manussasāṭheyye vattamāne sattānaṁ hitāhitaṁ jānāti.

How the Buddha knows what's best for sentient beings, even though people continue to be so shady, rotten, and tricky.

Gahanañhetaṁ, bhante, yadidaṁ manussā;

For human beings are shady, sir,

uttānakañhetaṁ, bhante, yadidaṁ pasavo.

while the animal is obvious.

Ahañhi, bhante, pahomi hatthidammaṁ sāretuṁ.

For I can drive an elephant in training,

Yāvatakena antarena campaṁ gatāgataṁ karissati sabbāni tāni sāṭheyyāni kūṭeyyāni vaṅkeyyāni jimheyyāni pātukarissati.

and while going back and forth in Campā it'll try all the tricks, bluffs, ruses, and feints that it can.

Amhākaṁ pana, bhante, dāsāti vā pessāti vā kammakarāti vā aññathāva kāyena samudācaranti aññathāva vācāya aññathāva nesaṁ cittaṁ hoti.

But my bondservants, employees, and workers behave one way by body, another by speech, and their minds another.

Acchariyaṁ, bhante, abbhutaṁ, bhante.

It's incredible, sir, it's amazing!

Yāvañcidaṁ, bhante, bhagavā evaṁ manussagahane evaṁ manussakasaṭe evaṁ manussasāṭheyye vattamāne sattānaṁ hitāhitaṁ jānāti.

How the Buddha knows what's best for sentient beings, even though people continue to be so shady, rotten, and tricky.

Gahanañhetaṁ, bhante, yadidaṁ manussā;

For human beings are shady, sir,

uttānakañhetaṁ, bhante, yadidaṁ pasavo"ti.

while the animal is obvious."

"Evametaṁ, pessa, evametaṁ, pessa.

"That's so true, Pessa! That's so true!

Gahanañhetaṁ, pessa, yadidaṁ manussā;

For human beings are shady,

uttānakañhetaṁ, pessa, yadidaṁ pasavo.

while the animal is obvious.

Cattārome, pessa, puggalā santo saṁvijjamānā lokasmiṁ.

Pessa, these four people are found in the world.

Katame cattāro?

What four?

Idha, pessa, ekacco puggalo attantapo hoti attaparitāpanānuyogamanuyutto;

One person mortifies themselves, committed to the practice of mortifying themselves.

idha pana, pessa, ekacco puggalo parantapo hoti paraparitāpanānuyogamanuyutto;

One person mortifies others, committed to the practice of mortifying others.

idha pana, pessa, ekacco puggalo attantapo ca hoti attaparitāpanānuyogamanuyutto, parantapo ca paraparitāpanānuyogamanuyutto;

One person mortifies themselves and others, committed to the practice of mortifying themselves and others.

idha pana, pessa, ekacco puggalo nevattantapo hoti nāttaparitāpanānuyogamanuyutto na parantapo na paraparitāpanānuyogamanuyutto.

One person doesn't mortify either themselves or others, committed to the practice of not mortifying themselves or others.

So anattantapo aparantapo diṭṭheva dhamme nicchāto nibbuto sītībhūto sukhappaṭisaṃvedī brahmabhūtena attanā viharati.

They live without wishes in the present life, extinguished, cooled, experiencing bliss, having become holy in themselves.

Imesaṃ, pessa, catunnaṃ puggalānaṃ katamo te puggalo cittaṃ ārādhetī"ti?

Which one of these four people do you like the sound of?"

"Yvāyaṃ, bhante, puggalo attantapo attaparitāpanānuyogamanuyutto, ayaṃ me puggalo cittaṃ nārādheti.

"Sir, I don't like the sound of the first three people.

Yopāyaṃ, bhante, puggalo parantapo paraparitāpanānuyogamanuyutto, ayampi me puggalo cittaṃ nārādheti.

Yopāyaṃ, bhante, puggalo attantapo ca attaparitāpanānuyogamanuyutto parantapo ca paraparitāpanānuyogamanuyutto, ayampi me puggalo cittaṃ nārādheti.

Yo ca kho ayaṃ, bhante, puggalo nevattantapo nāttaparitāpanānuyogamanuyutto na parantapo na paraparitāpanānuyogamanuyutto, so anattantapo aparantapo diṭṭheva dhamme nicchāto nibbuto sītībhūto sukhappaṭisaṃvedī brahmabhūtena attanā viharati—

ayameva me puggalo cittaṃ ārādhetī"ti.

I only like the sound of the last person, who doesn't mortify either themselves or others."

"Kasmā pana te, pessa, ime tayo puggalā cittaṃ nārādhentī"ti?

"But why don't you like the sound of those three people?"

"Yvāyaṁ, bhante, puggalo attantapo attaparitāpanānuyogamanuyutto so attānaṁ sukhakāmaṁ dukkhapaṭikkūlaṁ ātāpeti paritāpeti—

"Sir, the person who mortifies themselves does so even though they want to be happy and recoil from pain.

iminā me ayaṁ puggalo cittaṁ nārādheti.

That's why I don't like the sound of that person.

Yopāyaṁ, bhante, puggalo parantapo paraparitāpanānuyogamanuyutto so paraṁ sukhakāmaṁ dukkhapaṭikkūlaṁ ātāpeti paritāpeti—

The person who mortifies others does so even though others want to be happy and recoil from pain.

iminā me ayaṁ puggalo cittaṁ nārādheti.

That's why I don't like the sound of that person.

Yopāyaṁ, bhante, puggalo attantapo ca attaparitāpanānuyogamanuyutto parantapo ca paraparitāpanānuyogamanuyutto so attānañca parañca sukhakāmaṁ dukkhapaṭikkūlaṁ ātāpeti paritāpeti—

The person who mortifies themselves and others does so even though both themselves and others want to be happy and recoil from pain.

iminā me ayaṁ puggalo cittaṁ nārādheti.

That's why I don't like the sound of that person.

Yo ca kho ayaṁ, bhante, puggalo nevattantapo nāttaparitāpanānuyogamanuyutto na parantapo na paraparitāpanānuyogamanuyutto so anattantapo aparantapo diṭṭheva dhamme nicchāto nibbuto sītībhūto sukhappaṭisaṁvedī brahmabhūtena attanā viharati;

The person who doesn't mortify either themselves or others—living without wishes, extinguished, cooled, experiencing bliss, having become holy in themselves—does not torment themselves or others, both of whom want to be happy and recoil from pain.

so attānañca parañca sukhakāmaṁ dukkhapaṭikkūlaṁ neva ātāpeti na paritāpeti—

iminā me ayaṁ puggalo cittaṁ ārādheti.

That's why I like the sound of that person.

Handa ca dāni mayaṁ, bhante, gacchāma;

Well, now, sir, I must go.

bahukiccā mayaṁ bahukaraṇīyā"ti.

I have many duties, and much to do."

"Yassadāni tvaṁ, pessa, kālaṁ maññasī"ti.

"Please, Pessa, go at your convenience."

Atha kho pesso hatthārohaputto bhagavato bhāsitaṁ abhinanditvā anumoditvā uṭṭhāyāsanā bhagavantaṁ abhivādetvā padakkhiṇaṁ katvā pakkāmi.

And then Pessa the elephant driver's son approved and agreed with what the Buddha said. He got up from his seat, bowed, and respectfully circled the Buddha, keeping him on his right, before leaving.

Atha kho bhagavā acirapakkante pesse hatthārohaputte bhikkhū āmantesi:

Then, not long after he had left, the Buddha addressed the mendicants:

"paṇḍito, bhikkhave, pesso hatthārohaputto;

"Mendicants, Pessa the elephant driver's son is astute.

mahāpañño, bhikkhave, pesso hatthārohaputto.

He has great wisdom.

Sace, bhikkhave, pesso hatthārohaputto muhuttaṁ nisīdeyya yāvassāhaṁ ime cattāro puggale vitthārena vibhajissāmi, mahatā atthena saṁyutto abhavissa.

If he had sat here a little longer so that I could have analyzed these four people in detail, he would have greatly benefited.

Api ca, bhikkhave, ettāvatāpi pesso hatthārohaputto mahatā atthena saṁyutto"ti.

Still, even with this much he has already greatly benefited."

"Etassa, bhagavā, kālo, etassa, sugata, kālo,

"Now is the time, Blessed One! Now is the time, Holy One!

yaṁ bhagavā ime cattāro puggale vitthārena vibhajeyya. Bhagavato sutvā bhikkhū dhāressantī"ti.

May the Buddha analyze these four people in detail. The mendicants will listen and remember it."

"Tena hi, bhikkhave, suṇātha, sādhukaṁ manasi karotha, bhāsissāmī"ti.

"Well then, mendicants, listen and pay close attention, I will speak."

"Evaṁ, bhante"ti kho te bhikkhū bhagavato paccassosuṁ.

"Yes, sir," they replied.

Bhagavā etadavoca:

The Buddha said this:

"Katamo ca, bhikkhave, puggalo attantapo attaparitāpanānuyogamanuyutto? Idha, bhikkhave, ekacco puggalo acelako hoti muttācāro hatthāpalekhano naehibhaddantiko natiṭṭhabhaddantiko; nābhihaṭaṁ na uddissakataṁ na nimantanaṁ sādiyati;

"And what person mortifies themselves, committed to the practice of mortifying themselves? It's when someone goes naked, ignoring conventions. They lick their hands, and don't come or wait when called. They don't consent to food brought to them, or food prepared for them, or an invitation for a meal.

so na kumbhimukhā paṭigganhāti na kaḷopimukhā paṭigganhāti na eḷakamantaraṁ na daṇḍamantaraṁ na musalamantaraṁ na dvinnaṁ bhuñjamānānaṁ na gabbhiniyā na pāyamānāya na purisantaragatāya na saṅkittīsu na yattha sā upaṭṭhito hoti na yattha makkhikā saṇḍasaṇḍacārinī; na macchaṁ na maṁsaṁ na suraṁ na merayaṁ na thusodakaṁ pivati.

They don't receive anything from a pot or bowl; or from someone who keeps sheep, or who has a weapon or a shovel in their home; or where a couple is eating; or where there is a woman who is pregnant, breastfeeding, or who has a man in her home; or where there's a dog waiting or flies buzzing. They accept no fish or meat or liquor or wine, and drink no beer.

So ekāgāriko vā hoti ekālopiko, dvāgāriko vā hoti dvālopiko …pe… sattāgāriko vā hoti sattālopiko;

They go to just one house for alms, taking just one mouthful, or two houses and two mouthfuls, up to seven houses and seven mouthfuls.

ekissāpi dattiyā yāpeti, dvīhipi dattīhi yāpeti …pe… sattahipi dattīhi yāpeti;

They feed on one saucer a day, two saucers a day, up to seven saucers a day.

ekāhikampi āhāraṁ āhāreti, dvīhikampi āhāraṁ āhāreti …pe… sattāhikampi āhāraṁ āhāreti—iti evarūpaṁ aḍḍhamāsikaṁ pariyāyabhattabhojanānuyogamanuyutto viharati.

They eat once a day, once every second day, up to once a week, and so on, even up to once a fortnight. They live committed to the practice of eating food at set intervals.

So sākabhakkho vā hoti, sāmākabhakkho vā hoti, nīvārabhakkho vā hoti, daddulabhakkho vā hoti, haṭabhakkho vā hoti, kaṇabhakkho vā hoti, ācāmabhakkho vā hoti, piññākabhakkho vā hoti, tiṇabhakkho vā hoti, gomayabhakkho vā hoti; vanamūlaphalāhāro yāpeti pavattaphalabhojī.

They eat herbs, millet, wild rice, poor rice, water lettuce, rice bran, scum from boiling rice, sesame flour, grass, or cow dung. They survive on forest roots and fruits, or eating fallen fruit.

So sāṇānipi dhāreti, masāṇānipi dhāreti, chavadussānipi dhāreti, paṁsukūlānipi dhāreti, tirīṭānipi dhāreti, ajinampi dhāreti, ajinakkhipampi dhāreti, kusacīrampi dhāreti, vākacīrampi dhāreti, phalakacīrampi dhāreti, kesakambalampi dhāreti, vāḷakambalampi dhāreti, ulūkapakkhampi dhāreti;

They wear robes of sunn hemp, mixed hemp, corpse-wrapping cloth, rags, lodh tree bark, antelope hide (whole or in strips), kusa grass, bark, wood-chips, human hair, horse-tail hair, or owls' wings.

kesamassulocakopi hoti, kesamassulocanānuyogamanuyutto,

They tear out their hair and beard, committed to this practice.

ubbhaṭṭhakopi hoti āsanapaṭikkhitto,

They constantly stand, refusing seats.

ukkuṭikopi hoti ukkuṭikappadhānamanuyutto,

They squat, committed to the endeavor of squatting.

kaṇṭakāpassayikopi hoti kaṇṭakāpassaye seyyaṁ kappeti;

They lie on a mat of thorns, making a mat of thorns their bed.

sāyatatiyakampi udakorohanānuyogamanuyutto viharati—

They're committed to the practice of immersion in water three times a day, including the evening.

iti evarūpaṁ anekavihitaṁ kāyassa ātāpanaparitāpanānuyogamanuyutto viharati.

And so they live committed to practicing these various ways of mortifying and tormenting the body.

Ayaṁ vuccati, bhikkhave, puggalo attantapo attaparitāpanānuyogamanuyutto.

This is called a person who mortifies themselves, being committed to the practice of mortifying themselves.

Katamo ca, bhikkhave, puggalo parantapo paraparitāpanānuyogamanuyutto?

And what person mortifies others, committed to the practice of mortifying others?

Idha, bhikkhave, ekacco puggalo orabbhiko hoti sūkariko sākuṇiko māgaviko luddo macchaghātako coro coraghātako goghātako bandhanāgāriko, ye vā panaññepi keci kurūrakammantā.

It's when a person is a slaughterer of sheep, pigs, or poultry, a hunter or trapper, a fisher, a bandit, an executioner, a butcher, a jailer, or someone with some other kind of cruel livelihood.

Ayaṁ vuccati, bhikkhave, puggalo parantapo paraparitāpanānuyogamanuyutto.

This is called a person who mortifies others, being committed to the practice of mortifying others.

Katamo ca, bhikkhave, puggalo attantapo ca attaparitāpanānuyogamanuyutto parantapo ca paraparitāpanānuyogamanuyutto?

And what person mortifies themselves and others, being committed to the practice of mortifying themselves and others?

Idha, bhikkhave, ekacco puggalo rājā vā hoti khattiyo muddhāvasitto brāhmaṇo vā mahāsālo.

It's when a person is an anointed aristocratic king or a well-to-do brahmin.

So puratthimena nagarassa navaṁ santhāgāraṁ kārāpetvā kesamassuṁ ohāretvā kharājinaṁ nivāsetvā sappitelena kāyaṁ abbhañjitvā magavisāṇena piṭṭhiṁ kaṇḍuvamāno navaṁ santhāgāraṁ pavisati saddhiṁ mahesiyā brāhmaṇena ca purohitena.

He has a new temple built to the east of the city. He shaves off his hair and beard, dresses in a rough antelope hide, and smears his body with ghee and oil. Scratching his back with antlers, he enters the temple with his chief queen and the brahmin high priest.

So tattha anantarahitāya bhūmiyā haritupalittāya seyyaṁ kappeti.

There he lies on the bare ground strewn with grass.

Ekissāya gāviyā sarūpavacchāya yaṁ ekasmiṁ thane khīraṁ hoti tena rājā yāpeti, yaṁ dutiyasmiṁ thane khīraṁ hoti tena mahesī yāpeti, yaṁ tatiyasmiṁ thane khīraṁ hoti tena brāhmaṇo purohito yāpeti, yaṁ catutthasmiṁ thane khīraṁ hoti tena aggiṁ juhati, avasesena vacchako yāpeti.

The king feeds on the milk from one teat of a cow that has a calf of the same color. The chief queen feeds on the milk from the second teat. The brahmin high priest feeds on the milk from the third teat. The milk from the fourth teat is served to the sacred flame. The calf feeds on the remainder.

So evamāha:

He says:

'ettakā usabhā haññantu yaññatthāya, ettakā vacchatarā haññantu yaññatthāya, ettakā vacchatariyo haññantu yaññatthāya, ettakā ajā haññantu yaññatthāya, ettakā urabbhā haññantu yaññatthāya, ettakā assā haññantu yaññatthāya, ettakā rukkhā chijjantu yūpatthāya, ettakā dabbhā lūyantu barihisatthāyā'ti.

'Slaughter this many bulls, bullocks, heifers, goats, rams, and horses for the sacrifice! Fell this many trees and reap this much grass for the sacrificial equipment!'

Yepissa te honti dāsāti vā pessāti vā kammakarāti vā tepi daṇḍatajjitā bhayatajjitā assumukhā rudamānā parikammāni karonti.

His bondservants, employees, and workers do their jobs under threat of punishment and danger, weeping with tearful faces.

Ayaṁ vuccati, bhikkhave, puggalo attantapo ca attaparitāpanānuyogamanuyutto parantapo ca paraparitāpanānuyogamanuyutto.

This is called a person who mortifies themselves and others, being committed to the practice of mortifying themselves and others.

Katamo ca, bhikkhave, puggalo nevattantapo nāttaparitāpanānuyogamanuyutto na parantapo na paraparitāpanānuyogamanuyutto, so anattantapo aparantapo diṭṭheva dhamme nicchāto nibbuto sītībhūto sukhappaṭisaṁvedī brahmabhūtena attanā viharati?

And what person doesn't mortify either themselves or others, but lives without wishes, extinguished, cooled, experiencing bliss, having become holy in themselves?

Idha, bhikkhave, tathāgato loke uppajjati arahaṁ sammāsambuddho vijjācaraṇasampanno sugato lokavidū anuttaro purisadammasārathi satthā devamanussānaṁ buddho bhagavā.

It's when a Realized One arises in the world, perfected, a fully awakened Buddha, accomplished in knowledge and conduct, holy, knower of the world, supreme guide for those who wish to train, teacher of gods and humans, awakened, blessed.

So imaṁ lokaṁ sadevakaṁ samārakaṁ sabrahmakaṁ sassamaṇabrāhmaṇiṁ pajaṁ sadevamanussaṁ sayaṁ abhiññā sacchikatvā pavedeti.

He has realized with his own insight this world—with its gods, Māras and Brahmās, this population with its ascetics and brahmins, gods and humans—and he makes it known to others.

So dhammaṁ deseti ādikalyāṇaṁ majjhekalyāṇaṁ pariyosānakalyāṇaṁ sātthaṁ sabyañjanaṁ, kevalaparipuṇṇaṁ parisuddhaṁ brahmacariyaṁ pakāseti.

He teaches Dhamma that's good in the beginning, good in the middle, and good in the end, meaningful and well-phrased. And he reveals a spiritual practice that's entirely full and pure.

Taṁ dhammaṁ suṇāti gahapati vā gahapatiputto vā aññatarasmiṁ vā kule paccājāto.

A householder hears that teaching, or a householder's child, or someone reborn in some clan.

So taṁ dhammaṁ sutvā tathāgate saddhaṁ paṭilabhati.

They gain faith in the Realized One

So tena saddhāpaṭilābhena samannāgato iti paṭisañcikkhati:

and reflect:

'sambādho gharāvāso rajāpatho, abbhokāso pabbajjā.

'Living in a house is cramped and dirty, but the life of one gone forth is wide open.

Nayidaṁ sukaraṁ agāraṁ ajjhāvasatā ekantaparipuṇṇaṁ ekantaparisuddhaṁ saṅkhalikhitaṁ brahmacariyaṁ carituṁ.

It's not easy for someone living at home to lead the spiritual life utterly full and pure, like a polished shell.

Yannūnāhaṁ kesamassuṁ ohāretvā kāsāyāni vatthāni acchādetvā agārasmā anagāriyaṁ pabbajeyyan'ti.

Why don't I shave off my hair and beard, dress in ocher robes, and go forth from the lay life to homelessness?'

So aparena samayena appaṁ vā bhogakkhandhaṁ pahāya, mahantaṁ vā bhogakkhandhaṁ pahāya, appaṁ vā ñātiparivaṭṭaṁ pahāya, mahantaṁ vā ñātiparivaṭṭaṁ pahāya, kesamassuṁ ohāretvā, kāsāyāni vatthāni acchādetvā agārasmā anagāriyaṁ pabbajati.

After some time they give up a large or small fortune, and a large or small family circle. They shave off hair and beard, dress in ocher robes, and go forth from the lay life to homelessness.

So evaṁ pabbajito samāno bhikkhūnaṁ sikkhāsājīvasamāpanno pāṇātipātaṁ pahāya pāṇātipātā paṭivirato hoti nihitadaṇḍo nihitasattho, lajjī dayāpanno sabbapāṇabhūtahitānukampī viharati.

Once they've gone forth, they take up the training and livelihood of the mendicants. They give up killing living creatures, renouncing the rod and the sword. They're scrupulous and kind, living full of compassion for all living beings.

Adinnādānaṁ pahāya adinnādānā paṭivirato hoti dinnādāyī dinnapāṭikaṅkhī, athenena sucibhūtena attanā viharati.

They give up stealing. They take only what's given, and expect only what's given. They keep themselves clean by not thieving.

Abrahmacariyaṁ pahāya brahmacārī hoti ārācārī virato methunā gāmadhammā.

They give up unchastity. They are celibate, set apart, avoiding the vulgar act of sex.

Musāvādaṁ pahāya musāvādā paṭivirato hoti saccavādī saccasandho theto paccayiko avisaṁvādako lokassa.

They give up lying. They speak the truth and stick to the truth. They're honest and trustworthy, and don't trick the world with their words.

Pisuṇaṁ vācaṁ pahāya pisuṇāya vācāya paṭivirato hoti, ito sutvā na amutra akkhātā imesaṁ bhedāya, amutra vā sutvā na imesaṁ akkhātā amūsaṁ bhedāya— iti bhinnānaṁ vā sandhātā sahitānaṁ vā anuppadātā samaggārāmo samaggarato samagganandī samaggakaraṇiṁ vācaṁ bhāsitā hoti.

They give up divisive speech. They don't repeat in one place what they heard in another so as to divide people against each other. Instead, they reconcile those who are divided, supporting unity, delighting in harmony, loving harmony, speaking words that promote harmony.

Pharusaṁ vācaṁ pahāya pharusāya vācāya paṭivirato hoti, yā sā vācā nelā kaṇṇasukhā pemanīyā hadayaṅgamā porī bahujanakantā bahujanamanāpā tathārūpiṁ vācaṁ bhāsitā hoti.

They give up harsh speech. They speak in a way that's mellow, pleasing to the ear, lovely, going to the heart, polite, likable and agreeable to the people.

Samphappalāpaṁ pahāya samphappalāpā paṭivirato hoti kālavādī bhūtavādī atthavādī dhammavādī vinayavādī, nidhānavatiṁ vācaṁ bhāsitā kālena sāpadesaṁ pariyantavatiṁ atthasaṁhitaṁ.

They give up talking nonsense. Their words are timely, true, and meaningful, in line with the teaching and training. They say things at the right time which are valuable, reasonable, succinct, and beneficial.

So bījagāmabhūtagāmasamārambhā paṭivirato hoti,

They avoid injuring plants and seeds.

ekabhattiko hoti rattūparato virato vikālabhojanā;

They eat in one part of the day, abstaining from eating at night and food at the wrong time.

naccagītavāditavisūkadassanā paṭivirato hoti;

They avoid dancing, singing, music, and seeing shows.

mālāgandhavilepanadhāraṇamaṇḍanavibhūsanaṭṭhānā paṭivirato hoti;

They avoid beautifying and adorning themselves with garlands, perfumes, and makeup.

uccāsayanamahāsayanā paṭivirato hoti;

They avoid high and luxurious beds.

jātarūparajatapaṭiggahaṇā paṭivirato hoti;

They avoid receiving gold and money,

āmakadhaññapaṭiggahaṇā paṭivirato hoti;

raw grains,

āmakamaṁsapaṭiggahaṇā paṭivirato hoti;

raw meat,

itthikumārikapaṭiggahaṇā paṭivirato hoti;

women and girls,

dāsidāsapaṭiggahaṇā paṭivirato hoti;

male and female bondservants,

ajeḷakapaṭiggahaṇā paṭivirato hoti;

goats and sheep,

kukkuṭasūkarapaṭiggahaṇā paṭivirato hoti;

chickens and pigs,

hatthigavassavaḷavapaṭiggahaṇā paṭivirato hoti;

elephants, cows, horses, and mares,

khettavatthupaṭiggahaṇā paṭivirato hoti;

and fields and land.

dūteyyapahiṇagamanānuyogā paṭivirato hoti;

They avoid running errands and messages;

kayavikkayā paṭivirato hoti;

buying and selling;

tulākūṭakaṁsakūṭamānakūṭā paṭivirato hoti;

falsifying weights, metals, or measures;

ukkoṭanavañcananikatisāciyogā paṭivirato hoti;

bribery, fraud, cheating, and duplicity;

chedanavadhabandhanaviparāmosaālopasahasākārā paṭivirato hoti.

mutilation, murder, abduction, banditry, plunder, and violence.

So santuṭṭho hoti kāyaparihārikena cīvarena kucchiparihārikena piṇḍapātena. So yena yeneva pakkamati, samādāyeva pakkamati.

They're content with robes to look after the body and almsfood to look after the belly. Wherever they go, they set out taking only these things.

Seyyathāpi nāma pakkhī sakuṇo yena yeneva ḍeti, sapattabhārova ḍeti;

They're like a bird: wherever it flies, wings are its only burden.

evameva bhikkhu santuṭṭho hoti kāyaparihārikena cīvarena kucchiparihārikena piṇḍapātena. So yena yeneva pakkamati, samādāyeva pakkamati.

In the same way, a mendicant is content with robes to look after the body and almsfood to look after the belly. Wherever they go, they set out taking only these things.

So iminā ariyena sīlakkhandhena samannāgato ajjhattaṃ anavajjasukhaṃ paṭisaṃvedeti.

When they have this entire spectrum of noble ethics, they experience a blameless happiness inside themselves.

So cakkhunā rūpaṃ disvā na nimittaggāhī hoti nānubyañjanaggāhī.

When they see a sight with their eyes, they don't get caught up in the features and details.

Yatvādhikaraṇamenaṃ cakkhundriyaṃ asaṃvutaṃ viharantaṃ abhijjhādomanassā pāpakā akusalā dhammā anvāssaveyyuṃ tassa saṃvarāya paṭipajjati, rakkhati cakkhundriyaṃ, cakkhundriye saṃvaraṃ āpajjati.

If the faculty of sight were left unrestrained, bad unskillful qualities of desire and aversion would become overwhelming. For this reason, they practice restraint, protecting the faculty of sight, and achieving its restraint.

Sotena saddaṃ sutvā ...pe...

When they hear a sound with their ears ...

ghānena gandhaṃ ghāyitvā ...pe...

When they smell an odor with their nose ...

jivhāya rasaṃ sāyitvā ...pe...

When they taste a flavor with their tongue …

kāyena phoṭṭhabbaṁ phusitvā …pe…

When they feel a touch with their body …

manasā dhammaṁ viññāya na nimittaggāhī hoti nānubyañjanaggāhī.

When they know a thought with their mind, they don't get caught up in the features and details.

Yatvādhikaraṇamenaṁ manindriyaṁ asaṁvutaṁ viharantaṁ abhijjhādomanassā pāpakā akusalā dhammā anvāssaveyyuṁ tassa saṁvarāya paṭipajjati, rakkhati manindriyaṁ, manindriye saṁvaraṁ āpajjati.

If the faculty of mind were left unrestrained, bad unskillful qualities of desire and aversion would become overwhelming. For this reason, they practice restraint, protecting the faculty of mind, and achieving its restraint.

So iminā ariyena indriyasaṁvarena samannāgato ajjhattaṁ abyāsekasukhaṁ paṭisaṁvedeti.

When they have this noble sense restraint, they experience an unsullied bliss inside themselves.

So abhikkante paṭikkante sampajānakārī hoti, ālokite vilokite sampajānakārī hoti, samiñjite pasārite sampajānakārī hoti, saṅghāṭipattacīvaradhāraṇe sampajānakārī hoti, asite pīte khāyite sāyite sampajānakārī hoti, uccārapassāvakamme sampajānakārī hoti, gate ṭhite nisinne sutte jāgarite bhāsite tuṇhībhāve sampajānakārī hoti.

They act with situational awareness when going out and coming back; when looking ahead and aside; when bending and extending the limbs; when bearing the outer robe, bowl and robes; when eating, drinking, chewing, and tasting; when urinating and defecating; when walking, standing, sitting, sleeping, waking, speaking, and keeping silent.

So iminā ca ariyena sīlakkhandhena samannāgato, imāya ca ariyāya santuṭṭhiyā samannāgato, iminā ca ariyena indriyasaṁvarena samannāgato, iminā ca ariyena satisampajaññena samannāgato

When they have this noble spectrum of ethics, this noble contentment, this noble sense restraint, and this noble mindfulness and situational awareness,

vivittaṁ senāsanaṁ bhajati araññaṁ rukkhamūlaṁ pabbataṁ kandaraṁ giriguhaṁ susānaṁ vanapatthaṁ abbhokāsaṁ palālapuñjaṁ.

they frequent a secluded lodging—a wilderness, the root of a tree, a hill, a ravine, a mountain cave, a charnel ground, a forest, the open air, a heap of straw.

So pacchābhattaṁ piṇḍapātapaṭikkanto nisīdati pallaṅkaṁ ābhujitvā ujuṁ kāyaṁ paṇidhāya parimukhaṁ satiṁ upaṭṭhapetvā.

After the meal, they return from almsround, sit down cross-legged, set their body straight, and establish mindfulness in front of them.

So abhijjhaṁ loke pahāya vigatābhijjhena cetasā viharati, abhijjhāya cittaṁ parisodheti,

Giving up desire for the world, they meditate with a heart rid of desire, cleansing the mind of desire.

byāpādapadosaṁ pahāya abyāpannacitto viharati sabbapāṇabhūtahitānukampī, byāpādapadosā cittaṁ parisodheti;

Giving up ill will, they meditate with a mind rid of ill will, full of compassion for all living beings, cleansing the mind of ill will and malevolence.

thinamiddhaṁ pahāya vigatathinamiddho viharati ālokasaññī sato sampajāno, thinamiddhā cittaṁ parisodheti;

Giving up dullness and drowsiness, they meditate with a mind rid of dullness and drowsiness, perceiving light, mindful and aware, cleansing the mind of dullness and drowsiness.

uddhaccakukkuccaṁ pahāya anuddhato viharati ajjhattaṁ vūpasantacitto, uddhaccakukkuccā cittaṁ parisodheti;

Giving up restlessness and remorse, they meditate without restlessness, their mind peaceful inside, cleansing the mind of restlessness and remorse.

vicikicchaṁ pahāya tiṇṇavicikiccho viharati akathaṅkathī kusalesu dhammesu, vicikicchāya cittaṁ parisodheti.

Giving up doubt, they meditate having gone beyond doubt, not undecided about skillful qualities, cleansing the mind of doubt.

So ime pañca nīvaraṇe pahāya cetaso upakkilese paññāya dubbalīkaraṇe,

They give up these five hindrances, corruptions of the heart that weaken wisdom.

vivicceva kāmehi vivicca akusalehi dhammehi savitakkaṁ savicāraṁ vivekajaṁ pītisukhaṁ paṭhamaṁ jhānaṁ upasampajja viharati;

Then, quite secluded from sensual pleasures, secluded from unskillful qualities, they enter and remain in the first absorption, which has the rapture and bliss born of seclusion, while placing the mind and keeping it connected.

vitakkavicārānaṁ vūpasamā ajjhattaṁ sampasādanaṁ cetaso ekodibhāvaṁ avitakkaṁ avicāraṁ samādhijaṁ pītisukhaṁ dutiyaṁ jhānaṁ upasampajja viharati;

As the placing of the mind and keeping it connected are stilled, they enter and remain in the second absorption, which has the rapture and bliss born of immersion, with internal clarity and confidence, and unified mind, without placing the mind and keeping it connected.

pītiyā ca virāgā upekkhako ca viharati sato ca sampajāno sukhañca kāyena paṭisaṃvedeti, yaṃ taṃ ariyā ācikkhanti: 'upekkhako satimā sukhavihārī'ti tatiyaṃ jhānaṃ upasampajja viharati;

And with the fading away of rapture, they enter and remain in the third absorption, where they meditate with equanimity, mindful and aware, personally experiencing the bliss of which the noble ones declare, 'Equanimous and mindful, one meditates in bliss.'

sukhassa ca pahānā dukkhassa ca pahānā pubbeva somanassadomanassānaṃ atthaṅgamā adukkhamasukhaṃ upekkhāsatipārisuddhiṃ catutthaṃ jhānaṃ upasampajja viharati.

Giving up pleasure and pain, and ending former happiness and sadness, they enter and remain in the fourth absorption, without pleasure or pain, with pure equanimity and mindfulness.

So evaṃ samāhite citte parisuddhe pariyodāte anaṅgaṇe vigatūpakkilese mudubhūte kammaniye ṭhite āneñjappatte pubbenivāsānussatiñāṇāya cittaṃ abhininnāmeti.

When their mind has become immersed in samādhi like this—purified, bright, flawless, rid of corruptions, pliable, workable, steady, and imperturbable—they extend it toward recollection of past lives.

So anekavihitaṃ pubbenivāsaṃ anussarati, seyyathidaṃ—ekampi jātiṃ dvepi jātiyo tissopi jātiyo catassopi jātiyo pañcapi jātiyo dasapi jātiyo vīsampi jātiyo tiṃsampi jātiyo cattālīsampi jātiyo paññāsampi jātiyo jātisatampi jātisahassampi jātisatasahassampi anekepi saṃvaṭṭakappe anekepi vivaṭṭakappe anekepi saṃvaṭṭavivaṭṭakappe: 'amutrāsiṃ evaṃnāmo evaṅgotto evaṃvaṇṇo evamāhāro evaṃsukhadukkhappaṭisaṃvedī evamāyupariyanto, so tato cuto amutra udapādiṃ; tatrāpāsiṃ evaṃnāmo evaṅgotto evaṃvaṇṇo evamāhāro evaṃsukhadukkhappaṭisaṃvedī evamāyupariyanto, so tato cuto idhūpapanno'ti. Iti sākāraṃ sauddesaṃ anekavihitaṃ pubbenivāsaṃ anussarati.

They recollect many kinds of past lives, that is, one, two, three, four, five, ten, twenty, thirty, forty, fifty, a hundred, a thousand, a hundred thousand rebirths; many eons of the world contracting, many eons of the world expanding, many eons of the world contracting and expanding. They remember: 'There, I was named this, my clan was that, I looked like this, and that was my food. This was how I felt pleasure and pain, and that was how my life ended. When I passed away from that place I was reborn somewhere else. There, too, I was named this, my clan was that, I looked like this, and that was my food. This was how I felt pleasure and pain, and that was how my life ended. When I passed away from that place I was reborn here.' And so they recollect their many kinds of past lives, with features and details.

So evaṁ samāhite citte parisuddhe pariyodāte anaṅgaṇe vigatūpakkilese mudubhūte kammaniye ṭhite āneñjappatte sattānaṁ cutūpapātañāṇāya cittaṁ abhininnāmeti.

When their mind has become immersed in samādhi like this—purified, bright, flawless, rid of corruptions, pliable, workable, steady, and imperturbable—they extend it toward knowledge of the death and rebirth of sentient beings.

So dibbena cakkhunā visuddhena atikkantamānusakena satte passati cavamāne upapajjamāne hīne paṇīte suvaṇṇe dubbaṇṇe sugate duggate yathākammūpage satte pajānāti: 'ime vata bhonto sattā kāyaduccaritena samannāgatā vacīduccaritena samannāgatā manoduccaritena samannāgatā ariyānaṁ upavādakā micchādiṭṭhikā micchādiṭṭhikammasamādānā, te kāyassa bhedā paraṁ maraṇā apāyaṁ duggatiṁ vinipātaṁ nirayaṁ upapannā; ime vā pana bhonto sattā kāyasucaritena samannāgatā vacīsucaritena samannāgatā manosucaritena samannāgatā ariyānaṁ anupavādakā sammādiṭṭhikā sammādiṭṭhikammasamādānā, te kāyassa bhedā paraṁ maraṇā sugatiṁ saggaṁ lokaṁ upapannā'ti. Iti dibbena cakkhunā visuddhena atikkantamānusakena satte passati cavamāne upapajjamāne hīne paṇīte suvaṇṇe dubbaṇṇe sugate duggate yathākammūpage satte pajānāti.

With clairvoyance that is purified and superhuman, they see sentient beings passing away and being reborn—inferior and superior, beautiful and ugly, in a good place or a bad place. They understand how sentient beings are reborn according to their deeds: 'These dear beings did bad things by way of body, speech, and mind. They spoke ill of the noble ones; they had wrong view; and they chose to act out of that wrong view. When their body breaks up, after death, they're reborn in a place of loss, a bad place, the underworld, hell. These dear beings, however, did good things by way of body, speech, and mind. They never spoke ill of the noble ones; they had right view; and they chose to act out of that right view. When their body breaks up, after death, they're reborn in a good place, a heavenly realm.' And so, with clairvoyance that is purified and superhuman, they see sentient beings passing away and being reborn—inferior and superior, beautiful and ugly, in a good place or a bad place. They understand how sentient beings are reborn according to their deeds.

So evaṁ samāhite citte parisuddhe pariyodāte anaṅgaṇe vigatūpakkilese mudubhūte kammaniye ṭhite āneñjappatte āsavānaṁ khayañāṇāya cittaṁ abhininnāmeti.

When their mind has become immersed in samādhi like this—purified, bright, flawless, rid of corruptions, pliable, workable, steady, and imperturbable—they extend it toward knowledge of the ending of defilements.

So 'idaṁ dukkhan'ti yathābhūtaṁ pajānāti. 'Ayaṁ dukkhasamudayo'ti yathābhūtaṁ pajānāti. 'Ayaṁ dukkhanirodho'ti yathābhūtaṁ pajānāti. 'Ayaṁ dukkhanirodhagāminī paṭipadā'ti yathābhūtaṁ pajānāti.

They truly understand: 'This is suffering' … 'This is the origin of suffering' … 'This is the cessation of suffering' … 'This is the practice that leads to the cessation of suffering'.

'Ime āsavā'ti yathābhūtaṁ pajānāti. 'Ayaṁ āsavasamudayo'ti yathābhūtaṁ pajānāti. 'Ayaṁ āsavanirodho'ti yathābhūtaṁ pajānāti. 'Ayaṁ āsavanirodhagāminī paṭipadā'ti yathābhūtaṁ pajānāti.

They truly understand: 'These are defilements' ... 'This is the origin of defilements' ... 'This is the cessation of defilements' ... 'This is the practice that leads to the cessation of defilements'.

Tassa evaṁ jānato evaṁ passato kāmāsavāpi cittaṁ vimuccati, bhavāsavāpi cittaṁ vimuccati, avijjāsavāpi cittaṁ vimuccati.

Knowing and seeing like this, their mind is freed from the defilements of sensuality, desire to be reborn, and ignorance.

Vimuttasmiṁ vimuttamiti ñāṇaṁ hoti.

When they're freed, they know they're freed.

'Khīṇā jāti, vusitaṁ brahmacariyaṁ, kataṁ karaṇīyaṁ, nāparaṁ itthattāyā'ti pajānāti.

They understand: 'Rebirth is ended, the spiritual journey has been completed, what had to be done has been done, there is no return to any state of existence.'

Ayaṁ vuccati, bhikkhave, puggalo nevattantapo nāttaparitāpanānuyogamanuyutto, na parantapo na paraparitāpanānuyogamanuyutto.

This is called a person who neither mortifies themselves or others, being committed to the practice of not mortifying themselves or others.

So attantapo aparantapo diṭṭheva dhamme nicchāto nibbuto sītībhūto sukhappaṭisaṁvedī brahmabhūtena attanā viharatī"ti.

They live without wishes in the present life, extinguished, cooled, experiencing bliss, having become holy in themselves."

Idamavoca bhagavā.

That is what the Buddha said.

Attamanā te bhikkhū bhagavato bhāsitaṁ abhinandunti.

Satisfied, the mendicants were happy with what the Buddha said.

Kandarakasuttaṁ niṭṭhitaṁ paṭhamaṁ.

52 Atthakanagarasutta:

The Man From the City of Atthaka

Evaṁ me sutaṁ—

So I have heard.

ekaṁ samayaṁ āyasmā ānando vesāliyaṁ viharati beluvagāmake.

At one time Venerable Ānanda was staying near Vesālī in the little village of Beluva.

Tena kho pana samayena dasamo gahapati aṭṭhakanāgaro pāṭaliputtaṁ anuppatto hoti kenacideva karaṇīyena.

Now at that time the householder Dasama from the city of Aṭṭhaka had arrived at Pāṭaliputta on some business.

Atha kho dasamo gahapati aṭṭhakanāgaro yena kukkuṭārāmo yena aññataro bhikkhu tenupasaṅkami; upasaṅkamitvā taṁ bhikkhuṁ abhivādetvā ekamantaṁ nisīdi. Ekamantaṁ nisinno kho dasamo gahapati aṭṭhakanāgaro taṁ bhikkhuṁ etadavoca:

He went to the Chicken Monastery, approached a certain mendicant, bowed, sat down to one side, and said to him,

"kahaṁ nu kho, bhante, āyasmā ānando etarahi viharati?

"Sir, where is Venerable Ānanda now staying?

Dassanakāmā hi mayaṁ taṁ āyasmantaṁ ānandan"ti.

For I want to see him."

"Eso, gahapati, āyasmā ānando vesāliyaṁ viharati beluvagāmake"ti.

"Householder, Venerable Ānanda is staying near Vesālī in the little village of Beluva."

Atha kho dasamo gahapati aṭṭhakanāgaro pāṭaliputte taṁ karaṇīyaṁ tīretvā yena vesālī yena beluvagāmako yenāyasmā ānando tenupasaṅkami; upasaṅkamitvā āyasmantaṁ ānandaṁ abhivādetvā ekamantaṁ nisīdi. Ekamantaṁ nisinno kho dasamo gahapati aṭṭhakanāgaro āyasmantaṁ ānandaṁ etadavoca:

Then the householder Dasama, having concluded his business there, went to the little village of Beluva in Vesālī to see Ānanda. He bowed, sat down to one side, and said to Ānanda:

"atthi nu kho, bhante ānanda, tena bhagavatā jānatā passatā arahatā sammāsambuddhena ekadhammo akkhāto yattha bhikkhuno appamattassa ātāpino pahitattassa viharato avimuttañceva cittaṁ vimuccati, aparikkhīṇā ca āsavā parikkhayaṁ gacchanti, ananuppattañca anuttaraṁ yogakkhemaṁ anupāpuṇātī'ti?

"Honorable Ānanda, is there one thing that has been rightly explained by the Blessed One—who knows and sees, the perfected one, the fully awakened Buddha—practicing which a diligent, keen, and resolute mendicant's mind is freed, their defilements are ended, and they arrive at the supreme sanctuary?"

"Atthi kho, gahapati, tena bhagavatā jānatā passatā arahatā sammāsambuddhena ekadhammo akkhāto, yattha bhikkhuno appamattassa ātāpino pahitattassa viharato avimuttañceva cittaṁ vimuccati, aparikkhīṇā ca āsavā parikkhayaṁ gacchanti, ananuppattañca anuttaraṁ yogakkhemaṁ anupāpuṇātī'ti.

"There is, householder."

"Katamo pana, bhante ānanda, tena bhagavatā jānatā passatā arahatā sammāsambuddhena ekadhammo akkhāto, yattha bhikkhuno appamattassa ātāpino pahitattassa viharato avimuttañceva cittaṁ vimuccati, aparikkhīṇā ca āsavā parikkhayaṁ gacchanti, ananuppattañca anuttaraṁ yogakkhemaṁ anupāpuṇātī'ti?

"And what is that one thing?"

"Idha, gahapati, bhikkhu vivicceva kāmehi vivicca akusalehi dhammehi savitakkaṁ savicāraṁ vivekajaṁ pītisukhaṁ paṭhamaṁ jhānaṁ upasampajja viharati.

"Householder, it's when a mendicant, quite secluded from sensual pleasures, secluded from unskillful qualities, enters and remains in the first absorption, which has the rapture and bliss born of seclusion, while placing the mind and keeping it connected.

So iti paṭisañcikkhati:

Then they reflect:

'idampi kho paṭhamaṁ jhānaṁ abhisaṅkhataṁ abhisañcetayitaṁ.

'Even this first absorption is produced by choices and intentions.'

Yaṁ kho pana kiñci abhisaṅkhataṁ abhisañcetayitaṁ tadaniccaṁ nirodhadhamman'ti pajānāti.

They understand: 'But whatever is produced by choices and intentions is impermanent and liable to cessation.'

So tattha ṭhito āsavānaṁ khayaṁ pāpuṇāti.

Abiding in that they attain the ending of defilements.

No ce āsavānaṁ khayaṁ pāpuṇāti, teneva dhammarāgena tāya dhammanandiyā pañcannaṁ orambhāgiyānaṁ saṁyojanānaṁ parikkhayā opapātiko hoti tattha parinibbāyī anāvattidhammo tasmā lokā.

If they don't attain the ending of defilements, with the ending of the five lower fetters they're reborn spontaneously, because of their passion and love for that meditation. They are extinguished there, and are not liable to return from that world.

Ayampi kho, gahapati, tena bhagavatā jānatā passatā arahatā sammāsambuddhena ekadhammo akkhāto, yattha bhikkhuno appamattassa ātāpino pahitattassa viharato avimuttañceva cittaṁ vimuccati, aparikkhīṇā ca āsavā parikkhayaṁ gacchanti, ananuppattañca anuttaraṁ yogakkhemaṁ anupāpuṇāti.

This is one thing that has been rightly explained by the Blessed One—who knows and sees, the perfected one, the fully awakened Buddha—practicing which a diligent, keen, and resolute mendicant's mind is freed, their defilements are ended, and they arrive at the supreme sanctuary.

Puna caparaṁ, gahapati, bhikkhu vitakkavicārānaṁ vūpasamā ajjhattaṁ sampasādanaṁ ...pe... dutiyaṁ jhānaṁ upasampajja viharati.

Furthermore, as the placing of the mind and keeping it connected are stilled, they enter and remain in the second absorption ...

So iti paṭisañcikkhati:

'idampi kho dutiyaṁ jhānaṁ abhisaṅkhataṁ abhisañcetayitaṁ ...pe...

anuttaraṁ yogakkhemaṁ anupāpuṇāti.

Puna caparaṁ, gahapati, bhikkhu pītiyā ca virāgā ...pe... tatiyaṁ jhānaṁ upasampajja viharati.

third absorption ...

So iti paṭisañcikkhati:

'idampi kho tatiyaṁ jhānaṁ abhisaṅkhataṁ abhisañcetayitaṁ ...pe...

anuttaraṁ yogakkhemaṁ anupāpuṇāti.

Puna caparaṁ, gahapati, bhikkhu sukhassa ca pahānā ...pe... catutthaṁ jhānaṁ upasampajja viharati.

fourth absorption ...

So iti paṭisañcikkhati:

'idampi kho catutthaṁ jhānaṁ abhisaṅkhataṁ abhisañcetayitaṁ ...pe...

anuttaraṁ yogakkhemaṁ anupāpuṇāti.

Puna caparaṁ, gahapati, bhikkhu mettāsahagatena cetasā ekaṁ disaṁ pharitvā viharati, tathā dutiyaṁ, tathā tatiyaṁ, tathā catutthaṁ. Iti uddhamadho tiriyaṁ sabbadhi sabbattatāya sabbāvantaṁ lokaṁ mettāsahagatena cetasā vipulena mahaggatena appamāṇena averena abyābajjhena pharitvā viharati.

Furthermore, a mendicant meditates spreading a heart full of love to one direction, and to the second, and to the third, and to the fourth. In the same way above, below, across, everywhere, all around, they spread a heart full of love to the whole world—abundant, expansive, limitless, free of enmity and ill will.

So iti paṭisañcikkhati:

Then they reflect:

'ayampi kho mettācetovimutti abhisaṅkhatā abhisañcetayitā.

'Even this heart's release by love is produced by choices and intentions.'

Yaṁ kho pana kiñci abhisaṅkhataṁ abhisañcetayitaṁ tadaniccaṁ nirodhadhamman'ti pajānāti.

They understand: 'But whatever is produced by choices and intentions is impermanent and liable to cessation.' …

So tattha ṭhito …pe…

anuttaraṁ yogakkhemaṁ anupāpuṇāti.

Puna caparaṁ, gahapati, bhikkhu karuṇāsahagatena cetasā …pe…

Furthermore, a mendicant meditates spreading a heart full of compassion …

muditāsahagatena cetasā …pe…

rejoicing …

upekkhāsahagatena cetasā ekaṁ disaṁ pharitvā viharati, tathā dutiyaṁ, tathā tatiyaṁ, tathā catutthaṁ. Iti uddhamadho tiriyaṁ sabbadhi sabbattatāya sabbāvantaṁ lokaṁ upekkhāsahagatena cetasā vipulena mahaggatena appamāṇena averena abyābajjhena pharitvā viharati.

equanimity …

So iti paṭisañcikkhati:

'ayampi kho upekkhācetovimutti abhisaṅkhatā abhisañcetayitā.

Yaṁ kho pana kiñci abhisaṅkhataṁ abhisañcetayitaṁ tadaniccaṁ nirodhadhamman'ti pajānāti.

So tattha ṭhito …pe…

anuttaraṁ yogakkhemaṁ anupāpuṇāti.

Puna caparaṁ, gahapati, bhikkhu sabbaso rūpasaññānaṁ samatikkamā paṭighasaññānaṁ atthaṅgamā nānattasaññānaṁ amanasikārā 'ananto ākāso'ti ākāsānañcāyatanaṁ upasampajja viharati.

Furthermore, householder, a mendicant, going totally beyond perceptions of form, with the ending of perceptions of impingement, not focusing on perceptions of diversity, aware that 'space is infinite', enters and remains in the dimension of infinite space.

So iti paṭisañcikkhati:

Then they reflect:

'ayampi kho ākāsānañcāyatanasamāpatti abhisaṅkhatā abhisañcetayitā.

'Even this attainment of the dimension of infinite space is produced by choices and intentions.'

Yaṁ kho pana kiñci abhisaṅkhataṁ abhisañcetayitaṁ tadaniccaṁ nirodhadhamman'ti pajānāti.

They understand: 'But whatever is produced by choices and intentions is impermanent and liable to cessation.' ...

So tattha ṭhito …pe…

anuttaraṁ yogakkhemaṁ anupāpuṇāti.

Puna caparaṁ, gahapati, bhikkhu sabbaso ākāsānañcāyatanaṁ samatikkamma 'anantaṁ viññāṇan'ti viññāṇañcāyatanaṁ upasampajja viharati.

Furthermore, a mendicant, going totally beyond the dimension of infinite space, aware that 'consciousness is infinite', enters and remains in the dimension of infinite consciousness. ...

So iti paṭisañcikkhati:

'ayampi kho viññāṇañcāyatanasamāpatti abhisaṅkhatā abhisañcetayitā.

Yaṁ kho pana kiñci abhisaṅkhataṁ abhisañcetayitaṁ tadaniccaṁ nirodhadhamman'ti pajānāti.

So tattha ṭhito …pe…

anuttaraṁ yogakkhemaṁ anupāpuṇāti.

Puna caparaṁ, gahapati, bhikkhu sabbaso viññāṇañcāyatanaṁ samatikkamma 'natthi kiñcī'ti ākiñcaññāyatanaṁ upasampajja viharati.

Furthermore, a mendicant, going totally beyond the dimension of infinite consciousness, aware that 'there is nothing at all', enters and remains in the dimension of nothingness.

So iti paṭisañcikkhati:

Then they reflect:

'ayampi kho ākiñcaññāyatanasamāpatti abhisaṅkhatā abhisañcetayitā.

'Even this attainment of the dimension of nothingness is produced by choices and intentions.'

Yaṁ kho pana kiñci abhisaṅkhataṁ abhisañcetayitaṁ tadaniccaṁ nirodhadhamman'ti pajānāti.

They understand: 'But whatever is produced by choices and intentions is impermanent and liable to cessation.'

So tattha ṭhito āsavānaṁ khayaṁ pāpuṇāti.

Abiding in that they attain the ending of defilements.

No ce āsavānaṁ khayaṁ pāpuṇāti, teneva dhammarāgena tāya dhammanandiyā pañcannam orambhāgiyānaṁ saṁyojanānaṁ parikkhayā opapātiko hoti tattha parinibbāyī anāvattidhammo tasmā lokā.

If they don't attain the ending of defilements, with the ending of the five lower fetters they're reborn spontaneously because of their passion and love for that meditation. They are extinguished there, and are not liable to return from that world.

Ayampi kho, gahapati, tena bhagavatā jānatā passatā arahatā sammāsambuddhena ekadhammo akkhāto yattha bhikkhuno appamattassa ātāpino pahitattassa viharato avimuttañceva cittaṁ vimuccati, aparikkhīṇā ca āsavā parikkhayaṁ gacchanti, ananuppattañca anuttaraṁ yogakkhemaṁ anupāpuṇātī'ti.

This too is one thing that has been rightly explained by the Blessed One—who knows and sees, the perfected one, the fully awakened Buddha—practicing which a diligent, keen, and resolute mendicant's mind is freed, their defilements are ended, and they arrive at the supreme sanctuary."

Evaṁ vutte, dasamo gahapati aṭṭhakanāgaro āyasmantaṁ ānandaṁ etadavoca:

When he said this, the householder Dasama said to Venerable Ānanda,

"seyyathāpi, bhante ānanda, puriso ekaṁva nidhimukhaṁ gavesanto sakideva ekādasa nidhimukhāni adhigaccheyya;

"Honorable Ānanda, suppose a person was looking for an entrance to a hidden treasure. And all at once they'd come across eleven entrances!

evameva kho ahaṁ, bhante, ekaṁ amatadvāraṁ gavesanto sakideva ekādasa amatadvārāni alatthaṁ bhāvanāya.

In the same way, I was searching for the door to the deathless. And all at once I got to hear of eleven doors to the deathless.

Seyyathāpi, bhante, purisassa agāraṁ ekādasadvāraṁ, so tasmiṁ agāre āditte ekamekenapi dvārena sakkuṇeyya attānaṁ sotthiṁ kātuṁ;

Suppose a person had a house with eleven doors. If the house caught fire they'd be able to flee to safety through any one of those doors.

evameva kho ahaṁ, bhante, imesaṁ ekādasannaṁ amatadvārānaṁ ekamekenapi amatadvārena sakkuṇissāmi attānaṁ sotthiṁ kātuṁ.

In the same way, I'm able to flee to safety through any one of these eleven doors to the deathless.

Imehi nāma, bhante, aññatitthiyā ācariyassa ācariyadhanaṁ pariyesissanti, kimaṅgaṁ panāhaṁ āyasmato ānandassa pūjaṁ na karissāmī"ti.

Sir, those of other religions seek a fee for the teacher. Why shouldn't I make an offering to Venerable Ānanda?"

Atha kho dasamo gahapati aṭṭhakanāgaro pāṭaliputtakañca vesālikañca bhikkhusaṅghaṁ sannipātetvā paṇītena khādanīyena bhojanīyena sahatthā santappesi sampavāresi,

Then the householder Dasama, having assembled the Saṅgha from Vesālī and Pāṭaliputta, served and satisfied them with his own hands with delicious fresh and cooked foods.

ekamekañca bhikkhuṁ paccekaṁ dussayugena acchādesi, āyasmantañca ānandaṁ ticīvarena acchādesi, āyasmato ca ānandassa pañcasatavihāraṁ kārāpesīti.

He clothed each and every mendicant in a pair of garments, with a set of three robes for Ānanda. And he had a dwelling worth five hundred built for Ānanda.

Aṭṭhakanāgarasuttaṁ niṭṭhitaṁ dutiyaṁ.

53 Sekhasutta:

A Trainee

Evaṁ me sutaṁ—

So I have heard.

ekaṁ samayaṁ bhagavā sakkesu viharati kapilavatthusmiṁ nigrodhārāme.

At one time the Buddha was staying in the land of the Sakyans, near Kapilavatthu in the Banyan Tree Monastery.

Tena kho pana samayena kāpilavatthavānaṁ sakyānaṁ navaṁ santhāgāraṁ acirakāritaṁ hoti anajjhāvutthaṁ samaṇena vā brāhmaṇena vā kenaci vā manussabhūtena.

Now at that time a new town hall had recently been constructed for the Sakyans of Kapilavatthu. It had not yet been occupied by an ascetic or brahmin or any person at all.

Atha kho kāpilavatthavā sakyā yena bhagavā tenupasaṅkamiṁsu; upasaṅkamitvā bhagavantaṁ abhivādetvā ekamantaṁ nisīdiṁsu. Ekamantaṁ nisinnā kho kāpilavatthavā sakyā bhagavantaṁ etadavocuṁ:

Then the Sakyans of Kapilavatthu went up to the Buddha, bowed, sat down to one side, and said to him:

"idha, bhante, kāpilavatthavānaṁ sakyānaṁ navaṁ santhāgāraṁ acirakāritaṁ anajjhāvutthaṁ samaṇena vā brāhmaṇena vā kenaci vā manussabhūtena.

"Sir, a new town hall has recently been constructed for the Sakyans of Kapilavatthu. It has not yet been occupied by an ascetic or brahmin or any person at all.

Taṁ, bhante, bhagavā paṭhamaṁ paribhuñjatu. Bhagavatā paṭhamaṁ paribhuttaṁ pacchā kāpilavatthavā sakyā paribhuñjissanti.

May the Buddha be the first to use it, and only then will the Sakyans of Kapilavatthu use it.

Tadassa kāpilavatthavānaṁ sakyānaṁ dīgharattaṁ hitāya sukhāyā"ti.

That would be for the lasting welfare and happiness of the Sakyans of Kapilavatthu."

Adhivāsesi bhagavā tuṇhībhāvena.

The Buddha consented with silence.

Atha kho kāpilavatthavā sakyā bhagavato adhivāsanaṁ viditvā uṭṭhāyāsanā bhagavantaṁ abhivādetvā padakkhiṇaṁ katvā yena navaṁ santhāgāraṁ tenupasaṅkamiṁsu; upasaṅkamitvā sabbasanthariṁ santhāgāraṁ santharitvā āsanāni paññapetvā udakamaṇikaṁ upaṭṭhapetvā telappadīpaṁ āropetvā yena bhagavā tenupasaṅkamiṁsu;

Then, knowing that the Buddha had consented, the Sakyans got up from their seat, bowed, and respectfully circled the Buddha, keeping him on their right. Then they went to the new town hall, where they spread carpets all over, prepared seats, set up a water jar, and placed a lamp. Then they went back to the Buddha,

upasaṅkamitvā bhagavantaṁ abhivādetvā ekamantaṁ aṭṭhaṁsu.

bowed, stood to one side,

Ekamantaṁ ṭhitā kho kāpilavatthavā sakyā bhagavantaṁ etadavocuṁ:

and told him of their preparations, saying,

"sabbasanthariṁ santhataṁ, bhante, santhāgāraṁ, āsanāni paññattāni, udakamaṇiko upaṭṭhāpito, telappadīpo āropito.

Yassadāni, bhante, bhagavā kālaṁ maññatī"ti.

"Please, sir, come at your convenience."

Atha kho bhagavā nivāsetvā pattacīvaramādāya saddhiṁ bhikkhusaṅghena yena santhāgāraṁ tenupasaṅkami; upasaṅkamitvā pāde pakkhāletvā santhāgāraṁ pavisitvā majjhimaṁ thambhaṁ nissāya puratthābhimukho nisīdi.

Then the Buddha robed up and, taking his bowl and robe, went to the new town hall together with the Saṅgha of mendicants. Having washed his feet he entered the town hall and sat against the central column facing east.

Bhikkhusaṅghopi kho pāde pakkhāletvā santhāgāraṁ pavisitvā pacchimaṁ bhittiṁ nissāya puratthābhimukho nisīdi, bhagavantaṁyeva purakkhatvā.

The Saṅgha of mendicants also washed their feet, entered the town hall, and sat against the west wall facing east, with the Buddha right in front of them.

Kāpilavatthavāpi kho sakyā pāde pakkhāletvā santhāgāraṁ pavisitvā puratthimaṁ bhittiṁ nissāya pacchimābhimukhā nisīdiṁsu, bhagavantaṁyeva purakkhatvā.

The Sakyans of Kapilavatthu also washed their feet, entered the town hall, and sat against the east wall facing west, with the Buddha right in front of them.

Atha kho bhagavā kāpilavatthave sakye bahudeva rattiṁ dhammiyā kathāya sandassetvā samādapetvā samuttejetvā sampahaṁsetvā āyasmantaṁ ānandaṁ āmantesi:

The Buddha spent much of the night educating, encouraging, firing up, and inspiring the Sakyans with a Dhamma talk. Then he addressed Venerable Ānanda,

"paṭibhātu taṁ, ānanda, kāpilavatthavānaṁ sakyānaṁ sekho pāṭipado.

"Ānanda, speak about the practicing trainee to the Sakyans of Kapilavatthu as you feel inspired.

Piṭṭhi me āgilāyati;

My back is sore,

tamahaṁ āyamissāmī"ti.

I'll stretch it."

"Evaṁ, bhante"ti kho āyasmā ānando bhagavato paccassosi.

"Yes, sir," Ānanda replied.

Atha kho bhagavā catuggunam sanghātim paññāpetvā dakkhinena passena sīhaseyyam kappesi, pāde pādam accādhāya, sato sampajāno, utthānasaññam manasi karitvā.

And then the Buddha spread out his outer robe folded in four and laid down in the lion's posture—on the right side, placing one foot on top of the other—mindful and aware, and focused on the time of getting up.

Atha kho āyasmā ānando mahānāmam sakkam āmantesi:

Then Ānanda addressed Mahānāma the Sakyan:

"idha, mahānāma, ariyasāvako sīlasampanno hoti, indriyesu guttadvāro hoti, bhojane mattaññū hoti, jāgariyam anuyutto hoti, sattahi saddhammehi samannāgato hoti, catunnam jhānānam ābhicetasikānam ditthadhammasukhavihārānam nikāmalābhī hoti akicchalābhī akasiralābhī.

"Mahānāma, a noble disciple is accomplished in ethics, guards the sense doors, eats in moderation, and is dedicated to wakefulness. They have seven good qualities, and they get the four absorptions—blissful meditations in the present life that belong to the higher mind—when they want, without trouble or difficulty.

Kathañca, mahānāma, ariyasāvako sīlasampanno hoti?

And how is a noble disciple accomplished in ethics?

Idha, mahānāma, ariyasāvako sīlavā hoti, pātimokkhasamvarasamvuto viharati ācāragocarasampanno anumattesu vajjesu bhayadassāvī, samādāya sikkhati sikkhāpadesu.

It's when a noble disciple is ethical, restrained in the monastic code, conducting themselves well and seeking alms in suitable places. Seeing danger in the slightest fault, they keep the rules they've undertaken.

Evam kho, mahānāma, ariyasāvako sīlasampanno hoti.

That's how a noble disciple is ethical.

Kathañca, mahānāma, ariyasāvako indriyesu guttadvāro hoti?

And how does a noble disciple guard the sense doors?

Idha, mahānāma, ariyasāvako cakkhunā rūpam disvā na nimittaggāhī hoti nānubyañjanaggāhī.

When a noble disciple sees a sight with their eyes, they don't get caught up in the features and details.

Yatvādhikaranamenam cakkhundriyam asamvutam viharantam abhijjhādomanassā pāpakā akusalā dhammā anvāssaveyyuṁ tassa saṁvarāya paṭipajjati, rakkhati cakkhundriyaṁ, cakkhundriye saṁvaraṁ āpajjati.

If the faculty of sight were left unrestrained, bad unskillful qualities of desire and aversion would become overwhelming. For this reason, they practice restraint, protecting the faculty of sight, and achieving its restraint.

Sotena saddaṁ sutvā …pe…

When they hear a sound with their ears …

ghānena gandhaṁ ghāyitvā …pe…

When they smell an odor with their nose …

jivhāya rasaṁ sāyitvā …pe…

When they taste a flavor with their tongue …

kāyena phoṭṭhabbaṁ phusitvā …pe…

When they feel a touch with their body …

manasā dhammaṁ viññāya na nimittaggāhī hoti nānubyañjanaggāhī.

When they know a thought with their mind, they don't get caught up in the features and details.

Yatvādhikaraṇamenaṁ manindriyaṁ asaṁvutaṁ viharantaṁ abhijjhādomanassā pāpakā akusalā dhammā anvāssaveyyuṁ tassa saṁvarāya paṭipajjati, rakkhati manindriyaṁ, manindriye saṁvaraṁ āpajjati.

If the faculty of mind were left unrestrained, bad unskillful qualities of desire and aversion would become overwhelming. For this reason, they practice restraint, protecting the faculty of mind, and achieving its restraint.

Evaṁ kho, mahānāma, ariyasāvako indriyesu guttadvāro hoti.

That's how a noble disciple guards the sense doors.

Kathañca, mahānāma, ariyasāvako bhojane mattaññū hoti?

And how does a noble disciple eat in moderation?

Idha, mahānāma, ariyasāvako paṭisaṅkhā yoniso āhāraṁ āhāreti:

It's when a noble disciple reflects properly on the food that they eat:

'neva davāya na madāya na maṇḍanāya na vibhūsanāya; yāvadeva imassa kāyassa ṭhitiyā yāpanāya vihiṁsūparatiyā brahmacariyānuggahāya. Iti purāṇañca vedanaṁ paṭihaṅkhāmi, navañca vedanaṁ na uppādessāmi, yātrā ca me bhavissati anavajjatā ca phāsuvihāro cā'ti.

'Not for fun, indulgence, adornment, or decoration, but only to sustain this body, to avoid harm, and to support spiritual practice. In this way, I shall put an end to old discomfort and not give rise to new discomfort, and I will live blamelessly and at ease.'

Evaṁ kho, mahānāma, ariyasāvako bhojane mattaññū hoti.

That's how a noble disciple eats in moderation.

Kathañca, mahānāma, ariyasāvako jāgariyaṁ anuyutto hoti?

And how is a noble disciple dedicated to wakefulness?

Idha, mahānāma, ariyasāvako divasaṁ caṅkamena nisajjāya āvaraṇīyehi dhammehi cittaṁ parisodheti,

It's when a noble disciple practices walking and sitting meditation by day, purifying their mind from obstacles.

rattiyā paṭhamaṁ yāmaṁ caṅkamena nisajjāya āvaraṇīyehi dhammehi cittaṁ parisodheti,

In the evening, they continue to practice walking and sitting meditation.

rattiyā majjhimaṁ yāmaṁ dakkhiṇena passena sīhaseyyaṁ kappeti, pāde pādaṁ accādhāya, sato sampajāno, uṭṭhānasaññaṁ manasi karitvā,

In the middle of the night, they lie down in the lion's posture—on the right side, placing one foot on top of the other—mindful and aware, and focused on the time of getting up.

rattiyā pacchimaṁ yāmaṁ paccuṭṭhāya caṅkamena nisajjāya āvaraṇīyehi dhammehi cittaṁ parisodheti.

In the last part of the night, they get up and continue to practice walking and sitting meditation, purifying their mind from obstacles.

Evaṁ kho, mahānāma, ariyasāvako jāgariyaṁ anuyutto hoti.

That's how a noble disciple is dedicated to wakefulness.

Kathañca, mahānāma, ariyasāvako sattahi saddhammehi samannāgato hoti?

And how does a noble disciple have seven good qualities?

Idha, mahānāma, ariyasāvako saddho hoti, saddahati tathāgatassa bodhiṁ:

It's when a noble disciple has faith in the Realized One's awakening:

'itipi so bhagavā arahaṁ sammāsambuddho vijjācaraṇasampanno sugato lokavidū anuttaro purisadammasārathi satthā devamanussānaṁ buddho bhagavā'ti.

'That Blessed One is perfected, a fully awakened Buddha, accomplished in knowledge and conduct, holy, knower of the world, supreme guide for those who wish to train, teacher of gods and humans, awakened, blessed.'

Hirimā hoti, hiriyati kāyaduccaritena vacīduccaritena manoduccaritena, hiriyati pāpakānaṁ akusalānaṁ dhammānaṁ samāpattiyā.

They have a conscience. They're conscientious about bad conduct by way of body, speech, and mind, and conscientious about having any bad, unskillful qualities.

Ottappī hoti, ottappati kāyaduccaritena vacīduccaritena manoduccaritena, ottappati pāpakānaṁ akusalānaṁ dhammānaṁ samāpattiyā.

They exercise prudence. They're prudent when it comes to bad conduct by way of body, speech, and mind, and prudent when it comes to acquiring any bad, unskillful qualities.

Bahussuto hoti sutadharo sutasannicayo. Ye te dhammā ādikalyāṇā majjhekalyāṇā pariyosānakalyāṇā sātthā sabyañjanā kevalaparipuṇṇaṁ parisuddhaṁ brahmacariyaṁ abhivadanti tathārūpāssa dhammā bahussutā honti dhātā vacasā paricitā manasānupekkhitā diṭṭhiyā suppaṭividdhā.

They're very learned, remembering and keeping what they've learned. These teachings are good in the beginning, good in the middle, and good in the end, meaningful and well-phrased, describing a spiritual practice that's entirely full and pure. They are very learned in such teachings, remembering them, reinforcing them by recitation, mentally scrutinizing them, and comprehending them theoretically.

Āraddhavīriyo viharati akusalānaṁ dhammānaṁ pahānāya, kusalānaṁ dhammānaṁ upasampadāya, thāmavā daḷhaparakkamo anikkhittadhuro kusalesu dhammesu.

They live with energy roused up for giving up unskillful qualities and embracing skillful qualities. They're strong, staunchly vigorous, not slacking off when it comes to developing skillful qualities.

Satimā hoti, paramena satinepakkena samannāgato, cirakatampi cirabhāsitampi saritā anussaritā.

They're mindful. They have utmost mindfulness and alertness, and can remember and recall what was said and done long ago.

Paññavā hoti, udayatthagāminiyā paññāya samannāgato, ariyāya nibbedhikāya sammā dukkhakkhayagāminiyā.

They're wise. They have the wisdom of arising and passing away which is noble, penetrative, and leads to the complete ending of suffering.

Evaṁ kho, mahānāma, ariyasāvako sattahi saddhammehi samannāgato hoti.

That's how a noble disciple has seven good qualities.

Kathañca, mahānāma, ariyasāvako catunnaṁ jhānānaṁ ābhicetasikānaṁ diṭṭhadhammasukhavihārānaṁ nikāmalābhī hoti akicchalābhī akasiralābhī?

And how does a noble disciple get the four absorptions—blissful meditations in the present life that belong to the higher mind—when they want, without trouble or difficulty?

Idha, mahānāma, ariyasāvako vivicceva kāmehi …pe… paṭhamaṁ jhānaṁ upasampajja viharati;

It's when a noble disciple, quite secluded from sensual pleasures, secluded from unskillful qualities, enters and remains in the first absorption …

vitakkavicārānaṁ vūpasamā ajjhattaṁ sampasādanaṁ …pe… dutiyaṁ jhānaṁ upasampajja viharati;

second absorption …

pītiyā ca virāgā …pe… tatiyaṁ jhānaṁ upasampajja viharati;

third absorption …

sukhassa ca pahānā dukkhassa ca pahānā pubbeva somanassadomanassānaṁ atthaṅgamā …pe… catutthaṁ jhānaṁ upasampajja viharati.

fourth absorption.

Evaṁ kho, mahānāma, ariyasāvako catunnaṁ jhānānaṁ ābhicetasikānaṁ diṭṭhadhammasukhavihārānaṁ nikāmalābhī hoti akicchalābhī akasiralābhī.

That's how a noble disciple gets the four absorptions—blissful meditations in the present life that belong to the higher mind—when they want, without trouble or difficulty.

Yato kho, mahānāma, ariyasāvako evaṁ sīlasampanno hoti, evaṁ indriyesu guttadvāro hoti, evaṁ bhojane mattaññū hoti, evaṁ jāgariyaṁ anuyutto hoti, evaṁ sattahi saddhammehi samannāgato hoti, evaṁ catunnaṁ jhānānaṁ ābhicetasikānaṁ diṭṭhadhammasukhavihārānaṁ nikāmalābhī hoti akicchalābhī akasiralābhī, ayaṁ vuccati, mahānāma, ariyasāvako sekho pāṭipado apuccaṇḍatāya samāpanno, bhabbo abhinibbhidāya, bhabbo sambodhāya, bhabbo anuttarassa yogakkhemassa adhigamāya.

When a noble disciple is accomplished in ethics, guards the sense doors, eats in moderation, and is dedicated to wakefulness; and they have seven good qualities, and they get the four absorptions—blissful meditations in the present life that belong to the higher mind—when they want, without trouble or difficulty, they are called a noble disciple who is a practicing trainee. Their eggs are unspoiled, and they are capable of breaking out of their shell, becoming awakened, and achieving the supreme sanctuary.

Seyyathāpi, mahānāma, kukkuṭiyā aṇḍāni aṭṭha vā dasa vā dvādasa vā tānāssu kukkuṭiyā sammā adhisayitāni sammā pariseditāni sammā paribhāvitāni, kiñcāpi tassā kukkuṭiyā na evaṁ icchā uppajjeyya:

Suppose there was a chicken with eight or ten or twelve eggs. And she properly sat on them to keep them warm and incubated. Even if that chicken doesn't wish,

'aho vatime kukkuṭapotakā pādanakhasikhāya vā mukhatuṇḍakena vā aṇḍakosaṁ padāletvā sotthinā abhinibbhijjeyyun'ti,

'If only my chicks could break out of the eggshell with their claws and beak and hatch safely!'

atha kho bhabbāva te kukkuṭapotakā pādanakhasikhāya vā mukhatuṇḍakena vā aṇḍakosaṁ padāletvā sotthinā abhinibbhijjituṁ.

Still they can break out and hatch safely.

Evameva kho, mahānāma, yato ariyasāvako evaṁ sīlasampanno hoti, evaṁ indriyesu guttadvāro hoti, evaṁ bhojane mattaññū hoti, evaṁ jāgariyaṁ anuyutto hoti, evaṁ sattahi saddhammehi samannāgato hoti, evaṁ catunnaṁ jhānānaṁ ābhicetasikānaṁ diṭṭhadhammasukhavihārānaṁ nikāmalābhī hoti akicchalābhī akasiralābhī, ayaṁ vuccati, mahānāma, ariyasāvako sekho pāṭipado apuccaṇḍatāya samāpanno, bhabbo abhinibbhidāya, bhabbo sambodhāya, bhabbo anuttarassa yogakkhemassa adhigamāya.

In the same way, when a noble disciple is practicing all these things they are called a noble disciple who is a practicing trainee. Their eggs are unspoiled, and they are capable of breaking out of their shell, becoming awakened, and achieving the supreme sanctuary.

Sa kho so, mahānāma, ariyasāvako imaṁyeva anuttaraṁ upekkhāsatipārisuddhiṁ āgamma anekavihitaṁ pubbenivāsaṁ anussarati,

Relying on this supreme purity of mindfulness and equanimity, that noble disciple recollects their many kinds of past lives.

seyyathidaṁ—ekampi jātiṁ dvepi jātiyo ...pe... iti sākāraṁ sauddesaṁ anekavihitaṁ pubbenivāsaṁ anussarati,

That is: one, two, three, four, five, ten, twenty, thirty, forty, fifty, a hundred, a thousand, a hundred thousand rebirths; many eons of the world contracting, many eons of the world expanding, many eons of the world contracting and expanding. ... And so they recollect their many kinds of past lives, with features and details.

ayamassa paṭhamābhinibbhidā hoti kukkuṭacchāpakasseva aṇḍakosamhā.

This is their first breaking out, like a chick from an eggshell.

Sa kho so, mahānāma, ariyasāvako imaṁyeva anuttaraṁ upekkhāsatipārisuddhiṁ āgamma dibbena cakkhunā visuddhena atikkantamānusakena satte passati cavamāne upapajjamāne hīne paṇīte suvaṇṇe dubbaṇṇe sugate duggate ...pe...

yathākammūpage satte pajānāti,

Relying on this supreme purity of mindfulness and equanimity, that noble disciple, with clairvoyance that is purified and superhuman, sees sentient beings passing away and being reborn—inferior and superior, beautiful and ugly, in a good place or a bad place. ... They understand how sentient beings are reborn according to their deeds.

ayamassa dutiyābhinibbhidā hoti kukkuṭacchāpakasseva aṇḍakosamhā.

This is their second breaking out, like a chick from an eggshell.

Sa kho so, mahānāma, ariyasāvako imaṁyeva anuttaraṁ upekkhāsatipārisuddhiṁ āgamma āsavānaṁ khayā anāsavaṁ cetovimuttiṁ paññāvimuttiṁ diṭṭheva dhamme sayaṁ abhiññā sacchikatvā upasampajja viharati,

Relying on this supreme purity of mindfulness and equanimity, that noble disciple realizes the undefiled freedom of heart and freedom by wisdom in this very life. And they live having realized it with their own insight due to the ending of defilements.

ayamassa tatiyābhinibbhidā hoti kukkuṭacchāpakasseva aṇḍakosamhā.

This is their third breaking out, like a chick from an eggshell.

Yampi, mahānāma, ariyasāvako sīlasampanno hoti, idampissa hoti caraṇasmiṁ;

A noble disciple's conduct includes the following: being accomplished in ethics,

yampi, mahānāma, ariyasāvako indriyesu guttadvāro hoti, idampissa hoti caraṇasmiṁ;

guarding the sense doors,

yampi, mahānāma, ariyasāvako bhojane mattaññū hoti, idampissa hoti caraṇasmiṁ;

moderation in eating,

yampi, mahānāma, ariyasāvako jāgariyaṁ anuyutto hoti, idampissa hoti caraṇasmiṁ;

being dedicated to wakefulness,

yampi, mahānāma, ariyasāvako sattahi saddhammehi samannāgato hoti, idampissa hoti caraṇasmiṁ;

having seven good qualities,

yampi, mahānāma, ariyasāvako catunnaṁ jhānānaṁ ābhicetasikānaṁ diṭṭhadhammasukhavihārānaṁ nikāmalābhī hoti akicchalābhī akasiralābhī, idampissa hoti caraṇasmiṁ.

and getting the four absorptions when they want, without trouble or difficulty.

Yañca kho, mahānāma, ariyasāvako anekavihitaṁ pubbenivāsaṁ anussarati, seyyathidaṁ—ekampi jātiṁ dvepi jātiyo …pe… iti sākāraṁ sauddesaṁ anekavihitaṁ pubbenivāsaṁ anussarati, idampissa hoti vijjāya;

A noble disciple's knowledge includes the following: recollecting their past lives,

yampi, mahānāma, ariyasāvako dibbena cakkhunā visuddhena atikkantamānusakena satte passati cavamāne upapajjamāne hīne paṇīte suvaṇṇe dubbaṇṇe sugate duggate …pe… yathākammūpage satte pajānāti, idampissa hoti vijjāya.

clairvoyance that is purified and superhuman,

Yampi, mahānāma, ariyasāvako āsavānaṁ khayā anāsavaṁ cetovimuttiṁ paññāvimuttiṁ diṭṭheva dhamme sayaṁ abhiññā sacchikatvā upasampajja viharati, idampissa hoti vijjāya.

and realizing the undefiled freedom of heart and freedom by wisdom in this very life due to the ending of defilements.

Ayaṁ vuccati, mahānāma, ariyasāvako vijjāsampanno itipi caraṇasampanno itipi vijjācaraṇasampanno itipi.

This noble disciple is said to be 'accomplished in knowledge', and also 'accomplished in conduct', and also 'accomplished in knowledge and conduct'.

Brahmunāpesā, mahānāma, sanaṅkumārena gāthā bhāsitā:

And Brahmā Sanaṅkumāra also spoke this verse:

'Khattiyo seṭṭho janetasmiṁ,

ye gottapaṭisārino;

Vijjācaraṇasampanno,

so seṭṭho devamānuse'ti.

'The aristocrat is first among people

who take clan as the standard.

But one accomplished in knowledge and conduct

is first among gods and humans.'

Sā kho panesā, mahānāma, brahmunā sanaṅkumārena gāthā sugītā no duggītā, subhāsitā no dubbhāsitā, atthasaṁhitā no anatthasaṁhitā, anumatā bhagavatā"ti.

And that verse was well sung by Brahmā Sanaṅkumāra, not poorly sung; well spoken, not poorly spoken, beneficial, not harmful, and it was approved by the Buddha."

Atha kho bhagavā uṭṭhahitvā āyasmantaṁ ānandaṁ āmantesi:

Then the Buddha got up and said to Venerable Ānanda,

"sādhu sādhu, ānanda,

"Good, good, Ānanda!

sādhu kho tvaṁ, ānanda, kāpilavatthavānaṁ sakyānaṁ sekhaṁ pāṭipadaṁ abhāsī”ti.

It's good that you spoke to the Sakyans of Kapilavatthu about the practicing trainee."

Idamavocāyasmā ānando.

This is what Venerable Ānanda said,

Samanuñño satthā ahosi.

and the teacher approved.

Attamanā kāpilavatthavā sakyā āyasmato ānandassa bhāsitaṁ abhinandunti.

Satisfied, the Sakyans of Kapilavatthu were happy with what Venerable Ānanda said.

Sekhasuttaṁ niṭṭhitaṁ tatiyaṁ.

54 Potaliyasutta:

With Potaliya the Householder

Evaṁ me sutaṁ—

So I have heard.

ekaṁ samayaṁ bhagavā aṅguttarāpesu viharati āpaṇaṁ nāma aṅguttarāpānaṁ nigamo.

At one time the Buddha was staying in the land of the Northern Āpaṇas, near the town of theirs named Āpaṇa.

Atha kho bhagavā pubbaṇhasamayaṁ nivāsetvā pattacīvaramādāya āpaṇaṁ piṇḍāya pāvisi.

Then the Buddha robed up in the morning and, taking his bowl and robe, entered Āpaṇa for alms.

Āpaṇe piṇḍāya caritvā pacchābhattaṁ piṇḍapātapaṭikkanto yenaññataro vanasaṇḍo tenupasaṅkami divāvihārāya.

He wandered for alms in Āpaṇa. After the meal, on his return from almsround, he went to a certain forest grove for the day's meditation.

Taṁ vanasaṇḍaṁ ajjhogāhetvā aññatarasmiṁ rukkhamūle divāvihāraṁ nisīdi.

Having plunged deep into it, he sat at the root of a certain tree for the day's meditation.

Potaliyopi kho gahapati sampannanivāsanapāvuraṇo chattupāhanāhi jaṅghāvihāraṁ anucaṅkamamāno anuvicaramāno yena so vanasaṇḍo tenupasaṅkami; upasaṅkamitvā taṁ vanasaṇḍaṁ ajjhogāhetvā yena bhagavā tenupasaṅkami; upasaṅkamitvā bhagavatā saddhiṁ sammodi.

Potaliya the householder also approached that forest grove while going for a walk. He was well dressed in a cloak and sarong, with parasol and sandals. Having plunged deep into it, he went up to the Buddha, and exchanged greetings with him.

Sammodanīyaṁ kathaṁ sāraṇīyaṁ vītisāretvā ekamantaṁ aṭṭhāsi. Ekamantaṁ ṭhitaṁ kho potaliyaṁ gahapatiṁ bhagavā etadavoca:

When the greetings and polite conversation were over, he stood to one side, and the Buddha said to him,

"saṁvijjanti kho, gahapati, āsanāni; sace ākaṅkhasi nisīdā"ti.

"There are seats, householder. Please sit if you wish."

Evaṁ vutte, potaliyo gahapati "gahapativādena maṁ samaṇo gotamo samudācaratī"ti kupito anattamano tuṇhī ahosi.

When he said this, Potaliya was angry and upset. Thinking, "The ascetic Gotama addresses me as 'householder'!" he stayed silent.

Dutiyampi kho bhagavā ...pe...

For a second time ...

tatiyampi kho bhagavā potaliyaṁ gahapatiṁ etadavoca:

and a third time the Buddha said to him,

"saṁvijjanti kho, gahapati, āsanāni; sace ākaṅkhasi nisīdā"ti.

"There are seats, householder. Please sit if you wish."

Evaṁ vutte, potaliyo gahapati "gahapativādena maṁ samaṇo gotamo samudācaratī”ti kupito anattamano bhagavantaṁ etadavoca:

When he said this, Potaliya was angry and upset. Thinking, “The ascetic Gotama addresses me as ‘householder’!” he said to the Buddha,

“tayidaṁ, bho gotama, nacchannaṁ, tayidaṁ nappatirūpaṁ, yaṁ maṁ tvaṁ gahapativādena samudācarasī”ti.

“Master Gotama, it is neither proper nor appropriate for you to address me as ‘householder’.”

“Te hi te, gahapati, ākārā, te liṅgā, te nimittā yathā taṁ gahapatissā”ti.

“Well, householder, you have the features, attributes, and signs of a householder.”

“Tathā hi pana me, bho gotama, sabbe kammantā paṭikkhittā, sabbe vohārā samucchinnā”ti.

“Master Gotama, it’s because I have refused all work and cut off all judgments.”

“Yathā kathaṁ pana te, gahapati, sabbe kammantā paṭikkhittā, sabbe vohārā samucchinnā”ti?

“Householder, in what way have you refused all work and cut off all judgments?”

“Idha me, bho gotama, yaṁ ahosi dhanaṁ vā dhaññaṁ vā rajataṁ vā jātarūpaṁ vā sabbaṁ taṁ puttānaṁ dāyajjaṁ niyyātaṁ, tatthāhaṁ anovādī anupavādī ghāsacchādanaparamo viharāmi.

“Master Gotama, all the money, grain, gold, and silver I used to have has been handed over to my children as their inheritance. And in this matter I do not advise or reprimand them, but live with nothing more than food and clothes.

Evaṁ kho me, bho gotama, sabbe kammantā paṭikkhittā, sabbe vohārā samucchinnā”ti.

That’s how I have refused all work and cut off all judgments.”

“Aññathā kho tvaṁ, gahapati, vohārasamucchedaṁ vadasi, aññathā ca pana ariyassa vinaye vohārasamucchedo hotī”ti.

“The cutting off of judgments as you describe it is one thing, householder, but the cutting off of judgments in the noble one’s training is quite different.”

“Yathā kathaṁ pana, bhante, ariyassa vinaye vohārasamucchedo hoti?

“But what, sir, is cutting off of judgments in the noble one’s training?

Sādhu me, bhante, bhagavā tathā dhammaṁ desetu yathā ariyassa vinaye vohārasamucchedo hotī”ti.

Sir, please teach me this.”

"Tena hi, gahapati, suṇāhi, sādhukaṁ manasi karohi, bhāsissāmī"ti.

"Well then, householder, listen and pay close attention, I will speak."

"Evaṁ, bhante"ti kho potaliyo gahapati bhagavato paccassosi.

"Yes, sir," said Potaliya.

Bhagavā etadavoca:

The Buddha said this:

"aṭṭha kho ime, gahapati, dhammā ariyassa vinaye vohārasamucchedāya saṁvattanti.

"Householder, these eight things lead to the cutting off of judgments in the noble one's training.

Katame aṭṭha?

What eight?

Apāṇātipātaṁ nissāya pāṇātipāto pahātabbo;

Killing living creatures should be given up, relying on not killing living creatures.

dinnādānaṁ nissāya adinnādānaṁ pahātabbaṁ;

Stealing should be given up, relying on not stealing.

saccavācaṁ nissāya musāvādo pahātabbo;

Lying should be given up, relying on speaking the truth.

apisuṇaṁ vācaṁ nissāya pisuṇā vācā pahātabbā;

Divisive speech should be given up, relying on speech that isn't divisive.

agiddhilobhaṁ nissāya giddhilobho pahātabbo;

Greed and lust should be given up, relying on not being greedy and lustful.

anindārosaṁ nissāya nindāroso pahātabbo;

Blaming and insulting should be given up, relying on not blaming and not insulting.

akkodhūpāyāsaṁ nissāya kodhūpāyāso pahātabbo;

Anger and distress should be given up, relying on not being angry and distressed.

anatimānaṁ nissāya atimāno pahātabbo.

Arrogance should be given up, relying on not being arrogant.

Ime kho, gahapati, aṭṭha dhammā saṅkhittena vuttā, vitthārena avibhattā, ariyassa vinaye vohārasamucchedāya saṁvattantī"ti.

These are the eight things—stated in brief without being analyzed in detail—that lead to the cutting off of judgments in the noble one's training."

"Ye me, bhante, bhagavatā aṭṭha dhammā saṅkhittena vuttā, vitthārena avibhattā, ariyassa vinaye vohārasamucchedāya saṁvattanti, sādhu me, bhante, bhagavā ime aṭṭha dhamme vitthārena vibhajatu anukampaṁ upādāyā"ti.

"Sir, please teach me these eight things in detail out of compassion."

"Tena hi, gahapati, suṇāhi, sādhukaṁ manasi karohi, bhāsissāmī"ti.

"Well then, householder, listen and pay close attention, I will speak."

"Evaṁ, bhante"ti kho potaliyo gahapati bhagavato paccassosi.

"Yes, sir," said Potaliya.

Bhagavā etadavoca:

The Buddha said this:

"'Apāṇātipātaṁ nissāya pāṇātipāto pahātabbo'ti iti kho panetaṁ vuttaṁ, kiñcetaṁ paṭicca vuttaṁ?

"'Killing living creatures should be given up, relying on not killing living creatures.' That's what I said, but why did I say it?

Idha, gahapati, ariyasāvako iti paṭisañcikkhati:

It's when a noble disciple reflects:

'yesaṁ kho ahaṁ saṁyojanānaṁ hetu pāṇātipātī assaṁ, tesāhaṁ saṁyojanānaṁ pahānāya samucchedāya paṭipanno.

'I am practicing to give up and cut off the fetters that might cause me to kill living creatures.

Ahañceva kho pana pāṇātipātī assaṁ, attāpi maṁ upavadeyya pāṇātipātapaccayā, anuviccāpi maṁ viññū garaheyyuṁ pāṇātipātapaccayā, kāyassa bhedā paraṁ maraṇā duggati pāṭikaṅkhā pāṇātipātapaccayā.

But if I were to kill living creatures, because of that I would reprimand myself; sensible people, after examination, would criticize me; and when my body breaks up, after death, I could expect to be reborn in a bad place.

Etadeva kho pana saṁyojanaṁ etaṁ nīvaraṇaṁ yadidaṁ pāṇātipāto.

And killing living creatures is itself a fetter and a hindrance.

Ye ca pāṇātipātapaccayā uppajjeyyuṁ āsavā vighātapariḷāhā, pāṇātipātā paṭiviratassa evaṁsa te āsavā vighātapariḷāhā na honti'.

The distressing and feverish defilements that might arise because of killing living creatures do not occur in someone who does not kill living creatures.'

'Apāṇātipātaṁ nissāya pāṇātipāto pahātabbo'ti—

'Killing living creatures should be given up, relying on not killing living creatures.'

iti yantaṁ vuttaṁ idametaṁ paṭicca vuttaṁ.

That's what I said, and this is why I said it.

'Dinnādānaṁ nissāya adinnādānaṁ pahātabban'ti iti kho panetaṁ vuttaṁ, kiñcetaṁ paṭicca vuttaṁ?

'Stealing …

Idha, gahapati, ariyasāvako iti paṭisañcikkhati:

'yesaṁ kho ahaṁ saṁyojanānaṁ hetu adinnādāyī assaṁ, tesāhaṁ saṁyojanānaṁ pahānāya samucchedāya paṭipanno.

Ahañceva kho pana adinnādāyī assaṁ, attāpi maṁ upavadeyya adinnādānapaccayā, anuviccāpi maṁ viññū garaheyyuṁ adinnādānapaccayā, kāyassa bhedā paraṁ maraṇā duggati pāṭikaṅkhā adinnādānapaccayā.

Etadeva kho pana saṁyojanaṁ etaṁ nīvaraṇaṁ yadidaṁ adinnādānaṁ.

Ye ca adinnādānapaccayā uppajjeyyuṁ āsavā vighātapariḷāhā adinnādānā paṭiviratassa evaṁsa te āsavā vighātapariḷāhā na honti'.

'Dinnādānaṁ nissāya adinnādānaṁ pahātabban'ti—

iti yantaṁ vuttaṁ idametaṁ paṭicca vuttaṁ.

'Saccavācaṁ nissāya musāvādo pahātabbo'ti iti kho panetaṁ vuttaṁ, kiñcetaṁ paṭicca vuttaṁ?

lying …

Idha, gahapati, ariyasāvako iti paṭisañcikkhati:

'yesaṁ kho ahaṁ saṁyojanānaṁ hetu musāvādī assaṁ, tesāhaṁ saṁyojanānaṁ pahānāya samucchedāya paṭipanno.

Ahañceva kho pana musāvādī assaṁ, attāpi maṁ upavadeyya musāvādapaccayā, anuviccāpi maṁ viññū garaheyyuṁ musāvādapaccayā, kāyassa bhedā paraṁ maraṇā duggati pāṭikaṅkhā musāvādapaccayā.

Etadeva kho pana saṁyojanaṁ etaṁ nīvaraṇaṁ yadidaṁ musāvādo.

Ye ca musāvādapaccayā uppajjeyyuṁ āsavā vighātapariḷāhā, musāvādā paṭiviratassa evaṁsa te āsavā vighātapariḷāhā na honti'.

'Saccavācaṁ nissāya musāvādo pahātabbo'ti—

iti yantaṁ vuttaṁ idametaṁ paṭicca vuttaṁ.

'Apisuṇaṁ vācaṁ nissāya pisuṇā vācā pahātabbā'ti iti kho panetaṁ vuttaṁ, kiñcetaṁ paṭicca vuttaṁ?

divisive speech …

Idha, gahapati, ariyasāvako iti paṭisañcikkhati:

'yesaṁ kho ahaṁ saṁyojanānaṁ hetu pisuṇavāco assaṁ, tesāhaṁ saṁyojanānaṁ pahānāya samucchedāya paṭipanno.

Ahañceva kho pana pisuṇavāco assaṁ, attāpi maṁ upavadeyya pisuṇavācāpaccayā, anuviccāpi maṁ viññū garaheyyuṁ pisuṇavācāpaccayā, kāyassa bhedā paraṁ maraṇā duggati pāṭikaṅkhā pisuṇavācāpaccayā.

Etadeva kho pana saṁyojanam etaṁ nīvaraṇaṁ yadidaṁ pisuṇā vācā.

Ye ca pisuṇavācāpaccayā uppajjeyyuṁ āsavā vighātapariḷāhā, pisuṇāya vācāya paṭiviratassa evaṁsa te āsavā vighātapariḷāhā na honti'.

'Apisuṇaṁ vācaṁ nissāya pisuṇā vācā pahātabbā'ti—

iti yantaṁ vuttaṁ idametaṁ paṭicca vuttaṁ.

'Agiddhilobhaṁ nissāya giddhilobho pahātabbo'ti iti kho panetaṁ vuttaṁ, kiñcetaṁ paṭicca vuttaṁ?

greed and lust …

Idha, gahapati, ariyasāvako iti paṭisañcikkhati:

'yesaṁ kho ahaṁ saṁyojanānaṁ hetu giddhilobhī assaṁ, tesāhaṁ saṁyojanānaṁ pahānāya samucchedāya paṭipanno.

Ahañceva kho pana giddhilobhī assaṁ, attāpi maṁ upavadeyya giddhilobhapaccayā, anuviccāpi maṁ viññū garaheyyuṁ giddhilobhapaccayā, kāyassa bhedā paraṁ maraṇā duggati pāṭikaṅkhā giddhilobhapaccayā.

Etadeva kho pana saṁyojanam etaṁ nīvaraṇaṁ yadidaṁ giddhilobho.

Ye ca giddhilobhapaccayā uppajjeyyuṁ āsavā vighātapariḷāhā, giddhilobhā paṭiviratassa evaṁsa te āsavā vighātapariḷāhā na honti'.

'Agiddhilobhaṁ nissāya giddhilobho pahātabbo'ti—

iti yantaṁ vuttaṁ idametaṁ paṭicca vuttaṁ.

'Anindārosaṁ nissāya nindāroso pahātabbo'ti iti kho panetaṁ vuttaṁ, kiñcetaṁ paṭicca vuttaṁ?

blaming and insulting …

Idha, gahapati, ariyasāvako iti paṭisañcikkhati:

'yesaṁ kho ahaṁ saṁyojanānaṁ hetu nindārosī assaṁ, tesāhaṁ saṁyojanānaṁ pahānāya samucchedāya paṭipanno.

Ahañceva kho pana nindārosī assaṁ, attāpi maṁ upavadeyya nindārosapaccayā, anuviccāpi maṁ viññū garaheyyuṁ nindārosapaccayā, kāyassa bhedā paraṁ maraṇā duggati pāṭikaṅkhā nindārosapaccayā.

Etadeva kho pana saṁyojanaṁ etaṁ nīvaraṇaṁ yadidaṁ nindāroso.

Ye ca nindārosapaccayā uppajjeyyuṁ āsavā vighātapariḷāhā, anindārosissa evaṁsa te āsavā vighātapariḷāhā na honti'.

'Anindārosaṁ nissāya nindāroso pahātabbo'ti—

iti yantaṁ vuttaṁ idametaṁ paṭicca vuttaṁ.

'Akkodhūpāyāsaṁ nissāya kodhūpāyāso pahātabbo'ti iti kho panetaṁ vuttaṁ, kiñcetaṁ paṭicca vuttaṁ?

anger and distress …

Idha, gahapati, ariyasāvako iti paṭisañcikkhati:

'yesaṁ kho ahaṁ saṁyojanānaṁ hetu kodhūpāyāsī assaṁ, tesāhaṁ saṁyojanānaṁ pahānāya samucchedāya paṭipanno.

Ahañceva kho pana kodhūpāyāsī assaṁ, attāpi maṁ upavadeyya kodhūpāyāsapaccayā, anuviccāpi maṁ viññū garaheyyuṁ kodhūpāyāsapaccayā, kāyassa bhedā paraṁ maraṇā duggati pāṭikaṅkhā kodhūpāyāsapaccayā.

Etadeva kho pana saṁyojanaṁ etaṁ nīvaraṇaṁ yadidaṁ kodhūpāyāso.

Ye ca kodhūpāyāsapaccayā uppajjeyyuṁ āsavā vighātapariḷāhā, akkodhūpāyāsissa evaṁsa te āsavā vighātapariḷāhā na honti'.

'Akkodhūpāyāsaṁ nissāya kodhūpāyāso pahātabbo'ti—

iti yantaṁ vuttaṁ idametaṁ paṭicca vuttaṁ.

'Anatimānaṁ nissāya atimāno pahātabbo'ti iti kho panetaṁ vuttaṁ, kiñcetaṁ paṭicca vuttaṁ?

Arrogance should be given up, relying on not being arrogant.' That's what I said, but why did I say it?

Idha, gahapati, ariyasāvako iti paṭisañcikkhati:

It's when a noble disciple reflects:

'yesaṁ kho ahaṁ saṁyojanānaṁ hetu atimānī assaṁ, tesāhaṁ saṁyojanānaṁ pahānāya samucchedāya paṭipanno.

'I am practicing to give up and cut off the fetters that might cause me to be arrogant.

Ahañceva kho pana atimānī assaṁ, attāpi maṁ upavadeyya atimānapaccayā, anuviccāpi maṁ viññū garaheyyuṁ atimānapaccayā, kāyassa bhedā paraṁ maraṇā duggati pāṭikaṅkhā atimānapaccayā.

But if I were to be arrogant, because of that I would reprimand myself; sensible people, after examination, would criticize me; and when my body breaks up, after death, I could expect to be reborn in a bad place.

Etadeva kho pana saṁyojanaṁ etaṁ nīvaraṇaṁ yadidaṁ atimāno.

And arrogance is itself a fetter and a hindrance.

Ye ca atimānapaccayā uppajjeyyuṁ āsavā vighātapariḷāhā, anatimānissa evaṁsa te āsavā vighātapariḷāhā na honti'.

The distressing and feverish defilements that might arise because of arrogance do not occur in someone who is not arrogant.'

'Anatimānaṁ nissāya atimāno pahātabbo'ti—

'Arrogance should be given up by not being arrogant.'

iti yantaṁ vuttaṁ idametaṁ paṭicca vuttaṁ.

That's what I said, and this is why I said it.

Ime kho, gahapati, aṭṭha dhammā saṅkhittena vuttā, vitthārena vibhattā, ye ariyassa vinaye vohārasamucchedāya saṁvattanti;

These are the eight things—stated in brief and analyzed in detail—that lead to the cutting off of judgments in the noble one's training.

na tveva tāva ariyassa vinaye sabbena sabbaṁ sabbathā sabbaṁ vohārasamucchedo hotī"ti.

But just this much does not constitute the cutting off of judgments in each and every respect in the noble one's training."

"Yathā kathaṁ pana, bhante, ariyassa vinaye sabbena sabbaṁ sabbathā sabbaṁ vohārasamucchedo hoti?

"But, sir, how is there the cutting off of judgments in each and every respect in the noble one's training?

Sādhu me, bhante, bhagavā tathā dhammaṁ desetu yathā ariyassa vinaye sabbena sabbaṁ sabbathā sabbaṁ vohārasamucchedo hotī"ti.

Sir, please teach me this."

"Tena hi, gahapati, suṇāhi, sādhukaṁ manasi karohi, bhāsissāmī"ti.

"Well then, householder, listen and pay close attention, I will speak."

"Evaṁ, bhante"ti kho potaliyo gahapati bhagavato paccassosi.

"Yes, sir," said Potaliya.

Bhagavā etadavoca:

The Buddha said this:

1. Kamadinavakatha

1. The Dangers of Sensual Pleasures

"Seyyathāpi, gahapati, kukkuro jighacchādubbalyapareto goghātakasūnaṁ paccupaṭṭhito assa.

"Householder, suppose a dog weak with hunger was hanging around a butcher's shop.

Tamenaṁ dakkho goghātako vā goghātakantevāsī vā aṭṭhikaṅkalaṁ sunikkantaṁ nikkantaṁ nimmaṁsaṁ lohitamakkhitaṁ upasumbheyya.

Then a deft butcher or their apprentice would toss them a skeleton scraped clean of flesh and smeared in blood.

Taṁ kiṁ maññasi, gahapati,

What do you think, householder?

api nu kho so kukkuro amuṁ aṭṭhikaṅkalaṁ sunikkantaṁ nikkantaṁ nimmaṁsaṁ lohitamakkhitaṁ palehanto jighacchādubbalyaṁ paṭivineyyā"ti?

Gnawing on such a fleshless skeleton, would that dog still get rid of its hunger?"

"No hetaṁ, bhante".

"No, sir.

"Taṁ kissa hetu"?

Why not?

"Aduñhi, bhante, aṭṭhikaṅkalaṁ sunikkantaṁ nikkantaṁ nimmaṁsaṁ lohitamakkhitaṁ.

Because that skeleton is scraped clean of flesh and smeared in blood.

Yāvadeva pana so kukkuro kilamathassa vighātassa bhāgī assā"ti.

That dog will eventually get weary and frustrated."

"Evameva kho, gahapati, ariyasāvako iti paṭisañcikkhati:

"In the same way, a noble disciple reflects:

'aṭṭhikaṅkalūpamā kāmā vuttā bhagavatā bahudukkhā bahupāyāsā, ādīnavo ettha bhiyyo'ti.

'With the simile of a skeleton the Buddha said that sensual pleasures give little gratification and much suffering and distress, and they are all the more full of drawbacks.'

Evametaṁ yathābhūtaṁ sammappaññāya disvā yāyaṁ upekkhā nānattā nānattasitā taṁ abhinivajjetvā, yāyaṁ upekkhā ekattā ekattasitā yattha sabbaso lokāmisūpādānā aparisesā nirujjhanti tamevūpekkhaṁ bhāveti.

Having truly seen this with right understanding, they reject equanimity based on diversity and develop only the equanimity based on unity, where all kinds of grasping to the world's material delights cease without anything left over.

Seyyathāpi, gahapati, gijjho vā kaṅko vā kulalo vā maṁsapesiṁ ādāya uḍḍīyeyya.

Suppose a vulture or a crow or a hawk was to grab a lump of meat and fly away.

Tamenaṁ gijjhāpi kaṅkāpi kulalāpi anupatitvā anupatitvā vitaccheyyuṁ vissajjeyyuṁ.

Other vultures, crows, and hawks would keep chasing it, pecking and clawing.

Taṁ kiṁ maññasi, gahapati,

What do you think, householder?

sace so gijjho vā kaṅko vā kulalo vā taṁ maṁsapesiṁ na khippameva paṭinissajjeyya, so tatonidānaṁ maraṇaṁ vā nigaccheyya maraṇamattaṁ vā dukkhan"ti?

If that vulture, crow, or hawk doesn't quickly let go of that lump of meat, wouldn't that result in death or deadly suffering for them?"

"Evaṁ, bhante".

"Yes, sir." ...

"Evameva kho, gahapati, ariyasāvako iti paṭisañcikkhati:

'maṁsapesūpamā kāmā vuttā bhagavatā bahudukkhā bahupāyāsā, ādīnavo ettha bhiyyo'ti.

Evametaṁ yathābhūtaṁ sammappaññāya disvā yāyaṁ upekkhā nānattā nānattasitā taṁ abhinivajjetvā yāyaṁ upekkhā ekattā ekattasitā yattha sabbaso lokāmisūpādānā aparisesā nirujjhanti tamevūpekkhaṁ bhāveti.

Seyyathāpi, gahapati, puriso ādittaṁ tiṇukkaṁ ādāya paṭivātaṁ gaccheyya.

"Suppose a person carrying a blazing grass torch was to walk against the wind.

Taṁ kiṁ maññasi, gahapati,

What do you think, householder?

sace so puriso taṁ ādittaṁ tiṇukkaṁ na khippameva paṭinissajjeyya tassa sā ādittā tiṇukkā hatthaṁ vā daheyya bāhuṁ vā daheyya aññataraṁ vā aññataraṁ vā aṅgapaccaṅgaṁ daheyya, so tatonidānaṁ maraṇaṁ vā nigaccheyya maraṇamattaṁ vā dukkhan"ti?

If that person doesn't quickly let go of that blazing grass torch, wouldn't they burn their hands or arm or other limb, resulting in death or deadly suffering for them?"

"Evaṁ, bhante".

"Yes, sir." …

"Evameva kho, gahapati, ariyasāvako iti paṭisañcikkhati:

'tiṇukkūpamā kāmā vuttā bhagavatā bahudukkhā bahupāyāsā, ādīnavo ettha bhiyyo'ti.

Evametaṁ yathābhūtaṁ sammappaññāya disvā …pe… tamevūpekkhaṁ bhāveti.

Seyyathāpi, gahapati, aṅgārakāsu sādhikaporisā, pūrā aṅgārānaṁ vītaccikānaṁ vītadhūmānaṁ.

"Suppose there was a pit of glowing coals deeper than a man's height, full of glowing coals that neither flamed nor smoked.

Atha puriso āgaccheyya jīvitukāmo amaritukāmo sukhakāmo dukkhapaṭikkūlo.

Then a person would come along who wants to live and doesn't want to die, who wants to be happy and recoils from pain.

Tamenaṁ dve balavanto purisā nānābāhāsu gahetvā aṅgārakāsuṁ upakaḍḍheyyuṁ.

Then two strong men would grab them by the arms and drag them towards the pit of glowing coals.

Taṁ kiṁ maññasi, gahapati,

What do you think, householder?

api nu so puriso iticiticeva kāyaṁ sannāmeyyā"ti?

Wouldn't that person writhe and struggle to and fro?"

"Evaṁ, bhante".

"Yes, sir.

"Taṁ kissa hetu"?

Why is that?

"Viditañhi, bhante, tassa purisassa imañcāhaṁ aṅgārakāsuṁ papatissāmi, tatonidānaṁ maraṇaṁ vā nigacchissāmi maraṇamattaṁ vā dukkhan"ti.

For that person knows: 'If I fall in that pit of glowing coals, that'd result in my death or deadly pain.'" …

"Evameva kho, gahapati, ariyasāvako iti paṭisañcikkhati:

'aṅgārakāsūpamā kāmā vuttā bhagavatā bahudukkhā bahupāyāsā, ādīnavo ettha bhiyyo'ti.

Evametaṁ yathābhūtaṁ sammappaññāya disvā …pe… tamevūpekkhaṁ bhāveti.

Seyyathāpi, gahapati, puriso supinakaṁ passeyya ārāmarāmaṇeyyakaṁ vanarāmaṇeyyakaṁ bhūmirāmaṇeyyakaṁ pokkharaṇirāmaṇeyyakaṁ.

"Suppose a person was to see delightful parks, woods, meadows, and lotus ponds in a dream.

So paṭibuddho na kiñci paṭipasseyya.

But when they woke they couldn't see them at all. …

Evameva kho, gahapati, ariyasāvako iti paṭisañcikkhati:

'supinakūpamā kāmā vuttā bhagavatā bahudukkhā bahupāyāsā, ādīnavo ettha bhiyyo'ti …pe…

tamevūpekkhaṁ bhāveti.

Seyyathāpi, gahapati, puriso yācitakaṁ bhogaṁ yācitvā yānaṁ vā poriseyyaṁ pavaramaṇikuṇḍalaṁ.

Suppose a man had borrowed some goods—a gentleman's carriage and fine jewelled earrings—

So tehi yācitakehi bhogehi purakkhato parivuto antarāpaṇaṁ paṭipajjeyya.

and preceded and surrounded by these he proceeded through the middle of Āpaṇa.

Tamenaṁ jano disvā evaṁ vadeyya:

When people saw him they'd say:

'bhogī vata bho puriso, evaṁ kira bhogino bhogāni bhuñjantī'ti.

'This must be a wealthy man! For that's how the wealthy enjoy their wealth.'

Tamenaṁ sāmikā yattha yattheva passeyyuṁ tattha tattheva sāni hareyyuṁ.

But when the owners saw him, they'd take back what was theirs.

Taṁ kiṁ maññasi, gahapati, alaṁ nu kho tassa purisassa aññathattāyā"ti?

What do you think? Would that be enough for that man to get upset?"

"Evaṁ, bhante".

"Yes, sir.

"Taṁ kissa hetu"?

Why is that?

"Sāmino hi, bhante, sāni harantī"ti.

Because the owners took back what was theirs." …

"Evameva kho, gahapati, ariyasāvako iti paṭisañcikkhati:

'yācitakūpamā kāmā vuttā bhagavatā bahudukkhā bahupāyāsā, ādīnavo ettha bhiyyo'ti …pe…

tamevūpekkhaṁ bhāveti.

Seyyathāpi, gahapati, gāmassa vā nigamassa vā avidūre tibbo vanasaṇḍo.

"Suppose there was a dark forest grove not far from a town or village.

Tatrassa rukkho sampannaphalo ca upapannaphalo ca, na cassu kānici phalāni bhūmiyaṁ patitāni.

And there was a tree laden with fruit, yet none of the fruit had fallen to the ground.

Atha puriso āgaccheyya phalatthiko phalagavesī phalapariyesanaṁ caramāno.

And along came a person in need of fruit, wandering in search of fruit.

So taṁ vanasaṇḍaṁ ajjhogāhetvā taṁ rukkhaṁ passeyya sampannaphalañca upapannaphalañca.

Having plunged deep into that forest grove, they'd see that tree laden with fruit.

Tassa evamassa:

They'd think:

'ayaṁ kho rukkho sampannaphalo ca upapannaphalo ca, natthi ca kānici phalāni bhūmiyaṁ patitāni.

'That tree is laden with fruit, yet none of the fruit has fallen to the ground.

Jānāmi kho panāhaṁ rukkhaṁ ārohituṁ.

But I know how to climb a tree.

Yannūnāhaṁ imaṁ rukkhaṁ ārohitvā yāvadatthañca khādeyyaṁ ucchaṅgañca pūreyyan'ti.

Why don't I climb the tree, eat as much as I like, then fill my pouch?'

So taṁ rukkhaṁ ārohitvā yāvadatthañca khādeyya ucchaṅgañca pūreyya.

And that's what they'd do.

Atha dutiyo puriso āgaccheyya phalatthiko phalagavesī phalapariyesanaṁ caramāno tiṇhaṁ kuṭhāriṁ ādāya.

And along would come a second person in need of fruit, wandering in search of fruit, carrying a sharp axe.

So taṁ vanasaṇḍaṁ ajjhogāhetvā taṁ rukkhaṁ passeyya sampannaphalañca upapannaphalañca.

Having plunged deep into that forest grove, they'd see that tree laden with fruit.

Tassa evamassa:

They'd think:

'ayaṁ kho rukkho sampannaphalo ca upapannaphalo ca, natthi ca kānici phalāni bhūmiyaṁ patitāni.

'That tree is laden with fruit, yet none of the fruit has fallen to the ground.

Na kho panāhaṁ jānāmi rukkhaṁ ārohituṁ.

But I don't know how to climb a tree.

Yannūnāhaṁ imaṁ rukkhaṁ mūlato chetvā yāvadatthañca khādeyyaṁ ucchaṅgañca pūreyyan'ti.

Why don't I chop this tree down at the root, eat as much as I like, then fill my pouch?'

So taṁ rukkhaṁ mūlatova chindeyya.

And so they'd chop the tree down at the root.

Taṁ kiṁ maññasi, gahapati,

What do you think, householder?

amuko yo so puriso paṭhamaṁ rukkhaṁ ārūḷho sace so na khippameva oroheyya tassa so rukkho papatanto hatthaṁ vā bhañjeyya pādaṁ vā bhañjeyya aññataraṁ vā aññataraṁ vā aṅgapaccaṅgaṁ bhañjeyya, so tatonidānaṁ maraṇaṁ vā nigaccheyya maraṇamattaṁ vā dukkhan"ti?

If the first person, who climbed the tree, doesn't quickly come down, when that tree fell wouldn't they break their hand or arm or other limb, resulting in death or deadly suffering for them?"

"Evaṁ, bhante".

"Yes, sir."

"Evameva kho, gahapati, ariyasāvako iti paṭisañcikkhati:

"In the same way, a noble disciple reflects:

'rukkhaphalūpamā kāmā vuttā bhagavatā bahudukkhā bahupāyāsā, ādīnavo ettha bhiyyo'ti.

'With the simile of the fruit tree the Buddha said that sensual pleasures give little gratification and much suffering and distress, and they are all the more full of drawbacks.'

Evametaṁ yathābhūtaṁ sammappaññāya disvā yāyaṁ upekkhā nānattā nānattasitā taṁ abhinivajjetvā yāyaṁ upekkhā ekattā ekattasitā yattha sabbaso lokāmisūpādānā aparisesā nirujjhanti tamevūpekkhaṁ bhāveti.

Having truly seen this with right understanding, they reject equanimity based on diversity and develop only the equanimity based on unity, where all kinds of grasping to the world's material delights cease without anything left over.

Sa kho so, gahapati, ariyasāvako imaṁyeva anuttaraṁ upekkhāsatipārisuddhiṁ āgamma anekavihitaṁ pubbenivāsaṁ anussarati,

Relying on this supreme purity of mindfulness and equanimity, that noble disciple recollects their many kinds of past lives.

seyyathidaṁ—ekampi jātiṁ dvepi jātiyo ...pe... iti sākāraṁ sauddesaṁ anekavihitaṁ pubbenivāsaṁ anussarati.

That is: one, two, three, four, five, ten, twenty, thirty, forty, fifty, a hundred, a thousand, a hundred thousand rebirths; many eons of the world contracting, many eons of the world expanding, many eons of the world contracting and expanding. ... They recollect their many kinds of past lives, with features and details.

Sa kho so, gahapati, ariyasāvako imaṁyeva anuttaraṁ upekkhāsatipārisuddhiṁ āgamma dibbena cakkhunā visuddhena atikkantamānusakena satte passati cavamāne upapajjamāne hīne paṇīte suvaṇṇe dubbaṇṇe sugate duggate ...pe... yathākammūpage satte pajānāti.

Relying on this supreme purity of mindfulness and equanimity, that noble disciple, with clairvoyance that is purified and superhuman, sees sentient beings passing away and being reborn—inferior and superior, beautiful and ugly, in a good place or a bad place. ... They understand how sentient beings are reborn according to their deeds.

Sa kho so, gahapati, ariyasāvako imaṁyeva anuttaraṁ upekkhāsatipārisuddhiṁ āgamma āsavānaṁ khayā anāsavaṁ cetovimuttiṁ paññāvimuttiṁ diṭṭheva dhamme sayaṁ abhiññā sacchikatvā upasampajja viharati.

Relying on this supreme purity of mindfulness and equanimity, that noble disciple realizes the undefiled freedom of heart and freedom by wisdom in this very life. And they live having realized it with their own insight due to the ending of defilements.

Ettāvatā kho, gahapati, ariyassa vinaye sabbena sabbaṁ sabbathā sabbaṁ vohārasamucchedo hoti.

That's how there is the cutting off of judgments in each and every respect in the noble one's training.

Taṁ kiṁ maññasi, gahapati,

What do you think, householder?

yathā ariyassa vinaye sabbena sabbaṁ sabbathā sabbaṁ vohārasamucchedo hoti, api nu tvaṁ evarūpaṁ vohārasamucchedaṁ attani samanupassasī"ti?

Do you regard yourself as having cut off judgments in a way comparable to the cutting off of judgments in each and every respect in the noble one's training?"

"Ko cāhaṁ, bhante, ko ca ariyassa vinaye sabbena sabbaṁ sabbathā sabbaṁ vohārasamucchedo.

"Who am I compared to one who has cut off judgments in each and every respect in the noble one's training?

Ārakā ahaṁ, bhante, ariyassa vinaye sabbena sabbaṁ sabbathā sabbaṁ vohārasamucchedā.

I am far from that.

Mayañhi, bhante, pubbe aññatitthiye paribbājake anājānīyeva samāne ājānīyāti amaññimha, anājānīyeva samāne ājānīyabhojanaṁ bhojimha, anājānīyeva samāne ājānīyaṭhāne ṭhapimha;

Sir, I used to think that the wanderers following other religions were thoroughbreds, and I fed them and treated them accordingly, but they were not actually thoroughbreds.

bhikkhū pana mayaṁ, bhante, ājānīyeva samāne anājānīyāti amaññimha, ājānīyeva samāne anājānīyabhojanaṁ bhojimha, ājānīyeva samāne anājānīyaṭhāne ṭhapimha;

I thought that the mendicants were not thoroughbreds, and I fed them and treated them accordingly, but they actually were thoroughbreds.

idāni pana mayaṁ, bhante, aññatitthiye paribbājake anājānīyeva samāne anājānīyāti jānissāma, anājānīyeva samāne anājānīyabhojanaṁ bhojessāma, anājānīyeva samāne anājānīyaṭhāne ṭhapessāma.

But now I shall understand that the wanderers following other religions are not actually thoroughbreds, and I will feed them and treat them accordingly.

Bhikkhū pana mayaṁ, bhante, ājānīyeva samāne ājānīyāti jānissāma, ājānīyeva samāne ājānīyabhojanaṁ bhojessāma, ājānīyeva samāne ājānīyaṭhāne ṭhapessāma.

And I shall understand that the mendicants actually are thoroughbreds, and I will feed them and treat them accordingly.

Ajanesi vata me, bhante, bhagavā samaṇesu samaṇappemaṁ, samaṇesu samaṇappasādaṁ, samaṇesu samaṇagāravaṁ.

The Buddha has inspired me to have love, confidence, and respect for ascetics!

Abhikkantaṁ, bhante, abhikkantaṁ, bhante.

Excellent, sir! Excellent!

Seyyathāpi, bhante, nikkujjitaṁ vā ukkujjeyya, paṭicchannaṁ vā vivareyya, mūḷhassa vā maggaṁ ācikkheyya, andhakāre vā telapajjotaṁ dhāreyya, 'cakkhumanto rūpāni dakkhantī'ti; evamevaṁ kho, bhante, bhagavatā anekapariyāyena dhammo pakāsito.

As if he were righting the overturned, or revealing the hidden, or pointing out the path to the lost, or lighting a lamp in the dark so people with good eyes can see what's there, the Buddha has made the teaching clear in many ways.

Esāhaṁ, bhante, bhagavantaṁ saraṇaṁ gacchāmi dhammañca bhikkhusaṅghañca.

I go for refuge to the Buddha, to the teaching, and to the mendicant Saṅgha.

Upāsakaṁ maṁ bhagavā dhāretu ajjatagge pāṇupetaṁ saraṇaṁ gatan”ti.

From this day forth, may the Buddha remember me as a lay follower who has gone for refuge for life."

Potaliyasuttaṁ niṭṭhitaṁ catutthaṁ.

55 Jivakasutta:

With Jivaka

Evaṁ me sutaṁ—

So I have heard.

ekaṁ samayaṁ bhagavā rājagahe viharati jīvakassa komārabhaccassa ambavane.

At one time the Buddha was staying near Rājagaha in the Mango Grove of Jīvaka Komārabhacca.

Atha kho jīvako komārabhacco yena bhagavā tenupasaṅkami; upasaṅkamitvā bhagavantaṁ abhivādetvā ekamantaṁ nisīdi. Ekamantaṁ nisinno kho jīvako komārabhacco bhagavantaṁ etadavoca:

Then Jīvaka went up to the Buddha, bowed, sat down to one side, and said to the Buddha:

"sutaṁ metaṁ, bhante:

"Sir, I have heard this:

'samaṇaṁ gotamaṁ uddissa pāṇaṁ ārabhanti, taṁ samaṇo gotamo jānaṁ uddissakataṁ maṁsaṁ paribhuñjati paṭiccakamman'ti.

'They slaughter living creatures specially for the ascetic Gotama. The ascetic Gotama knowingly eats meat prepared on purpose for him: this is a deed he caused.'

Ye te, bhante, evamāhaṁsu: 'samaṇaṁ gotamaṁ uddissa pāṇaṁ ārabhanti, taṁ samaṇo gotamo jānaṁ uddissakataṁ maṁsaṁ paribhuñjati paṭiccakamman'ti, kacci te, bhante, bhagavato vuttavādino, na ca bhagavantaṁ abhūtena abbhācikkhanti, dhammassa cānudhammaṁ byākaronti, na ca koci sahadhammiko vādānuvādo gārayhaṁ ṭhānaṁ āgacchatī"ti?

I trust that those who say this repeat what the Buddha has said, and do not misrepresent him with an untruth? Is their explanation in line with the teaching? Are there any legitimate grounds for rebuke and criticism?"

"Ye te, jīvaka, evamāhaṁsu: 'samaṇaṁ gotamaṁ uddissa pāṇaṁ ārabhanti, taṁ samaṇo gotamo jānaṁ uddissakataṁ maṁsaṁ paribhuñjati paṭiccakamman'ti na me te vuttavādino, abbhācikkhanti ca maṁ te asatā abhūtena.

"Jīvaka, those who say this do not repeat what I have said. They misrepresent me with what is false and untrue.

Tīhi kho ahaṁ, jīvaka, ṭhānehi maṁsaṁ aparibhoganti vadāmi.

In three cases I say that meat may not be eaten:

Diṭṭhaṁ, sutaṁ, parisaṅkitaṁ—

it's seen, heard, or suspected.

imehi kho ahaṁ, jīvaka, tīhi ṭhānehi maṁsaṁ aparibhoganti vadāmi.

These are three cases in which meat may not be eaten.

Tīhi kho ahaṁ, jīvaka, ṭhānehi maṁsaṁ paribhoganti vadāmi.

In three cases I say that meat may be eaten:

Adiṭṭhaṁ, asutaṁ, aparisaṅkitaṁ—

it's not seen, heard, or suspected.

imehi kho ahaṁ, jīvaka, tīhi ṭhānehi maṁsaṁ paribhoganti vadāmi.

These are three cases in which meat may be eaten.

Idha, jīvaka, bhikkhu aññataraṁ gāmaṁ vā nigamaṁ vā upanissāya viharati.

Take the case of a mendicant living supported by a town or village.

So mettāsahagatena cetasā ekaṁ disaṁ pharitvā viharati, tathā dutiyaṁ, tathā tatiyaṁ, tathā catutthaṁ. Iti uddhamadho tiriyaṁ sabbadhi sabbattatāya sabbāvantaṁ lokaṁ mettāsahagatena cetasā vipulena mahaggatena appamāṇena averena abyābajjhena pharitvā viharati.

They meditate spreading a heart full of love to one direction, and to the second, and to the third, and to the fourth. In the same way above, below, across, everywhere, all around, they spread a heart full of love to the whole world—abundant, expansive, limitless, free of enmity and ill will.

Tamenaṁ gahapati vā gahapatiputto vā upasaṅkamitvā svātanāya bhattena nimanteti.

A householder or their child approaches and invites them for the next day's meal.

Ākaṅkhamānova, jīvaka, bhikkhu adhivāseti.

The mendicant accepts if they want.

So tassā rattiyā accayena pubbaṇhasamayaṁ nivāsetvā pattacīvaramādāya yena tassa gahapatissa vā gahapatiputtassa vā nivesanaṁ tenupasaṅkamati;

upasaṅkamitvā paññatte āsane nisīdati.

When the night has passed, they robe up in the morning, take their bowl and robe, and approach that householder's home, where they sit on the seat spread out.

Tamenaṁ so gahapati vā gahapatiputto vā paṇītena piṇḍapātena parivisati.

That householder or their child serves them with delicious almsfood.

Tassa na evaṁ hoti:

It never occurs to them,

'sādhu vata māyaṁ gahapati vā gahapatiputto vā paṇītena piṇḍapātena pariviseyyāti.

'It's so good that this householder serves me with delicious almsfood!

Aho vata māyaṁ gahapati vā gahapatiputto vā āyatimpi evarūpena paṇītena piṇḍapātena pariviseyyā'ti—

I hope they serve me with such delicious almsfood in the future!'

evampissa na hoti.

They don't think that.

So taṁ piṇḍapātaṁ agathito amucchito anajjhopanno ādīnavadassāvī nissaraṇapañño paribhuñjati.

They eat that almsfood untied, uninfatuated, unattached, seeing the drawback, and understanding the escape.

Taṁ kiṁ maññasi, jīvaka,

What do you think, Jīvaka?

api nu so bhikkhu tasmiṁ samaye attabyābādhāya vā ceteti, parabyābādhāya vā ceteti, ubhayabyābādhāya vā cetetī'ti?

At that time is that mendicant intending to hurt themselves, hurt others, or hurt both?"

"No hetaṁ, bhante".

"No, sir."

"Nanu so, jīvaka, bhikkhu tasmiṁ samaye anavajjaṁyeva āhāraṁ āhāretī'ti?

"Aren't they eating blameless food at that time?"

"Evaṁ, bhante.

"Yes, sir.

Sutaṁ metaṁ, bhante:

Sir, I have heard that

'brahmā mettāvihārī'ti.

Brahmā abides in love.

Taṁ me idaṁ, bhante, bhagavā sakkhidiṭṭho;

Now, I've seen the Buddha with my own eyes,

bhagavā hi, bhante, mettāvihārī''ti.

and it is the Buddha who truly abides in love."

"Yena kho, jīvaka, rāgena yena dosena yena mohena byāpādavā assa so rāgo so doso so moho tathāgatassa pahīno ucchinnamūlo tālāvatthukato anabhāvaṅkato āyatiṁ anuppādadhammo.

"Any greed, hate, or delusion that might give rise to ill will has been given up by the Realized One, cut off at the root, made like a palm stump, obliterated, and is unable to arise in the future.

Sace kho te, jīvaka, idaṁ sandhāya bhāsitaṁ anujānāmi te etan''ti.

If that's what you were referring to, I acknowledge it."

"Etadeva kho pana me, bhante, sandhāya bhāsitaṁ".

"That's exactly what I was referring to."

"Idha, jīvaka, bhikkhu aññataraṁ gāmaṁ vā nigamaṁ vā upanissāya viharati.

"Take the case, Jīvaka, of a mendicant living supported by a town or village.

So karuṇāsahagatena cetasā …pe…

They meditate spreading a heart full of compassion …

muditāsahagatena cetasā …pe…

They meditate spreading a heart full of rejoicing …

upekkhāsahagatena cetasā ekaṁ disaṁ pharitvā viharati, tathā dutiyaṁ, tathā tatiyaṁ, tathā catutthaṁ.

They meditate spreading a heart full of equanimity to one direction, and to the second, and to the third, and to the fourth.

Iti uddhamadho tiriyaṁ sabbadhi sabbattatāya sabbāvantaṁ lokaṁ upekkhāsahagatena cetasā vipulena mahaggatena appamāṇena averena abyābajjhena pharitvā viharati.

In the same way above, below, across, everywhere, all around, they spread a heart full of equanimity to the whole world—abundant, expansive, limitless, free of enmity and ill will.

Tamenaṁ gahapati vā gahapatiputto vā upasankamitvā svātanāya bhattena nimanteti.

A householder or their child approaches and invites them for the next day's meal.

Ākankhamānova, jīvaka, bhikkhu adhivāseti.

The mendicant accepts if they want.

So tassā rattiyā accayena pubbaṇhasamayaṁ nivāsetvā pattacīvaramādāya yena gahapatissa vā gahapatiputtassa vā nivesanaṁ tenupasankamati; upasankamitvā paññatte āsane nisīdati.

When the night has passed, they robe up in the morning, take their bowl and robe, and approach that householder's home, where they sit on the seat spread out.

Tamenaṁ so gahapati vā gahapatiputto vā paṇītena piṇḍapātena parivisati.

That householder or their child serves them with delicious almsfood.

Tassa na evaṁ hoti:

It never occurs to them,

'sādhu vata māyaṁ gahapati vā gahapatiputto vā paṇītena piṇḍapātena pariviseyyāti.

'It's so good that this householder serves me with delicious almsfood!

Aho vata māyaṁ gahapati vā gahapatiputto vā āyatimpi evarūpena paṇītena piṇḍapātena pariviseyyā'ti—

I hope they serve me with such delicious almsfood in the future!'

evampissa na hoti.

They don't think that.

So taṁ piṇḍapātaṁ agathito amucchito anajjhopanno ādīnavadassāvī nissaraṇapañño paribhuñjati.

They eat that almsfood untied, uninfatuated, unattached, seeing the drawback, and understanding the escape.

Taṁ kiṁ maññasi, jīvaka,

What do you think, Jīvaka?

api nu so bhikkhu tasmiṁ samaye attabyābādhāya vā ceteti, parabyābādhāya vā ceteti, ubhayabyābādhāya vā cetetī"ti?

At that time is that mendicant intending to hurt themselves, hurt others, or hurt both?"

"No hetaṁ, bhante".

"No, sir."

"Nanu so, jīvaka, bhikkhu tasmiṁ samaye anavajjaṁyeva āhāraṁ āhāretī"ti?

"Aren't they eating blameless food at that time?"

"Evaṁ, bhante.

"Yes, sir.

Sutaṁ metaṁ, bhante:

Sir, I have heard that

'brahmā upekkhāvihārī'ti.

Brahmā abides in equanimity.

Taṁ me idaṁ, bhante, bhagavā sakkhidiṭṭho;

Now, I've seen the Buddha with my own eyes,

bhagavā hi, bhante, upekkhāvihārī'ti.

and it is the Buddha who truly abides in equanimity."

"Yena kho, jīvaka, rāgena yena dosena yena mohena vihesavā assa arativā assa paṭighavā assa so rāgo so doso so moho tathāgatassa pahīno ucchinnamūlo tālāvatthukato anabhāvaṅkato āyatiṁ anuppādadhammo.

"Any greed, hate, or delusion that might give rise to cruelty, discontent, or repulsion has been given up by the Realized One, cut off at the root, made like a palm stump, obliterated, and is unable to arise in the future.

Sace kho te, jīvaka, idaṁ sandhāya bhāsitaṁ, anujānāmi te etan"ti.

If that's what you were referring to, I acknowledge it."

"Etadeva kho pana me, bhante, sandhāya bhāsitaṁ".

"That's exactly what I was referring to."

"Yo kho, jīvaka, tathāgataṁ vā tathāgatasāvakaṁ vā uddissa pāṇaṁ ārabhati so pañcahi ṭhānehi bahuṁ apuññaṁ pasavati.

"Jīvaka, anyone who slaughters a living creature specially for the Realized One or the Realized One's disciple makes much bad karma for five reasons.

Yampi so, gahapati, evamāha:

When they say:

'gacchatha, amukaṁ nāma pāṇaṁ ānethā'ti, iminā paṭhamena ṭhānena bahuṁ apuññaṁ pasavati.

'Go, fetch that living creature,' this is the first reason.

Yampi so pāṇo galappaveṭhakena ānīyamāno dukkhaṁ domanassaṁ paṭisaṁvedeti, iminā dutiyena ṭhānena bahuṁ apuññaṁ pasavati.

When that living creature experiences pain and sadness as it's led along by a collar, this is the second reason.

Yampi so evamāha:

When they say:

'gacchatha imaṁ pāṇaṁ ārabhathā'ti, iminā tatiyena ṭhānena bahuṁ apuññaṁ pasavati.

'Go, slaughter that living creature,' this is the third reason.

Yampi so pāṇo ārabhiyamāno dukkhaṁ domanassaṁ paṭisaṁvedeti, iminā catutthena ṭhānena bahuṁ apuññaṁ pasavati.

When that living creature experiences pain and sadness as it's being slaughtered, this is the fourth reason.

Yampi so tathāgataṁ vā tathāgatasāvakaṁ vā akappiyena āsādeti, iminā pañcamena ṭhānena bahuṁ apuññaṁ pasavati.

When they provide the Realized One or the Realized One's disciple with unallowable food, this is the fifth reason.

Yo kho, jīvaka, tathāgataṁ vā tathāgatasāvakaṁ vā uddissa pāṇaṁ ārabhati so imehi pañcahi ṭhānehi bahuṁ apuññaṁ pasavatī'ti.

Anyone who slaughters a living creature specially for the Realized One or the Realized One's disciple makes much bad karma for five reasons."

Evaṁ vutte, jīvako komārabhacco bhagavantaṁ etadavoca:

When he had spoken, Jīvaka said to the Buddha:

"acchariyaṁ, bhante, abbhutaṁ, bhante.

"It's incredible, sir, it's amazing!

Kappiyaṁ vata, bhante, bhikkhū āhāraṁ āhārenti;

The mendicants indeed eat allowable food.

anavajjaṁ vata, bhante, bhikkhū āhāraṁ āhārenti.

The mendicants indeed eat blameless food.

Abhikkantaṁ, bhante, abhikkantaṁ, bhante …pe…

Excellent, sir! Excellent! …

upāsakaṁ maṁ bhagavā dhāretu ajjatagge pāṇupetaṁ saraṇaṁ gatan"ti.

From this day forth, may the Buddha remember me as a lay follower who has gone for refuge for life."

Jīvakasuttaṁ niṭṭhitaṁ pañcamaṁ.

56 Upalisutta:

With Upali

Evaṁ me sutaṁ—

So I have heard.

ekaṁ samayaṁ bhagavā nāḷandāyaṁ viharati pāvārikambavane.

At one time the Buddha was staying near Nāḷandā in Pāvārika's mango grove.

Tena kho pana samayena nigaṇṭho nāṭaputto nāḷandāyaṁ paṭivasati mahatiyā nigaṇṭhaparisāya saddhiṁ.

At that time the Jain ascetic of the Ñātika clan was residing at Nāḷandā together with a large assembly of Jain ascetics.

Atha kho dīghatapassī nigaṇṭho nāḷandāyaṁ piṇḍāya caritvā pacchābhattaṁ piṇḍapātapaṭikkanto yena pāvārikambavanaṁ yena bhagavā tenupasaṅkami; upasaṅkamitvā bhagavatā saddhiṁ sammodi.

Then the Jain ascetic Dīgha Tapassī wandered for alms in Nāḷandā. After the meal, on his return from almsround, he went to Pāvārika's mango grove. There he approached the Buddha, and exchanged greetings with him.

Sammodanīyaṁ kathaṁ sāraṇīyaṁ vītisāretvā ekamantaṁ aṭṭhāsi. Ekamantaṁ ṭhitaṁ kho dīghatapassiṁ nigaṇṭhaṁ bhagavā etadavoca:

When the greetings and polite conversation were over, he stood to one side. The Buddha said to him,

"saṁvijjanti kho, tapassi, āsanāni; sace ākaṅkhasi nisīdā"ti.

"There are seats, Tapassī. Please sit if you wish."

Evaṁ vutte, dīghatapassī nigaṇṭho aññataraṁ nīcaṁ āsanaṁ gahetvā ekamantaṁ nisīdi.

When he said this, Dīgha Tapassī took a low seat and sat to one side.

Ekamantaṁ nisinnaṁ kho dīghatapassiṁ nigaṇṭhaṁ bhagavā etadavoca:

The Buddha said to him,

"kati pana, tapassi, nigaṇṭho nātaputto kammāni paññapeti pāpassa kammassa kiriyāya pāpassa kammassa pavattiyā"ti?

"Tapassī, how many kinds of deed does the Jain ascetic of the Ñātika clan describe for performing bad deeds?"

"Na kho, āvuso gotama, āciṇṇaṁ nigaṇṭhassa nātaputtassa 'kammaṁ, kamman'ti paññapetuṁ;

"Reverend Gotama, the Jain Ñātika doesn't usually speak in terms of 'deeds'.

'daṇḍaṁ, daṇḍan'ti kho, āvuso gotama, āciṇṇaṁ nigaṇṭhassa nātaputtassa paññapetun"ti.

He usually speaks in terms of 'rods'."

"Kati pana, tapassi, nigaṇṭho nātaputto daṇḍāni paññapeti pāpassa kammassa kiriyāya pāpassa kammassa pavattiyā"ti?

"Then how many kinds of rod does the Jain Ñātika describe for performing bad deeds?"

"Tīṇi kho, āvuso gotama, nigaṇṭho nātaputto daṇḍāni paññapeti pāpassa kammassa kiriyāya pāpassa kammassa pavattiyāti, seyyathidaṁ—

"The Jain Ñātika describes three kinds of rod for performing bad deeds:

kāyadaṇḍaṁ, vacīdaṇḍaṁ, manodaṇḍan"ti.

the physical rod, the verbal rod, and the mental rod."

"Kiṁ pana, tapassi, aññadeva kāyadaṇḍaṁ, aññaṁ vacīdaṇḍaṁ, aññaṁ manodaṇḍan"ti?

"But are these kinds of rod all distinct from each other?"

"Aññadeva, āvuso gotama, kāyadaṇḍaṁ, aññaṁ vacīdaṇḍaṁ, aññaṁ manodaṇḍan"ti.

"Yes, each is quite distinct."

"Imesaṁ pana, tapassi, tiṇṇaṁ daṇḍānaṁ evaṁ paṭivibhattānaṁ evaṁ paṭivisiṭṭhānaṁ katamaṁ daṇḍaṁ nigaṇtho nātaputto mahāsāvajjataraṁ paññapeti pāpassa kammassa kiriyāya pāpassa kammassa pavattiyā, yadi vā kāyadaṇḍaṁ, yadi vā vacīdaṇḍaṁ, yadi vā manodaṇḍan"ti?

"Of the three rods thus analyzed and differentiated, which rod does the Jain Ñātika describe as being the most blameworthy for performing bad deeds: the physical rod, the verbal rod, or the mental rod?"

"Imesaṁ kho, āvuso gotama, tiṇṇaṁ daṇḍānaṁ evaṁ paṭivibhattānaṁ evaṁ paṭivisiṭṭhānaṁ kāyadaṇḍaṁ nigaṇtho nātaputto mahāsāvajjataraṁ paññapeti pāpassa kammassa kiriyāya pāpassa kammassa pavattiyā, no tathā vacīdaṇḍaṁ, no tathā manodaṇḍan"ti.

"The the Jain Ñātika describes the physical rod as being the most blameworthy for performing bad deeds, not so much the verbal rod or the mental rod."

"Kāyadaṇḍanti, tapassi, vadesi"?

"Do you say the physical rod, Tapassī?"

"Kāyadaṇḍanti, āvuso gotama, vadāmi".

"I say the physical rod, Reverend Gotama."

"Kāyadaṇḍanti, tapassi, vadesi"?

"Do you say the physical rod, Tapassī?"

"Kāyadaṇḍanti, āvuso gotama, vadāmi".

"I say the physical rod, Reverend Gotama."

"Kāyadaṇḍanti, tapassi, vadesi"?

"Do you say the physical rod, Tapassī?"

"Kāyadaṇḍanti, āvuso gotama, vadāmī"ti.

"I say the physical rod, Reverend Gotama."

Itiha bhagavā dīghatapassiṁ nigaṇthaṁ imasmiṁ kathāvatthusmiṁ yāvatatiyakaṁ patiṭṭhāpesi.

Thus the Buddha made Dīgha Tapassī stand by this point up to the third time.

Evaṁ vutte, dīghatapassī nigaṇṭho bhagavantaṁ etadavoca:

When this was said, Dīgha Tapassī said to the Buddha,

"tvaṁ panāvuso gotama, kati daṇḍāni paññapesi pāpassa kammassa kiriyāya pāpassa kammassa pavattiyā"ti?

"But Reverend Gotama, how many kinds of rod do you describe for performing bad deeds?"

"Na kho, tapassi, āciṇṇaṁ tathāgatassa 'daṇḍaṁ, daṇḍan'ti paññapetuṁ;

"Tapassī, the Realized One doesn't usually speak in terms of 'rods'.

'kammaṁ, kamman'ti kho, tapassi, āciṇṇaṁ tathāgatassa paññapetun"ti?

He usually speaks in terms of 'deeds'."

"Tvaṁ panāvuso gotama, kati kammāni paññapesi pāpassa kammassa kiriyāya pāpassa kammassa pavattiyā"ti?

"Then how many kinds of deed do you describe for performing bad deeds?"

"Tīṇi kho ahaṁ, tapassi, kammāni paññapemi pāpassa kammassa kiriyāya pāpassa kammassa pavattiyā, seyyathidaṁ—

"I describe three kinds of deed for performing bad deeds:

kāyakammaṁ, vacīkammaṁ, manokamman"ti.

physical deeds, verbal deeds, and mental deeds."

"Kiṁ panāvuso gotama, aññadeva kāyakammaṁ, aññaṁ vacīkammaṁ, aññaṁ manokamman"ti?

"But are these kinds of deed all distinct from each other?"

"Aññadeva, tapassi, kāyakammaṁ, aññaṁ vacīkammaṁ, aññaṁ manokamman"ti.

"Yes, each is quite distinct."

"Imesaṁ panāvuso gotama, tiṇṇaṁ kammānaṁ evaṁ paṭivibhattānaṁ evaṁ paṭivisiṭṭhānaṁ katamaṁ kammaṁ mahāsāvajjataraṁ paññapesi pāpassa kammassa kiriyāya pāpassa kammassa pavattiyā, yadi vā kāyakammaṁ, yadi vā vacīkammaṁ, yadi vā manokamman"ti?

"Of the three deeds thus analyzed and differentiated, which deed do you describe as being the most blameworthy for performing bad deeds: physical deeds, verbal deeds, or mental deeds?"

"Imesaṁ kho ahaṁ, tapassi, tiṇṇaṁ kammānaṁ evaṁ paṭivibhattānaṁ evaṁ paṭivisiṭṭhānaṁ manokammaṁ mahāsāvajjataraṁ paññapemi pāpassa kammassa kiriyāya pāpassa kammassa pavattiyā, no tathā kāyakammaṁ, no tathā vacīkamman"ti.

"I describe mental deeds as being the most blameworthy for performing bad deeds, not so much physical deeds or verbal deeds."

"Manokammanti, āvuso gotama, vadesi"?

"Do you say mental deeds, Reverend Gotama?"

"Manokammanti, tapassi, vadāmi".

"I say mental deeds, Tapassī."

"Manokammanti, āvuso gotama, vadesi"?

"Do you say mental deeds, Reverend Gotama?"

"Manokammanti, tapassi, vadāmi".

"I say mental deeds, Tapassī."

"Manokammanti, āvuso gotama, vadesi"?

"Do you say mental deeds, Reverend Gotama?"

"Manokammanti, tapassi, vadāmī"ti.

"I say mental deeds, Tapassī."

Itiha dīghatapassī nigaṇṭho bhagavantaṁ imasmiṁ kathāvatthusmiṁ yāvatatiyakaṁ patiṭṭhāpetvā uṭṭhāyāsanā yena nigaṇṭho nāṭaputto tenupasaṅkami.

Thus the Jain ascetic Dīgha Tapassī made the Buddha stand by this point up to the third time, after which he got up from his seat and went to see the Jain Ñātika.

Tena kho pana samayena nigaṇṭho nāṭaputto mahatiyā gihiparisāya saddhiṁ nisinno hoti bālakiniyā parisāya upālipamukhāya.

Now at that time the Jain Ñātika was sitting together with a large assembly of laypeople of Bālaka headed by Upāli.

Addasā kho nigaṇṭho nāṭaputto dīghatapassiṁ nigaṇṭhaṁ dūratova āgacchantaṁ;

The Jain Ñātika saw Dīgha Tapassī coming off in the distance

disvāna dīghatapassiṁ nigaṇṭhaṁ etadavoca:

and said to him,

"handa kuto nu tvaṁ, tapassi, āgacchasi divā divassā"ti?

"So, Tapassī, where are you coming from in the middle of the day?"

"Ito hi kho ahaṁ, bhante, āgacchāmi samaṇassa gotamassa santikā"ti.

"Just now, sir, I've come from the presence of the ascetic Gotama."

"Ahu pana te, tapassi, samaṇena gotamena saddhiṁ kocideva kathāsallāpo"ti?

"But did you have some discussion with him?"

"Ahu kho me, bhante, samaṇena gotamena saddhiṁ kocideva kathāsallāpo"ti.

"I did."

"Yathā kathaṁ pana te, tapassi, ahu samaṇena gotamena saddhiṁ kocideva kathāsallāpo"ti?

"And what kind of discussion did you have with him?"

Atha kho dīghatapassī nigaṇṭho yāvatako ahosi bhagavatā saddhiṁ kathāsallāpo taṁ sabbaṁ nigaṇṭhassa nāṭaputtassa ārocesi.

Then Dīgha Tapassī informed the Jain Ñātika of all they had discussed.

Evaṁ vutte, nigaṇṭho nāṭaputto dīghatapassiṁ nigaṇṭhaṁ etadavoca:

When he had spoken, the Jain Ñātika said to him,

"sādhu sādhu, tapassi.

"Good, good, Tapassī!

Yathā taṁ sutavatā sāvakena sammadeva satthusāsanaṁ ājānantena evameva dīghatapassinā nigaṇṭhena samaṇassa gotamassa byākataṁ.

Dīgha Tapassī has answered the ascetic Gotama like a learned disciple who rightly understands their teacher's instructions.

Kiñhi sobhati chavo manodaṇḍo imassa evaṁ oḷārikassa kāyadaṇḍassa upanidhāya.

For how impressive is the measly mental rod when compared with the substantial physical rod?

Atha kho kāyadaṇḍova mahāsāvajjataro pāpassa kammassa kiriyāya pāpassa kammassa pavattiyā, no tathā vacīdaṇḍo, no tathā manodaṇḍo"ti.

Rather, the physical rod is the most blameworthy for performing bad deeds, not so much the verbal rod or the mental rod."

Evaṁ vutte, upāli gahapati nigaṇṭhaṁ nāṭaputtaṁ etadavoca:

When he said this, the householder Upāli said to him,

"sādhu sādhu, bhante dīghatapassī.

"Good, sir! Well done, Dīgha Tapassī!

Yathā taṁ sutavatā sāvakena sammadeva satthusāsanaṁ ājānantena evamevaṁ bhadantena tapassinā samaṇassa gotamassa byākataṁ.

The Honorable Tapassī has answered the ascetic Gotama like a learned disciple who rightly understands their teacher's instructions.

Kiñhi sobhati chavo manodaṇḍo imassa evaṁ oḷārikassa kāyadaṇḍassa upanidhāya.

For how impressive is the measly mental rod when compared with the substantial physical rod?

Atha kho kāyadaṇḍova mahāsāvajjataro pāpassa kammassa kiriyāya pāpassa kammassa pavattiyā, no tathā vacīdaṇḍo, no tathā manodaṇḍo.

Rather, the physical rod is the most blameworthy for performing bad deeds, not so much the verbal rod or the mental rod.

Handa cāhaṁ, bhante, gacchāmi samaṇassa gotamassa imasmiṁ kathāvatthusmiṁ vādaṁ āropessāmi.

I'd better go and refute the ascetic Gotama's doctrine regarding this point.

Sace me samaṇo gotamo tathā patiṭṭhahissati yathā bhadantena tapassinā patiṭṭhāpitaṁ; seyyathāpi nāma balavā puriso dīghalomikaṁ eḷakaṁ lomesu gahetvā ākaḍḍheyya parikaḍḍheyya samparikaḍḍheyya; evamevāhaṁ samaṇaṁ gotamaṁ vādena vādaṁ ākaḍḍhissāmi parikaḍḍhissāmi samparikaḍḍhissāmi.

If he stands by the position that he stated to Dīgha Tapassī, I'll take him on in debate and drag him to and fro and round about, like a strong man would drag a fleecy sheep to and fro and round about!

Seyyathāpi nāma balavā soṇḍikākammakāro mahantaṁ soṇḍikākilañjaṁ gambhīre udakarahade pakkhipitvā kaṇṇe gahetvā ākaḍḍheyya parikaḍḍheyya samparikaḍḍheyya; evamevāhaṁ samaṇaṁ gotamaṁ vādena vādaṁ ākaḍḍhissāmi parikaḍḍhissāmi samparikaḍḍhissāmi.

Taking him on in debate, I'll drag him to and fro and round about, like a strong brewer's worker would toss a large brewer's sieve into a deep lake, grab it by the corners, and drag it to and fro and round about!

Seyyathāpi nāma balavā soṇḍikādhutto vālaṁ kaṇṇe gahetvā odhuneyya niddhuneyya nipphoṭeyya; evamevāhaṁ samaṇaṁ gotamaṁ vādena vādaṁ odhunissāmi niddhunissāmi nipphoṭessāmi.

Taking him on in debate, I'll shake him down and about and give him a beating, like a strong brewer's mixer would grab a strainer by the corners and shake it down and about, and give it a beating!

Seyyathāpi nāma kuñjaro saṭṭhihāyano gambhīraṁ pokkharaṇiṁ ogāhetvā sāṇadhovikaṁ nāma kīḷitajātaṁ kīḷati; evamevāhaṁ samaṇaṁ gotamaṁ sāṇadhovikaṁ maññe kīḷitajātaṁ kīḷissāmi.

I'll play a game of ear-washing with the ascetic Gotama, like a sixty-year-old elephant would plunge into a deep lotus pond and play a game of ear-washing!

Handa cāhaṁ, bhante, gacchāmi samaṇassa gotamassa imasmiṁ kathāvatthusmiṁ vādaṁ āropessāmī”ti.

Sir, I'd better go and refute the ascetic Gotama's doctrine on this point.”

“Gaccha tvaṁ, gahapati, samaṇassa gotamassa imasmiṁ kathāvatthusmiṁ vādaṁ āropehi.

“Go, householder, refute the ascetic Gotama's doctrine on this point.

Ahaṁ vā hi, gahapati, samaṇassa gotamassa vādaṁ āropeyyaṁ, dīghatapassī vā nigaṇṭho, tvaṁ vā”ti.

For either I should do so, or Dīgha Tapassī, or you.”

Evaṁ vutte, dīghatapassī nigaṇṭho nigaṇṭhaṁ nāṭaputtaṁ etadavoca:

When he said this, Dīgha Tapassī said to the Jain Ñātika,

“na kho metaṁ, bhante, ruccati yaṁ upāli gahapati samaṇassa gotamassa vādaṁ āropeyya.

“Sir, I don't believe it's a good idea for the householder Upāli to rebut the ascetic Gotama's doctrine.

Samaṇo hi, bhante, gotamo māyāvī āvaṭṭaniṁ māyaṁ jānāti yāya aññatitthiyānaṁ sāvake āvaṭṭetī”ti.

For the ascetic Gotama is a magician. He knows a conversion magic, and uses it to convert the disciples of other religions.”

“Aṭṭhānaṁ kho etaṁ, tapassi, anavakāso yaṁ upāli gahapati samaṇassa gotamassa sāvakattaṁ upagaccheyya.

“It is impossible, Tapassī, it cannot happen that Upāli could become Gotama's disciple.

Ṭhānañca kho etaṁ vijjati yaṁ samaṇo gotamo upālissa gahapatissa sāvakattaṁ upagaccheyya.

But it is possible that Gotama could become Upāli's disciple.

Gaccha tvaṁ, gahapati, samaṇassa gotamassa imasmiṁ kathāvatthusmiṁ vādaṁ āropehi.

Go, householder, refute the ascetic Gotama's doctrine on this point.

Ahaṁ vā hi, gahapati, samaṇassa gotamassa vādaṁ āropeyyaṁ, dīghatapassī vā nigaṇṭho, tvaṁ vā”ti.

For either I should do so, or Dīgha Tapassī, or you.”

Dutiyampi kho dīghatapassī …pe…

For a second time …

tatiyampi kho dīghatapassī nigaṇṭho nigaṇṭhaṁ nāṭaputtaṁ etadavoca:

and a third time, Dīgha Tapassī said to the Jain Ñātika,

“na kho metaṁ, bhante, ruccati yaṁ upāli gahapati samaṇassa gotamassa vādaṁ āropeyya.

“Sir, I don’t believe it’s a good idea for the householder Upāli to rebut the ascetic Gotama’s doctrine.

Samaṇo hi, bhante, gotamo māyāvī āvaṭṭaniṁ māyaṁ jānāti yāya aññatitthiyānaṁ sāvake āvaṭṭetī”ti.

For the ascetic Gotama is a magician. He knows a conversion magic, and uses it to convert the disciples of other religions.”

“Aṭṭhānaṁ kho etaṁ, tapassi, anavakāso yaṁ upāli gahapati samaṇassa gotamassa sāvakattaṁ upagaccheyya.

“It is impossible, Tapassī, it cannot happen that Upāli could become Gotama’s disciple.

Ṭhānañca kho etaṁ vijjati yaṁ samaṇo gotamo upālissa gahapatissa sāvakattaṁ upagaccheyya.

But it is possible that Gotama could become Upāli’s disciple.

Gaccha tvaṁ, gahapati, samaṇassa gotamassa imasmiṁ kathāvatthusmiṁ vādaṁ āropehi.

Go, householder, refute the ascetic Gotama’s doctrine on this point.

Ahaṁ vā hi, gahapati, samaṇassa gotamassa vādaṁ āropeyyaṁ, dīghatapassī vā nigaṇṭho, tvaṁ vā”ti.

For either I should do so, or Dīgha Tapassī, or you.”

“Evaṁ, bhante”ti kho upāli gahapati nigaṇṭhassa nāṭaputtassa paṭissutvā uṭṭhāyāsanā nigaṇṭhaṁ nāṭaputtaṁ abhivādetvā padakkhiṇaṁ katvā yena pāvārikambavanaṁ yena bhagavā tenupasaṅkami; upasaṅkamitvā bhagavantaṁ abhivādetvā ekamantaṁ nisīdi. Ekamantaṁ nisinno kho upāli gahapati bhagavantaṁ etadavoca:

"Yes, sir," replied the householder Upāli to the Jain Ñātika. He got up from his seat, bowed, and respectfully circled him, keeping him on his right. Then he went to the Buddha, bowed, sat down to one side, and said to him,

"āgamā nu khvidha, bhante, dīghatapassī nigaṇṭho"ti?

"Sir, did the Jain ascetic Dīgha Tapassī come here?"

"Āgamā khvidha, gahapati, dīghatapassī nigaṇṭho"ti.

"He did, householder."

"Ahu kho pana te, bhante, dīghatapassinā nigaṇṭhena saddhiṁ kocideva kathāsallāpo"ti?

"But did you have some discussion with him?"

"Ahu kho me, gahapati, dīghatapassinā nigaṇṭhena saddhiṁ kocideva kathāsallāpo"ti.

"I did."

"Yathā kathaṁ pana te, bhante, ahu dīghatapassinā nigaṇṭhena saddhiṁ kocideva kathāsallāpo"ti?

"And what kind of discussion did you have with him?"

Atha kho bhagavā yāvatako ahosi dīghatapassinā nigaṇṭhena saddhiṁ kathāsallāpo taṁ sabbaṁ upālissa gahapatissa ārocesi.

Then the Buddha informed Upāli of all they had discussed.

Evaṁ vutte, upāli gahapati bhagavantaṁ etadavoca:

When he said this, the householder Upāli said to him,

"sādhu sādhu, bhante tapassī.

"Good, sir, well done by Tapassī!

Yathā taṁ sutavatā sāvakena sammadeva satthusāsanaṁ ājānantena evamevaṁ dīghatapassinā nigaṇṭhena bhagavato byākataṁ.

The Honorable Tapassī has answered the ascetic Gotama like a learned disciple who rightly understands their teacher's instructions.

Kiñhi sobhati chavo manodaṇḍo imassa evaṁ oḷārikassa kāyadaṇḍassa upanidhāya?

For how impressive is the measly mental rod when compared with the substantial physical rod?

Atha kho kāyadaṇḍova mahāsāvajjataro pāpassa kammassa kiriyāya pāpassa kammassa pavattiyā, no tathā vacīdaṇḍo, no tathā manodaṇḍo"ti.

Rather, the physical rod is the most blameworthy for performing bad deeds, not so much the verbal rod or the mental rod."

"Sace kho tvaṁ, gahapati, sacce patiṭṭhāya manteyyāsi siyā no ettha kathāsallāpo"ti.

"Householder, so long as you debate on the basis of truth, we can have some discussion about this."

"Sacce ahaṁ, bhante, patiṭṭhāya mantessāmi;

"I will debate on the basis of truth, sir.

hotu no ettha kathāsallāpo"ti.

Let us have some discussion about this."

"Taṁ kiṁ maññasi, gahapati,

"What do you think, householder?

idhassa nigaṇṭho ābādhiko dukkhito bāḷhagilāno sītodakapaṭikkhitto uṇhodakapaṭisevī.

Take a Jain ascetic who is sick, suffering, gravely ill. They reject cold water and use only hot water.

So sītodakaṁ alabhamāno kālaṁ kareyya.

Not getting cold water, they might die.

Imassa pana, gahapati, nigaṇṭho nāṭaputto katthūpapattiṁ paññapetī"ti?

Now, where does the Jain Ñātika say they would be reborn?"

"Atthi, bhante, manosattā nāma devā tattha so upapajjati".

"Sir, there are gods called 'mind-bound'. They would be reborn there.

"Taṁ kissa hetu"?

Why is that?

"Asu hi, bhante, manopaṭibaddho kālaṁ karotī"ti.

Because they died with mental attachment."

"Manasi karohi, gahapati, manasi karitvā kho, gahapati, byākarohi.

"Think about it, householder! You should think before answering.

Na kho te sandhiyati purimena vā pacchimaṁ, pacchimena vā purimaṁ.

What you said before and what you said after don't match up.

Bhāsitā kho pana te, gahapati, esā vācā:

But you said that you would debate on the basis of truth."

'sacce ahaṁ, bhante, patiṭṭhāya mantessāmi,

hotu no ettha kathāsallāpo'"ti.

"Kiñcāpi, bhante, bhagavā evamāha, atha kho kāyadaṇḍova mahāsāvajjataro pāpassa kammassa kiriyāya pāpassa kammassa pavattiyā, no tathā vacīdaṇḍo, no tathā manodaṇḍo"ti.

"Even though the Buddha says this, still the physical rod is the most blameworthy for performing bad deeds, not so much the verbal rod or the mental rod."

"Taṁ kiṁ maññasi, gahapati,

"What do you think, householder?

idhassa nigaṇṭho nāṭaputto cātuyāmasaṁvarasaṁvuto sabbavārivārito sabbavāriyutto sabbavāridhuto sabbavāriphuṭo.

Take a Jain ascetic who is restrained in the fourfold restraint: obstructed by all water, devoted to all water, shaking off all water, pervaded by all water.

So abhikkamanto paṭikkamanto bahū khuddake pāṇe saṅghātaṁ āpādeti.

When going out and coming back they accidentally injure many little creatures.

Imassa pana, gahapati, nigaṇṭho nāṭaputto kaṁ vipākaṁ paññapetī"ti?

Now, what result does the Jain Ñātika say they would incur?"

"Asañcetanikaṁ, bhante, nigaṇṭho nāṭaputto no mahāsāvajjaṁ paññapetī"ti.

"Sir, the Jain Ñātika says that unintentional acts are not very blameworthy."

"Sace pana, gahapati, cetetī"ti?

"But if they are intentional?"

"Mahāsāvajjaṁ, bhante, hotī"ti.

"Then they are very blameworthy."

"Cetanaṁ pana, gahapati, nigaṇṭho nāṭaputto kismiṁ paññapetī"ti?

"But where does the Jain Ñātika say that intention is classified?"

"Manodaṇḍasmiṁ, bhante"ti.

"In the mental rod, sir."

"Manasi karohi, gahapati, manasi karitvā kho, gahapati, byākarohi.

"Think about it, householder! You should think before answering.

Na kho te sandhiyati purimena vā pacchimaṁ, pacchimena vā purimaṁ.

What you said before and what you said after don't match up.

Bhāsitā kho pana te, gahapati, esā vācā:

But you said that you would debate on the basis of truth."

'sacce ahaṁ, bhante, patiṭṭhāya mantessāmi;

hotu no ettha kathāsallāpo'"ti.

"Kiñcāpi, bhante, bhagavā evamāha, atha kho kāyadaṇḍova mahāsāvajjataro pāpassa kammassa kiriyāya pāpassa kammassa pavattiyā, no tathā vacīdaṇḍo, no tathā manodaṇḍo"ti.

"Even though the Buddha says this, still the physical rod is the most blameworthy for performing bad deeds, not so much the verbal rod or the mental rod."

"Taṁ kiṁ maññasi, gahapati,

"What do you think, householder?

ayaṁ nāḷandā iddhā ceva phītā ca bahujanā ākiṇṇamanussā"ti?

Is this Nāḷandā successful and prosperous and full of people?"

"Evaṁ, bhante, ayaṁ nāḷandā iddhā ceva phītā ca bahujanā ākiṇṇamanussā"ti.

"Indeed it is, sir."

"Taṁ kiṁ maññasi, gahapati,

"What do you think, householder?

idha puriso āgaccheyya ukkhittāsiko.

Suppose a man were to come along with a drawn sword

So evaṁ vadeyya:

and say:

'ahaṁ yāvatikā imissā nāḷandāya pāṇā te ekena khaṇena ekena muhuttena ekaṁ maṁsakhalaṁ ekaṁ maṁsapuñjaṁ karissāmī'ti.

'In one moment I will reduce all the living creatures within the bounds of Nālandā to one heap and mass of flesh!'

Taṁ kiṁ maññasi, gahapati,

What do you think, householder?

pahoti nu kho so puriso yāvatikā imissā nālandāya pāṇā te ekena khaṇena ekena muhuttena ekaṁ maṁsakhalaṁ ekaṁ maṁsapuñjaṁ kātun"ti?

Could he do that?"

"Dasapi, bhante, purisā, vīsampi, bhante, purisā, tiṁsampi, bhante, purisā, cattārīsampi, bhante, purisā, paññāsampi, bhante, purisā nappahonti yāvatikā imissā nālandāya pāṇā te ekena khaṇena ekena muhuttena ekaṁ maṁsakhalaṁ ekaṁ maṁsapuñjaṁ kātuṁ.

"Sir, even ten, twenty, thirty, forty, or fifty men couldn't do that.

Kiñhi sobhati eko chavo puriso"ti.

How impressive is one measly man?"

"Taṁ kiṁ maññasi, gahapati,

"What do you think, householder?

idha āgaccheyya samaṇo vā brāhmaṇo vā iddhimā cetovasippatto.

Suppose an ascetic or brahmin with psychic power, who has achieved mastery of the mind, were to come along

So evaṁ vadeyya:

and say:

'ahaṁ imaṁ nālandaṁ ekena manopadosena bhasmaṁ karissāmī'ti.

'I will reduce Nālandā to ashes with a single malevolent act of will!'

Taṁ kiṁ maññasi, gahapati,

What do you think, householder?

pahoti nu kho so samaṇo vā brāhmaṇo vā iddhimā cetovasippatto imaṁ nālandaṁ ekena manopadosena bhasmaṁ kātun"ti?

Could he do that?"

"Dasapi, bhante, nālandā, vīsampi nālandā, tiṁsampi nālandā, cattārīsampi nālandā, paññāsampi nālandā pahoti so samaṇo vā brāhmaṇo vā iddhimā cetovasippatto ekena manopadosena bhasmaṁ kātuṁ.

"Sir, an ascetic or brahmin with psychic power, who has achieved mastery of the mind, could reduce ten, twenty, thirty, forty, or fifty Nāḷandās to ashes with a single malevolent act of will.

Kiñhi sobhati ekā chavā nāḷandā"ti.

How impressive is one measly Nāḷandā?"

"Manasi karohi, gahapati, manasi karitvā kho, gahapati, byākarohi.

"Think about it, householder! You should think before answering.

Na kho te sandhiyati purimena vā pacchimaṁ, pacchimena vā purimaṁ.

What you said before and what you said after don't match up.

Bhāsitā kho pana te, gahapati, esā vācā:

But you said that you would debate on the basis of truth."

'sacce ahaṁ, bhante, patiṭṭhāya mantessāmi;

hotu no ettha kathāsallāpo'"ti.

"Kiñcāpi, bhante, bhagavā evamāha, atha kho kāyadaṇḍova mahāsāvajjataro pāpassa kammassa kiriyāya pāpassa kammassa pavattiyā, no tathā vacīdaṇḍo, no tathā manodaṇḍo"ti.

"Even though the Buddha says this, still the physical rod is the most blameworthy for performing bad deeds, not so much the verbal rod or the mental rod."

"Taṁ kiṁ maññasi, gahapati,

"What do you think, householder?

sutaṁ te daṇḍakīraññaṁ kāliṅgāraññaṁ majjhāraññaṁ mātaṅgāraññaṁ araññaṁ araññabhūtan"ti?

Have you heard how the wildernesses of Daṇḍaka, Kaliṅga, Mejjha, and Mātaṅga came to be that way?"

"Evaṁ, bhante, sutaṁ me daṇḍakīraññaṁ kāliṅgāraññaṁ majjhāraññaṁ mātaṅgāraññaṁ araññaṁ araññabhūtan"ti.

"I have, sir."

"Taṁ kiṁ maññasi, gahapati, kinti te sutaṁ kena taṁ daṇḍakīraññaṁ kāliṅgāraññaṁ majjhāraññaṁ mātaṅgāraññaṁ araññaṁ araññabhūtan"ti?

"What have you heard?"

"Sutaṁ metaṁ, bhante, isīnaṁ manopadosena taṁ daṇḍakīraññaṁ kāliṅgāraññaṁ majjhāraññaṁ mātaṅgāraññaṁ araññaṁ araññabhūtan”ti.

"I heard that it was because of a malevolent act of will by hermits that the wildernesses of Daṇḍaka, Kaliṅga, Mejjha, and Mātaṅga came to be that way."

"Manasi karohi, gahapati, manasi karitvā kho, gahapati, byākarohi.

"Think about it, householder! You should think before answering.

Na kho te sandhiyati purimena vā pacchimaṁ, pacchimena vā purimaṁ.

What you said before and what you said after don't match up.

Bhāsitā kho pana te, gahapati, esā vācā:

But you said that you would debate on the basis of truth."

'sacce ahaṁ, bhante, patiṭṭhāya mantessāmi;

hotu no ettha kathāsallāpo'"ti.

"Purimenevāhaṁ, bhante, opammena bhagavato attamano abhiraddho.

"Sir, I was already delighted and satisfied by the Buddha's very first simile.

Api cāhaṁ imāni bhagavato vicitrāni pañhapaṭibhānāni sotukāmo, evāhaṁ bhagavantaṁ paccanīkaṁ kātabbaṁ amaññissaṁ.

Nevertheless, I wanted to hear the Buddha's various solutions to the problem, so I thought I'd oppose you in this way.

Abhikkantaṁ, bhante, abhikkantaṁ, bhante.

Excellent, sir! Excellent!

Seyyathāpi, bhante, nikkujjitaṁ vā ukkujjeyya, paṭicchannaṁ vā vivareyya, mūḷhassa vā maggaṁ ācikkheyya, andhakāre vā telapajjotaṁ dhāreyya: 'cakkhumanto rūpāni dakkhantī'ti; evamevaṁ bhagavatā anekapariyāyena dhammo pakāsito.

As if he were righting the overturned, or revealing the hidden, or pointing out the path to the lost, or lighting a lamp in the dark so people with good eyes can see what's there, the Buddha has made the teaching clear in many ways.

Esāhaṁ, bhante, bhagavantaṁ saraṇaṁ gacchāmi dhammañca bhikkhusaṅghañca.

I go for refuge to the Buddha, to the teaching, and to the mendicant Saṅgha.

Upāsakaṁ maṁ bhagavā dhāretu ajjatagge pāṇupetaṁ saraṇaṁ gatan"ti.

From this day forth, may the Buddha remember me as a lay follower who has gone for refuge for life."

"Anuviccakāraṁ kho, gahapati, karohi, anuviccakāro tumhādisānaṁ ñātamanussānaṁ sādhu hotī'ti.

"Householder, you should act after careful consideration. It's good for well-known people such as yourself to act after careful consideration."

"Imināpāhaṁ, bhante, bhagavato bhiyyoso mattāya attamano abhiraddho yaṁ maṁ bhagavā evamāha: 'anuviccakāraṁ kho, gahapati, karohi, anuviccakāro tumhādisānaṁ ñātamanussānaṁ sādhu hotī'ti.

"Now I'm even more delighted and satisfied with the Buddha, since he tells me to act after careful consideration.

Mañhi, bhante, aññatitthiyā sāvakaṁ labhitvā kevalakappaṁ nāḷandaṁ paṭākaṁ parihareyyuṁ:

For if the followers of other religions were to gain me as a disciple, they'd carry a banner all over Nāḷandā, saying:

'upāli amhākaṁ gahapati sāvakattaṁ upagato'ti.

'The householder Upāli has become our disciple!'

Atha ca pana maṁ bhagavā evamāha:

And yet the Buddha says:

'anuviccakāraṁ kho, gahapati, karohi, anuviccakāro tumhādisānaṁ ñātamanussānaṁ sādhu hotī'ti.

'Householder, you should act after careful consideration. It's good for well-known people such as yourself to act after careful consideration.'

Esāhaṁ, bhante, dutiyampi bhagavantaṁ saraṇaṁ gacchāmi dhammañca bhikkhusaṅghañca.

For a second time, I go for refuge to the Buddha, to the teaching, and to the mendicant Saṅgha.

Upāsakaṁ maṁ bhagavā dhāretu ajjatagge pāṇupetaṁ saraṇaṁ gatan"ti.

From this day forth, may the Buddha remember me as a lay follower who has gone for refuge for life."

"Dīgharattaṁ kho te, gahapati, niganṭhānaṁ opānabhūtaṁ kulaṁ yena nesaṁ upagatānaṁ piṇḍakaṁ dātabbaṁ maññeyyāsī"ti.

"For a long time now, householder, your family has been a well-spring of support for the Jain ascetics. You should consider giving to them when they come."

"Imināpāhaṁ, bhante, bhagavato bhiyyoso mattāya attamano abhiraddho yaṁ maṁ bhagavā evamāha: 'dīgharattaṁ kho te, gahapati, niganṭhānaṁ opānabhūtaṁ kulaṁ yena nesaṁ upagatānaṁ piṇḍakaṁ dātabbaṁ maññeyyāsī'ti.

"Now I'm even more delighted and satisfied with the Buddha, since he tells me to consider giving to the Jain ascetics when they come.

Sutaṁ metaṁ, bhante, samaṇo gotamo evamāha:

I have heard, sir, that the ascetic Gotama says this:

'mayhameva dānaṁ dātabbaṁ, nāññesaṁ dānaṁ dātabbaṁ;

'Gifts should only be given to me, not to others.

mayhameva sāvakānaṁ dānaṁ dātabbaṁ, nāññesaṁ sāvakānaṁ dānaṁ dātabbaṁ;

Gifts should only be given to my disciples, not to the disciples of others.

mayhameva dinnaṁ mahapphalaṁ, nāññesaṁ dinnaṁ mahapphalaṁ;

Only what is given to me is very fruitful, not what is given to others.

mayhameva sāvakānaṁ dinnaṁ mahapphalaṁ, nāññesaṁ sāvakānaṁ dinnaṁ mahapphalan'ti.

Only what is given to my disciples is very fruitful, not what is given to the disciples of others.'

Atha ca pana maṁ bhagavā niganthesupi dāne samādapeti.

Yet the Buddha encourages me to give to the Jain ascetics.

Api ca, bhante, mayamettha kālaṁ jānissāma.

Well, sir, we'll know the proper time for that.

Esāhaṁ, bhante, tatiyampi bhagavantaṁ saraṇaṁ gacchāmi dhammañca bhikkhusaṅghañca.

For a third time, I go for refuge to the Buddha, to the teaching, and to the mendicant Saṅgha.

Upāsakaṁ maṁ bhagavā dhāretu ajjatagge pāṇupetaṁ saraṇaṁ gatan"ti.

From this day forth, may the Buddha remember me as a lay follower who has gone for refuge for life."

Atha kho bhagavā upālissa gahapatissa anupubbiṁ kathaṁ kathesi, seyyathidaṁ—

Then the Buddha taught the householder Upāli step by step, with

dānakathaṁ sīlakathaṁ saggakathaṁ, kāmānaṁ ādīnavaṁ okāraṁ saṅkilesaṁ, nekkhamme ānisaṁsaṁ pakāsesi.

a talk on giving, ethical conduct, and heaven. He explained the drawbacks of sensual pleasures, so sordid and corrupt, and the benefit of renunciation.

Yadā bhagavā aññāsi upālim gahapatim kallacittam muducittam vinīvaraṇacittam udaggacittam pasannacittam, atha yā buddhānam sāmukkaṁsikā dhammadesanā tam pakāsesi—

And when he knew that Upāli's mind was ready, pliable, rid of hindrances, elated, and confident he explained the special teaching of the Buddhas:

dukkham, samudayam, nirodham, maggam.

suffering, its origin, its cessation, and the path.

Seyyathāpi nāma suddham vattham apagatakāḷakam sammadeva rajanam paṭiggaṇheyya;

Just as a clean cloth rid of stains would properly absorb dye,

evameva upālissa gahapatissa tasmiṁyeva āsane virajam vītamalam dhammacakkhum udapādi:

in that very seat the stainless, immaculate vision of the Dhamma arose in Upāli:

"yam kiñci samudayadhammam sabbam tam nirodhadhamman"ti.

"Everything that has a beginning has an end."

Atha kho upāli gahapati diṭṭhadhammo pattadhammo viditadhammo pariyogāḷhadhammo tiṇṇavicikiccho vigatakathaṅkatho vesārajjappatto aparappaccayo satthusāsane bhagavantam etadavoca:

Then Upāli saw, attained, understood, and fathomed the Dhamma. He went beyond doubt, got rid of indecision, and became self-assured and independent of others regarding the Teacher's instructions.

"handa ca dāni mayam, bhante, gacchāma, bahukiccā mayam bahukaraṇīyā"ti.

He said to the Buddha, "Well, now, sir, I must go. I have many duties, and much to do."

"Yassadāni tvam, gahapati, kālam maññasī"ti.

"Please, householder, go at your convenience."

Atha kho upāli gahapati bhagavato bhāsitam abhinanditvā anumoditvā uṭṭhāyāsanā bhagavantam abhivādetvā padakkhiṇam katvā yena sakam nivesanam tenupasaṅkami; upasaṅkamitvā dovārikam āmantesi:

And then the householder Upāli approved and agreed with what the Buddha said. He got up from his seat, bowed, and respectfully circled the Buddha, keeping him on his right. Then he went back to his own home, where he addressed the gatekeeper,

"ajjatagge, samma dovārika, āvarāmi dvāraṁ niganthānaṁ niganthīnaṁ, anāvataṁ dvāraṁ bhagavato bhikkhūnaṁ bhikkhunīnaṁ upāsakānaṁ upāsikānaṁ.

"My good gatekeeper, from this day forth close the gate to Jain monks and nuns, and open it for the Buddha's monks, nuns, laymen, and laywomen.

Sace koci nigantho āgacchati tamenaṁ tvaṁ evaṁ vadeyyāsi:

If any Jain ascetics come, say this to them:

'tittha, bhante, mā pāvisi.

'Wait, sir, do not enter.

Ajjatagge upāli gahapati samaṇassa gotamassa sāvakattaṁ upagato.

From now on the householder Upāli has become a disciple of the ascetic Gotama.

Āvataṁ dvāraṁ niganthānaṁ niganthīnaṁ, anāvataṁ dvāraṁ bhagavato bhikkhūnaṁ bhikkhunīnaṁ upāsakānaṁ upāsikānaṁ.

His gate is closed to Jain monks and nuns, and opened for the Buddha's monks, nuns, laymen, and laywomen.

Sace te, bhante, piṇḍakena attho, ettheva tittha, ettheva te āharissantī'"ti.

If you require almsfood, wait here, they will bring it to you.'"

"Evaṁ, bhante"ti kho dovāriko upālissa gahapatissa paccassosi.

"Yes, sir," replied the gatekeeper.

Assosi kho dīghatapassī nigantho:

Dīgha Tapassī heard that

"upāli kira gahapati samaṇassa gotamassa sāvakattaṁ upagato"ti.

Upāli had become a disciple of the ascetic Gotama.

Atha kho dīghatapassī nigantho yena nigantho nātaputto tenupasaṅkami; upasaṅkamitvā nigantaṁ nātaputtaṁ etadavoca:

He went to the Jain Ñātika and said to him,

"sutaṁ metaṁ, bhante, upāli kira gahapati samaṇassa gotamassa sāvakattaṁ upagato"ti.

"Sir, they say that the householder Upāli has become a disciple of the ascetic Gotama."

"Aṭṭhānaṁ kho etaṁ, tapassi, anavakāso yaṁ upāli gahapati samaṇassa gotamassa sāvakattaṁ upagaccheyya.

"It is impossible, Tapassī, it cannot happen that Upāli could become Gotama's disciple.

Ṭhānañca kho etaṁ vijjati yaṁ samaṇo gotamo upālissa gahapatissa sāvakattaṁ upagaccheyyā"ti.

But it is possible that Gotama could become Upāli's disciple."

Dutiyampi kho dīghatapassī nigaṇṭho …pe…

For a second time …

tatiyampi kho dīghatapassī nigaṇṭho nigaṇṭhaṁ nāṭaputtaṁ etadavoca:

and a third time, Dīgha Tapassī said to the Jain Ñātika,

"sutaṁ metaṁ, bhante …

"Sir, they say that the householder Upāli has become a disciple of the ascetic Gotama."

pe…

"It is impossible, Tapassī, it cannot happen that Upāli could become Gotama's disciple.

upālissa gahapatissa sāvakattaṁ upagaccheyyā"ti.

But it is possible that Gotama could become Upāli's disciple."

"Handāhaṁ, bhante, gacchāmi yāva jānāmi yadi vā upāli gahapati samaṇassa gotamassa sāvakattaṁ upagato yadi vā no"ti.

"Well, sir, I'd better go and find out whether or not Upāli has become Gotama's disciple."

"Gaccha tvaṁ, tapassi, jānāhi yadi vā upāli gahapati samaṇassa gotamassa sāvakattaṁ upagato yadi vā no"ti.

"Go, Tapassī, and find out whether or not Upāli has become Gotama's disciple."

Atha kho dīghatapassī nigaṇṭho yena upālissa gahapatissa nivesanaṁ tenupasaṅkami.

Then Dīgha Tapassī went to Upāli's home.

Addasā kho dovāriko dīghatapassiṁ nigaṇṭhaṁ dūratova āgacchantaṁ.

The gatekeeper saw him coming off in the distance

Disvāna dīghatapassiṁ nigaṇṭhaṁ etadavoca:

and said to him,

"tiṭṭha, bhante, mā pāvisi.

"Wait, sir, do not enter.

Ajjatagge upāli gahapati samaṇassa gotamassa sāvakattaṁ upagato.

From now on the householder Upāli has become a disciple of the ascetic Gotama.

Āvaṭaṁ dvāraṁ nigaṇṭhānaṁ nigaṇṭhīnaṁ, anāvaṭaṁ dvāraṁ bhagavato bhikkhūnaṁ bhikkhunīnaṁ upāsakānaṁ upāsikānaṁ.

His gate is closed to Jain monks and nuns, and opened for the Buddha's monks, nuns, laymen, and laywomen.

Sace te, bhante, piṇḍakena attho, ettheva tiṭṭha, ettheva te āharissantī"ti.

If you require almsfood, wait here, they will bring it to you."

"Na me, āvuso, piṇḍakena attho"ti vatvā tato paṭinivattitvā yena nigaṇṭho nāṭaputto tenupasaṅkami; upasaṅkamitvā nigaṇṭhaṁ nāṭaputtaṁ etadavoca:

Saying, "No, mister, I do not require almsfood," he turned back and went to the Jain Ñātika and said to him,

"saccaṁyeva kho, bhante, yaṁ upāli gahapati samaṇassa gotamassa sāvakattaṁ upagato.

"Sir, it's really true that Upāli has become Gotama's disciple.

Etaṁ kho te ahaṁ, bhante, nālatthaṁ, na kho me, bhante, ruccati yaṁ upāli gahapati samaṇassa gotamassa vādaṁ āropeyya.

Sir, I couldn't get you to accept that it wasn't a good idea for the householder Upāli to rebut the ascetic Gotama's doctrine.

Samaṇo hi, bhante, gotamo māyāvī āvaṭṭaniṁ māyaṁ jānāti yāya aññatitthiyānaṁ sāvake āvaṭṭetīti.

For the ascetic Gotama is a magician. He knows a conversion magic, and uses it to convert the disciples of other religions.

Āvaṭṭo kho te, bhante, upāli gahapati samaṇena gotamena āvaṭṭaniyā māyāyā"ti.

The householder Upāli has been converted by the ascetic Gotama's conversion magic!"

"Aṭṭhānaṁ kho etaṁ, tapassi, anavakāso yaṁ upāli gahapati samaṇassa gotamassa sāvakattaṁ upagaccheyya.

"It is impossible, Tapassī, it cannot happen that Upāli could become Gotama's disciple.

Ṭhānañca kho etaṁ vijjati yaṁ samaṇo gotamo upālissa gahapatissa sāvakattaṁ upagaccheyyā"ti.

But it is possible that Gotama could become Upāli's disciple."

Dutiyampi kho dīghatapassī nigaṇṭho nigaṇṭhaṁ nāṭaputtaṁ etadavoca:

For a second time …

"saccaṁyeva, bhante …pe…

upālissa gahapatissa sāvakattaṁ upagaccheyyā"ti.

Tatiyampi kho dīghatapassī nigaṇṭho nigaṇṭhaṁ nāṭaputtaṁ etadavoca:

and a third time, Dīgha Tapassī told the Jain Ñātika

"saccaṁyeva kho, bhante …

that it was really true.

pe…

"It is impossible …

upālissa gahapatissa sāvakattaṁ upagaccheyyā"ti.

"Handa cāhaṁ, tapassi, gacchāmi yāva cāhaṁ sāmaṁyeva jānāmi yadi vā upāli gahapati samaṇassa gotamassa sāvakattaṁ upagato yadi vā no"ti.

Well, Tapassī, I'd better go and find out for myself whether or not Upāli has become Gotama's disciple."

Atha kho nigaṇṭho nāṭaputto mahatiyā nigaṇṭhaparisāya saddhiṁ yena upālissa gahapatissa nivesanaṁ tenupasaṅkami.

Then the Jain Ñātika went to Upāli's home together with a large following of Jain ascetics.

Addasā kho dovāriko nigaṇṭhaṁ nāṭaputtaṁ dūratova āgacchantaṁ.

The gatekeeper saw him coming off in the distance

Disvāna nigaṇṭhaṁ nāṭaputtaṁ etadavoca:

and said to him:

"tiṭṭha, bhante, mā pāvisi.

'Wait, sir, do not enter.

Ajjatagge upāli gahapati samaṇassa gotamassa sāvakattaṃ upagato.

From now on the householder Upāli has become a disciple of the ascetic Gotama.

Āvaṭaṃ dvāraṃ niganthānaṃ niganthīnaṃ, anāvaṭaṃ dvāraṃ bhagavato bhikkhūnaṃ bhikkhunīnaṃ upāsakānaṃ upāsikānaṃ.

His gate is closed to Jain monks and nuns, and opened for the Buddha's monks, nuns, laymen, and laywomen.

Sace te, bhante, piṇḍakena attho, ettheva tiṭṭha, ettheva te āharissantī"ti.

If you require almsfood, wait here, they will bring it to you."

"Tena hi, samma dovārika, yena upāli gahapati tenupasaṅkama; upasaṅkamitvā upāliṃ gahapatiṃ evaṃ vadehi:

"Well then, my good gatekeeper, go to Upāli and say:

'niganṭho, bhante, nāṭaputto mahatiyā niganṭhaparisāya saddhiṃ bahidvārakoṭṭhake ṭhito;

'Sir, the Jain Ñātika is waiting outside the gates together with a large following of Jain ascetics.

so te dassanakāmo'"ti.

He wishes to see you.'"

"Evaṃ, bhante"ti kho dovāriko niganṭhassa nāṭaputtassa paṭissutvā yena upāli gahapati tenupasaṅkami; upasaṅkamitvā upāliṃ gahapatiṃ etadavoca:

"Yes, sir," replied the gatekeeper. He went to Upāli and relayed what was said.

"niganṭho, bhante, nāṭaputto mahatiyā niganṭhaparisāya saddhiṃ bahidvārakoṭṭhake ṭhito;

so te dassanakāmo"ti.

"Tena hi, samma dovārika, majjhimāya dvārasālāya āsanāni paññapehī"ti.

Upāli said to him, "Well, then, my good gatekeeper, prepare seats in the hall of the middle gate."

"Evaṃ, bhante"ti kho dovāriko upālissa gahapatissa paṭissutvā majjhimāya dvārasālāya āsanāni paññapetvā yena upāli gahapati tenupasaṅkami; upasaṅkamitvā upāliṃ gahapatiṃ etadavoca:

"Yes, sir," replied the gatekeeper. He did as he was asked, then returned to Upāli and said,

"paññattāni kho, bhante, majjhimāya dvārasālāya āsanāni.

"Sir, seats have been prepared in the hall of the middle gate.

Yassadāni kālaṁ maññasī"ti.

Please go at your convenience."

Atha kho upāli gahapati yena majjhimā dvārasālā tenupasaṅkami; upasaṅkamitvā yaṁ tattha āsanaṁ aggañca seṭṭhañca uttamañca paṇītañca tattha sāmaṁ nisīditvā dovārikaṁ āmantesi:

Then Upāli went to the hall of the middle gate, where he sat on the highest and finest seat. He addressed the gatekeeper,

"tena hi, samma dovārika, yena nigaṇṭho nāṭaputto tenupasaṅkama; upasaṅkamitvā nigaṇṭhaṁ nāṭaputtaṁ evaṁ vadehi:

"Well then, my good gatekeeper, go to the Jain Ñātika and say to him:

'upāli, bhante, gahapati evamāha—

'Sir, Upāli says

pavisa kira, bhante, sace ākaṅkhasī'"ti.

you may enter if you wish.'"

"Evaṁ, bhante"ti kho dovāriko upālissa gahapatissa paṭissutvā yena nigaṇṭho nāṭaputto tenupasaṅkami; upasaṅkamitvā nigaṇṭhaṁ nāṭaputtaṁ etadavoca:

"Yes, sir," replied the gatekeeper. He went to the Jain Ñātika and relayed what was said.

"upāli, bhante, gahapati evamāha:

'pavisa kira, bhante, sace ākaṅkhasī'"ti.

Atha kho nigaṇṭho nāṭaputto mahatiyā nigaṇṭhaparisāya saddhiṁ yena majjhimā dvārasālā tenupasaṅkami.

Then the Jain Ñātika went to the hall of the middle gate together with a large following of Jain ascetics.

Atha kho upāli gahapati—

yaṁ sudaṁ pubbe yato passati nigaṇṭhaṁ nāṭaputtaṁ dūratova āgacchantaṁ disvāna tato paccuggantvā yaṁ tattha āsanaṁ aggañca seṭṭhañca uttamañca paṇītañca taṁ uttarāsaṅgena sammajjitvā pariggahetvā nisīdāpeti so—

Previously, when Upāli saw the Jain Ñātika coming, he would go out to greet him and, having wiped off the highest and finest seat with his upper robe, he would put his arms around him and sit him down.

dāni yaṃ tattha āsanaṃ aggañca seṭṭhañca uttamañca paṇītañca tattha sāmaṃ nisīditvā nigaṇṭhaṃ nāṭaputtaṃ etadavoca:

But today, having seated himself on the highest and finest seat, he said to the Jain Ñātika,

"saṃvijjanti kho, bhante, āsanāni;

"There are seats, sir.

sace ākaṅkhasi, nisīdā"ti.

Please sit if you wish."

Evaṃ vutte, nigaṇṭho nāṭaputto upāliṃ gahapatiṃ etadavoca:

When he said this, the Jain Ñātika said to him:

"ummattosi tvaṃ, gahapati, dattosi tvaṃ, gahapati.

"You're mad, householder! You're a moron!

'Gacchāmahaṃ, bhante, samaṇassa gotamassa vādaṃ āropessāmī'ti gantvā mahatāsi vādasaṅghāṭena paṭimukko āgato.

You said: 'I'll go and refute the ascetic Gotama's doctrine.' But you come back caught in the vast net of his doctrine.

Seyyathāpi, gahapati, puriso aṇḍahārako gantvā ubbhatehi aṇḍehi āgaccheyya, seyyathā vā pana gahapati puriso akkhikahārako gantvā ubbhatehi akkhīhi āgaccheyya;

Suppose a man went to deliver a pair of balls, but came back castrated. Or they went to deliver eyes, but came back blinded.

evameva kho tvaṃ, gahapati, 'gacchāmahaṃ, bhante, samaṇassa gotamassa vādaṃ āropessāmī'ti gantvā mahatāsi vādasaṅghāṭena paṭimukko āgato.

In the same way, you said: 'I'll go and refute the ascetic Gotama's doctrine.' But you come back caught in the vast net of his doctrine.

Āvaṭṭosi kho tvaṃ, gahapati, samaṇena gotamena āvaṭṭaniyā māyāyā"ti.

You've been converted by the ascetic Gotama's conversion magic!"

"Bhaddikā, bhante, āvaṭṭanī māyā;

"Sir, this conversion magic is excellent.

kalyāṇī, bhante, āvaṭṭanī māyā;

This conversion magic is lovely!

piyā me, bhante, ñātisālohitā imāya āvaṭṭaniyā āvaṭṭeyyuṁ; piyānampi me assa
ñātisālohitānaṁ dīgharattaṁ hitāya sukhāya; `

If my loved ones—relatives and kin—were to be converted by this, it would be for
their lasting welfare and happiness.

sabbe cepi, bhante, khattiyā imāya āvaṭṭaniyā āvaṭṭeyyuṁ; sabbesānampissa
khattiyānaṁ dīgharattaṁ hitāya sukhāya; sabbe cepi, bhante, brāhmaṇā ...pe...
vessā ...pe... suddā imāya āvaṭṭaniyā āvaṭṭeyyuṁ; sabbesānampissa suddānaṁ
dīgharattaṁ hitāya sukhāya;

If all the aristocrats, brahmins, merchants, and workers were to be converted by
this, it would be for their lasting welfare and happiness.

sadevako cepi, bhante, loko samārako sabrahmako sassamaṇabrāhmaṇī pajā
sadevamanussā imāya āvaṭṭaniyā āvaṭṭeyyuṁ; sadevakassapissa lokassa
samārakassa sabrahmakassa sassamaṇabrāhmaṇiyā pajāya sadevamanussāya
dīgharattaṁ hitāya sukhāyāti.

If the whole world—with its gods, Māras and Brahmās, this population with its
ascetics and brahmins, gods and humans—were to be converted by this, it would
be for their lasting welfare and happiness.

Tena hi, bhante, upamaṁ te karissāmi.

Well then, sir, I shall give you a simile.

Upamāyapidhekacce viññū purisā bhāsitassa atthaṁ ājānanti.

For by means of a simile some sensible people understand the meaning of what
is said.

Bhūtapubbaṁ, bhante, aññatarassa brāhmaṇassa jiṇṇassa vuḍḍhassa mahallakassa
daharā māṇavikā pajāpatī ahosi gabbhinī upavijaññā.

Once upon a time there was an old brahmin, elderly and senior. His wife was a
young brahmin lady who was pregnant and about to give birth.

Atha kho, bhante, sā māṇavikā taṁ brāhmaṇaṁ etadavoca,

Then she said to the brahmin,

'gaccha tvaṁ, brāhmaṇa, āpaṇā makkaṭacchāpakaṁ kiṇitvā ānehi, yo me
kumārakassa kīḷāpanako bhavissatī'ti.

'Go, brahmin, buy a baby monkey from the market and bring it back so it can be
a playmate for my child.'

Evaṁ vutte, so brāhmaṇo taṁ māṇavikaṁ etadavoca:

When she said this, the brahmin said to her,

'āgamehi tāva, bhoti, yāva vijāyati.

'Wait, my dear, until you give birth.

Sace tvaṁ, bhoti, kumārakaṁ vijāyissasi, tassā te ahaṁ āpaṇā makkaṭacchāpakaṁ kiṇitvā ānessāmi, yo te kumārakassa kīḷāpanako bhavissati.

If your child is a boy, I'll buy you a male monkey,

Sace pana tvaṁ, bhoti, kumārikaṁ vijāyissasi, tassā te ahaṁ āpaṇā makkaṭacchāpikaṁ kiṇitvā ānessāmi, yā te kumārikāya kīḷāpanikā bhavissatī'ti.

but if it's a girl, I'll buy a female monkey.'

Dutiyampi kho, bhante, sā māṇavikā …pe…

For a second time,

tatiyampi kho, bhante, sā māṇavikā taṁ brāhmaṇaṁ etadavoca:

and a third time she said to the brahmin,

'gaccha tvaṁ, brāhmaṇa, āpaṇā makkaṭacchāpakaṁ kiṇitvā ānehi, yo me kumārakassa kīḷāpanako bhavissatī'ti.

'Go, brahmin, buy a baby monkey from the market and bring it back so it can be a playmate for my child.'

Atha kho, bhante, so brāhmaṇo tassā māṇavikāya sāratto paṭibaddhacitto āpaṇā makkaṭacchāpakaṁ kiṇitvā ānetvā taṁ māṇavikaṁ etadavoca:

Then that brahmin, because of his love for the brahmin lady, bought a male baby monkey at the market, brought it to her, and said,

'ayaṁ te, bhoti, āpaṇā makkaṭacchāpako kiṇitvā ānīto, yo te kumārakassa kīḷāpanako bhavissatī'ti.

'I've bought this male baby monkey for you so it can be a playmate for your child.'

Evaṁ vutte, bhante, sā māṇavikā taṁ brāhmaṇaṁ etadavoca:

When he said this, she said to him,

'gaccha tvaṁ, brāhmaṇa, imaṁ makkaṭacchāpakaṁ ādāya yena rattapāṇi rajakaputto tenupasaṅkama; upasaṅkamitvā rattapāṇiṁ rajakaputtaṁ evaṁ vadehi—

'Go, brahmin, take this monkey to Rattapāṇi the dyer and say,

icchāmahaṁ, samma rattapāṇi, imaṁ makkaṭacchāpakaṁ pītāvalepanaṁ nāma raṅgajātaṁ rajitaṁ ākoṭitapaccākoṭitaṁ ubhatobhāgavimaṭṭhan'ti.

"Mister Rattapāṇi, I wish to have this monkey dyed the color of yellow greasepaint, pounded and re-pounded, and pressed on both sides."'

Atha kho, bhante, so brāhmaṇo tassā māṇavikāya sāratto paṭibaddhacitto tam makkaṭacchāpakam ādāya yena rattapāṇi rajakaputto tenupasaṅkami; upasaṅkamitvā rattapāṇim rajakaputtam etadavoca:

Then that brahmin, because of his love for the brahmin lady, took the monkey to Rattapāṇi the dyer and said,

'icchāmaham, samma rattapāṇi, imam makkaṭacchāpakam pītāvalepanam nāma raṅgajātam rajitam ākoṭitapaccākoṭitam ubhatobhāgavimaṭṭhan'ti.

'Mister Rattapāṇi, I wish to have this monkey dyed the color of yellow greasepaint, pounded and re-pounded, and pressed on both sides.'

Evam vutte, bhante, rattapāṇi rajakaputto tam brāhmaṇam etadavoca:

When he said this, Rattapāṇi said to him,

'ayam kho te, bhante, makkaṭacchāpako raṅgakkhamo hi kho, no ākoṭanakkhamo, no vimajjanakkhamo'ti.

'Sir, this monkey can withstand a dying, but not a pounding or a pressing.'

Evameva kho, bhante, bālānam niganṭhānam vādo raṅgakkhamo hi kho bālānam no paṇḍitānam, no anuyogakkhamo, no vimajjanakkhamo.

In the same way, the doctrine of the foolish Jains looks fine initially—for fools, not for the astute—but can't withstand being scrutinized or pressed.

Atha kho, bhante, so brāhmaṇo aparena samayena navam dussayugam ādāya yena rattapāṇi rajakaputto tenupasaṅkami; upasaṅkamitvā rattapāṇim rajakaputtam etadavoca:

Then some time later that brahmin took a new pair of garments to Rattapāṇi the dyer and said,

'icchāmaham, samma rattapāṇi, imam navam dussayugam pītāvalepanam nāma raṅgajātam rajitam ākoṭitapaccākoṭitam ubhatobhāgavimaṭṭhan'ti.

'Mister Rattapāṇi, I wish to have this new pair of garments dyed the color of yellow greasepaint, pounded and re-pounded, and pressed on both sides.'

Evam vutte, bhante, rattapāṇi rajakaputto tam brāhmaṇam etadavoca:

When he said this, Rattapāṇi said to him,

'idam kho te, bhante, navam dussayugam raṅgakkhamañceva ākoṭanakkhamañca vimajjanakkhamañcā'ti.

'Sir, this pair of garments can withstand a dying, a pounding, and a pressing.'

Evameva kho, bhante, tassa bhagavato vādo arahato sammāsambuddhassa raṅgakkhamo ceva paṇḍitānaṁ no bālānaṁ, anuyogakkhamo ca vimajjanakkhamo cā"ti.

In the same way, the doctrine of the Buddha looks fine initially—for the astute, not for fools—and it can withstand being scrutinized and pressed."

"Sarājikā kho, gahapati, parisā evaṁ jānāti:

"Householder, the king and his retinue know you as

'upāli gahapati niganṭhassa nāṭaputtassa sāvako'ti.

a disciple of the Jain Ñātika.

Kassa taṁ, gahapati, sāvakaṁ dhāremā"ti?

Whose disciple should we remember you as?"

Evaṁ vutte, upāli gahapati uṭṭhāyāsanā ekaṁsaṁ uttarāsaṅgaṁ karitvā yena bhagavā tenañjaliṁ paṇāmetvā niganṭhaṁ nāṭaputtaṁ etadavoca:

When he had spoken, the householder Upāli got up from his seat, arranged his robe over one shoulder, raised his joined palms in the direction of the Buddha, and said to the Jain Ñātika,

"tena hi, bhante, suṇohi yassāhaṁ sāvako"ti:

"Well then, sir, hear whose disciple I am:

"Dhīrassa vigatamohassa,

Pabhinnakhīlassa vijitavijayassa;

Anīghassa susamacittassa,

Vuddhasīlassa sādhupaññassa;

Vesamantarassa vimalassa,

Bhagavato tassa sāvakohamasmi.

The wise one, free of delusion,

rid of barrenness, victor in battle;

he's untroubled and so even-minded,

with the virtue of an elder and the wisdom of a saint,

immaculate in the midst of it all:

he is the Buddha, and I am his disciple.

Akathaṅkathissa tusitassa,

Vantalokāmisassa muditassa;

Katasamaṇassa manujassa,

Antimasārīrassa narassa;

Anopamassa virajassa,

Bhagavato tassa sāvakohamasmi.

He has no indecision, he's content,

joyful, he has spat out the world's bait;

he has completed the ascetic's task as a human,

a man who bears his final body;

he's beyond compare, he's stainless:

he is the Buddha, and I am his disciple.

Asaṁsayassa kusalassa,

Venayikassa sārathivarassa;

Anuttarassa ruciradhammassa,

Nikkaṅkhassa pabhāsakassa;

Mānacchidassa vīrassa,

Bhagavato tassa sāvakohamasmi.

He's free of doubt, he's skillful,

he's a trainer, an excellent charioteer;

supreme, with brilliant qualities,

confident, his light shines forth;

he has cut off conceit, he's a hero:

he is the Buddha, and I am his disciple.

Nisabhassa appameyyassa,

Gambhīrassa monapattassa;

Khemaṅkarassa vedassa,

Dhammaṭṭhassa saṁvutattassa;

Saṅgātigassa muttassa,

Bhagavato tassa sāvakohamasmi.

The chief bull, immeasurable,

profound, sagacious;

he is the builder of sanctuary, knowledgeable,

firm in principle and restrained;

he has got over clinging and is liberated:

he is the Buddha, and I am his disciple.

Nāgassa pantasenassa,

Khīṇasaṁyojanassa muttassa;

Paṭimantakassa dhonassa,

Pannadhajassa vītarāgassa;

Dantassa nippapañcassa,

Bhagavato tassa sāvakohamasmi.

He's a giant, living remotely,

he's ended the fetters and is liberated;

he's skilled in dialogue and cleansed,

with banner put down, desireless;

he's tamed, and doesn't proliferate:

he is the Buddha, and I am his disciple.

Isisattamassa akuhassa,

Tevijjassa brahmapattassa;

Nhātakassa padakassa,

Passaddhassa viditavedassa;

Purindadassa sakkassa,

Bhagavato tassa sāvakohamasmi.

He is the seventh sage, free of deceit,

with three knowledges, he has attained to holiness,

he has bathed, he knows philology,

he's tranquil, he understands what is known;

he crushes resistance, he is the lord:

he is the Buddha, and I am his disciple.

Ariyassa bhāvitattassa,

Pattipattassa veyyākaraṇassa;

Satimato vipassissa,

Anabhinatassa no apanatassa;

Anejassa vasippattassa,

Bhagavato tassa sāvakohamasmi.

The noble one, evolved,

he has attained the goal and explains it;

he is mindful, discerning,

neither leaning forward nor pulling back,

he's unstirred, attained to mastery:

he is the Buddha, and I am his disciple.

Samuggatassa jhāyissa,

Ananugatantarassa suddhassa;

Asitassa hitassa,

Pavivittassa aggappattassa;

Tiṇṇassa tārayantassa,

Bhagavato tassa sāvakohamasmi.

He has risen up, he practices absorption,

not following inner thoughts, he is pure,

independent, and fearless;

secluded, he has reached the peak,

crossed over, he helps others across:

he is the Buddha, and I am his disciple.

Santassa bhūripaññassa,

Mahāpaññassa vītalobhassa;

Tathāgatassa sugatassa,

Appaṭipuggalassa asamassa;

Visāradassa nipuṇassa,

Bhagavato tassa sāvakohamasmi.

He's peaceful, his wisdom is vast,

with great wisdom, he's free of greed;

he is the Realized One, the Holy One,

unrivaled, unequaled,

assured, and subtle:

he is the Buddha, and I am his disciple.

Taṇhacchidassa buddhassa,

Vītadhūmassa anupalittassa;

Āhuneyyassa yakkhassa,

Uttamapuggalassa atulassa;

Mahato yasaggapattassa,

Bhagavato tassa sāvakohamasmī"ti.

He has cut off craving and is awakened,

free of fuming, unsullied;

a mighty spirit worthy of offerings,

best of men, inestimable,

grand, he has reached the peak of glory:

he is the Buddha, and I am his disciple."

"Kadā saññūḷhā pana te, gahapati, ime samaṇassa gotamassa vaṇṇā"ti?

"But when did you compose these praises of the ascetic Gotama's beautiful qualities, householder?"

"Seyyathāpi, bhante, nānāpupphānaṃ mahāpuppharāsi, tamenaṃ dakkho mālākāro vā mālākārantevāsī vā vicittaṃ mālaṃ gantheyya;

"Sir, suppose there was a large heap of many different flowers. A deft garland-maker or their apprentice could tie them into a colorful garland.

evameva kho, bhante, so bhagavā anekavaṇṇo anekasatavaṇṇo.

In the same way, the Buddha has many beautiful qualities to praise, many hundreds of such qualities.

Ko hi, bhante, vaṇṇārahassa vaṇṇaṃ na karissatī"ti?

Who, sir, would not praise the praiseworthy?"

Atha kho nigaṇṭhassa nāṭaputtassa bhagavato sakkāraṃ asahamānassa tattheva uṇhaṃ lohitaṃ mukhato uggacchīti.

Unable to bear this honor paid to the Buddha, the Jain Ñātika spewed hot blood from his mouth there and then.

Upālisuttaṃ niṭṭhitaṃ chaṭṭhaṃ.

57 Kukkuravatikasutta:

The Ascetic Who Behaved Like a Dog

Evaṃ me sutaṃ—

So I have heard.

ekaṃ samayaṃ bhagavā koliyesu viharati haliddavasanaṃ nāma koliyānaṃ nigamo.

At one time the Buddha was staying in the land of the Koliyans, where they have a town named Haliddavasana.

Atha kho puṇṇo ca koliyaputto govatiko acelo ca seniyo kukkuravatiko yena bhagavā tenupasaṅkamiṃsu; upasaṅkamitvā puṇṇo koliyaputto govatiko bhagavantaṃ abhivādetvā ekamantaṃ nisīdi. Acelo pana seniyo kukkuravatiko bhagavatā saddhiṃ sammodi. Sammodanīyaṃ kathaṃ sāraṇīyaṃ vītisāretvā kukkurova palikujjitvā ekamantaṃ nisīdi.

Then Puṇṇa Koliyaputta, who had taken a vow to behave like a cow, and Seniya, a naked ascetic who had taken a vow to behave like a dog, went to see the Buddha. Puṇṇa bowed to the Buddha and sat down to one side, while Seniya exchanged greetings and polite conversation with him before sitting down to one side curled up like a dog.

Ekamantaṁ nisinno kho puṇṇo koliyaputto govatiko bhagavantaṁ etadavoca:

Puṇṇa said to the Buddha,

"ayaṁ, bhante, acelo seniyo kukkuravatiko dukkarakārako chamānikkhittaṁ bhojanaṁ bhuñjati.

"Sir, this naked dog ascetic Seniya does a hard thing: he eats food placed on the ground.

Tassa taṁ kukkuravataṁ dīgharattaṁ samattaṁ samādinnaṁ.

For a long time he has undertaken that observance to behave like a dog.

Tassa kā gati, ko abhisamparāyo"ti?

Where will he be reborn in his next life?"

"Alaṁ, puṇṇa, tiṭṭhatetaṁ; mā maṁ etaṁ pucchī"ti.

"Enough, Puṇṇa, let it be. Don't ask me that."

Dutiyampi kho puṇṇo koliyaputto govatiko …pe…

For a second time …

tatiyampi kho puṇṇo koliyaputto govatiko bhagavantaṁ etadavoca:

and a third time, Puṇṇa said to the Buddha,

"ayaṁ, bhante, acelo seniyo kukkuravatiko dukkarakārako chamānikkhittaṁ bhojanaṁ bhuñjati.

"Sir, this naked dog ascetic Seniya does a hard thing: he eats food placed on the ground.

Tassa taṁ kukkuravataṁ dīgharattaṁ samattaṁ samādinnaṁ.

For a long time he has undertaken that observance to behave like a dog.

Tassa kā gati, ko abhisamparāyo"ti?

Where will he be reborn in his next life?"

"Addhā kho te ahaṁ, puṇṇa, na labhāmi.

"Clearly, Puṇṇa, I'm not getting through to you when I say:

Alaṁ, puṇṇa, tiṭṭhatetaṁ; mā maṁ etaṁ pucchīti;

'Enough, Puṇṇa, let it be. Don't ask me that.'

api ca tyāhaṁ byākarissāmi.

Nevertheless, I will answer you.

Idha, puṇṇa, ekacco kukkuravataṁ bhāveti paripuṇṇaṁ abbokiṇṇaṁ, kukkurasīlaṁ bhāveti paripuṇṇaṁ abbokiṇṇaṁ, kukkuracittaṁ bhāveti paripuṇṇaṁ abbokiṇṇaṁ, kukkurākappaṁ bhāveti paripuṇṇaṁ abbokiṇṇaṁ.

Take someone who develops the dog observance fully and uninterruptedly. They develop a dog's ethics, a dog's mentality, and a dog's behavior fully and uninterruptedly.

So kukkuravataṁ bhāvetvā paripuṇṇaṁ abbokiṇṇaṁ, kukkurasīlaṁ bhāvetvā paripuṇṇaṁ abbokiṇṇaṁ, kukkuracittaṁ bhāvetvā paripuṇṇaṁ abbokiṇṇaṁ, kukkurākappaṁ bhāvetvā paripuṇṇaṁ abbokiṇṇaṁ kāyassa bhedā paraṁ maraṇā kukkurānaṁ sahabyataṁ upapajjati.

When their body breaks up, after death, they're reborn in the company of dogs.

Sace kho panassa evaṁdiṭṭhi hoti: 'imināhaṁ sīlena vā vatena vā tapena vā brahmacariyena vā devo vā bhavissāmi devaññataro vā'ti, sāssa hoti micchādiṭṭhi.

But if they have such a view: 'By this precept or observance or mortification or spiritual life, may I become one of the gods!' This is their wrong view.

Micchādiṭṭhissa kho ahaṁ, puṇṇa, dvinnaṁ gatīnaṁ aññataraṁ gatiṁ vadāmi—nirayaṁ vā tiracchānayoniṁ vā.

An individual with wrong view is reborn in one of two places, I say: hell or the animal realm.

Iti kho, puṇṇa, sampajjamānaṁ kukkuravataṁ kukkurānaṁ sahabyataṁ upaneti, vipajjamānaṁ nirayan"ti.

So if the dog observance succeeds it leads to rebirth in the company of dogs, but if it fails it leads to hell."

Evaṁ vutte, acelo seniyo kukkuravatiko parodi, assūni pavattesi.

When he said this, Seniya cried and burst out in tears.

Atha kho bhagavā puṇṇaṁ koliyaputtaṁ govatikaṁ etadavoca:

The Buddha said to Puṇṇa,

"etaṁ kho te ahaṁ, puṇṇa, nālatthaṁ.

"This is what I didn't get through to you when I said:

Alaṁ, puṇṇa, tiṭṭhatetaṁ; mā maṁ etaṁ pucchī"ti.

'Enough, Puṇṇa, let it be. Don't ask me that.'"

"Nāhaṁ, bhante, etaṁ rodāmi yaṁ maṁ bhagavā evamāha;

"Sir, I'm not crying because of what the Buddha said.

api ca me idaṁ, bhante, kukkuravataṁ dīgharattaṁ samattaṁ samādinnaṁ.

But, sir, for a long time I have undertaken this observance to behave like a dog.

Ayaṁ, bhante, puṇṇo koliyaputto govatiko.

Sir, this Puṇṇa has taken a vow to behave like a cow.

Tassa taṁ govataṁ dīgharattaṁ samattaṁ samādinnaṁ.

For a long time he has undertaken that observance to behave like a cow.

Tassa kā gati, ko abhisamparāyo"ti?

Where will he be reborn in his next life?"

"Alaṁ, seniya, tiṭṭhatetaṁ; mā maṁ etaṁ pucchī"ti.

"Enough, Seniya, let it be. Don't ask me that."

Dutiyampi kho acelo seniyo …pe…

For a second time …

tatiyampi kho acelo seniyo kukkuravatiko bhagavantaṁ etadavoca:

and a third time Seniya said to the Buddha,

"ayaṁ, bhante, puṇṇo koliyaputto govatiko.

"Sir, this Puṇṇa has taken a vow to behave like a cow.

Tassa taṁ govataṁ dīgharattaṁ samattaṁ samādinnaṁ.

For a long time he has undertaken that observance to behave like a cow.

Tassa kā gati, ko abhisamparāyo"ti?

Where will he be reborn in his next life?"

"Addhā kho te ahaṁ, seniya, na labhāmi.

"Clearly, Seniya, I'm not getting through to you when I say:

Alaṁ, seniya, tiṭṭhatetaṁ; mā maṁ etaṁ pucchīti;

'Enough, Seniya, let it be. Don't ask me that.'

api ca tyāhaṁ byākarissāmi.

Nevertheless, I will answer you.

Idha, seniya, ekacco govataṁ bhāveti paripuṇṇaṁ abbokiṇṇaṁ, gosīlaṁ bhāveti paripuṇṇaṁ abbokiṇṇaṁ, gocittaṁ bhāveti paripuṇṇaṁ abbokiṇṇaṁ, gavākappaṁ bhāveti paripuṇṇaṁ abbokiṇṇaṁ.

Take someone who develops the cow observance fully and uninterruptedly. They develop a cow's ethics, a cow's mentality, and a cow's behavior fully and uninterruptedly.

So govataṁ bhāvetvā paripuṇṇaṁ abbokiṇṇaṁ, gosīlaṁ bhāvetvā paripuṇṇaṁ abbokiṇṇaṁ, gocittaṁ bhāvetvā paripuṇṇaṁ abbokiṇṇaṁ, gavākappaṁ bhāvetvā paripuṇṇaṁ abbokiṇṇaṁ kāyassa bhedā paraṁ maraṇā gunnaṁ sahabyataṁ upapajjati.

When their body breaks up, after death, they're reborn in the company of cows.

Sace kho panassa evaṁdiṭṭhi hoti: 'imināhaṁ sīlena vā vatena vā tapena vā brahmacariyena vā devo vā bhavissāmi devaññataro vā'ti, sāssa hoti micchādiṭṭhi.

But if they have such a view: 'By this precept or observance or mortification or spiritual life, may I become one of the gods!' This is their wrong view.

Micchādiṭṭhissa kho ahaṁ, seniya, dvinnaṁ gatīnaṁ aññataraṁ gatiṁ vadāmi—nirayaṁ vā tiracchānayoniṁ vā.

An individual with wrong view is reborn in one of two places, I say: hell or the animal realm.

Iti kho, seniya, sampajjamānaṁ govataṁ gunnaṁ sahabyataṁ upaneti, vipajjamānaṁ nirayan"ti.

So if the cow observance succeeds it leads to rebirth in the company of cows, but if it fails it leads to hell."

Evaṁ vutte, puṇṇo koliyaputto govatiko parodi, assūni pavattesi.

When he said this, Puṇṇa cried and burst out in tears.

Atha kho bhagavā acelaṁ seniyaṁ kukkuravatikaṁ etadavoca:

The Buddha said to Seniya,

"etaṁ kho te ahaṁ, seniya, nālatthaṁ.

"This is what I didn't get through to you when I said:

Alaṁ, seniya, tiṭṭhatetaṁ; mā maṁ etaṁ pucchī"ti.

'Enough, Seniya, let it be. Don't ask me that.'"

"Nāhaṁ, bhante, etaṁ rodāmi yaṁ maṁ bhagavā evamāha;

"Sir, I'm not crying because of what the Buddha said.

api ca me idaṁ, bhante, govataṁ dīgharattaṁ samattaṁ samādinnaṁ.

But, sir, for a long time I have undertaken this observance to behave like a cow.

Evaṁ pasanno ahaṁ, bhante, bhagavati;

I am quite confident that the Buddha

pahoti bhagavā tathā dhammaṁ desetuṁ yathā ahaṁ cevimaṁ govataṁ pajaheyyaṁ, ayañceva acelo seniyo kukkuravatiko taṁ kukkuravataṁ pajaheyyā"ti.

is capable of teaching me so that I can give up this cow observance, and the naked ascetic Seniya can give up that dog observance."

"Tena hi, puṇṇa, suṇāhi, sādhukaṁ manasi karohi, bhāsissāmī"ti.

"Well then, Puṇṇa, listen and pay close attention, I will speak."

"Evaṁ, bhante"ti kho puṇṇo koliyaputto govatiko bhagavato paccassosi.

"Yes, sir," he replied.

Bhagavā etadavoca:

The Buddha said this:

"Cattārimāni, puṇṇa, kammāni mayā sayaṁ abhiññā sacchikatvā paveditāni.

"Puṇṇa, I declare these four kinds of deeds, having realized them with my own insight.

Katamāni cattāri?

What four?

Atthi, puṇṇa, kammaṁ kaṇhaṁ kaṇhavipākaṁ;

There are dark deeds with dark results;

atthi, puṇṇa, kammaṁ sukkaṁ sukkavipākaṁ;

bright deeds with bright results;

atthi, puṇṇa, kammaṁ kaṇhasukkaṁ kaṇhasukkavipākaṁ;

dark and bright deeds with dark and bright results; and

atthi, puṇṇa, kammaṁ akaṇhaṁ asukkaṁ akaṇhaasukkavipākaṁ, kammakkhayāya saṁvattati.

neither dark nor bright deeds with neither dark nor bright results, which lead to the ending of deeds.

Katamañca, puṇṇa, kammaṁ kaṇhaṁ kaṇhavipākaṁ?

And what are dark deeds with dark results?

Idha, puṇṇa, ekacco sabyābajjhaṁ kāyasaṅkhāraṁ abhisaṅkharoti, sabyābajjhaṁ vacīsaṅkhāraṁ abhisaṅkharoti, sabyābajjhaṁ manosaṅkhāraṁ abhisaṅkharoti.

It's when someone makes hurtful choices by way of body, speech, and mind.

So sabyābajjhaṁ kāyasaṅkhāraṁ abhisaṅkharitvā, sabyābajjhaṁ vacīsaṅkhāraṁ abhisaṅkharitvā, sabyābajjhaṁ manosaṅkhāraṁ abhisaṅkharitvā, sabyābajjhaṁ lokaṁ upapajjati.

Having made these choices, they're reborn in a hurtful world,

Tamenaṁ sabyābajjhaṁ lokaṁ upapannaṁ samānaṁ sabyābajjhā phassā phusanti.

where hurtful contacts strike them.

So sabyābajjhehi phassehi phuṭṭho samāno sabyābajjhaṁ vedanaṁ vedeti ekantadukkhaṁ, seyyathāpi sattā nerayikā.

Touched by hurtful contacts, they experience hurtful feelings that are exclusively painful—like the beings in hell.

Iti kho, puṇṇa, bhūtā bhūtassa upapatti hoti;

This is how a being is born from a being.

yaṁ karoti tena upapajjati,

For your deeds determine your rebirth,

upapannamenaṁ phassā phusanti.

and when you're reborn contacts strike you.

Evampāhaṁ, puṇṇa, 'kammadāyādā sattā'ti vadāmi.

This is why I say that sentient beings are heirs to their deeds.

Idaṁ vuccati, puṇṇa, kammaṁ kaṇhaṁ kaṇhavipākaṁ.

These are called dark deeds with dark results.

Katamañca, puṇṇa, kammaṁ sukkaṁ sukkavipākaṁ?

And what are bright deeds with bright results?

Idha, puṇṇa, ekacco abyābajjhaṁ kāyasaṅkhāraṁ abhisaṅkharoti, abyābajjhaṁ vacīsaṅkhāraṁ abhisaṅkharoti, abyābajjhaṁ manosaṅkhāraṁ abhisaṅkharoti.

It's when someone makes pleasing choices by way of body, speech, and mind.

So abyābajjhaṁ kāyasaṅkhāraṁ abhisaṅkharitvā, abyābajjhaṁ vacīsaṅkhāraṁ abhisaṅkharitvā, abyābajjhaṁ manosaṅkhāraṁ abhisaṅkharitvā abyābajjhaṁ lokaṁ upapajjati.

Having made these choices, they are reborn in a pleasing world,

Tamenaṁ abyābajjhaṁ lokaṁ upapannaṁ samānaṁ abyābajjhā phassā phusanti.

where pleasing contacts strike them.

So abyābajjhehi phassehi phuṭṭho samāno abyābajjhaṁ vedanaṁ vedeti ekantasukhaṁ, seyyathāpi devā subhakiṇhā.

Touched by pleasing contacts, they experience pleasing feelings that are exclusively happy—like the gods replete with glory.

Iti kho, puṇṇa, bhūtā bhūtassa upapatti hoti;

This is how a being is born from a being.

yaṁ karoti tena upapajjati,

For your deeds determine your rebirth,

upapannamenaṁ phassā phusanti.

and when you're reborn contacts strike you.

Evampāhaṁ, puṇṇa, 'kammadāyādā sattā'ti vadāmi.

This is why I say that sentient beings are heirs to their deeds.

Idaṁ vuccati, puṇṇa, kammaṁ sukkaṁ sukkavipākaṁ.

These are called bright deeds with bright results.

Katamañca, puṇṇa, kammaṁ kaṇhasukkaṁ kaṇhasukkavipākaṁ?

And what are dark and bright deeds with dark and bright results?

Idha, puṇṇa, ekacco sabyābajjhampi abyābajjhampi kāyasaṅkhāraṁ abhisaṅkharoti, sabyābajjhampi abyābajjhampi vacīsaṅkhāraṁ abhisaṅkharoti, sabyābajjhampi abyābajjhampi manosaṅkhāraṁ abhisaṅkharoti.

It's when someone makes both hurtful and pleasing choices by way of body, speech, and mind.

So sabyābajjhampi abyābajjhampi kāyasaṅkhāraṁ abhisaṅkharitvā, sabyābajjhampi abyābajjhampi vacīsaṅkhāraṁ abhisaṅkharitvā, sabyābajjhampi abyābajjhampi manosaṅkhāraṁ abhisaṅkharitvā sabyābajjhampi abyābajjhampi lokaṁ upapajjati.

Having made these choices, they are reborn in a world that is both hurtful and pleasing,

Tamenaṁ sabyābajjhampi abyābajjhampi lokaṁ upapannaṁ samānaṁ sabyābajjhāpi abyābajjhāpi phassā phusanti.

where hurtful and pleasing contacts strike them.

So sabyābajjhehipi abyābajjhehipi phassehi phuṭṭho samāno sabyābajjhampi abyābajjhampi vedanaṁ vedeti vokiṇṇasukhadukkhaṁ, seyyathāpi manussā ekacce ca devā ekacce ca vinipātikā.

Touched by both hurtful and pleasing contacts, they experience both hurtful and pleasing feelings that are a mixture of pleasure and pain—like humans, some gods, and some beings in the underworld.

Iti kho, puñña, bhūtā bhūtassa upapatti hoti;

This is how a being is born from a being.

yaṁ karoti tena upapajjati.

For what you do brings about your rebirth,

Upapannamenaṁ phassā phusanti.

and when you're reborn contacts strike you.

Evampāhaṁ, puñña, 'kammadāyādā sattā'ti vadāmi.

This is why I say that sentient beings are heirs to their deeds.

Idaṁ vuccati, puñña, kammaṁ kaṇhasukkaṁ kaṇhasukkavipākaṁ.

These are called dark and bright deeds with dark and bright results.

Katamañca, puñña, kammaṁ akaṇhaṁ asukkaṁ akaṇhaasukkavipākaṁ, kammakkhayāya saṁvattati?

And what are neither dark nor bright deeds with neither dark nor bright results, which lead to the ending of deeds?

Tatra, puñña, yamidaṁ kammaṁ kaṇhaṁ kaṇhavipākaṁ tassa pahānāya yā cetanā, yamidaṁ kammaṁ sukkaṁ sukkavipākaṁ tassa pahānāya yā cetanā, yamidaṁ kammaṁ kaṇhasukkaṁ kaṇhasukkavipākaṁ tassa pahānāya yā cetanā—

It's the intention to give up dark deeds with dark results, bright deeds with bright results, and both dark and bright deeds with both dark and bright results.

idaṁ vuccati, puṇṇa, kammaṁ akaṇhaṁ asukkaṁ akaṇhaasukkavipākaṁ, kammakkhayāya saṁvattatīti.

These are called neither dark nor bright deeds with neither dark nor bright results, which lead to the ending of deeds.

Imāni kho, puṇṇa, cattāri kammāni mayā sayaṁ abhiññā sacchikatvā paveditānī”ti.

These are the four kinds of deeds that I declare, having realized them with my own insight.”

Evaṁ vutte, puṇṇo koliyaputto govatiko bhagavantaṁ etadavoca:

When he had spoken, Puṇṇa Koliyaputta the observer of cow behavior said to the Buddha,

“abhikkantaṁ, bhante, abhikkantaṁ, bhante.

“Excellent, sir! Excellent! …

Seyyathāpi, bhante …pe…

upāsakaṁ maṁ bhagavā dhāretu ajjatagge pāṇupetaṁ saraṇaṁ gatan”ti.

From this day forth, may the Buddha remember me as a lay follower who has gone for refuge for life.”

Acelo pana seniyo kukkuravatiko bhagavantaṁ etadavoca:

And Seniya the naked dog ascetic said to the Buddha,

“abhikkantaṁ, bhante, abhikkantaṁ, bhante.

“Excellent, sir! Excellent! …

Seyyathāpi, bhante …pe… pakāsito.

Esāhaṁ, bhante, bhagavantaṁ saraṇaṁ gacchāmi dhammañca bhikkhusaṅghañca.

I go for refuge to the Buddha, to the teaching, and to the mendicant Saṅgha.

Labheyyāhaṁ, bhante, bhagavato santike pabbajjaṁ, labheyyaṁ upasampadan”ti.

Sir, may I receive the going forth, the ordination in the Buddha's presence?”

“Yo kho, seniya, aññatitthiyapubbo imasmiṁ dhammavinaye ākaṅkhati pabbajjaṁ, ākaṅkhati upasampadaṁ so cattāro māse parivasati. Catunnaṁ māsānaṁ accayena āraddhacittā bhikkhū pabbājenti, upasampādenti bhikkhubhāvāya.

"Seniya, if someone formerly ordained in another sect wishes to take the going forth, the ordination in this teaching and training, they must spend four months on probation. When four months have passed, if the mendicants are satisfied, they'll give the going forth, the ordination into monkhood.

Api ca mettha puggalavemattatā viditā"ti.

However, I have recognized individual differences in this matter."

"Sace, bhante, aññatitthiyapubbā imasmiṁ dhammavinaye ākaṅkhantā pabbajjaṁ ākaṅkhantā upasampadaṁ te cattāro māse parivasanti catunnaṁ māsānaṁ accayena āraddhacittā bhikkhū pabbājenti upasampādenti bhikkhubhāvāya, ahaṁ cattāri vassāni parivasissāmi catunnaṁ vassānaṁ accayena āraddhacittā bhikkhū pabbājentu, upasampādentu bhikkhubhāvāyā"ti.

"Sir, if four months probation are required in such a case, I'll spend four years on probation. When four years have passed, if the mendicants are satisfied, let them give me the going forth, the ordination into monkhood."

Alattha kho acelo seniyo kukkuravatiko bhagavato santike pabbajjaṁ, alattha upasampadaṁ.

And the naked dog ascetic Seniya received the going forth, the ordination in the Buddha's presence.

Acirūpasampanno kho panāyasmā seniyo eko vūpakaṭṭho appamatto ātāpī pahitatto viharanto nacirasseva—yassatthāya kulaputtā sammadeva agārasmā anagāriyaṁ pabbajanti, Tadanuttaraṁ—brahmacariyapariyosānaṁ diṭṭheva dhamme sayaṁ abhiññā sacchikatvā upasampajja vihāsi.

Not long after his ordination, Venerable Seniya, living alone, withdrawn, diligent, keen, and resolute, soon realized the supreme end of the spiritual path in this very life. He lived having achieved with his own insight the goal for which gentlemen rightly go forth from the lay life to homelessness.

"Khīṇā jāti, vusitaṁ brahmacariyaṁ, kataṁ karaṇīyaṁ, nāparaṁ itthattāyā"ti abbhaññāsi.

He understood: "Rebirth is ended; the spiritual journey has been completed; what had to be done has been done; there is no return to any state of existence."

Aññataro kho panāyasmā seniyo arahataṁ ahosīti.

And Venerable Seniya became one of the perfected.

Kukkuravatikasuttaṁ niṭṭhitaṁ sattamaṁ.

58 Abhayarajakumarasutta:

With Prince Abhaya

Evaṁ me sutaṁ—

So I have heard.

ekaṁ samayaṁ bhagavā rājagahe viharati veḷuvane kalandakanivāpe.

At one time the Buddha was staying near Rājagaha, in the Bamboo Grove, the squirrels' feeding ground.

Atha kho abhayo rājakumāro yena nigaṇṭho nāṭaputto tenupasaṅkami; upasaṅkamitvā nigaṇṭhaṁ nāṭaputtaṁ abhivādetvā ekamantaṁ nisīdi. Ekamantaṁ nisinnaṁ kho abhayaṁ rājakumāraṁ nigaṇṭho nāṭaputto etadavoca:

Then Prince Abhaya went up to the Jain ascetic of the Ñātika clan, bowed, and sat down to one side. The Jain Ñātika said to him,

"ehi tvaṁ, rājakumāra, samaṇassa gotamassa vādaṁ āropehi.

"Come, prince, refute the ascetic Gotama's doctrine.

Evaṁ te kalyāṇo kittisaddo abbhuggacchissati:

Then you will get a good reputation:

'abhayena rājakumārena samaṇassa gotamassa evaṁ mahiddhikassa evaṁ mahānubhāvassa vādo āropito'"ti.

'Prince Abhaya refuted the doctrine of the ascetic Gotama, so mighty and powerful!'"

"Yathā kathaṁ panāhaṁ, bhante, samaṇassa gotamassa evaṁ mahiddhikassa evaṁ mahānubhāvassa vādaṁ āropessāmī"ti?

"But sir, how am I to do this?"

"Ehi tvaṁ, rājakumāra, yena samaṇo gotamo tenupasaṅkama; upasaṅkamitvā samaṇaṁ gotamaṁ evaṁ vadehi:

"Here, prince, go to the ascetic Gotama and say to him:

'bhāseyya nu kho, bhante, tathāgato taṁ vācaṁ yā sā vācā paresaṁ appiyā amanāpā'ti?

'Sir, might the Realized One utter speech that is disliked by others?'

Sace te samaṇo gotamo evaṁ puṭṭho evaṁ byākaroti:

When he's asked this, if he answers:

'bhāseyya, rājakumāra, tathāgato taṁ vācaṁ yā sā vācā paresaṁ appiyā amanāpā'ti, tamenaṁ tvaṁ evaṁ vadeyyāsi:

'He might, prince,' say this to him,

'atha kiñcarahi te, bhante, puthujjanena nānākaraṇaṁ?

'Then, sir, what exactly is the difference between you and an ordinary person?

Puthujjanopi hi taṁ vācaṁ bhāseyya yā sā vācā paresaṁ appiyā amanāpā'ti.

For even an ordinary person might utter speech that is disliked by others.'

Sace pana te samaṇo gotamo evaṁ puṭṭho evaṁ byākaroti:

But if he answers,

'na, rājakumāra, tathāgato taṁ vācaṁ bhāseyya yā sā vācā paresaṁ appiyā amanāpā'ti, tamenaṁ tvaṁ evaṁ vadeyyāsi:

'He would not, prince,' say this to him:

'atha kiñcarahi te, bhante, devadatto byākato:

'Then, sir, why exactly did you declare of Devadatta:

"āpāyiko devadatto, nerayiko devadatto, kappaṭṭho devadatto, atekiccho devadatto"ti?

"Devadatta is going to a place of loss, to hell, there to remain for an eon, irredeemable"?

Tāya ca pana te vācāya devadatto kupito ahosi anattamano'ti.

Devadatta was angry and upset with what you said.'

Imaṁ kho te, rājakumāra, samaṇo gotamo ubhatokoṭikaṁ pañhaṁ puṭṭho samāno neva sakkhiti uggilituṁ na sakkhiti ogilituṁ.

When you put this dilemma to him, the Buddha won't be able to either spit it out or swallow it down.

Seyyathāpi nāma purisassa ayosiṅghāṭakaṁ kaṇṭhe vilaggaṁ, so neva sakkuṇeyya uggilituṁ na sakkuṇeyya ogilituṁ;

He'll be like a man with an iron cross stuck in his throat, unable to either spit it out or swallow it down."

evameva kho te, rājakumāra, samaṇo gotamo imaṁ ubhatokoṭikaṁ pañhaṁ puṭṭho samāno neva sakkhiti uggilituṁ na sakkhiti ogilitun"ti.

"Evaṁ, bhante"ti kho abhayo rājakumāro nigaṇṭhassa nāṭaputtassa paṭissutvā utthāyāsanā nigaṇṭhaṁ nāṭaputtaṁ abhivādetvā padakkhiṇaṁ katvā yena bhagavā tenupasaṅkami; upasaṅkamitvā bhagavantaṁ abhivādetvā ekamantaṁ nisīdi.

"Yes, sir," replied Abhaya. He got up from his seat, bowed, and respectfully circled the Jain Ñātika, keeping him on his right. Then he went to the Buddha, bowed, and sat down to one side.

Ekamantaṁ nisinnassa kho abhayassa rājakumārassa sūriyaṁ ulloketvā etadahosi:

Then he looked up at the sun and thought,

"akālo kho ajja bhagavato vādaṁ āropetuṁ.

"It's too late to refute the Buddha's doctrine today.

Sve dānāhaṁ sake nivesane bhagavato vādaṁ āropessāmī"ti bhagavantaṁ etadavoca:

I shall refute his doctrine in my own home tomorrow." He said to the Buddha,

"adhivāsetu me, bhante, bhagavā svātanāya attacatuttho bhattan"ti.

"Sir, may the Buddha please accept tomorrow's meal from me, together with three other monks."

Adhivāsesi bhagavā tuṇhībhāvena.

The Buddha consented with silence.

Atha kho abhayo rājakumāro bhagavato adhivāsanaṁ viditvā utthāyāsanā bhagavantaṁ abhivādetvā padakkhiṇaṁ katvā pakkāmi.

Then, knowing that the Buddha had consented, Abhaya got up from his seat, bowed, and respectfully circled the Buddha, keeping him on his right, before leaving.

Atha kho bhagavā tassā rattiyā accayena pubbaṇhasamayaṁ nivāsetvā pattacīvaramādāya yena abhayassa rājakumārassa nivesanaṁ tenupasaṅkami; upasaṅkamitvā paññatte āsane nisīdi.

Then when the night had passed, the Buddha robed up in the morning and, taking his bowl and robe, went to Abhaya's home, and sat down on the seat spread out.

Atha kho abhayo rājakumāro bhagavantaṁ paṇītena khādanīyena bhojanīyena sahatthā santappesi sampavāresi.

Then Abhaya served and satisfied the Buddha with his own hands with delicious fresh and cooked foods.

Atha kho abhayo rājakumāro bhagavantaṁ bhuttāviṁ onītapattapāṇiṁ aññataraṁ nīcaṁ āsanaṁ gahetvā ekamantaṁ nisīdi.

When the Buddha had eaten and washed his hand and bowl, Abhaya took a low seat, sat to one side,

Ekamantaṁ nisinno kho abhayo rājakumāro bhagavantaṁ etadavoca:

and said to him,

"bhāseyya nu kho, bhante, tathāgato taṁ vācaṁ yā sā vācā paresaṁ appiyā amanāpā"ti?

"Sir, might the Realized One utter speech that is disliked by others?"

"Na khvettha, rājakumāra, ekaṁsenā"ti.

"This is no simple matter, prince."

"Ettha, bhante, anassuṁ nigaṇṭhā"ti.

"Then the Jains have lost in this, sir."

"Kiṁ pana tvaṁ, rājakumāra, evaṁ vadesi:

"But prince, why do you say that

'ettha, bhante, anassuṁ nigaṇṭhā'"ti?

the Jains have lost in this?"

"Idhāhaṁ, bhante, yena nigaṇṭho nāṭaputto tenupasaṅkami; upasaṅkamitvā nigaṇṭhaṁ nāṭaputtaṁ abhivādetvā ekamantaṁ nisīdiṁ. Ekamantaṁ nisinnaṁ kho maṁ, bhante, nigaṇṭho nāṭaputto etadavoca:

Then Abhaya told the Buddha all that had happened.

'ehi tvaṁ, rājakumāra, samaṇassa gotamassa vādaṁ āropehi.

Evaṁ te kalyāṇo kittisaddo abbhuggacchissati—

abhayena rājakumārena samaṇassa gotamassa evaṁ mahiddhikassa evaṁ mahānubhāvassa vādo āropito'ti.

Evaṁ vutte, ahaṁ, bhante, nigaṇṭhaṁ nāṭaputtaṁ etadavocaṁ:

'yathā kathaṁ panāhaṁ, bhante, samaṇassa gotamassa evaṁ mahiddhikassa evaṁ mahānubhāvassa vādaṁ āropessāmī'ti?

'Ehi tvaṁ, rājakumāra, yena samaṇo gotamo tenupasaṅkama; upasaṅkamitvā samaṇaṁ gotamaṁ evaṁ vadehi:

"bhāseyya nu kho, bhante, tathāgato taṁ vācaṁ yā sā vācā paresaṁ appiyā amanāpā"ti?

Sace te samaṇo gotamo evaṁ puṭṭho evaṁ byākaroti:

"bhāseyya, rājakumāra, tathāgato taṁ vācaṁ yā sā vācā paresaṁ appiyā amanāpā"ti, tamenaṁ tvaṁ evaṁ vadeyyāsi:

"atha kiñcarahi te, bhante, puthujjanena nānākaraṇaṁ?

Puthujjanopi hi taṁ vācaṁ bhāseyya yā sā vācā paresaṁ appiyā amanāpā"ti.

Sace pana te samaṇo gotamo evaṁ puṭṭho evaṁ byākaroti:

"na, rājakumāra, tathāgato taṁ vācaṁ bhāseyya yā sā vācā paresaṁ appiyā amanāpā"ti, tamenaṁ tvaṁ evaṁ vadeyyāsi—

atha kiñcarahi te, bhante, devadatto byākato:

"āpāyiko devadatto, nerayiko devadatto, kappaṭṭho devadatto, atekiccho devadatto"ti?

Tāya ca pana te vācāya devadatto kupito ahosi anattamano'ti.

Imaṁ kho te, rājakumāra, samaṇo gotamo ubhatokoṭikaṁ pañhaṁ puṭṭho samāno neva sakkhiti uggilituṁ na sakkhiti ogilituṁ.

Seyyathāpi nāma purisassa ayosiṅghāṭakaṁ kaṇṭhe vilaggaṁ, so neva sakkuṇeyya uggilituṁ na sakkuṇeyya ogilituṁ;

evameva kho te, rājakumāra, samaṇo gotamo imaṁ ubhatokoṭikaṁ pañhaṁ puṭṭho samāno neva sakkhiti uggilituṁ na sakkhiti ogilitun"ti.

Tena kho pana samayena daharo kumāro mando uttānaseyyako abhayassa rājakumārassa aṅke nisinno hoti.

Now at that time a little baby boy was sitting in Prince Abhaya's lap.

Atha kho bhagavā abhayaṁ rājakumāraṁ etadavoca:

Then the Buddha said to Abhaya,

"Taṁ kiṁ maññasi, rājakumāra,

"What do you think, prince?

sacāyaṁ kumāro tuyhaṁ vā pamādamanvāya dhātiyā vā pamādamanvāya kaṭṭhaṁ vā kaṭhalaṁ vā mukhe āhareyya, kinti naṁ kareyyāsī'ti?

If—because of your negligence or his nurse's negligence—your boy were to put a stick or stone in his mouth, what would you do to him?"

"Āhareyyassāhaṁ, bhante.

"I'd try to take it out, sir.

Sace, bhante, na sakkuṇeyyaṃ ādikeneva āhattuṃ, vāmena hatthena sīsaṃ pariggahetvā dakkhiṇena hatthena vaṅkaṅguliṃ karitvā salohitampi āhareyyaṃ.

If that didn't work, I'd hold his head with my left hand and take it out using a hooked finger of my right hand, even if it drew blood.

Taṃ kissa hetu?

Why is that?

Atthi me, bhante, kumāre anukampā"ti.

Because I have compassion for the boy, sir."

"Evameva kho, rājakumāra, yaṃ tathāgato vācaṃ jānāti abhūtaṃ atacchaṃ anatthasaṃhitaṃ sā ca paresaṃ appiyā amanāpā, na taṃ tathāgato vācaṃ bhāsati.

"In the same way, prince, the Realized One does not utter speech that he knows to be untrue, false, and pointless, and which is disliked by others.

Yampi tathāgato vācaṃ jānāti bhūtaṃ tacchaṃ anatthasaṃhitaṃ sā ca paresaṃ appiyā amanāpā, tampi tathāgato vācaṃ na bhāsati.

The Realized One does not utter speech that he knows to be true and correct, but which is harmful and disliked by others.

Yañca kho tathāgato vācaṃ jānāti bhūtaṃ tacchaṃ atthasaṃhitaṃ sā ca paresaṃ appiyā amanāpā, tatra kālaññū tathāgato hoti tassā vācāya veyyākaraṇāya.

The Realized One knows the right time to speak so as to explain what he knows to be true, correct, and beneficial, but which is disliked by others.

Yaṃ tathāgato vācaṃ jānāti abhūtaṃ atacchaṃ anatthasaṃhitaṃ sā ca paresaṃ piyā manāpā, na taṃ tathāgato vācaṃ bhāsati.

The Realized One does not utter speech that he knows to be untrue, false, and pointless, but which is liked by others.

Yampi tathāgato vācaṃ jānāti bhūtaṃ tacchaṃ anatthasaṃhitaṃ sā ca paresaṃ piyā manāpā tampi tathāgato vācaṃ na bhāsati.

The Realized One does not utter speech that he knows to be true and correct, but which is harmful, even if it is liked by others.

Yañca tathāgato vācaṃ jānāti bhūtaṃ tacchaṃ atthasaṃhitaṃ sā ca paresaṃ piyā manāpā, tatra kālaññū tathāgato hoti tassā vācāya veyyākaraṇāya.

The Realized One knows the right time to speak so as to explain what he knows to be true, correct, and beneficial, and which is liked by others.

Taṃ kissa hetu?

Why is that?

Atthi, rājakumāra, tathāgatassa sattesu anukampā”ti.

Because the Realized One has compassion for sentient beings.”

“Yeme, bhante, khattiyapaṇḍitāpi brāhmaṇapaṇḍitāpi gahapatipaṇḍitāpi samaṇapaṇḍitāpi pañhaṁ abhisaṅkharitvā tathāgataṁ upasaṅkamitvā pucchanti,

“Sir, there are clever aristocrats, brahmins, householders, or ascetics who come to see you with a question already planned.

pubbeva nu kho, etaṁ, bhante, bhagavato cetaso parivitakkitaṁ hoti ‘ye maṁ upasaṅkamitvā evaṁ pucchissanti tesāhaṁ evaṁ puṭṭho evaṁ byākarissāmī’ti, udāhu ṭhānasovetaṁ tathāgataṁ paṭibhātī’ti?

Do you think beforehand that if they ask you like this, you’ll answer like that, or does the answer just appear to you on the spot?”

“Tena hi, rājakumāra, taññevettha paṭipucchissāmi, yathā te khameyya tathā naṁ byākareyyāsi.

“Well then, prince, I’ll ask you about this in return, and you can answer as you like.

Taṁ kiṁ maññasi, rājakumāra,

What do you think, prince?

kusalo tvaṁ rathassa aṅgapaccaṅgānan”ti?

Are you skilled in the various parts of a chariot?”

“Evaṁ, bhante, kusalo ahaṁ rathassa aṅgapaccaṅgānan”ti.

“I am, sir.”

“Taṁ kiṁ maññasi, rājakumāra,

“What do you think, prince?

ye taṁ upasaṅkamitvā evaṁ puccheyyuṁ:

When they come to you and ask:

‘kiṁ nāmidaṁ rathassa aṅgapaccaṅgan’ti?

‘What’s the name of this chariot part?’

Pubbeva nu kho te etaṁ cetaso parivitakkitaṁ assa ‘ye maṁ upasaṅkamitvā evaṁ pucchissanti tesāhaṁ evaṁ puṭṭho evaṁ byākarissāmī’ti, udāhu ṭhānasovetaṁ paṭibhāseyyā”ti?

Do you think beforehand that if they ask you like this, you'll answer like that, or does the answer appear to you on the spot?"

"Ahañhi, bhante, rathiko saññāto kusalo rathassa aṅgapaccaṅgānaṁ.

"Sir, I'm well-known as a charioteer skilled in a chariot's parts.

Sabbāni me rathassa aṅgapaccaṅgāni suviditāni.

All the parts are well-known to me.

Ṭhānasovetaṁ maṁ paṭibhāseyyā"ti.

The answer just appears to me on the spot."

"Evameva kho, rājakumāra, ye te khattiyapaṇḍitāpi brāhmaṇapaṇḍitāpi gahapatipaṇḍitāpi samaṇapaṇḍitāpi pañhaṁ abhisaṅkharitvā tathāgataṁ upasaṅkamitvā pucchanti, ṭhānasovetaṁ tathāgataṁ paṭibhāti.

"In the same way, when clever aristocrats, brahmins, householders, or ascetics come to see me with a question already planned, the answer just appears to me on the spot.

Taṁ kissa hetu?

Why is that?

Sā hi, rājakumāra, tathāgatassa dhammadhātu suppaṭividdhā yassā dhammadhātuyā suppaṭividdhattā ṭhānasovetaṁ tathāgataṁ paṭibhātī"ti.

Because the Realized One has clearly comprehended the principle of the teachings, so that the answer just appears to him on the spot."

Evaṁ vutte, abhayo rājakumāro bhagavantaṁ etadavoca:

When he had spoken, Prince Abhaya said to the Buddha,

"abhikkantaṁ, bhante, abhikkantaṁ, bhante …pe…

"Excellent, sir! Excellent! …

ajjatagge pāṇupetaṁ saraṇaṁ gatan"ti.

From this day forth, may Master Gotama remember me as a lay follower who has gone for refuge for life."

Abhayarājakumārasuttaṁ niṭṭhitaṁ aṭṭhamaṁ.

59 Bahuvedaniyasutta:

The Many Kinds of Feeling

Evaṁ me sutaṁ—

So I have heard.

ekaṁ samayaṁ bhagavā sāvatthiyaṁ viharati jetavane anāthapiṇḍikassa ārāme.

At one time the Buddha was staying near Sāvatthī in Jeta's Grove, Anāthapiṇḍika's monastery.

Atha kho pañcakaṅgo thapati yenāyasmā udāyī tenupasaṅkami; upasaṅkamitvā āyasmantaṁ udāyiṁ abhivādetvā ekamantaṁ nisīdi. Ekamantaṁ nisinno kho pañcakaṅgo thapati āyasmantaṁ udāyiṁ etadavoca:

Then the master builder Pañcakaṅga went up to Venerable Udāyī, bowed, sat down to one side, and said to him,

"kati nu kho, bhante udāyi, vedanā vuttā bhagavatā"ti?

"Sir, how many feelings has the Buddha spoken of?"

"Tisso kho, thapati, vedanā vuttā bhagavatā.

"Master builder, the Buddha has spoken of three feelings:

Sukhā vedanā, dukkhā vedanā, adukkhamasukhā vedanā—

pleasant, painful, and neutral.

imā kho, thapati, tisso vedanā vuttā bhagavatā"ti.

The Buddha has spoken of these three feelings."

Evaṁ vutte, pañcakaṅgo thapati āyasmantaṁ udāyiṁ etadavoca:

When he said this, Pañcakaṅga said to Udāyī,

"na kho, bhante udāyi, tisso vedanā vuttā bhagavatā;

"Sir, Udāyī, the Buddha hasn't spoken of three feelings.

dve vedanā vuttā bhagavatā—

He's spoken of two feelings:

sukhā vedanā, dukkhā vedanā.

pleasant and painful.

Yāyaṁ, bhante, adukkhamasukhā vedanā santasmiṁ esā paṇīte sukhe vuttā bhagavatā”ti.

The Buddha said that neutral feeling is included as a peaceful and subtle kind of pleasure.”

Dutiyampi kho āyasmā udāyī pañcakaṅgaṁ thapatiṁ etadavoca:

For a second time, Udāyī said to Pañcakaṅga,

“na kho, gahapati, dve vedanā vuttā bhagavatā;

“The Buddha hasn’t spoken of two feelings,

tisso vedanā vuttā bhagavatā.

he’s spoken of three.”

Sukhā vedanā, dukkhā vedanā, adukkhamasukhā vedanā—

imā kho, thapati, tisso vedanā vuttā bhagavatā”ti.

Dutiyampi kho pañcakaṅgo thapati āyasmantaṁ udāyiṁ etadavoca:

For a second time, Pañcakaṅga said to Udāyī,

“na kho, bhante udāyi, tisso vedanā vuttā bhagavatā;

“The Buddha hasn’t spoken of three feelings,

dve vedanā vuttā bhagavatā—

he’s spoken of two.”

sukhā vedanā, dukkhā vedanā.

Yāyaṁ, bhante, adukkhamasukhā vedanā santasmiṁ esā paṇīte sukhe vuttā bhagavatā”ti.

Tatiyampi kho āyasmā udāyī pañcakaṅgaṁ thapatiṁ etadavoca:

And for a third time, Udāyī said to Pañcakaṅga,

“na kho, thapati, dve vedanā vuttā bhagavatā;

“The Buddha hasn’t spoken of two feelings,

tisso vedanā vuttā bhagavatā.

he’s spoken of three.”

Sukhā vedanā, dukkhā vedanā, adukkhamasukhā vedanā—

imā kho, thapati, tisso vedanā vuttā bhagavatā”ti.

Tatiyampi kho pañcakaṅgo thapati āyasmantaṁ udāyiṁ etadavoca:

And for a third time, Pañcakaṅga said to Udāyī,

"na kho, bhante udāyi, tisso vedanā vuttā bhagavatā,

"The Buddha hasn't spoken of three feelings,

dve vedanā vuttā bhagavatā—

he's spoken of two."

sukhā vedanā, dukkhā vedanā.

Yāyaṁ, bhante, adukkhamasukhā vedanā santasmiṁ esā paṇīte sukhe vuttā bhagavatā"ti.

Neva kho sakkhi āyasmā udāyī pañcakaṅgaṁ thapatiṁ saññāpetuṁ, na panāsakkhi pañcakaṅgo thapati āyasmantaṁ udāyiṁ saññāpetuṁ.

But neither was able to persuade the other.

Assosi kho āyasmā ānando āyasmato udāyissa pañcakaṅgena thapatinā saddhiṁ imaṁ kathāsallāpaṁ.

Venerable Ānanda heard this discussion between Udāyī and Pañcakaṅga.

Atha kho āyasmā ānando yena bhagavā tenupasaṅkami; upasaṅkamitvā bhagavantaṁ abhivādetvā ekamantaṁ nisīdi.

Then he went up to the Buddha, bowed, sat down to one side,

Ekamantaṁ nisinno kho āyasmā ānando yāvatako ahosi āyasmato udāyissa pañcakaṅgena thapatinā saddhiṁ kathāsallāpo taṁ sabbaṁ bhagavato ārocesi.

and informed the Buddha of all they had discussed.

Evaṁ vutte, bhagavā āyasmantaṁ ānandaṁ etadavoca:

When he had spoken, the Buddha said to him,

"santaññeva kho, ānanda, pariyāyaṁ pañcakaṅgo thapati udāyissa nābbhanumodi, santaññeva ca pana pariyāyaṁ udāyī pañcakaṅgassa thapatissa nābbhanumodi.

"Ānanda, the explanation by the mendicant Udāyī, which the master builder Pañcakaṅga didn't agree with, was quite correct. But the explanation by Pañcakaṅga, which Udāyī didn't agree with, was also quite correct.

Dvepānanda, vedanā vuttā mayā pariyāyena, tissopi vedanā vuttā mayā pariyāyena, pañcapi vedanā vuttā mayā pariyāyena, chapi vedanā vuttā mayā pariyāyena, aṭṭhārasapi vedanā vuttā mayā pariyāyena, chattiṁsapi vedanā vuttā mayā pariyāyena, aṭṭhasatampi vedanā vuttā mayā pariyāyena.

In one explanation I've spoken of two feelings. In another explanation I've spoken of three feelings, or five, six, eighteen, thirty-six, or a hundred and eight feelings.

Evaṁ pariyāyadesito kho, ānanda, mayā dhammo.

I've explained the teaching in all these different ways.

Evaṁ pariyāyadesite kho, ānanda, mayā dhamme ye aññamaññassa subhāsitaṁ sulapitaṁ na samanujānissanti na samanumaññissanti na samanumodissanti tesametaṁ pāṭikaṅkhaṁ—bhaṇḍanajātā kalahajātā vivādāpannā aññamaññaṁ mukhasattīhi vitudantā viharissanti.

This being so, you can expect that those who don't concede, approve, or agree with what has been well spoken will argue, quarrel, and fight, continually wounding each other with barbed words.

Evaṁ pariyāyadesito kho, ānanda, mayā dhammo.

I've explained the teaching in all these different ways.

Evaṁ pariyāyadesite kho, ānanda, mayā dhamme ye aññamaññassa subhāsitaṁ sulapitaṁ samanujānissanti samanumaññissanti samanumodissanti tesametaṁ pāṭikaṅkhaṁ—samaggā sammodamānā avivadamānā khīrodakībhūtā aññamaññaṁ piyacakkhūhi sampassantā viharissanti.

This being so, you can expect that those who do concede, approve, or agree with what has been well spoken will live in harmony, appreciating each other, without quarreling, blending like milk and water, and regarding each other with kindly eyes.

Pañca kho ime, ānanda, kāmaguṇā.

There are these five kinds of sensual stimulation.

Katame pañca?

What five?

Cakkhuviññeyyā rūpā iṭṭhā kantā manāpā piyarūpā kāmūpasaṁhitā rajanīyā,

Sights known by the eye that are likable, desirable, agreeable, pleasant, sensual, and arousing.

sotaviññeyyā saddā …pe…

Sounds known by the ear …

ghānaviññeyyā gandhā …pe…

Smells known by the nose …

jivhāviññeyyā rasā …pe…

Tastes known by the tongue …

kāyaviññeyyā phoṭṭhabbā iṭṭhā kantā manāpā piyarūpā kāmūpasaṁhitā rajanīyā—

Touches known by the body that are likable, desirable, agreeable, pleasant, sensual, and arousing.

ime kho, ānanda, pañca kāmaguṇā.

These are the five kinds of sensual stimulation.

Yaṁ kho, ānanda, ime pañca kāmaguṇe paṭicca uppajjati sukhaṁ somanassaṁ idaṁ vuccati kāmasukhaṁ.

The pleasure and happiness that arise from these five kinds of sensual stimulation is called sensual pleasure.

Yo kho, ānanda, evaṁ vadeyya: ‘etaparamaṁ sattā sukhaṁ somanassaṁ paṭisaṁvedentī’ti, idamassa nānujānāmi.

There are those who would say that this is the highest pleasure and happiness that sentient beings experience. But I don’t grant them that.

Taṁ kissa hetu?

Why is that?

Atthānanda, etamhā sukhā aññaṁ sukhaṁ abhikkantatarañca paṇītatarañca.

Because there is another pleasure that is finer than that.

Katamañcānanda, etamhā sukhā aññaṁ sukhaṁ abhikkantatarañca paṇītatarañca?

And what is that pleasure?

Idhānanda, bhikkhu vivicceva kāmehi vivicca akusalehi dhammehi …pe… paṭhamaṁ jhānaṁ upasampajja viharati.

It’s when a mendicant, quite secluded from sensual pleasures, secluded from unskillful qualities, enters and remains in the first absorption, which has the rapture and bliss born of seclusion, while placing the mind and keeping it connected.

Idaṁ kho, ānanda, etamhā sukhā aññaṁ sukhaṁ abhikkantatarañca paṇītatarañca.

This is a pleasure that is finer than that.

Yo kho, ānanda, evaṁ vadeyya: ‘etaparamaṁ sattā sukhaṁ somanassaṁ paṭisaṁvedentī’ti, idamassa nānujānāmi.

There are those who would say that this is the highest pleasure and happiness that sentient beings experience. But I don’t grant them that.

Taṁ kissa hetu?

Why is that?

Atthānanda, etamhā sukhā aññaṁ sukhaṁ abhikkantatarañca paṇītatarañca.

Because there is another pleasure that is finer than that.

Katamañcānanda, etamhā sukhā aññaṁ sukhaṁ abhikkantatarañca paṇītatarañca?

And what is that pleasure?

Idhānanda, bhikkhu vitakkavicārānaṁ vūpasamā …pe… dutiyaṁ jhānaṁ upasampajja viharati.

It's when, as the placing of the mind and keeping it connected are stilled, a mendicant enters and remains in the second absorption, which has the rapture and bliss born of immersion, with internal clarity and confidence, and unified mind, without placing the mind and keeping it connected. …

Idaṁ kho, ānanda, etamhā sukhā aññaṁ sukhaṁ abhikkantatarañca paṇītatarañca.

Yo kho, ānanda, evaṁ vadeyya …

pe….

There is another pleasure that is finer than that.

Katamañcānanda, etamhā sukhā aññaṁ sukhaṁ abhikkantatarañca paṇītatarañca?

And what is that pleasure?

Idhānanda, bhikkhu pītiyā ca virāgā …pe… tatiyaṁ jhānaṁ upasampajja viharati.

It's when, with the fading away of rapture, a mendicant enters and remains in the third absorption, where they meditate with equanimity, mindful and aware, personally experiencing the bliss of which the noble ones declare, 'Equanimous and mindful, one meditates in bliss.' …

Idaṁ kho, ānanda, etamhā sukhā aññaṁ sukhaṁ abhikkantatarañca paṇītatarañca.

Yo kho, ānanda, evaṁ vadeyya …

pe….

There is another pleasure that is finer than that.

Katamañcānanda, etamhā sukhā aññaṁ sukhaṁ abhikkantatarañca paṇītatarañca?

And what is that pleasure?

Idhānanda, bhikkhu sukhassa ca pahānā …pe… catutthaṁ jhānaṁ upasampajja viharati.

It's when, giving up pleasure and pain, and ending former happiness and sadness, a mendicant enters and remains in the fourth absorption, without pleasure or pain, with pure equanimity and mindfulness. …

Idaṁ kho, ānanda, etamhā sukhā aññaṁ sukhaṁ abhikkantatarañca paṇītatarañca.

Yo kho, ānanda, evaṁ vadeyya …

pe.…

There is another pleasure that is finer than that.

Katamañcānanda, etamhā sukhā aññaṁ sukhaṁ abhikkantatarañca paṇītatarañca?

And what is that pleasure?

Idhānanda, bhikkhu sabbaso rūpasaññānaṁ samatikkamā, paṭighasaññānaṁ atthaṅgamā, nānattasaññānaṁ amanasikārā 'ananto ākāso'ti ākāsānañcāyatanaṁ upasampajja viharati.

It's when a mendicant, going totally beyond perceptions of form, with the ending of perceptions of impingement, not focusing on perceptions of diversity, aware that 'space is infinite', enters and remains in the dimension of infinite space. …

Idaṁ kho, ānanda, etamhā sukhā aññaṁ sukhaṁ abhikkantatarañca paṇītatarañca.

Yo kho, ānanda, evaṁ vadeyya …

pe.…

There is another pleasure that is finer than that.

Katamañcānanda, etamhā sukhā aññaṁ sukhaṁ abhikkantatarañca paṇītatarañca?

And what is that pleasure?

Idhānanda, bhikkhu sabbaso ākāsānañcāyatanaṁ samatikkamma 'anantaṁ viññāṇan'ti viññāṇañcāyatanaṁ upasampajja viharati.

It's when a mendicant, going totally beyond the dimension of infinite space, aware that 'consciousness is infinite', enters and remains in the dimension of infinite consciousness. …

Idaṁ kho, ānanda, etamhā sukhā aññaṁ sukhaṁ abhikkantatarañca paṇītatarañca.

Yo kho, ānanda, evaṁ vadeyya …

pe.…

There is another pleasure that is finer than that.

Katamañcānanda, etamhā sukhā aññaṁ sukhaṁ abhikkantatarañca paṇītatarañca?

And what is that pleasure?

Idhānanda, bhikkhu sabbaso viññāṇañcāyatanaṁ samatikkamma 'natthi kiñcī'ti ākiñcaññāyatanaṁ upasampajja viharati.

It's when a mendicant, going totally beyond the dimension of infinite consciousness, aware that 'there is nothing at all', enters and remains in the dimension of nothingness. ...

Idaṁ kho, ānanda, etamhā sukhā aññaṁ sukhaṁ abhikkantatarañca paṇītatarañca.

Yo kho, ānanda, evaṁ vadeyya ...

pe....

There is another pleasure that is finer than that.

Katamañcānanda, etamhā sukhā aññaṁ sukhaṁ abhikkantatarañca paṇītatarañca?

And what is that pleasure?

Idhānanda, bhikkhu sabbaso ākiñcaññāyatanaṁ samatikkamma nevasaññānāsaññāyatanaṁ upasampajja viharati.

It's when a mendicant, going totally beyond the dimension of nothingness, enters and remains in the dimension of neither perception nor non-perception.

Idaṁ kho, ānanda, etamhā sukhā aññaṁ sukhaṁ abhikkantatarañca paṇītatarañca.

This is a pleasure that is finer than that.

Yo kho, ānanda, evaṁ vadeyya: 'etaparamaṁ sattā sukhaṁ somanassaṁ paṭisaṁvedentī'ti, idamassa nānujānāmi.

There are those who would say that this is the highest pleasure and happiness that sentient beings experience. But I don't grant them that.

Taṁ kissa hetu?

Why is that?

Atthānanda, etamhā sukhā aññaṁ sukhaṁ abhikkantatarañca paṇītatarañca.

Because there is another pleasure that is finer than that.

Katamañcānanda, etamhā sukhā aññaṁ sukhaṁ abhikkantatarañca paṇītatarañca?

And what is that pleasure?

Idhānanda, bhikkhu sabbaso nevasaññānāsaññāyatanaṁ samatikkamma saññāvedayitanirodhaṃ upasampajja viharati.

It's when a mendicant, going totally beyond the dimension of neither perception nor non-perception, enters and remains in the cessation of perception and feeling.

Idaṃ kho, ānanda, etamhā sukhā aññaṃ sukhaṃ abhikkantatarañca paṇītatarañca.

This is a pleasure that is finer than that.

Ṭhānaṃ kho panetaṃ, ānanda, vijjati yaṃ aññatitthiyā paribbājakā evaṃ vadeyyuṃ:

It's possible that wanderers of other religions might say,

'saññāvedayitanirodhaṃ samaṇo gotamo āha; tañca sukhasmiṃ paññapeti.

'The ascetic Gotama spoke of the cessation of perception and feeling, and he includes it in happiness.

Tayidaṃ kiṃsu, tayidaṃ kathaṃsū'ti?

What's up with that?'

Evaṃvādino, ānanda, aññatitthiyā paribbājakā evamassu vacanīyā:

When wanderers of other religions say this, you should say to them,

'na kho, āvuso, bhagavā sukhaṃyeva vedanaṃ sandhāya sukhasmiṃ paññapeti;

'Reverends, when the Buddha describes what's included in happiness, he's not just referring to pleasant feeling.

api ca, āvuso, yattha yattha sukhaṃ upalabbhati yahiṃ yahiṃ taṃ taṃ tathāgato sukhasmiṃ paññapetī'"ti.

The Realized One describes pleasure as included in happiness wherever it's found, and in whatever context.'"

Idamavoca bhagavā.

That is what the Buddha said.

Attamano āyasmā ānando bhagavato bhāsitaṃ abhinandīti.

Satisfied, Venerable Ānanda was happy with what the Buddha said.

Bahuvedanīyasuttaṃ niṭṭhitaṃ navamaṃ.

60 Apannakasutta:

Guaranteed

Evaṁ me sutaṁ—

So I have heard.

ekaṁ samayaṁ bhagavā kosalesu cārikaṁ caramāno mahatā bhikkhusaṅghena saddhiṁ yena sālā nāma kosalānaṁ brāhmaṇagāmo tadavasari.

At one time the Buddha was wandering in the land of the Kosalans together with a large Saṅgha of mendicants when he arrived at a village of the Kosalan brahmins named Sālā.

Assosuṁ kho sāleyyakā brāhmaṇagahapatikā:

The brahmins and householders of Sālā heard:

"samaṇo khalu bho gotamo sakyaputto sakyakulā pabbajito kosalesu cārikaṁ caramāno mahatā bhikkhusaṅghena saddhiṁ sālaṁ anuppatto.

"It seems the ascetic Gotama—a Sakyan, gone forth from a Sakyan family—wandering in the land of the Kosalans has arrived at Sālā, together with a large Saṅgha of mendicants.

Taṁ kho pana bhavantaṁ gotamaṁ evaṁ kalyāṇo kittisaddo abbhuggato:

He has this good reputation:

'itipi so bhagavā arahaṁ sammāsambuddho vijjācaraṇasampanno sugato lokavidū anuttaro purisadammasārathi satthā devamanussānaṁ buddho bhagavā'ti.

'That Blessed One is perfected, a fully awakened Buddha, accomplished in knowledge and conduct, holy, knower of the world, supreme guide for those who wish to train, teacher of gods and humans, awakened, blessed.'

So imaṁ lokaṁ sadevakaṁ samārakaṁ sabrahmakaṁ sassamaṇabrāhmaṇiṁ pajaṁ sadevamanussaṁ sayaṁ abhiññā sacchikatvā pavedeti.

He has realized with his own insight this world—with its gods, Māras and Brahmās, this population with its ascetics and brahmins, gods and humans—and he makes it known to others.

So dhammaṁ deseti ādikalyāṇaṁ majjhekalyāṇaṁ pariyosānakalyāṇaṁ sātthaṁ sabyañjanaṁ, kevalaparipuṇṇaṁ parisuddhaṁ brahmacariyaṁ pakāseti.

He teaches Dhamma that's good in the beginning, good in the middle, and good in the end, meaningful and well-phrased. And he reveals a spiritual practice that's entirely full and pure.

Sādhu kho pana tathārūpānaṁ arahataṁ dassanaṁ hotī"ti.

It's good to see such perfected ones."

Atha kho sāleyyakā brāhmaṇagahapatikā yena bhagavā tenupasaṅkamiṁsu; upasaṅkamitvā appekacce bhagavantaṁ abhivādetvā ekamantaṁ nisīdiṁsu. Appekacce bhagavatā saddhiṁ sammodiṁsu; sammodanīyaṁ kathaṁ sāraṇīyaṁ vītisāretvā ekamantaṁ nisīdiṁsu. Appekacce yena bhagavā tenañjaliṁ paṇāmetvā ekamantaṁ nisīdiṁsu. Appekacce bhagavato santike nāmagottaṁ sāvetvā ekamantaṁ nisīdiṁsu. Appekacce tuṇhībhūtā ekamantaṁ nisīdiṁsu. Ekamantaṁ nisinne kho sāleyyake brāhmaṇagahapatike bhagavā etadavoca:

Then the brahmins and householders of Sālā went up to the Buddha. Before sitting down to one side, some bowed, some exchanged greetings and polite conversation, some held up their joined palms toward the Buddha, some announced their name and clan, while some kept silent. The Buddha said to them:

"atthi pana vo, gahapatayo, koci manāpo satthā yasmiṁ vo ākāravatī saddhā paṭiladdhā"ti?

"So, householders, is there some other teacher you're happy with, in whom you have acquired grounded faith?"

"Natthi kho no, bhante, koci manāpo satthā yasmiṁ no ākāravatī saddhā paṭiladdhā"ti.

"No, sir."

"Manāpaṁ vo, gahapatayo, satthāraṁ alabhantehi ayaṁ apaṇṇako dhammo samādāya vattitabbo.

"Since you haven't found a teacher you're happy with, you should undertake and implement this guaranteed teaching.

Apaṇṇako hi, gahapatayo, dhammo samatto samādinno, so vo bhavissati dīgharattaṁ hitāya sukhāya.

For when the guaranteed teaching is undertaken, it will be for your lasting welfare and happiness.

Katamo ca, gahapatayo, apaṇṇako dhammo?

And what is the guaranteed teaching?

Santi, gahapatayo, eke samaṇabrāhmaṇā evaṁvādino evaṁdiṭṭhino:

There are some ascetics and brahmins who have this doctrine and view:

'natthi dinnaṁ, natthi yiṭṭhaṁ, natthi hutaṁ; natthi sukatadukkaṭānaṁ kammānaṁ phalaṁ vipāko, natthi ayaṁ loko, natthi paro loko; natthi mātā, natthi pitā; natthi sattā opapātikā; natthi loke samaṇabrāhmaṇā sammaggatā sammā paṭipannā ye imañca lokaṁ parañca lokaṁ sayaṁ abhiññā sacchikatvā pavedentī'ti.

'There's no meaning in giving, sacrifice, or offerings. There's no fruit or result of good and bad deeds. There's no afterlife. There's no such thing as mother and father, or beings that are reborn spontaneously. And there's no ascetic or brahmin who is well attained and practiced, and who describes the afterlife after realizing it with their own insight.'

Tesaṁyeva kho, gahapatayo, samaṇabrāhmaṇānaṁ eke samaṇabrāhmaṇā ujuvipaccanīkavādā.

And there are some ascetics and brahmins whose doctrine directly contradicts this.

Te evamāhaṁsu:

They say:

'atthi dinnaṁ, atthi yiṭṭhaṁ, atthi hutaṁ; atthi sukatadukkaṭānaṁ kammānaṁ phalaṁ vipāko; atthi ayaṁ loko, atthi paro loko; atthi mātā, atthi pitā; atthi sattā opapātikā; atthi loke samaṇabrāhmaṇā sammaggatā sammā paṭipannā ye imañca lokaṁ parañca lokaṁ sayaṁ abhiññā sacchikatvā pavedentī'ti.

'There is meaning in giving, sacrifice, and offerings. There are fruits and results of good and bad deeds. There is an afterlife. There are such things as mother and father, and beings that are reborn spontaneously. And there are ascetics and brahmins who are well attained and practiced, and who describe the afterlife after realizing it with their own insight.'

Taṁ kiṁ maññatha, gahapatayo:

What do you think, householders?

'nanume samaṇabrāhmaṇā aññamaññassa ujuvipaccanīkavādā'"ti?

Don't these doctrines directly contradict each other?"

"Evaṁ, bhante".

"Yes, sir."

"Tatra, gahapatayo, ye te samaṇabrāhmaṇā evaṁvādino evaṁdiṭṭhino:

"Since this is so, consider those ascetics and brahmins whose view is that

'natthi dinnaṁ, natthi yiṭṭhaṁ …pe… ye imañca lokaṁ parañca lokaṁ sayaṁ abhiññā sacchikatvā pavedentī'ti

there's no meaning in giving, etc.

tesametaṁ pāṭikaṅkhaṁ—yamidaṁ kāyasucaritaṁ, vacīsucaritaṁ, manosucaritaṁ—ime tayo kusale dhamme abhinivajjetvā yamidaṁ kāyaduccaritaṁ, vacīduccaritaṁ, manoduccaritaṁ—ime tayo akusale dhamme samādāya vattissanti.

You can expect that they will reject good conduct by way of body, speech, and mind, and undertake and implement bad conduct by way of body, speech, and mind.

Taṁ kissa hetu?

Why is that?

Na hi te bhonto samaṇabrāhmaṇā passanti akusalānaṁ dhammānaṁ ādīnavaṁ okāraṁ saṅkilesaṁ, kusalānaṁ dhammānaṁ nekkhamme ānisaṁsaṁ vodānapakkhaṁ.

Because those ascetics and brahmins don't see that unskillful qualities are full of drawbacks, sordidness, and corruption, or that skillful qualities have the benefit and cleansing power of renunciation.

Santaṁyeva pana paraṁ lokaṁ 'natthi paro loko' tissa diṭṭhi hoti; sāssa hoti micchādiṭṭhi.

Moreover, since there actually is another world, their view that there is no other world is wrong view.

Santaṁyeva kho pana paraṁ lokaṁ 'natthi paro loko'ti saṅkappeti; svāssa hoti micchāsaṅkappo.

Since there actually is another world, their thought that there is no other world is wrong thought.

Santaṁyeva kho pana paraṁ lokaṁ 'natthi paro loko'ti vācaṁ bhāsati; sāssa hoti micchāvācā.

Since there actually is another world, their speech that there is no other world is wrong speech.

Santaṁyeva kho pana paraṁ lokaṁ 'natthi paro loko'ti āha; ye te arahanto paralokaviduno tesamayaṁ paccanīkaṁ karoti.

Since there actually is another world, in saying that there is no other world they contradict those perfected ones who know the other world.

Santaṁyeva kho pana paraṁ lokaṁ 'natthi paro loko'ti paraṁ saññāpeti; sāssa hoti asaddhammasaññatti.

Since there actually is another world, in convincing another that there is no other world they are convincing them to accept an untrue teaching.

Tāya ca pana asaddhammasaññattiyā attānukkaṁseti, paraṁ vambheti.

And on account of that they glorify themselves and put others down.

Iti pubbeva kho panassa susīlyaṁ pahīnaṁ hoti, dussīlyaṁ paccupaṭṭhitaṁ—

So they give up their former ethical conduct and are established in unethical conduct.

ayañca micchādiṭṭhi micchāsaṅkappo micchāvācā ariyānaṁ paccanīkatā asaddhammasaññatti attukkaṁsanā paravambhanā. Evamassime aneke pāpakā akusalā dhammā sambhavanti micchādiṭṭhipaccayā.

And that is how these many bad, unskillful qualities come to be with wrong view as condition—wrong view, wrong thought, wrong speech, contradicting the noble ones, convincing others to accept untrue teachings, and glorifying oneself and putting others down.

Tatra, gahapatayo, viññū puriso iti paṭisañcikkhati:

A sensible person reflects on this matter in this way:

'sace kho natthi paro loko evamayaṁ bhavaṁ purisapuggalo kāyassa bhedā sotthimattānaṁ karissati;

'If there is no other world, when this individual's body breaks up they will keep themselves safe.

sace kho atthi paro loko, evamayaṁ bhavaṁ purisapuggalo kāyassa bhedā paraṁ maraṇā apāyaṁ duggatiṁ vinipātaṁ nirayaṁ upapajjissati.

And if there is another world, when their body breaks up, after death, they will be reborn in a place of loss, a bad place, the underworld, hell.

Kāmaṁ kho pana māhu paro loko, hotu nesaṁ bhavataṁ samaṇabrāhmaṇānaṁ saccaṁ vacanaṁ;

But let's assume that those who say that there is no other world are correct.

atha ca panāyaṁ bhavaṁ purisapuggalo diṭṭheva dhamme viññūnaṁ gārayho— dussīlo purisapuggalo micchādiṭṭhi natthikavādo'ti.

Regardless, that individual is still criticized by sensible people in the present life as being an immoral individual of wrong view, a nihilist.'

Sace kho attheva paro loko, evaṁ imassa bhoto purisapuggalassa ubhayattha kaliggaho—

But if there really is another world, they lose on both counts.

yañca diṭṭheva dhamme viññūnaṁ gārayho, yañca kāyassa bhedā paraṁ maraṇā apāyaṁ duggatiṁ vinipātaṁ nirayaṁ upapajjissati.

For they are criticized by sensible people in the present life, and when their body breaks up, after death, they will be reborn in a place of loss, a bad place, the underworld, hell.

Evamassāyaṁ apaṇṇako dhammo dussamatto samādinno, ekaṁsaṁ pharitvā tiṭṭhati, riñcati kusalaṁ ṭhānaṁ.

They have wrongly undertaken this guaranteed teaching in such a way that it encompasses the positive outcomes of one side only, leaving out the skillful premise.

Tatra, gahapatayo, ye te samaṇabrāhmaṇā evaṁvādino evaṁdiṭṭhino:

Since this is so, consider those ascetics and brahmins whose view is that

'atthi dinnaṁ …pe… ye imañca lokaṁ parañca lokaṁ sayaṁ abhiññā sacchikatvā pavedentī'ti

there is meaning in giving, etc.

tesametaṁ pāṭikaṅkhaṁ—yamidaṁ kāyaduccaritaṁ, vacīduccaritaṁ, manoduccaritaṁ—ime tayo akusale dhamme abhinivajjetvā yamidaṁ kāyasucaritaṁ, vacīsucaritaṁ, manosucaritaṁ—ime tayo kusale dhamme samādāya vattissanti.

You can expect that they will reject bad conduct by way of body, speech, and mind, and undertake and implement good conduct by way of body, speech, and mind.

Taṁ kissa hetu?

Why is that?

Passanti hi te bhonto samaṇabrāhmaṇā akusalānaṁ dhammānaṁ ādīnavaṁ okāraṁ saṅkilesaṁ, kusalānaṁ dhammānaṁ nekkhamme ānisaṁsaṁ vodānapakkhaṁ.

Because those ascetics and brahmins see that unskillful qualities are full of drawbacks, sordidness, and corruption, and that skillful qualities have the benefit and cleansing power of renunciation.

Santaṁyeva kho pana paraṁ lokaṁ 'atthi paro loko' tissa diṭṭhi hoti; sāssa hoti sammādiṭṭhi.

Moreover, since there actually is another world, their view that there is another world is right view.

Santaṁyeva kho pana paraṁ lokaṁ 'atthi paro loko'ti saṅkappeti; svāssa hoti sammāsaṅkappo.

Since there actually is another world, their thought that there is another world is right thought.

Santaṁyeva kho pana paraṁ lokaṁ 'atthi paro loko'ti vācaṁ bhāsati; sāssa hoti sammāvācā.

Since there actually is another world, their speech that there is another world is right speech.

Santaṁyeva kho pana paraṁ lokaṁ 'atthi paro loko'ti āha; ye te arahanto paralokaviduno tesamayaṁ na paccanīkaṁ karoti.

Since there actually is another world, in saying that there is another world they don't contradict those perfected ones who know the other world.

Santaṁyeva kho pana paraṁ lokaṁ 'atthi paro loko'ti paraṁ saññāpeti; sāssa hoti saddhammasaññatti.

Since there actually is another world, in convincing another that there is another world they are convincing them to accept a true teaching.

Tāya ca pana saddhammasaññattiyā nevattānukkaṁseti, na paraṁ vambheti.

And on account of that they don't glorify themselves or put others down.

Iti pubbeva kho panassa dussīlyaṁ pahīnaṁ hoti, susīlyaṁ paccupaṭṭhitaṁ—

So they give up their former unethical conduct and are established in ethical conduct.

ayañca sammādiṭṭhi sammāsaṅkappo sammāvācā ariyānaṁ apaccanīkatā saddhammasaññatti anattukkaṁsanā aparavambhanā. Evamassime aneke kusalā dhammā sambhavanti sammādiṭṭhipaccayā.

And that is how these many skillful qualities come to be with right view as condition—right view, right thought, right speech, not contradicting the noble ones, convincing others to accept true teachings, and not glorifying oneself or putting others down.

Tatra, gahapatayo, viññū puriso iti paṭisañcikkhati:

A sensible person reflects on this matter in this way:

'sace kho atthi paro loko, evamayaṁ bhavaṁ purisapuggalo kāyassa bhedā paraṁ maraṇā sugatiṁ saggaṁ lokaṁ upapajjissati.

'If there is another world, when this individual's body breaks up, after death, they will be reborn in a good place, a heavenly realm.

Kāmaṁ kho pana māhu paro loko, hotu nesaṁ bhavataṁ samaṇabrāhmaṇānaṁ saccaṁ vacanaṁ;

But let's assume that those who say that there is no other world are correct.

atha ca panāyaṁ bhavaṁ purisapuggalo diṭṭheva dhamme viññūnaṁ pāsaṁso— sīlavā purisapuggalo sammādiṭṭhi atthikavādo'ti.

Regardless, that individual is still praised by sensible people in the present life as being a moral individual of right view, who affirms a positive teaching.'

Sace kho attheva paro loko, evaṁ imassa bhoto purisapuggalassa ubhayattha kaṭaggaho—

So if there really is another world, they win on both counts.

yañca diṭṭheva dhamme viññūnaṁ pāsaṁso, yañca kāyassa bhedā paraṁ maraṇā sugatiṁ saggaṁ lokaṁ upapajjissati.

For they are praised by sensible people in the present life, and when their body breaks up, after death, they will be reborn in a good place, a heavenly realm.

Evamassāyaṁ apaṇṇako dhammo susamatto samādinno ubhayaṁsaṁ pharitvā tiṭṭhati, riñcati akusalaṁ ṭhānaṁ.

They have rightly undertaken this guaranteed teaching in such a way that it encompasses the positive outcomes of both sides, leaving out the unskillful premise.

Santi, gahapatayo, eke samaṇabrāhmaṇā evaṁvādino evaṁdiṭṭhino:

There are some ascetics and brahmins who have this doctrine and view:

'karoto kārayato, chindato chedāpayato, pacato pācāpayato, socayato socāpayato, kilamato kilamāpayato, phandato phandāpayato, pāṇamatipātayato, adinnaṁ ādiyato, sandhiṁ chindato, nillopaṁ harato, ekāgārikaṁ karoto, paripanthe tiṭṭhato, paradāraṁ gacchato, musā bhaṇato; karoto na karīyati pāpaṁ.

'The one who acts does nothing wrong when they punish, mutilate, torture, aggrieve, oppress, intimidate, or when they encourage others to do the same. They do nothing wrong when they kill, steal, break into houses, plunder wealth, steal from isolated buildings, commit highway robbery, commit adultery, and lie.

Khurapariyantena cepi cakkena yo imissā pathaviyā pāṇe ekaṁ maṁsakhalaṁ ekaṁ maṁsapuñjaṁ kareyya, natthi tatonidānaṁ pāpaṁ, natthi pāpassa āgamo.

If you were to reduce all the living creatures of this earth to one heap and mass of flesh with a razor-edged chakram, no evil comes of that, and no outcome of evil.

Dakkhiṇañcepi gaṅgāya tīraṁ gaccheyya hananto ghātento, chindanto chedāpento, pacanto pācento; natthi tatonidānaṁ pāpaṁ, natthi pāpassa āgamo.

If you were to go along the south bank of the Ganges killing, mutilating, and torturing, and encouraging others to do the same, no evil comes of that, and no outcome of evil.

Uttarañcepi gaṅgāya tīraṁ gaccheyya dadanto dāpento, yajanto yajāpento; natthi tatonidānaṁ puññaṁ, natthi puññassa āgamo.

If you were to go along the north bank of the Ganges giving and sacrificing and encouraging others to do the same, no merit comes of that, and no outcome of merit.

Dānena damena saṁyamena saccavajjena natthi puññaṁ, natthi puññassa āgamo'ti.

In giving, self-control, restraint, and truthfulness there is no merit or outcome of merit.'

Tesaṁyeva kho, gahapatayo, samaṇabrāhmaṇānaṁ eke samaṇabrāhmaṇā ujuvipaccanīkavādā te evamāhaṁsu:

And there are some ascetics and brahmins whose doctrine directly contradicts this. They say:

'karoto kārayato, chindato chedāpayato, pacato pācāpayato, socayato socāpayato, kilamato kilamāpayato, phandato phandāpayato, pāṇamatipātayato, adinnaṁ ādiyato, sandhiṁ chindato, nillopaṁ harato, ekāgārikaṁ karoto, paripanthe tiṭṭhato, paradāraṁ gacchato, musā bhaṇato; karoto karīyati pāpaṁ.

'The one who acts does a bad deed when they punish, mutilate, torture, aggrieve, oppress, intimidate, or when they encourage others to do the same. They do a bad deed when they kill, steal, break into houses, plunder wealth, steal from isolated buildings, commit highway robbery, commit adultery, and lie.

Khurapariyantena cepi cakkena yo imissā pathaviyā pāṇe ekaṁ maṁsakhalaṁ ekaṁ maṁsapuñjaṁ kareyya, atthi tatonidānaṁ pāpaṁ, atthi pāpassa āgamo.

If you were to reduce all the living creatures of this earth to one heap and mass of flesh with a razor-edged chakram, evil comes of that, and an outcome of evil.

Dakkhiṇañcepi gaṅgāya tīraṁ gaccheyya hananto ghātento, chindanto chedāpento, pacanto pācento; atthi tatonidānaṁ pāpaṁ, atthi pāpassa āgamo.

If you were to go along the south bank of the Ganges killing, mutilating, and torturing, and encouraging others to do the same, evil comes of that, and an outcome of evil.

Uttarañcepi gaṅgāya tīraṁ gaccheyya dadanto dāpento, yajanto yajāpento; atthi tatonidānaṁ puññaṁ, atthi puññassa āgamo.

If you were to go along the north bank of the Ganges giving and sacrificing and encouraging others to do the same, merit comes of that, and an outcome of merit.

Dānena damena saṁyamena saccavajjena atthi puññaṁ, atthi puññassa āgamo'ti.

In giving, self-control, restraint, and truthfulness there is merit and outcome of merit.'

Taṁ kiṁ maññatha, gahapatayo,

What do you think, householders?

nanume samaṇabrāhmaṇā aññamaññassa ujuvipaccanīkavādā"ti?

Don't these doctrines directly contradict each other?"

"Evaṁ, bhante".

"Yes, sir."

"Tatra, gahapatayo, ye te samaṇabrāhmaṇā evaṁvādino evaṁdiṭṭhino:

"Since this is so, consider those ascetics and brahmins whose view is that

'karoto kārayato, chindato chedāpayato, pacato pācāpayato, socayato socāpayato, kilamato kilamāpayato, phandato phandāpayato, pāṇamatipātayato, adinnaṁ ādiyato, sandhiṁ chindato, nillopaṁ harato, ekāgārikaṁ karoto, paripanthe tiṭṭhato, paradāraṁ gacchato, musā bhaṇato; karoto na karīyati pāpaṁ.

the one who acts does nothing wrong when they punish, etc.

Khurapariyantena cepi cakkena yo imissā pathaviyā pāṇe ekaṁ maṁsakhalaṁ ekaṁ maṁsapuñjaṁ kareyya, natthi tatonidānaṁ pāpaṁ, natthi pāpassa āgamo.

Dakkhiṇañcepi gaṅgāya tīraṁ gaccheyya hananto ghātento …pe… dānena damena saṁyamena saccavajjena natthi puññaṁ, natthi puññassa āgamo'ti

tesametaṁ pāṭikaṅkhaṁ—yamidaṁ kāyasucaritaṁ, vacīsucaritaṁ, manosucaritaṁ—ime tayo kusale dhamme abhinivajjetvā yamidaṁ kāyaduccaritaṁ, vacīduccaritaṁ, manoduccaritaṁ—ime tayo akusale dhamme samādāya vattissanti.

You can expect that they will reject good conduct by way of body, speech, and mind, and undertake and implement bad conduct by way of body, speech, and mind.

Taṁ kissa hetu?

Why is that?

Na hi te bhonto samaṇabrāhmaṇā passanti akusalānaṁ dhammānaṁ ādīnavaṁ okāraṁ saṅkilesaṁ, kusalānaṁ dhammānaṁ nekkhamme ānisaṁsaṁ vodānapakkhaṁ.

Because those ascetics and brahmins don't see that unskillful qualities are full of drawbacks, sordidness, and corruption, or that skillful qualities have the benefit and cleansing power of renunciation.

Santaṁyeva kho pana kiriyaṁ 'natthi kiriyā' tissa diṭṭhi hoti; sāssa hoti micchādiṭṭhi.

Moreover, since action actually does have an effect, their view that action is ineffective is wrong view.

Santaṁyeva kho pana kiriyaṁ 'natthi kiriyā'ti saṅkappeti; svāssa hoti micchāsaṅkappo.

Since action actually does have an effect, their thought that action is ineffective is wrong thought.

Santaṁyeva kho pana kiriyaṁ 'natthi kiriyā'ti vācaṁ bhāsati; sāssa hoti micchāvācā.

Since action actually does have an effect, their speech that action is ineffective is wrong speech.

Santaṁyeva kho pana kiriyaṁ 'natthi kiriyā'ti āha, ye te arahanto kiriyavādā tesamayaṁ paccanīkaṁ karoti.

Since action actually does have an effect, in saying that action is ineffective they contradict those perfected ones who teach that action is effective.

Santaṁyeva kho pana kiriyaṁ 'natthi kiriyā'ti paraṁ saññāpeti; sāssa hoti asaddhammasaññatti.

Since action actually does have an effect, in convincing another that action is ineffective they are convincing them to accept an untrue teaching.

Tāya ca pana asaddhammasaññattiyā attānukkaṁseti, paraṁ vambheti.

And on account of that they glorify themselves and put others down.

Iti pubbeva kho panassa susīlyaṁ pahīnaṁ hoti, dussīlyaṁ paccupaṭṭhitaṁ—

So they give up their former ethical conduct and are established in unethical conduct.

ayañca micchādiṭṭhi micchāsaṅkappo micchāvācā ariyānaṁ paccanīkatā asaddhammasaññatti attukkaṁsanā paravambhanā. Evamassime aneke pāpakā akusalā dhammā sambhavanti micchādiṭṭhipaccayā.

And that is how these many bad, unskillful qualities come to be with wrong view as condition—wrong view, wrong thought, wrong speech, contradicting the noble ones, convincing others to accept untrue teachings, and glorifying oneself and putting others down.

Tatra, gahapatayo, viññū puriso iti paṭisañcikkhati:

A sensible person reflects on this matter in this way:

'sace kho natthi kiriyā, evamayaṁ bhavaṁ purisapuggalo kāyassa bhedā sotthimattānaṁ karissati;

'If there is no effective action, when this individual's body breaks up they will keep themselves safe.

sace kho atthi kiriyā evamayaṁ bhavaṁ purisapuggalo kāyassa bhedā paraṁ maraṇā apāyaṁ duggatiṁ vinipātaṁ nirayaṁ upapajjissati.

And if there is effective action, when their body breaks up, after death, they will be reborn in a place of loss, a bad place, the underworld, hell.

Kāmaṁ kho pana māhu kiriyā, hotu nesaṁ bhavataṁ samaṇabrāhmaṇānaṁ saccaṁ vacanaṁ;

But let's assume that those who say that there is no effective action are correct.

atha ca panāyaṁ bhavaṁ purisapuggalo diṭṭheva dhamme viññūnaṁ gārayho—dussīlo purisapuggalo micchādiṭṭhi akiriyavādo'ti.

Regardless, that individual is still criticized by sensible people in the present life as being an immoral individual of wrong view, one who denies the efficacy of action.'

Sace kho attheva kiriyā, evaṁ imassa bhoto purisapuggalassa ubhayattha kaliggaho—

But if there really is effective action, they lose on both counts.

yañca diṭṭheva dhamme viññūnaṁ gārayho, yañca kāyassa bhedā paraṁ maraṇā apāyaṁ duggatiṁ vinipātaṁ nirayaṁ upapajjissati.

For they are criticized by sensible people in the present life, and when their body breaks up, after death, they will be reborn in a place of loss, a bad place, the underworld, hell.

Evamassāyaṁ apaṇṇako dhammo dussamatto samādinno, ekaṁsaṁ pharitvā tiṭṭhati, riñcati kusalaṁ ṭhānaṁ.

They have wrongly undertaken this guaranteed teaching in such a way that it encompasses the positive outcomes of one side only, leaving out the skillful premise.

Tatra, gahapatayo, ye te samaṇabrāhmaṇā evaṁvādino evaṁdiṭṭhino:

Since this is so, consider those ascetics and brahmins whose view is that

'karoto kārayato, chindato chedāpayato, pacato pācāpayato, socayato socāpayato, kilamato kilamāpayato, phandato phandāpayato, pāṇamatipātayato, adinnaṁ ādiyato, sandhiṁ chindato, nillopaṁ harato, ekāgārikaṁ karoto, paripanthe tiṭṭhato, paradāraṁ gacchato, musā bhaṇato; karoto karīyati pāpaṁ.

the one who acts does a bad deed when they punish, etc.

Khurapariyantena cepi cakkena yo imissā pathaviyā pāṇe ekaṁ maṁsakhalaṁ ekaṁ maṁsapuñjaṁ kareyya, atthi tatonidānaṁ pāpaṁ, atthi pāpassa āgamo.

Dakkhiṇañcepi gaṅgāya tīraṁ gaccheyya hananto ghātento, chindanto chedāpento, pacanto pācento, atthi tatonidānaṁ pāpaṁ, atthi pāpassa āgamo.

Uttarañcepi gaṅgāya tīraṁ gaccheyya dadanto dāpento, yajanto yajāpento, atthi tatonidānaṁ puññaṁ, atthi puññassa āgamo. Dānena damena saṁyamena saccavajjena atthi puññaṁ, atthi puññassa āgamo'ti

tesametaṁ pāṭikaṅkhaṁ yamidaṁ kāyaduccaritaṁ, vacīduccaritaṁ, manoduccaritaṁ—ime tayo akusale dhamme abhinivajjetvā yamidaṁ kāyasucaritaṁ, vacīsucaritaṁ, manosucaritaṁ—ime tayo kusale dhamme samādāya vattissanti.

You can expect that they will reject bad conduct by way of body, speech, and mind, and undertake and implement good conduct by way of body, speech, and mind.

Taṁ kissa hetu?

Why is that?

Passanti hi te bhonto samaṇabrāhmaṇā akusalānaṁ dhammānaṁ ādīnavaṁ okāraṁ saṅkilesaṁ, kusalānaṁ dhammānaṁ nekkhamme ānisaṁsaṁ vodānapakkhaṁ.

Because those ascetics and brahmins see that unskillful qualities are full of drawbacks, sordidness, and corruption, and that skillful qualities have the benefit and cleansing power of renunciation.

Santaṁyeva kho pana kiriyaṁ 'atthi kiriyā' tissa diṭṭhi hoti; sāssa hoti sammādiṭṭhi.

Moreover, since action actually does have an effect, their view that action is effective is right view.

Santaṁyeva kho pana kiriyaṁ 'atthi kiriyā'ti saṅkappeti; svāssa hoti sammāsaṅkappo.

Since action actually does have an effect, their thought that action is effective is right thought.

Santaṁyeva kho pana kiriyaṁ 'atthi kiriyā'ti vācaṁ bhāsati; sāssa hoti sammāvācā.

Since action actually does have an effect, their speech that action is effective is right speech.

Santaṁyeva kho pana kiriyaṁ 'atthi kiriyā'ti āha; ye te arahanto kiriyavādā tesamayaṁ na paccanīkaṁ karoti.

Since action actually does have an effect, in saying that action is effective they don't contradict those perfected ones who teach that action is effective.

Santaṁyeva kho pana kiriyaṁ 'atthi kiriyā'ti paraṁ saññāpeti; sāssa hoti saddhammasaññatti.

Since action actually does have an effect, in convincing another that action is effective they are convincing them to accept a true teaching.

Tāya ca pana saddhammasaññattiyā nevattānukkaṁseti, na paraṁ vambheti.

And on account of that they don't glorify themselves or put others down.

Iti pubbeva kho panassa dussīlyaṁ pahīnaṁ hoti, susīlyaṁ paccupaṭṭhitaṁ—

So they give up their former unethical conduct and are established in ethical conduct.

ayañca sammādiṭṭhi sammāsaṅkappo sammāvācā ariyānaṁ apaccanīkatā saddhammasaññatti anattukkaṁsanā aparavambhanā. Evamassime aneke kusalā dhammā sambhavanti sammādiṭṭhipaccayā.

And that is how these many skillful qualities come to be with right view as condition—right view, right thought, right speech, not contradicting the noble ones, convincing others to accept true teachings, and not glorifying oneself or putting others down.

Tatra, gahapatayo, viññū puriso iti paṭisañcikkhati:

A sensible person reflects on this matter in this way:

'sace kho atthi kiriyā, evamayaṁ bhavaṁ purisapuggalo kāyassa bhedā paraṁ maraṇā sugatiṁ saggaṁ lokaṁ upapajjissati.

'If there is effective action, when this individual's body breaks up, after death, they will be reborn in a good place, a heavenly realm.

Kāmaṁ kho pana māhu kiriyā, hotu nesaṁ bhavataṁ samaṇabrāhmaṇānaṁ saccaṁ vacanaṁ;

But let's assume that those who say that there is no effective action are correct.

atha ca panāyaṁ bhavaṁ purisapuggalo diṭṭheva dhamme viññūnaṁ pāsaṁso— sīlavā purisapuggalo sammādiṭṭhi kiriyavādo'ti.

Regardless, that individual is still praised by sensible people in the present life as being a moral individual of right view, who affirms the efficacy of action.'

Sace kho attheva kiriyā, evaṁ imassa bhoto purisapuggalassa ubhayattha kaṭaggaho—

So if there really is effective action, they win on both counts.

yañca diṭṭheva dhamme viññūnaṁ pāsaṁso, yañca kāyassa bhedā paraṁ maraṇā sugatiṁ saggaṁ lokaṁ upapajjissati.

For they are praised by sensible people in the present life, and when their body breaks up, after death, they will be reborn in a good place, a heavenly realm.

Evamassāyaṁ apaṇṇako dhammo susamatto samādinno, ubhayaṁsaṁ pharitvā tiṭṭhati, riñcati akusalaṁ ṭhānaṁ.

They have rightly undertaken this guaranteed teaching in such a way that it encompasses the positive outcomes of both sides, leaving out the unskillful premise.

Santi, gahapatayo, eke samaṇabrāhmaṇā evaṁvādino evaṁdiṭṭhino:

There are some ascetics and brahmins who have this doctrine and view:

'natthi hetu, natthi paccayo sattānaṁ saṅkilesāya;

'There is no cause or reason for the corruption of sentient beings.

ahetū appaccayā sattā saṅkilissanti.

Sentient beings are corrupted without cause or reason.

Natthi hetu, natthi paccayo sattānaṁ visuddhiyā;

There's no cause or reason for the purification of sentient beings.

ahetū appaccayā sattā visujjhanti.

Sentient beings are purified without cause or reason.

Natthi balaṁ, natthi vīriyaṁ, natthi purisathāmo, natthi purisaparakkamo;

There is no power, no energy, no human strength or vigor.

sabbe sattā sabbe pāṇā sabbe bhūtā sabbe jīvā avasā abalā avīriyā niyatisaṅgatibhāvapariṇatā chasvevābhijātīsu sukhadukkhaṁ paṭisaṁvedentī'ti.

All sentient beings, all living creatures, all beings, all souls lack control, power, and energy. Molded by destiny, circumstance, and nature, they experience pleasure and pain in the six classes of rebirth.'

Tesaṁyeva kho, gahapatayo, samaṇabrāhmaṇānaṁ eke samaṇabrāhmaṇā ujuvipaccanīkavādā.

And there are some ascetics and brahmins whose doctrine directly contradicts this.

Te evamāhaṁsu:

They say:

'atthi hetu, atthi paccayo sattānaṁ saṅkilesāya;

'There is a cause and reason for the corruption of sentient beings.

sahetū sappaccayā sattā saṅkilissanti.

Sentient beings are corrupted with cause and reason.

Atthi hetu, atthi paccayo sattānaṁ visuddhiyā;

There is a cause and reason for the purification of sentient beings.

sahetū sappaccayā sattā visujjhanti.

Sentient beings are purified with cause and reason.

Atthi balaṁ, atthi vīriyaṁ, atthi purisathāmo, atthi purisaparakkamo;

There is power, energy, human strength and vigor.

na sabbe sattā sabbe pāṇā sabbe bhūtā sabbe jīvā avasā abalā avīriyā niyatisaṅgatibhāvapariṇatā chasvevābhijātīsu sukhadukkhaṁ paṭisaṁvedentī'ti.

It is not the case that all sentient beings, all living creatures, all beings, all souls lack control, power, and energy, or that, molded by destiny, circumstance, and nature, they experience pleasure and pain in the six classes of rebirth.'

Taṁ kiṁ maññatha, gahapatayo,

What do you think, householders?

nanume samaṇabrāhmaṇā aññamaññassa ujuvipaccanīkavādā"ti?

Don't these doctrines directly contradict each other?"

"Evaṁ, bhante".

"Yes, sir."

"Tatra, gahapatayo, ye te samaṇabrāhmaṇā evaṁvādino evaṁdiṭṭhino:

"Since this is so, consider those ascetics and brahmins whose view is that

'natthi hetu, natthi paccayo sattānaṁ saṅkilesāya;

there's no cause or reason for the corruption of sentient beings, etc.

ahetū appaccayā sattā saṅkilissanti.

Natthi hetu, natthi paccayo sattānaṁ visuddhiyā;

ahetū appaccayā sattā visujjhanti.

Natthi balaṁ, natthi vīriyaṁ, natthi purisathāmo, natthi purisaparakkamo; sabbe sattā sabbe pāṇā sabbe bhūtā sabbe jīvā avasā abalā avīriyā niyatisaṅgatibhāvapariṇatā chasvevābhijātīsu sukhadukkhaṁ paṭisaṁvedentī'ti

tesametaṁ pāṭikaṅkhaṁ—yamidaṁ kāyasucaritaṁ, vacīsucaritaṁ, manosucaritaṁ—ime tayo kusale dhamme abhinivajjetvā yamidaṁ kāyaduccaritaṁ, vacīduccaritaṁ, manoduccaritaṁ—ime tayo akusale dhamme samādāya vattissanti.

You can expect that they will reject good conduct by way of body, speech, and mind, and undertake and implement bad conduct by way of body, speech, and mind.

Taṁ kissa hetu?

Why is that?

Na hi te bhonto samaṇabrāhmaṇā passanti akusalānaṁ dhammānaṁ ādīnavaṁ okāraṁ saṅkilesaṁ, kusalānaṁ dhammānaṁ nekkhamme ānisaṁsaṁ vodānapakkhaṁ.

Because those ascetics and brahmins don't see that unskillful qualities are full of drawbacks, sordidness, and corruption, or that skillful qualities have the benefit and cleansing power of renunciation.

Santaṁyeva kho pana hetuṁ 'natthi hetū' tissa diṭṭhi hoti; sāssa hoti micchādiṭṭhi.

Moreover, since there actually is causality, their view that there is no causality is wrong view.

Santaṁyeva kho pana hetuṁ 'natthi hetū'ti saṅkappeti; svāssa hoti micchāsaṅkappo.

Since there actually is causality, their thought that there is no causality is wrong thought.

Santaṁyeva kho pana hetuṁ 'natthi hetū'ti vācaṁ bhāsati; sāssa hoti micchāvācā.

Since there actually is causality, their speech that there is no causality is wrong speech.

Santaṁyeva kho pana hetuṁ 'natthi hetū'ti āha; ye te arahanto hetuvādā tesamayaṁ paccanīkaṁ karoti.

Since there actually is causality, in saying that there is no causality they contradict those perfected ones who teach that there is causality.

Santaṁyeva kho pana hetuṁ 'natthi hetū'ti paraṁ saññāpeti; sāssa hoti asaddhammasaññatti.

Since there actually is causality, in convincing another that there is no causality they are convincing them to accept an untrue teaching.

Tāya ca pana asaddhammasaññattiyā attānukkaṁseti, paraṁ vambheti.

And on account of that they glorify themselves and put others down.

Iti pubbeva kho panassa susīlyaṁ pahīnaṁ hoti, dussīlyaṁ paccupaṭṭhitaṁ—

So they give up their former ethical conduct and are established in unethical conduct.

ayañca micchādiṭṭhi micchāsaṅkappo micchāvācā ariyānaṁ paccanīkatā asaddhammasaññatti attānukkaṁsanā paravambhanā. Evamassime aneke pāpakā akusalā dhammā sambhavanti micchādiṭṭhipaccayā.

And that is how these many bad, unskillful qualities come to be with wrong view as condition—wrong view, wrong thought, wrong speech, contradicting the noble ones, convincing others to accept untrue teachings, and glorifying oneself and putting others down.

Tatra, gahapatayo, viññū puriso iti paṭisañcikkhati:

A sensible person reflects on this matter in this way:

'sace kho natthi hetu, evamayaṁ bhavaṁ purisapuggalo kāyassa bhedā paraṁ maraṇā sotthimattānaṁ karissati;

'If there is no causality, when this individual's body breaks up they will keep themselves safe.

sace kho atthi hetu, evamayaṁ bhavaṁ purisapuggalo kāyassa bhedā paraṁ maraṇā apāyaṁ duggatiṁ vinipātaṁ nirayaṁ upapajjissati.

And if there is causality, when their body breaks up, after death, they will be reborn in a place of loss, a bad place, the underworld, hell.

Kāmaṁ kho pana māhu hetu, hotu nesaṁ bhavataṁ samaṇabrāhmaṇānaṁ saccaṁ vacanaṁ;

But let's assume that those who say that there is no causality are correct.

atha ca panāyaṁ bhavaṁ purisapuggalo diṭṭheva dhamme viññūnaṁ gārayho— dussīlo purisapuggalo micchādiṭṭhi ahetukavādo'ti.

Regardless, that individual is still criticized by sensible people in the present life as being an immoral individual of wrong view, one who denies causality.'

Sace kho attheva hetu, evaṁ imassa bhoto purisapuggalassa ubhayattha kaliggaho—

But if there really is causality, they lose on both counts.

yañca diṭṭheva dhamme viññūnaṁ gārayho, yañca kāyassa bhedā paraṁ maraṇā apāyaṁ duggatiṁ vinipātaṁ nirayaṁ upapajjissati.

For they are criticized by sensible people in the present life, and when their body breaks up, after death, they will be reborn in a place of loss, a bad place, the underworld, hell.

Evamassāyaṁ apaṇṇako dhammo dussamatto samādinno, ekaṁsaṁ pharitvā tiṭṭhati, riñcati kusalaṁ ṭhānaṁ.

They have wrongly undertaken this guaranteed teaching in such a way that it encompasses the positive outcomes of one side only, leaving out the skillful premise.

Tatra, gahapatayo, ye te samaṇabrāhmaṇā evaṁvādino evaṁdiṭṭhino:

Since this is so, consider those ascetics and brahmins whose view is that

'atthi hetu, atthi paccayo sattānaṁ saṅkilesāya;

there is a cause and reason for the corruption of sentient beings, etc.

sahetū sappaccayā sattā saṅkilissanti.

Atthi hetu, atthi paccayo sattānaṁ visuddhiyā;

sahetū sappaccayā sattā visujjhanti.

Atthi balaṁ, atthi vīriyaṁ, atthi purisathāmo, atthi purisaparakkamo; na sabbe sattā sabbe pāṇā sabbe bhūtā sabbe jīvā avasā abalā avīriyā niyatisaṅgatibhāvapariṇatā chasvevābhijātīsu sukhadukkhaṁ paṭisaṁvedentī'ti

tesametaṁ pāṭikaṅkhaṁ—yamidaṁ kāyaduccaritaṁ, vacīduccaritaṁ, manoduccaritaṁ—ime tayo akusale dhamme abhinivajjetvā yamidaṁ kāyasucaritaṁ, vacīsucaritaṁ, manosucaritaṁ—ime tayo kusale dhamme samādāya vattissanti.

You can expect that they will reject bad conduct by way of body, speech, and mind, and undertake and implement good conduct by way of body, speech, and mind.

Taṁ kissa hetu?

Why is that?

Passanti hi te bhonto samaṇabrāhmaṇā akusalānaṁ dhammānaṁ ādīnavaṁ okāraṁ saṅkilesaṁ, kusalānaṁ dhammānaṁ nekkhamme ānisaṁsaṁ vodānapakkhaṁ.

Because those ascetics and brahmins see that unskillful qualities are full of drawbacks, sordidness, and corruption, and that skillful qualities have the benefit and cleansing power of renunciation.

Santaṁyeva kho pana hetuṁ 'atthi hetū' tissa diṭṭhi hoti; sāssa hoti sammādiṭṭhi.

Moreover, since there actually is causality, their view that there is causality is right view.

Santaṁyeva kho pana hetuṁ 'atthi hetū'ti saṅkappeti; svāssa hoti sammāsaṅkappo.

Since there actually is causality, their thought that there is causality is right thought.

Santaṁyeva kho pana hetuṁ 'atthi hetū'ti vācaṁ bhāsati; sāssa hoti sammāvācā.

Since there actually is causality, their speech that there is causality is right speech.

Santaṁyeva kho pana hetuṁ 'atthi hetū'ti āha, ye te arahanto hetuvādā tesamayaṁ na paccanīkaṁ karoti.

Since there actually is causality, in saying that there is causality they don't contradict those perfected ones who teach that there is causality.

Santaṁyeva kho pana hetuṁ 'atthi hetū'ti paraṁ saññāpeti; sāssa hoti saddhammasaññatti.

Since there actually is causality, in convincing another that there is causality they are convincing them to accept a true teaching.

Tāya ca pana saddhammasaññattiyā nevattānukkaṁseti, na paraṁ vambheti.

And on account of that they don't glorify themselves or put others down.

Iti pubbeva kho panassa dussīlyaṁ pahīnaṁ hoti, susīlyaṁ paccupaṭṭhitaṁ—

So they give up their former unethical conduct and are established in ethical conduct.

ayañca sammādiṭṭhi sammāsaṅkappo sammāvācā ariyānaṁ apaccanīkatā saddhammasaññatti anattukkaṁsanā aparavambhanā. Evamassime aneke kusalā dhammā sambhavanti sammādiṭṭhipaccayā.

And that is how these many skillful qualities come to be with right view as condition—right view, right thought, right speech, not contradicting the noble ones, convincing others to accept true teachings, and not glorifying oneself or putting others down.

Tatra, gahapatayo, viññū puriso iti paṭisañcikkhati: 'sace kho atthi hetu, evamayaṁ bhavaṁ purisapuggalo kāyassa bhedā paraṁ maraṇā sugatiṁ saggaṁ lokaṁ upapajjissati.

A sensible person reflects on this matter in this way: 'If there is causality, when this individual's body breaks up, after death, they will be reborn in a good place, a heavenly realm.

Kāmaṁ kho pana māhu hetu, hotu nesaṁ bhavataṁ samaṇabrāhmaṇānaṁ saccaṁ vacanaṁ;

But let's assume that those who say that there is no causality are correct.

atha ca panāyaṁ bhavaṁ purisapuggalo diṭṭheva dhamme viññūnaṁ pāsaṁso— sīlavā purisapuggalo sammādiṭṭhi hetuvādo'ti.

Regardless, that individual is still praised by sensible people in the present life as being a moral individual of right view, who affirms causality.'

Sace kho atthi hetu, evaṁ imassa bhoto purisapuggalassa ubhayattha kaṭaggaho—

So if there really is causality, they win on both counts.

yañca diṭṭheva dhamme viññūnaṁ pāsaṁso, yañca kāyassa bhedā paraṁ maraṇā sugatiṁ saggaṁ lokaṁ upapajjissati.

For they are praised by sensible people in the present life, and when their body breaks up, after death, they will be reborn in a good place, a heavenly realm.

Evamassāyaṁ apaṇṇako dhammo susamatto samādinno, ubhayaṁsaṁ pharitvā tiṭṭhati, riñcati akusalaṁ ṭhānaṁ.

They have rightly undertaken this guaranteed teaching in such a way that it encompasses the positive outcomes of both sides, leaving out the unskillful premise.

Santi, gahapatayo, eke samaṇabrāhmaṇā evaṁvādino evaṁdiṭṭhino:

There are some ascetics and brahmins who have this doctrine and view:

'natthi sabbaso āruppā'ti.

'There are no totally formless states of meditation.'

Tesaṁyeva kho, gahapatayo, samaṇabrāhmaṇānaṁ eke samaṇabrāhmaṇā ujuvipaccanīkavādā.

And there are some ascetics and brahmins whose doctrine directly contradicts this.

Te evamāhaṁsu:

They say:

'atthi sabbaso āruppā'ti.

'There are totally formless states of meditation.'

Taṁ kiṁ maññatha, gahapatayo,

What do you think, householders?

nanume samaṇabrāhmaṇā aññamaññassa ujuvipaccanīkavādā"ti?

Don't these doctrines directly contradict each other?"

"Evaṁ, bhante".

"Yes, sir."

"Tatra, gahapatayo, viññū puriso iti paṭisañcikkhati—

"A sensible person reflects on this matter in this way:

ye kho te bhonto samaṇabrāhmaṇā evaṁvādino evaṁdiṭṭhino:

'Some ascetics and brahmins say that

'natthi sabbaso āruppā'ti, idaṁ me adiṭṭhaṁ;

there are no totally formless meditations, but I have not seen that.

yepi te bhonto samaṇabrāhmaṇā evaṁvādino evaṁdiṭṭhino:

Some ascetics and brahmins say that

'atthi sabbaso āruppā'ti, idaṁ me aviditaṁ.

there are totally formless meditations, but I have not known that.

Ahañceva kho pana ajānanto apassanto ekaṁsena ādāya vohareyyaṁ—

Without knowing or seeing, it would not be appropriate for me to take one side and declare,

idameva saccaṁ, moghamaññanti, na metaṁ assa patirūpaṁ.

'This is the only truth, other ideas are silly.'

Ye kho te bhonto samaṇabrāhmaṇā evaṁvādino evaṁdiṭṭhino:

If those ascetics and brahmins who say that

'natthi sabbaso āruppā'ti, sace tesaṁ bhavataṁ samaṇabrāhmaṇānaṁ saccaṁ vacanaṁ, ṭhānametaṁ vijjati—

there are no totally formless meditations are correct, it is possible

ye te devā rūpino manomayā, apaṇṇakaṁ me tatrūpapatti bhavissati.

that I will be guaranteed rebirth among the gods who possess form and made of mind.

Ye pana te bhonto samaṇabrāhmaṇā evaṁvādino evaṁdiṭṭhino:

If those ascetics and brahmins who say that

'atthi sabbaso āruppā'ti, sace tesaṁ bhavataṁ samaṇabrāhmaṇānaṁ saccaṁ vacanaṁ, ṭhānametaṁ vijjati—

there are totally formless meditations are correct, it is possible

ye te devā arūpino saññāmayā, apaṇṇakaṁ me tatrūpapatti bhavissati.

that I will be guaranteed rebirth among the gods who are formless and made of perception.

Dissanti kho pana rūpādhikaraṇaṁ

daṇḍādānasatthādānakalahaviggahavivādatuvaṁtuvaṁpesuññamusāvādā.

Now, owing to form, bad things are seen: taking up the rod and the sword, quarrels, arguments, and disputes, accusations, divisive speech, and lies.

'Natthi kho panetaṁ sabbaso arūpe'ti.

But those things don't exist where it is totally formless.'

So iti paṭisaṅkhāya rūpānaṁyeva nibbidāya virāgāya nirodhāya paṭipanno hoti.

Reflecting like this, they simply practice for disillusionment, dispassion, and cessation regarding forms.

Santi, gahapatayo, eke samaṇabrāhmaṇā evaṁvādino evaṁdiṭṭhino:

There are some ascetics and brahmins who have this doctrine and view:

'natthi sabbaso bhavanirodho'ti.

'There is no such thing as the total cessation of future lives.'

Tesaṁyeva kho, gahapatayo, samaṇabrāhmaṇānaṁ eke samaṇabrāhmaṇā ujuvipaccanīkavādā.

And there are some ascetics and brahmins whose doctrine directly contradicts this.

Te evamāhaṁsu:

They say:

'atthi sabbaso bhavanirodho'ti.

'There is such a thing as the total cessation of future lives.'

Taṁ kiṁ maññatha, gahapatayo,

What do you think, householders?

nanume samaṇabrāhmaṇā aññamaññassa ujuvipaccanīkavādā"ti?

Don't these doctrines directly contradict each other?"

"Evaṁ, bhante".

"Yes, sir."

"Tatra, gahapatayo, viññū puriso iti paṭisañcikkhati—

"A sensible person reflects on this matter in this way:

ye kho te bhonto samaṇabrāhmaṇā evaṁvādino evaṁdiṭṭhino:

'Some ascetics and brahmins say that

'natthi sabbaso bhavanirodho'ti, idaṁ me adiṭṭhaṁ;

there is no such thing as the total cessation of future lives, but I have not seen that.

yepi te bhonto samaṇabrāhmaṇā evaṁvādino evaṁdiṭṭhino:

Some ascetics and brahmins say that

'atthi sabbaso bhavanirodho'ti, idaṁ me aviditaṁ.

there is such a thing as the total cessation of future lives, but I have not known that.

Ahañceva kho pana ajānanto apassanto ekaṁsena ādāya vohareyyaṁ—

Without knowing or seeing, it would not be appropriate for me to take one side and declare,

idameva saccaṁ, moghamaññanti, na metaṁ assa patirūpaṁ.

'This is the only truth, other ideas are silly.'

Ye kho te bhonto samaṇabrāhmaṇā evaṁvādino evaṁdiṭṭhino:

If those ascetics and brahmins who say that

'natthi sabbaso bhavanirodho'ti, sace tesaṁ bhavataṁ samaṇabrāhmaṇānaṁ saccaṁ vacanaṁ, ṭhānametaṁ vijjati—

there is no such thing as the total cessation of future lives are correct, it is possible

ye te devā arūpino saññāmayā apaṇṇakaṁ me tatrūpapatti bhavissati.

that I will be guaranteed rebirth among the gods who are formless and made of perception.

Ye pana te bhonto samaṇabrāhmaṇā evaṁvādino evaṁdiṭṭhino:

If those ascetics and brahmins who say that

'atthi sabbaso bhavanirodho'ti, sace tesaṁ bhavataṁ samaṇabrāhmaṇānaṁ saccaṁ vacanaṁ, ṭhānametaṁ vijjati—

there is such a thing as the total cessation of future lives are correct, it is possible

yaṁ diṭṭheva dhamme parinibbāyissāmi.

that I will be fully extinguished in the present life.

Ye kho te bhonto samaṇabrāhmaṇā evaṁvādino evaṁdiṭṭhino:

The view of those ascetics and brahmins who say that

'natthi sabbaso bhavanirodho'ti, tesamayaṁ diṭṭhi sārāgāya santike, saṁyogāya santike, abhinandanāya santike, ajjhosānāya santike, upādānāya santike.

there is no such thing as the total cessation of future lives is close to greed, approving, attachment, and grasping.

Ye pana te bhonto samaṇabrāhmaṇā evaṁvādino evaṁdiṭṭhino:

The view of those ascetics and brahmins who say that

'atthi sabbaso bhavanirodho'ti, tesamayaṁ diṭṭhi asārāgāya santike, asaṁyogāya santike, anabhinandanāya santike, anajjhosānāya santike, anupādānāya santiketi.

there is such a thing as the total cessation of future lives is close to non-greed, non-approving, non-attachment, and non-grasping.'

So iti paṭisaṅkhāya bhavānaṁyeva nibbidāya virāgāya nirodhāya paṭipanno hoti.

Reflecting like this, they simply practice for disillusionment, dispassion, and cessation regarding future lives.

Cattārome, gahapatayo, puggalā santo saṁvijjamānā lokasmiṁ.

Householders, these four people are found in the world.

Katame cattāro?

What four?

Idha, gahapatayo, ekacco puggalo attantapo hoti attaparitāpanānuyogamanuyutto.

One person mortifies themselves, committed to the practice of mortifying themselves.

Idha, gahapatayo, ekacco puggalo parantapo hoti paraparitāpanānuyogamanuyutto.

One person mortifies others, committed to the practice of mortifying others.

Idha, gahapatayo, ekacco puggalo attantapo ca hoti attaparitāpanānuyogamanuyutto parantapo ca paraparitāpanānuyogamanuyutto.

One person mortifies themselves and others, committed to the practice of mortifying themselves and others.

Idha, gahapatayo, ekacco puggalo nevattantapo hoti nāttaparitāpanānuyogamanuyutto naparantapo naparaparitāpanānuyogamanuyutto;

One person doesn't mortify either themselves or others, committed to the practice of not mortifying themselves or others.

so anattantapo aparantapo diṭṭheva dhamme nicchāto nibbuto sītībhūto sukhappaṭisaṁvedī brahmabhūtena attanā viharati.

They live without wishes in the present life, extinguished, cooled, experiencing bliss, having become holy in themselves.

Katamo ca, gahapatayo, puggalo attantapo attaparitāpanānuyogamanuyutto?

And what person mortifies themselves, committed to the practice of mortifying themselves?

Idha, gahapatayo, ekacco puggalo acelako hoti muttācāro hatthāpalekhano …pe…

It's when someone goes naked, ignoring conventions. …

iti evarūpaṁ anekavihitaṁ kāyassa ātāpanaparitāpanānuyogamanuyutto viharati.

And so they live committed to practicing these various ways of mortifying and tormenting the body.

Ayaṁ vuccati, gahapatayo, puggalo attantapo attaparitāpanānuyogamanuyutto.

This is called a person who mortifies themselves, being committed to the practice of mortifying themselves.

Katamo ca, gahapatayo, puggalo parantapo paraparitāpanānuyogamanuyutto?

And what person mortifies others, committed to the practice of mortifying others?

Idha, gahapatayo, ekacco puggalo orabbhiko hoti sūkariko …pe… ye vā panaññepi keci kurūrakammantā.

It's when a person is a butcher of sheep, pigs, poultry, or deer, a hunter or fisher, a bandit, an executioner, a butcher of cattle, a jailer, or has some other cruel livelihood.

Ayaṁ vuccati, gahapatayo, puggalo parantapo paraparitāpanānuyogamanuyutto.

This is called a person who mortifies others, being committed to the practice of mortifying others.

Katamo ca, gahapatayo, puggalo attantapo ca attaparitāpanānuyogamanuyutto parantapo ca paraparitāpanānuyogamanuyutto?

And what person mortifies themselves and others, being committed to the practice of mortifying themselves and others?

Idha, gahapatayo, ekacco puggalo rājā vā hoti khattiyo muddhāvasitto …pe…

It's when a person is an anointed aristocratic king or a well-to-do brahmin. …

tepi daṇḍatajjitā bhayatajjitā assumukhā rudamānā parikammāni karonti.

His bondservants, servants, and workers do their jobs under threat of punishment and danger, weeping, with tearful faces.

Ayaṁ vuccati, gahapatayo, puggalo attantapo ca attaparitāpanānuyogamanuyutto parantapo ca paraparitāpanānuyogamanuyutto.

This is called a person who mortifies themselves and others, being committed to the practice of mortifying themselves and others.

Katamo ca, gahapatayo, puggalo nevattantapo nāttaparitāpanānuyogamanuyutto na parantapo na paraparitāpanānuyogamanuyutto;

And what person doesn't mortify either themselves or others, committed to the practice of not mortifying themselves or others,

so anattantapo aparantapo diṭṭheva dhamme nicchāto nibbuto sītībhūto sukhappaṭisaṁvedī brahmabhūtena attanā viharati?

living without wishes in the present life, extinguished, cooled, experiencing bliss, having become holy in themselves?

Idha, gahapatayo, tathāgato loke uppajjati arahaṁ sammāsambuddho …

It's when a Realized One arises in the world, perfected, a fully awakened Buddha …

pe…

A householder hears that teaching, or a householder's child, or someone reborn in some good family. …

so ime pañca nīvaraṇe pahāya cetaso upakkilese paññāya dubbalīkaraṇe

They give up these five hindrances, corruptions of the heart that weaken wisdom.

vivicceva kāmehi vivicca akusalehi dhammehi savitakkaṁ savicāraṁ vivekajaṁ pītisukhaṁ paṭhamaṁ jhānaṁ upasampajja viharati.

Then, quite secluded from sensual pleasures, secluded from unskillful qualities, they enter and remain in the first absorption …

Vitakkavicārānaṁ vūpasamā ajjhattaṁ sampasādanaṁ cetaso ekodibhāvaṁ avitakkaṁ avicāraṁ samādhijaṁ pītisukhaṁ dutiyaṁ jhānaṁ …pe…

second absorption …

tatiyaṁ jhānaṁ …pe…

third absorption …

catutthaṁ jhānaṁ upasampajja viharati.

fourth absorption.

So evaṁ samāhite citte parisuddhe pariyodāte anaṅgaṇe vigatūpakkilese mudubhūte kammaniye ṭhite āneñjappatte pubbenivāsānussatiñāṇāya cittaṁ abhininnāmeti.

When their mind has become immersed in samadhi like this—purified, bright, flawless, rid of corruptions, pliable, workable, steady, and imperturbable—they extend it toward recollection of past lives. …

So anekavihitaṁ pubbenivāsaṁ anussarati seyyathidaṁ—ekampi jātiṁ dvepi jātiyo …pe… iti sākāraṁ sauddesaṁ anekavihitaṁ pubbenivāsaṁ anussarati.

They recollect their many kinds of past lives, with features and details.

So evaṁ samāhite citte parisuddhe pariyodāte anaṅgaṇe vigatūpakkilese mudubhūte kammaniye ṭhite āneñjappatte sattānaṁ cutūpapātañāṇāya cittaṁ abhininnāmeti.

When their mind has become immersed in samadhi like this—purified, bright, flawless, rid of corruptions, pliable, workable, steady, and imperturbable—they extend it toward knowledge of the death and rebirth of sentient beings.

So dibbena cakkhunā visuddhena atikkantamānusakena satte passati cavamāne upapajjamāne hīne paṇīte suvaṇṇe dubbaṇṇe, sugate duggate …pe… yathākammūpage satte pajānāti.

With clairvoyance that is purified and superhuman, they see sentient beings passing away and being reborn—inferior and superior, beautiful and ugly, in a good place or a bad place. … They understand how sentient beings are reborn according to their deeds.

So evaṁ samāhite citte parisuddhe pariyodāte anaṅgaṇe vigatūpakkilese mudubhūte kammaniye ṭhite āneñjappatte āsavānaṁ khayañāṇāya cittaṁ abhininnāmeti.

When their mind has become immersed in samadhi like this—purified, bright, flawless, rid of corruptions, pliable, workable, steady, and imperturbable—they extend it toward knowledge of the ending of defilements.

So 'idaṁ dukkhan'ti yathābhūtaṁ pajānāti …pe…

They truly understand: 'This is suffering' … 'This is the origin of suffering' … 'This is the cessation of suffering' … 'This is the practice that leads to the cessation of suffering'.

'ayaṁ āsavanirodhagāminī paṭipadā'ti yathābhūtaṁ pajānāti.

They truly understand: 'These are defilements' … 'This is the origin of defilements' … 'This is the cessation of defilements' … 'This is the practice that leads to the cessation of defilements'.

Tassa evaṁ jānato evaṁ passato kāmāsavāpi cittaṁ vimuccati, bhavāsavāpi cittaṁ vimuccati, avijjāsavāpi cittaṁ vimuccati.

Knowing and seeing like this, their mind is freed from the defilements of sensuality, desire to be reborn, and ignorance.

Vimuttasmiṁ vimuttamiti ñāṇaṁ hoti.

When they're freed, they know they're freed.

'Khīṇā jāti, vusitaṁ brahmacariyaṁ, kataṁ karaṇīyaṁ, nāparaṁ itthattāyā'ti pajānāti.

They understand: 'Rebirth is ended, the spiritual journey has been completed, what had to be done has been done, there is no return to any state of existence.'

Ayaṁ vuccati, gahapatayo, puggalo nevattantapo nāttaparitāpanānuyogamanuyutto na parantapo na paraparitāpanānuyogamanuyutto;

This is called a person who neither mortifies themselves or others, being committed to the practice of not mortifying themselves or others.

so anattantapo aparantapo diṭṭheva dhamme nicchāto nibbuto sītībhūto sukhappaṭisaṁvedī brahmabhūtena attanā viharatī'ti.

They live without wishes in the present life, extinguished, cooled, experiencing bliss, having become holy in themselves."

Evaṁ vutte, sāleyyakā brāhmaṇagahapatikā bhagavantaṁ etadavocuṁ:

When he had spoken, the brahmins and householders of Sālā said to the Buddha,

"abhikkantaṁ, bho gotama, abhikkantaṁ, bho gotama.

"Excellent, Master Gotama! Excellent!

Seyyathāpi, bho gotama, nikkujjitaṁ vā ukkujjeyya, paṭicchannaṁ vā vivareyya, mūḷhassa vā maggaṁ ācikkheyya, andhakāre vā telapajjotaṁ dhāreyya 'cakkhumanto rūpāni dakkhantī'ti; evamevaṁ bhotā gotamena anekapariyāyena dhammo pakāsito.

As if he were righting the overturned, or revealing the hidden, or pointing out the path to the lost, or lighting a lamp in the dark so people with good eyes can see what's there, Master Gotama has made the teaching clear in many ways.

Ete mayaṁ bhavantaṁ gotamaṁ saraṇaṁ gacchāma dhammañca bhikkhusaṅghañca.

We go for refuge to Master Gotama, to the teaching, and to the mendicant Saṅgha.

Upāsake no bhavaṁ gotamo dhāretu ajjatagge pāṇupetaṁ saraṇaṁ gate"ti.

From this day forth, may Master Gotama remember us as lay followers who have gone for refuge for life."

Apaṇṇakasuttaṁ niṭṭhitaṁ dasamaṁ.

Gahapativaggo niṭṭhito paṭhamo.

Tassuddānaṁ

Kandaranāgarasekhavato ca,

Potaliyo puna jīvakabhacco;

Upālidamatho kukkuraabhayo,

Bahuvedanīyāpaṇṇakato dasamo.